THE
ALL ENGLAND
LAW REPORTS
1981

Volume 3

Editor
PETER HUTCHESSON LL M
Barrister, New Zealand

Assistant Editor
BROOK WATSON
of Lincoln's Inn, Barrister
and of the New South Wales Bar

Consulting Editor
WENDY SHOCKETT
of Gray's Inn, Barrister

London
BUTTERWORTHS

ENGLAND: Butterworth & Co (Publishers) Ltd
                London: 88 Kingsway, WC2B 6AB

AUSTRALIA: Butterworths Pty Ltd
                Sydney: 271–273 Lane Cove Road, North Ryde, NSW 2113
                Also at Melbourne, Brisbane, Adelaide and Perth

CANADA: Butterworth & Co (Canada) Ltd
                Toronto: 2265 Midland Avenue, Scarborough M1P 4S1

NEW ZEALAND: Butterworths of New Zealand Ltd
                Wellington: 33–35 Cumberland Place

SOUTH AFRICA: Butterworth & Co (South Africa) (Pty) Ltd
                Durban: 152–154 Gale Street

USA: Butterworth & Co (Publishers) Inc
                Boston: 10 Tower Office Park, Woburn, Mass 01801

©

Butterworth & Co (Publishers) Ltd

1981

ISBN 0 406 85142 5

Typeset by CCC, printed and bound in Great Britain by William Clowes (Beccles) Limited, Beccles and
London

House of Lords

The Lord High Chancellor: Lord Hailsham of St Marylebone

Lords of Appeal in Ordinary

Lord Wilberforce
Lord Diplock
Lord Edmund-Davies
(retired 30th September 1981)
Lord Fraser of Tullybelton
Lord Russell of Killowen

Lord Keith of Kinkel
Lord Scarman
Lord Roskill
Lord Bridge of Harwich
Lord Brandon of Oakbrook
(appointed 24th September 1981)

Court of Appeal

The Lord High Chancellor

The Lord Chief Justice of England: Lord Lane

The Master of the Rolls: Lord Denning

The President of the Family Division: Sir John Lewis Arnold

Lords Justices of Appeal

Sir John Frederick Eustace Stephenson
Sir Frederick Horace Lawton
Sir Roger Fray Greenwood Ormrod
Sir Sebag Shaw
Sir George Stanley Waller
Sir James Roualeyn Hovell-Thurlow-
Cumming-Bruce
Sir Edward Walter Eveleigh
Sir Henry Vivian Brandon
(appointed Lord of Appeal in Ordinary,.
24th September 1981)
Sir Sydney William Templeman

Sir John Francis Donaldson
Sir John Anson Brightman
Sir Desmond James Conrad Ackner
Sir Robin Horace Walford Dunn
Sir Peter Raymond Oliver
Sir Tasker Watkins VC
Sir Patrick McCarthy O'Connor
Sir William Hugh Griffiths
Sir Michael John Fox
Sir Michael Robert Emanuel Kerr
(appointed 24th September 1981)

Chancery Division

The Lord High Chancellor

The Vice-Chancellor: Sir Robert Edgar Megarry

Sir Peter Harry Batson Woodroffe Foster
Sir John Norman Keates Whitford
Sir Ernest Irvine Goulding
Sir Raymond Henry Walton
Sir Christopher John Slade
Sir Nicolas Christopher Henry Browne-
    Wilkinson

Sir John Evelyn Vinelott
Sir George Brian Hugh Dillon
Sir Martin Charles Nourse
Sir Douglas William Falconer
Sir Jean-Pierre Frank Eugene Warner
Sir Peter Leslie Gibson

Queen's Bench Division

The Lord Chief Justice of England

Sir John Thompson
Sir Helenus Patrick Joseph Milmo
Sir Joseph Donaldson Cantley
Sir Hugh Eames Park
Sir Bernard Caulfield
Sir Hilary Gwynne Talbot
Sir William Lloyd Mars-Jones
Sir Ralph Kilner Brown
Sir Peter Henry Rowley Bristow
Sir Hugh Harry Valentine Forbes
Sir Robert Hugh Mais
Sir Neil Lawson
Sir David Powell Croom-Johnson
Sir John Raymond Phillips
Sir Leslie Kenneth Edward Boreham
Sir John Douglas May
Sir Michael Robert Emanuel Kerr
    (appointed Lord Justice of Appeal,
    24th September 1981)
Sir Alfred William Michael Davies
Sir John Dexter Stocker
Sir Kenneth George Illtyd Jones
Sir Haydn Tudor Evans
Sir Peter Richard Pain
Sir Kenneth Graham Jupp
Sir Robert Lionel Archibald Goff
Sir Stephen Brown

Sir Roger Jocelyn Parker
Sir Ralph Brian Gibson
Sir Walter Derek Thornley Hodgson
Sir James Peter Comyn
Sir Anthony John Leslie Lloyd
Sir Frederick Maurice Drake
Sir Brian Thomas Neill
Sir Michael John Mustill
Sir Barry Cross Sheen
Sir David Bruce McNeill
Sir Harry Kenneth Woolf
Sir Thomas Patrick Russell
Sir Peter Edlin Webster
Sir Thomas Henry Bingham
Sir Iain Derek Laing Glidewell
Sir Henry Albert Skinner
Sir Peter Murray Taylor
Sir Murray Stuart-Smith
Sir Christopher Stephen Thomas Jonathan
    Thayer Staughton
Sir Donald Henry Farquharson
Sir Anthony James Denys McCowan
Sir Iain Charles Robert McCullough
Sir Hamilton John Leonard
    (appointed 15th September 1981)
Sir Alexander Roy Asplan Beldam
    (appointed 24th September 1981)

Family Division

The President of the Family Division

Sir John Brinsmead Latey
Sir Alfred Kenneth Hollings
Sir Charles Trevor Reeve
Sir Francis Brooks Purchas
Dame Rose Heilbron
Sir Brian Drex Bush
Sir Alfred John Balcombe
Sir John Kember Wood

Sir Ronald Gough Waterhouse
Sir John Gervase Kensington Sheldon
Sir Thomas Michael Eastham
Dame Margaret Myfanwy Wood Booth
Sir Christopher James Saunders French
Sir Anthony Leslie Julian Lincoln
Dame Ann Elizabeth Oldfield Butler-Sloss
Sir Anthony Bruce Ewbank

CITATION

These reports are cited thus:

[1981] 3 All ER

REFERENCES

These reports contain references to the following major works of legal reference described in the manner indicated below.

Halsbury's Laws of England

The reference 35 Halsbury's Laws (3rd Edn) 366, para 524, refers to paragraph 524 on page 366 of volume 35 of the third edition, and the reference 26 Halsbury's Laws (4th Edn) para 577 refers to paragraph 577 on page 296 of volume 26 of the fourth edition of Halsbury's Laws of England.

Halsbury's Statutes of England

The reference 5 Halsbury's Statutes (3rd Edn) 302 refers to page 302 of volume 5 of the third edition of Halsbury's Statutes of England.

The Digest

References are to the replacement volumes (including reissue volumes) of The Digest (formerly the English and Empire Digest), and to the continuation volumes of the replacement volumes.

The reference 44 Digest (Repl) 144, *1240*, refers to case number 1240 on page 144 of Digest Replacement Volume 44.

The reference 28(1) Digest (Reissue) 167, *507*, refers to case number 507 on page 167 of Digest Replacement Volume 28(1) Reissue.

The reference Digest (Cont Vol D) 571, *678b*, refers to case number 678b on page 571 of Digest Continuation Volume D.

Halsbury's Statutory Instruments

The reference 12 Halsbury's Statutory Instruments (Third Reissue) 125 refers to page 125 of the third reissue of volume 12 of Halsbury's Statutory Instruments; references to subsequent reissues are similar.

CORRIGENDA

[1981] 2 All ER
pp 386, 393. **A v Liverpool City Council.** The case referred to on p 386 line *b* 1 and p 393 line *d* 3 should be *Re D (a minor) (justices' decision: review)* [1977] 3 All ER 481, [1977] Fam 158.
p 1066. **I Congreso del Partido.** Counsel for the respondents should read *'Brian Davenport QC, Robert Jennings QC and Timothy Saloman'*.

[1981] 3 All ER
p 45. **Royal Borough of Windsor and Maidenhead v Brandrose Investments Ltd.** Solicitors for the defendants: *Gamlens* were agents for *Lovegrove & Durant,* Windsor.
p 244. **Exxon Corpn v Exxon Insurance Consultants International Ltd.** Line *f* 3: the reference should be to Lewis Carroll's Nonsense poem.
p 291. **JEB Fasteners Ltd v Marks, Bloom & Co (a firm).** Counsel for the defendants should read *'Quintin J Iwi and Andrew Jordan'.*
p 548. **Edwards (Insp. of Taxes) v Clinch.** Line *c* 4: the words from 'For example, the assessment' to the end of the paragraph should be omitted.
p 680. **Harrison v British Railways Board.** Counsel for the second defendant was *Peter Leighton.*

Cases reported in volume 3

Page

Air Canada v Secretary of State for Trade [QBD] 336
Akehurst, Weller v [ChD] 411
Alan Estates Ltd v WG Stores Ltd [CA] 481
Albanese, ex parte, R v Wells Street Magistrates' Court [QBD] 769
Albert v Lavin [HL] 878
Alex Lawrie Factors Ltd v Modern Injection Moulds Ltd [QBD] 658
Allied Collection Agencies Ltd v Wood [QBD] 176
Allwork, ex parte, R v Rochdale Justices [QBD] 434
Amalgamated Investment & Property Co Ltd (in liquidation) v Texas Commerce International Bank Ltd [CA] 577
Arun District Council, Routhan v [CA] 752
Ashcroft v Cambro Waste Products Ltd [QBD] 699
Aspinall v Sterling Mansell Ltd [QBD] 866
Attorney General, McGovern v [ChD] .. 493
Banque de l'Indochine et de Suez SA v Euroseas Group Finance Co Ltd [QBD] .. 198
Barclays Bank Trust Co Ltd v Bluff [ChD] 232
Barge v Graham Brown (Oasis Trading) Ltd [QBD] 360
Beirne, Latchford v [QBD] 705
Bickenhall Engineering Ltd, Selim Ltd v [ChD] 210
Blacklocks v JB Developments (Godalming) Ltd [ChD] 392
Bluff, Barclays Bank Trust Co Ltd v [ChD] .. 232
Brandrose Investments Ltd, Royal Borough of Windsor and Maidenhead v [ChD] .. 38
British Railways Board, Harrison v [QBD] 679
Brown, Easton v [ChD] 278
Brown (Graham) (Oasis Trading) Ltd, Barge v [QBD] 360
Bulk Oil International Ltd, Nereide SpA di Navigazione [HL] 737
Bulldog Tools Ltd, Prescott v [QBD] .. 869
Burditt v Joslin [QBD] 203
Buttes Gas and Oil Co v Hammer (Nos 2 & 3) [HL] 616
Buttes Gas and Oil Co, Occidental Petroleum Corpn v (Nos 1 & 2) [HL] 616
Cambro Waste Products Ltd, Ashcroft v [QBD] 699
Camden and Islington Area Health Authority, Connolly v [QBD] 250
Central Electricity Generating Board, ex parte, R v Chief Constable of the Devon and Cornwall Constabulary [CA] 826
Cerealmangimi SpA v Alfred C Toepfer [QBD] 533
Cerrahogullari TAS, Tradax Internacional SA v [QBD] 344
Chief Constable of West Midlands, Hunter v [HL] 727
China Pacific SA v Food Corpn of India [HL] 688
Claire Cleaners (Holdings) Ltd, Oakacre Ltd v [ChD] 667
Clinch, Edwards (Inspector of Taxes) v [HL] 543
Clipper Maritime Co Ltd v Mineralimportexport [QBD] 664
Cohen v Nessdale Ltd [QBD] 118
Comr of Police of the Metropolis, ex parte, R v Uxbridge Justices [CA] 129
Connolly v Camden and Islington Area Health Authority [QBD] 250
Copas, Wheeler v [QBD] 405
Cottingham, Marshall v [ChD] .. 8
Crédit Suisse, Trendtex Trading Corpn v [HL] 520
Croke (a minor) v Wiseman [CA] .. 852
Crossley v Rawlinson [QBD] 674
Crown Court at Knightsbridge, R v, ex parte International Sporting Club (London) Ltd [QBD] 417
Cummins Engine Co Ltd v Davis Freight Forwarding (Hull) Ltd [CA] 567
Davis Freight Forwarding (Hull) Ltd, Cummins Engine Co Ltd v [CA] 567
de Vere, R v [CA] 473
Devon and Cornwall Constabulary (Chief Constable), R v, ex parte Central Electricity Generating Board [CA] 826

Page

Din v London Borough of Wandsworth [HL] 881
Duke of Norfolk's Settlement Trusts, Re [CA] 220
Dunkley v Evans [QBD] 285
East Midlands Housing Association Ltd, North West Leicestershire District Council v [CA] 364
Easton v Brown [ChD] 278
Edwards (Inspector of Taxes) v Clinch [HL] 543
Edwin Evans & Sons (a firm), Yianni v [QBD] 592
Eggleton, Sudbrook Trading Estate Ltd v [CA] 105
Elaghill Trading Co, Syros Shipping Co SA v [QBD] 189
Eurometal, The [QBD] 533
Euroseas Group Finance Co Ltd, Banque de l'Indochine et de Suez SA v [QBD] .. 198
Evans, Dunkley v [QBD] 285
Exxon Corpn v Exxon Insurance Consultants International Ltd [QBD] 241
Exxon Insurance Consultants International Ltd, Exxon Corpn v [CA] 241
Ezedinma, London Borough of Hackney v [QBD] 438
Faulkner v Talbot [QBD] 468
Folkestone and Hythe Juvenile Court, R v, ex parte R (a juvenile) [QBD] 840
Food Corpn of India, China Pacific SA v [HL] 688
Francesco of Jermyn Street Ltd, Regent OHG Aisenstadt und Barig v [QBD] .. 327
Gaskill v Preston [QBD] 427
Goldup v John Manson Ltd [QBD] .. 257
Governor of Pentonville Prison, R v, ex parte Singh [QBD] 23
Greater London Council, Tate & Lyle Food and Distribution Ltd v [QBD] 716
Green, Midland Bank Trust Co Ltd v (No 3) [CA] 744
H (a barrister), Re [Visitors of Gray's Inn] .. 205
Hackney (London Borough) v Ezedinma [QBD] 438
Hammer, Buttes Gas and Oil Co v (Nos 2 & 3) [HL] 616
Hanson, ex parte, R v Leeds Justices [QBD] 72
Harrison v British Railways Board [QBD] .. 679
Haw Tua Tau v Public Prosecutor [PC] 14
Hay's Settlement Trusts, Re [ChD] .. 786
Hayward v Thompson [CA] 450
Helen Slater Charitable Trust Ltd, Inland Revenue Comrs v [CA] 98
Heron, R v [CA] 641
Hillingdon (London Borough), Islam v [HL] 901
Hodson-Pressinger, Sampson v [CA] 710
Holder, Reel v [CA] 321
Howell, R v [CA] 383
Hunter v Chief Constable of West Midlands [HL] 727
Immigration Appeal Tribunal, R v, ex parte Shaikh [QBD] 29
Inland Revenue Comrs v Helen Slater Charitable Trust Ltd [CA] 98
International Sporting Club (London) Ltd, ex parte, R v Crown Court at Knightsbridge [QBD] 417
Islam v London Borough of Hillingdon [HL] 901
JB Developments (Godalming) Ltd, Blacklocks v [ChD] 392
JEB Fasteners Ltd v Marks, Bloom & Co (a firm) [QBD] 289
Janov v Morris [CA] 780
Jogoo, The [QBD] 634
Joslin, Burditt v [QBD] 203
Kooragang Investments Pty Ltd v Richardson & Wrench Ltd [PC] 65
Lane, Phonogram Ltd v [CA] 182
Latchford v Beirne [QBD] 705
Laura Prima, The [HL] 737
Lavin, Albert v [HL] 878
Law Society, Swain v [CA] 797
Leeds Justices, R v, ex parte Hanson [QBD] 72
Lewisham (London Borough) v M [FamD] .. 307
Littell, R v [CA] 1

	Page
London Borough of Hackney v Ezedinma [QBD]	438
London Borough of Hillingdon, Islam v [HL]	901
London Borough of Lewisham v M [FamD]	307
London Borough of Wandsworth, Din v [HL]	881
Lowrie (a bankrupt), Re, ex parte the trustee of the bankrupt v The bankrupt [ChD]	353
M, London Borough of Lewisham v [FamD]	307
M Eregli, The [QBD]	344
McGovern v Attorney General [ChD]	493
Manson (John) Ltd, Goldup v [QBD]	257
Marie Leonhardt, The [QBD]	664
Marks, Bloom & Co (a firm), JEB Fasteners Ltd v [QBD]	289
Marshall v Cottingham [ChD]	8
Midland Bank Trust Co Ltd v Green (No 3) [CA]	744
Miller v F A Sadd & Son Ltd [QBD]	265
Miller v Pickering Bull & Co Ltd [QBD]	265
Mineralimportexport, Clipper Maritime Co Ltd v [QBD]	664
Modern Injection Moulds Ltd, Alex Lawrie Factors Ltd v [QBD]	658
Morris, Janov v [CA]	780
Munro and anor (bankrupts), (Trustee of the property of), Singer v [ChD]	215
National Bank of Kuwait SAK, Power Curber International Ltd v [CA]	607
Nereide SpA di Navigazione v Bulk Oil International Ltd [HL]	737
Nessdale Ltd, Cohen v [QBD]	118
North West Leicestershire District Council v East Midlands Housing Association Ltd [CA]	364
Oakacre Ltd v Claire Cleaners (Holdings) Ltd [ChD]	667
Occasions Textiles Ltd, Suedeclub Co Ltd v [ChD]	671
Occidental Petroleum Corpn v Buttes Gas and Oil Co (Nos 1 & 2) [HL]	616
Olugboja, R v [CA]	443
Patel, R v [CA]	94
Phekoo, R v [CA]	84
Phonogram Ltd v Lane [CA]	182
Pickering Bull & Co Ltd, Miller v [QBD]	265
Pieck, R v [CJEC]	46
Power Curber International Ltd v National Bank of Kuwait SAK [CA]	607
Practice Direction (Commercial Court: Urgent matters) [QBD]	864
Practice Direction (Counsel: Fees: Accident cases) [Sup Ct Taxing Office]	480
Practice Direction (Criminal Law: Costs: Acquittal) [CA]	703
Practice Direction (Crown Court: Bail) [LCJ]	433
Practice Direction (Tape recorder) [SupCt]	848
Practice Direction (Trial: London) [QBD]	61
Prescott v Bulldog Tools Ltd [QBD]	869
Preston, Gaskill v [QBD]	427
Procedure Direction (House of Lords: Security for costs) [HL]	7
Proodos C, The [QBD]	189
Public Prosecutor, Haw Tua Tau v [PC]	14
R v Chief Constable of the Devon and Cornwall Constabulary, ex parte Central Electricity Generating Board [CA]	826
R v Crown Court at Knightsbridge, ex parte International Sporting Club (London) Ltd [QBD]	417
R v de Vere [CA]	473
R v Folkestone and Hythe Juvenile Court, ex parte R (a juvenile) [QBD]	840
R v Governor of Pentonville Prison, ex parte Singh [QBD]	23
R v Heron [CA]	641
R v Howell [CA]	383
R v Immigration Appeal Tribunal, ex parte Shaikh [QBD]	29
R v Leeds Justices, ex parte Hanson [QBD]	72
R v Littell [CA]	1
R v Olugboja [CA]	443
R v Patel [CA]	94

	Page
R v Phekoo [CA]	84
R v Pieck [CJEC]	46
R v Reynolds [CA]	849
R v Rochdale Justices, ex parte Allwork [QBD]	434
R v Uxbridge Justices, ex parte Comr of Police of the Metropolis [CA]	129
R v Wells Street Magistrates' Court, ex parte Albanese [QBD]	769
R (a juvenile), ex parte, R v Folkestone and Hythe Juvenile Court [QBD]	840
Rawlinson, Crossley v [QBD]	674
Reel v Holder [CA]	321
Regent OHG Aisenstadt und Barig v Francesco of Jermyn Street Ltd [QBD]	327
Reynolds, R v [CA]	849
Richardson & Wrench Ltd, Kooragang Investments Pty Ltd v [PC]	65
Rochdale Justices, R v, ex parte Allwork [QBD]	434
Routhan v Arun District Council [CA]	752
Royal Bank of Canada, United City Merchants (Investments) Ltd v [CA]	142
Royal Borough of Windsor and Maidenhead v Brandrose Investments Ltd [ChD]	38
Sadd (F A) & Son Ltd, Miller v [QBD]	265
Sampson v Hodson-Pressinger [CA]	710
Savoy Hotel Ltd, Re [ChD]	646
Secretary of State for Trade, Air Canada v [QBD]	336
Selim Ltd v Bickenhall Engineering Ltd [ChD]	210
Shaikh, ex parte, R v Immigration Appeal Tribunal [QBD]	29
Singer v Trustee of the property of Munro and anor (bankrupts) [ChD]	215
Singh, ex parte, R v Governor of Pentonville Prison [QBD]	23
Sony Corpn v Time Electronics [ChD]	376
St Piran Ltd, Re [ChD]	270
Sterling Mansell Ltd, Aspinall v [QBD]	866
Sudbrook Trading Estate Ltd v Eggleton [CA]	105
Suedeclub Co Ltd v Occasions Textiles Ltd [ChD]	671
Swain v Law Society [CA]	797
Syros Shipping Co SA v Elaghill Trading Co [QBD]	189
Talbot, Faulkner v [QBD]	468
Tate & Lyle Food and Distribution Ltd v Greater London Council [QBD]	716
Texas Commerce International Bank Ltd, Amalgamated Investment & Property Co Ltd (in liquidation) v [CA]	577
Thompson, Hayward v [CA]	450
Time Electronics, Sony Corpn v [ChD]	376
Toepfer (Alfred C), Cerealmangimi SpA v [QBD]	533
Tradax Internacional SA v Cerrahogullari TAS [QBD]	344
Trendtex Trading Corpn v Crédit Suisse [HL]	520
Trustee of the Property of Munro and anor (bankrupts), Singer v [ChD]	215
United City Merchants (Investments) Ltd v Royal Bank of Canada [CA]	142
Uxbridge Justices, R v, ex parte Comr of Police of the Metropolis [CA]	129
W (a minor), Re [CA]	401
WG Stores Ltd, Alan Estates Ltd v [CA]	481
Wagener, West Mercia Constabulary v [QBD]	378
Wandsworth (London Borough), Din v [HL]	881
Warden v Warden [CA]	193
Weller v Akehurst [ChD]	411
Wells Street Magistrates' Court, R v, ex parte Albanese [QBD]	769
West Mercia Constabulary v Wagener [QBD]	378
West Midlands (Chief Constable), Hunter v [HL]	727
Wheeler v Copas [QBD]	405
Windsor and Maidenhead (Royal Borough) v Brandrose Investments Ltd [ChD]	38
Winson, The [HL]	688
Wiseman, Croke (a minor) v [CA]	852
Wood, Allied Collection Agencies Ltd v [QBD]	176
Yianni v Edwin Evans & Sons (a firm) [QBD]	592

R v Littell

COURT OF APPEAL, CRIMINAL DIVISION
WATKINS LJ, CANTLEY AND HOLLINGS JJ
22nd, 26th JANUARY, 6th MARCH 1981

Road traffic – Breath test – Inflation of bag in requisite manner – Provision of specimen of breath in sufficient quantity to enable test to be carried out – Provision of specimen in more than one breath – Specimen so provided not of quality required to give reliable indication of proportion of alcohol in blood – Whether failure to provide specimen of breath – Road Traffic Act 1972, s 12(1) (3).

A police constable stopped the appellant when he noticed that the appellant had been driving his car in a markedly erratic manner. The appellant smelled of drink, was unsteady and appeared to be under the influence of alcohol. He was arrested pursuant to s 5(5) of the Road Traffic Act 1972 as being unfit to drive through drink or drugs and taken to a police station, where, pursuant to s 8(7) of the 1972 Act, he was given an opportunity to provide a specimen of breath for a breath test. The appellant agreed to provide a specimen, the breath test device was assembled and the appellant was told, in accordance with the manufacturer's instructions issued with the device, to inflate the bag in one breath in not less than 10 or more than 20 seconds. It was emphasised that the bag had to be inflated in one breath. The appellant took ten short puffs of breath and fully inflated the bag. The result did not indicate an alcohol proportion above the prescribed limit. The inspector at the police station took the view that a proper test had not been carried out. The appellant was given three more opportunities to provide a specimen, on each of which the appellant took at least five short puffs and in none of which was the bag fully inflated. The inspector decided that the appellant had failed to provide a specimen of breath for the purposes of the 1972 Act and accordingly required him under s 9 thereof to provide a specimen of blood or urine for a laboratory test. The appellant provided a specimen of blood which subsequent analysis showed to contain nearly twice the permitted proportion of alcohol. Following a ruling by the judge that the appellant had failed to provide a proper specimen of breath for a breath test by failing to inflate the bag in one breath and that the evidence of the analysis of the specimen of blood was therefore admissible, the appellant pleaded guilty to a charge of driving a motor vehicle when he had a blood-alcohol concentration above the prescribed limit, contrary to s 6(1) of the 1972 Act, and was convicted accordingly. He appealed against conviction on the ground that the judge's ruling was wrong.

Held – Since s 12(1)[a] of the 1972 Act provided that a 'breath test' meant a test for the purpose of obtaining an indication of the proportion of alcohol in a person's blood carried out by means of an approved device on a specimen of breath provided by that person and

---

a Section 12, so far as material, provides:
    '(1) In sections 6 to 11 of this Act, except so far as the context otherwise requires—"breath test" means a test for the purpose of obtaining an indication of the proportion of alcohol in a person's blood carried out by means of a device of a type approved for the purpose of such a test by the Secretary of State, on a specimen of breath provided by that person . . .
    '(3) References in sections 8, 9 and 11 of this Act to providing a specimen of breath for a breath test are references to providing a specimen thereof in sufficient quantity to enable that test to be carried out . . .'

since by s 12(3) of that Act a 'specimen of breath for a breath test' referred to a specimen
in sufficient quantity to enable that test to be carried out, it followed that to hold that a
specimen of breath, which had been provided in such a way as to defeat the purpose of *a*
the breath test by making it impossible to obtain by means of the approved device a
reliable indication whether the proportion of alcohol in the tested person's blood
exceeded the prescribed limit, constituted a 'specimen of breath for a breath test' would
be to ignore the declared purpose which was part of the definition of a 'breath test' within
s 12(1). Accordingly, even though s 12(3) referred to the quantity of the specimen and *b*
not to its quality, it followed that, if a person provided the quantity asked for but, by
ignoring the instructions he had been given for its provision, provided it in such a way
that it was of a quality which did not and could not indicate the proportion of alcohol in
his blood and was no reliable indication of whether that proportion exceeded the
prescribed limit, the test contemplated by the 1972 Act had not been carried out. Since
it was clear from the subsequent laboratory test on the specimen of blood provided by *c*
the appellant that the specimen of breath he had provided was useless for the purpose of
indicating the proportion of alcohol in his blood, it followed that he had failed to provide
a specimen of breath and the police inspector had accordingly been entitled to require
the appellant to provide a specimen of blood for a laboratory test, evidence of the result
of which was admissible. The appeal would therefore be dismissed (see p 4 *j* to p 5 *b* and
p 7 *a* to *c*, post). *d*

Dicta of Lord Pearson and of Lord Diplock in *Director of Public Prosecutions v Carey*
[1969] 3 All ER at 1674, 1678 and of Lord Diplock and of Lord Kilbrandon in *Walker v
Lovell* [1975] 3 All ER at 113–114, 131 applied.

Dicta of Viscount Dilhorne in *Director of Public Prosecutions v Carey* [1969] 3 All ER at
1670–1671 and in *Walker v Lovell* [1975] 3 All ER at 120, 122 not followed.

Notes *e*

For the power to require a breath test and the effect of failure to take a test, see
Supplement to 33 Halsbury's Laws (3rd Edn) para 1061A.3-6.

For the Road Traffic Act 1972, ss 5, 6, 8, 9, 12, see 42 Halsbury's Statutes (3rd Edn)
1646, 1648, 1651, 1655, 1660.

Cases referred to in judgment *f*

Attorney General's Reference (No 1 of 1978) (1978) 67 Crim App R 387, [1978] RTR 377,
    CA.
Brennan v Farrell 1969 JC 45, Digest (Cont Vol D) 889, *1035qppp.
Director of Public Prosecutions v Carey [1969] 3 All ER 1662, [1970] AC 1072, [1969] 3
    WLR 1169, 134 JP 59, [1970] RTR 14, HL, Digest (Cont Vol C) 936, 322aa.
R v Chapman [1969] 2 All ER 321, [1969] 2 QB 436, [1969] 2 WLR 1004, 133 JP 405, 53 *g*
    Cr App R 336, CA, Digest (Cont Vol C) 933, 322m.
R v Holah [1973] 1 All ER 106, [1973] 1 WLR 127, 137 JP 106, 57 Cr App R 186, [1973]
    RTR 74, CA, Digest (Cont Vol D) 879, 322oc.
Walker v Lovell [1975] 3 All ER 107, [1975] 1 WLR 1141, 139 JP 708, [1974] RTR 377,
    HL, Digest (Cont Vol D) 883, 322llq.
  h

Cases also cited

R v Thorpe [1974] RTR 465, CA.
Rendell v Hooper [1970] 2 All ER 72, [1970] 1 WLR 747, DC.
Shepherd v Kavulock [1978] RTR 85, DC.

Appeal *j*

On 25th July 1979 at the Crown Court at Chelmsford before his Honour Judge Hill-
Smith the appellant, Ronald Arthur Littell, pleaded guilty to a charge of driving a motor
vehicle when he had a blood-alcohol concentration above the prescribed limit contrary
to s 6(1) of the Road Traffic Act 1972. He was sentenced to be fined £50, ordered to pay
£75 towards the prosecution costs and £100 towards his legal aid costs. The appellant
was also disqualified for holding a driving licence for 12 months. He appealed against his

a conviction on the ground that the trial judge had wrongly ruled that he had failed to provide a specimen of breath for a breath test. The facts are set out in the judgment of the court.

The appellant appeared in person.
Justin Philips for the Crown.

b   *Cur adv vult*

6th March. **CANTLEY J** read the following judgment of the court: This appeal directly raises for decision yet another entirely technical point in the lamentable jurisprudence of the breathalyser law.

Section 5(1) of the Road Traffic Act 1972 provides that a person who when driving a
c motor vehicle on a road or other public place is unfit to drive through drink or drugs shall be guilty of an offence. Section 5(5) provides that a constable may arrest without warrant a person committing an offence under this section.

Section 8(7) provides that a person arrested under s 5(5) shall while at a police station be given an opportunity to provide a specimen of breath for a breath test there.

Section 9(1) provides that a person who has been arrested under s 5(5) may while at a
d police station be required by a constable to provide a specimen for a laboratory test (which may be a specimen of blood or urine) if he has previously been given an opportunity to provide a specimen of breath for a breath test at that station under s 8(7) and either (a) it appears to a constable in consequence of the breath test that the device by means of which the test is carried out indicates that the proportion of alcohol in his blood exceeds the prescribed limit, or (b) when given the opportunity to provide that specimen
e he fails to do so.

Section 12(1) states that a breath test means a test for the purpose of obtaining an indication of the proportion of alcohol in a person's blood, carried out by means of a device of a type approved for the purpose of such a test by the Secretary of State, on a specimen of breath provided by that person. Section 12(3) provides that references in ss 8 and 9 of the 1972 Act to providing a specimen of breath for a breath test are
f 'references to providing a specimen thereof in sufficient quantity to enable that test to be carried out'.

On the evening of 20th January 1978 a police constable off duty and in plain clothes was driving his motor car along Barking Road, London E6 when he noticed a motor car ahead of him being driven in a markedly erratic manner. He drew alongside, caused the driver to stop and showed him his warrant card. The driver was the appellant. He
g smelled of drink, was unsteady and appeared to be under the influence of alcohol. The constable arrested him pursuant to the provision of s 5(5) of the 1972 Act as being unfit to drive through drink or drugs and the appellant was taken to Barking Police Station. At the police station the appellant as is required by s 8(7) was given an opportunity to provide a specimen of breath for a breath test and agreed to do so. The official Alcotest equipment was duly assembled and the appellant was told, in accordance with the
h manufacturer's instructions issued with the equipment, to inflate the bag in one breath in not less than 10 or more than 20 seconds. It was emphasised that the bag had to be inflated in one breath. The appellant then took ten short puffs of breath and fully inflated the bag. The result was negative; it did not indicate alcohol above the prescribed limit. The inspector did not regard this as a proper test. He gave the appellant further opportunities. On the second attempt the appellant took eight short puffs. The bag was
j not fully inflated. At the third attempt the appellant took seven short puffs and at the fourth attempt five short puffs. In none of these was the bag fully inflated. The inspector decided that the appellant had failed to provide a specimen of breath for the purposes of the 1972 Act and accordingly required him under s 9 to provide a specimen of blood or urine for a laboratory test. The appellant provided a specimen of blood which subsequent analysis showed contained not less than 152 mg of alcohol in 100 ml of blood. The legal limit is 80.

The appellant elected trial by jury and eventually appeared at the Crown Court at Chelmsford. He pleaded not guilty to an indictment containing two counts under the 1972 Act. The first alleged that he drove a motor vehicle when he had a blood-alcohol concentration above the prescribed limit contrary to s 6(1).

During the trial counsel for the appellant asked the judge to exclude the evidence of the result of the analysis of the blood sample on the ground that it had been unlawfully or unfairly obtained. His submission was that the appellant had not failed to provide a specimen of breath nor had the specimens he had provided indicated that the proportion of alcohol in his blood exceeded the prescribed limit and accordingly there was no power under the 1972 Act to require him to provide the specimen of blood, which it was said was unfairly obtained because the appellant had been warned under s 9(7) that his failure to provide a specimen of blood or urine would make him liable to prosecution.

The judge ruled that on the undisputed evidence the appellant had failed to provide a proper specimen of breath for a breath test by failing to inflate the bag in one breath and the evidence of the analysis of the blood test was therefore admissible. The ruling effectively deprived the appellant of his only defence to the charge under s 6(1). He therefore withdrew his plea of not guilty to that charge and admitted it and was sentenced accordingly. He now appeals against his conviction on the ground that the judge's ruling was wrong.

In *R v Chapman* [1969] 2 All ER 321, [1969] 2 QB 436 it was held that if the bag was not fully inflated in one breath that in itself constituted a failure to provide a specimen of breath for a breath test as required by the 1972 Act, with the result that the consequences of such failure prescribed by the Act would follow. A more practical view of the purpose of this legislation has since prevailed and it can now be taken as finally settled, despite some powerful dissent to the contrary on the way, that if a specimen of breath is provided which indicates a proportion of alcohol above the prescribed limit there has been no failure to provide a specimen of breath in sufficient quantity to enable the test to be carried out even though the bag has not been fully inflated and has been inflated with more than one breath. Failure to comply with the instructions for providing a specimen of breath does not of itself invalidate the test if the test result is positive: see *Director of Public Prosecutions v Carey* [1969] 3 All ER 1662, [1970] AC 1072, *R v Holah* [1973] 1 All ER 106, [1973] 1 WLR 127; *Walker v Lovell* [1975] 3 All ER 107, [1975] 1 WLR 1141 and *Attorney General's Reference (No 1 of 1978)* (1978) 67 Cr App R 387.

In this appeal we have to consider a situation where the test results were negative. At his first attempt this appellant fully inflated the bag but he did not do so in one breath as instructed. At his subsequent attempts he did not fully inflate the bag. None of his attempts produced a positive result but it was contended that, as he did fully inflate the bag the first time, he did not fail to provide a specimen of breath as required by the 1972 Act, although it is clear from the subsequent laboratory test that the specimen he provided was useless for the purpose of indicating the proportion of alcohol in his blood. It is said that he filled the bag by blowing into it and the fact that he took more than one breath to do so is a mere breach of the manufacturer's instructions and of no legal consequence. The test proved negative. It is claimed that he did not fail the test; he passed it.

So far as we have discovered there is no reported authority directly dealing with this particular point, although one would expect of this fruitful branch of litigation, where it seems that no arguable defence, however technical, is ever overlooked or abandoned, that it must have arisen before.

In our view some guidance as to the true meaning of a 'breath test' in the 1972 Act is provided in s 12(1). A 'breath test' is stated in that subsection to mean a test for the purpose of obtaining an indication of the proportion of alcohol in a person's blood. The test for this purpose must be carried out by means of an approved device on 'a specimen of breath' provided by that person. By s 12(3) that person has to provide a specimen of breath in sufficient quantity to enable the test to be carried out.

Has the stated purpose of all this procedure to be wholly ignored? We do not think so.

Section 12(3) refers to quantity and not quality; but, if the person provides the quantity
he is asked for (one bag full) but, by ignoring the instructions he has been given, provides
a it in such a way that it is of a quality which does not and could not indicate the
proportion of alcohol in his blood and is no reliable indication of whether the proportion
of alcohol in his blood exceeds the prescribed limit, has the test contemplated by the
1972 Act been carried out? Some would think not, but judicial opinion has not all been
one way.

b There are powerful dicta on either side in the speeches in the House of Lords in
Director of Public Prosecutions v Carey and *Walker v Lovell*. In *Director of Public Prosecutions
v Carey* [1969] 3 All ER 1662 at 1670–1671, [1970] AC 1072 at 1086–1087 Viscount
Dilhorne referred to *R v Chapman* and to a decision to the contrary effect in the High
Court of Justiciary in Scotland (*Brennan v Farrell* 1969 JC 45) and continued:

c 'The question which of these two decisions is right does not arise for decision in
this case, but it is to be observed that the only obligation imposed by the Act is to
provide a sufficient quantity of breath to enable the test to be made ... not a
sufficient quantity in a single breath. I do not myself find it easy to see how a breach
of the manufacturer's instructions to inflate in a single breath can be regarded as a
failure or refusal to take a test when the Act making it by s. 2(3) an offence without
reasonable excuse to provide a quantity of breath for the test does not stipulate that
d it must be in a single breath.'

He referred to the question again in *Walker v Lovell* [1975] 3 All ER 107 at 120, 122,
[1975] 1 WLR 1141 at 1156, 1158 where he said:

'In my opinion these statutory provisions make it clear that a sufficient quantity
of breath to enable a test to be carried out means in relation to the alcotest a
e sufficient quantity to inflate the bag ... Parliament could have enacted that a
failure by the motorist to comply with the maker's instructions rendered him liable
to arrest and prosecution. It did not do so. All that it provided was that failure to
provide a specimen of breath in sufficient quantity to enable a test to be carried out
rendered him liable to arrest and if without reasonable excuse, to prosecution. It
may well be that in not stipulating that a specimen must be provided in a single
f breath, Parliament left a lacuna in the Act. If so, it is not one which in my view it
would be proper for this House in its judicial capacity to attempt to fill.'

A different approach to the problem was made by Lord Pearson, Lord Diplock and
Lord Kilbrandon. In *Director of Public Prosecutions v Carey* [1969] 3 All ER 1662 at 1674,
[1970] AC 1072 at 1090 Lord Pearson said:

g 'My opinion is that there is not in this Act any absolute requirement, express or
implied, that a test in order to be a "breath test" within the meaning of the Act must
be carried out in perfect compliance with the maker's instructions. There is an
express requirement that the test must be carried out for the purpose of obtaining
an indication of the proportion of alcohol in the blood, and it follows that the police
officer must be trying to use the device correctly in order to obtain a true indication.
h I think also that there probably is an implied requirement (not adding much for
practical purposes to the express requirement) that the test must be carried out with
such accuracy as is reasonably attainable in the circumstances.'

In the same case Lord Diplock said ([1969] 3 All ER 1662 at 1678, [1970] AC 1072 at
1096):
j
'The constable conducting the test must do his honest best to see that this
instruction is complied with, but it should be treated in a common-sense way. In
the circumstances in which the first breath test at any rate is carried out little
purpose would generally be served by telling the suspect that he must take between
10 and 20 seconds to fill the bag, nor can the constable be expected to time him with
a stop watch. The sensible thing to do, and it appears to be the common practice,

is to tell the suspect to fill the bag with a single deep breath. It is, in my view,
sufficient if in the constable's bona fide judgment the way in which the bag is in fact   *a*
inflated by the suspect does not depart so widely from the instructions that it is
likely to show a significantly greater proportion of alcohol in the suspect's blood
than is actually there. There was no evidence in the present case as to what would
be the effect on the indication given by the device of a departure from this
instruction either by taking more than one breath or by taking less than ten seconds
or more than 20 seconds to fill the bag. Any departure, however, which to the   *b*
constable's knowledge would result in the device giving a lower reading of the
blood-alcohol content than the true reading can be ignored by him if the result of
the test is positive, since the test would still provide a sufficient indication that the
proportion of alcohol exceeds the prescribed limit. If, on the other hand, the
constable is not possessed of this knowledge and the departure is one which he
thinks may be sufficient to make the reading given by the device lower than the   *c*
true reading, he may require the suspect to repeat the test in accordance with the
instructions and if the suspect fails to do so the constable may arrest him under s.
2(5). If the suspect's failure is without reasonable excuse, e.g., physical disability not
due to alcohol, he also commits an offence under s. 2(3).'

Lord Diplock in that passage was referring to sections in the Road Safety Act 1967 which
contained provisions corresponding with those in the 1972 Act.   *d*

In *Walker v Lovell* [1975] 3 All ER 107 at 113–114, [1975] 1 WLR 1141 at 1147–1148
Lord Diplock referred to the approved form of breathalyser, Alcotest® 80, and continued:

'It makes use of the phenomenon that alcohol present in a person's bloodstream
passes into the air in his lungs where, almost but not quite immediately, it reaches
a state of equilibrium at which the proportion of vapourised alcohol in that air   *e*
reflects with a reasonable degree of accuracy the proportion of alcohol in his blood.
So a "specimen of breath" to be provided for a breath test as defined in s 12(1) must
mean air that has been drawn into and exhaled from the lungs of the person
undergoing the test ... The reason why the constable should communicate this
instruction to the person on whom the breath test is to be carried out, is because the
constable does not know in advance whether the proportion of alcohol in that   *f*
person's blood does not exceed or slightly exceeds or greatly exceeds the prescribed
limit. If the excess is only slight, failure to provide enough breath to inflate the bag
may defeat the purpose of a "breath test" by making it impossible to obtain by
means of the Alcotest R80 an indication that the proportion of alcohol in his blood
exceeds the prescribed limit, though such is indeed the fact. The same consequence
may follow from using more than a single breath to inflate the bag; for to take a   *g*
fresh breath may result in the specimen of breath provided containing a larger
proportion of air that has not been drawn into and exhaled from the lungs than
would be the case if it were provided in a single breath. Mere failure by a person on
whom a breath test has been carried out to have followed the instructions of the
constable is not an offence under the Act; nor does it, in my view, constitute a
failure to provide a specimen of breath for a breath test within the meaning of s 8(5),   *h*
unless the result of his departing from those instructions has been to defeat the
purpose of the breath test by making it impossible to obtain by means of the
Alcotest R80 a reliable indication whether or not the proportion of alcohol in *his*
blood exceeds the prescribed limit.'

Lord Kilbrandon in the same case said ([1975] 3 All ER 107 at 131, [1975] 1 WLR 1141
at 1167):   *j*

'If too little air is put into the bag, and the crystals do not change colour, the test
has not been properly conducted, because the conclusion to be drawn from the non-
change may be either that the proportion in the body is less than that forbidden, or
that the amount of air exhaled has been inadequate to cause the change of colour to
occur, although the forbidden proportion be present. The same is true, mutatis

a   mutandis, if the bag has been inflated in short puffs. In such circumstances a constable would be entitled to arrest the motorist for failing to take the test.'

We respectfully agree with the opinions of Lord Pearson, Lord Diplock and Lord Kilbrandon, which we believe correctly interpret what is meant by a 'breath test' in s 12(1) of the 1972 Act. To hold that the negative specimen of breath, provided in the way in which it was provided by the appellant in the present case, constituted 'a specimen of breath for a breath test' would, in our view, be to ignore the declared purpose which is
b   part of the definition of a 'breath test' in s 12(1).

The inspector was right when he decided that the appellant had failed to provide a specimen of breath for the breath test. Accordingly he was entitled to require the specimen of blood for a laboratory test, and the evidence of the result of that test was admissible.

The appeal is dismissed.
c

Appeal dismissed.

Solicitors: *R E T Birch* (for the Crown).

Sepala Munasinghe Esq   Barrister.
d

Procedure Direction

e   HOUSE OF LORDS
House of Lords – Costs – Security for costs – Increase in amount of security.

House of Lords – Costs – Taxation – Bills of costs lodged for taxation to be drawn in accordance with revised scales.

f   (1) *Security for costs*
    The House of Lords has ordered the doubling of all forms of security lodged by appellants in appeals to the House of Lords presented on or after 1st October 1981 as follows: (a) by payment into the House of Lords' Security Fund Account of the sum of four thousand pounds, such sum to be subject to the order of the House in regard to the costs of the appeal; or (b) by payment of the sum of two thousand pounds into the House
g   of Lords' Security Fund Account, and by entering into a recognisance, in person or by substitute, to the amount of two thousand pounds; or (c) by procuring two sufficient sureties, to the satisfaction of the Clerk of the Parliaments, to enter into a joint and several bond to the amount of two thousand pounds, and by entering a recognisance, in person or by substitute, to the amount of two thousand pounds.

These increases were approved by the House of Lords' Offices Committee (Fourth
h   Report, 21st July 1981) and subsequently by the House of Lords on 30th July 1981.

(2) *Forms of bills of costs*
    The House of Lords has also ordered a revision of the Forms of Bill of Costs applicable to Judicial Taxations in the House of Lords.

From 1st October 1981 and until 31st March 1982 bills drawn on the revised and the
j   1977 scales will be accepted for taxation but thereafter all bills of costs lodged for taxation in the House of Lords should be drawn in accordance with the revised scales.

This revision was approved by the Appeal Committee and agreed to by the House of Lords on 23rd July 1981.

PETER HENDERSON
Clerk of the Parliaments.

30th July 1981

Marshall v Cottingham   *a*

CHANCERY DIVISION

SIR ROBERT MEGARRY V-C

11th, 12th DECEMBER 1980, 30th JANUARY 1981

Mortgage – Receiver – Appointment under debenture – Remuneration – Debenture not specifying   *b*
rate of commission – Debenture extending statutory powers of receiver by giving power of sale
and providing that receiver's remuneration 'and the costs of realisation' to be paid out of proceeds
of sale – Whether receiver entitled to retain commission at rate of 5% out of gross proceeds of sale
without application to court – Whether agents' fees and expenses, costs of conveyance and
caretaker's wages pending sale deductible from commission as part of 'costs, charges, and
expenses' incurred by receiver – Law of Property Act 1925, s 109(6).

   c

A company which owned premises issued a debenture to a bank to secure money due
from it to the bank. Clause 8 of the debenture, which was expressed to take effect by way
of variation and extension of the provisions of ss 99 to 109 of the Law of Property Act
1925, gave the bank power, after demanding payment of money secured by the
debenture, to appoint a receiver of the 'premises hereby charged', gave the receiver a   *d*
power of sale and provided that all money received by him should be applied 'first in
payment of his . . . remuneration and the costs of realisation'. The debenture did not
specify the receiver's rate of commission. Subsequent to the issuing of the debenture the
company executed a legal charge on the premises in favour of the plaintiff to secure
money he had paid to the company. The bank, having demanded payment of money
secured by the debenture, appointed a receiver of the premises under the debenture and   *e*
later the receiver sold the premises for £125,000. In proceedings brought by the
plaintiff seeking payment by the receiver of the balance of the net proceeds of the sale in
his hands, the receiver applied by summons for determination of the questions (i)
whether on the true construction of s 109(6)[a] of the 1925 Act he was entitled, in the
absence of a specified rate of commission in the debenture, to retain a commission of 5%
on the gross amount of the money received by him, for his remuneration and in   *f*
satisfaction of all costs, charges and expenses incurred by him as receiver, without
applying to the court, and (ii) whether the agents' fees and expenses on the sale, the
conveyancing costs of the sale and the wages paid to a caretaker of the premises pending
the sale were to be treated as part of the 'costs, charges, and expenses incurred by him as
receiver', within s 109(6), and were therefore payable out of his commission.

   g

Held – (1) On the true construction of s 109(6) of the 1925 Act a receiver appointed
under an instrument which did not specify his rate of commission was entitled without
applying to the court to retain commission at the rate of 5% on the gross amount of the
money he received, as his remuneration and in satisfaction of all costs, charges and
expenses incurred by him as receiver, and s 109(6) only required an application to the
court where the receiver wished to obtain a rate of commission higher than 5% (see p 12   *h*
e f, post).

(2) Since the receiver had not been appointed solely under the 1925 Act but under a
debenture which extended the provisions of that Act by appointing him a receiver of the
premises charged, and not merely a receiver of the income, and by giving him a power
of sale, and since the debenture expressly provided that money received by the receiver
was, after payment of his remuneration, to be applied in payment of 'the costs of   *j*
realisation' and that phrase included the agents' fees and expenses on the sale of the
premises, the conveyancing costs and the caretaker's wages pending the sale, those items

---

a   Section 109(6) is set out at p 10 g, post

did not fall to be paid out of the receiver's commission as part of the 'costs, charges, and
a expenses incurred by him as receiver' within s 109(6) (see p 13 *e* to *g*, post).

Notes
For a receiver's right to remuneration, see 32 Halsbury's Laws (4th Edn) para 748.
For the Law of Property Act 1925, s 109, see 27 Halsbury's Statutes (3rd Edn) 516.

b **Cases referred to in judgment**
Hanlon v Law Society [1980] 2 All ER 199, [1981] AC 124, [1980] 2 WLR 756, HL; *affg in
part, rvsg in part* [1980] 1 All ER 763, [1981] AC 124, [1980] 2 WLR 756, CA.
Steel (deceased), Re, Public Trustee v Christian Aid Society [1978] 2 All ER 1026, [1979] Ch
218, [1978] 2 WLR 950, Digest (Cont Vol E) 650, 3688a.

c **Summons**
Barrie Cottingham, the receiver under a debenture dated 2nd April 1974, who was the
defendant in proceedings by originating summons brought by the plaintiff, Brian
Marshall, for payment of the balance in the receiver's hands of the proceeds of sale of
premises at Spitalgate Mill, Grantham, Lincolnshire, applied by a summons dated 17th
October 1980 for the following relief: (1) the determination of the following questions:
d (i) whether on the true construction of s 109(6) of the Law of Property Act 1952 he was
entitled, in default of application to the court, to retain for his remuneration and in
satisfaction of all costs, charges and expenses incurred by him as a receiver a commission
at the rate of 5% on the gross amount of all money received by him, and, if so, (ii)
whether he was required to treat agents' fees and expenses on the sale of Spitalgate Mill,
the conveyancing costs of the sale and the costs of a caretaker pending the sale as
e deductible from his commission as part of the costs, charges and expenses incurred by
him as receiver, (2) further or alternatively that the rate of commission be determined by
the court, and (3) that provision be made for the costs of the application. The facts are set
out in the judgment.

William Blackburne for the plaintiff.
f *B C Maddocks* for the receiver.

Cur adv vult

30th January. **SIR ROBERT MEGARRY V-C** read the following judgment: This
summons raises two questions about a receiver appointed by a mortgagee. The first is
g purely on the construction of the Law of Property Act 1925, s 109(6), and the second is
a mixed question of the construction and application of that subsection as incorporated
in a debenture and extended by it. There appears to be no authority on or near either
question, and although some authorities were put before me, I was able to derive little
assistance from any of them. In essence, the first question is whether, in the absence of
any rate specified in his appointment or in any order of the court, the receiver is entitled,
h in the language of the subsection, to retain 'a commission' at the rate of 'five per centum'
on the gross amount of all money received, as his 'remuneration', and 'in satisfaction of
all costs, charges, and expenses incurred by him as receiver'. The second question is
whether, on the receiver selling buildings included in the receivership, he is required to
treat the agents' fees and expenses, the conveyancing costs and the wages paid to a
caretaker pending the sale as part of the 'costs, charges, and expenses incurred by him as
j receiver', and so as being payable out of his commission. To these questions counsel for
the receiver answers Yes and No respectively, whereas counsel for the second mortgagee,
the plaintiff, who is entitled to the balance after paying the receiver, gives the opposite
answers. The summons, which was taken out by the receiver, also asks further or
alternatively for the determination of the rate of commission by the court. The
summons, I should add, was taken out by the receiver in proceedings by way of

originating summons brought against him by the second mortgagee, the plaintiff, seeking payment to him of the balance of moneys in the hands of the receiver.

    a

The premises in question are known as Spitalgate Mill, at Grantham in Lincolnshire. A company called Spitalgate Ltd was incorporated in May 1973, and bought the mill in July of that year: the plaintiff was a director of the company. The mill was converted into a combination of hotel, restaurant, public house and discotheque; and on 2nd April 1974 the company issued a debenture to a bank to secure all money and liabilities then or thereafter to become due. In January 1975 the company executed a legal charge in *b*
favour of the plaintiff to secure £34,750 paid by him to the company. The venture did not prosper, and on 4th August 1975 the bank demanded payment of the money secured by the debenture; and the next day, by an instrument in writing, the bank, as it was entitled to do under the debenture, appointed the receiver to be the receiver of all the property subject to the debenture. This instrument did not specify any rate of commission for the receiver. The debenture gave the receiver a power of sale without *c*
the restrictions imposed by the Law of Property Act 1925, s 103, as well as many other powers. On 25th November 1975 the receiver accepted an offer of £125,000 for the mill, and the sale was duly completed on 20th February 1976 by a conveyance by the company and the receiver to the purchaser. A compulsory winding-up order against the company was made on 15th July 1977; and in October 1978 the receiver paid the plaintiff £10,000 on account of the surplus proceeds of sale. *d*

I think that I can now turn to the Law of Property Act 1925. Section 101(1)(iii) provides that a mortgagee is to have power, when the mortgage money has become due, to appoint a receiver of the income of the mortgaged property. Section 109(1) provides that a mortgagee entitled to appoint a receiver under the power conferred by the Act is not to appoint a receiver until he has become entitled to exercise the power of sale conferred by the Act, but that he may then appoint a receiver by writing under his *e*
hand. The section continues with various other provisions relating to 'a receiver appointed under the powers conferred by this Act' and 'the receiver'. I pause there to say that in the present case, cl 8 of the debenture gave the bank power, as soon as it had demanded payment of any money secured by the debenture, to appoint a receiver of 'the premises hereby charged', and not merely the income thereof, and that the appointment of the receiver was expressed in like terms. Further, all the provisions of cl 8 were *f*
expressed as taking effect by way of variation and extension of the provisions of ss 99 to 109 (inclusive) of the Law of Property Act 1925, which provisions, as so varied and extended, were to be regarded as incorporated in the debenture. I then come to s 109(6). That reads as follow:

> 'The receiver shall be entitled to retain out of any money received by him, for his *g*
> remuneration, and in satisfaction of all costs, charges, and expenses incurred by him
> as receiver, a commission at such rate, not exceeding five per centum on the gross
> amount of all money received, as is specified in his appointment, and if no rate is so
> specified, then at the rate of five per centum on that gross amount, or at such other
> rate as the court thinks fit to allow, on application made by him for that purpose.'

    h

Apart from substituting 'other rate' for 'higher rate', this provision reproduces the Conveyancing Act 1881, s 24(6), down to the last comma; and it was on the last comma that counsel for the plaintiff placed considerable reliance. Two things seem plain. First, what is being considered is the 'commission' that the receiver is entitled to retain out of the money received by him; and that commission is to include two distinct matters, (a) 'his remuneration', and (b) the 'satisfaction of all costs, charges, and expenses incurred by *j*
him as receiver'. Second, the mortgagee is entitled to specify the rate of the commission in the instrument appointing the receiver, though this must not exceed 5%. That, of course, was not done in the present case: if it had been, then this case would not have arisen. Banks and other mortgagees will doubtless bear this in mind when considering the wording of their instruments of appointment.

_a_ What raises the difficulty is the last limb of the subsection, which applies 'if no rate is so specified'. In that case, the receiver may retain commission at the rate of—

'five per centum on that gross amount, or at such other rate as the court thinks fit to allow, on application made by him for that purpose.'

Omit the last comma, said counsel for the plaintiff, and it would be clear that there was a simple alternative: the rate was either to be 5%, in which case there was to be no _b_ application to the court, or else it was to be such other rate as was fixed on an application to the court. But the last comma was there, and it produced a parenthetical effect: the rate was to be 5% (or such other rate as the court allows) on application made by the receiver for that purpose. On this reading, in every case where the instrument of appointment has failed to specify a rate an application to the court to fix a rate, whether that rate is 5% or anything else, must be made by the receiver, unless, indeed, the parties _c_ agree a rate.

The primary submission of counsel for the plaintiff was on the punctuation: but he supported it by other contentions. If the receiver was entitled to 5% in any event, without any application to the court, the phrase 'such other rate' could refer only to a higher rate, since the application is to be made by the receiver, and he would not be likely to ask for less. Why, then, should the draftsman have used the word 'other' instead of _d_ 'higher'? On the other hand, if the receiver must apply to the court to get even 5%, then his opponent would be able to contend for some lower rate, and 'other' was the mot juste. Counsel for the plaintiff also referred me to some authorities cited in Daniell's Chancery Practice (8th Edn, 1914, p 1485) in support of his contention that in days gone by there was no fixed rule of a rate of 5% for receivers, but that lesser rates were sometimes fixed by the court. The book provides no direct authority on the operation _e_ of the Conveyancing Act 1881, s 24(6), for it does not mention that subsection. Indeed, there is no reference to s 24 anywhere in the chapter on receivers; but this is hardly surprising, since the chapter is directed to the appointment of receivers by the court, rather than by a mortgagee.

For the receiver, counsel in effect contended that grammatical sense must prevail over punctuation. Take a receiver who is content with 5% and does not seek any 'other _f_ rate'. On counsel for the plaintiff's parenthetic construction, the subsection provides that the commission of such a receiver is to be 'at the rate of five per centum on that gross amount ... on application made by him for that purpose.' This suffers from two grammatical defects. First, there is no verb; and legislation, though often complex, is usually grammatically orthodox. There is no 'if the court so allows' or any corresponding phrase between 'amount' and 'on application', or, indeed, anywhere else; for on this _g_ reading the phrase 'as the court thinks fit to allow', with its operative verb, stands securely tucked away in the parenthesis. Second, the words 'for that purpose' obviously refer back to the alleged parenthesis. In that parenthesis, the court is thinking fit to allow a rate other than 5%, so that 'for that purpose' must then be referring to an application made for a rate other than 5%. In the result, on this reading the court is being authorised to allow 5% if the receiver applies not for 5% but for some other rate; and, put at its _h_ lowest, that would be an eccentricity which should not lightly be imputed to Parliament.

In addition, it is to be borne in mind that the mortgagee is free, without restriction, to fix a rate of 5% (or, of course, less) in the instrument appointing the receiver, and that those who are entitled to the equity in the property have no control over this. I think it improbable that Parliament intended to provide that in every case where the mortgagee had omitted to do this an application to the court must be made, even if the receiver _j_ seeks a rate of 5% or less, and that those interested in the equity of redemption will then be able to argue the point. Why require the expense of an application to the court and confer the opportunity of opposition when the mortgagee could have unilaterally imposed the rate ab initio? What purpose is served by requiring an application to the court to be made merely because the mortgagee has omitted to take the opportunity of fixing the rate?

As for counsel for the plaintiff's point on the comma, I accept, of course, that the day is long past when the courts would pay no heed to punctuation in an Act of Parliament: *a* see *Hanlon v Law Society* [1980] 2 All ER 199 at 221, [1981] AC 124 at 197–198 per Lord Lowry. Nor do I say that a mere comma can have little force; indeed, I would be the last to deny that its presence or absence may be highly significant: see e g *Re Steel* (*deceased*), *Public Trustee v Christian Aid Society* [1978] 2 All ER 1026, [1979] Ch 218. Over two centuries ago James Burrow, the law reporter, in his Essay on Punctuation (1772, p 11), gave an illustration of the potency of punctuation in a little jingle: *b*

> 'Every lady in this land
> Hath twenty nails upon each hand
> Five and twenty on hands and feet
> And this is true, without deceit.'

Leave this unpunctuated, or with punctuation only at the end of the lines, and it seems *c* plainly untrue. Insert a comma or semi-colon at the beginning and end of the phrase 'upon each hand five', and nonsense becomes sense, albeit at the cost of some impairment of the rhythm. Yet throughout, one must remember that punctuation is normally an aid, and no more than an aid, towards revealing the meaning of the phrases used, and the sense that they are to convey when put in their setting. Punctuation is the servant and not the master of substance and meaning. Furthermore, although a pair of commas may *d* of course be used to enclose a parenthetic phrase, there is no rule of grammar, usage or common sense that requires words so enclosed to be treated as a parenthesis. If examples be required, one has to look no further than any volume of Vesey Junior's comma-encrusted reports of Lord Eldon's judgments.

In the result, therefore, I think that the submissions of counsel for the plaintiff on this point fail and the submissions of counsel for the receiver are right. If no rate of *e* commission is specified in the instrument which appoints a receiver, he is entitled to retain out of money received by him, for his remuneration, and in satisfaction of all costs, charges and expenses incurred by him as receiver, a commission at the rate of 5% on the gross amount of all moneys received, without any application to the court being needed for the purpose. If he wishes to obtain some other rate, then he must make an application to the court for that purpose. I accordingly answer Yes to question (1)(i) in the summons *f* before me.

I turn to the second question, that of the agents' fees and expenses on the sale of the property, the conveyancing costs on that sale, and the 'payroll costs', being wages paid to a caretaker pending the sale. There were also some items for rates and other matters under the head 'Various Costs', but in the end it was agreed that these were no longer in issue. Counsel for the plaintiff argued strenuously that all three items were included in *g* the phrase 'costs, charges, and expenses' which were incurred by the receiver 'as receiver' within the meaning of s 109(6), and so must be borne by the receiver out of the 5% commission that I have held him to be entitled to receive. He emphasised that all three items of expense had been incurred by the receiver acting as such, and so fell within the statutory language. He further contended that if this were wrong, and the items did not have to come out of the receiver's commission under s 109(6), they would have to be *h* fitted into s 109(8), which deals with the application of money received by the receiver. In s 109(8), the only possible home for these items was in para (i) which runs 'In discharge of all rents, taxes, rates, and outgoings whatever affecting the mortgaged property': and in this, even the word 'outgoings' was not apt for the three items. Accordingly, since s 109(8) formed a complete code for the application of money received by the receiver, the absence of any suitable place in it for the three items indicated that they were to be *j* borne by the receiver out of his commission under s 109(6).

It will be observed that this argument is based on the terms of s 109. As such, I can see some force in it, though I am far from being convinced that it is right. But even if it is, I do not think that it would be decisive of this case. What I have to consider is the position of a receiver who has been appointed not under the Law of Property Act 1925

a simpliciter, but under a debenture which incorporates and extends ss 99 to 109 of that Act. By itself, the Act gives the receiver no power of sale, and all that s 109(3) authorises the receiver to receive is the 'income of which he is appointed receiver'. Apart from the limited instance given by s 101(1)(iii), which is not relevant here, the receiver is not made a receiver of the capital or corpus.

For these reasons it has long been common in debentures to extend the statutory

b powers; and this is what has been done by cl 8 of the debenture in this case. In addition to strengthening s 109(2) as to the receiver being the agent of the morgagor, and making the company solely responsible for the receiver's acts or defaults and for his remuneration, the debenture confers not merely a power to appoint a receiver of the income, but a power to appoint a receiver 'of the premises hereby charged'. Furthermore, the receiver is given an express power to sell 'any of the property hereby charged'. As I have

c indicated, these and the other provisions of cl 8 are expressed to—

> 'take effect as and by way of variation and extension of the provisions of sections 99 to 109 inclusive of the said Act which provisions so varied and extended shall be regarded as incorporated herein.'

As s 109 is framed in relation to a power to appoint a receiver of the income who has no

d power of sale, the debenture inserts provisions to make the power appropriate to a receiver who is a receiver of the property itself and has a power of sale. One provision operates by way of adaptation of s 109(8), the subsection on which counsel for the plaintiff relied. This provision, which is inserted after the other provisions giving a power of sale and other powers, is that all money received by the receiver 'shall be applied first in payment of his . . . remuneration and the costs of realisation . . .'; and then come

e the matters specified in the first three paragraphs of s 109(8), with the reference to 'outgoings' in the first of them.

The result, in my judgment, is that if the phrase 'costs of realisation' in cl 8 include the agents' fees and expenses on the sale of the property, the conveyancing costs of that sale, and the caretaker's wages pending the sale, then the debenture has expressly provided for them to be paid out of any money received by the receiver; and as they are to be paid in

f this way, then it cannot be contended that they are nevertheless to be borne by the receiver out of his commission as part of the 'costs, charges, and expenses incurred by him as receiver' within s 109(6). It seems to me perfectly plain that these items are included in the 'costs of realisation', and that there is no ground on which it could be said that the receiver's commission must bear them. To this contention I have heard no answer. Counsel for the plaintiff, if I may say so, was barking up the wrong tree; and

g when in his reply counsel for the receiver indicated the right tree, counsel for the plaintiff had no bark left. That is the end of the matter. Counsel for the plaintiff urged on me that the receiver was doing very well in getting 5% on the gross proceeds of sale; and I can well see that a rate of 5% which would be reasonable if charged only on income might be more than is reasonable if charged on capital. However, that is a matter for the parties in agreeing the terms of the debenture, and in any case it cannot affect the

h decision on the points before me. I shall accordingly answer question (1)(ii) in the summons by saying No. On the two answers that I have given, question 2 does not arise, and I shall now hear what is to be said about costs under question 3.

Determination accordingly.

j Solicitors: *Oxley & Coward*, Rotherham (for the plaintiff); *Collyer-Bristow* (for the receiver).

Azza M Abdallah   Barrister.

Haw Tua Tau v Public Prosecutor and other appeals

PRIVY COUNCIL

LORD DIPLOCK, LORD FRASER OF TULLYBELTON, LORD SCARMAN, LORD ROSKILL AND SIR NINIAN STEPHEN

29th, 30th APRIL, 22nd JUNE 1981

Criminal evidence – Statement of accused – Cross-examination on statement – Singapore – Right of accused to make unsworn statement without subjecting himself to cross-examination abolished – Accused charged with capital offence – Accused called on to give evidence on oath or affirmation and thereby submit to cross-examination if he wished to do so – Accused warned of adverse inference from failure to exercise right to give evidence – Whether procedure for trial in breach of rules of natural justice – Whether abolition of an accused's former rights valid – Constitution of Singapore, arts 4, 9(1) – Criminal Procedure Code of Singapore (as amended by the Criminal Procedure Code (Amendment) Act 1976), ss 188(2), 195.

The three appellants were charged in Singapore with capital offences. At their trials, the presiding judge, at the conclusion of the prosecution's case, formally called on the appellants in accordance with s 188(2)[a] of the Criminal Procedure Code, as amended by the Criminal Procedure Code (Amendment) Act 1976, to give evidence on oath or affirmation in their defence if they wished to do so, warning them that if they elected to give evidence they would be liable to cross-examination and that if after being called by the court to give evidence they refused to be sworn or affirmed, or having been sworn or affirmed they, without good cause, refused to answer any question, the court in determining whether they were guilty of the offence charged might, in accordance with s 195[b] of the Code, draw inferences from such refusal. The appellants, after consulting counsel, elected to give evidence. The appellants were convicted and their appeals against their convictions were dismissed by the Court of Criminal Appeal of Singapore. The appellants appealed to the Privy Council contending that the amendments made to the Code by the 1976 Act, by which the previously existing right of an accused to make an unsworn statement of fact without subjecting himself to cross-examination was abolished, were void by virtue of art 4 of the Constitution of Singapore as being inconsistent with the provision of art 9(1) of the Constitution that 'No person shall be deprived of his life or personal liberty save in accordance with law' because the procedure for the trial of criminal offences violated a fundamental rule of natural justice, ie the privilege against self-incrimination.

Held – (1) In considering whether a particular practice adopted by a court of law offended against a fundamental rule of natural justice, that practice had to be looked at not in isolation but in the light of the part which it played in the complete judicial process. Accordingly, although it would not be regarded as contrary to natural justice to compel an accused to answer questions put to him by the judge under a system of justice in which the court itself was invested with what were in part inquisitorial functions, that did not necessarily justify compelling the accused to submit to hostile interrogation by the prosecution at a trial if the procedure was predominantly, if not exclusively, adversarial. Moreover, what might properly be regarded as rules of natural justice changed with the times (see p 21 h j, post).

(2) However, under the Criminal Procedure Code of Singapore an accused was not compelled in law to give evidence on his own behalf, although the fact that adverse

---

a   Section 188(2) is set out at p 18 c, post
b   Section 195 is set out at p 18 e to h, post

a inferences might be drawn from his failure to do so might be a strong inducement for him to do so. In any event, adverse inferences could have been drawn from the failure of an accused to go into the witness box even before the 1976 Act withdrew the former option to make an unsworn statement; that Act did not enlarge the inferences the court might draw from the failure of the accused to testify but limited them, as they had always been, to such inferences as appeared to the decider of fact to be proper in the particular case having regard to all its circumstances. It followed therefore that the

b amendments made to the Code by the 1976 Act were consistent with the Constitution of Singapore and were valid (see p 22 d to h, post).

Observations on the attitude of mind to be adopted by the decider of fact in criminal trials towards the prosecution's evidence at the conclusion of the prosecution's case (see p 19 f to p 20 c, post).

c **Notes**
For evidence of defendant as witness for defence in criminal proceedings, see 11 Halsbury's Laws (4th Edn) paras 465, 468.

Cases referred to in judgment
Ong Ah Chuan v Public Prosecutor [1980] 3 WLR 855, PC.

d *Ong Kiang Kek v Public Prosecutor* [1970] 2 MLJ 283.

Appeals
Haw Tua Tau v Public Prosecutor
Haw Tua Tau appealed pursuant to leave granted by the Board on 17th December 1980 against the decision of the Court of Criminal Appeal of Singapore (Wee Chong Jin CJ,

e Kulasekarem and D'Cotta JJ) on 7th September 1979 dismissing the appellant's appeal against his conviction on 17th April 1978 in the High Court of Singapore (Chua and Rajah JJ) of two offences of murder and his sentence of death. The facts are set out in the judgment of the Board.

Tan Ah Tee and another v Public Prosecutor
f Tan Ah Tee son of Tan Kok Ser and Low Hong Eng appealed pursuant to leave granted by the Board on 1st April 1981 against the decision of the Court of Criminal Appeal of Singapore (Wee Chong Jin CJ, Kulasekarem and Chua JJ) on 10th October 1979 dismissing the appellants' appeals against their convictions for trafficking in a controlled drug, namely diamorphine, contrary to s 3(a) of the Misuse of Drugs Act 1973 read with s 34 of the Penal Code, and sentence of death in the High Court of Singapore (Choor

g Singh and Rajah JJ) on 22nd September 1978. The facts are set out in the judgment of the Board.

Louis Blom-Cooper QC and *Alan Newman* for the appellant Haw.
George Newman QC for the appellant Tan.
George Newman QC and *George Warr* for the appellant Low.

h *Stuart McKinnon QC, Jonathan Harvie* and *Richard King* for the respondent.

30th April. At the conclusion of argument their Lordships stated that they were of the opinion that the appeals should be dismissed and that they would give their reasons for their decision at a later date.

j **LORD DIPLOCK.** These three appeals from the Court of Criminal Appeal of Singapore, which were heard together because they raised a single and identical point of law, arise out of two separate trials for different capital offences that were tried before two judges of the High Court under s 193 in the 1980 reprint of the Criminal Procedure Code. Throughout these reasons for their decision dismissing the appeals, which was given orally on 30th April 1981, their Lordships will refer to the relevant sections of the Criminal Procedure Code as they are numbered in the current reprint.

Haw Tua Tau was charged with the murder of two persons. He was convicted of both offences by the unanimous decision of the two High Court judges (Chua and Rajah JJ). He appealed against his conviction to the Court of Criminal Appeal, and his appeal was dismissed on 7th September 1979. Low Hong Eng and Tan Ah Tee were charged jointly with trafficking in 459·3g of diamorphine, a quantity that attracts a mandatory death penalty under the Misuse of Drugs (Amendment) Act 1975. They were convicted of that offence by the unanimous decision of Choor Singh and Rajah JJ, and their appeals against their convictions were dismissed by the Court of Criminal Appeal on 10th October 1979.

It is unnecessary for their Lordships to say anything about the various grounds relied on by any of the appellants in the Court of Criminal Appeal. They were plainly without merit and none of them was pursued before this Board. Nor is it necessary to say anything more about the evidence at either of the trials that led to the convictions of the appellants, except that in each of them, at the conclusion of the prosecution's case, the presiding judge addressed to the accused what since the passing of the Criminal Procedure Code (Amendment) Act 1976 has become the standard allocution, and formally called on them to give evidence; each of the accused, after consulting counsel, did in fact give evidence in his or her defence.

The standard allocution, which their Lordships will set out later in these reasons, follows closely the terms of ss 188(2) and 195(1), (2) and (3) of the Criminal Procedure Code which were inserted in the code by the 1976 Act and abolished the previously existing right of the accused to make an unsworn statement without subjecting himself to cross-examination. The only question argued before this Board was the contention, common to all three appellants, that the amendments made to the Criminal Procedure Code by the 1976 Act were inconsistent with art 9(1) of the Constitution of Singapore that 'No person shall be deprived of his life or personal liberty save in accordance with law' and, being inconsistent, were rendered void by art 4.

The whole foundation of the argument on which this contention was based was the interpretation that this Board had placed on the expression 'law' in the context of art 9(1) in *Ong Ah Chuan v Public Prosecutor* [1980] 3 WLR 855. The Board's judgment in that case was delivered on 15th October 1980, more than a year after the judgments of the Court of Criminal Appeal of Singapore in the instant appeals; so the point about the unconstitutionality of the 1976 amending Act for inconsistency with art 9(1) of the Constitution, in the form that it was presented to their Lordships in the instant appeals, was not available to be taken by the appellants in the Court of Criminal Appeal.

It was this exceptional circumstance, coupled with the fact that these are capital cases, that induced this Board to give special leave to appeal in order to raise the question of the inconsistency of the 1976 Act with art 9(1) of the Constitution of Singapore, notwithstanding that the point was not taken in the courts in Singapore. In doing so their Lordships had no intention of departing from the policy declared in *Ong Ah Chuan v Public Prosecutor* (at 859) that if at the conclusion of the argument they had entertained any doubt as to the constitutionality of an impugned Act of the Singapore Parliament they would have remitted the case to the Court of Criminal Appeal to hear argument on the constitutional point so that this Board might have the benefit of that court's opinion before reaching its own final decision. In the result, however, the arguments that have been addressed to them have not succeeded in raising in their Lordships' minds any doubt as to the constitutionality of ss 188(2) and 195(1), (2) and (3) of the Criminal Procedure Code; so no prior remission to the Court of Criminal Appeal was needed in order to enable the decision to be given on 30th April 1981 at the conclusion of the argument in these appeals.

The passage in the judgment of this Board in *Ong Ah Chuan v Public Prosecutor*, on which the appellants relied, appeared in a part of that judgment that was disposing of an extreme contention that had been made on behalf of the Public Prosecutor: that so long as the deprivation of life or personal liberty was authorised by a written law passed by the Parliament of Singapore there could be no breach of art 9(1) of the Constitution, however arbitrary and procedurally unfair that written law might be. What the Board said (at 865) in answer to that extreme contention was:

'In a Constitution founded on the Westminster model and particularly in that

a part of it that purports to assure to all individual citizens the continued enjoyment of fundamental liberties or rights, references to "law" in such contexts as "in accordance with law", "equality before the law", "protection of the law" and the like, in their Lordships' view, refer to a system of law which incorporates those fundamental rules of natural justice that had formed part and parcel of the common law of England that was in operation in Singapore at the commencement of the

b Constitution. It would have been taken for granted by the makers of the Constitution that the "law" to which citizens could have recourse for the protection of fundamental liberties assured to them by the Constitution would be a system of law that did not flout those fundamental rules. If it were otherwise it would be misuse of language to speak of law as something which affords "protection" for the individual in the enjoyment of his fundamental liberties, and the purported

c entrenchment (by article 5) of articles 9(1) and 12(1) would be little better than a mockery.'

The subsequent paragraphs of the judgment made clear their Lordships' view that neither art 9(1) nor art 12(1) called for the perpetuation of the rules of criminal procedure or of evidence as they existed in Singapore when the Constitution came into force on

d 16th September 1963. So no amendment to the Constitution is needed to empower the legislature of Singapore (the President and Parliament) to enact whatever laws it thinks appropriate to regulate the procedure to be followed at the trial of criminal offences by courts in Singapore, subject only to the limitation that so long as art 9(1) remains unamended such procedure does not offend against some fundamental rule of natural justice. It must not be obviously unfair. So the question for their Lordships is not

e whether the 1976 Act made a significant alteration to the disadvantage of accused persons in the procedure previously followed in criminal trials in Singapore (as indisputably it does), but whether the consequence of the alteration is a procedure for the trial of criminal offences that is contrary to some fundamental rule of natural justice.

It would be imprudent of their Lordships to attempt to make a comprehensive list of what constitute fundamental rules of natural justice applicable to procedure for

f determining the guilt of a person charged with a criminal offence. Nor is this necessary in order to dispose of these three appeals. The only rule alleged to be the fundamental rule of natural justice against which the appellants claim the 1976 Act offends is the so-called privilege against self-incrimination as expressed in the latin maxim nemo debet se ipsum prodere.

Under the Code of Criminal Procedure as it stood when the Constitution came into

g force in 1963, the accused had the option of either making an unsworn statement from the dock on which he could not be cross-examined, or of giving evidence on oath or affirmation and thereby submitting himself for cross-examination too. This option had been enjoyed in England since the Criminal Evidence Act 1898 first made persons accused of felony competent, though not compellable, witnesses in their own defence. The continued retention of this option on the part of the accused has been the subject of

h consideration and report in England by the Criminal Law Revision Committee in 1972 (11th Report, Evidence (General), Cmnd 4991). They strongly recommended its abolition and made provision for this in cll 4 and 5 of the draft Bill annexed to their report. No effect has yet been given to this recommendation by the Parliament of the United Kingdom; and in the meantime the recommendation has been reinforced by the approval of the Royal Commission on Criminal Procedure (in England) which reported

j as recently as January 1981 (Cmnd 8092). That the Parliament of Singapore for its part was aware of and approved and adopted this recommendation of the English Criminal Law Revision Committee as applicable to criminal procedure in Singapore is evident from the fact that the scheme and actual language of the amendments to the Criminal Procedure Code made by the 1976 Act are based on and follow closely the wording of cll 4 and 5 of the draft Bill annexed to that committee's report in 1972. Although recognising that it is not impossible, their Lordships would regard it as surprising if the distinguished English judges, jurists and legal practitioners who composed that committee should have recommended for adoption in England a procedure that was *a* contrary to a fundamental rule of natural justice.

To put the matter in perspective the provisions of the Criminal Procedure Code which it is convenient to set out are ss 188(1) and (2), 189(1) to (3), 190 and 195(1) to (3), of which ss 188(2) and 195(1) to (3) were inserted by the 1976 Act.

These provisions read as follows:

'**188.**—(1) When the case for the prosecution is concluded the court, if it finds *b* that no case against the accused has been made out which if unrebutted would warrant his conviction, shall record an order of acquittal or, if it does not so find, shall call on the accused to enter on his defence.

'(2) Before any evidence is called for the defence, the court shall tell the accused that he will be called upon by the court to give evidence in his own defence and shall tell him in ordinary language what the effect will be if, when so called upon, he *c* refuses to be sworn or affirmed, and thereupon the court shall call upon the accused to give evidence.

'**189.**—(1) The accused or his advocate may then open his case, stating the facts or law on which he intends to rely and making such comments as he thinks necessary on the evidence for the prosecution.

'(2) He may then examine his witnesses (if any) and after their cross-examination *d* and re-examination (if any) may sum up his case.

'(3) If any accused person elects to be called as a witness, his evidence shall be taken before that of other witnesses for the defence.

'**190.** In all cases the counsel for the Public Prosecutor shall have the right to reply on the whole case, whether the accused adduces evidence or not.

'**195.**—(1) In any criminal proceedings except an inquiry preliminary to *e* committal for trial, the accused shall not be entitled to make a statement without being sworn or affirmed, and accordingly, if he gives evidence, he shall do so on oath or affirmation and be liable to cross-examination; but this subsection shall not affect the right of the accused, if not represented by an advocate, to address the court otherwise than on oath or affirmation on any matter on which, if he were so represented, the advocate could address the court on his behalf. *f*

'(2) If the accused—(*a*) after being called upon by the court to give evidence or after he or the advocate representing him has informed the court that he will give evidence, refuses to be sworn or affirmed; or (*b*) having been sworn or affirmed, without good cause refuses to answer any question, the court, in determining whether the accused is guilty of the offence charged, may draw such inferences from the refusal as appear proper. *g*

'(3) Nothing in this section shall be taken to render the accused compellable to give evidence on his own behalf, and he shall accordingly not be guilty of contempt of court by reason of a refusal to be sworn or affirmed in the circumstances described in paragraph (*a*) of subsection (2).'

What has become the standard allocution given to the accused pursuant to s 188(2) was *h* given by the presiding judge to each of the appellants at their trials. Chua J addressed Haw Tua Tau in the following terms:

'... we find that the prosecution has made out a case against you on both the charges on which you are being tried which if unrebutted would warrant your conviction. Accordingly, we call on you to enter on your defence on both the charges. Before any evidence is called for the defence we have to inform you that *j* you will be called on by the court to give evidence in your own defence. You are not entitled to make a statement without being sworn or affirmed and accordingly, if you give evidence, you will do so on oath or affirmation and be liable to cross-examination. If after being called by the court to give evidence you refuse to be sworn or affirmed or having been sworn or affirmed you, without good cause,

a   refuse to answer any question, the court in determining whether you are guilty of the offence charged, may draw such inferences from the refusal as appear proper. There is nothing in the Criminal Procedure Code which renders you compellable to give evidence on your own behalf and you shall accordingly not be guilty of contempt of court by reason of a refusal to be sworn or affirmed when called on by the court to give evidence. We now call on you to give evidence in your own defence. If you have any difficulty in deciding whether or not you wish to give
b   evidence on your own behalf you may consult your counsel.'

Section 188(1) states the conditions precedent to the right and duty of the judge of trial to call on the accused to enter on his defence. It takes the form of a double negative: if the court does *not* find that *no* case against the accused has been made out which, if unrebutted, would warrant his conviction. For reasons that are inherent in the adversarial character of criminal trials under the common law system, it does not place
c   on the court a positive obligation to make up its mind at that stage of the proceedings whether the evidence adduced by the prosecution has by then already satisfied it beyond reasonable doubt that the accused is guilty. Indeed it would run counter to the concept of what is a fair trial under that system to require the court to do so.

The crucial words in s 188(1) are the words 'if unrebutted', which make the question that the court has to ask itself a purely hypothetical one. The prosecution makes out a
d   case against the accused by adducing evidence of primary facts. It is to such evidence that the words 'if unrebutted' refer. What they mean is that for the purpose of reaching the decision called for by s 188(1) the court must act on the presumptions (a) that all such evidence of primary fact is true, unless it is inherently so incredible that no reasonable person would accept it as being true, and (b) that there will be nothing to displace those inferences as to further facts or to the state of mind of the accused which would
e   reasonably be drawn from the primary facts in the absence of any further explanation. Whoever has the function of deciding facts on the trial of a criminal offence should keep an open mind about the veracity and accuracy of recollection of any individual witness, whether called for the prosecution or the defence, until after all the evidence to be tendered in the case on behalf of either side has been heard and it is possible to assess to what extent (if any) that witness's evidence has been confirmed, explained or contradicted
f   by the evidence of other witnesses.

The proper attitude of mind that the decider of fact ought to adopt towards the prosecution's evidence at the conclusion of the prosecution's case is most easily identified by considering a criminal trial before a judge and jury, such as occurs in England and occurred in Singapore until its final abolition in capital cases in 1969. Here the decision-making function is divided; questions of law are for the judge, questions of fact are for
g   the jury. It is well established that in a jury trial at the conclusion of the prosecution's case it is the judge's function to decide for himself whether evidence has been adduced which, *if it were to be accepted by the jury as accurate*, would establish each essential element in the alleged offence, for what are the essential elements in any criminal offence is a question of law. If there is no evidence (or only evidence that is so inherently incredible that no reasonable person could accept it as being true) to prove any one or more of those
h   essential elements, it is the judge's duty to direct an acquittal, for it is only on evidence that juries are entitled to convict; but, if there is *some* evidence, the judge must let the case go on. It is not the function of the jurors, as sole deciders of fact, to make up their minds at that stage of the trial whether they are so convinced of the accuracy of the only evidence that is then before them that they have no reasonable doubt as to the guilt of the accused. If this were indeed their function, since any decision that they reach must be
j   a collective one, it would be necessary for them to retire, consult together and bring in what in effect would be a conditional verdict of guilty before the accused had any opportunity of putting before them any evidence in his defence. On the question of the accuracy of the evidence of any witness jurors would be instructed that it was their duty to suspend judgment until all the evidence of fact that either party wished to put before the court had been presented. Then and then only should they direct their minds to the

question whether the guilt of the accused had been proved beyond reasonable doubt.

In their Lordships' view the same principle applies to criminal trials where the combined roles of decider of law and decider of fact are vested in a single judge (or in two judges trying capital cases). At the conclusion of the prosecution's case what has to be decided remains a question of law only. As decider of law, the judge must consider whether there is some evidence (not inherently incredible) which, if he were to accept it as accurate, would establish each essential element in the alleged offence. If such evidence as respects any of those essential elements is lacking, then, and then only, is he justified in finding 'that no case against the accused has been made out which if unrebutted would warrant his conviction', within the meaning of s 188(1). Where he has not so found, he must call on the accused to enter on his defence, and as decider of fact must keep an open mind as to the accuracy of any of the prosecution's witnesses until the defence has tendered such evidence, if any, by the accused or other witnesses as it may want to call and counsel on both sides have addressed to the judge such arguments and comments on the evidence as they may wish to advance.

Although s 188(1) first became law in 1960 and so forms no part of the amendments made by the 1976 Act, their Lordships have dealt with its interpretation at some length because in the judgment of the Court of Criminal Appeal of Singapore in *Ong Kiang Kek v Public Prosecutor* [1970] 2 MLJ 283 there are certain passages that seem, on a literal reading, to suggest that unless at the end of the prosecution's case the evidence adduced has already satisfied the judge beyond a reasonable doubt that the accused is guilty, the judge must order his acquittal. But this can hardly have been what that court intended, for it ignores the presence in the section of the crucial words 'if unrebutted', to which in other passages the court refers, and it converts the hypothetical question of law which the judge has to ask himself at that stage of the proceeding, 'If I were to accept the prosecution's evidence as accurate *would* it establish the case against the accused beyond a reasonable doubt?' into an actual and quite different question of fact, 'Has the prosecution's evidence already done so?' For the reasons already discussed their Lordships consider this to be an incorrect statement of the effect of s 188(1).

Turning now to the amendments made by the 1976 Act. Section 195(1) withdraws from accused persons the anomalous privilege which they previously enjoyed of making unsworn statements of fact without subjecting themselves to cross-examination. It was not contended on behalf of any appellant that this of itself involved a breach of any fundamental rule of natural justice.

Section 195(2) provides expressly that the court may draw such inferences as may appear proper from the failure of the accused to give evidence on oath. This, in their Lordships' view, made no change in the existing law. The Criminal Procedure Code was previously silent on the matter, and consequently s 5 made applicable the law of England relating to criminal procedure where it was not inconsistent with the code. English law has always recognised the right of the deciders of fact in a criminal trial to draw inferences from the failure of a defendant to exercise his right to give evidence and thereby submit himself to cross-examination. It would in any event be hopeless to expect jurors or judges, as reasonable men, to refrain from doing so. Although the Criminal Evidence Act 1898 prohibited the prosecution itself from inviting the jury to draw inferences from the accused's failure to testify in his own defence, it did not prohibit judges from commenting on such failure; very often the judge did comment and draw to the attention of the jury inferences that they might properly draw, if they thought fit, from the failure of the accused to go into the witness box to contradict the evidence of the prosecution on matters that were within his own knowledge or to displace a natural inference as to his mental attitude at the time of the alleged offence that, in the absence of some other explanation, would properly be drawn by any reasonable person from his conduct at that time.

Their Lordships do not find it useful to refer to recent English authorities on this subject. They are directed to the propriety of comments made by English judges to English juries in particular cases, under a system of procedure under which the jury and not the judge is the sole decider of primary facts and inferences to be drawn from them,

and the accused still has the option to make an unsworn statement instead of giving
a evidence. Neither of these features of a criminal trial in England continues to exist in
Singapore. What inferences are proper to be drawn from an accused's refusal to give
evidence depend on the circumstances of the particular case, and is a question to be
decided by applying ordinary common sense, on which the judiciary of Singapore needs
no instruction by this Board.

Section 195(3) makes it clear that the accused has a legal right to refuse to give evidence
b at his trial; no legal sanctions can be imposed on him if he chooses to remain silent. It
is only if he elects to give evidence that he exposes himself to the risk of being compelled,
under threat of legal sanctions, to answer questions put in cross-examination which, if
answered truthfully, might tend to show that he was guilty of the offence with which he
was charged. Subsection (4), which is not reproduced above, preserves to him
substantially the same protection as a defendant had previously enjoyed from being
c compelled to answer questions which would elicit his criminal record or which, if
answered, might tend to show that he had committed any crime other than that for
which he was being tried.

So, in the absence of any legal compulsion on the accused to give evidence, the
appellants are driven to base their argument on the contention that the procedure for
which s 188(2) provides of calling on the accused at the conclusion of the prosecution's
d case to give evidence and informing him of the consequences of a refusal to do so has the
practical effect of putting the accused under a compulsion to give evidence no less than
if he were compelled by law to do so, despite his being told in the course of the standard
allocution that he is not. Fundamental rules of natural justice, say the appellants, are
concerned with the practical effect on the defendant of the procedure followed, not with
its legal technicalities; and if, as the appellants claim, the maxim nemo debet se ipsum
e prodere enshrines a fundamental rule of natural justice the procedure prescribed by
s 188(2) infringes it.

In order to dispose of these appeals, however, their Lordships do not find it necessary
to decide whether by virtue of that maxim it should be recognised, as a fundamental rule
of natural justice under the common law system of criminal procedure, that a person
who is standing trial before a court of justice charged with an offence which he does not
f admit must not be ordered by the court, under threat of legal sanctions in the event of
disobedience, to disclose what he knows about the matter which is the subject of the
charge. Such a rule finds no place in the Universal Declaration of Human Rights
proclaimed by the United Nations in 1948 (UN 2 (1949); Cmd 7662) or in the European
Convention for the Protection of Human Rights and Fundamental Freedoms of 1950 (TS
71 (1953); Cmd 8969). Its non-observance involves no conflict with the undoubted
g fundamental rule of natural justice stated in art 6(2) of the convention: 'Everyone
charged with a criminal offence shall be presumed innocent until proved guilty according
to law'; and in many countries of the non-communist world, whose legal systems are not
derived from the common law, the court itself has an investigatory role to play in the
judicial process for the trial of criminal offences. In such systems interrogation of the
accused by a judge, though not direct interrogation by the prosecution, forms an essential
h part of the proceedings.

Nevertheless, in considering whether a particular practice adopted by a court of law
offends against a fundamental rule of natural justice, that practice must not be looked at
in isolation but in the light of the part which it plays in the complete judicial process.
Their Lordships accordingly recognise that the fact that, under a system of justice in
which the court itself is invested with what are in part inquisitorial functions, compelling
j an accused to answer questions put to him by a judge would not be regarded as contrary
to natural justice does not necessarily justify compelling the accused to submit to hostile
interrogation by the prosecution at a trial in which the procedure is predominantly, if
not exclusively, adversarial.

Their Lordships recognise, too, that what may properly be regarded by lawyers as rules
of natural justice change with the times. The procedure for the trial of criminal offences
in England at various periods between the abolition of the Court of Star Chamber and

High Commission in the seventeenth century and the passing of the Criminal Evidence
Act in 1898 involved practices, particularly in relation to the trial of felonies, that
nowadays would unhesitatingly be regarded as flouting fundamental rules of natural
justice. Deprivation until 1836 of the right of the accused to legal representation at his
trial and, until 1898, of the right to give evidence on his own behalf are obvious
examples. Nevertheless, throughout all that period the rule that an accused person could
not be *compelled* to submit to hostile interrogation even in trials for misdemeanours, at
which he was a competent witness on his own behalf, remained intact; and if their
Lordships had been of the opinion that there was any substance in the argument that the
effect of the amendments made to the Criminal Procedure Code by the 1976 Act was to
create a genuine *compulsion* on the accused to submit himself at his trial to cross-
examination by the prosecution, as distinguished from creating a strong *inducement* to
him to do so, at any rate if he were innocent, their Lordships, before making up their
own minds, would have felt it incumbent on them to seek the views of the Court of
Criminal Appeal whether the practice of treating the accused as not compellable to give
evidence on his own behalf had become so firmly based in the criminal procedure of
Singapore that it would be regarded there by lawyers as having evolved into a
fundamental rule of natural justice by 1963 when the constitution came into force.

There is, however, in their Lordships' view, no substance in the appellants'
argument. The accused is not compelled in law to give evidence on his own behalf.
Section 195(3) says so, and s 188(2) requires that the accused be told so. Even before
s 195(1) withdrew the former option to make an unsworn statement, instead of going
into the witness box to give evidence, the accused, if he were properly advised by counsel,
would be aware that adverse inferences might well be drawn if he failed to go into the
witness box, the strength of those inferences depending on the nature of the evidence
that had been adduced against him in the particular case. This in itself would be a strong
inducement to an accused to give evidence, particularly if he were innocent. The only
added inducement consequent on the removal of the option is the withdrawal of the
hope that he can get away with a story the truth of which cannot be tested by cross-
examination. The inferences that the court may draw from his failure to testify are not
enlarged by the amendments to the code: they are limited, as they have always been, to
such inferences as appear to the decider of fact to be proper in the particular case having
regard to all its circumstances.

It was suggested on behalf of the appellants that the fact that the accused is formally
'called on' by the court itself to give evidence provides in itself an element of compulsion;
but this occurs only after he has been told by the court that he is not compelled to do so
and there has been explained to him what the effect of a refusal will be, ie that such
adverse inferences as are proper may be drawn from his refusal. In their Lordships' view
it is only fair that an accused who is not legally represented should be warned of the risks
he runs by failing to give evidence. Where the accused is legally represented the
standard allocution ends with a recommendation to the accused to consult with his own
counsel who can advise him (as he would have done even if there had been no formal
'calling on') whether or not it is in the accused's own interests to testify on his own behalf.

Inducement there is and always has been since the accused first became a competent
witness on his own behalf; compulsion there is not. Their Lordships have no doubt at
all that the amendments to the Criminal Procedure Code made by the 1976 Act are
consistent with the Constitution of Singapore and are valid.

Finally their Lordships would mention briefly, lest it be thought that they had
overlooked it, the suggestion that at the trial of Haw Tua Tau the judge may have taken
literally those Delphic passages in the judgment of the Court of Criminal Appeal in *Ong
Kiang Kek v Public Prosecutor* to which their Lordships have had occasion to refer. If this
be so the only effect can be that the judges applied to the prosecution's evidence a more
rigorous test of credibility than they need have done before deciding to call on Haw Tua
Tau to give evidence. The error, if there was one, and there is nothing in the judges'
reasons for judgment to indicate what was the standard that they did apply, can only

have been in favour of the accused. In the other two appeals where the offence was
a trafficking in diamorphine, the statutory presumptions which this Board upheld in *Ong
Ah Chuan v Public Prosecutor* have the effect of making the two standards the same as
respects inferences to be drawn as to the guilty knowledge of the accused from the fact
of their being in possession of the drugs.

Appeals dismissed.

b

Solicitors: *Kingsford, Dorman* (for the appellant Haw); *Coward Chance* (for the appellant
Tan); *Phillip Conway, Thomas & Co* (for the appellant Low); *Jaques & Co* (for the
respondent).

Mary Rose Plummer   Barrister.

c

R v Governor of Pentonville Prison, ex parte Singh

d QUEEN'S BENCH DIVISION
ACKNER LJ AND SKINNER J
18th DECEMBER 1980, 21st JANUARY 1981

*Extradition – Committal – Evidence – Evidence sufficient to justify committal – Evidence relied
on not given under oath in requesting state – Affirmation – Statement of witness not made on oath
e – Witness acknowledging after making statement that he was aware of consequences of giving
perjured evidence – Whether 'sworn deposition or statement of witness' including affirmation –
Whether witness's statement amounting to affirmation – Whether evidence given in third state
admissible in holding state – Extradition Act 1870, s 14 – Extradition Act 1873, s 4.*

The applicant was accused of committing certain drug offences within the jurisdiction of
f Norway and the government of Norway sought his extradition under the Extradition
Acts 1870 and 1873 and the relevant extradition treaty between Norway and the United
Kingdom. At the extradition proceedings the magistrate, having heard evidence
produced by the government of Norway and submissions on behalf of both the applicant
and that government, found that there was a case to answer and committed the applicant
to await extradition to Norway. The evidence before the magistrate consisted of, inter
g alia, (i) evidence on oath before a court in Norway, (ii) statements by four persons, who
were accomplices in the alleged crimes, and (iii) evidence on oath before a court in
Denmark. The statements of the four accomplices had been given before a Norwegian
court, not under oath, and they had subsequently been reminded of a provision in the
Norwegian Penal Code which made them liable to punishment if they gave perjured
evidence in court. Three of the accomplices had stated that they had been aware of the
h provision in the code when giving their evidence. The fourth declared that, although he
had not been aware of that provision, his evidence would have been the same had he
known of it and repeated that he had told the truth. The applicant applied for a writ of
habeas corpus in respect of the warrant of committal made by the magistrate and
submitted that the material in classes (ii) and (iii) was not admissible evidence in
extradition proceedings in England and that the remaining evidence was not sufficient
j to justify the committal on the grounds that (i) s 14*a* of the 1870 Act and s 4*b* of the 1873
Act read together with the relevant extradition treaty required that the evidence of the
requesting state, ie Norway, had to be taken on oath if it was to be admissible in the

---

a Section 14 is set out at p 26 *c*, post
b Section 4 is set out at p 26 *e*, post

courts of the United Kingdom, (ii) alternatively, if evidence could be taken on
affirmation, the procedure which took place in Norway was deficient to such a degree as
to make the material inadmissible in the United Kingdom because it did not comply
with the 1870 and 1873 Acts or the treaty and neither did it comply with the United
Kingdom rules as to the competence of witnesses or admissibility of evidence, and (iii)
art Xᶜ of the treaty did not permit evidence on oath or otherwise given in a third state to
be admissible in a holding state.

Held – (1) Article X of the treaty did not permit evidence, whether on oath or otherwise,
given in a third state to be admissible in a holding state, and accordingly the evidence
given in court in Denmark was not admissible in proceedings in the United Kingdom for
the extradition of a person to Norway (see p 26 *b*, post).

(2) Having regard to the fact that one of the effects of the treaty was to avoid the
necessity of bringing witnesses from overseas, the words 'sworn deposition or statement
of witnesses' in art X of the treaty were to be given a liberal interpretation and included
an affirmation (see p 26 *f* to *j* and p 28 *f g*, post); dicta of Lord Russell CJ in *Re Arton (No
2)* [1896] 1 QB at 517 and of Lord Widgery CJ in *R v Governor of Pentonville Prison, ex parte
Ecke* [1974] Crim LR 102 applied.

(3) The question of what amounted to an affirmation was a matter of fact and degree
dependent on the particular circumstances of the case, and it need not have taken place
prior to the making of the statement. Where the statement had been made and later
accepted or adopted, its adoption had to be made in circumstances which recognised the
gravity and importance of the truth being told on the particular occasion. Although a
mere acknowledgment, albeit before a judicial authority, that what had been previously
said was the truth could not amount to an affirmation, in the circumstances the
acknowledgment made by the accomplices had been made before the judicial authority
after the terms of the substance of the Norwegian Penal Code had been drawn to their
attention. Accordingly the subsequent acknowledgment of the truth of what they had
previously said amounted to a sufficient acknowledgment. The application for a writ of
habeas corpus would therefore be dismissed (see p 27 *f* to *j* and p 29 *a* to *e*, post).

Notes

For evidence required for extradition, see 18 Halsbury's Laws (4th Edn) para 225 and for
cases on the subject, see 24 Digest (Reissue) 1137–1138, 12,055–12,074.

For the Extradition Act 1870, s 14, see 13 Halsbury's Statutes (3rd Edn) 259.

For the Extradition Act 1873, s 4, see ibid 270. •

Cases referred to in judgments

Arton, Re (No 2) [1896] 1 QB 509, 65 LJMC 50, 74 LT 249, 60 JP 132, 18 Cox CC 177, DC,
24 Digest (Reissue) 1125, 11946.

R v Governor of Brixton Prison, ex parte Twena (27th November 1980, unreported), DC.

R v Governor of Pentonville Prison, ex parte Ecke [1974] Crim LR 102, DC.

Cases also cited

R v Bitterlin (1913) 48 L Jo 371.

R v Governor of Ashford Remand Centre, ex parte Beese [1973] 3 All ER 250, [1973] 1 WLR
969, DC; *affd* [1973] 3 All ER 689, [1973] 1 WLR 1426, HL. •

R v Governor of Gloucester Prison, ex parte Miller [1979] 2 All ER 1103, [1979] 1 WLR 539,
DC.

R v Governor of Pentonville Prison, ex parte Kirby [1979] 2 All ER 1094, [1979] 1 WLR 541,
DC.

Application

Harmohan Singh applied for a writ of habeas corpus directed to the Governor of
Pentonville Prison, where the applicant was detained in respect of a warrant of committal

a issued by the Chief Metropolitan Stipendiary Magistrate at Bow Street on 23rd October 1980. The government of Norway, which was also a respondent to the application, had sought the applicant's extradition under the Extradition Acts 1870 and 1873 in respect of drug offences committed within the jurisdiction of the government of Norway. The evidence relied on by the Norwegian government at the extradition proceedings consisted of, inter alia, (i) statements made by four accomplices who had subsequently acknowledged their statements and (ii) evidence on oath by witnesses before a court in

b Copenhagen. The facts are set out in the judgment of Ackner LJ.

Richard Du Cann QC and *Andrew Trollope* for the applicant.
David Tudor Price and *Clive Nicholls* for the respondents.

Cur adv vult

c
21st January. The following judgments were read.

ACKNER LJ. Harmohan Singh applies for a writ of habeas corpus in respect of a warrant of committal issued by the Chief Metropolitan Stipendiary Magistrate at Bow Street on 23rd October 1980. The government of Norway allege that the applicant is

d accused of the commission of the crimes of conspiring to supply a dangerous drug, supplying a dangerous drug and being knowingly concerned in carrying, removing, depositing, harbouring, keeping or concealing or in any manner dealing with a dangerous drug in respect of which a prohibition on importation is, for the time being, in force within the jurisdiction of the government of Norway. The drugs involved are alleged to be morphine and heroin. The magistrate, having heard evidence produced by

e the government of Norway and submissions on behalf of both the applicant and that government, held that there was a case to answer, and committed the applicant to prison to await his extradition to Norway.

Counsel for the applicant in his most helpful, clear and concise submissions has pointed out that the evidence fell into four different classes: (1) evidence on oath before the court in Oslo; (2) statements by four persons, two Norwegians and two Indians, who

f were accomplices to the alleged crimes; they had all been arrested in Norway prior to signing their statements; (3) evidence on oath by witnesses who gave evidence before a court in Copenhagen; (4) evidence of English police officers given under s 9 of the Criminal Justice Act 1967.

Counsel submitted that the material in classes (2) and (3) was not admissible evidence in extradition proceedings in England, and the remaining evidence was not sufficient to

g justify the committal. He made four submissions. (1) The Extradition Acts 1870 and 1873 read together with the relevant treaty required that the evidence taken in the requesting state, that is Norway, has to be taken on oath if it is to be admissible in the courts in this country. (2) Alternatively, if the above proposition is too wide and evidence can be taken on affirmation, then the procedure which took place in Norway was deficient to such a degree as to make the material inadmissible in this country. The

h procedure was deficient because, (a) it did not comply with the Acts and the treaty and (b) it did not comply with United Kingdom rules as to competence of witnesses or admissibility of evidence. (3) In relation to the evidence given in the court in Copenhagen, the treaty did not permit evidence, whether on oath or otherwise, given in a third state to be admissible in a holding state. (4) On the assumption that the above three submissions were correct, or alternatively that the first two submissions were

j correct, the remaining evidence was insufficient to justify the committal.

It is convenient to deal first of all with the third submission. The treaty relied on, concluded on 26th June 1873 and the subject matter of an Order in Council made on 13th September 1873, provided in art X as follows:

'In the examinations which they have to make, in accordance with the foregoing stipulations, the authorities of the State applied to shall admit as entirely valid evidence the sworn depositions or statements of witnesses taken in the other State,

or copies thereof, and likewise the warrants and sentences issued therein, provided
such documents are signed or certified by a Judge, Magistrate, or Officer of such *a*
State, and are authenticated by the oath of some witness, or by being sealed with the
official seal of the Minister of Justice or some other Minister of State.'

Counsel for the applicant submits, and counsel for the prison governor and the
government of Norway, the respondents, concedes, that the words 'taken in the other
State' make inadmissible the sworn depositions or statements taken in Denmark.
However, it is common ground that the exclusion of the evidence given in Copenhagen *b*
leaves an adequacy of material to establish a prima facie case, and I therefore turn to deal
with the first two submissions.

As to the first submission, s 14 of the Extradition Act 1870 provides:

> 'Depositions or statements on oath, taken in a foreign state, and copies of such
> original depositions or statements, and foreign certificates of or judicial documents
> stating the fact of conviction, may, if duly authenticated, be received in evidence in *c*
> proceedings under this Act.'

Lord Brougham's Act (13 & 14 Vict c 21 (1850)), whose worthy object is entitled 'An
Act for shortening the Language used in Acts of Parliament', provided in s 4, inter alia:

> 'That in all Acts ... the Words "Oath", "swear" and "Affidavit" shall include
> Affirmation, Declaration, affirming, and declaring, in the Case of Persons by Law *d*
> allowed to declare or affirm instead of swearing.'

Nevertheless shortly before the Order in Council referred to above, namely on 5th
August 1873, the Extradition Act 1873 was passed and this provided by s 4:

> 'The provisions of the principal Act relating to depositions and statements on oath
> taken in a foreign state, and copies of such original depositions and statements, do *e*
> and shall extend to affirmations taken in a foreign state, and copies of such
> affirmations.'

Counsel for the applicant rightly points out that Lord Brougham's Act only applies to
Acts of Parliament and not to treaties. Article X makes no reference to affirmations and
he therefore contends that there is no justification for construing the words 'sworn *f*
depositions or statements of witnesses' to include affirmations.

In relation to the interpretation of treaties, counsel for the respondents reminded us of
the well-known observation of Lord Russell CJ in *Re Arton (No 2)* [1896] 1 QB 509 at 517:
'In my judgment these treaties ought to receive a liberal interpretation, which means no
more than that they should receive their true construction according to their language,
object and intent.'   *g*

In *R v Governor of Pentonville Prison, ex parte Ecke* [1974] Crim LR 102 Lord Widgery
CJ, after reciting that part of the judgment of Lord Russell CJ referred to above,
emphasised that an extradition treaty is not to be construed as though it were a domestic
statute. He said:

> 'The words used in a treaty of this kind are to be given their general meaning,
> general to lawyer and layman alike. They are to be given, as it were, the meaning *h*
> of the diplomat rather than the lawyer, and they are to be given their ordinary
> international meaning and not a particular meaning which they may have attracted
> in England or in certain branches of activity in England.'

Bearing in mind that the 1873 Act came into effect before the Order in Council and
further that one of the intents of the treaty was to avoid the necessity of bringing *j*
witnesses from overseas, I consider that a justifiable liberal interpretation of the treaty
involves construing the words 'sworn depositions or statements of witnesses' as extending
to affirmations. I therefore turn to the second submission, namely that the statements
of the four accomplices did not amount to affirmations.

Under s 186 of the Norwegian Penal Code an oath must not be taken by a witness who
has been found guilty of the act or guilty of complicity in the act which is the subject of

the investigation or who is under suspicion of such guilt. Thus there could be no
a question of any of the four accomplices taking the oath. All four alleged accomplices
were willing to give evidence. What took place in each case was that their previous
statements, or one or more of them, was read and each accepted before the court that it
was accurate, subject in one case to certain corrections. These verbal acceptances were
dictated by the judges into the court record which was then signed by these witnesses.

It is provided by s 168 of the Norwegian Penal Code that:

b   'Anybody who by false accusation, report, or testimony before a court, the
prosecution or any other public authority, by distortion or removal of evidence or
by establishment of false evidence, or otherwise against his better conscience,
attempts to cause somebody else to be charged with or convicted of an offence, or is
assessory thereto, shall be punished by imprisonment from six months to eight
years if the offence concerned is a felony, and by imprisonment up to four years if
c   the offence is a misdemeanour.'

Within two to three days of giving their evidence it was apparently thought desirable
by the authorities to remind the alleged accomplices of the provisions of this section.
They were accordingly brought back before the judge and informed of the terms of the
code. Three of them stated that in giving their evidence they were each aware that they
d would be liable to punishment if they gave 'perjurious evidence in court'. One of the
Indians, Mr Hardial Singh, declared that he did not know of the provision when he gave
his evidence, but declared that his evidence would be the same even if he had known of
the provision. He repeated that he had told the whole and full truth.

Counsel for the applicant submits that there are three requirements for a valid
affirmation: (1) a solemn undertaking has to be given to the judicial authority; (2) it
e must be given prior to the giving of evidence to the court; (3) the undertaking ought to
include some reference to a promise to tell the truth, however expressed.

The right to affirm was introduced in 1838 for the benefit of Quakers and Moravians
and the essential part of the declaration is still retained today, namely 'I . . . do solemnly,
sincerely, and truly declare and affirm'. Although neither party suggests that this or any
closely comparable formula has to be used, it is agreed that the mere signature to a
f document or the verbal acknowledgment that its contents are correct cannot amount to
an affirmation. Where then is the line to be drawn?

The answer cannot be precise: it must be a matter of fact and degree dependent on the
particular circumstances of the case. I do not consider that the affirmation need take
place prior to the making of the statement. What is required, where the statement has
been made, is its adoption in circumstances which recognise the gravity and importance
g of the truth being told on the particular occasion. I would not necessarily accept that the
mere acknowledgment, albeit before a judicial authority, that what has been previously
said is the truth would amount to an affirmation. But in this case the acknowledgment
before the judicial authority was made after the terms or the substance of s 168 of the
Norwegian Penal Code was drawn to the attention of each of the alleged accomplices.
The fact that the provisions of this section were not drawn to their attention initially
h when they appeared before the judge does not seem to me, in the circumstances of this
case, to make any material difference. They were brought back before the court within
a very short time of their initial appearance and their subsequent acknowledgment in the
circumstances which I have described of the truth of what they had previously said
amounted, in my judgment, to a sufficient acknowledgment.

It is conceded that, if the evidence of the alleged accomplices was properly before the
j Chief Metropolitan Stipendiary Magistrate, there was sufficient evidence to justify his
conclusion that a prima facie case had been made out by the Norwegian government. I
would accordingly dismiss this appeal.

SKINNER J. Of the four submissions made so clearly by counsel for the applicant and
referred to by Ackner LJ, I need only consider two.

The first is that the committing magistrates can only act on sworn testimony in

deciding whether the evidence is such as would, in the words of s 10 the Extradition Act
1870, '. . . according to the law of England justify the committal for trial of the prisoner   *a*
if the crime of which he is accused had been committed in England . . .' This argument
depends first on the 1873 treaty (Order in Council dated 30th September 1873) and, in
particular, on art X which provides that '. . . the authorities of the State applied to shall
admit as entirely valid evidence the sworn depositions or statements of witnesses taken
in the other State, or copies thereof . . .' Any domestic legislation has to be read in the
light of those words. The relevant domestic legislation lies in the Oaths Act 1838, Lord   *b*
Brougham's Act (13 & 14 Vict c 21 (1850)), s 14 of the 1870 Act and s 4 of the Extradition
Act 1873, to all of which Ackner LJ has already referred. Counsel for the applicant
submits that, however inconvenient or out of date it might be, and whatever the position
may have been in English law either in 1873 or now, sworn statements alone can be
received.

Counsel for the respondents concedes that the treaty is the determining factor. He   *c*
relies on the well-known words of Lord Russell CJ in *Re Arton (No 2)* [1896] 1 QB 509 at
517: '. . . treaties ought to receive a liberal interpretation, which means no more than
that they should receive their true construction according to their language, object and
intent.'

Lord Widgery CJ in *R v Governor of Pentonville Prison, ex parte Ecke* [1974] Crim LR 102
helpfully put the correct approach in the following words: *d*

'The words used in a treaty of this kind are to be given their general meaning,
general to lawyer and layman alike. They are to be given, as it were, the meaning
of the diplomat rather than the lawyer, and they are to be given their ordinary
international meaning and not a particular meaning which they may have attracted
in England or in certain branches of activity in England.'

e
Counsel for the respondents asks us to look at this treaty in the light of events at the
time it was signed and ratified. It was concluded on 26th June 1873. On 5th August
1873 the Extradition Act 1873 received the royal assent, thereby widening the scope of
s 10 of the 1870 Act to include affirmations despite the fact that the English courts could
only hear affirmed evidence if given by a Quaker or Moravian. On 28th August 1873
the treaty was ratified. Lord Brougham's Act, though not directly relevant to   *f*
interpretation of the treaty, had been in force for nearly a quarter of a century. In the
light of this, what is the general meaning, general to lawyer and layman alike, of 'sworn
depositions or statements of witnesses' in the treaty? Does it include an affirmation? In
my judgment it does.

Thus counsel's argument for the respondents succeeds on the first point, and as to the
second he concedes that, to be within the treaty, the evidence submitted must either be   *g*
on oath or affirmation; unsworn or unaffirmed evidence cannot be received.

That brings me to counsel's second submission for the applicant that the crucial
statements in this case, namely those given by four alleged accomplices of the applicant,
were not affirmations. What is meant by an affirmation in this context? Ackner LJ has
recited what in fact occurred in the Norwegian court and the relevant sections of the
Norwegian Penal Code. The difference between the parties is a narrow one. They agree   *h*
(a) that an affirmation need not follow the wording of the Oaths Act 1838 (which has
remained unchanged since that date), (b) that there must be a solemn undertaking given
to the court to tell the truth. Counsel for the applicant would add (c) that it ought to
contain a promise to tell the truth, (d) that the promise ought to be given before the
evidence is recorded.

In my judgment, there has been some confusion caused by failure to differentiate   *j*
between the verb 'to affirm' and the noun 'affirmation'. Within the context of the
Extradition Act 1873 an affirmation must be a document like a deposition or statement
on oath (see per Donaldson LJ and Hodgson J in *R v Twena* (27th November 1980,
unreported)). I do not accept counsel's submission on this point that that court wrongly
made a differentiation. In my judgment the document put forward as an affirmation

a must contain, or show on its face, a solemn declaration by the witness before a judicial authority that its contents are true. The document might consist of a record of what the witness had said or might refer to a record of something said on another occasion and acknowledged or adopted in solemn form before the judicial authority. The vital constituent is the solemn declaration of the truth, which might be expressed in a number of different ways. For example, in the present case the reference in the case of each witness to section 168 of the Norwegian Penal Code clearly emphasises the solemnity of
b what the witness is adopting and accepting in the document.

Here, each of the witnesses appeared in court before a judge on 20th or 21st May 1980. Because he was an accomplice Norwegian law precluded him from taking the oath. Each was informed of his right to refuse to give evidence. He than accepted or confirmed earlier statements he had made and this was recorded. The two Indian witnesses are both recorded as saying that their statements were in accordance with the
c truth. On 23rd May, because it was felt that perhaps all the formalities had not been observed, each was brought back to the court before the judge and informed (in one case) and reminded (in the other three cases) of the provisions of s 168. The three 'reminded' all said that they had been aware of the section at the previous hearing. The one 'informed' said that, had he been aware, he would have given the same evidence and it was the truth. In order to decide whether there was an affirmation in any particular case,
d the documents recording the witnesses' evidence have to be looked at as a whole. Doing so here, I have no hesitation in saying that, in each of these cases, the documents reveal a solemn declaration, reinforced by penal sanctions, that their contents are true and they amount to affirmations within s 4 of the 1873 Act. For these reasons I agree that this application should be dismissed.

e *Application dismissed. Leave to appeal to the House of Lords refused.*

12th May. The Appeal Committee of the House of Lords (Lord Frazer of Tullybelton, Lord Scarman and Lord Roskill) dismissed a petition by the applicant for leave to appeal.

Solicitors: *Hallinan, Blackburn Gittings & Co* (for the applicant); *Director of Public*
f *Prosecutions.*

April Weiss   Barrister.

R v Immigration Appeal Tribunal, ex parte
g # Shaikh

QUEEN'S BENCH DIVISION (DIVISIONAL COURT LIST)
BINGHAM J
19th FEBRUARY 1981

h *Immigration – Leave to enter – Non-patrial – Student – Variation of leave for purpose of study – Intention to leave at end of studies – Whether applicant must prove intention to leave at end of studies when he applies for variation of leave to enter – Whether applicant must prove merely that he wishes to remain as bona fide student – Whether applicant's wish to remain after end of studies if permitted disentitling him to apply for variation of leave to enter in order to complete studies – Whether applicant must prove requisite intention at time of application for variation or at time*
j *of hearing of appeal from refusal to grant variation – Immigration Rules for Control on Entry: EEC and Other Non-Commonwealth Nationals (1972–73), para 17 – Immigration Rules for Control after Entry: EEC and Other Non-Commonwealth Nationals (1972–73), para 12.*

The applicant, a student, was granted leave to enter the United Kingdom for 12 months from October 1973 to attend a course of study. In October 1974 his leave to stay was extended and was subsequently further extended in 1975, 1976 and 1977. In June 1978 notice was given to the Home Office that the applicant had been accepted to commence *a* a further three-year course in a field that was related to his previous course of study. The applicant wrote to the Home Office and stated in his letter that, if granted permission, he would like to work in the United Kingdom to gain experience in his particular field of work. The Home Office refused an extension of permission to remain as a student in January 1979 on the grounds that the Secretary of State was not satisfied that the applicant intended to leave the United Kingdom on completion of his studies in *b* accordance with para 12^{*a*} of the immigration rules for control after entry of EEC and other non-commonwealth nationals read with para 17^{*b*} of the immigration rules for control on entry of such nationals. The applicant appealed against the refusal and in January 1980 the adjudicator allowed the appeal. The Secretary of State appealed against that decision to the Immigration Appeal Tribunal, which found that, in the light of the applicant's stated intention to start his career in the United Kingdom and his desire for *c* permission to start work there, the Secretary of State had rightly refused a further extension to remain. The tribunal also found that the adjudicator's determination on the applicant's intention to remain in this country was unsatisfactory as it had not been based on his intention at the time when the Secretary of State had made his decision to refuse a further extension. The applicant sought an order of certiorari to quash the tribunal's order on the grounds (i) that, although para 17 required that on entry an applicant had *d* to show an intention to leave at the end of his studies, para 12 did not require him to prove the same intention when he applied for an extension, (ii) that the purpose of the rules governing admission and continuing stay as a student, in so far as they were concerned with the student's intentions, were concerned with those intentions in order to make sure that leave given for a temporary purpose was not used for a collateral purpose, and the mere fact that it was the applicant's intention if permitted to gain work *e* experience did not disentitle him to an extension, and (iii) that the tribunal had been wrong in law to overturn the adjudicator's finding of fact that the applicant intended to leave on completion of his studies.

Held – (1) While para 17 of the rules for control on entry contained a clear requirement that on entry an applicant had to show an intention to leave at the end of his studies, he *f* was not required by para 12 of the rules for control after entry to prove the same intention when he applied for an extension, but was merely required to prove that he wished to remain as a bona fide student (see p 35 h j, post).

(2) The fact that the applicant wished to stay in the United Kingdom after the completion of his course of studies if his extension was granted and if he was permitted to do so did not of itself disentitle him to the extension which he sought (see p 37 b c, *g* post); dictum of Lord Widgery CJ in *R v Immigration Appeals Adjudicator, ex parte Perween Khan* [1972] 3 All ER at 300 applied; *R v Chief Immigration Officer, Gatwick Airport, ex parte Kharrazi* [1980] 3 All ER 373 distinguished.

(3) Although the tribunal had been justified in criticising the adjudicator's finding of fact because he had reached his decision on the basis of the applicant's intention at the time of the hearing before him and not at the time of the application to the Secretary of *h* State, there had not in the circumstances been any material before the adjudicator on which he could have concluded that the applicant intended to stay unlawfully in the United Kingdom after the completion of his studies or that he had any ulterior or collateral purpose. It followed that an order of certiorari would issue and the case would be remitted to the tribunal (see p 37 g h, post).

Per Curiam. It is clear that the Secretary of State has power under the immigration *j* rules to exclude an applicant who has some collateral purpose and in particular an unlawful purpose, or any intention of abusing, flouting or breaching in any way the conditions on which he was permitted to enter (see p 36 c d, post).

---

a   Paragraph 12 is set out at p 35 *c*, post
b   Paragraph 17 is set out at p 34 *j* to p 35 *a*, post

Notes

a For the entry of non-patrial students, see 4 Halsbury's Laws (4th Edn) para 948.

Cases referred to in judgment

Harding v Secretary of State for the Home Department (7th January 1976, unreported), Immigration Appeal Tribunal.

R v Chief Immigration Officer, Gatwick Airport, ex parte Kharrazi [1980] 3 All ER 373,

b [1980] 1 WLR 1396, CA.

R v Immigration Appeals Adjudicator, ex parte Perween Khan [1972] 3 All ER 297, [1972] 1 WLR 1058, 136 JP 770, DC, 2 Digest (Reissue) 198, 1149.

Tagbo v Entry Clearance Officer, Lagos (5th June 1977, unreported), Immigration Appeal Tribunal.

Visa Officer, Karachi v Hassan Mohammad [1978] Imm AR 168.

c
Application for judicial review

Muneer Ahmed Shaikh applied, with the leave of Russell J on 29th August 1980 for, inter alia, an order of certiorari to quash an order of the Immigration Appeal Tribunal made on 2nd June 1980 whereby it allowed an appeal by the Secretary of State against the decision of the adjudicator on 2nd January 1980 allowing an appeal by the applicant

d against the refusal of the Secretary of State to grant him a variation of his leave to enter the United Kingdom. The facts are set out in the judgment.

Ian Macdonald for the applicant.
Simon D Brown for the Secretary of State.

e **BINGHAM J.** The applicant seeks an order of judicial review, namely an order of certiorari to quash an order of the Immigration Appeal Tribunal made on 2nd June 1980 and an order of mandamus instructing that tribunal to dismiss the Secretary of State's appeal to it. The decision it is sought to challenge before me is the decision of the Immigration Appeal Tribunal, and the essential question which that tribunal had to determine was whether the Secretary of State in deciding not to extend the applicant's

f right to remain in this country as a student made a correct decision reached by a correct procedure on 24th January 1979.

I shall have to recite a little of the history in order to make it clear how this question arises. With effect from 27th October 1973 the applicant was given leave to enter this country for 12 months with a restriction on his right to accept employment, in order to attend a three-year course at the University of Essex. In fact, it appears that on attending

g at the University of Essex he found that the course which he was due to attend there overlapped with a degree course which he had already attended in his own country, and consequently he instead went to the polytechnic in Manchester and embarked on a Higher National Diploma course in computer studies.

In October 1974 his leave was extended until 27th October 1975, and there were subsequent extensions granted until the same date in 1976, and in 1977, and finally until

h 31st July 1978. The reason that the course took so long, it would appear, was not that the applicant was an idle or frivolous student but just that he was not a very successful one, with the result that the course took longer than it should have done.

On 22nd June 1978 notice was given by the Manchester Polytechnic that the applicant had been accepted and was due to embark on a three-year full-time course leading to the polytechnic's diploma in printing. At this time the polytechnic confirmed very much

j what I have said, namely that the applicant's attendance as a student had been good, and the polytechnic further said that he was considered to be a good candidate for the printing course.

The Home Office at that point, on 26th July 1978, wrote to the applicant a letter directed to ascertain from him what his future intentions were, and the letter ended up by saying: 'In which country do you intend to pursue your career? What are your long-term plans?'

The applicant answered that letter on 3rd August 1978, and in the course of his answer made various statements which are of importance in these proceedings. He said:

'This printing diploma deals with computers, printing in way that helps me to use computer in printing field as well as in photography. I intend to start a career in computing field. I like to start my computer career in this country. If you grant me permission to start work in this country, then I can join evening classes in advance computing/printing. My long-term ambition lies in a good career in computing field and long-term service for United Kingdom Industries.'

Following the receipt of that letter by the Home Office, an extension of permission to remain in this country as a student was refused on 4th October 1978, and that notification, having gone apparently astray, was repeated on 24th January 1979, which is being treated as the relevant date for the purposes of these proceedings.

The grounds on which the Secretary of State refused permission to remain emerges, I think, from the Home Office statement which reads as follows:

'The Secretary of State now considered the application for further leave to remain. The appellant had been treated as a genuine, though obviously not particularly talented student since his arrival in 1973. He had been admitted for a 3 year BA course but had evidently "lowered his sights" and taken a 2 year HND course which he had passed successfully after 4 years study. He had applied to continue his studies by taking a 3 year printing course, but had then made it clear that he considered his future lay in the United Kingdom and had also said he would like to commence employment and continue his studies at evening classes. In these circumstances the Secretary of State was not satisfied that the appellant intended to leave the United Kingdom on completion of his studies and he decided to refuse his application in accordance with paragraph 12 of [the Statement of Immigration Rules for Control after Entry: EEC and other Non-Commonwealth Nationals (HC Paper (1972–73) no 82)] read with paragraph 17 of [the Statement of Immigration Rules for Control on Entry: EEC and other Non-Commonwealth Nationals (HC Paper (1972–73) no 81)]. He originally did so on 4 October 1978 but the recorded delivery package was lost in the post and a fresh notice of refusal and appeal forms were sent on 24 January 1979.'

Perhaps I may interrupt the narrative to mention one part of that paragraph that has been the subject of comment. It is quite true that the applicant had, in his letter, said that he would like to commence employment and continue his studies at evening classes, but the paragraph also contains the statement that the applicant 'had then', that is in his letter, 'made it clear that he considered his future lay in the United Kingdom', and that statement is the subject of some criticism as being something not fairly to be extracted from the letter which the applicant wrote.

The applicant, having received notice of refusal, appealed by a notice given on 31st January 1979, and on 2nd January 1980, very nearly a year later, the adjudicator gave his decision. The adjudicator summarised the history very much in the way that I have done and recorded, as was then agreed, that the applicant's printing course had a direct occupational link with the computer course that he had previously done. The adjudicator clearly formed a very favourable view of the applicant, saying that he was a good witness and that he accepted his credibility. He then, in the course of his decision, went on as follows:

'Whilst on this course [that is the first course] he was informed by his family that, as a result of a change of government policy, many fewer computer installations were being imported into Pakistan and in consequence job opportunities were greatly reduced. Employment was being given only to persons with experience and it was for this reason that he referred in his correspondence with the Home Office to his wish to gain experience in employment with computers in this country. He said that by using the expression "long term service for United Kingdom Industries" he meant service abroad by using computer installations manufactured here. He decided to undertake his present course in computer techniques in the printing industry because he had learnt that this was a field in which there was no shortage of job opportunities in his own country and in consequence through pursuing it the necessity for him to obtain work experience in this country prior to leaving was removed. He assured me that he had no intention of remaining here beyond the end of his course. He has no relations here; as he put it, "I am alone." He has five sisters and two brothers in Pakistan and is the oldest son of the family and was clearly aware of his traditional responsibilities as the eldest son and considered that these required him to return at the end of his course. His testimony satisfied me that he is a genuine student with an intention to return at the end of his present course. I, therefore, allow the appeal and direct that he be granted permission to remain until the conclusion of his course subject to his progress being satisfactory.'

It is, I think, fair to infer from the terms of this decision that when the adjudicator has set out what he was told by the applicant he believed it to be true, having, as I have pointed out, already indicated his acceptance of the applicant's credibility.

From that decision the Secretary of State appealed to the Immigration Appeal Tribunal and their decision is dated 2nd June 1980. Again, a careful and accurate summary of the history is set out. There is a reference to the evidence given before the adjudicator, to which I will return subsequently, and the tribunal make reference to the terms of the rules, para 17 of HC Paper (1972–73) no 81 and para 12 of HC Paper (1972–73) no 82, which have already been referred to.

The crux of the tribunal's decision, I think, is to be found on the last three pages of it, and I shall read such parts as appear to be necessary whilst omitting quite a lot which is inessential for present purposes. The contention on behalf of the Secretary of State is recorded as having been—

'that the Secretary of State had no option but to refuse the [applicant] a further extension in the light of the latter's expression in his letter of 26th July 1978 of a wish to start his computer career in this country and his desire for permission to start work in this country. The Secretary of State could not possibly be satisfied, having received this letter, that once the [applicant] had completed his new course of study, he would depart from the United Kingdom. The onus was on the [applicant] to satisfy the Secretary of State that he would then depart; he had not discharged that onus. He was not entitled to stay for work experience on the conclusion of his studies.'

There was a criticism of the adjudicator's factual findings. The applicant's representative's submissions were summarised and, in particular, the submission that it was not for the tribunal to substitute their findings of fact for those of the adjudicator who had seen and heard the applicant. The tribunal then continued:

'In deciding the appeal to us, it is well to have in mind what was the essential issue the adjudicator had to decide. It was not whether the [applicant] was at the time of the hearing before the adjudicator a genuine student with an intention to return to Pakistan, but whether the decision the Secretary of State made was correct or wrong. No question of discretion arises under the relevant immigration rules; the adjudicator's function was to decide judicially whether the Secretary of State's decision was or was not in accordance with the law and those rules, and in so deciding he was entitled to review any question of fact on which that decision was based (s 19 of the Immigration Act 1971). An adjudicator is, as it was emphasised in *Visa Officer, Karachi v Hassan Mohammad* [1978] Imm AR 168, an appellate authority and not some kind of super immigration officer. In the present appeal, the adjudicator's function was to decide whether on the facts in existence at the time of the Secretary of State's refusal he should or should not have been satisfied, on a balance of probability, by [the applicant] that he would depart on conclusion of his studies. On the facts as put before the Secretary of State by [the applicant] in his letter (and his state of mind and intention are facts) no reasonable officer in the Home Office could have been satisfied that [the applicant] so intended. He expressly stated that he had in mind, if permitted, staying on to work in the first instance in this country. He had an intention not to depart but to remain at any rate for a time and the facts that he had no intention of remaining illegally and that his purpose was to gain experience do not qualify him to stay. (See *Harding v Secretary of State for the Home Department* (7th January 1976, unreported) and *Tagbo v Entry Clearance Officer, Lagos* (5th June 1977, unreported).) The tribunal must reject [the applicant's representative's] submission that he could, on this evidence, be held to have an intention to depart on conclusion of his studies. We have noted that in his grounds of appeal to the adjudicator [the applicant] reiterated that he had no intention to remain without permission of the Home Office. Thus the principal question raised by the grounds of appeal was similar to that raised and decided in *Harding*, but the adjudicator's determination makes no reference to it. The tribunal has considered the record of [the applicant's] evidence to the adjudicator and it is noted that he said that he had thought he should get a job in the United Kingdom to get experience to enable him to get a job at home. He thought he would get experience by working during the day and studying at evening classes. The tribunal is well conscious of the principle enunciated by the Court of Appeal in the case to which [the applicant's representative] referred us. It is a principle which it has consistently followed. It has always been reluctant to disturb a finding of fact made by an adjudicator provided there was sufficient evidence to support it and has always been particularly so reluctant when the finding of fact is based on the adjudicator's judgment of the credibility of a witness whom he has seen and heard, even though on the papers before it the tribunal felt it might have itself reached a different conclusion. It may be possible that by the time [the applicant] gave evidence to the adjudicator he had abandoned the intention of remaining in this country after his further studies to gain experience, but the evidence is that he had this intention at the time when the Secretary of State made his decision to refuse him a further extension of his leave to be in this country. It follows that the Secretary of State's refusal was in accordance with the law and the immigration rules. Further the tribunal considers that the adjudicator's determination is generally an unsatisfactory one. It does not sufficiently deal with or do justice to the Secretary of State's case. The Secretary of State's appeal to the tribunal is allowed and his refusal is affirmed.'

That, therefore, was the decision which the applicant before me seeks to challenge, and counsel for the applicant makes three substantial criticisms of that decision. The first is based on the language of the rules themselves, that is para 17 of HC Paper (1972–73) no 81 dealing with control of those seeking to enter the country as students, and para 12 of HC Paper (1972–73) no 82 laying down the conditions for control after entry. The effect of counsel's submission is that so far as an intention to leave at the end of a period of study is concerned, while para 17 of HC Paper (1972–73) no 81 contains a clear requirement that on entry an applicant must show an intention to leave at the end of his studies, he is not required by the language of para 12 of HC Paper (1972–73) no 82 to prove the same intention at the later stage. The decision was therefore wrong in imposing a burden to prove the fact on the applicant.

In order to understand that submission it is necessary to look at the language of the rules, and the entry provision contained in para 17 of HC Paper (1972–73) no 81 reads as follows:

'An applicant is to be refused an entry clearance as a student if the officer is not satisfied that the applicant is able, and intends, to follow a full-time course of study and to leave the country on completion of it. In assessing the case the officer should consider such points as whether the applicant's qualifications are adequate for the

a
    course he proposes to follow, and whether there is any evidence of sponsorship by his home government or any other official body. As a general rule an entry clearance is not to be granted unless the applicant proposes to spend not less than 15 hours a week in organised day-time study of a single subject or of related subjects, and is not to be granted for the taking of a correspondence course.'

    The important language in that rule is, of course, the reference to the requirement that the officer should be satisfied that the applicant intends to leave the country on
b completion of the course of study.

    When one looks at para 12 of HC Paper (1972–73) no 82, the provision reads as follows:

c
    'Applications from students or would-be students for variation of their leave will consist mainly of applications for extension of stay as a student. An extension for an appropriate period, normally up to 12 months, may be granted if the applicant produces evidence, which is verified on a check being made, that he has enrolled for a full-time course of daytime study which meets the requirements for admission as a student; that he is giving regular attendance; and that he has adequate funds available for his maintenance and that of any dependants. When an extension is granted the student may be reminded that he will be expected to leave at the end of
d his studies.'

    The submission made on behalf of the applicant emerges clearly from the language of the rules themselves, and rests on the fact that whereas in para 17 the officer is to refuse entry if not satisfied that the applicant intends to leave the country on completion of his studies, in para 12 the only express provision is that when an extension is granted the
e student may be reminded that he will be expected to leave at the end of his studies. In the light of that wording, so it is submitted, it would be quite inconsistent to infer that the student is required at the later stage to discharge the same burden of satisfying the authorities of his intention to leave once his course is completed.

    Counsel for the Secretary of State, in rejecting that submission, argues that one must read the rules together in order to make sense of them, and that it would be irrational to
f have different rules operating at the two stages at which application may be made. I entirely agree that the rules must be read together since they form part of a coherent scheme governing immigration into the country and permission to remain within it, and it would indeed be absurd to attempt to read the rules in isolation. I further agree with counsel's submission that one should not construe these rules as if they were a statute. On the other hand, it is, in my judgment, incumbent on anybody seeking to
g give effect to these rules to read what they say and, so far as possible, give effect to the language used, unless of course that leads to absurdity or inconvenience so gross as to have been clearly outside anyone's contemplation.

    It is not, in my judgment, irrational that there should be a burden imposed on an applicant seeking to enter the country which is not in terms imposed on him if he seeks to extend his stay. It is, of course, necessary for him to satisfy the authorities on the latter
h occasion that he is a bona fide student, and if the Secretary of State had real ground for believing either that he was not a bona fide student, or that he had some ulterior motive in seeking to stay, even for the purpose of carrying out a course of study, I can well understand that a different situation entirely would arise. But it does seem to me, as a matter of looking at these rules and seeking to give effect to what they say, that it is reading into para 12 language which is not there to read it as if it imposes on an applicant
j for extension a duty to satisfy the Home Office of something which does not, in terms, appear in the paragraph at all.

    Accordingly, I agree, in broad terms, with counsel's submission for the applicant and do not think it was incumbent on the applicant to satisfy the Home Office, at that stage, although, for reasons I have just mentioned, that would by no means necessarily be the end of the matter.

The second submission that counsel for the applicant made was that, in any event, the purpose of the rules governing admission and continuing stay as a student, in so far as the rules were concerned with the student's intentions, were concerned with those intentions in order to make sure that leave given for a temporary purpose was not used for a collateral purpose and, in particular, was not used so as to enable the student to remain in the country on a longer-term basis illegally. It is right, I think, to say that in his reply counsel laid more stress on the collateral purpose than the avoidance of illegality.

The real question that arises in this case is this: if the applicant's intention at the relevant time was to leave at the end of his studies but to remain here, if he was permitted to do so, in order to gain work experience, did the mere fact that he harboured the latter intention, that is, to remain if permitted for the gaining of work experience, of itself disable him as a candidate for extension? Was the mere fact that he acknowledged that desire enough to keep him out? Counsel says the rules should be administered with common sense and flexibility and, no doubt, a measure of humanity.

It is, I think, quite clear, and indeed scarcely needs stating, that, in the case of any applicant whose real ambition is to enter under cover of one nominal purpose and to remain for a much longer term for a different illegitimate purpose, the Secretary of State, under these rules, should have, and clearly has, power to exclude him. But should the Secretary of State have power to exclude him, and is it the intention of the rules that he should, if somebody, while having no intention to abuse the rules, or flout them, or disobey them, or breach any condition imposed on him, does wish, if allowed, to remain for a longer period than the strict period allowed for the course of study on which he is embarked?

This is, I think, a difficult question, and it may very well be that some distinction falls to be drawn between what a person intends to do willy-nilly and that which he desires to do but has no intention whatever to do without permission. In this context some assistance is, I think, to be drawn from the judgment of Lord Widgery CJ in *R v Immigration Appeals Adjudicator, ex parte Perween Khan* [1972] 3 All ER 297 at 300, [1972] 1 WLR 1058 at 1062, where he said:

'The fact that the immigrant has in mind the possibility, amongst other things, of being allowed to stay in this country should not, in my judgment, affect his or her right of entry, provided that the course of instruction is the primary purpose with which the entry into this country is made. I think that there should be no real difficulty for immigration officers to distinguish between these two cases, the case where the course of instruction, although genuinely intended, is really no more than a convenient key to obtain entry into the country, and the case where the course of instruction is the primary or overriding purpose for which the immigrant seeks to obtain entry. I hesitate to suggest yet another form of test, or yet another construction of the [Commonwealth Immigrants Act 1962], but in many cases it seems to me that much will turn on whether the immigrant attaches so much importance to the course that he or she will come to the course anyway, regardless whether she can stay in the country afterwards, or not, or whether the course played such a relatively minor part in his or her calculations that she would not dream of coming for the course alone, but merely regards it as a stepping stone to other and more permanent sojourn here.'

Counsel for the Secretary of State points out, quite rightly, that one should approach this decision with caution, since it not only relates to different rules but to a different Act as well, and I fully accept that one cannot apply it as it stands to the present case. It does, I think, none the less, give some assistance as disavowing the view that a would-be immigrant, under the provision then in force, must show, at the point of entry, a positive intention to go home again, and the view that he is debarred if he has in mind the possibility, amongst other things, of being allowed to stay in this country. Counsel contended that if this approach was correct much of the argument and decision in *R v Chief Immigration Officer, Gatwick Airport, ex parte Kharrazi* [1980] 3 All ER 373, [1980] 1

WLR 1396 would have been unnecessary. The issue in that case was, however, quite
_a_ different from that in this case, and there had in the meantime been a very significant
alteration in the wording of the rules.

It has been pointed out that under some circumstances the Home Office can give
permission to those lawfully in this country as students to remain for an additional
period as trainees, and it would, I think, be both harsh, and in many ways unrealistic, if
a student who admitted to a desire to take advantage of those possibilities should be
_b_ excluded whereas one who kept his hopes dark profited from that concealment.
Accordingly, in my judgment, the disclosure and the fact, if it was a fact, that this
applicant would have wished to stay in this country after his completion of his course of
studies, if his extension were granted, and if he were permitted to do so, should not of
itself disentitle him to the extension which he sought. In saying that, I emphasise that
in a case where somebody was suspected of having some collateral purpose, and in
_c_ particular an unlawful purpose, or had any intention of abusing, flouting or breaching
in any way the conditions on which he was permitted to enter, a different situation
entirely would arise.

Counsel's third submission for the applicant was that the Immigration Appeal
Tribunal was wrong in law to overturn the adjudicator's finding of fact that the applicant
did intend to leave on completion of his studies. This submission was based on the
_d_ familiar and acknowledged principle that an appellate tribunal will only in very rare
circumstances substitute its view of the facts for those of the primary fact-finding
tribunal. For my part, I think that the tribunal's criticism of the adjudicator's finding of
fact was justified because it does appear to me from the terms of his decision that the
adjudicator was concentrating on the applicant's intention at the time that he was giving
evidence before the adjudicator, about a year after his notice of appeal, and not on his
_e_ intention at the earlier and appropriate date. Furthermore, it is to be noted that in his
evidence to the adjudicator the applicant did say, 'I thought I should get job in U.K. to get
experience to enable me to get job at home'. So it seems to me really quite clear, as the
tribunal thought, that whatever the position at the time he was giving evidence before
the adjudicator there was, none the less, an inference to be drawn that at the earlier stage,
that is at the stage when the Secretary of State refused permission, it had been the
_f_ applicant's desire to remain in this country if permitted.

It seems to me, looking at the letter which he wrote, and accepting the adjudicator's
interpretation of what the applicant said about his reference to long-term service in
United Kingdom industries, that the applicant did betray a desire to remain in this
country to gain work experience, if permitted. On the other hand, I think that the
qualification 'if permitted' was clearly to be read in the letter because he said, 'I _like_ to start
_g_ my computer career in this country. If you grant me permission to start work in this
country, then I can join evening classes in advance computing/printing'.

Accordingly, although I think that the tribunal's criticism of the adjudicator's finding
of fact was justified, I do not think that there was any material before the adjudicator on
which he could have concluded that the applicant intended to stay in this country willy-
nilly or had any ulterior or collateral purpose and, indeed, it is acknowledged in the
_h_ tribunal's decision that the applicant had no intention to remain here unlawfully.

On those grounds, it is my conclusion that the Immigration Appeal Tribunal
misdirected itself in certain important respects and its decision should be quashed.

Order of certiorari granted. Case remitted to Immigration Appeal Tribunal.

Solicitors: _Sushma Lal_, Manchester (for the applicant); _Treasury Solicitor._

N P Metcalfe Esq   Barrister.

Royal Borough of Windsor and Maidenhead v Brandrose Investments Ltd

CHANCERY DIVISION

FOX J

22nd, 23rd JANUARY, 6th FEBRUARY 1981

Town and country planning – Conservation area – Control of demolition – Agreement between planning authority and developer allowing development of land in conservation area – Agreement not specifically prohibiting demolition of buildings on land – Development not capable of being carried out without demolition of buildings – Developer demolishing buildings without consent of planning authority – Whether consent of authority necessary for demolition of buildings – Whether agreement containing implied consent of authority to demolition – Whether authority able to prohibit demolition in spite of implied consent in agreement – Town and Country Planning Act 1971, ss 52(3), 277A.

The defendants owned property, consisting of buildings and land within a conservation area, which they intended to develop. There was no development plan or direction of the Secretary of State which affected the property. In 1976, following a compulsory purchase inquiry at which the defendants were objectors, an agreement was entered into by the defendants and the local planning authority under s 52[a] of the Town and Country Planning Act 1971 which provided, inter alia, in sub-s (1) that a local planning authority could enter into an agreement with any person interested in land in their area for the purpose of restricting or regulating the development or use of that land and in sub-s (3)(a) that nothing in s 52 or in any agreement made thereunder was to be construed as restricting any powers exercisable by, inter alios, the authority so long as those powers were exercised in accordance with a development plan or directions of the Secretary of State. In October 1976 the defendants were granted planning permission by the local planning authority for the development of the property. The development contemplated could not be carried out without the demolition of the buildings. Under s 277A[b] of the 1971 Act a building in a conservation area could not be demolished without the consent of the local planning authority. The defendants commenced demolition of the buildings on the land in the summer of 1979 without the consent of the local planning authority. In July 1979 the authority were granted an interlocutory injunction to restrain the defendants from proceeding with the demolition without their consent and they further sought a declaration that the defendants were not entitled to demolish the building without consent and an injunction to restrain the defendants from demolishing the buildings. The authority also by motion sought an order to restrain the demolition of the buildings until the trial of the action. At the hearing of the motion in July 1979 the order was refused and the motion dismissed. No further steps were taken in the action until January 1980 when the defendants issued a summons to dismiss the action for want

---

a Section 52, so far as material, is set out at p 41 g to p 42 a, post

b Section 277A, so far as material, provides:

'(1) This section applies to all buildings in conservation areas other than—(a) listed buildings; (b) excepted buildings within the meaning of section 58(2) above; and (c) buildings in relation to which a direction under subsection (4) below is for the time being in force.

'(2) A building to which this section applies shall not be demolished without the consent of the appropriate authority.

'(3) An application for consent to the demolition of such a building may be made as a separate application or as part of an application for planning permission to redevelop the site of the building, but consent to demolition shall not be taken to have been given as part of planning permission for redevelopment of the site unless the appropriate authority, on granting the planning permission, states that it includes consent to demolish the building ...'

a of prosecution. In February the plaintiffs delivered a statement of claim seeking only the declaration originally sought, and at the same time withdrew two enforcement notices in respect of the buildings. In March the Secretary of State confirmed the withdrawal of the enforcement notices and stated that he would take no further steps in relation to the buildings. In October the defendants issued a further summons to strike out the statement of claim as disclosing no cause of action. By the time of the hearing all the buildings had been demolished, and the only questions to be determined were (i)

b whether the local planning authority could lawfully enter into an agreement having the effect of disentitling them from requiring consent under s 277A to the demolition of the buildings and (ii) if so, whether the agreement they had entered into with the defendants under s 52 had that effect.

c **Held** – (1) On the true construction of s 52(3) of the 1971 Act there was no restriction on the exercise of a local planning authority's powers in relation to the development of land but only so far as they were exercised in accordance with a development plan or the appropriate direction of the Secretary of State. The wording of s 52(3)(*a*) was inconsistent with a general saving of the authority's right to exercise its powers contrary to the provisions of an agreement entered into under s 52. Since there was no development

d plan or direction by the Secretary of State, it followed that there was nothing in law to prevent the agreement having the effect of limiting the authority's power to take steps to prevent the demolition of the buildings (see p 43 *d h j* and p 44 *a* to *c*, post); *Ransom & Luck Ltd v Surbiton Borough Council* [1949] 1 All ER 185 distinguished.

(2) The agreement entered into by the defendants and the local planning authority under s 52 contained an obvious implied agreement by the authority to the demolition of the buildings and there was to be implied into it a provision by the authority not to

e require their consent under their statutory powers to such demolition nor to do anything that would impede the demolition. In the absence of any development plan, the authority could not have used any of their statutory powers to prevent the demolition, and accordingly the authority could not enforce their powers under s 277A in relation to the conservation area so as to prevent the demolition of the buildings (see p 45 *b c f*, post).

f Per Curiam. (1) There is in principle nothing which prevents the exercise of a statutory power being limited by the previous exercise of another statutory power (see p 44 *d* to *f*, post); dictum of Pennycuick V-C in *Dowty Boulton Paul Ltd v Wolverhampton Corpn* [1971] 2 All ER at 282 applied.

(2) There is nothing in s 52 to prevent a local planning authority inserting in an agreement entered into under that section a provision preserving all or any of its powers in full (see p 45 *g h*, post).

g

Notes

For demolition of buildings in conservation areas, see 34 Halsbury's Laws (4th Edn) para 686.

For agreements with a local planning authority regulating development or use of land,

h see 37 Halsbury's Laws (3rd Edn) 276, para 374, and for cases on the subject, see 45 Digest (Repl) 334–335, 31–32.

For the Town and Country Planning Act 1971, s 52, see 41 Halsbury's Statutes (3rd Edn) 1648, and for s 277A of that Act (as inserted by the Town and Country Amenities Act 1974, s 1), see 44 ibid 1744.

As from 13th November 1980 s 277A(3) was repealed and s 277A(4) was amended by

j the Local Government, Planning and Land Act 1980, ss 90, 194, Sch 15, para 26(2), Sch 34, Part X.

Cases referred to in judgment

Dowty Boulton Paul Ltd v Wolverhampton Corpn [1971] 2 All ER 277, [1971] 1 WLR 204, 135 JP 333, 69 LGR 192, 13 Digest (Reissue) 286, 2567.

Ransom & Luck Ltd v Surbiton Borough Council [1949] 1 All ER 185, [1949] Ch 180, [1949] LJR 809, 113 JP 95, 47 LGR 467, CA, 45 Digest (Repl) 335, 32.

Southend-on-Sea Corpn v Hodgson (Wickford) Ltd [1961] 2 All ER 46, [1962] 1 QB 416, [1961] 2 WLR 806, 125 JP 348, 59 LGR 193, 12 P & CR 165, DC, 45 Digest (Repl) 346, 76.

Case also cited

Ayr Harbour Trustees v Oswald (1883) 8 App Cas 623, HL.

Summons

By summons dated 3rd July 1979 the plaintiffs, the Royal Borough of Windsor and Maidenhead, having been granted ex parte relief by Foster J on 2nd July 1979 and having given the usual undertakings as to damages, sought as against the defendants, Brandrose Investments Ltd, a declaration that the defendants were not entitled to demolish the buildings known as 107–111 Peascod Street, Windsor without obtaining the consent of the plaintiffs, the local planning authority, pursuant to s 277A of the Town and Country Planning Act 1971 and an injunction restraining the defendants by themselves or their servants, agents or contractors from demolishing or continuing to demolish the buildings. Also on 3rd July 1979 by notice of motion the plaintiffs sought an order in terms similar to those of the injunction sought granting relief until further order or trial of the action. On 11th July Walton J dismissed the motion and refused the relief sought. The plaintiffs did not appeal. On 30th January 1980 the defendants issued a summons to dismiss the action for want of prosecution. In February the plaintiffs delivered a statement of claim and withdrew certain enforcement notices which they had served in respect of the demolition of the buildings. In March the Secretary of State confirmed the withdrawal of the enforcement notice and stated that he would be taking no steps in relation to the buildings. On 7th October the defendants issued a summons under RSC Ord 18, r 19 to strike out the statement of claim as disclosing no cause of action. The summons also sought an inquiry into what damages if any the plaintiffs should pay pursuant to their undertaking given to Foster J on 2nd July 1979. By agreement the hearing of the summons was treated as the trial of the action. The facts are set out in the judgment.

Lionel Read QC and *Timothy F M Stow* for the plaintiffs.
K R Bagnall QC and *Kirk Reynolds* for the defendants.

Cur adv vult

6th February. **FOX J** read the following judgment: This is an application by the defendants to strike out the statement of claim as disclosing no cause of action.

The matter arises out of proposals for the development of property at 107–111 Peascod Street, Windsor. The defendants have been the owners of the site since about 1973. The site adjoins land which is owned by the plaintiffs who are the local planning authority. In 1976 there was a compulsory purchase inquiry at which the defendants were objectors.

A compromise was reached in consequence of which three agreements were entered into between the parties. These were (1) a land exchange agreement, (2) an agreement dated 22nd January 1976 under s 52 of the Town and Country Planning Act 1971, which I will call 'the s 52 agreement', and (3) a side letter.

In October 1976 planning permission was granted by the plaintiffs to the defendants for the development of 107–111 Peascod Street. On 29th March 1979 the plaintiffs amended the boundaries of the conservation areas in Windsor so as to include, inter alia, 107–111 Peascod Street. In general, if property is lawfully designated as within a conservation area, the consent of the planning authority, the plaintiffs in this case, is necessary for the demolition of buildings thereon under s 277A of the Town and Country Planning Act 1971.

The defendants commenced to demolish 107–111 Peascod Street in the summer of
1979. On 2nd July 1979 the plaintiffs applied ex parte for an interlocutory injunction to
restrain the defendants from proceeding with the demolition without the plaintiffs'
consent. Foster J granted that injunction.

The writ was issued on 3rd July 1979. It claimed (1) a declaration that the defendants
were not entitled to demolish the premises without the plaintiffs' consent and (2) an
injunction to restrain the defendants from demolishing the premises. A notice of
motion by the plaintiffs to restrain the defendants from demolishing until the trial of the
action was issued on 3rd July. That motion was heard by Walton J. The defendants
resisted the application for an injunction. They contended, inter alia, that the terms of
the s 52 agreement were such that the plaintiffs were not entitled to require the
defendants to obtain their consent before demolishing the premises. Walton J gave
judgment on 11th July 1979. He refused to grant an injunction and dismissed the
motion. The plaintiffs did not appeal.

Between 11th July 1979 and 30th January 1980 no step was taken in the action. On
30th January 1980 the defendants issued a summons to dismiss the action for want of
prosecution. In February 1980 the plaintiffs delivered a statement of claim. The relief
sought therein differed from that sought in the writ in that the claim for an injunction
has been abandoned. The only substantive relief sought is a declaration that the
defendants are not and/or have at no time since the land was included in a conservation
area been entitled to demolish the buildings thereon known as 107–111 Peascod Street,
without obtaining the consent of the plaintiffs as the local planning authority pursuant
to s 277A of the Town and Country Planning Act 1971.

On delivery of the statement of claim the plaintiffs withdrew two enforcement notices
which they had served in respect of the premises in relation to the demolition. In March
1980 the Secretary of State confirmed the withdrawal of the enforcement notices and
stated that he would be taking no steps in relation to the premises.

The present summons to strike out the statement of claim was issued in October 1980.

It is common ground that none of the buildings was of any historic or architectural
interest at all. All the buildings have in fact now been demolished. The present
proceedings are, therefore, of no practical importance save as to costs and, possibly, the
question of liability on the implied undertaking for damages given on the grant of the
ex parte injunction by Foster J.

Whether this is a proper case for striking out I need not consider. It is agreed that,
since the parties are before me, it is convenient that I should determine the question
whether the defendants are correct in their contention as to the effect of the s 52
agreement. That in turn will determine whether the plaintiffs have a case for the grant
of a declaration as sought. Section 52 of the Town and Country Planning Act 1971,
provides as follows:

'(1) A local planning authority may enter into an agreement with any person
interested in land in their area for the purpose of restricting or regulating the
development or use of the land, either permanently or during such period as may
be prescribed by the agreement; and any such agreement may contain such
incidental or consequential provisions (including provisions of a financial character)
as appear to the local planning authority to be necessary or expedient for the
purposes of the agreement.

'(2) An agreement made under this section with any person interested in land
may be enforced by the local planning authority against persons deriving title under
that person in respect of that land, as if the local planning authority were possessed
of adjacent land and as if the agreement had been expressed to be made for the
benefit of such land.

'(3) Nothing in this section or in any agreement made thereunder shall be
construed—(a) as restricting the exercise, in relation to land which is the subject of
any such agreement, of any powers exercisable by any Minister or authority under

this Act so long as those powers are exercised in accordance with the provisions of
the development plan, or in accordance with any directions which may have been
given by the Secretary of State as to the provisions to be included in such a plan; or
(b) as requiring the exercise of any such powers otherwise than as mentioned in
paragraph (a) of this subsection . . .'

Subsection (4) I need not read.

The s 52 agreement is in the following terms, so far as material:

'WHEREAS:—

'(1) THE DEVELOPER [that is the defendants] is or shortly will be the owner in fee
simple of all that land edged purple on Plan No. 1 attached hereto

'(2) THE CORPORATION [that is the plaintiffs] are or shortly will be the owners in fee
simple of inter alia all that land edged blue on the said plan

'(3) IT IS INTENDED that the development of the land of the Developer and the
incidental development of the Corporation's land shall be regulated in accordance
with the provisions of Section 52 of the Town and Country Planning Act 1971

'NOW THEREFORE IT IS AGREED as follows:—

'1. FOR THE PURPOSES OF THIS DEED IT IS AGREED between the parties hereto that the
line marked "X" "Y" "Z" on the said plan is the boundary between the respective
developments of the Corporation and the Developer

'2. THE CORPORATION and the Developer hereby covenant in respect of the
following rights and restrictions and by reference to the said plan and Plan No. 2
attached hereto as follows:—(a) THE CORPORATION hereby covenants and agrees with
the Developer that the Developer may build up to the said line "X" "Y" "Z" and
along its length at levels "B" "D" and "E" on the said plan No. 2 (b) THE DEVELOPER
hereby covenants and agrees with the Corporation that the Corporation may build
up to the said line "X" "Y" "Z" and along its whole length at levels "B" and "D" . . .
(c) THE CORPORATION hereby further covenants and agrees with the Developer that
above level "E" the Developer may build as follows:—(i) BETWEEN points "X" and
"Y" to a level of 5·3 metres above level "E" or higher if the point is contained within
an angle of 50° measured from a point 5·3 metres above level "E" along the line "X"
"Y" as shown in Section AA of the said plan No. 2 (ii) BETWEEN points "Y" and "Z"
to a height contained within an angle of 50° measured from a point 3 metres from
the boundary "Y" "Z" and at a height of 800 mm above level "E" as shown in Section
BB on the said plan No. 2

'3. THE DEVELOPER hereby further covenants and agrees with the Corporation that
the Developer will not build on its land edged purple on Plan No. 1 to a height
exceeding 16 metres above the present ground level at point "X" shown on the said
Plan No. 1.'

There are, I think, two questions to be determined: (1) could the plaintiffs lawfully
enter into an agreement which has the effect of disentitling the plaintiffs to require
consent under s 277A to the demolition of the buildings? (2) if so, did the s 52 agreement
have that effect? As to the first question I was referred by counsel for the plaintiffs, by
way of preliminary, to the decision of the Court of Appeal in *Ransom & Luck Ltd v Surbiton
Borough Council* [1949] 1 All ER 185, [1949] Ch 180. That case related to s 34 of the Town
and Country Planning Act 1932, which provides:

'(1) Where any person is willing to agree with any such authority as is mentioned
in subsection (2) of this section that his land, or any part thereof, shall, so far as his
interest in the land enables him to bind it, be made subject, either permanently or
for a specified period, to conditions restricting the planning, development, or use
thereof in any manner in which those matters might be dealt with by or under a
scheme, the authority may, if they think fit, enter into an agreement with him to
that effect, and shall have power to enforce the agreement against persons deriving
title under him in the like manner and to the like extent as if the authority were

a possessed of, or interested in, adjacent land and as if the agreement had been entered into for the benefit of that adjacent land . . .'

In *Ransom & Luck Ltd v Surbiton Borough Council* the parties had entered into an agreement under s 34. The action was a claim by the plaintiffs for damages on the grounds that the council had refused liberty to develop their land in breach of the provisions of the s 34 agreement, it being contended that under the agreement the council, as authorised by s 34, assumed a contractual obligation not to exercise statutory

b powers to restrict the planning development and use of the land in accordance with the agreement. The council had refused an application for planning permission. The claim failed. It was held that s 34 only enabled the landowner to enter into an agreement with the local authority restricting the user of land so that the local authority could enforce the restrictions against the successor in title of the landowner, and that it was not competent to the council to incorporate into a s 34 agreement any restrictions on its statutory

c powers. Lord Greene MR made observations to which I was referred as to the improbability that Parliament by such a section would authorise a local authority to tie its hands with regard to its statutory duties and to contract itself out of them (see [1949] 1 All ER 185 at 189, [1949] Ch 180 at 195).

I bear those observations in mind, but plainly Parliament could by appropriate language authorise a planning authority to enter into agreements which limit the

d subsequent exercise of the authority's powers. The question is whether Parliament has done so in s 52.

It is clear that s 52 is very different in its language from s 34. I observe that while s 34 is only dealing with the case where a landowner is willing to agree to conditions restricting the planning development or use of the land, s 52, on the other hand, opens with a wide general authority to the planning authority to enter into any agreement

e with any person interested in the land for the purpose of restricting or regulating the development or use of the land. However, that is by the way. The fundamental difference between the two sections is to be found in the provisions of s 52(3) which have no counterpart in s 34. Subsection (3)(a) deals with the restriction of the authority's powers. It provides that nothing in s 52 or in any agreement entered into under it shall

f be construed—

'as restricting the exercise, in relation to land which is the subject of any such agreement, of any powers exercisable by any Minister or authority under this Act so long as those powers are exercised in accordance with the provisions of the development plan, or in accordance with any directions which may have been given by the Secretary of State as to the provisions to be included in such a plan . . .'

g If that provision was intended to operate so as to save fully the right of the authority to exercise any of its powers and discretions the paragraph could have stopped after the words 'this Act', but the subsequent part, which begins 'so long as' is, it seems to me, quite plainly intended to place a limitation on the saving provision. The saving only operates to a limited extent. The extent is that there is no restriction on the exercise of

h the planning authority's powers in relation to the land *so long as* they are exercised in accordance with the development plan or the appropriate direction of the Secretary of State, but not further.

It seems to me that the only sensible construction of the wording of sub-s (3)(a) is that an exercise of the authority's power is *not* preserved, contrary to provisions of the agreement, save to the extent that the exercise is in accordance with the development

j plan or a direction of the Secretary of State in relation to the contents of the plan. The language of sub-s (3)(a) seems to me to be quite inconsistent with a general saving of the authority's right to exercise its powers contrary to the provisions of the agreement.

I turn to sub-s (3)(b). That provides that nothing in the section or any agreement made thereunder 'shall be construed . . . as requiring the exercise of any such powers otherwise than as mentioned in paragraph (a) of this subsection'.

In my judgment that provision does require a positive exercise of the authority's powers in certain circumstances. The circumstances are (i) that the provisions of the relevant s 52 agreement are such as to require such exercise and (ii) that the exercise is in accordance with the provisions of the development plan or a relevant direction of the Secretary of State in relation to the contents of the plan.

The result it seems to me is that both paras (*a*) and (*b*) in sub-s (3) contemplate the existence, in consequence of a s 52 agreement, of fetters on the powers of the local planning authority. I do not think that s 52 is merely concerned with enabling the authority to enforce the agreement; the section seems to me to go a long way beyond that.

Now, so far as the present case is concerned it is common ground that there was no development plan or direction by the Secretary of State. In the circumstances it follows in my view that, if, on its true construction, the s 52 agreement limits the exercise of the plaintiffs' powers to take steps to prevent the demolition of 107–111 Peascod Street, there is nothing in law to prevent the agreement having that effect. It is, of course, well established that a person on whom a statutory power is conferred cannot simply fetter its future exercise. Thus in *Southend-on-Sea Corpn v Hodgson (Wickford) Ltd* [1961] 2 All ER 46 at 48–49, [1962] 1 QB 416 at 424 Lord Parker CJ said:

> 'There is a long line of cases to which we have not been specifically referred which lay down that a public authority cannot by contract fetter the exercise of its discretion.'

There is nothing, it seems to me, in principle to prevent the exercise of a statutory power being limited by the previous exercise of another statutory power. As Pennycuick V-C observed in *Dowty Boulton Paul Ltd v Wolverhampton Corpn* [1971] 2 All ER 277 at 282, [1971] 1 WLR 204 at 210:

> 'The cases are concerned with attempts to fetter in advance the future exercise of statutory powers otherwise than by the valid exercise of a statutory power. The cases are not concerned with the position which arises after a statutory power has been validly exercised.'

Walton J in his judgment on the motion for an interlocutory injunction reached the same conclusion as to the effect of s 52(3). He said:

> 'Before the predecessor of s 52 (which I think was s 25 of the Town and Country Planning Act 1947) was enacted with equivalent provisions to those in sub-s (3), one of the very obvious difficulties in the way of effecting any such agreement restricting or regulating the development or use of the land as a permanent matter or during such period as may be prescribed by the agreement, from the point of view of the landowner entering into the agreement, was that the local planning authority was able in a good many ways to change the rules of the game in its own favour if it so thought fit. The reason for that was that it was well established under the old law, and, indeed, apart from special provisions still is, that anybody (and this includes a planning authority) on whom statutory obligations and discretions are conferred in general (because there are exceptions and I am simply talking about the general case) cannot do one of either of two things; first of all, contract not to exercise its statutory powers in the future or, second, contract as to the manner in which it will exercise its statutory powers in the future. Those restrictions meant of course that the attractions from the point of view of the landowner of entering into any such agreement would be minimal. It is obviously, within certain general limits, therefore highly desirable that a local planning authority should be able to do both of those things, and that is provided for by sub-s (3) [Then, after setting out sub-s (3) Walton J continued:] So that, although I freely confess it is a rather curious method of legislating, there can be no doubt really about it ... So that sub-s (3)(*b*) in a curiously negative way provides that the local planning authority may bind itself to exercise its powers in the future provided that they are exercised in accordance with

a

the provisions of the development plan and not otherwise. That is a very considerable breach in the existing law, and so is sub-s (3)(a).'

Walton J concluded:

b

'So that the situation now is when a developer enters into a s 52 agreement he must be taken to know that any powers, for example the powers of extending a conservation area, may properly be exercised as against him provided that they are in accordance with the provisions of the development plan.'

I respectfully agree with the views expressed by Walton J.

The next question is the effect of the s 52 agreement itself. Walton J took the view that there was an obvious implied agreement contained in the s 52 agreement by the plaintiffs to the demolition of the buildings, and, indeed, that it was the foundation of what the defendants were going to do thereafter. I agree with that, and, in fact, counsel

c

for the plaintiffs accepts that, as he says, the whole premise of the s 52 agreement was that the buildings should be demolished. Counsel says, however, that it does not follow that there is to be implied into the agreement any provision by the plaintiffs not to require their consent under statutory powers to such demolition.

That seems to me to be quite unreal. It is conceded that the basis on which the agreement proceeded was that the buildings on the site should be demolished. A

d

purpose of the agreement was, in the language of s 52, to regulate the development of the land. One of the parties is the planning authoriy. It must have been implied that the plaintiffs so far as they were entitled to do so would do nothing to impede the demolition. I treat the s 52 agreement as if it provided in terms that the defendants be at liberty to demolish the Peascod Street houses. In the context of an agreement executed under a section which authorises the local planning authority to restrict the future

e

exercise of its powers, it does not seem to me sensible to infer that the authority was doing other than restricting its power to prevent the very thing that it was authorising and agreeing to.

My conclusion, therefore, is the same as that of Walton J, namely that in view of s 52(3) the plaintiffs cannot use any of their statutory powers against the defendants to prevent the demolition of the buildings, unless what the plaintiffs are proposing is in

f

accordance with the development plan. There was not and is not any development plan. The result, in my view, is that the plaintiffs could not enforce their powers under s 277A in relation to the extension of the conservation area, so as to prevent the demolition of these Peascod Street buildings.

There are two further matters to which I should refer. First, the extension of the conservation area was perfectly lawful; the only question is whether the plaintiffs were

g

entitled to apply the consequences of that extension against the defendants in relation to the demolition of the buildings on 107–111 Peascod Street, having regard to the s 52 agreement. As I have indicated I think they are not. Second, there is nothing in s 52 to prevent a local planning authority stipulating for the insertion into a s 52 agreement of a provision preserving all or any of its powers in full. How far a landowner would be prepared to enter into a s 52 agreement on that basis is another matter.

h

The result, it seems to me, is that the defendants have at all time since the execution of the s 52 agreement been entitled to demolish the buildings standing on 107–111 Peascod Street, at the date of the s 52 agreement without the consent of the plaintiffs under s 277A of the Town and Country Planning Act 1971. In the circumstances it seems to me that the action fails.

Declaration accordingly. Action dismissed.

Solicitors: *S G Hazelton,* Maidenhead (for the plaintiffs); *Gamlens* (for the defendants).

Azza M Abdallah   Barrister.

R v Pieck

(Case 157/79)

COURT OF JUSTICE OF THE EUROPEAN COMMUNITIES (FIRST CHAMBER)
JUDGES O'KEEFFE (PRESIDENT OF CHAMBER), BOSCO AND KOOPMANS
ADVOCATE-GENERAL J-P WARNER
8th MAY, 4th JUNE, 3rd JULY 1980

European Economic Community – Workers – Freedom of movement – Frontier checks – Presentation of passport or identity card – Prohibition on requirement of visa or equivalent document – Visa or equivalent document – Whether administrative measures at frontier going beyond passport or identity card check a restriction on freedom of movement – Whether indorsement of passport granting leave to enter equivalent to requirement of visa or equivalent document – Whether grant of leave to enter only for an initial period a restriction on freedom of movement – EEC Treaty, arts 7, 48 – EEC Council Directive 68/360, art 3.

European Economic Community – Workers – Freedom of movement – Right of residence – Proof of right of residence – Compliance with formalities required as proof of right of residence – Failure to obtain prescribed residence permit – Penalty for failure – Whether deportation or imprisonment for failure compatible with right of workers to move freely within Community – EEC Council Directive 68/360, art 4.

The defendant, a Netherlands national, was employed as a printer in Wales. When he entered the United Kingdom the immigration authorities indorsed his passport 'Given leave to enter the United Kingdom for six months'. After the expiration of the six months the defendant continued to reside in the United Kingdom without having in the meantime obtained a residence permit. He was charged under s 24(1)(b)(i)[a] of the Immigration Act 1971 with knowingly remaining in the United Kingdom beyond the time limited by the leave given to him. Section 24(1) provided that such an offence was punishable with a fine of up to £200 or up to six months' imprisonment or both, and in addition an offender was, by virtue of s 3(5)(a)[b] of the 1971 Act, liable to be deported. In the magistrates' court the defendant pleaded not guilty on the grounds (i) that the indorsement of his passport was invalid under Community law as being 'an entry visa or equivalent document' and accordingly prohibited by art 4[c] of EEC Council Directive 68/360, (ii) that the limitation of his right to stay in the United Kingdom to six months was in derogation of the right under art 48[d] of the EEC Treaty of workers to move freely

---

a   Section 24(1), so far as material, is set out at p 53 c, post
b   Section 3(5), so far as material, is set out at p 52 h, post
c   Article 4, so far as material, is set out at p 49 j to p 50 a, post
d   Article 48, so far as material, provides:

  '1. Freedom of movement for workers shall be secured within the Community by the end of the transitional period at the latest.

  '2. Such freedom of movement shall entail the abolition of any discrimination based on nationality between workers of the Member States as regards employment, remuneration and other conditions of work and employment.

  '3. It shall entail the right, subject to limitations justified on grounds of public policy, public security or public health: (a) to accept offers of employment actually made; (b) to move freely within the territory of Member States for this purpose; (c) to stay in a Member State for the purpose of employment in accordance with the provisions governing the employment of nationals of that State laid down by law, regulation or administrative action; (d) to remain in the territory of a Member State after having been employed in that State, subject to conditions which shall be embodied in implementing regulations to be drawn up by the Commission . . .'

a within the Community and was inconsistent with art 7^e of the Treaty and with the directive, and (iii) that in any event, even if an initial leave of six months could be imposed on entry into the United Kingdom, breach of it could not be punished by deportation or imprisonment. On a reference to the Court of Justice of the European Communities of certain questions concerning the interpretation of art 48 of the Treaty and the directive,

b **Held** – (1) Since the right of nationals of an EEC member state to enter the territory of another member state and reside therefor the purposes intended by the Treaty was a right conferred directly by the Treaty or by the provisions adopted for its implementation, and since the aim of Directive 68/360 was to abolish any remaining restrictions concerning movement and residence within the Community, in which connection art $3(1)^f$ of the directive provided that member states were to allow workers within the *c* Community to enter their territory on production of a valid identity card or passport and art 3(2) of which further provided that no entry visa or equivalent requirement could be demanded from those workers, it followed that any administrative measures requiring in a general way formalities at the frontier other than simply the production of a valid identity card or passport were prohibited by art 3(2). The indorsement on the defendant's passport was therefore illegal (see p 59 c to g and p 60 j to p 61 a, post).

d (2) The issue of the special residence document provided for in art 4 of Directive 68/360 only had a declaratory effect, and it could not, in the case of aliens to whom art 48 of the Treaty applied, be assimilated to a residence permit such as was prescribed for aliens in general, in connection with the issue of which the national authorities had a discretion. Accordingly, a member state could not require a person enjoying the protection of Community law to possess a general residence permit instead of the *e* document provided for in art 4 of the directive. It followed that the granting to the defendant of an initial leave to remain in the United Kingdom for a period limited to six months was incompatible with arts 7 and 48 of the Treaty and Directive 68/360 (see p 59 j to p 60 a and p 61 a b, post); *Sagulo, Brenca and Bakhouche* [1977] ECR 1495 applied.

(3) Deportation for failure to comply with the formalities required as proof of the right of residence of a worker enjoying the protection of Community law was *f* incompatible with the provisions of the EEC Treaty since such a measure negated the very right conferred and guaranteed by the Treaty. Although national authorities were entitled to impose penalties for such failures which were comparable to those attaching to minor offences by nationals, they were not justified in imposing penalties so disproportionate to the gravity of the infringement that they became an obstacle to the free movement of workers. It followed that such failures could not be punished by a *g* recommendation for deportation or by measures which went as far as imprisonment (see p 60 e to g and p 61 b, post).

Per Curiam. The restriction contained in art 48(3) of the EEC Treaty on the freedom of movement for workers within the Community on grounds of public policy, public security or public health is to be regarded not as a condition precedent to the acquisition of the right of entry and of residence but as providing the possibility, in individual cases *h* where there is sufficient justification, of imposing restrictions on the exercise of a right derived directly from the Treaty (see p 59 e, post).

Per the Advocate-General. In punishing an EEC worker for refusal to obtain the residence permit prescribed by art 4 of Directive 68/360, the court should not take into account any wholly separate offence (see p 57 j to p 58 a, post).

j ───

e   Article 7, so far as material, provides: 'Within the scope of application of this Treaty, and without prejudice to any special provisions contained therein, any discrimination on grounds of nationality shall be prohibited . . .'

f   Article 3 is set out at p 49 e, post

Notes

For the freedom of movement for workers within the EEC and the implementation of
that right, see Supplement to 39A Halsbury's Laws (3rd Edn) paras 108, 111, 113, and for
cases on the subject, see 21 Digest (Reissue) 252–267, 1675–1742.

For control within the United Kingdom of immigration of EEC nationals, see 4
Halsbury's Laws (4th Edn) para 1001.

For entry in contravention of the immigration laws, see ibid para 1027.

For the Immigration Act 1971, ss 3, 24, see 41 Halsbury's Statutes (3rd Edn) 20, 43.

For the EEC Treaty, arts 7, 48, see 42A ibid 126, 751.

Cases cited

Devred (Evelyn) née Kenny-Levick v EC Commission Case 257/78 [1979] ECR 3767, CJEC.

International Fruit Co NV v Produktschap voor Groenten en Fruit Cases 51–54/71 [1971] ECR
    1107, CJEC.

R v Bouchereau Case 30/77 [1981] 2 All ER 924, [1978] QB 732, [1978] 2 WLR 250, [1977]
    ECR 1999, CJEC, 21 Digest (Reissue) 254, 1686.

R v Secretary of State for the Home Department, ex parte Santillo Case 131/79 [1981] 2 All ER
    897, [1981] 2 WLR 362, CA, CJEC.

Royer (Jean Noël) Case 48/75 [1976] ECR 497, [1976] 2 CMLR 619, [1977] ICR 314,
    CJEC, 21 Digest (Reissue) 254, 1685.

Sagulo (Concetta), Gennaro Brenca and Addelmadjid Bakhouche Case 8/77 [1977] ECR 1495,
    [1977] 2 CMLR 585, CJEC, 21 Digest (Reissue) 255, 1687.

Watson (Lynne) and Alessandro Belmann Case 118/75 [1976] ECR 1185, [1976] 2 CMLR
    552, CJEC, 21 Digest (Reissue) 251, 1670.

Reference

The Pontypridd Magistrates' Court, Mid Glamorgan, Wales, by an order dated 5th
September 1979 referred certain questions set out at p 55, post, as to the interpretation
of arts 7 and 48 of the EEC Treaty, EEC Council Directive 64/221 and art 3(2) of EEC
Council Directive 68/360 to the Court of Justice of the European Communities for a
preliminary ruling under art 177 of the Treaty. The questions arose as a result of a plea
of not guilty entered by the defendant, Stanislaus Pieck, to a charge that, being a person
who was not a patrial and only having a limited leave to remain in the United Kingdom,
he knowingly remained in the United Kingdom beyond 29th January 1979, the time
limited by the leave. The defendant had also been served with a notice pursuant to s 6(2)
of the Immigration Act 1971 to the effect that if he was convicted of the offence charged
the court would have power to recommend his deportation under s 3(6) of the 1971
Act. The United Kingdom, the defendant and the Commission of the European
Communities submitted written observations to the European Court. The Director of
Public Prosecutions indicated that he indorsed the observations of the United Kingdom,
but he did not submit separate observations and was not represented in the
proceedings. The language of the case was English. The facts are set out in the opinion
of the Advocate-General.

Alan Newman for the defendant.
Simon D Brown for the United Kingdom.
Anthony McClellan, agent for the EC Commission, *Richard Plender* with him, for the
    Commission.

4th June. **The Advocate-General (J-P Warner)** delivered the following opinion: My
Lords, this case comes before the court by way of a reference for a preliminary ruling by
a stipendiary magistrate sitting in the Pontypridd Magistrates' Court, in Wales. It arises
from the prosecution before that court of a Dutch worker, Mr Stanislaus Pieck, for an

offence under United Kingdom immigration law and it raises questions as to the
a compatibility of that law with Community law.

The relevant provisions of Community law are, first, those of the EEC Treaty on
freedom of movement for persons and in particular for workers, the terms of which are
so familiar that I refrain from rehearsing them, and secondly the provisions of EEC
Council Regulation 1612/68 'on freedom of movement for workers within the
Community', of EEC Council Directive 68/360 'on the abolition of restrictions on
b movement and residence within the Community for workers of Member States and
their families', and of EEC Council Directive 64/221 'on the co-ordination of special
measures concerning the movement and residence of foreign nationals which are
justified on grounds of public policy, public security or public health'. The combined
effect of those instruments cannot, however, in my opinion, properly be appreciated
unless one also takes into account EEC Council Directive 73/148 'on the abolition of
c restrictions on movement and residence within the Community for nationals of Member
States with regard to establishment and the provision of services'.

Of Regulation 1612/68 I need say little. Its terms too are familiar. It applies of course
not only to workers but also to their families. It is of direct relevance only in that
Directive 68/360 refers to it.

Directive 68/360 is the instrument with the interpretation of which this case is mainly
d concerned. It replaced an earlier directive (64/240), which had itself replaced an earlier
one still, dated 16th August 1961. The provisions of Directive 68/360 that are
particularly in point are these:

> '*Article 3*
> '1. Member States shall allow the persons referred to in Article 1 [ie persons to
e whom Regulation 1612/68 applies] to enter their territory simply on production of
> a valid identity card or passport.
> '2. No entry visa or equivalent document may be demanded save from members
> of the family who are not nationals of a Member State. Member States shall accord
> to such persons every facility for obtaining any necessary visas.'

I pause there to observe that the words 'No entry visa or equivalent document may be
f demanded' in the English text of para 2 of that article differ somewhat from the
corresponding words in the other texts of it. Thus the French text has 'Aucun visa
d'entrée ni obligation équivalente ne peut être imposé', which literally means 'No entry
visa or equivalent requirement may be imposed'. The Danish, Dutch and Italian texts
have exactly the same meaning as the French. The German has 'Für die Einreise darf
weder ein Sichtvermerk noch ein gleichartiger Nachweis verlangt werden'. That is close
g to the English, but 'Nachweis' is less vague a term than 'document'. The particular
wording of the English text led counsel in this case to concentrate unduly, in my
opinion, on the question what sort of document art 3(2) was about, rather than on the
question what sort of requirement it was about. It is noteworthy that the English text
of art 3(2) of Directive 73/148, which is the parallel provision relating to the abolition of
restrictions on movement and residence within the Community of nationals of member
h states with regard to freedom of establishment and freedom to provide services, uses the
phrase 'No entry visa or equivalent requirement'.

Article 4 of Directive 68/360 provides:

> '1. Member States shall grant the right of residence in their territory to the
> persons referred to in Article 1 who are able to produce the documents listed in
j paragraph 3.
> '2. As proof of the right of residence, a document entitled "Residence Permit for
> a National of a Member State of the EEC" shall be issued. This document must
> include a statement that it has been issued pursuant to Regulation (EEC) No.
> 1612/68 and to the measures taken by the Member States for the implementation
> of the present Directive . . .

'3. For the issue of a Residence Permit for a National of a Member State of the EEC, Member States may require only the production of the following documents; —by the worker: (a) the document with which he entered their territory; (b) a confirmation of engagement from the employer or a certificate of employment . . .'

I pause again because there too there is a slight discrepancy between the English text and most of the other texts. Your Lordships will have observed that in the English text art 4(1) opens with the words 'Member States shall grant the right . . .' In such a context 'grant' can mean either 'confer' or simply 'recognise'. The same ambiguity is present in the German text, which uses the word 'gewähren'. But it is absent from the texts in the other languages and they show, in my opinion, that 'recognise' is the correct meaning. In art 8 of the directive (to which I shall come) the English text unambiguously has 'recognise'.

Article 6 provides:

'1. The residence permit . . . (b) must be valid for at least five years from the date of issue and be automatically renewable . . .

'3. Where a worker is employed for a period exceeding three months but not exceeding a year in the service of an employer in the host State or in the employ of a person providing services, the host Member State shall issue him a temporary residence permit, the validity of which may be limited to the expected period of the employment . . .'

Article 8 provides that 'Member States shall, without issuing a residence permit, recognize the right of residence in their territory' of three kinds of worker: (a) 'a worker pursuing an activity as an employed person, where the activity is not expected to last for more than three months; in the case of such a person, 'the document with which [he] entered the territory and a statement by the employer on the expected duration of the employment shall be sufficient to cover his stay'; (b) 'a worker who, while having his residence in the territory of a Member State to which he returns as a rule each day or at least once a week, is employed in the territory of another Member State'; the competent authority of the state where such a worker is employed may, however, issue him 'a special permit valid for five years and automatically renewable'; (c) 'a seasonal worker who holds a contract of employment stamped by the competent authority of the Member State on whose territory he has come to pursue his activity'.

Article 10 provides that member states shall not derogate from the provisions of the directive save on the grounds of public policy, public security or public health.

Your Lordships thus see that art 3 of Directive 68/360 is concerned with the right of a person to whom Regulation 1612/68 applies to enter a member state's territory, whilst the subsequent articles of the directive are concerned with his right to reside there. That right exists independently of his possession of a residence permit, which is only 'proof' of the right, and is not appropriate in all cases, for instance not if his stay is to be of less than three months.

The United Kingdom government referred to a declaration recorded in the minutes of the Council when Directive 68/360 was under consideration, to the effect that a national of a member state seeking employment in another member state should have a minimum of three months to achieve that purpose, and that, if he had not found employment on the expiry of that period, his stay might be terminated. That declaration does not appear to be officially published, though it is referred to in a number of published works (see for instance T Hartley on EEC Immigration Law (1978, pp 105–106). In the *Royer* case [1976] ECR 497 this court clearly expressed the view that such a person came within the category of those on whom the Treaty conferred the right of free movement.

Directive 73/148 is, as I have said, the parallel directive about freedom of movement for persons within the Community in connection with freedom of establishment and freedom to provide services. It replaced EEC Council Directive 64/220. Essentially it applies to 'nationals of a Member State who are established or wish to establish themselves

a in another Member State in order to pursue activities as self-employed persons, or who wish to provide services in that State', to nationals of a member state 'wishing to go to another Member State as recipients of services', and to members of the families of any of them. Its provisions, particularly art 3 about the right of entry, and arts 4 ff about the right of residence and residence permits, correspond closely to those of Directive 68/360. Your Lordships will remember that, in the *Watson and Belmann* case [1976] ECR

b 1185 at 1202–1205, the Advocate-General (A Trabucchi) discussed the application of the provisions of the Treaty on freedom of movement for persons to 'recipients of services', and expressed doubt as to the scope of the category of recipients of services, particularly whether it could include tourists. He said that the practical effect of a 'broad interpretation' of that concept would be to 'extend the right of freedom of movement to all nationals of the Member States because everyone is actually or potentially a recipient

c of services'. I will not take up your Lordships' time on that, except to say that it should not be assumed that I share the Advocate-General's hesitations.

I come lastly to Directive 64/221, which remains applicable both in relation to Directive 68/360 and to Directive 73/148, and in particular in relation to the issue of residence permits under both of them. Article 5 of Directive 64/221 provides:

d
> '1. A decision to grant or to refuse a first residence permit shall be taken as soon as possible and in any event not later than six months from the date of application for the permit. The person concerned shall be allowed to remain temporarily in the territory pending a decision either to grant or to refuse a residence permit . . .'

Articles 6 to 9 provide for safeguards, by way of appeal and the like, for a person who is refused a residence permit. The grounds of refusal can only be grounds of public

e policy, public security or public health.

Decisions of this court to which we have been referred, in particular the *Royer* case the *Watson and Belmann* case and the *Sagulo, Brenca and Bakhouche* case [1977] ECR 1495, underline or clarify certain points.

1. Persons entitled to freedom of movement within the Community, whether it be as workers or members of their families or by virtue of the provisions relating to

f freedom of establishment or freedom to provide services, derive their rights (to enter the territories of member states other than their own and to reside there) directly from the relevant provisions of the Treaty, as refined on by the acts of the Council implementing them. Accordingly no act of any member state is necessary to confer those rights on such a person, and no member state may restrict or hinder his exercise of them.

2. A residence permit of the kind provided for by Directive 68/360 'has only a

g declaratory effect'. It is no more than evidence of the holder's entitlement to those rights, and a member state is under an obligation to issue such a permit to anyone who provides the appropriate documentary proof that he is entitled to them.

3. It follows among other things that a member state must recognise the right to reside on its territory of a worker who is able to prove his entitlement to that right by producing the two documents specified in art 4(3) of Directive 68/360, ie his identity

h card or passport and a confirmation of employment from his employer or a certificate of employment.

4. That is not to say that a member state may not require the worker concerned to comply with the formalities prescribed by its own law for the control of aliens, in so far as those formalities are reasonable and do not limit the rights of entry and of residence conferred on him by the Treaty. A member state may for instance require the worker

j to register with, or report his presence to, a prescribed authority in that state; and it may require him to apply for a residence permit of the kind provided for by the directive where the directive makes that appropriate, though it may not require him to have any other sort of residence permit prescribed by its law for aliens in general (the issue of which may be discretionary). Nor is a member state precluded from prescribing sanctions for failure to comply with such formalities.

5. Those sanctions may not however include deportation, for that amounts to a denial of the right conferred by the Treaty, and may only be resorted to on grounds of public policy, public security or public health. Mere disregard of formalities relating to the control of aliens cannot constitute such grounds.

6. Other sanctions, such as fines and imprisonment, must not be so disproportionate to the gravity of the offence as to become obstacles to the exercise, by those entitled to them, of the rights conferred by the Treaty. Where a member state has not adapted its law to the requirements of Community law in that respect, it is for the courts of that state to exercise their sentencing powers so as to avoid any conflict with those requirements.

The relevant United Kingdom law and practice are to be found in the Immigration Act 1971 and in the immigration rules made by the Secretary of State. Those rules lay down the practice to be followed in the administration of the Act. They do not, strictly speaking, have legislative force, but they must, by virtue of s 3(2) of the Act, be laid before Parliament and may be disapproved by resolution of either House of Parliament.

Sections 1 and 2 of the 1971 Act, between them, define a category of persons called 'patrials', who have 'the right of abode in the United Kingdom', and who are thereby—

'free to live in, and to come and go into and from, the United Kingdom without let or hindrance except such as may be required . . . to enable their right to be established . . .'

(Your Lordships will remember that I dealt with the complexities of the law in that respect in my opinion in *Devred v EC Commission* [1979] ECR 3767.)

Section 3(1) of the 1971 Act provides that, subject to exceptions that are not here material—

'where a person is not patrial—(a) he shall not enter the United Kingdom unless given leave to do so in accordance with this Act; (b) he may be given leave to enter the United Kingdom (or, when already there, leave to remain in the United kingdom) either for a limited or for an indefinite period; (c) if he is given a limited leave to enter or remain in the United kingdom, it may be given subject to conditions restricting his employment or occupation in the United Kingdom, or requiring him to register with the police, or both.'

Section 3(3) provides, so far as material:

'In the case of a limited leave to enter or remain in the United Kingdom—(a) a person's leave may be varied, whether by restricting, enlarging or removing the limit on its duration, or by adding, varying or revoking conditions . . .

Subsections (5) and (6) of s 3 are about deportation. Your Lordships are familiar with them because the court had to consider them *R v Bouchereau* [1981] 2 All ER 924, [1978] QB 732 and they were of some relevance also in the *Santillo* case [1981] 2 All ER 897, [1981] 2 WLR 362. Those subsections are, so far as material, in these terms:

'(5) A person who is not patrial shall be liable to deportation from the United Kingdom—(a) if, having only a limited leave to enter or remain, he does not observe a condition attached to the leave or remains beyond the time limited by the leave . . .

'(6) Without prejudice to the operation of subsection (5) above, a person who is not patrial shall also be liable to deportation from the United Kingdom if . . . he is convicted of an offence for which he is punishable with imprisonment and on his conviction is recommended for deportation by a court empowered by this Act to do so.'

The court empowered by the Act to recommend a person for deportation is, your Lordships remember, the court empowered to sentence him for the offence in question. By virtue of s 6(2) of the 1971 Act a court may not recommend a person for deportation

unless he has been given not less than seven days' notice in writing of certain things
a specified in the subsection.

Section 4(1) of the Act provides:

'The power under this Act to give or refuse leave to enter the United Kingdom
shall be exercised by immigration officers, and the power to give leave to remain in
the United Kingdom, or to vary any leave under section 3(3)(*a*) (whether as regards
duration or conditions), shall be exercised by the Secretary of State; and . . . those
b powers shall be exercised by notice in writing given to the person affected . . .'

Section 24(1) provides:

'A person who is not patrial shall be guilty of an offence punishable on summary
conviction with a fine of not more than £200 or with imprisonment for not more
than six months, or with both, in any of the following cases—(*a*) if contrary to this
c Act he knowingly enters the United Kingdom in breach of a deportation order or
without leave; (*b*) if, having only a limited leave to enter or remain in the United
Kingdom, he knowingly either—(i) remains beyond the time limited by the leave;
or (ii) fails to observe a condition of the leave . . .'

Schedule 2 to the Act, which is entitled 'Administrative Provisions as to Control on
d Entry etc', provides among other things, by para 2(1):

'An immigration officer may examine any persons who have arrived in the
United Kingdom by ship or aircraft . . . for the purpose of determining—(*a*) whether
any of them is or is not patrial; and (*b*) whether, if he is not, he may or may not enter
the United Kingdom without leave; and (*c*) whether, if he may not, he should be
given leave and for what period and on what conditions (if any), or should be
e refused leave.'

Two sets of rules made by the Secretary of State and laid before Parliament under s 3(2)
of the Act are here in point. They are the Immigration Rules for Control on Entry: EEC
and other Non-Commonwealth Nationals and the Immigration Rules for Control after
Entry: EEC and other Non-Commonwealth Nationals (HC Papers (1972–73) nos 81 and
f 82). Both were laid before Parliament on 25th January 1973. Both have been amended
from time to time since, but not in ways that affect this case.

The rules for control on entry (which do not apply to citizens of Ireland, who are
afforded more favourable treatment) provide that a person must, on arrival in the United
Kingdom, produce on request to the immigration officer 'a valid national passport or
other document satisfactorily establishing his identity and nationality' and that nationals
g of other member states of the Community 'may use valid national identity cards instead
of passports' (see r 3 and the footnote thereto). The rules also provide that nationals of
certain countries, which are listed in an appendix and do not include any member state
of the Community, must produce to the immigration officer 'a passport or other identity
document endorsed with a United Kingdom visa and should be refused leave to enter if
they have no current visa' (see r 8). Part V of the rules contains special provisions as to the
h admission of nationals of other member states of the Community. Those provisions,
where they apply, override any other relevant provisions of the rules (see r 49). They
include rr 51 and 52, which provide:

'51. When an EEC national is given leave to enter, no condition is to be imposed
restricting his employment or occupation in the United Kingdom. Admission
should normally be for a period of six months, except in the case of a returning
j resident or the holder of a valid resident's permit.

'52. An EEC national who wishes to enter the United Kingdom in order to take
or seek employment, set up in business or work as a self-employed person is to be
admitted without a work permit or other prior consent.'

The rules for control after entry are divided into two parts, Part A, which is headed

'Variation of Leave to Enter or Remain', and Part B, headed 'Deportation'. I need not trouble with anything in Part B. Part A has two sections, section I, which applies generally to non-Commonwealth nationals, and section II, which applies specifically to EEC nationals (again other than Irish). The rules in section II, where they apply, override those in section I. Of the rules in section II, r 34 is particularly in point. It reads:

'If a person admitted for six months enters employment he should be issued with a residence permit. The residence permit should be limited to the duration of the employment if this is expected to be less than 12 months. Otherwise the permit should be for five years. But a permit should not normally be granted if the person has not found employment at the end of the six months period for which he was admitted, nor if during that time he has become a charge on public funds.'

The effect of those provisions, so far as here material, appears to be that every national of a member state (other than Ireland) seeking entry into the United Kingdom must produce either his passport or his identity card and obtain leave to enter from the immigration officer. Unless he is a returning resident or the holder of a valid resident's permit, he will normally be given leave to enter for a period of six months, whatever the purpose of his journey to the United Kingdom may be. That leave must be given to him 'by notice in writing'. Thereafter he may apply to the Secretary of State for his leave to be varied, by enlarging or removing the limit on its duration. If he enters employment, the application to vary the leave will result in the issue to him of a residence permit valid for five years, or for the duration of the employment if this is expected to be less than 12 months.

It was explained to us on behalf of the United Kingdom that the object of the system was to avoid delay at the port or airport of entry. It avoided the immigration officer having to examine each national of a member state as he arrived in order to ascertain whether the purpose of his coming to the United Kingdom was or was not one giving him a right of entry under the Treaty. It meant that there was a period of six months in which an entrant could decide whether he wished to remain longer and, if appropriate, apply for a residence permit. I confess that, to my mind, that seems a sensible system, particularly for a country that has no 'population registers', does not issue identity cards, and requires aliens to register with the police only in certain cases. That is not to say, however, that the system, as applied in the present case, accords with Community law.

The facts of the present case are set out in a statement accompanying the order for reference and are not in dispute. Mr Pieck is a Dutch national and the holder of a Dutch passport. He is not patrial. It appears from his passport that he first entered the United Kingdom on 3rd August 1973 and that he subsequently left and re-entered it on several occasions. On 12th April 1976 his passport was renewed at the Dutch consulate in London, on which occasion he gave his residence as 'Cardiff (GB)'. He entered the United Kingdom again on 3rd December 1977, left on 22nd July 1978 and re-entered one week later, on 29th July 1978. On each occasion that he entered the United Kingdom, including 29th July 1978, his passport was stamped by the immigration officer with the date and place of entry into the United Kingdom and with an indorsement consisting of the words 'Given leave to enter the United Kingdom for six months'. At all times since his entry into the United Kingdom on 3rd December 1977, Mr Pieck has been, and he still is, employed as a printer by a firm called Graphic Prints at Taffs Well, near Cardiff. The six months' leave of entry into the United Kingdom granted to him on 29th July 1978 expired on 29th January 1979. In March 1979 he went of his own accord to the South Wales Constabulary, explained that he had overstayed his leave and asked for advice. He was advised to send his passport to the Home Office together with an application for a further stay, but he did nothing. On 3rd May 1979, when required by a police officer to produce his passport, he said, 'I was going to send it off but I forgot.' He was then charged with an offence under s 24(1)(b)(i) of the Immigration Act 1971 and served with a notice as regards liability to deportation pursuant to s 6(2) of the Act. The charge against him reads as follows:

'For that you being a person who is not patrial and only having a limited leave to
remain in the United Kingdom knowingly remained in the United Kingdom
beyond 29 January 1979, the time limited by the leave.'

On 12th July 1979 Mr Pieck appeared before the stipendiary magistrate and pleaded
not guilty to the charge. It was argued on his behalf (a) that the stamp in his passport
relating to his entry into the United Kingdom on 29th July 1978 amounted to an 'entry
visa or equivalent document' contrary to the provisions of Directive 68/360, (b) that
under art 48(3)(b) and (c) of the Treaty, Mr Pieck had a right to move freely within and
stay in the United Kingdom for the purpose of employment, and that the purported
grant of leave to enter the United Kingdom limited to six months on 29th July 1978 was
in derogation of those rights, and further inconsistent with art 7 of the Treaty, (c) that the
initial grant of six months' leave to enter the United Kingdom was inconsistent with the
provisions of Directive 68/360 and (d) that even if an initial leave of six months stay could
be imposed on entry into the United Kingdom, breach of it could not be punished by
deportation or imprisonment. Arguments to the contrary were submitted on behalf of
the Crown. As a result, the magistrate has referred three questions to this court. In
slightly abbreviated form they are these:

1. What is the meaning of 'entry visa or equivalent document' in art 3(2) of Council
Directive 68/360?

2. On entry into a member state by an EEC national, is the grant by that member state
of an initial leave to remain for a period limited to six months consistent with the rights
secured to such a national by arts 7 and 48 of the EEC Treaty and the provisions of
Directives 64/221 and 68/360?

3. If the answer to question 2 is affirmative, where such a national is given a six
months' limited leave to remain in a member state, and being employed as a worker but
having failed to apply for a residence permit he overstays that leave, can such a breach of
law be punished in that member state by measures which include imprisonment and/or
a recommendation for deportation?

The argument before us on the first question was, as I mentioned earlier, coloured by
the fact that the English text of art 3(2) of Directive 68/360 refers to a 'document' being
'demanded' rather than to a requirement being imposed. This led to its being emphasised
on behalf of the United Kingdom government that EEC nationals were not called on to
'produce', on their arrival at United Kingdom ports or airports, anything other than their
identity cards or passports. It also led to a learned discussion of the etymology of the
word 'visa', and of the meaning of that word in consular usage and in international
agreements for the abolition of visas. Basing itself on the meaning of 'visa' in such
contexts the United Kingdom government submitted that the phrase 'entry visa or
equivalent document' in art 3(2) connoted 'a documentary clearance or consent which an
intending entrant is required to obtained from the proposed host member state's
representative(s) abroad prior to arrival at the intended time and point of entry into the
host country'.

In my opinion that is too narrow an interpretation of the phrase. Article 3 of the
directive must in my opinion be interpreted as a whole and with due regard to the
purpose of the directive, which is the abolition of restrictions on the free movement of
workers and their families within the Community. It appears to me, from the wording
of art 3(2), that it is intended to do three things: (i) to underline and reinforce the terms
of art 3(1) which require a member state to allow a person to whom the directive applies
to enter its territory 'simply on production of a valid identity card or passport'; (ii) to
make an exception to that requirement in the case of any member of a worker's family
who is not a national of a member state; and (iii) to require a member state to accord to
such a member of a worker's family 'every facility for obtaining any necessary visas'.

It would therefore in my opinion be inconsistent both with the purpose and with the
wording of art 3 to interpret it as allowing a member state to impose on a worker a
requirement additional to the production of his identity card or passport so long as that

requirement was to be met at the point of entry into its territory and not previously by
application to its representatives abroad.

a

On the other hand art 3 obviously does not envisage that, on production of a worker's
identity card or passport to the immigration officer or other responsible official of a
member state, that official should necessarily remain mute and passive. At least a smile,
a nod or a wave of the hand must be permitted. If that be so, I can see no possible
objection to a stamp in the man's passport, or to the issue to him of a separate document,
acknowledging his right to enter the territory of the member state concerned. Thus, in
my opinion, if in the present case the stamp in Mr Pieck's passport had simply said 'Given
leave to enter the United Kingdom', and if, as a matter of United Kingdom law, that
stamp had meant no more than that his right to enter the United Kingdom was
acknowledged, there could have been no objection to it.

b

On that analysis, there are two difficulties in this case.

The first and the most obvious is that in fact the stamp in Mr Pieck's passport went on
to say 'for six months'. I propose to leave that aside for the moment.

c

The second difficulty arises because it looks from the provisions of the Immigration
Act 1971 and of the Immigration Rules for Control on Entry as though, as a matter of
United Kingdom law, the giving of leave to enter may not be a mere acknowledgement
of a right, but may be discretionary. It is not of course for this court, but for the courts
of the United Kingdom, to determine whether that is so. As to the relevant Community
law, with which this court is concerned, it was submitted on behalf of the United
Kingdom government that a member state must have such a discretion because freedom
of movement for persons was, under that law, subject to limitations. It is of course
subject to limitations in that, on the one hand, it does not extend to nationals of a
member state wishing to go to another member state for a purpose not envisaged by the
Treaty and in that, on the other hand, it may be denied to a particular person on grounds
of public policy, public health or public security. At first sight that means that a
member state may deny entry to a person in whose case either of those limitations
applies.

d

e

Does it follow that a member state is entitled (or perhaps even bound), when a national
of another member state seeks entry into its territory, to examine his case to see whether
or not he has a right to enter, to do, in other words, precisely that which the United
Kingdom system, as it was explained to us, is designed to avoid? As to that art 3 of the
directive contains within itself an apparent contradiction. It applies only to persons to
whom Regulation 1612/68 applies, yet it requires member states to allow such persons
to enter their territory simply on production of a valid identity card or passport, a
document which is inherently unlikely to show whether the holder is a person to whom
the regulation applies. There are two possible avenues of escape from that dilemma.
One is to hold that it is implicit in art 3 that the person concerned must, in order to
obtain entry, produce, in addition to his identity card or passport, evidence that he is a
person to whom the regulation applies. The other is to hold that the authors of the
directive intended that, subject to possible derogation on grounds of public policy, public
security or public health, members states should allow each other's nationals to enter
their territories simply on proof of their nationality and that any question as to their
right to be there under the Treaty should be examined after entry. In my opinion the
latter solution is to be preferred, for two reasons. Firstly, it is more consistent than the
former with the terms of the directive. It is under art 4 and 8, which are concerned with
the right of residence, that evidence is to be furnished by a person concerned that he is
a person to whom the regulation applies. That that is something which he is to do after
entry, and not at the time of entry, is shown by, for instance, the use of the past tense in
the phrase 'the document with which he entered their territory' in arts 4(3) and 8(1)(a).
Secondly, it accords with common sense, as indeed the United Kingdom practice
evinces. The authors of the directive must have been aware that it and the successive
directives relating to free movement of persons in connection with freedom of
establishment and freedom to provide services would, between them, cover many if not

f

g

h

j

most nationals of member states travelling to other member states. They cannot have
intended that all should be delayed at the internal frontiers of the Community while the
a sheep were sorted from the goats. Nor does it seem to me that it was beyond the powers
conferred on the Council by arts 49, 54 and 63 of the Treaty to legislate so as to avoid that
result.

Thus, in my opinion, the answer to the magistrate's first question is that art 3(2) of
Directive 68/360, in so far as it provides that 'No entry visa or equivalent document may
b be demanded', means that a member state may not impose on a national of another
member state any requirement beyond the production of a valid identity card or passport
as a condition of allowing him to enter its territory.

As to the fact that the stamp in Mr Pieck's passport went on to say 'for six months', it
seems to me that that cannot be relevant to any question relating to art 3, which is
concerned only with entry. It affected Mr Pieck's right to remain in the United Kingdom
c after entry, which is the subject matter of the magistrate's second question.

As regards that question I think that I have said enough about the provisions of the
Treaty and of the relevant Council legislation, and in my summary of the effect of the
decisions of this court interpreting them, to show that a member state may not, save on
grounds of public policy, public security or public health, limit the right of a worker who
is a national of another member state to remain on its territory, but that it may require
d him to establish, in accordance with arts 4 ff of Directive 68/360 and arts 5 ff of Directive
64/221, his right to remain there.

We were told on behalf of the United Kingdom government that the sole effect of a
stamp such as that in Mr Pieck's passport was to indicate to the entrant that he had duly
been given leave to enter and that he had a period of six months within which to obtain
a residence permit, to which he would have an absolute right subject to considerations
e of public policy, public security and public health. The stamp was in no way, so it was
said, restrictive of the entrant's rights; it allowed him a period of six months in which to
decide whether, because he wished to remain, to seek a residence permit. It is of course
for the courts of the United Kingdom, not for this court, to say whether that
interpretation of the stamp is correct. I confine myself to observing that the charge
against Mr Pieck is that 'being a person who is not patrial and only having a limited leave
f to remain in the United Kingdom [he] knowingly remained in the United Kingdom
beyond . . . the time limited by the leave'. The charge is not that, being under an
obligation to apply for a residence permit, he failed to do so.

In that connection, we were handed at the hearing copies of a printed notice (HO Form
IS.120) which, we were told, has since 1st January 1980 been given to nationals of other
member states on their entry into the United Kingdom, in lieu of any stamp in their
g passports. No question arises in this case as to the compatibility of the terms of that
notice with Community law. After some hesitation I have come to the conclusion that
it will be best if I say nothing about it.

So I turn lastly to the magistrate's third question.

The answer to that too is to be found in the decisions of the court the effect of which
I have summarised. It could, it seems to me, possibly be relevant if the charge against Mr
h Pieck were to be interpreted, as the United Kingdom government suggested that it
should be, as being that he failed to apply for a residence permit when he should have
done so. For that, he clearly could not be deported. So much indeed is common
ground. Whether he could be imprisoned would depend on the sentencing court's
assessment of the gravity of the offence. On behalf of the United Kingdom government
it was submitted that such an offence could be punished by imprisonment in exceptional
j circumstances, for instance if it were persistent and constituted a wilful refusal to comply
with the law. I see no reason to differ from that.

We were told on behalf of the United Kingdom government that Mr Pieck, when he
appeared before the magistrate on 12th July 1979, was charged also with stealing a lady's
handbag, an offence to which he pleaded guilty and for which he was placed on probation
and ordered to pay compensation of £1·50 and costs of £15. The United Kingdom

government suggested, as I understood it, that his conviction for that offence could properly be taken into account by the magistrate in considering whether to sentence him to imprisonment for the offence under the Immigration Act 1971. I think not, but, since the magistrate has asked this court no question about that, I say no more about it.

In the result I am of the opinion that, in answer to the questions referred to the court by the magistrate, your Lordships should rule as follows:

1. Article 3(2) of Directive 68/360, in so far as it provides that 'No entry visa or equivalent document may be demanded', means that a member state may not impose on a national of another member state any requirement beyond the production of a valid identity card or passport as a condition of allowing him to enter its territory.

2. A member state may not, otherwise than on grounds of public policy, public security or public health, limit the stay on its territory of a national of another member state to a period shorter than that for which he is entitled to reside there by virtue of art 48 of the EEC Treaty and of the provisions of Directive 68/360; but it may, in a case where the provisions of that directive render the issue of a residence permit appropriate, require him to apply for such a permit within six months of his entry into its territory or within any other reasonable period.

3. Where a member state has validly imposed on a national of another member state an obligation to apply for a residence permit, his failure to comply with that obligation may not be punished by deportation and may be punished by imprisonment only where the circumstances of the offence make it one of exceptional gravity.

3rd July.   **THE COURT OF JUSTICE** delivered its judgment which, having summarised the facts, procedure and submissions of the parties, dealt with the law as follows:

1. By order of 5th September 1979, which was received at the court on 15th October 1979, the Pontypridd Magistrates' Court under art 177 of the EEC Treaty asked three questions on the interpretation of arts 7 and 48 of the Treaty and of EEC Council Directives 64/221 of 25th February 1964 on the co-ordination of special measures concerning the movement and residence of foreign nationals which are justified on grounds of public policy, public security or public health and 68/360 of 15th October 1968 on the abolition of restrictions on movement and residence within the Community for workers of members states and their families.

2. Criminal proceedings were brought in the national court against a Netherlands national, residing in Cardiff, Wales, and pursuing an activity as an employed person, who was charged that, being a person who was not a 'patrial' (a British national having a right of abode in the United Kingdom) and having only been granted leave to enter the United Kingdom or to remain there for a limited period, knowingly remained beyond the time limited by the leave. The accused held no residence permit; when he last entered the territory of the United Kingdom, on 29th July 1978, an indorsement containing the words 'Given leave to enter the United Kingdom for six months' was stamped on his passport.

The first question

3. In its first question the national court asks what is the meaning of 'entry visa or equivalent document' in art 3(2) of Council Directive 68/360?

4. This court has already stated on several occasion that the right of nationals of a member state to enter the territory of another member state and reside there for the purposes intended by the Treaty is a right conferred directly by the Treaty or, as the case may be, by the provisions adopted for its implementation.

5. The aim of Directive 68/360, as the recitals in the preamble thereto show, is to adopt measures for the abolition of restrictions which still exist concerning movement and residence within the Community, which conform to the rights and privileges accorded to nationals of member states by EEC Council Regulation 1612/68 in freedom of movement for workers within the Community. To this end the directive lays down

the conditions on which nationals of member states may exercise their right to leave
a their state of origin to take up activities as employed persons in the territory of another
member state and their right to enter the territory of that state and to reside there.

6. In this connection art 3(1) of the directive provides that member states shall allow
the persons to whom Regulation 1612/68 applies to enter their territory on production
of a valid identity card or passport. Article 3(2) contains the further provision that no
entry visa or equivalent requirement may be demanded from these workers.

b 7. In the course of the procedure before the court the United Kingdom government
maintained that the phrase 'entry visa' means exclusively a documentary clearance issued
before the traveller arrives at the frontier in the form of an indorsement on his passport
or of a separate document. On the contrary an indorsement stamped on a passport at the
time of arrival giving leave to enter the territory may not be regarded as an entry visa or
equivalent document.

c 8. This argument cannot be upheld. For the purpose of applying the directive, the
object of which is to abolish restrictions on movement and residence for Community
workers within the Community, the time at which clearance to enter the territory of a
member state has been given and indicated on a passport or by another document is
immaterial. Furthermore the right of Community workers to enter the territory of a
member state which Community law confers may not be made subject to the issue of a
d clearance to this effect by the authorities of that member state.

9. Admittedly the right of entry for the workers in question is not unlimited.
Nevertheless the only restriction which art 48 of the Treaty lays down concerning
freedom of movement in the territory of member states is that of limitations justified on
grounds of public policy, public security or public health. This restriction must be
regarded not as a condition precedent to the acquisition of the right of entry and
e residence but as providing the possibility, in individual cases where there is sufficient
justification, of imposing restrictions on the exercise of a right derived directly from the
Treaty. It does not therefore justify administrative measures requiring in a general way
formalities at the frontier other than simply the production of a valid identity card or
passport.

10. The answer to the first question should therefore be that art 3(2) of Directive
f 68/360 prohibiting member states from demanding an entry visa or equivalent
requirement for Community workers moving within the Community must be
interpreted as meaning that the phrase 'entry visa or equivalent requirement' covers any
formality for the purpose of granting leave to enter the territory of a member state which
is coupled with a passport or identity card check at the frontier, whatever may be the
place or time at which that leave is granted and in whatever form it may be granted.

g *The second question*

11. In its second question the national court seeks to ascertain whether, on entry into
a member state by an EEC national, the granting by that member state of an initial leave
to remain for a period limited to six months is compatible with arts 7 and 48 of the
Treaty and with Council Directives 64/221 and 68/360.

h 12. Article 4 of Directive 38/360 provides that member states shall grant the right of
residence in their territory to the persons referred to in the directive and goes on to say
that as 'proof' of this right a special residence permit shall be issued. This provisions
must be interpreted in the light of the recitals in the preamble to the directive, according
to which the rules applicable to residence should, as far as possible, bring the position of
workers from other member states into line with that of nationals.

j 13. The court has already stated in its judgment in *Sagulo, Brenca and Bakhouche* [1977]
ECR 1495 that the issue of a special residence document provided for in art 4 above-
mentioned has only a declaratory effect and that, for aliens to whom art 48 of the Treaty
or parallel provisions give rights, it cannot be assimilated to a residence permit such as is
prescribed for aliens in general, in connection with the issue of which the national
authorities have a discretion. The court went on to say that a member state may not

therefore require from a person enjoying the protection of Community law that he should possess a general residence permit instead of the document provided for in art 4 of Directive 68/360.

14. It follows that the answer to the second question has already been given by the court in the above-mentioned judgment.

The third question

15. The third question asks whether a national of a member state of the Community who has overstayed the leave granted in the residence permit may be punished in that member state by measures which include imprisonment and/or a recommendation for deportation.

16. In the above-mentioned judgment in *Sagulo, Brenca and Bakhouche* the court has already decided that the imposition of penalties or other coercive measures is ruled out in so far as a person protected by the provisions of Community law does not comply with national provisions which prescribe for such a person possession of a general residence permit instead of the document provided for in Directive 68/360, since the national authorities should not impose penalties for disregard of a provision which is incompatible with Community law.

17. Having regard however to the circumstances of this case as stated by the national court and in the light of the answer just given to the second question, the third question may also be understood as raising the problem whether the failure on the part of a national of a member state of the Community, to whom the rules on freedom of movement for workers apply, to obtain the special residence permit prescribed in art 4 of Directive 68/360 may be punished by measures which include imprisonment or a recommendation for deportation.

18. Among the penalties attaching to a failure to comply with the formalities required as proof of the right of residence of a worker enjoying the protection of Community law, deportation is certainly incompatible with the provisions of the Treaty since, as the court has already confirmed in other cases, such a measure negates the very right conferred and guaranteed by the Treaty.

19. As regards other penalties such as fines and imprisonment, whilst the national authorities are entitled to impose penalties in respect of failure to comply with the terms of provisions relating to residence permits which are comparable to those attaching to minor offences by nationals, they are not justified in imposing a penalty so disproportionate to the gravity of the infringement that it becomes an obstacle to the free movement of persons. This would be especially so if that penalty included imprisonment.

20. It follows that the failure on the part of a national of a member state of the Community, to whom the rules on freedom of movement for workers apply, to obtain the special residence permit prescribed in art 4 of Directive 68/360 may not be punished by a recommendation for deportation or by measures which go as far as imprisonment.

Costs

21. The costs incurred by the government of the United Kingdom and by the Commission of the European Communities which have submitted observations to the court are not recoverable. As these proceedings are, in so far as the parties to the main proceedings are concerned, in the nature of a step in the proceedings pending before the national court, the decision on costs is a matter for that court.

On those grounds, the court (First Chamber) in answer to the questions referred to it by the Pontypridd Magistrates' Court, Mid Glamorgan, Wales, by order of 5th September 1979 hereby rules: 1. art 3(2) of Council Directive 68/360 of 15th October 1958 prohibiting member states from demanding an entry visa or equivalent requirement from Community workers moving within the Community must be interpreted as meaning that the phrase 'entry visa or equivalent requirement' covers any formality for the purpose of granting leave to enter the territory of a member state which is coupled with a passport or identity card check at the frontier, whatever may be the place or time a   at which that leave is granted and in whatever form it may be granted; (2)(a) the issue of a special residence document provided for in art 4 of Council Directive 68/360 of 15th October 1968 has only a declaratory effect, and for aliens to whom art 48 of the Treaty or parallel provisions give rights it cannot be assimilated to a residence permit such as is prescribed for aliens in general, in connection with the issue of which the national authorities have a discretion; (b) a member state may not require from a person enjoying the protection of Community law that he should possess a general residence permit

b   instead of the document provided for in art 4(2) of Directive 68/360 in conjunction with the annex thereto; (3) the failure on the part of a national of a member state of the Community, to whom the rules on freedom of movement for workers apply, to obtain the special residence permit prescribed in art 4 of Directive 68/360 may not be punished by a recommendation for deportation or by measures which go as far as imprisonment.

c   Agents: *Spicketts*, Pontypridd (for the defendant); *G Dagtoglou*, Treasury Solicitor's Department (for the United Kingdom); *Anthony McClellan*, Legal Service of the EC Commission (for the Commission).

Andrew Durand Esq   Barrister.

d

Practice Direction

QUEEN'S BENCH DIVISION

e   *Practice – Trial – Setting down action – Setting down action for trial in London – Lists – Administrative provisions.*

All proceedings in the Queen's Bench Division for hearing in London shall be set down in the appropriate list and administered as follows.   •

f   1. *The Crown Office list*
     (a) Proceedings required to be heard by or applications required to be made to a Divisional Court of the Queen's Bench Division.
     (b) Proceedings pursuant to RSC Ord 53, Ord 54 and Ord 56 which may be heard by a single judge.
     (c) Actions directed to be set down in the Crown Office list.
g   (d) Proceedings pursuant to RSC Ord 55, Ord 94 and Ord 111.
     (e) Save as is otherwise expressly provided, any other special case or case stated under any statute or order.

2. *Administrative provisions in respect of the Crown Office list*
     Without prejudice to any party's right to apply for direction to a judge for the time h   being hearing matters in the Crown Office list and the right of the Master of the Crown Office to refer such a matter to a judge, the Crown Office list shall be administered by the Crown Office under the direction of the Master of the Crown Office.

3. *The jury list*
     Actions ordered to be tried by a judge and jury.

j
     4. *The non-jury list*
     (a) Actions other than jury actions or short causes set down under the provisions of RSC Ord 34, r 3.
     (b) Preliminary questions or issues ordered to be tried under RSC Ord 33, rr 3 and 4(2).

(c) Motions to commit other than those required to be heard by a Divisional Court of the Queen's Bench Division.

(d) Motions for judgment.

5. The short cause list

Actions ordered to be tried by a judge alone where the time estimated for the trial does not exceed four hours.

Administrative provisions: jury, non-jury and short cause lists

6. (a) All actions in the non-jury list shall in the first instance be set down in a non-jury general list, numbered in sequence and show the setting down date.

(b) Subject to the provisions of para 6(c), (d) and (e) hereof, non-jury actions shall be liable to come into the warned list (see para 11 below) at any time after the expiration of 28 days from the date of setting down.

(c) (i) As soon as a non-jury action is set down for trial in the general list, and within four weeks of such setting down, any party may, on obtaining an appointment from the Clerk of the Lists for this purpose, give notice in writing to the other party or parties of his intention to apply to the Clerk of the Lists to fix a date for the trial of the action. Suitable forms of notice (form B 14d) may be obtained from the forms room (room 278) or from law stationers. (ii) Where an application to fix a date for the trial of the action is not taken out within four weeks of setting down for trial, the parties may, by consent, apply to the Clerk of the Lists to extend the time within which to take out such an application. Any opposed application for such an extension of time must be made to the judge in charge of the non-jury list.

(d) On the hearing of an application for a fixed date the Clerk of the Lists may, after taking into account the wishes of the parties, the circumstances of the case and the state of the non-jury list, (i) fix a date for the trial of the action, or (ii) direct that the case shall come on for trial on a date specified by him, subject to the case or cases already fixed for hearing on that date, or (iii) direct that the case be marked not to come on for trial before a date specified by him, keeping its numerical order in the general list, or (iv) direct that the case be returned to the general list, or (v) direct that the case be placed in the warned list, or (vi) direct that the case be stood over generally, or (vii) direct that the application be referred to the judge in charge of the non-jury list.

(e) If any party is dissatisfied with the date fixed by the Clerk of the Lists or with his direction under sub-paras (ii) to (vi) of para 6(d) hereof, or with his direction under para 7(b) hereof, that party may, on giving two days' notice in writing to the other party or parties, apply to the judge in charge of the non-jury list to vary the date so fixed or the direction so given. Such application to the judge shall be made within seven days of the hearing before the Clerk of the Lists, or the date of his decision under para 7(b) hereof, as the case may be. On the hearing of such application the judge may vary the date fixed, or the direction given by the Clerk of the Lists, or may make such other order or give such other directions on such terms as to costs or otherwise as he shall think fit.

(f) If an application under sub-para (c) of this paragraph be not made the action shall remain in the non-jury general list and be subject to the provisions of sub-para (b) of this paragraph.

(g) When an action or other proceeding in the Jury List and the non-jury list is settled, withdrawn, or discontinued, or where the estimate of length of trial is varied, it shall be the duty of the solicitors for the parties so to inform the Clerk of the Lists in writing forthwith.

7. (a) Once an action in the non-jury list has been allocated a fixed date for trial, every opposed application to vacate, alter or otherwise determine the date of trial shall be made to the judge in charge of the non-jury list and be made in accordance with the provisions of para 10 hereof.

(b) Where all the parties to a non-jury action agree to vacate, alter or otherwise determine the date of trial, they may apply to the Clerk of the Lists. The application *a*   should be by way of a written consent signed by all the parties. The consent shall specify the nature of the application and the grounds thereof. The Clerk of the Lists shall deal with the application in accordance with the provisions of para 6(d) hereof, and his decision shall be subject to the provisions of para 6(e) hereof.

8. (a) On the hearing of the summons for directions the court may, if it appears that the action ought to have an early trial, give a direction (to be called 'an order for speedy trial') that an application be made to the Clerk of the Lists to fix a date for the hearing.

b   (b) Within one week from setting down for trial or within such other time as may be specified in the order the parties shall apply for a date to the Clerk of the Lists, who shall deal with the application in accordance with the provisions of para 6(d) hereof, his decision being subject to the provisions of para 6(e) hereof.

9. (a) For each week of each sittings there shall be published a list of non-jury actions to be called the 'Weekly List of Non-Jury Actions'.

c   (b) The weekly list shall be printed on the first day and on every subsequent Monday of each sittings.

(c) The weekly list shall contain: (i) a number of actions in both the non-jury general list and the non-jury fixture list which are likely to be tried or have been fixed for trial during the next succeeding week which will be listed together under the denomination

d   of the 'Week's List'; (ii) the remaining actions in the non-jury general list which have been set down on or before the end of the previous week, except actions which have by order or consent been stood out from the non-jury general list. The weekly list will, if possible, contain an intimation that actions in the non-jury general list will not be taken before a date or dates to be specified; (iii) the remaining actions in the non-jury fixtures list fixed for hearing during the current sittings (or directed to be heard on a particular

e   day in the sittings subject to fixtures).

10. (a) So far as appropriate the Clerk of the Lists shall administer the jury and short cause lists in like manner to the non-jury list.

(b) Except in cases dealt with above every application to fix, vacate, alter or otherwise determine the date of trial of an action in the jury, non-jury and short cause list shall be made to the judge in charge of that list.

f   (c) Any party making an application under this paragraph shall give the other party or parties notice of his intention to apply to the judge in charge of the appropriate list. The notice shall not be less than one clear day before the date on which such application is proposed to be made and shall specify the nature of the application and the grounds thereof.

(d) All applications to the judge in charge of the appropriate list shall be made at the

g   sitting of the court or at such other time or times as may be specified by such judge for the time being.

11. (a) A number of actions which are likely to be taken on the following day will be listed together and printed in the Daily Cause List under the denomination of the 'Warned List'. Such actions will be taken from those standing at the head of the week's

h   list.

(b) No action in the warned list will be removed from it by stay or postponement or will have its position altered except in accordance with the provisions of paras 7 and 10 hereof.

12. *The commercial list*

j   (a) Actions for trial in the Commercial Court.

(b) Any matter in para 4 hereof which appertains to a matter in the Commercial Court.

13. *The arbitration case list*

Proceedings under RSC Ord 73, r 2.

14. *Administrative provisions: commercial and arbitration case lists*
    Actions or other proceedings in the Commercial Court will be dealt with as follows.
    (a) Any party to an action to be tried in the Commercial Court may at any stage in the proceedings apply to the Commercial Judge by summons to fix a date for the trial or to vary or vacate such a date.
    (b) An order made by the court fixing the date of hearing will normally also provide for a date by which the cause must be set down for trial in the commercial list.
    (c) When a party to an action who has set it down for trial notifies the other parties to the action that he has done so, he should also inform the Commercial Court Listing Office to the same effect.
    (d) If any action which has been set down for trial in the Commerical Court is settled or withdrawn, or if the estimate of length of trial is revised, it shall be the duty of all parties to notify the court of the fact without delay.
    (e) (i) Any proceeding in the arbitration case list shall in the first instance be referred to the judge in charge of the commercial list for his consideration as to its suitability for retention in that list. (ii) Where the judge directs that such a matter shall be heard by a Commercial Judge any party may thereafter apply to fix a date for trial.

15. *The Admiralty list*
    Proceedings under RSC Ord 75.

16. *Administrative provisions: Admiralty list*
    Actions or other proceedings in the Admiralty Court will be dealt with as follows.
    (a) All motions will be listed for hearing by the Admiralty Registry.
    (b) In all actions the mode and date of trial will be fixed by the judge of the Admiralty Court at the hearing of the summons for directions unless the judge otherwise orders.

17. *General administrative provision*
    The lists of actions in the Queen's Bench Division for trial in London shall be kept by the Head Clerk of the Crown Office and shall be included in the general lists of appeals and causes in the Supreme Court of Judicature published for each sittings.

18. The directions for London issued by the Lord Chief Justice on 9th December 1958 ([1958] 3 All ER 678, [1958] 1 WLR 1291) are hereby revoked.

LANE CJ

31st July 1981

a
Kooragang Investments Pty Ltd v Richardson & Wrench Ltd

PRIVY COUNCIL
LORD WILBERFORCE, LORD SIMON OF GLAISDALE, LORD ELWYN-JONES, LORD EDMUND-DAVIES AND
LORD BRIDGE OF HARWICH
b 9th, 10th, 11th, 15th, 16th JUNE, 27th JULY 1981

Vicarious liability – Master and servant – Act of a class servant authorised to do – Act done negligently – Real estate valuations – Servant doing valuations for group of companies during period when ordered not to do business with them – Ultimate client not knowing of servant's existence or authority as a valuer – Whether servant had actual authority – Whether actual *c* *authority could be inferred from fact that valuations were a class of act which servant was authorised to do – Liability of master for negligence of servant in making valuations.*

The respondents were real estate agents and valuers. One of the respondents' clients was the GB Group and valuations for it were carried out by R and another valuer. All valuers had to follow a definite and strict internal procedure within the respondent company and *d* all documentation was kept on file. The paper on which the valuations were made was headed with the respondents' name and address, and the names of the five valuers appeared in the margin. The valuation itself was signed in the name of the respondents and R had authority so to sign valuations made by him for clients of the respondents. On 20th November 1972 the respondents issued a memorandum to all their valuers instructing them not to do further valuation work for the GB Group as substantial sums *e* of money remained unpaid for completed valuations. R signed the memorandum in acknowledgment. In 1973 R, who had become a director of a company in the GB Group, prepared, on instructions from companies in the group, valuations at the offices of the group. Two of the valuations were for the appellants, a finance or moneylending company which lent money on mortgage. The valuations were typed by a secretary of the group on headed paper of the respondents provided by R and R signed the *f* respondents' name. A photocopy was sent to the appellants. In the process of photocopying, the names of the valuers were cut off and accordingly the appellants had no knowledge of the identity of the valuers or that the valuation had been done by R. Furthermore, the valuations were not recorded with the respondents and no fee was charged by or paid to the respondents for them. The appellants made two advances on mortgage of real property in the suburbs of Sydney in reliance on the valuations. The *g* valuations were done negligently and resulted in a loss to the appellants. The appellants brought an action against the respondents in the Supreme Court of New South Wales claiming damages for negligence in and about the issue of the valuations. At the trial the appellants disclaimed reliance on any ostensible authority of R; the issue was one of actual authority. The trial judge dismissed the action on the ground that R had not made the valuations in the course of his employment with the respondents. The appellants *h* appealed to the Privy Council.

Held – (1) In determining whether an act done by a servant or agent was done in the course or within the scope of his employment in cases where there was no dealing by the injured third party with the servant or agent and where the issue was one not of ostensible authority but of actual authority or total absence of authority, it was necessary *j* in order to render the master liable to prove that he had authorised the act, and authority could not be inferred from the fact that the acts done were of a class which the servant or agent was authorised to do on the master's behalf (see p 71 *b*, post); *Uxbridge Permanent Benefit Building Society v Pickard* [1939] 2 All ER 344 distinguished.

(2) On the facts it was clear that R had had no authority to make the valuations in question and in making them he had acted totally outside the course and scope of his

employment. He had made them not as an employee of the respondents but as an
employee or associate of the GB Group and on their instructions. It followed therefore
that the respondents were not liable to the appellants for R's negligence, and the appeal
would accordingly be dismissed (see p 68 *g h* and p 71 *c* to *g*, post).

Notes

For the liability of a principal for the acts of his agent which are not expressly authorised,
see 1 Halsbury's Laws (4th Edn) para 847, and for cases on a principal's liability for his
agent's negligence, see 1(2) Digest (Reissue) 816–818, 5280–5291.

Cases referred to in judgment

Barwick v English Joint Stock Bank (1867) LR 2 Exch 259, [1861–73] All ER Rep 194, 36 LJ
    Ex 147, 16 LT 461, Ex Ch, 1(2) Digest (Reissue) 801, 5208.
Hedley Byrne & Co Ltd v Heller & Partners Ltd [1963] 2 All ER 575, [1964] AC 465, [1963]
    3 WLR 101, [1963] 1 Lloyd's Rep 485, HL, 36(1) Digest (Reissue) 24, 84.
Lloyd v Grace, Smith & Co [1912] AC 716, [1911–13] All ER Rep 51, 81 LJKB 1140, 107
    LT 531, HL, 1(2) Digest (Reissue) 802, 5210.
Mackay v Commercial Bank of New Brunswick (1874) LR 5 PC 394, 43 LJPC 31, 30 LT 180,
    38 JP 296, PC, 1(2) Digest (Reissue) 803, 5211.
Swift v Winterbotham and Goddard (1873) LR 8 QB 244, 42 LJQB 111; varied sub nom
    Swift v Jewsbury (1874) LR 9 QB 301, 43 LJQB 56, Ex Ch, 1(1) Digest (Reissue) 420,
    2949.
Swire v Francis (1877) 3 App Cas 106, [1874–80] All ER Rep 601, 47 LJPC 18, 37 LT 554,
    PC, 1(2) Digest (Reissue) 813, 5255.
Uxbridge Permanent Benefit Building Society v Pickard [1939] 2 All ER 344, [1939] 2 KB 248,
    108 LJKB 757, 160 LT 407, CA, 34 Digest (Repl) 170, 1198.

Appeal

The plaintiffs, Kooragang Investments Pty Ltd, appealed against the decision of Rogers
J in the Supreme Court of New South Wales, Common Law Division, Commercial List,
given on 4th July 1980 whereby he dismissed the plaintiffs' action against the defendants,
Richardson & Wrench Ltd, for damages for loss sustained as a consequence of advancing
money in reliance on two valuations of real property prepared by Thomas George
Rathborne who was employed by the defendants as a valuer. The facts are set out in the
judgment of the Board.

David Hirst QC, Michael McHugh QC and *John J Garnsey* (both of the New South Wales Bar)
    with him, for the appellants.
Robert Alexander QC, J M N Rolfe QC and *S B Austin* (both of the New South Wales Bar)
    with him, for the respondents.

LORD WILBERFORCE. This is an appeal from a judgment of Rogers J in the
Supreme Court of New South Wales, Common Law Division, Commercial List, whereby
he dismissed the appellants' action with costs.

The appellants are a finance or moneylending company which (inter alia) lends money
on mortgage. In March and June 1973 they made two advances on mortgage of real
property in suburbs of Sydney, one of property in Glebe, the other of property at
McMahons Point. Both of these advances were made in reliance on valuations made by
Thomas George Rathborne ('Rathborne') and it is not now disputed that they were made
negligently. They resulted in a loss to the appellants. The respondents are real estate
agents and valuers. They employed valuers, of whom Rathborne was one. The issues in
this action now remaining for decision are (a) whether the respondents are vicariously
responsible for Rathborne's negligence, (b) whether the respondents owed a duty of care
to the appellants in respect of either or both of the two valuations. Both issues were
decided in favour of the respondents at the trial.

a The first issue depends on whether the valuations in question were made by Rathborne in the course of his employment by the respondents. Evidence as to the authority of valuers employed by the respondents was given by a director, Mr Hodgson. Rathborne himself was not called by either side.

When the respondents received instructions to value property, the work was allocated by Mr Hodgson to one of five valuers of whom Rathborne was one; a Mr Rowan was another. Usually work was allotted on a geographical basis, but in some cases where a

b particular client called for a number of valuations the same valuer would deal with those valuations, irrespective of location. One such instance was work done for the Giles Bourke group of companies ('GB Group') which played a critical role in this matter; valuations for them were carried out by Mr Rowan and Rathborne.

There was a definite and strict internal procedure within the respondents which valuers had to follow. All documentation including instructions, field-notes and other

c material was kept in a file. When the valuer was ready to make his valuation, it was typed by one of three secretaries. In relation to valuations exceeding £100,000, Mr Hodgson was to be informed. All valuations were prepared in one original, one carbon copy on white paper and one on pink. The latter copy was bound in a valuation book, which was kept as a permanent record. The client was given the original and white carbon and, unless he paid immediately, he was sent at the same time an invoice. Copies

d of this invoice were retained by the respondents and used to give reminders to the client. The paper on which the valuations were made was headed with the respondents' name and address, and the names of the five valuers appeared in the left-hand margin. In a box on the right there would normally appear the initials of the valuer concerned, in Rathborne's case 'TGR', followed by the initials of the typist. There was a cover sheet in front of the valuation, stating the name of the client and the property; it bore at the

e foot the name of the respondents. The valuation itself was signed in the name of the respondents, ie 'Richardson & Wrench Ltd', without indicating who had actually signed. Rathborne had authority so to sign valuations made by him for clients of the respondents.

As regards the appellants, relations between them and the respondents started in 1972. The appellants were a dormant subsidiary of a large public company, Australian

f Fertilizers Ltd ('AFL'). AFL caused the appellants to change their name to their present designation and to obtain a moneylending licence; it was to lend money made available by AFL, under directions from that company. The respondents had a long established relationship with AFL and were naturally consulted by the appellants when they entered the moneylending business.

On 21st February 1972 the appellants wrote a letter to Mr Hodgson, of the respondents,

g setting out the procedure to be followed; this was to apply 'in all applications which appear suitable to us'. The procedure involved a preliminary inspection of the property to be charged, followed by a general comment by the respondents on its suitability; a fee of about $25 then became payable. The letter continued that thereafter 'we [sc the appellants] will advise you by letter when an applicant may seek a valuation on a property. It is expected that you will provide your normal valuation which will show

h land and buildings separately'. There was to be a separate letter in which the respondents were to supply information under a number of listed headings.

It is now necessary to turn to the GB Group. This was a group of companies which, as stated, was a client of the respondents. A Mr John Bourke seems to have handled the matters relevant to this case.

In 1972, before 20th November, there were approximately twenty valuations done by

j the respondents for the GB Group; all of these were done by Rathborne or Mr Rowan. On 20th November 1972 Mr Hodgson issued a memorandum to all the respondents' valuers, expressed as referring to 'Giles Bourke Holdings, Fidelity Acceptance Corporation, Feutron Interiors, Group Unity Securities [sic] and Associated Companies' (ie members of the GB Group), instructing them that as substantial sums of money remained unpaid for completed valuations, further valuation work from this client was to be refused until

payment was made. Rathborne signed this memorandum in acknowledgment. This
instruction was not revoked during the critical period, November 1972 to September
1973. What happened thereafter was the subject of some contention before their
Lordships which involved careful examination of a number of valuations and
correspondence. Their Lordships will not set this out in detail. They are satisfied, and
this is the vital conclusion, that, with the exception of two valuations made in December
1972, themselves not paid for during the period, no genuine valuations were made for
the GB Group during the critical period. By 'genuine valuations' are meant valuations
carried out in a regular manner for the respondents, entered in the respondents' books,
and paid for.

On the other hand, there were some thirty valuations, including the two now in issue,
which were carried out by Rathborne for the GB Group which were not 'genuine' in the
sense just referred to. The circumstances of these were as follows.

In November 1972 Rathborne had become a director of Group Unity Syndications Pty
Ltd, a company of the GB Group. In 1973, on instructions from companies in the group,
he prepared valuations, two of which were those the subject of the present proceedings.
All these valuations were prepared by Rathborne at the offices of the GB Group. They
were dictated by Rathborne to a secretary of the group put at Rathborne's disposal by Mr
J Bourke and typed by her on headed paper of the respondents (see above) provided by
Rathborne. Rathborne then signed the respondents' corporate name. In the case of the
Glebe valuation the identifying box was left blank; in the McMahons Point valuation it
was filled in with TGR/SC. The initials SC, not those of the typist, were inserted on
Rathborne's instructions. Only one version of the valuation was made. This was then
photocopied; the result of the photocopying in the case of the Glebe and McMahons
Point valuations was to cut off the left-hand margin, including, whether by accident or
design, the names of the valuers. The ultimate client, ie the appellants, who received a
photocopy, thus had no knowledge of the identity of the respondents' valuers and no
knowledge that the valuation had been done by Rathborne. This is obviously crucial in
relation to a possible contention of 'holding out'.

Furthermore, as to the 'non-genuine' valuations, (1) no instructions to carry them out
were recorded with the respondents, (2) neither Mr Hodgson, nor any other director of
the respondents, knew that Rathborne was being instructed to make these valuations,
nor did Mr Hodgson allocate the valuers or supervise them, (3) no file was opened, or
documentation prepared, in relation to the valuations, (4) no fee was charged by or paid
to the respondents for these valuations.

These circumstances, taken together, establish a high degree of irregularity and, to
understate, of suspicious behaviour. The learned judge did not so characterise them, as
their Lordships might be tempted to do. He confined himself to a consideration whether
these valuations were made by Rathborne in the course of his employment by the
respondents and found that they were not.

It is clear from what has been stated above that no question of ostensible authority or
of 'holding out' arises. The appellants did not deal with Rathborne, or know of his
existence, or rely on his authority as a valuer. Reliance on any ostensible authority of
Rathborne was in fact disclaimed by leading counsel for the appellants at the trial. The
issue is one of actual authority, or nothing. An issue of actual authority includes one of
action within the course of employment.

The manner in which the common law has dealt with the liability of employers for
acts of employees (masters for servants, principals for agents) has been progressive: the
tendency has been toward more liberal protection of innocent third parties. At the same
time recognition has been given by the law to the movement which has taken place from
a relationship, akin to that of slavery, in which all actions of the servant were dictated by
the master, to one in which the servant claimed and was given some liberty of action.
In recent times it is common knowledge that many employees supplement their wages
by independent use in their own interests of the skills, and sometimes the tools, which
they use in their employment. These activities may be above-board and legitimate or
they may be surreptitious. Problems of authority and the course of employment must
be approached in the light of these realities.

a   Beyond cases of actual authority to commit a wrongful act, of which only rare instances appear, to hold the employer liable for negligent acts was simple and uncontroversial. Negligence is a method of performing an act: instead of it being done carefully, it is done negligently. So liability for negligent acts in the course of employment is clear. Cases of fraud present at first sight more difficulty, for if fraudulent acts are not directly forbidden, most relationships would carry an implied prohibition against them. If committed for the benefit of the employer and while doing his business, principle and logic demand that the employer should be held liable, and for

b   some time the law rested at this point. The classic judgment of Willes J in *Barwick v English Joint Stock Bank* (1867) LR 2 Exch 259 at 266, [1861–73] All ER Rep 194 at 198 stated the principle thus:

'In all these cases it may be said . . . that the master has not authorized the act. It is true, he has not authorized the particular act, but he has put the agent in his place

c   to do that class of acts, and he must be answerable for the manner in which the agent has conducted himself in doing the business which it was the act of his master to place him in.'

That was a case where the wrong was committed for the master's (viz the bank's) benefit, and Willes J stated this as an ingredient of liability ((1867) LR 2 Exch 259 at 265,

d   [1861–73] All ER Rep 194 at 198):

'. . . the master is answerable for every such wrong of the servant or agent as is committed in the course of the service and for the master's benefit, though no express command or privity of the master be proved.'.

This judgment (a) did not cover the case where the wrongful act was committed solely

e   for the servant's benefit, and (b) is no authority as regards acts done by the servant outside the scope of his employment.

What then if the wrong was committed solely for the benefit of the employee? Although Willes J did not so state, or even imply, it took the decision of the House of Lords in *Lloyd v Grace, Smith & Co* [1912] AC 716, [1911–13] All ER Rep 51 to dispel the suggestion that there was no liability of the employer for frauds or wrongs committed

f   for the benefit of the employee. Earl Loreburn LC said ([1912] AC 716 at 725, [1911–13] All ER Rep 51 at 54):

'Willes J cannot have meant that the principal is absolved whenever his agent intended to appropriate for himself the proceeds of his fraud. Nearly every rogue intends to do that';

g   and this point was elaborated in the classic opinion of Lord Macnaghten. Since then it has never been held, or contended, that for liability to exist, the act must be done for the benefit of the master. If the act was in fact done for the master's benefit, that is a valuable indication that it was done in the course of employment; the converse was thenceforth not true.

So the fact, here, that Rathborne was acting exclusively for himself and the GB Group

h   does not determine the case.

The second point remains for examination. The appellants' contention, indeed their main argument, was that based on the words (see above) 'he has put the agent in his place to do that class of acts'; so the respondents, they argued, set Rathborne up as a valuer to prepare valuations which would be placed before intending lenders and to sign them in the name of the respondents: this is enough to fix the respondents with liability.

j   Emphasising, once again, that there is no question in this case of any 'holding out' of Rathborne by the respondents (if there were, the case would be wholly different), the appellants' argument involves the proposition that, so long as a servant is doing the acts of the same kind as those which it was within his authority to do, the master is liable, and that he is not entitled to show that in fact the servant had no authority to do them. This is an extreme proposition and carries the principle of vicarious liability further than it has been carried hitherto. It is necessary, first, to consider whether it is supported by authority.

There is no doubt that the proposition contended for is contradicted, as a matter of principle, by that group of cases which is concerned with the use of motor vehicles. These are cases (i) where a servant has, without authority, permitted another person to drive the master's vehicle, (ii) where a servant has, without authority, invited another person on to the vehicle, who suffers injury, (iii) where a servant has embarked on an unauthorised detour, or, as lawyers like to call it, a 'frolic of his own'.

These cases have given rise to a number of fine distinctions, the courts in some cases struggling to find liability, in others to avoid it, which it is not profitable here to examine. It remains true to say that, whatever exceptions or qualifications may be introduced, the underlying principle remains that a servant, even while performing acts of the class which he was authorised, or employed, to do, may so clearly depart from the scope of his employment that his master will not be liable for his wrongful acts.

In the present case, their Lordships are admittedly in a different factual area: the appellants say so different that a fresh approach must be made. A number of authorities have been invoked. Their Lordships consider it profitable to confine their attention to five.

It has already been pointed out that *Barwick's* case itself does not support the appellants' argument: the bank manager there was clearly acting within the scope of his employment, and the contrary was not examined or discussed. *Swift v Winterbotham and Goddard* (1873) LR 8 QB 244 too did not raise any issue as to the course of employment: the bank manager was clearly so acting and the issue was whether the inquiry as to credit made by one bank of another bank was to be taken as having been made for a customer of the inquiring bank. *Mackay v Commercial Bank of New Brunswick* (1874) LR 5 PC 394 was relied on as a parallel to the present case in that there, as here, the third party and ultimate plaintiff did not know of the existence or identity of the (fraudulent) agent: but the parallel stops there. There was no question but that Sancton, the agent in question, was doing the bank's business for the benefit of the bank and that the bank benefited by his fraudulent act. It was a clear case of actual authority to do the act in question, albeit honestly, so that it was plainly in the course of Sancton's employment by the bank.

In *Swire v Francis* (1877) 3 App Cas 106, [1874–80] All ER Rep 601 Shaw, the fraudulent agent, was in charge of the respondent's business at Kiukiang, with authority to make advances and to enter them when made in the account. He had a general authority to draw bills on behalf of the respondent: he did so, and the respondent received the money, which Shaw then misappropriated. It was as clear as could be that Shaw was throughout acting in the course of his employment.

The authority most relied on by the appellants was *Uxbridge Permanent Benefit Building Society v Pickard* [1939] 2 All ER 344, [1939] 2 KB 248. The case itself decides no more than that it is not necessary, in order to enable a third party to hold a solicitor liable for the fraud of his clerk, that the third party should be, as in *Lloyd v Grace, Smith & Co* she was, a client of the firm. The third party there was an intending mortgagee. That the clerk Conway was acting in the course of his employment was clear, and all that could be suggested to the contrary was that he acted fraudulently and did not comply with some internal requirements of his master's business. In the course of his judgment Greene MR said ([1939] 2 All ER 344 at 348, [1939] 2 KB 248 at 254–5):

'. . . in the case of the servant who goes off on a frolic of his own, no question arises of any actual or ostensible authority upon the faith of which some third person is going to change his position. The very essence of the present case is that the actual authority and the ostensible authority . . . were of a kind which, in the ordinary course of an everyday transaction, was going to lead third persons, on the faith of it, changing their position, just as a purchaser from an apparent client or a mortgagee lending money to a client is going to change his position by being brought into contact with that client. That is within the actual and ostensible authority of the clerk. It is totally different in the case of a servant driving a motor car, or in cases of that kind, where there is no question of the action of third parties being affected in the least degree by any apparent authority on the part of the servant.'

The distinction thus drawn between the 'driving' cases, to which reference has been
a made, and cases where a third party deals with an agent is no doubt valid and useful; it
is so because it enables, in the latter cases, an argument to be based on ostensible or
apparent authority. In the *Uxbridge* case the third party (the building society) was
dealing with the (fraudulent) servant; that was the essence of the case. To quote again
Greene MR ([1939] 2 All ER 344 at 347, [1939] 2 KB 248 at 253): '. . . the authority of
a clerk occupying the position of the principal to deal with third parties . . . cannot be
b denied.'

But where, as here, there was no dealing with the servant or agent, and where the issue
is one of actual authority or total absence of authority, the case gives no support for an
argument that authority need not be proved but is to be inferred from the fact that the
acts done are of a class which the master could himself have done or have entrusted to the
servant.
c   In the present case, the respondents did carry out valuations. Valuations were a class
of acts which Rathborne could perform on their behalf. To argue from this that any
valuation done by Rathborne, without any authority from the respondents, not on
behalf of the respondents but in his own interest, without any connection with the
respondents' business, is a valuation for which the respondents must assume responsibility
is not one which principle or authority can support. To indorse it would strain the
d doctrine of vicarious responsibility beyond breaking point and in effect introduce into
the law of agency a new principle equivalent to one of strict liability.

If one then inquires, as their Lordships think it correct to do, whether Rathborne had
any authority to make the valuations in question, the answer is clear; it is given in clear
and convincing terms by the learned judge. Rathborne was not authorised to make
them; he made them during a period when the GB Group were not in a client relationship
e with the respondents, when valuers were ordered not to do business with them.
Rathborne did them, not as an employee of the respondents, but as an employee, or
associate, in the GB Group and on their instructions. They were done at the premises of
the GB Group, and using the staff of the GB Group; they were not processed through the
respondents and no payment in respect of them was made to the respondents. Mr
Hodgson, the responsible director, knew nothing of them. They had no connection with
f the respondents except through the use, totally unauthorised, to say nothing more, of the
respondents' stationery. A clearer case of departure from the course or scope of
Rathborne's employment cannot be imagined: it was total. The judge's conclusion on
this part of the case was, in their Lordships' opinion, entirely correct.

If the conclusion had been reached (contrary to what has been said) that the
respondents were responsible for Rathborne's negligence in connection with the
g valuations, it would have been necessary to consider whether they owed a duty of care in
respect of them to the appellants. This would be on the principle established by the
House of Lords in *Hedley Byrne & Co Ltd v Heller & Partners Ltd* [1963] 2 All ER 575,
[1964] AC 465, a case followed in Australia.

It was not disputed by the respondents that as a matter of principle that case was
capable of invocation here, but reliance was placed on certain special circumstances
h affecting the valuations in question, including the letter written by the appellants to the
respondents on 21st February 1972, as excluding liability. In view of their decision on
the first and main question of the authority of Rathborne, and since, moreover, no
question of principle arises, their Lordships do not think it necessary to express any
opinion as to the correctness of the learned judge's opinion, in favour of the respondents,
on this point. Nor is any conclusion necessary on the cross-appeal of the respondents
j raising a case of contributory negligence.

Their Lordships will humbly advise Her Majesty that the appeal be dismissed. The
appellants must pay the costs of the appeal, and the costs, if any, of the cross-appeal.

Appeal dismissed.

Solicitors: *Clifford-Turner* (for the appellants); *Linklaters & Paines* (for the respondents).

Mary Rose Plummer   Barrister.

R v Leeds Justices, ex parte Hanson
and other cases

QUEEN'S BENCH DIVISION
GRIFFITHS LJ AND WOOLF J
2nd, 3rd, 4th, 22nd JUNE 1981

Magistrates – Jurisdiction – Trial of information – Validity of information – Laying of information – Invalid process issued on invalidly laid information – Defendant not required to attend court on first hearing of information and not present – Court having before it register setting out particulars of offence on which prosecution intended to proceed – Court at first hearing not considering information for purpose of issuing process in belief that valid process already issued – Case adjourned – Adjourned hearing taking place after time limit for commencing proceedings – Whether court having jurisdiction at adjourned hearing to try case – Whether information 'laid' at first hearing – Whether consideration of information for purpose of issuing process an essential ingredient of laying information – Magistrates' Courts Act 1952, s 104.

Magistrates – Appeal – Appeal to Divisional Court – Mode of appeal – Case stated or application for judicial review – Case stated inappropriate where defendant seeking to have conviction quashed and not answer to question whether magistrates had power to quash conviction.

Magistrates – Information – Computer used for issuing process – Summons produced from information fed into computer – No need for production of separate information – Unsigned summons to be treated as information – Information 'laid' on date contents of summons brought to attention of magistrate or justices' clerk – Magistrates' Courts Act 1952, s 104.

Informations against three defendants were improperly laid before the administrative staff of magistrates' courts instead of before the justices' clerk or a magistrate, and the summonses issued on the informations were also improperly issued by the administrative staff and were consequently invalid. The procedure of each court was that a defendant who pleaded not guilty to a summons was not required to attend court on the first hearing of the summons. Each of the three defendants pleaded not guilty and therefore did not attend court on the first hearing of his summons. At the first hearing of each of the summonses, which in each case took place within six months of the offence, the court had before it a copy of the court register which set out the particulars of the offence on which the prosecutor wished to proceed and identified the informant. In each case, as a summons had already been issued and the court, on the first hearing of the summons, believed that proper consideration had been given to its issue, the court did not on the occasion of the first hearing consider the informations before it for the purpose of issuing process. At the end of the first hearing each case was adjourned. At the adjourned hearings, which took place more than six months after the commission of the offences, each of the three defendants submitted that the court had no jurisdiction to try his case on the ground that no information had been 'laid' within six months of the commission of the offence, as prescribed by s 104[a] of the Magistrates' Courts Act 1952. At the adjourned hearings it was held that, whilst no informations had been laid for the purpose of s 104 before the summonses were issued, informations had been 'laid' within six months of the offences, within s 104, on the occasions of the first hearing of each of the summonses. In the first two cases the magistrates' court further adjourned the cases to allow the defendants to apply to the Divisional Court for orders of prohibition to prevent the magistrates' courts from trying the cases on the ground of want of jurisdiction. In the third case the magistrates' court tried the case and convicted the defendant, who

a   Section 104 is set out at p 78 a, post

applied to the Divisional Court for an order of certiorari to quash the conviction. In the
a Divisional Court the defendants submitted that consideration of an information for the
purpose of issuing process was an essential ingredient of laying an information within
s 104 and that therefore informations had not been laid within s 104 on the occasions of
the first hearing of each of the summonses, with the consequence that at the adjourned
hearings there had been no jurisdiction to try the cases.

b **Held** – An information was 'laid' for the purpose of s 104 of the 1952 Act when the
contents of the information and the fact that the prosecutor wished to pursue criminal
process were brought to the attention of a magistrate or clerk to the justices, as part of the
prosecution process, and not when the magistrate or clerk considered the information for
the purpose of issuing process. Since on the first hearing of each summons the
magistrates' court had been aware that the case was in its list because the prosecution
wished to proceed on it and had had before it the register containing all the relevant
c information relating to the offence, and since the first hearings had taken place within six
months of each offence, an information had been 'laid' within s 104 on the occasion of
the first hearing of each summons and accordingly at the adjourned hearings the
magistrates' courts had had jurisdiction to try the cases. It followed that the defendants'
applications would be refused (see p 80 *j* and p 81 *f* to *j*, post).

d R v Brentford Justices, ex part Catlin [1975] 2 All ER 201 applied.
Dictum of Donaldson LJ in R v Gateshead Justices, ex parte Tesco Stores Ltd [1981] 1 All
ER at 1030, 1032 considered.
Per Curiam. (1) Although in most cases a magistrate will consider an information for
the purpose of issuing process at the time when the information is first placed before
him, this will not always be so and consideration of the information by a magistrate or
e clerk to the justices for the purpose of issuing process can take place after the information
has been laid even though more than six months from the offence has elapsed (see p 80
j to p 81 *b*, post).
(2) Where the substantive relief sought by a defendant is the quashing of his
conviction rather than an answer to the question whether the magistrates' court had
power to quash the conviction, the defendant should apply for judicial review by way of
f an order of certiorari and should not proceed by way of case stated (see p 82 *f g*, post).
(3) Where a computer system is used for issuing process and a summons is produced
from information fed into a computer and contains on its face all the detail required to
be contained in an information, a separate information need not be produced by the
computer and the unsigned copy of the summons can be treated as the information.
Such an information is laid on the date that its contents are brought to the attention of
g the clerk to the justices or a magistrate and not on the date that the information is fed
into the computer. Consideration should therefore be given to amending the form of
summons or the computer program to show that the date of an information is the date
on which it is laid before the clerk or a magistrate (see p 83 *e* to *g*, post).

Notes
For the laying of an information and the time in which it must be laid, see 29 Halsbury's
h Laws (4th Edn) paras 242, 291, and for cases on the subject, see 33 Digest (Repl) 205, 441–
445.
For appeals from a magistrates' court to the High Court and for the control of
magistrates' proceedings by prerogative orders, see 29 Halsbury's Laws (4th Edn) paras
473–474, and for cases on the subject, see 33 Digest (Repl) 330–338, 1535–1636.
For the Magistrates' Courts Act 1952, s 104, see 21 Halsbury's Statutes (3rd Edn) 273.
j As from 6th July 1981 s 104 of the 1952 Act has been replaced by s 127(1) of the
Magistrates' Courts Act 1980.

Cases referred to in judgment
Brooks v Bagshaw [1904] 2 KB 798, 73 LJKB 839, 91 LT 535, 68 JP 514, 20 Cox CC 727,
2 LGR 1007, DC, 14(1) Digest (Reissue) 181, 1294.

R v Brentford Justices, ex parte Catlin [1975] 2 All ER 201, [1975] QB 455, [1975] 2 WLR
506, 139 JP 516, DC, Digest (Cont Vol D) 631, *476a*.
R v Fairford Justices, ex parte Brewster [1975] 2 All ER 757, [1976] QB 600, [1975] 3 WLR
59, 139 JP 574, DC, Digest (Cont Vol D) 631, *463a*.
*R v Gateshead Justices, ex parte Tesco Stores Ltd, R v Birmingham Justices, ex parte D W Parkin
Construction Ltd* [1981] 1 All ER 1027, [1981] 2 WLR 419, DC.
R v Uxbridge Justices, ex parte Clark [1968] 2 All ER 992, 132 JP 464, 52 Cr App R 578, DC,
16 Digest (Reissue) 434, *4793*.
R v West London Justices, ex parte Klahn [1979] 2 All ER 221, [1979] 1 WLR 933, DC,
Digest (Cont Vol E) 397, *467a*.

Applications for judicial review and case stated

R v Leeds Justices, ex parte Hanson

John Andrew Jones Hanson applied, with the leave of Woolf J granted on 28th April
1981, for an order of certiorari to quash the decision of the Leeds justices made on 26th
March 1981 convicting him of a driving offence committed on 17th September 1980.
The ground on which the relief was sought was that the justices had had no jurisdiction
to adjudicate as the information had not been laid before a person authorised to act as a
justice of the peace. The facts are set out in the judgment of the court.

R v Edmonton Justices, ex parte Hughes

Stephen Hughes applied, with the leave of Woolf J granted on 28th April 1981, for an
order of prohibition prohibiting the justices of the peace for the petty sessional division
of Edmonton from further proceeding with his trial on a summons issued against him
under s 3 of the Road Traffic Act 1972. The grounds on which the relief was sought were
that the justices' decision on 17th March 1981 to adjourn the case for trial on 7th April
1981 exceeded their jurisdiction because the information purported to be laid on 6th
August 1980 on which the summons was issued was laid before an administrative officer
of the justices' clerk's office and was not considered or approved by a magistrate or the
clerk to the justices and the summons merely bore the facsimile signature of the justices'
clerk, and the information was not considered by a magistrate or clerk to the justices and
accordingly, a valid information was not laid within six months of the commission of the
offence, as prescribed by s 104 of the Magistrates' Courts Act 1952. The facts are set out
in the judgment of the court.

R v Manchester Stipendiary Magistrate, ex parte Hill

Leonard Hill applied, with the leave of Woolf J granted on 13th April 1981, for an order
of prohibition prohibiting the Manchester City stipendiary magistrate from proceeding
to try him on an allegation brought against him under s 6(1) of the Road Traffic Act
1972. The ground on which the relief was sought was that the decision of the stipendiary
magistrate made on 6th March 1981 that Mr Hill should be tried on the allegation
exceeded the magistrate's jurisdiction because no information had been properly laid and
judicially considered by a magistrate or justices' clerk within six months of the
commission of the alleged offence. The facts are set out in the judgment of the court.

R v Gateshead Justices, ex parte Ives

Derek Ives applied, with the leave of Woolf J granted on 30th April 1981, for an order of
certiorari to quash a decision of the Gateshead justices sitting at Blaydon on 22nd January
1981 convicting him of two offences contrary to s 146 of the Social Security Act 1975.
The grounds on which the relief was sought were that informations on which the
summonses were issued were not considered by a magistrate or justices' clerk and that
defect was not remedied within the period prescribed by s 104 of the Magistrates' Courts
Act 1952 for the institution of the proceedings.

R v Dartford Justices, ex parte Dhesi

a   Gian Singh Dhesi applied, with the leave of Woolf J granted on 1st May 1981, for an order of certiorari to quash the determination of the Dartford justices on 7th April 1981 purporting to convict him on two summonses alleging that on 17th July 1980 he failed without reasonable excuse to provide a specimen of blood or urine, contrary to s 9(3) of the Road Traffic Act 1972, and on the same date failed to give his name and address to a police constable, contrary to s 162 of that Act. The grounds on which the relief was

b   sought were that the informations on which the summonses were issued were not considered by a justices' clerk, and the summonses were not authorised to be issued by a magistrate or justices' clerk, and accordingly the informations were not properly laid, within six months of the offences being committed. The facts are set out in the judgment of the court.

c   *Moody v Anderton*

Carl Philip Moody appealed by way of case stated by the justices for the County of Greater Manchester acting in and for the petty sessional division of Eccles in respect of their adjudication as a magistrates' court on 19th March 1981. On 5th March 1981 two informations preferred by the respondent, Cyril James Anderton, the Chief Constable of Greater Manchester, against the appellant, alleging certain motoring offences were heard

d   by the justices. Mr Moody pleaded guilty and on 5th March was convicted and sentenced. On that occasion no issue as to the justices' jurisdiction was raised. On 19th March Mr Moody applied to the justices to set aside the order of 5th March convicting and sentencing him on the ground that the informations had not been laid before a qualified person and the summonses issued on them were defective so that on 5th March the justices lacked jurisdiction. The justices decided that although the summonses were

e   defective and although on 5th March there had been want of jurisdiction, they were functus officio on 19th March and furthermore had no inherent power to quash the order of 5th March. Accordingly the justices agreed to state a case for the opinion of the High Court raising the questions (i) whether, where a magistrates' court had ordered a conviction and sentence without jurisdiction, it had inherent power to quash the order without the necessity of an appeal and (ii) if the justices did not have inherent power to

f   quash the order of 5th March, whether the High Court would quash that order because of the justices' lack of jurisdiction on that date. During the course of the hearing the Divisional Court gave Mr Moody leave to apply for an order of certiorari. The facts are set out in the judgment of the court.

David Mitchell for Mr Hanson.
g   *John Hitchen* for the West Yorkshire Metropolitan Police.
Adrian Salter for Mr Hughes.
Michael Kershaw QC and *Roger Stout* for Mr Hill.
Nicholas Simmonds for the Chief Constable of Greater Manchester.
Michael Hodson for Mr Ives.
Andrew Collins for Mr Dhesi.
h   *Richard Aikens* for the Dartford justices.
Gregory Stone for the Kent County Constabulary.
John Reide for Mr Moody.
Simon D Brown as amicus curiae in all the cases.
The respondents to Mr Hughes's and Mr Ives's applications did not appear.

j   *Cur adv vult*

22nd June. **GRIFFITHS LJ** read the following judgment of the court: These five cases all come before this court as a result of the recent decision in *R v Gateshead Justices, ex parte Tesco Stores Ltd* [1981] 1 All ER 1027, [1981] 2 WLR 419 in which it was held that a judicial function could not be delegated, with the result that a summons to appear

before a magistrates' court could only be issued by a justice of the peace or a clerk to the
justices who had considered the information containing the charge. The point of the   *a*
case was that the consideration of the information for the purpose of deciding whether
or not to issue the summons could not be delegated to an official in the magistrates'
court.

We decided to hear all five cases together so that we might have the benefit of all the
arguments of counsel to enable us to see the full implication of the *Gateshead* decision.
We are grateful to all counsel for the parties for their arguments and to counsel who   *b*
assisted us as amicus curiae.

It has turned out that the most important and difficult question that this court has to
decide in the present proceedings is what constitutes the laying of an information within
the meaning of the Magistrates' Courts Act 1952. The point arises directly in *R v
Manchester Stipendiary Magistrates, ex parte Hill, R v Edmonton Justices, ex parte Hughes* and
R v Dartford Justices, ex parte Dhesi. We will, therefore, deal first with these three cases   *c*
and we commence by setting out the essential facts in each case.

Mr Hill's case
The prosecution allege against Mr Hill that on 29th November 1979 he drove a motor car
in the wrong direction down a one-way street, and at a time when he had an excess of the
permitted limit of alcohol in his blood contrary to s 1 of the Road Traffic Regulation Act   *d*
1967 and s 6(1) of the Road Traffic Act 1972.

In May 1980 Mr Hill received summonses in respect of those offences requiring him
to attend court to answer them on 29th May 1980. The summonses bore the facsimile
signature of the clerk to the justices for the City of Manchester but they had not been
considered by him and they had been issued by a member of his staff to whom he had
delegated that task. It is conceded that the summonses were consequently invalid.   *e*

At the same time as he received the summonses, Mr Hill also received a notice in the
following terms:

> 'Important notice to Defendant. In order to avoid the unnecessary attendance of
> persons at court, the prosecution have been advised NOT to bring any witnesses to
> court on the hearing date set down on your summons. Therefore, the case will only
> be able to be dealt with on that day if you attend (either personally or by counsel or   *f*
> solicitor) and plead "guilty". If you intend to plead "not guilty" you should complete
> the attached form and return it to me at the above address as soon as possible and,
> in any event, not less than seven days before the hearing on the date of your
> summons. You would not then have to attend court on that date and arrangements
> would be made to adjourn the hearing and to fix a new date of hearing when you
> would have to attend here, and, subject to any unforeseen circumstances arising, the   *g*
> case should be heard on the new date.'

On 20th May Mr Hill's solicitor wrote to the court saying that Mr Hill would plead not
guilty to the offences, and asking that the matter should be adjourned. On 29th May Mr
Hill's case was listed in no 1 court of the Manchester Magistrates' Court, but of course
neither he nor his solicitor appeared. Although neither the magistrates nor the court   *h*
clerk now have any personal recollection of the matter, there seems no reason to doubt
that the normal procedure was followed, namely that the clerk told the magistrates that
there was a plea of not guilty and asked them to adjourn the case to a suitable date. The
magistrates would not have a copy of the summons before them but they would have a
copy of the court register which sets out the particulars of the offence, the date of the
offence, and the identity of the informant. The magistrates then announce that the case   *j*
is adjourned either sine die or to a particular date. It appears from the entry in the
register that in this case it was adjourned to 15th August 1980.

There were then further adjournments and eventually the case came for trial before
the Manchester stipendiary magistrate on 6th March 1981. It was then submitted on
behalf of Mr Hill that the stipendiary magistrate had no jurisdiction to try the case

because the information had not been laid within six months of the date of the offence
as required by s 104 of the Magistrates' Courts Act 1952. The stipendiary magistrate,
however, held that although the information had not been laid before a magistrate or the
clerk to the justices before the issue of the summons it was laid before the magistrates on
29th May when they adjourned the case and, as that date was within the six-month
period, he had jurisdiction to try the case. The case was then adjourned to give Mr Hill
the opportunity to test the magistrate's decision by applying to this court for an order of
prohibition to prevent him from hearing the case on the ground that he has no
jurisdiction to do so.

Mr Hughes's case

The prosecution allege that on 25th April 1980 Mr Hughes drove a motor car without
due care and attention, contrary to s 3 of the Road Traffic Act 1972. Mr Hughes received
a summons dated 6th August 1980 requiring him to attend court on 13th October
1980. The summons bore the signature of the clerk to the justices, but its issue had been
delegated to a member of his staff and it is conceded that it was not a valid summons.
The Tottenham Magistrates' Court follows the same procedure as the Manchester
Magistrates' Court. You are only required to attend on the first hearing if you are
pleading guilty. Mr Hughes informed the court he was pleading not guilty and did not
attend on 13th October.

The Tottenham magistrates went through the same exercise as the Manchester
magistrates. Mr Hughes's case was in the list for 13th October. The magistrates were
told that there was a plea of not guilty and they adjourned it sine die. The court register
containing a statement of the offence, the date on which it was alleged to have been
committed and that the police were the informants, was in court and signed by the
chairman at the end of the court sitting.

On 17th March 1981 when Mr Hughes appeared on the adjourned hearing, it was
submitted that the magistrates had no jurisdiction to hear the case as no information had
been laid within six months of the offence. But the Tottenham magistrates took the
same view as the Manchester stipendiary magistrate and held that the information was
laid before the magistrates on 13th October and, as this was within the six-month period,
they had jurisdiction. So, Mr Hughes also applies for an order of prohibition.

Mr Dhesi's case

The prosecution allege that on 17th July 1980 Mr Dhesi failed without reasonable
excuse to give a sample of blood or urine for a laboratory test, contrary to s 6(3) of the
Road Traffic Act 1972 and on the same day failed to give his name and address to a police
constable contrary to s 162 of the Road Traffic Act 1972. Mr Dhesi received a summons
dated 22nd October 1980 returnable on 27th November. Again, although the summons
bore the facsimile signature of the clerk to the justices, the information had not been
considered by him or any justice and it was an invalid summons.

The Dartford Magistrates' Court follows the same procedure as the Manchester and
Tottenham courts. Mr Dhesi's solicitor wrote to the court indicating that the plea would
be not guilty. Neither he nor Mr Dhesi attended court on 27th November and the
magistrates on that day were told by their clerk of the letter indicating a not guilty plea
and adjourned the case sine die.

The magistrates had before them a copy of the court register containing the particulars
of the offences. The informations were available in court if they wished to see them.

The case came on for hearing on 7th April 1981. Mr Dhesi's solicitor submitted that
the magistrates had no jurisdiction to hear the matter because more than six months had
elapsed since the date of the offence. But again, this bench of magistrates held that they
had jurisdiction because the case had been before the court on 27th November which was
within the six-month period. The magistrates heard the case and convicted Mr Dhesi of
both offences. Accordingly in this case an order of certiorari to quash their decision is
sought on the ground that they had no jurisdiction to try the case.

Section 104 of the Magistrates' Courts Act 1952 provides:

> 'Except as otherwise expressly provided by any enactment, a magistrates' court *a* shall not try an information or hear a complaint unless the information was laid, or the complaint made, within six months from the time when the offence was committed, or the matter of complaint arose.'

Six months is the appropriate period for all the offences in these three cases. I now set out the terms of s 1 of the 1952 Act: *b*

> '(1) Upon an information being laid before a justice of the peace for any county or borough that any person has, or is suspected of having, committed an offence, the justice may, in any of the events mentioned in subsection (2) of this section—(*a*) issue a summons directed to that person requiring him to appear before a magistrates' court for the county or borough to answer to the information; or (*b*) issue a warrant to arrest that person and bring him before a magistrates' court for *c* the county or borough or such magistrates' court as is provided in subsection (2) of this section: Provided that the justice shall not issue a warrant unless the information is in writing and substantiated on oath.
>
> '(2) A justice of the peace for a county or borough may issue a summons or warrant under this section—(*a*) if the offence was committed or is suspected to have been committed within the county or borough; or (*b*) if it appears to the justice *d* necessary or expedient, with a view to the better administration of justice, that the person charged should be tried jointly with, or in the same place as, some other person who is charged with an offence, and who is in custody, or is being or is to be proceeded against, within the county or borough; or (*c*) if the person charged resides or is, or is believed to reside or be, within the county or borough; or (*d*) if under any enactment a magistrates' court for the county or borough has jurisdiction to try the *e* offence: Provided that where the offence charged is not an indictable offence—(i) a summons shall not be issued by virtue only of paragraph (*c*) of this subsection, and (ii) any warrant issued by virtue only of that paragraph shall require the person charged to be brought before a magistrates' court having jurisdiction to try the offence.'
>
> *f*

These provisions provide the citizen with a twofold protection against prosecution for summary offences. First he is not to be harassed by accusations of stale offences. This is achieved by s 104 which provides that the prosecutor must start the prosecution by laying the information within six months of the date of the offence, or such other period as may have been specially provided by the Act creating the offence. For example, in one of the cases before us (*Ex parte Ives*) the relevant period is that prescribed by s 147(3) of *g* the Social Security Act 1975 which provides:

> 'Notwithstanding any enactment prescribing the period within which summary proceedings may be commenced, proceedings for an offence under this Act may in England and Wales be commenced at any time within the period of three months from the date on which evidence, sufficient in the opinion of the Secretary of State to justify a prosecution for the offence, comes to his knowledge, or within the *h* period of 12 months after the commission of the offence, whichever period last expires.'

Proceedings are commenced for the purposes of such a statute when the information is laid: see *Brooks v Bagshaw* [1904] 2 KB 798. So, in all cases concerning the statutory time limit within which the jurisdiction of the justices must be exercised the crucial *j* question is on what date was the information laid.

The other protection is provided by the duty of a magistrate or the clerk to the justices to give judicial consideration to the information before he authorises the issue of a summons or a warrant, pursuant to s 1. In *R v West London Justices, ex parte Klahn* [1979] 2 All ER 221, [1979] 1 WLR 933 it was said that the magistrate should consider the whole of the relevant circumstances including, but without attempting an exhaustive definition of all relevant circumstances, (1) whether the allegation is of an offence known to the law and, if so whether the essential ingredients of the offence are prima facie present, (2) whether the offence alleged is not 'out of time', (3) whether the court has jurisdiction, (4) whether the informant has the necessary authority to prosecute and also whether the allegation is vexatious.

If it was shown that a magistrate had issued a summons without giving judicial consideration to the information and that in the result the defendant had suffered injustice, no doubt this court could intervene to quash the conviction. But there is no requirement that the summons must be issued within a particular time after the information has been laid) (see *R v Fairford Justices, ex parte Brewster* [1975] 2 All ER 757, [1976] QB 600) although again this court would have power to quash a conviction if there had been excessive delay between the laying of the information and the issue of the summons and the defendant had thereby suffered injustice.

With these considerations in mind we turn now to the question when is the information laid so as to stop time running for the purposes of s 104.

The applicants submit that the information is not laid until it is considered by the magistrate or the clerk to the justices for the purposes of issuing criminal proceedings. They say that the laying of the information and the consideration of it by the magistrate are all part of one process and they rely on two passages to that effect in the judgment of Donaldson LJ in *R v Gateshead Justices, ex parte Tesco Stores Ltd* [1981] 1 All ER 1027 at 1030, [1981] 2 WLR 419 at 423: 'An information is laid when it is considered by a person authorised to do so.' Later he said ([1981] 1 All ER 1027 at 1032, [1981] 2 WLR 419 at 425):

> 'An information is not "laid" within the meaning of the Magistrates' Courts Act 1952, and is certainly not "laid before a justice of the peace" unless it is laid before and considered by either a justice of the peace or the clerk to the justices acting as a justice of the peace pursuant to the [Justices' Clerks Rules 1970] and, incidentally, no summons can be issued by any other person or without a prior judicial consideration by that person of the information upon which the summons is based.'

If an information is not laid until the magistrate considers it for the purpose of issuing a summons or warrant, they were clearly not laid on the occasion that these three cases were adjourned. The magistrates were not then putting their minds to any of those matters that they were under a duty to consider when deciding whether or not to issue a summons. There was no reason why they should do so. They believed that consideration had already been given to these matters when the summons was issued. So, if such consideration is a necessary ingredient of the laying of the information, we are led to the strange conclusion that although the cases appeared in the list, were called and dealt with in open court, nevertheless the prosecutor had not yet commenced proceedings.

It is submitted on behalf of the magistrates with the support of counsel as amicus, that those passages in Donaldson LJ's judgment are obiter and were uttered without the benefit of argument on the question of what constitutes the laying of an information. The whole argument in the *Gateshead* case turned on the question of whether or not the consideration of an information was a judicial or administrative function and whether it could be delegated. The informations in the *Gateshead* case had never come to the attention of a magistrate or the clerk to the justices within the time limits provided for commencing proceedings; they had been dealt with by administrative staff in the magistrates' court. If the informations had never been near a magistrate or the clerk to the justices, they had clearly not been laid before them unless they were entitled to delegate their duty, and the court held they were not. It was thus not necessary for the court to consider precisely what was involved in laying an information.

It was further submitted that to hold that an information was not laid until it had been considered for the purpose of issuing process would be inconsistent with the earlier *a* decision of this court in *R v Brentford Justices, ex parte Catlin* [1975] 2 All ER 201, [1975] QB 455. In that case the applicant had received a document that bore a justice's facsimile signature and was in the form of a summons to answer an information on a specific date within six months of an alleged offence of careless driving. The applicant appeared at court on that date unrepresented, she was granted legal aid and the case was adjourned. At the adjourned hearing which was more than six months after the alleged offence, her *b* counsel submitted that the justices had no jurisdiction to hear the case on the grounds that no information was laid within the six-month period, alternatively, that the summons was invalid in that it had been signed by a justice who had not considered the information in breach of r 81 of the Magistrates' Courts' Rules 1968, SI 1968 No 1920. The justices did not accept the submissions and tried and convicted the applicant. Her application for certiorari to quash her conviction failed. As we understand that decision *c* of the Divisional Court it was held that even assuming that the summons was invalid because it was issued by a justice before whom an information had not been laid, nevertheless the information was laid before the justices on the occasion that they adjourned the case and, as that was within the six-month period, it gave them jurisdiction.

Michael Davies J said ([1975] 2 All ER 201 at 206, [1975] QB 455 at 463):   *d*

'It is practical common sense, the respondents say, and I agree with them, that on 4th October 1973 in the circumstances which I have described the applicant did in fact appear before the justices, the document called a summons was laid before the justices then sitting, as the affidavit of the court inspector proves, and that document or summons did contain the charge. So that, therefore, the justices on 4th October had placed before them the charge within six months of the offence. The *e* respondents concede that if the six months had expired and the summons which had been issued was for any reason invalid, the placing of it before the justices on 4th October would be insufficient to found jurisdiction, but the six months had not expired.'

The only factual differences between the situation in *Catlin's* case and these three cases are that the particulars of the offence were contained in the summons placed before the *f* justices, whereas in the present cases they were contained in the court registers, and the presence of the defendant before the court. Michael Davies J does refer to the presence of the defendant before the court but does not suggest that it was material to the question whether or not the information was laid before the justices. What he said was ([1975] 2 All ER 201 at 207, [1975] QB 455 at 463):

'The appellant was there. She was before the court, the summons was before the *g* court—and by summons I mean the document—and that contained sufficient to constitute the information against her.'

We do not read his judgment as suggesting that the mere presence of the applicant would have been sufficient if there had been no document before the court containing sufficient particulars of the offence to constitute an information. The presence of the *h* defendant was material because it allowed the justices to hear the case even though the summons was defective. The presence of the defendant cured the defect in the summons not in the laying of the information.

We have come to the conclusion that we are free to regard the passages already cited from the judgment of Donaldson LJ in the *Gateshead* decision as obiter and that we are not bound by that decision to hold that the laying of the information necessarily involves *j* the consideration of the issue of criminal process.

No doubt as a matter of practice the magistrate will in most cases give his consideration to an information at the same time as it is first placed before him. But it does not necessarily follow that this will always be so. It is not difficult to envisage situations in which an information is brought to the attention of a magistrate shortly before the

expiration of a statutory time limit but either through pressure of work or illness the
a magistrate is unable to give it his attention until after the time limit has elapsed. In such
a case the prosecutor has done all that he can to commence the proceedings within the
time limit and we can see no reason why it should not be held that he laid the
information, or in civil proceedings made the complaint, at the time he brought the
matter to the attention of the magistrate.

The commencement of proceedings lies in the hands of the prosecutor; it is his duty
b to lay the information; he can do no more than place it before a magistrate. He cannot
force the magistrate to consider it. Suppose the magistrate in dereliction of his duty
issues a summons without giving proper consideration to the information, is it to be said
that the prosecutor never laid the information? Surely not.

At one stage in the argument we considered whether it could be said that the
information was laid when it was delivered to the magistrates' court. As a matter of
c practical reality there is a good deal to be said for that view. In the case of written
informations we have little doubt that the matter is out of the hands of the prosecutor
once he has posted or delivered his information to the court. Thereafter, in practice, the
prosecutor is unlikely to have any control over the destination of his information. The
decision as to when and by whom the information is to be considered will be out of the
prosecutor's hands and will be decided in accordance with the procedures of the particular
d magistrates' court. However, such a view would not fit well with the historical
development of summary prosecutions before justices which we think undoubtedly
involved a personal approach by a prosecutor to a justice to commence proceedings, nor
can it stand with the *Gateshead* decision, for in that case although the informations were
never placed before a magistrate or the justices' clerk they had undoubtedly been
received by the court within the statutory period.

e The applicants in the course of their argument in support of the proposition that
consideration of the information was an essential ingredient of the laying, said that
merely placing an information before a magistrate could not amount to laying the
information, for his mind might not go to the purpose of the document. We would
agree that it must be made clear to the magistrate that the information is placed before
him because the prosecutor wishes to pursue a criminal process. But we do not accept
f the applicants' submission that the information is not laid unless and until it is considered
by a magistrate for the purpose of issuing a summons. The consideration of the
information is the judicial function that has to be performed by the magistrate or the
clerk to the justices after the information has been laid, pursuant to his judicial duty not
to issue a criminal process unless he is satisfied that there are sufficient grounds to
warrant it.

g In our view an information is laid when its contents are brought to the attention of a
magistrate or the clerk to the justices as a part of the prosecution process.

An information can be in writing or oral. It does not have to be in any prescribed
form. If in writing it has to be a document identifying the informant and giving
particulars of the offence on which the prosecutor wishes to proceed. In each of the three
cases we are considering, the justices had before them a register containing all this
h information. They were well aware that the cases were in the lists because the
prosecution wished to proceed on them and, in our opinion, the informations were laid
before them on the dates of these hearings when they adjourned the proceedings.

All these dates were within the six-month period and, accordingly, we agree with the
magistrates that they had jurisdiction. These applications must be refused.

j Mr Ives's and Mr Moody's cases
We will now turn to R v Gateshead Justices, ex parte Ives and the case stated of Moody v
Anderton.

Although one case comes before us by way of an application for certiorari and one by
way of case stated, they both raise the same point. In each case, after the applicant had
been convicted by the magistrates, it was discovered that the issue of the summons had

been delegated and the information had not been placed before or considered by a magistrate or the clerk to the justices within the relevant statutory period. In each case the relevant statutory period had expired before the case was first listed in the magistrates court. The situation of each applicant is indistinguishable from the applicants in *R v Gateshead Justices, ex parte Tesco Stores Ltd.*

There can be no doubt that in both cases the magistrates acted without jurisdiction. No purpose is served by setting out the facts at length. Certiorari will go to quash the conviction in both cases.

But one word of general warning. We do not wish this decision to give any encouragement to others to think that at a late stage they can climb on this particular bandwagon. The practice of delegating the issue of the summons that came to light as a result of the *Gateshead* decision has, we are sure, now ceased. We draw attention to the wording of RSC Ord 53, r 4. Applications for judicial review must be brought without delay and an order for certiorari is a discretionary remedy. It is unlikely that this court would look favourably on any further applications based on a practice that we presume has now been corrected.

We wish, however, to observe that to proceed by way of case stated in *Moody v Anderton* was not the appropriate procedure. It arose in this way. Mr Moody on 5th March 1981 pleaded guilty and was convicted and sentenced for two motoring offences. The magistrates did not at that date realise that they had no jurisdiction. On 19th March, after the report of the *Gateshead* decision, an application was made on behalf of Mr Moody to the magistrates to quash the convictions and sentence because they had no jurisdiction. The magistrates declined to do so. They held that Mr Moody's pleas of guilty were unequivocal and that they were functus officio, although they acknowledged that had they known the true facts on 5th March 1981 they would have held that they had no jurisdiction. The magistrates were right to hold that they were functus officio: see *R v Uxbridge Justices, ex parte Clark* [1968] 2 All ER 992. They considered s 41 of the Criminal Justice Act 1972 (now s 142 of the Magistrates' Courts Act 1980) and rightly decided that the section did not give them power to quash a conviction after an unequivocal plea of guilty. They could have rescinded the sentence they had passed but that would have left the conviction on the defendant's record which would be a manifestly unsatisfactory state of affairs. In all the circumstances the magistrates rightly declined to take any action leaving it to this court to quash the conviction if it saw fit to do so. As the substantive relief sought by the applicant was the quashing of his conviction rather than the answer to the question of whether or not the magistrates had power to quash it, the applicant should have applied for judicial review and asked for an order of certiorari. Therefore, we gave leave to the applicant to apply for an order of certiorari during the course of the hearing.

Mr Hanson's case

Finally, there is the case of *R v Leeds Justices, ex parte Hanson* in which Mr Hanson asks for an order of certiorari to quash his conviction for exceeding the speed limit.

This case has afforded us an interesting insight into the use of computers in the legal process but it comes before this court as a result of a misunderstanding at the Leeds Magistrates' Court and raises no question of law.

On 26th March 1981 Mr Hanson appeared before Leeds Magistrates' Court in answer to a summons that alleged he had exceeded the speed limit on 17th September 1980. His solicitor who had read the *Gateshead* decision asked to see the information to see if he could take the point that the information had not been laid within six months of the offence. It is clear from the affidavits of the applicant's solicitor and the justices' clerk's assistant that there was a misunderstanding between them which left the solicitor with the impression that the summons was issued as a result of an oral information which could not be identified. It also seems that the justices' clerk's assistant was not familiar with the practice by which informations were laid and summonses issued in the Leeds Magistrates' Court. If he had been able to explain it to the applicant's solicitor we are sure that these proceedings would not have been before us. The justices inspected the summons and declared that they were satisfied that the information had been laid in time and accepted jurisdiction. They convicted Mr Hanson, fined him £40 and his licence was endorsed.

The affidavit of Mr Whitehead, the clerk to the justices, sets out fully and clearly the computer system used for issuing process in the Leeds Magistrates' Court since 1st October 1980. Every day the police feed into the computer details of offences for which they wish summonses to be issued. The details will show the name, age and occupation of the defendant, details of the alleged offence, particulars of the officer concerned with the case and the police division. In the case of other prosecutions, the details are put into the computer by the court staff.

The computer produces two lists, one of the police cases and one of all other cases. The police check their list and the court staff check their list. If necessary, amendments are fed into the computer.

After the lists have been checked and amended the computer prints out three copies of every summons. No separate 'information' is printed but each summons contains on its face all the detail required to be contained in an information. It shows as the date of the information/complaint the date on which the detail was first fed into the computer, in this case 24th October 1980. It shows the date of summons, in this case 28th October 1980. It contains full particulars of the date and place of the alleged offence, in this case exceeding the speed limit on 17th September 1980 on the M1, northbound, Holbeck.

After the summonses have been printed by the computer, they are placed on the same day before the clerk to the justices or a magistrate for his consideration. If the clerk to the justices or the magistrate authorises the issue of summonses, his signature is placed on the summons and it is issued. The summons in this case bears the signature of Mr Whitehead, the clerk to the justices.

There is no reason why a separate information should be produced by the computer. It is sensible and sufficient to treat the unsigned copy of the summons as the information. We are quite satisfied that in this case an information was laid before the clerk to the justices on 28th September 1980 which was well within the six-month limitation period and this application must be refused.

In the light of our decision in this case the information is laid not on the date that the information is put into the computer but on the date that its contents are brought to the attention of the clerk to the justices or a magistrate. Although it is of no significance in this case, there may in the future be a case in which time expires between the first computer input and the printing of the summons. In such circumstances, it would be seriously misleading to show on the summons the date of the information as the date of the computer input rather than the date on which it was laid. Consideration should be given to an amendment to the form of summons or the computer program so that the date of the information is shown as the date on which it is laid before a magistrate or the clerk to the justices.

Applications by Mr Hanson, Mr Hughes, Mr Hill and Mr Dhesi refused. Orders of certiorari granted to Mr Ives and Mr Moody.

31st July. The court refused applications by Mr Hughes, Mr Hill and Mr Dhesi for leave to appeal to the House of Lords but certified, under s 1(2) of the Administration of Justice Act 1960, that the following point of law of general public importance was involved in the decision: what constitutes a laying of an information for the purposes of s 104 of the Magistrates' Courts Act 1952 (now s 127 of the Magistrates' Courts Act 1980)?

Solicitors: *Ward Bowie*, agents for *A V Hammond & Co*, Bradford (for Mr Hanson); *Hewitt, Woollacott & Chown*, agents for *M D Shaffner*, Wakefield (for the West Yorkshire Metropolitan Police); *Shepherd, Harris & Co*, Enfield (for Mr Hughes); *Betesh & Co*, Manchester (for Mr Hill); *D S Gandy*, Manchester (for the Chief Constable of Greater

Manchester); *Park Nelson & Doyle Devonshire*, agents for *John Foley & Co*, Newcastle upon Tyne (for Mr Ives); *Hatten, Wyatt & Co*, Gravesend (for Mr Dhesi); *A H Lewin*, Dartford (for the Dartford justices); *R A Crabb*, Maidstone (for the Kent County Constabulary); *Douglas-Mann & Co*, agents for *Casson & Co*, Salford (for Mr Moody); Treasury Solicitor.

April Weiss   Barrister.

R v Phekoo

COURT OF APPEAL, CRIMINAL DIVISION
WATKINS LJ, CANTLEY AND HOLLINGS JJ
16th JANUARY, 27th FEBRUARY 1981

Criminal law – Unlawful eviction and harassment of residential occupier of premises – Harassment – Mens rea – Defendant believing that person harassed was not a residential occupier – Whether sufficient for Crown to prove that person harassed was in fact a residential occupier – Whether Crown required to disprove defendant's belief – Whether defendant required to have reasonable grounds for his belief – Whether sufficient if defendant's belief honestly held – Protection from Eviction Act 1977, s 1(3).

The defendant, who was the owner of a house, believed that two men who were in the house were squatters and had no right to be there. He therefore called on them and asked them to leave and, it was alleged, was abusive to them and threatened them with violence if they did not leave. The defendant was charged with doing acts calculated to interfere with the peace or comfort of 'residential occupiers' of the house, ie the two men, with intent to cause them, as residential occupiers, to give up their occupation, contrary to s 1(3)(a)[a] of the Protection from Eviction Act 1977. At the conclusion of the evidence at the trial the defence conceded that the two men were in fact 'residential occupiers' within s 1(1) of the 1977 Act but submitted that it was a defence to the charges that the defendant believed the men to be merely squatters. The trial judge ruled that if the person harassed by a defendant was in fact a residential occupier within s 1(1) the defendant's belief regarding the status of the person harassed was irrelevant, and accordingly, as it had been conceded that the two men were in fact residential occupiers, in his direction to the jury the judge did not refer to the defendant's belief that they were squatters. The defendant was convicted. He appealed against his conviction on the ground that the judge's ruling and direction to the jury were wrong.

Held – Since the acts which could constitute harassment under s 1(3) of the 1977 Act might be of a serious nature, eg tantamount to blackmail, and since s 1(4) of that Act

---

a Section 1, so far as material, provides:
    '(1) In this section "residential occupier", in relation to any premises, means a person occupying the premises as a residence, whether under a contract or by virtue of any enactment or rule of law giving him the right to remain in occupation or restricting the right of any other person to recover possession of the premises . . .
    '(3) If any person with intent to cause the residential occupier of any premises—(a) to give up the occupation of the premises or any part thereof; or (b) to refrain from exercising any right or pursuing any remedy in respect of the premises or part thereof; does acts calculated to interfere with the peace or comfort of the residential occupier or members of his household, or persistently withdraws or withholds services reasonably required for the occupation of the premises as a residence, he shall be guilty of an offence.
    '(4) A person guilty of an offence under this section shall be liable—(a) on summary conviction, to a fine not exceeding £400 or to imprisonment for a term not exceeding 6 months or to both; (b) on conviction on indictment, to a fine or to imprisonment for a term not exceeding 2 years or to both . . .'

a provided for substantial penal consequences to follow conviction of an offence under
s 1(3), it followed that such an offence was truly criminal and could not be regarded
merely as a quasi-criminal offence prohibited under a penalty in the interests of the
public's safety. Under general principles of criminal law, therefore, proof of mens rea
was required, and the intent required by s 1(3) was an intent to do acts in relation to 'the
residential occupier' of premises. Accordingly, on the true construction of s 1(3), where
the issue of a defendant's belief about the status of the person harassed was raised, the
b Crown was required to prove an intent on the part of the defendant to harass someone
he knew to be a residential occupier and also to prove that his belief that that person was
not a residential occupier was not an honest belief; it was not sufficient for the Crown to
prove merely that the person harassed was in fact a residential occupier. In ruling and in
directing the jury as he did, the judge had therefore been wrong, and the appeal would
accordingly be allowed and the conviction quashed (see p 92 c to h and p 93 h, post).
c   Dicta of Wright J in Sherras v De Rutzen [1895–99] All ER Rep at 1169–1170, of Lord
Reid, of Lord Pearce and of Lord Diplock in Sweet v Parsley [1969] 1 All ER at 349–350,
356, 361 and of James LJ in R v Miller [1975] 2 All ER at 976 applied.
      Per Curiam. Where a defendant to a charge under s 1(3) asserts his belief that the
person harassed was not a residential occupier the jury should be directed that there must
be reasonable grounds for that belief (see p 93 h, post).
d   R v Tolson [1886–90] All ER Rep 26 applied.
      Director of Public Prosecutions v Morgan [1975] 2 All ER 347 considered.

Notes

For unlawful eviction and harassment of a residential occupier of premises, see 11
Halsbury's Laws (4th Edn) para 867.
e   For the Protection from Eviction Act 1977, s 1, see 47 Halsbury's Statutes (3rd Edn)
662.

Cases referred to in judgment

Albert v Lavin [1981] 1 All ER 628, [1981] 2 WLR 1070, 72 Cr App R 178, DC.
f Alphacell Ltd v Woodward [1972] 2 All ER 475, [1972] AC 824, [1972] 2 WLR 1320, 136
      JP 505, 70 LGR 455, HL, Digest (Cont Vol D) 1019, 321Ab.
Attorney General v Lockwood (1842) 9 M & W 378, 152 ER 160; affd 10 M & W 464, Ex
      Ch, 44 Digest (Repl) 364, 2015.
Bank of New South Wales v Piper [1897] AC 383, 66 LJPC 73, 76 LT 572, 61 JP 660, PC,
      14(1) Digest (Reissue) 19, 47.
g Director of Public Prosecutions v Morgan [1975] 2 All ER 347, [1976] AC 182, [1975] 2
      WLR 913, 139 JP 476, 61 Cr App R 136, HL, 15 Digest (Reissue) 1212, 10,398.
Lim Chin Aik v Reginam [1963] 1 All ER 223, [1963] AC 160, [1963] 2 WLR 42, PC, 2
      Digest (Reissue) 194, *839.
M'Naghten's Case (1843) 10 Cl & Fin 200, [1843–60] All ER Rep 229, 4 State Tr NS 847,
      1 Town St Tr 314, 1 Car & Kir 130n, 8 Scott NR 595, 8 ER 718, HL, 14(1) Digest
h (Reissue) 38, 156.
Norton v Knowles [1967] 3 All ER 1061, [1969] 1 QB 572, [1968] 3 WLR 183, 132 JP 200,
      19 P & CR 57, [1968] RA 1, DC, 31(2) Digest (Reissue) 923, 7631.
R v Davidson-Acres [1980] Crim LR 50, CA.
R v Gould [1968] 1 All ER 849, [1968] 2 QB 65, [1968] 2 WLR 643, 132 JP 209, 52 Cr App
      R 152, CA, 15 Digest (Reissue) 1030, 8937.
j R v Miller [1975] 2 All ER 974, [1975] 1 WLR 1222, 139 JP 613, 61 Cr App R 182, [1975]
      RTR 479, CA, Digest (Cont Vol D) 895, 413f.
R v Sheppard [1980] 3 All ER 899, [1981] AC 394, [1980] 3 WLR 960, 72 Cr App R 82,
      HL.
R v Smith (David Raymond) [1974] 1 All ER 632, [1974] QB 354, [1974] 2 WLR 20, 138
      JP 236, 58 Cr App R 320, CA, 14(2) Digest (Reissue) 746, 6263.

R v Tolson (1889) 23 QBD 168, [1886–90] All ER Rep 26, 58 LJMC 97, 60 LT 899, 54 JP
4, 20, 16 Cox CC 629, CCR, 15 Digest (Reissue) 1028, 8922.

R v Twose (1879) 14 Cox CC 327, 14(1) Digest (Reissue) 33, 127.

Sherras v De Rutzen [1895] 1 QB 918, [1895–99] All ER Rep 1167, 64 LJMC 218, 72 LT
839, 59 JP 440, 18 Cox CC 157, 15 R 388, DC, 30 Digest (Reissue) 110, 791.

Sweet v Parsley [1969] 1 All ER 347, [1970] AC 132, [1969] 2 WLR 470, 133 JP 188, 53
Cr App R 221, HL, 15 Digest (Reissue) 1084, 9179.

Woolmington v Director of Public Prosecutions [1935] AC 462, [1935] All ER Rep 1, 104
LJKB 433, 153 LT 232, 25 Cr App R 72, 30 Cox CC 234, HL, 14(2) Digest (Reissue)
474, 3919.

Case also cited

McCall v Abelesz [1976] 1 All ER 727, [1976] QB 585, CA.

Appeal

On 17th May 1979 in the Crown Court at Croydon before his Honour Judge Thomas and
a jury the appellant, Harold Phekoo, was convicted on two counts of an indictment
charging him with doing acts calculated to interfere with the peace or comfort of a
residential occupier of premises with intent to cause him to give up occupation of those
premises, contrary to s 1(3)(a) of the Protection from Eviction Act 1977. He was
convicted and fined £100 on each count, with 21 days' imprisonment in default of
payment. He appealed against his conviction on the grounds that the trial judge was
wrong (1) in holding that the appellant's honest, or honest and reasonable, belief that the
persons in the premises were not residential occupiers within the meaning of s 1(1) of the
1977 Act was not a defence to the offences charged in the counts, (2) in holding that
'intent' for the purpose of s 1(3)(a) of the 1977 Act meant an intent to cause any person
actually in the premises who was in fact a residential occupier to give up the occupation
of the premises, whether or not the defendant knew or believed such a person to be a
residential occupier, and (3) in holding that the appellant's honest, or honest and
reasonable, belief that the persons in the premises were not residential occupiers did not
(a) negative intent for the purpose of s 1(3)(a) and/or (b) constitute the defence of mistake
of fact, and on the ground (4) that on a proper construction of s 1(3)(a) intent meant an
intent to cause a person whom the defendant knew or believed to be a residential
occupier to give up the occupation of the premises. The facts are set out in the judgment
of the court.

Evan Stone QC and *M J Segal* for the appellant.
David Van Hee for the Crown.

Cur adv vult

27th February. **HOLLINGS J** read the following judgment of the court: On 17th May
1979 in the Crown Court at Croydon before his Honour Judge Thomas the appellant was
convicted on two counts of an indictment of offences under s 1(3) of the Protection from
Eviction Act 1977. He was acquitted under a third count of possessing an offensive
weapon (a knife) in a public place. He was fined £100 on each count with 21 days'
imprisonment in default. The appellant applied for leave to appeal against conviction;
leave has been granted and with counsel's agreement this hearing, in which the Crown
is represented, is being treated as the appeal.

Section 1 of the 1977 Act repeals and replaces s 30 of the Rent Act 1965. Section 1(3)
(a) makes it an offence for any person, with intent to cause the residential occupier of any
premises to give up his occupation of the premises or any part thereof, to do acts
calculated to interfere with the peace or comfort of the residential occupier. Section 1(1)
defines residential occupier as meaning in relation to any premises a person occupying
the premises as a residence, whether under a contract or by virtue of any enactment or

rule of law giving him the right to remain in occupation or restricting the right of any
other person to recover possession of the premises.

a   The appellant was the owner of a house, 67 Chatham Avenue, Hayes. It was common
ground that on the day in question, 15th January 1978, there were two persons in the
house, Trevillion, named in the first count, and Broster, named in the second count, and
that on that day the appellant called on them and asked each of them to leave. Until the
conclusion of the evidence for the Crown and the defence that was the total extent of the

b common ground. Trevillion and Broster each alleged that the appellant was abusive and
uttered threats to 'be back with his friends' or 'would bring his mates round' and, in the
case of Trevillion, threatened to 'carve him up' with a knife which he had in his pocket,
part of which was visible, if he did not leave, conduct which, if accepted by the jury, was
clearly calculated to interfere with their peace or comfort, and from which the jury could
(and did) infer the necessary intent to cause the two men to give up their occupation of

c the house. The appellant said he uttered no threats and, in effect, that he simply asked
them to leave. The jury's verdict showed that they disbelieved the appellant.

    Part of the evidence was directed to the question, put in issue by the defence, whether
these two men were residential occupiers within the meaning of the Act; the appellant's
evidence was that on the day in question the only person whom he knew was living in
the house was one Agate. He had never seen Trevillion or Broster before. The day

d before his wife had told him (as she confirmed when she gave evidence herself) that
Agate had called, left a set of two keys with her and told her that the house had been
vacated, or would be by 6 pm that evening. He also told her that other people had keys
and the house should be secured.

    At the conclusion of the evidence counsel for the defence conceded that Trevillion and
Broster had indeed been residential occupiers within the meaning of the Act. There had
been evidence that they had been given subtenancies by Agate or another former tenant,

e Cassidy, and it is to be assumed that the concession was based on the fact that the two
men's occupation was protected under the Rent Acts, although effective notices to quit
had previously been given to Cassidy and Agate. It was however at the same time
submitted that, in the words used by the judge in his ruling, 'on the wording of [s 1(3)
of the 1977 Act] it is a defence for the defendant to say that he lacked the belief that these

f two men were residential occupiers'.

    The judge ruled against this submission, saying:

> 'I think it matters not whether the defendant, in this or in any other case, thinks
> that a person is a residential occupier or squatter. If he is a residential occupier
> within s 1 then no question of the state of mind of the defendant arises in relation
> to what he believes the residential occupier to be. The state of mind as to the intent,

g   which relates to the acts set out in sub-s 3 is very relevant.'

    The direction to the jury accordingly made no reference to the defendant's belief, the
judge saying:

> 'As far as these two counts are concerned the prosecution must prove first of all
> that Trevillion, who is mentioned in count 1, or Broster, mentioned in count 2, was

h   a residential occupier within the meaning of the 1977 Act. We now know, because
> the defence concede it, that is not an issue. It is accepted they were residential
> occupiers. The next thing the prosecution must prove is that the defendant did the
> acts alleged in the counts. The prosecution must prove that those acts were
> calculated to interfere with the comfort and peace of Trevillion or Broster, and they
> were done with the intention alleged in the count. That is to say, with intention of

j   causing Trevillion or Broster to give up occupation of 67 Chatham Avenue. The
> defendant, of course, denies he did those alleged acts at all.'

    This forms the basis of the appeal. It is the fact that the appellant stated in evidence
that he thought both men were squatters and had no right at all to be in the house. If
therefore the judge had ruled and summed up on this issue as the defence submitted that

he should there was plainly an issue of fact as to the appellant's belief for the jury to decide. In other words the evidential burden of disproving honest belief would have *a* been on the Crown. We prefer to express it in this way for, since *Woolmington v Director of Public Prosecutions* [1935] AC 462, [1935] All ER Rep 1, the burden would be on the prosecution to negative honest belief and it is incorrect or at least misleading to refer to the 'defence' of honest belief. If the appellant's submission is right then plainly the conviction cannot stand and it is accepted by the Crown that this is not a case for the application of the proviso. The question for the court therefore is whether, on a proper *b* construction of the subsection and in the light of the decided cases where the issue has been raised, the Crown has to prove that the appellant did not honestly believe that the person 'harassed' (to put it shortly) was not a residential occupier. This is quite apart from the specific intent required by the subsection, namely, intent to cause the residential occupier to give up occupation of the premises.

We will leave for later consideration the question whether the jury should also have *c* been directed that such belief should be on reasonable grounds for, since consideration of the appellant's belief, whether reasonably held or not, was wholly withheld from the jury, it is not strictly material to the appeal. It must be emphasised also that what is in question is not the appellant's ignorance of the law (that of course is no defence or excuse) but his alleged ignorance of the facts relating to the status of the persons the appellant was seeking to evict. *d*

Counsel for the appellant has supplied the court with a transcript of the judgment in *R v Davidson-Acres* [1980] Crim LR 50. Since that decision concerned an offence under s 1(2) it has no direct relevance, but sub-s (2) itself has or may have relevance, however, to the construction of sub-s (3). Subsection (2) is as follows:

> 'If any person unlawfully deprives the residential occupier of any premises of his occupation of the premises or any part thereof, or attempts to do so, he shall be *e* guilty of an offence unless he proves that he believed, and had reasonable cause to believe, that the residential occupier had ceased to reside in the premises.'

('Unlawfully' clearly refers to the following ss 2 and 3.) It is to be observed that in s 1(2) Parliament has seen fit to provide expressly for a particular defence; but it has also provided that the onus of establishing that defence (no doubt on a balance of probability) *f* is to be on the defendant, contrary to the general principles. In any event this defence only relates to one aspect: belief that the occupier has ceased to reside. It does not assist in deciding the present question, which can be posed in respect of s 1(2) also, ie what if the appellant says he believed the occupier was in fact a squatter? In this connection there is a relevant passage in the judgment of Wills J in *R v Tolson* (1889) 23 QBD 168, [1886–90] All ER Rep 26 (a case to which further reference will be made later). *g*

The most relevant and authoritative guidance is to be found, we consider, in the decision in the House of Lords in *Sweet v Parsley* [1969] 1 All ER 347, [1970] AC 132. There the mens rea of the offence created by s 5 of the Dangerous Drugs Act 1965 was in question. The decision of the House rested strictly on the construction of the words of the section and in particular on the meaning and effect of the phrase 'permits premises to be used for the purpose of smoking cannabis resin', but some of the Law Lords gave *h* general guidance in respect of mens rea in statutory offences.

Lord Reid said ([1969] 1 All ER 347 at 349–350, [1970] AC 132 at 148–149):

> 'Our first duty is to consider the words of the Act; if they show a clear intention to create an absolute offence, that is an end of the matter. But such cases are very rare. Sometimes the words of the section which creates a particular offence make it *j* clear that mens rea is required in one form or another. Such cases are quite frequent. But in a very large number of cases there is no clear indication either way. In such cases there has for centuries been a presumption that Parliament did not intend to make criminals of persons who were in no way blameworthy in what they did. That means that, whenever a section is silent as to mens rea, there is a

a

presumption that, in order to give effect to the will of Parliament, we must read in words appropriate to require mens rea. [After referring to the words of Alderson B in *Attorney General v Lockwood* (1842) 9 M & W 378 at 398 152 ER 160 at 168 Lord Reid continued:] It is also firmly established that the fact that other sections of the Act expressly require mens rea, for example because they contain the word "knowingly", is not in itself sufficient to justify a decision that a section which is silent as to mens rea creates an absolute offence. In the absence of a clear indication in the Act that an offence is intended to be an absolute offence, it is necessary to go outside the Act and examine all relevant circumstances in order to establish that this must have been the intention of Parliament. I say "must have been", because it is a universal principle that if a penal provision is reasonably capable of two interpretations, that interpretation which is most favourable to the accused must be adopted. What, then, are the circumstances which it is proper to take into account? In the well-known case of *Sherras* v. *De Rutzen* ([1895] 1 QB 918 at 922, [1895–99] All ER Rep 1167 at 1169), Wright J., only mentioned the subject-matter with which the Act deals. But he was there dealing with something which was one of a class of acts which "are not criminal in any real sense, but are acts which in the public interest are prohibited under a penalty". It does not in the least follow that, when one is dealing with a truly criminal act, it is sufficient merely to have regard to the subject-matter of the enactment. One must put oneself in the position of a legislator. It has long been the practice to recognise absolute offences in this class of quasi-criminal acts, and one can safely assume that, when Parliament is passing new legislation dealing with this class of offences, its silence as to mens rea means that the old practice is to apply. But when one comes to acts of a truly criminal character, it appears to me that there are at least two other factors which any reasonable legislator would have in mind. In the first place, a stigma still attaches to any person convicted of a truly criminal offence, and the more serious or more disgraceful the offence the greater the stigma. So he would have to consider whether, in a case of this gravity, the public interest really requires that an innocent person should be prevented from proving his innocence in order that fewer guilty men may escape.'

b

c

d

e

Lord Pearce said ([1969] 1 All ER 347 at 356, [1970] AC 132 at 156):

f

'Before the court will dispense with the necessity for mens rea it has to be satisfied that Parliament so intended. The mere absence of the word "knowingly" is not enough. But the nature of the crime, the punishment, the absence of social obloquy, the particular mischief and the field of activity in which it occurs, and the wording of the particular section and its context, may show that Parliament intended that the act should be prevented by punishment regardless of intent or knowledge.'

g

Lord Diplock said ([1969] 1 All ER 347 at 361, [1970] AC 132 at 156):

'But only too frequently the actual words used by Parliament to define the prohibited conduct are in themselves descriptive only of a physical act and bear no connotation as to any particular state of mind on the part of the person who does the act. Nevertheless, the mere fact that Parliament has made the conduct a criminal offence gives rise to *some* implication about the mental element of the conduct proscribed. It has, for instance, never been doubted since *M'Naghten's Case* ((1843) 10 Cl & Fin 200, [1843–60] All ER Rep 229) that one implication as to the mental element in any statutory offence is that the doer of the prohibited act should be sane within the M'Naghten rules; yet this part of the full definition of the offence is invariably left unexpressed by Parliament. Stephen, J., in *R.* v. *Tolson* ((1889) 23 QBD 168, [1886–90] All ER Rep 26) suggested other circumstances never expressly dealt with in the statute where a mental element to be implied from the mere fact that the doing of an act was made a criminal offence would be absent, such as where it was done in a state of somnambulism or under duress, to which one might add inevitable accident. But the importance of the actual decision of the nine judges

h

j

who constituted the majority in *R. v. Tolson* which concerned a charge of bigamy under s. 57 of the Offences Against the Person Act 1861, was that it laid down as a general principle of construction of any enactment, which creates a criminal offence that, even where the words used to describe the prohibited conduct would not in any other context connote the necessity for any particular mental element, they are nevertheless to be read as subject to the implication that a necessary element in the offence is the absence of a belief held honestly and on reasonable grounds in the existence of facts which, if true, would make the act innocent. As was said by the Privy Council in *Bank of New South Wales* v. *Piper* ([1897] AC 383), the absence of mens rea really consists in such a belief by the accused. This implication stems from the principle that it is contrary to a rational and civilised criminal code, such as Parliament must be presumed to have intended, to penalise one who has performed his duty as a citizen to ascertain what acts are prohibited by law (ignorantia juris non excusat) and has taken all proper care to inform himself of any facts which would make his conduct lawful. Where penal provisions are of general application to the conduct of ordinary citizens in the course of their everyday life, the presumption is that the standard of care required of them in informing themselves of facts which would make their conduct unlawful, is that of the familiar common law duty of care. But where the subject-matter of a statute is the regulation of a particular activity involving potential danger to public health, safety or morals, in which citizens have a choice whether they participate or not, the court may feel driven to infer an intention of Parliament to impose, by penal sanctions, a higher duty of care on those who choose to participate and to place on them an obligation to take whatever measures may be necessary to prevent the prohibited act, without regard to those considerations of cost or business practicability which play a part in the determination of what would be required of them in order to fulfil the ordinary common law duty of care. But such an inference is not lightly to be drawn, nor is there any room for it unless there is something that the person on whom the obligation is imposed can do directly or indirectly, by supervision or inspection, by improvement of his business methods or by exhorting those whom he may be expected to influence or control, which will promote the observance of the obligation (see *Lim Chin Aik* v. *Reginam* ([1963] All ER 223, [1963] AC 160)).'

In *Sherras v De Rutzen* [1895] 1 QB 918 at 921–922, [1895–99] All ER Rep 1167 at 1169–1170, referred to by Lord Reid, Wright J gave examples of the kind of offences which might truly be considered 'absolute' (or perhaps more properly of strict liability: see eg Smith and Hogan's Criminal Law (4th Edn, 1978, pp 79, 92)) in the sense of the mens rea not being an essential ingredient and suggests that there are three possible classes: acts not criminal in any real sense but which in the public interest are prohibited under penalties, acts which are public nuisances and, thirdly cases in which, although the proceeding is criminal in form it is really only a summary mode of enforcing a civil right.

The maximum punishment for an offence under s 1 of the Protection from Eviction Act 1977 is, on summary conviction, a fine of £400 or six months' imprisonment or both or, on indictment, a fine without express limit or two years' imprisonment or both; in neither case can the sanction be said to be light.

In *R v Smith (David Raymond)* [1974] 1 All ER 632, [1974] QB 354, an appeal to this court, it was held that no offence is committed under s 1(1) of the Criminal Damage Act 1971 when a person damages property belonging to another if he does so in the honest though mistaken belief that the property was his own. The offence created by this statute, includes, as James LJ said in the judgment of the court, the elements of intention or recklessness and the absence of lawful excuse (ss 1 and 5 of the Act). The court, in arriving at its decision that the issue of honest belief that the property was his own should have been left to the jury, expressly gave as its reason that the actus reus of the offence was 'destroying or damaging property belonging to another' and said that it was not possible to exclude the words 'belonging to another', which described the property, and

so, applying the ordinary principle of mens rea, the intention of recklessness and the
a absence of lawful excuse required to constitute the offence have reference to property
belonging to another, so that no offence is committed if the defendant honestly but
mistakenly believes that the property is his own. It is true that in that case there were
earlier cases and earlier Acts indicating that this had been the law before the 1971 Act (see
R v Twose (1879) 14 Cox CC 327 and the Malicious Damage Act 1861, s 13). No reference
seems to have been made to *Sweet v Parsley*.

b   In *R v Miller* [1975] 2 All ER 974, [1975] 1 WLR 1222 (James LJ again giving
judgment) it was held in this court that s 99 of the Road Traffic Act 1972 created an
'absolute' offence which did not require proof of mens rea and which was proved when
the prosecution established that there was a driving of a motor vehicle on a road by a
person who was disqualified at the time, so that the judge ruled correctly that the
defendant's state of mind as to the nature of the place on which he was admittedly
c driving, namely his belief that the place was not a 'road' within the meaning of the Act,
ie a place to which the public had access, was irrelevant. *Sweet v Parsley* was considered
but the court concluded that offences under the Road Traffic Act came within the
category of 'absolute' or 'strict liability' offences. James LJ said ([1975] 2 All ER 974 at
976, [1975] 1 WLR 1222 at 1224–1225):

d   'Secondly, we observe that the offence created is in an Act of Parliament dealing
with the regulation of road traffic, and we ask ourselves whether that offence created
in that statute by this section is one that would properly be called a truly "criminal"
offence as distinct from an offence which is prohibited under the sanction of
penalties in the interests of the safety of the public. The answer to that question
appears quite clearly, and counsel for the appellant would not argue strenuously to
the contrary, that this does not create what would normally be called a truly
e   criminal offence, but does make provision for safeguarding the safety of the public
by prohibiting an act under sanction of a penalty.'

Cases under earlier Road Traffic Acts to similar effect were followed; other provisions of
the 1972 Act itself were also deemed relevant (see [1975] 2 All ER 974 at 978, [1975] 1
WLR 1222 at 1226).
f   In *Alphacell Ltd v Woodward* [1972] 2 All ER 475 at 483, [1972] AC 824 at 839, a case
concerning pollution of a river contrary to the Rivers (Prevention of Pollution) Act 1951,
Viscount Dilhorne said:

        'This Act is, in my opinion, one of those Acts to which my noble and learned
friends, Lord Reid and Lord Diplock, referred in *Sweet v Parsley* [1969] 1 All ER 347
at 350, 361, [1970] AC 132 at 149, 162 which, to apply the words of Wright J in
g   *Sherras v De Rutzen* [1895] 1 QB 918 at 922, [1895–99] All ER Rep 1169 at 1169
deals with acts which "are not criminal in any real sense, but are acts which in the
public interest are prohibited under a penalty".'

Lord Pearson also referred to the passage in Lord Diplock's speech and to Lord Pearce's
speech (see [1972] 2 All ER 475 at 487, [1972] AC 824 at 844). Lord Salmon said ([1972]
h 2 All ER 475 at 490–491, [1972] AC 824 at 848):

        'The offences created by the Act of 1951 seem to me to be prototypes of offences
which "are not criminal in any real sense, but are acts which in the public interest
are prohibited under a penalty": *Sherras v De Rutzen* referred to with approval by my
noble and learned friends, Lord Reid and Lord Diplock, in *Sweet v Parsley*.'

j   We have been referred to a further, more recent, decision in the House of Lords, *R v
Sheppard* [1980] 3 All ER 899 at 906, [1981] AC 394 at 407–408, (concerning an offence
under s 1(1) of the Children and Young Persons Act 1933, wilful neglect of a child). Lord
Diplock said:

        'The climate of both parliamentary and judicial opinion has been growing less
favourable to the recognition of absolute offences over the last few decades, a trend

to which s 1 of the Homicide Act 1957 and s 8 of the Criminal Justice Act 1967 bear
witness in the case of Parliament, and in the case of the judiciary is illustrated by the *a*
speeches in this House in *Sweet v Parsley*.'

We refer also to Lord Edmund-Davies's speech (see [1980] 3 All ER 899 at 909, [1981]
AC 394 at 411).

It is of interest finally on this aspect to consider the case of *Norton v Knowles* [1967] 3
All ER 1061, [1969] 1 QB 572, which concerned the identical offence of harassment
under the Rent Act 1965, s 30. Here the complainant lived in his own caravan on land *b*
owned by the defendant. The defendant (the appellant in the Divisional Court)
contended that since the complainant did not occupy his, the defendant's, land as a
residence but only the caravan, in respect of which there was no contract, the complainant
was not a 'resident occupier'. This submission failed. We refer to this case only to
illustrate the distinction between a mistaken belief as to fact and a mistaken belief as to
the law, which is of course not relevant or available as a defence, for the appellant in that *c*
case was under no mistake as to the facts and so it could not be and was not put forward
as a ground of defence or appeal.

We return to the circumstances of the present appeal. Counsel for the Crown has
submitted that the Protection from Eviction Act 1977 is in essence an adjunct to 'social
legislation' relating to the protection of tenants and so is really in the category of quasi-
criminal offences or offences which are not truly criminal, such as were referred to in the *d*
speeches in *Sweet v Parsley* and by this court in *R v Miller*. We cannot take that view. Not
only are substantial penal consequences provided for by s 1 of the 1977 Act but also
conviction for such an offence must in our view be considered as a conviction of a truly
criminal offence and as attaching serious stigma to the offender. Nor is there absence of
social obloquy. It is true that the gravity of an offence of harassment can vary very
greatly; at one end of the scale the relevant acts may be no more than intermittent but *e*
persistent withdrawal by the landlord of services (specifically referred to in s 1(3)). At the
other end of the scale however the acts may amount to more serious threats which are
tantamount to the statutory crime of blackmail though not chargeable as such. We
consider that these factors far outweigh the other factors mentioned in the passages
quoted above.

Further, the specific intent required by s 1(3) is an intent to do certain acts in relation *f*
to 'the residential occupier'. Counsel for the Crown has argued that the use of 'the' rather
than 'a' gives an indication of the meaning that should be attached to this section, namely
that all that suffices is that the person harassed should be 'the' residential occupier,
whatever the belief of the alleged offender. We consider this too fine a point to be of real
assistance. We consider that, general principle apart, the requirement of this specific,
guilty intent does, or ought, when the issue is raised, to comprise proof of intent to harass *g*
someone who is known or believed by the offender to be a person who, in effect, is not
just a 'squatter'. This, in our judgment, is consistent with the decision in *R v Smith* [1974]
1 All ER 632, [1974] QB 354. For these reasons, based on general principles and on the
construction of the section, we consider that the judge was in error in ruling and
summing up as he did.

As has been said earlier it is not strictly necessary for the purposes of this appeal to *h*
decide whether, in his summing up, the judge should have ruled that honest belief,
whether reasonably held or justified on the facts or not, had to be disproved by the
Crown or whether he should have ruled that such belief should have been held reasonably
and on reasonable grounds. Although reference was made in the course of the appeal to
this aspect, no argument was in fact addressed to us on this point. We consider however
that, having reached the decision which we have, we ought to give guidance on this *j*
aspect.

Until the decision of the House of Lords in *Director of Public Prosecutions v Morgan*
[1975] 2 All ER 347, [1976] AC 182, *R v Tolson* (1889) 23 QBD 168, [1886–90] All ER 26
has generally been accepted by the court as governing this aspect of mens rea. In *R v*

Tolson Cave J, in concurring with the majority of the judges that a belief on reasonable
a grounds that the first spouse is dead is a good defence to bigamy, said (23 QBD 168 at
181, [1886–90] All ER Rep 26 at 34):

> 'At common law an honest and reasonable belief in the existence of circumstances,
> which, if true, would make the act for which a prisoner is indicted an innocent act
> has always been held to be a good defence. This doctrine is embodied in the
> somewhat uncouth maxim "actus non facit reum, nisi mens sit rea". Honest and
> *b* reasonable mistake stands in fact on the same footing as absence of the reasoning
> faculty, as in infancy, or perversion of that faculty, as in lunacy. Instances of the
> existence of this common law doctrine will readily occur to the mind. So far as I am
> aware it has never been suggested that these exceptions do not equally apply in the
> case of statutory offences unless they are excluded expressly or by necessary
> implication.'

c
Strong support for this view was given by Lord Diplock in his speech in *Sweet v Parsley*
[1969] 1 All ER 347 at 360–364, [1970] AC 132 at 161–166. See also *Bank of New South
Wales v Piper* [1897] AC 383 and *R v Gould* [1968] 1 All ER 849, [1968] 2 QB 65.

Director of Public Prosecutions v Morgan [1975] 2 All ER 347, [1976] AC 182 concerned
the offence of rape and whether belief that the complainant was consenting should be on
d reasonable grounds or whether the test was subjective. The majority decided that in the
case of rape the Crown must disprove an actual belief, however unreasonable it appeared,
but it seems to us clear that this decision was confined and intended to be confined to the
offence of rape (see [1975] 2 All ER 347 at 351–353, 361–362, 381–383, [1976] AC 182
at 199–201, 214–215, 237–238 per Lord Cross, Lord Hailsham and Lord Fraser). Lord
Cross (who was otherwise in agreement with the other two who with him made up the
e majority), and Lord Simon and Lord Edmund-Davies, who dissented, all confirmed the
general application of the principles in *R v Tolson*.

Director of Public Prosecutions v Morgan was considered by the Divisional Court in *Albert
v Lavin* [1981] 1 All ER 628, [1981] 2 WLR 1070. That case concerned a charge of
assaulting a constable in the course of his duty. The Divisional Court answered the
question whether a belief that the person resisted by the appellant was not a constable
f must be held on reasonable grounds for there to be an acquittal in the affirmative.

The Divisional Court refused leave to appeal but certified a point of law of general
public importance ([1981] 1 All ER 628 at 640, [1981] 2 WLR 1070 at 1085):

> 'Whether a person charged with an offence of assault may properly be convicted
> if the court finds that he acted in the belief that facts existed which if true would
> justify his conduct on the basis of self-defence but that there were in fact no
> *g* reasonable grounds for so believing.'

The Appeal Committee of the House of Lords on 19th February 1981 gave leave to
appeal. We do not think it necessary to defer this judgment for the decision of the House
of Lords since for the reasons already given it would not affect the result of this appeal.

In considering therefore, as we do, that there must be a reasonable basis for the asserted
h belief, we also have regard to the nature and object of the statutory offence, and, though
of lesser influence, to the fact that in s 1(2) of the 1977 Act, where the onus is placed on
the defence, Parliament has deemed it right to provide that the defendant must show
reasonable cause for his belief.

For these reasons we allow the appeal and the conviction is quashed.

Appeal allowed. Conviction quashed.

Solicitors: *Judge & Priestley*, Bromley (for the appellant); *R E T Birch*.

N P Metcalfe Esq   Barrister.

R v Patel

a

COURT OF APPEAL, CRIMINAL DIVISION
SHAW LJ, BRISTOW AND HODGSON JJ
16th, 26th JANUARY 1981

Criminal evidence – Hearsay – Document – Home Office records – Evidence as to contents of
records given by person other than officer responsible for compiling and keeping records – *b*
Defendant charged with assisting illegal entry into United Kingdom – Home Office records
showing person assisted was illegal entrant – Immigration officer giving evidence that he had
examined records – Whether evidence admissible – Whether records proof of facts contained
therein – Criminal Evidence Act 1965, s 1(1).

The defendant was charged with assisting the illegal entry of A into the United Kingdom, *c*
contrary to s 25(1) of the Immigration Act 1971. To prove that A was an illegal entrant
the Crown called an immigration officer, who gave evidence that he had examined
Home Office records which showed that A's name was not in the records as being
entitled to a certificate of registration in the United Kingdom and that therefore at the
material time he was an illegal entrant. On a submission by the defendant that the
Home Office records were inadmissible evidence, the trial judge ruled that the records *d*
were admissible to prove that A was an illegal entrant. The defendant was convicted.
He, appealed against the conviction on the ground that the judge's ruling was wrong.

Held – The Home Office records relied on by the Crown were hearsay evidence, and,
since they were not within the class of documents which were made admissible in
criminal proceedings as evidence of the facts contained in them under s 1(1)[a] of the *e*
Criminal Evidence Act 1965, an officer responsible for their compilation and custody
should have been called by the Crown to give evidence that the method of compilation
was such that if A's name was not in the records he must be an illegal entrant. Since the
immigration officer was not such an officer, his evidence about the records had been
wrongly admitted and, as no other evidence had been adduced by the Crown to prove
that A was an illegal entrant, the defendant's conviction would be quashed (see p 96 e to *f*
h and p 97 e, post).

Myers v Director of Public Prosecutions [1964] 2 All ER 881 applied.
Per Curiam. Where there are a large number of counts in an indictment dealing with
several different offences in respect of several different matters, even though there may
be a common thread running through them all, it is important that in his summing up
the trial judge should deal clearly and distinctly with the case on each count in order to *g*
avoid the possibility of confusion in the jury's mind (see p 97 d e, post).

Notes
For the inadmissibility of hearsay evidence and exceptions to the rule under the Criminal

h

a Section 1(1) provides: 'In any criminal proceedings where direct oral evidence of a fact would be
admissible, any statement contained in a document and tending to establish that fact shall, on
production of the document, be admissible as evidence of that fact if—(a) the document is, or
forms part of, a record relating to any trade or business and compiled, in the course of that trade
or business, from information supplied (whether directly or indirectly) by persons who have, or
may reasonably be supposed to have, personal knowledge of the matters dealt with in the
information they supply; and (b) the person who supplied the information recorded in the *j*
statement in question is dead, or beyond the seas, or unfit by reason of his bodily or mental
condition to attend as a witness, or cannot with reasonable diligence be identified or found, or
cannot reasonably be expected (having regard to the time which has elapsed since he supplied the
information and to all the circumstances) to have any recollection of the matters dealt with in the
information he supplied.'

Evidence Act 1965 in regard to certain documents, see 11 Halsbury's Laws (4th Edn)
a paras 437, 439, 442.
For the Criminal Evidence Act 1965, s 1, see 12 Halsbury's Statutes (3rd Edn) 907.
For the Immigration Act 1971, s 25, see 41 ibid 45.

Cases referred to in judgment
Myers v Director of Public Prosecutions [1964] 2 All ER 881, [1965] AC 1001, [1964] 3 WLR
b   145, 128 JP 481, 48 Cr App R 348, HL; *affg* sub nom *R v Myers* [1964] 1 All ER 877,
CCA, 22 Digest (Reissue) 63, 388.
R v Mehet and Hayr (21st March 1980, unreported), CA.

Application for leave to appeal
On 22nd November 1979 in the Crown Court at Preston before his Honour Judge
c Openshaw the appellant, Abdul Hamid Ibrahim Patel, was convicted on, inter alia,
counts 4 and 5 of an indictment of assisting the illegal entry of Mohammed Ashraf into
the United Kingdom, contrary to s 25(1) of the Immigration Act 1971, and was sentenced
on each of those counts to three years' imprisonment to run consecutively. He applied for
leave to appeal against the convictions on the ground that the trial judge had erred in law
in admitting Home Office records as evidence that Ashraf was an illegal entrant when
d that evidence was hearsay. The facts are set out in the judgment of the court.

N J Ley for the appellant.
Philip Cattan for the Crown.

Cur adv vult

e 26th January. **BRISTOW J** read the following judgment of the court: On 22nd
November 1979 the appellant, then aged 32, was tried in the Crown Court at Preston
before his Honour Judge Openshaw on an indictment containing ten counts, as
follows. Counts 1 and 2 were handling stolen goods. He was convicted and sentenced
to six months on each count concurrent. Count 3 was obtaining a policy of insurance by
f deception. This count was not proceeded with and was ordered to lie on the file, not to
be proceeded with without leave. Counts 4 and 5 were assisting illegal entry into the
United Kingdom, contrary to s 25(1)(d) of the Immigration Act 1971. He was convicted
and sentenced to three years on each count concurrent with each other, and with the
sentences on counts 1 and 2. Count 6 was assisting illegal entry into the United Kingdom,
contrary to s 25(1) of the 1971 Act, and he was acquitted. Count 7 was possession of a
g false document, contrary to s 26(1)(d) of the 1971 Act. He was convicted and sentenced
to three months concurrent. Count 8 was assisting illegal entry into the United Kingdom,
contrary to s 25(1) of the 1971 Act. He was convicted and sentenced to four years'
imprisonment concurrent. Count 9 was harbouring an illegal entrant, contrary to
s 25(2) of the 1971 Act. He was sentenced to three months concurrent. Count 10 was
inciting someone to enter the office of the Registrar of Births, Deaths and Marriages at
h Chorley and steal registration certificates. He was acquitted of that.
In passing sentence, the trial judge observed that it was quite plain that the appellant
was running some sort of ghastly racket, and that it was conduct which could not be
tolerated since it created ill-will between the various races, and racial prejudice. The
judge made it clear that the sentences which he passed were intended, in total, to be
exemplary.
j The appellant now applies to this court for leave to appeal against conviction and
sentence. This court has given leave to appeal and, since counsel for both the appellant
and the Crown have been present and have presented argument to the court, has treated
the hearing as the hearing of the appeal.
No argument has been presented by counsel for the appellant in respect of his
convictions on counts 1 and 2. In so far as his appeal relates to conviction and sentence on

those counts, it is dismissed. Not only were the sentences proper, but they have already been served. This court does not interfere with those sentences. Counsel for the Crown *a* rightly does not seek to support the convictions on counts 7 and 9. It is accepted that the offences charged in these counts are offences triable only summarily, not on indictment, see *R v Mehet and Hayr* (21st March 1980, unreported), a case which does not appear to have been cited for the assistance of the trial judge when asked to rule on the question of the jurisdiction of the Crown Court in relation to counts 7 and 9. The convictions on those counts are therefore quashed.   *b*

So there remain the appeals in respect of counts 4, 5 and 8. Count 4 charged the appellant and Mohammed Ashraf with being knowingly concerned in making arrangements for facilitating the entry into the United Kingdom of Ashraf, who he knew, or had reasonable cause to believe, was an illegal entrant. Count 5 charged the appellant with being knowingly concerned in making arrangements for securing or facilitating the entry into the United Kingdom of Mohammed Ashraf, who he knew, or *c* had reasonable cause to believe, was an illegal entrant. Count 8 charged him similarly in respect of Masoud Akhtar.

The evidence led by the Crown to prove that Ashraf was an illegal immigrant was that of Brian Stone, the chief immigration officer at Manchester airport. His evidence was that his examination of Home Office records showed that Ashraf was not entitled to a certificate of registration in the United Kingdom and was, at the time with which count *d* 4 is concerned, an illegal entrant. Counsel for the appellant submitted to the trial judge that the Home Office records were inadmissible to prove that Ashraf was an illegal entrant. The trial judge ruled that they were clearly admissible. Counsel for the appellant submits to this court that he was wrong, relying on the decision in the House of Lords in *Myers v Director of Public Prosecutions* [1964] 2 All ER 881, [1965] AC 1001, and in particular on the observations of Lord Morris and Lord Hodson ([1964] 2 All ER 881 at *e* 890, 896, [1965] AC 1001 at 1028, 1033).

In the judgment of this court, the Home Office records relied on by the Crown in this case are hearsay, just as were the commercial records in question in *Myers v Director of Public Prosecutions*, and since they cannot therefore speak for themselves in criminal proceedings, and are not within those classes of documents which, since the Criminal Evidence Act 1965 have been allowed to speak for themselves in criminal proceedings, *f* an officer responsible for their compilation and custody should have been called to give evidence that the method of compilation and custody is such that if Ashraf's name is not there, he must be an illegal entrant. It is not suggested that Mr Stone is such an officer. In our judgment, the trial judge was wrong in law to admit the evidence about the state of the records for the purpose for which it was tendered. Ashraf failed to appear at the trial and give evidence. The appellant made no admission about whether Ashraf was an *g* illegal entrant or not. There was, therefore, in the judgment of this court, no admissible evidence to support the proposition that he was, a proposition which was an essential element in the offence charged in count 4. The conviction on count 4 is therefore quashed.

In support of count 5, the evidence was that a blank passport application form was found bearing the name of Arif, together with letters addressed to the appellant from a *h* man called Butt, in the appellant's house. The appellant said he knew nothing about them, and the forensic evidence shed no light on who had written the Arif application form. As far as this court has been able to discover, there was no other evidence about whether Arif was an illegal entrant or not, or indeed that the appellant did anything about him. Of course, the finding of the application form in the appellant's house arouses suspicion, but, in our judgment, there was no more evidence in respect of count 5 and *j* Arif than there was in respect of count 6 and Kurishid, where the judge rightly directed the jury to return a verdict of not guilty. The conviction on count 5 is accordingly quashed.

In respect of count 8, Masood Akhtar, the position is very different. When the appellant's house was searched on 17th July 1979 the police found taped to the back of

a picture in the fireplace a completed application form bearing two photographs in the
name of Akhtar. The appellant said he knew nothing about it. But Akhtar was called,
a and gave evidence that the appellant agreed to get a British passport for him for a fee of
£200 plus £11, the passport office fee, and that he could go out on his Pakistan passport,
and return on the bogus British passport and stay permanently. On his own story,
Akhtar was a party to a deal intended to get him into the United Kingdom as an illegal
entrant, and so an accomplice of whose evidence the jury ought to look for corroboration,
b without which it would be dangerous to convict. The trial judge, taking the view, in our
judgment erroneously, that Akhtar was not an accomplice, did not give the jury the
classic direction on corroboration, although he warned them that Akhtar might have an
axe to grind. Had he done so, the jury would no doubt have concluded that the finding
of the passport application corroborated Akhtar's story up to the hilt.

Counsel for the appellant very candidly told this court that if he had been charged on
c count 8 alone, he would have had difficulty in saying that the conviction on count 8 was
unsatisfactory. But he submits that having regard to the course the trial took, we ought
so to regard it. It was part of a complex story, some of which ought not to have been
before the Crown Court at all, some of which was supported by inadmissible evidence,
some of which was really insufficiently supported by evidence, a story which, if all taken
at its face value, added up to the black picture spoken of by the trial judge in sentencing.

d This court has found the case made at trial difficult to follow because of the way in
which the trial judge summed up to the jury. Where you have ten counts dealing with
several different offences in respect of several different people, even though there may be
a common thread running through them all, it is important to deal clearly and distinctly
with the case on each count in order to avoid the possibility of confusion in the jury's
mind.

In our judgment, the trial judge for once fell short of his usual high standard. For
e these reasons, we have come to the conclusion that, in spite of the strength of the Crown
case on count 8, this court must regard the conviction on count 8 as unsafe, and it must
be quashed.

Accordingly, to that extent this appeal succeeds.

f *Appeal allowed in part.*

Solicitors: *J S Siergant & Co*, Chorley (for the appellant); *Leo B Wallwork & Co*, Chorley
(for the Crown).

N P Metcalfe Esq   Barrister.

Inland Revenue Commissioners v Helen   *a*
Slater Charitable Trust Ltd

COURT OF APPEAL, CIVIL DIVISION
WALLER, OLIVER AND FOX LJJ
5th, 6th, 19th MAY 1981

         b

Income tax – Exemption – Charity – Donations from one charity to another – Donations accumulated by recipient charity – Whether donations 'applied to charitable purposes' – Income and Corporation Taxes Act 1970, s 360(1)(c).

Capital gains tax – Exemptions and reliefs – Charity – Donations from one charity to another – Donations accumulated by recipient charity – Whether donations 'applied to charitable   *c purposes' – Finance Act 1965, s 35(1).*

In 1970 a trust and a foundation were each incorporated as a company limited by guarantee. Both companies were registered charities and had been set up to work in tandem, the trust's main function being to raise funds for the foundation. Their general objects were identical, save that the trust's objects specifically included the making of *d* grants to other bodies established for charitable purposes. The same persons were at all material times directors of both companies. In the years 1973 to 1975 the trust donated substantially the whole of its income to the foundation, most of which the foundation added to its general funds, which were not distributed. A claim by the trust for exemption from income tax under s 360(1)[a] of the Income and Corporation Taxes Act 1970 and capital gains tax under s 35(1)[b] of the Finance Act 1965 in respect of its *e* donations to the foundation as money applicable to and applied for charitable purposes was rejected on the ground that the money had not been 'applied' to charitable purposes. The Special Commissioners upheld the trust's contention that it was entitled to the exemption claimed, and on appeal the judge ([1980] 1 All ER 785) affirmed their determination. The Crown appealed, contending that the money donated to the foundation had not been 'applied' for charitable purposes since (i) the money had not *f* been expended 'in the field' or appropriated for a specific charitable purpose by the foundation and (ii) the trust, in making the donations, had merely transferred the money to the foundation to be held on substantially the same trusts as those on which it had previously been held and there had been no significant change in the beneficial ownership of the money transferred.

         g

Held – Any charitable corporation which, pursuant to its trust deed or constitution, made an outright transfer of money applicable for charitable purposes to any other corporation established exclusively for charitable purposes, in such manner as to pass to the transferee full title to the money, had to be said, by the transfer itself, to have 'applied' such money for charitable purposes, within s 35(1) of the 1965 Act and s 360(1)(c)(iii) of the 1970 Act, notwithstanding the fact that the transferee added the money to its general *h* reserves for expenditure in the future and that the funds of both the transferee and the transferor were held on similar trusts by the same trustees or directors, unless the transferor knew or ought to have known that the money would be misapplied by the transferee. Accordingly, since there was no question of lack of bona fides on the part of the trust or of any moneys having been misapplied by the foundation, it followed that the money transferred by the trust to the foundation was exempt from income tax under *j* s 360(1) of the 1970 Act and from capital gains tax under s 35(1) of the 1965 Act. The

---

a   Section 360(1), so far as material, is set out at p 100 *b*, post
b   Section 35(1) is set out at p 100 *d*, post

appeal would therefore be dismissed (see p 101 c d h j, p 102 a, p 104 e to h and p 105 b to
a f, post).
   Decision of Slade J [1980] 1 All ER 785 affirmed.

Notes
For the exemption of charities from income tax and capital gains tax, see 23 Halsbury's
Laws (4th Edn) paras 1066–1071 and 5 ibid para 137.
b For the Finance Act 1965, s 35, see 34 Halsbury's Statutes (3rd Edn) 906.
   For the Income and Corporation Taxes Act 1970, s 360, see 33 ibid 477.
   Section 35 of the Finance Act 1965 was replaced by s 145 of the Capital Gains Tax Act
1979 with effect from 6th April 1979.

Cases referred to in judgments
c *General Nursing Council for Scotland v Inland Revenue Comrs* 1929 SC 664, 14 Tax Cas 645,
      28(1) Digest (Reissue) 486, *1238.
   Inland Revenue Comrs v Educational Grants Association Ltd [1967] 2 All ER 893, [1967] Ch
      993, [1967] 3 WLR 41, 44 Tax Cas 93, 46 ATC 71, [1967] TR 79, CA, 28(1) Digest
      (Reissue) 478, 1727.
   Mostyn (Lord) v London (Surveyor of Taxes) [1895] 1 QB 170, 3 Tax Cas 294, 64 LJQB 106,
d   71 LT 760, 59 JP 390, 15 R 49, DC, 28(1) Digest (Reissue) 249, 782.
   Peel, Re, Tattersall v Peel [1936] Ch 161, [1935] All ER Rep 179, 105 LJ Ch 65, 154 LT 373,
      47 Digest (Repl) 276, 2392.
   Vestey's Settlement, Re, Lloyds Bank Ltd v O'Meara [1950] 2 All ER 891, [1951] Ch 209, CA,
      47 Digest (Repl) 275, 2388.
   Williams v Papworth [1900] AC 563, 69 LJPC 129, 83 LT 184, PC, 47 Digest (Repl) 282,
e   2454.

Case also cited
George Drexler Ofrex Foundation Trustees v Inland Revenue Comrs [1965] 3 All ER 529,
   [1966] Ch 675, 42 Tax Cas 524.

f **Appeal**
The Crown appealed against the decision of Slade J ([1980] 1 All ER 785, [1981] Ch 79,
[1980] STC 150) whereby he dismissed an appeal by the Crown by way of a case (set out
at [1980] 1 All ER 786–789, [1980] STC 151–154) stated by the Commissioners for the
Special Purposes of the Income Tax Acts in respect of their decision on 9th November
1978 whereby they allowed an appeal by Helen Slater Charitable Trust Ltd against
g assessments to tax in respect of income and gains for the accounting periods ended 31st
March 1973 to 1975 inclusive. The facts are set out in the judgment of Oliver LJ.

D C Potter QC and *C H McCall* for the Crown.
Andrew Park QC and *W A Blackburne* for the trust.

h   *Cur adv vult*

19th May. The following judgments were read.

OLIVER LJ (delivering the first judgment at the invitation of Waller LJ). This is an
appeal by the Crown against a judgment of Slade J ([1980] 1 All ER 785, [1981] Ch 79,
[1980] STC 150) delivered on 30th November 1979 and dismissing the Crown's appeal
j by way of case stated from a decision of the Special Commissioners which had allowed
the taxpayer's appeal against a decision of the Board of Inland Revenue disallowing the
taxpayer's claim to exemption from tax in respect of income and gains received in the
accounting periods ending on 31st March in each of the years 1973, 1974 and 1975.
   The point at issue in the appeal can be shortly stated; it is whether the taxpayer
company as a charitable body is entitled to claim exemption from tax in respect of

moneys representing income and capital gains which were received by it during the
relevant accounting periods and were paid by it to another charitable body but which   *a*
were not distributed by the recipient body.

Before I come to the relevant facts, it will be convenient to refer to the sections of the
relevant statutes under which the taxpayer claims exemption. As regards income, the
exemption is claimed under s 360(1) of the Income and Corporation Taxes Act 1970,
which provides that on a claim made to the Board there shall be granted, inter alia—

> '(c) exemption—(i) from tax under Schedule C in respect of any interest, annuities,   *b*
> dividends or shares of annuities, (ii) from tax under Schedule D in respect of any
> yearly interest or other annual payment, and (iii) from tax under Schedule F in
> respect of any distribution, [and here come the important words] where the income
> in question forms part of the income of a charity, or is, according to rules or
> regulations established by Act of Parliament, charter, decree, deed of trust or will,
> applicable to charitable purposes only, and so far as it is applied to charitable   *c*
> purposes only.'

So far as chargeable gains are concerned, s 360(2) as amended provides that a charity
shall in respect of tax on chargeable gains be allowed exemption in accordance with s 35
of the Finance Act 1965, which was the statute in force at the material time, although it
has subsequently been superseded by a consolidating enactment. Section 35(1) reads as   *d*
follows:

> 'Subject to subsection (2) of this section [which does not matter for present
> purposes] a gain shall not be a chargeable gain if it accrues to a charity and is
> applicable and applied for charitable purposes.'

So the framework of both the relevant sections is substantially the same. There are   *e*
two requirements for exemption. The income or the gain (as the case may be) must both
be applicable for charitable purposes only under the relevant trusts, and it must be
applied for charitable purposes.

The relevant facts for the purposes of the present appeal are set out in the stated case
and are as follows. The respondent company, Helen Slater Charitable Trust Ltd ('the
trust'), is a company limited by guarantee without a share capital and is a registered   *f*
charity. Its general objects are (i) to relieve suffering among the aged, impotent or poor,
(ii) to advance education, and (iii) to further such other charitable objects as the trust may
think fit and in particular but without prejudice to the generality of the foregoing to
make grants to such associations, trusts, societies or corporations as are established for
charitable purposes only. It was founded by Mrs Helen Slater, and incorporated in
February 1970 under the name Univale Ltd, and adopted its present name on 6th July   *g*
1970. At the same time another charitable body, Slater Foundation Ltd ('the foundation'),
was formed by Mrs Slater's husband, Mr J D Slater. That was also a company limited by
guarantee, was originally incorporated under the name Basilicon Ltd and likewise
adopted its present name on 6th July 1970. Its general objects are identical to those of the
trust, save that object (iii) does not contain the specific object of making grants to other
bodies, being confined simply to furthering 'such other charitable objects as the company   *h*
may think fit'.

There is an important paragraph in the case stated which reads as follows (see [1980]
1 All ER 785 at 787, [1980] STC 150 at 152):

> 'It is an agreed fact that the Trust and the Foundation were established as a joint
> operation whereby money would from time to time, pass from the Trust to the
> Foundation. They were intended to operate in tandem and the trustee/directors   *j*
> have, in practice, at all material times been common to both companies. Mr and
> Mrs Slater have been directors throughout the companies' existence: there have
> been some changes among the other directors.'

Additionally, counsel for the trust has helpfully conceded before us that, although
there is no specific evidence of the composition of the respective boards, he is content that

a the matter should be argued on the assumption that the boards of both companies were at all material times composed of the same individuals.

In the accounting period to 31st March 1973 the trust had a net income of £739,219 of which £24,901 was undistributed, the remainder being comprised in two donations of which one, a sum of £639,318, was paid to the foundation.

In the following two years its net income was £5,050 and £12,225 the whole of which, in each case, was donated to the foundation. There are some figures of the b foundation's income and distributions which are not altogether easy to follow, but they can be ignored for present purposes since it has been agreed that, for the purposes of the appeal, the trust accepts the Revenue's calculation that a sum of £578,479 out of the first donation, and the whole of the two subsequent donations, were added to the foundation's funds and were not distributed.

It is not in dispute that the income and gains of the trust were income and gains which c were, under the trust's constitution, applicable for charitable purposes only; nor is it contested that the trusts of the foundation are trusts for charitable purposes only. Equally I should say at once that there is no question of any lack of bona fides or of any breach of trust on anybody's part. It is not in question that the donations from the trust to the foundation were a perfectly proper disposition of the trust's charitable funds and the only question is whether, having regard to the fact that the funds when received were d not distributed but were accumulated as part of the foundation's general funds subject to the charitable trusts declared in its constitution, they can be said to have been 'applied' by the trust for charitable purposes so as to fulfil the second condition on which exemption from tax depends.

Counsel's first submission on behalf of the Crown is that, contrary to what was conceded before the learned judge and the Special Commissioners, money subject to e charitable trusts is not 'applied' for the purposes of the relevant subsections unless it is actually expended, as counsel for the Crown puts it, 'in the field', that is to say, on the expenses of managing the charity and distributions for the attainment of particular charitable objects. Thus, according to this submission, a charity which is a grant-making charity, that is to say, one whose object is or includes the making of donations to other charitable bodies, does not 'apply' its funds for charitable purposes when it makes a f payment to another charitable body. The funds paid over are 'applied' only when the recipient body expends them on one or more of its specific charitable purposes. Thus, if the recipient merely invests the fund received and adds to its general reserves for expenditure in the future, there is no 'application' and hence no relief under the subsections.

Counsel for the Crown suggests that 'application' must not be confused with mere g payment. Money may be paid without being applied. For instance, if all the trustees of a charity retired and the funds subject to the trusts were transferred or paid to a body of new trustees, there would be no 'application' for charitable purposes. There would be merely a payment of an administrative nature. That may be true, although I am not, speaking for myself, entirely convinced that even such a payment of a purely administrative nature made in the carrying on of a charitable trust is not an 'application' h of the money for the charitable purposes of the trust (take, for instance, the salary paid to a full time secretary of a charity). But it does not in any event follow, and I do not think that counsel for the Crown so contends, that, because payment and application are not necessarily synonyms, a payment cannot also be an application; and, where the trusts on which the funds are held envisage the accomplishment of the charitable purpose by a payment to some other organisation, I cannot for my part see why such a payment is j not an application of the funds.

The Crown's proposition is a startling one; it involves this, that the trustees of a grant-making charity, although they may discharge themselves as a matter of law by making a grant to another properly constituted charity, are obliged, if they wish to claim exemption under the subsections, to inquire into the application of the funds given and to demonstrate to the Revenue how those funds have been dealt with by other trustees over whom they have no control and for whose actions they are not answerable.

Anything more inconvenient would be difficult to imagine, and I find myself quite unable to accept that Parliament, in enacting these sections, can possibly have intended *a* such a result. For my part, I entertain no doubt whatever that, as a general proposition, funds which are donated by charity A pursuant to its trust deed or constitution to charity B are funds which are 'applied' by charity A for charitable purposes.

Counsel's second submission for the Crown is a much more limited one; it accepts the proposition that a payment by charity A to an independent charity B pursuant to the objects of charity A may, in general, be an application within the terms of the relevant *b* subsections. It is, however, submitted that, in order to qualify as an 'application', the payment must have some further characteristic than this, that it is simply a payment made pursuant to the declared objects of the trust. It must, counsel for the Crown submits, be a payment which produces a change of what, for want of a better expression, he calls 'the beneficial ownership'. There must be some mental element of dedication to a particular charitable purpose beyond the mere retention of funds, as funds, generally *c* subject to the applicable charitable trusts.

Essentially the argument proceeds in two stages. First, counsel for the Crown submits, a charity which invests the income which it receives (or the gains which it makes on capital transactions; there is no difference in principle) and simply retains the investments so made as an accumulation to its general funds does not 'apply' the income for charitable purposes. The income is already devoted to charitable purposes and some more positive *d* act is required before it can be said to be 'applied', although counsel was disposed to concede, as possibly a borderline case, that an accumulation revocably devoted to some specific charitable object which might or might not be accomplished in the future might properly be said to be 'applied'. Second, it is said, where money, instead of being accumulated by charity A, is passed by charity A to charity B and is accumulated by charity B as part of *its* general funds, the money will have been applied for charitable *e* purposes by charity A only if there has been not only a change in the legal ownership but also a significant change in the 'beneficial ownership', that being a convenient phrase to describe the trusts on which it is held. Thus, it is argued, if the result of the transfer is merely that charity B holds the funds transferred on substantially the same trusts as those on which it was previously held by charity A, then there will not, by reason of the transfer alone, have been any 'application' of the funds by charity A. To find whether *f* there has been such an application, one has to look to see what was done with the funds by charity B and if one finds that no more has happened than an investment of the funds and a retention of them by way of accumulation as part of the funds of charity B, then the position is exactly the same as if they had been retained and accumulated by charity A itself.

The final stage of this argument is that when one looks at the facts of the case stated in *g* the instant case, the agreed fact that the two charities were set up as a joint operation and intended to work in tandem, the identity of the directorate and the close similarity of the trusts of the two bodies, then one sees that there was no application here by the trust, but merely what was tantamount to an arrangement for the accumulation of the trust's money as part of general funds held on charitable trusts common to both bodies.

This was, in substance, the argument which was advanced before the learned judge *h* and which he found himself unable to accept. As regards the first limb of the argument, namely that a simple accumulation by way of investment and addition to the general reserves of a charity does not constitute an application, some support for this can be derived from the opinion of Lord Blackburn in *General Nursing Council for Scotland v Inland Revenue Comrs* 1929 SC 664 at 674–675, 14 Tax Cas 645 at 656, which was concerned with the substantially similar wording of s 37(1)(b) of the Income Tax Act *j* 1918, although the views expressed were obiter since the body there applying for exemption was held not to be a charity. Lord Blackburn said:

'Reaching that conclusion it is perhaps unnecessary to consider the other question which was discussed, namely, whether the income of the surplus fund is entitled to exemption seeing that it is devoted to no other purpose than the increase of the surplus fund. The income is taxed under Schedule D, and the claim to exemption is based on the terms of Sub-head (b) of Section 37(1) of the Act of 1918. This sub-head ends with the words "and so far as the same are applied to charitable purposes only". Some income then which otherwise would be entitled to exemption is not to be exempt unless it is actually applied to charitable purposes, and I agree with Lord Sands that these words are apt to apply to the income in question, assuming that the Council was itself a charitable institution. I should hesitate to give them so strict a construction as to attach to small sums necessarily carried forward in the accounts of a charitable trust from one year to another to enable the trust to be conducted in a businesslike manner. But it seems to me that they do require that the income, if not actually expended on a charitable purpose during the year of assessment, must at least be appropriated to expenditure on charity in the immediate future.'

That is to be contrasted with the contrary view expressed in the opinion of Lord Sands in the same case. He said (1929 SC 664 at 671, 14 Tax Cas 645 at 653–654):

'But even if the construction be as indicated, the limitation is, in my opinion, of very small application. It does not import that the exemption is to be allowed only when the income has been spent, or falls immediately to be spent, for some charitable purpose. If the directors of a charitable trust deem it desirable that a capital sum should be accumulated for the service of the trust or that a reserve fund should be formed for the greater security of the trust, the income carried to the credit of any such account is, in my view, applied to a charitable purpose. If testamentary trustees were directed to apply part of an estate to charitable purposes, it would, as it appears to me, be quite unreasonable to suggest that they had failed so to apply it if they made it over to the capital fund of a charitable institution. Surplus income of the charity which the managing body find it possible to use in the same way seems to me to be on the same footing and to be applied to a charitable purpose.'

A number of other authorities were referred to, but they do not, I think, help very much. In Re Vestey's Settlement [1950] 2 All ER 891, [1951] Ch 209 the question was as to the effect of a resolution by the trustees of a private settlement that certain sums of undistributed income be allocated to infant beneficiaries absolutely and accumulated for their respective benefits pursuant to s 31 of the Trustee Act 1925. That was resolved on pursuant to a discretionary power to 'pay or apply' income for the benefit of, inter alios, the infant beneficiaries, and the question was whether the resolution constituted either a payment or an application. The argument, based on the decision of Eve J in Re Peel [1936] Ch 161, [1935] All ER Rep 179, was that the mere retention of the sums by way of accumulation did not constitute a compliance with a trust to 'pay or apply' to or for the support or benefit of identified beneficiaries, since it certainly was not a payment and it could not constitute an 'application'. This court held that there was an application of the moneys, inasmuch as the trustees' resolution allocating them irrevocably to the individual beneficiaries constituted more than a mere retention, and distinguished the case from Re Peel. Counsel for the Crown argues that the importance attached in that case to the change of title underlines his central proposition that a mere retention of income by way of accumulation without any change of title cannot constitute an 'application' of the income retained. Certainly Re Peel is authority for the proposition that where a fund is already contingently settled on X a trust 'to pay or apply' the income for the maintenance education or benefit of X does not authorise an accumulation for his ultimate benefit, for that is retention, not application. It has, however, to be borne in mind that in those cases the word was being construed against the background of the trusts of the settlement as a whole and that the meaning of an ordinary English word such as 'pay' or 'apply' may vary greatly according to the context in which it falls to be construed, a matter very clearly brought out in the judgment of Jenkins LJ in the Vestey case. The question whether any given act constitutes an 'application' of a fund may receive quite a different answer according to whether what is sought to be elicited is whether income is being 'applied for the benefit' of a particular beneficiary or whether the fund is being 'applied *a* in accordance with' the trusts of the settlement. Thus, for instance, in one case cited to Slade J (*Williams v Papworth* [1900] AC 563), where the question was whether a trust to 'apply' funds for maintenance of a class of beneficiaries authorised the trustees to select those members of the class who would benefit, Lord Macnaghten expressed the view that 'applied' meant only 'devoted to' or 'employed for the special purpose of'. On the other hand in *Lord Mostyn v London (Surveyor of Taxes)* [1895] 1 QB 170, 3 Tax Cas 294 a *b* Divisional Court consisting of Wright and Collins JJ held that the proceeds of a fine received on the renewal of a lease which were placed on temporary deposit pending permanent investment had not been 'applied as productive capital' within s 60, Sch (A), No II, r 5 of the Income Tax Act 1842. I find these cases of little assistance in determining the meaning of the word 'applied' in the context of the relevant subsections. Manifestly Parliament, in enacting them in the form in which they are, intended to impose some *c* additional qualification for the exemption of income beyond that of merely being applicable for charitable purposes. On the narrow view of the matter that additional qualification could be no more than this, that the income be not actually applied for non-charitable purposes (as, for instance, occurred in *Inland Revenue Comrs v Educational Grants Association Ltd* [1967] 2 All ER 893, [1967] Ch 993, 44 Tax Cas 93); but I agree with the learned judge that it imports more than that, some affirmative requirement *d* that the income should have been dealt with in some way or other. Speaking for myself I am, however, disposed to favour the view expressed by Lord Sands that the limitation is of small application. Charitable trustees who simply leave surplus income uninvested cannot, I think, be said to have 'applied' it at all and, indeed, would be in breach of trust. But if the income is reinvested by them and held, as invested, as part of the funds of the charity, I would be disposed to say that it is no less being applied for charitable *e* purposes than it is if it is paid out in wages to the secretary. I share the learned judge's difficulty in seeing why an accumulation for a specific charitable purpose resolved on by the trustees as being a desirable way of carrying out their charitable objects should be, as it is conceded it is, an 'application' whereas an accumulation for the general purposes of the charity is not. I agree, however, with the learned judge that it is not in fact necessary to decide the point because, in my judgment, the argument breaks down at its second *f* stage.

I do not think that I can express it better than it was expressed by the learned judge. He said ([1980] 1 All ER 785 at 795, [1981] Ch 79 at 88–89, [1980] STC 150 at 160):

'Whatever other doubts may arise in other contexts as to the meaning of the phrase "applied for charitable purposes", it seems to me that, ordinarily, income must be said to have been thus "applied" by charitable corporation A, if it is *g* transferred outright to charitable corporation B, being itself a corporation with exclusively charitable objects. A disposition of assets by one corporation in favour of another corporation, in such manner as to pass the whole title in such assets to the transferee, must, in my judgment, ordinarily amount to an "application" of such assets within the normal use of legal terminology.'

h

He went on to reject the Crown's argument based on para 8(11) of the stated case (see [1980] 1 All ER 785 at 788, [1980] STC 150 at 152), which was a reflection of the argument advanced by counsel for the Crown before this court, namely that the foundation is what was described in the court below as a 'parallel body' and that although there was a change in the bare legal title there was no significant change in the trusts on which the income transferred was held. I am not for myself convinced that it would *j* matter if the declared charitable objects of both corporations were absolutely identical (although they were not in fact). The fact is that the charitable objects of the trust included an express object of making donations to other charitable institutions (whether or not 'parallel' institutions). The only question is whether, in making the payment in fact made by the trust, it was applying the money paid for charitable purposes, and in my judgment it clearly was.

a It is, of course, the fact that there was a common directorate and that the money transferred to the foundation was, in the event, accumulated and added to the capital of the foundation and held for *its* charitable purposes, and I am content to assume, although I think this is not clearly established, that it was known at the date of the transfer that this would occur. The answer that I would give to this is the same as that given by the learned judge, and again I do not think that I can do better than to adopt his judgment on this point. He said ([1980] 1 All ER 785 at 795–796, [1981] Ch 79 at 89, [1980] STC
b 150 at 160–161):

'The [Finance Act 1965] and the [Income and Corporation Taxes Act 1970] could well have contained provisions ancillary to the two subsections providing, in effect, that a transfer of income or gains to a connected body should not be treated as an "application" for the purposes of the two subsections. In many other contexts the Income Tax Acts contain special provisions designed to cover dealings between
c connected persons or bodies. There are, however, no such special provisions applicable in the present case. In their absence, the following general proposition is in my judgment correct in law. Any charitable corporation which, acting intra vires, makes an outright transfer of money applicable for charitable purposes to any other corporation established exclusively for charitable purposes, in such manner as to pass to the transferee full title to the money, must be taken, by the transfer itself,
d to have "applied" such money for "charitable purposes", within the meaning of the two subsections, unless the transferor knows or ought to know that the money will be misapplied by the transferee. In such circumstances, and subject to the last-mentioned exception, the transferor corporation is in my judgment entitled to claim exemption under the two subsections, without having to show how the money has been dealt with by the transferee.'

e As the learned judge pointed out, and as I have already emphasised, there is no question of lack of bona fides here or of any moneys having been misapplied by the foundation.

Accordingly, for the reasons stated, I would dismiss the appeal.

FOX LJ. I agree.

f **WALLER LJ.** I also agree.

Appeal dismissed. Leave to appeal to the House of Lords refused.

Solicitors: *Solicitor of Inland Revenue; Clifford-Turner* (for the trust).

Edwina Epstein   Barrister.

g
Sudbrook Trading Estate Ltd v Eggleton and others

COURT OF APPEAL, CIVIL DIVISION

h CUMMING-BRUCE, TEMPLEMAN AND OLIVER LJJ
18th, 19th, 23rd FEBRUARY, 17th MARCH 1981

Option – Option to purchase – Tenant's option conferred by lease – Uncertainty of option – Agreement to agree – Option to purchase at price to be fixed by valuers nominated by parties – Tenant seeking to exercise option – Landlord refusing to appoint valuer – Tenant asking court to
j *order specific performance or to appoint valuer – Whether option uncertain – Whether court should order specific performance – Whether court having power to appoint valuer.*

By a lease dated 23rd March 1949 the predecessors in title of the landlords granted the tenants' predecessors in title a lease of property to expire on 24th December 1997. A clause gave the tenants an option to purchase the reversion in fee simple at a price to be agreed by two valuers, one to be nominated by the landlords and the other by the tenants and, in default of agreement, by an umpire to be appointed by the valuers, a minimum purchase price being specified in the clause. By three other leases in 1956, 1966 and 1968, adjoining properties were demised by the landlords' predecessors in title to the tenants' predecessors in title for varying terms ending on 24th December 1997. Each lease contained an option to purchase the reversion on almost identical terms, save for differences in the minimum purchase price. When the tenants sought to exercise the options in December 1979 the landlords claimed that the option clauses were void for uncertainty and refused to appoint a valuer. On the tenants' application, the judge declared that the options to purchase were valid and had been effectively exercised. On the landlords' appeal, the tenants contended that the court should direct the landlords to appoint a valuer, or should itself appoint one if they refused, or should remedy the machinery provided in the leases and determine a fair purchase price. The landlords contended that the options were unenforceable as there was no contract of sale since the purchase price had not been fixed. The landlords further contended that the court had no power to grant a mandatory order and could not itself appoint a valuer or determine a fair price.

Held – The appeal would be allowed and the declarations quashed for the following reasons—

(1) It was settled law that in ascertaining an essential term of a contract (a) the court would not substitute its own machinery for ascertaining that term for the machinery agreed by the parties, however defective that might be, (b) the court would not decree specific performance until the parties' own machinery had operated successfully to ascertain an essential term, because until then no contract existed to be performed, and (c) where the operation of the machinery agreed by the parties was stultified by one party's refusal to appoint a valuer or arbitrator, the court would not compel that party, by a partial grant of specific performance, to make the appointment. Accordingly, since the parties had left the essential issue of the option price to be decided by their nominees in a clearly uncertain formula by merely agreeing to agree or to accept such price as other persons (the valuers and/or the umpire) might agree, the court had no power to intervene by substituting its own machinery, and neither could it grant full or part specific performance because no contract existed to be enforced (see p 112 *g h*, p 114 *f* to p 115 *b*, p 117 *a* to *h* and p 118 *a*, post); *Agar v Macklew* (1825) 2 Sim & St 418, *Morgan v Milman* (1853) 3 De GM & G 24, *Darbey v Whitaker* (1857) 4 Drew 134, *Hart v Hart* (1881) 18 Ch D 670 and *Re Smith & Service and Nelson & Sons* (1890) 25 QBD 545 applied; *Morse v Merest* (1821) 6 Madd 26, *Smith v Peters* (1875) LR 20 Eq 511, *Talbot v Talbot* [1967] 2 All ER 920 and *Brown v Gould* [1971] 2 All ER 1505 distinguished.

(2) Although in recognised exceptional circumstances, as, for example, where an agreement containing an uncertain express stipulation had been partly performed so that intervention was required to aid a grant that had taken place or where the uncertain term was construed as relating to a subsidiary part only of a wider contract in which no uncertainty existed, the court would provide substitute machinery for ascertaining an essential term, the option clause in the leases did not come within the recognised exceptions because it could not be described as such an essential stipulation of the lease as to compel the court to provide certainty to make sense of the grant and neither was it merely subsidiary, since machinery for fixing the price went to the root of the contract (see p 115 *b* to *d f* to *j*, p 116 *c d*, p 117 *h j* and p 118 *a*, post); *Gregory v Mighell* (1811) 18 Ves 328, *Dinham v Bradford* (1869) LR 5 Ch App 519, *Smith v Peters* (1875) LR 20 Eq 511, *Hordern v Hordern* [1910] AC 465 and *Beer v Bowden* [1981] 1 All ER 1070 distinguished; *Vickers v Vickers* (1867) LR 4 Eq 529 and *Richardson v Smith* (1870) LR 5 Ch App 648 considered.

Notes

For the need for certainty in the terms of a contract, see 9 Halsbury's Laws (4th Edn) para 266, and for cases on the subject, see 12 Digest (Reissue) 24–26, 13–21.

Cases referred to in judgment

Agar v Macklew (1825) 2 Sim & St 418, 4 LJOS Ch 16, 57 ER 405, 44 Digest (Repl) 9, 25.

Beer v Bowden [1981] 1 All ER 1070, [1981] 1 WLR 522, CA.

a *Blundell v Brettargh* (1810) 17 Ves 232, [1803–13] All ER Rep 496, 34 ER 90, LC, 40 Digest (Repl) 16, 51.

Brown v Gould [1971] 2 All ER 1505, [1972] Ch 53, [1971] 3 WLR 334, 22 P & CR 871, 31(1) Digest (Reissue) 285, 2351.

Collins v Collins (1858) 26 Bear 306, 28 LJ Ch 184, 32 LTOS 233, 5 Jur NS 30, 53 ER 916, 3 Digest (Reissue) 17, 71.

b *Darbey v Whitaker* (1857) 4 Drew 134, 29 LTOS 351, 62 ER 52, 40 Digest (Repl) 79, 603.

Dinham v Bradford (1869) LR 5 Ch App 519, LC, 36(2) Digest (Reissue) 727

Firth v Midland Railway Co (1875) LR 20 Eq 100, 44 LJ Ch 313, 32 LT 219, 40 Digest (Repl) 16, 52.

Gregory v Mighell (1811) 18 Ves 328, 34 ER 341, 31(1) Digest (Reissue) 67, 500.

Hart v Hart (1881) 18 Ch D 670, 50 LJ Ch 697, 45 LT 13, 44 Digest (Repl) 42, 293.

c *Hordern v Hordern* [1910] AC 465, 80 LJPC 15, 102 LT 867, PC, 36(2) Digest (Reissue) 761, 1372.

Milnes v Gery (1807) 14 Ves 400, [1803–13] All ER Rep 369, 33 ER 574, 40 Digest (Repl) 16, 46.

Morgan v Milman (1853) 3 De GM & G 24, 22 LJ Ch 897, 20 LTOS 285, 43 ER 10, 40 Digest (Repl) 17, 59.

d *Morse v Merest* (1821) 6 Madd 26, 56 ER 999, 40 Digest (Repl) 16, 53.

Paris Chocolate Co v Crystal Palace Co (1855) 3 Sm & G 119, 25 LTOS 7, 1 Jur NS 720, 65 ER 588, 31(1) Digest (Reissue) 102, 821.

Pritchard v Ovey (1820) 1 Jac & W 396, 37 ER 426, 44 Digest (Repl) 96, 780.

Richardson v Smith (1870) LR 5 Ch App 648, 39 LJ Ch 877, LC and LJ, 40 Digest (Repl) 79, 605.

e *Smith v Peters* (1875) LR 20 Eq 511, 44 LJ Ch 613, 40 Digest (Repl) 80, 605.

Smith & Service and Nelson & Sons, Re (1890) 25 QBD 545, 59 LJQB 533, 63 LT 475, CA, 3 Digest 104, 545.

Talbot v Talbot [1967] 2 All ER 920, [1968] Ch 1, [1967] 3 WLR 438, CA, Digest (Cont Vol C) 1060, 427a.

Tillett v Charing Cross Bridge Co (1859) 26 Beav 419, 28 LJ Ch 863, 34 LTOS 42, 5 Jur NS f 994, 53 ER 959, 3 Digest (Reissue) 103, 531.

Vickers v Vickers (1867) LR 4 Eq 529, 36 LJ Ch 964, 40 Digest (Repl) 17, 55.

Cases also cited

Bates (Thomas) & Son Ltd v Wyndham's (Lingerie) Ltd [1981] 1 All ER 1077, [1981] 1 WLR 505, CA.

g *Courtney and Fairbairn Ltd v Tolaini Brothers (Hotels) Ltd* [1975] 1 All ER 716, [1975] 1 WLR 297, CA.

Dallman v King (1837) 4 Bing NC 105, 132 ER 729.

Emery v Wase (1801) 5 Ves 846, 31 ER 889; *affd* 8 Ves 505, 32 ER 451, LC.

Gaskarth v Lord Lowther (1804) 12 Ves 107, 33 ER 41, LC.

Gourlay v Duke of Somerset (1815) 19 Ves 429, 34 ER 576.

h *Johnson v Agnew* [1979] 1 All ER 883, [1980] AC 367, HL.

King's Motors (Oxford) Ltd v Lax [1969] 3 All ER 665, [1970] 1 WLR 426.

Panamena Europea Navigacion (Compania Limitada) v Leyland & Co (J Russell & Co), [1947] AC 428, HL.

R v Bradford (1869) LR 5 Ch App 51.

Radnor (Earl) v Shafto (1805) 11 Ves 448, 32 ER 1160, LC.

j *Tito v Waddell (No 2)* [1977] 3 All ER 129, [1977] Ch 106.

Appeal

William Vernon Eggleton, Thomas Harraden Drew Keck and Alan Gibson Keddie ('the landlords') appealed against the judgment of Lawson J sitting as an additional judge of the Chancery Division at Bristol on 17th November 1980 whereby he granted the respondents, Sudbrook Trading Estate Ltd ('the tenants'), declarations (i) that the option clauses in four leases dated 23rd March 1949, 18th November 1955, 30th August 1966 *a* and 26th July 1968 and made between the respective predecessors in title of the landlords and of the tenants conferred on the tenants valid options to purchase the reversions in fee simple of properties in High Orchard Street, Gloucester and (ii) that the options in the 1955, 1966 and 1968 leases had been validly and effectively exercised. By a respondent's notice dated 18th February 1981 the tenants contended that the decision of Lawson J should be affirmed on grounds other than those relied on by the judge. The facts are set out in the judgment of the court. *b*

Roger Kaye for the landlords.
Gerald Godfrey QC and *Martin Roth* for the tenants.

Cur adv vult

c

17th March. **TEMPLEMAN LJ** read the following judgment of the court: In these proceedings the tenants seek to enforce an option in a lease which enables them to purchase the reversion at a valuation and the landlords contend that the option is unenforceable.

The option is contained in a lease dated 23rd March 1949 and made between the respective predecessors in title of the present landlords and tenants. By the lease a *d* property at High Orchard Street, Llanthony in the City of Gloucester was demised for a term expiring on 24th December 1997 at a yearly rent of £2,750 subject to periodical rent reviews. Clause II of the lease conferred on the tenants an option—

> 'to purchase the reversion in fee simple in the premises hereby demised ... at such price not being less than seventy-five thousand pounds as may be agreed upon by two valuers one to be nominated by the Lessor and the other by the Lessee or in *e* default of such an agreement by an Umpire appointed by the said Valuers ...'

By three further leases dated 18th November 1955, 30th August 1966 and 26th July 1968 adjoining properties were also demised by the predecessors in title of the present landlords to the predecessors in title of the present tenants for terms ending on 24th December 1997 and each lease contained an option to purchase the reversion on terms *f* identical with the option contained in the 1949 lease, save that different minimum purchase prices are specified in the 1955 and 1968 leases, and no minimum price appears in the 1966 lease.

The tenants having exercised their options to purchase the reversions, the defendant appellants, as landlords, have declined to appoint a valuer. The tenants claim that there exists a contract for the sale of the reversion. In the court below Lawson J, sitting as an *g* additional judge of the Chancery Division, made an order dated 17th November 1980 whereby he declared that the clauses in the leases to which we have referred conferred on the tenants valid options to purchase the reversions in fee simple and that the options had been validly exercised. In this court the tenants have argued that the court will direct the landlords to appoint a valuer if the landlords continue to refuse to do so and will if necessary appoint a valuer and an umpire to determine the price; alternatively if the *h* machinery for the ascertainment of the purchase price indicated in the lease fails for any reason, because the landlords refuse to appoint a valuer or because the valuers can neither agree on a price or on an umpire or because the umpire fails to determine a price, the court will remedy the defective machinery and will carry out the original intentions of the parties by determining the fair price of the reversion which the machinery provided by the lease was obviously intended to produce.

j

The landlords appeal from the order of Lawson J and in this court claim that there is no contract for the sale of the reversion because the price has not been fixed and the court will not make a contract where none exists. If there is a contract for the appointment of valuers, which appointment might lead to a contract for the sale of the reversion, the court will not make a mandatory order or take any other step to require performance of

the contract to appoint a valuer and cannot itself appoint a valuer or an umpire or
a determine a fair value. The court cannot decree specific performance and has no power
to alter or modify the express terms of the contractual relations between the parties
embodied in the lease. The tenants cannot demonstrate any damage, and are therefore
without remedy. The option is unenforceable.

The ground is encumbered with authority, more ancient than modern. In *Milnes v
Gery* (1807) 14 Ves 400, [1803–13] All ER Rep 369 there was a contract for sale at a price
b to be determined by two valuers or an umpire chosen by the valuers. The valuers were
appointed but were unable to agree on the choice of an umpire. The vendors sued for
specific performance and asked the court to appoint a valuer or to make a valuation.
Grant MR dismissed the action, saying (14 Ves 400 at 406, 409, [1803–13] All ER Rep
369 at 370, 371):

> *c* 'The only agreement, into which the Defendant entered, was to purchase at a
> price, to be ascertained in a specified mode. No price having ever been fixed in that
> mode, the parties have not agreed upon any price . . . If you go into a Court of Law
> for damages, you must be able to state some valid legal contract, which the other
> party wrongfully refuses to perform; if you come to a Court of Equity for a specific
> performance, you must also be able to state some contract, legal or equitable,
> concluded between the parties; which the one refuses to execute. In this case the
> *d* Plaintiff seeks to compel the Defendant to take this estate at such price as a Master
> of this Court shall find it to be worth; admitting, that the Defendant never made
> that agreement; and my opinion is, that the agreement he has made is not
> substantially, or in any fair sense, the same with that; and it could only be by an
> arbitrary discretion that the Court could substitute the one in the place of the other.'

e That was a case in which there had been no misconduct either on the part of the
contracting parties or on the part of the valuers appointed by them. The machinery had
broken down and the court was powerless to substitute other machinery.

In *Gregory v Mighell* (1811) 18 Ves 328, 34 ER 341 a tenant had been in possession for
11 years under an agreement for a lease for 21 years at 'a fair and just annual rent', to be
fixed and ascertained by two valuers to be chosen by the landlord and the tenant
f respectively or their umpire. Valuers were chosen but the landlord refused to sign
arbitration bonds and the valuers refused to proceed unless such bonds were signed.
Grant MR made an order for specific performance of the agreement for a lease and
directed the master to ascertain the fair rent, saying (18 Ves 328 at 333, 34 ER 341 at
343):

> *g* 'After it was known, that the arbitrators had not fixed any rent, and that none of
> the other means, provided by the agreement, were resorted to, the Defendant still
> acquiesced in the Plaintiff's retaining possession of these lands. That is a case in
> which the failure of the arbitrators to fix the rent can never affect the agreement.
> It is in part performed; and the Court must find some means of completing its
> execution . . . the Plaintiff is not to be considered as a trespasser. Some rent he must
> pay: the amount must be fixed in some other mode . . . it should be ascertained by
> *h* the Master, without sending it to another arbitration; which might possibly end in
> the same way.'

That was a case in which it could not be said that there was no agreement because the
parties had acted for eleven years on the basis that the agreement subsisted. It was also
a case in which one of the contracting parties was at fault in not performing his duty to
j ensure that the valuers duly valued.

In *Blundell v Brettargh* (1810) 17 Ves 232, [1803–13] All ER Rep 496 there was a
contract for sale at a price to be fixed by two valuers or their umpire in writing under seal
before 1st July. The valuers agreed the valuation by 10th June, but did not complete the
written award until 24th June by which time one of the contracting parties had died.
Lord Eldon LC held that on the construction of the agreement the award was required

to be made during the joint lives of both contracting parties. He refused to order specific
performance, saying (17 Ves 232 at 243, [1803–13] All ER Rep 496 at 499–500):   *a*

> 'There is no instance, where the medium of arbitration or umpirage, resorted to
> for settling the terms of a contract, having failed, this Court has assumed jurisdiction
> to determine, that, though there is no contract at Law ... there is a contract in
> Equity; and this Court will specifically execute that contract, to which the parties
> never agreed.'

This was another case in which the machinery for fixing the price agreed between the   *b*
parties failed without any default on either side.

In *Morse v Merest* (1821) 6 Madd 26, 56 ER 999 there was a contract for sale of an estate
at 25 years' purchase based on an annual value to be fixed by three named valuers on or
before a certain day. The vendor refused to allow the valuers to enter the estate and they
were therefore unable to make their valuation before the time expired. Leach V-C
granted an injunction ordering the vendor to permit the valuation to be made, saying   *c*
that 'in equity a Defendant was not permitted to set up a legal defence which grew out
of his own misconduct, and ... this agreement was now to be acted upon as if no time
were limited, or the time was not passed' (see 6 Madd 26 at 27, 56 ER 999). This was a
case where one of the contracting parties was in default and the machinery for fixing a
price was still capable of operating, and could be made to operate by a negative injunction.

In *Agar v Macklew* (1825) 2 Sim & St 418, 57 ER 405 tenants exercised an option in a   *d*
lease to purchase the reversion at a price to be determined by two persons, as surveyors
or appraisers to be chosen by the landlords and the tenants respectively or the umpire
appointed by the valuers. The landlords refused to appoint their valuer. The tenants
asked for an injunction directing the landlords to appoint their valuer or for an order that
if the landlords persisted in refusing to nominate a valuer the value should be ascertained
by the master. Leach V-C dismissed the action, saying (2 Sim & St 418 at 423, 57 ER 405   *e*
at 407):

> 'I consider it to be quite settled that this Court will not entertain a Bill for the
> specific performance of an agreement to refer to arbitration; nor will, in such case,
> substitute the Master for the arbitrators which will be to bind the parties contrary
> to their agreement.'
          f
If this case was good law in 1825 and remains good law, the tenants in the present case
must fail.

In *Morgan v Milman* (1853) 3 De GM & G 24, 43 ER 10 a vendor agreed to sell to a
railway company property at a price to be ascertained at the option of the vendor by
arbitration or a jury. The vendor died before directing how the property should be
valued. Lord Cranworth LC said (3 De GM & G 24 at 34, 43 ER 10 at 14) that the   *g*
authorities—

> 'enunciate the proposition in the strongest language, that where the parties have
> stipulated that the price should be ascertained by arbitration ... that in such case, if
> the arbitration does not proceed, the price is not ascertained according to the mode
> in which the parties stipulated, [and] this Court has no right to make a different
> contract from that which the parties have entered into, and ascertain it for them in   *h*
> some different mode.'

This was a case where neither contracting party was in default and where the
machinery chosen by them to ascertain the price irretrievably broke down.

In *Darbey v Whitaker* (1857) 4 Drew 134, 62 ER 52 a vendor agreed to sell the lease and
the goodwill of a public house at a fixed price and to take the fixtures and stock in trade   *j*
at a valuation to be made by two named valuers or their umpire. One of the named
valuers refused to proceed because the purchaser said he did not intend to complete.
Kindersley V-C refused to grant specific performance of the agreement in whole or in
part so that the vendor lost the sale of the public house because he could not enforce the
sale of the fixtures and stock in trade at a valuation. Kindersley V-C said (4 Drew 134 at
140, 62 ER 52 at 55):

a
'Now I assume it to be clear that this Court has no power to decree specific performance of a contract for sale or purchase at a price to be fixed by arbitration, unless the arbitrators have actually fixed the price. It appears to me that that is implied by the very nature of a decree for specific performance. What would it be? A decree that directs payment to the Plaintiff of such a sum of money as A. and B. shall fix. I never saw such a decree, and I think the Court cannot make it, on the ground that this Court will never make a decree that it cannot see its way to

b
enforce. Now, how could I enforce such a decree? What is the time to be allowed for arbitration? How can I compel the arbitration? It appears in this case as a fact, that one of the arbitrators has refused to go on, because he was told by the Defendant that he did not mean to complete. How can I be sure that he will go on? And even if the arbitrators do go on, and differ, how can I compel the appointment of an umpire?'

c
In that case, notwithstanding that the purchase of the fixtures and the stock in trade was subsidiary to the main agreement for the sale of the public house at a fixed price and notwithstanding that the valuation machinery broke down as a result of default on the part of the purchaser, the court refused the vendor any remedy on the grounds that the court will not make a decree for specific performance which it cannot supervise, control and carry into effect.

d
In *Collins v Collins* (1858) 26 Beav 306, 53 ER 916 there was an agreement to sell at a price to be fixed by named valuers or by an umpire chosen by the valuers before making their valuation. The valuers were unable to agree on an umpire and the vendor sought an order from the court appointing an umpire, and relied for that purpose on the arbitration provisions of the Common Law Procedure Act 1854. Romilly MR held that the Act did not apply to a valuation and made no order. His judgment makes it clear that

e
he regarded the law as settled in the line of authorities from *Milnes v Gery* to *Darbey v Whitaker*, and the only question for his decision was whether the court had power to make an order under the 1854 Act.

In *Tillett v Charing Cross Bridge Co* (1859) 26 Beav 419, 53 ER 959, where the authorities were reviewed, the court refused specific performance of a contract which included a term that named nominees or their umpire should decide what kind of housing should

f
be built on the land comprised in the agreement. The decision was put on the grounds that—

'this Court cannot decree the specific performance of a contract which it does not see its way to enforce eventually; and if it should turn out hereafter that these persons will not fix the character of the houses, and will have nothing to do with it, then the result will be, that the Court ought not to have decreed a specific

g
performance, and it ought not now to make such a decree hypothetically on an event which may or may not happen hereafter.'

(See 26 Beav 419 at 426, 53 ER 959 at 962.)

In that case the task which the court was asked to perform was more difficult and more vague than an order directing a contracting party to appoint a valuer or an order

h
appointing a valuer.

In *Vickers v Vickers* (1867) LR 4 Eq 529 it was agreed that in certain circumstances which happened, a retired partner should have the option to purchase the former partnership business to be valued 'in the usual way' by two valuers, one to be named by the vendor and one by the purchaser or by their umpire. The valuers were appointed but the purchaser then changed his mind and would not allow the valuation to proceed. The

j
purchaser sought a declaration that he was entitled to become the purchaser of the business and of the property connected with the valuation and also sought specific performance of the agreement. Page Wood V-C refused to grant any relief on the grounds that until the price was fixed the contract was not a complete contract and there was nothing upon which the court could act and said (at 536): '. . . because the Courts have decided, we must take it to be positive law, that there is no existing contract until the valuation has taken place . . .'

That was a case in which the machinery chosen by the parties broke down because of the default of the vendor. The fact that there was no contract for the sale of the property *a* in existence was logically no reason why the court should not injunct the vendor against a breach of his obligation to allow the valuation to proceed but nevertheless the purchaser failed.

In *Dinham v Bradford* (1869) LR 5 Ch App 519 a partnership agreement contained a provision that on the determination of the partnership one partner should purchase the share of the other at a valuation to be made by two persons, one appointed by each *b* partner. There was no express provision for the appointment of an umpire. The vendor sought a winding up of the partnership in the usual way. The purchaser sought specific performance of the provisions in the partnership agreement which enabled him to purchase the share of the vendor. Lord Hatherley LC affirmed the decision of Stuart V-C who declared that the purchaser was entitled to purchase the share of the vendor and directed the value of the vendor's share to be ascertained by the court. The provision *c* which enabled one partner to purchase the share of the other when the partnership determined was part of a partnership agreement which had been carried into effect. Lord Hatherley LC said (at 523):

> 'This case is not like that of the sale of an estate the price of which is to be settled by arbitration, but is a case in which the whole scope and object of the deed would be entirely frustrated if the Court were to apply the well-known doctrine to the *d* present state of circumstances. In cases of specific performance the matter is very plain and simple. One person agrees to sell his estate in a given way, and no rights are changed by the circumstance of that method of selling the estate having failed. The estate remains where it was, and the money where it was. But here is a man who has had the whole benefit of the partnership in respect of which this agreement was made, and now he refuses to have the rest of the agreement performed, on *e* account of the difficulty which has arisen. It is much more like the case of an estate sold, and the timber, on a part, to be taken at a valuation, the adjusting of matters of that sort forming part of the arrangement, but being by no means the substance of the agreement; and in such cases the Court has found no difficulty. If the valuation cannot be made *modo et formâ*, the Court will substitute itself for the arbitrators. It is not the very essence and substance of the contract, so that no *f* contract can be made out except through the medium of the arbitrators. Here the property has been had and enjoyed, and the only question now is, what is right and proper to be done in settling the price?'

In the present case the option to purchase the reversion was part of the terms whereby the tenants agreed to enter and pay rent and to enjoy the property. The landlords *g* contend that the option to purchase the reversion is a separate agreement and that the lease, unlike the partnership agreement in *Dinham v Bradford* will continue to operate. If the option does not create enforceable rights and obligations, the court has no power to intervene.

In *Richardson v Smith* (1870) LR 5 Ch App 648 it was agreed that an estate should be purchased for £24,000 and certain articles worth about £2,000 should be purchased for *h* a price to be determined by two valuers appointed by the parties. But the vendor declined to nominate a valuer and the purchaser sought and obtained an order for specific performance. Stuart V-C made an order for specific performance. Lord Hatherley LC and Giffard LJ in effect severed the agreement and ordered specific performance limited to the estate on the grounds that the agreement with regard to the articles was a minor and subsidiary part of the agreement and not at all essential. To hold *j* otherwise, said Lord Hatherley LC (at 651–652)—

> 'would induce vendors who are desirous of retaining the power of escaping from their contracts to introduce provisions for the valuation of some minor part of the subject matter of the contract in such a mode that they might at any time escape from the performance of the agreement as to the main subject of the contract

a   simply by setting up an act of their own in wrong of the purchaser, and refusing to appoint a valuer.'

In the present case we do not regard the option to purchase the reversion as being minor or inessential, but if the landlords are correct it is severable, thus leaving in force the lease without the unenforceable option to purchase the reversion.

b   In *Smith v Peters* (1875) LR 20 Eq 511 there was an agreement for the sale of a house at a fixed price and of the fixtures and furniture at a valuation by a specified valuer who was willing to carry out the valuation but was not allowed by the vendor to enter the premises in order to value. Jessel MR made an order for specific performance of the agreement and a mandatory order compelling the vendor to allow the valuer to enter on the premises. He said (at 513): 'There is no evidence that the value of the fixtures and furniture was so large as to be an essential portion of the contract.' Clearly Jessel MR saw no difficulty in the fact that a concluded contract for the sale and purchase of the fixtures c   and fittings could not come into existence until the valuation was made. He obliged the vendor to comply with his implied obligation not to prevent the valuation being taken.

In *Re Smith & Services and Nelson & Sons* (1890) 25 QBD 545 shipowners claimed damages for a breach of a charterparty which contained an arbitration clause providing for one arbitrator to be appointed by the shipowners and one by the charterers and for a third arbitrator to be appointed by the first two arbitrators. The shipowners appointed d   an arbitrator but the charterers refused to do so. The shipowners asked the court to order the charterers to appoint an arbitrator, relying on the Arbitration Act 1889 or an inherent power in the court. The Court of Appeal held that there was no statutory power to order the appointment of an arbitrator and that the courts of equity had always refused the grant specific performance of an obligation to appoint an arbitrator. Lindley LJ said (at 553) that the order sought was 'opposed to all the practice of the last 200 years'.

e   If the court had no authority to order a contracting party to appoint an arbitrator, then clearly it had no power to order a contracting party to appoint a valuer. There are, however, different consequences from failure to achieve arbitration. If arbitration machinery fails the parties may have recourse to the courts of law to obtain a remedy. In *Re Smith & Service and Nelson & Sons*, for example, the shipowners' claim for damages for breach of the charterparty was presumably sustainable in the courts. In the case of a f   valuation, however, if the machinery breaks down and if the court cannot interfere, then neither party has any remedy.

In *Talbot v Talbot* [1967] 2 All ER 920, [1968] Ch 1 a testator gave two of his sons the option of purchasing the farms in which they lived together 'at a reasonable valuation'. There was no provision in the will for the mode of valuation of the farms and the Court of Appeal affirmed the decision of Burgess V-C that the court itself would undertake the g   task and direct a special inquiry as to what was a reasonable price for the farms. Harman LJ referred to *Milnes v Gery*, where the testator had directed a valuation by two arbitrators and an umpire, and continued ([1967] 2 All ER 920 at 922–923, [1968] Ch 1 at 11–12):

'Those means broke down and SIR WILLIAM GRANT came to the conclusion that the court, where the means pointed out by the testator had broken down, would not h   create others as that would be something which the court had no jurisdiction to do, but that, where the matter was left open, as SIR WILLIAM GRANT said, and no machinery was provided, there is no reason why the court should not step in and lend its benevolent aid. That seems to me to be good sense and good law ... Therefore there is good authority for saying that an option to purchase "at a fair valuation" or "at a fair price" is an option which the court will enforce ...'

j   In the present case there is no reference to 'a fair valuation'. Counsel for the tenants submitted that in the context of the lease the parties intended that there should be a fair valuation resulting in a fair price on the footing of a bargain between the landlords owning the reversion and willing to sell, and the tenants owning the leasehold interest and willing to buy the freehold reversion. The implication of a fair valuation does not however relieve counsel of the difficulty that in this case, as in *Milnes v Gery*, express provision was made for the ascertainment of a fair valuation by two arbitrators and an umpire.

In *Brown v Gould* [1971] 2 All ER 1505 at 1057, [1972] Ch 53 at 56 Megarry J upheld *a* the validity of an option to renew a lease—

'for a further term of Twenty one years at a rent to be fixed having regard to the market value of the premises at the time of exercising this option taking into account to the advantage of the Tenant any increased value of such premises *b* attributable to structural improvements made by the Tenant . . .'

Megarry J held, consistently with *Talbot v Talbot*, that, where an option is expressed to be exercisable at a price to be determined according to some stated formula without any effective machinery in terms provided for working out that formula, the court has jurisdiction to determine it. In the present case the parties themselves have provided the machinery. *c*

Finally *Beer v Bowden* [1981] 1 All ER 1070, [1981] 1 WLR 522 concerned a lease for ten years which fixed a rent of £1,250 per annum for the first five years and thereafter 'such rent as shall thereupon be agreed between the landlords and the tenant but no account shall be taken of any improvements carried out by the tenant in computing the amount of increase . . .' This court implied a term that the rent to be agreed and fixed on the rent review should be a fair rent. Geoffrey Lane LJ said ([1981] 1 All ER 1070 at *d* 1075–1076, [1981] 1 WLR 522 at 527):

'Had this been a contract of sale or an ordinary commercial contract of some sort, there would have been a great deal to be said for the view that from the date of the first rent review in March 1973 the contract was void for uncertainty, the parties having failed to agree on a vital term of the contract. But here there is a subsisting estate, *e* and a subsisting estate in land, the lease, which is to continue until 1982, 14 years from the date of the lease itself. It is conceded by the tenant that some rent must be paid in respect of these premises by the tenant, and therefore it follows that the court must imply something, some term which will enable a rent to be fixed.'

In the present case the lease can continue without any difficulty, without any *f* implication or intervention by the court to make effective the option to purchase the reversion.

The instant case is one of an option which contains in express terms machinery for ascertaining the option price. That is the machinery which the parties selected when they entered into the agreement and it is clear from the cases that if the machinery breaks down, the court will not force on the parties an agreement which they did not *g* make, by substituting some other machinery. We can therefore put on one side those authorities which support the proposition that the court can supply the absence of certainty by itself ascertaining the 'fair' or the 'reasonable' or the 'market' price or rent. Counsel for the tenants seeks to imply into the option the word 'fair', but even assuming that this is possible (and we are by no means persuaded that it is) it seems to us to be of no help here because it is inherent in this option that the price, whether it be described *h* as 'fair', 'reasonable', 'market' or anything else, is to be arrived at only by means of the agreed machinery. The questions are (a) what is the effect of a failure in the agreed machinery and (b) does it make any difference that that failure is induced by one of the parties?

The principles which emerge from the authorities may be summarised thus. First, in ascertaining the essential terms of a contract, the court will not substitute machinery of *j* its own for machinery provided by the parties, however defective that machinery may prove to be. Second, where machinery is agreed for the ascertainment of an essential term, then until the agreed machinery has operated successfully, the court will not decree specific performance, since there is not yet any contract to perform. Third, where the operation of the machinery is stultified by the refusal of one of the parties to appoint a valuer or an arbitrator, the court will not, by way of partial specific performance, compel him to make an appointment.

a   All three of these principles stem from one central proposition, that where the agreement on the face of it is incomplete until something else has been done, whether by further agreement between the parties or by the decision of an arbitrator or valuer, the court is powerless, because there is no complete agreement to enforce (see *Hart v Hart* (1881) 18 Ch D 670 at 689 per Kay J).

b   It is clear, however, that there are circumstances in which the courts have made exceptions, the most striking of which are cases such as *Gregory v Mighell* (1811) 18 Ves 328, 34 ER 341 and *Beer v Bowden*. This exception may be expressed thus: where an agreement which would otherwise be unenforceable for want of certainty or finality in an essential stipulation has been partly performed so that the intervention of the court is necessary in aid of a grant that has already taken effect, the court will strain to the utmost

c   to supply the want of certainty even to the extent of providing substitute machinery.

A second exception, not perhaps always easily defensible in logic, is the case where the term which is uncertain or in respect of which the machinery has broken down, is construed as relating to a subsidiary part only of a wider contract in respect of which no such problem arises. In *Richardson v Smith* (1870) LR 5 Ch App 648 the court adopted the more logical course of severing that part of the contract from the remainder and

d   decreeing specific performance of all but the severed part. In *Smith v Peters* (1875) LR 20 Eq 511 Jessel MR decreed specific performance and made a mandatory order compelling the vendor to operate the machinery. It should, however, be noted that in that case reference was to a single named valuer and that once the valuer had been allowed to enter and make his valuation there was no further possibility of any uncertainty. The contract was certain. The court made an interlocutory order in order to restrain the defendant

e   from obstructing its performance.

Subject to these exceptions, however, the general principle has stood for over a century and a half and was clearly recognised by the Court of Appeal in Chancery in *Richardson v Smith*. In *Firth v Midland Railway Co* (1875) LR 20 Eq 100 at 112 Bacon V-C said:

f   'It is in vain to say that the Court has it in its power of itself to enforce such an agreement as this, or any agreement for a valuation; unless the valuation be a matter wholly subsidiary to, and not of the essence of, the agreement.'

Plainly the instant case cannot be said to be one of a stipulation which is subsidiary: the machinery for arriving at a price goes to the very root of the transaction. Equally, we find great difficulty in seeing how it can properly be brought under the umbrella of the *Gregory v Mighell* principle. It is of course true that the lease in which the option appears

g   has been partly peformed in the sense that the term of years has been granted and the tenants are in possession and paying the agreed rent. But the circumstances which prompted the court to substitute its own machinery in *Gregory v Mighell* and *Beer v Bowden* are entirely absent in the present case. In those cases the tenant was in possession and, as was acknowledged on all hands, bound to pay a rent. The grant of the term of years could not be undone and some formula had to be found for ascertaining the rent

h   which the tenant had to pay for the balance of the term if he was not to occupy either rent free or at a rent which did not accord with any possible construction of the lease. Here the court is concerned solely with the construction of a collateral option to purchase. *Dinham v Bradford* (1869) LR 5 Ch App 519 is perhaps a case rather nearer on the facts, although that was a partnership case. Lord Hatherley LC there upheld the decree of Stuart V-C directing that the price at which the outgoing partner's share was to

j   be bought in was to be ascertained by the court, the agreed arbitration procedure having failed. He seems to have treated the stipulation for fixing the price as not being of the essence and undoubtedly he was influenced by the fact that the property (the plaintiff's benefit from the partnership) had been had and enjoyed. That case was approved by the Privy Council in *Hordern v Hordern* [1910] AC 465 at 474 where Lord Shaw, giving the judgment of the Board, adverted to—

'The distinction between a case where a transaction fails because an operation in the nature of a valuation upon which the conclusion of the transaction depended *a* fails and a case like the present, in which the transaction of sale and transfer of the business is already concluded by the contract and the detail of a particular method of fixing the price may have to be in some respect altered . . .'

We confess that we do not find the distinction self-evident and the case is not easily reconcilable with *Vickers v Vickers* (1867) LR 4 Eq 529 but it may be that the ratio was *b* that since the agreement, which had, of course, been fully performed except for the final disposition of the partnership assets, contemplated only one method of winding up, namely the acquisition by one partner of the other's share, the method of valuation could properly be treated as subsidiary and inessential, if it was not to result in the parties being held to an agreement quite different from that which they had made. Whatever may be the explanation of *Dinham v Bradford*, we find it difficult to see how it can be prayed in *c* aid in the instant case. The price is clearly an essential stipulation of the option, but the option cannot, we think, be said to be an essential stipulation of the lease such that the court is compelled to provide certainty in order to make sense of the grant. The term of years continues and the terms of the lease are unequivocal and clear, quite regardless of the validity or invalidity of the option.

The question then arises: if the court cannot, on authority, substitute its own *d* machinery for that on which the parties have agreed, can it nevertheless, by granting injunctive relief, decree a partial specific performance to the extent of compelling one of the parties at least to take such steps as lie within his power to make the agreed machinery operate? Counsel for the tenants points to two authorities which suggest that such a course is possible. The first is the decision of Leach V-C in *Morse v Merest* (1821) 6 Madd 26, 56 ER 999 where the agreement was for a valuation to be carried out by three *e* named persons by a particular date. It does not appear that any difficulty was anticipated if the valuers could once inspect the land, but the defendant had prevented the entry until the contract date had passed. Leach V-C held that the defendant, having prevented the valuers from inspecting, could not rely on the passage of time occasioned by his own default and he enjoined him from further preventing the inspection. He clearly recognised that the relief capable of being granted at that stage was only partial, for the *f* valuers might prove unable to agree a valuation, but he indicated that if they did produce a valuation, that could be used as the foundation for a supplemental bill. It is not easy to reconcile this with the mainstream of the authorities, and it has this distinction from the other cases, that the valuers named were not agents for, or in any way under the control of, the defendant. All that he was required to do was to give them an opportunity to inspect. Nevertheless it is difficult to see how this case stands together with those cases *g* where the courts have said in terms that until the valuation is made there is no completed agreement. It can only be based on the implication of a term that a party to a subsisting contract will not himself impede its completion, and that postulates a subsisting and enforceable contract in the first place.

The other case is *Smith v Peters* (1875) LR 20 Eq 511. That case had two distinguishing features. In the first place, as in *Morse v Merest*, there was nothing further to be done *h* beyond carrying out the valuation and, as we pointed out in our summary of the case, the contract was certain by its terms. Secondly, Jessel MR made it plain that by his interlocutory order he was only enforcing a term which he regarded as a minor and subsidiary part of the contract.

These two cases do not help the tenants a great deal. It may be that where the completion of the agreement is frustrated by one of the parties and the court can see that *j* no further intervention on its part will be required beyond negativing the frustrating act, specific performance can be decreed and the defaulting party will not be permitted to pray in aid his own wrong to resist the performance (see, for instance, *Pritchard v Ovey* (1820) 1 Jac & W 396, 37 ER 426). But that is a long way from saying that where, even without the act or omission of a defaulting party, there still remains an uncertainty as to

an essential term, the court will enforce one or more of a series of steps which may, but
a equally well may not, lead to certainty.

There are, in our judgment, two considerations which rule out such a course in the
instant case. In the first place, it is, we think, unarguable that an option granted by A to
B to purchase at such price as they shall agree could be enforced, and it would be rendered
no more enforceable by a further provision that if A and B could not agree they should
refer the matter to some other person to be agreed between them. That is simply the
b classic case of an agreement to agree, which is no contract. That defective contract is not
improved simply by putting the agreement to be arrived at at one remove and leaving
it to be negotiated between other persons (whether designated as valuers, arbitrators or
by any other description) to be nominated in the future, and in case of disagreement
between them to be settled by such person as *they* shall agree. It remains equally
uncertain. The court cannot force the parties to agree; it cannot, a fortiori, force their
c nominees to agree; and it will not decree what it cannot see its way to enforce. We think
that the words of Kindersley V-C in *Darbey v Whitaker*, which have already been quoted,
are as true today as they were in 1857. If the court cannot decree specific performance
now, then equally it seems to us that it cannot do indirectly, by way of partial specific
performance, that which it cannot do directly. The objection to the order which the
judge made is, in our judgment, summed up in his own words 'wait and see', because
d those words indicate in themselves that the court cannot see that there ever will be an
agreement to enforce. Thus, on any analysis, the first declaration which the judge made
must, in our judgment, be wrong, because it cannot at this moment be said whether
there is a valid option in the sense of an option which has ripened into a contract.

The second point is, in essence, an extension of the first. It has been established for
well over 150 years that the court will not decree specific performance of an agreement
e to name an arbitrator to fix the amount of a purchase price. In *Agar v Macklew* (1825) 2
Sim & St 418, 57 ER 405 Leach V-C considered it well settled. So did Stuart V-C in *Paris
Chocolate Co v Crystal Palace Co* (1855) 3 Sm & Giff 119 at 124, 65 ER 588 at 590. It was
affirmed by Lord Cranworth LC in *Morgan v Milman* (1853) 3 De GM & G 24, 43 ER 10,
and by Kindersley V-C in *Darbey v Whitaker* in 1857. Equally it is clearly established by
the authority of this court, in *Re Smith & Service and Nelson & Sons* (1890) 25 QBD 545,
f that the court will not order a party to appoint an arbitrator even though he is party to
a submission and capriciously refuses to do so. The judge in the instant case declined to
follow *Agar v Macklew*, which was in fact a case which applied the same principle to a
valuer, really on the grounds (a) that there has been a change in the attitude of the courts
to arbitration and (b) that valuation is a professional exercise which involves no control
by the court and therefore falls to be governed by a different principle. As to the former,
g there has no doubt been a change, and the court's power to appoint arbitrators or umpires
is now regulated by statute. But that in no way impinges on the authority of *Re Smith
& Service and Nelson & Sons* as regards cases not within the statute. That case bound the
judge and is binding on this court. We do not see our way to distinguish the case of a
valuer, and it seems to us that the same principle must apply.

So we are driven to the conclusion that this appeal should be allowed. We arrive at
h that conclusion regretfully because this option was clearly intended to be effective and
was at the time thought to be effective. No doubt the formula seemed a sensible one.
Nevertheless, it seems to us that in leaving the essential matter of the price to be left to
be fixed by the agreement of persons who have to be nominated by the parties and who
themselves have to agree on some third person to resolve any variance between them, the
parties succeeded in selecting a classically uncertain formula which the court cannot
j assist them to operate.

We take the view that both the effect in law of a contract expressed in these terms, and
the rule that equity will not grant specific performance thereof, have been settled for so
long that it is not open to this court now to make declarations inconsistent with such
settled principles. The landlords are entitled to a decision that the settled law is in their
favour.

For those reasons we allow the appeal. We quash the declarations made by the judge, and for his judgment substitute an order that in the action judgment be entered for the defendants.   *a*

Appeal allowed. Leave to appeal to the House of Lords refused.

Solicitors: *Taynton & Son*, Gloucester (for the landlords); *Rickerbys*, Cheltenham (for the tenants).

Henrietta Steinberg   Barrister.   *b*

Cohen v Nessdale Ltd

QUEEN'S BENCH DIVISION

KILNER BROWN J   *c*

15th, 16th, 19th, 21st, 22nd JANUARY, 11th FEBRUARY 1981

Specific performance – Sale of land – Conditional contract – Waiver of conditions – Oral agreement for sale of lease not expressed to be subject to contract – Letter from vendor confirming terms of oral agreement but stated to be subject to contract – Letter from purchaser confirming terms of oral agreement but not stated to be subject to contract – Purchaser making payment of *d* *ground rent provided for in agreement – Vendor accepting payment but crediting it to purchaser's arrears of rent under former lease – Whether agreement between parties remaining 'subject to contract' – Whether parties agreeing to waive condition that agreement was 'subject to contract' – Whether letters constituting sufficient note or memorandum of agreement for sale of lease – Whether payment of rent sufficient part performance to entitle purchaser to specific performance of agreement for sale of lease – Law of Property Act 1925, s 40(1).*   *e*

In 1970 the plaintiff was occupying a flat owned by the defendants as a statutory tenant holding over after expiry of a long lease. The defendants appointed H as negotiator for the sale of long leases to sitting tenants, and appointed agents for the collection of rents of their various properties. In March 1977 H wrote to the plaintiff, offering to sell the lease of the flat for £20,000 'subject to contract'. Negotiations ensued between the parties for the sale of the lease of the flat but came to a halt in May 1977 with no   *f* agreement having been reached. On 2nd November 1977 H wrote to the plaintiff, referring to the negotiations and suggesting further consideration of the purchase of the leasehold interest. The letter was expressed to be 'without prejudice', but did not contain the words 'subject to contract'. A meeting was held on 18th November 1977, when the plaintiff and H orally agreed to the sale of the lease for a term of 99 years from December 1968 on terms that the plaintiff was to pay a premium of £17,000, a service charge of   *g* £100 a year and a ground rent of £50 a year. No reference was made by either party to the terms as being 'subject to contract'. It was mutually understood that the documentation would be completed by their respective solicitors by the end of the year. On the same day, H confirmed the agreement in writing, but 'subject to contract'. On 24th November, in an open letter without the words 'subject to contract', the plaintiff confirmed the agreement. Both the plaintiff and H understood the sale to   *h* be proceeding pursuant to the agreement reached. In accordance with the agreement, the plaintiff sent a cheque for £50 for ground rent to the defendants' agents who credited it to his general account for rack rent which was in arrears. No further steps to complete the contract were taken by the defendants. In September 1978 the defendants informed the plaintiff that they would not be proceeding with the sale of the lease of the flat. The plaintiff brought an action against the defendants, seeking, inter alia, specific performance   *j* of the contract. He contended that the letter of 18th November 1977 was a sufficient note or memorandum of the agreement within s 40(1) of the Law of Property Act 1925 or, alternatively, that it was evidence of an oral agreement of which the payment of the £50 for ground rent constituted part performance.

Held – The use of the words 'subject to contract' in the letter of 18th November 1977 *a* indicated that there had been no acknowledgment of a binding agreement and accordingly the letter could not constitute a sufficient note or memorandum within s 40(1) of the 1925 Act. However, the agreement of 18th November 1977 contained sufficient agreement as to essential terms to be capable of specific performance and the payment of the ground rent amounted to part performance if there was an agreement capable of being part performed. Although in exceptional circumstances the conclusive and well-established effect of the words 'subject to contract' would be treated as being

b waived if there was a new and distinct agreement waiving the 'subject to contract' qualification, that only applied in the strictly limited case where an express or implied agreement to waive was obvious not merely from the subsequent agreement but also from the circumstances leading up to it. Having regard to the facts that the negotiations had not been irrevocably broken off in May 1977 and that the meeting on 18th November 1977 was merely a resumption of discussions which had not previously

c resulted in agreement, it could not be said that when the discussions were resumed on 18th November there was an implied or express agreement that the previous 'subject to contract' qualification was to be regarded as no longer applicable. That qualification accordingly remained and the oral agreement of 18th November was not a contract which was capable of being part performed. Specific performance would therefore not be ordered (see p 126 *f* to *h*, p 127 *b c* and p 128 *b* to *g*, post).

d *Sherbrooke v Dipple* (1980) 255 Estates Gazette 1203 applied.

Law v Jones [1973] 2 All ER 437 not followed.

Notes

For the need for a note or memorandum in writing if action is to be brought on a contract for sale of land, see 34 Halsbury's Laws (3rd Edn) 207–210, paras 346–348, and

e for cases on the subject, see 40 Digest (Repl) 21–38, 82–205.

For exceptions from the requirement for a note or memorandum in cases of part performance, see 34 Halsbury's Laws (3rd Edn) 209, para 348, and for cases on the subject, see 40 Digest (Repl) 39–44, 218–264.

For the Law of Property 1925, s 40, see 27 Halsbury's Statutes (3rd Edn) 399.

Cases referred to in judgment

f *Daulia Ltd v Four Millbank Nominees Ltd* [1978] 2 All ER 557, [1978] Ch 231, [1978] 2 WLR 621, 36 P & CR 244, CA, Digest (Cont Vol E) 528, 8 *1b*.

Law v Jones [1973] 2 All ER 437, [1974] Ch 112, [1973] 2 WLR 994, 26 P & CR 42, CA, Digest (Cont Vol D) 795, *120a*.

Sherbrooke v Dipple (1980) 255 Estates Gazette 1203, CA.

Steadman v Steadman [1974] 2 All ER 977, [1976] AC 536, [1974] 3 WLR 56, 29 P & CR

g 46, HL, Digest (Cont Vol D) 795, 8 *1a*.

Tevanan v Norman Brett (Builders) Ltd (1972) 223 Estates Gazette 1945.

Tiverton Estates Ltd v Wearwell Ltd [1974] 1 All ER 209, [1975] Ch 146, [1974] 2 WLR 176, 27 P & CR 24, CA, Digest (Cont Vol D) 116, *602b*.

Action and counterclaim

h By a writ dated 19th December 1978 the plaintiff, Ronald Cohen, brought an action against the defendants, Nessdale Ltd, seeking damages for breach of an oral contract for the sale of flat 2, 11 Rutland Gate, Kensington, London, by the defendants to the plaintiff, or alternatively for specific performance of the contract. The plaintiff also sought a declaration that he held the flat as a statutory tenant under the Rent Acts. By their defence served on 26th April 1979 the defendants denied that the agreement was

j enforceable because of the absence of a sufficient note or memorandum thereof within s 40(1) of the Law of Property Act 1925 and they counterclaimed for possession of the flat, £1,735·20 arrears of rent up to and including 12th April 1979, and rent from 12th April 1979 at the rate of £754 pa until possession. The facts are set out in the judgment.

Nigel Murray for the plaintiff.

David Neuberger for the defendants.

Cur adv vult

11th February. **KILNER BROWN J** read the following judgment: In this action the plaintiff seeks specific performance of an alleged agreement of 18th November 1977 to   *a*
grant a lease for the term of 99 years of a flat of which he was the statutory tenant. The defendants resist the claim on the basis that the alleged agreement was not a contract capable of being specifically enforced because the note or memorandum relied on contained the words 'subject to contract', which phrase had been introduced in earlier negotiations. With complete integrity and admirable common sense counsel for the defendants recognised that it might be said that his clients had behaved without decency   *b*
and that any judge would within the framework of the law strive to find against them. Nevertheless, it is said that however reluctant the court might be it would be constrained to reject the claim. The difficult problem is to ascertain the state of the law when negotiations are resumed without specifically restoring the previous use of the term 'subject to contract' and where payment of money is said to be an act of part performance.

There now follows a full and detailed recital of the evidence which is summarised at   *c*
a later stage of this judgment. Number 11 Rutland Gate in the immediate post-war years had become somewhat shorn of its pristine elegance and had been turned into a block of six flats. Flat 2 was occupied by the plaintiff under the terms of a lease dated 7th March 1963 granted by the defendants' predecessors in title, the benefit of which was assigned to the plaintiff at the end of that year. The plaintiff remained in occupation after the expiry of his lease and thereby became a statutory tenant at the beginning of 1970. In   *d*
1970 the defendant company became the landlords. They set about a reorganisation of the existing arrangements for occupancy. At some time, and it matters not when, agreements were made with reference to four of the six tenancies whereby long leases were granted on payment of a substantial premium and the terms included an annual payment of ground rent and an apportionment of outgoings which was expressed as a service charge. The plaintiff was not of like mind. This is not surprising as he was not   *e*
ignorant of his bargaining power in view of the fact that he carried on business as a consultant in commerce and the law. He was not qualified to practice in either branch of the legal profession but presumably he was better qualified than most to resist the blandishments of the defendants' representatives. So far as he was concerned, the first move was a visit by a representative of the landlords and the possible alternative considerations were embodied in a letter dated 14th August 1970 sent to him by way of   *f*
confirmation of the discussion. One suggestion was that he should give up possession in return for a payment of £500; the other which was expressed to be 'subject to contract' was that he should be granted a 76½-year lease on payment of a premium of £7,000, an annual ground rent of £75 and an annual service charge calculated at one-sixth of the total outgoings. The plaintiff made a counter offer of £4,500 which was rejected by the defendants' agents who in turn increased the offer of payment for vacant possession. In   *g*
the meantime, the plaintiff was withholding rent and was contending that the condition of dilapidation, which was serious, was structural and in breach of the landlords' covenant. He was also calling on the defendants to honour in more reasonable fashion their proposal to grant a new lease. This dispute was partially resolved by a county court order to pay arrears of rent which was complied with, and by active steps on the part of the landlords through their agents to attend to their obligations as to quiet enjoyment   *h*
and structural repair. The plaintiff remained in occupation and the abortive negotiations of 1971 play no further part in this case and have no relevance to the issues I have to decide. By 1976 the defendants' agents for this property had become Goddard & Smith. Two partners, Mr Adams and Mr Brooks, gave evidence which was not only most helpful but dignified and impressive.

The evidence given by Mr Sadleir, a director, and Mr Henderson, a negotiator   *j*
employed by the defendant company, was by contrast quite deplorable. Goddard & Smith were agents of the defendants with reference to (1) the collection of rent, (2) the inspection and maintenance of the premises, and (3) advice as to fixing and apportionment of service charges. The amount of premium to be paid in return for the grant of a lease was reserved to the defendants themselves. In view of the fact that they employed a

a negotiator in the person of Mr Henderson for this specific purpose, I conclude that they preferred to haggle for terms most favourable to them without much regard for a professionally assessed fair market value. By reason of this allocation of responsibility and the volume of work handled by Goddard & Smith it is not surprising that as agents they were not fully acquainted with the different problems which concerned the plaintiff and the defendants with reference to this property and this particular flat.

b Thus it was that side by side with arguments about the compliance by the defendants with their covenants and with a reopening of discussion about the sale of a lease there were applications for increase of rent before the fair rent tribunal. There was an application in May 1977 which was adjudicated on in July 1977 and the rent was increased. This matter operated very strongly on the mind of the plaintiff as can be seen from a recital of other facts.

c At some time in 1976 the defendants took up again the question of the grant of a new lease of the flat. This appears to have been due to the keenness of Mr Henderson to justify his employment as negotiator, an office which he had assumed several years after the breakdown and complete termination of the negotiations which took place in 1971. There was an interview, but nothing came of it. Once again Mr Henderson entered the fray. On 15th March 1977 he wrote to the plaintiff. After referring to the discussion of the previous year he included this sentence: 'We are prepared to sell a term

d of 99 years from 25.12.1968 for the sum of £20,000 subject to contract.' At the foot of the page and for good measure, there appeared in large capital letters the words 'subject to contract and without prejudice'. Before the plaintiff replied to that letter he received a letter from Goddard & Smith dated 23rd March 1977 which requested his co-operation along with that of the other tenants whilst new carpeting was to be installed in the ground floor hall and lobby, and the price was mentioned presumably to give notification

e of a proportionate maintenance charge to be levied against him.

It is convenient to observe at this point that both Mr Sadleir and Mr Henderson stated in evidence that the plaintiff was on the whole very unco-operative and could rarely be found either on a visit or on attempts to get in touch with him by telephone. However, in marked contrast to Mr Sadleir, who never replied once to a series of letters over a period of many months from the plaintiff and the plaintiff's solicitors, the plaintiff did

f reply to the letter of 15th March, albeit not until 2nd May. In that reply the plainitff rejected the figure of £20,000 and made a tentative proposal in these words: 'However I would be prepared to consider subject to contract a figure of £15,000 on the same conditions subject to clarification of the Service Charge which I don't at the moment quite follow.' Understandably enough, counsel for the defendants places considerable store on the wording used by the plaintiff.

g The next day, still under the 'umbrella' of the words 'subject to contract', the defendants by another director, Mr Glover, put forward what was called 'a compromise' figure of £18,500. That was rejected by the plaintiff and then he said: 'I think the best course would be to proceed along the second alternative suggested in your letter of 15th March.' That was a reference to a suggestion that he should vacate the premises. The plaintiff then proceeded to put forward the sum of £12,000 by way of consideration. On

h 6th May Mr Glover countered with a valuation of £5,000 coupled in the alternative with a final offer of £17,500 for a new lease, again 'subject to contract'. On 10th May the plaintiff sent off a short letter which after acknowledging receipt of the latest proposal continued in these words: 'In the meantime I have received notice from the Rent Registration Office upon your application for an increase in the rent. In these circumstances obviously there is nothing further we can do in the matter.'

j As he explained in a letter to Goddard & Smith dated 7th July 1977 he was, to quote his own words, 'quite flabbergasted to find myself firstly in negotiation with my landlord at his instigation and then he applies to have the rent increased'. He made it plain in that letter that he regarded the negotiations as terminated. Of course he was not to know that the right hand of the defendants, wearing a glove labelled 'Glover', acted quite independently of the left hand, wearing a glove labelled 'Goddard & Smith Rent

Department'. Furthermore, in that letter he complained that no representative of the defendants had had the courtesy to turn up at the fair rent tribunal and that there had *a* been another serious inroad into his quiet enjoyment by reason of a flood of water descending from upstairs.

In the ensuing correspondence he tried to enlist the sympathy of Mr Onglay, the senior partner of Goddard & Smith, by reciting his woes and quoting the inspecting officer from the fair rent tribunal who gave her opinion that the premises were in such a state that a premium for the grant of a new lease should be no more than £10,000. *b* However, Goddard & Smith very wisely kept within their terms of their agency and made no comment about the negotiations or the fair market value, but did assist the plaintiff to the extent of forwarding copies of his letter to the defendants. Goddard & Smith concentrated on the complaints with reference to structural dilapidation and damage by water.

After a long delay the defendants in the person of Mr Henderson reopened discussion *c* about the granting of a new lease. A letter was sent to the plaintiff on 2nd November 1977 inviting further consideration of a possible sale of a lease. This referred to the previous meeting and discussions but was not said to be 'subject to contract' but merely 'without prejudice'. As a result it was arranged that the plaintiff and Mr Henderson should meet at the latter's office on the morning of 18th November 1977. There is a conflict of evidence as to what was said at that meeting and I accept the plaintiff's *d* evidence and reject that given by Mr Henderson. The plaintiff's evidence was to the effect that there was a general discussion trying to get the whole thing settled. He acknowledged that rent for the year 1977 had not been paid because in his opinion he was entitled to withold this rent because the landlords had defaulted on their obligations and that the negotiations for sale of the lease had broken down because the landlords were wholly unreasonable.
                                                                                                    e
Therefore, taking all these matters into consideration a figure of £17,000 by way of premium was agreed. It was further agreed that the maintenance charge should be £100 a year, being 25% of the outgoings, and that the ground rent should be £50 a year payable as from 1st January next. The lease and contract were to be drawn up and completed by the end of the year. At the end of the discussion Mr Henderson said that he was so glad that everything was agreed and they shook hands on it. Nothing was said *f* at any time about the decisions reached being subject to contract. I find as a fact that that is what happened. I do not believe Mr Henderson when he gave evidence to the effect that he made it plain that whole discussion was subject to contract in the accepted sense. The contemporary and subsequent documents indicate that he regarded the agreement as final and binding and he gave a very significant answer when giving evidence as to his understanding of the words 'subject to contract'. He said and I quote *g* from the transcript, as well as relying on my note: 'I understand them to mean subject to the terms being reduced in an agreement which would be finalised by the solicitors or in writing at a later date.'

On the afternoon of the same day, 18th November, Mr Henderson sent a letter in the following terms:

'Further to our discussion, I have pleasure in confirming the sale of the above to *h* you for the sum of £17,000 subject to contract. This is for a term of 99 years from 25th December 1968 with a service charge of £100 per annum payable on account being 25% of the landlords' outgoings. The ground rent will be £50 per annum for the first 33 years doubling every 33 thereafter. I have requested our solicitors Messrs. Harold Stern and Company of 6 Holborn Viaduct London EC1R (Mr. Thompson) to submit a draft contract to Messrs. Kood Kingdom Sompen [sic] *j* attention Mr. J. M. Davies for their approval.'

In fact Mr Henderson wrote to Harold Stern & Co not on that day but by letter dated 21st November. This began with the significant words, 'I have pleasure in advising that I have sold the above flat to the tenant, Mr. R. Cohen subject to contract'. Then after setting out the details agreed it concluded with these words: 'The solicitors acting on his

behalf are Messrs. Kood Kingdom and Somper [sic] London EC4 and if you would
a submit to them a draft contract for the attention of Mr. J. M. Davies I would be most
grateful.'

According to both Mr Sadleir and Mr Henderson the usual internal practice was for Mr
Sadleir to see such outgoing correspondence before it was dispatched. Although he did
not see the letter of 18th November Mr Sadleir did see the letter of 21st November and
stopped it, although apparently without taking the trouble to tell Mr Henderson. The
b reason why Mr Sadleir stopped it was because he thought the price of £17,000 was too
low. However he did nothing by way of explanation to anyone, giving the explanation
that he wanted to inspect the flat, an explanation which I found totally unacceptable. He
also said that Mr Henderson had got the wrong firm of solicitors because he had another
firm of solicitors who did his conveyancing work. I do not understand why he could not
at least have told Mr Henderson. He himself wrote to Mr Brooks of Goddard & Smith
c on 15th December and began his letter saying: 'Mr Henderson of this office has now
agreed the sale of the above flat to Mr Cohen.' The queries that were raised were as to the
standard length of lease, the ground rent and the apportionment of service charges. Mr
Sadleir explained this by saying that the valuation of the premium was his own concern
but he wanted assurance from Mr Brooks that the other terms were in order.

In the meantime, on 24th November, the plaintiff had confirmed the terms set out in
d the letter of 18th November in an open letter without any reference to the words 'subject
to contract'. This would have been a sufficient note or memorandum to bind the
plaintiff and supports his evidence that he considered that a firm agreement had been
reached at the meeting between him and Mr Henderson.

For his part Mr Henderson, in ignorance of what Mr Sadleir was doing or not doing,
wrote a personal letter to Mr Thompson of Harold Stern & Co enclosing a copy of the
e letter of 18th November asking him to get on as quickly as possible. This letter was also
stopped by Mr Sadleir. It is clear that both the plaintiff and Mr Henderson believed that
all that was necessary was for the agreement to be formalised by the solicitors acting for
the parties. In fact all that was happening was an exchange of correspondence between
Mr Sadleir and Goddard & Smith who were the only people, as far as I can see, that he
treated with any courtesy or sense of urgency. To judge from a letter dated 14th
f December 1977, which the plaintiff wrote to his solicitors, he spoke to someone at the
defendants who assured him that the draft lease would be shortly sent as the only reason
for delay was a question concerning the service charge.

As there had been no submission of any draft lease to the plaintiff's solicitors by the
New Year, the plaintiff ultimately managed to speak to Mr Sadleir in the middle of
January 1978. Mr Sadleir never acknowledged this conversation but the plaintiff wrote
g on 7th February referring to this conversation which in my judgment undoubtedly took
place. I accept the plaintiff's evidence that Mr Sadleir said nothing about any hold-up but
on the contrary gave the impression that matters were proceeding and that he would get
on to the solicitors to hurry them up. The plaintiff would not go as far as to say that Mr
Sadleir acknowledged that there was a firm binding contract. My impression of Mr
Sadleir is such that I do not think that he would have relaxed his guard to that extent
h however deceptive he may have been.

In the meantime, believing that he would be granted a new lease, the plaintiff
arranged for considerable alterations and improvements to be carried out by builders and
decorators and he took steps to find a purchaser who would pay a considerably larger sum
than the £17,000 for an assignment of the lease. Mr Sadleir would not have it that such
a possibility, which I would have thought was an obvious consequence, in any way
j operated on his mind when he deliberately prevented any steps to pursue the agreement
reached on 18th November. To put it mildly, I was suspicious of his testimony. In fact
he continued to stall.

Not only did the plaintiff attempt to get some response from Mr Sadleir, but he turned
again to Goddard & Smith. On 7th February 1978, the same day as he wrote to Mr
Sadleir, the plaintiff wrote with reference to arrears of rent, pointing out that there was
an agreement for the grant of a new lease and that the matter was in the hands of the

respective solicitors. On 28th February the plaintiff appealed to Mr Onglay, the senior
partner of Goddard & Smith, referring to the fact that repeated telephone calls elicited no
response from the defendants. On 7th March Mr Onglay replied that it was not within
his province to persuade Mr Sadleir to do anything about the matter. The agents
confined themselves to the area of their instructions and the rent department wrote a
warning letter on 22nd March with reference to the accumulated arrears of rent.

The plaintiff realised that matters were getting out of hand and that he must do more
to assert his position. I accept his evidence that he realised that if there was an agreement,
as he believed, he should honour his obligation to pay the £50 ground rent which was
due on 1st January 1980. He typed and signed a letter and drew a cheque for £50.
Although the existence of this letter was challenged by the defendants and although the
plaintiff left it to his secretary to post, I am satisfied that it was sent and received by
Goddard & Smith. The cheque was undoubtedly received and credited to the plaintiff's
rent account. The letter was sent to the rent officer at Goddard & Smith and was dated
31st March 1978. It read: 'Re Flat 2, 11 Rutland Gate London SW7. Herewith Ground
Rent £50 for the year 1978. Kindly acknowledge receipt.' Although the cheque was
paid and debited against the plaintiff's account he did not press for an acknowledgment
realising that he could prove its receipt, as he did.

He also went ahead with arrangements to assign the lease at considerable profit to
himself. Goddard & Smith continued to press for arrears of rent and also sent the
appropriate notice of increased registered rent. But Goddard & Smith would not get
involved in the failure of the defendants to proceed with the grant of a new lease to the
plaintiff. So the plaintiff tried again to get some response from the defendants. On 31st
May 1978 he wrote to Mr Henderson following a visit that same day. It was a firm,
reasonable letter putting on record that Mr Henderson was very surprised that nothing
had been done for over six months and referring to the plaintiff's repeated attempts to
get some response from the defendants and the various excuses and explanations put
forward. It closed with the statement that the matter was now in the hands of the
plaintiff's solicitors.

The solicitors wrote on 1st June 1978 in terms which plainly called for a reply. No
reply was forthcoming; nor was there any acknowledgment of reminders sent on 26th
June or 10th July. A letter dated 1st August was replied to by Mr Glover who said Mr
Sadleir would deal with it on return from holiday. He did not; so the solicitors wrote
again on 6th September and to this, Mr Sadleir curtly replied that the defendants would
not be proceeding with the sale of a lease to the plaintiff. This letter was subscribed with
the usual shibboleth at the foot of the page that it was 'subject to contract and without
prejudice'. The plaintiff's solicitors naturally inquired whether these words meant that
there was no definite refusal to grant a new lease in an open letter. Then the plaintiff's
solicitors discovered that Mr Sadleir was merely repudiating the original agreed price of
£17,000 and was wanting more because he had heard that the plaintiff had made a very
lucrative arrangement for assignment. Mr Sadleir confirmed this in writing and said he
would consider the sale to the plaintiff if a larger amount was agreed, The plaintiff's
solicitors treated this as an act of repudiation of a previous agreement and these
proceedings are the result.

It is necessary to extract from this very lengthy and detailed recital of facts, either
disclosed or ascertained from the evidence, those matters which are relevant and material
to the issues which call for decision. These can be summarised as follows.

1. In 1970 the plaintiff was occupying flat 2, 11 Rutland Gate as a statutory tenant
holding over after expiry of a long lease. The defendants were the landlords.

2. Negotiations for the grant of a long lease on payment of a premium broke down in
1971 and were terminated altogether.

3. From 1971 onwards there were continuing disputes between the plaintiff and the
defendants about non-payment of rent on the one hand and non-compliance with
covenants as to quiet enjoyment and maintenance of structural repair on the other hand.

4. The defendants appointed and employed a Mr Henderson as a negotiator for the
sale of long leases to sitting tenants and appointed Goddard & Smith as agents for the

collection of rent and for maintenance and repair of their various properties. Goddard
a & Smith had no authority to negotiate or evaluate the commercial value of the grant of
a long lease to a sitting statutory tenant.

5. On 15th March 1977 Mr Henderson wrote to the plaintiff in these terms: 'We are
prepared to sell a term of 99 years from 25th December 1968 for the sum of £20,000
subject to contract.' The plaintiff rejected this offer on 2nd May 1977 and put forward
the proposal: 'However I would be prepared to consider, subject to contract, a figure of
b £15,000 on the same conditions.' The defendants suggested £18,500 which was rejected
by the plaintiff and there followed some exchange of views as to the appropriate sum to
be paid for vacant possession culminating in a final offer by the defendants, subject to
contract, of £17,500 for the grant of a new lease.

6. In a letter dated 10th May 1977 the plaintiff referred to the fact that he had received
notice of an application for an increase in the rent. He concluded by saying, with
c reference to the negotiations: 'In these circumstances there is nothing we can do in the
matter.'

7. The plaintiff entered into correspondence with Goddard & Smith suggesting that
they should assist by reopening discussions on a much lower evaluation, but the agents
having no authority to act merely forwarded the letters to the defendants.

8. On 2nd November 1977 Mr Henderson wrote to the plaintiff referring to the
d previous meeting and suggesting further consideration of the purchase of a leasehold
interest. The letter was expressed to be 'without prejudice' but nowhere contained the
words 'subject to contract'.

9. A meeting was held on 18th November. No reference was made by either party to
the proposals and counter-proposals which were discussed as being 'subject to contract'.

10. At the end of the meeting the plaintiff and Mr Henderson shook hands on an oral
e agreement in the following terms. The defendants would sell a long lease of 99 years
from 25th December 1968 on payment by the plaintiff of the sum of £17,000. The
plaintiff would pay a service charge of £100 a year and a ground rent of £50 a year
doubling every 33 years. It was mutually understood that the 'documentation' would be
completed by the respective solicitors by the end of the year.

11. Later the same day, 18th November, Mr Henderson confirmed the agreement in
f writing but introduced the words 'subject to contract' in that confirmatory letter.

12. Instructions to the defendants' solicitors to proceed along the lines of the
confirmatory letter were set out in a letter written and signed by Mr Henderson but it
was never sent because Mr Sadleir, a director of the defendant company, stopped it
without informing the plaintiff or Mr Henderson that he was not honouring the
agreement.

g 13. On 24th November in an open letter without the words 'subject to contract' the
plaintiff for his part confirmed the terms of the agreement of 18th November and he
informed his solicitors of the agreement and that they could expect the draft lease very
shortly from the defendants' solicitors. They never did get it.

14. The plaintiff and Mr Henderson both understood that the matter was proceeding
pursuant to the agreement already reached. The plaintiff took steps by telephone
h inquiries and by a letter of 7th February 1978 to ascertain the reason for delay but was
never told that the defendants had no intention of proceeding. He either was told
nothing or was fobbed off with excuses.

15. In the meantime, believing that he would be granted a new lease, the plaintiff
arranged for builders to carry out substantial alterations and improvements to the flat
and took steps to find someone who would take an assignment of the lease on payment
j of a sum considerably in excess of the £17,000.

16. In February and March 1978 the plaintiff was in touch with a senior partner of
Goddard & Smith who were fully informed that the defendants had agreed the sale of a
lease but had not instructed solicitors to proceed.

17. Pursuant to his understanding that he was under an obligation to pay ground rent
of £50 as from 1st January 1978 the plaintiff wrote on 31st March 1978 to the rent
officer at Goddard & Smith: 'Re Flat 2, 11 Rutland Gate . . . Herewith Ground Rent £50

for the year 1978.' The cheque for £50 was received, debited against the plaintiff and credited to his general account for rack rent, which was considerably in arrears.

18. Despite many letters either from the plaintiff himself or his solicitors there was no explanation given by the defendants of their failure to honour the agreement.

19. On 6th September 1978 Mr Sadleir wrote to the plaintiff's solicitors that the defendants would not be proceeding with the sale of a lease to the plaintiff but marked the letter 'subject to contract and without prejudice'.

20. After inquiry whether this was intended to be a final repudiation of the agreement or whether Mr Sadleir was seeking to vary the original sum by a demand for an increase, Mr Sadleir confirmed that the latter was the case. The plaintiff's solicitors treated this correspondence as a repudiation of the original agreement by the defendants and these proceedings for specific performance were commenced.

It is common ground that the transaction was 'for the sale or other disposition of land or any interest in land' and therefore s 40(1) of the Law of Property Act 1925 applies. Consequently no action can be brought on an agreement unless there was some note or memorandum in writing of that agreement.

On behalf of the plaintiff it is contended that the letter of 18th November 1977 either was a sufficient note or memorandum of an agreement or alternatively was evidence of an oral agreement which was subsequently part performed by the plaintiff. In the light of well-established authority it is clear beyond argument that the use of the term 'subject to contract' in that letter means that it indicates that there was no acknowledgment of a binding agreement and therefore it cannot be a sufficient note or memorandum. So that part of the plaintiff's argument must be rejected. The alternative proposition can only be examined on the hypothesis that there was an agreement capable of being enforced and the defendants' strongest submission is that the discussion of 18th November can only be considered in the light of the previous negotiations which may well lead to the conclusion that the alleged oral agreement was only a discussion on a subject to contract basis. It is convenient however to leave that question to the last, as it requires much more detailed analysis.

The law as to part performance requires that I should look first at the act relied on and to determine whether it indicated the existence of and refers to a prior contract. In my judgment the sending of a cheque for £50 accompanied by a letter indicating that it was for ground rent for the year 1978 with reference to flat 2, 11 Rutland Gate clearly indicates that there was in existence an agreement in the form of a lease of that flat which required annual payment of ground rent amongst the terms. The purported ground rent was received by the defendants' agents. The person who dealt with the cheque should have known that the sum of £50 bore no relation to the normal instalments of rent and that it was plainly said to be for ground rent and not for ordinary rent. The senior partner of the agents knew that the plaintiff was alleging that there was an agreement for a lease which involved the obligation to pay ground rent. The agents therefore received the money with knowledge of what it was intended for and the defendants are bound by their agents' action in accepting it.

The old authorities which indicated that payment of money was an equivocal act and not capable of being an act of part performance have been largely overruled by the House of Lords in *Steadman v Steadman* [1974] 2 All ER 977, [1976] AC 536. This was a decision which caused dismay to many including the learned authors of Megarry and Wade on the Law of Real Property (4th Edn, 1975, p 567), just as the decision of the Court of Appeal in *Law v Jones* [1973] 2 All ER 437, [1974] Ch 112 caused dismay to traditionalist conveyancers until their fears were allayed by Lord Denning MR in *Tiverton Estates Ltd v Wearwell Ltd* [1974] 1 All ER 209, [1975] Ch 146. *Steadman v Steadman* was applied and followed in *Daulia Ltd v Four Millbank Nominees Ltd* [1978] 2 All ER 557 at 564–565, [1978] 1 Ch 231 at 243–244 per Goff LJ, and is doubly binding on me. As one brought up and educated in the common law I am gratified to be so directed.

My conclusion as to the nature and effect of the alleged act of part performance entitles me to turn back to the evidence as to the meeting between the plaintiff and Mr

Henderson on 18th November. Subject to the possibility that the effect of the words
a 'subject to contract' used throughout the earlier negotaitions still extended and applied
to the meeting, I have no doubt at all about the nature and effect of the discussion which
took place. By reference back to the findings of fact under paras 8 to 15 inclusive I am
quite satisfied that both the plaintiff and Mr Henderson believed that they had reached
firm agreement as to the terms set out in the letters exchanged and dated 18th and 24th
November. I fully appreciate that had they been solicitors each would have known that
b there could not be a final and conclusive agreement until the respective landlord's and
tenant's covenants had been drafted, but they were not and it is important to bear in
mind throughout this case that what would be plain to a professional expert need not be
held against persons such as these two gentlemen. Even though there would have had
to have been further consideration of the appropriate covenants to be included in the
draft lease there was, in my view, agreement as to sufficient essential terms to make it
c one enforceable by an order for specific performance.

Nevertheless, I am fully conscious of the need to maintain the conclusive and well-
established effect of the words 'subject to contract'. I remind myself that the Law
Commission when asked to consider the immorality and socially disruptive effect of the
practice known as 'gazumping' came to the decision that even frequent instances of such
a practice were not sufficiently socially disruptive to outweigh the chaos which would be
d created if the well-established reliance on the phrase were to be undermined (Transfer of
Land Report on 'Subject to Contract' Agreements (Law Com 65; HC Paper (1974–75) no
119)). If I were to disregard or endeavour to escape the consequences of its application to
this case because I thought, as I do, that the defendants behaved dishonourably I would
fall into error and contribute to chaos.

In the light of this reminder, I turn to that part of the case which I have found to be
e much the most difficult. The problem can be simply and shortly stated: did the words
'subject to contract', introduced and relied on by both parties in earlier negotiations, still
continue to apply to the agreement reached orally on 18th November? Counsel for the
plaintiff relies strongly on a passage in the judgment of Buckley LJ, with which Orr LJ
specifically concurred, in *Daulia Ltd v Four Millbank Nominees Ltd* [1978] 2 All ER 557 at
570, [1978] 1 Ch 231 at 250. Buckley LJ was referring to *Law v Jones* in which the same
f two Lords Justices gave the effective judgment of the court and which was strongly
disapproved in *Tiverton Estates Ltd v Wearwell Ltd*. Taken as a whole the passage, without
conceding error, seeks to reiterate the correctness of part of the judgment of the court in
Law v Jones and to repudiate the wholesale condemnation expressed in the *Tiverton Estates*
case. The particular sentence on which reliance is placed is this:

g 'What it did decide was that, if the parties subsequently enter into a new and
distinct oral agreement, the facts may be such that the earlier letter may form part
of a sufficient note or memorandum of the later oral agreement notwithstanding
that it was "subject to contract" in relation to the earlier bargain.'

Counsel for the plaintiff contends, and counsel for the defendants concedes, that this
sentence would appear to indicate that the mere entry into a new and distinct oral
h agreement can remove the effect of the phrase 'subject to contract' which appeared in
earlier negotiations. Counsel for the defendants contended that the words were obiter
dicta. That may technically be so, but effectively they were restoring part of the decision
in *Law v Jones*.

He was on stronger ground when he relied on the subsequent authority of *Sherbrooke
v Dipple* (1980) 255 Estates Gazette 1203. This was a decision of the Court of Appeal in
j which Lord Denning MR was joined and supported by Templeman and Watkins LJJ.
The court adopted and applied the words used by Brightman J in *Tevanan v Norman Brett
(Builders) Ltd* (1972) 223 Estates Gazette 1945: '. . . parties could get rid of the qualification
of "subject to contract" only if they both expressly agreed that it should be expunged or
if such an agreement was to be necessarily implied'. This decision would appear to be in
conflict with the interpretation put on *Law v Jones* by Buckley and Orr LJJ and both

counsel recognise that such is the case and with manifest relief pass the resultant problem for me to resolve.

The discomfort which I have experienced is analogous to that of the soldier who, confused by the smoke of battle, finds himself caught in the cross-fire of opposing forces. I have to try and reach the safety of neutral ground. Is it possible to reconcile the apparent conflict of superior judicial opinion? Without in any way wishing to appear presumptuous, I believe this to be possible. It seems to me that in the light of *Sherbrooke's* case the words 'if the parties subsequently enter into a new and distinct oral agreement the facts may be such . . .' must be applied in strictly limited fashion and in exceptional cases if they are to lead to an escape from the effect of a previous use of the phrase 'subject to contract'. Put another way, the oral agreement must take place in circumstances where the 'umbrella' has by express or implied agreement obviously been pulled down. It is not merely the fact of oral agreement to which one must have regard. One must equally have regard to the circumstances leading up to the oral agreement.

An application of these principles and this approach to the facts of the instant case indicate that the plaintiff is faced with a difficult task. There was no evidence of an expressed agreement to expunge the effect of the words 'subject to contract'. There remains the possibility of an implied agreement so to do. Now the negotiations of March and May 1977 were clearly made subject to contract by both parties. The furthest that the plaintiff went was to say in his letter of 10th May that because of the proposals to increase rent there was in the circumstances nothing that could be done in the matter. If nothing more had happened for a year or so it would be simple to say that the negotiations had been irrevocably broken off. But the plaintiff did not regard the negotiations as irrevocably broken off because he tried to reopen them with the assistance of the agents, Goddard & Smith.

The next thing that happened was the letter of 2nd November which was plainly expressed to be 'without prejudice' and was on the face of it an invitation to resume discussion which had not previously resulted in agreement. In my judgment it is impossible to say that when the discussion was resumed on 18th November there was to be implied an agreement that the previous qualification of 'subject to contract' was to be regarded as no longer being applicable. This means that the qualification remained and the oral agreement of 18th November was not a contract which was capable of being part performed and therefore specific performance cannot be ordered.

I am driven to this conclusion with great regret. It illustrates only too clearly that the overriding need to maintain the effectiveness of the well-established concept of the words 'subject to contract' can provide a dishonourable vendor with the lawful excuse to resile from an agreement which the ordinary reasonable person would regard as binding. The practice of 'gazumping' is not, as the Law Commission believed, a temporary phenomenon. To judge from the evidence in this case it remains a social and moral blot on the law relating to the disposition of real property.

There must be judgment for the defendants.

Judgment for the defendants on the claim. Counterclaim, by consent, to be remitted to the appropriate county court.

Solicitors: *Coode, Kingdon, Somper & Co* (for the plaintiff); *Harold Stern & Co* (for the defendants).

K Mydeen Esq   Barrister.

R v Uxbridge Justices, ex parte Commissioner of Police of the Metropolis

COURT OF APPEAL, CIVIL DIVISION

LORD DENNING MR, SIR GEORGE BAKER AND SIR STANLEY REES

5th, 12th JUNE 1981

Police – Property in possession of police – Delivery to owner – Costs of application for order for delivery to owner – Jurisdiction of justices to make order for costs – Justices having power to award costs where proceedings initiated by way of complaint – Whether 'application' by claimant for order for delivery of property to him properly made by way of complaint – Whether justices having power to order police to pay costs – Police (Property) Act 1897, s 1(1) – Magistrates' Courts Act 1952, s 55(1).

The respondent claimed a number of currency notes worth over £1,000 which came into the possession of the police during a criminal investigation. He applied, by way of complaint, to magistrates for an order under s 1(1)[a] of the Police (Property) Act 1897 that the notes should be handed over to him. A summons was then issued by the magistrates ordering the police to appear before the magistrates to answer the complaint. The police were not legally represented at the hearing of the complaint, but a detective constable informed the court that they did not oppose the application. The magistrates made the order and, at the respondent's request and in the purported exercise of their power under s 55(1)[b] of the Magistrates' Courts Act 1952, awarded the respondent £350 costs against the police. The police sought an order of certiorari to quash the order for costs on the ground that the magistrates had no power to make such an order on an 'application' under s 1(1) of the 1897 Act because their jurisdiction under s 55 of the 1952 Act was limited to proceedings initiated by complaint and an application under s 1(1) of the 1897 Act was not a complaint. The Divisional Court refused to grant an order of certiorari, on the ground that the magistrates were entitled under s 55(1) of the 1952 Act to order costs against the police on the respondent's complaint under s 1(1) of the 1897 Act because the magistrates had been required to exercise a judicial function, ie to determine property rights between the parties, and the procedure by complaint was the appropriate method of initiating proceedings in which their judicial function would have to be exercised. The police appealed.

Held (Lord Denning MR dissenting) – Where proceedings were initiated by way of complaint and summons before magistrates for the return of property under s 1(1) of the 1897 Act, the magistrates had power under s 55(1) of the 1952 Act to make an order for costs because, even though s 1(1) of the 1897 Act referred only to an 'application', the procedure by complaint and summons could properly be used to begin proceedings under s 1(1) of the 1897 Act. It followed that all the requirements of s 55(1) of the 1952 Act had been complied with, and the appeal would accordingly be dismissed (see p 136 h j, p 137 g h, p 138 d e, p 139 b to d, p 141 f g and p 142 a, post).

Irving v National Provincial Bank Ltd [1962] 1 All ER 157 and *Raymond Lyons & Co Ltd v Metropolitan Police Comr* [1975] 1 All ER 335 considered.

Per Curiam. (1) It is inappropriate to make an order for costs in proceedings under the 1897 Act where the police do not object to the order sought (see p 133 g, p 139 d and p 141 g to p 142 a, post).

(2) An application under s 1(1) of the 1897 Act need not be made by complaint but can be made by application only, that being the practice in the metropolitan magistrates'

---

a   Section 1(1), so far as material, is set out at p 131 h, post

b   Section 55(1), so far as material, is set out at p 134 b, post

courts, and in that case the magistrates have no power to order costs (see p 134 *g h*, p 135 *j* to p 136 *a* and *e*, p 137 *f g* and p 140 *j* to p 141 *b*, post).

Decision of the Divisional Court of the Queen's Bench Division [1981] 1 All ER 940 affirmed.

Notes

For property in the possession of the police, see 29 Halsbury's Laws (4th Edn) para 422, and for costs between parties in magistrates' courts, see ibid para 392.

For the Police (Property) Act 1897, s 1, see 25 Halsbury's Statutes (3rd Edn) 280.

For the Magistrates' Courts Act 1952, s 55, see 21 ibid 231.

As from 6th July 1981 s 55 of the 1952 Act has been replaced by s 64 of the Magistrates' Courts Act 1980.

Cases referred to in judgments

Chic Fashions (West Wales) Ltd v Jones [1968] 1 All ER 229, [1968] 2 QB 299, [1968] 2 WLR 201, 132 JP 175, CA, 14(1) Digest (Reissue) 215, *1573*.

Irving v National Provincial Bank Ltd [1962] 1 All ER 157, [1962] 2 QB 73, [1962] 2 WLR 503, 126 JP 76, CA, 46 Digest (Reissue) 522, *671*.

Raymond Lyons & Co Ltd v Metropolitan Police Comr [1975] 1 All ER 335, [1975] QB 321, [1975] 2 WLR 197, 139 JP 213, DC, Digest (Cont Vol D) 723, *115Aa*.

Cases also cited

Boulter v Kent Justices [1897] AC 556, HL.
Trathan v Trathan [1955] 2 All ER 701, [1955] 1 WLR 805, DC.

Appeal

The Commissioner of Police of the Metropolis appealed against the decision of the Divisional Court of the Queen's Bench Division (Donaldson LJ and Kilner Brown J) ([1981] 1 All ER 940, [1981] 1 WLR 112) given on 2nd July 1980 whereby it refused an application for an order of certiorari, the court holding that the Uxbridge justices in exercising their powers under the Police (Property) Act 1897 on 11th January 1979 had had jurisdiction to direct that the commissioner should pay the costs of the respondent, Sukh Deo Prasad, in the sum of £350. The facts are set out in the judgment of Lord Denning MR.

Alan Rawley QC and *Stuart Sleeman* for the appellant.
John Lloyd QC and *Michael Harington* for the respondent.

Cur adv vult

12th June. The following judgments were read.

LORD DENNING MR. This case raises a dry point of law about the meaning of the word 'complaint' in an Act of Parliament. But dry points of law can be illuminated by the facts which give rise to them. So I will tell the story behind it all.

The stolen currency notes

Sukh Deo Prasad was a frequenter of Heathrow airport. He got into touch with thieves. They stole currency notes from the wallets or packages of travellers. They handed them to Mr Prasad. He dishonestly received them and gave the thieves a reward. The police kept watch on him. They arrested him and found a lot of currency notes on him. They suspected that the currency notes had been stolen. They charged him with dishonestly handling stolen currency notes and with corruption.

They went to his house and found there quite a hoard of currency notes of all kinds,
a worth over £1,000. This is what they found: 12 Bank of England £5 notes, 92 Bank of
England £10 notes, 67 Bank of England £1 notes, 4 Bank of Clydesdale £5 notes, 3
United States $10 notes, one United States $5 note, 27 United States $1 notes. 2 Fijian
£10 notes. 5 Fijian $5 notes, 3 Fijian $2 notes and 2 Fijian $1 notes.

Those currency notes, coming as they did from countries far and wide, aroused the
suspicions of the police. Very reasonably. It looked very much as if they also had been
b stolen from travellers. So the police took possession of them as they were entitled by law
to do, pending further investigation: see *Chic Fashions (West Wales) Ltd v Jones* [1968] 1 All
ER 229, [1968] 2 QB 299.

The trial

In May 1978 Mr Prasad was tried at the Crown Court at Reading in respect of the
c stolen currency notes *found on him*. He was convicted on six counts of dishonestly
handling stolen currency and one count of corruption. He was sentenced to 18 months'
imprisonment.

At the trial the judge was satisfied that the currency notes *found on him* were stolen
property which had been used to facilitate the offence. So he made an order under
s 43(3) of the Powers of Criminal Courts Act 1973 depriving Mr Prasad of any right to
d them.

Mr Prasad's counsel then applied to the judge for the currency notes which were found
in the house to be given to him. He said that they belonged to Mr Prasad and that there
was no proof that they had been stolen. He suggested that Mr Prasad might have come
by them quite honestly, as, for instance, savings from his wages or gifts by travellers.

The judge took the usual course in such cases. He refused to make an order for the
e currency notes to be returned to Mr Prasad. He said that if Mr Prasad wished to claim
these currency notes he should apply to the appropriate magistrates' court under the
provisions of the Police (Property) Act 1897. That is a procedure which is available in
straightforward, simple cases where there is no difficulty of law and the matter is clear:
see *Raymond Lyons & Co Ltd v Metropolitan Police Comr* [1975] 1 All ER 335, [1975] QB
321. It is a very necessary procedure for the protection of the police. If these currency
f notes were stolen property, and the police had handed them over to Mr Prasad without
a court order, the true owners could have come down on the police for conversion and
damages. So it was absolutely essential that Mr Prasad should get a court order in his
favour.

The Police (Property) Act 1897

g Mr Prasad's lawyers followed the advice of the judge. They laid claim to the
currency. On 17th November 1978 they applied to the Uxbridge Magistrates Court
under s 1(1) of the 1897 Act, as amended by the Theft Act 1968 and the Criminal Justice
Act 1972. It says:

> 'Where any property has come into the possession of the police in connexion with
> their investigation of a suspected offence . . . a court of summary jurisdiction may,
h > *on application, either by an officer of police or by a claimant of the property,* make an order
> for the delivery of the property to the person appearing to the magistrate or court
> to be the owner thereof, or, if the owner cannot be ascertained, make such order
> with respect to the property as to the magistrate or court may seem meet.'

I have emphasised the words *'on application, either by an officer of police or by a claimant
j of the property'* because in this case the lawyers for Mr Prasad went to the clerk to the
magistrates and got a form of application for making a *complaint*, as distinct from an
application. It was not an appropriate form because they had to leave some spaces
blank. Particularly the spaces for inserting 'against' whom the complaint was made and
'for' what cause were not filled in. They were left blank. The lawyers adapted it so that
it read as follows:

'In the Middlesex Commission Area of Greater London

PETTY SESSIONAL DIVISION OF UXBRIDGE

TO   Commissioner of Police of the Metropolis,
                      Prisoner's Property Office,
                      Unit 6,
                      Cricklewood Trading Estate,
                      Claremont Road,
                      London N.W.2. 1SY.
                      (Ref. L.78/2697/RAD)

COMPLAINANT   Sukh Deoprasad

Address   :—   House Block One, H.M.P. The Verne, Portland, Dorset OT5
                      1EQ, formerly of 29 Leamington Road, Southall, Middlesex.

Who states that :—   certain property

, namely,   :—   See Schedule overleaf
                      has come into the possession of the Metropolitan Police in
                      connection with the investigation of a criminal offence

against   :—   [left blank]

for   :—   [left blank]

Wherefore the said complainant applies for the delivery of the said property to him,
he being the owner thereof (or for the disposal of the said property).

Pursuant to the Police (Property) Act 1897.

Above are particulars of a complaint which was made by the within mentioned
Complainant,

on the   :—   17th November 1978.

YOU ARE THEREFORE HEREBY SUMMONED TO APPEAR BEFORE THE MAGISTRATES' COURT
SITTING AT THE COURTHOUSE, HAREFIELD ROAD, UXBRIDGE

on   :—   Thursday, 11th January 1979
AT 10.00 a.m. TO ANSWER TO THE SAID COMPLAINT.

                                                 [Signature]
                                        CLERK TO THE JUSTICES.

per Solicitors,
Edward Mackie & Co.,
39 The Mall,
Ealing, W5.

Any communication with respect to this summons should be addressed to the CLERK
TO THE JUSTICES, UXBRIDGE, accompanied by a stamped addressed envelope.

SCHEDULE

Twelve £5 Bank of England notes, ninetytwo £10 Bank of England notes,
sixtyseven £1 Bank of England notes, four £5 Bank of Clydesdale notes, three US 10
dollar notes, one US 5 dollar note, twentyseven US 1 dollar notes, 2 ten dollar Fijian
notes, 5 five dollar Fijian notes, 3 two dollar Fijian notes & 2 one dollar Fijian notes.'

The hearing

On 11th January 1979 the application was heard by the magistrates sitting at
Uxbridge. The police had made inquiries and had not been able to trace any of the true
owners of the currency notes. No doubt if the currency notes were stolen the true
owners were travellers who had gone on their way. So the police had no evidence to
refute the evidence of Mr Prasad. They decided not to oppose his application. They told
the clerk to the justices that they were not opposing the application.

At the hearing Mr Prasad was represented by counsel. The police were represented, not by lawyers, but by Det Con Leonard from the Heathrow police station and by Mrs Pawley, a civilian executive officer of the police property department. Mr Prasad had been brought from prison for the hearing. He gave evidence to the effect that the currency notes belonged to him. The police representatives said that they did not wish to cross-examine him nor did they object to the order being made.

Counsel for Mr Prasad then asked for an order against the police that they should pay costs. He said that they amounted to £350. The police representative opposed. They submitted that there was no power in such a case to order costs. They produced an extract from the Justices of the Peace and Local Government Review ((1968) 132 JP Jo 586) in which the opinion was expressed that there was no power to make such an order.

The justices retired. Their clerk advised them that they had power to make an order for costs. They ordered the police to pay £350 costs. Their order was drawn up and concluded in this way:

'AND the said Complainant applies for the delivery of the said property to him, he being the owner thereof. Pursuant to the Police (Property) Act 1897.

'IT IS THIS DAY adjudged that the said complaint is true and it is ordered that the said property be delivered to Mr. Deo Prasad and that the Defendant should pay £350 costs to the Complainant.

'DATED the 11th day of January 1979.'

A surprising order.

I must say that I am most surprised by the order of the magistrates. The police had done nothing wrong at all. They had taken possession of these currency notes, absolutely properly, because they were reasonably suspected by them to have been stolen. They retained them pending trial equally properly. They were absolutely right not to deliver them without a court order. If they had given them up to Mr Prasad and the true owners had turned up afterwards, the police would have been liable in damages to the true owners. Only by a court order would they be protected. Viewed in the eyes of the civil law, the police were bailees of the goods. Their custody was like that of a sheriff: custodia legis. Faced with a claimant, the sheriff is entitled to interplead and to get his costs as a first charge so long as he acts properly, but he is never bound to pay any costs. So also when the police have goods in custodia legis, and act perfectly properly in regard to them, they should not be ordered to pay costs.

Another point was made forcibly by counsel for the applicant. Suppose that, after the £350 had been paid to Mr Prasad's solicitors, the true owners had turned up and demanded the currency notes from Mr Prasad. At any time within six months these owners could have brought proceedings against Mr Prasad and recovered their notes: see s 1(2) of the 1897 Act. Yet the police could not have got back their £350 from Mr Prasad's solicitors.

All this satisfies me that, even if (a big *if*) the magistrates had jurisdiction to order costs, they ought not to have ordered the police to pay any. Even more serious, the police had no right of appeal at all. There is no provision at all for any appeal from an order under the Police (Property) Act 1897. So the police took the only course open to them. They applied for judicial review; and they did it on the only ground open to them, namely that the magistrates had no jurisdiction to make an order as to costs. The Divisional Court held that the magistrates had jurisdiction. The police appeal to this court.

The point of jurisdiction

One thing is clear. The magistrates have no inherent jurisdiction to award costs in any proceedings before them, either judicial or administrative. Their jurisdiction, if it exists, must be found in a statute.

Another thing is equally clear. Neither the Police (Property) Act 1897 (nor its predecessor the Metropolitan Police Courts Act 1839) gave any jurisdiction to the magistrates to make an order as to costs. Their only jurisdiction under those statutes was to make an order for delivery of the property to the person appearing to them to be the owner thereof.

The only statute which is said to give the magistrates jurisdiction to award costs is the Magistrates' Courts Act 1952 re-enacting in shortened form s 18 of the Summary Jurisdiction Act 1848. It says in s 55(1):

'On the hearing of a complaint a magistrates' court shall have power in its discretion to make such order as to costs—(a) on making the order for which the complaint is made, to be paid by the defendant to the complainant; (b) on dismissing the complaint, to be paid by the complainant to the defendant, as it thinks just and reasonable . . .'

Note the word 'complaint'. It is only on the hearing of a 'complaint' that an order can be made. Not on the hearing of an 'application'. The police say that that section does not cover in any way an application under the Police (Property) Act 1897. An application under that Act is not a 'complaint' within the 1952 Act.

'Complaint' or 'application'

The 1952 Act does not define 'complaint'. Nor does it define 'application'. In the absence of any definition I would state these as the essential features of a *complaint* as disclosed in the statute. There must be a complainant and a defendant. There must be a grievance alleged by the complainant against the defendant. There must be an application for an order to be made against the defendant. There must be a summons to be served on the defendant requiring him to appear.

Whereas the essential feature of an *application* is that there may not be a defendant, there may be no grievance, there may be no order made against a defendant. There need be no summons. These features can be seen running through the 1952 Act. Under that Act there are many cases where it is provided that an application can be made 'by complaint'. For instance, s 51(1) says that an 'application' for an affiliation order 'shall be made by complaint', whereas s 94 contemplates an 'application' which is not made by complaint. Again, it is quite clear that an order may be made 'on complaint'. For instance, s 50(1) says: 'A magistrates' court shall have power to make an order on complaint' for the payment of money; see also ss 53, 54(2), 73(1), 74(1), 91(1), 96(2).

Applications

Taking the above features as significant it is plain to me that an application under the Police (Property) Act 1897 can be made as an application simpliciter and not as a complaint. It does not require anyone to be summoned to appear. Often there may be no one as defendant at all. It is simply a request for an order. Counsel for Mr Prasad admitted as much. He acknowledged that if an application is made simpliciter then there is no power to order costs because there is no 'complaint' so as to bring the case within s 55(1) of the 1952 Act. That is indeed the practice in the Metropolitan Police District. We were shown a standard form of application which does not attract any order for costs. It is in this form:

'IN THE INNER LONDON AREA AND IN THE METROPOLITAN POLICE DISTRICT

TO THE COMMISSIONER OF POLICE, NEW SCOTLAND YARD.

WHEREAS application has this day been made to the undersigned, Metropolitan Stipendiary Magistrate sitting at the   Magistrates Court by
              of   to make an order under the provisions of the "Police (Property) Act 1897", respecting certain Property, to wit
which Property has come into the possession of the Police under the circumstances mentioned in the said Act:

YOU ARE THEREFORE HEREBY SUMMONED to appear before me, or such other of the

said Magistrates as may then be sitting at the said Magistrates' Court on
day, the   day of   at the hour of Two in the afternoon
if you desire to shew cause why an order should not then be made for the delivery
of the said Property to the person appearing to be the owner thereof, or such other
order as to me, or such other Magistrate as aforesaid, may seem meet.

Dated the   day of   19   .'

That is a very good precedent. If it had been used in the present case the magistrates
could have made no order for costs against the police. Counsel for Mr Prasad admitted
as much.

Form of application
But in this case Mr Prasad's lawyers did not use that form. I expect that the Uxbridge
Magistrates' Court had no such form. They only had a complaints form. So Mr Prasad's
lawyers filled it in as best they could, leaving blanks, as I have shown, in the spaces which
were inappropriate. Counsel for Mr Prasad submitted that, by using the complaints
form, it made all the difference. It enabled the magistrates at Uxbridge to make an order
for costs against the police.

I cannot think this is right. It cannot be that the applicant can confer jurisdiction on
the magistrates by using an inappropriate form in which to make his application. In
these days jurisdiction depends on the substance of the application, not on the form of
it. Although Mr Prasad's application was set out on a 'complaints' form, it was, and is, in
substance an application simpliciter, not an application on complaint. And the order
made by the magistrates was an 'order on application' and not an 'order on complaint'.
So it did not give any jurisdiction to award costs.

This view is supported by Mr Brian Harris in his excellent book on the Criminal
Jurisdiction of Magistrates (7th Edn, 1979, p 287). He points out that the 1897 Act does
not even give authority to issue a summons. He says of the 1897 Act:

'There would appear to be no authority for the issue of a summons in these
proceedings. It is suggested that the interests of justice would be satisfied by a
notice being served upon interested parties giving them an opportunity to appear
and make representations. There would appear to be no power to order costs in
these proceedings—see the Practical Point at 132 J.P.N. 586.'

Thus well supported, I am of opinion that the magistrates at Uxbridge had no
jurisdiction to order costs against the police.

Conclusion
Looking at the general legislative purpose of the 1897 Act, I am quite clear that it was
not intended that the magistrates should have jurisdiction to award costs. If there had
been, there would have been provision for an appeal, but admittedly there is none. The
procedure of the Act should be confined to straightforward, simple cases where there is
no difficulty of law or fact, and where there is no need for much in the way of legal
costs. If the case is in any way complicated in law or in fact, the applicant should take
civil proceedings in the High Court or county court. He will then get his costs if he
deserves them, but not if he does not deserve them. In the present case it was quite
unnecessary for Mr Prasad to spend £350 in costs. All he had to do was to make a simple
application himself to the magistrates. It would not have been opposed, and he would
have got the currency notes back. He preferred to leave it to his lawyers who managed
to run up costs of £350 in doing it. They should get that sum out of Mr Prasad or out
of the currency notes they recovered for him, not out of the police who have done
nothing whatever.

Sir George Baker and Sir Stanley Rees take a different view. They hold that an
application under the 1897 Act can be made by complaint and, if so made, the magistrates
have jurisdiction to make an order as to costs. But Sir George Baker holds (with me) that
the application need not be made by complaint, and that it can be made by application

as is done in the Metropolitan Police District, in which case the magistrates have no
jurisdiction to order costs.

This opens a way in which to avoid any trouble in the future. The clerk to the justice
should not accept any application under the 1897 Act which is made by 'complaint'. He
should only accept an application which is made in the form used in the Metropolitan
Police District, or by way of a notice such as is suggested by Mr Brian Harris in his
book. By insisting on this procedure the clerk to the justices will be able to ensure the
result, which to my mind is the right result, that the magistrates have no jurisdiction to
make an order as to costs.

I would allow the appeal accordingly.

SIR GEORGE BAKER. When proceedings are begun by the making of a complaint
to a magistrate, and the court for which he acts has power to make an order against any
person, the magistrate may issue a summons directed to that person requiring him to
appear (see s 43 of the Magistrates' Courts Act 1952; now s 51 of the Magistrates' Courts
Act 1980). Then, on the hearing of the complaint, the magistrates' court has power to
make an order for costs (see s 55 of the 1952 Act; now s 64 of the 1980 Act). As the
jurisdiction of magistrates is founded entirely on statute there is no other process or
proceeding in which justices are able to award costs.

Section 1(1) of the Police (Property) Act 1897, as amended, provides:

'Where any property has come into the possession of the police in connexion with
their investigation of a suspected offence . . . a court of summary jurisdiction may,
on application, either by an officer of police or by a claimant of the property, make
an order for the delivery of the property . . . or . . . make such order with respect to
the property as to the . . . court may seem meet.'

The magistrates have no jurisdiction to award costs on an application under that Act
unless such an application can be, and is, made by complaint and summons.

The question whether a complaint can properly be made to initiate such an application
has been much discussed, and it is at first sight surprising that there is no reported
decision. It appears that in metropolitan magistrates' courts the practice is for application
to be made on a form specifically so headed. Elsewhere the 'complaint' procedure has
been used to initiate process (eg as in *Raymond Lyons & Co Ltd v Metropolitan Police Comr*
[1975] 1 All ER 335, [1975] QB 321, where no objection seems to have been made to such
procedure, and *Irving v National Provincial Bank Ltd* [1962] 1 All ER 157, [1962] 2 QB 73,
where the proceedings are said to have been on summons for an order under the Police
(Property) Act 1897, and again no point was taken).

In the present case the respondent 'complained' on 17th November 1978 that money
in notes belonging to him had come into the possession of the Metropolitan Police in
connection with the investigation of a criminal offence and he, the complainant, and
owner, applied for the delivery of the property to him pursuant to the Police (Property)
Act 1897. A summons was issued ordering the Commissioner of Police of the Metropolis
to appear before the Uxbridge Magistrates' Court on 16th January to 'answer the said
complaint'.

It is said that an 'application' for an order for delivery of his money is not a 'complaint'
in the ordinary sense but is akin to an application to a court for an order that fingerprints
of a person in custody may be taken (see s 40 of the Magistrates' Courts Act 1952) or for
the return of property taken from an accused (see s 39). I think this is wrong on two
grounds: first, the applications under ss 39 and 40 relate to persons who are already
before the court; they are not initiating process; and, second, and more important, the
respondent was saying: 'You the police have my money. You will not, perhaps cannot,
give it to me without an order of the court. That is my grievance. I apply for an order
to remedy that grievance.' In my opinion that is a 'complaint' in ordinary language, and
is certainly a 'complaint' within a definition of the Shorter Oxford Dictionary: 'A

statement of—grievance laid before a court for the purpose of—redress.' See also Pugh's
Matrimonial Proceedings before Magistrates (3rd Edn, 1974, p 256):

> 'Note: Complaint. This expression is now used exclusively for describing an act
> corresponding to an information by which proceedings not in respect of an offence
> are set in motion.'

Justices sitting at Uxbridge heard the summons on 11th January 1979. The police
were not legally represented. But on behalf of the commissioner a detective constable
who was present with a civilian executive officer of the police property department
informed the court that the application was not opposed and that they wished neither to
cross-examine the respondent nor to object to the making of an order for the delivery of
the property to him. At the conclusion of the hearing counsel for the respondent asked
for costs. The police opposed that application, contending that there was no power to
make any such order. The magistrates found the complaint true, ordered delivery of the
notes to the respondent and payment to him of £350 costs.

There is no right of appeal against this order. The only remedy is by judicial review.
So it is not surprising that the police are aggrieved. On their behalf it is said they could
not safely pay the money without an order; they were involuntary bailees who did not
oppose, but were, so to speak, interpleading, and in principle if they pay costs on a claim
held to be false in later legal proceedings taken within six months from the date of the
order (this right is preserved by s 1(2) of the Police (Property) Act 1897) there is no way
in which they can recover such costs. I have sympathy with their grievance but apart
from having been told that £100 had to be paid by the respondent to the prison
authorities to bring him from Portland, where he was serving a sentence, we do not
know why the justices gave a further £250 and I suppose we must assume in the absence
of such knowledge that they exercised discretion reasonably. There may be other cases
in which the property is urgently required, eg to pay the owner's creditors or to provide
for his family while he is incarcerated, and in which he has had to incur some expense to
obtain the order. It might be very unfair and cause hardship to an owner to be out of
pocket by having to incur costs in obtaining his own property. All such matters are
within the discretion of the magistrates if, but only if, they have jurisdiction to award
costs.

The Police (Property) Act 1897 does not say how the application is to be made to
invoke the power to make an order. It is simply 'a court . . . may, on application . . .
make an order'. I agree that a notice as used in the metropolitan magistrates' courts
served on interested parties giving them an opportunity to appear will suffice, and if the
police seek an order they will no doubt use such procedure. There is no formality
prescribed such as is required in an application for adoption which 'shall be in Form 1'
(see the Magistrates Courts (Adoption) Rules 1976, SI 1976 No 1768, r 4(1)).

But the question is whether an application by complaint is precluded by the words of
s 1(1) of the 1897 Act or by any other enactment. Unless it is so precluded it seems to me
that it is and was in 1897 available by the provisions of s 1 of the Summary Jurisdiction
Act 1848 and s 51(3) of the Summary Jurisdiction Act 1879.

The former, so far as relevant, is:

> '. . . and also in all Cases where a Complaint shall be made to any such Justice or
> Justices upon which he or they have or shall have Authority by Law to make any
> Order for the Payment of Money or otherwise, then and in every such Case it shall
> be lawful for such . . . Justices . . . to issue [a] Summons directed to such Person,
> stating shortly the Matter of such . . . Complaint, and requiring him to appear . . .'

The s 51(3) of the 1879 Act which is to facilitate the application of the Summary
Jurisdiction Acts to future Acts reads:

> 'Where in any future Act a court of summary jurisdiction is authorised to order
> . . . a person to do . . . any act . . . the Summary Jurisdiction Acts shall apply
> accordingly.'

Many modern Acts provide for application by complaint. Examples are: the Matrimonial Proceedings (Magistrates' Courts) Act 1960, s 1, by which a spouse 'may *a* apply by way of complaint' for a matrimonial order; the Domestic Proceedings and Magistrates' Courts Act 1978, s 30(2): 'Any application for an order under this Part of this Act, including an application for the variation or revocation of such an order, shall be made by way of complaint'; and the Attachment of Earnings Act 1971, s 19(1): 'an application to a magistrates' court for an attachment of earnings order . . . shall be made by complaint.'
b

Then there are provisions that certain events cannot happen except when an order has been made on complaint (see the Magistrates' Courts Act 1952, s 73(1): committal for default of payment of civil debt), and of course the order for costs, and there are numerous provisions in the Magistrates' Courts Rules 1968, SI 1968 No 1920, made under s 15 of the Justices of the Peace Act 1949 for regulating and prescribing the procedure and practice to be followed in magistrates' courts, that proceedings shall be by *c* complaint. For example, r 30 (appeals), r 35 (affiliation payments to persons having custody), r 70 (application to vary sureties), r 84 (road traffic disqualifications), r 85 (food and drugs) and r 86 (conditional discharge).

But nowhere can I find any provision or even suggestion that because an Act refers only to an 'application' and does not mention a 'complaint' then application is the only process by which an order can be obtained, and complaint followed by summons is *d* barred, or at least not available. That it seems to me would be contrary to the quoted provisions of the Summary Jurisdiction Acts 1848 and 1879. Moreover if reference in an Act to application(s) and not to complaints was held to bar or to prohibit the complaint procedure it is at least arguable that a rule made under s 15 of the Justices of the Peace Act 1949 that such proceedings are to be by complaint would be ultra vires. An example of this is in the Guardianship of Minors Acts 1971 and 1973 where 'apply' and 'application' *e* are used throughout, but s 16(5) of the 1971 Act appears to assume by the words 'whatever adjudication the court makes on the complaint' that a 'complaint' has been made. Section 5(1) of the 1971 Act provides:

'Where a minor has no parent, no guardian of the person, and no other person having parental rights with respect to him, the court, on the application of any person, may, if it thinks fit, appoint the applicant to be the guardian of the minor.' *f*

It requires some imagination to construe such an application as a complaint, but by complaint it must be, for r 4 of the Magistrates' Courts (Guardianship of Minors) Rules 1974, SI 1974 No 706, provides:

'Except as provided in rule 8 [representations regarding a supervision order], an application to a court under any provision of the Act of 1971 or 1973 shall be made *g* by way of complaint.'

These 1974 rules supplanted the Guardianship of Infants (Summary Jurisdiction) Rules 1925, SR & O 1925 No 960, which had been made under s 7(2) of the Guardianship of Infants Act 1925. That Act extended to magistrates a jurisdiction in guardianship by providing that with certain exceptions they could 'entertain any application . . . relating *h* to an infant'.

It is I think helpful to refer to the 1925 rules because they provided that power to do anything authorised by the Act except consent to a marriage should be exercised by 'an order on complaint made personally either verbally or in writing'. Then there was provision for an application for consent to marriage to be made personally either verbally or in writing directed to and served on the person refusing consent, and heard in the *j* same manner as a complaint, but in camera. The law relating to consents was then taken into s 3 of the Marriage Act 1949 with the 1925 guardianship rules on consent surviving (see s 79(2) of the 1949 Act) to 1974 when it was substantially re-enacted in the Magistrates' Courts (Guardianship of Minors) Rules 1974, SI 1974 No 706, r 5. So there is a procedure laid down for process by application. It differs little from the complaint procedure, except of course that no summons is issued and no costs could be awarded. Apart from the adoption application it is the only provision regulating a process by application, as distinct from a process by complaint, known to me. The relevance is that provision is made by rule for the application for consent to be made in one way, and other applications arising out of the same Act to be by complaint. It follows in my judgment that without a rule either method could have been used for any application made under the Act.

The Magistrates' Courts Rule Committee might profitably consider whether the time has now come when all civil proceedings in magistrates' courts should be the subject of one provision, viz every order to be sought by complaint with such specific exceptions as are thought necessary.

My conclusion is that the complaint procedure is and has for long been simply a convenient and accepted manner of bringing a civil matter before magistrates for an order. It has always been an alternative to an application and used as such to obtain orders under the Police (Property) Act 1897. The Police (Disposal of Property) Regulations 1975, SI 1975 No 1474, are silent as to procedure, referring only to 'an application' having been made (see r 4(4)). It cannot be improper to use the complaint procedure, nor is its use prohibited. For these reasons I agree with the conclusion reached by Donaldson LJ and Kilner Brown J.

I have had the advantage of reading the judgment about to be delivered by Sir Stanley Rees and wish to say that I entirely agree with him about the undesirability of magistrates making orders for costs in cases like the present.

I would dismiss the appeal.

SIR STANLEY REES. I have had the advantage of reading the drafts of the judgments delivered by Lord Denning MR and Sir George Baker. In those judgments the relevant facts are reviewed and the reasons for the differing conclusions which have been arrived at are fully stated. Nevertheless, since there is a difference of opinion I have felt it right to set out as briefly as possible my own conclusion and the reasons for it.

The issue which arises for decision in this appeal is whether justices have power to make an order for costs in proceedings brought by a claimant for the delivery of property in the possession of the police pursuant to the Police (Property) Act 1897. Since justices have no power to make any order for costs by common law it is conceded that if there is such power it can only have been under the provisions of s 55(1) of the Magistrates' Courts Act 1952, which was then the operating statute. The relevant terms of that subsection are these:

'On the hearing of a complaint, a magistrates' court shall have power in its discretion to make such order as to costs—(a) on making the order for which the complaint is made, to be paid by the defendant to the complainant; (b) on dismissing the complaint, to be paid by the complainant to the defendant, as it thinks just and reasonable . . .'

It is noteworthy that an order for costs under this subsection can only be made in favour of the party who suceeds, but it by no means follows that the successful party shall always be awarded costs; that is a matter of discretion. So to empower the magistrates to make an order for costs the requirements of the statute are that there must have been a hearing of a complaint for an order in which a complainant and a defendant were involved. There is not, and there cannot be, any dispute that in the proceedings before the magistrates which gave rise to the present appeal all the requirements of s 55(1) were fulfilled. But it is argued on behalf of the police that procedure by complaint is not an appropriate way to initiate proceedings under the Police (Property) Act 1897 and that the appropriate course would have been to make an application to the magistrates having given prior notice to any persons who might be concerned. Reliance was strongly placed on these words in s 1(1) of the 1897 Act:

'. . . a court of summary jurisdiction may, *on application*, either by an officer of police or by a claimant of the property, make an order for the delivery of the property to the person appearing to the magistrate or court to be the owner thereof . . .'

It was argued that this Act prescribes a procedure by way of an 'application' and that no other form of procedure is permissible. I shall consider shortly what form of procedure exists or could be devised to constitute an 'application' in a magistrates' court.

The procedure which was followed by the respondent is not in dispute and was as follows. He made a complaint for an order for the delivery to him of the currency held by the police to a justice of the peace under s 43 of the 1952 Act and the justice duly issued a summons directed to the Commissioner of Police of the Metropolis. That summons recorded that the respondent was the complainant who had *applied* (and I emphasise that word) for the delivery of the said property pursuant to the Police (Property) Act 1897. This recital concluded with the words: 'ABOVE are particulars of a complaint which was made by the within mentioned complainant on the 17th November 1978.' The Commissioner of Police was duly summoned to appear before the magistrates' court on 11th January 1979. The summons was in common form and the certificate of service properly described the Commissioner of Police as 'the Defendant'.

On 11th January 1979 the respondent was represented by counsel and the Commissioner of Police was not legally represented, but a police officer and a civilian executive officer of the police property department attended on his behalf. The respondent gave evidence on oath and the police did not oppose the making of the order sought on behalf of the respondent. An application was made for costs and this was resisted by the police on the grounds that they had not opposed the application and also that the court had no power to make an order for costs. The magistrates, after retirement, made the order sought and also an order for £350 costs in favour of the respondent. As I have already indicated all the requirements of s 55(1) of the 1952 Act were fully implemented.

I now turn to consider the argument that the use of the words 'on application' in s 1 of the 1897 Act not only prescribe a procedure by way of an application, whether oral or in writing, but prohibit any other form of procedure.

Counsel for the police helpfully referred us to a number of the provisions of the 1952 Act in which reference is made to a complaint. Many of them referred to an 'order' which the court could make on a 'complaint'. One at least of them, namely s 54(2), provides that the court may 'by order made on complaint' suspend or rescind certain orders. Counsel also referred to the Magistrates' Courts Rules 1968, SI 1968 No 1920, of which a number, eg rr 85 and 86, include the phrase 'application by complaint'. Speaking for myself I did not derive any great assistance from this exercise in deciding the issue before us but am nevertheless grateful to counsel for drawing our attention to these sections and rules. Despite his researches counsel was not able to find any statutory provisions prescribing the procedure for an 'application'. So far as 'civil' matters are concerned the procedure appears to be by way of 'complaint for an order', and may sometimes be by way of 'an application made by complaint'. The absence of any prescribed procedure by way of application is illustrated by the need to invent a form of notice of the hearing of an application which can be sent to possible claimants or to the police. We were shown such a document and were told that it is in use in the Inner London area. The need for such a 'notice' is that the provisions of s 43 of the 1952 Act do not permit the issue of a summons save 'where a complaint is made'.

The strongest argument presented to us in favour of the police was that in some cases the application for an order under the 1897 Act may be made by the police when neither the owner nor any other claimant can be ascertained. So that there will be no other party to the proceedings. In such circumstances the police would no doubt apply orally and ex parte to the magistrates and be granted the order sought if the police are able to establish that no other party interested can be ascertained. In such cases, of course, no 'lis' exists nor any party against whom an order for costs could be made. It does therefore follow that in certain cases an application under the 1897 Act could be made to the magistrates' court otherwise than by complaint and by summons. In my judgment this factor does not necessarily override a conclusion that where these are ascertainable and necessary parties involved in the application the normal procedure by way of complaint and summons could, and in my view must, be adopted.

I can deal shortly with two further points. The first is that it was argued that because by s 47 of the 1952 Act the magistrates are given the power in certain circumstances to issue a warrant for the arrest of a defendant who fails to appear in answer to a summons the procedure by complaint and summons is plainly inappropriate for an application under the 1897 Act. It is not easy to envisage any circumstances in which magistrates would ever exercise this power in proceedings under the 1897 Act. But the mere existence of this power would not in my view inhibit the adoption of the normal procedure.

The second point was that any order which could be made under the 1897 Act is only in its nature an order nisi (see the judgment of Holroyd Pearce LJ in *Irving v National Provincial Bank Ltd* [1962] 1 All ER 157, [1962] 2 QB 73, to which I shall refer in a moment) since by s 1(2) of that Act an owner may within six months of the order claim the property in question despite the magistrates' court order. Again I do not consider that this nisi quality of the order made by the magistrates prevents the issue being regarded as a 'lis' between the parties concerned, particularly if one bears in mind that after six months it becomes absolute. And the value of the property at stake may be large; even in the present case it exceeds £1,000.

We were referred to two cases in which the provisions of the 1897 Act were considered, namely *Irving v National Provincial Bank Ltd* in the Court of Appeal and *Raymond Lyons & Co Ltd v Metropolitan Police Comr* [1975] 1 All ER 335, [1975] QB 321 in a Queen's Bench Divisional Court. In the former the magistrates' court proceedings were instituted by 'summons' and in the latter a 'complaint was made'. Accordingly in each case there must have been a complaint and a summons. In neither was it argued, nor did the appellate court concerned suggest, that the procedure followed was inapt.

My conclusion for the reasons I have attempted to state is that the procedure by way of complaint and summons adopted by the applicant in the instant case was not only permissible but was compulsory and that accordingly the magistrates did have the power to make an order for costs under s 55 of the Magistrates' Courts Act 1952. In a case in which the police seek an order under the 1897 Act and are able to satisfy the magistrates that no claimant can be traced, I would agree that it would be the appropriate, and the only, course for an ex parte application to be made to the magistrates.

The proceedings before us do not include any issue or argument as to the propriety of the exercise of the discretion of the magistrates to make the order for costs which they did in favour of the complainant. Nevertheless, I share the considerable degree of unease in regard to the order for costs which is evident in the judgments delivered by Lord Denning MR in this court and in the judgments delivered in the Divisional Court by Donaldson LJ and Kilner Brown J. If, as I am satisfied is the case, the magistrates are empowered to make an order for costs in proceedings by complaint and summons under the Police (Property) Act 1897 where there is a complainant and a defendant, their discretion must be exercised having regard to the exceptional and perhaps even unique nature of the order sought and to the respective roles of the parties concerned. In a case in which the police have clearly indicated that they do not oppose the making of the order sought and are merely attending before the magistrates to confirm their attitude and to ensure that an appropriate order is made before the property is delivered to the applicant, it would indeed be difficult to justify any order for costs against the police. Even in a case in which the police do not consent to the order sought by the claimant or claimants but attend the hearing and the magistrates are satisfied that it was reasonable for them to do so in order to assist the court to assess the validity of the claim or claims made to the ownership of the property, it would be proper for no order for costs to be made against the police, even if the order for delivery of the property sought by a claimant were made. In short, in my judgment, the proper approach to an application for costs in such proceedings should most certainly not be on the basis that costs should simply follow the event, but rather that the discretion to award them should be sparingly exercised, having regard to the exceptional nature of the role of the police as custodians of the property in issue, who require an order of the court to protect them before delivering up of the property to a claimant.

For the reasons I have attempted to state and for those set out in the judgment of Sir George Baker, I would dismiss the appeal.

Appeal dismissed. Leave to appeal to the House of Lords.

Solicitors: *R E T Birch* (for the appellant); *Edmund Mackie & Co*, Ealing (for the respondent).

Henrietta Steinberg   Barrister.

United City Merchants (Investments) Ltd and others v Royal Bank of Canada (Vitrorefuerzos SA and others, third parties)

COURT OF APPEAL, CIVIL DIVISION

STEPHENSON, ACKNER AND GRIFFITHS LJJ

26th, 27th, 28th, 29th, 30th JANUARY, 2nd, 3rd, 4th, 5th, FEBRUARY, 13th MARCH 1981

Currency control – Exchange control – Bretton Woods Agreements – Exchange contracts – Enforceability – Exchange contracts involving currency of member of International Monetary Fund and contrary to exchange control regulations of that member – Meaning of 'exchange contracts' – Contract for sale of goods – Peruvian resident buying goods from English company at inflated US dollar price and requesting excess to be deposited in bank in United States of America – Peruvian exchange control regulations prohibiting Peruvian residents from maintaining foreign currency accounts in Peru or abroad – Whether 'exchange contract' and therefore unenforceable in England – Whether contract only partly an 'exchange contract' – Whether contract enforceable as to part relating to genuine price of goods and freight – Bretton Woods Agreements Order in Council 1946 (SR & O 1946 No 36), Sch, Part I, art VIII, s 2(b).

Bank – Documentary credit – Irrevocable credit – Duty of bank on presentation of documents – Non-conforming documents – Bill of lading falsely and fraudulently completed by shipping agent – Beneficiary presenting documents in good faith – Bank aware of falseness – Whether bank obliged to refuse payment – Whether beneficiary's good faith relevant.

In 1975 the seller, an English company, contracted to sell fibreglass making machinery to the buyer, a Peruvian company concerned in the glass fibre industry. The terms of the contract, although having all the appearances of a genuine sale fob United Kingdom port, involved (i) the buyer (at its suggestion) paying the seller double the price originally quoted, (ii) the seller agreeing to remit the excess price to the credit of an associate company of the buyer at a bank in the United States of America, and (iii) the price being paid by an irrevocable letter of credit issued by a Peruvian bank. Payment was to be made as to 20% with the order, as to 70% against shipping documents and as to 10% on completion of erection of the machinery. The buyer arranged the transaction in that way so that not only could it acquire the machinery but also its associate company could acquire in the United States of America a large quantity of United States dollars for which the buyer, through the Peruvian bank, would pay in Peruvian currency. The excess price was to be held beneficially for the buyer by its associate company. Such a scheme was not illegal in the United Kingdom, but it was illegal under Peruvian law which made it an offence for Peruvian residents to maintain or establish foreign currency accounts in Peru or abroad or to overvalue imports and obligations payable in foreign currency in violation of Peruvian exchange control regulations. In accordance with the scheme the buyer, using the inflated invoice, obtained permission to buy the United States dollars; it then opened a letter of credit with the Peruvian bank, which in turn arranged with the defendant, a bank in England, to open a confirmed irrevocable letter of credit in favour of the seller, payable in London. The seller collected the first 20% of the inflated price under the terms of the letter of credit and duly remitted half the dollars to the buyer's associate company at its bank in the United States of America. The machinery was shipped on 16th December 1976, but the shipping agent, who was aware that the letter of credit required shipment no later than 15th December 1976, falsely and fraudulently, but not as agent of the seller or of a merchant bank to which it had assigned the letter of credit, entered the date of shipment on the bill of lading as 15th December 1976. When the merchant bank presented the shipping documents to the defendant's London branch it refused to pay because it had discovered that the date on the bill of lading was false and that the machinery had been shipped after the contract date. At that stage the defendant was unaware that the transaction infringed Peruvian exchange control regulations. The seller and the assignee of the letter of credit brought an action against the defendant seeking payment of the 70% of the purchase price which was to be paid against the shipping documents. The trial judge rejected the defendant's defence that it was entitled to reject the documents for non-conformity with the terms of the credit and fraud, but he refused to give judgment for the plaintiffs on the ground that the letter of credit was unenforceable under the Bretton Woods Agreements Order in Council 1946, which gave force to art VIII, s 2(b)[a] of the Bretton Woods Agreement establishing the International Monetary Fund. He did not decide a further submission that the transaction was illegal and/or unenforceable at common law as intended to achieve an object which was contrary to Peruvian exchange control regulations. The plaintiffs appealed.

Held – (1) Although when considered in isolation the letter of credit contract was a contract to pay dollars against documents, it was in fact a monetary transaction in disguise, namely an agreement to exchange United States dollars for Peruvian currency. The doubling of the purchase price and the payment of half the doubled price to the buyer's associate company in the United States of America constituted an overpayment and disposition of the surplus, and were thus contrary to the Peruvian exchange control regulations. The court was therefore bound to refuse to give its assistance to the parties and to decline to give judgment for that part of the claim which related to the exchange contract. In the absence of other considerations, there was, however, no reason why the court should not give judgment on the letter of credit (which was not itself illegal or void or unenforceable at common law as intended to achieve an object which was illegal or contrary to public policy) for that sum which constituted payment for the machinery and freight, since that sum was easily identifiable, there was nothing in the 1946 order which rendered that part of the claim unenforceable and the object of the 1946 order would be achieved by refusing judgment for so much of the claim as would frustrate the performance of the exchange contract. Furthermore, the courts of a country which was a party to the Bretton Woods Agreement ought to do their best to promote both international comity and international trade, and that duty could in the circumstances best be carried out by enforcing that part of the contract which did not offend against the law of Peru and refusing to enforce that part of it which was a disguised monetary transaction. It followed that if that had been the only defence to the plaintiffs' claim the

---

a   Section 2(b) is set out at p 149 c, post

court would have allowed the appeal to that extent (see p 150 *c d f* to *j*, p 151 *a* to *c*, p 155 *h* to p 156 *b h j*, p 157 *d* to *f*, p 158 *c*, p 165 *f g*, p 166 *c h j*, p 167 *c f g*, p 168 *c*, p 171 *g h* and p 173 *g* to p 174 *a* and *f* to *h*, post); dicta of Viscount Simonds and of Lord Reid in *Regazzoni v K C Sethia (1944) Ltd* [1957] 3 All ER at 290, 293 applied; *Sharif v Azad* [1966] 3 All ER 785 distinguished.

(2) However, with regard to a letter of credit, a bank was only obliged to pay on the presentation of genuine documents in accordance with the requirements of the letter of credit. Where the documents presented were to the bank's knowledge fraudulently false they were not genuine conforming documents and the bank was obliged to refuse to pay, and the fact that the person who presented the documents had acted in good faith was irrelevant. It followed that, since the date of shipment had been falsely and fraudulently entered on the bill of lading and since the defendant knew that it had been intentionally deceived as to a date material to its liability to pay, it had been right to refuse to honour the plaintiffs' credit. The appeal would accordingly be dismissed (see p 159 *d* to *h*, p 161 *b c*, p 163 *j* to p 165 *b*, p 167 *g* to *j*, p 170 *a* to *j*, p 171 *b*, p 175 *c* to *e* and p 176 *c* to *e*, post); *Edward Owen Engineering Ltd v Barclays Bank International Ltd* [1978] 1 All ER 976 followed.

Notes

For unenforceability of contracts contravening exchange control regulations of countries which are members of the International Monetary Fund, see 32 Halsbury's Laws (4th Edn) para 267.

For tender of documents under a letter of credit, see 3 ibid para 141, and for cases on letters of credit, see 3 Digest (Reissue) 665–670, 4121–4136.

For the Bretton Woods Agreements Act 1945, see 22 Halsbury's Statutes (3rd Edn) 886.

Cases referred to in judgments

Alan (W J) & Co Ltd v El Nasr Export & Import Co [1972] 2 All ER 127, [1972] 2 QB 189, [1972] 2 WLR 800, [1972] 1 Lloyd's Rep 313, CA, Digest (Cont Vol D) 124, 4170a.
Bank of East Asia Ltd v Pang (1926) 249 P 1060.
Bank of Taiwan v Union National Bank of Philadelphia (1924) 1 F 2d 65.
Bank Russo-Iran v Gordon Woodroffe & Co Ltd (1972) Times, 4th October.
Batra v Ebrahim [1977] Court of Appeal Transcript 197B
Buchanan (James) & Co Ltd v Babco Forwarding & Shipping (UK) Ltd [1977] 3 All ER 1048, [1978] AC 141, [1977] 3 WLR 967, [1978] RTR 59, [1978] 1 Lloyd's Rep 119, [1978] CMLR 156, HL; *affg* [1977] 1 All ER 158, [1977] 2 WLR 107, [1977] RTR 457, [1977] 2 CMLR 455, [1977] 1 Lloyd's Rep 234, CA, Digest (Cont Vol E) 36, 1435.
Chao (trading as Zung Fu Co) v British Traders and Shippers Ltd (NV Handelmaatschappij J Smits Import-Export, third party) [1954] 1 All ER 779, [1954] 2 QB 459, [1954] 2 WLR 365, [1954] 1 Lloyd's Rep 16, 39 Digest (Repl) 720, 2047.
Clifford (Frank W) Ltd v Garth [1956] 2 All ER 323, [1956] 1 WLR 570, CA, 17 Digest (Reissue) 504, 184.
Continental National Bank v National City Bank of New York (1934) 69 F 2d 312.
De Beeche v South American Stores (Gath & Chaves) Ltd [1935] AC 148, [1934] All ER Rep 284, 104 LJKB 101, 152 LT 309, 40 Com Cas 157, HL, 11 Digest (Reissue) 485, 894.
Dennis & Co Ltd v Munn [1949] 1 All ER 616, [1949] 2 KB 327, [1949] LJR 857, CA, 17 Digest (Reissue) 503, 179.
Equitable Trust Co of New York v Dawson & Partners Ltd (1927) 27 Ll L Rep 49, HL.
Etablissement Esefka International Anstalt v Central Bank of Nigeria [1979] 1 Lloyd's Rep 445, CA, Digest (Cont Vol E) 334, 79f.
Fielding & Platt Ltd v Najjar [1969] 2 All ER 150, [1969] 1 WLR 357, CA, 6 Digest (Reissue) 139, 994.
Foster v Driscoll [1929] KB 470, [1928] All ER Rep 130, 98 LJKB 282, 140 LT 479, CA, 6 Digest (Reissue) 66, 578.

Gian Singh & Co Ltd v Banque de l'Indochine [1974] 2 All ER 754, [1974] 1 WLR 1234,
a   [1974] 1 Lloyd's Rep 1, PC, 3 Digest (Reissue) 670, *3138.
Guaranty Trust Co of New York v Van Den Berghs Ltd (1925) 22 Ll L Rep 58.
Harbottle (R D) (Mercantile) Ltd v National Westminster Bank Ltd [1977] 2 All ER 862,
    [1978] QB 146, [1977] 3 WLR 752, 3 Digest (Reissue) 669, *4134.*
Intraworld Industries Inc v Girard Trust Bank (1975) 336 A 2d 316
Jackson Stansfield & Sons v Butterworth [1948] 2 All ER 558, 112 JP 377, 46 LGR 410, CA,
b   17 Digest (Reissue) 503, *178.*
Laudisi v American Exchange National Bank (1924) 239 NY 234, 146 NE 347.
Malas (trading as Hamzeh Malas & Sons) v British Imex Industries Ltd [1958] 1 All ER 262,
    [1958] 2 QB 127, [1958] 2 WLR 100, [1957] 2 Lloyd's Rep 549, CA, 3 Digest (Reissue)
    667, *4129.*
Napier v National Business Agency Ltd [1951] 2 All ER 264, 44 R & IT 413, 30 ATC 180,
c   CA, 12 Digest (Reissue) 302, *2177.*
New York Life Insurance Co v Hartford National Bank & Trust Co (1977) 173 Conn 492, 378
    A 2d 562.
North Wales Produce and Supply Co Ltd, Re [1922] 2 Ch 340, [1922] All ER Rep 730, 91 LJ
    Ch 415, 127 LT 288, [1922] B & CR 12, 7 Digest (Reissue) 32, *160.*
Old Colony Trust Co v Lawyers Title & Trust Co (1924) 297 F 152.
d   *O'Meara (Maurice) Co v National Park Bank of New York* (1925) 239 NY 386, 39 ALR 747,
    146 NE 636.
Owen (Edward) Engineering Ltd v Barclays Bank International Ltd [1978] 1 All ER 976,
    [1978] QB 159, [1977] 3 WLR 764, CA, Digest (Cont Vol E) 18, *4136a.*
Ralli Brothers v Compañia Naviera Sota y Aznar [1920] 2 KB 287, [1920] All ER Rep 427,
    89 LJKB 999, 123 LT 375, 15 Asp MLC 33, 25 Com Cas 227, CA, 11 Digest (Reissue)
e   476, *843.*
Regazzoni v K C Sethia (1944) Ltd [1957] 3 All ER 286, [1958] AC 301, [1957] 3 WLR 572,
    [1957] 2 Lloyd's Rep 289, HL, 11 Digest (Reissue) 484, *892.*
Schlisselman v Rubin [1951] WN 530.
Sharif v Azad [1966] 3 All ER 785, [1967] 1 QB 605, [1966] 3 WLR 1285, CA, 17 Digest
    (Reissue) 512, *213.*
f   *Société Métallurgique d'Aubrives & Villerupt v British Bank for Foreign Trade* (1922) 11 Ll L
    Rep 168.
Southwestern Shipping Corpn v National City Bank of New York (1959) 6 NY 2d 454, 190 NY
    2d 352.
Stanton v Brown [1900] 1 QB 671, 69 LJQB 301, 64 JP 326, DC, 12 Digest (Reissue) 328,
    2368.
g   *Sztejn v J Henry Schroder Banking Corpn* (1941) 31 NYS 2d 631.
Toprak Mahsulleri Ofisi v Finagrain Compagnie Commerciale, Agricole et Financière SA [1979]
    2 Lloyd's Rep 98, CA, Digest (Cont Vol E) 111, *3344a.*
United Bank Ltd v Cambridge Sporting Goods Corpn (1976) 41 NY 2d 254, 360 NE 2d 943,
    392 NYS 2d 265.
United Railways of Havana and Regla Warehouses Ltd, Re [1960] 2 All ER 332, [1961] AC
h   1007, [1960] 2 WLR 969, HL, 11 Digest (Reissue) 489, *919.*
United Technologies Corpn v Citibank NA (1979) 469 F Supp 473.
Wilson, Smithett & Cope Ltd v Terruzzi [1976] 1 All ER 817, [1976] QB 683, [1976] 2 WLR
    418, [1976] 1 Lloyd's Rep 509, CA; affg [1975] 2 All ER 649, [1976] QB 638, [1975] 2
    WLR 1009, [1975] 1 Lloyd's Rep 642, Digest (Cont Vol E) 178, *213a.*

j   **Cases also cited**
Basse and Selve v Bank of Australasia (1904) 90 LT 618.
Bowes v Shand (1877) 2 App Cas 455, [1874–80] All ER Rep 174, HL.
British Imex Industries Ltd v Midland Bank Ltd [1958] 1 All ER 264, [1958] 1 QB 542.
Discount Records Ltd v Barclays Bank Ltd [1975] 1 All ER 1071, [1975] 1 WLR 315.

Howe Richardson Scale Co Ltd v Polimex-Cekop and National Westminster Bank Ltd [1978] 1
  Lloyd's Rep 161, CA   *a*
Stein v Hambro's Bank of Northern Commerce (1921) 9 Ll L Rep 433, 507; *rvsd* 10 Ll L Rep
  529, CA.
Urquhart Lindsay & Co Ltd v Eastern Bank Ltd [1922] 1 KB 318, [1921] All ER Rep 340.

Appeal

By a writ dated 17th January 1977 the plaintiffs, United City Merchants (Investments) *b*
Ltd ('United City Merchants') and Glass Fibres and Equipments Ltd ('Glass Fibres')
brought an action against the defendants, Royal Bank of Canada, a bank incorporated in
Canada and carrying on business in London and other places, claiming $US494,537·59
or alternatively, damages in respect of an irrevocable transferable letter of credit issued
by Banco Continental SA of Lima, Peru ('Banco') on instructions from Vitrorefuerzos SA
of Lima, Peru ('Vitro') and confirmed by the defendants for $US794,502·20 in favour of *c*
Glass Fibres, which, on 22nd July 1976, assigned all their rights, entitlements, benefits
and payments thereunder to United City Merchants. By notice dated 15th June 1977
and subsequently amended the defendants joined Vitro as first third parties to the action,
and by notice dated 7th July 1977 the defendants added Banco as second third parties.
On 18th May 1978 Mocatta J rejected the defendants' defence that they had been entitled
to reject the shipping documents presented to them by United City Merchants on the *d*
grounds of non-conformity with the terms of the credit and fraud, but he adjourned the
trial in order to hear argument on an amendment to their defence sought by Banco,
which amendment the judge granted on 21st February 1978. On 12th October 1978 at
the direction of Mocatta J Vitro's solicitors, who had received no further instructions and
had been provided with no further funds, ceased to act for Vitro and Vitro thereafter
took no further part in the proceedings. On 12th March 1979 Mocatta J gave judgment *e*
for the defendants on the ground that the letter of credit was unenforceable by virtue of
the Bretton Woods Agreements Act 1945 and the Bretton Woods Agreements Order in
Council 1946 but he did not decide whether the letter of credit was illegal and/or
unenforceable at common law as intended to achieve an object which was contrary to
Peruvian law relating to foreign currency. The plaintiffs appealed. By an agreement
between the defendants and Banco, and with the leave of the court, Banco was the *f*
respondent to the appeal and the defendants were not represented thereat. By a
respondent's notice dated 2nd December 1980 Banco sought to uphold Mocatta J's
judgment on the grounds (i) that the letter of credit was illegal and/or unenforceable at
common law as being intended to achieve an object which was illegal and/or contrary to
public policy and (ii) that the defendants had been entitled to reject the shipping
documents. The facts are set out in the judgment of Stephenson LJ.   *g*

David Hirst QC and *Anthony Blair* for the plaintiffs.
Christopher Staughton QC and *Richard Wood* for Banco.

                                                                       Cur adv vult
                                                                              h
13th March. The following judgments were read.

STEPHENSON LJ. On 12th March 1979 Mocatta J dismissed an action by the
plaintiffs ('United City Merchants' and 'Glass Fibres') against the defendants, the Royal
Bank of Canada. The action was brought by writ dated 17th January 1977 for payment
under an irrevocable transferable letter of credit, issued by the second third party *j*
('Banco') on instructions from the first third party ('Vitro') and confirmed by the
defendants, for the amount of $US794,502·20 in favour of Glass Fibres for the account of
Vitro. Vitro, a Peruvian company, had agreed in 1975 to buy plant and equipment for
manufacturing glass fibre from Glass Fibres, an English company. The purchase was to
be financed by this letter of credit. Shipment was to be from London to Callao in Peru

on or before (after an extension) 15th December 1976; payment was to be made in
a London by the defendants' London branch by sight drafts against clean bills of lading on
or before (after an extension) 31st December 1976.

On 22nd July 1976 Glass Fibres assigned the rights and benefits of the letter of credit
to United City Merchants. On 16th December 1976 the goods were shipped in the
American Accord, not from London but from Felixstowe, not on 15th December 1976
but on 16th December 1976. On 20th December 1976 United City Merchants presented
b the documents to the defendants, who rejected them. On 22nd December United City
Merchants presented amended documents to the defendants, who again rejected them.
So the writ was issued by the plaintiffs, and the defendants got leave in RSC Ord 14
proceedings to defend and joined the third parties. The trial of the action began on 6th
February 1978 on the defendants' arguable defence that they were entitled to reject the
documents on two grounds, non-conformity with the terms of the credit and fraud, and
c after 32 days and two further defences Mocatta J rejected that defence. His judgment on
all those issues is reported in *The American Accord* [1979] 1 Lloyd's Rep 267. But he was
unable to give judgment for the plaintiffs on their claim because of an amendment asked
for by the second third party and granted on 21st February 1978.

This amendment was adopted by the defendants, and by agreement the judge
proceeded to decide the other issues and postponed the trial of the issues raised by the
d amendment. The second trial took place a year later in January 1979. The issues were
argued between United City Merchants standing in the shoes of Glass Fibres and Banco
standing in the shoes of the defendants. They were that the letter of credit was
unenforceable by virtue of the Bretton Woods Agreements Act 1945 and the Bretton
Woods Agreements Order in Council 1946, SR & O 1946 No 36, and was illegal and/or
unenforceable at common law as intended to achieve an object which was contrary to
e Peruvian law relating to foreign currency.

In a reserved judgment given on 12th March 1979 ([1979] 2 Lloyd's Rep 498) Mocatta
J 'after considerable hesitation' decided the first issue in favour of Banco and without
deciding the second issue gave judgment for the defendants. Hence this appeal.

By the respondent's notice Banco, still in the defendants' shoes, ask that if the plaintiffs
succeed in persuading this court that the judge was wrong on the first issue his judgment
f should be affirmed on the ground that Banco's argument on the second issue should be
accepted or that the judge's first judgment in the plaintiffs' favour was wrong and the
defendants should succeed on the issues there decided against them.

The first question to be decided is whether the judge was right in holding in his second
judgment 'that the court should not, by enforcing the confirmed credit, enable the
Bretton Woods Agreements Order in Council to be avoided'. The main argument of
g counsel for the plaintiffs was that the judge and this court are bound by the authority of
Sharif v Azad [1966] 3 All ER 785, [1967] 1 QB 605 to enforce the letter of credit in this
case and the judge was wrong to distinguish that case. But if that authority was
distinguishable counsel submitted that the judge was wrong not to give effect to the
autonomy of an irrevocable letter of credit, clearly recognised in his first judgment, by
giving his second judgment in the plaintiffs' favour.

h The judge summarised the facts relevant to the issues canvassed at the second trial in
his second judgment. Neither these facts nor the inferences he drew from them are
challenged by either party to this appeal. They can be shortly restated.

In October 1975 Mr Olguin, a resident in Peru, a director, general manager and
majority shareholder of Vitro, the Peruvian company, and apparently also manager of an
associated company called Nanke International Corpn of Panama ('Nanke'), with offices
j in Miami in the United States of America called on Glass Fibres London office and met
their sales director Mr McFarlane. After a visit to Glass Fibres' factory at Malvern, a
further meeting resulted in Glass Fibres submitting a quotation to another of Mr Olguin's
companies for one glass fibre forming plant, output 225 tons per annum, total fob UK
port $US256,043. Mr Olguin then asked Mr McFarlane to double the price of the
quotation and make it out to Nanke, giving as his reason that it would simplify matters

for him to open only one letter of credit and the balance could be used to purchase other equipment. Mr Hadi, Glass Fibres' managing director, to whom Mr McFarlane referred *a* the matter, regarded the suggestion as unusual, but was told by Mr McFarlane that Mr Olguin had explained that it would make it easier for him to get the necessary consents and permissions in one go, and Mr Hadi agreed to the project going forward on Mr Olguin's terms, which Mr Olguin then requested should be altered by substituting Vitro for Nanke.

The result was a revised quotation of 14th October 1975 submitted to Vitro for exactly *b* the same 12 items each priced double and a resulting total fob UK port of $US512,086, increased by another $150,000 for glass making equipment fob UK port to $662,086.

The terms of payment were 30% with order, 60% against shipping documents and 10% on completion of erection. Then came a telex from Vitro to Glass Fibres that Peruvian government regulations permitted only 20% with the order and 70% against shipping documents. This was followed by Mr McFarlane in November visiting Vitro *c* and Banco in Peru and Banco arranging to find credit for $662,086, and Mr McFarlane and Mr Olguin meeting in Miami in the office of Nanke. The result was a letter to Glass Fibres signed by Mr Olguin for Vitro and dated 20th November 1975 in these terms (it is headed Nanke International Corpn and addressed to Glass Fibres and Equipment Ltd):

'Dear Sirs,

'Re: Our order for 225 Ton Glass Fibre Plant   *d*

'We are pleased to confirm that credit as agreed is being opened by our bankers – BANCO CONTINENTAL – LIMA – PERU. We shall be obliged if you will kindly confirm that 50% of the credit value (excluding that part being cost of freight) is remitted within 10 days of negotiation of credit (including draw down as arranged), to.— NANKE INTERNATIONAL CORPORATION for account no 205–00067 BANKERS TRUST INTERNATIONAL (MIAMI) CORP. 1 Biscayne Tower – Miami – Florida 233131. Thank *e* you for your cooperation,

'Signed for – VITRO REFUERZOS S.A.

'Eudoro A. Olguin
'DIRECTOR.'

In capital letters there is then typed: *f*

'WE CONFIRM THAT THE ORDER IS ACCEPTED SUBJECT TO THE ABOVE MENTIONED TERMS AND CONDITIONS – AND GLASS FIBRES AND EQUIPMENT LTD. OF ENGLAND UNDERTAKES TO REMIT THE RESPECTIVE AMOUNTS AS AGREED –

'signed for and on behalf of Glass Fibres and Equipment Ltd.

'J. T. McFarlane
'Director' *g*

Mr Hadi and Mr McFarlane for Glass Fibres, signed this addition at the foot of the letter, as I have said.

So came about four contracts: (1) the contract between Glass Fibres and Vitro, on its face a contract for the sale and purchase of goods; (2) a contract between Vitro and Banco in December 1975 for the opening of an irrevocable transferable letter of credit in favour *h* of Glass Fibres for account of Vitro up to the sum of $662,086, 'for financing with 80% F.O.B. plus freight, at 5 years'; (3) a contract between Banco and the defendants in March 1976 by which the defendants agreed to confirm the letter of credit, which Banco opened; (4) the contract between the defendants as confirming bankers and Glass Fibres as beneficiaries of the letter of credit of 30th March 1976, which is the contract sued on.

United City Merchants drew on the letter of credit by arranging for one half of the *j* 'draw down' of 20% of the fob value, namely $66,208.60, to be paid to Nanke in dollars in accordance with the first contract. The 10% has been remitted to the United States of America, all the goods have reached Peru, but Vitro have not taken delivery of any of them and the plaintiffs have not received any payment for them. The balance the defendants have refused to pay, and I now consider the first of the grounds on which they ask the court to uphold their refusal.

The defendants claim that—

'the sale Contract and the letter of credit opened pursuant thereto were monetary transactions involving the manipulation of currencies disguised as an agreement for the sale and purchase of goods. In the premises, the said contract and credit were exchange contracts within Art VIII 2(b) of the Bretton Woods Agreement; and are unenforceable in England by reason of the Bretton Woods Agreements Order in Council 1946, being contrary to the Exchange Control Regulations of a signatory to the said Agreement, namely Peru . . .'

That Order in Council made under the Bretton Woods Agreements Act 1945, gives by art 3 and the schedule the force of law to art VIII, s 2(b) of the agreement for the establishment of the International Monetary Fund. That article provides:

'Exchange contracts which involve the currency of any Member and which are contrary to the exchange control regulations of that member maintained or imposed consistently with this Agreement shall be unenforceable in the territories of any member . . .'

The defendants claim that the regulations of Peru which will be contravened if the letter of credit is enforced are the following:

(1) Articles 1 and 18 of Decree Law 18275 of 15th May 1970 which provides:

'1. From the date hereafter it is prohibited for individuals or corporations resident in Peru, with the exception of Banco Central de Reserva del Peru and Banco de la Nacion, to maintain or establish deposits in a foreign currency in banks and other institutions in this country and/or abroad.

'18. It is an offence of fraud against the State to maintain foreign currency or to perform any type of operation prohibited by this Decree Law.

'19. The offence referred to in the preceding article shall be punished with imprisonment for not less than one year nor more than five years, with the additional penalty of forfeiture to the State of the sums which are the subject matter of the offence plus a fine of ten times the amount of the fraud. Directors administrators or managers who have legal representation of a corporation responsible for the maintenance or operations aforesaid shall be penalised as principals . . .'

(2) Article 7 of Decree Law 18891 of 17th June 1971 which provides:

'The over-valuing of imports and obligations payable in a foreign currency, as well as the under-valuing of exports, in violation of what is provided for in the Foreign Currency Certificates Regulations, constitutes the offence of fraud damaging to the State. Any offence referred to in the previous paragraph shall be penalised as stated in Article 19 of Decree Law 18275.'

There is no challenge to the judge's findings on the facts and the evidence of Dr Rodriguez, a Peruvian lawyer, that if the whole of the letter of credit transaction had been carried through, $331,043 would have found its way to the account of Nanke in the Bankers Trust at Miami, that the $66,208·60 which did reach Nanke—

'was held beneficially for Vitro and that, as Dr. Rodriguez said, would constitute a breach of art. 1 [and] that if Vitro, as they did, initiated from Peru the letter of credit by Banco, which was confirmed by the Royal Bank of Canada, under arrangements made by them for siphoning off about half the amount of credit in dollars to an account in Miami held to their benefit, they thereby committed a breach of art. 1 in Peru.'

(See [1979] 2 Lloyd's Rep 498 at 502.)

I would also hold, if it were necessary to do so, that implicit in his judgment is a finding that in doubling the dollar price of these goods there was a violation of art 7 in accordance with the Peruvian lawyer's evidence.

These violations of Peruvian law were going to result, as the judge found (at 503) in 'the receipt by Nanke on behalf of Vitro of a large quantity of United States dollars which Vitro, through Banco, would have had to repay over a period of five years by selling Peruvian soles for dollars'. How far Glass Fibres knowingly abetted or participated in those violations may be to some extent uncertain, but there can be no quarrel with his findings that Mr Hadi and Mr McFarlane were prepared to close their eyes to the obvious implications of what Mr Olguin was asking them to do. Both plaintiffs knew that they were required to hold to the order of Bankers Trust International (Miami) Corpn the sum of not less than $200,000 from the net proceeds of full production and negotiation of documents as called for under the letter of credit and United City Merchants, after being asked by Glass Fibres to treat the agreements relating to that sum as 'very strictly confidential', described it to the defendants as 'commission monies' to be remitted to Nanke, to enable the defendants to obtain the Bank of England's permission to remit it. On these facts and findings is the court now being asked by enforcing the confirmed credit to enforce an exchange contract (or exchange contracts) declared unenforceable by art VIII, s 2(b)?

If the letter of credit contract between Glass Fibres and the defendants is considered in isolation, it is a contract to pay dollars against documents. It contains no agreement to exchange one currency for another. And that is what an 'exchange contract' is. In *Sharif v Azad* Lord Denning MR adopted a wider definition suggested by Dr Mann, but in *Wilson, Smithett & Cope Ltd v Terruzzi* [1976] 1 All ER 817, [1976] QB 683 he recanted and with the concurrence of the other members of the court preferred a narrower definition accepted by Kerr J ([1975] 2 All ER 649 at 658–663, [1976] QB 683 at 696–702) and derived from the judgment of Lord Radcliffe in *Re United Railways of Havana and Regla Warehouses Ltd* [1960] 2 All ER 322 at 350, [1961] AC 1007 at 1059 and from an article by Dr Nussbaum in 1949 (59 Yale LJ 421). Exchange contracts are not 'contracts which in any way affect a country's exchange resources' (as Dr Mann defined them in the Legal Aspect of Money (3rd Edn, 1971 p 441)); but 'contracts to exchange the currency of one country for the currency of another', and 'contracts involving securities or merchandise cannot be considered as exchange contracts except when they are monetary transactions in disguise'.

I accept, as we are bound to accept, that a contract will be an exchange contract if it is a monetary transaction in disguise, that is in reality an agreement to exchange currencies though disguised as an agreement to do something else. But considered in isolation the plaintiffs' contract with the defendants is not that: it is what it seems, an agreement to pay money against documents.

But it has come into existence to pay the dollars required by the underlying contract of sale. It is a necessary step on the way towards an ultimate exchange of United States dollars for Peruvian soles. It is part and parcel of a scheme to defeat the Peruvian exchange control regulations. If it is enforced by ordering the defendants to pay dollars to the plaintiffs, its enforcement would enable Vitro through Banco to exchange currencies contrary to the laws of Peru. True it is that the first contract between Glass Fibres and Vitro is a contract of sale and purchase of goods, but that contract itself contains two terms which betray the wolf of an unenforceable exchange contract in the sheep's clothing of an enforceable sale contract: the doubling of the genuine purchase price and the payment of half the doubled price to Nanke in the United States of America. These terms, the overpayment and the disposition of the surplus, are contrary to the exchange control regulations of Peru, and those regulations are admittedly maintained or imposed consistently with the Bretton Woods Agreement. Those terms therefore make the sale agreement a monetary transaction in disguise, at least in part. If that mixed contract is not in itself an exchange contract it is one if considered as another necessary step in carrying out the scheme to defeat the Peruvian currency regulations.

I venture to doubt whether it is right to split up art VIII, s 2(b) into compartments and ask: is it an exchange contract? If it is, does it involve the currency of any member? I would ask whether a contract is an exchange contract involving the currency of Peru, and

I would answer that both the first and the last contracts are such contracts because they involve ultimately the exchange of soles for the dollars which they stipulated, and so, in the words of Shaw LJ in *Wilson, Smithett & Cope Ltd v Terruzzi* [1976] 1 All ER 817 at 832, [1976] QB 683 at 725, 'though ostensibly made for other purposes, had the object and ultimate outcome of bringing about an exchange of currencies'. But I would agree that the connection between the contract and the exchange is closer in the sale contract than in the letter of credit contract and that the unusual provisions of the sale contract call for explanation by the surrounding circumstances whereas there is nothing unusual in the provisions of the contract sued on.

I accordingly agree with Mocatta J ([1979] 2 Lloyd's Rep 498 at 504) that the sale contract 'can be described as constituting an exchange contract by being a monetary transaction in disguise contrary to the exchange control regulations of Peru and as being rendered unenforceable by the 1946 Order in Council'. But that, though in the forefront of the plaintiffs' notice of appeal, is not their counsel's main submission in this court. His main submission for the plaintiffs is that, whatever the nature of the sale contract, it has no relevance to the contract sued on. That is a separate, independent, autonomous contract, and the defendants are not concerned with the sale contract or any underlying contract or anything but the documents against which they have promised to pay.

The independence of an irrevocable letter of credit contract is well established and commercially important. It is one of a number of irrevocable obligations assumed by bankers, of which guarantees and performance bonds are others.

'Credits, by their nature, are separate transactions from the sales or other contracts on which they may be based and banks are in no way concerned with or bound by such contracts.' So much is clearly stated in the general provisions and definitions of the Uniform Customs and Practice for Documentary Credits of the International Chamber of Commerce (1974 revision, ICC Publication 290), art 8(a) of which declares: 'In documentary credit operations all parties concerned deal in documents and not in goods.' The nature of a confirmed letter of credit is expounded in a classic passage of the judgment of Jenkins LJ in *Malas (trading as Hamzeh Malas & Sons) v British Imex Industries Ltd* [1958] 1 All ER 262 at 263, [1958] 2 QB 127 at 129:

'We were referred to several authorities, and it seems to be plain that the opening of a confirmed letter of credit constitutes a bargain between the banker and the vendor of the goods, which imposes on the banker an absolute obligation to pay, irrespective of any dispute which there may be between the parties whether the goods are up to contract or not. An elaborate commercial system has been built up on the footing that bankers' confirmed credits are of that character, and, in my judgment, it would be wrong for this court in the present case to interfere with that established practice. It has also to be remembered that a vendor of goods selling against a confirmed letter of credit is selling under the assurance that nothing will prevent him from receiving the price. That is of no mean advantage when goods manufactured in one country are being sold in another. Furthermore, vendors are often re-selling goods bought from third parties. When they are doing that, and when they are being paid by a confirmed letter of credit, their practice—and I think it was followed by the defendants in this case—is to finance the payments necessary to be made to their suppliers against the letter of credit. That system of financing these operations, as I see it, would break down completely if a dispute as between the vendor and the purchaser was to have the effect of "freezing", if I may use that expression, the sum in respect of which the letter of credit was opened.'

Such irrevocable obligations assumed by banks as irrevocable confirmed letters of credit, guarantees and performance bonds are 'the lifeblood of international commerce, ... collateral to the underlying rights and obligations between the merchants at either end of the banking chain', and are to be honoured by banks free from interference by the courts 'if the documents are in order and the terms of the credit are satisfied', except in cases of fraud, an exception to be considered later: see *R D Harbottle (Mercantile) Ltd v*

National Westminster Bank Ltd [1977] 2 All ER 862 at 870, [1978] QB 146 at 155 per Kerr J and *Edward Owen Engineering Ltd v Barclays Bank International Ltd* [1978] 1 All ER 976 esp at 981, [1978] QB 159 esp at 169 per Lord Denning MR.

A letter of credit may be not only irrevocable but transferable, as was this confirmed letter of credit; it is then, as art 46(*a*) of the Uniform Customs and Practice explains—

'a credit under which the beneficiary has the right to give instructions to the bank called upon to, effect payment or acceptance or to any bank entitled to effect negotiation to make the credit available in whole or in part to one or more third parties (second beneficiaries),'

but transferable once only: see art 46(*e*). It is not a negotiable instrument, though it resembles a bill of exchange or a cheque in some respects, for instance, in that, if honoured, payment under it discharges a buyer's debt for the purchase price: see *W J Alan & Co Ltd v El Nasr Export & Import Co* [1972] 2 All ER 127 at 139, [1972] 2 QB 189 at 212 per Lord Denning MR.

We have been referred to a considerable body of authorities, English and American, which state the absolute and unqualified nature of a banker's obligation under a letter of credit to examine with reasonable care the documents which the beneficiary is required to present for payment in order to make sure that they appear on their face to conform to the terms and conditions of the letter of credit, irrespective of whether they conform to the terms of any underlying contract between the beneficiary and the bank's customer, to pay promptly and without question on presentation if they do so conform, and not to pay if they do not conform, however minor the non-conformity. The banker is not obliged to go behind the documents and to consider whether the terms of the underlying contract conform to the terms of the letter of credit or whether they have been or will be performed; he is concerned with documents and what the credit requires them to be, not with goods or the contract which requires them to be paid for. If he does what he is told he is safe; if he refuses to do anything else he is safe; if he departs from the terms and conditions of the credit he acts at his own risk: see *Equitable Trust Co of New York v Dawson & Partners Ltd* (1927) 27 Ll L Rep 49 at 52 per Viscount Sumner and *Gian Singh & Co Ltd v Banque de l'Indochine* [1974] 2 All ER 754 at 757–758, [1974] 1 WLR 1234 at 1238–1239 per Lord Diplock.

This special character of irrevocable letters of credit and a bank's contractual obligations thereunder would, counsel for the plaintiffs submits, be undermined if the court upheld a banker's refusal to honour a particular letter of credit by looking behind, beyond and beneath it to its object and ultimate outcome, or to other contracts connected with it, including exchange contracts. That submission in effect adopts the opinion of Dr Mann in the Legal Aspect of Money (3rd Edn, 1971, p 422) and seeks support in the two authorities to which Dr Mann there refers. Indeed counsel argues that the second case is indistinguishable from this one and binds us to allow his appeal on this point. Dr Mann writes:

'Moreover the test must be complied with by the specific contract in issue so that the existence of an exchange contract cannot be inferred from a variety of different contracts, taken as a whole, none or only some of which, regarded separately, come within the definition. In other words, it is necessary to consider each contract separately rather than the totality of a scheme or an arrangement. In effect the Court of Appeals in New York so decided as early as 1959; a debt of dollars due from a New York bank to a New York corporation is not an exchange contract, even though the dollars held by the bank as well as the assignment to the corporation of the title to the debt were derived from a transaction between other parties involving Italian lira and contrary to Italian law. Similarly the English Court of Appeal held that a sterling cheque drawn on an English bank by a resident of England in favour of another resident of England was not an exchange contract, although it was drawn as a result of and in connection with a transaction involving the currency and infringing the law of Pakistan.'

The words are directed to the erroneous test of what is in an exchange contract which
a was rejected in *Wilson, Smithett & Cope Ltd v Terruzzi*. If they mean what I think they say,
almost every contract constituting a step towards an exchange contract would be
enforceable and the currencies would in fact be illegally exchanged unless the last
contract necessary to carrying out the unlawful exchange required the help of a court of
law to enforce it.   That consequence might be thought to undermine to a surprising
extent this important provision of the Bretton Woods Agreement.   Does either decision
b compel us to adopt it?

In the American case of *South Western Shipping Corpn v National City Bank of New York*
(1959) 6 NY 2d 454, cited by Dr Mann, all the judges of the court seem to have been of
opinion that the defendant bank could have relied on the rule that the court would not
assist a party to an illegal contract to carry out this illegal object, as a defence to the
plaintiffs' claim in negligence and breach of contract in paying out to the wrong person
c (in fact the party to the illegal contract) money deposited with the defendant bank in
furtherance of a breach of Italian currency regulations and art VIII, s 2(*b*) of the Bretton
Woods Agreement.   But the majority, overriding the decisions of both inferior courts,
held that the rule was subject to the applicable exception, supported by citation of
American authorities, that if a party to the illegal transaction (as they regarded an
exchange contract offending against art VIII, s 2(*b*)) turns over money or property to a
d third person (there the defendant bank) for use of the other party to the transaction (there
the plaintiffs) the latter can enforce the express or implied promise or trust of the third
party and the third person, as a mere depository or conduit, has no defence of illegality
to the plaintiffs' claim.

The majority certainly were able to isolate the contract there sued on from the
connected contracts which infringed the Bretton Woods Agreement, but held that the
e Bretton Woods Agreement added nothing to the common law rule and did not prevail
against the relevant exception.   I find the decision of little help in deciding whether we
should isolate this contract sued on.

Nearer the present case and less easily distinguishable is the English decision to which
Dr Mann refers, *Sharif v Azad* [1966] 3 All ER 785, [1967] 1 QB 605.   There the plaintiff,
a Pakistani citizen resident in England, claimed against the defendant, another Pakistani
f citizen resident in England, £300 on a dishonoured cheque for £300, or alternatively
two dishonoured cheques for £200 and £100 substituted for the original cheque drawn
by him on a bank in England.   Behind this transaction between the plaintiff and the
defendant was an earlier agreement resulting from the desire of one Latif, a Pakistani
resident in Pakistan but on a visit to England, to take rupees out of Pakistan without the
permission of the Pakistan State Bank contrary to Pakistan currency regulations.   To
g enable him to do this the plaintiff had given him £300 in sterling in cash and received
in return a cheque for 6,000 Pakistan rupees drawn on Latif's bank in Pakistan by Latif,
but with the payee's name left blank.   That rupees cheque the plaintiff took to the
defendant who, or perhaps someone on his behalf, filled in the name of the payee as his
brother, an Azad resident in Pakistan, and sent it out to him there to collect the rupees
from Latif's bank.   The defendant's defence in the county court was that the plaintiff had
h agreed with him to deliver to him the rupees cheque in consideration of the defendant's
delivering to the plaintiff the £stg300 cheque sued on; the object of the transactions, as
the plaintiff well knew, was to enable Latif to take money out of Pakistan contrary to
Pakistan currency regulations and they were therefore illegal in that they had that illegal
object and/or were contrary to public policy.   The county court judge decided that there
was nothing illegal in the cheque transaction in that it took place wholly in England, and
j he gave judgment for the plaintiff.

The defendant appealed, mainly on the ground that the judge was wrong in holding
that the transaction between the plaintiff and the defendant was not tainted with this
illegality.   But at the hearing his counsel referred the court to the Bretton Woods
Agreements Act 1945 and the Order in Council, and after adjourning to consider further
submissions on art VIII, s 2(*b*) the court in reserved judgments dismissed the appeal.

The similarities between that case and this are striking. Looked at in isolation the
contract sued on was legal and enforceable, as the judge held. Underlying it was the *a*
contract between the plaintiff and Latif to exchange cheques, which constituted a breach
of the currency regulations by Latif as a resident in Pakistan. To come into being was the
collection of the rupees from Latif's bank in Pakistan and their remittances from
Pakistan contrary to the laws of Pakistan unless permitted by the state bank. But there
are also striking differences. The defendant's brother in Pakistan did get permission to
have the rupees cheque credited, though the rupees were put into a blocked account and *b*
not paid out to him. Though the defendant postdated his sterling cheque to give time
for his brother to get paid on the rupees cheque, payment of the £300 to the plaintiff was
not a necessary step towards the breach of the Pakistan currency regulations and so
unenforceable by art VIII, s 2(*b*). Finally the action was on a cheque, not a letter of
credit. A cheque is a negotiable instrument; a letter of credit, though transferable, is
not. A cheque is a bill of exchange to which special provisions of the Bills of Exchange *c*
Act 1882 apply. It was pointed out by counsel for the plaintiffs that a letter of credit
more easily separates itself from a series of connected transactions than a cheque because
the confirming bank is a stranger to the sale transaction and its obligation to pay is not
defeated by absence of consideration. But the legal effects of treating bills of exchange
such as cheques as equivalent to cash are well known, and all three judges, most clearly
Diplock LJ, appear to have rested their judgments on the fact that the plaintiff was suing *d*
not on any contract but on the cheque issued in performance of the contract between the
plaintiff and the defendant (see [1966] 3 All ER 785 at 787, 790, 791, [1967] 1 QB 605 at
614, 619, 620). Diplock LJ regarded the plaintiff as a holder in due course for value of a
bill of exchange not affected with illegality. And both Diplock and Russell LJJ attached
importance to the rupees cheque being met, though blocked (see [1966] 3 All ER 785 at
790, 791, [1967] 1 QB 605 at 619, 620). They all appear to have held, as stated in the *e*
headnote (see [1967] 1 QB 605 at 606) but contrary to Dr Mann's interpretation of the
decision, that the £300 cheque transaction, or the contract represented by that cheque,
was an exchange contract (in Dr Mann's wider sense), as were the contracts relating to the
rupees cheque between Latif and the plaintiff and between Latif and successive holders
of it.

I find the decision and its ratio not altogether easy to follow in more senses than one. *f*

This court has twice since considered *Sharif's* case and the effect of this article on
contracts sued on. In *Wilson, Smithett & Cope Ltd v Terruzzi* [1976] 1 All ER 817, [1976]
QB 683 the court decided that contracts for the sale and purchase of metals between
brokers on the London Metal Exchange and a dealer in Italy, who entered into them in
breach of Italian exchange control regulations, were legitimate commercial contracts
and, though involving the currency of Italy, were not contracts to exchange one currency *g*
for another and were therefore enforceable by the brokers. As they were not 'exchange
contracts', art VIII, s 2(*b*) had no application. But *Sharif's* case was considered both by
Kerr J and the Court of Appeal. I have already mentioned the substitution of the
narrower definition of exchange contracts for that adopted in *Sharif's* case. Kerr J
referred also to Azad's defence of art VIII, s 2(*b*) in this way ([1975] 2 All ER 649 at 661,
[1976] QB 683 at 699):   *h*

'The unanimous decision of the court was that this defence failed because the
contracts between the plaintiff and defendant represented by the sterling cheques
were not in contravention of the Pakistan foreign exchange regulations since both
of these parties were resident in England. To a continental lawyer this might
appear as a somewhat surprising result, because the giving of these cheques was *j*
clearly part of an overall exchange transaction which might well be considered as
falling within the object of art VIII, s 2(*b*). But to an English lawyer the decision
would appear correct and logical because we tend to favour a more precise analytical
approach to construction and interpretation. One must then go to the judgments
to see to what extent they assist in a case such as the present, bearing in mind that

a on the facts of that case the contracts in question were clearly "exchange contracts" in the ordinary sense of that term.'

In the Court of Appeal Lord Denning MR said that Kerr J had 'covered the whole subject most satisfactorily'. Ormrod LJ said that in *Sharif*'s case 'this court was concerned with contracts which, quite clearly, were "exchange contracts" in the sense in which the phrase was sued by Lord Radcliffe'. And Shaw LJ said: 'On the facts of that case the

b contracts under consideration did amount to exchange contracts in the narrower sense of the expression; therefore they *did* affect the country's exchange resources.' (See [1976] 1 All ER 817 at 823, 824, 832, [1976] QB 683 at 714, 715, 725.)

These references to contracts by the Lords Justices must, I think, refer, like Kerr J's reference, to the two contracts represented by the two cheques given by Azad to Sharif, and if so support my interpretation of the *Sharif* decision to some extent. All three

c judges who dealt with the decision in *Sharif*'s case treated it as unanimously deciding that an exchange contract represented by two cheques was not in contravention of the Pakistan foreign exchange regulations because both parties were resident in England, although the giving of the cheques was clearly part of an overall exchange transaction which might well be considered within the object of art VIII, s 2 (*b*).

In *Batra v Ebrahim* [1977] Court of Appeal Transcript 197B this court held, when the

d point was taken for the first time, that art VIII, s 2(*b*) applied. They held that two contracts by each of which the plaintiff, an Indian in England, agreed to pay cheques in sterling to the defendant, another Indian in England, and the defendant agreed to pay in exchange Indian rupees in India to him or for his benefit when he went to India, contrary to the Indian foreign exchange regulations, were exchange contracts offending against art VIII, s 2(*b*) and unenforceable here for that reason.

e Both Lord Denning MR and Lawton LJ held that it was the duty of the court to take the point of unenforceability under the article, like illegality and not like unenforceability in the contrasting sense in the Statute of Frauds for instance, where it is only for the court to consider the point if it is taken by the defendant. The plaintiff was not suing on either of his cheques but on the defendant's promises to repay him in rupees, yet Lord Denning MR seems to speak of the two transactions (meaning the plaintiff's payments by cheque

f and the defendant's agreement to repay in rupees) as contrary to the Indian regulations and the Bretton Woods Agreement, though he regarded money paid under such agreements as probably recoverable if the consideration had wholly failed. The only reference to *Sharif v Azad* throws no light on its ratio decidendi but gives valuable guidance on what 'unenforceable' means.

I think that *Sharif*'s case depended on its special facts and the law applicable to cheques

g and should not be applied to enforce every action on a letter of credit. I agree with the judge that the case was considered in relation to s 30 of the Bills of Exchange Act 1882, and on this basis the court found no difficulty in giving effect to the cheque. The case does not decide that every contract made in England by parties resident in England is outside art VIII, s 2(*b*), as *Batra v Ebrahim* demonstrates. The court must examine the particular contract sued on and its connection with the alleged breach of foreign currency

h regulations. If its 'involves' those regulations and their breach (and 'involves' is a wide word: see *Regazzoni v K C Sethia (1944) Ltd* [1957] 3 All ER 286 at 297, [1958] AC 301 at 330 per Lord Somervell) it may offend against the article and be unenforceable, whether or not it is an exchange contract when looked at in isolation.

For these reasons I feel free to distinguish *Sharif*'s case and to consider whether the court is required by the nature of a letter of credit to look at it in all cases and

j circumstances, including the circumstances of this case, in isolation from those circumstances and so lend its aid to the enforcement of a contract declared unenforceable by art VIII, s 2(*b*). I do not think that the court is required or entitled to do so. International trade requires the enforcement of letters of credit but international comity requires the enforcement of the Bretton Woods Agreement.

I do not see why a court should shut its eyes to the object of the contract and with its eyes shut fall over backwards to avoid complying with the demands of international comity. On the contrary, the courts of this country should incline the other way and do *a* their best to prevent breaches of the Bretton Woods Agreement, to which this country is a party. In my judgment the courts of a country which is a party to the agreement should do its best to promote both international comity and international trade. I have come to the conclusion that this court could best carry out this double duty in this case by enforcing the part of the sale agreement which does not offend against the law of Peru, and refusing to enforce the part of it which is a disguised monetary transaction by *b* which currencies are to be exchanged in breach of that law. If this were the only defence to the plaintiffs' claim I would therefore proceed to allow the plaintiffs part of their claim.

Before stating my reasons for that conclusion I can however, dispose shortly of counsel's second submission for Banco. This is that the letter of credit was illegal and/or void and/or unenforceable by the common law of England, being intended and designed to achieve an object which was illegal and/or contrary to public policy. This submission *c* was not the subject of a decision by Mocatta J because he upheld counsel's first submission. It is raised by Banco's respondent's notice as the first further ground on which the judge's judgment should be affirmed.

It seeks to apply to this letter of credit the principle stated by this court in *Foster v Driscoll* [1929] 1 KB 470, [1928] All ER Rep 130 and approved and applied by the House of Lords in *Regazzoni v K C Sethia (1944) Ltd*. In the former case no partner in a joint *d* venture, which had as its object the running of whisky into the United States of America contrary to the American prohibition legislation then in force, was allowed to enforce contracts on their face lawfully performable in England. In the latter case, an apparently innocent sale by the defendant to the plaintiff of jute in India cif Genoa was held unenforceable because its purpose was to send it to South Africa in contravention of Indian law.   *e*

The reason for the common law principle and its application is international comity (see [1929] 1 KB 470 at 510, 521, [1928] All ER Rep 130 at 143, 148 per Lawrence and Sankey LJJ and [1957] 3 All ER 286 at 289, 293, 295, [1958] AC 301 at 318, 323, 327 per Viscount Simonds, Lord Reid and Lord Keith); as is the allied but distinct principle that the courts will not enforce a contract in a foreign country if performance has become illegal by the laws of that country: see *Ralli Brothers v Compañía Naviera Sota y Aznar* *f* [1920] 2 KB 287, [1920] All ER Rep 427 and *De Beeche v South American Stores (Gath & Chaves) Ltd* [1935] AC 148, [1934] All ER Rep 284. The principles are helpfully discussed by Robert Goff J in a judgment approved by this court on other points in *Toprak Mahsulleri Ofisi v Finagrain Compagnie Commerciale Agricole et Financière SA* [1979] 2 Lloyd's Rep 98 at 106–107. But, in my judgment, the first principle is no more applicable to this case than the second; even if it were applicable to this case on the facts, *g* it has no application to it in law. Counsel for the plaintiffs is right in submitting that the Bretton Woods Agreement lays down the standard, or requirement, of comity in the area of exchange control which it covers; whether it extends to states who are not members of the International Monetary Fund or parties to the agreement we do not have to consider. Article VIII, s 2(b) displaces the common law principle, as was clearly the opinion of Diplock LJ in *Sharif v Azad* [1966] 3 All ER 785 at 789, [1967] 1 QB 605 at *h* 617, with which I respectfully agree.

There is consequently nothing in these authorities which conflicts with the interpretation put on art VIII, 2(b) in *Batra v Ebrahim* or compels us to regard the breaches of Peruvian exchange control law as so infecting the whole series of contracts with that illegality as to deprive the plaintiffs of their contractual right to any payment. Indeed one of counsel for Banco's own cases furnishes a contrary instance. In *Ralli Brothers v* *j* *Compañía Naviera Sota y Aznar* English charterers chartered a Spanish ship from Spanish shipowners under an English charterparty in London to carry a cargo of jute from Calcutta to Barcelona at a freight of £50 per ton, some of it payable at Barcelona at the current rate of exchange. The charterers were liable under the charterparty to pay the freight to the shipowners if the receivers of the cargo did not pay. A supervening decree of the Spanish Commission of Supplies confirmed by a Royal Proclamation made it

unlawful for the freight on jute to exceed 875 pesetas a tonne, which this freight did.   It
a was therefore illegal by the law of the place of performance, Barcelona, to pay or receive
more than 875 pesetas a tonne and the receivers of the cargo tendered a lawful amount
only; but the shipowners claimed to be paid the full amount including the illegal
excess.   This court decided that the shipowners could not recover the excess.   The
judgments appear to justify the report of the decision in the headnote that the part of the
contract which required the payment of freight in excess of 875 pesetas per tonne was
b invalid and could not be enforced against the charterers, and to imply that the other part
was valid and could be enforced (see [1920] 2 KB 287).   The figure for freight at £50 per
ton had apparently been divided by the receivers of the cargo (though incorrectly
according to the aribitrator) between the lawful and the unlawful parts.

After the last war the courts became familiar with cases in which builders entered into
lump sum contracts to do work in excess of the amount for which licences had been
c granted and so were in breach of Defence (General) Regulations 1939, SR & O 1939 No
927, reg 56A.   In such cases as *Jackson Stansfield & Sons v Butterworth* [1948] 2 All ER 558
and *Dennis & Co Ltd v Munn* [1949] 1 All ER 616, [1949] 2 KB 327, plaintiff builders
recovered the licensed amount (by concession of the defendant building owners, it is
true) but could not enforce the claim to the unlicensed excess.   In *Frank W Clifford Ltd v
Garth* [1956] 2 All ER 323, [1956] 1 WLR 570 the cost in excess of the limit was allowed,
d but Denning LJ doubted whether a lump sum contract 'for a single and indivisible work'
would not be wholly illegal and irrecoverable.   But when the work is divisible into its
component items I see no reason why the court should not divide it and its cost; and the
court should not be disabled from dividing it by its being claimed in one total.   Then it
is a matter of form only.   So might it be with a claim for an agreed rent in excess of the
standard rent: the standard rent would be recoverable, whether or not it had been
e separated in the claim from the excess: see *Schlisselman v Rubin* [1951] WN 530.

Here the composition of the total is obvious and its division presents no difficulty; and
I would have held it should be made, were it not for the second ground on which counsel
for Banco asks us to uphold the judge's rejection of the plaintiffs' claim, by allowing the
plaintiffs to recover the agreed real price of the goods sold to Vitro less the proper credit
and by disallowing the fictitious part of the total price agreed to be paid over to Nanke.
f This figure can be easily calculated and has been agreed, not at the amount of $319,537·59
claimed in the notice of appeal, but at the revised figure of $262,807·49.

It was contended for Banco that the judge was right to reject this severance (if it is
rightly so called) and to hold as he did that the letter of credit was 'either enforceable in
full according to its terms or not at all'.   He preferred to apply the decision of this court
in *Napier v National Bankers Agency Ltd* [1951] 2 All ER 264 to applying the decision in
g *Fielding & Platt Ltd v Najjar* [1969] 2 All ER 150, [1969] 1 WLR 357.

There are of course long-standing objections to severing entire contracts as there are to
enforcing any part of a contract tainted with illegality.   But the authorities are not easy
to reconcile, and the further argument on this point in this court has not brought to light
any single principle or even any clear guidelines on when a court can award a plaintiff
half a loaf and when it is bound to refuse him any bread.

h We were referred to the discussion of the problem in Chitty on Contracts (24th Edn,
1977, vol 1, para 1049, p 494, in particular para 1051, p 495, on 'General principles' and
para 1055, p 497, on 'Illegality of part of the consideration').   Paragraph 1051 reads as
follows:

'Although a number of authorities on the application of the doctrine of severance
cannot easily be reconciled, it is submitted that two underlying principles have
j throughout guided the courts.   First, the courts will not make a new contract for the
parties, whether by rewriting the existing contract, or by bascially altering its
nature; secondly, the courts will not sever the unenforceable parts of a contract,
unless it accords with public policy to do so.'

But any alteration of a contract for the purposes of enforcement of less than all of it
involves making a new contract or rewriting the old and the justice of enforcing part

ought not to depend on the precise form in which the parts of the whole are originally put together. Ease of excision or alteration is one consideration; their extent is *a* another. Public policy introduces distinctions between the immoral and the illegal and between the void and the illegal.

If exchange contracts were illegal, it would be harder to confine the contamination to a part only of the sale contract and to enforce the other part and the letter of credit contract. But here we are concerned with unenforceability, as it was explained in *Batra v Ebrahim*, and should try to enforce as much of these contracts as is proper and *b* practicable. How far judges have been prepared to go towards rewriting contracts and using the blue pencil not merely to strike out is illustrated by the cases to which counsel for the plaintiffs referred us of *Stanton v Brown* [1900] 1 QB 671 and *Re North Wales Produce and Supply Society* [1922] 2 Ch 340, [1922] All ER Rep 730.

I would follow them in giving effect to so much of the plaintiffs' contract with the defendants as would not involve breaches of Peruvian law, were it not for the opinion I *c* have formed that the defendants have a complete answer to the whole claim on the branch of the case which remains to be considered.

That is the defendants' cross-appeal against the judge's first judgment in favour of the plaintiffs.

This now raises the question whether the defendants are entitled to judgment and the plaintiffs to recover nothing since, on the facts found by Mocatta J, the defendants are *d* entitled not to pay under the letter of credit because they were presented with a bill of lading which conformed on its face with the terms of the credit but was false and made fraudulently by the person who issued it, to the knowledge of the defendants but not to the knowledge of the plaintiffs.

The unchallenged findings of fraud are these: the bills of lading presented by United City Merchants on 22nd December 1976 were prepared and issued by an employee of E *e* H Mundy & Co (Freight Agencies) Ltd named Baker. That company were loading brokers for an American corporation, Prudential Lines Inc, who were the carriers. Baker made out the bills of lading on 16th December, fraudulently altered the date to 15th December and fraudulently dated 15th December a signed notation stamped on the bills 'These goods are actually on board', falsely representing the date of shipment (which was in fact 16th December) without belief in its truth or recklessly, careless whether it was *f* true or false. Neither plaintiff knew of his fraud and he and E H Mundy & Co were not their agents, but the agents of the carriers who paid them. These facts give rise to a shorter and simpler question than that which the judge was asked to decide, but it is the point added to Banco's respondent's notice by leave and indeed at the invitation of the court, and in my opinion the answer to it determines this appeal in the defendants' favour without requiring the court to pronounce on the wider questions raised in *g* argument before the judge and this court. The amendment reads:

> 'that the defendants were entitled to refuse payment against the documents presented to them because one of the documents so presented (namely, the bill of lading or a part of it) was a false document and was made fraudulently by the person who issued it.'   *h*

The form in which the issue was first raised is to be found in para 5 of the defendants' original points of defence:

> 'Further or alternatively, the documents presented by the First Plaintiffs to the Defendants were by reason of the facts alleged in paragraph 4 hereof false, in that the Bill of Lading: (a) was dated 15th December, 1976 (b) stated that London was *j* the port of loading (c) bore an "on board notation" representing that the goods were placed on board the vessel on 15th December, 1976.'

But that was elaborated in written submissions on what was regarded, rightly in my judgment, by the judge as 'a half-way house' between fraud and accuracy, namely inaccuracy in a material particular. The judge set out what was counsel's sixth written submission for Banco (see [1979] 1 Lloyd's Rep 267 at 277) and proceeded to review some of the authorities in support of that 'wide reaching submission' before rejecting it and

a returning to the effect of Baker's fraud.   The point appeared to be put in equally wide-reaching terms in Banco's unamended respondent's notice.

In the court below it appears that counsel for Banco drew no distinction between a document which was inaccurate and a document which was false, or between a document which was false to the knowledge of its maker and a document which he forged.   There is an ambiguity in describing a document as truthful or genuine or as untruthful or false,

b which is illustrated by an American case, *Old Colony Trust Co v Lawyers' Title & Trust Co* (1924) 297 F 152.   A document may tell a lie about itself, e g about the person who made it, or the time or place of making.   If it tells a lie about the maker, it is a forgery; if it tells a lie about the time or place of making 'where either is material', it is a forgery: see the Forgery Act 1913, s 1(2).   In the former case it may be a nullity; in the latter not: see *Chao (trading as Zung Fu Co) v British Traders and Shippers Ltd (NV Handelsmaatschappij J Smits*

c *Import-Export, third party)* [1954] 1 All ER 779 at 787, [1954] 2 QB 459 at 476 and *Gian Singh & Co Ltd v Banque de l'Indochine* [1974] 2 All ER 754 at 757–758, [1974] 1 WLR 1234 at 1238–1239.   Or the document may tell a lie about its contents.   Then it is no forgery, but the maker or utterer of it may commit a criminal offence of some kind of fraud.   Or a document may be untrue in the sense of inaccurate by mistake and without any intention to deceive by its maker or anyone who puts it forward.

d Here we are not required by the facts to go into these distinctions or to consider counsel's submission for Banco that an inaccurate statement when material in a document is in itself a ground for a banker refusing to pay the beneficiary who presents the document under a letter of credit.   This bill of lading did in fact tell a lie about itself, that it was executed on 15th December, when in fact it was executed on 16th December, and two lies about its contents, that the goods were received on board the American

e Accord on 15th December when they were received on 16th December and that they were shipped in London when they were shipped in Felixstowe.   The second 'lie' deceived nobody and interested nobody; on the judge's findings the requirement of the credit as to London was clearly waived.   But, if the bill of lading had stated the truth that the goods were received on board on 16th December, the defendants would have been entitled and indeed bound to refuse payment because the bill of lading did not conform

f to the requirements of the credit.   On these facts the wider issues raised by counsel only arise if the exception of fraud does not apply when the fraud is not the fraud of the seller or beneficiary who tenders the documents.   In my judgment it does, and I therefore express no opinion on the effect of material inaccuracy honestly included in a document presented to a bank under a letter of credit, except that I would follow the judge in adopting the statement of the Court of Appeals, Ninth Circuit, in *Continental National*

g *Bank v National City Bank of New York* (1934) 69 F 2d 312 at 317 and say that to accept counsel's submission 'would practically undermine the general principle that the bank must honor the draft if the documents comply with the terms of the letter of credit' and, in the judge's own words, 'might greatly hold up the smooth running of international trade and might place on banks exceptionally onerous investigations': see [1979] 1 Lloyd's Rep 267 at 277–278.

h The fraud exception is stated by Lord Denning MR in *Edward Owen Engineering Ltd v Barclays Bank International Ltd* [1978] 1 All ER 976 at 981, [1978] QB 159 at 169.   In an interlocutory appeal upholding Kerr J's decision to discharge an injunction restraining a bank from paying under a performance bond, Lord Denning MR quoted Jenkin LJ's statement of the principle governing confirmed letters of credit in *Malas (trading as Hamzeh Malas & Sons) v British Imex Industries Ltd* and said:

j 'To this general principle there is an exception in the case of what is called established or obvious fraud to the knowledge of the bank.   The most illuminating case is of *Sztejn v J Henry Schroder Banking Corpn* (1941) 31 NYS 2d 631 at 633 which was heard in the New York Supreme Court in 1941.   After citing many cases Shientag J said this: "It is well established that a letter of credit is independent of the primary contract of sale between the buyer and the seller.   The issuing bank agrees to pay upon presentation of documents, not goods.   This rule is necessary to preserve the efficiency of the letter of credit as an instrument for the financing of trade." He said (at 634) that in that particular case it was different because—". . . on the present *a* motion, it must be assumed that the seller has intentionally failed to ship any goods ordered by the buyer. In such a situation, where the seller's fraud has been called to the bank's attention before the drafts and documents have been presented for payment, the principle of the independence of the bank's obligation under the letter of credit should not be extended to protect the unscupulous seller." That case shows that there is this exception to the strict rule; the bank ought not to pay under the *b* credit if it knows that the documents are forged or that the request for payment is made fraudulently in circumstances when there is no right to payment. I would in this regard quote the words of Browne LJ in an unreported case when he was sitting at first instance. It is *Bank Russo-Iran v Gordon Woodroffe & Co Ltd* (1972) Times, 4th October. He said: "In my judgment, if the documents are presented by the beneficiary himself, and are forged or fraudulent, the bank is entitled to refuse *c* payment if the bank finds out before payment, and is entitled to recover the money as paid under a mistake of fact if it finds out after payment." But as Kerr J said in this present case: ". . . in cases of obvious fraud to the knowledge of the banks, the courts may preclude banks from fulfilling their obligation to third parties." Such is the law as to a confirmed letter of credit.'

In agreeing Browne LJ said ([1978] All ER 976 at 984, [1978] QB 159 at 172):   *d*

'As Lord Denning MR has said, it is well established that in the case of a confirmed irrevocable credit in respect of a contract for the sale of goods the confirming bank is not in any way concerned with disputes between the buyers and the sellers under the contract of sale which underlies the credit. But I agree also that it is established that there is at any rate one exception to this rule. Lord Denning *e* MR has already referred to the New York case of *Sztejn v H Henry Schroder Banking Corpn* and has quoted what I said in *Bank Russo-Iran v Gordon Woodroffe & Co Ltd*. That exception is that where the documents under the credit are presented by the beneficiary himself and the bank knows when the documents are presented that they are forged or fraudulent, the bank is entitled to refuse payment.'

And Geoffrey Lane LJ said ([1978] 1 All ER 796 at 986, [1978] QB 159 at 175):   *f*

'The only circumstances which would justify the bank not complying with a demand made under that agreement would be those which would exonerate them under similar circumstances if they had entered into a letter of credit, and that is this, if it had been clear and obvious to the bank that the buyers had been guilty of fraud.'   *g*

The unanimous decision of the court was that fraud on the part of the buyers (who were the beneficiaries) or their Libyan bank was not clearly enough established or evidenced to justify the defendants in withholding payment at the order of the court.

Counsel for the plaintiffs calls attention to Shientag J's reference to not protecting 'the unscrupulous seller' (the beneficiary under a letter of credit) to Lord Denning MR's statement that the bank ought not to pay 'if it knows that the request for payment is *h* made fraudulently', to Browne LJ's reference to the documents being 'presented by the beneficiary himself' and to Geoffrey Lane LJ's observation that the circumstances which would justify the bank not paying would be 'if it had been clear and obvious to the bank that the buyers had been guilty of fraud'. But fraud on the part of the beneficiary was all that the court was concerned with both in the American case and in the English case, and there is no limitation to the fraud in the statements quoted by Lord Denning MR from *j* the judgments of Browne LJ in *Bank Russo-Iran v Gordon Woodroffe & Co Ltd* and of Kerr J in *Edward Owen Engineering Ltd v Barclays Bank International Ltd* itself.

Counsel for the plaintiff's, however, submits that those were both cases of fraud on the part of the beneficiary and that the limitation to the beneficiary's own fraud is supported by other American authorities, by textbook writers and by legal principle and commercial convenience, whereas the unlimited exception is unsupported by any authority or textbook writer, except the writer of an article criticising Mocatta J's decision on the point.

The judge accepted that the exception rests on the principle ex turpi causa non oritur actio.   It was because he held that there was no fraud on the part of the plaintiffs, or knowledge that the date on the bills of lading was false when they presented the documents, that the plaintiffs were, apart from the Bretton Woods Agreement Order in Council, entitled to succeed.   I would agree that that is a good ground for dismissing a beneficiary's claim to be paid under a letter of credit.   I would agree also that the fewer the cases in which a bank is entitled to hold up payment the better for the smooth running of international trade.   But I do not think that the courts have a duty to assist international trade to run smoothly if it is fraudulent any more than when it violates an international agreement.   Banks trust beneficiaries to present honest documents; if beneficiaries go to others (as they have to) for the documents they present, it is important to all concerned that those documents should accord not merely with the requirements of the credit but with the facts, and if they do not because of the intention of anyone concerned with them to deceive I see good reason when the choice is between two innocent parties putting the loss on the beneficiary, not the bank or its customer.

There is, I think it is conceded, no authority, English or American, directly deciding that the fraud of a third party such as the maker of a false document is or is not a good defence to a claim to be paid in accordance with the terms of a letter of credit.   Most of the cases of fraud are, as is to be expected, cases of fraud by a seller hoping to be paid for rubbish or, at the least, defective goods before the true state of affairs is known which his own misdescription has concealed.   It is in the context of such facts that Bailhache J's statement about misdescription, fraudulent or (where the buyer had rejected the goods before payment by the bank) innocent, in *Société Métallurgique d'Aubrives & Villerupt v British Bank for Foreign Trade* (1922) 11 Ll L Rep 168 at 170 and the statements I have quoted from *Edward Owen Engineering Ltd v Barclays International Ltd* have to be considered.

In *Bank of Taiwan v Union National Bank of Philadelphia* (1924) 1 F 2d 65 at 66 the Circuit Court of Appeals, Third Circuit, stated: 'That the date of the bills of lading did not truthfully represent the date of the beginning of actual transportation would be a defense, if it can constitute a defense, if *and only if* the plaintiff knew that fact when it acquired the draft.'   But there the plaintiff was not the seller, a Japanese company, but the bank in whose favour it drew its draft on the defendant bank, who agreed by a term added to the letter of credit 'with the drawers, indorsers, and bona fide holders of bills' to honour them.   So the court was saying that the bone fide holder must know of the false date before payment could be refused to it under that particular credit, and neither the decision nor that sentence in the judgment throws any light on the true limits of a bank's defence to a claim to be paid under a letter of credit.

Maurice O'Meara Co v National Park Bank of New York (1925) 239 NY 386 in the New York Court of Appeals contains an interesting dissenting judgment of Cardozo J (with which Crane J concurred).   It was not a case of fraud and counsel for Banco relied on it, as on Bailhache J's judgment in the *Société Métallurgique* case, in support of his wider propositions.   But counsel for the plaintiffs can rely on what that great judge there said about fraud (at 401):

'I assume that no duty is owing from the bank to its depositor which *requires* it to investigate the quality of the merchandise. (*Laudisi v American Exchange National Bank* 239 NY 234.) I dissent from the view that if it chooses to investigate and discovers thereby that the merchandise tendered is not in truth the merchandise which the documents describe, it may be forced by the delinquent seller to make payment of the price irrespective of its knowledge. We are to bear in mind that this controversy is not one between the bank on the one side and on the other a holder of the drafts who has taken them without notice and for value. The controversy arises between the bank and a seller who has misrepresented the security upon which advances are demanded. Between parties so situated, payment may be resisted if the documents are false.'

That was a claim by the seller's assignee and it was the seller's conduct alone which was alleged to give the defendant bank a defence and to which those observations were *a* accordingly directed. I cannot guess what Cardozo J would have said if the security had been misrepresented, but not by the seller. In *Bank of East Asia Ltd v Pang* (1926) 249 P 1060 the Supreme Court of Washington preferred the decision of the majority in *O'Meara's* case, as did Mocatta J, and it was followed as a leading case in the Circuit Court of Appeals, Ninth Circuit, in *Continental National Bank v National City Bank of New York* (1934) 69 F 2d 312 and in *Sztejn's* case.   *b*

There are in the judgment of Shientag J in *Sztejn's* case other references to intentional or active fraud on the part of the seller, but they add no support to counsel's submission for the plaintiffs in the light of the facts, which had to be assumed for the purposes of the motion to restore a payment to the buyer, that the seller had intentionally failed to ship any bristles, the goods required by the contract of sale, but had shipped cowhair and other rubbish instead.   *c*

Counsel for the plaintiffs relied also on a statement in the opinion of six judges of the Supreme Court of Pennsylvania in *Intraworld Industries Inc v Girard Trust Bank* (1975) Pa 336 A 2d 316 at 324 that—

> 'the circumstances which will justify an injunction against honor [of a letter of credit] must be narrowly limited to situations of fraud in which the wrongdoing of the beneficiary has so vitiated the entire transaction that the legitimate purposes of *d* the independence of the issuer's obligation would no longer be served.'

But the Pennsylvania court was considering whether to apply the decision in the leading case of *Sztejn* to a case where the documents presented by the beneficiary were 'genuine in the sense of having some basis in fact', and as it was not a case of cowhair for bristles the injunction was refused.   *e*

We were referred to a case of *New York Life Insurance Co v Hartford National Bank and Trust Co* (1977) 378 A 2d 562 at 567 where the Supreme Court of Connecticut approved that statement.

United Bank Ltd v Cambridge Sporting Goods Corpn (1976) 392 NYS 2d 265 was a case not of cowhair for bristles, but old, unpadded, ripped and mildewed gloves instead of new boxing gloves as ordered by the appellant, Cambridge Sporting Goods, from a Pakistani *f* corporation. The respondents, the Pakistani sellers' Pakistani bank, asserted that they, as holders in due course of the drafts made payable to them by the sellers, were entitled to be paid under a letter of credit issued by a New York bank the money which that bank had paid to the sheriff after the appellant had obtained judgment for the amount of the drafts against the sellers. The first question was stated by the court (at 267–268) to be 'whether fraud on the part of a seller-beneficiary of an irrevocable letter of credit may be *g* successfully asserted as a defense against holders of drafts drawn by the seller pursuant to the credit'. The Court of Appeals of New York, reversing the trial court's decision, held that the shipment of the esentially worthless gloves constituted 'fraud in the transaction' within the meaning of $\S5-114(2)$ of the Uniform Commercial Code, and in that circumstance the burden shifted to the respondent bank to prove that they were holders in due course for value, in good faith and without notice of any fraud on the part of the *h* seller under another section of the code. That burden the respondent bank failed to discharge.

It was therefore a case of seller's fraud, but the report is of great interest and relevance, in my opinion, to our problem in its references to the Uniform Commercial Code. Section 5-114(2) reads:

> 'Unless otherwise agreed when documents appear on their face to comply with *j* the terms of a credit but a required document . . . is forged or fraudulent or there is fraud in the transaction (a) the issuer must honor the draft or demand for payment if honor is demanded by a negotiating bank or other holder of the draft or demand which has taken the draft or demand under the credit and under circumstances which would make it a holder in due course (Section 3–302) . . . and (b) in all other cases as against its customer, an issuer acting in good faith may honor

a   the draft or demand for payment despite notification from the customer of fraud, forgery or other defect not apparent on the face of the documents but a court of appropriate jurisdiction may enjoin such honor.'

This code apparently resulted from a 1955 report of a New York Law Revision Committee and has now been adopted, we were told by counsel, by every state in the Union except parts of Louisiana. The original version contained the words 'fraud in a required document'. The rule in this section represents an attempt to codify the *S*ʒ*tejn*

b   case and the drafters of it 'have eschewed a dogmatic approach and adopted a flexible standard to be applied to the circumstances of a particular situation mandate' (see 392 NYS 2d 265 at 271). I do not think that a later case, in which the United States District Court, SD New York followed the boxing gloves case and refused to find 'fraud in the transaction', helps to provide an answer to this issue between the parties before us: see *United Technologies Corpn v Citibank NA* (1979) 469 F Supp 473.

c   Of the textbooks, Professor Davis in the Law relating to Commercial Letters of Credit (3rd Edn, 1963, pp 145–146) speaks first of forgery or fraud in connection with false documents without differentiation. Then he states:

'If a draft drawn under a credit is forged, the issuing banker is undoubtedly entitled to refuse payment, his undertaking being to pay a valid draft. The position is the same even if the person presenting the draft is a bona fide purchaser for

d   value. If the banker pays a forged draft he cannot claim reimbursement from the buyer, for he has not acted in accordance with the terms of his mandate ... Whether a banker who has paid a person who presents a draft bearing a forged signature can never pay the payee is a matter of doubt.'

His language is wide enough to cover fraud or forgery by a third person other than the beneficiary/seller. Not so the language of Benjamin's Sale of Goods (1974, para 2074, p

e   1060) where the editors, citing *S*ʒ*tejn*'s case, treat the fraud exception as applying 'where the seller has committed a fraud, such as the tender of forged documents or documents which, to the seller's knowledge, contain a false and fraudulent description of the goods.'

Similarly Gutteridge and Megrah in the Law of Bankers' Commercial Credits (6th Edn, 1979, p 137) deal only with documents which are forged or false in the sense that

f   they wrongly describe the goods, and so go on to state: 'If to the knowledge of the bank the beneficiary was responsible for the forgery or falseness the bank could refuse to pay.' There is here too an express limitation to fraud or forgery on the part of the beneficiary/seller; but such descriptions will usually be false to the knowledge of the seller and, if the misdescription is so thorough as to represent worthless rubbish as valuable cargo, there must generally be fraud on the part of the seller.

Article 9 of the Uniform Customs and Practice, however, distinguishes between 'the

g   form, sufficiency, accuracy, genuineness, falsification or legal effect of any documents' and 'the description, quantity, weight, quality, condition, packing, delivery, value or existence of the goods represented thereby. For neither category is the bank liable or responsible, but there is no indication that it matters who falsifies a document presented to it or who misrepresents the description of the goods in a document presented to it.

h   The only writer who gives clear support to the exception including the fraud of a third party is Professor R M Goode in a recent article in Centre Point, 'Reflections on Letters of Credit—1' [1980] JBL 291. There he discusses the position of the bona fide plaintiff such as the plaintiffs in the instant case and criticises the decision of Mocatta J for holding that Baker's fraud did not defeat their claim. He states (at p 294):

'Is a plaintiff who seeks to enforce a letter of credit affected by forgery of the

j   documents or other fraud in the transaction if he himself acted in good faith? There is a remarkable dearth of authority on this question. Let us start with the beneficiary. He himself has a duty to tender documents which are in order, and the fact that he acted in good faith in tendering forged documents is thus irrelevant. This fundamental point appears to have been overlooked by Mocatta J in The American Accord when he held that the beneficiary was entitled to collect payment despite the insertion of a fraudulent shipping date on the bill of lading, since the fraud had been committed by the loading broker who was the agent of the carrier, not of the seller/beneficiary. But this, with respect, is not to the point. The beneficiary under a credit is not like a holder in due course of a bill of exchange; he is only entitled to be paid if the documents are in order. A fraudulently completed bill of lading does not become a conforming document merely because the fraud is that of a third party.'

For that he cites *United Technologies Corpn v Citibank NA* (1979) 469 F Supp 473, one of the cases which applied New York's Uniform Commercial Code.

It will be seen that this is the point to which counsel has in his amendment to Banco's respondent's notice fined down the wider arguments which he addressed to Mocatta J and this court. It is the only version of those arguments which I find it necessary to consider because I hold it to be well founded and to determine this appeal in the defendants' favour. We cannot dispose of the argument on the short ground that this bill of lading is a forgery because we ruled that the point, not having been pleaded or argued below or raised in Banco's respondent's notice, was not open to them in this court. Counsel for the plaintiffs submitted that, if it had been raised below, evidence might have been directed to the question whether the date of the bill itself was material, as the time of making has to be, for Baker to have committed forgery; Baker seems to have thought it material or he would not have put the false date at the foot of the bill, but if it was material the forgery point might have been expected to have been taken earlier; the court should not, however, speculate or admit a point to which evidence could have been but was not directed. We found this submission irresistible.

But whether or not a forged document is a nullity, it is not a genuine or valid document entitling the presenter of it to be paid, and if the banker to which it is presented under a letter of credit knows it to be forged he must not pay. We do not have to consider the complications which may arise when a claim is made under a letter of credit by a bona fide holder for value of, for example, a draft, because what was forged and false here was not a draft but a bill of lading and the point that the plaintiffs were bona fide holders for value was not raised at the trial. But we do have to decide whether a document fraudulent as was this bill of lading is likewise not a genuine or valid document, no more entitled than a forgery to require payment and equally to be rejected by the banker who knows it to be fraudulent.

If a document false in the sense that it is forged by a person other than the beneficiary can entitle a bank to refuse payment, I see no reason why a document in any way false to the knowledge of a person other than the beneficiary should not have the same effect. Here again we do not have to decide such wider questions raised in argument as whether the falsity of the document amounts to clearly established fraud or only points to fraud, or whether a bank is bound to its customer to refuse payment or only entitled to refuse payment. For we are not concerned with an application for an interlocutory injunction to restrain payment or for leave to defend RSC Ord 14 proceedings, but with a bank's refusal to pay on discovering a fraud established on a balance of probabilities to the satisfaction of the trial judge and not disputed to be such by the plaintiffs.

There was fraud in the transaction, and our courts should adopt 'the flexible standard to be applied as the circumstances of a particular situation mandate', as did the Uniform Commercial Code now ruling in the United States of America. We should not apply it only to 'situations . . . in which the wrongdoing of the beneficiary has so vitiated the entire transaction that the legitimate purposes of the independence of the issuer's obligation would no longer be served' (see *Intraworld Industries Inc v Girard Trust Bank* (1975) Pa 336 A 2d 316 at 324–325), of which there appears to have been a striking illustration in the case of *Etablissement Esefka International Anstalt v Central Bank of Nigeria* [1979] 1 Lloyd's Rep 445. It should also be applied to any fraud which, if known to the issuing or confirming bank, would entitle it to refuse payment. In that situation the bank owes no duty to the beneficiary to pay and, I would say, owes a duty to the customer not to pay. So here the defendants, when they knew, on the judge's findings, that they had been intentionally deceived as to a date material to their liability to pay, were right

to refuse to honour the plaintiffs' credit. Even though the judge was not able to find that
a Baker was the plaintiffs' agent in making the bill of lading for presentation to the
defendants, the plaintiffs were the innocent party who put him in the position in which
he made the bill, and made it fraudulently, and in my judgment it is they rather than the
defendants, already improverished by the dollars remitted to the United States of
America, who should bear the loss.

For these reasons, which differ from those of the judge, I would affirm his judgment
b in favour of the defendants and dismiss the appeal.

ACKNER LJ. The second plaintiffs, Glass Fibres, manufacture small glass fibre making
machines. In 1975 Glass Fibres entered into a contract to sell fibreglass equipment to
Vitro, a Peruvian company concerned in the glass fibre industry. The terms of that
contract, although having all the appearances of a genuine sale fob United Kingdom
c port, involved: (1) Vitro (at its suggestion) paying Glass Fibres double the price originally
quoted; (2) Glass Fibres agreeing to remit the excess price to the credit of Nanke
International Corpn, Panama at Bankers Trust, Miami (Nanke were closely associated
with Vitro); (3) the price being paid by an irrevocable letter of credit issued by the second
third party, Banco Continental SA, a Peruvian bank. This letter of credit was
subsequently confirmed by the Royal Bank of Canada, the defendants in the action and
d the respondents to this appeal.

Glass Fibres would have been perfectly content to have sold its machinery to Vitro for
the sum set out in its quotation. However, Vitro, apart from acquiring the machinery,
desired to use the transaction as a means of Nanke acquiring a large quantity of United
States dollars which Vitro, through Banco, would have to pay for in Peruvian currency.
The relevant provisions of Peruvian law are as follows.
e 1. Article 1 of Decree Law 18275 of 15th May 1975 provides:

'From the date hereafter it is prohibited for individuals or corporations resident
in Peru . . . to maintain or establish deposits in a foreign currency in banks and other
institutions in this country and/or abroad.'

2. Article 18 of the same Decree Law provides:

f
'It is an offence of fraud against the State to maintain foreign currency or to
perform any type of operation prohibited by this Decree Law.'

On the facts the judge found that the excess price was to be held by Nanke beneficially
for Vitro. Accordingly, the judge held, and this is not challenged, that Vitro, by
initiating from Peru the letter of credit by Banco, which was confirmed by the Royal
g Bank of Canada, under arrangements made by them for siphoning off about half the
amount of credit in dollars to an account in Miami held to their benefit, thereby
committed a breach of art 1 in Peru.
3. Article 7 of Decree Law 18891 of 17th June 1971 provides:

'The over-valuing of imports and obligations payable in foreign currency, as well
as the under-valuing of exports, in violation of what is provided for in the Foreign
h Currency Certificates Regulations, constitutes the offence of fraud, damaging to the
State.'

The judge accepted the expert evidence called by Banco that an overvaluing of imports
payable in a foreign currency would be an offence under art 7, because such action would
be contrary to the principle that the regime's foreign exchange control was seeking to
j preserve. On 19th November Mr McFarlane, the sales director of Glass Fibres, met in
Lima a Mr Duncan, who was the manager of the international department of Banco,
whose special duty was to ascertain where lines of credit might be found for the purpose
of enabling Banco to open letters of credit to pay for imports into Peru. Mr Duncan was
asked whether he could find credit for $662,086, which was the inflated fob price of the
goods. It is not disputed that Vitro committed a breach of art 7. To my mind, although
the judge made no finding, Glass Fibres also committed a breach of this article.

Both the United Kingdom and Peru are parties to the Bretton Woods Agreement. By
the Bretton Woods Agreements Order in Council 1946, SR & O 1946 No 36, made under   *a*
the Bretton Woods Agreements Act 1945, it is provided in Part I of the schedule to the
order, giving effect to art VIII, s 2(b) of the agreement:

> 'Exchange contracts which involve the currency of any Member and which are
> contrary to the exchange control regulations of that member maintained or imposed
> consistently with this Agreement shall be unenforceable in the territories of any   *b*
> member . . .'

It was held by this court in *Wilson, Smithett & Cope Ltd v Terruzzi* [1976] 1 All ER 817,
[1976] QB 683 that an 'exchange contract' meant a contract to exchange the currency of
one country for that of another, and that contracts involving securities or merchandise
are not exchange contracts *except* where they are monetary transactions in disguise.

The judge held, and in my view rightly so held, that this contract, although involving   *c*
merchandise, was an 'exchange contract' because in the circumstances which I have
described above it was a monetary transaction in disguise.

Had the plaintiffs been seeking to enforce the merchandise contract, what would have
been the effect of the order making such contracts 'unenforceable'? In *Batra v Ebrahim*
[1977] Court of Appeal Transcript 197B the Court of Appeal had to consider a case in
which there were exchange contracts involving the currencies in England and India, and   *d*
concluded that they were contrary to the exchange control regulations of the latter
country. However, the Bretton Woods Agreement was not raised in the defence and the
question which the court had to decide was whether the court itself should take the
point. Lord Denning MR drew attention to the fact that the word used in art VIII, s 2(b)
is 'unenforceable'; it is not 'illegal'. He went on to say:
                                                                                        e
> 'If the word "unenforceable" was used in the strict sense in which an English
> lawyer uses that word, the court could leave it to the parties to decide whether or not
> to raise the point, just as they did in the Statute of Frauds. If the defendant did not
> raise art VIII, 2(b) in his defence, the court would take no notice of it. I cannot think
> that would be right. We should construe this article in the same way as we construe
> other international agreements. We should adopt such a construction as will   *f*
> promote the general legislative purpose: see *James Buchanan & Co Ltd v Babco
> Forwarding and Shipping (UK) Ltd* [1977] 1 All ER 518 at 522, [1977] QB 208 at 213–
> 214. On this basis it seems to me that if it appears to the court that a party is suing
> on a contract which is made unenforceable by art VIII, s 2(b) then the court must
> itself take the point and decline to enforce the contract . . . If money has been paid
> under it and the consideration has failed, then the money can probably be recovered   *g*
> back: see Mann, the Legal Aspect of Money (3rd Edn, 1971, pp 448–449).'

Batra's case, however, leaves undecided whether the consequence of the plaintiffs
seeking to enforce the merchandise contract, if this had been the course which they had
decided to adopt, would have been a failure to recover the *whole* contract price, or merely
the excess contract price, ie that part of the price which represented the disguise. The   *h*
facts of this case enable one to isolate and identify with precision how much of the
consideration was, as a matter of reality, attributable to the machinery and was to be
retained by Glass Fibres and how much represented the money which was to find its way
back to Vitro but to be held in Miami. The agreement, not being 'illegal', we do not have
to consider whether the whole contract can be said to be 'tainted' because that part which
is a monetary transaction in disguise was contrary to the exchange control regulations of   *j*
Peru. The monetary transaction in disguise being clearly identifiable, I can see no
problem in the court refusing to enforce the merchandise contract to the extent that it
was an exchange contract. Accordingly, if the plaintiffs had sued on the merchandise
contract, they would have been entitled to recover so much of the true and genuine price
of the goods as was then due and owing.

I do not consider that *Foster v Driscoll* [1929] 1 KB 470, [1928] All ER Rep 130 and

Regazzoni v K C Sethia (1944) *Ltd* [1957] 3 All ER 286, [1958] AC 301 have any application
in the present case where the foreign law which is relied on as affecting the contractual
rights of the parties is the exchange control regulations of a state which is a party to the
Bretton Woods Agreement. I respectfully agree with the statement of Diplock LJ in
Sharif v Azad [1966] 3 All ER 785, [1967] 1 QB 605 (a case to which I shall have to refer
in greater detail later) that in such a situation the matter is regulated not by the general
rules of English conflict of laws but by an English statute, namely the Bretton Woods
Agreements Act 1945 and an English statutory order made under that statute. Although
Diplock LJ was the only member of the court expressly to make that observation, Lord
Denning MR and Russell LJ must be taken to have proceeded on that basis, *Regazzoni's*
case having been specifically cited.

Were I wrong in the view expressed above and the merchandise contract fell to be
considered as illegal on the grounds of public policy, based on international comity, then,
none the less, the plaintiffs would in my judgment have been able to recover in an action
on the merchandise contract the selfsame sum. In *Ralli Brothers v Compañía Naviera Sota
y Aznar* [1922] KB 287, [1920] All ER Rep 427 this court was concerned with an English
charterparty to be construed according to English law, but that part of the contract
dealing with the obligation of the charterers with regard to the payment of the balance
of freight had to be performed in Spain. Spanish law provided that the freight was not
to exceed 875 pesetas per tonne. However, owing to alterations in the rate of exchange
the freight reserved by the charterparty was, at the date of the arrival at Barcelona, largely
in excess of this figure. It was accordingly held that the freight above 875 pesetas per
tonne was illegal and that part of the contract which required payment of freight in
excess of that figure was invalid and could not be enforced against the charterers. It was
not suggested that the whole contract was so tainted by the illegality attaching to the
excess as to make nothing recoverable. The post-war building licences cases have some
materiality. In those cases where work had been actually licenced it was held that if work
was done in excess of the licence it was only the excess which was unlawful. The builder
could recover payment for the licenced figure, but not for the excess: see *Frank W Clifford
Ltd v Garth* [1956] 2 All ER 323 at 325, [1956] 1 WLR 570 at 572.

But the plaintiffs did not sue on the merchandise contract. They sued the Royal Bank
of Canada under their confirmed letter of credit. In my judgment, for the following
reasons, the consequences are the same.

(1) I respectfully agree with the judge that, once any payment is made by the Royal
Bank of Canada under the confirmed letter of credit, effect is, *to some extent*, being given
to an exchange contract contrary to the exchange control regulations in Peru. This in
fact happened in relation to the initial or 'draw down' payment of 20% of the contract
price, half of which found its way into Nanke's account in Miami. The same proportion
of subsequent payments was to reach the same destination.

(2) It is, of course, well settled that the opening of a confirmed letter of credit
constitutes a bargain between the banker and the vendor of the goods, which imposes on
the banker an obligation to pay, irrespective of any dispute there may be between the
parties whether the goods are up to contract or not. Under a letter of credit, the contract
is to buy documents not goods. The established exception to this general rule, to which
I must refer in greater detail when dealing with Banco's respondent's notice, is that the
bank ought not to pay under the credit if it knows that the documents are forged or that
the request for payment is made fraudulently in circumstances where there is no right
of payment: see *Malas (trading as Hamzeh Malas & Sons) v British Imex Industries Ltd* [1958]
1 All ER 262 at 263, [1958] 2 QB 127 at 129 per Jenkins LJ and *Edward Owen Engineering
Ltd v Barclays Bank International Ltd* [1978] 1 All ER 976 at 981–982, [1978] QB 159 at
169. To my mind, however, these cases are concerned with the relevance or irrelevance
of disputes between the buyer and the seller of the goods, the general rule being that they
must settle these amongst themselves and that they are no concern of the bank. We,
however, are concerned with a situation in which *the court*, by virtue of an international
agreement, has an obligation not to enforce a certain species of agreement: see the *Batra*
case.

(3) The *Sharif* case was a decision on very unusual facts and I agree with Stephenson LJ that it can be properly distinguished from this case. In that case there was no *a* contravention of the foreign exchange regulations, both parties being resident in England. Moreover, there was no question that the payment under the cheques had the result of effect being given to an exchange contract which was contrary to the Pakistani currency regulations. Payment had already been made to the defendant's brother prior to the plaintiff bringing his action. This payment must have been authorised by the state bank, although apparently on terms that blocked the payee's account. I agree with *b* Mocatta J that the claim, being based on a bill of exchange, was considered in relation to s 30 of the Bills of Exchange Act 1882, whereas the autonomy of a banker's letter of credit from the underlying sale contract is of a different character.

I would have accordingly allowed the appeal to the extent of enabling the plaintiffs to recover no more than the amount due and owing at the time of their action in respect of the true and proper purchase price of the goods and the cost of the freight, but for the *c* point raised in Banco's respondent's notice, to which I now turn.

Banco's respondent's notice

The bill of lading was inaccurate in three respects. (1) It contained the notation 'these goods are actually on board 15th December 1976'. The goods were not on board until 16th December. (2) The port of loading was said to be the port of London. It was in fact *d* Felixstowe. (3) The date of issue of the bill of lading was said to be 15th December. It was in fact 16th December.

The inaccuracy in regard to the port of loading was of no significance. It was known and accepted by all parties that the goods had been loaded at Felixstowe. However, the letter of credit, as amended, permitted shipment up to 15th December. Mr Baker, an employee of E H Mundy & Co (Freight Agencies) Ltd, who were the loading brokers for *e* the Prudential Line and who had signed the notation that the goods were actually on board on 15th December, knew that statement to be untrue. He knew that the correct date was a matter of importance in relation to the letter of credit. Mocatta J accordingly held him guilty of fraudulent misrepresentation, the motive no doubt being to cover up his employer's failure to arrange the shipping on time.

Mr Baker was also aware that the date of issue of the bill of lading was not 15th *f* December, but precisely why he resorted to that misstatement is not apparent. It may have been to give verisimilitude to the false date of shipment. However, no importance was attached to this misstatement, no doubt because if the correct date had been stated it would have made no difference to the attitude of the bank. Of course if it had been a 'material' date then the document would have been a forgery by virtue of s 1(2) of the Forgery Act 1913. The document would have told a lie about itself.

g The judge held that neither Mr Baker nor his company were acting on behalf of the plaintiffs. Mundy & Co were acting as loading brokers on behalf of Prudential Lines, from whom they received their remuneration in the form of a commission on the freight. The plaintiffs did not know that the date of shipment was false.

On the presentation of the documents on 22nd December they were rejected, the reasons given including, 'information in our possession suggests that shipment was not *h* in fact effected as it appears by the Bill of Lading'. Before this rejection there had been various communications from South America, Vitro through Banco taking the view that as the ship left England on 17th December, after the expiration of the credit, they had instructed Banco not to honour the documentation.

Counsel for Banco, when he addressed the judge, was of course unaware of the findings of fact at which the judge would arrive. He did not have the advantage, which *j* we have had in this court, of knowing, in advance of his submissions, the findings which the judge would ultimately make. The judge had been invited to find that Mr Baker's alteration of the date of the bill of lading by the use of Snopake and his superimposing 15th December on the date which had originally been 16th December had been done at the express request of United City Merchants. If that had been found by the judge to have occurred, and he expressly negatived this suggestion, then it is clear, on the authority of *Edward Owen Engineering Ltd v Barclays Bank International Ltd* [1978] 1 All ER 976, [1978] QB 159, that the defendants would have been entitled to reject the documents. The principle of the independence of the bank's obligations under the letter of credit does not extend to protect the unscrupulous seller. The same result would of course have followed if the submission that Mr Baker, although receiving no such express instructions, was nevertheless acting on behalf of either of the plaintiffs had been accepted. There was the further possibility, which had to be covered by counsel in his submissions, that while in fact providing an inaccurate date of shipment in the bill of lading Mr Baker had not appreciated that he was incorporating anything inaccurate in the document or if appreciating the inaccuracy he had not provided the inaccurate notation with intent to defraud. To cover what the judge referred to as 'a half-way house', counsel submitted that the bank might refuse to pay if it knows that any of the documents are inaccurate in a material particular. He developed this in a written submission, referring to a number of American decisions. With all these possible permutations and combinations it appears to have been overlooked that the very situation as found by the judge on the facts raised a much narrower point. This has now been covered in an amendment to Banco's respondent's notice in these terms:

> 'that the defendants were entitled to refuse payment against the documents presented to them because one of the documents so presented (namely, the bill of lading or a part of it) was a false document and was made fraudulently by the person who issued it.'

In short, is the fraud exception to the strict rule that the bank must pay if the documents are, on their face, in order limited to the case where the fraud is that of the seller/presenter, or does it apply in all cases of fraud to the knowledge of the bank?

I am most grateful to counsel for their industry in bringing to our attention all possible relevant authorities, but, since this important question has never arisen for decision heretofore, not surprisingly these cases are of very little assistance. The letter of credit in this case was expressly made subject to the Uniform Customs and Practice for Documentary Credits issued by the International Chamber of Commerce. Certainly, from the point of view of this appeal, these do no more than restate the duty of the bank at common law. In the ordinary case visual inspection of the actual documents presented is all that is called for. Banks must examine all documents with reasonable care to ascertain that they appear on their face to be in accordance with the terms and conditions of credit. Thus, for example, the bank is under no duty to take further steps to investigate the genuineness of a signature which, on the face of it, purports to be the signature of the person named or described in the letter of credit: see *Gian Singh & Co Ltd v Banque de l'Indochine* [1974] 2 All ER 754, [1974] 1 WLR 1234 and art 7 of the Uniform Customs and Practice for Documentary Credits.

But this is no ordinary case. There is a finding of fraud in relation to the bill of lading. Had it been the seller who fraudulently misrepresented in the bill of lading the date of shipment, the Uniform Customs and Practice would not protect the bank, who had knowledge of the fraud. The American authorities referred to by Stephenson LJ and by Mocatta J, in so far as they approach the question at issue, all focus on the fraud of the 'unscrupulous seller'. In *Sztejn v J Henry Schroder Banking Corpn* (1941) 31 NYS 2d 631, cited with approval in *Edward Owen Engineering Ltd v Barclays Bank International Ltd* [1978] 1 All ER 976, [1978] QB 159 and referred to in subsequent American authorities as a 'landmark' case, the seller intentionally failed to ship any goods ordered by the buyer. The documents accompanying the draft were fraudulent in that they did not represent actual merchandise but instead covered boxes fraudulently filled with worthless material by the seller of the goods; instead of bristles, there was cow hair and other worthless rubbish. In *United Bank Ltd v Cambridge Sports Goods Corpn* (1976) 392 NYS 2d 265 instead of boxing gloves the seller shipped old unpadded, ripped and mildewed gloves.

What is the justification for allowing the fraud exception? Counsel for the plaintiffs, relying on the latin maxim ex turpi causa non oritur actio, contends that the basis of the

exception is the inability of the fraudulent seller to rely on his own wrongdoing. It does
not seem to me that this can be an exhaustive explanation. If the signature on the bill of   *a*
lading had been forged, a fact of which the sellers were ex hypothesi ignorant, but of
which the bank were aware when the document was presented, I can see no valid basis
on which the bank would be entitled to take up the drafts and debit their customer.
Counsel was virtually obliged to accept this. A banker cannot be compelled to honour
a credit unless all the conditions precedent have been performed, and he ought not to be
under an obligation to accept or pay against documents which he knows to be waste   *b*
paper. To hold otherwise would be to deprive the banker of that security for his
advances, which is a cardinal feature of the process of financing carried out by means of
the credit: see Gutteridge and Megrah on the Law of Bankers' Commercial Credits (6th
Edn, 1979, p 142).

Counsel for the plaintiffs, however, contends that such a forgery would render the bill
of lading a nullity. However, a bill of lading on which the date of shipment has been   *c*
forged is not a nullity, since such a forgery would not go to the essence of the document,
the primary purpose of which is to evidence a contract of affreightment and to enable the
buyer to remove the goods from the ship (see per Devlin J in *Chao (trading as Zung Fu Co)
v British Traders and Shippers Ltd (NV Handelsmaatschappij J Smits Import-Export, third
party)* [1954] 1 All ER 779 at 787, [1954] 2 QB 459 at 476. Nevertheless, the buyer,
unless otherwise agreed, cannot be deemed to have authorised the banker to pay against   *d*
documents which are known to be forged: see Gutteridge and Megrah (p 142). If the
documents are forged, then obviously they are not valid. The buyer's instructions to the
banker must be construed as requiring the acceptance of valid documents only, and the
banker's promise to the seller must be similarly construed: see Davis on the Law Relating
to Commercial Letters of Credit (3rd Edn, 1963, p 149).

If I am right about the view I have expressed in relation to forged documents, where   *e*
the forgery is not the responsibility of the seller, then the ex turpi causa justification for
the fraud exception is not adequate and one must therefore search for what is the
acceptable basis for the exception. In order to do so it is necessary to go back to first
principles. The buyer has arranged with the bank to provide finance for the seller, in the
seller's country, on delivery of certain documents. The banker's authority or mandate is
to pay against genuine documents and that is what the bank has undertaken to do. It is   *f*
the character of the document, not its origin, that must decide whether or not it is a
'conforming' document, that is a document which complies with the terms of the credit.

Moreover, the bank is prepared to provide finance to the exporter because it holds
shipping documents as collateral security for the advance and, if necessary, can take
recourse to the buyer as instructing customer and the exporter as drawer of the bill. The
bank invariably asks for the delivery of a full set of original bills of lading; otherwise a   *g*
fraudulent shipper would be able to obtain payment under the documentary credit on
one of them and advances from other banks on the security of the other originals
constituting the set: see Schmitthoff, The Export Trade (6th Edn, 1975, p 216). It is
therefore of vital importance to the bank not to take up worthless documents.

The above reasons seem to me adequately to explain why the bank would have been
equally entitled to refuse to pay were it to be aware that the bill of lading was forged, as   *h*
it would have been entitled, on the authority of *Edward Owen Engineering Ltd v Barclays
Bank International Ltd*, to have refused payment had it been aware that the bill of
exchange had been fraudulently completed by the seller. But should a fraudulently
completed bill of lading by a third party be treated by a bank as a conforming document
if it is aware of such fraud and its source? It would indeed be a very odd situation if that
were to be the case. How can there be a difference in principle between a document   *j*
forged by a third party and a document *fraudulently completed* by a third party? Can there
be any valid basis for a rule which obliges a bank with knowledge of the material facts
to be obliged to refuse to pay on the former and yet to be obliged to pay on the latter?
Consider how narrow the line was on the present facts. The bill of lading in this case
only escaped being a forgery because the date the goods were said to be on board was the
subject of a special notation. Such a notation was by no means essential nor even usual.

The bill of lading could, as is often the case, have merely recorded that the goods were shipped on board on the date of issue of the bill of lading, that is the date the bill was signed. Had that been the case then the bill of lading would have been a forgery, since the date of the issue of the bill would have been a material date (see the Forgery Act 1913, s 1(2)), and, on the view which I have expressed above, the bank, given knowledge of the forgery, would have been obliged to refuse payment. However, if I am correct in my view that it is the character of the document that decides whether it is a conforming document and not its origin, then it must follow that, if the bank knows that a bill of lading has been fraudulently completed by a third party, it must treat that as a non-conforming document in the same way as if it knew that the seller was party to the fraud. I would also dismiss the appeal.

GRIFFITHS LJ (read by Stephenson LJ). A Peruvian company, Vitro, or possibly its owner, had two objectives: the first was to buy manufacturing equipment from an English company, Glass Fibres; the second was to buy a large number of US dollars with Peruvian soles and lodge those dollars in a bank account in Miami. Peruvian exchange control law prohibited the second objective: individuals or corporations resident in Peru were prohibited from maintaining or establishing deposits in foreign currency in banks abroad by art 1 of Decree Law 18275 of 15th May 1970.

Vitro accepted Glass Fibres' dollar quotation for the machinery. In order to achieve their second objective they asked Glass Fibres to double their quotation. This inflated quotation would enable Vitro to obtain permission from the Peruvian government to buy double the number of dollars they needed to pay for the machinery and Glass Fibres would then collect, by means of a letter of credit, both the price of the machinery which they would keep, and the extra dollars which they would remit to a bank in Miami for the credit of Vitro.

Glass Fibres fell in with this scheme. They were not going to make any direct profit out of it but I suppose they feared that unless they did so they would lose the contract for the machinery. The scheme was not illegal in this country but it was illegal in Peru for it involved a breach of art 1 of Decree Law 18275 and it also was in breach of art 7 of Decree Law 18891 of 17th June 1971 which made it an offence to overvalue imports payable in foreign currency.

The deal between Vitro and Glass Fibres involved two agreements: first, the agreement for the purchase of the machinery, and, second, a collateral agreement by which the Glass Fibres agreed to provide an inflated invoice and to collect dollars on behalf of the Peruvian company through the letter of credit and remit them to a bank in Miami. The sole purpose of the second agreement was to enable the Peruvian company to exchange Peruvian soles for dollars in breach of the Peruvian exchange control regulations; it was the device by which an exchange contract was disguised by inflating the invoice to make it appear all part of the commercial transaction for the purchase of machinery. It was precisely the type of agreement that Professor Nussbaum calls a 'monetary transaction in disguise' ((1949) 59 Yale LJ 421 at 427) and which Lord Denning MR in *Wilson, Smithett and Cope Ltd v Terruzzi* [1976] 1 All ER 817 at 823, [1976] QB 683 at 714 said would be an exchange contract within art VIII, s 2(b) of the Bretton Woods Agreement and made a part of our own domestic law by the Bretton Woods Agreements Acts 1945 and Bretton Woods Agreements Order in Council 1946, SR & O 1946 No 36.

At first all went well with the deal. Vitro armed with their inflated invoice obtained permission to buy the dollars, then they opened a letter of credit with their bank in Peru, Banco Continental, who in turn arranged for the Royal Bank of Canada to open a confirmed irrevocable letter of credit in favour of Glass Fibres, payable in London. The English company collected the first 20% of the inflated price under the terms of the letter of credit and duly remitted half the dollars to Miami. But when the machinery was shipped the bank refused to pay the next tranche of 70% due on presentation of the shipping documents. The reasons for the refusal of the bank were wholly unconnected with the exchange contract because at that time the banks were unaware of its existence; they thought that they were financing a straightforward commercial transaction. Glass

Fibres had assigned their letter of credit to an English merchant bank and together they sued the Royal Bank of Canada on the letter of credit.

During the course of the trial the true nature of the arrangement emerged and leave was given to Banco, who had been joined as a third party by the Royal Bank of Canada, to plead that the sale contract and the letter of credit were illegal and contrary to public policy as their object was to transfer funds from Peru in breach of that country's foreign exchange control regulations and alternatively that they were exchange contracts and unenforceable by reason of the 1946 Order In Council.

Mocatta J found in favour of the bank on the ground that the sale contract was an exchange contract being a monetary transaction in disguise, contrary to the exchange control regulations of Peru and thus rendered unenforceable by the Order in Council, and that if he enforced the letter of credit he would enable the Order in Council to be avoided. He rejected an argument that he should give judgment for half the sum claimed which represented payment for the machinery on the grounds that the court could not sever the letter of credit; it was either enforceable in full according to its terms or not at all. Accordingly he gave judgment for the Royal Bank of Canada.

Counsel for the plaintiffs submits that a letter of credit is an autonomous contract entirely separate from the underlying contract of sale and that when an action is brought on a letter of credit it is impermissible to look at the contract that underlies it. For this proposition he cited a number of authorities that establish that, fraud apart, a bank that has issued an irrevocable letter of credit is not concerned with any dispute between buyer and seller as to the nature or quality of the goods which are the subject of the contract of sale: see *Malas (trading as Hamzeh Malas & Sons) v British Imex Industries Ltd* [1958] 1 All ER 262, [1958] 2 QB 127, *R D Harbottle (Mercantile) Ltd v National Westminster Bank Ltd* [1977] 2 All ER 862, [1978] QB 146 and *Edward Owen Engineering Ltd v Barclays Bank International Ltd* [1978] 1 All ER 976, [1978] QB 159.

Counsel for the plaintiffs submits that the judge should have looked at the letter of credit in isolation and if he had done that he could not have held that it was an exchange contract. If it is right to look at the letter of credit in isolation from the matrix of the arrangement in which it operated, I accept that it was not an exchange contract, for it did not involve Peruvian currency but was concerned solely with dollars. It was a contract between two parties neither of whom was resident in Peru and its performance did not involve any infringement of Peruvian exchange regulations. But is it right to look at the letter of credit in isolation, in the circumstances of this case?

There are compelling commercial reasons for isolating the obligations owed by a bank to the holder of a letter of credit from disputes about the goods between the buyer and the seller under the sale contract. These reasons are fully discussed in the authorities and in the leading textbooks. The letter of credit is regarded as almost equivalent to cash in the seller's hand. It is his guarantee that payment for his goods will not be held up by the buyer on some pretext as to their quality. The holder of an irrevocable letter of credit need not fear that he may have to bring an action to recover the price and be met with a specious counterclaim that enables the buyer to get leave to defend and so keep him out of his money for the months or years that may pass before the action can be brought to trial. The seller can use the letter of credit to finance other business; it is, as has been said more than once, part of the lifeblood of commerce.

But in this case the court is not dealing with a letter of credit that has been opened solely to pay for goods under a sale contract, nor is it dealing with a dispute between buyer and seller under the sale contract. The facts reveal that the buyer and the seller have conspired together to use the letter of credit as a means of giving effect to an exchange contract in breach of the foreign exchange regulations of Peru. Is the court to refuse to recognise the reality of the situation and allow effect to be given to the exchange contract because it sits in blinkers looking at the letter of credit in isolation? I find nothing in any of the decisions dealing with letters of credit that leads to this conclusion. They do no more than establish that the bank is not concerned with possible breaches of the underlying sale contract.

If counsel's argument for the plaintiffs is right then the Order in Council relating to

the unenforceability of exchange contracts will scarcely be worth the paper it is written
_a_ on. In this case it so happens that there was a genuine sale contract which disguised the
exchange contract, but it would not be difficult to envisage the use of a completely
spurious sale contract to disguise the exchange contract.

Unless constrained by authority to do otherwise, the court, in my view, ought to look
at the whole arrangement and if it sees that the sale contract disguises an exchange
contract it should refuse to enforce it through the medium of the letter of credit.

_b_   Counsel, however, submits that there is a decision of this court that requires us to look
solely at the letter of credit and ignore what was really going on between the parties. He
relies on _Sharif v Azad_ [1966] 3 All ER 785, [1967] 1 QB 605. In that case one Latif, a
native of Pakistan, came to this country and sold a cheque drawn on a bank in Pakistan
for a total of 6,000 rupees to Sharif for £300. Latif did this in breach of the Pakistan
exchange control regulations. Sharif then sold the cheque to Azad. Azad paid by two
_c_ postdated cheques for a total of £300 drawn on an English bank. Azad gave the
Pakistani cheque to his brother to cash in Pakistan. In Pakistan the authorities apparently
became suspicious and the rupees were paid into a blocked account so Azad's brother was
unable to collect the money. Azad thereupon stopped his cheques. Sharif then sued
Azad in the county court on the cheques. This court held that Sharif was entitled to
recover on the cheques. I confess I do not find this an easy case. I recognise the
_d_ strength of counsel's argument for the plaintiff that a bill of exchange and a letter of
credit are both means of honouring international commercial obligations which a court
should strive to uphold, and that if the court in _Sharif v Azad_ was prepared to look in
isolation at the English cheque so also in this case it should concern itself only with the
terms of the letter of credit. But the following features distinguish _Sharif v Azad_ from
the present case. Neither Sharif nor Azad was in breach of Pakistan's exchange control
_e_ regulations, because they were both resident in England and the regulations only applied
to residents in Pakistan, whereas Glass Fibres, by providing the false invoice, were
themselves in breach of the Peruvian exchange control regulations. Secondly, it was an
action on an English bill of exchange which was not tainted by illegality in English law
and for which consideration had been given. Finally, by giving judgment on the cheque
the court was not assisting a breach of the Pakistan exchange control regulations, for the
_f_ proceeds of the Pakistani cheque had already been blocked in Pakistan, whereas, if the
letter of credit is enforced in this case, active assistance will be given to the breach of the
Peruvian regulations.

I have, after some hesitation, concluded that this case does not bind me to follow a
course which would, I think, do a grave disservice to the obligations that this country
accepted as a party to the Bretton Woods Agreement. As Lord Denning MR pointed out
_g_ in _Batra v Ebrahim_ [1977] Court of Appeal Transcript 197B the court itself has a duty to
take the point of unenforceability under the 1946 Order in Council irrespective of the
wishes of the parties to the litigation. In my opinion the court should not shirk this duty
by turning its back on the reality of the situation. Once it sees that the real purpose of
the letter of credit is in part to give effect to an exchange contract in breach of the
Peruvian exchange control regulations the court should refuse its assistance and decline
_h_ to give judgment for such part of the claim as relates to the exchange contract.

I do not however see why the court should not give judgment on the letter of credit
for that sum which is in payment for the machinery and freight. These sums are easily
identifiable, and nothing in the Order in Council renders them unenforceable. In
refusing to give judgment for so much of the claim that relates to the unenforceable
exchange contract the court would be following the precedents set in _Ralli Brothers v_
_j_ _Compañia Naviera Sota y Aznar_ [1922] 2 KB 187, [1920] All ER Rep 427, in which
judgment was given for freight up to 875 pesetas per tonne but refused as to the excess
which was illegal under Spanish law, and the building contract cases in which judgment
was given for that part of the work for which a licence had been obtained but refused for
the unlicensed excess: see _Jackson Stransfield & Sons v Butterworth_ [1948] 2 All ER 558 and
Dennis & Co Ltd v Munn [1949] 1 All ER 616, [1949] 2 KB 327. The object of the Order
in Council will be achieved by refusing judgment for so much of the claim as will

frustrate the performance of the exchange contract. I see no reason why the court should go further and prevent the plaintiff from recovering payment for the machinery which has been lying in a warehouse in Peru for the last five years.

Counsel for Banco submits that comity requires the court to refuse judgment on any part of the letter of credit because it forms part of a transaction that was intended to achieve an end that was illegal in a friendly state. He relied on *Foster v Driscoll* [1929] 1 KB 470, [1928] All ER Rep 130, in which the court refused any relief to the parties to an agreement to sell whisky in the United States in the days of prohibition. Lawrence LJ founded his judgment on the illegality of the enterprise ([1929] 1 KB 470 at 510, [1928] All ER Rep 130 at 143):

> 'The ground upon which I rest my judgment that such a partnership is illegal is that its recognition by our Courts would furnish a just cause for complaint by the United States Government against our Government (of which the partners are subjects) and would be contrary to our obligation of international comity as now understood and recognized, and therefore would offend against our notions of public morality.'

Sankey LJ expressed his views in similar language (see [1929] 1 KB 470 at 520, [1928] All ER Rep 130 at 148). In *Regazzoni v K C Sethia (1944) Ltd* [1957] 3 All ER 286, [1958] AC 301 the courts refused to enforce a contract for the purchase of jute from India for resale in South Africa when the parties knew that the exporting of jute from India to South Africa was prohibited by Indian law. The contract was held to be unenforceable. Viscount Simonds said ([1957] 3 All ER 286 at 290, [1958] AC 301 at 319):

> 'Just as public policy avoids contracts which offend against our own law, so it will avoid at least some contracts which violate the laws of a foreign state, and it will do so because public policy demands that deference to international comity.'

Lord Reid said ([1957] 3 All ER 286 at 293, [1958] AC 301 at 323):

> 'The real question is one of public policy in English law; but, in considering this question, we must have in mind the background of international law and international relationships often referred to as the comity of nations.'

Do considerations of comity and public policy require that the English sellers should be deprived of the purchase price of their goods in this case? I think not. They are certainly not in pari delicto with the buyers; it was the buyers who thought up the scheme to break the exchange control regulations and who were to reap the benefit of it; the sellers weakly fell in with the request for the inflated invoice. Provided judgment is only given for the cost of the machinery and freight, nothing will be done under the letter of credit that involves a breach of the Peruvian exchange regulations and our courts will have honoured the Bretton Woods obligation to give their assistance in the protection of the currency of another country that was party to the agreement. It seems to me that in these circumstances comity requires no more. So if matters rested here I should have given judgment for the cost of the machinery and freight but refused judgment in respect of the surplus dollars destined for Miami.

However, Banco's notice raises this further question: is the holder of an irrevocable letter of credit entitled to payment by the bank if the supporting documents, although appearing on their face to conform to the requirements of the letter of credit, have in fact been fraudulently prepared to present false information? The plaintiffs say, 'Yes, unless the holder of the letter of credit is himself a party to the fraud.' The bank say, 'No, its obligation is to pay on the production of genuine documents and not on false documents.'

We have had the advantage of elaborate citation of both English and American authorities, but I find only limited assistance from the reports because in no case was the court considering the problem with which we are now confronted. This does not surprise me unduly as the facts of this case are most unusual.

The latest date for shipment of the machinery was 15th December 1976. The machinery was in fact shipped on 16th December 1976, and if the bill of lading had

shown that date the bank would have refused to pay on presentation of the documents
because of the strict rule that the documents must comply in every respect with the
terms of the letter of credit: see *Guaranty Trust Co of New York v Van Den Berghs Ltd* (1925)
22 Ll L Rep 58. The shipping agent who knew this therefore falsely and, as the judge
found, fraudulently entered the date of shipment as 15th December on the bill of
lading. But the judge also held that the shipping agent was not acting as the agent of the
seller or the merchant bank to whom the seller had assigned the letter of credit. The
judge held that the shipping agent was acting on behalf of the shipping line and that
therefore there was no fraud on the part of the sellers or their assignees. The bank
refused to pay because they discovered that the date on the bill of lading was false and
that the goods had in fact been shipped on 16th December.

Were the bank wrong to refuse payment in these circumstances? It seems to me that
it would be a strange rule that required a bank to refuse payment if the document
correctly showed the date of shipment as 16th December, yet obliged the bank to make
payment if it knew that the document falsely showed the date of shipment as 15th
December and that the true date was 16th December. It is argued that this consequence
flows from the cases that establish the rule that the bank undertakes to pay against
documents and is not concerned with disputes as to the nature or quality of goods that
may arise between buyer and seller. It must be accepted that, in so far as the documents
contain a description of the goods, the bank is not concerned with whether or not the
goods in fact conform to the description on the documents. To that extent it can be said
that the bank is obliged to pay on the presentation of documents that it may suspect or
even know contain a misdescription of the goods. But this rule is not carried so far as to
apply to a misdescription that amounts to a fraud on the part of the seller: see *Sztejn v J
Henry Schroder Banking Corpn* (1941) 31 NYS 2d 631 and *Edward Owen Engineering Ltd v
Barclays Bank International Ltd* [1978] 1 All ER 976, [1978] QB 159.

What is the position if the bank is presented with documents that appear on their face
to be in order but which the bank knows to be forgeries? The bank takes the documents
as its security for payment. It is not obliged to take worthless documents. If the bank
knows that the documents are forgeries it must refuse to accept them: see *Edward Owen
Engineering Ltd v Barclays Bank International Ltd* and *Bank Russo-Iran v Gordon Woodroffe
& Co Ltd* (1972) Times, 4th October. It may be that the party presenting the documents
has himself been duped by the forger and believes the documents to be genuine, but that
surely cannot affect the bank's right to refuse to accept the forgeries. The identity of the
forger is immaterial. It is the fact that the documents are worthless that matters to the
bank. In such a case the right of the bank to refuse payment does not rest on the
application of the maxim ex turpi causa non oritur actio but on the fact that the bank's
obligation is to pay on the presentation of genuine documents in accordance with the
requirements of the letter of credit. If the documents presented are fraudulently false,
they are not genuine conforming documents and the bank has no obligation to pay.

This proposition seems to me self-evident, but if authority is required support for it is
to be found in the American cases. In *Old Colony Trust Co v Lawyers' Title & Trust Co*
(1924) 297 F 152, a decision of the Circuit Court of Appeals, Second Circuit, it was a
requirement of the letter of credit that it should be accompanied by a warehouse receipt
showing that the goods were landed and in the warehouse. A warehouse receipt falsely
showed the goods as in the warehouse. The defendant knew that the goods were not in
the warehouse and refused to honour the draft. In giving its judgment for the defendants
the court said (at 157–158):

> 'The matter is very simple when colloquially stated. It was as if defendant trust
> company said, "With your draft, deliver to us a truthful warehouse receipt which
> will inform us that the goods are in the warehouse" . . . Obviously, when the issuer
> of a letter of credit knows that a document, although correct in form, is, in point of
> fact, false or illegal, he cannot be called upon to recognize such a document as
> complying with the terms of a letter of credit.'

In *Maurice O'Meara Co v National Park Bank of New York* (1925) 239 NY 386 at 395, a
decision of the New York Court of Appeals, McLaughlin J said: 'The bank's obligation

was to pay sight drafts when presented, if accompanied by genuine documents specified in the letter of credit.'

In *Sztejn v J Henry Schroder Banking Corpn* (1941) 31 NYS 2d 631 at 633–634 the judge said:

'It would be a most unfortunate interference with business transactions if a bank before honoring drafts drawn upon it was obliged or even allowed to go behind the documents, at the request of the buyer and enter into controversies between the buyer and the seller regarding the quality of the merchandise shipped ... Of course, the application of this doctrine presupposes that the documents accompanying the draft are genuine and conform in terms to the requirements of the letter of credit.'

I am unable to draw any distinction between a false document which is a forgery according to English criminal law and a document which fraudulently conveys false information but is not technically a forgery. It would be most unfortunate if we had to look to the technicalities of our criminal law to determine the validity of international commercial transactions. As Ackner LJ has pointed out, if the bill of lading had been in a different form it would have been a forgery, but the mischief remained the same whichever form of bill of lading was used: the date of shipment was falsely and fraudulently stated to be 15th December. It was a dishonest document, it was not a genuine document, and, in my view, the bank were entitled to reject it.

Accordingly, I would dismiss the appeal.

Appeal dismissed. No order for costs. Leave to appeal to the House of Lords granted.

Solicitors: *Nicholson, Graham & Jones* (for the plaintiffs); *Thomas Cooper & Stibbard* (for Banco).

Patricia Hargrove   Barrister.

Allied Collection Agencies Ltd v Wood and another

QUEEN'S BENCH DIVISION
NEILL J
11th, 20th JUNE 1980

Costs – Order for costs – Interlocutory application – Order for 'costs in any event' – Effect of order – Party concerned to have costs of interlocutory application irrespective of final outcome of substantive action but taxation deferred until conclusion of action – RSC Ord 14, r 7(1), Ord 62, rr 4(1), 11(1), Ord 86, r 7.

Costs – Order for costs – Interlocutory application – Order for 'defendant's costs' or 'plaintiff's costs' – No reference to 'in any event' – Effect of order – Party concerned entitled to immediate taxation – RSC Ord 14, r 7(1), Ord 62, rr 4(1), 11(1), Ord 86, r 7.

Where on an interlocutory application the court intends that one party is to have the costs of that application irrespective of the outcome of the substantive action, the usual form of order is 'costs in any event', in which case taxation is deferred until the conclusion of the substantive action. The words 'defendant's costs' and the words 'plaintiff's costs', which are only used in exceptional circumstances, have the effect of entitling the party concerned to obtain an immediate taxation (see p 181 *b c e* to *g*, post).

Adam & Harvey Ltd v International Maritime Supplies Co Ltd [1967] 1 All ER 533, _J T_
a _Stratford & Son Ltd v Lindley_ (No 2) [1969] 3 All ER 1122 and _Settlement Corpn v Hochschild_
(1967) 111 Sol Jo 354 followed.

There is an apparent inconsistency between RSC Ord 62, r 11(1)[a], on the one hand, and
Ord 62, r 4(1)[b], Ord 14, r 7(1)[c] and Ord 86, r 7[d], on the other, which requires attention
so that the present formulae for orders for costs in interlocutory applications can be
replaced and a form of order prescribed to cover the exceptional case where immediate
b taxation is intended (see p 181 _g h_, post).

Notes

For an order for costs of an application, see 30 Halsbury's Laws (3rd Edn) 479, para 900,
for taxation pursuant to an order for costs, see ibid 426, para 805, and for cases on the
taxation of and entitlement to costs, see 51 Digest (Repl) 884–885, 4368–4379.

c
Cases referred to in judgment

Adams & Harvey Ltd v International Maritime Supplies Co Ltd [1967] 1 All ER 533, [1967]
1 WLR 445, CA, Digest (Cont Vol C) 1091, 2006a.
Settlement Corpn v Hochschild (1967) 111 Sol Jo 354, CA.
Stratford (J T) & Son Ltd v Lindley (No 2) [1969] 3 All ER 1122, [1969] 1 WLR 1547, [1969]
d 2 Lloyd's Rep 309, CA, Digest (Cont Vol C) 1091, 2080a.

Case also cited

Phillips v Phillips (1879) 5 QBD 60, CA.

Interlocutory application

e By summons dated 15th May 1980 the defendants, Ian Alexander Wood and Universal
Collections and Investigations Ltd, applied under RSC Ord 20, r 11 for the correction of
an order of the court made on 21st August 1979 in an action brought against the
defendants by the plaintiff company, Allied Collection Agencies Ltd. The summons was
heard in chambers but judgment was given by Neill J in open court. The facts are set out
in the judgment.

f
M J Segal for the plaintiff company.
Peter Birts for the defendants.

Cur adv vult

g 20th June. **NEILL J** read the following judgment: This is an application by the
defendants pursuant to RSC Ord 20, r 11 to correct what is said to be a clerical error in
an order made by Mars-Jones J on 21st August 1979 during the last long vacation.

The matter first came before the court on 3rd June 1980 when, after hearing some
argument, Wien J adjourned the case for a special appointment. The adjourned hearing
took place before me on 11th June, when I was asked by the parties to give judgment in
h open court.

The facts of the matter can be stated shortly. At all material times before 23rd July
1979 the first defendant was employed by the plaintiff company. His contract of
employment, dated 28th June 1977, contained a number of stipulations, including

---

_a_   Rule 11(1) is set out at p 180 _j_, post
. _b_   Rule 4(1) is set out at p 180 _e_, post
j _c_   Rule 7(1) is set out at p 180 _g_, post
_d_   Rule 7 provides: 'If the plaintiff makes an application under rule 1 [for summary judgment in
certain actions in the Chancery Division] where the case is not within this Order, or if it appears
to the Court that the plaintiff knew that the defendant relied on a contention which would entitle
him to unconditional leave to defend, then, without prejudice to Order 62, and, in particular, to
rule 4(1) thereof, the Court may dismiss the application with costs and may, if the plaintiff is not
an assisted person, require the costs to be paid by him forthwith.'

undertakings by the first defendant not to disclose the plaintiff company's private affairs, nor to use any confidential information which he acquired during his employment. *a*

The contract did not contain any express term as to dealings between the first defendant and the plaintiff company's customers after he ceased to be employed.

At about the end of July 1979 the first defendant went to work for the defendant company, Universal Collections and Investigations Ltd, which, as its name suggests, was engaged in a business similar to that carried on by the plaintiff company. It was suspected that the first defendant was approaching customers of the plaintiff company. *b*

On 14th August 1979 the plaintiff company applied ex parte for an injunction. On that day an injunction was granted by Mars-Jones J restraining the first defendant and the defendant company from approaching or having any dealings with a number of named customers of the plaintiff company. A summons was then issued so that the matter could come back again before the court inter partes.

Before the case was called on before Mars-Jones J on 21st August 1979 there was a *c* discussion between counsel for the defendants (who are not counsel who appeared before me) and counsel for the plaintiff company. It was soon accepted by counsel for the plaintiff company that in the absence of any express term in the contract of employment the application to continue the injunction could not be pursued. It was therefore agreed between counsel that the application should be dismissed. Accordingly, when the case was called on, the matter was mentioned only very briefly to the judge and the *d* application was duly dismissed.

No difficulty arises in relation to any of the matters which I have so far recounted. I am concerned in the present summons solely with the form of the order which was made as to costs. The order as initialled by the judge was in these terms:

'Application dismissed. Defendants' costs in any event. Certificate for two counsel for the Defendants.' *e*

Later a formal order was drawn up by the plaintiff's solicitors as follows:

'It is ordered that this application be dismissed and that the costs of this application be the Defendants' costs in any event. Certificate for two counsel for the Defendants.' *f*

The words with which I am concerned are 'Defendants' costs in any event'. It is common ground that the words of the order were intended to reflect what had been agreed between counsel before the case was called on. There was no argument as to costs before Mars-Jones J and, indeed, as the matter had been resolved, counsel for the plaintiff company was not actually present in chambers when the case was mentioned to the judge. *g*

It was submitted before me on behalf of the defendants that the order as initialled by the judge and as subsequently drawn up by the plaintiff company did not reflect what had been agreed. It is therefore necessary for me to consider what was agreed as to costs, and in particular what the effect is of the form of words which the parties employed. Fortunately, there is no dispute as to the form of words which was used by counsel.

I shall now refer to the affidavit of Mr Martin Shaw, sworn on 2nd June 1980. He *h* deposed as follows:

'I am a solicitor and partner in the firm of Firth & Co of the above address and I have the conduct of this action on behalf of the First and Second Defendants. I was present on the 21st August 1979 when the Plaintiffs' application for an order that the injunction granted on the 14th August 1979 be continued until the trial of this *j* action came before the Court. Before the said application was called before the Court, the Plaintiffs through their Counsel and solicitors had indicated that they would not proceed with the application and accordingly when it came before the Court the application was dismissed. On the dismissal of the application the Defendants applied to the Court for their costs, and this application was granted. To a   the best of my recollection, none of the Counsel who appeared for the parties used the expression "in any event" when the question of costs came before the Court. Further, to the best of my recollection the learned Judge did not use that expression in making the order that the Defendants should have their costs. The Defendants were represented by both Leading and Junior Counsel, and my recollection is reinforced by the fact that both Counsel in endorsing their briefs have used the expressions "costs to Defendants" and "with costs" respectively, and have not used

b   the expression "in any event".'

He exhibited to the affidavit the two back sheets of the briefs.

I have seen the indorsements made by both counsel who appeared before Mars-Jones J for the defendants; they were respectively 'Application withdrawn. Costs to the Defendants' and 'Application dismissed with costs. Certificate for two counsel'.

c   Counsel for the plaintiff company told me that he accepted Mr Shaw's version of the facts, and said that he indorsed his brief in these terms: 'Application dismissed with costs. Certificate for two counsel for Defendants.'

From this recital of the facts it is therefore clear that I must proceed on the basis that neither the judge nor counsel used the words 'in any event' and that these words were added by the clerk to the court when the order was written out to be initialled by the

d   judge. In these circumstances, it would be open to me merely to delete the words 'in any event' as being a clerical error and to leave the question as to the meaning of the order without these words to be debated before the taxing master and perhaps in further proceedings.

I have been urged not to take that course but to deal in my judgment with the effect of the order with the words 'in any event' omitted; in other words, I am asked to express a view on the effect of an order made on an interlocutory application, 'defendants' costs'.

e   Counsel for the defendants submitted that there was a well-recognised distinction between 'defendants' costs' and 'defendants' costs in any event'. Under the first form of order the defendants are entitled to proceed to tax their costs immediately; under the second form of order taxation is postponed until the conclusion of the proceedings.

Counsel drew my attention to two authorities. In *Adam & Harvey Ltd v International*

f   *Maritime Supplies Co Ltd* [1967] 1 All ER 533, [1967] 1 WLR 445 an application was made to the Court of Appeal by motion under RSC Ord 20, r 11 to correct an order in the terms 'Appeal allowed with costs' so as to add the words 'in any event'. The application succeeded.

In his judgment Harman LJ referred to the fact that in the course of the interlocutory observations he had used the words 'No immediate taxation' and all the members of the court were of the view that the order as drawn did not express the intention of the

g   court. Harman LJ said ([1967] 1 All ER 533 at 534, [1967] 1 WLR 445 at 448):

'. . . I did not intend that there should be this exceptional order for payment of costs at once, but that costs should be in any event those of the successful appellant.'

The second case to which counsel referred was *J T Stratford & Son Ltd v Lindley (No 2)*

h   [1969] 3 All ER 1122 at 1123, [1969] 1 WLR 1547 at 1553. In the course of his judgment, Lord Denning MR referred to the meaning of the phrase 'costs in the cause' and continued:

'"Plaintiff's costs in any event" means that, no matter who wins or loses when the case is decided, the plaintiff is to have the costs of those interlocutory proceedings. "Plaintiff's costs" means that the plaintiff is to have the costs of the interlocutory

j   proceedings without waiting for a decision.'

Counsel also drew my attention to Bullen and Leake's Precedents of Pleadings (9th Edn, 1935, p 53, note 6) which included these words:

'If the Master orders the costs to be "Defendant's costs in any event," the Plaintiff will have to pay the costs of the application on both sides, whatever the result of the action, but not at once: they will be taken into account in the ultimate taxation. It is only where the application is dismissed 'with costs' that the successful party is *a* entitled to an immediate taxation.'

Accordingly, counsel submitted that as the parties had omitted the words 'in any event' the effect of their agreement was that the defendants were entitled to an order which would give them the right to an immediate taxation. The words 'defendants' costs' would give them that right.

Counsel for the plaintiff company did not seek to contend that the words 'in any event' *b* should be allowed to remain merely because that was the usual form or order, or because he himself had in contemplation that the normal form of order as to costs would follow. He recognised that the words 'defendants' costs' or words to the same effect had been employed on both sides. He was therefore constrained to put forward the following arguments, which he advanced with force and clarity: (1) that since the coming into force of r 4(1) of the Supreme Court Costs Rules 1959, which is now RSC Ord 62, r 4(1), *c* an order which requires costs to be paid forthwith must say so in terms. The all-important word, said counsel, is 'forthwith'; if that word is omitted the order does not give the relevant party the right to an immediate taxation; (2) that the decision in *Adam & Harvey Ltd v International Maritime Supplies Co Ltd* was reached per incuriam and without regard to the wording of Ord 62, r 4(1), or the corresponding words in the 1959 rules; (3) that I was entitled not to follow the guidance of Lord Denning MR in *J T* *d* *Stratford & Son Ltd v Lindley (No 2)* because what the Master of the Rolls had said on the matter was plainly obiter.

I shall deal first with counsel's argument based on Ord 62, r 4(1). That rule is in these terms:

'Costs may be dealt with by the Court at any stage of the proceedings or after the *e* conclusion of the proceedings; and any order of the Court for the payment of any costs may, if the Court thinks fit, and the person against whom the order is made is not an assisted person, require the costs to be paid forthwith notwithstanding that the proceedings have not been concluded.'

Counsel submitted that this rule plainly contemplates a form of words in the order *f* which make it clear to the paying party that the payment is to be made forthwith.

In this context, I was also referred to Ord 86, r 7 (which deals with dismissal of an application for summary judgment in an action for specific performance) and to Ord 14, r 7(1). It is sufficient if I read the terms of Ord 14, r 7(1). This provides:

'If the plaintiff makes an application under Rule 1 where the case is not within this Order or if it appears to the Court that the plaintiff knew that the defendant *g* relied on a contention which would entitle him to unconditional leave to defend, then without prejudice to Order 62, and, in particular, to Rule 4(1) thereof, the Court may dismiss the application with costs and may, if the plaintiff is not an assisted person, require the costs to be paid by him forthwith.'

In each of these rules, ie Ord 14, r 7, Ord 62, r 4 and Ord 86, r 7, the word 'forthwith' *h* is used. Moreover, it would appear that by Ord 14, r 7 and Ord 86, r 7 two separate discretions are conferred: a discretion to dismiss the application with costs and a further discretion, where the plaintiff is not an assisted person, to require the costs to be paid by the plaintiff forthwith.

I should now refer to Ord 62, r 11 (formerly r 11 of the 1959 rules). That rule provides as follows: *j*

'(1) Where an action, petition or summons is dismissed with costs, or a motion is refused with costs, or an order of the Court directs the payment of any costs, or any party is entitled under rule 10 to tax his costs, no order directing the taxation of those costs need be made . . .'

a In the light of that rule, it can be argued that if a summons is dismissed with costs under Ord 14, r 7 or Ord 86, r 7 the defendant can proceed to taxation without any further order. Why then is it necessary to include in these two rules the words 'as to payment forthwith', unless it is intended that a mere dismissal with costs would not be sufficient to secure immediate taxation and payment, notwithstanding the wording of Ord 62, r 11(1).

b I see the force of this argument, but I am satisfied that in the course of time the words 'defendant's costs' have acquired a special meaning. The words constitute, as counsel for the plaintiff company put it, a formula. The formula is used where the court or, as in this case, the parties intend or must be deemed to intend that the defendant should be entitled to tax his costs immediately. Moreover, I see no escape from the plain words of Ord 62, r 11(1) that where a summons is dismissed with costs no order directing the taxation of those costs need be made. The opening words of this rule are the same as *c* those in RSC 1883, Ord 65, r 27(33) which was the corresponding rule before the Supreme Court Costs Rules 1959 came into force. Regulation (33) was itself based on the old practice laid down in Consolidated Order 40, r 38.

I can deal with counsel's other arguments for the plaintiff company more briefly. I am afraid I am quite unable to accept the argument that I can regard the decision in the *Adam & Harvey Ltd* case as decided per incuriam; nor would I wish to disregard the *d* guidance of Lord Denning MR in *J T Stratford & Son Ltd v Lindley (No 2)*. It is further to be observed that a few weeks after the judgments in the *Adam & Harvey Ltd* case were delivered an application was made following an interlocutory appeal in *Settlement Corpn v Hochschild* (1967) 111 Sol Jo 354, where the report says:

'. . . some doubt arose as to whether the appeal had been dismissed "with costs" or "with costs in any event", the briefs of leading and junior counsel having been *e* differently endorsed in that respect.'

In the course of the application to ascertain the intention of the court, reference was made to the *Adam & Harvey Ltd* case, which dealt with the respective effects of the orders. Lord Denning MR said the appeal had been dismissed 'with costs in any event'. He desired to say that that was the usual order in interlocutory appeals, save in exceptional *f* circumstances.

I can therefore state my conclusion as follows. (1) Where on an interlocutory application the court intends that one party is to have the costs, the usual form of order is 'costs in any event'. It is only in exceptional circumstances that the words 'defendant's costs' or the words 'plaintiff's costs' are used. (2) If the words 'plaintiff's costs' or 'defendant's costs' are used they are effective to entitle the party concerned to obtain an *g* immediate taxation.

I would only add this. I have been forced to conclude on the material which has been put before me that the words 'defendant's costs' have the meaning for which counsel for the defendants contends. One cannot, however, regard the present situation as satisfactory. There is an apparent inconsistency between RSC Ord 62, r 11(1), on the one hand, and Ord 62, r 4(1), Ord 14, r 7(1) and Ord 86, r 7, on the other hand. I would hope *h* that the matter can be brought to the attention of the Rule Committee so that the present formula can be replaced and a form of order can be prescribed to cover the exceptional case where immediate taxation is intended. I regard the present formula as a source of confusion.

Order accordingly.

Solicitors: *Judge & Priestley*, Bromley (for the plaintiff company); *Penningtons*, agents for *Firth & Co*, Woking (for the defendants).

K Mydeen Esq   Barrister.

Phonogram Ltd v Lane   *a*

COURT OF APPEAL, CIVIL DIVISION
LORD DENNING MR, SHAW AND OLIVER LJJ
9th, 10th MARCH 1981

Contract – Parties – Unformed company – Liability of person purporting to contract as agent for
unformed company – Defendant signing contract 'for and on behalf of' company not yet in course *b*
of formation – Whether defendant personally liable on contract under European Communities
legislation – Whether legislation applying to contract made as agent for company about to be
formed but not yet in course of formation – Whether person 'purports' to contract as agent for
unformed company only where he represents that company already in existence – Whether a
company can be 'a person' purporting to contract as agent for unformed company – Whether
there is an 'agreement to the contrary', ie that person purporting to contract not to be personally *c*
liable, where he signs contract as agent for unformed company – Whether contract must contain
an express exclusion of personal liability – Whether formula adopted for signing contract
affecting personal liability under European Communities legislation – European Communities Act
1972, s 9(2).

Prior to the formation of a company to be called F Ltd, which was going to manage a pop *d*
music group, negotiations took place between the defendant, an artistes' manager, on
behalf of F Ltd, and the plaintiff company regarding financing the pop group which
resulted in an arrangement that the plaintiffs would finance the group in the sum of
£12,000 to be payable in two instalments of £6,000 each. In pursuance of that
arrangement the plaintiffs, on 4th July 1973, wrote a letter to the defendant, which was
addressed to him at F Ltd, stating that a cheque for £6,000 was therewith sent to 'you' in *e*
anticipation of a contract to exploit the services of the pop group being signed between
the plaintiffs and F Ltd. The letter went on to state that if that contract was not
completed within a certain period 'you [ie the defendant] will undertake to repay us the
£6000'. For administrative reasons the cheque for the £6,000 was made payable to a
company called J Ltd of which the defendant was a director. The defendant, as requested
by the letter, signed a copy of the letter, 'for and on behalf of' F Ltd, and returned the *f*
signed copy to the plaintiffs. The cheque for £6,000, together with a further sum of
£600 paid by the plaintiffs in respect of value added tax, was paid into J Ltd's account.
The contract to exploit the pop group's services was never completed and therefore under
the terms of the letter of 4th July 1973 the £6,600 became repayable to the plaintiffs.
However, the money was not repaid, and in October 1976 the plaintiffs issued a writ
against the defendant claiming repayment of the £6,600 from him. By his defence the *g*
defendant denied that he was personally liable to repay that sum. At the trial of the
action the judge found on the facts that the agreement to repay contained in the letter of
4th July 1973 did not make the defendant personally liable to repay the £6,600 but held
that he was personally liable to repay that sum under s 9(2)[a] of the European
Communities Act 1972 because the agreement to repay was 'a contract [purporting] to
be made . . . by a person [ie the defendant] as agent of a company [ie F Ltd], at a time *h*
when the company has not been formed', and accordingly, in the absence of 'any
agreement to the contrary', the contract to repay had effect under s 9(2) as a contract
entered into by the defendant under which he was personally liable. The defendant
appealed, submitting that s 9(2) did not apply on the grounds (i) that the section was to
be construed in accordance with the French text of EEC Council Directive 68/151[b],
which led to the enactment of s 9, and s 9(2) was, thereunder, limited to a contract *j*
purporting to be made on behalf of a company which was already in the course of
formation, which was not the case in regard to F Ltd, (ii) that the word 'purports' in s 9(2)
meant there had to be a representation that the unformed company was already in

---

a Section 9(2) is set out at p 185 *j*, post
b The French text of the directive, so far as material, is set out at p 186 *c*, post

a existence and (iii) that a company could be the 'person' who purported to contract on behalf of the unformed company, within s 9(2), and that in the circumstances J Ltd, and not the defendant, was the person who had purported to contract on behalf of F Ltd and was personally liable for the repayment under s 9(2).

Held – The defendant was personally liable to repay the £6,600 by virtue of s 9(2) of the 1972 Act, and the appeal would be dismissed, for the following reasons—

b (1) Under art 189^c of the EEC Treaty only the spirit and intent of an EEC Council directive was binding on a member state. Accordingly, as s 9(2) was in accordance with the spirit and intent of Directive 68/151, it fell to be construed in accordance with its own terms, and therefore applied to a contract purporting to be made by a person as agent for a company which was about to be formed but which was not then in the course of formation (see p 186 e to g, p 187 f and p 188 a b j, post).

c (2) A contract was 'purported' to be made on behalf of an unformed company, within s 9(2), even though both parties to the contract knew that the company had not then been formed and was only about to be formed, and accordingly there did not have to be a representation that the company was already in existence for s 9(2) to apply (see p 186 g, p 187 f and p 188 j, post).

(3) As J Ltd had not itself entered into the contract to repay in the letter of 4th July *d* 1973 it was not the 'person' which had purported to contract as agent for F Ltd, for the purpose of s 9(2), and therefore it could not be argued that J Ltd, rather than the defendant, was personally liable under s 9(2) to repay the £6,600 (see p 186 h, p 187 f and p 188 j, post).

Per Curiam. An 'agreement to the contrary' within s 9(2), ie an agreement that the person purporting to contract as agent for an unformed company is not to be personally *e* liable on the contract, cannot be inferred by the fact that the contract is signed by that person as agent for the company, for that would defeat the purpose of s 9(2), and (per Lord Denning MR) in all cases where a person purports to contract on behalf of a company not yet formed then, unless there is a clear exclusion of his personal liability, he is personally liable on the contract however he expresses his signature (see p 187 e f and p 188 b h, post).

f Per Lord Denning MR. Section 9(2) applies whatever formula is adopted for signing a contract on behalf of an unformed company, for the distinction under the common law between the effect of a signature as 'agent for' or 'for and on behalf of' an unformed company on the one hand and a signature in the name of the company on the other is obliterated by s 9(2) (see p 187 b c, post); *Hollman v Pullin* (1884) Cab & El 254, *Kelner v Baxter* (1886) LR 2 CP 174, *Newborne v Sensolid (Great Britain) Ltd* [1953] 1 All ER 708 and *g* *Black v Smallwood* (1965) 117 CLR 51 considered.

Per Oliver LJ. Although at common law the contractual liability of an agent depended on the real intent revealed by the contract, namely on whether the agent intended himself to be a party to the contract and not on the narrow distinction between a signature 'for and on behalf of' a company and a signature in the name of the company, any distinctions depending on the form of the signature which might have been raised *h* at common law have been rendered irrelevant by s 9(2) of the 1972 Act in any case where a contract is either with a company or with the agent of a company (see p 188 b to d and h, post); *Hollman v Pullin* (1884) Cab & El 254, *Kelner v Baxter* (1886) LR 2 CP 174, *Newborne v Sensolid (Great Britain) Ltd* [1953] 1 All ER 708 and *Black v Smallwood* (1965) 117 CLR 51 considered.

Notes

j For liability in contract where the contract purports to be made by a person as agent for an unformed company, see 9 Halsbury's Laws (4th Edn) para 1366, and for cases on the subject, see 9 Digest (Reissue) 712, 4211–4215.

For the European Communities Act 1972, s 9, see 42 Halsbury's Statutes (3rd Edn) 60.

For EEC Council Directive 68/151 (in the English text), see 42A ibid 277.

---

c Article 189 is set out at p 186 f, post

Cases referred to in judgments

Black v Smallwood (1965) 117 CLR 51, [1966] ALR 744, 39 ALJR 405 (Aust HC), 9 Digest *a*
(Reissue) 715, *2107.

Hollman v Pullin (1884) Cab & El 254, 1(2) Digest (Reissue) 841, 5440.

Kelner v Baxter (1866) LR 2 CP 174, 36 LJCP 94, 15 LT 213, 12 Jur NS 1016, 9 Digest
(Reissue) 712, 4211.

Newborne v Sensolid (Great Britain) Ltd [1953] 1 All ER 708, [1954] 1 QB 45, [1953] 2 WLR
596, CA, 1(2) Digest (Reissue) 840, 5433.   *b*

Appeal

By a writ and statement of claim dated 14th October 1976 the plaintiffs, Phonogram Ltd,
alleged that by a contract made on or about 4th July 1973 they agreed with the
defendant, Mr Brian Lane, that in consideration of the payment by them of £6,000,
together with the further sum of £600 in respect of value added tax, to a company called *c*
Jelly Music Ltd on behalf of Mr Lane, in anticipation and/or in furtherance of a contract
to be entered into between Phonogram Ltd and a company called Fragile Management
Ltd, Mr Lane agreed and/or undertook to repay the sum of £6,600 to Phonogram Ltd in
the event of that contract not being entered into in a binding form within one month of
4th July 1973, that that contract was not entered into within one month of 4th July 1973
or at all and that wrongfully and in breach of the agreement of 4th July 1973 Mr Lane *d*
had refused and/or failed to repay to Phonogram Ltd the £6,600 or any part thereof, and
Phonogram Ltd claimed from him that sum and interest thereon. By his defence Mr
Lane denied that he had agreed and/or undertaken to repay the sum of £6,600 to
Phonogram Ltd and therefore denied that he was indebted to Phonogram Ltd in that
sum or at all. On 12th July 1977 Phillips J gave judgment for Phonogram Ltd for the
sum claimed on the ground that, whilst the events of 4th July 1973 did not give rise to *e*
a contract between Phonogram Ltd and Mr Lane personally, Phonogram Ltd's claim
against Mr Lane succeeded under s 9(2) of the European Communities Act 1972. Mr
Lane appealed on the ground that the judge had erred in law in holding that Mr Lane was
personally liable to Phonogram Ltd under s 9(2). The facts are set out in the judgment
of Lord Denning MR.

f

Anthony Thompson QC and *Ian Grainger* for Mr Lane.
Peter Leaver for Phonogram Ltd.

LORD DENNING MR. In 1973 there was a group of 'pop' artists. They included two
gentlemen called Brian Chatton and John McBurnie. The suggestion was that they
should perform under the name 'Cheap Mean and Nasty'. A company was going to be *g*
formed to run the group. It was to be called 'Fragile Management Ltd'.

Before the company was formed, negotiations took place for the financing of the
group. It was to be financed by one of the subsidiaries of a big organisation called the
Hemdale Group. It was eventually arranged that money should be provided by
Phonogram Ltd. The agreed amount was £12,000, and the first instalment was to be *h*
£6,000. The first instalment of £6,000 was paid.

But the new company was never formed. The group never performed under it. And
the £6,000 was due to be repaid. But it was never repaid. Phonogram Ltd then tried to
discover who was liable to repay the money. Mr Roland Rennie was the man who had
negotiated on behalf of Phonogram. Mr Brian Lane was the man who had negotiated on
behalf of the new company which was to be formed. I will read the letter from Mr *j*
Rennie to Mr Lane of 4th July 1973. It is the subject matter of this action:

'Brian Lane, Esq.,
Fragile Ltd.,
39 South Street,
London, W.1.

'Dear Brian,

'In regard to the contract now being completed between Phonogram Ltd and Fragile Management Ltd concerning recordings of a group consisting of Brian Chatton, John McBurnie and one other with a provisional title of "Cheap Mean and Nasty" and further to our conversation this morning, I send you herewith our cheque for £6000 in anticipation of the contract signing, this being the initial payment for the initial LP called for in the contract. In the unlikely event that we fail to complete within, say, one month you will undertake to repay us the £6000. As per our telephone conversation the cheque has been made payable to Jelly Music Ltd. For good orders sake, Brian, I should be appreciative if you could sign the attached copy of this letter and return it to me so that I can keep our accounts people informed of what is happening.

'Yours sincerely,
'Roland G. Rennie

'SIGNED BY . . . .
for and on behalf of FRAGILE MANAGEMENT LTD.'

That was signed by Mr Lane. So there is the written contract embodying the agreement between those concerned. An invoice was sent forward by Phonogram Ltd:

'Invoice

'To contract between Fragile Management
and Phonogram Ltd.
Re.   "Cheap Mean & Nasty"   6000·00
                                          VAT   600·00
                                                   £6600·00

Initial Payment for first album as
in contract.'

The money was paid over. According to the accounts, it went into the account of Jelly Music Ltd, which was one of the subsidiaries of the Hemdale Group of which Mr Lane, with others, was a director.

The first question is whether, on the true construction of the contract, Mr Lane made himself personally liable. As I read the words of the contract, 'I send you herewith our cheque for £6000' and 'In the unlikely event that we fail to complete within, say, one month you will undertake to repay us the £6000', the word 'you' referred to Mr Lane personally. The cheque was made out in favour of Jelly Music Ltd only as a matter of administrative convenience (as the judge found). It did not affect the fact that the agreement to repay was made by Brian Lane, especially when it is realised that it was known to all concerned that Fragile Management Ltd had not been formed. So I would have construed the contract, without recourse to any other aids, as making Mr Lane personally liable.

But Phillips J construed the contract differently. He had heard a lot of evidence. He said in his judgment: 'But I am quite satisfied that the events of 4th July did not of themselves involve a contract with Mr Lane personally.'

I will accept for the moment that the judge was correct in so holding. Even so Phonogram Ltd say that the law of England has been much altered by s 9(2) of the European Communities Act 1972. It says:

'Where a contract purports to be made by a company, or by a person as agent for a company, at a time when the company has not been formed, then subject to any agreement to the contrary the contract shall have effect as a contract entered into by the person purporting to act for the company or as agent for it, and he shall be personally liable on the contract accordingly.'

That seems to me to cover this very case. The contract purports to be made on behalf of Fragile Management Ltd, at a time when the company had not been formed. It **a** purports to be made by Mr Lane on behalf of the company. So he is to be personally liable for it.

Counsel for Mr Lane argued very skilfully that s 9(2) did not apply. First, he said: 'Look at the directive under the European Community law which led to this section being introduced.' It is the directive of 9th March 1968 (EEC Council Directive 68/151). It was written in French. (In 1968 English was not one of the official languages **b** of the European Community.) So counsel for Mr Lane referred us to the French text of art 7 of the directive:

'Si des actes ont été accomplis au nom d'une société en formation, avant l'acquisition par celle-ci de la personnalité morale, et si la société ne reprend pas les engagements résultant de ces actes, les personnes qui les ont accomplis en sont solidairement et indéfiniment responsables, sauf convention contraire.'   **c**

Mr Lane's counsel says that, according to the French text, that directive is limited to companies which are 'en formation', that is companies which have already started to be formed. His submission is reinforced by a passage from a French textbook, Ripert et Roblot, Traité Elémentaire de Droit Commercial (1970). As I read the passages at pp 601 and 604 of that treatise, interpreting the French as best I can, in the case of a French **d** company or société there may be, recognised by law, a period of time while a company is in the course of formation when people have put their signatures to what I may call 'the articles of association'. That period is called the period when the société is 'en formation'. A parallel is drawn (at p 604) with a baby at the time of gestation, ie between the time of conception and the time of birth, and a company when it is 'en formation'.

I reject the submission of counsel for Mr Lane. I do not think we should go by the **e** French text of the directive. It was drafted with regard to a different system of company law from that in this country. We should go by s 9(2) of our own statute, the European Communities Act 1972. Under art 189 of the EEC Treaty, these directives are to be binding only in so far as the spirit and intent are concerned. Article 189 says:

'A directive shall be binding, as to the result to be achieved, upon each Member State to which it is addressed, but shall leave to the national authorities the choice of **f** form and methods.'

Section 9(2) is in accordance with the spirit and intent of the directive. We should go by our own statute, and not by the directive.

That brings me to the second point. What does 'purports' mean in this context? Counsel for Mr Lane suggests that there must be a representation that the company is **g** already in existence. I do not agree. A contract can purport to be made on behalf of a company, or by a company, even though that company is known by both parties not to be formed and that it is only about to be formed.

The third point made by counsel for Mr Lane was that a company can be 'a person' within the meaning of that expression where it first occurs in s 9(2). He says that Jelly Music Ltd was 'a person' which was purporting to contract on behalf of Fragile **h** Management Ltd. I do not agree. Jelly Music Ltd were not entering into a contract. Mr Lane was purporting to do so.

So all three points made by Mr Lane's counsel fail.

But I would not leave the matter there. This is the first time the section has come before us. It will have much impact on the common law. I am afraid that before 1972 the common law had adopted some fine distinctions. As I understand Kelner v Baxter **j** (1866) LR 2 CP 174, it decided that, if a person contracted on behalf of a company which was non-existent, he himself would be liable on the contract. Just as, if a man signs a contract for and on behalf 'of his horses', he is personally liable. But, since that case was decided, a number of distinctions have been introduced by Hollman v Pullin (1884) Cab & El 254, Newborne v Sensolid (Great Britain) Ltd [1953] 1 All ER 708, [1954] 1 QB 45 and

Black v Smallwood (1965) 117 CLR 51 in the High Court of Australia. Those three cases seem to suggest that there is a distinction to be drawn according to the way in which an agent signs a contract. If he signs it as 'agent for X company', or 'for and on behalf of X company', and there is no such body as X company, then he himself can be sued on it. On the other hand, if he signs it as X company per pro himself the managing director, then the position may be different: because he is not contracting personally as an agent. It is the company which is contracting.

That distinction was disliked by Windeyer J in *Black v Smallwood*. It has been criticised in Treitel on the Law of Contract (5th Edn, 1979, p 559). In my opinion the distinction has been obliterated by s 9(2) of the European Communities Act 1972. We now have the clear words, 'Where a contract purports to be made by a company, or by a person as agent for a company, at a time when the company has not been formed'. That applies whatever formula is adopted. The person who purports to contract for the company is personally liable.

There is one further point on s 9(2) which I must mention. In Cheshire and Fifoot's Law of Contract (9th Edn, 1976, p 462), after reciting s 9(2), it says:

'How far [s 9(2)] in fact [increases the number of cases where the agent is personally liable] will depend on the meaning given to the words "subject to any agreement to the contrary" since it could be argued that words showing that A signs as agent express an agreement that he is not to be personally liable. If this were correct *Newborne v. Sensolid (Great Britain), Ltd.* would still be decided the same way. But it may be suspected that the courts will try to give more content to the subsection.'

We certainly will. The words 'subject to any agreement to the contrary' mean, as Shaw LJ suggested in the course of the argument, 'unless otherwise agreed'. If there was an express agreement that the man who was signing was not to be liable, the section would not apply. But, unless there is a clear exclusion of personal liability, s 9(2) should be given its full effect. It means that in all cases such as the present, where a person purports to contract on behalf of a company not yet formed, then however he expresses his signature he himself is personally liable on the contract.

I think Phillips J was right on the s 9(2) point. I would dismiss the appeal.

SHAW LJ. I agree. Like Lord Denning MR I would have read into the letter of 4th July 1973 an undertaking on the part of Mr Lane to be personally liable for the repayment of the £6,000 if the contemplated contract with Fragile Management Ltd was not in the event entered into. But the judge found otherwise on the facts, and it is not open to this court, as there is no cross-notice in regard to this, to depart from that finding. So one has to look to the basis on which the judge himself came to the conclusion in favour of the plaintiffs.

The general principle is, of course, that a person who makes a contract ostensibly as an agent cannot afterwards sue or be sued on it, subject to some qualification where there is a foreign principal or a del credere agent. The real problem in any given situation is to determine the status of the persons who enter into the argument. Are they entering into it, whatever form of description they may use, as agents or as principals? It may be that similar formulae in different cases will lead to a different conclusion because the surrounding facts have a different impact on the interpretation of phrases such as 'for and on behalf of', as in *Kelner v Baxter* (1866) LR 2 CP 174. There, notwithstanding the use of that phrase, the judgment proceeded on the basis that the reality of the matter was that the parties so subscribing themselves were acting as principals, and this was so notwithstanding that reference was made to a company which was in contemplation though not incorporated when the contract was signed.

It could of course happen, and did happen, that in some cases where an agent enters into a contract for a company whose incorporation is contemplated but which had not yet been effected, the third party would be left without redress. He could not sue the agent on the contract itself because the agent had acted as such; nor could the third party sue the agent for breach of warranty of authority if it was known to the third party that *a* the ostensible principal was not in existence. Section 9(2) of the European Communities Act 1972 gives a remedy in such a situation.

Counsel for Mr Lane, in his careful analysis of it, put forward a number of propositions, but I agree with the result described by Lord Denning MR in dealing with the effect of of s 9(2) in the light of EEC Council Directive 68/151. I also think that the note in Cheshire and Fifoot's Law of Contract (9th Edn, 1976, p 462) requires to be reconsidered. *b* I would dismiss this appeal.

OLIVER LJ. I also agree. Speaking for myself I am not convinced that the common law position apart from the European Communities Act 1972 depends on the narrow distinction between a signature 'for and on behalf of' and a signature in the name of a company or an association. The question I think in each case is what is the real intent as *c* revealed by the contract? Does the contract purport to be one which is directly between the supposed principal and the other party, or does it purport to be one between the agent himself, albeit acting for a supposed principal, and the other party? In other words, what you have to look at is whether the agent intended himself to be a party to the contract. So in *Kelner v Baxter* (1866) LR 2 CP 174, where the correspondence was directed to the agents and referred to 'the proposed company' which everybody knew *d* was not yet in existence, there really was no room for the suggestion that the purchasers were acting in any other capacity than personally. On the other hand, in *Newborne v Sensolid (Great Britain) Ltd* [1953] 1 All ER 708, [1954] 1 QB 45, where the contract was on the company's notepaper, it was clearly intended to be a company's contract (nobody realising that it had not yet been registered) and it could not be said that the individual plaintiff's signature in the company's name could possibly have been intended to make *e* him a party to the contract. The case, in my judgment, does not rest on any narrow point as to the way in which the contract was actually signed. The result would have been exactly the same, in my judgment, if the signature there had been accompanied by some such formula as 'for and on behalf of' or 'per pro'. The judgment of Parker J ([1954] 1 QB 45 at 47) and the judgments in the Court of Appeal of Lord Goddard CJ and Morris LJ show that the case turned on what the contract purported to do; and precisely the *f* same applies I think in *Hollman v Pullin* (1884) Cab & El 254, where a contract, albeit signed by the plaintiff as chairman of the association, was clearly intended to be, and intended only to be, a contract directly with the association by which the defendant's services were intended to be retained. The same again I think applies to the Australian case of *Black v Smallwood* (1965) 117 CLR 51. The contract there on its face purported to be a contract between the vendor and the company as purchaser and nothing else, *g* nobody then realising that the company had not been incorporated.

Whether that is right or not, any such subtle distinctions which might have been raised are rendered now irrelevant by s 9(2) of the European Communities Act 1972 in a case where a contract is either with a company or with the agent of a company. It has been suggested that an agreement to the contrary may still be inferred by the fact that the contract was signed by a person acting as agent so as to exclude the section. That I am *h* bound to say seems to me to be wholly unarguable when the section itself in terms provides 'Where a contract purports to be made ... by a person as agent for a company', and to interpret it in the way suggested would defeat the whole purpose of the section.

For the reasons which Lord Denning MR and Shaw LJ have given in the instant case, I agree that the appeal should be dismissed.

j

Appeal dismissed. Leave to appeal to the House of Lords refused.

Solicitors: *Wright & Webb, Syrett & Sons* (for Mr Lane); *Denton, Hall & Burgin* (for Phonogram Ltd).

Sumra Green   Barrister.

Syros Shipping Co SA v Elaghill Trading Co
The Proodos C

QUEEN'S BENCH DIVISION (COMMERCIAL COURT)

LLOYD J

24th, 25th MARCH 1980

Contract – Consideration – Performance of existing duty – Shipowners required under existing contract to discharge cargo – Shipowners diverting vessel because of congestion at original port of discharge – Shipowners requiring further payment from consignees before agreeing to discharge at original port of discharge – Consignees agreeing to make further payment – Cargo discharged but consignees refusing to make further payment – Whether consignees estopped from refusing to pay.

The shipowners chartered their vessel to the charterers who used it to carry a consignment of tractors from Sweden to the Yemen. The freight was prepaid by the Yemeni consignees to the charterers and bills of lading signed by the master of the vessel and binding on the owners were issued to the consignees. In the course of the voyage the charterers became insolvent and defaulted in the payment of hire to the owners. Because of congestion in the port when the vessel reached the port of discharge in the Yemen, the owners ordered the vessel to proceed to other ports to discharge the rest of her cargo. Before the vessel returned to the port of discharge the owners negotiated with the consignees for an extra payment for the discharge of the cargo free of any liens. The consignees agreed to pay an extra $US31,000 over and above the freight already paid. However when the cargo had been discharged the consignees refused to pay the $31,000. The dispute was referred to an arbitrator who held that there was no consideration for the agreement, but that the consignees were nevertheless estopped from departing from the agreement. The arbitrator therefore upheld the owners' claim. The consignees applied to have award set aside on the ground that it contained an error of law on its face.

Held – The shipowners had no claim, other than by virtue of the agreement, for the $31,000 they were seeking to recover from the consignees, and in the absence of consideration they could not enforce that agreement or rely on equitable estoppel as creating an independent cause of action. The award would therefore, in the circumstances, be remitted to the arbitrator (see p 190 j to p 191 a and d to g and p 192 e f, post).

Central London Property Trust Ltd v High Trees House Ltd (1946) [1956] 1 All ER 256 and *Combe v Combe* [1951] 1 All ER 767 applied.

Panchaud Frères SA v Etablissements General Grain Co [1970] 1 Lloyd's Rep 53 considered.

Notes

For equitable estoppel, see 9 Halsbury's Laws (4th Edn) paras 575–579 and 16 ibid paras 1513–1514, and for cases on the subject, see 21 Digest (Reissue) 8–16, 52–74.

Cases referred to in judgment

Central London Property Trust Ltd v High Trees House Ltd (1946) [1956] 1 All ER 256, [1947] 1 KB 130, [1947] LJR 77, 175 LT 332, 31(1) Digest (Reissue) 477, 3933.

Combe v Combe [1951] 1 All ER 767, [1951] 2 KB 215, CA, 12 Digest (Reissue) 219, 1411.

London Dock Co v Shadwell Parish (1862) 1 New Rep 91, 32 LJQB 30, 7 LT 381, 27 JP 324, 3 Digest (Reissue) 178, 1084.

North Ocean Shipping Co Ltd v Hyundai Construction Co Ltd, The Atlantic Baron [1978] 3 All ER 1170, [1979] 3 WLR 419, [1979] 1 Lloyd's Rep 89, Digest (Cont Vol E) 104, 673a.

Panchaud Frères SA v Etablissements General Grain Co [1970] 1 Lloyd's Rep 53, CA, Digest (Cont Vol C) 856, 1046a.

Pao On v Lau Yiu [1979] 3 All ER 65, [1980] AC 614, [1979] 3 WLR 435, PC, Digest (Cont Vol E) 107, 1899a.

Application

The respondents, Elaghill Trading Co, applied to have an award of $US31,000 made by a sole arbitrator, Mr Donald Davies, on 23rd July 1978 in favour of the applicants, Syros Shipping SA ('the owners'), set aside on the grounds of errors of law on the face of the award. The facts are set out in the judgment.

Martin Moore-Bick for the respondents.
Peter Digney for the owners.

LLOYD J. This is an application to set aside an award made by Mr Donald Davies, as sole arbitrator, on 23rd July 1978. The dispute relates to a consignment of 82 Volvo tractors shipped at Uddevala, Sweden, in October 1976, for carriage to Hodeidah, in the Yemen, on the claimants' vessel, the Proodos C. The vessel was under time charter at the time to a company called Kinglade Ltd. But the time charterers, having issued freight prepaid bills of lading on behalf of the owners, became insolvent in the course of the voyage. The question is therefore the familiar one: which of two innocent parties, the claimants as owners of the vessel or the respondents as receivers of the cargo and holders of the bill of lading, is to suffer by reason of the insolvency of a third?

The vessel arrived at Hodeidah on 9th November 1976. The port was congested at the time so the vessel proceeded to other ports to discharge the rest of her cargo first. She did not return to Hodeidah until nearly six months later, on 14th April 1977. Meanwhile, on 28th February 1977, the owners had entered into an agreement with certain of the consignees, including the respondents, as to the terms on which the vessel would return to Hodeidah. The agreement is set out in full in the award. Each of the consignees who signed the agreement agreed to pay an additional $US12·50 per ton; in the case of the respondents that came to a total of $US31,000.

The owners duly delivered the respondents' cargo, but the respondents have refused to pay the $US31,000 saying that there was no consideration for the agreement of 28th February 1977, or, alternatively, that the agreement is voidable for duress. The agreement of 28th February 1977 contained a London arbitration clause. The owners appointed Mr Donald Davies as their arbitrator. In due course he became sole arbitrator under the provisions of s 7(b) of the Arbitration Act 1950. No point has been taken before me as to the arbitrator's jurisdiction to deal with the matters in dispute.

The arbitrator has held, first, that there was no consideration for the agreement of 28th February 1977, second, that the agreement was not voidable for duress, and, third, that the owners are, despite the absence of consideration, entitled to succeed on the basis of equitable estoppel. The respondents now seek to set aside the award on the grounds that there are errors of law on the face of the award.

The owners seek to support the award. They say that there are no errors of law on the face of the award; alternatively, if there are, then the arbitrator was wrong in holding that there was no consideration. Thus he came to the right result, albeit for the wrong reason. This was, it was said, a ground on which I should exercise my discretion against setting aside the award. As a last resort the owners invited me to remit the award, rather than set it aside, with the direction that the arbitrator was wrong in law in holding that there was no consideration.

I shall deal first with the ground on which the arbitrator decided in favour of the owners, namely, equitable estoppel. What is said about that is to be found in para 14(d) of his award:

'While it may be that the receivers are the respondents in this case it does not mean that the doctrine of equitable estoppel is not available to the claimant owners.'

For myself, and with great respect to the arbitrator, I do not see how that can be right in law. It is unnecessary to go back to the cases decided in the last century; it is sufficient to start with *Central London Property Trust Ltd v High Trees House Ltd* (1946) [1956] 1 All ER 256, [1947] 1 KB 130, the case which marked a turning point in the modern law of

equitable estoppel. In that case, Denning J made it clear that the principle cannot be used
a   to create a new cause of action; in the time-honoured phrase, it can be used as a shield, not
as a sword. He used similar language as Denning LJ in *Combe v Combe* [1951] 1 All ER
767 at 769–770, [1951] 2 KB 215 at 219–220:

> 'That principle does not create new causes of action where none existed before
> [and then, after a reference to a number of decided cases, he said:] In none of these
b   > cases was the defendant sued on the promise, assurance, or assertion as a cause of
> action in itself. He was sued for some other cause, for example, a pension or a
> breach of contract, or possession, and the promise, assurance, or assertion only
> played a supplementary role, though, no doubt, an important one. That is, I think,
> its true function. It may be part of a cause of action, but not a cause of action in itself
> ... Seeing that the principle never stands alone as giving a cause of action in itself,
c   > it can never do away with the necessity of consideration when that is an essential
> part of the cause of action. The doctrine of consideration is too firmly fixed to be
> overthrown by a side-wind. Its ill effects have been largely mitigated of late, but it
> still remains a cardinal necessity of the formation of a contract, although not of its
> modification or discharge.'

d   In the present case the owners could have had no claim for the $US31,000 which they
are seeking to recover from the respondents in these proceedings if it were not for the
'agreement' of 28th February 1977. They have no independent cause of action: they are
suing on the naked promise to pay the $US31,000: they are using equitable estoppel as
a sword and not as a shield; and that they cannot do.
Counsel for the respondents tried to bring the case within the ordinary scope of
e   equitable estoppel by arguing that the respondents had led the owners to believe that
they would not insist on their strict legal rights whereby they were entitled to have the
cargo delivered at Hodeidah free of expense; and that they cannot now go back on that
promise. But that is to stand equitable estoppel on its head. The reality is that the
owners are suing on the 'agreement' of 28th February 1977. If, as the arbitrator has
found, there was no consideration for that 'agreement' then it is unenforceable in law.
f   The arbitrator also referred in his award to *Panchaud Frères SA v Etablissements General
Grain Co* [1970] 1 Lloyd's Rep 53. The arbitrator stated the principle in that case as being
that 'It would be unfair or unjust to allow a person to depart from a particular state of
affairs which another has taken to be settled or correct'. The principle established in
Panchaud Frères has not yet been fully worked out by the courts; in particular it is
uncertain whether it is to be regarded as based on estoppel or whether it is a kind of
g   waiver, and if so, what its limits are. But one thing is quite certain. It cannot be used to
create a new cause of action. That is how the owners are seeking to use it here. For those
reasons it is, in my view, inescapable that the award contains an error of law on its face.
But that is not the end of the case. For counsel for the respondents argues that, even
so, I am not bound to set aside the award; the power of the court to set aside, like the
power to remit, is discretionary. He submits that I ought not to exercise my discretion
h   to set aside in the present case for two reasons. In the first place the nature of the dispute
cried aloud for the award to be stated in the form of a special case; having not asked for
a special case when they had the opportunity to do so, the respondents are now too late:
see *London Dock Co v Shadwell Parish* (1862) 1 New Rep 91. Second, counsel says that the
respondents left it to the very last day of the six weeks allowed before applying to set
aside. I have given those two matters my best consideration. But they do not amount
j   to very much.
A more substantial point is whether I should refuse to set aside the award,
notwithstanding the error of law on its face, on the grounds that the arbitrator reached
the right result despite the error. I agree with counsel for the respondents' submission
this far, that if I could be certain that the arbitrator had reached the right result, albeit for
the wrong reason, then it would be a waste of time and money to compel the parties to

start again. In such a case I would not hesitate to exercise my discretion against setting the award aside. The real question here, as I see it, is whether I can be certain that the arbitrator reached the right result. Counsel for the respondents submitted that the arbitrator was plainly wrong in his conclusion that there was no consideration for the agreement. He relied on the reasons given by the arbitrator in para 14(a) of his award for reaching his conclusion, namely, first, that the bill of lading did not, on its true construction, entitle the owners to deliver at any port other than Hodeidah, and, second, that the owners had no right of lien against the respondents' cargo. Counsel for the respondents submitted that those reasons are bad reasons; for the question is not whether the owners were entitled to discharge the cargo elsewhere but whether they honestly believed that they were entitled to discharge the cargo elsewhere. The compromise of a doubtful claim is good consideration even though that claim is bad in law, provided there is an honest belief in the claim and an intention to pursue it.

Once again I am prepared to go much of the way with counsel for the respondents. I agree with him that the reasons given by the arbitrator in para 14(a) are not in themselves sufficient to support his conclusion that there was no consideration for the agreement of 28th February; but I am not prepared to go the next step and say that the arbitrator was therefore wrong in concluding that there was no consideration. He may have been right. For there may well have been other reasons which do not appear in the award; and if I cannot be certain that there was consideration for the agreement then I cannot be certain that the arbitrator reached the right result despite the error on the face of the award. It follows that there are no convincing reasons, in my view, why I should exercise my discretion in favour of upholding the award; on the contrary there are strong reasons why I should exercise my discretion the other way.

In those circumstances, counsel for the respondents submitted as an argument of last resort that the more convenient course was for the award to be remitted rather than set aside. Counsel for the owners, to whose argument I am much indebted, did not resist that suggestion. Accordingly the award will be remitted to the arbitrator with a direction that the facts as disclosed in the award do not in law give rise to any equitable estoppel or analogous remedy in favour of the owners. The arbitrator will no doubt wish also to reconsider his conclusion that there was no consideration for the agreement of 28th February in the light of my comments in this judgment, and any further argument which he may invite. It may be that he will reach the same conclusion as before; it may be that he will reach a different conclusion; it is a matter entirely for him.

On the question of duress on which the respondents also relied, I would say only this: that I heard nothing in the course of the argument which suggested to me that the arbitrator's decision on duress was wrong in law, or that there is any error in that respect on the face of his award. However, the arbitrator will perhaps wish to reconsider the question of duress also and, if he does so, to bear in mind the decision of the Privy Council in *Pao On v Lau Yiu* [1979] 3 All ER 65, [1980] AC 614, as well as the decision in *North Ocean Shipping Co Ltd v Hyundai Construction Co Ltd, The Atlantic Baron* [1978] 3 All ER 1170, [1979] QB 705, to which he refers in his award. From those decisions it appears that the question of duress turns on whether the commercial pressure exercised by one party on the other was such as to vitiate the other party's consent by coercion of his will. If not, then the agreement is not voidable for duress.

On the question of mistake on which the respondents also sought to rely by way of a last minute amendment to their notice of motion, I need say nothing at all.

Award remitted to arbitrator with direction that the facts set out in the award in law did not give rise to equitable estoppel.

Solicitors: *Max Bitel, Greene & Co* (for the respondents); *Holman, Fenwick & Willan* (for the owners).

K Mydeen Esq   Barrister.

Warden v Warden

COURT OF APPEAL, CIVIL DIVISION
ORMROD, DUNN LJJ AND WATERHOUSE J
4th JUNE 1981

Husband and wife – Variation of maintenance agreement – Backdating of order – Jurisdiction of court to backdate order – Matrimonial Causes Act 1973, s 35(2).

Under s 35(2)[a] of the Matrimonial Causes Act 1973 the court has power to backdate an order made thereunder varying a maintenance agreement since the provision in s 35(2) that the agreement shall have effect 'thereafter', ie after the variation order is made, as if the variation had been made by agreement between the parties for valuable consideration is to be construed as meaning that the agreement shall 'then' have that effect, and thus the purpose of the provision is simply to make clear that although a variation order has been made the parties' obligations (subject to the variation) remain contractual and are not converted by the variation order into some other kind of legal obligation, and accordingly the provision does not prevent the variation from having retrospective effect (see p 195 *e f*, p 196 *e f j* and p 197 *a* to *e*, post).

Carr (G A) v Carr (D V) [1974] 3 All ER 366 overruled.

Notes

For the court's power to vary maintenance agreements, see 22 Halsbury's Laws (4th Edn) paras 1153–1157 and for cases on the subject, see 27(1) Digest (Reissue) 85–86 652–653.

For the Matrimonial Causes Act 1973, s 35, see 43 Halsbury's Statutes (3rd Edn) 580.

Cases referred to in judgments

Carr (G A) v Carr (D V) [1974] 3 All ER 366, [1974] Fam 65, [1974] 3 WLR 449, Digest (Cont Vol D) 420, 6709a.

Macdonald v Macdonald [1963] 2 All ER 857, [1964] P 1, [1963] 3 WLR 350, CA, 27(2) Digest (Reissue) 843, 6709.

Style v Style and Keiller [1954] 1 All ER 442, [1954] P 209, [1954] 2 WLR 306, CA, 27(2) Digest (Reissue) 871, 6949.

Appeal

The husband, Peter William Warden, pursuant to leave granted by the judge on the day of the hearing, appealed against an order made by Balcombe J on 27th March 1981 declaring that the court had no power under s 35 of the Matrimonial Causes Act 1973 to backdate variations of maintenance agreements before the date of the variation order. The husband was seeking to vary retrospectively a maintenance agreement executed by himself and his wife, Jean Barbara Warden, on 17th October 1975. The facts are set out in the judgment of Ormrod LJ.

Peter Ralls for the husband.
Bruce Coleman for the wife.

ORMROD LJ. This is an appeal from a judgment on a preliminary issue by Balcombe J on 27th March of this year in the Family Division. He had before him a point of considerable general importance on the construction of a section which not often comes before the court, s 35 of the Matrimonial Causes Act 1973, which is the section which gives the court power to vary maintenance agreements. The section is a reproduction without change of a provision which was first introduced by the Maintenance Agreements Act 1957, up to which time maintenance agreements and separation

---

a   Section 35(2) is set out at p 194 *j* to p 195 *b*, post

agreements could not be altered by the court in any circumstances. In the light of the difficulties which had arisen, usually from the drafting of these agreements, great hardship had been caused to parties where financial circumstances had changed unexpectedly and so Parliament gave the court a limited power to vary financial arrangements under such agreements. Section 34 defines maintenance agreements for these purposes and it is common ground in this case that the agreement in question is a maintenance agreement.

It is perhaps convenient to briefly refer to the agreement. It is a deed executed on 17th October 1975 between the appellant in this court, Peter William Warden, and his wife, Jean Barbara Warden. They are still husband and wife, though separated. The first part recites the agreement to part and then the fact that they have three children. Clause 1 is the agreement to live apart and provides for the wife having the custody of the children. Clause 2 is a covenant by the husband to provide the wife with a yearly gross sum of £2,678 payable by equal monthly instalments and those payments are to continue until the death of the wife or—

> '(i) the making of a Court Order whereby the Husband is ordered to make any payment to or for the benefit of the Wife or give any security for any such payment or (ii) the Wife shall at any time live with another man or (iii) such change in taxation law that the amount of the said payments is no longer deductible from the Husband's income for the purposes of Income Tax and Surtax.'

The rest of the deed goes on to deal with the occupation of the matrimonial home, the use of the furniture, and the usual indemnity at the end.

The facts of the case, in so far as they are relevant, are that within a very short time of the execution of the deed the husband lost what had been an extremely good job and he has been in continuing financial difficulties ever since. Negotiations took place in 1977 to revise the agreement but those negotiations failed. In 1980 the wife issued a writ and on 13th February 1981 she obtained a judgment for £3,796 in RSC Ord 14 proceedings. At that stage the master took the view that the husband had no defence to the claim because, on the authority of the decision of Hollings J in *Carr (G A) v Carr (D V)* [1974] 3 All ER 366, [1974] Fam 65, under s 35 the court had no power to backdate any variation of the financial provisions of the agreement so that the amount prima facie outstanding under the deed was due and owing on that interpretation of the law and as the authorities then stood.

We are told by counsel for the husband that the wife has been in full-time employment for some time, the children are now grown up and off her hands, and that the execution of that judgment of the master has been stayed pending the determination of the preliminary issue whether or not the court has power to backdate any variation in the terms of the maintenance agreement which it thinks right to make on the facts.

The problem arises in a very short compass and the arguments which we have had have been admirably succinct and to the point. But it does not make the point that we have to decide any easier.

Section 35, so far as it is relevant, reads as follows:

> '(1) Where a maintenance agreement is for the time being subsisting and each of the parties to the agreement is for the time being either domiciled or resident in England and Wales, then, subject to subsection (3) below, either party may apply to the court or to a magistrates' court for an order under this section.
> '(2) If the court to which the application is made is satisfied either—(a) that by reason of a change in the circumstances in the light of which any financial arrangements contained in the agreement were made or, as the case may be, financial arrangements were omitted from it (including a change foreseen by the parties when making the agreement), the agreement should be altered so as to make different, or, as the case may be, so as to contain, financial arrangements, or (b) that the agreement does not contain proper financial arrangements with respect to any

child of the family, then subject to subsections (3), (4) and (5) below, that court may by order make such alterations in the agreement—(i) by varying or revoking any financial arrangements contained in it, or (ii) by inserting in it financial arrangements for the benefit of one of the parties to the agreement or of a child of the family, as may appear to that court to be just having regard to all the circumstances, including, if relevant, the matters mentioned in section 25(3) above; and the agreement shall have effect thereafter as if any alteration made by the order had been made by agreement between the parties and for valuable consideration . . .'

The submission which is made on behalf of the wife is that those concluding words '. . . and the agreement shall have effect thereafter as if any alteration made by the order had been made by agreement between the parties and for valuable consideration' mean that no change in the obligations created by the agreement can be made or take effect until the order of the court is made. That argument found favour with Hollings J in the case I have mentioned of Carr (G A) v Carr (D V). He construed those words as meaning what they said, in effect, and held that he had no power to backdate the order at all. Balcombe J, faced with the same problem, took the same view, but he was at pains in the course of giving his judgment in this case to make it clear that he was not simply following Hollings J, he was forming his own view which was in agreement with the view that Hollings J had formed.

In his argument before this court and also before the judge in the court below, counsel for the husband has submitted that this is a misconstruction of s 35(2). He says that the words in question mean simply that, the court having intervened to vary the financial terms of the agreement, the agreement itself will continue thereafter in effect, subject only to that alteration, and he points to the concluding words of the subsection which provide that 'the agreement shall have effect thereafter as if any alteration made by the order had been made by agreement between the parties and for valuable consideration.' Counsel's main submission is that the word 'thereafter' at the end of sub-s (2) is put in to demonstrate that the legal obligations on the parties remain contractual and are not converted by the variation order into any other kind of legal obligation. They remain contractual, subject to the change. He says that the concluding words have no other meaning. He points out also that there is nothing to stop the parties to such an agreement making, by agreement, a variation in the financial terms of the original agreement retrospective in character if they so wish, and for valuable consideration. And that must be right.

Then counsel for the husband submits that in general the court has power in the exercise of its various jurisdictions under the Matrimonial Causes Act 1973 to vary its own orders retrospectively. He relies on two cases in this court, Macdonald v Macdonald [1963] 2 All ER 857, [1964] P 1 and Style v Style and Keiller [1954] 1 All ER 442, [1954] P 209, and there is no doubt that both of those cases establish beyond any possibility of doubt that the court, in so far as its own orders are concerned, has an almost unrestricted power to vary them retrospectively and, moreover, retrospectively beyond the date of the application for variation, so that in the case of periodical payments the power to vary extends backwards in the case of an order for periodical payments after divorce to the date of decree nisi, or in the case of an order for alimony pending suit, to the date of the petition. Counsel's submission is that it would be anomalous if, when it passed the 1957 Act Parliament had given the court a more restricted power, or to put it in another way, if it had been intended to restrict the court's power in respect of varying maintenance agreements in the way suggested, one would have expected to see it in the forefront of the section rather than tucked away in a sub-clause.

For my part I am impressed by that argument. It strikes me as being, at least, surprising that the draftsman, had he intended to restrict the court's power in this way, should have done it by a clause right at the end of sub-s (2) and not put it in the forefront of the section.

The next point is that the drafting of sub-ss (1) and (2) of s 35, apart from the words which are in dispute at the moment, follows very closely indeed the lines of the corresponding section, now s 31, which deals with variation orders. Section 31(1) gives the court—

'power to vary or discharge the order or to suspend any provision thereof temporarily and to revive the operation of any provision so suspended.'

Section 35(2)(i) gives the court power—

'by varying or revoking any financial arrangements contained in it, or (ii) by inserting in it financial arrangements . . .'

They are closely parallel in structure and it is only when one reaches the final subsection that one finds any difference.

If the construction of Balcombe and Hollings JJ is right it leads, as has been pointed out, to this extraordinary anomaly that the moment when the variation takes effect, no matter what the justice of the case, must be the date on which the court makes its order which, in some ways, is a wholly irrelevant date. It means that a husband would be deprived of the benefit of the variation to which he is entitled in so far as justice is concerned, by a freak of being unable to get his case heard owing to court arrangements, for a month or two months, or as the case may be, and I find it difficult to accept, unless the section is explicit, that the power of the court in such circumstances is restricted to the moment when the order itself is made. It is highly anomalous that the relief should not be capable of being granted at least from the date of the application for that relief. That makes me question the correctness of the construction adopted by Hollings J in *Carr (G A) v Carr (D V)* and the judge in the present case.

I think, therefore, that counsel for the husband is right and that those words '. . . and the agreement shall have effect thereafter as if any alteration made by the order had been made by agreement between the parties and for valuable consideration' can properly be read, as suggested by Waterhouse J in the course of argument, as if the word 'then' appeared instead of 'thereafter' and if the word 'then' appeared, I doubt that there would be any difficulty about it. It would then read 'and the agreement shall have effect *then* as if any alteration . . .', meaning clearly that the agreement is to continue in force with the variation inserted by the court. I see no difficulty in reading the section in that way and I see grave disadvantages in treating those words as imposing so severe a limitation on the jurisdiction and powers of the court as to cause inevitably severe injustice. One has only got to take this case, for example. The wife has got a judgment which she can execute at any time she wishes once this preliminary point has been settled, for £3,000 odd, in circumstances in which it may well be quite clear that the agreement is bound to be changed radically and her rights under the agreement are bound to be severely diminished, and it would be a very strange thing if Parliament had produced a situation where it is accepted by the court that a radical variation in the agreement is required and yet a wife can execute for the full amount of the arrears simply because the court is powerless to backdate the variation to the point at which in justice it should be made. I would be disinclined to accept any construction of the section which led to that conclusion unless there were no alternatives. In my judgment counsel for the husband has provided us with an alternative and I would accept it.

Accordingly I would allow the appeal.

DUNN LJ. I agree. If the construction which the judge put on s 35(2) of the Matrimonial Causes Act 1973 is right there is a further anomaly which arises from the section itself. Subsection (6) provides:

'For the avoidance of doubt it is hereby declared that nothing in this section or in section 34 above affects any power of a court before which any proceedings between the parties to a maintenance agreement are brought under any other enactment (including a provision of this Act) to make an order containing financial arrangements or any right of either party to apply for such an order in such proceedings.'

The effect of that subsection is that the court has power under s 35 to vary a maintenance agreement, and at the same time to consider an application to make an order for financial provision under one of the other sections of the 1973 Act. So far as the orders for financial provision are concerned, the court would have power to backdate the order, but if the construction of the judge is right it would have no power to vary the maintenance agreement so as to bring it into line with the financial provision which the court is proposing to make under one of the other sections. Speaking for myself I cannot believe that that was the intention of Parliament and for that reason, and for the reasons given by Ormrod LJ, I, too, would allow this appeal.

WATERHOUSE J. I also agree. Whilst I differ with hesitation from Hollings and Balcombe JJ in their construction of the word 'thereafter' in s 35(2) of the Matrimonial Causes Act 1973, I think that it fails to give adequate effect to the words that immediately follow, namely 'as if any alteration made by the order had been made by agreement between the parties and for valuable consideration.' It is clear that the parties may themselves agree to vary a maintenance agreement retrospectively for valuable consideration and I can see no compelling interpretative reason for withholding from the court a power to do so by an order within the framework of s 35(2). I respectfully agree with Ormrod LJ that the wide powers conferred on the court by the earlier provisions of s 35(2) point against a restrictive interpretation of the last clause of the subsection. In my judgment the word 'thereafter' means no more than 'then' in this context, and the effect of the last clause is simply to make clear that the agreement survives and continues, once the order has been made, in its varied form: thus the variation by order may be retrospective, just as an agreed variation might have been retrospective. The practical advantages of this construction have already been stressed; and I agree that the appeal should be allowed for the reasons stated by Ormrod and Dunn LJJ.

Appeal allowed. Leave to appeal to the House of Lords refused.

Solicitors: *Kenwright & Cox*, Ilford (for the husband); *Parker, Fogg & Pinsent*, Hornchurch (for the wife).

Avtar S Virdi Esq   Barrister.

Banque de l'Indochine et de Suez SA v Euroseas Group Finance Co Ltd and others

QUEEN'S BENCH DIVISION

ROBERT GOFF J

28th JANUARY 1981

Company – Name – Use of name – Use of abbreviation – Registered name containing word 'Company' in full – 'Company' abbreviated to 'Co' on cheque drawn by company – Cheque signed by officers of company – Whether officers personally liable for amount of cheque – Whether abbreviation 'Co' constituting proper mention of name on cheque – Companies Act 1948, s 108(1)(c)(4)(b).

The registered name of a company was 'Euroseas Group Finance Company Limited'. Two cheques drawn by the company in favour of the plaintiff bore the printed words 'Per pro Euroseas Group Finance Co Ltd' and were signed, beneath the printed words, by the defendants as officers of the company on behalf of the company. The cheques were dishonoured on presentation for payment. The plaintiff brought an action against the defendants claiming that they were personally liable for the amount of the cheques under s 108(4)[d] of the Companies Act 1948 because the use of the abbreviation 'Co' on the cheques did not constitute proper mention of the company's name within s 108(1)(c) and (4)(b). The plaintiff applied for summary judgment against the defendants.

Held – Where an abbreviation of a word was generally accepted and treated as equivalent to that word and there was no other word so abbreviated and, further, where there was no possibility that the companies registrar would accept for registration two companies having the same name except that one contained the full word and the other used an abbreviation of it, the use of the abbreviation as part of a company's name in a document specified in s 108(1)(c) of the 1948 Act was not a breach of s 108(1)(c), for there was no possibility of confusion arising from use of the abbreviation. Since 'Co' was so generally accepted as an abbreviation of 'Company' as to be treated as equivalent to 'Company' and could not be taken to mean anything else and since there was no practical possibility that the companies registrar would accept for registration two companies with the same name where one contained the word 'Company' and the other 'Co', the use of the abbreviation 'Co' on the cheques was not a breach of s 108(1)(c) and, accordingly, the defendants were not in breach of s 108(4)(b) and were not personally liable to the plaintiff under s 108(4). It followed that the application would be dismissed (see p 201 a to f and p 202 e to j, post).

Dictum of Scrutton J in *Stacey & Co Ltd v Wallis* (1912) 106 LT at 547 applied.

Dictum of Donaldson J in *Durham Fancy Goods Ltd v Michael Jackson (Fancy Goods) Ltd* [1968] 2 All ER at 990 considered.

Notes

For requirements as to use of a company's name, see 7 Halsbury's Laws (4th Edn) para 733, for liability of a company's officers, see ibid para 745, and for cases on a company's name, see 9 Digest (Reissue) 48–49, 180–184.

For the Companies Act 1948, s 108, see 5 Halsbury's Statutes (3rd Edn) 198.

Cases referred to in judgment

Durham Fancy Goods Ltd v Michael Jackson (Fancy Goods) Ltd [1968] 2 All ER 987, [1968] 2 QB 839, [1968] 3 WLR 225, [1968] 2 Lloyd's Rep 98, 1(2) Digest (Reissue) 870, 5646.

---

a Section 108, so far as material, is set out at p 199 199 g to j, post.

Penrose v Martyr (1858) EB & E 499, 28 LJQB 28, 5 Jur NS 362, 120 ER 595, 1(2) Digest (Reissue) 870, 5640.
Stacey & Co Ltd v Wallis (1912) 106 LT 544, 1(2) Digest (Reissue) 871, 5648.

Action

By a writ dated 17th April 1980 the plaintiff, Banque de l'Indochine et de Suez SA, claimed in the Commercial Court against the defendants, Euroseas Group Finance Co Ltd, Mr G Thorley and Miss B A O'Donnell, £50,000 in respect of two cheques dated 13th and 20th February 1980, each for £25,000, drawn by the first defendant on the National Westminster Bank Ltd in favour of the plaintiff and signed by the second and third defendants as officers of the first defendant. The claim against the second and third defendants was that they were personally liable to the plaintiff for the amount of the cheques by virtue of s 108(4) of the Companies Act 1948. By summons dated 13th May 1980 the plaintiff applied for summary judgment against the defendants. The first defendant was in liquidation by the time the summons came on for hearing and took no further part in the proceedings. The summons was heard in chambers but judgment was given by Robert Goff J in open court. The facts are set out in the judgment.

Michael Crystal for the plaintiff.
Michael E Jones for the second and third defendants.

ROBERT GOFF J. There is before the court a summons under RSC Ord 14 in which the plaintiff, Banque de l'Indochine et de Suez SA, are claiming summary judgment against the second and third defendants in this case. The claim of the plaintiff is on two cheques. Each cheque is in the sum of £25,000 and each is made payable to the plaintiff drawn on the National Westminster Bank. Each one is signed as follows. There are printed, no doubt by the bank, on the cheque itself, the words, 'Per pro Euroseas Group Finance Co Ltd', and under those printed words the second and third defendants as signatories have signed their names on behalf of the defendant company. I understand that the defendant company has no assets to meet this claim, and so the plaintiff is proceeding against the second and third defendants as signatories of the cheque, relying on the provisions of s 108 of the Companies Act 1948. When the matter was presented to me by counsel for the plaintiff, it appeared at once that the summons raised a question of law arising out of the construction of s 108 which, if decided first, might be decisive of the matter, and therefore I was invited to consider first this problem, which is the subject matter of this judgment.

Section 108 provides, inter alia:

'(1) Every company . . . (c) shall have its name mentioned in legible characters in all business letters of the company and in all notices and other official publications of the company, and in all bills of exchange, promissory notes, endorsements, cheques and orders for money or goods purporting to be signed by or on behalf of the company, and in all bills of parcels, invoices, receipts and letters of credit of the company . . .

'(4) If an officer of a company or any person on its behalf . . . (b) issues or authorises the issue of any business letter of the company or any notice or other official publication of the company, or signs or authorises to be signed on behalf of the company any bill of exchange, promissory note, endorsement, cheque or order for money or goods wherein its name is not mentioned in manner aforesaid . . . he shall be liable to a fine not exceeding fifty pounds, and shall further be personally liable to the holder of the bill of exchange, promissory note, cheque or order for money or goods for the amount thereof unless it is duly paid by the company.'

Now the case for the plaintiff is as follows. The defendant company's registered name is 'Euroseas Group Finance Company Limited', and the words 'Company' and 'Limited' are written out in full. On the two cheques signed by the second and third defendants the word 'Company' is abbreviated to 'Co'. It is said by the plaintiff that in these

circumstances there has been a breach by the company of the provisions of s 108(1)(c) in
that the name of the company has not been mentioned in legible characters on the two
cheques; therefore by virtue of s 108(4), this is a case where the second and third
defendants have signed a cheque wherein the name of the company was not mentioned
in the manner set out in s 108(1)(c) and, this being a case where the company has not
fully paid the cheques, the second and third defendants are each personally liable to the
holder of the cheques for the amount of the cheques. So this case raises the question,
which is a question of construction of the 1948 Act, whether the way in which the
company's name is printed on the cheques, in particular the use of the abbreviation 'Co'
in place of the word 'Company' in its name, constitutes a breach of s 108(1)(c) of the 1948
Act in that the company has not had its name mentioned in legible characters on the
cheque.

I was referred to certain authorities. The first one I propose to refer to is *Stacey & Co
Ltd v Wallis* (1912) 106 LT 544, a case in which Scrutton J considered a comparable case
where the relevant abbreviation was not of 'Company' to 'Co' but of 'Limited' to 'Ltd'.
He held that in that case there was no failure to comply with the relevant provision of the
Companies (Consolidation) Act 1908, which was the predecessor of the section with
which I am now concerned. He said (at 547):

> 'In the present case the name is correct except that part of it is abbreviated with
> what is a very common English abbreviation for the word "Limited." I had the
> curiosity as I walked down Queen Victoria-street this morning, to examine the
> names that appeared on the shops down that thoroughfare, and for every one that
> had "Limited" five or six had "Ltd." The same point might have been raised by
> counsel—and I suppose this decision may also be taken as a decision on the same
> point—whether "Co." instead of "Company" would be a legal description of a
> company's name. In my view the name here is so expressed that any commercial
> man of ordinary intelligence would read the description accurately, but it might be
> different if the abbreviation was "L." or "Li."; but "Ltd.," using my ordinary
> knowledge of commerce, is such a constant abbreviation that every commercial
> man of intelligence would know that by "Ltd.," "Limited" was meant. The English
> way of abbreviating "Limited" is just as common as the whole word "Limited"
> itself, and with every sympathy for the intelligent foreigner whom counsel for the
> plaintiffs referred to, I think he must be taken to have the same knowledge as an
> ordinary Englishman would have of the way in which the English word is expressed
> in print. The reason pointed out by Crompton, J. in the case I have referred to
> [*Penrose v Martyr* (1858) EB & E 499 at 503, 120 ER 595 at 597], and the reasons for
> the other decisions on the question, appear to me to be satisfied when it is said that
> there are in the name of the company marks and signs which to every ordinary
> Englishman would convey the knowledge that the company was a limited one and
> not an unlimited one. I am, therefore, of opinion that the company's name is
> correctly described in the address.'

It seems to me plain from what Scrutton J said in that particular case that he would
have decided the present case in precisely the same way as he decided *Stacey v Wallis*, as
may be inferred from his remark—

> 'I suppose this decision may also be taken as a decision on the same point—
> whether "Co." instead of "Company" would be a legal description of a company's
> name.'

I approach the matter as follows. It seems to me that under the section the company
is required to have its name mentioned in legibile characters on, inter alia, cheques, and
the question is whether on a true construction of the section that has been done in the
present case. Every word in the company's name forms part of its name, and so whether
it is Euroseas, Group, Finance, or Company or Limited, each one of those words forms
part of the company's name. Obviously, as we all know, just as 'Ltd' is a common
abbreviation of 'Limited', so 'Co' is a common abbreviation of 'Company'; and the

question is whether using such an abbreviation is permissible under this subsection
which requires that the company's name shall be mentioned in legible characters on the
relevant document. One thing is plain from the decision of Scrutton J, and that is that
in certain circumstances an abbreviation will be permissible, because he so held by
holding that the abbreviation 'Ltd' was permissible for the word 'Limited'. As I
understand his judgment he is saying that in the English language in ordinary
commercial usage the expression 'Ltd' is accepted not merely as an abbreviation of
'Limited', but accepted in common parlance as actually being equivalent to the word
'Limited'; so there could be no possible confusion if that abbreviation was used in place
of the full word 'Limited'. When I come to look at the word 'Company' it seems to me
that exactly the same thing applies. First of all, 'Co' is an abbreviation of 'Company';
second, and we all know this to be true as a matter of ordinary commercial usage, 'Co' is
a generally and commonly accepted abbreviation of the word 'Company', and is so to
such an extent that it is treated as equivalent to 'Company' and there is no possibility of
it meaning anything else.

Counsel for the plaintiff urged on me that there are other words which might be
abbreviated to 'Co' and therefore there was some possibility of confusion. The words he
cited to me were 'corporation', 'constitution', 'co-operative' and 'consideration'. I am
bound to say that I have never in my experience ever known any of those four words
abbreviated in this way; and indeed taking 'corporation' as being really the most relevant
of the four words he mentioned, there is a generally accepted abbreviation of the word
'corporation' to 'corp'. I have never heard of 'corporation' being abbreviated to 'co'.
Furthermore, there is no practical possibility as I understand it, and I think this is
common ground, of the companies registrar accepting for registration the names of two
companies which were precisely the same except that in one name the full word
'Company' was used, and in another name the abbreviation 'Co' was used. So having
regard to the fact that no other word, as far as I am aware, is abbreviated to 'Co', having
regard to the fact that 'Co' is so generally accepted as an abbreviation of 'Company' as to
be treated as equivalent to 'Company', and having regard to the fact that there is no
practical possibility of the companies registrar registering the companies in the manner
I have described, it seems to me that there is no possibility of confusion arising from
using the abbreviation, which in my judgment is not merely a generally accepted
abbreviation of the word 'Company' but is treated as equivalent to 'Company'. For what
it is worth I notice that this is the view taken in the Land Registry; my attention has been
drawn to a particular reference to this in the New Law Journal where it is stated that the
abbreviation 'Co' is treated in the Land Registry as being the same as the word 'Company'
(see (1981) 131 NLJ at 11). It seems to me that the same point would arise in relation to
the use of an ampersand in place of the word 'and'. An ampersand is an abbreviation, it
is a symbolic abbreviation of the word 'and', and is used simply because it is shorter to
write or print than to write out or print out the full word 'and'. It seems to me that on
exactly the same principle it would be legitimate to abbreviate the word 'and' in a
company's name to '&' because in the first place it is a generally accepted abbreviation of
the word 'and', so much so that it is treated as equivalent to the word 'and'; second,
nothing else, so far as I know, is abbreviated to an ampersand except the word 'and'; and
finally there can be no practical possibility of the companies registrar registering two
companies which were precisely the same except in one the word 'and' is used and in the
other the symbol '&' is used.

Counsel for the plaintiff in support of his argument, in opposition to what I have just
indicated to be my view, relied on the judgment of Donaldson J in *Durham Fancy Goods
Ltd v Michael Jackson (Fancy Goods) Ltd* [1968] 2 All ER 987, [1968] 2 QB 839 where a
question arose whether in relation to the name 'Michael Jackson (Fancy Goods) Ltd' it
would be permissible for the word 'Michael' to be abbreviated to 'M'. He held that it
would not, and said as follows ([1968] 2 All ER 987 at 990, [1968] 2 QB 839 at 846):

'Counsel for Mr. Jackson also submitted that just as "Ltd." was an acceptable
abbreviation for "Limited", so "M" was an acceptable abbreviation for "Michael".
This I do not accept. The word "Limited" is included in a company's name by way

of description and not identification. Accordingly a generally accepted abbreviation will serve this purpose as well as the word in full. The rest of the name, by contrast, *a* serves as a means of identification and may be compounded of or include initials or abbreviations. The use of any abbreviation of the registered name is calculated to create problems of identification which are not created by an abbreviation of "Limited". I should therefore be prepared to hold that no abbreviation was permissible of any part of a company's name other than "Ltd." for "Limited" and, possibly, the ampersand for "and". However it is not necessary to go as far as this. *b* Any abbreviation must convey the full word unambiguously and the intitial "M" neither shows that it is an abbreviation nor does it convey "Michael".'

Counsel for the plaintiff, of course, relied on the sentence (which he agrees is an obiter dictum) in that passage where the judge said, 'I should therefore be prepared to hold that no abbreviation was permissible of any part of a company's name other than "Ltd." for "Limited" and, possibly, the ampersand for "and".' Now first of all this is indeed an *c* obiter dictum. Having regard to the fact that the word 'Company' did not appear in the name of the company in that particular case, the judge was not necessarily addressing his mind to the question whether 'Co' would be an acceptable abbreviation of the word 'Company'. Second, if the judge was seeking to suggest that 'Co' would not be an acceptable abbreviation for the word 'Company' it seems to me that his obiter dictum to that effect would be in conflict with the obiter dictum of Scrutton J in the earlier case of *d* *Stacey v Wallis*. If so, then with the greatest respect I prefer the approach of Scrutton J. I would add this, that if one is going to treat '&' as an acceptable abbreviation for 'and' the ampersand of course may occur in any part of the company's name, and it seems to me therefore that one has to look at the whole name, including every word of it, and try to establish what is the general principle on which an abbreviation will be allowed. It seems to me that in those circumstances the general principle, which I derive from the *e* words of Scrutton J, is that where there is an abbreviation of a word which is not merely an accepted abbreviation but is treated as equivalent to that word, and where there is no other word which is abbreviated to that particular abbreviation, and where there is no question of the companies registrar accepting for registration two companies, both of which have the same name, except that one contains the full word and the other the abbreviated word, then in those circumstances there is absolutely no possibility of any *f* confusion arising by reason of the abbreviation, and in those circumstances where the abbreviation is used it is proper to hold that the company has its name mentioned in the relevant document in legible characters, as required by s 108(1)(c) of the 1948 Act.

Of course, in the *Durham Fancy Goods* case the test was not complied with, because the letter 'M' can mean many things besides Michael, and it is possible to conceive of a case where the companies registrar might accept registration of one company whose name *g* contained the full word, and of another company having the same name save that it merely contains the initial letter of that word. So it can readily be understood that where a word in a company's name is abbreviated to its initial letter, as where Michael is abbreviated to 'M', the court should hold that the subsection is not complied with. Finally I would add that, if the submission of counsel for the plaintiff is right and the expression 'Co' is not an acceptable abbreviation of 'Company', then there is a rich harvest *h* of uncollected fines to be collected throughout the land, and so far as I know no steps have yet been taken to gather in that harvest.

In all the circumstances I am unable to accept counsel for the plaintiff's submission, and the plaintiff's application for summary judgment must be dismissed.

Application dismissed.   *j*

Solicitors: *Durrant, Piesse* (for the plaintiff); *Gershon, Young & Co* (for the second and third defendants).

K Mydeen Esq   Barrister.

Burditt v Joslin

QUEEN'S BENCH DIVISION
DONALDSON LJ AND BINGHAM J
12th FEBRUARY 1981

Firearms – Certificate – Application – Residence qualification – Application for firearm certificate to be made to chief officer of police for area in which applicant 'resides' – Resides – Applicant owning house in United Kingdom but not entitled to occupy it – Applicant residing for time being overseas – Whether applicant entitled to apply to chief officer of police for area in which he owns house in United Kingdom – Firearms Act 1968, s 26(1).

The applicant was a regular serving officer in the Army stationed in Germany. He owned a house in Warwickshire which he had let and accordingly had no right to occupy. He applied to the chief constable of Warwickshire for a firearm certificate under s 26(1)[a] of the Firearms Act 1968, but his application was refused on the ground that he did not 'reside' within the area of the chief constable. The applicant's appeal to the Crown Court against the refusal of his application was dismissed. He appealed to the Divisional Court.

Held – A residential connection arising out of the ownership of property which did not carry with it the right of occupation was not sufficient to show that an applicant for the grant of a firearm certificate under s 26 of the 1968 Act resided within the area in which he applied for the certificate. The application made by the applicant had therefore been properly refused and his appeal would be dismissed (see p 204 *f g* and p 205 *a* to *d*, post).

Notes

For restrictions on possession of firearms without a certificate, see 11 Halsbury's Laws (4th Edn) para 875, and for cases on the subject, see 15 Digest (Reissue) 930–932, 8040–8049.

For the Firearms Act 1968, s 26, see 8 Halsbury's Statutes (3rd Edn) 744.

Case stated

Colonel Brian Sedgley Burditt appealed by way of case stated from the decision of Mr Recorder Alan de Piro QC and justices of the County of Warwick dismissing his appeal against a refusal by the respondent, the Chief Constable of Warwickshire, to grant him a firearm certificate under s 26 of the Firearms Act 1968. The facts are set out in the judgment of Donaldson LJ.

Brian Leech for Colonel Burditt.
D E Roberts for the chief constable.

DONALDSON LJ. This is an appeal by case stated from the decision of the Crown Court at Warwick, Mr Recorder Alan de Piro QC presiding, which dismissed an appeal from the refusal of the Chief Constable, Warwick Constabulary, to grant a firearm certificate to Colonel Burditt under the Firearms Act 1968.

Let it be made abundantly clear, as it was made clear in the decision of the Crown Court and the contrary was never suggested for one moment by the police, that Colonel Burditt is an experienced handler of firearms. He is a fit and proper person to hold a firearm certificate, and indeed he has since this case been granted a firearm certificate. The difficulty which arose in this case is a different one. It is whether the Chief Constable of Warwickshire had any jurisdiction to grant a firearm certificate in the circumstances in which Colonel Burditt found himself.

---

a   Section 26(1) is set out at p 204 *b*, post.

The relevant sections of the Firearms Act 1968 are ss 7 and 26. Section 7 is headed 'Police permit' and provides:

> '(1) A person who has obtained from the chief officer of police for the area in which he resides a permit for the purpose in the prescribed form may, without holding a certificate under this Act, have in his possession a firearm and ammunition in accordance with the terms of the permit . . .'

The important words there are 'the chief officer of police for the area in which he resides'. Section 26(1) provides:

> 'An application for the grant of a firearm or shot gun certificate shall be made in the prescribed form to the chief officer of police for the area in which the applicant resides and shall state such particulars as may be required by the form.'

Again the important words are 'the chief officer of police for the area in which [he] resides.'

The point which troubled the chief constable, and which led him to refuse this application, was that in his view Colonel Burditt did not reside in the County of Warwick. The facts at the date of the application were that Colonel Burditt owned a house in Rugby. He was a permanent professional regular serving officer in the Army stationed with the British Army of the Rhine. At the time of the application he had let his house. It must follow that, subject to any covenant that there may be in the tenancy permitting the landlord to inspect and make sure that the tenant was not breaking the place up, he had no right to occupation at all in the house at that time.

It is said by counsel for Colonel Burditt that this section must receive a wide construction, that it has only an administrative purpose, namely to identify which chief constable shall deal with an application for a firearm certificate and that all the very necessary precautions and limitations on the right to bear firearms are contained in s 27, which provides for conditions to be inserted in firearm certificates and so on.

I think there is force in that submission, but I cannot get away from the fact that Parliament has decided that in general no one shall possess a firearm in this country unless they are authorised in accordance with the procedures laid down by Parliament. It follows that Colonel Burditt and anybody else in his position has to bring himself within some authorisation procedure. Parliament could have said that anybody who has a residential base in this country, or anybody who owns property in this country, shall be entitled to apply to the chief officer of police where that property is situated. But what it has said is that the application must be to the chief officer of police for the area in which applicant resides, and it must follow from that that the only people who can apply are people who are actually residing in this country.

Again I would accept that people can have two residences. An obvious example is somebody who has a weekend cottage in the country and a mid-week flat in London. He resides in both of them.

But if Colonel Burditt is to succeed in this case the sections have to have a wider meaning than that. It is not even sufficient to say 'ordinarily resides' because at the time of the application he did not ordinarily reside in Rugby. What counsel suggested was that 'resides' in this context means (and I quote from the note that I made), 'the place with which you have a residential connection at the present time or have had such a connection in the past coupled with an intention to reside at that place in the future'. That would certainly get over the problem which afflicts people in Colonel Burditt's position, and I am bound to say that I would have liked to assist Colonel Burditt because it seems to me that if Parliament has made it impossible for serving officers who have let their homes to obtain a firearm certificate it must be because those concerned never applied their minds to the problem. Had they applied their minds to the problem, I am sure they would have made provision for it.

I am not averse to applying a broad construction in order to remedy any deficiencies in an Act of Parliament which would be apparent if one applied a narrow construction.

But there are, I think, limits to the extent to which there can be judicial amendment of *a* Acts of Parliament, and I fear that in Colonel Burditt's case it would go beyond the accepted limits to hold (and this decision as far as I am concerned is entirely confined to this) that somebody resides at an address for the purpose of s 26 at a time at which that address is let to others and therefore he has no right to occupy it.

I am very far from saying that, for instance, a young soldier who on his leave always stays with his parents cannot be said to reside with his parents. That would have to be *b* decided on some other occasion. But this decision, I think, must be limited to the question of a house which is let, and for that purpose I do not think on the facts that Colonel Burditt can say that at the date of his application he resided in Rugby. Accordingly I would dismiss the appeal.

BINGHAM J. I agree. Like Donaldson LJ I would wish to seek to give a broad *c* construction to the word 'resides', given the degree of control which the police can subsequently exercise for ensuring that there is no risk to the public in the possession by any person of firearms. It is, however, the case that at the relevant time here Colonel Burditt did not physically live in Warwickshire. Moreover he could not do so because his house was let to tenants and he had no right to occupy the house himself.

Accordingly, sympathetic though I am to his predicament, I feel bound to regard those *d* conclusions as fatal to his success on this appeal.

Appeal dismissed. Leave to appeal granted.

Solicitors: *Driver & Co*, Bishop Waltham (for Colonel Burditt); *Sarginson & Co*, Coventry (for the chief constable).

e

                                                        April Weiss   Barrister.

Re H (a barrister)

f
VISITORS OF GRAY'S INN
LATEY J, SIR ROBERT MEGARRY V-C AND RALPH GIBSON J
12th, 25th JUNE 1981

Counsel – Disciplinary proceedings – Sentence – Conduct unbecoming a barrister, not being *g* *professional misconduct – Criminal conviction – Barrister unsuccessfully pleading not guilty – Whether distinction to be drawn between professional misconduct and misconduct outside profession – Whether unsuccessful plea of not guilty a matter to be taken into consideration by disciplinary tribunal.*

The appellant, a practising barrister of some eight years' standing, was charged with *h* persistently importuning for immoral purposes in a public lavatory on one occasion. The case for the prosecution was not that he had importuned by words or by any direct physical approach but that it was to be inferred from certain gestures that he had been doing so. He pleaded not guilty and gave evidence. After a lengthy retirement the jury returned a verdict of guilty. The appellant was fined £250. Subsequently, before a disciplinary committee of the Senate of the Inns of Court and the Bar, the appellant *j* admitted one charge of conduct unbecoming a barrister arising from the conviction. He was sentenced to a period of suspension for three months from practice as a barrister. The appellant appealed against the sentence to the judges of the High Court as visitors of his Inn of Court. He contended (i) that a distinction was to be drawn between misconduct by a barrister in his professional capacity and misconduct in his private life, (ii) that the disciplinary tribunal should have been cautious about the weight it placed on the fact that the appellant had unsuccessfully pleaded not guilty in the criminal court, and (iii) that the sentence was out of proportion to that imposed in comparable cases.

Held – (1) A distinction was to be drawn between professional misconduct and misconduct outside the profession; and, although in a case of professional misconduct it would take a very strong case to induce the visitors to interfere with a sentence passed by a disciplinary tribunal, in a case where there was no suggestion of professional misconduct the visitors were bound to consider whether in their opinion the sentence passed by the disciplinary tribunal was in proportion to the misconduct which had been proved (see p 207 h to p 208 b, post); Re a solicitor [1956] 3 All ER 516 applied.

(2) Although, in weighing the consequences of pleading guilty or not guilty in court to criminal offences outside the bounds of their professional practice, members of professions and occupations were faced with the pressure of considering the effect of failure of a plea of not guilty not only on the sentence passed on them by the court but also on that which would later be passed by a disciplinary tribunal of their profession, and although in that context a barrister could not expect to be put in a special position, nevertheless an unsuccessful plea of not guilty was a factor which it was proper for the disciplinary tribunal to weigh with all others, but, in the absence of aggravating circumstances, it should not be the predominant factor leading to the very heavy sentence of suspension from practice where otherwise there would have been the lighter one of reprimand (see p 208 d to h, post).

(3) In all the circumstances, and bearing in mind that in similar cases solicitors were not usually suspended from practice, the appeal would be allowed and for the sentence of suspension there would be substituted a reprimand without publication (see p 209 a to i, post).

Per the Visitors. Where barristers have been convicted by criminal courts of offences not involving professional misconduct, it is desirable that there should be consistency of sentences imposed by disciplinary tribunals in comparable cases. For this purpose the record of the decisions ought to state matters such as the penalty imposed by the criminal court, the approximate length of the barrister's standing at the Bar, whether or not he is a practising barrister and any other matters material to the sentence which can readily be stated (see p 208 j to p 209 a, post).

Notes

For disciplinary authority over barristers, see 3 Halsbury's Laws (4th Edn) para 1134, and for cases on the subject, see 3 Digest (Reissue) 746–748, 4452–4461.

Case referred to in decision

Solicitor, Re a [1956] 3 All ER 516, [1956] 1 WLR 1312, DC, 43 Digest (Repl) 434, 4614.

Appeal

H, a barrister, admitted before the disciplinary tribunal of the Senate of the Inns of Court and the Bar on 23rd February 1981 one charge of conduct unbecoming a barrister arising out of his conviction in the Crown Court of an offence of persistently importuning for immoral purposes in a public lavatory on one occasion for which he was fined £250. The disciplinary tribunal sentenced him to a period of suspension for three months from practice as a barrister and from the enjoyment of all rights and privileges as a member of his Inn of Court. He appealed against the sentence to Her Majesty's Judges sitting as visitors of the Honourable Society of Gray's Inn. The respondent to the appeal was the Professional Conduct Committee of the Bar Council. The visitors heard the appeal in private but, at the request of the parties, stated their reasons in public. The facts are set out in the decision of the visitors.

John Hazan QC for the appellant.
Nicholas R Davidson for the respondent.

Cur adv vult

25th June. **LATEY J** read the following decision of the visitors: The appellant, a practising barrister of some eight years' standing, was convicted of an offence of persistently importuning for immoral purposes in a public lavatory on one occasion. The case for the prosecution was not that he importuned by words or by any direct physical approach, but that it should be inferred from certain gestures that he was doing so. He pleaded not guilty and gave evidence. After a lengthy retirement the jury returned a verdict of guilty, and he was fined £250.

Before the disciplinary tribunal of the Senate he admitted one charge of conduct unbecoming a barrister arising from the conviction. He was sentenced to a period of suspension for three months from practice as a barrister and from the enjoyment of all rights and privileges as a member of his Inn of Court. The tribunal's retirement also was a lengthy one. From that sentence he appeals to Her Majesty's Judges as visitors of the Inns of Court. Before the tribunal he did not seek to go behind the conviction, nor has he sought to do so before us. Counsel who represented him and counsel who represented the Senate appeared also before us. This has been helpful as they have been able to inform us of some matters which do not appear in the papers.

Moreover, material, some of it important, has been put before us which the tribunal did not have. Examples are a comparable case which has been heard by the tribunal since the instant one, and the approach and practice of the Law Society concerning solicitors in comparable cases. The Senate, through counsel, not only did not object to this new material being put before us but is anxious that the visitors should be supplied with all material which might help them reach a just result. This is consistent with the jurisdiction and role of the visitors. Their powers are not restricted. It is not necessary, for example, that they should find that the tribunal has erred in principle as a condition precedent of allowing an appeal or altering a sentence. We emphasise that in saying this we do not mean that the decision of the tribunal should be ignored. Far from it. The tribunal is chaired by a High Court Judge and comprises a lay representative and three members of the Bar. It is there to have regard to the interests of the public and is in close touch with the Bar. As such, its findings and views should be and are important factors to be weighed as such with all else.

Counsel for the appellant submitted that the case raises matters of moment and principle important to the Bar generally. Counsel for the Senate said that the Senate is anxious for any guidance which we may feel able to give as to the approach to be adopted so that consistency can be achieved so far as possible in cases of this nature. Rule 5(3) of the Hearings before the Visitors Rules 1980 provides: 'In an appeal against sentence the petition may refer to any factors which it is contended make the sentence unduly severe in relation to the appellant's record or to sentence in other similar cases.' On counsel's invitation, and because we agree that it is the right course in his case, we are stating our reasons in public.

At the heart of the matter are three general questions regarding the approach to sentencing. First, is there a distinction to be drawn between misconduct by a barrister in his professional practice and misconduct in his private life? Second, where the misconduct is in the commission of a criminal offence, to what extent should the fact that he has unsuccessfully pleaded not guilty affect the sentence of the disciplinary tribunal? Third, to what extent should the disciplinary tribunal have regard to sentences imposed in comparable cases?

As to the first question, we are in no doubt that a distinction should be drawn between professional misconduct and misconduct outside the profession. In *Re a solicitor* [1956] 3 All ER 516, [1956] 1 WLR 1312 a solicitor had been convicted of two indecent assaults and sentenced to three months' imprisonment. The Disciplinary Committee under the Solicitors Act 1932 ordered his name to be struck off the roll of solicitors. He appealed to the Divisional Court. Giving the judgment of the court Lord Goddard CJ said ([1956] 3 All ER 516 at 517, [1956] 1 WLR 1312 at 1314):

> 'This court is always, and always has been, very loth to interfere with the findings of the Disciplinary Committee either on a matter of fact, because they understand these matters so well, or with regard to penalty. If a matter were one of professional

misconduct, it would take a very strong case to induce this court to interfere with the sentence passed by the Disciplinary Committee, because obviously the Disciplinary Committee are the best possible people for weighing the seriousness of professional misconduct. There is no suggestion of professional misconduct in this case. That being so, this court is bound to consider, as the Court of Criminal Appeal would have to do, whether or not in its opinion the sentence is in proportion or out of proportion to the misconduct which has been proved.'

That, in our opinion, lays down the approach today as correctly as it did in 1956, and is equally appropriate to the disciplinary tribunal of the Senate and the visitors, though the sentence which the Divisional Court imposed in that case (suspension from practice for two years) in what counsel have aptly described as the pre-Wolfenden era would in the ordinary run of cases be inappropriate in the changed climate of the post-Wolfenden era.

As to the second question (the unsuccessful plea of not guilty), this, counsel for the appellant submits, is of major importance to any barrister who is charged with an offence against the law. In the instant case, as counsel are agreed and as is plain from the statement of decision and sentence of the chairman of the tribunal, the facts that the appellant unsuccessfully pleaded not guilty and that his evidence was evidently rejected by the jury caused the tribunal to pass a sentence of suspension instead of imposing a reprimand, which would have been the sentence had he pleaded guilty.

This, in counsel's submission, is of general concern to barristers who may find themselves charged with a criminal offence outside the bounds of their professional practice, who may wish to contest the charge and plead not guilty, and who then have to consider the effect of failure not only on the sentence passed on them by the court but also, and later, on that imposed by the disciplinary tribunal.

The relevant ground of the petition of appeal appears to contend that the tribunal should pay no attention at all in any case to the barrister's choice of plea in the court. Counsel for the appellant does not put it so high. He accepts that it is a factor which the tribunal is entitled to give weight to. He accepts that there may be cases where it may be weighty, indeed decisive, and he instanced the case where the accused barrister fabricates a false alibi. But, he says, such cases apart, cases where the defence advanced is scandalous or without merit, the disciplinary tribunal should be cautious about the weight to be attached to a plea of not guilty. He suggests that, if the approach adopted by the disciplinary tribunal in the instant case is correct, it places improper pressure on a barrister who is innocent to plead guilty and so preserve his right to practise. It would put a barrister defendant in a worse position than any other member of the public. As to this last point, counsel for the Senate suggests that a barrister is not in a unique position. In weighing the consequences of pleading guilty or not guilty, members of other professions and occupations are faced with somewhat similar pressure for the reason, among others, that a contested trial usually attracts more publicity.

We agree that in this context a barrister cannot expect to be put in a special position. But that does not destroy the generality of counsel's submission for the appellant. We agree with it. An unsuccessful plea of not guilty is a factor which it is proper for the disciplinary tribunal to weigh with all others, but it should not be the predominant factor leading to the very heavy sentence of suspension from practice where otherwise there would have been the lighter one of reprimand, unless there are aggravating circumstances.

We may add that in the instant case the weight to be attached to the plea of not guilty was raised by a member of the disciplinary tribunal at the very end of the hearing, and so the tribunal did not have the benefit of the full and researched submissions which we have had from counsel.

As to the third question, namely the extent to which the disciplinary tribunal should have regard to sentences imposed in comparable cases, in general it is desirable that there should be consistency, and r 5(3), already quoted, underlines that desirability. For this purpose we think that the record of the decisions ought to state matters such as the penalty imposed by the criminal court, the approximate length of the barrister's standing

at the Bar, whether or not he is a practising barrister, and any other matters material to
a the sentence which can readily be stated. We say this because, in the records of the three
comparable cases put before us, only one stated the penalty imposed by the criminal
court, only one disclosed the barrister's standing at the Bar, and none stated whether or
not he was practising. In fact, two were practising and one was not; and in deciding
whether or not to impose a sentence of suspension the tribunal must obviously bear in
mind the greater severity of such a sentence in the case of a practising barrister as
b compared with a non-practising barrister. No doubt in many cases some of these matters
could be discovered by consulting the Bar List; but decisions which are to be used as
precedents ought to be self-contained.

Is there yet an established pattern or norm for barristers in this type of case? Of the
three comparable cases, one was decided after this case was heard. One of the three was
a case of importuning and the other two were cases of gross indecency. In all three cases
c the sentence imposed was a reprimand, with no recommendation for publication. There
were, as there always are, some differences between one case and another, and counsel for
the Senate says that there is not yet an established pattern. Counsel for the appellant
suggests that there is already something of a pattern. We agree and consider that it is the
appropriate one.

But the matter does not stop there. Counsel for the appellant has made inquiry of the
d Law Society and is authorised to inform us that in this category of case where solicitors
are involved it is the established practice not to suspend the solicitor from practice but to
impose a reprimand or a fine or both. (The Senate tribunal has no power to impose a
fine, as distinct from ordering fees to be repaid or foregone.) In this context we can see
no reason in logic or principle to draw a distinction between members of the two
branches of the profession, and counsel for the Senate accepted this.

e Finally, the mitigation in the instant case was described by the tribunal as
impressive. Indeed it is. The appellant is spoken of in the highest terms by judges before
whom he practices, by the head and all members of his chambers, by leading counsel
who was his pupil-master and by solicitors regularly instructing him. The appellant's
offence, isolated though it is, is not trivial. But neither is a reprimand a trivial penalty,
and we consider it the appropriate one to meet and mark the offence.

f We have then had to consider whether, having decided that the appropriate penalty is
a reprimand and not suspension, the reprimand should be with or without publication.
It is to be noted that the original offence of importuning received in the neighbourhood
where this barrister lives and practises the considerable publicity that such convictions
commonly receive in the case of a professional man. The solicitors who normally
employ his professional services, or are likely to do so, or who may be opposed by him
in legal proceedings, have undoubtedly learned about the conviction and, in professional
g circles, that knowledge will persist. Unlike a case of misconduct in professional practice,
where the profession and public may hear nothing of the wrongdoing unless the
profession publishes it, this conviction has been fully reported.

The function of these proceedings in bringing home to the barrister the fact that the
conduct which brought about the conviction will not be passed over or tolerated by the
h profession has been achieved in this case without the accentuation of the penalty of
reprimand by publication of it. Further, all that we have heard of the conduct of this
barrister since the offence, and of the continued confidence in him expressed by both
clients and colleagues, has persuaded us that publication is not necessary either as a
warning and deterrent to him or as a marking by the profession of its view of the
commission of such an offence by a barrister. On the facts of this case the reprimand
j alone is sufficient.

For all these reasons we have allowed the appeal, set aside the sentence and substituted
for it a reprimand without publication.

*Appeal allowed ; sentence of suspension set aside and reprimand without publication substituted
therefor.*

Sepala Munasinghe Esq   Barrister.

Selim Ltd v Bickenhall Engineering Ltd   *a*

CHANCERY DIVISION
SIR ROBERT MEGARRY V-C
8th, 15th MAY 1981

Land charge – Pending action – Registration – Pending land action – Application for leave to   *b*
commence action for breach of repairing covenant in lease – Whether application registrable –
Whether application a proceeding 'relating to' land – Whether a proceeding which if successful
would destroy an interest in land can 'relate to' land – Leasehold Property (Repairs) Act 1938,
s 1(3) – Land Charges Act 1972, ss 5(1), 17(1).

In about May 1980 the landlords of two houses comprised in registered leasehold titles   *c*
served on the lessees forfeiture notices under s 146 of the Law of Property Act 1925 for
breach of the repairing covenants in the leases. The lessees, as they were entitled to do,
served counter-notices under the Leasehold Property (Repairs) Act 1938 which, by
s 1(3)[d], had the effect of prohibiting the landlords from taking proceedings by action
without leave of the court to enforce any right of forfeiture or to claim damages for
breach of the covenants. On 17th October 1980 the leases were assigned to the   *d*
plaintiffs. On 9th December the landlords issued an application in the county court
under the 1938 Act for leave to commence an action against the plaintiffs for breach of
the repairing covenants in the leases. If leave was given the landlords intended to claim
forfeiture of the leases and not merely damages for breach of the repairing covenants.
Since the leasehold titles were registered a pending action was required to be entered on
the register against the titles as a caution against dealings with the titles. The plaintiffs   *e*
wished to sell the leases and requested the landlords to remove the cautions but they
refused to do so. The plaintiffs sold the leases and in order to be able to convey a clear title
issued a writ and a notice of motion seeking an order that the cautions be vacated. On
the hearing of the motion they submitted that the application in the county court for
leave to bring an action against them was not a 'pending land action' within s 17(1)[b] of
the Land Charges Act 1972 because it was not a proceeding 'relating to' land within   *f*
s 17(1) and therefore it was not registrable as a pending action under s 5(1)[c] of the 1972
Act and the cautions should be vacated.

Held – Proceedings which if successful would destroy an interest in land 'related to' the
land, within s 17(1) of the 1972 Act, just as much as proceedings for the acquisition of
land, and accordingly proceedings for forfeiture of a lease were proceedings which   *g*
'related to' land within s 17(1). Since an application under the 1938 Act for leave to
commence an action was, where it was intended that the action should include a claim
for forfeiture of the lease, a preliminary stage in forfeiture proceedings, such an

---

a   Section 1, so far as material, provides:
     '(1) Where a lessor serves on a lessee under subsection (1) of section one hundred and forty-six   *h*
of the Law of Property Act, 1925, a notice that relates to a breach of a covenant or agreement to
keep or put in repair during the currency of the lease all or any of the property comprised in the
lease, and at the date of the service of the notice three years or more of the term of the lease remain
unexpired, the lessee may within twenty-eight days from that date serve on the lessor a counter-
notice to the effect that he claims the benefit of this Act . . .
     '(3) Where a counter-notice is served by a lessee under this section, then, notwithstanding
anything in any enactment or rule of law, no proceedings, by action or otherwise, shall be taken   *j*
by the lessor for the enforcement of any right of re-entry or forfeiture under any proviso or
stipulation in the lease for breach of the covenant or agreement in question, or for damages for
breach thereof, otherwise than with the leave of the court.'
b   Section 17(1), so far as material, is set out at p 211 j, post
c   Section 5(1), so far as material, provides: 'There may be registered in the register of pending
actions—(a) a pending land action . . .'

application was also a proceeding 'relating to' the land, within s 17(1). It followed that
a the landlords' application in the county court was a 'pending land action' within s 17(1)
and was therefore registrable under s 5(1) of the 1972 Act. The claim in the motion for
an order vacating the cautions would accordingly be refused (see p 213 j, p 214 c to e g j
and p 215 a, post).
   Calgary and Edmonton Land Co Ltd v Dobinson [1974] 1 All ER 484, *Whittingham v
Whittingham (National Westminster Bank Ltd intervening)* [1978] 3 All ER 805 and *Allen v
b Greenhi Builders Ltd* [1978] 3 All ER 1163 considered.
   Per Curiam. It is doubtful whether an action for damages for breach of a repairing
covenant in a lease is, by itself, a 'pending land action' (see p 214 j, post).

Notes
For what may be registered as a pending land action, see 26 Halsbury's Laws (4th Edn)
c para 747. For vacation of a registration, see ibid, para 753.
   For the Leasehold Property (Repairs) Act 1938, s 1, see 18 Halsbury's Statutes (3rd Edn)
473.
   For the Land Charges Act 1972, ss 5, 17, see 42 Halsbury's Statutes (3rd Edn) 1604,
1618.

d ## Cases referred to in judgment
Allen v Greenhi Builders Ltd [1978] 3 All ER 1163, [1979] 1 WLR 156, 37 P & CR 176,
   Digest (Cont Vol E) 502, 925g.
Calgary and Edmonton Land Co Ltd v Dobinson [1974] 1 All ER 484, [1974] Ch 102, [1974]
   2 WLR 143, 26 P & CR 516, Digest (Cont Vol D) 757, 926eb.
Heywood v BDC Properties Ltd (No 2) [1964] 2 All ER 702, [1964] 1 WLR 971, CA; *rvsg in
e part* [1964] 1 All ER 180, [1964] 1 WLR 267, Digest (Cont Vol B) 548, 285a.
Pips (Leisure Productions) Ltd v Walton (23rd May 1980, unreported).
Taylor v Taylor [1968] 1 All ER 843, [1968] 1 WLR 378, 19 P & CR 193, CA, Digest (Cont
   Vol C) 436, 2133e.
Whittingham v Whittingham (National Westminster Bank Ltd intervening) [1978] 3 All ER
   805, [1979] Fam 9, [1978] 2 WLR 936, 36 P & CR 164, Ch D & CA, Digest (Cont Vol
f E) 275, 6962Aq(iv).

Motion
By a notice of motion dated 5th May 1981 the plaintiff company, Selim Ltd, moved in
an action by them against the defendant company, Bickenhall Engineering Ltd, for
orders under s 82 of the Land Registration Act 1925, or alternatively under the court's
g inherent jurisdiction, vacating the registration in the Land Registry by the defendant
company of cautions against the registered leasehold title to two houses, 58 and 74
Taybridge Road, Battersea, against dealings with those leasehold interests because of
pending actions relating to them. The facts are set out in the judgment.

M M *Pascoe* for the plaintiff company.
h W *Elland* for the defendant company.

Cur adv vult

15th May. **SIR ROBERT MEGARRY V-C** read the following judgment: This
motion raises a single question of law. That question is whether certain proceedings fall
j within the definition of 'a pending land action' in the Land Charges Act 1972, and so is
registrable as a 'pending action' under s 5 of the 1972 Act. By s 17(1), unless the context
otherwise requires, the expression 'pending land action' means 'any action or proceeding
pending in court relating to land or any interest in or charge on land'. The question is
whether this definition includes proceedings in a county court under the Leasehold
Property (Repairs) Act 1938 which seek leave to commence an action against an assignee
of a lease for breach of the repairing covenants.

The matter arises in this way. The two houses in question, 58 and 74 Taybridge Road, Battersea, were demised by separate leases for 99 years from 24th June 1890, each at a rent of £7 a year. On 17th October 1980 each lease was assigned to the plaintiff company. Some five months earlier the defendant company, the landlords, had served on the assignors notices under s 146 of the Law of Property Act 1925 in respect of the disrepair of the premises, accompanied by schedules of dilapidations. As over three years of each lease was unexpired, the assignors were entitled to serve on the defendant company a counter-notice under the 1938 Act, and this they did on 10th June 1980 in respect of each house. By s 1(3) of the 1938 Act, the effect of this was to prohibit the defendant company from taking any proceedings, by action or otherwise, for the enforcement of any right of re-entry or forfeiture for breach of the repairing covenants, or for damages for such breach, without the leave of the court. On 9th December 1980, after the assignment to the plaintiff company, the defendant company issued originating applications in the Wandsworth County Court in respect of each house, seeking, inter alia, 'leave to commence an action' against the plaintiff company 'for breach of the repairing covenants' in the leases.

The title to each leasehold registered at the Land Registry with good leasehold title. By virtue of s 59(1) and (5) of the Land Registration Act 1925, a pending action which for unregistered land is required to be protected under the Land Charges Act 1972 is, for registered land, required to be protected by the entry of a caution against dealings with the land instead. The plaintiff company wished to sell the leasehold interest in both houses, and gave instructions for them to be sold at auction on 27th April 1981. However, on 2nd April 1981 the defendant company's solicitors wrote to the plaintiff company's solicitors to say that they had registered cautions against each of the houses. Despite the protests of the plaintiff company's solicitors, the defendant company refused to remove the cautions. At the auction on 27th April an announcement was made about the service of the schedules of dilapidations and the commencement of proceedings to enforce them; and it was stated that the purchasers would have to deal with all problems relating to these. Despite this, both houses were sold at the auction (one with part vacant possession), and the plaintiff company expects that the purchasers will require the cautions to be vacated before they will complete. The plaintiff company accordingly issued a writ and notice of motion on 5th May 1981 seeking in respect of each house, either under s 82 of the Land Registration Act 1925 or the inherent jurisdiction, an order that the cautions be vacated. The writ also claims damages.

Counsel for the plaintiff company and counsel for the defendant company were in agreement on every point save the one in dispute. For the purposes of the motion only, counsel for the plaintiff company accepted that there were breaches of the repairing covenants and that leave under the 1938 Act will be granted by the county court. No question was raised on the power of the court to grant on motion the relief sought by the plaintiff company, or on the jurisdiction (whether inherent or under s 82 of the Land Registration Act 1925) to make the order sought, or on the form of the order, whether personal or impersonal. On both hands it was accepted that the only question was whether the application to the Wandsworth County Court was or was not a 'pending land action', and so a 'pending action', within ss 5 and 17(1) of the Land Charges Act 1972. Counsel for the plaintiff company, of course, says that it is not, whereas counsel for the defendant company says that it is.

The meaning of 'pending land action' has been discussed in five recent cases to which I should refer. In *Heywood v BDC Properties Ltd (No 2)* [1964] 1 All ER 180, [1964] 1 WLR 267 the defendants alleged that the plaintiffs had agreed to sell certain land to them, and registered estate contracts as land charges in respect of the alleged contracts. The plaintiffs then issued a writ seeking vacation of the land charges on the ground that there were no contracts in existence; and on motion they obtained the order that they sought. The defendants then registered the plaintiffs' action as a pending action, and the plaintiffs applied for the vacation of this registration. Plowman J held that the action was not a pending action because neither party was making any claim to land against the

other. The plaintiffs were doing no more than seeking a declaration that there was no
a contract relating to the land between the parties, and there was old authority which
showed that a pending action was an action asserting a claim to land or an interest in
land. The Court of Appeal reversed this decision on a procedural point, but the decision
on the pending action point was not affected (see [1964] 2 All ER 702, [1964] 1 WLR
971). In *Taylor v Taylor* [1968] 1 All ER 843, [1968] 1 WLR 378 a wife took out a
summons under s 17 of the Married Women's Property Act 1882, in which she sought
b an order for the sale of the matrimonial home and a declaration that she was entitled to
half the proceeds of sale. Both in s 20(6) of the Land Charges Act 1925, and in s 17(1) of
the Land Charges Act 1972, 'land' is defined as excluding an undivided share in land.
The Court of Appeal held that the wife's summons was not a pending action. Then in
Calgary and Edmonton Land Co Ltd v Dobinson [1974] 1 All ER 484, [1974] Ch 102 I
followed *Heywood v BDC Properties Ltd (No 2)*, and held that a summons in the Companies
c Court to restrain the liquidator from disposing of certain land belonging to a company
was not a pending land action, for it claimed no proprietary right in land, and sought
merely to restrain a disposition of land.

The other two decisions were on the other side of the line. In *Whittingham v
Whittingham (National Westminster Bank Ltd intervening)* [1978] 3 All ER 805, [1979] Fam
9, on a divorce the wife applied for an order transferring her husband's house to her; and
d the Court of Appeal, affirming Balcombe J, held that this application was a 'pending land
action' and so was registrable as a pending action. It mattered not that the wife had no
existing proprietary right in the house; it sufficed that she was seeking an order that
would give her such a right. Finally, there was *Allen v Greenhi Builders Ltd* [1978] 3 All
ER 1163, [1979] 1 WLR 156. There, a number of houseowners brought separate actions
against some builders, claiming, inter alia, that they had easements of support for their
e houses which were being interfered with by the builders. They sought an injunction to
restrain future interferences, with a mandatory order to make good past interferences,
and damages. Browne-Wilkinson J held that an action claiming an easement was a
'pending land action', especially when it included a claim to the mandatory order
sought. I should mention that this case, and *Taylor v Taylor* were not cited in argument
before me.

f   If one returns to the definition of 'pending land action', it seems plain that in this case
the opening words are satisfied, namely 'any action or proceeding pending in court'; and
no contention to the contrary has been put forward. Nor is there much difficulty about
the concluding words, 'land or any interest in or charge on land'. 'Land', I may say, is
given a wide definition in s 17(1) of the 1972 Act. The difficulty lies in the two words
'relating to'. As was mentioned in a passage in *Calgary and Edmonton Land Co Ltd v
g Dobinson* [1974] 1 All ER 484 at 487, [1974] Ch 102 at 105, which was cited in *Whittingham
v Whittingham* [1978] 3 All ER 805 at 814, [1979] Fam 9 at 22, there must be some
restriction on the literal width of these words, for otherwise an action to restrain a
nuisance alleged to emanate from X's land would be registrable. The question is what
that restriction is.

In *Calgary and Edmonton Land Co Ltd v Dobinson* I did not seek to lay down any
h exhaustive definition, and I do not seek to do so now. (In view of what Stamp LJ said in
Whittingham v Whittingham [1978] 3 All ER 805 at 815, [1979] Fam 9 at 23, I may also say
that I certainly did not intend to suggest that only a claim to an existing interest in land
would suffice, so that a claim to have a new right granted would not: I would respectfully
adopt what Eveleigh LJ said about this: see [1978] 3 All ER 805 at 816, [1979] Fam 9 at
24.) What are in question in this case are not proceedings which merely seek to restrain
j any disposition of the land, or to obtain a declaration that no contract to sell it exists. On
the other hand, the proceedings do not seek to obtain a transfer of the land or to assert an
easement over it. The proceedings are a first step towards launching further proceedings
which may merely claim damages or may seek forfeiture of the lease, or may do both.

I propose to take the matter by stages. First, if the proceedings were direct proceedings
for forfeiture, would they be registrable as a pending action? Plainly they would not be

proceedings which claim some proprietary right in the land, in any ordinary sense of the words. What they would seek would be to destroy an estate in the land. Yet I think that one must consider the effect of such a distinction. If the immediate reversioner on a lease purchases that lease, the normal result will be that the lease will perish by surrender, and the reversion will become an interest in possession; and if the reversioner seeks to enforce the agreement, that plainly would fall within the authorities as being a pending land action. If instead the reversioner sues for forfeiture, the result, if he succeeds, will be much the same: the lease will disappear and the reversion will become an interest in possession. Thus although the forfeiture is in one sense an act of destruction, from another aspect it may be regarded as an act of acquisition; for it augments the reversioner's interest in the land.

Even if I am wrong in this view, I have to remember that what I am primarily concerned with is the phrase 'relating to land'; and on any ordinary meaning of those words, proceedings for the forfeiture of a lease of land seem to me to fall within that expression. I do not think that there is anything in the authorities which precludes me from giving effect to this view. The cases which speak in terms of a claim to specific property, or the recovery or assertion of title to specific property, or a claim to some proprietary right in land (see Calgary and Edmonton Land Co Ltd v Dobinson [1974] 1 All ER 484 at 488–489, [1974] Ch 102 at 107) do not seem to me to connote that proceedings to destroy an interest in land cannot be a pending land action. After all, the statutory words 'relate to' are very general in their meaning, and although there must be some limit to this meaning, I would have thought that proceedings for the destruction of an interest in land 'relate to' the land as much as proceedings for the acquisition of an interest in the land. In each case the proceedings directly affect an estate or interest in the land; and without aspiring to any definition, exhaustive or otherwise, I would regard such an approach as providing a helpful guide to proceedings which fall within the statutory definition.

There is a further consideration. In Whittingham v Whittingham [1978] 3 All ER 805 at 815, [1979] Fam 9 at 23, and in Allen v Greenhi Builders Ltd [1978] 3 All ER at 1165, [1979] 1 WLR 156 at 159, there is some discussion of it being material to take into account whether, if the action is not registered, a third party, acquiring the land before judgment in the action and without notice, will take free from the plaintiff's claim. In the case of leaseholds, it seems to me to be important that a purchaser should, by searching, be able to discover pending proceedings for forfeiture, for otherwise he might be purchasing something which, on service of the proceedings for forfeiture, had ceased to exist. Nearly a year ago I had such a case (Pips (Leisure Productions) Ltd v Walton (23rd May 1980, unreported)); and it was a striking warning to purchasers of leaseholds. It seems to me that this consideration supports the view that proceedings which, if successful, will destroy an interest in land ought on any fair reading of the words to be regarded as proceedings which 'relate to' that land.

That, however, is not the end of the matter. The present proceedings in the county court are not proceedings for forfeiture of the lease, but at any rate on one view are at best at one remove from such proceedings. Each originating application merely seeks 'leave to commence an action' against the plaintiff company 'for breach of the repairing covenant' in the lease. Under s 1(3) of the 1938 Act, such leave is needed both for proceedings for forfeiture and for proceedings claiming damages. There is nothing in the originating application to show that, if leave is given, it is proceedings for forfeiture that will be commenced, with or without a claim for damages. The probability, however, is that forfeiture would be sought, and in any case the affidavit of a solicitor filed on behalf of the defendant company states in terms that the defendant company is seeking leave 'to take forfeiture proceedings'. The next paragraph, indeed, refers to the prospects 'of obtaining forfeiture itself of both leases'. In those circumstances, it seems to me that the proceedings in the county court may fairly be regarded as a preliminary stage in the forfeiture proceedings which the defendant company wishes to take. I doubt whether an action for damages for breach of covenant is, by itself, a 'pending land action', *a* but I think that proceedings for leave to commence an action which may include a claim for forfeiture of a lease, and is intended to do so, sufficiently relate to the land under lease for them to be a 'pending land action'. I so hold. It follows that the claim in the motion for an order vacating the registrations fails, and so the motion will be dismissed.

Motion dismissed.

b Solicitors: *L B Marks & Co* (for the plaintiff company); *Slowes* (for the defendant company).

Azza M Abdallah   Barrister.

---

c # Singer v Trustee of the property of Munro and another (bankrupts)

CHANCERY DIVISION
WALTON J
23rd MARCH 1981

d *Bankruptcy – Trustee in bankruptcy – Release of trustee – Application to set aside release – Release improperly obtained – Notice required to be sent to creditor not sent to creditor's address on proof but to his solicitors – Creditor applying to court to reverse order releasing trustee – Effect of release – Whether trustee obliged to send notice to creditor at address on proof – Whether trustee can send notice to different address provided he clearly indicates exactly what he has done* *e* *– Whether court should reverse order releasing trustee – Bankruptcy Act 1914, s 93(1)(3) – Bankruptcy Rules 1952 (SI 1952 No 2113), r 341.*

Solicitor – Authority – Notices – Receipt of notices on behalf of client – Solicitor having no authority to receive notices on behalf of client in absence of express authority.

f The applicant was a creditor of a firm of solicitors which went into liquidation in 1970. The respondent was the trustee in bankruptcy of the firm and of the individual partners. In 1978 an order was made allowing the applicant's proof for about £80,000 and also allowing him to put in additional claims either in the bankruptcy of the partnership or in the bankruptcy of the individual partners. In fact the assets of the partnership were minimal and no payment of any dividend was ever made to any of the *g* creditors. In 1980 the respondent applied for and was granted a release from his trusteeship under s 93(1)[a] of the Bankruptcy Act 1914. Before applying for the release the trustee, as required by r 341[b] of the Bankruptcy Rules 1952, sent notices of his intention to all the creditors. In an affidavit sworn in support of his application for release the respondent stated that he had sent the required notices to the creditors at their respective addresses set out in their respective proofs, but, although the applicant's *h* address in his proof was in France, notice had in fact been sent to him care of his solicitors in England. The applicant applied for an order that the decision to grant the release of the respondent from his trusteeship be reversed or otherwise varied or modified. The respondent opposed the application, contending that he had merely committed a technical slip.

j **Held** – (1) If a trustee in bankruptcy served notice on creditors other than at their respective addresses set out in their respective proofs, which he might do with good reason, he was bound to inform the court of precisely what he had done. Since the

---

a   Section 93(1) is set out at p 217 *f g*, post
b   Rule 341, so far as material, is set out at p 217 *h*, post

respondent had not informed the court that he had not sent notice to the applicant at the address in his proof, it followed that he had obtained his discharge as trustee improperly, in that it had been obtained on evidence which in part was untrue (see p 218 *e* to *g*, post).

(2) Since s 93(3)ᶜ of the 1914 Act provided that the effect of an order under s 93(1) releasing a trustee in bankruptcy was to discharge him from all liability for his actions as trustee, it followed that, if the respondent's release were to stand, the applicant would be deprived completely of any redress against the respondent in respect of his conduct as trustee. Since the release had been improperly obtained, the court would reverse the order granting the release of the respondent from his office as trustee of the property of the bankrupts (see p 219 *b* to *f*, post).

Per Curiam. In general a solicitor does not have any authority to receive notices on behalf of a client, although he may be given express authority to do so (see p 218 *c d*, post).

Notes

For application by a trustee in bankruptcy for release and for the effect of such release, see 3 Halsbury's Laws (4th Edn) paras 518–519.

For the Bankruptcy Act 1914, s 93, see 3 Halsbury's Statutes (3rd Edn) 126.

For the Bankruptcy Rules 1952, r 341, see 3 Halsbury's Statutory Instruments (Fourth Reissue) 294.

Case referred to in judgment

Re Harris, ex parte Hasluck [1899] 2 QB 97, 68 LJQB 769, 80 LT 499, 6 Mans 259, 4 Digest (Reissue) 273, 2433.

Motion

By a notice of motion dated 20th November 1980 David Mortimer Singer, a creditor in the bankruptcies of Donald Edward Munro and Lionel Rowe, lately practising in partnership as Donald Munro, Tudor & Rowe, applied for an order that the decision of the Secretary of State for Trade granting the release of the respondent, George Albert Auger, from his office as trustee of the property of the bankrupts be reversed or otherwise varied or modified. The facts are set out in the judgment.

David Marks for the applicant.
The respondent appeared in person.

WALTON J. This is an unusual application by a creditor in bankruptcy of Donald Edward Munro and Lionel Rowe, lately practising in partnership as Donald Munro, Tudor & Rowe, a firm of solicitors, for an order that the decision of the Secretary of State for Trade granting the release of the respondent from his office as trustee of the property of the bankrupts may be reversed or otherwise varied or modified, for an order that the respondent do pay the costs of and incidental to this motion, and such further or other relief as to the court shall seem just.

The situation is a little complicated, and I desire to say as little about the complications as I can because in so doing I might be appearing to slant the facts one way or the other. The position is that the applicant, whose address at all material times has been Vieux Cagnes, France, had a very intimate relation with the firm of Donald Munro, Tudor & Rowe in the sense that, apparently, all of his assets were in some way or other looked after by or bound up with that firm. There were a large number of transactions indeed between himself and that firm. When that firm went into liquidation, the trustee in bankruptcy originally took the view that the applicant was largely indebted to

---

c   Section 93(3) is set out at p 219 *a*, post.

that firm, whereas, as we now know, the fact is that the firm was very largely indebted
a to the applicant. I certainly think that part of the blame is to be found in the fact that
that firm did not, apparently, maintain their records in the form that solicitors ought to
maintain them; indeed, probably not in the form that any reputable firm ought to
maintain them. This may very well, I know not, have initially put the trustee off the
scent. Although the bankruptcy took place as long ago as 1970, it was not until the year
1978 that the trustee in bankruptcy finally, as it were, threw in his hand and admitted
b the proof of the applicant in the bankruptcy for the sum of £79,926 10s 4d. The order
of Goulding J, which allowed that to happen, also allowed the applicant to put in
additional claims either in the bankruptcy of the partnership or in the bankruptcy of the
individuals. I gather that recently he has put in a revised proof of debt of the order of
about £185,000. However, he may put in proofs of debt until he is blue in the face, but
the assets of the partnership were absolutely minimal and have not resulted and will not
c result in any payment of any dividend to any of the creditors.

The real hope of the applicant recovering any part of his money lies in the Law
Society's Compensation Fund, which has already paid to him a sum of £34,000 without
prejudice to any other payments which may be made, it being stated in the
correspondence with the Law Society (I have no other evidence so I do not know how
true this is) that the applicant's claim is the largest single claim with which the Law
d Society down to the date of its being made had ever had to deal.

In order that there should be no possible get-out, as it were, on any other basis than
that the bankrupt firm were thoroughly fraudulent in their dealings with the applicant,
the applicant has commenced proceedings in the Queen's Bench Division to which,
among others, the respondent trustee in bankruptcy is a party, for the purpose of being
able to say that it has been established by action that the bankrupts were in fact
e fraudulent. Whether that is strictly necessary or not, seems to be a matter of some
dispute with the Law Society who appear, and for all I know, quite properly, over a
period of time to have changed their stance in that regard.

However that may be, what has now happened is that the respondent, the former
trustee of the property of the firm, applied to the Department of Trade for his release
under the provisions of s 93(1) of the Bankruptcy Act 1914 which reads:

f 'When the trustee has realised all the property of the bankrupt, or so much
thereof as can, in his opinion, be realised without needlessly protracting the
trusteeship, and distributed a final dividend, if any, or has ceased to act by reason of
a composition having been approved, or has resigned, or has been removed from his
office, the [Department] of Trade shall, on his application, cause a report on his
accounts to be prepared, and, on his complying with all the requirements of the
g [Department], shall take into consideration the report, and any objection which
may be urged by any creditor or person interested against the release of the trustee,
and shall either grant or withhold the release accordingly, subject nevertheless to an
appeal to the High Court.'

That is, to some extent, fleshed out by r 341 of the Bankruptcy Rules 1952, SI 1952 No
h 2113, which provides:

'Before applying to the [Department] of Trade for his release, a trustee shall send
notice of his intention so to do, accompanied by a summary of his receipts and
payments as trustee, to all creditors who have proved their debts and to the debtor
...'

j Then there is a proviso which is not material, and I do not read. That rule is quite clearly
intended to enable the creditors to know that the trustee is applying for his release and
so to take objection against the release if they have any ground on which they are
properly entitled to so object.

What has happened in the present case is that in all three cases, because the respondent
was trustee not only of the property of the firm but also of the individual bankrupts, the

common form affidavit was sworn by the trustee in bankruptcy in which he makes oath
and says:

'1. That I did on the 4th day of August 1980, send to the Debtor and to each
Creditor who has proved in this matter a Notice of the Trustee's intention to Apply
for Release together with a Summary of the Accounts in the form hereunto annexed
marked "A."

'2. That such Notices were addressed to the Debtor at his last known address and
to such of the Creditors who have proved their debts according to the addresses in
their respective proofs.'

As regards the applicant, that last statement just is not true, because the applicant's
address in his proof was Vieux Cagnes in France. In fact, it transpires that the notice to
him was not sent to Vieux Cagnes in France at all but was sent to the applicant care of his
solicitors, who at that time were Messrs Payne, Hicks Beach & Co.

It is, of course, a common fallacy to think that solicitors have an implied authority on
behalf of their clients to receive notices. They may have express authority so to receive
them, but in general a solicitor does not have any authority to accept a notice on behalf
of his client. However, if the situation had been that in the affidavit relating to the
partnership, the respondent had sworn to that which in fact is said on his behalf did
happen, that is to say, that the notice went to the applicant care of his solicitors, I should
at the least have required very detailed explanation from Messrs Payne, Hicks Beach &
Co as to exactly what they did with that notice when they received it and what the
applicant's reaction was. But I am here confronted with the fact that half of the evidence
on which the respondent obtained the release from the Department of Trade was just not
so. The respondent submitted to me that it was, after all, only a technical slip at the
highest and that there are other forms which are in use which show that the trustee can
modify the requirements of the affidavit as to service so as to indicate precisely and
exactly what he did.

So far from in any way supporting the respondent's proposition, that evidence is
exactly and entirely against him, because it does show that if the trustee in bankruptcy,
for whatever reason (and there may very well be in many cases very good reasons why
notices have to be served in some peculiar way) serves them on creditors other than at
their respective addresses as set out in their respective proofs, he must and is entitled to,
indeed is bound, to inform the court of precisely and exactly what he has done. So the
position is crystal clear in that the respondent has obtained his discharge on evidence
which in part, and maybe in vital part, is untrue.

What ought I to do about it? It is quite clear from the provisions of s 93(1) that there
is an appeal to the High Court against the decision of the Department of Trade. It is also
clear from the Bankruptcy Rules 1952, r 8(1)(d) that the appeal must be heard and
determined in open court. It is also clear that the period is a period of 21 days (see
s 108(3) of the 1914 Act). The notice of motion is dated 20th November 1980 and is,
indeed, in time.

If the only matter in issue had been the continuance of the respondent as a defendant
in the action in the Queen's Bench Division to which I have already referred, I do not
think that the situation would have demanded such a drastic alteration as reversion or
cancellation of the decision of the Secretary of State for Trade, because it seems to me that
quoad that action the Official Receiver, who now steps into the shoes of the trustee in
bankruptcy as a result of his release under s 90(5) of the Bankruptcy Act 1914, would for
the purpose of that action do just as well as the respondent himself, bearing more
particularly in mind that there are no funds available in the bankruptcy whatsoever, and
that at this stage when the situation is pretty well known nobody is going to supply the
trustee in bankruptcy with any money for the purpose of defending that action, which
I also understand is in the event indefensible, and the trustee would not in fact seek to
defend it.

Unfortunately, the matter does not stop there. Section 93(3) reads as follows:

a

'An order of the [Department of Trade] releasing the trustee shall discharge him from all liability in respect of any act done or default made by him in the administration of the affairs of the bankrupt, or otherwise in relation to his conduct as trustee, but any such order may be revoked on proof that it was obtained by fraud or by suppression or concealment of any material fact.'

b Nobody, of course, suggests for one moment that the respondent has been fraudulent or has intentionally attempted to suppress or conceal any material fact. The situation, therefore, is that if the order stands it would be, in my judgment, quite impossible for the applicant to sue the trustee in respect of his conduct between the time when the order of adjudication was made in 1970 and the date in 1978 when the trustee threw in his hand quoad the applicant.

c Of course, I know nothing more than an outline of what happened then, and I have not either practically, judicially or actually the slightest idea whether there is any possible claim by the applicant against the trustee or not. What is in my judgment crystal clear is that on a true construction of s 93(3), which interestingly does not ever appear to have been previously construed, although the proviso thereto was construed in *Re Harris, ex parte Hasluck* [1899] 2 QB 97, it appears to me that the intention of that subsection, and *d* it is a very right, proper and wholesome intention, is to wipe the slate completely clean so far as the trustee is concerned so that he may thereafter pay no thought to the previous course of his actions as the trustee in bankruptcy. Of course, that means that if the release is now allowed to stand, the applicant would be deprived completely of any redress whatsoever against the trustee in bankruptcy in respect of the whole of the conduct of the trustee in bankruptcy in relation to the applicant's own proof of debt. *e* Having regard to many factors which I need not go into, the attitude of the trustee to the applicant's proofs may very well have been, so far as the applicant was concerned, most material in a large number of respects.

It, therefore, appears to me that at the end of the day in order to enable justice to be done I must carry the fact that the release has been improperly obtained to its logical conclusion and discharge or reverse the order of the Secretary of State for Trade granting *f* the release of the respondent from his office as trustee of the property of the bankrupt.

Order accordingly.

Solicitors: *Payne, Hicks, Beach & Co* (for the applicant).

Hazel Hartman　　Barrister.

Re Duke of Norfolk's Settlement Trusts   *a*

COURT OF APPEAL, CIVIL DIVISION
CUMMING-BRUCE, BRIGHTMAN AND FOX LJJ
2nd, 3rd, 4th, 5th MARCH, 15th APRIL 1981

Trust and trustee – Remuneration of trustee – Approval by court for increase in fees of corporate   *b*
trustee – Provision in settlement for remuneration to be in accordance with trustee's usual scale
of fees at date of settlement – Remuneration inadequate for work being done 20 years later – No
fundamental change in nature or assets of trust – Whether court having inherent jurisdiction to
alter general level of scale of fees.

On 1st April 1958 the settlor executed a settlement whereby he set up a discretionary   *c*
trust for the benefit of certain of his relatives and their descendants. The settled property
consisted mainly of shares, certain agricultural land and a block of an estate in London
known as 'the Strand estate'. The settlor appointed three trustees, including a trust
company. The settlement provided that the trust company was to be entitled to
remuneration for its services as trustee in accordance with its usual scale of fees in force
at the date of the settlement, which included a management fee of 2/- per £100 of capital   *d*
held in the trust annually, payable out of capital, the capital values being 'the book value
as shown in the last audited accounts of the trust'. In the late 1960s the settlor added to
the settlement two further blocks of the Strand estate and received in return from the
trustees some of the agricultural land which they held. The addition to the settlement
of the two extra blocks of the Strand estate made possible the execution of a scheme for
the comprehensive redevelopment of that estate. The execution of the scheme involved   *e*
the plaintiffs, who were the two surviving trustees of the settlement, one of whom was
the trust company, in an exceptional amount of additional work which enhanced the
value of the trust property and which could not have been foreseen when they accepted
office. The introduction of capital transfer tax in 1975 subsequently caused the plaintiffs
extra work in that it caused them to consider the form of the settlement closely and
whether they should execute an appointment to produce an 'interest in possession' for   *f*
capital transfer tax purposes. Such an appointment was in fact executed on 30th March
1976.
The plaintiffs applied to the court for an order under its inherent jurisdiction
authorising them to charge, be paid for and retain remuneration for their services. They
proposed, inter alia, that the trust company should be authorised (i) to operate a revised
scale of charges as from 31st March 1977 to raise the general level of remuneration fixed   *g*
by the trust instrument, (ii) to receive £25,000 for services performed outside the scope
of its duties, (iii) to receive an annual sum of £25,000 for its services to the trust during
the years ending 31st March 1976 and 31st March 1977, and (iv) to receive remuneration
for services of an exceptional nature or which were outside the scope of a trustee's duties
performed in the future. There was evidence that the general level of the trust company's
fees was low compared with that of similar institutions, that the proposed new scale   *h*
would be below that charged by such institutions, especially the Public Trustee, and that
the trust company was incurring a substantial and continuing financial loss as a result of
its trusteeship. The beneficiaries under the settlement were highly satisfied with the way
in which the plaintiffs had discharged their duties and did not oppose the application.
The judge ([1978] 3 All ER 907) held that the plaintiffs were entitled to a proper
allowance for the work done in connection with the redevelopment of the Strand estate   *j*
because their services were outside the scope of their normal duties and were only
rendered on the basis of an implied promise that they would be remunerated. The judge
further held, however, on the grounds that the court's inherent jurisdiction would only
be exercised to award remuneration in exceptional cases and that once a trust had been
unconditionally accepted the court would only rarely alter the general level of

a remuneration fixed by the trust instrument, that the plaintiffs were not entitled to claim for the work done following the fiscal changes effected by the introduction of capital transfer tax, since that work was inherent in the trusteeship of a discretionary trust, and that there were no grounds for altering the general level of the trust company's fees because there had not been such a fundamental change in the nature or the assets of the trust as to enable the court to exercise its inherent jurisdiction. The trust company appealed, seeking a declaration that the court had, inter alia, inherent jurisdiction to b authorise the trust company to charge remuneration at a higher rate than that permitted under the settlement.

Held – The court had an inherent jurisdiction to authorise the payment of remuneration to trustees if such an increase would be beneficial to the administration of the trust, and that jurisdiction extended to increasing the remuneration authorised by a trust c instrument. The jurisdiction was to be exercised by balancing, on the one hand, the fact that the office of trustee was essentially gratuitous and beneficiaries had to be protected against spurious claims by trustees and, on the other, that it was most important that the trust should be properly administered. The court would therefore first have regard to the nature of the trust, the experience and skill of the particular trustee, the sums that he wished to charge when compared with those of other trustees and all the surrounding d facts, and, having done so, could then exercise its jurisdiction to increase the trustee's remuneration if that was in the best interests of the beneficiaries. Accordingly, the court would grant the declaration sought and would remit the case to the Chancery Division to decide whether the jurisdiction should be exercised (see p 230 b to d f g and j to p 231 c and p 232 c d, post).

Marshall v Holloway (1820) 2 Swan 432, *Brocksopp v Barnes* (1820) 5 Madd 90, *Bainbrigge* e *v Blair* (1845) 8 Beav 588, *Re Masters (deceased)* [1953] 1 All ER 19 and *Re Worthington (deceased)* [1954] 1 All ER 677 considered.

Robinson v Pett (1734) 3 P Wms 249, *Re Salmen* (1912) 107 LT 108 and *Chapman v Chapman* [1954] 1 All ER 798 distinguished.

Decision of Walton J [1978] 3 All ER 907 reversed in part.

Notes
f For the remuneration of trustees, see 38 Halsbury's Laws (3rd Edn) 958–961, paras 1659–1662, and for cases on the subject, see 47 Digest (Repl) 251–255, 2207–2235.

Cases referred to in judgments
Bainbrigge v Blair (1845) 8 Beav 588, 1 New Pract Cas 283, 14 LJ Ch 405, 5 LTOS 454, 9 Jur 765, 50 ER 231, 23 Digest (Reissue) 59, 732.
g *Barbour's Settlement, Re, National Westminster Bank Ltd v Barbour* [1974] 1 All ER 1188, [1974] 1 WLR 1198, Digest (Cont Vol D) 1013, 2219a.
Brocksopp v Barnes (1820) 5 Madd 90, 56 ER 829, 23 Digest (Reissue) 52, 580.
Chapman v Chapman [1954] 1 All ER 798, [1954] AC 429, [1954] 2 WLR 723, [1954] TR 93, 33 ATC 84, 47 R & IT 310, HL, 47 Digest (Repl) 329, 2973.
Codd (deceased), Re [1975] 2 All ER 1051n, [1975] 1 WLR 1139, Digest (Cont Vol D) h 1013, 2219b.
Dale v Inland Revenue Comrs [1953] 2 All ER 671, [1954] AC 11, [1953] 3 WLR 448, 34 Tax Cas 468, [1953] TR 269, 32 ATC 294, 46 R & IT 513, HL, 28(1) Digest (Reissue) 583, 2163.
Forster v Ridley (1864) 4 De GJ & Sm 452, 4 New Rep 417, 11 LT 200, 46 ER 993, LJJ, 47 Digest (Repl) 255, 2231.
j *Freeman's Settlement Trusts, Re* (1887) 37 Ch D 148, 57 LJ Ch 160, 57 LT 798, 23 Digest (Reissue) 52, 586.
Inland Revenue Comrs v Lord Rennell [1963] 1 All ER 803, [1964] AC 173, [1963] 2 WLR 745, 42 ATC 55, [1963] TR 73, HL, 26 Digest (Reissue) 20, 75.
Macadam, Re, Dallow and Moscrop v Codd [1945] 2 All ER 664, [1946] Ch 73, 115 LJ Ch 14, 173 LT 395, 47 Digest (Repl) 366, 3293.

Marshall v Holloway (1820) 2 Swan 432, 36 ER 681, LC, 23 Digest (Reissue) 52, 584.

Masters (deceased), Re, Coutts & Co v Masters [1953] 1 All ER 19, [1953] 1 WLR 81, 47 Digest (Repl) 253, 2219. *a*

Morison v Morison (1838) 4 My & Cr 215, 3 Jur 528, 41 ER 85, LC, 23 Digest (Reissue) 52, 585.

Pooley, Re (1888) 40 Ch D 1, [1886–90] All ER Rep 157, 58 LJ Ch 1, 60 LT 73, CA, 43 Digest (Repl) 133, 1211.

Robinson v Pett (1734) 3 P Wms 249, 2 Eq Cas Abr 454, 24 ER 1049, sub nom *Robinson v Lorkin* 2 Barn KB 435, LC, 23 Digest (Reissue) 51, 579. *b*

Salmen, Re, Salmen v Bernstein (1912) 107 LT 108, Ch D and CA, 23 Digest (Reissue) 570, 6358.

Thorley, Re, Thorley v Massam [1891] 2 Ch 613, 60 LJ Ch 537, 64 LT 515, CA.

White, Re, Pennell v Franklin [1898] 2 Ch 217, 67 LJ Ch 502, 78 LT 770, CA, 23 Digest (Reissue) 61, 741.

Worthington (deceased), Re, ex parte Leighton v MacLeod [1954] 1 All ER 677, [1954] 1 WLR 526, 23 Digest (Reissue) 59, 733. *c*

Cases also cited

Allot, Re [1924] 2 Ch 498, [1924] All ER Rep 810, CA.

Bignell, Re [1892] 1 Ch 59, CA.

Campbell (deceased), In the Estate of [1954] 1 All ER 448, [1954] 1 WLR 516. *d*

Denton v Davy (1836) 1 Moo PCC 15, 12 ER 716.

Duncan v Watts (1852) 16 Beav 204, 51 ER 756.

Hallett v Hallett (1879) 13 Ch D 232.

McConnell, Re [1956] NI 151.

Pearson v Inland Revenue Comrs [1980] 2 All ER 479, [1980] 2 WLR 872.

Roberts, Re [1937] Ch 274. *e*

Spedding (deceased), Re [1966] NZLR 447.

Turner v Hancock (1882) 20 Ch D 303, CA.

Appeal

By an originating summons dated 10th January 1975, the plaintiffs, the Rt Hon John *f* David, Earl of Perth, and Schroder Executor and Trustee Co Ltd, the trustees of a settlement dated 1st April 1958 and made by the first defendant, the Most Noble Bernard Marmaduke, Duke of Norfolk EM ('the settlor'), sought the following relief: that the court might in exercise of its inherent jurisdiction authorise the plaintiffs to charge, be paid, and retain remuneration for their services as trustees of the settlement in accordance with the draft minutes of order intended to be exhibited to an affidavit of Alan William Lewis White intended to be sworn and filed, or in accordance with such other provisions *g* as should seem fit to the court. The defendants were (1) the settlor, (2) the Hon Ann Elizabeth Fitzalan-Howard, commonly called Lady Ann Fitzalan-Howard, (3) the Hon Mary Katherine Fitzalan-Howard, commonly called Lady Mary Fitzalan-Howard, (4) the Hon Sarah Margaret Fitzalan-Howard, commonly called Lady Sarah Fitzalan-Howard, (5) the Hon Theresa Jane Fitzalan-Howard, commonly called Lady Jane Fitzalan-Howard, (6) the Hon Edward William Fitzalan-Howard, (7) the Hon Gerald Fitzalan-Howard, (8) *h* the Rt Hon Miles Francis, Baron Beaumont, (9) the Hon Sir Michael Fitzalan-Howard, (10) the Hon Martin Fitzalan-Howard and (11) the Hon Mark Fitzalan-Howard, all of whom were beneficially interested under the settlement. The settlor died on 31st January 1975 and was succeeded by the eighth defendant. The summons was adjourned into open court for judgment. The second plaintiff appealed from so much of the judgment of Walton J ([1978] 3 All ER 907, [1979] Ch 37) as adjudged that no general *j* increase should be authorised in its remuneration. By an amended originating summons the second plaintiff also sought a declaration that the court had jurisdiction, under its inherent jurisdiction or under s 57 of the Trustee Act 1925, to authorise it to charge a higher rate of remuneration than that provided for under the settlement. None of the living beneficiaries opposed the second plaintiff's application for increased remuneration,

but, because unborn beneficiaries might have been affected by the appeal, counsel for the
sixth and seventh defendants (who were the only beneficiaries appearing on the appeal)
was requested to act as amicus curiae. The facts are set out in the judgment of Fox LJ.

Robert Walker for the trustees.
Ian Romer for the sixth and seventh defendants and as amicus curiae.

Cur adv vult

15th April. The following judgments were read.

FOX LJ (delivering the first judgment at the invitation of Cumming-Bruce LJ). This is
an appeal from Walton J ([1978] 3 All ER 907, [1979] Ch 37). It is concerned with the
jurisdiction of the court to authorise the payment out of trust property of remuneration
to a trustee.

By a settlement of 1st April 1958, made between the sixteenth Duke of Norfolk, as
settlor, of the one part, and Lord Perth, George Bellord (who has since died) and Schroder
Executor and Trustee Co Ltd ('SETCO'), as trustees, of the other part, certain property
was settled on, in effect, discretionary trusts during a lengthy period (which might, in
fact, endure until January 2038).

The provisions for remuneration of the trustees are contained in cll 11 and 12 of the
settlement and are as follows:

'11. ANY trustee hereof who shall be an individual engaged in any profession or
business shall be entitled to charge and be paid all professional or other reasonable
and proper charges for any business done or time spent or services rendered by him
in connection with the trusts of this settlement ... whether or not of a nature
requiring the employment of a person so engaged and no trustee shall be liable to
account for any benefits received by him through the employment by the trustees
of any firm or company of which he is a member or officer or in which he is
otherwise interested

'12. i. Schroder Executor and Trustee Company Limited hereinafter called "the
Company" shall be entitled to remuneration for its services as trustee hereof ... in
accordance with its usual scale of fees in force at the date hereof ii. The Company
may employ or consent to employing Messrs. J. Henry Schroder & Co. (hereinafter
called "the Bank") to act as banker to the trust and the Bank may make advances to
the trust estate as fully and with the like protections and rights including non-
accountability for profits made as a banker as if the Company were not a trustee
hereof iii. Lord Perth shall not be liable to account for any remuneration or other
benefits received by him either from the Company or from the Bank.'

The sixteenth Duke died in 1975; I shall refer to him as the settlor. The property
settled by the 1958 settlement consisted in the main of three items: (a) the issued share
capital of Fitzalan Howard Estates Ltd; the main asset of that company was the settlor's
life interest in certain freehold land; (b) an agricultural estate in Yorkshire of some 3,000
acres; (c) the south-east block of the settlor's Strand Estate in London; that estate consisted
of four blocks of property lying between the Strand and the river.

As a result of certain transactions (including the winding up of Fitzalan Howard
Estates Ltd) the trustees became entitled to certain agricultural estates and cash. In 1966
the settlor added to the settlement the north-east block of the Strand Estate. In 1968 the
settlor added the south-west block of the Strand Estate in exchange for some of the
agricultural land.

This concentration of the greater part of the Strand Estate in the hands of the trustees
led to the substantial redevelopment of the Strand Estate which took place in recent
years. This development, as the judge found, involved the trustees in work which was
entirely outside anything which would reasonably have been foreseen when they
accepted office.

The originating summons was issued by Lord Perth and SETCO as plaintiffs. The relief sought by the summons was, in essence, twofold. (1) The payment of an annual sum to Lord Perth as remuneration for his services as trustee. Clause 11 of the settlement had never applied to Lord Perth. (2) The establishment of a new scale of charges for SETCO. Under the settlement SETCO's remuneration was as follows: (i) an acceptance fee which was paid when the settlement was created; (ii) a management fee of 2/- (10p) per £100 of capital held in trust (the capital being valued at book values in the last audited accounts); (iii) a change of investment fee of 2/- per £100 on the amount involved in the transaction; (iv) a withdrawal fee of 5/- per £100.

The summons so far as SETCO is concerned asked, so far as material, for remuneration as follows: (i) a sum in respect of services performed prior to the issue of the summons (the services being services alleged to be outside the ordinary scope of a trustee's duties); (ii) sums in respect of its services to the trust during the two years ending 31st March 1976 and 1977 (which were periods after the issue of the summons but before the hearing); (iii) an increase in the management fee to 40p per £100 on the aggregate amount of the market values of the trust property (the investment fee and the withdrawal fee were to be left broadly as they were under cl 12 of the settlement); (iv) additional remuneration for any services performed by SETCO after the date of the order on the originating summons, which are exceptional or outside the ordinary scope of a trustee's duties, such additional remuneration to be of such amounts as should from time to time be certified in writing as reasonable by Messrs Cooper & Lybrands (or another firm of chartered accountants of similar standing) having regard to the difficulty of the work and to the time spent on it.

The evidence is that the general level of SETCO's fees is low compared with that of similar institutions and that the new scale proposed would still be below that charged by such institutions, especially the Public Trustee. There is also evidence that the amount of work transacted by SETCO as a trustee of the settlement is such that SETCO is incurring a substantial and continuing financial loss in consequence of its trusteeship. That, it is said, is because the amount of work now involved in administering the trust is so greatly in excess of anything contemplated when the trust was established.

The judge came to the conclusion that he had jurisdiction to authorise the payment of additional remuneration, both to Lord Perth and to SETCO, in respect of work which they had done in the past which was outside the scope of any duties which could reasonably have been expected to be rendered by them as trustees. He made certain orders authorising payments accordingly. Those orders are not appealed from and I need not refer to them further.

The judge also decided, however, that he had no inherent jurisdiction to authorise for the future any general increase in SETCO's remuneration as provided by cl 12 of the settlement. It is against that decision that this appeal is brought.

The living beneficiaries do not oppose SETCO's application for an increased scale of remuneration. The only beneficiaries who in fact appear on this appeal are the sixth and seventh defendants (the latter of whom was a minor when the proceedings started but is now of full age) who appear by counsel. As unborn beneficiaries may be affected, the court invited counsel for the sixth and seventh beneficiaries to act as amicus and he has addressed to us a full and helpful argument in support of the judge's decision.

At the request of the parties this court will decide the question of jurisdiction only. We are not asked to decide whether, if any jurisdiction exists, it should be exercised. The originating summons has accordingly been amended to ask for a declaration that the court has jurisdiction (whether under its inherent jurisdiction or under s 57 of the Trustee Act 1925 or otherwise) to authorise SETCO to charge remuneration at a rate higher than that to which it has previously been entitled under cl 12 of the settlement. I should mention that, before the judge, the discussion extended to the inherent jurisdiction only.

I turn to consider the inherent jurisdiction. That depends, in the main, on authority. An examination of a number of decisions is, therefore, necessary.

I start with *Robinson v Pett* 3 P Wms 249, 24 ER 1049 which was decided in 1734 by Lord Talbot LC. In that case the issue was whether—

> 'an excutor who had renounced but had yet been assisting in the trust according to the request of the testator should have any additional consideration, when he had an expressed legacy (£100) for such his assistance.'

The application was refused. The Lord Chancellor, after saying that it was an established rule that a trustee should have no allowance for his care and trouble, said (3 P Wms 249 at 251, 24 ER 1049 at 1050):

> 'But further; in the present case, the testator has by his will expressly directed what should be the defendant's recompense for his trouble, in case of his refusing the executorship, *viz.* that he still should have the £100 legacy, to which I can make no addition.'

Thus the Lord Chancellor felt that he was not entitled to increase the benefit given by the trust instrument to the trustee.

In 1818 *Marshall v Holloway* 2 Swan 432, 36 ER 681 came before Lord Eldon LC. The judgment itself is not of assistance on the present question but the order, of which there is a full report, is of value. The material part is as follows (2 Swan 432 at 452–454, 36 ER 681 at 689):

> '. . . and it being alleged by the said Plaintiffs, the trustees, that the nature and circumstances of the estate of the said testator require the application of a great proportion of time, by and on the part of the said trustees, for the due execution of the trusts of his said will, in regard to his estate, and that they cannot undertake to continue the execution of the trusts without the aid and assistance of the said *Faithful Croft*, as a co-trustee, he having, during the life of the said testator, had the principal and confidential management thereof, and being better acquainted therewith than any other person, and therefore it will be for the benefit of the said testator's estate that he should continue to be a trustee thereof; and the said *Faithful Croft*, alleging, that due attention to the affairs and concerns of the said testator will require so much of his time and attention as will be greatly prejudicial to his other pursuits and concerns in business, and therefore that he would not have undertaken to act therein, but under the assurance that an application would be made to this Court to authorise the allowance and payment of a reasonable compensation out of the said testator's estate for such his labour and time, and that he cannot continue to act therein without such reasonable allowance being made to him, it is ordered, that it be referred to the said Master to settle a reasonable allowance to be made to the said *Faithful Croft* out of the testator's estate, for his time, pains and trouble, in the execution of the said trusts, for the time past, and, in settling such allowance, the said Master is to have regard to the legacy of two hundred pounds given and bequeathed to the said *Faithful Croft* by the said will of the said testator, on the execution of the trusts thereby reposed in him: and it is ordered, that the said Master do inquire whether it will be for the benefit of the said testator's estate that the said *Faithful Croft* should continue to be a trustee under the said will, and to receive a compensation for the future employment of his time and trouble; and in case the said Master shall be of opinion that it will be for the benefit of the said testator's estate that the said *Faithful Croft* should be continued a trustee, then the said Master is to settle a reasonable allowance to be made to the said *Faithful Croft* therein . . .'

I make two observations on that order. First, it authorised the payment of remuneration in respect both of past and future services as trustee. Second, it appears to have authorised additional remuneration to that given by the will, since the master was directed to take into account in respect of past services the legacy of £200 given to Croft by the will; it is, I think, a reasonable inference that Lord Eldon LC regarded the £200 as remuneration for undertaking the trusteeship.

In *Brocksopp v Barnes* (1820) 5 Madd 90, 56 ER 829 the will appointed executors and trustees but gave them no remuneration. Barnes, one of the trustees, petitioned the court for payment out of the estate of an amount as recompense for his loss of time, personal trouble and expenses in the management of the estate. Leach V-C held that, while Barnes was entitled to his out-of-pocket expenses, he was entitled to no more since 'a trustee is not entitled to compensation for personal trouble or loss of time'. The Vice-Chancellor added: 'If the nature of the trust be such that a trustee ought not to undertake it without compensation, a special case must be made in this Court before the trust is accepted.' If that proposition is to be applied strictly, it would preclude such an application as SETCO makes in this case. And indeed it would also preclude the order made by Lord Eldon LC in *Marshall v Holloway* since Croft was already a trustee when the order was made.

In *Morison v Morison* (1838) 4 My & Cr 215 at 224, 41 ER 85 at 88 Lord Cottenham LC said that it would not be doubted that the court could appoint an executor or trustee as a consignee (which I take to be an agent to manage trust property abroad) with the usual profits. He regarded *Marshall v Holloway* as authority for that.

Bainbridge v Blair (1845) 8 Beav 558, 50 ER 231 is a case of importance. The testator, by his will, appointed Mr Blair and two others to be trustees and executors, and he gave Mr Blair a legacy of £200 'as compensation for his trouble in acting as one of the executors of the will'. The estate was involved in much litigation, in which Mr Blair acted as attorney for the trustees. He claimed, out of the trust property, the amount of his various bills of costs. The taxing master held that Mr Blair was only entitled to his disbursements and was not entitled to any remuneration for his services. Lord Langdale MR upheld that. But he said (8 Beav 558 at 596–597, 50 ER 231 at 234–235):

'It is very different from the case, where a trust being in the course of execution, and many things remaining to be done, which can be done beneficially only by a particular trustee, who cannot, from his situation, do it without grievous personal loss, and that party comes to the Court, and states, that he is in a situation and is willing to do these things, but that he cannot consistently with his own interest, proceed with such duties, and gratuitously devote his time for the benefit of the trust. In such a case, it is competent for the Court considering what is beneficial to the *cestuis que trust*, and is calculated to promote their interest, to take the matter into consideration, and to give proper remuneration to that person who alone, by his own exertion, can produce that benefit.'

This seems to me to be an explicit recognition by Lord Langdale MR that, even where a trustee has accepted the trusts, the court would have jurisdiction, if it was in the interests of the beneficiaries and if the trustee felt unable gratuitously to devote his time to trust affairs, to authorise payment of remuneration to him.

In *Forster v Ridley* (1864) 4 De GJ & Sm 452, 46 ER 993 the Court of Appeal authorised payment of remuneration, retrospectively, to trustees of a will who, for two years, had managed the testator's leaseholds and carried on his business.

Re Freeman's Settlement Trusts (1887) 37 Ch D 148 was a petition to the court to appoint two Canadians and an English agent to be trustees and to authorise payment to the English agent of commission on rents of various farms receivable as receiver and manager. North J authorised the appointment and remuneration on the production of an affidavit as to the propriety of the remuneration.

There are a number of more modern authorities, to which I should now refer. I put aside for the moment *Re Salmen* (1912) 107 LT 108, to which I shall refer later.

In *Re Masters* [1953] 1 All ER 19 at 20, [1953] 1 WLR 81 at 83 Danckwerts J, after holding that the court had jurisdiction under s 42 of the Trustee Act 1925 to authorise proper remuneration to be paid to a corporate body appointed by the court to be administrator and trustee of the estate of the intestate, went on to comment on the inherent jurisdiction. He said:

'Apart from the statutory jurisdiction conferred by s. 42 [of the Trustee Act 1925], it is also plain that there is inherent jurisdiction in the court to authorise remuneration of the trustee, whether appointed by the court or not. Authority for that is to be found in *Re Freeman's Settlement Trusts* and *Marshall* v. *Holloway*. [He then referred to *Re Macadam* [1945] 2 All ER 664, [1946] Ch 73 and an unreported case in which he had appeared at the Bar, and concluded:] There is, in my view, no doubt whatever about the inherent jurisdiction of this court to authorise remuneration.'

I should observe that in *Re Masters* the trustee corporation which was seeking remuneration had been appointed administrators in 1949. The summons seeking remuneration was not issued until April 1951.

In *Re Worthington (deceased)* [1954] 1 All ER 677 at 678, [1954] 1 WLR 526 at 528, an application by an administrator for remuneration, Upjohn J said that the law was clear:

'He cannot charge for work done as administrator, but must give his services gratuitously. On the other hand, it cannot be doubted that the court has a jurisdiction to direct that remuneration shall, in a proper case, be allowed to the administrator. That, I think is clear from the recent decision in *Re Masters* and from the speech of Lord Cohen in *Dale* v. *Inland Revenue Comrs*. ([1953] 2 All ER 671 at 678, [1954] AC 11 at 33–34) . . . Equally, I think it is clear that, although there is a jurisdiction in the court to allow remuneration to trustees, that jurisdiction should be exercised only sparingly and in exceptional cases.'

Upjohn J referred to Lord Langdale MR's judgment in *Bainbrigge v Blair* as giving an example of the sort of circumstances in which the jurisdiction could be exercised, namely the case of a trustee who said that he would be prepared to carry out certain matters for the trust but that he was not prepared to spend the time unless he received some remuneration (see [1954] 1 All ER 677 at 679, [1954] 1 WLR 526 at 528).

Re Barbour's Settlement [1974] 1 All ER 1188, [1974] 1 WLR 1198 was an application to the court to approve terms of compromise of a dispute relating to beneficial interests under the trust. There were included in the terms of compromise provisions which increased the existing scale of remuneration of the corporate trustee of the trust; the existing scale was the scale authorised in the settlement itself in 1942. Megarry J, having expressed doubts, inter alia, on the propriety of including such a provision in terms of compromise of a dispute quite unrelated to the question of remuneration, the proposal to increase the remuneration was abandoned. Megarry J, however, said ([1974] 1 All ER 1188 at 1192, [1974] 1 WLR 1198 at 1203):

'Let me add that I am not saying that such an application, if properly supported by compelling evidence, is doomed to failure. The words "exceptional cases" used by Upjohn J in *Re Worthington (deceased)* may require further explanation: I very much doubt whether that phrase was intended by the judge to exclude disastrous consequences following from inflation merely because inflation is not an exception but, unhappily, the rule. Yet there must at least be proper evidence before the court of consequences of such weight and gravity as to justify the exercise of the jurisdiction.'

In *Re Codd (deceased)* [1975] 2 All ER 1051n, [1975] 1 WLR 1139 the Westminster Bank was the sole trustee of the will. The bank's authorised remuneration under the will was £10 a year. It applied for authority to charge remuneration in accordance with its usual scale for trust business. The beneficiaries did not resist the application. Graham J said that it was in the interest of the trust as a whole that the remuneration should be increased, and he allowed the application.

In the present case the conclusions which Walton J reached were broadly as follows. (1) Subject to (2) below the only ground on which the court has ever acted in relation to remuneration has been the necessity of obtaining the services of some particular individual trustee whose services were of special value to the trust or of obtaining the services of some particular kind of trustee. (2) It was indicated by Eve J in *Re Salmen* (1912) 107 LT 108 that remuneration might be awarded if the circumstances were such as to raise an implied promise to pay it on behalf of the beneficiaries. (3) There has never been a case in which the court has ever altered the general level of remuneration fixed by the trust instrument, unless it be *Re Codd (deceased)* where there was no argument. (4) The only conceivable ground on which he would be justified in authorising any additional remuneration would be (2) above. And, while that justified the authorising of payments for work of a wholly exceptional nature, it gave no basis for any inherent jurisdiction to increase the level of SETCO's fees for the future.

In my opinion the judge took too narrow a view of the inherent jurisdiction. There is, in my judgment, no doubt that the court has an inherent jurisdiction to authorise payment of remuneration to trustees. Danckwerts J in *Re Masters* [1953] 1 All ER 19, [1953] 1 WLR 81 and Upjohn J in *Re Worthington (deceased)* [1954] 1 All ER 677, [1954] 1 WLR 526 accepted that. The older authorities lead me to the same conclusion. In *Marshall v Holloway* Lord Eldon LC himself authorised remuneration for both past and future services. The existence of the jurisdiction is also supported by *Morison v Morison* (1838) 4 My & Cr 215, 41 ER 85, *Bainbrigge v Blair* (1845) 8 Beav 588, 50 ER 231, *Forster v Ridley* (1864) 4 De GJ & Sm 452, 46 ER 993 and *Re Freeman's Settlement Trusts* (1887) 37 Ch D 148.

The question is the extent of that jurisdiction. There can, in my view, be no doubt that there is an inherent jurisdiction on the appointment of a trustee to direct that he be remunerated; that was accepted by Leach V-C in *Brocksopp v Barnes* (1820) 5 Madd 90, 56 ER 829 and must be inherent in what was said in *Re Masters* and *Re Worthington (deceased)*. Indeed, it is not really in dispute at all. In the present case, however, what is sought is the increase of remuneration authorised by the trust instrument. The judge said that there had never been a case in which that was done, unless it was *Re Codd (deceased)* [1975] 2 All ER 1051n, [1975] 1 WLR 1139, where the matter was not argued. I feel much doubt whether that proposition is in fact correct. Most cases relating to trustees' remuneration are dealt with in chambers and are not reported. My own impression, and, I understand, that of Brightman LJ also, is that since the early 1950s orders have been made in chambers, under the inherent jurisdiction, authorising increases in remuneration given by the trust instrument. But I do not rely on that. I will approach the matter as one of principle and on the reported cases. If it be the law, as I think it clearly is, that the court has inherent jurisdiction on the appointment of a trustee to authorise payment of remuneration to him, is there any reason why the court should not have jurisdiction to increase the remuneration already allowed by the trust instrument?

Two reasons are suggested. First, it is said that a trustee's right to remuneration under an express provision of the settlement is based on a contract between the settlor and the trustee which the trustee is not entitled to avoid; the benefit of that contract is to be regarded as settled by the trust instrument for the benefit of the beneficiaries. I find that analysis artificial. It may have some appearance of reality in relation to a trustee who, at the request of the settlor, agrees to act before the settlement is executed and approves the terms of the settlement. But very frequently executors and trustees of wills know nothing of the terms of the will until the testator is dead; sometimes in the case of corporate trustees such as banks, they have not even been asked by the testator whether they will act. It is difficult to see with whom, in such cases, the trustees are to be taken as contracting. The appointment of a trustee by the court also gives rise to problems as to the identity of the contracting party.

The position, it seems to me, is this. Trust property is held by the trustees on the trusts and subject to the powers conferred by the trust instrument and by law. One of those powers is the power to the trustee to charge remuneration. That gives the trustee certain rights which equity will enforce in administering the trust. How far those rights can properly be regarded as beneficial interests I will consider later. But it seems to me to be quite unreal to regard them as contractual. So far as they derive from any order of the court they simply arise from the court's jurisdiction and so far as they derive from the trust instrument itself they derive from the settlor's power to direct how this property should be dealt with.

I appreciate that in *Re Salmen* (1912) 107 LT 108 Eve J, whose decision was upheld by the Court of Appeal, said in the course of his judgment that the jurisdiction must be founded on some such proposition as that the circumstances of the case raise an implied contract on the part of the persons against whom the claim for remuneration is made, to pay such remuneration. I observe that Upjohn J in *Re Worthington (deceased)* [1954] 1 All ER 677 at 680, [1954] 1 WLR 526 at 529 disagreed with that altogether. He said that the true rule was that the court had an inherent jurisdiction to authorise remuneration, even against creditors. He pointed out that the Court of Appeal did not consider the question of inherent jurisdiction; in the Court of Appeal the case was treated as governed by *Re White* [1898] 1 Ch 297. I agree with that; *Re White* says nothing about contract. Further, I think it necessary to bear in mind that *Re Salmen* was a case of an insolvent estate (as was *Re White*). In such a case, the court might, whatever the jurisdiction, be unwilling to impose on the creditors a liability to remunerate in the absence of some circumstances that made it equitable that the creditors should bear the remuneration. A provision in a will authorising trustees to charge does not bind the creditors. As Chitty LJ said in *Re White* [1898] 2 Ch 217 at 218–219: 'The declaration made by the testator is bounty on his part. No one can claim the bounty until the creditors are satisfied.' I do not regard *Re Salmen* as establishing a contractual basis for the remuneration of trustees, and I do not think such a basis is sound in principle.

I come to the second objection. It is said that the right to remuneration is a beneficial interest in the trust property and can only be varied by an order under the Variation of Trusts Act 1958 or (in accordance with the principles established in *Chapman v Chapman* [1954] 1 All ER 798, [1954] AC 429) under a compromise of a dispute as to beneficial interests or by way of salvage.

I do not doubt that, to some extent, the right of a trustee to remuneration is to be regarded as a beneficial interest. Thus, in *Re Pooley* (1888) 40 Ch D 1, [1886–90] All ER Rep 157, it was held that a trustee who was an attesting witness of a will was not entitled to claim remuneration under the express provisions of the will because s 15 of the Wills Act 1837 precluded an attesting witness from claiming benefits under the will; the benefit of the remuneration clause was, in effect, a legacy. Again, in *Re Thorley* [1891] 2 Ch 613, trustees were entitled to £250 per annum each under the provisions of the will while they carried on the testator's business. It was held that those benefits were legacies and subject to legacy duty.

And, as I have mentioned, in *Re White* the benefits given by a trustee remuneration clause were treated as bounty.

In *Re Thorley* and *Re White* there were substantial reasons of policy why the remuneration should be treated as a beneficial interest. It would not be acceptable that a testator should be able to confer on trustees such benefits as he might choose, in the guise of remuneration, to the disadvantage of creditors and in avoidance of death duties. I observe that when the law as to estate duty on marriage settlements was altered by s 53 of the Finance Act 1963 in consequence of the decision in *Inland Revenue Comrs v Lord Rennell* [1963] 1 All ER 803, [1964] AC 173 the exemption in relation to trustees' remuneration was restricted to 'a reasonable amount'.

But, accepting that a trustee's right to remuneration may for certain purposes be treated as a beneficial interest in the trust property, I do not think that it comes within the principle laid down in *Chapman v Chapman* as to the general inability of the court under its inherent jurisdiction to vary beneficial interests. The question of trustees' remuneration was not discussed in *Chapman v Chapman*, and, in my judgment, the law as to such remuneration, as it admittedly stands at present, is not consistent with the proposition that it is governed by the *Chapman* principles. Thus there is no doubt that the court has, on the appointment of a trustee, jurisdiction to authorise the payment of remuneration to him. But that is a variation of the existing beneficial interests because it entrenches on the existing interests of the beneficiaries. There is no difference, in principle, in that respect between a power in the court to authorise remuneration on appointment and a power to increase existing remuneration. In both cases the extent of the rights of the beneficiaries in the trust property is reduced.

Chapman v Chapman, it seems to me, was concerned with the power of the court to authorise variations in beneficial interests as such. The present problem is different. It is concerned not with beneficial interests as such, but with the administration of the trust fund. When the court authorises payment of remuneration to a trustee under its inherent jurisdiction it is, I think, exercising its ancient jurisdiction to secure the competent administration of the trust property just as it has done when it appoints or removes a trustee under its inherent jurisdiction. The result, in my view, is that there is nothing in the principles stated in *Chapman v Chapman* which is inconsistent with the existence of an inherent jurisdiction in the court to increase the remuneration payable to trustees under the trust instrument. In my view, therefore, neither of the two objections which have been raised as to existence of such a jurisdiction is well founded.

There remains the question whether, on principle and authority, we can properly infer that the jurisdiction does exist. As to principle, it seems to me that, if the court has jurisdiction, as it has, on the appointment of a trustee to authorise remuneration though no such power exists in the trust instrument, there is no logical reason why the court should not have power to increase the remuneration given by the instrument. In many cases the latter may involve a smaller interference with the provisions of the trust instrument than the former. Further, the law has not stopped short at authorising remuneration to a trustee only if he seeks the authority at the time when he accepts the trusts. That, in my view, appears from the observations of Lord Langdale MR in *Bainbrigge v Blair* (1845) 8 Beav 588, 50 ER 231 and from *Re Masters* [1953] 1 All ER 19, [1953] 1 WLR 81, in which it is clear that Danckwerts J would have been prepared to make the order which he did (and which authorised payment of remuneration to an administrator who had taken a grant some years previously) under the inherent jurisdiction.

I appreciate that the ambit of the court's inherent jurisdiction in any sphere may, for historical reasons, be irrational and that logical extensions are not necessarily permissible. But I think that it is the basis of the jurisdiction that one has to consider. The basis, in my view, in relation to a trustee's remuneration is the good administration of trusts. The fact that in earlier times, with more stable currencies and with a plenitude of persons with the leisure and resources to take on unremunerated trusteeships, the particular problem of increasing remuneration may not have arisen does not, in my view, prevent us from concluding that a logical extension of admitted law which is wholly consistent with the apparent purpose of the jurisdiction is permissible. If the increase of remuneration be beneficial to the trust administration, I do not see any objection to that in principle.

As to authority, I do not find in the English authorities any decision which positively excludes any inherent jurisdiction to increase remuneration, unless it be *Robinson v Pett* (1734) 3 P Wms 249, 24 ER 1049. But that was a case of a renouncing executor who was expressly given a legacy for his trouble if he did renounce. Lord Talbot LC said that he was unable to give him any more. I do not think *Robinson v Pett* really touches the present case. On the other hand, Lord Eldon LC's order in *Marshall v Holloway* (1820) 2 Swan 432, 36 ER 681 seem to have increased the benefit given by the will, and in *Re Barbour's Settlement* [1974] 1 All ER 1188, [1974] 1 WLR 1198 Megarry J did not really doubt that, on an application in proper form and supported by appropriate evidence, the court would on have had jurisdiction to increase the remuneration of the corporate trustee.

I conclude that the court has an inherent jurisdiction to authorise the payment of remuneration of trustees and that that jurisdiction extends to increasing the remuneration authorised by the trust instrument. In exercising that jurisdiction the court has to balance two influences which are to some extent in conflict. The first is that the office of trustee is, as such, gratuitous; the court will accordingly be careful to protect the interests of the beneficiaries against claims by the trustees. The second is that it is of great importance to the beneficiaries that the trust should be well administered. If therefore the court concludes, having regard to the nature of the trust, to the experience and skill of a particular trustee and to the amounts which he seeks to charge when compared with what other trustees might require to be paid for their services and to all the other circumstances of the case, that it would be in the interests of the beneficiaries to increase the remuneration, then the court may properly do so.

Having regard to the view which I take as to the inherent jurisdiction, it is not necessary to consider the extent of the court's jurisdiction under s 57 of the Trustee Act 1925 or otherwise.

I would allow the appeal, and make the declaration sought by the amended summons so far as it relates to the inherent jurisdiction. The matter should, I think, be remitted to the Chancery Division to enable the trustees to make such application and on such further evidence as they think fit.

BRIGHTMAN LJ. I entirely agree with the judgment of Fox LJ and wish to add only a few words of my own.

In this appeal we are concerned with the power of the High Court to authorise a trust corporation, which has been in office for some twenty years, to charge fees for its future services in excess of those laid down in the trust instrument. In his admirable submissions in the unwelcome role of advocatus diaboli which this court imposed on him, counsel for the sixth and seventh defendants confined himself to that narrow issue. He did not dispute that the High Court can, in the exercise of its inherent jurisdiction, authorise a trustee to retain remuneration where none is provided by the terms of the trust. What the court has no jurisdiction to do, he submitted, was to authorise an increase in the general level of remuneration of a paid trustee by way of addition to the remuneration which is allowed by the trust, once the trust has been unconditionally accepted.

Where the court appoints a trust corporation to be a trustee, it has a statutory power to authorise it to charge remuneration: see the Trustee Act 1925, s 42. The inherent power of the court to authorise a prospective trustee to charge remuneration is exemplified by such cases as *Re Freeman's Settlement Trusts* (1887) 37 Ch D 148. The inherent power to authorise an unpaid trustee to charge remuneration, notwithstanding prior acceptance of the unpaid office, was regarded by Lord Langdale MR in *Bainbrigge v Blair* (1845) 8 Beav 588, 50 ER 231 as undoubted.

If the court has an inherent power to authorise a prospective trustee to take remuneration for future services, and has a similar power in relation to an unpaid trustee who has already accepted office and embarked on his fiduciary duties on a voluntary basis, I have some difficulty in appreciating the logic of the principle that the court has no power to increase or otherwise vary the future remuneration of a trustee who has already accepted office. It would mean that, if the remuneration specified in the trust instrument were lower than was acceptable to the incumbent trustee or any substitute who could be found, the court would have jurisdiction to authorise a substitute to charge an acceptable level of remuneration, but would have no jurisdiction to authorise the incumbent to charge precisely the same level of remuneration. Such a result appears to me bizarre, and to call in question the validity of the principle on which it is supposedly based.

Two foundations for the principle are suggested. One is that the right to remuneration is based on contract, and the court has no power to vary the terms of a contract. The contractual conception suffers from the difficulties explained in the judgment of Fox LJ. It also seems to me, in the context of the present debate, to give little weight to the fact that a trustee, whether paid or unpaid, is under no obligation, contractual or otherwise, to provide future services to the trust. He can at any time express his desire to be discharged from the trust and in that case a new trustee will in due course be appointed under s 36 or s 41 of the 1925 Act. The practical effect therefore of increasing the remuneration of the trustee (if the contractual conception is correct) will merely be to amend for the future, in favour of a trustee, the terms of a contract which the trustee has a unilateral right to determine. The interference of the court in such circumstances can hardly be said, in any real sense, to derogate from the contractual rights of the settlor or the beneficiaries if he or they are to be regarded as entitled to the benefit of the contract.

The other foundation suggested for the supposed principle is that the remuneration allowed to a trustee under the terms of the trust is a beneficial interest, and the court has no inherent jurisdiction to vary that beneficial interest save in special circumstances not here material (see *Chapman v Chapman* [1954] 1 All ER 798, [1954] AC 429). I agree that the remuneration given to a trustee by a will is an 'interest' within the meaning of s 15 of the Wills Act 1837, that it is a 'gift' on a condition for the purposes of the legislation which formerly charged legacy duty on testamentary gifts and that an executor or trustee remunerated by the will cannot retain such remuneration against creditors if the estate turns out to be insolvent. There are obvious arguments why a testator should not be able to circumvent the provisions of the Wills Act 1837, or avoid legacy duty, or defeat his creditors, by the award of remuneration to his executors or trustees. It does not follow that a remunerated trustee is to be considered as a cestui que trust for the purposes of the principles laid down in *Chapman v Chapman*. If he were it is difficult, as Fox LJ says, to see what right the court would have to authorise remuneration to be charged by a prospective trustee, since such authority will have the inevitable effect of adding a new beneficiary to the trust at the expense of the existing beneficiaries.

I would allow the appeal.

CUMMING-BRUCE LJ. I agree with the order proposed by Fox LJ and with the reasons expressed in the judgments of both Fox and Brightman LJJ.

Appeal allowed. Declaration granted. Summons to be remitted to the Chancery Division for further application by trustees.

Solicitors: *Witham, Weld & Co* (for the trustees); *Fisher, Dowson & Wasbrough* (for the sixth and seventh defendants).

Henrietta Steinberg   Barrister.

Barclays Bank Trust Co Ltd v Bluff

CHANCERY DIVISION
H E FRANCIS QC SITTING AS A DEPUTY JUDGE OF THE HIGH COURT
27th, 28th, 30th JANUARY 1981

Partnership – Dissolution – Death – Partnership at will – Death of partner – Profits – Estate entitled pending final settlement to receive share of profits or interest on deceased's share of assets – Executor electing to take interest – Value of assets of partnership business increasing after date of death – Whether executor's election to take interest depriving estate of right to receive share of increased value of assets – Whether 'profits' of partnership business after date of death including increase in value of assets – Partnership Act 1890, s 42(1).

The father carried on a farming business with his son on terms that they were to share the profits equally under a partnership at will. The father died in 1972 and accordingly the partnership was dissolved at the date of his death. The son continued to carry on the farming business and entered into negotiations with the father's executor for the purchase of the father's share of the partnership business, but no settlement was reached. The aggregate net value of the partnership assets at the date of the father's death was £41,500, but had since increased to in excess of £100,000. The executor issued a summons seeking, inter alia, a declaration that in the event of the executor electing *a*   under s 42(1)[a] of the Partnership Act 1890 for payment of interest the executor would not thereby deprive the estate of the right to receive that part of the proceeds of a sale of the partnership assets which was attributable to the increase in value of the assets between the father's death and the sale of the assets. Under s 42(1) if a member of a partnership died and the surviving partners carried on the partnership business with its capital or assets pending final settlement of accounts, then in the absence of any agreement to the contrary the estate had the option of receiving either that share of the

b   profits made since the dissolution which the court found to be attributable to the use of the deceased partner's share of the assets or interest at the rate of 5% p a on that share of the assets. The son contended (i) that the profits made by the partnership since it was dissolved by the father's death included the increase in the value of the partnership assets occurring since the dissolution, (ii) that the executor had by certain letters during the negotiations made an election under s 42(1) of the 1890 Act to take interest at 5% p a in

c   lieu of a share of the profits made since the dissolution, and (iii) that as a consequence of such election the father's estate was no longer entitled to claim a share of the profits made since the dissolution, including the increase in the value of the assets.

Held – (1) On the true construction of s 42(1) of the 1890 Act the term 'profits' referred to profits accruing in the ordinary course of carrying on the partnership business pending

d   realisation. Accordingly, for the purpose of s 42(1), the profits of the farming business carried on by the son using the partnership's assets following the dissolution caused by the father's death consisted of the earnings of the business derived from the disposal in the ordinary course of trade of livestock and produce, and did not include any increase in value of the partnership assets occurring after the father's death. Thus, even if the father's executor had made an election under s 42(1) to take 5% interest instead of a share

e   of the profits (which on the facts he had not), such an election would not have affected the estate's right to a share of the increase in value of the assets (see p 238 *h j*, p 239 *f* to *j* and p 240 *g*, post).

(2) Until realisation of the partnership business and assets the son was trustee of the business for the deceased's estate and himself. Accordingly, the increase in the value of the assets was held by him for the benefit of both the estate and himself (see p 239 *j*, post);

f   dictum of Kingsmill Moore J in *Meagher v Meagher* [1961] IR at 110 applied.

(3) Since the executor had not elected to take 5% interest on the deceased's share under s 42(1) of the 1890 Act rather than a share of the profits since dissolution of the partnership, it was still open to him to make such an election and, if he did so, that would not deprive the estate of the right to receive one-half of the net proceeds of sale of the assets of the partnership business after making a proper allowance to the son for the management of the partnership business since the death of the deceased (see p 239 *d* and

g   p 240 *e* to *h*, post); *Meagher v Meagher* [1961] IR 96 not followed.

Notes

For the dissolution of a partnership on death, see 28 Halsbury's Laws (3rd Edn) 563, para 1097, and for cases on the subject, see 36(2) Digest (Reissue) 783, 1590–1602.

For the Partnership Act 1890, s 42, see 24 Halsbury's Statutes (3rd Edn) 523.

h

Cases referred to in judgment

Bourne, Re [1906] 2 Ch 427, 75 LJ Ch 779, 95 LT 131, CA, 36(2) Digest (Reissue) 673, 652.

Meagher v Meagher [1961] IR 96, 36(2) Digest (Reissue) 784, *701.

Stevenson (Hugh) & Sons Ltd v Aktiengesellschaft für Cartonagen-Industrie [1918] AC 239, [1918–19] All ER Rep 600, 87 LJKB 416, 118 LT 126, HL, 1(2) Digest (Reissue) 920,

j   5972.

Cases also cited

Ammonia Soda Co Ltd v Chamberlain [1918] 1 Ch 266, [1916–17] All ER Rep 708, CA.

Robinson v Ashton (1875) LR 20 Eq 25.

---

a   Section 42(1) is set out at p 238 *c d*, post

Spanish Prospecting Co Ltd, Re [1911] 1 Ch 92, [1908–10] All ER Rep 573, CA.
Young v Bristol Aeroplane Co Ltd [1946] 1 All ER 98, [1946] AC 163, HL.   *a*

Summons

By a summons dated 23rd June 1977 and subsequently amended, the plaintiff, Barclays
Bank Trust Co Ltd, sought the following relief: (1) a declaration that the partnership
between Francis Arthur Bluff, deceased, and the defendant, Aubrey Bluff, in respect of
the farming business carried on by them was dissolved by reason of the death of the   *b*
deceased on 13th May 1972; (2) an order that the affairs of the partnership be wound up;
(3) an order that the following accounts and inquiries be made: (1) an account of the
partnership debts and liabilities at 13th May 1972, (ii) an account of all receipts,
payments, dealings and transactions of the defendant in respect of the partnership
business from 13th May 1972 and (iii) an inquiry into what had become of the property
and assets of the partnership business since 13th May 1972; (4) that it be declared   *c*
whether in the events which had happened the plaintiff (a) had or (b) had not elected in
respect of the period between the death of the deceased and the final settlement of
accounts between the defendant and the plaintiff to take interest at the rate of 5% p a on
the amount of the share of the deceased in the partnership assets; (5) that it be declared
(whether the answer to the foregoing paragraph was in sense (a) or (b)) whether the
amount due to the plaintiff in respect of the share of the deceased in the net partnership   *d*
assets was to be calculated by reference to the value of such assets as at (a) the date of death
of the deceased or (b) the date on which the accounts between the defendant and the
plaintiff were settled or (c) at some other, and if so what, date; (6) an order for sale of (i)
the freehold land known as Grange Farm, Bolton upon Dearne, South Yorkshire, (ii) the
freehold land known as Black Banks, Bolton upon Dearne and (iii) any other assets of the
partnership between the deceased and the defendant which remained unsold. The facts   *e*
are set out in the judgment.

Dirik Jackson for the plaintiff.
Kenneth Farrow for the defendant.

                                                        Cur adv vult   *f*

30th January. **H E FRANCIS QC** read the following judgment: The plaintiff, is the
executor of Francis Arthur Bluff (hereinafter called 'the deceased') who died on 13th May
1972 and whose will was proved by the plaintiff on 23rd August 1972. Until his death
the deceased carried on a farming business at Bolton upon Dearne in South Yorkshire
with his son, the defendant, on the terms that they should share the profits equally. It   *g*
is common ground that the partnership was a partnership at will and that it was dissolved
by the death of the deceased. By his will the deceased gave his half share in the
partnership business to his son Mervyn Bluff. The farming business was carried on at
Grange Farm and a small piece of land known as Black Banks which together comprised
about 61 acres at the deceased's death. These properties were freehold. The business was
also carried on under eight separate agricultural tenancies on various parcels of land   *h*
amounting in all to some 150 acres. It is common ground that the market value of the
freehold property at the deceased's death was of the order of £30,000 and that of the
tenanted property about £784. It is also agreed, as I gather, that at the deceased's death
the aggregate value of the other assets of the partnership was of the order of £11,430.
The aggregate net value, after deducting sums due to creditors and for income tax, of the
partnership assets of the firm as now agreed between the parties was of the order of   *j*
£41,500. The farm accounts which have been put in evidence show that the earnings of
the business were derived from sales of cattle, pigs, milk and other produce such as
potatoes and barley. The net profits as shown in the accounts increased over the years
from £1,669 for the period 6th April 1971 until 13th May 1972 to some £4,500 for the
year ended 5th April 1977, but for some reason not apparent it fell in the next year to

£1,259. I have no information as to the amount of the net profits in the years ended 5th April 1979 and 5th April 1980. Since the death of the deceased the defendant has continued to carry on the farming business on the land as in his father's lifetime, except that in 1974 some 13 acres of the freehold property were sold to the National Coal Board for the sum of £13,927, which was divided equally between the defendant and the deceased's estate, and that in 1973 one of the agricultural tenancies comprising just over 4 acres came to an end. There has been no final settlement of accounts between the parties, and, apart from the half share of proceeds of sale of the land sold to the National Coal Board, the only payment made by the defendant to the estate has been that of a sum of £1,000 paid to the plaintiff in 1973 on account of the deceased's share.

It is obvious that there has been a great deal of delay in winding up the affairs of the partnership, but it is fair to say that the initial delay was attributable, at any rate in part, to the fact that the parties expected to be able to obtain planning permission for the residential development of part of Grange Farm, which no doubt would have greatly increased the value of that land. Eventually however it transpired that there was no prospect of obtaining such planning permission. Thereafter the defendant was pressed to make further payments to the estate, and the trading accounts of the farm business were called for by the plaintiff's solicitors. Thus, on 10th April 1974 the plaintiff's solicitors, Attey, Bower & Jones of Doncaster, wrote to the defendant's solicitors, Dibb & Clegg of Barnsley, as follows:

'. . . our Client is concerned that the Estate should receive from [the defendant] on his Father's share of the partnership assets which he continues to use in the business. We are not aware of the arrangement your Client has made for payment of the interest but we assume that the Farming Accounts for the period following death are now available.'

I should mention that at this time Attey, Bower & Jones acted not only for the plaintiff but also for Mr Mervyn Bluff, and the letter of 10th April may have been written by them as much on behalf of Mervyn Bluff as on behalf of the plaintiff.

Curiously enough the defendant's solicitors in their reply of 24th April stated: 'Whilst we appreciate the point you are making we do not really see the relevance of our Client's trading accounts.'

On 3rd May the plaintiff's solicitors wrote again to the defendant's solicitors and said:

'With regard to the Trading Accounts we consider that the Executors of a deceased Partner are entitled to know how the partnership assets have been dealt with in a case where those assets continue to be used in the business. We note that the Partnership Act provides for interest to be paid at a rate of 5% and since Mr. Bluff died two years ago we should be glad to know when your Client proposes to make the first payment.'

On 20th May the defendant's solicitors replied as follows:

'We have seen our Client with regard to the Bank's claim for interest and would think the fairest way of dealing with this would be for our Client to pay interest on the value of the implements etc. as valued for Probate and to pay one half of the agricultural rental (say £7 per acre) in respect of the 61 acres which he is farming. This is based upon the rentals paid for adjoining land and such an arrangement would also have the advantage of putting matters on a regular footing whilst the question of a sale of the farming land (which seems to be becoming rather hypothetical) is resolved.'

Then on 10th June the plaintiff's solicitors wrote again to the defendant's solicitors in these terms:

'We refer to your letter of 20th May on which we are seeking the Bank's instructions. They say that they are prepared to accept interest rather than the alternative of a share of the profits, and they are at present considering your suggested rent of £7 per acre. We do not yet appear to have received your comments on the second paragraph of our letter of 3rd May. The Bank shares our view that as Executors they are entitled to see the Trading Accounts which have been prepared since death on the ground that assets belonging to the Estate continue to be employed by your Client, and the Bank naturally feels that they have a right to know how they are being utilised.'

This letter was acknowledged by the defendant's solicitors on 11th June and they said that they would take their client's instructions.

On 10th July a meeting was held at the Barnsley offices of the defendant's solicitors which was attended by Mr Hattrell of the firm of Attey, Bower & Jones, Mr Kay and Mr Bowers of the plaintiff, Mr Birch of the firm of S T Johnson & Co who had valued the deceased's estate for probate purposes and Mr Moore of the firm of Dibb & Clegg. A note of the meeting was made by Mr Moore which so far as relevant read as follows:

'Discussion took place upon the future administration of the estate and it was agreed . . . 2. It was thought that it would be possible to conclude matters by [the defendant] paying his brother in one of 3 ways namely:—(a) a straight share of the profits. (b) a cash payment for the stock in trade coupled with a rental payment for the land. (c) a cash payment for the stock in trade coupled with an interest payment calculated upon an agreed value for the land.'

On 4th September there was another meeting between the interested parties or their advisers and this time Mr Mervyn Bluff, who as I have said had previously been represented by the plaintiff's solicitors, was represented by separate solicitors, that is by Sir John Renwick of the firm of Renwick & Co, Eckington, nr Sheffield. The meeting was attended by Sir John, Mr Moore, Mr Hattrell and two representatives of the plaintiff and was held at Sir John's offices. Much of the discussion related to proceedings brought by the deceased's daughter under the Inheritance (Family Provision) Act 1938 which were then pending, but I am not concerned with those proceedings. A note of the meeting made by Mr Moore, which so far as relevant to this action is accepted as correct, stated:

'After the present position was outlined it was put forward by Mr. Moore that it would be to the benefit of all parties if the estate was wound up on an agreed basis . . . [The defendant] was prepared to pay five % on the live and dead stock valuation for Probate and also to pay a rental of £8. per acre (i.e. £4. would be his half share) for the remaining land amounting to something like 61 acres . . . It was agreed that Sir John would take his Client's instructions on [the defendant's] offer and ascertain his wishes for the future . . .'

Then a note was added by Mr Moore stating:

'Since the meeting Mr. Moore has spoken to [the defendant] who would be prepared to buy out the live and dead stock and to pay the said figure of £4. for the resultant acreage (this is likely to be in the region of 61 acres but this is only an approximation). It is understood that the planning application has been refused and [the defendant] feels that the Valuers ought not to proceed further and should be asked to render their account.'

On 4th August 1975 there was a further meeting at Sir John's offices attended by Sir John, Mr Hattrell, Mr Moore and by a representative of the plaintiff. There was a note of this meeting, again made by Mr Moore, which includes the following paragraphs:

'5. Sir John said that his client would prefer to be paid out in full on a negotiated figure but if this cannot be achieved then his client would be prepared to accept payment for the implements etc. and to take a rental based on a valuation of £8.00 per acre ie [the defendant] would pay at the rate of £4.00 per acre . . .
6. It was further agreed that:—(a) the partnership ceased on death and that there

was no possibility of a continuing partnership . . . (b) that [the defendant's]
responsibility was to discharge his father's interest in the business as at the date of
death and to pay interest upon the capital he had utilised since the date of death
from date of death to date of payment or, alternatively, to pay a share of
profits . . . J.R.M. pointed out that he had no instructions to do other than offer to
buy out the deceased's share at agricultural value at date of death, but he agreed to
take instructions upon what had been put forward.'

On 18th August Renwick & Co made a proposal to the defendant's solicitors to the
effect that the defendant should purchase the deceased's share for the sum of £19,429
calculated on the basis of the value of the whole farm as agreed with the district valuer,
that is £44,900, together with interest at 6% pa from 13th May 1972 up to payment. A
dispute then arose as to the market value of the farm at the deceased's death. No
agreement for settlement was reached. By May 1976, not unnaturally, Mr Mervyn Bluff
was getting very impatient at the delay, and on 24th May 1976 the plaintiff wrote to the
defendant's solicitors as follows:

'In the absence of agreement the, Trust Company as Executor would seem to have
little option other than to consider an application for the winding up of the former
partnership under the terms of the Partnership Act, 1890, and for the sight of
Accounts from the date of Mr Bluff's death and a clear indication of the present
position of the business. Despite previous requests for sight of Accounts we are no
better informed concerning the business than at the date of Mr Bluff's death, and,
such being the case, we cannot see how it can be contended that we have elected for
interest on the share of the partnership capital. Only when we have the necessary
information from your client will we be in any position to determine how to
exercise the option available to us under the 1890 Act.'

On 2nd June 1976 the defendant's solicitors replied to the plaintiff by a letter which
stated:

'Whilst we note your comment as to proceedings under the Partnership Act as a
last resort we would have thought that such proceedings would not be in the best
interests of the parties. Surely the situation is basically a simple one; our Client has
to pay his father's Executor the value of his father's share in the partnership assets as
at the date of father's death and this our Client is prepared to do. If agreement can
be reached upon a figure then the question of interest and/or share of profits can
follow on. We do however reserve our views upon the Bank's course of conduct
which may have resulted in an election.'

That paragraph contains a misconception as to the legal position in this case. The
defendant had no right to purchase at a valuation. The representatives of the deceased
partner had a right in a case such as the present to insist on the assets of the partnership
being sold on the open market. The significance of the last sentence in the same
paragraph will emerge presently when I deal with the claims made in this action on
behalf of the defendant. Further attempts were made to reach an amicable settlement of
the matter but unfortunately these attempts were of no avail, and on 23rd June 1977 the
present proceedings were commenced by originating summons.

On 16th November 1977, it being agreed between the parties that the partnership had
been dissolved from 13th May 1972, the master made an order for the usual partnership
accounts and inquiry in the terms of para 3 of the originating summons. In April 1980
the originating summons was amended by the addition of the following paragraphs:

'4. That it may be declared whether in the events which have happened the
Plaintiff (a) has or (b) has not elected in respect of the period between the death of
the said Francis Arthur Bluff and the final settlement of accounts between the
Defendant and the Plaintiff to take interest at the rate of 5 per cent. per annum on
the amount of the share of the said Francis Arthur Bluff of the partnership assets.

'5. That it may be declared (whether the answer to the foregoing paragraph is in sense (a) or (b)) whether the amount due to the Plaintiff in respect of the share of the *a* said Francis Arthur Bluff of the net partnership assets is to be calculated by reference to the value of such assets as at (a) the date of death of the said Francis Arthur Bluff or (b) the date on which the accounts between the defendant and the plaintiff are settled, or (c) at some other, and if so what, date.

'6. An Order for sale of (1) the freehold land known as Grange Farm, Bolton-on-Dearne, South Yorkshire, (2) the freehold land known as Black Banks, Bolton-on- *b* Dearne, aforesaid and (3) any other assets of the partnership between the said Francis Arthur Bluff and the Defendant which remain unsold.'

The contentions between the parties as developed before me raise a very important question as to the operation of s 42(1) of the Partnership Act 1890 which reads as follows:

'Where any member of a firm has died or otherwise ceased to be a partner, and *c* the surviving or continuing partners carry on the business of the firm with its capital or assets without any final settlement of accounts as between the firm and the outgoing partner or his estate, then, in the absence of any agreement to the contrary, the outgoing partner or his estate is entitled at the option of himself or his representatives to such share of the profits made since the dissolution as the Court may find to be attributable to the use of his share of the partnership assets, or to *d* interest at the rate of five per cent. per annum on the amount of his share of the partnership assets.'

Now it has been argued by counsel for the defendant, first, that the plaintiff in the year 1974 by certain letters to which I shall refer in a moment has exercised the option given by s 42(1) of the 1890 Act by electing to take interest at 5% pa on the amount of the deceased's share of the partnership assets, that is to say on the value of that share as at the *e* deceased's death, which I gather the parties have agreed as being of the order of £20,750, being one-half of the figure of £41,500 to which I have referred above, second, that as a consequence of such election the plaintiff can no longer claim any part of the profits of the partnership business which have arisen since the death, and, third, that such profits include the difference between the value of the partnership assets at death and their value at the date of sale. If these contentions are correct their effect with respect to the *f* distribution of the net proceeds of sale of Grange Farm would be enormous. I am told that the market value of the farm today is in excess of £100,000. The value of Grange Farm at the deceased's death including the land sold to the National Coal Board is apparently agreed as having been of the order of £30,000. It would follow on the basis of these contentions that, making allowance for the sale to the National Coal Board, the deceased's estate would receive something less than £15,000 out of the proceeds of sale *g* of Grange Farm. All the remainder would go to the defendant. On the face of it, this result would appear to be both extraordinary and unjust, but counsel in his skilful argument has called in aid an Irish authority, *Meagher v Meagher* [1961] IR 96 which although not binding on me is plainly a case to which I must pay proper regard.

I will deal first with the contention that the plaintiff in 1974 exercised the s 42 option by electing to take interest at 5% pa on the amount of the deceased's share. The letters *h* relied on by counsel are the two letters dated respectively 3rd May 1974 and 10th June 1974 which I have already read. Both these letters were written by the plaintiff's solicitors, Attey, Bower & Jones. In my judgment these letters did not constitute an election and were not intended to do so. I say this for the following reasons. First, the terms of the letters are ambiguous. The last paragraph of the letter of 3rd May makes a reference to the provision in the 1890 Act about interest and an inquiry when the *j* defendant proposed to make the first payment. The letter of 10th June merely indicates that the plaintiff was prepared to accept interest rather than the alternative share of profits, but it is plain that the interest contemplated was something different from the 5% interest referred to in the 1890 Act and remained to be negotiated. Second, the option had to be exercised by the plaintiff as executor. There is no evidence that the

plaintiff gave any specific authority to its solicitors to exercise the option. The affidavit
a of Mr Thomas Allen Kay sworn on 25th July 1980 (Mr Kay I should say was a trust officer
who was concerned with the administration of the deceased's estate at this time) shows
that the executor never reached a decision how the option should be exercised. The
executor's concern at this time was to bring about an amicable arrangement between the
two sides without regard to the strict legal position under the 1890 Act. Third, the
option which the executor had under s 42 was a fiduciary right and could not properly
b be exercised without regard to the advantage or disadvantage of electing in one way or
the other. For this purpose the executor would need to have information whether any
and what profits had been made in the conduct of the partnership business since the
death; in other words the plaintiff would need to see the farm accounts, but in fact they
were being withheld from the estate. Fourth, it is plain from the subsequent
communications between the parties that they regarded the mode of winding up the
c partnership affairs as being completely at large and in particular they considered that it
was still open to the plaintiff to claim either interest or a share of profits in respect of the
period between the death and the sale of the partnership business (see the extracts which
I have already read from the notes of the meetings of 10th July 1974, 4th September
1974 and 4th August 1975). The first hint of a claim by the defendant (at any rate in the
correspondence) that the plaintiff had made an election to take interest is to be found in
d the defendant's solicitor's letter of 2nd June 1976, that is, after the negotiations for an
amicable settlement had virtually broken down.

It follows therefore that it is still open to the plaintiff, if it so wishes, to elect for a share
of profits under s 42 instead of for interest at 5% pa on the amount of the deceased's
share. However, it appears that interest at 5% pa would greatly exceed such share of the
profits as might be found attributable to the use of the deceased's share of the partnership
e assets. The plaintiff therefore wants me to decide whether in the event of the plaintiff's
electing for payment of interest under s 42 the plaintiff would thereby deprive itself of
any right to receive any part of the proceeds of a sale of Grange Farm which were
attributable to the increase in value of the farm between the deceased's death and the sale
of the farm.

I propose in the first instance to consider this question apart from authority. In my
f judgment the word 'profits' in s 42(1) of the 1890 Act means profits which have accrued
in the ordinary course of carrying on the partnership business pending realisation. The
profits in this case arise from the carrying on of a farming business. This involves the use
of farm land and buildings for rearing livestock and growing agricultural produce. The
earnings of the business derive from the disposal in the ordinary course of trade of the
livestock and produce. The profits consist of the excess of these earnings over the
g expenditure incurred in carrying on the businees. These profits are brought about by the
use of the farm land and buildings. These, as it seems to me, are the profits referred to
in s 42(1). An increase in the market value of Grange Farm between the deceased's death
and the sale of the farm, whether resulting from a general increase in the market price
of agricultural property or from the possibility of obtaining planning permission for the
development of part of the land does not in my view fall within the ambit of the word
h 'profits' as used in s 42(1). Such increase in value cannot be regarded as having been
brought about by the efforts of the defendant and it is difficult to see any rhyme or reason
why he should have the whole benefit of it even if the plaintiff has chosen to take interest
of 5% pa in lieu of a share of profits by way of income for the period between dissolution
and sale of the partnership business. After all the defendant is not the sole beneficial
owner of the farm. He is a trustee of it for the deceased's estate and himself. In that
j situation a fortuitous accretion to the value of the farm ought surely to enure to the
benefit of all the beneficiaries interested in the property.

In this connection I refer to a passage in the judgment of Kingsmill Moore J in *Meagher
v Meagher* [1961] IR 96 at 110, with which I respectfully agree. He said this:

> 'The claim made in this case is that the representatives of the deceased have no
> right to take the benefit of a general rise in prices occurring between the dissolution

and sale, but that the whole advantage of such a rise should go to the surviving partner. This appears to me to be contrary to the principles of equity and the *a* provisions of the Partnership Act. Surviving partners stand in a fiduciary relationship to the representatives of a deceased partner (*Hugh Stevenson & Sons Ltd v Aktiengesellschaft für Cartonagen-Industrie* [1918] AC 239 at 248, 250–251, 252, [1918–19] All ER Rep 600 at 604, 605, 606 per Lord Dunedin and Lord Atkinson). It is the right and duty of surviving partners to realise the assets (*Re Bourne* [1906] 2 Ch 427 at 430, 431 per Vaughan Williams and Romer LJJ). A person in a fiduciary *b* position cannot make a profit out of this trusteeship by appropriating to himself the rising value of assets which he holds as a trustee.'

In *Meagher v Meagher* however it was held that if the personal representative of a deceased partner chose under s 42 of the 1890 Act to accept interest at the rate of 5% pa on the deceased partner's share from the date of death to the date of dissolution in lieu of a share of profits for the same period, such share must in the circumstances be calculated *c* as at the death of the deceased. The court in that case made an order for the sale of the partnership property including the goodwill. Kingsmill Moore J said this ([1961] IR 96 at 112):

'If, however, the plaintiff elects to take five per cent per annum on the deceased's share from dissolution there must be an inquiry as to the value of his share on *d* dissolution. In the conduct of this inquiry, regard must be had to the prices fetched on sale, but those must be reduced by any amounts ascertained as a result of [the] inquiry . . . and also by such amount as is attributable to the enhancement of value due to the retention of the assets unsold from the date of dissolution to the date of sale of the relevant assets.'

It would follow therefore that if the plaintiff in that case elected to take 5% interest he *e* would not be entitled to any part of the proceeds of sale of the partnership property so far as such proceeds were attributable to the enhancement in value of the partnership assets between the date of dissolution and the date of sale. With the greatest respect to the Irish Supreme Court I am quite unable to take the view that s 42(1) of the 1890 Act has the effect of producing such an inequitable result. In *Meagher v Meagher* the main business *f* of the partnership consisted of acquiring premises, increasing their value by suitable repairs, alterations and improvements and then renting them to business or other tenants or reselling them at a profit. It is plain that while the partnership business was a going concern profits arising from the sale of improved premises were profits within s 42, but on the sale of the entire partnership business lock, stock and barrel as a going concern it does not seem to me that any part of the proceeds of sale can properly be regarded as profits within the meaning of s 42. *g*

I will therefore declare: (1) that the plaintiff has not heretofore exercised the option conferred on it by s 42(1) of the 1890 Act and (2) that if the plaintiff elects to take interest at 5% pa on the amount of the deceased's share such election will not deprive it of the right to receive in respect of the deceased's share one-half of the net proceeds of sale of Grange Farm and Black Banks and the live and dead stock belonging to the partnership business after paying or discharging the debts and liabilities of the firm and after making *h* a proper allowance to the defendant for the management of the partnership business since the death of the deceased.

Declaration and order accordingly.

Solicitors: *Sharpe, Pritchard & Co*, agents for *Attey, Bower & Jones*, Doncaster (for the plaintiff); *Oxley & Coward*, Rotherham (for the defendant).

Hazel Hartman   Barrister.

a # Exxon Corpn and others v Exxon Insurance Consultants International Ltd

COURT OF APPEAL, CIVIL DIVISION
STEPHENSON, OLIVER LJJ AND SIR DAVID CAIRNS
11th, 12th JUNE 1981

b *Copyright – Literary work – Original literary work – Single invented word – Time and labour spent on inventing word – Word forming part of plaintiff company's name – Defendant company incorporating word in its name – Whether infringement of copyright – Whether word an 'original literary work' – Copyright Act 1956, s 2(1).*

c The first plaintiff, a multinational oil company, decided to devise a new corporate name and trade mark for itself and its associated companies and after considerable research and consultation selected the word 'Exxon' for use as part of the corporate name of itself and its associated companies, including the second, third and fourth plaintiffs. The word 'Exxon' was registered as a trade mark in the United Kingdom and elsewhere. The defendant company, which had no connection with the plaintiffs, subsequently used the d word 'Exxon' as part of its corporate name without the plaintiffs' licence or consent. The plaintiffs brought an action against the defendant seeking, inter alia, (i) an injunction to restrain infringement of their copyright in the name 'Exxon' and (ii) an injunction to restrain the defendant from passing off its goods or services as the plaintiffs' goods or services by using the word 'Exxon'. The judge ([1981] 2 All ER 495) granted the injunction restraining the defendant from passing off but held that the plaintiffs were e not entitled to copyright in the word 'Exxon' and therefore were not entitled to an injunction restraining infringement of copyright. The plaintiffs appealed, contending that 'Exxon' was an 'original literary work' in which, by virtue of s 2(1)[a] of the Copyright Act 1956, they held the copyright. The plaintiffs submitted that 'Exxon' was first used by the plaintiffs and was therefore 'original', that it was expressed in letters or writing and was therefore 'literary', and that research and effort had been involved in its creation, f making it a 'work'. Accordingly, they submitted, 'Exxon' was an 'original literary work'.

Held – On a commonsense construction of s 2(1) of the 1956 Act, the term 'original literary work' was a composite expression denoting a written literary work of one or more words intended to offer information, instruction or pleasure in the form of literary enjoyment. To bring an expression within the term 'original literary work' it was not g sufficient that it could separately be described as 'original', 'literary' and 'work', and although the term 'Exxon' could thus be separately described, it was not an original literary work because it conveyed no information, provided no instruction and gave no pleasure. Accordingly, the term 'Exxon' was not an original literary work in which copyright could subsist and the judge had been right to refuse an injunction restraining infringement of copyright. The appeal would accordingly be dismissed (see p 248 g to h j and p 249 b to e and g to p 250 a, post).

Dictum of Davey LJ in *Hollinrake v Truswell* [1894] 3 Ch at 427–428 applied.
Decision of Graham J [1981] 2 All ER 495 affirmed.

Notes
For copyright in an original literary work, see 9 Halsbury's Laws (4th Edn) para 934, and j for cases on the subject, see 13 Digest (Reissue) 54–56, 572–581.
For the Copyright Act 1956, s 2, see 7 Halsbury's Statutes (3rd Edn) 132.

Cases referred to in judgments
Anderson (D P) & Co Ltd v Lieber Code Co [1917] 2 KB 469, 86 LJKB 1220, 117 LT 361, 13 Digest (Reissue) 55, 579.

---

a   Section 2(1), so far as material, is set out at p 245 a, post

British Northrop Ltd v Texteam Blackburn Ltd [1974] RPC 57, 13 Digest (Reissue) 81, 717.
Burberry's v J C Cording & Co Ltd (1909) 100 LT 985, 26 RPC 693, 46 Digest (Repl) 264, 1710.
Davis & Co v Comitti (1885) 54 LJ Ch 419, 52 LT 539, CA, 13 Digest (Reissue) 72, 666.
Day v Brownrigg (1878) 10 Ch D 294, 48 LJ Ch 173, 39 LT 553, CA, 28(2) Digest (Reissue) 1096, 973.
Francis, Day and Hunter Ltd v Twentieth Century Fox Corpn Ltd [1939] 4 All ER 192, [1940] AC 112, 109 LJPC 11, 161 LT 396, [1939] 4 DLR 353, PC, 13 Digest (Reissue) 130, 1079.
Hollinrake v Truswell [1894] 3 Ch 420, 63 LJ Ch 719, 71 LT 419, 7 R 568, CA, 13 Digest (Reissue) 72, 667.
Ladbrooke (Football) Ltd v William Hill (Football) Ltd [1964] 1 All ER 465, [1964] 1 WLR 273, HL, 13 Digest (Reissue) 62, 623.
Karo Step Trade Mark [1977] RPC 255, Digest (Cont Vol E) 627, 631a.
Tavener Rutledge Ltd v Trexapalm Ltd [1977] RPC 275, [1975] FSR 479.
University of London Press Ltd v University Tutorial Press Ltd [1916] 2 Ch 601, 86 LJ Ch 107, 115 LT 301, 13 Digest (Reissue) 55, 578.
Wombles Ltd v Wombles Skips Ltd [1977] RPC 99, [1975] FSR 488, Digest (Cont Vol E) 116, 1054a.

Appeal

The plaintiffs, Exxon Corpn, Esso Petroleum Co Ltd, Exxon Ltd and Exxon International Ltd, appealed against that part of the judgment of Graham J ([1981] 2 All ER 495, [1981] 1 WLR 624) given on 22nd January 1981 dismissing their claim against the defendant, Exxon Insurance Consultants International Ltd, for an injunction restraining the defendant from infringing the plaintiffs' copyright in the name 'Exxon'. The facts are set out in the judgment of Stephenson LJ.

Vivian Price QC and *J V Fitzgerald* for the plaintiffs.
John Mummery for the Attorney General as amicus curiae.
The defendants were not represented.

STEPHENSON LJ. This appeal is concerned with the word 'Exxon', and a claim by four companies or corporations against a fifth. The claim is firstly for breach of contract, secondly for passing off and thirdly for infringement of copyright. The defendant company failed to appear, or to deliver a defence to the claim; the four plaintiffs accordingly moved the court for such judgment as they appeared entitled to on the statement of claim under RSC Ord 19, r 7(1). Graham J on 22nd January 1981 ([1981] 2 All ER 495, [1981] 1 WLR 624) heard counsel for the plaintiff, and counsel as amicus curiae for the Attorney General; he ordered, firstly, that the defendants be restrained from passing off and ancillary relief; secondly, he ordered an inquiry as to damages; but he held that the plaintiffs could not succeed on the ground of copyright and so gave them no relief against infringement. Not content with the protection that they derived from the learned judge's order, the plaintiffs have appealed to this court, and we have heard counsel for the plaintiffs in support of the view that there is here a copyright in this word Exxon to be protected, and counsel supporting, not on behalf of the non-appearing defendants but as amicus curiae, the conclusion of the learned judge.

The first plaintiff, Exxon Corpn, is incorporated in the USA, and it carries on business throughout the USA. It has associated, or subsidiary, companies in almost a hundred other countries. Until 1st November 1972 it called itself Standard Oil Co (New Jersey). On that date it adopted the name Exxon Corpn; it registered that name as a trade mark, and itself as proprietor of it, in the United Kingdom and elsewhere; its associates and subsidiaries followed suit and adopted the same word as part of their names. That was not true of the second plaintiff, which retained the name Esso Petroleum Co Ltd, Esso being an onomatopoeic version of the first two initials (or so I have always assumed) of

Standard Oil. Their function, or their business, is that of producing, transporting, refining and marketing, through motor garage outlets and so on, 'petroleum products in all parts of the United Kingdom, together with all goods and services connected therewith and a wide variety of other goods displaying the name EXXON together with the name ESSO'. The third and fourth plaintiffs, incorporated in 1969 and 1973 respectively, carry on business in this country and their names are respectively Exxon Ltd and Exxon International Ltd.

The claim relevant to this appeal is made first of all under para 19 of the statement of claim, which reads as follows:

'The word EXXON is an original literary work falling within the provisions of section 2(1) of the Copyright Act 1956 and the First Plaintiff is the owner of the copyright therein and the Second, Third and Fourth Plaintiffs licensees thereof.'

The defendant company was formed in 1977 and it is alleged in para 21 of the statement of claim that it 'has, without the licence or consent of the Plaintiffs, adopted the name EXXON as part of its corporate name'. Then, in para 22, the statement of claim alleges:

'Further the Defendant has, without the licence or consent of the Plaintiffs, reproduced and/or authorised the reproduction of the Plaintiffs' copyright work EXXON in the Defendants corporate name.'

And then, in para 23:

'By reason of the matters referred to . . . the Defendant has infringed the Plaintiffs' copyright in the word EXXON, and threatens to continue to do so.'

The basis of the claim is contained in paras 9 and 10 of the statement of claim, which read as follows:

'(9) Prior to 1970 the First Plaintiff set up a committee to devise and select a new name and trade mark for itself and which could also be used by overseas associates and subsidiary companies when appropriate. The said committee concluded that the said new name must satisfy the following three basic conditions namely: (a) was capable of being readily identified with the First Plaintiff and its associate or subsidiary companies their goods and services, (b) was invented and was devoid of any meaning in English or in any other language spoken in any place in which the goods and/or services of the First Plaintiff and/or its associates and/or subsidiary companies were marketed or likely to be marketed, (c) was short distinctive and easily memorised.'

'(10) Following considerable research and testing the said Committee selected the word "EXXON", devised by them.'

Graham J referred to the short and simple arguments on both sides by which counsel for the plaintiffs supported the claim and by which counsel as amicus curiae opposed it. He considered a number of cases; in particular he referred to *University of London Press Ltd v University Tutorial Press Ltd* [1916] 2 Ch 601 and the judgment of Peterson J in that case (at 608). He referred also to the approval of Peterson J's comments on a literary work by three members of the House of Lords in *Ladbroke (Football) Ltd v William Hill (Football) Ltd* [1964] 1 All ER 465, [1964] 1 WLR 273, to the Privy Council decision in *Francis, Day and Hunter Ltd v Twentieth Century Fox Corpn Ltd* [1939] 4 All ER 192, [1940] AC 112 and to *D P Anderson & Co Ltd v Lieber Code Co* [1917] 2 KB 469. He also heard the submissions of counsel as amicus curiae, particularly as to the possible consequences of upholding the plaintiffs' claim.

Graham J in his judgment posed the basic question, and in my judgment posed it rightly, as being the question—

'whether it is proper to construe "original literary work" in s 2 of the Copyright Act 1956 as covering a single invented word even if considerable time and work were expended on it and, if so, whether the word Exxon here is such a work. There are, I think no decided cases which deal specifically with the precise point that I have to decide. The answer, therefore, must in the end depend on the proper construction of the words in the 1956 Act according to general principles and the facts of the case.'

(See [1981] 2 All ER 495 at 502, [1981] 1 WLR 624 at 632.)

He answered the question in this way ([1981] 2 All ER 495 at 503, [1981] 1 WLR 624 at 634–635):

'As I have already stated, the question that I have to decide is, shortly stated, whether Exxon is an "original literary work" within s 2 of the 1956 Act? I do not think it is. What is it then, one may ask. It is a word which, though invented and therefore original, has no meaning and suggests nothing in itself. To give it substance and meaning, it must be accompanied by other words or used in a particular context or juxtaposition. When used as part of any of the plaintiffs' corporate names, it clearly has a denominative characteristic as denoting the company in question. When used, as I assume it is, with the plaintiffs' goods, it would clearly have the effect of denoting origin or quality. It is in fact an invented word with no meaning, which is a typical subject for trade mark registration, and which no doubt, with adequate user, is capable also of becoming, if it has not already become, distinctive of the plaintiffs and their goods at common law. It is not in itself a title or distinguishing name and, as I have said, only takes on meaning or significance when actually used with other words, for example indicating that it is the name of a company, or in a particular juxtaposition as, for example, on goods. Nothing I have said above is intended to suggest that I consider that a word which is used as a title can, as a matter of law, never in any circumstances be the subject of copyright, and I would disagree with dicta in previous cases to the contrary effect. Such a word would, however, I think have to have qualities or characteristics in itself, if such a thing is possible, which would justify its recognition as an original literary work rather than merely as an invented word . . . the mere fact that a single word is invented and that research or labour was involved in its invention does not in itself in my judgment necessarily enable it to qualify as an original literary work within s 2 of the 1956 Act.'

The learned judge then went on to consider an analogy with Lewis Carroll's Nonsense poem 'Jabberwocky', and came to the conclusion that the words 'Jabberwock' or 'Jabberwocky', if used alone without any poem, could not form the subject of copyright, the legal reason being—

'that the word alone and by itself cannot properly be considered as a "literary work", the subject of copyright under the Act. It becomes part of a "literary work" within the Act when it is embodied in the poem, but it is the poem as a composition which is a work within the Act and not the word itself.'

(See [1981] 2 All ER 495 at 504, [1981] 1 WLR 624 at 635; Graham J's emphasis.)

I have quoted extensively from Graham J's judgment in order to adopt it gratefully. It seems to me that the learned judge asked the right question and gave it the right answer; but I would be doing less than justice to counsel for the plaintiffs' vigorous argument if I left the matter there.

The Copyright Act 1956 is the third of a series of statutes. The Copyright Act 1911 greatly extended the range of copyright, particularly of literary copyright, beyond that which had been protected by the Copyright Act 1842. There is, I think, no difference material to this case between the 1911 and 1956 Acts, and I go straight to the 1956 Act, and to s 2, on which this appeal turns.

Section 1 states the nature of copyright under the 1956 Act as meaning the exclusive right, by virtue and subject to the provisions of the Act, to do and to authorise other persons to do certain acts.

Section 2 provides:

'(1) Copyright shall subsist, subject to the provisions of this Act, in every original literary, dramatic or musical work which is unpublished . . .
'(2) Where an original literary, dramatic or musical work has been published then, subject to the provisions of this Act, copyright shall subsist in the work . . .'

Subsection (5) sets out the acts restricted by the copyright in a literary, dramatic or musical work and states them to be:

'(a) reproducing the work in any material form; (b) publishing the work; (c) performing the work in public; (d) broadcasting the work; (e) causing the work to be transmitted to subscribers to a diffusion service; (f) making any adaptation of the work; (g) doing, in relation to an adaptation of the work, any of the acts specified in relation to the work in paragraphs (a) to (e) of this subsection.'

Subsection (6) defines 'adaptation'—

'(a) in relation to a literary or dramatic work, means any of the following, that is to say . . . (iii) a translation of the work; (iv) a version of the work in which the story or action is conveyed wholly or mainly by means of pictures in a form suitable for reproduction in a book or in a newspaper, magazine or similar periodical . . .'

There is no definition in this Act or in any earlier Act of the word 'work' but there is, in s 48, as there was in s 35 of the 1911 Act, a definition of 'literary work'. What sub-s (1) of the interpretation section, s 48, of the 1956 Act, says is '"literary work" includes any written table or compilation', and '"writing" includes any form of notation, whether by hand or by printing, typewriting or any similar process'.

The question, therefore, is whether this word Exxon is an original literary work. It was invented, as the statement of claim alleges, after research and testing to find a suitable word, apparently over a period of more than a year. It is therefore difficult, if not impossible, to say that it is not original. It was invented and devised by and originated with the first plaintiff. Is it an original literary work? Counsel for the plaintiffs has submitted that it is. He says that the 1842 Act, by its preamble, was concerned to protect literary works of lasting benefit to the world, but such literary works were confined by the Act, as is clear from all its sections, to printed books; there is no such limitation in copyright in literary works since 1911 in this country. What is now protected as an original literary work is anything which can be, and has been, written down for the first time, any combination of letters thought out and written down, any tangible product of intellectual endeavour. Counsel referred us to Webster's Dictionary, in which 'work' is defined in one place as 'something produced or accomplished by effort, exertion, or exercise of skill . . . something produced by the exercise of creative talent or expenditure of creative effort'. He says that this word satisfies those conditions. It does not matter how much work went into it, subject, perhaps, to the principle de minimis lex non curat; it does not matter how poor the quality of the work is; if it was the result, or the product, of creative effort, the exercise of some skill and effort, it is a work, and if it is a work which is written down and consists of letters it is a literary work. If you take the phrase 'original literary work' to pieces, this word Exxon is original for the reason that I have given, it is literary and it is a work. Why, then, is it not an original literary work? But he concedes, although he submits that it is helpful to split the phrase up into its three component words, that it is the expression as a whole in the context of the Act which has to be construed. 'Literary' is given a broader meaning in the 1956 Act than it was given in the 1842 Act, and that broader meaning must colour and extend the meaning of 'work'. Some skill and care having been exerted in inventing this word by selecting these 4 letters out of the alphabet of 26, the word qualifies as an original literary work. Admittedly there is no authority for treating such a word as the subject of copyright, but counsel submits that in its plain and natural meaning this one word, meaningless though it is unless applied to a company or to goods, is an original literary work.

The only help from the authorities which I have found is the judgment of Peterson J in *University of London Press Ltd v University Tutorial Press Ltd* [1916] 2 Ch 601 which *a* Graham J cited. In that case, Peterson J had to consider whether examination papers were the subject of copyright under s 1(1) of the Copyright Act 1911, which provided, exactly in the way provided by s 2 of the 1956 Act, for copyright in 'every original literary dramatic musical and artistic work'. Peterson J pointed out (at 608) that the 1842 Act protected books, and many things which had no pretensions to literary style acquired copyright— *b*

'for example, a list of registered bills of sale, a list of foxhounds and hunting days, and trade catalogues; and I see no ground for coming to the conclusion that the present Act was intended to curtail the rights of authors. In my view the words "literary work" cover work which is expressed in print or writing, irrespective of the question whether the quality or style is high. The word "literary" seems to be used in a sense somewhat similar to the use of the word "literature" in political or *c* electioneering literature and refers to written or printed matter. Papers set by examiners are, in my opinion, "literary work" within the meaning of the present Act.'

Later the learned judge said (at 609–610):

'The objections with which I have dealt do not appear to me to have any substance, *d* and, after all, there remains the rough practical test that what is worth copying is prima facie worth protecting.'

Those observations of Peterson J were approved by Lord Reid, Lord Hodson and Lord Pearce in *Ladbrooke (Football) Ltd v William Hill (Football) Ltd* [1964] 1 All ER 465 at 469, 475, 479, [1964] 1 WLR 273 at 277, 285, 291, where their Lordships were concerned *e* with the originality of certain football coupons and with the question whether a substantial part of them had been copied. So there is nothing in the decision in that case which assists either counsel's argument or this court in considering what the right answer to the question is; but the majority of their Lordships indicated their approval of what Peterson J had said in the *London University Press* case.

I think counsel was also entitled to rely on the 'code' case of *D P Anderson & Co Ltd v* *f* *Lieber Code Co* [1917] 2 KB 469. In that case Mr Worrall had selected from an enormous number of words 100,000 five-letter words to form a suitable code for cabling purposes and Bailhache J was pressed with the argument that, these words being meaningless, except so far as they were fixed with the arbitrary meaning which the devisor of the code gave them in the so-called 'Empire cipher code', they could not be literary, or a literary work. The learned judge rejected that argument and said (at 471): *g*

'The words—I call them so for want of a better name—are for use for telegraphic purposes, and to each of them a meaning can be attached by the person sending the message and also by the addressee, provided, of course, he is informed of the meaning attached to it by the sender,'

and he came to the conclusion that copyright did exist and that the defendants had *h* infringed it, although it was a copyright in those very numerous and meaningless code words, meaningless only in the sense which I have described.

Counsel also referred us to observations of two learned judges, first of all observations made by Megarry J, in *British Northrop Ltd v Texteam Blackburn Ltd* [1974] RPC 57 at 68 in which he said:

'I do not think that the mere fact that a drawing is of an elementary and *j* commonplace article makes it too simple to be the subject of copyright.'

He also referred us to an observation of Whitford J in *Karo Step Trade Mark* [1977] RPC 255 at 273:

'No doubt a drawing may be so simple that it cannot be said to be "a work"—for example, a straight line or a circle—for the word "work" itself carries with it the idea of the exercise of some degree of skill and labour; but I am unable to accept the submission of counsel for [the appellant] that the artistic part of this device is of so simple a nature that no copyright can reside in it.'

With those observations I do not, of course, quarrel, but I do not find them of much assistance in deciding whether this word Exxon qualifies as an original literary work, when I give those words in their context as ordinary a meaning as I can.

The submissions of counsel as amicus curiae were these: first of all he called our attention to sub-ss (5) and (6) of s 2 of the 1956 Act, which I have read, as indicating the sorts of literary works which copyright is concerned with, and which the statute was seeking to protect. It would be possible to reproduce this word in a material form; it would be impossible to perform it in public; it would be impossible, or almost impossible, to make any adaptation of it, certainly to translate it or to provide a version of it with a story or action being conveyed by means of pictures. But, as counsel for the plaintiffs pointed out, not all of these different provisions in these two subsections do relate to all kinds of work, literary, dramatic or musical, and although I think counsel as amicus curiae is right to call our attention to those subsections they do not seem to me to provide any compelling reason for rejecting counsel for the plaintiff's submissions. It does, I think, appear from the 1956 Act that its object is the encouragement of creative work; for that I would need no authority.

The authorities to which counsel as amicus curiae next referred us are dicta, first of all of Parker J in *Burberry's v J C Cording & Co Ltd* (1909) 26 RPC 693 at 701, in which that learned judge said: 'Apart from the law as to trade marks, no one can claim monopoly rights in the use of a word or name'; and to dicta of Walton J in two more recent cases, the first being the 'Wombles' case, *Wombles Ltd v Wombles Skips Ltd* [1977] RPC 99 at 101–102 where the learned judge said:

'It seems to me that the only conceivable ground for suggesting any business connection between the plaintiff and the defendant is that the characters, albeit mythical, are characters who clean up premises, but I do not think that anybody seeing a "Womble" skip, albeit in the road, albeit on one of the defendant's lorries, would think that there really was any connection between that and any business carried on by the plaintiff. The plaintiff's business is simply to license copyright reproductions. It may be a defect in the law that, having invented the characters known as the "Wombles", the authoress has not a complete monopoly of the use of that invented word, which she could then assign to the plaintiffs, but such is the law and that being so it seems to me I must in fact dismiss this motion.'

Very shortly after considering that matter, Walton J had to pass from considering the word 'Wombles' to considering the work 'Kojak', and in *Tavener Rutledge Ltd v Trexapalm Ltd* [1977] RPC 275 at 278 he said:

'... it may very well be that in the United States of America there are rights in invented names or invented fictional characters which are not recognised in this country because, so far as the law of England is concerned, we do not recognise any copyright or other species of property in any names or words, whether invented or not. I think that for that I need only quote two cases, *Day v. Brownrigg* ((1878) 10 Ch D 294), and the well-known case of *Burberrys v. J. Cording & Co. Ltd*.'

Those are dicta, and, as counsel for the plaintiff pointed out, in the first of those cases they were dicta in connection with the 1842 Act, and the second two cases were passing-off cases, where copyright was not directly in point. Nevertheless, it seems to have been assumed, both by Parker J in 1904 and by Walton J in 1975, that there could be no copyright in a name or a word, including an invented name or word.

As I read the judgment of Graham J, he was not prepared to accept those dicta as a full and complete statement of the law, and I find it unnecessary to decide whether what *a* those learned judges said can be accepted without qualification. It is, however, certain that this is the first time, as far as the researches of counsel go, that any court has been asked to hold that there could be copyright in a single invented word or name. It was for that reason, as I understand it, that in this case Graham J sought the assistance of the Attorney General and invited counsel as amicus curiae to befriend the court. He felt that this claim raised a matter which might affect the public interest adversely in other cases *b* and, as he said, it might be far-reaching in its consequences if granted.

I find rather more assistance in the last case to which counsel as amicus curiae referred us; in particular, the observations of Davey LJ in *Hollinrake v Truswell* [1894] 3 Ch 420 at 427–428. That case was concerned with copyright in a cardboard pattern sleeve with scales and figures and descriptive words on it. In his judgment Davey LJ said:

'The preamble of the Act [that was referring to the 1842 Act, of course] recites *c* that it is expedient "to afford greater encouragement to the production of literary works of lasting benefit to the world": and although I agree that the clear enactment of a statute cannot be controlled by the preamble, yet I think that the preamble may be usefully referred to for the purpose of ascertaining the class of works it was intended to protect. Now, a literary work is intended to afford either information and instruction, or pleasure, in the form of literary enjoyment. The sleeve chart *d* before us gives no information or instruction. It does not add to the stock of human knowledge or give, and is not designed to give, any instruction by way of description or otherwise; and it certainly is not calculated to afford literary enjoyment or pleasure. It is a representation of the shape of a lady's arm, or more probably of a sleeve designed for a lady's arm, with certain scales for measurement upon it. It is intended, not for the purpose of giving information or pleasure, but for practical use *e* in the art of dressmaking. It is, in fact, a mechanical contrivance, appliance or tool, for the better enabling a dressmaker to make her measurments for the purpose of cutting out the sleeve of a lady's dress, and is intended to be used for that purpose. In my opinion it is no more entitled to copyright as a literary work than the scale attached to the barometer in *Davis v. Comitti* ((1885) 54 LJ Ch 419).'

He agreed with Lindley LJ, I think, that the plaintiffs in that case were attempting to use *f* the 1842 Act for a purpose to which it was not properly applicable.

Counsel for the plaintiffs says that those observations of Davey LJ as to what is a literary work must be considered in the light of the preamble to the 1842 Act, to which Davey LJ expressly referred. The words of Davey LJ do, however, appeal to me as stating the ordinary meaning of the words 'literary work'. I would have thought, unaided or *g* unhampered by authority, that, unless there is something in the context of the 1956 Act which forbids it, a literary work would be something which was intended to afford either information and instruction or pleasure in the form of literary enjoyment, whatever those last six words may add to the word 'pleasure'. Counsel has not convinced me that this word Exxon was intended to do, or does do, either of those things; nor has he convinced me that it is not of the essence of a literary work that it should do one of those *h* things. Nor has he convinced me that there is anything in the 1956 Act, or in what Peterson J said about the words in the earlier Act, or in any authority, or in principle, which compels me to give a different construction from Davey LJ's to the words 'literary work'. As I have already said, I agree with the way in which Graham J put the matter; I am not sure whether this can be said to be a 'work' at all; I am clearly of the opinion that it cannot be said to be a literary work. I therefore agree with Graham J, and I would *j* dismiss this appeal.

I should add a reference to the final submissions of counsel as amicus curiae that if we were to accede to this claim we should be endangering freedom of speech, and we should be ignoring the protection already given by the Trade Marks Act 1938.

a   I attach little weight to the first submission, because in my view counsel for the plaintiffs is right in saying that the plaintiffs have clearly impliedly licensed the world to use this word properly.

As to his second submission, it is noticeable that s 9(1)(c) of the Trade Marks Act 1938 does give protection to an invented word, or invented words; nevertheless I agree with Graham J that no great weight should be attached to the fact that adequate protection, or apparently adequate protection, is already provided to the plaintiffs under the Trade
b   Marks Act 1938.

OLIVER LJ. I entirely agree.

Section 2 of the 1956 Act provides that copyright should subsist in every original literary work, and in essence counsel for the plaintiffs submissions are very simple. First,
c   he says that the name Exxon is undoubtedly original; it had not been thought of before or, so far as is known, used before; it is an artificial word, which does not appear in any known language. It is, he says, literary; it is composed of letters and it is written, typed or printed. It is a 'work' because work or effort went into its invention and its selection as a suitable name for the plaintiff group which had no meaning, offensive or otherwise, in any other language.

d   But 'original literary work' as used in the 1956 Act is a composite expression, and for my part I do not think that the right way to apply a composite expression is, or at any rate is necessarily, to ascertain whether a particular subject matter falls within the meaning of each of the constituent parts, and then to say that the whole expression is merely the sum total of the constituent parts. In my judgment it is not necessary, in construing a statutory expression, to take leave of one's common sense, and the result to which
e   counsel seeks to drive us is one which, to my mind, involves doing just that.

Stephenson LJ has already referred to the judgment of Davey LJ in *Hollinrake v Truswell* [1894] 3 Ch 420 at 428 where he said: 'Now, a literary work is intended to afford either information and instruction, or pleasure, in the form of literary enjoyment'. Admittedly, that was said in relation to the preamble to the Copyright Act 1842, which referred to affording 'greater encouragement to the production of literary works of
f   lasting benefit to the world'. But it does seem to me, as it seems to Stephenson LJ, that what Davey LJ said was a fair summary of what the expression means in ordinary language.

We have been referred to a number of cases in which copyright has been successfully claimed in, for instance, examination papers, football coupons and tables of ciphers; but all these (and I do not exclude the case of the telegraphic code in *D P Anderson & Co Ltd*
g   *v Lieber Code Co* [1917] 2 KB 469) seem to me to fall fairly within Davey LJ's commonsense formulation.

But that for which protection is sought in the instant case does not appear to me to have any of the qualities which common sense would demand. It conveys no information; it provides no instruction; it gives no pleasure that I can conceive; it is simply an artificial combination of four letters of the alphabet which serves a purpose
h   only when it is used in juxtaposition with other English words, to identify one or other of the companies in the plaintiff group. Whether, as might perhaps be the case if one followed up the suggestion made in the judgment of Graham J, the insertion of the extra 'x' was to avoid the risk of involving the Bishop of Exeter in proceedings for infringement every time he wrote to The Times newspaper I do not pause to inquire.

I am clearly of the opinion that Graham J arrived at the correct conclusion when he
j   held that this was not an original literary work in which copyright subsists, and I agree that the appeal should be dismissed.

SIR DAVID CAIRNS. I agree with everything that has been said by Stephenson and

Oliver LJJ in the two judgments that have already been delivered; for those reasons I too would dismiss the appeal.

a

Appeal dismissed. Leave to appeal to House of Lords refused.

Solicitors: *Needham & Grant* (for the plaintiffs); *Treasury Solicitor.*

Patricia Hargrove   Barrister. *b*

Connolly v Camden and Islington Area Health Authority

c

QUEEN'S BENCH DIVISION
COMYN J
6th, 7th, 8th APRIL 1981

Damages – Personal injury – Loss of future earnings – Shortened expectation of life – Loss of *d* *earnings in lost years – Young child – Action by child aged five in respect of injury sustained in course of operation performed shortly after birth – Child rendered mentally abnormal and unlikely to be able to earn a living – Whether a young child able to claim damages for loss of earnings in lost years – Whether claim proved.*

The plaintiff, a child aged nearly five years, was reduced to a severely mentally abnormal *e* state as a result of an overdose of anaesthetic given to him while undergoing an operation in hospital shortly after his birth. As a result of his condition he would never be able to earn a living and his life expectancy was shortened to 27½ years. The hospital authority admitted liability. The question arose whether the plaintiff was entitled to damages for loss of earnings in the lost years during which he would have lived but for his injury.

f

Held – A young child could claim damages under the head of damage for loss of earnings in the lost years, subject to proof of loss, and such a claim was not limited to exceptional cases, e g where the child was already earning as a television star. Accordingly, the plaintiff qualified to claim under that head of damage but on the material before the court the claim would be assessed at nil (see p 254 c, p 255 g h and p 256 d to h, post).

Pickett v British Rail Engineering Ltd [1979] 1 All ER 774 and dictum of Lord Scarman *g* in *Gammell v Wilson* [1981] 1 All ER at 593 considered.

Notes

For damages for lost years, see 12 Halsbury's Laws (4th Edn) para 1154.

Cases referred to in judgment

h

Benham v Gambling [1941] 1 All ER 7, [1941] AC 157, 110 LJKB 49, 164 LT 290, HL, 36(1) Digest (Reissue) 383, 1544.

Gammell v Wilson, Furness v B & S Massey Ltd [1981] 1 All ER 578, [1981] 2 WLR 248, HL.

Pickett v British Rail Engineering Ltd, British Rail Engineering Ltd v Pickett [1979] 1 All ER 774, [1980] AC 136, [1978] 3 WLR 955, [1979] 1 Lloyd's Rep 519, HL, Digest (Cont Vol E) 459, 1314b.

j

Action

By a writ issued on 23rd April 1979 the plaintiff, Liam Connolly, a minor suing by his father and next friend, Frank Brendan Connolly, brought an action against the defendants, Camden and Islington Area Health Authority and a surgeon at one of the *a* health authority's hospitals, claiming damages for personal injury sustained by him during the course of an operation. By notice dated 5th September 1980 the action against the second defendant was wholly discontinued. The facts are set out in the judgment.

G H Rooke QC and *W G B Hungerford* for the plaintiff.
J R S Adams for the health authority.

b
COMYN J. I am not going to keep any of the parties, particularly the parents of this little boy, in suspense, and I will announce straightaway the total sum of damages which I have arrived at, to which there will have to be added interest, on which I will hear counsel at the end. The total sum, to which interest will have to be added, is an award of £220,007.

c Little Liam Connolly will be five years old in three months' time, on 24th July 1981. I have seen him and met him and he is a delightful little boy, despite the horrifying handicaps which he suffers and which I will have to deal with. He has quite exceptionally devoted and dedicated parents: a mother, who is 27 years of age, and a father, who is 37 years of age. The father is fully qualified in the plastering trade, but unhappily for some time now has been out of work.

d Liam is the middle of five children, all under ten, that the parents have. No praise can be too high for them, both of them, for what they have been doing for Liam and for their determination to keep him out of an institution and in their loving care. But for them he would alas be fully qualified for institutional care for the remainder of his life. I am well satisfied, not only of their determination to bring him up themselves, but also of their ability to do so.

e When Liam was born he was, as I find and is not now seriously disputed, a normal, healthy child. His two parents are of normal health and his brothers and sister are entirely normal. When he was a few days old, that is to say towards the end of July 1976, he had persistent vomiting, and he was accordingly admitted to hospital on 4th August. Six days later, when he was only 17 days old, preparations were made for an operation to cure this condition, and for the purpose of that operation he was accordingly anaesthetised. Tragically he was given a serious overdose of anaesthetic, and I need say

f no more about that painful fact than that liability is admitted for it on behalf of the first defendant, that is to say the Camden and Islington Area Health Authority, the authority in charge of University College Hospital where this tragedy occurred and where in fact Liam had been born.

The consequences of what happened were and are quite dreadful. I will summarise

g them from the medical evidence I have heard, four very distinguished specialists, and from their reports and from the reports of speech therapists and, though only for a matter of about ten minutes, from my own observation. The medical evidence and reports are of the highest standard. Put shortly, Liam has been reduced to a very severely mentally abnormal child with a mental age which I put at between 15 and 18 months. He is subject to epilepsy, has had four or five attacks already and one of those lasted for

h an hour and a half. He will never be able to earn his living in any real sense. He will not be in a position to marry. He will need constant care and perpetual supervision. He has been walking since he was about two years of age, but he is a bit bandy legged and only walks up to about 100 yards or so at the very most. He falls over frequently, he stumbles, he hurts himself when he falls and he constantly bruises himself. He is incontinent of urine and faeces day and night. He is only capable of speaking a very few words. He has

j little sustained attention. He frequently looks vacant. He cannot feed himself and he slobbers. His concentration is very poor. He can be aggressive to his brothers. He needs full assistance in washing and dressing. He has become hyperactive and also rather obstructive and destructive. For example, he will prevent other members of his family watching the television, he will break crockery or glass if any of it is to hand and he has the passion that many small children have of wanting to open doors and drawers. The parents have had to fit special locks, but the danger here, which does not exist with normal children, is, for example, if he gets into the bathroom he can fill up the bath to **a** the point of its overflowing and can damage the room and possibly himself also. He has to be watched all the time. He has a squint which is attributable to the brain damage he suffered as a result of the anaesthetic. When he goes to bed in the evening he has to have his mother to lie down with him for half an hour to three-quarters in order to get him off to sleep at all. He wakes frequently during the night and it is his habit to wake up the whole family at about 5.30 in the morning. At present he is in his parent's bedroom and **b** they look after him, not only during the day, but during these disturbing periods at night too. It is little wonder that I find words difficult in which to express one's praise of them. He is restless, he will not settle for any period of time and the only peace which the parents have is when, during term time, he attends a special school for handicapped children. He is liable to colds and coughs and consequent respiratory trouble. He is also, unfortunately, liable to ear infections. **c**

I make the following specific findings, which, for reasons which will appear, I regard as very important indeed. I find that he is very affectionate and very friendly, especially towards his parents and those whom he knows. I believe that his feelings run to knowledge of the affection shown towards him and also any disapproval shown to him by his parents or others. I am quite certain that now, and as time goes on, he will appreciate that other children, particularly his brothers and sister, are different to him **d** and able to do things that he cannot do. In my judgment, he will not only know this but feel this, with a feeling of unhappiness and frustration. In my judgment also, he will feel, and feel deeply, his inability to participate with his brothers and sister and with other children. He will notice and he will feel changes around him of whatever sort they are and as his strength grows so, in my judgment, will he feel the deeper his inability to do what his strength should allow. **e**

His mother and father have managed between themselves for much of the time since this tragic occurrence, but recently have had the benefit of help. Contrary to the submission made, if I may say so, most ably by counsel for the health authority, I consider that his brothers and sister will not be able or, if able, will not be willing to help in bringing him up. His surroundings and tradition are such that older children would help to bring up the younger children to a certain extent, but I do not regard that as at **f** all likely here where (a) they will become increasingly conscious of, and probably impatient of, his condition; and (b) they are likely to be impatient when he acts, as act he will, provocatively.

It is very difficult to dip into the human mind even when it is a normal human mind. It is all the more difficult to dip into it when it is, alas as here, a mind retarded to the extent of the mental ability of 15 to 18 months. But, doing the best I can and **g** weighing everything up, I consider that this little boy now appreciates and feels things; not everything but many things, and will do so increasingly. He will, in my judgment, for example, both feel and worry about his incontinence of urine and faeces. He has a degree of feeling and appreciation which I think has perhaps been rather underplayed in this case.

I have had four distinguished, careful and, may I stress this word because I mean it **h** most sincerely, sympathetic medical witnesses called before me, two on each side, all four accompanied by their reports. When I say sympathetic I mean just that. It was a matter of great gratification for me to find that the care of their reports and evidence was also shown by their truly sympathetic attitude in regard to their little patient, Liam, plus their unbounded admiration for the parents. As an illustration of the matter, one of them said in a report that an hour or so with the little boy had exhausted him completely **j** for some time, whereas the mother, who accompanied the little boy, appeared to take it in her stride.

I have had Professor Illingworth, an emeritus professor of child health in the University of Sheffield and also Professor Holt, a paediatrician in the University of London, for the

health authority. I have had Dr Hierons, a consultant neurologist at a number of
a hospitals, and I have had Dr Lawrence, a consultant paediatrician; Dr Hierons and Dr
Lawrence being highly qualified and having long experience. The same is of course true
of the two professors, but I stress it in regard to Dr Hierons and Dr Lawrence, because
they do not possess professorships as such.

   I have drawn on their evidence and the reports for the picture I have given of little
Liam. The most important question they dealt with was the expectation of life, because
b of course that governs pretty well every other process in this case. Liam will be five in
July. Expectation of life for the average young, middle-aged or spritely elderly person is
literally in the lap of God, but in the courts we have to do our best to deal with difficult
questions about expectation of life. May I say immediately that none could be more
difficult than this particular case. The question of expectation of life here I approach
with humility, and by that I mean with a consciousness that I may be seriously wrong
c one way or the other. The medical witnesses themselves appreciate that, but perhaps
their appreciation cannot be quite as great as that of a judge who has to find the right
number of years on which to hang everything else.

   Very broadly, the medical evidence split this way: the two professors for the health
authority put the expectation of life at maximum 20 years from now; the two physicians
put it at 30. This is no matter where you split differences. This is a matter where one has
d to look with great care. There is literature on the subject which all four medical
gentlemen consulted very carefully, but I think that literature is subject to one criticism
which they made, and which I make, which is that it relates to statistics in respect of the
whole class of mentally afflicted young people in their twenties and thirties, and the
range, as we know, is depressingly and awfully wide. Reliance, for example, was put on
a statistic that the figures showed an increased expectancy in recent years from mid-
e thirties to early forties, but that is taking, as I say, the whole broad spectrum.

   I believe that in this case, although we may all be wildly wrong, I must start with the
situation that this little boy almost certainly will not live beyond the age of 30. So I
therefore set that at one end of my approach. I am well conscious that two very
experienced professors in giving the figure of 20 are giving really what they consider to
be their extremity and that they are pledging themselves to 20 in a rather stronger way
f than the two physicians are, or can be, to 30. Dr Hierons impressed me very much
indeed on this subject. They all impressed me, but he impressed me more perhaps than
the others. He, in weighing everything up and taking into account such factors as one
can, hit on $27\frac{1}{2}$ years as being the likely lifetime of this little boy, that is to say another $22\frac{3}{4}$
years life.

   I have thought about that a very great deal, and I have brought into play the knowledge
g one accumulates in these courts and in the world of handicapped children. Eighty years
ago and earlier they were virtually hidden away. They were regarded all too often as
being some sort of disgrace to the family. But with the years a lot of things have come
about, a more tolerant attitude, a huge amount of help from the state and voluntary
organisations, an immensity of goodwill from ordinary people, a willingness to help
from ordinary people and also a great increase in medical knowledge and medical care.

h   I can well see that this little boy is exposed to infections which others would not be and
that such infections with him could have more serious consequences. I also have very
much in mind his epilepsy, directly caused by the anaesthetic accident, as I would call
it. These and other factors go to make his risks of continued life high. There is a lot to
be balanced against it. I have seen him and seen him in motion. He is a picture of
perpetual motion, even more so than ordinary children aged five. Observing him and
j going to the reports and listening to the evidence, I think there is a lot to be put into the
other side of the scale against the risks of infection and epilepsy. I think there may be
sturdiness and there may well be increasing strength, especially with loving care from his
parents, and one knows of course all too well in these courts and elsewhere that people
with handicaps very often do live on far, far beyond what is expected.

Doing the best I can in all the circumstances, I have come to the conclusion that Dr Hierons has given me the most reliable guide as to expectation of life, namely a total life *a* of 27½ years, which means a life from now of 22¾ years.

I want to end on this subject as I began, by saying that I approach it with humility and well conscious of the fact (a) that I may be, as medical men may be, seriously wrong one way or the other and (b) that of course financially speaking that will be of importance one way or the other. I have taken every consideration I can think of into account. I have, after reaching my provisional view, gone back over all the evidence and all the other *b* reports. I have sought to approach the matter in many different ways, but I have come to the firm conclusion that 27½ years total life, 22¾ years expectation of life, is the right approach here.

Turning to the question of damages, they have to be assessed under the following heads: pain, suffering and loss of amenities, future care, loss of earnings, special damage and what I would call the lost years point. To anticipate a little, I am going to find that *c* this little boy qualifies for a lost years calculation, but, pursuant to the argument of counsel for the health authority, my assessment of that is nil.

Pain, suffering and loss of amenities. I think that they amount to more than, with respect, counsel or the medical witnesses really suggested. The figures put before me for a bracket were £60,000 at the top end, well below £30,000 at the bottom end, a suggestion by counsel for the health authority that £30,000 was the right sum and a *d* suggestion on behalf of Liam that perhaps £40,000 was the right sum. To this matter I have given the most anxious thought and have come to the conclusion that the right sum is £50,000. This is this little boy's money, peculiarly his, whilst the future care money is not. I may say that in assessing the figure of £50,000 I consider that the feeling and appreciation of this little boy and the indignities to which he will find himself subjected and the frustration which he will feel all have to go into this calculation. I feel, *e* with respect to counsel on both sides, that it is not just in the end loss of amenities; there is quite an element of pain and suffering. I revert there simply to an awareness day and night, constantly, of incontinence of faeces. It is but one example.

In my judgment, a little boy who has suffered as this little boy has to date and who will continue to suffer for 20 years or more, as I believe, is entitled to £50,000 under that head. It is never easy to assess damages, but, in my judgment, no objective test could *f* fault the figure of £50,000 here in the light of the evidence and the reports, not only of the doctors, but of the speech therapist too. So item 1 is £50,000 for pain, suffering and loss of amenities.

For future care I have been provided with a helpful schedule of care and attendance, which is listed under four heads: daily during school term time, daily during school holidays, a night sitter from 11 pm to 6 am and a holiday help. The term time hours are *g* five hours a day, the school holidays time is eight hours a day, the night sitter time seven hours, the holiday help a fortnight at £70 a week.

Counsel for the health authority has not quarrelled with the term time or the holidays or the holiday help. I find the hourly rate given for all of these (£2·50) as frankly modest in the extreme. Without taking any account at all of inflation, I believe that £2·50 an hour to attend to this little boy of perpetual motion by day and fairly regular intervention *h* by night is indeed a modest sum. I find, contrary to a submission at one time by counsel for the health authority, that a night sitter can be found. There are people prepared to undertake this work. Miss Smalley of the British Nursing Association, who gave evidence before me, told me of the type of people, namely those who sought work at night but were not anxious to do light factory work or anything of that sort.

What counsel for the health authority said was, firstly, that night sitters were not *j* necessary at all and were indeed, on the medical evidence of his medical experts, unnecessary and undesirable. He further suggested that seven hours was all right, but for seven nights a week at least two nights could be left off, and he got, by perfectly proper questioning, what might be termed an admission from Miss Smalley to that effect. But I would not have called it an enthusiastic admission and certainly not one that

a I feel binds me.

Having heard this case and having outlined the facts I have, I have no doubt whatever that there should be a night sitter and that the night sitter should be for seven nights a week. I believe that in the interests of the child and in the interests of the mother to a greater extent, the father to a lesser extent, this is essential right into the future. The mother comes into the matter very acutely, because she has a family to run; she has got

b to be ready to look after this little boy at other times. At the present moment her sleep is subject to perpetual interruption, and the whole family are woken at about 5.30 in the morning. So I have no doubt whatever in holding that a night sitter is essential for seven nights a week. As I have said, I am also satisfied that one would be and is available.

The annual figure produced by the four items put forward on the schedule is £11,480 per year. There has been agreed as an additional annual figure to cover washing of

c clothes, nappies indeed, and general expenses a sum of £400, making £11,880 a year.

What is the correct multiplier here, bearing in mind that I have assessed the future loss of expectation of life occurring at 27½ years of age, ie 22¾ years time? I have come to the conclusion that the proper multiplier is 13 years, plus one quarter, being the quarter from 24th April 1981 to 24th July and the two weeks also to be added between now and 24th April, because my calculations are all based on this child from the age of five. So

d that everyone can understand it, the figures as calculated by me come down to 13 years: £153,400; quarter year: £2,950; two weeks plus: £490; the total of £156,840. So that is the second item I find in relation to future care.

I now come to the question of future earnings. The only yardstick, if it can even be dignified with that word, that could be taken was in the plastering trade, following in father's footsteps. It is all very problematical, all very artificial, all very hypothetical, all

e very difficult. Both counsel arrived at a loss of earnings figure, based on £60 a week or thereabouts, of £15,000. They differed entirely whether that should be reduced and, if so, by how much. It was suggested to me that there ought really in the circumstances to be no deduction at all. I do not accept that view. Counsel for Liam pressed it very diligently and very charmingly, if I may say so, but on that I prefer the argument advanced by counsel for the health authority, and I prefer his figure of £7,500, being one

f half of the anticipated total.

To those figures has got to be added agreed special damage of £5,667. That brings the grand total, to which interest has got to be added, to £220,007, made up of £50,000, £156,840, £7,500, £5,667, total £220,007.

I will hear argument on interest in a moment, but I have got to deal, finally, and I am afraid I can deal with it rather quickly, with counsel for Liam's point about the lost years,

g as they were known, I think, even before *Pickett v British Rail Engineering Ltd* [1979] 1 All ER 774, [1980] AC 136 was decided in the House of Lords. There has been since in the House of Lords another case connected with *Pickett*, namely *Gammell v Wilson* [1981] 1 All ER 578, [1981] 2 WLR 248. *Pickett* established the principle that, enormously difficult though it might be, there was an element of damages to be considered and to be judged by the High Court (that case was remitted to the High Court accordingly) for the years

h when a man would have been working in the future, mayhap the distant future, but for the accident. It is a loss of earnings situation in a very different and long-term setting. Their Lordships in both these cases, between both these cases, applied it as being the law and applicable in regard not only to living plaintiffs but those who had died or those claiming on behalf of those who had died. I have, before this case, read and reread these two decisions. I say, with profound respect, that I do not find either of them easy for the

j purposes of this case. It is noticeable that it is said more than once by way of comment on *Benham v Gambling* [1941] 1 All ER 7, [1941] AC 157 way back in 1941 that there are advantages in having more than one speech in the House of Lords. I have found the speeches in these two cases difficult so far as I am concerned in looking at the problem that I have to look at. It seems to me that what their Lordships say with clarity is that a young man, or even a middle-aged man, well fixed on a professional or trade course can rightly expect for himself or his estate or dependants the financial benefit of the years *a* that he would have worked or would have been likely to have worked but for the accident and that that calculation has to be done although it involves necessarily a great many hypothetical considerations and a good deal of guess work. But running as an undercurrent in some of the speeches in these two cases is the fact that a child is in a different position. With great respect, I agree that there are obvious differences not only in age but in the question of actual future occupation, the age at which the lost years are *b* to begin, how many lost years are to be taken, what rate they are to be taken at and so forth.

Lord Scarman said in *Gammell v Wilson* [1981] 1 All ER 578 at 593, [1981] 2 WLR 248 at 265:

> '... the court must make the best estimate it can. In civil litigation it is the balance of probabilities which matters. [Then there follow these words:] In the case *c* of a young child, the lost years of earning capacity will ordinarily be so distant that assessment is mere speculation. No estimate being possible, no award, not even a "conventional" award, should ordinarily be made. Even so, there will be exceptions: a child television star, cut short in her prime at the age of five, might have a claim; it would depend on the evidence. A teenage boy or girl, however, as in *Gammell's* case may well be able to show either actual employment or real prospects ...' *d*

What am I to deduce from these cases in regard to a child of, to take the present case, nearly five? Is it being said by their Lordships as a matter of law binding on me that there is no claim possible in respect of such a child except in purely exceptional circumstances, such as I would call, perhaps somewhat old-fashionedly, the Shirley Temple type of case? I do not think that can be so. Other courts in this building deal *e* with children up to the age of 16, sometimes to 18 and exceptionally beyond. I do not think, with respect, that any hard and fast rule can be laid down, and I think a child qualifies as such under this head of damage dependent on the ability to prove. It is difficult enough in the case of a teenager or a middle-aged person to prove something for lost years. It is more difficult for a child, but I can envisage, with respect, far more examples than the Shirley Temple case or that of a television star. I can envisage the only *f* son of a father who owns a prosperous business. I can envisage the son who is born to a farmer who is able to leave the estate to the son. I can envisage a number of situations where the court can look at something and find that there are lost years to be compensated for.

It is not my intention in this judgment to seek to contribute to the wealth of learning on this subject or to turn my judgment into a sort of Law Quarterly Review article on this subject. But what I hold, and hold clearly, is that *Pickett v British Rail Engineering Ltd* *g* and *Gammell v Wilson* give this little boy a head of claim for lost years, but on the material before me I am going to follow precisely the way counsel for the health authority put it, which I believe expressly states the law, not that there is no claim but that there is a claim but I assess it at nil.

In those circumstances there will be judgment for £220,007.

h

Judgment for the plaintiff for £220,007.

Solicitors: *Bindman & Partners* (for the plaintiff); *Hempsons* (for the health authority).

K Mydeen Esq   Barrister.

Goldup v John Manson Ltd and another

QUEEN'S BENCH DIVISION

ORMROD LJ AND WEBSTER J

26th, 27th MARCH, 15th APRIL 1981

Food and drugs – Not of quality demanded – Evidence – Standard of quality – No statutory standard – Expert's opinion of standard – Minced beef – Proportion of fat in minced beef – Both cheap and more expensive quality of minced beef on sale in shop – Notice in shop that minced beef sold containing up to 30% fat – High demand in area for cheap quality – Purchaser buying cheap quality which on analysis found to contain 33% fat – Expert opinion that minced beef should contain no more than 25% fat – Evidence not contradicted – Magistrates acquitting owner and manager of shop of selling food not of quality demanded by purchaser – Whether expert's opinion amounting to evidence of quality demanded by purchaser – Whether sale to prejudice of purchaser – Food and Drugs Act 1955, s 2(1).

At a butcher's shop owned and managed respectively by the first and second defendants a cheap quality and a more expensive quality of minced beef were displayed for sale priced at 58p per pound and 74p per pound. A notice in the shop stated that minced beef sold in the shop contained up to 30% of fat. There was a demand in the area for the cheap minced beef and 400 lb of it were sold per week as compared to 100 lb of the more expensive quality. The maximum percentage of fat in minced beef was not prescribed by statute or regulation. A portion of the cheap minced beef bought by a local authority sampling officer was found on analysis to contain 33% fat. The defendants were charged with selling to the prejudice of a purchaser food, namely minced beef, which was not of the quality demanded by the purchaser in that it contained 33% fat, contrary to s 2(1)[a] of the Food and Drugs Act 1955. At the trial in the magistrates' court the prosecutor called three analysts who gave evidence that according to a number of samples of minced beef they had examined most minced beef on sale contained 25% or less fat and that minced beef should contain no more than 25% fat, but their evidence did not indicate whether those samples were sold as first or second quality minced beef or the prices charged for the samples. The magistrates acquitted the defendants, holding that the price at which minced beef was sold was crucial in determining the quality demanded by the purchaser and that in view of the price of the cheap minced beef it was not beyond reasonable doubt that mince sold at that price which contained 33% fat was not of the quality demanded by a purchaser. The prosecutor appealed, contending that where the standard for food was not prescribed by statute or regulation the magistrates were required to find a standard and could do so only on the evidence called before them, and therefore, where there was expert evidence establishing a standard which was not contradicted, the magistrates ought to accept that evidence and act on it.

Held – The appeal would be dismissed for the following reasons—

(1) Since the standard of the 'quality' of food, for the purpose of s 2(1) of the 1955 Act, was defined in s 2(1) in terms of the quality demanded by the purchaser rather than being prescribed by statute or regulation, the bare opinion of an expert witness as to the standard could not be evidence of the quality demanded by a purchaser, since the standard was then determined by the express terms of the contract of sale or, more often, by implication or inference from all the surrounding circumstances, and the expert's standard was not evidence of, and could not be substituted for, the standard demanded by the purchaser. Since the analysts' evidence had not indicated whether the samples on which they based their opinion was first or second quality minced beef or the prices charged for the samples, but amounted to a bare statement of opinion, it was not

---

a   Section 2(1), so far as material, provides: 'If a person sells to the prejudice of the purchaser any food ... which is not of the nature, or not of the substance, or not of the quality, of the food ... demanded by the purchaser, he shall, subject to the provisions of the next following section, be guilty of an offence.'

evidence of the quality demanded by the purchaser. Accordingly, the magistrates had been entitled to find that they were not satisfied that the minced beef in question was not *a* of the quality demanded by the purchaser (see p 263 *j*, p 264 *c* to *j* and p 265 *b*, post); *Morton v Green* (1881) 8 R (Ct of Sess) 36, *Anness v Grivell* [1915] 3 KB 685, *Hunt v Richardson* [1916–17] All ER Rep 64 and *Collins Arden Products Ltd v Barking Corpn* [1943] 2 All ER 249 applied; dictum of Shearman J in *Bowker v Woodroffe* [1927] All ER Rep at 420 explained.

(2) Furthermore, in view of the notice in the shop that minced beef contained up to *b* 30% fat, a purchaser who selected the cheap minced beef impliedly asked for minced beef containing that quantity of fat and since the 3% excess fat which the minced beef was found to contain was de minimis, it did not amount to prejudice to the purchaser within s 2(1) (see p 264 *j* to p 265 *b*, post); dictum of Lord Parker CJ in *Hall v Owen-Jones and Jones (trading as Central Dairies)* [1967] 3 All ER at 212 applied.

Notes
c
For the sale of food not of the proper nature, substance or quality see 18 Halsbury's Laws (4th Edn) paras 10, 69, 1074 and for cases on the subject, see 25 Digest (Reissue) 103–111, 901–942.

For the Food and Drugs Act 1955, s 2, see 14 Halsbury's Statutes (3rd Edn) 21.

Cases referred to in judgment
d
Anness v Grivell [1915] 3 KB 685, 85 LJKB 121, 113 LT 995, 79 JP 558, 13 LGR 1215, 25
   Cox CC 190, 25 Digest (Reissue) 107, 916.
Bowker v Woodroffe [1928] 1 KB 217, [1927] All ER Rep 415, 96 LJKB 750, 137 LT 347,
   91 JP 118, 25 LGR 306, 28 Cox CC 397, DC, 25 Digest (Reissue) 89, 788.
Broughton v Whittaker [1944] 2 All ER 544, [1944] KB 269, 113 LJKB 248, 170 LT 298,
   108 JP 75, 42 LGR 88, DC, 25 Digest (Reissue) 105, 908.   *e*
Collins Arden Products Ltd v Barking Corpn [1943] 2 All ER 249, [1943] KB 419, 112 LJKB
   406, 169 LT 12, 107 JP 117, 41 LGR 161, DC, 25 Digest (Reissue) 108, 922.
Hall v Owen-Jones and Jones (trading as Central Dairies) [1967] 3 All ER 209, [1967] 1 WLR
   1362, 131 JP 405, 65 LGR 511, DC, 25 Digest (Reissue) 121, 1012.
Hunt v Richardson [1916] 2 KB 446, [1916–17] All ER Rep 64, 85 LJKB 1360, 115 LT 114,
   80 JP 305, 14 LGR 854, 25 Cox CC 441, DC, 25 Digest (Reissue) 144, 1184.   *f*
Mills (A J) & Co Ltd v Williams (1964) 62 LGR 354, [1964] Crim LR 533, DC, 25 Digest
   (Reissue) 104, 905.
Morton v Green (1881) 8 R (Ct of Sess) 36, 18 Sc LR 570, 25 Digest (Reissue) 150, 1225.
Roberts v Leeming (1905) 69 JP 417, 3 LGR 1031, 25 Digest (Reissue) 105, 906.
Tonkin v Victor Value Ltd [1962] 1 All ER 821, [1962] 1 WLR 339, 126 JP 169, 60 LGR
   149, DC, 25 Digest (Reissue) 100, 878.   *g*
Webb v Jackson Wyness Ltd [1948] 2 All ER 1054, 113 JP 38, 47 LGR 172, DC, 25 Digest
   (Reissue) 105, 909.

Case stated
Rodney Charles Goldup, on behalf of the Hampshire County Council, appealed by way of case stated by the justices for the County of Hampshire, acting in and for the petty *h* sessional division of Odiham, in respect of their adjudication as a magistrates' court sitting at Aldershot on 11th August 1980 whereby they dismissed informations laid by the appellant against the respondents, John Manson Ltd and Daniel James Hassall, alleging that on 22nd November 1979 the respondents contravened s 2 of the Food and Drugs Act 1955 by selling, to the prejudice of a purchaser, food, namely minced beef, which was not of the quality demanded by the purchaser. The facts are set out in the *j* judgment of the court.

Richard Dening for the appellant.
Cyril W F Newman for the first respondent.
The second respondent did not appear.

Cur adv vult

15th April. **ORMROD LJ** read the following judgment of the court: This is an appeal by the prosecutor by case stated from the dismissal, on 11th August 1980 by the justices for the petty sessional division of Odiham, of two informations against the first and second respondents, who are respectively the owners and manager of a butcher's shop, alleging offences under s 2 of the Food and Drugs Act 1955. The respondents were alleged to have sold to the prejudice of the purchaser $1\frac{1}{2}$ lb of minced beef, which was not of the quality demanded by the purchaser, in that it contained not less than 33% of fat.

On 22nd November 1979 a sampling officer entered the shop and purchased $1\frac{1}{2}$ lb of minced beef at 58p per pound. Two qualities of minced beef were on sale, at 58p per pound and 74p per pound respectively. The sampling officer asked for and was sold the cheaper quality. There was a notice displayed in the shop stating that minced beef contained up to 30% of fat. On analysis the sample was found to contain not less than 33% of fat. The analyst's certificate stated that: 'In my opinion a sample described as minced beef must contain not more than 25 per cent of fat.'

The witnesses for the prosecution were Mr King, the analyst to whom the sample was submitted, Mr Allen, the quality food controller for Hampshire County Council, Mr Shelton, another public analyst, and the sampling officer.

Mr King said that 40 samples of minced beef had been analysed in his department in November 1979; 33 contained less than 25% of fat. Since 1974, 162 samples had been analysed in his department, the average content of fat being 20·1%. He expressed the opinion, as in his certificate, that minced beef should not contain more than 25% of fat. Mr Allen said that a 'natural' joint is 'not expected' to have a fat content in excess of 25%. Mr Shelton, in a written statement, said that in 1976 he had done a survey of minced beef. The average content of fat was 17·5%; 2·6% of the samples contained more than 30% of fat. He too expressed the opinion that minced beef should not contain more than 25% of fat.

Three witnesses for the company gave evidence to the effect that the policy of the company was to work to the 25% limit, though the only check on the fat content was a visual one. There was, however, a demand in the area for a cheaper quality of minced beef. One witness explained that the 25% limit was aimed at because of cases brought against butchers' shops by the local authority. The manager, Mr Hassall, said that there was a strong demand for the cheaper quality. He sold 400 lb a week of the cheaper quality as compared to 100 lb of the more expensive quality.

The justices concluded that the price of minced beef was crucial in determining the quality demanded by the customer and that they were unable to find beyond reasonable doubt that minced beef containing 33% of fat was not of the quality demanded by the purchaser, notwithstanding the opinions of the experts. The justices ask whether, in these circumstances, they erred in not convicting the respondents.

Counsel for the appellant in this court, submitted that on the evidence the justices were bound to convict the respondents. He relied on a line of cases, beginning with *Bowker v Woodroffe* [1928] 1 KB 217, [1927] All ER Rep 415 supported by *Broughton v Whittaker* [1944] 2 All ER 544, [1944] KB 269, *Webb v Jackson Wyness Ltd* [1948] 2 All ER 1054 and *Mills v Williams* (1964) 62 LGR 354.

His argument may be summarised in this way. Where no standard for the article in question has been prescribed by statute or regulation, the justices must find a standard for themselves. This they can only do on the evidence before them. Therefore, where there is expert evidence which establishes a standard, which is neither qualified nor contradicted by other evidence, they ought to accept that evidence and act on it. They should, therefore, have convicted.

Counsel for the respondents, submitted that this line of cases was distinguishable from the instant case on two grounds. In the first place, all the cases relied on were concerned with the substance of the article sold and not with its quality, ie the informations were all laid in the conjunctive form, alleging that the article was not of the nature, substance and quality demanded, and on their facts were concerned with substance rather than with quality, whereas the present case was concerned with quality only. In the second place, the articles concerned in all these cases were non-natural manufactured preparations, sold under trade names, and not, as in the present case, a natural product.

He relied on another line of cases, beginning with the Scots case of *Morton v Green* (1881) 8 R (Ct of Sess) 36, and including *Anness v Grivell* [1915] 3 KB 685 and *Hunt v Richardson* [1916] 2 KB 446, [1916–17] All ER Rep 64 and submitted that the question was whether the purchaser received an article of the quality which he asked for or was entitled to expect. The purchaser was entitled to expect that the article would be of commercial quality or of merchantable quality. Price was, therefore, a relevant factor. Accordingly, he submitted that there was no evidence in the present case that the purchaser received an article which was not of the quality demanded in that there was no evidence that the minced beef was not of commercial or merchantable quality, having regard to the price, and that the purchaser had selected the cheaper quality. Furthermore, the evidence established that the cheaper quality was very popular. His argument was also supported by one case to which we were referred by counsel for the appellant in order to distinguish it, *Collins Arden Products Ltd v Barking Corpn* [1943] 2 All ER 249, [1943] KB 419.

These two lines of authority appear to be in conflict and we do not think that they can be reconciled by distinguishing between substance and quality, or between manufactured and natural products. (Is minced beef a natural or manufactured product?) It is remarkable that, apart from a brief contact in *Broughton v Whittaker*, in which the *Collins Arden Products Ltd* case was dismissed as 'exceptional', these two lines of authorities appear never to have touched before the present case. Since the outcome of this appeal virtually depends on which of them governs it, we are compelled to examine the judgments in these cases in some detail in an attempt to reconcile them. The question to be decided is the extent to which quantitative evidence by analysts is evidence of the nature or substance or quality of the article 'demanded by the purchaser' for the purposes of s 2 of the 1955 Act.

The foundation of counsel's argument for the appellant is a passage in the judgment of Shearman J in *Bowker v Woodroffe* [1928] 1 KB 217 at 226, [1927] All ER Rep 415 at 420 which is reproduced verbatim in the headnote ([1928] 1 KB 217):

'That principle is that the analyst is entitled to express his opinion as to what the standard of any article should be, in order that the thing sold should not be sold to the prejudice of the purchaser, and if he expresses his opinion in his analysis, the Court is bound to accept it unless it is contradicted.'

This unequivocal and unqualified statement of principle is not supported by the other two judgments in the case. Lord Hewart CJ's opinion was much more qualified. After referring to the judgment of Ridley J in *Roberts v Leeming* (1905) 69 JP 417 to the effect that justices in these cases must 'fix some standards' of their own, Lord Hewart CJ said ([1928] 1 KB 217 at 224, [1927] All ER Rep 415 at 419):

'Now undoubtedly the words "fix some standard" are ambiguous. I do not think that those learned judges meant that there must be a quantitative standard, drawing a hard and fast line. That is, of course, one way of fixing a standard, and in some cases it may be the best way, but there is clearly another way of doing so, and that is, to have regard to a minimum and to say with regard to the contents of a particular admixture that, upon any reasonable view of the true minimum, this compound must fall short of it.'

Avory J treated the case as essentially one of fact, holding that the opinion of an analyst expressed in his certificate was to be regaarded as evidence of fact.

The question at issue in *Bowker v Woodroffe* was whether a preparation sold as 'extract of meat and malt wine', which on analysis was found to consist almost entirely of water and sugar, with possibly 2% of meat and malt extracts and no wine at all, was sold to the prejudice of the purchaser as not being of the nature, substance or quality demanded. The analyst's opinion was that it was not a meat and malt wine extract and that a genuine extract of meat and malt wine should contain not less than 5% of a mixture of equal parts of meat and malt extracts with a wine basis.

It was held that this expression of opinion was admissible in evidence and, there being no evidence to the contrary, the defendant having elected to call no evidence, it established that the article was not of the nature, substance and quality demanded by the purchaser and was, therefore, sold to the prejudice of the purchaser. Accordingly, the justices ought to have convicted. Notwithstanding the headnote, we do not think that this case is authority for any wider proposition than that.

It was followed in *Broughton v Whittaker*. In that case the defendant was prosecuted under the section for selling a beverage labelled 'sweetened lemon flavouring cordial, not made from lemons'. The analyst gave evidence that a preparation which contains neither alcohol nor sugar could not be called a 'cordial'. The justices declined to convict, giving as their reason that there was no proof that when an ordinary person purchased a non-alcoholic beverage marked 'cordial', he meant to purchase a beverage which contained sugar. Not perhaps an unreasonable doubt, since sugar was strictly rationed at the time, and they were referred to the *Collins Arden Products Ltd* case which had been decided the year before, in which this definition of cordial had been rejected. The court, however, allowed the prosecutor's appeal on the ground that the only evidence before the court was the analyst's opinion, and that they were, therefore, obliged to accept it. Once again the defendant elected to call no evidence.

Counsel for the appellant referred us to three other cases. In *Webb v Jackson Wyness Ltd* [1948] 2 All ER 1054 the defendants were charged in the conjunctive form with selling vinegar containing less than 4% acetic acid. In that case the prosecution did not rely on the evidence of the analyst alone, but called a body of evidence, including a representative of the Vinegar Manufacturing Association which proved that the minimum content of acetic acid in non-brewed vinegar was 4%. In other words, a preparation containing less than this percentage of acetic acid was not of the standard or quality recognised by the trade and others, and so the prosecution had proved that the vinegar supplied was not of commercial quality and, therefore, by inference, not of the nature, substance and quality demanded by the purchaser.

In *Tonkin v Victor Value Ltd* [1962] 1 All ER 821, [1962] 1 WLR 339 the product was 'mock salmon cutlette', which on analysis proved to contain 33% of fish. The Food Standards (Fish Cakes) Order 1950, SI 1950 No 589, had specified a minimum content of fish of 35%. The analyst gave evidence that he thought that an article described as a 'fish cutlette' should contain not less fish than a fish cake. The justices dismissed the information on the ground that the analyst's evidence did not go far enough. This court held that the analyst was entitled to say that however much fish a fish cutlette should contain, it must be more than the minimum prescribed for fish cakes, and that the justices ought to have convicted.

In *A J Mills & Co Ltd v Williams* (1964) 62 LGR 354 the court was concerned with tins of what was described as 'steak and gravy'. The tins were found to contain only 60% of meat. The analyst expressed the opinion that such tins ought to contain at least 75% of meat, basing his view on a report of the British Food Standards Committee in 1962. The justices accepted this evidence and convicted the defendants. This court dismissed their appeal. Lord Parker CJ expressly dealt with the case as a question of substance, not of quality, and agreed with the view expressed by the justices that they were precluded from taking into account the reduced price at which the tins were being sold. He stated the principle of law involved in these words (at 355):

'This is a case in which there is no standard or minimum standard fixed by any regulation or order, and in those circumstances it is for the justices to fix what they consider is the proper minimum standard, it being, as I understand it, the standard which those in the trade would recognise as the proper standard. The justices can only fix the standard on the evidence before them.'

At the end of his judgment he said (at 356):

'. . . if a man clearly indicates that the tin does not contain the accepted standard
of the substance in question, then he commits no offence at all, and all that is
necessary here is to state on the tin what its content is.'

Turning now to the line of cases of counsel for the respondents, the first is *Morton v
Green* (1881) 8 R (Ct of Sess) 36, a judgment of the Court of Justiciary. In that case the
defendant was charged with selling cream which was not of the nature, substance and
quality demanded. The case for the prosecution was that the purchaser bought four gills
of cream for 4d, which on analysis was found to contain 10·5% butter fat. The analyst
stated that cream contained an average of 25% butter fat. Evidence was given for the
defence that it was the practice in the trade to sell two qualities of cream, one at 2d per
gill, 'good' cream, and a cheaper quality at 1d per gill, which was the cream sold to the
purchaser. The sheriff convicted but the court allowed the appeal. Lord Young held that
no prejudice to the purchaser had been proved, and said (at 39):

'. . . I am clearly of opinion that a delivery of that article, which was sold at a
penny per gill satisfies a demand for "cream" on the streets of Paisley, there being no
suggestion that the article was adulterated or unwholesome or not worth the money
that was paid for it.'

He also said that the court was not called on to say what quantity of fat is necessary to
justify the use of the term 'cream'. The Lord Justice-Clerk said (at 40):

'Here, however, we have to consider two questions relative to the construction of
this clause of the statute, first, What is the true meaning of "quality demanded"? and
second, What is the meaning of "to the prejudice of the buyer"? Now, on the
matter of quality, I am of opinion that this term implies that the demand made was
for an article different in quality from that furnished, and that the words used by
the purchaser were intended by him and understood by the seller to mean an article
of a different grade in quality, although identical in substance . . . Now, here the
trader has different qualities of the same generic substance. They are marked by
different prices, and their difference is well known, and perfectly discernible by any
ordinary buyer.'

Anness v Grivell [1915] 3 KB 685 is clear authority that the quality contemplated in the
section is the commercial quality and that, where quality is in issue, price is a relevant
consideration in determining the 'quality demanded' by the purchaser. The case also
illustrates the care which needs to be taken in the quantitative approach, especially where
percentages are used to compare the sample with the standard suggested. The court had
no hesitation in that case in ignoring the difference between 10% and 4% of butter in the
article sold as a mixture of butter and margarine.

The most important of this line of cases is *Hunt v Richardson* [1916] 2 KB 446, [1916–
17] All ER Rep 64, a case which was heard by the full court consisting of Avory, Scrutton,
Lawrence, Bray and Darling JJ, all of whom delivered reserved judgments. That case
clearly established that in a prosecution for selling milk which was not of the nature,
substance and quality demanded, it had to be proved that the milk was not of the quality
actually demanded or, alternatively, not of merchantable quality. Merchantable quality
is a question of fact to be determined by the evidence of those who deal in the article,
sellers and buyers (see [1916] 2 KB 446 at 471, [1916–17] All ER Rep 64 at 69–70 per
Bray J).

The judgment of Scrutton J contains a most valuable analysis of the law which is
relevant to the present case. It is conveniently summarised in the following extract
([1916] 2 KB 446 at 466, [1916–17] All ER Rep 64 at 78):

'The same question arises when quality is demanded. What has happened to the
milk, whether by intentional faulty feeding or by subsequent addition or abstraction,
may explain why the article supplied is not of the quality demanded; but the real

questions are What is the quality demanded? and Has it been supplied? If it has not, it is immaterial that there has been no adulteration or abstraction. New laid eggs are asked for; bad eggs are supplied; an offence against s. 6 has been committed. The quality demanded is a question of fact; it may be a question of the interpretation of a trade description; it may be a question of evidence of the commercial quality spoken of by the Court in *Anness* v. *Grivell*; it may be a question of evidence of merchantable quality implied by the Sale of Goods Act, 1893, in goods sold by description. But it is a question of fact for the magistrates, not of law for the Court, who are not judges of fact and may not know accurately what they think they know about it. A natural product may be so poor in quality, though the genuine product of Nature, that it does not possess the commercial or merchantable quality which is required by the custom of buyers and sellers, which is a question of evidence. It is, I think, common knowledge that some milk is so poor from the poor condition of the animal that it will not nourish; some meat so poor from the poor condition of the animal that no consumer except the poorest would have it on his table. In my view to supply such products will be an offence though the products have not been tampered with.'

It is clear from all the judgments that the court rejected the contention of the prosecution that on proof that the milk, sold as 'new morning milk', contained a deficiency of 9% milk fat (the difference between 2·73% found in the sample and the analyst's standard of 3·0%) the defendant must be convicted. The majority were in favour of allowing the appeal and quashing the conviction, the minority (Scrutton and Bray JJ) thinking that it should go back to the justices to answer the question of fact, whether the milk supplied was of the nature, substance and quality demanded, in view of the principles laid down in the judgments.

The same approach was adopted by this court in *Collins Arden Products Ltd v Barking Corpn* [1943] 2 All ER 249, [1943] KB 419. The question was whether an offence against the corresponding section in the 1938 Act had been committed by selling a product which was described as 'orange-citric flavoured cordial', which contained no sugar, being sweetened with saccharin (it was wartime). The analyst gave evidence for the prosecution that 'non-alcoholic cordials should contain a quantity of sugar'. The justices convicted, but the appeal was allowed on the ground that the justices had not considered the proper question, namely whether when the purchaser asked for a cordial he meant only a liquid containing alcohol or sugar. Hallett J said ([1943] 2 All ER 249 at 252, [1943] KB 419 at 424): 'It is the demand by the purchaser which, to my mind, is the determining factor in deciding what ought to be supplied.' He then referred to *Morton v Green*.

Finally, in *Hall v Owen Jones and Jones (trading as Central Dairies)* [1967] 3 All ER 209 at 212, [1967] 1 WLR 1362 at 1368 Lord Parker CJ, after referring to *Hunt v Richardson*, said:

'. . . the basis of those decisions [is] that, if the natural constituents are not present in the proper proportions, it is a matter of quality not of substance, and, if the purchaser has not demanded milk of a particular quality containing a percentage of solids and fats, then he has got what he asked for, namely, the substance, genuine milk.'

These two lines of authority can be reconciled by defining more precisely the 'standards' which the justices must determine before finding that an offence has been committed under s 2 of the 1955 Act. The standard prescribed by the section is defined in terms of the purchaser's demand, which, ultimately, is a question of fact. It may be determined by the express terms of the contract, eg 'new morning milk' as in *Hunt v Richardson*. More often the nature or substance or quality demanded by the purchaser will be a matter of implication or inference from all the surrounding circumstances of the case. A purchaser who asked for 'cream' in the streets of Paisley in 1881, and accepted 'cream' at the price of 1d per gill, impliedly demanded the cheaper quality normally sold in Paisley at that price, even though it contained half as much milk fat as the more expensive quality: see *Morton v Green*. In other cases, in the absence of evidence of *a* specific circumstances, it will be inferred that the purchaser demanded an article which corresponds in substance or quality with that normally sold in the trade, eg non-brewed vinegar, containing not less than 4% acetic acid: see *Webb v Jackson Wyness Ltd* [1948] 2 All ER 1054. In that case evidence from the trade established the standard of commercial quality or merchantability.

When the article is sold by description, eg 'extract of meat and malt wine' or 'lemon *b* flavoured cordial containing no lemon', the purchaser impliedly demands a product which is of merchantable quality, ie which corresponds to the description by trade standards. The disparity between the composition of the article sold and the description may be so great as to raise a prima facie case of unmerchantable quality and, in the absence of evidence to the contrary, prove the case for the prosecution: see *Bowker v Woodroffe* [1928] 1 KB 217, [1927] All ER Rep 415. Similarly if the unchallenged *c* evidence is that a 'cordial' must contain either alcohol or sugar and the product sold contains neither: see *Broughton v Whittaker* [1944] 2 All ER 544, [1944] KB 269.

Counsel's argument for the appellant goes, and must go, further than this. To succeed in this appeal he must go all the way with Shearman J's dictum in *Bowker v Woodroffe* [1928] 1 KB 217 at 226, [1927] All ER Rep 415 at 420, namely that the analyst is entitled to express his opinion as to what the standard should be, and that the court is bound to *d* accept it, unless contradicted. In our judgment counsel's argument goes too far because it inevitably leads to the conclusion that where no standard has been prescribed by statute or regulation, the analyst can make good the deficiency by himself determining the standard, subject of course to evidence to the contrary. (The evidence in this case tends to show that this is what is actually happening. The analyst's opinion leads to prosecutions, justices convict, and butchers adapt their standards to avoid conviction.) *e* But this involves redrafting s 2 of the 1955 Act by substituting the analyst's standard for the standard demanded by the purchaser. In other words, Shearman J's statement of principle was incomplete and, therefore, misleading because it did not identify the nature of the standard or standards to which he was referring. It is quite clear from the context that the judge did not intend the concluding words of his judgment to be read as a comprehensive statement of principle. In any event, it goes much further than was *f* necessary for the decision in that case and was, therefore, obiter.

The apparent conflict between these two lines of authority can be explained in procedural terms. In all the cases relied on by counsel for the appellant the defence elected to call no evidence and relied on a submission of no case to answer. This court had, therefore, to decide whether the prosecution had made out a prima facie case. If so, conviction was inevitable. If some of the results seem unreasonable from a common *g* sense point of view, the fault lies with the tactic adopted by the defence, which is prone to produce artificial results.

If the evidence in the present case is approached in this way the *bare* statement by the analyst 'In my opinion minced beef must not contain more than 25% of fat' is irrelevant since by itself it is not evidence of the quality demanded by the purchaser. The evidence given by the analyst and other witnesses as to the composition of other samples of *h* minced beef is relevant as far as it goes. It proves that most samples of minced beef on sale contain 25% or less of fat which is some evidence of the commercial quality of minced beef. But, in this case, it does not go far enough because there is no indication of whether the samples were sold as first or second quality minced beef, and there is no evidence of the prices charged for the samples. This is particularly important where the cheaper of two qualities is chosen by the purchaser. The prosecution have to prove that *j* a purchaser of minced beef at 58p per pound is, in effect, demanding minced beef, the commercial quality of which contains significantly less than 33% of fat.

There is a further difficulty in the way of the prosecution. The seller was displaying a notice saying that minced beef contained 'up to 30% of fat'. A purchaser who selects the cheaper quality is impliedly asking for minced beef of that specification. In Lord

Parker CJ's words in *Hall v Owen-Jones and Jones* [1967] 3 All ER 209 at 212, [1967] 1 WLR 1362 at 1368, he got what he asked for, namely minced beef containing 30% of fat. The prosecution, rightly, did not attempt to rely on the difference between 30% and 33% of fat. The difference in real terms is half an ounce of fat in the pound which could not possibly amount to prejudice to the purchaser.

Accordingly, the justices were entitled to hold that they were not satisfied that the minced beef containing 33% of fat was not of the quality demanded by the purchaser. The appeal, therefore, fails.

Appeal dismissed.

Solicitors: *Theodore Goddard & Co*, agents for *R A Leyland*, Winchester (for the appellant); *Warren & Co*, Streatham (for the respondents).

Sepala Munasinghe Esq   Barrister.

Miller v F A Sadd & Son Ltd
Miller v Pickering Bull & Co Ltd

QUEEN'S BENCH DIVISION
ACKNER LJ AND MCNEILL J
15th APRIL, 18th MAY 1981

Trade description – False or misleading indication as to price of goods – Contract to supply goods at price calculated according to agreed formula as and when purchaser calling for delivery – Purchaser calling for delivery of goods and vendor appropriating those goods to contract and delivering them – Delivery accompanied by invoice charging higher price than contract price – Whether vendor 'supplying' or 'offering to supply' goods – Whether separate offences – Whether vendor 'offering to supply' goods and giving 'indication' in contract that goods were offered at price lower than that charged – Whether vendor 'supplying goods' and merely stating wrong price in invoice – Trade Descriptions Act 1968, ss 1(1)(b), 6, 11(2).

The respondents contracted with a local authority to supply fruit and vegetables to schools at a price calculated by reference to the prices quoted in the fruit trade's official journal. In accordance with the contract the local authority requested delivery of 6 lb of apples to a school and these were delivered by the respondents to the school on the same day. The delivery was accompanied by an invoice or delivery note charging the local authority with a price for the apples which was higher than the contract price. An information was laid against the respondents alleging that in offering to supply goods, ie the apples, they gave an indication (namely, in the contract) likely to be taken as an indication that the goods were being offered at a price less than that in the invoice at which they were in fact offered, contrary to s 11(2)[a] of the Trade Description Act 1968. The magistrates dismissed the information. The prosecutor appealed, contending that (i) when the respondents appropriated the apples to the contract, for delivery, they then had them in their 'possession for supply' and were 'deemed to offer to supply them', within s 6[b] of the 1968 Act, and (ii) the formula in the contract for calculating the price of the fruit and vegetables to be delivered amounted to a continuing indication, which

---

a   Section 11(2) is set out at p 267 f, post
b   Section 6, so far as material, is set out at p 267 g, post

was referable to each delivery made under the contract, that the goods were being offered (ie delivered) at a price calculated in accordance with the contract formula.

Held – The 1968 Act, by s 1(1)(b)^c, created separate offences of 'supplying' and 'offering to supply' goods to which a false trade description was applied. In the circumstances there was a concluded contract, and therefore a 'supply of goods', rather than an 'offer to supply' within s 11(2). Moreover, even though the goods were falsely described in the invoice as being at a higher price than that specified in the contract that did not amount to a false trade description within s 1(1)(b). Accordingly, no offence had been committed by the respondents under the 1968 Act and the appeal would be dismissed (see p 269 *e f* and p 270, post).

Per Curiam. (1) When goods are appropriated under a contract by the vendor to the purchaser and invoiced, they cannot be said to be 'in [the vendor's] possession for supply' within s 6 of the 1968 Act, when they are merely held by him for the purpose of delivery or collection pursuant to the contract. The words 'in his possession for supply' in s 6 are to be read sui generis with the words 'exposing . . . for supply' in s 6 and in the context of an offer to supply goods, as opposed to a concluded contract (see p 269 *h j*, post).

(2) The concept of a false 'indication' in s 11(2) is inapplicable in the context of a concluded contract. If the price stated in a contract is the correct price and the only false or misleading price is that contained in a delivery note, the vendor when appropriating the goods to the contract cannot be said to give a false 'indication' that the goods are being offered or supplied at any price other than the contract price, since the purchaser is only obliged to pay the contract price and not the wrongly stated price in the invoice (see p 269 *j* and p 270 *b*, post).

Notes

For false or misleading indications as to the price of goods, see 18 Halsbury's Laws (4th Edn) para 1011.

For the Trade Descriptions Act 1968, ss 1, 6, 11, see 37 Halsbury's Statutes (3rd Edn) 949, 955, 957.

Cases referred to in judgment

Doble v David Greig Ltd [1972] 2 All ER 195, [1972] 1 WLR 703, 136 JP 469, 70 LGR 411, DC, Digest (Cont Vol D) 990, 1118a.

Great Northern Railway Co v Witham (1873) LR 9 CP 16, 43 LJCP 1, 29 LT 471, 12 Digest (Reissue) 254, 1176.

Nattras v Marks & Spencer Ltd (25th June 1980, unreported), DC.

Cases stated

Charles Miller, the consumer protection officer for the North Yorkshire County Council, appealed by way of cases stated by the justices for the County of North Yorkshire acting in and for the petty sessional division of Allertonshire in respect of their adjudications as a magistrates' court at Northallerton on 26th November 1980 whereby they dismissed informations laid by the appellant against F A Sadd & Son Ltd and Pickering Bull & Co Ltd respectively, alleging that the respondents in offering to supply goods to the county council gave an indication likely to be taken as an indication that the price of the goods being offered was less than the price at which the goods were in fact being offered, contrary to s 11(2) of the Trade Descriptions Act 1968. The facts are set out in the judgment of the court.

J A Swanson for the appellant.
Michael Mettyear for the respondents in both cases.

Cur adv vult

---

c   Section 1(1), so far as material, is set out at p 269 *e*, post

18th May. **McNEILL J** read the following judgment of the court: These are appeals by way of cases stated by justices for the County of North Yorkshire in respect of their adjudications as magistrates' courts sitting at Northallerton when on 26th November 1980 they dismissed informations preferred by the appellant, who is the county consumer protection officer for the North Yorkshire County Council, against the respondents alleging breaches of s 11(2) of the Trade Descriptions Act 1968. The informations were heard and determined separately by the justices, but as the same point of law arises on both and the parties are respectively represented by the same counsel we consented to an application by both to hear the appeals together.

The terms of the several informations were as follows. In the Pickering Bull case: that they on 3rd March 1980 at Scarborough in offering to supply goods, namely vegetables and fruit, to the North Yorkshire County Council gave an indication likely to be taken as an indication that the price at which French Golden Delicious Apples, class I, were being offered for delivery to Pindar School, Moor Lane Kitchen, Eastfield, Scarborough on 3rd March 1980 was 10p per pound less 5% discount, such price being less than that at which the goods were in fact being offered, namely 13p per pound less 4·9% discount.

In the F A Sadd case: that they on 6th March 1980 at York in offering to supply goods, namely vegetables and fruit, to the North Yorkshire County Council gave an indication likely to be taken as an indication that the price at which United Kingdom topped round beetroot was being offered for delivery to Huntington Comprehensive School, Mill Hill, Huntington, York on 6th March 1980 was 46p per stone less 5% discount, such price being less than that at which the goods were in fact being offered, namely 54p per stone less 5% discount.

We turn later to the facts found in respect of each information but, as we have said, each raises the same point of law, that is to say yet another problem on the construction, and the application to the particular facts, of s 11(2) of the Trade Descriptions Act 1968. The subsection reads:

> 'If any person offering to supply any goods gives, by whatever means, any indication likely to be taken as an indication that the goods are being offered at a price less than that at which they are in fact being offered he shall, subject to the provisions of this Act, be guilty of an offence.'

In construing this subsection the court has to apply the definition of 'offer to supply' in s 6:

> 'A person exposing goods for supply or having goods in his possession for supply shall be deemed to offer to supply them.'

Moreover, the words 'likely to be taken as an indication' are to be construed as Ashworth J said in *Doble v David Greig Ltd* [1972] 2 All ER 195 at 198–199, [1972] 1 WLR 703 at 707:

> 'But in order to spread its net more widely, and as I think to protect customers more carefully, Parliament chose wider language, and what was enacted was that a person who "gives, by whatever means, any indication likely to be taken as an indication that the goods are being offered at a price", and so on. The words "likely to be taken as an indication" seem to me quite plainly to involve a wider consideration than the single word "indication". One is looking, if I may say so, at the customers and the effect on the customers of whatever is said or done or displayed. If it is likely to be taken as an indication to the effect stated, then the conditions of the subsection are fulfilled.'

Melford Stevenson and Forbes JJ, the other members of the court, stressed similarly the intended extension of the words used beyond precise legal words such as 'offer' and 'representation'. Forbes J put it in this way ([1972] 2 All ER 195 at 201, [1972] 1 WLR 703 at 710):

'If it is reasonably possible that some customers might interpret the label as an indication of that kind, it seems to me that an offence is committed, even though *a* many more customers might in fact take the opposite view.'

It is to be noted that in that case the 'indication' was, by concession, capable of alternative meanings, one involving falsity, the other not.

There is little difficulty in applying s 11(2) to the cases which may be regarded as straightforward and to which Parliament clearly intended it to apply; the obvious example is the shelf of goods in a supermarket above which is a notice 'These goods are *b* sold at the reduced price of 35p' but where some of the goods are individually labelled 35p and others, for whatever reason, are labelled 40p, the likelihood being that when taken to the cash desk the assistant will charge the price on the label. There is present on those facts a clear offer to supply in the words 'exposing . . . for supply' and a clear 'indication that the goods are being offered at a price less than that at which (some of them at least) are in fact being offered'.   *c*

This court has had to deal with such a case in *Nattrass v Marks & Spencer Ltd* (25th June 1980, unreported). The inspector there entered the defendant's premises and observed freezer cabinets containing foodstuffs. There were display cards indicating prices. One said: 'Lower Price 10 Cod Fish Fingers'; the price of 53p was struck out and the price of 40p substituted. Inside the cabinets were packets of fish fingers and a few packets in each cabinet had the former price stuck on 'no doubt because someone had either forgotten *d* to check the tickets or had put in a batch of packets from some other place showing the higher price'. Some examples of those with the higher price were taken to the check-out where the inspector was charged the higher price shown on the ticket. This was plainly a prima facie case of an offence under s 11(2) and may, according to the court then sitting, have justified, if proved, and if no statutory defence were established, an absolute discharge.   *e*

It is to be noted that the statutory defence, expressly reserved in the subsection by the words 'subject to the provisions of this Act', might be available to the person charged, and in the case in point Ormrod LJ commented on the ill-advisability in such a case of a submission of no case to answer.

Similar straightforward factual situations may be found where the goods not being exposed are 'in possession for supply'; for example, the goods in the storeroom behind *f* the shop labelled with the higher and not the reduced price. So too, as in *Doble's* case, the indication may be ambiguous or capable of alternative meanings. Sometimes of course difficult questions of fact may have to be resolved but, once resolved, the applicability or non-applicability of the subsection becomes apparent.

The present cases are in no sense straightforward 'offer' cases as a summary of the facts will show. The facts of only one need to be set out in detail; we set out those of the *g* Pickering Bull case. Any differences are recorded in brackets.

On 6th (8th) August 1979 the Yorkshire Purchasing Authority, on behalf of the North Yorkshire County Council, accepted the respondents' tenders of June or July 1979 to provide apples (beetroot) at a price based on the mean 'official' prices quoted in the Fruit Traders' Journal less a discount of 5%. The justices found that the acceptance of the tenders created a binding contract for the supply of the goods concerned to the *h* establishments concerned for a period up to 30th September 1981. Thus the respondents, so the justices found and as was accepted by counsel on both sides of the case in the argument, became obliged to supply to the schools in accordance with the tenders such quantities of apples (beetroot) as were called for at a price to be calculated in accordance with the agreed formula. Early in the hearing before us counsel for the appellant was asked what the obligations of the parties were under this agreement so found.   *j*

There was, it appears from what he said, no obligation on the authority whatsoever to require or accept any particular quantity of goods save to pay at the price calculated as agreed for the goods which it requisitioned to an unspecified and unlimited extent. The respondents' obligation was to deliver the quantities required from time to time.

In the events which happened, on dates before 3rd (6th) March 1980 the county council called for the delivery of 6 lb of apples (4 stones of beetroot). The respondents delivered those quantities to the schools and the deliveries on those dates were accompanied by an invoice or delivery note charging the county council with prices which, by concession, were in each case greater than the prices properly calculated in accordance with the formula. It was said on the appellant's behalf that in those circumstances the county council's finance or accounting department would simply have paid the respondents the sums on the invoice and would not have checked it against the formula, and so, it was argued, the situation was analogous to that of the assistant at the supermarket cash desk. This is a surprising proposition when a public authority is concerned, but so be it.

Counsel for the appellant contended that he could successfully establish the charges laid against the respondents under s 11(2) of the 1968 Act on the following premises. (1) When the respondents appropriated the apples (beetroot) to the delivery they then had them in their possession for supply and therefore by reason of s 6 of the Act were 'deemed to offer to supply them'. (2) At that time, and until delivery to the schools, the apples (beetroot) were in fact being so offered at a price which was higher than the price which would have been charged if properly calculated in accordance with the formula. (3) The agreement to deliver apples (beetroot) at a price to be calculated in accordance with the formula was, or contained, a continuing indication, that is to say an indication referable to each delivery, and in particular to the instant deliveries, that the goods then being offered (as so defined) were being offered at the prices calculated in accordance with the formula which was less than the price at which they were in fact being offered.

We are not persuaded by this argument. However, it is not its artificiality alone which leads us to the conclusion that Parliament cannot have intended the subsection to be so construed or applied.

In the first place, Parliament determined to create separate offences, severally identified as 'supply' and 'offer to supply' by s 1(1)(b) of the Act:

> 'Any person who, in the course of a trade or business . . . (b) supplies or offers to supply any goods to which a false trade description is applied; shall . . . be guilty of an offence.'

The present facts disclose what might be regarded as a classic case of 'supply', and it is clear that no false trade description was applied to the goods when supplied save in so far as they were falsely described as being at a higher price than was in fact the case. This itself is clearly *not* an offence. The appellant confuses and erroneously confuses a 'supply' case with an 'offer to supply' case and attempts to apply to the former rules applicable to the latter.

Secondly, the 'supply' was pursuant to a contract. Where, as here, the respondents' tender is a standing offer, each requisition by the county council was an individual act of acceptance in respect of the definite quantity of goods called for at the contract price, that is to say, the price agreed to be calculated in accordance with the formula: see *Great Northern Railway v Witham* (1873) LR 9 CP 16. Accordingly, the price on the invoice whether erroneously above or below the contract price not only had no force or effect whatsoever but was no part of the respondents' offer even in the extended sense imported by s 6 of the Act. It would be straining language to say that when goods were appropriated by a vendor to a purchaser, priced and invoiced, they nevertheless were 'in his possession for supply' when they were merely held by him for the purposes of delivery or collection pursuant to the contract of sale; in our view, the words 'in his possession for supply' must be read sui generis with 'exposing . . . for supply' and in the context of a definition of 'offering to supply'. Moreover, as counsel for the respondents put it in the course of argument, the word 'indication' makes no sense in the context of a concluded contract.

Thirdly, on the facts of this case the justices were entitled to find, as they did, that 'the correct price was the contract price, as contained in the original tender of July 1979. From that it follows that the only false or misleading price was that which was contained in the delivery note . . .' Accordingly, the indication in the tenders, which was continuing to the extent that the county council's requisitions concluded contracts at the prices based on the formula, was not false; the respondents did not give any indication *a* at that time (whether likely to be taken as an indication or not) that the goods were being offered or were to be supplied at any price other than the price calculated in accordance with the formula. It was, at worst against the respondents, the invoice which was false, not the indication. The appellant was at all times obliged to pay only the contract price and was neither bound nor, if competently served by the officers of the county council, likely to be misled by the wrongly priced invoice. The correct answer was not these *b* proceedings but a sharp reminder that the contract price was not accurately stated on the document.

Once again the difficulty in this case has arisen because the appellant has sought to treat a 'supply' case as an 'offer to supply' case; the two must be kept separate as, in our view, Parliament intended.

Whilst the Trade Descriptions Act 1968 is a statute for the protection of consumers, it *c* is also a penal statute; unless Parliament has made it plain that particular conduct is criminal, the courts and the enforcement officers should not seek artificial constructions of the statutory words to make it so. In this case the relevant conduct was supplying goods; the supply was in no sense coloured by misdescription. The justices were right to refuse to engraft on to this straightforward transaction rules inappropriate to it.

Appeals dismissed.   *d*

Solicitors: *Sharpe, Pritchard & Co*, agents for *W A Harrison*, Northallerton (for the appellants); *Lucien A Isaacs & Co*, agents for *Gosschalk, Wheldon & Co*, Hull (for the respondents).

Sepala Munasinghe Esq   Barrister. *e*

f

Re St Piran Ltd

CHANCERY DIVISION
DILLON J
29th JUNE, 1st, 7th JULY 1981   *g*

Company – Compulsory winding up – Petition by contributory – Evidence – Report of Department of Trade inspectors – Secretary of State declining to present petition himself – Contributory petitioning on basis of findings in inspectors' report – Petitioner criticising conduct of director but not alleging misconduct or breach of legal duty – Petitioner filing no other evidence – Whether petitioner entitled to rely on inspectors' report – Whether petition required to identify **f** *specific matters in inspectors' report relied on – Whether failure to allege misconduct or breach of legal duty a ground for striking out allegation criticising director's conduct.*

The activities of a company and its directors were investigated by inspectors appointed by the Secretary of State under ss 165 and 172 of the Companies Act 1948. In their report to the Secretary of State the inspectors recommended that he should petition the court to **h** wind up the company. The Secretary of State declined to act on that recommendation on the ground that the company was active, solvent and conducting its affairs without any evidence of criminality. The petitioner, a contributory of the company, presented a petition for the compulsory winding up of the company on the ground that it was just and equitable to do so. The petitioner relied largely on the inspectors' report and adopted as its own allegations the findings of the inspectors in their report. The petitioner alleged that as a result of the conduct of one of the directors of the company and the findings of the inspector, stock exchange quotation of the shares of the company had been suspended, to the detriment of the petitioner. The petitioner filed no further evidence in support of the petition. The company moved to have the petition struck out, contending (i) that only the Secretary of State was entitled to rely on the findings in a report of inspectors to support a petition and that any other petitioner suing in his own right as a creditor or a contributory had to make out his case on evidence admissible by the ordinary rules of evidence, (ii) that, since there was no allegation of misconduct or breach of legal duty on the part of the company or its management as such, the mere allegation relating to the director's conduct was insufficient to justify the winding up of the company and (iii) that, in any event, it was embarrassing to the company for the petitioner to adopt the inspectors' report as a whole without classifying or identifying the matters therein which were said by the petitioner to warrant the making of a compulsory winding-up order.

Held – (1) Although a report of inspectors appointed by the Secretary of State under ss 165 and 172 of the 1948 Act was hearsay evidence, it was not ordinary hearsay evidence because the inspectors acted in a statutory fact-finding capacity and were only appointed where there were facts about some aspect of the company's activities which were not readily available and there appeared to the Secretary of State to be a need for an inquiry. Since one reason for appointing inspectors was to protect the interests of minority shareholders in a company, and although in such a case it might not be expedient for the Secretary of State to petition for winding up, it would defeat the object of the inspectors' inquiry if a minority shareholder who wished to petition could not rely on the inspectors' report. It followed that a contributory was entitled to rely on a report of inspectors appointed by the Secretary of State to investigate the affairs of a company to support a petition for the winding up of that company (see p 276 a to g and j, post); Re Travel & Holiday Clubs Ltd [1967] 2 All ER 606, Re SBA Properties Ltd [1967] 2 All ER 615 and Re Armvent Ltd [1975] 3 All ER 441 applied.

(2) The court's jurisdiction to order the winding up of a company on a contributory's petition if it was just and equitable to do so was wide, and whether, in any case, a winding-up order ought to be made depended on a full investigation of the facts of the particular case at the hearing of the petition. It was accordingly appropriate to leave the matter until the hearing of the petition for the company to show if it could, and as part of the material to be considered by the court, that there had been no conduct on the part of the company or its management which would justify the company's winding up (see p 277 a to e, post).

(3) The petition was, however, embarrassing in the form in which it had been presented in that it did not make it sufficiently clear what case the petitioner thought it could make out and it failed to identify the specific matters in the inspectors' report on which the petitioner intended to rely. The motion would accordingly be adjourned to give the petitioner an opportunity to amend the petition (see p 277 g to j, post).

Per Curiam. (1) Although an application to strike out a petition to wind up a company should be made at the earliest opportunity, each case must depend on its own facts, and it is not necessarily too late to apply when the petition has already been given an agreed date for effective hearing (see p 273 b c, post.)

(2) A point that a winding-up petition has not been presented in good faith or that the petitioner does not come to the court with clean hands should be taken in an affidavit, so that the petitioner can direct evidence to the issues it raises which, like other issues of fact, will normally be decided on the effective hearing of the petition, and not by way of motion to strike out the petition (see p 273 f g, post).

(3) It is always open to a company, without filing any evidence to challenge the inspectors' findings, to submit that the findings, even if accepted as wholly correct, are not sufficient to make out that it is just and equitable that the company should be wound up (see p 276 j, post).

Notes

For proceedings arising out of a report of inspectors appointed by the Secretary of State for Trade, see 7 Halsbury's Laws (4th Edn) para 975.

For the admissibility of hearsay evidence in relation to winding-up petitions, see ibid para 1023.

For affidavits in support of a petition, see ibid para 1022, and for cases on the subject, see 10 Digest (Reissue) 959–963, 5667–5691.

For the Companies Act 1948, ss 165, 172, see 5 Halsbury's Statutes (3rd Edn) 243, 248.

Cases referred to in judgment

Armvent Ltd, Re [1975] 3 All ER 441, [1975] 1 WLR 1679, Digest (Cont Vol D) 98, 5690a.

Davis Investments (East Ham) Ltd, Re [1961] 3 All ER 926, [1961] 1 WLR 1396, 10 Digest (Reissue) 926, 5397.

Koscot Interplanetary (UK) Ltd, Re, Re Koscot AG [1972] 3 All ER 829, 10 Digest (Reissue) 962, 5691.

Lubin, Rosen and Associates Ltd, Re [1975] 1 All ER 577, [1975] 1 WLR 122, 10 Digest (Reissue) 942, 5525.

SBA Properties Ltd, Re [1967] 2 All ER 615, [1967] 1 WLR 799, 10 Digest (Reissue) 962, 5690.

Travel & Holiday Clubs Ltd, Re [1967] 2 All ER 606, [1967] 1 WLR 711, 10 Digest (Reissue) 962, 5689.

Cases also cited

ABC Coupler and Engineering Co Ltd (No 2), Re [1962] 3 All ER 68, [1962] 1 WLR 1236.

Allied Produce Co Ltd, Re [1967] 3 All ER 399, [1967] 1 WLR 1469.

Briman Properties Ltd v Barclays Bank [1978] Court of Appeal Transcript 708.

Willcocks (W R) & Co Ltd, Re [1973] 2 All ER 93, [1974] 1 Ch 163.

Motion

By notice of motion, St Piran Ltd ('St Piran') moved for an order to dismiss a petition presented by Runic Nominees Ltd on 12th May 1981 to wind up St Piran on the grounds, inter alia, that it disclosed no reasonable grounds for a winding-up order, that it might prejudice or embarrass a fair trial of the application to wind up St Piran and that it was an abuse of the process of the court. Gasco Investments (Netherlands) BV ('Gasco'), the principal shareholder in St Piran, supported the motion. The facts are set out in the judgment.

Alan Steinfeld for the petitioner.
Charles Aldous for St Piran.
Ralph Instone for Gasco.

Cur adv vult

7th July.   **DILLON J** read the following judgment: I have before me a motion issued on 24th June 1981 whereby St Piran Ltd ('St Piran') seeks to have a petition for the compulsory winding up of St Piran which was presented by a company called Runic Nominees Ltd struck out and dismissed on the grounds that it is embarrassing and an abuse of the process of the court and discloses no reasonable grounds for the relief claimed. The motion is supported by Gasco Investments (Netherlands) BV ('Gasco'), which is the principal shareholder in St Piran.

The winding-up petition was presented on 12th May 1981 by the petitioner as a contributory. It is common ground that St Piran is solvent and there would be a surplus for the contributories in a winding up. The petitioner is the holder of 70,000 shares at 25p each out of a total issued share capital of St Piran of £2,916,746. The basis of the petition is that it is alleged that it is just and equitable that St Piran should be compulsorily a wound up. The petition also refers to relief under s 75 of the Companies Act 1980, but counsel for the petitioner has made it plain that no form of relief other than a compulsory winding-up order is sought. Had other relief been desired it would have been incumbent on the petitioner to indicate the nature of the relief in the petition and that has not been done.

b The petition thus issued on 12th May was mentioned to me in the ordinary Companies List on Monday, 22nd June, that is two days before the present motion was issued, and I then adjourned the petition by consent for effective hearing on a number of days at the end of July 1981 fixed through the usual channels. Counsel for the petitioner has therefore submitted that the motion comes too late. Any application to strike out ought to be made at the earliest opportunity and it is, said counsel for the petitioners, far too late to apply when the petition has already been given an agreed date for effective hearing. I do not take that view. Each case must depend on its own facts and in the circumstances

c of this present case I have no doubt at all that it is expedient that the three main points on which St Piran relies should be considered by the court in advance of any effective hearing of the petition.

Before I come to those points however I should notice briefly a fourth point taken by counsel on behalf of Gasco. Counsel says, no doubt correctly, that any petitioner who comes to the court seeking to have a company wound up on just and equitable grounds

d must come with clean hands, and he submits that the petitioner does not come with clean hands. He hints that the petition may have been presented for ulterior and improper reasons. He puts this forward as a further reason why the petition should be struck out now. In support he refers to two paragraphs in an affidavit of Mr Stone, who is a director of St Piran and also of Gasco, in which it is asserted, and the assertions are admitted, firstly, that the petition was presented and served without any letter before

e action and, secondly, that the filed accounts of the petitioner show, as indeed its name suggests, that it holds its shares in St Piran as a nominee for a third party and has only nominal assets of its own. He adds that the petitioner and its principal have failed to offer any explanation why they seek a winding-up order rather than the much less drastic relief of an order under s 75 that their shares be bought by Gasco at a price fixed by the court. This in my judgment is altogether too oblique a way of taking such a point as that

f a petition is not presented in good faith or that the petitioner does not come to the court with clean hands. If it is desired to take such a point the point should be taken fairly and squarely in an affidavit so that the petitioner can direct evidence to the issues it raises. Those issues, like other issues of fact, will then normally be decided on the effective hearing of the petition and not on a motion to strike out. I should add that I am told that the petitioner in fact holds its shares in St Piran as nominee for its own parent company,

g a substantial South African mining finance company, and that the parent company, which has no locus standi itself as a petitioner, has offered an undertaking in respect of costs.

I turn to the main issues. The activities of St Piran and its directors and in particular of a Mr Raper in relation to the affairs of St Piran have over recent years attracted a good deal of publicity in the financial press, and on 18th December 1979 Her Majesty's

h Secretary of State for Trade appointed inspectors, a Queen's Counsel and a chartered accountant, to investigate the affairs of St Piran under ss 165 and 172 of the Companies Act 1948. The inspectors made their final report on 31st March 1981 and that report has been published by the Secretary of State.

Section 35 of the Companies Act 1967 provides, so far as material, as follows:

j 'If, in the case of any body corporate liable to be wound up under the principal Act, it appears to the Board of Trade from any report made under section 168 . . . that it is expedient in the public interest that the body should be wound up, the Board may, unless the body is already being wound up by the court, present a petition for it to be wound up if the court thinks it just and equitable for it to be so wound up . . .'

In the final sentence of their report the inspectors after referring to s 35 submitted that the Secretary of State might think after considering the report that he had not only the power but the duty to petition the court, thus enabling the shareholders to express their views to the court and the court to reach its own conclusion. This invitation the Secretary of State declined to accept. He made his position clear in a letter released on 7th May 1981. He is not willing to present a petition for the winding up of St Piran or to countenance the expenditure of public money which that would entail. He regards it as no light matter to seek to wind up an active trading company which is solvent and apparently conducting its relations with the outside world without any evidence of criminality.

However, the petitioner has rushed in where the Secretary of State feared to tread and the petition is very largely founded on the inspectors' report. That report is referred to in para 6 of the petition and the allegations on which the petitioner submits that it is just and equitable that St Piran should be wound up by the court are contained in paras 7 and 8 of the petition. These read as follows:

'7. Since in or about March 1973 one John James Raper (hereinafter called Mr. Raper) became a director of the Company and a company or companies acting apparently under his control acquired a substantial shareholding in the Company, the affairs of the Company have been conducted and are continuing to be conducted by or at the direction of Mr. Raper and his associates as identified in the Report in a manner unfairly prejudicial to the interests of your Petitioner and all other shareholders in the Company other than those shareholders who are controlled by Mr. Raper. Full particulars of the manner in which the affairs of the Company have been conducted and are continuing to be conducted as aforesaid and the manner in which the same is unfairly prejudicial to the interests of your Petitioner and the other said shareholders are contained in the findings of the Inspectors in the Report, a copy of which is annexed hereto. Your Petitioner adopts as its own allegations all the findings of the Inspectors in the Report.

'8. In consequence of the refusal of Mr Raper, both individually and through companies controlled by him to comply with a direction of the City Panel on Takeovers and Mergers to make an offer to purchase the whole of the issued share capital in the Company not already owned by Mr Raper and/or any such companies as aforesaid at a price of 85p per share and/or in consequence of the said findings of the Inspectors, the quotation of the shares in the Company on the Stock Exchange has been and continues to be suspended and in consequence of the bid for the whole of the issued share capital of the Company by Gasco Investments (Netherlands) B.V. (one of the companies controlled by Mr. Raper) at 60p per share becoming unconditional on Friday 8th May, 1981 and/or in consequence of the said findings of the Inspectors the quotation on the Stock Exchange of the shares of Milbury Ltd. and South Crofts Ltd., both subsidiaries of the Company was suspended on 8th May, 1981. The marketability of some of the major assets of the Company is thus seriously impaired to the detriment of your Petitioner and other minority shareholders in the Company.'

By way of evidence these allegations and the rest of the petition are merely supported by the usual statutory affidavit in the form required by the Companies (Winding-Up) Rules 1949, SI 1949 No 330, and by an affidavit producing certain documents. There is also a short affidavit by the chairman of a company which formerly held shares in St Piran as to the reasons for that company's accepting the offer by Gasco referred to in para 8 of the petition. The statutory affidavit, being sworn by an officer of the petitioner who has no personal knowledge of the matters dealt with by the inspectors in their report, affords no evidence at all in the normal sense of that word of the matters recorded by the inspectors or of the validity of the inspectors' findings and conclusions.

There is no doubt at all that the general rule is that allegations in a winding-up petition must be proved by proper evidence in accordance with the ordinary rules as to the admissibility of evidence in civil litigation and not by hearsay: see *Re Koscot*

Interplanetary (UK) Ltd [1972] 3 All ER 829. In addition it is a rule of practice, though not
a an inflexible rule of law, that a contributory's winding-up petition in which allegations
of fraud or serious misconduct are made should be supported by affidavits to prove the
fraud or misconduct in addition to the statutory affidavit. There are however two well-
established exceptions to the rule about hearsay evidence. The first is that the court is
entitled to act on the statutory affidavit, although it is often hearsay, because the statutory
affidavit is required by the 1949 rules. Even so however it is open to the court in its
b discretion in an appropriate case to decline to accept a mere statutory affidavit as sufficient
to warrant making a compulsory winding-up order: see *Re Davis Investments (East Ham)
Ltd* [1961] 3 All ER 926, [1961] 1 WLR 1396. The second exception to the hearsay rule
is that the court hearing a winding-up petition can accept the contents of a report by
inspectors appointed by the Secretary of State under the Companies Act 1948 as material
which it is proper for the court to take into consideration if, at any rate, the petition has
c been presented by the Secretary of State under s 35 of the Companies Act 1967 or its
predecessor, s 169(3) of the Companies Act 1948.

The first point therefore taken by St Piran on this motion is that only the Secretary of
State is entitled to rely in support of a petition on the findings in a report of inspectors.
Any other petitioner, it is submitted, suing in his own right as a creditor or contributory
must make out his case by evidence admissible by the ordinary rules. Therefore, as the
d petitioner does not intend to file any further evidence in support of the petition, para 7
which depends entirely on the inspectors' report should be struck out.

The second point taken is that para 8 alleges no misconduct or breach of legal duty on
the part of St Piran or its management as such. Therefore, it is said, an order for the
compulsory winding up of St Piran could not conceivably be made on the allegations in
para 8, and so para 8 also, and therefore the petition as a whole, should be struck out.

e The final point taken is that even if St Piran is wrong on the first point, it is highly
embarrassing for the inspectors' report, which runs to over 200 pages, to be thrown at St
Piran as a whole, as it is by para 7 of the petition, without any attempt by way of
particulars to classify or pick out the matters canvassed in the report which are said by the
petitioners to warrant the making of a compulsory winding-up order.

The leading modern authority on the use of an inspectors' report on a winding-up
f petition presented by the Secretary of State is the decision of Pennycuick J in *Re Travel
& Holiday Clubs Ltd* [1967] 2 All ER 606, [1967] 1 WLR 711. He there held on an
unopposed petition that the court could look at the inspectors' report and, being satisfied
on the report, in the absence of any evidence to the contrary adduced by the company,
that on the basis of the findings in the report it was just and equitable for a company to
be wound up, could make the usual compulsory winding-up order. He pointed out in
g the course of his judgment that under s 169(3) of the Companies Act 1948 there were
two requirements. First, it must appear to the Board of Trade, now the Secretary of State,
from the report that it is expedient by reason of the specified circumstances to present a
winding-up petition, and, second, the court must think it just and equitable to make a
winding-up order. As to the first requirement, under the wording of s 35 which I have
already read it must appear to the Secretary of State to be expedient in the public interest
h that the company should be wound up. That a petition presented by the Secretary of
State is presented because a responsible officer of state is of the view that it is in the public
interest that the petition should be presented or that the company should be wound up
is a factor to which the court always attaches importance in reaching its own decision
whether it is just and equitable that the company concerned should be wound up: see *Re
Lubin, Rosen & Associates Ltd* [1975] 1 All ER 577, [1975] 1 WLR 122. The petitioner
j cannot of course pray that factor in aid in support of this petition. But it is not, as it
seems to me, a factor directly relevant to the question whether or not the petitioner is
entitled to rely on the inspectors' report at all on this petition.

As I understand the judgments of Pennycuick J in *Re Travel & Holiday Clubs Ltd* and
in *Re SBA Properties Ltd* [1967] 2 All ER 615, [1967] 1 WLR 799, which was decided
shortly afterwards, the reason why he held that the Secretary of State was entitled to rely
on the inspectors' report to support his petition was a combination of two factors, first,

that the report was not ordinary hearsay evidence because the inspectors acted in a statutory fact-finding capacity, and, second, that it would be nonsensical if the court *a* could not take the report into consideration in deciding whether it was just and equitable that the company should be wound up when by the very terms of s 169(3) of the 1948 Act, as of s 35 of the 1967 Act, it is on the basis of his consideration of the report that the Secretary of State has concluded that it is expedient that the winding-up petition should be presented or that the company should be wound up. It would be strange in that context if Parliament had intended that the Secretary of State should have to rely on *b* entirely fresh evidence and should not be able to present the report to the court and rely on the findings of the inspectors.

Even if the Secretary of State decides not to present a petition in reliance on the inspectors' report, the inspectors will still have been acting in a statutory fact-finding capacity in making their report. Inspectors will only be appointed where facts about some aspect of a company's activities are not readily available and there appears to be a *c* need for inquiry. The object of the appointment of inspectors is partly in the public interest, particularly where there is suspicion of criminal activities, for instance that the company has been trading in fraud of the public, and it is the Secretary of State in particular who is in this field concerned to protect the public interest. But the object of the appointment may also be to protect the interests of minority shareholders. The circumstances in which inspectors may be appointed are set out in s 165(b) of the *d* Companies Act 1948 and these include in sub-paras (ii) and (iii) the following:

> '(ii) that persons concerned with its formation or the management of its affairs have in connection therewith been guilty of fraud, misfeasance or other misconduct towards it or towards its members; or (iii) that its members have not been given all the information with respect to its affairs which they might reasonably expect.'

e

If inspectors are appointed because there is ground for suspecting that material information has been withheld from shareholders in a company and the inspectors by questioning the directors and examining documents not available to the general body of shareholders establish that this is so and report accordingly, there may well be little public interest involved to make it expedient for the Secretary of State to present a petition. A minority shareholder aggrieved by consistent withholding of material *f* information might none the less wish to petition, and it would to a considerable extent, as it seems to me, defeat the object of having the inspectors' inquiry if the aggrieved shareholder could not rely on their report.

Accordingly I see no valid reason why the inspectors' report cannot be used to support a contributory's petition to the same extent that it can be used to support a petition by the Secretary of State. In his judgment in *Re Travel & Holiday Clubs Ltd* [1967] 2 All ER 606 at 609, [1967] 1 WLR 711 at 715 Pennycuick J stated that a different position would arise *g* if the findings in the inspectors' report were to be challenged by evidence adduced on behalf of the company. That aspect was discussed by Templeman J in *Re Armvent* [1975] 3 All ER 441, [1975] 1 WLR 1679, where he ruled that the opponents of a petition could not exclude a report of inspectors simply by asserting by counsel that the inspectors' findings were challenged. Any challenge had to be by evidence disputing the particular *h* findings which were challenged. If such evidence were adduced then it would be for the judge hearing the petition to weigh all the material before him at the end of the hearing including the report and decide then whether a winding-up order should be made (see [1975] 3 All ER 441 esp at 446, [1975] 1 WLR 1679 esp at 1685). *Re Armvent* is in my judgment as applicable to the petition presented by a contributory in the present case as it is to any petition presented by the Secretary of State.

j

I should add for completeness that it is always open to a company, without filing any evidence to challenge the inspectors' findings, to submit that the findings, even if accepted as wholly correct, are not sufficient to make out that it is just and equitable that the company should be wound up.

For the foregoing reasons I reject the first point taken by St Piran on this motion.

I turn to the second point which is directed at para 8 of the petition. It is said for St Piran that the directions of the City Takeover Panel have no legislative sanction and that the failure of Mr Raper and Gasco or their associates to make a bid for the entire share capital of St Piran as directed by the panel was not an act or omission, let alone a default or misconduct, on the part of St Piran itself or on the part of its management as such. Therefore, it is said, para 8 could never provide grounds for a winding-up order and should be struck out. I do not take such a narrow view. The court has jurisdiction to order the winding up of a company on a contributory's petition if it is just and equitable that the company should be wound up. The words 'just and equitable' are wide general words to be construed generally and taken at their face value. The provisions of the City Code set out a code of conduct which has been laid down by responsible and experienced persons in the City as being fair and reasonable conduct in relation to companies which like St Piran have obtained the benefit of a public quotation on the Stock Exchange. If the directors of a publicly quoted company or the principal shareholders in such a company choose to flout that code of fair and reasonable conduct and to ignore without good reason the consequent directions of the City Takeover Panel, and minority shareholders are injured by the withdrawal of the Stock Exchange quotation for the company's shares, then it seems to me that it could very well be just and equitable in the natural sense of those words that the company should be wound up. Whether in any case a winding-up order should be made would depend on a full investigation of the facts of the particular case. That is a matter for the hearing of the petition and not for this motion.

It is sufficient for the present for me to say that para 8, in my judgment, is not demurrable and to say also that as the concept of justice and equity is a very wide concept it must, in my view, be open to St Piran to show if it can at the hearing of the petition and as a part of the material to be then considered by the court that the panel misdirected itself in making the findings of fact which led to the direction which was disobeyed.

I therefore reject counsel's second point on behalf of St Piran and turn to his third point, that the way the whole of the inspectors' report has been incorporated into para 7 of the petition is highly embarrassing because it does not make it sufficiently clear what case the petitioner thinks it can make out of the report and does not identify the specific matters in the report on which the petitioner intends to rely. Therefore St Piran cannot wholly know what case it has to meet. Oddly, though this point loomed large in counsel's submissions on behalf of St Piran, it was not suggested in Mr Stone's affidavit that the form of the petition is embarrassing for want of particularity. As I have already mentioned, the report runs to over 200 pages. What the inspectors have done, and given their terms of reference it is a sensible approach whether their conclusions be correct or not, is to review the history of St Piran and its affairs in detail since 1973. The report ends with a section headed 'Principal conclusions' which seems to be a summary of the more important matters that are to be found in earlier paragraphs. This section itself runs to some 17 pages and even this section contains many matters as to which I do not as at present advised see how they can be relevant to the petition. This is not a report which paints a picture of unmitigated villainy on the part of everyone concerned with the management of St Piran. What appears from the report, whether or not it is enough if unchallenged to warrant a compulsory winding-up order, is a much more complex picture with some former directors exonerated from all criticism. With such a report it is in my judgment for the petitioner's advisers to do the necessary work of selection and identify the matters discussed in the report on which the petitioner is really relying to establish, on the inspectors' findings, that it is just and equitable that St Piran should be wound up by the court. I therefore find the petition embarrassing in its present form, but the difficulty may well be capable of being cured by amendment.

Accordingly, I propose to adjourn the present motion, if counsel for the petitioner wishes, to give him an opportunity of bringing forward suggested amendments to the petition to particularise the complaints in para 7.

Order accordingly.

Solicitors: *Herbert Smith & Co* (for the petitioner); *Hancock & Willis* (for St Piran and Gasco).

Evelyn M C Budd   Barrister.

Easton and another v Brown

a

CHANCERY DIVISION
GOULDING J
26th, 27th, 28th, 29th JANUARY 1981

Specific performance – Order – Delay in enforcing order – Summons to proceed on order –
Extension of time for proceeding where long period elapsing from date of order – Refusal of b
extension of time – Purchaser obtaining order for specific performance for sale of property with
vacant possession – Purchaser intending to redevelop property – Order not enforced for nearly
eight years because vendor's former wife in occupation of property – Purchaser reaching
agreement with wife to provide her with alternative accommodation – Purchaser applying for
leave to issue summons to proceed on specific performance order – Purchaser having reasonable
explanation for delay – Whether detriment to vendor justifying refusal of extension of time for c
enforcing order – Whether extension of time to be refused only if both insufficient explanation for
delay and detriment to vendor – Whether purchaser entitled to supplemental order for inquiry
as to damage suffered after date of specific performance order by reason of vendor's delay – RSC
Ord 3, r 5(1), Ord 44, r 2(1).

On 1st September 1971 the defendant contracted to sell to the plaintiffs a house and land d
with vacant possession. The plaintiffs wanted the property for the purposes of demolition
and redevelopment. The defendant failed to complete the contract and on 16th
September 1971 the plaintiffs issued a writ against him claiming specific performance of
the contract. They then applied for summary judgment and on 10th August 1972
specific performance of the contract was ordered. The defendant's former wife and the
nine children of the marriage were in occupation of the house. The defendant took no e
steps to get them out of the house because the wife's solicitors contended that she had a
right to remain there. The plaintiffs received legal advice that it was unlikely that they
would succeed in litigation against her. The plaintiffs could not therefore obtain vacant
possession of the property and were consequently unable to obtain the finance they
needed to carry out the redevelopment. Accordingly, for some eight years they took no
steps to enforce the 1972 order for specific performance. In July 1979 they made an f
agreement with the wife whereby she agreed to give up possession of the house in return
for alternative accommodation provided by the plaintiffs. The difficulty in the way of
enforcing the 1972 specific performance order being thus removed, the plaintiffs, on 3rd
June 1980, took out a summons seeking leave to proceed on the 1972 order
notwithstanding that the ten day limit for proceeding on the order prescribed by RSC
Ord 44, r 2(1)[a] had expired. On 27th February 1980 the plaintiffs had applied by another g
summons for orders supplementing the 1972 order including an order for an inquiry as
to the damage they had suffered by the defendant's failure to complete the contract of
sale after the 1972 order. The defendant applied by summons for an order staying all
further proceedings in the plaintiffs' action for specific performance because of their
inordinate delay in prosecuting their claim. He contended that, having regard to the
length of time which had elapsed since the 1972 order and in all the circumstances, an h
extension of the time to proceed should not be granted under RSC Ord 3, r 5(1)[b], or,
alternatively, that it would be inequitable to grant an extension of time because of the
detriment the defendant would suffer because of the delay, since the decrease in the value

---

a   Rule 2(1), so far as material, provides: 'Where in order to carry out any directions contained in a
     judgment given in a cause or matter in the Chancery Division it is necessary to proceed in
     chambers under the judgment, the party entitled to prosecute the judgment must, within 10 days   j
     after entry of the judgment, leave a copy of it at the judge's chambers with a certificate that it is
     a true copy of the judgment as entered.'
b   Rule 5(1), so far as material, provides: 'The Court may, on such terms as it thinks just, by order
     extend . . . the period within which a person is required . . . by these rules . . . to do any act in any
     proceedings.'

of the purchase price made him less able to carry out his duty to house his former wife
a and children.

Held – (1) It was a principle of equity that leave to enforce a decree of specific
performance would be refused where a long period of time had elapsed since the decree
was made and there was both an insufficient explanation by the plaintiff for the delay in
enforcing the decree and detriment to the defendant arising from the delay. Since the
b plaintiffs had acted reasonably in waiting until they obtained the wife's co-operation
before attempting to enforce the 1972 specific performance order and therefore had a
reasonable explanation for their delay, both elements for a refusal of the order were not
present, and therefore the mere fact that there might be detriment to the defendant
through the lapse of time in enforcing the order did not justify a refusal to extend the
time for enforcing the order. In any event the defendant would not suffer detriment
since alternative accommodation for his wife was being provided at the plaintiffs' expense
c so that the defendant would be relieved of any duty he had to house her (see p 282 *j* to
p 283 *b* and *e* to *h*, post); *McKenna v Richey* [1950] VLR 360 applied.

(2) The plaintiffs' summons of 3rd June 1980 would be granted by extending the time
for issuing a summons to proceed on the 1972 order, and the plaintiffs' summons of 27th
February 1980 would stand as the summons to proceed. Moreover, the order on that
d summons could include, as a supplement to the 1972 order, an order for an inquiry
whether the plaintiffs had suffered any damage after 10th August 1972 by reason of the
defendant's delay in completing the contract for sale, because the plaintiffs had proved
that their reasonable delay in enforcing the 1972 order had for several years held up their
development scheme and that, in the circumstances, was sufficient for the court to order
an inquiry as to damages. It followed that the defendant's summons would be dismissed
e (see p 283 *h j* and p 284 *d* to *f*, post); *Ford-Hunt v Raghbir Singh* [1973] 2 All ER 700
applied.

Notes
For extension of the time appointed by the Rules of the Supreme Court for taking any
proceedings, see 30 Halsbury's Laws (3rd Edn) 402, para 755.

f ### Cases referred to in judgment
Ford-Hunt v Raghbir Singh [1973] 2 All ER 700, [1973] 1 WLR 738, Digest (Cont Vol D)
1056, 2035*a*.
McKenna v Richey [1950] VLR 360, [1950] ALR 773.

Cases also cited
g *Dixon v Kennaway & Co* [1900] 1 Ch 833.
Lamb (W T) & Sons v Rider [1948] 2 All ER 402, [1948] 2 KB 331, CA.
McIlkenny v Chief Constable of West Midlands Police Force [1980] 2 All ER 227, [1980] QB
283, CA.
Quennell v Maltby [1979] 1 All ER 568, [1979] 1 WLR 318, CA.

h ### Summonses
On 10th August 1972 May J ordered specific performance of a contract for the sale of a
house and land made on 1st September 1971 between the defendant, Oscar Ebenezer
Brown, as the vendor, and the plaintiffs, Jack Arthur Easton and his wife, Beryl Eileen
Easton, as the purchasers. By a summons dated 27th February 1980 the plaintiffs applied
for the following relief: (1) an order that on their paying into court to the credit of the
j action between them and the defendant the sum of £18,900, being the balance certified
as due from them in accordance with a certificate dated 10th August 1972, and on
production to the defendant of the certificate of lodgement in court of the money, the
defendant should forthwith deliver conveyances duly executed in accordance with the
order of 10th August 1972 and forthwith deliver all deeds and writings in his possession
or power relating solely to the property in question; (2) that in the event of non-

compliance by the defendant with the 1972 order there should be execution of
conveyances by a person appointed by the court, under s 47 of the Supreme Court of **a**
Judicature (Consolidation) Act 1925; and (3) an order for an inquiry as to the damage
caused to the plaintiffs by the defendant's failure to procure the release of all charges
affecting the property which should have been released prior to completion. By a
summons dated 12th May 1980 the defendant applied for an order staying all further
proceedings in the action because of the plaintiffs' inordinate delay in prosecuting their
claims and the prejudice which would be caused to the defendant's former wife, Mrs **b**
Mary Helen Spurge, and to the children of the marriage. By a further summons dated
16th May 1980, the plaintiffs applied for liberty to pay the sum of £18,900 into court
and not to the defendant, as ordered on 10th August 1972. On 3rd June 1980 the
plaintiffs took out a summons applying for leave to issue a summons to proceed on the
order of 10th August 1972 notwithstanding the expiry of the time limited for so doing
under RSC Ord 44, r 2. The facts are set out in the judgment. **c**

Robert Reid QC for the plaintiffs.
Jonathan Fulthorpe for the defendant.

GOULDING J. This is, as has been said, an extraordinary case. It all arose from a
contract in writing for the sale and purchase of a house and land which was made as long **d**
ago as 1st September 1971. It was made between the defendant, Oscar Ebenezer Brown,
of the one part and the plaintiffs, Jack Arthur Easton and his wife, Beryl Eileen Easton,
of the other part. The defendant was the vendor; the plaintiffs were the purchasers. The
property sold, as I have said, was a house and land at Warblington, near Havant. The
purchase money was £21,000. A 10% deposit was paid to the solicitors, Messrs Coffin,
Mew & Clover, as stakeholders. Those solicitors originally acted for both vendor and **e**
purchasers. The property was sold with vacant possession on completion, and completion
within 28 days was contemplated.

On the face of it, that seems quite an ordinary and straightforward contract. However,
although the conveyancing by the solicitors got to an advanced stage, completion did not
take place and the plaintiffs began this action by writ. The writ is dated 16th September
1971. It was specially endorsed with a claim for specific performance of the contract; **f**
further or alternatively, damages for breach of contract; alternatively, rescission of the
contract and repayment of the deposit, with a declaration of lien.

The plaintiffs applied for summary judgment, pursuant to RSC Ord 86. That
application was opposed by the defendant, and he made his case for leave to defend by
affidavit in the usual way. I think that his proposed defence really contained three
elements. First, that he denied that he had signed the contract in such a way as to make **g**
it binding on him. I need not go into the details of his contention in that respect.
Second, he alleged that there had been at the best negligence, and at the worst some
dishonest conduct, on the part of the solicitors acting for both sides because one of their
partners was, through a company, indirectly interested in the deal. The third matter,
put forward in a very jejune way in the last paragraph of the defendant's affidavit in the
Ord 86 proceedings, is this: 'The property is now the home of my former wife Helen **h**
Mary Spurge and our nine children who divorced me approximately five years ago.' The
affidavit does not contain any allegation as to any right or interest of Mrs Spurge or the
children, nor an assertion that the defendant was unable to give vacant possession, but
that, I think, must have been the force of the allegation, that if specific performance were
ordered, in effect he would be ordered to do the impossible because he could not get his
former wife out.

However that may be, the plaintiffs' application for judgment came before May J, **j**
sitting as vacation judge, in 1972, and he made an order on 10th August 1972. He
declared that the contract ought to be specifically performed and ordered the same
accordingly. He in the ordinary way directed the plaintiffs' costs to be assessed in
chambers and, when assessed, to be deducted from the balance of purchase money. Then

his order recorded that the plaintiffs, on behalf of themselves and of a sub-purchaser of
a part of the property, named Bridgewalk Construction Ltd, had accepted the defendant's
title and that draft conveyances, one to the plaintiffs and one to the company, Bridgewalk
Construction Ltd, had been approved on behalf of all parties. The judge finally, in
common form, ordered execution of the conveyances by the defendant, the fixing of an
appointment for completion, and the delivery of the conveyances and other documents
of title by the defendant to the plaintiffs on payment of the certified balance of purchase
b money less costs. The order ended:

> 'And it is ordered that the defendant do give to the plaintiffs on behalf of
> themselves and of the said Bridgewalk Construction Limited vacant possession of
> the said property And the parties are to be at liberty to apply.'

So the contract was made on 1st September 1971 and the decree of specific
c performance, in terms that I have summarised, on 10th August 1972.

Nearly eight years after the latter date, on 3rd June 1980, the plaintiffs have taken out
a summons for leave to issue a summons to proceed notwithstanding the expiry of the
time limited for so doing. The time in question is limited by the RSC Ord 44, r 2, which
requires the plaintiffs to take out a summons to proceed within ten days after entry of the
judgment. So the plaintiffs come nearly eight years late asking for an extension of time
d under the general provisions of the rules, no special directions being given in Ord 44.
The relevant general provision is contained in Ord 3, r 5.

It is common ground that the court has a discretion whether to extend the time or
not. It is common ground that it is for the plaintiffs to explain and excuse the
extraordinary delay that has taken place. It is common ground that in exercising its
discretion, the court must consider what, at the present time when the discretion is to be
e exercised, is equitable between the plaintiffs and the defendant.

The nature of the court's discretion and duty was considered by O'Bryan J of the
Supreme Court of Victoria in *McKenna v Richey* [1950] VLR 360 which, so far as counsel's
researches have disclosed, seems to be the nearest reported case to the present. I will read
only a short passage from it. The judge, having cited certain 19th century English
authorities on the making of a decree of specific performance, continued (at 367):

f
> 'These cases illustrate how a Court of Equity will not decree specific performance
> if the plaintiff's delay in coming for such relief makes it inequitable to the defendant
> who has broken his contract, so to decree. In this case, of course, we are dealing with
> what took place after judgment. But, in my opinion, the Court, in its equitable
> jurisdiction, would be as careful to preserve the equities between the parties as well
> after the decree as before it, and if the plaintiff has been guilty after judgment of
g > delays which now make it equitable [sic] to make further orders for the purpose of
> specifically enforcing the contract, the Court, even after the decree, will refuse to
> her its aid by making further ancillary orders. In my opinion this result follows
> even if the plaintiff's delays have been induced by the belief, reasonably founded on
> the defendant's conduct, that the defendant was still unwilling to fulfil her
> obligations under the contract and the judgment. On the principle of the cases last
h > referred to, if she delayed for an unreasonable time to enforce her judgment because
> she thought the defendant would not help to get her son out of the premises and the
> defendant has been prejudiced thereby, Equity will not help her.'

The explanations for delay given by the plaintiffs in the present case turn essentially on
the position of Mrs Spurge, the former wife of the defendant. She was at all material
j times resident in the house which forms part of the property sold and that was known
at all material times to both sides. After obtaining the order of May J, the plaintiffs,
through their solicitors, entered into correspondence with Mrs Spurge's solicitors. They
invited particulars of Mrs Spurge's claim to remain in the property and they did not get
them. Mrs Spurge's solicitors (perhaps wisely, for I do not know to this day what the
nature of her claim, if any, was) refrained from giving any particulars and, after some

few months of correspondence, in February 1973, they said: 'In our view our client has a right to continue in occupation of the premises', and, in effect, they challenged the *a* plaintiffs and their sub-purchaser (a company in which the first plaintiff is interested) to proceed against Mrs Spurge by litigation.

Thereupon, the plaintiffs were in a difficulty. They and their sub-purchaser wanted the property to build houses on it in accordance with planning permission which had already been obtained. But they were not people with big financial resources. They could only embark on the development operations with finance from the bank and the *b* bank, not unnaturally, was unwilling to assist them until it was clear that they had, or could obtain, vacant possession of the whole of the property. At all times it was contemplated, so it would appear, that the demolition of the existing dwelling-house would be part of the necessary development.

Accordingly, the plaintiffs took legal advice through their solicitors from a number of different counsel practising in different branches of the law. They were under the *c* difficulty that they did not really know what rights Mrs Spurge might have. They seem to have been unable to obtain any legal advice sanguine enough to encourage them to sue her. So no summons to proceed under May J's order was taken out and the years passed by, with Mrs Spurge and her children still living in the house and the defendant still not performing his contract. The deposit has at all times remained in the hands of Messrs Coffin, Mew & Clover so far as appears from any evidence before me.   *d*

Those are the reasons given by the plaintiffs for their delay to proceed under the judgment for many years. The defendant has suggested another and less creditable reason. He goes back to his allegations against the solicitors who acted for him and the plaintiffs in 1971. They are of course not open to him now by way of challenge to the validity of May J's order, against which the defendant did not appeal. He made the allegations then and they were by necessary implication rejected. But he does say that *e* the plaintiffs were anxious to avoid embarrassment to Messrs Coffin, Mew & Clover and that was, or may have been, the real reason for their not proceeding with the judgment which they had obtained against the defendant. On the evidence of witnesses who have been cross-examined before me, I wholly reject that contention. It is the more improbable in that the solicitors themselves, when the defendant did not pay their charges against him, sued him in the Portsmouth County Court, where he again raised *f* this matter of their alleged negligence or misconduct.

Then the situation changed at the beginning of 1978. A son of Mrs Spurge got in touch with the plaintiffs and their sub-purchaser. It appears that he and his mother, or both of them, were anxious about the continued existence of the decree of specific performance and the insecurity to which it exposed their occupation of the house, and wanted to see if they could improve their position. I do not believe on the evidence that *g* the occurrences that prompted Mrs Spurge's approach to the plaintiffs were in any way provoked by the plaintiffs. However that may be, she did in fact, at first in person with one or more of her sons and later through solicitors, negotiate with the plaintiffs and the sub-purchaser. In the end an agreement was drawn up and executed under which, at the expense of the plaintiffs or their sub-purchaser, alternative accommodation is to be provided for Mrs Spurge in the form of a house that she is to be able to occupy and, more *h* than that, if she ceases to occupy it and it is sold, she is to get half the proceeds of sale. That is all at the expense of the plaintiffs or the sub-purchaser and, accordingly, that agreement having been made on 9th July 1979, the difficulty in the way of enforcing the decree of specific performance was removed and so the plaintiffs came back and took out their summons. Mrs Spurge gave evidence herself. She said, in effect, that she had repented of the agreement she had made in 1979, but she did not claim not to be bound *j* by it, and I myself think that her discontent arises in part from an insufficient understanding of certain provisions of the agreement. However that may be, there it is and the parties have the benefit of it today.

I think that the plaintiffs have given a reasonable explanation of and excuse for

allowing the judgment to remain unenforced for so long. The defendant had in the
a plainest possible terms contracted to give vacant possession and the court had ordered
him to give it. It appeared that there was a third party who might have rights and who
might present difficulties. The defendant did nothing, and clearly was not going to do
anything, to get her out. In all those circumstances, it seems to me that the plaintiffs
cannot be said, as between themselves and the defendant, to have acted unreasonably. I
think there was no point in taking out a summons to proceed in the circumstances. It
b is no good taking a pilot on board if the weather outside is too bad to pass through the
harbour mouth.

However, the defendant, while maintaining in the first place that a delay of this length
and in these circumstances is fatal of itself, submits that if that argument is rejected, as
I do reject it, then at any rate it is not equitable to give the plaintiffs the extension of time
they now seek if meanwhile the defendant has altered his position to his detriment. The
c detriment suggested is this, that the defendant has at all times accepted a moral duty to
house his former wife, with whom the numerous progeny of their union reside.
Whether he is under any legal duty to provide a home for that family is not in
evidence. But at least, it is said, he has and accepts a moral duty to provide that home.
Had the order of 1972 been promptly enforced, then, it is said, the purchasing power of
£21,000 being what it then was, he could have provided an alternative home for Mrs
d Spurge and the children. Today, with the rise in value of all property, including that of
the subject matter of the contract, he will get no part of the enhanced value and the
£21,000 will not find an alternative home for the family today. Counsel for the
plaintiffs doubts on the evidence that the defendant's financial position was such in 1972
that he could have retained enough of the purchase money to provide the alternative
accommodation. Those doubts may or may not be well founded. I do not propose to
e decide the case on them. Counsel, I think, is on firm ground when, in the alternative, he
says that there is no detriment to the defendant because the plaintiffs or their sub-
purchaser have now at their own expense provided alternative accommodation that will
relieve the defendant of the duty he is so anxious to fulfil. That I think is a sound answer.

Moreover, I think there may be another answer. As I understand the equitable
principle involved and the words of the Australian judgment from which I read an
f extract, the enforcement of the decree after a long lapse of time will be refused on the
coincidence of two elements, namely the lack of a sufficient explanation of the delay by
the plaintiffs and the suffering of some detriment by the defendant. If, as between the
plaintiffs and the defendant, the plaintiffs have acted reasonably (as here I hold that the
plaintiffs did) the defendant, having full knowledge of whatever difficulties there may
have been, contracted to give vacant possession and made no attempt to do so. If they
g acted reasonably in waiting until they could get co-operation from Mrs Spurge, then I
think the mere fact that there may have been detriment to the defendant through the
lapse of time is not sufficient ground for refusing enforcement of the order that the court
has made. Of course, all these matters turn on the whole facts of the particular case.
Here, in my judgment, there is no sufficient equity to refuse the extension of time
sought.

h In an endeavour to avoid unnecessary delay or avoidable expense, I propose on
summons no 4, as it is numbered before me (that is to say, the plaintiffs' summons dated
3rd June 1980) to extend the time for the issue of a summons to proceed on the order of
1972 over to today and to order also that the summons taken out by the plaintiffs on 27th
February 1980, which is the summons no 1 in the bundle before me, do stand as the
summons to proceed. It appears to me that the corollary to those orders is that the
j defendant's summons, which is no 3 in the bundle, dated 12th May 1980, seeking a stay
of all further proceedings in the action because of inordinate delay on the part of the
plaintiffs in the prosecution of their claims and prejudice to Mrs Spurge and her children,
must be dismissed.

If that order is right, then it remains for me to hear submissions on the summons no a that I have ordered to stand as the summons to proceed, on which the plaintiffs seek certain supplemental orders or directions, and the summons no 2, dated 16th May 1980, relating simply to payment of the balance of purchase money into court.

[After a short adjournment, his Lordship continued:] Now I shall give judgment on the two remaining summonses that are before me.

I should perhaps say by way of introduction that on 10th August 1972 May J gave the plaintiffs a decree for specific performance of a contract for the sale of land with vacant possession by the defendant to the plaintiffs in the usual form where the title has been accepted and the form of the conveyance previously agreed. A short time ago I gave leave to the plaintiffs to take out a summons to proceed on the order of 1972, notwithstanding the great lapse of time. I also directed that a summons dated 27th February 1980 do stand as the summons to proceed. I now propose to give judgment in the first place on that summons of 27th February 1980.

Apart from the costs of the application, it seeks relief under three heads. It will be convenient to deal with the third first. That seeks an inquiry as to the damage caused to the plaintiffs by the defendant's failure to procure the release of charges affecting the property free of which he should have conveyed, but not discharged on completion. Then there is a mention of a certain mortgage to Barclays Bank, which I was told on instructions no longer exists, and the occupation of the property by the defendant's former wife.

It is submitted, in the first place, that it is not shown that the plaintiffs have suffered any damage by the defendant's long failure after the date of the decree to complete the contract. However, it was proved by one of the plaintiffs that the delay held up a scheme of building development on the land for several years and I think that is sufficient for the court, in the circumstances, to order an inquiry as to damages, if any. I propose to follow precisely the precedent (although I can see certain theoretical difficulties about it which may be due to my own lack of understanding) in *Ford-Hunt v Raghbir Singh* [1973] 2 All ER 700, [1973] 1 WLR 738, a reserved judgment of Brightman J. I shall do as he did. As a supplement to the order of 1972, I shall direct an inquiry whether the plaintiffs have suffered any and what damage after 10th August 1972 by reason of the defendant's delay in completing the agreement in the order of 10th August 1972 referred to. And whatever else I say about costs of these applications hereafter, the costs of the inquiry will be reserved.

Continuing backwards to the second paragraph of the summons of 27th February 1980, that paragraph seeks an order that, in the event of non-compliance by the defendant with the order of 1972, under the provisions of s 47 of the Supreme Court of Judicature (Consolidation) Act 1925 there should be execution of conveyances by a person appointed by the court. I am not going to assume that the defendant will disobey the order of the court and I shall direct that paragraph of the summons to stand over generally.

Then in the first paragraph of the summons the plaintiffs seek what is purely, to my mind, a variation (in the light of subsequent circumstances) of the order of 1972, because they seek a direction that instead of payment on completion to the defendant of the balance of purchase money less costs, they, the plaintiffs, should be permitted to pay that balance into court. They also desire (and I am now going back to the third paragraph) directions for the payment out of that money of any damages found due from the defendant. I am bound to say that, no precedent having been cited, I am of opinion that the court has no jurisdiction to vary the order of 1972 in that way, although, as in other matters affecting the breadth of equitable jurisdiction, I do not regard the matter as obvious or easy.

So, then, I decline to make an order on para 1 of this summons. That also involves dismissal of a summons dated 16th May 1980, which is a formal application on the part of the plaintiffs for liberty to pay money into court. The order that I make today should contain (I cannot give a time or place now but that can be done in chambers) a statement of a time and place for completion in pursuance of the order of 1972. That should, in my view, be not less than one calendar month and not more than two calendar months

ahead. If the parties cannot agree a time and place, it will have to be appointed by the
master before the order is drawn up.

Order accordingly.

Solicitors: *Robbins, Olivey & Lake*, agents for *Blake, Lapthorn, Rea & Williams*, Portsmouth
(for the plaintiffs); *Thomas Eggar & Son*, Chichester (for the defendant).

Evelyn M C Budd   Barrister.

Dunkley v Evans and another

QUEEN'S BENCH DIVISION
ORMROD LJ AND WEBSTER J
24th MARCH, 15th APRIL 1981

*Statutory instrument – Validity – Part of instrument invalid – Severance of invalid part –
Invalid part not inextricably interconnected with valid part – Whether whole instrument invalid
– Whether invalid part may be severed leaving valid part in force – West Coast Herring
(Prohibition of Fishing) Order 1978 (SI 1978 No 930).*

Where it is possible to sever an invalid part of an order, rule or regulation made in
exercise of a power conferred by an Act of Parliament from a valid part of that order, rule
or regulation then, unless the invalid part is inextricably interconnected with the valid
part, the court is entitled to set aside or disregard the invalid part, leaving the rest intact.
Accordingly the West Coast Herring (Prohibition of Fishing) Order 1978 which was
made under the Sea Fish (Conservation) Act 1967 and which purports to prohibit herring
fishing within a defined area is not invalidated by the inclusion in the defined area of an
area of sea adjacent to the coast of Northern Ireland which, by virtue of s 23(1) of the
1967 Act, as amended by the Fishery Limits Act 1976, is excluded from the waters in
which the 1967 Act gives power to prohibit fishing (see p 287 *g* to *j* and p 288 *e f*, post).
Dictum of Cussen J in *Olsen v City of Camberwell Corpn* [1926] VLR at 68 adopted.
Hotel and Catering Industry Training Board v Automobile Pty Ltd [1969] 2 All ER 582 and
Agricultural, Horticultural and Forestry Industry Training Board v Aylesbury Mushrooms Ltd
[1972] 1 All ER 280 followed.

Notes

For severance of partly invalid orders or other instruments, see 1 Halsbury's Laws (4th
Edn) para 26.
For fishery limits, see 18 ibid para 745, for general restrictions on sea fishing, see ibid
para 764, and for power to restrict fishing for sea fish, see ibid paras 776–777.
For the Sea Fish (Conservation) Act 1967, ss 5, 23, see 13 Halsbury's Statutes (3rd Edn)
1028.
For the Fishery Limits Act 1976, see 46 ibid 598.

Cases referred to in judgment

Agricultural, Horticultural and Forestry Industry Training Board v Aylesbury Mushrooms Ltd
[1972] 1 All ER 280, [1972] 1 WLR 190, [1972] ITR 16, Digest (Cont Vol D) 937,
37 *ja.*
Carltona Ltd v Comrs of Works [1943] 2 All ER 560, CA, 17 Digest (Reissue) 490, *131.*
Hotel and Catering Industry Training Board v Automobile Pty Ltd [1969] 2 All ER 582, [1969]
1 WLR 697, [1969] TR 177, 6 KIR 447, HL, Digest (Cont Vol C) 981 *37c.*

Olsen v City of Camberwell Corpn [1926] VLR 58, 47 ALT 116, [1926] Argus LR 40, 38
  Digest (Repl) 241, *674.   *a*
Point of Ayr Colleries v Lloyd-George [1943] 2 All ER 546, CA, 17 Digest (Reissue) 540, *313*.
Potato Marketing Board v Merricks [1958] 2 All ER 538, [1958] 2 QB 316, [1958] 3 WLR
  135, 2 Digest (Reissue) 159, *976*.
Strickland v Hayes [1896] 1 QB 290, 65 LJMC 55, 74 LT 137, 60 JP 164, 18 Cox CC 244,
  DC, 38 Digest (Repl) 178, *103*.
                                                                                                                   b
Case also cited
Hoffman-La Roche (F) & Co AG v Secretary of State for Trade and Industry [1974] 2 All ER
  1128, [1975] AC 295, HL.

Case stated
The prosecutor, Daniel John Dunkley, appealed by way of case stated by the justices for   *c*
the county of Humberside acting in and for the petty sessional division of Great Grimsby
Borough in respect of their adjudication as a magistrates' court sitting at the Law Courts,
Great Grimsby on 16th December 1980, whereby they dismissed certain informations
laid by the appellant against the respondents, Raymond Evans and Sandy Fishing Co Ltd.
   On 12th November 1979 informations were preferred by the appellant against the
respondents that they had, on or about 14th October 1979, within British fishery limits,   *d*
and within the area specified in the schedule to the West Coast Herring (Prohibition of
Fishing) Order 1978, SI 1978 No 930, as being an area in which such fishing is prohibited,
being the master/owners of the British fishing vessel Grimsby Lady (Gy 430), fished for
herring contrary to art 2 of the 1978 order and s 5(1) of the Sea Fish (Conservation) Act
1967. The justices heard the informations on 16th December 1980 and found the
following facts which had been formally admitted on behalf of the respondents: (i)   *e*
Raymond Evans was, from 3rd October 1979, the master of the British fishing vessel
Grimsby Lady; (ii) Sandy Fishing Co Ltd was, at all material times, the owner of the
vessel; (iii) on or about 14th October 1979, Raymond Evans fished for herring from the
vessel within British fishery limits at position 56°30′ N, 10°00′ W. It was contended by
the appellant that, although the order was invalid as to part of the area included in the
schedule to the order, ie an area adjacent to Northern Ireland, any offence committed in   *f*
the remainder of the area should result in a conviction. The Northern Ireland waters
were clearly defined and severable. The Grimsby Lady was fishing in that area for which
the minister had power to make the order. The part of the area which was invalid could
be separated without altering the character of the rest of the order. It was contended by
the respondents that where the good law was inextricably inseparable from the bad law
in the order, whereby the order needed rewriting, then the order would be invalid. The
wording of the schedule to the 1978 order and s 23(1) of the 1967 Act needed   *g*
amendment, and could not be made valid by striking out words in the schedule. The
justices were of the opinion that the area described in the schedule to the order was
unambiguous, but that it included Northern Ireland waters which the minister had no
power to include in the order and that the order was ultra vires. They preferred the
contention of the respondents that severance of the invalid area from the area described   *h*
in the schedule could not be supported by case law. They accordingly dismissed the
informations. The prosecutor appealed. The question for the opinion of the High Court
was whether the justices were right in holding the 1978 order to be invalid.

John Davies QC and *Peter Langdon-Davies* for the appellant.
Nicholas Phillips QC and *Mark Cran* for the respondents.
                                                                                                                   j

                                                                                          Cur adv vult

15th April. **ORMROD LJ** read the following judgment of the court: This is an appeal
by case stated by the prosecutor from the dismissal on 16th December 1980 by the

justices for the county of Humberside, sitting at Great Grimsby, of informations alleging
a that the respondents, on 14th October 1979, had fished for herring in a prohibited area,
contrary to art 2 of the West Coast Herring (Prohibition of Fishing) Order 1978, SI 1978
No 930.

It was admitted by the respondents that they had been fishing for herring at a position
56°30′ N, 10°00′ W, which is within the area referred to in the order, contrary to art 2.
The defence was that this order was ultra vires the ministers who purported to make it
b under the terms of the Sea Fish (Conservation) Act 1967.

The justices accepted this submission and dismissed the informations. They now ask
if they were right to do so. The point arises in this way. Under s 5(2) of the Sea Fish
(Conservation) Act 1967, the ministers concerned may make orders prohibiting fishing
within the area of the British fishery limits as defined in the Act, as amended.

The 1978 order prohibited fishing for herring within the area of the sea defined in the
c schedule, that is, the area lying within British fishery limits and bounded by a line
defined by a series of co-ordinates set out in the schedule. It was conceded that the
respondents were fishing for herring at a point which was within British fishery limits
and within the area defined by the co-ordinates.

However, s 23(1) of the 1967 Act, as amended by the Fishery Limits Act 1976,
provides that the minister's powers under the 1967 Act shall not extend over a defined
d area of the sea adjacent to the coast of Northern Ireland 40 miles long by 9 miles wide.

The prosecutor conceded that the minister's power to make regulations did not extend
over this relatively small area of the sea, notwithstanding that the Secretary of State for
Northern Ireland was one of the ministers who made the order. Powers over this area
were reserved to the government of Northern Ireland. We understand that at present
the power to make prohibition orders in respect of this area of the sea is vested in the
e Department of Agriculture (Northern Ireland), a statutory corporation which can make
the necessary orders itself. The Secretary of State for Northern Ireland has no power
personally to make such orders.

The prosecutor submits that the fact that this order is ultra vires in so far as this area
off the coast of Northern Ireland is concerned does not render the whole order ultra
vires. Counsel for the respondents contends that the whole order is rendered invalid by
f including this area of the sea. The offending area represents 0·8% of the area covered by
the order.

The only question, therefore, is whether it is possible to sever the invalid part from the
valid part of the order, or whether the whole order is invalidated by the inclusion of this
small area.

The general principle is stated in 1 Halsbury's Laws (4th Edn) para 26 thus:

g   'Unless the invalid part is inextricably interconnected with the valid, a court is
    entitled to set aside or disregard the invalid part, leaving the rest intact.'

The principle is more fully formulated in the judgment of Cussen J in the Supreme
Court of Victoria in *Olsen v City of Camberwell Corpn* [1926] VLR 58 at 68, where he said:

    'If the enactment with the invalid portion omitted is so radically or substantially
h   different a law as to the subject matter dealt with by what remains from what it
    would be with the omitted portions forming part of it as to warrant the belief that
    the legislative body intended it as a whole only, or in other words, to warrant belief
    that if all could not be carried into effect, the legislative body would not have
    enacted the remainder independently, then the whole must fail.'

j   We respectfully agree with and adopt this statement of the law. It would be difficult
to imagine a clearer example than the present case of a law which the legislative body
would have enacted independently of the offending portion and which is so little affected
by eliminating the invalid portion. This is clearly, therefore, an order which the court
should not strive officiously to kill to any greater extent that it is compelled to do.

Counsel for the respondents submitted that the court must confine the ministers 'within the four corners of the powers given by the legislature', and referred us to two judgments by Lord Greene MR in *Point of Ayr Collieries Ltd v Lloyd-George* [1943] 2 All ER **a** 546 and *Carltona Ltd v Comrs of Works* [1943] 2 All ER 560. That will be the precise effect of eliminating the invalid portion of the order in question.

He also submitted that the ministers did not apply their minds to the right question. With respect, the question was the prohibition of herring fishing in an area off the west coast to which they clearly applied their minds. Someone, however, overlooked the powers of the Department of Agriculture (Northern Ireland) and probably failed to **b** appreciate the niceties of the present constitutional position of the Secretary of State for Northern Ireland.

His main point, however, was that the court could not sever the invalid portion of this order from the remainder because it was not possible to excise from the text of the order the words which rendered part of it invalid. This is the so-called 'blue pencil test'.

This test has been elaborated mainly in connection with covenants in restraint of **c** trade. No doubt the court will not and cannot rewrite contracts, and so confines itself to deleting part of the text when it is able to do so. The same policy has been followed in relation to byelaws where the text permitted (see *Strickland v Hayes* [1896] 1 QB 290) and to a demand for a return, part of which could be struck out from a form (see *Potato Marketing Board v Merricks* [1958] 2 All ER 538, [1958] 2 QB 316).

We can see no reason why the powers of the court to sever the invalid portion of a **d** piece of subordinate legislation from the valid should be restricted to cases where the text of the legislation lends itself to judicial surgery or textual emendation by excision. It would have been competent for the court in an action for a declaration that the provisions of the order in this case did not apply to the area of the sea off Northern Ireland reserved by s 23(1) of the 1967 Act, as amended, to make the declaration sought, without in any way affecting the validity of the order in relation to the remaining 99·2% of the area **e** referred to in the schedule to the order.

Such an order was made, in effect, by the House of Lords in *Hotel and Catering Industry Training Board v Automobile Pty Ltd* [1969] 2 All ER 582, [1969] 1 WLR 697 and by Donaldson J in *Agricultural, Horticultural and Forestry Industry Training Board v Aylesbury Mushrooms Ltd* [1972] 1 All ER 280, [1972] 1 WLR 190.

Accordingly we hold that the West Coast Herring (Prohibition of Fishing) Order 1978 **f** is not ultra vires the ministers who made the order, save in so far as it affects the area of the sea reserved by s 23(1) of the Sea Fish (Conservation) Act 1967, as amended, and answer the question put at the end of the case in the negative.

The appeal is, therefore, allowed. The case will be remitted to the justices to convict the respondents and impose the appropriate penalty or penalties.

g

Appeal allowed. Case remitted to the justices.

The court refused leave to appeal to the House of Lords but certified, under s 1(2) of the Administration of Justice Act 1960, that the following points of law of general public importance were involved in the decision: 1. whether where a statutory instrument (on the true construction of which criminal liability depends) has been made partly ultra vires, the court can construe it and give effect to it in so far as it would probably have applied had it been made intra vires; 2. if so, in what circumstances and on what principles should the court act in deciding whether so to construe and give effect to it? In particular, is the doctrine of severance applicable? If so, should the court apply the 'blue pencil test' or some other, and if so what, test?

Solicitors: *Solicitor to the Ministry of Agriculture, Fisheries and Food* (for the appellant); *Sinclair, Roche & Temperley* (for the respondents).

N P Metcalfe Esq   Barrister.

JEB Fasteners Ltd v Marks, Bloom & Co (a firm)

QUEEN'S BENCH DIVISION

WOOLF J

20th, 21st, 22nd, 23rd, 24th, 27th, 28th, 29th OCTOBER, 19th DECEMBER 1980

Negligence – Information or advice – Knowledge third party might rely on information – Auditor – Preparation of company's accounts – Duty to prospective investor – Auditor negligent in preparing accounts – Auditor aware when preparing accounts that company requiring outside financial support – Accounts made available to plaintiffs – Plaintiffs taking over company – Whether auditor owing duty of care to plaintiffs in preparation of accounts.

In April 1975 the defendants, a firm of accountants, prepared an audited set of accounts for a manufacturing company for the year ended 31st October 1974. The company's stock, which had been purchased for some £11,000, was shown as being worth £23,080, that figure being based on the company's own valuation of the net realisable value of the stock. The defendants nevertheless described the stock in the accounts as being 'valued at lower of cost and net realisable value'. On the basis of the inflated stock figure the accounts showed a net profit of £11·25, whereas if the stock had been included at cost with a discount for possible errors the accounts would have shown a loss of over £13,000. The defendants were aware when they prepared the accounts that the company faced liquidity problems and was seeking outside financial support from, inter alios, the plaintiffs, who manufactured similar products and were anxious to expand their business. The accounts prepared by the defendants were made available to the plaintiffs, who, although they had reservations about the stock valuation, decided to take over the company in June 1975 for a nominal amount, because they would thereby obtain the services of the company's two directors who had considerable experience in the type of manufacturing carried on by the plaintiffs. In discussions between the plaintiffs and the defendants during the take-over the defendants failed to inform the plaintiffs that the stock had been put in the accounts at an inflated value. The plaintiffs' take-over of the company proved to be less successful than they had anticipated and they brought an action for damages against the defendants alleging that the defendants had been negligent in preparing the company's accounts, that they had relied on the accounts when purchasing the company, and that they would not have purchased the company had they been aware of its true financial position. The plaintiffs contended that an auditor when preparing a set of accounts owed a duty of care to all persons whom he ought reasonably to have foreseen would rely on the accounts. The defendants contended that if a duty of care existed it was only owed to persons who made a specific request for information.

Held – (1) Whether the defendants owed a duty of care to the plaintiffs in regard to their preparation of the accounts of the company depended on whether they knew or ought reasonably to have foreseen at the time the accounts were prepared that persons such as the plaintiffs might rely on the accounts for the purpose of deciding whether to take over the company and might suffer loss if the accounts were inaccurate. Since the defendants knew at the time the accounts were prepared that the company needed outside financial support and ought reasonably to have foreseen that a take-over was a possible means of obtaining finance and that a person effecting a take-over might rely on those accounts, it followed that the defendants owed the plaintiffs a duty of care in the preparation of the accounts. The defendants were in breach of that duty by negligently including in the accounts stock at a value of some £13,000 over the discounted cost without appending a note in the accounts to that effect (see p 296 h j, p 300 j to p 301 d and g to p 302 c and j to p 303 a and f to p 304 a, post); dicta of Lord Wilberforce and of Lord Salmon in *Anns v London Borough of Merton* [1977] 2 All ER at 498–499, 512–513, *Scott Group Ltd v McFarlane* [1978] 1 NZLR 553 and *Ross v Caunters* (a firm) [1979] 3 All ER 580 applied.

(2) However, even though the plaintiffs had relied on the accounts, they would not have acted differently had they known the true position, since they knew the company **a** was in financial difficulties, their reason for taking over the company was to obtain the services of its directors and the consideration paid for the company was only nominal. Accordingly, the defendants' negligence in preparing the accounts was not a cause of any loss suffered by the plaintiffs as a result of taking over the company. The plaintiffs' action would therefore be dismissed (see p 305 *e* to *h*, post).

b

Note

For damages for negligent statements in precontractual negotiations, see 31 Halsbury's Laws (4th Edn) paras 1099–1102.

Cases referred to in judgment

Anns v London Borough of Merton [1977] 2 All ER 492, [1978] AC 728, [1977] 2 WLR 1024, **c** 191 JP 526, 75 LGR 555, HL, Digest (Cont Vol E) 449, 99*b*.

Barton v Armstrong (1973) [1975] 2 All ER 465, [1976] AC 104, [1975] 2 WLR 1050, 3 ALR 355, PC, 12 Digest (Reissue) 117, *486*a.

Candler v Crane, Christmas & Co [1951] 1 All ER 426, [1951] 2 KB 164, CA, 36(1) Digest (Reissue) 22, 75.

Derry v Peek (1889) 14 App Cas 337, [1886–90] All ER Rep 1, 58 LJ Ch 864, 61 LT 265, **d** 54 JP 148, 1 Meg 292, HL, 9 Digest (Reissue) 123, 650.

Donoghue (or M'Alister) v Stevenson [1932] AC 562, [1932] All ER Rep 1, 101 LJPC 119, 37 Com Cas 350, 1932 SC (HL) 31, 1932 SLT 317, HL, 36(1) Digest (Reissue) 144, 562.

Everett v Griffiths [1920] 3 KB 163, 89 LJKB 929, 123 LT 280, 84 JP 161, CA; *affd* [1921] 1 AC 631, 90 LJKB 737, 125 LT 230, 85 JP 149, 19 LGR 283, HL, 33 Digest (Repl) 709, 1659.

e

Grover Industrial Holdings Ltd v Newman Harris & Co (12th January 1976, unreported).

Haig v Bamford, Hagan, Wicken and Gibson [1976] WWR 331.

Hedley Byrne & Co Ltd v Heller & Partners Ltd [1963] 2 All ER 575, [1964] AC 465, [1963] 3 WLR 101, [1963] 1 Lloyd's Rep 485, HL, 36(1) Digest (Reissue) 24, 84.

Le Lievre v Gould [1893] 1 QB 491, 62 LJQB 353, 68 LT 626, 57 JP 484, CA, 36(1) Digest (Reissue) 9, 27.

f

Low v Bouverie [1891] 3 Ch 82, [1891–4] All ER Rep 348, 60 LJ Ch 594, 65 LT 533, CA, 35 Digest (Repl) 34, 258.

Home Office v Dorset Yacht Co Ltd [1970] 2 All ER 294, [1970] AC 1004, [1970] 2 WLR 1140, [1970] 1 Lloyd's Rep 453, HL, 36(1) Digest (Reissue) 27, 93.

Rhode Island Hospital Trust National Bank v Swartz, Bresenoff, Yavner & Jacobs (1972) 455 F 2d 847.

g

Ross v Caunters (a firm) [1979] 3 All ER 580, [1980] Ch 297, [1979] 3 WLR 605, Digest (Cont Vol E) 451, 158*b*.

SCM (UK) Ltd v W J Whittall & Son Ltd [1970] 3 All ER 245, [1971] 1 QB 337, [1970] 3 WLR 494, CA, 36(1) Digest (Reissue) 28, 94.

Scott Group Ltd v McFarlane [1978] 1 NZLR 553.

Spartan Steel & Alloys Ltd v Martin & Co (Contractors) Ltd [1972] 3 All ER 557, [1973] QB **h** 27, [1972] 3 WLR 502, CA, 17 Digest (Reissue) 149, 403.

Sykes v Midland Bank Executor & Trustee Co Ltd [1970] 2 All ER 471, [1971] 1 QB 113, [1970] 3 WLR 273, CA, Digest (Cont Vol C) 897, 862*a*.

Ultramares Corpn v Touche (1931) 174 NE 441.

Weller & Co v Foot and Mouth Disease Research Institute [1965] 3 All ER 560, [1966] 1 QB 569, [1965] 3 WLR 1082, [1965] Lloyd's Rep 414, 36(1) Digest (Reissue) 45, 143.   **j**

Action

By a writ issued on 31st May 1978, the plaintiffs, JEB Fasteners Ltd, claimed against the defendants, Marks, Bloom & Co (a firm), damages for loss suffered by the plaintiffs *a* following the acquisition of the issued share capital of a company, BG Fasteners Ltd, which the plaintiffs claimed to have done in reliance on the accounts of the company negligently prepared by the defendants as accountants and auditors of the company. The facts are set out in the judgment.

Murray Pickering for the plaintiffs.
Quintin J Iwi and *Andrew Jordan* for the defendants.

b

Cur adv vult

19th December. **WOOLF J** read the following judgment: In this action the plaintiffs are claiming damages from the defendants who are a firm of chartered accountants, in respect of the alleged negligence of the defendants in preparing the audited accounts of *c* a company called BG Fasteners Ltd.

In June 1975 the plaintiffs acquired the entire share capital of that company. They contend that they would not have purchased the company if they had known its true financial position, but that they did so relying on its audited accounts for the year ending 31st October 1974, prepared by the defendants, which did not give a true and fair view of the state of the company. The plaintiffs allege that they have suffered substantial loss *d* and damage as a result of the purchase of the company.

Before going into the facts in great detail it is desirable if I indicate my views as to the legal issues involved which have been in dispute before me.

In order to succeed in this case, the plaintiffs have to establish as a matter of law that the defendants owed them a duty of care so as to give rise to liability if they were negligent in the preparation of the accounts. It is not alleged that at the time the *e* accounts were audited the defendants knew that the accounts would be relied on by the plaintiffs. Indeed, no takeover was then contemplated, and counsel for both the plaintiffs and the defendants agree that there is no direct English authority on the question whether the defendants owe such a duty in those circumstances.

The plaintiffs contend that an auditor, in preparing the audited accounts of a company, owes a duty of care to all persons who he ought to know could rely on the accounts, and *f* the test is one of reasonable foresight or contemplation based on status and proximity. Furthermore, the duty is not limited by the absence of a request for information by the person relying on the accounts, or the fact that at the time of the audit the person is unidentified, or the fact that that person only suffers financial loss.

Before the decision of the House of Lords in *Hedley Byrne & Co Ltd v Heller & Partners Ltd* [1963] 2 All ER 575, [1964] AC 465 it could not have been argued before a judge of *g* first instance that there was any possible liability in such circumstances. However, in that case the House of Lords overruled the majority judgment of the Court of Appeal in *Candler v Crane, Christmas & Co* [1951] 1 All ER 426, [1951] 2 KB 164 and approved the dissenting judgment of Denning LJ, expressly in the case of Lord Devlin (see [1963] 2 All ER 575 at 611, [1964] AC 465 at 530).

In his judgment in *Candler v Crane, Christmas & Co* Denning LJ dealt with the question *h* of whether or not accountants owed a duty. First he said ([1951] 1 All ER 426 at 433, [1951] 2 KB 164 at 179–180):

'Let me now be constructive and suggest the circumstances in which I say that a duty to use care in making a statement does exist apart from a contract in that behalf. First, what persons are under such duty? My answer is those persons, such as accountants, surveyors, valuers and analysts, whose profession and occupation it *j* is to examine books, accounts, and other things, and to make reports on which other people—other than their clients—rely in the ordinary course of business. Their duty is not merely a duty to use care in their reports. They have also a duty to use care in their work which results in their reports. Herein lies the difference between these professional men and other persons who have been held to be under no duty to use care in their statements, such as promoters who issue a prospectus: *Derry* v. *Peek* ((1889) 14 App Cas 337, [1886–90] All ER Rep 1) (now altered by statute *a* [Companies Act 1948, s. 43]), and trustees who answer inquiries about the trust funds: *Low* v. *Bouverie* ([1891] 3 Ch 82, [1891–4] All ER Rep 348). Those persons do not bring, and are not expected to bring, any professional knowledge or skill into the preparation of their statements. They can only be made responsible by the law affecting persons generally, such as contract, estoppel, innocent misrepresentation or fraud. It is, however, very different with persons who engage in a calling which *b* requires special knowledge and skill. From very early times it has been held that they owe a duty of care to those who are closely and directly affected by their work apart altogether from any contract or undertaking in that behalf.'

Further on Denning LJ continued as follows ([1951] 1 All ER 426 at 433–434, [1951] 2 KB 164 at 180–181):

c

'The same reasoning has been applied to medical men who make reports on the sanity of others: see *Everett* v. *Griffiths* ([1920] 3 KB 163 at 182, 217). It is, I think, also applicable to professional accountants. They are not liable, of course, for casual remarks made in the course of conversation, nor for other statements made outside their work, or not made in their capacity as accountants . . . but they are, in my opinion, in proper cases, apart from any contract in the matter, under a duty to use *d* reasonable care in the preparation of their accounts and in the making of their reports. Secondly, to whom do these professional people owe this duty? I will take accountants, but the same reasoning applies to the others. They owe the duty, of course, to their employer or client and also, I think, to any third person to whom they themselves show the accounts, or to whom they know their employer is going to show the accounts so as to induce him to invest money or take some other action *e* on them. I do not think, however, the duty can be extended still further so as to include strangers of whom they have heard nothing and to whom their employer without their knowledge may choose to show their accounts. Once the accountants have handed their accounts to their employer, they are not, as a rule, responsible for what he does with them without their knowledge or consent.'

Denning LJ then referred to *Le Lievre* v *Gould* [1893] 1 QB 491 and then continued *f* ([1951] 1 All ER 426 at 434, [1951] 2 KB 164 at 181):

'Excluding such cases as those, however, there are some cases—of which the present is one—where the accountants know all the time, even before they present their accounts, that their employer requires the accounts to show to a third person so as to induce him to act on them, and then they themselves, or their employers, *g* present the accounts to him for the purpose. In such cases I am of opinion that the accountants owe a duty of care to the third person. The test of proximity in these cases is: Did the accountants know that the accounts were required for submission to the plaintiff and use by him?'

Denning LJ continued ([1951] 1 All ER 426 at 436, [1951] 2 KB 164 at 184–185):

h

'One final word. I think the law would fail to serve the best interests of the community if it should hold that accountants and auditors owe a duty to no one but their client. Its influence would be most marked in cases where the client is a company or firm controlled by one man. It would encourage accountants to accept the information which the one man gives them without verifying it, and to prepare and present the accounts rather as a lawyer prepares and presents a case, putting the *j* best appearance on the accounts they can without expressing their personal opinion of them. This is, to my way of thinking, an entirely wrong approach. There is a great difference between the lawyer and the accountant. The lawyer is never called on to express his personal belief in the truth of his client's case, whereas the accountant, who certifies the accounts of his client, is always called on to express his personal opinion whether the accounts exhibit a true and correct view of his client's affairs, and he is required to do this, not so much for the satisfaction of his own client, but more for the guidance of shareholders, investors, revenue authorities, and others who may have to rely on the accounts in serious matters of business. If we should decide this case in favour of the defendants, there will be no reason why accountants should ever verify the word of the one man in a one-man company, because there will be no one to complain about it. The one man who gives them wrong information will not complain if they do not verify it. He wants their backing for the misleading information he gives them, and he can only get it if they accept his word without verification. It is just what he wants so as to gain his own ends. And the persons who are misled cannot complain because the accountants owe no duty to them. If such be the law, I think it is to be regretted, for it means that the accountants' certificate, which should be a safeguard, becomes a snare for those who rely on it. I do not myself think that it is the law. In my opinion, accountants owe a duty of care not only to their own clients, but also to all those whom they know will rely on their accounts in the transactions for which those accounts are prepared.'

In *Candler*, although the facts are in some respects similar to those in the present case, it was clear that the accountants concerned had knowledge that the accounts were to be supplied to the plaintiffs, and of the specific purpose for which they were required. It is therefore understandable that Denning LJ, having dealt with liability of accountants who had such knowledge and the position of strangers to the accountants to whom their employer without their knowledge chose to show their accounts, did not deal specifically with the position where the accountants had no actual knowledge that the accounts would be shown to a particular person, but should reasonably have foreseen that the accounts could be shown to a third person who would rely on them.

However, in *Grover Industrial Holdings Ltd v Newman Harris & Co* (12th January 1976, unreported) (a transcript of which was placed before me), Stocker J makes it clear that he could see no good reason in principle why negligent accountants should not owe a duty of care 'to those who can be foreseen as likely to sustain damage if carelessness existed'. However, having examined the authorities, including the judgment of Cardozo CJ in the American case of *Ultramares Corpn v Touche* (1931) 174 NE 441, he felt he was precluded from confirming there was such a duty, though on the facts of that case he was able to come to the conclusion that a duty existed.

In the *Ultramares* case the accountants had no prior knowledge of the plaintiffs and were held not liable in negligence to a company which had extended credit in reliance on certified accounts prepared by the accountants. The situation was one where the range of the transactions in which the certificate of audit might be expected to play a part was not confined in any way, and it was in that situation that Cardozo CJ (at 444) made his important statement of principle that—

'If liability for negligence exists, a thoughtless slip or blunder, the failure to detect a theft or forgery beneath the cover of deceptive entries, may expose accountants to a liability in an indeterminate amount for an indeterminate time to an indeterminate class. The hazards of a business conducted on these terms are so extreme as to enkindle doubt whether a flaw may not exist in the implication of a duty that exposes to these consequences.'

If there had been no further decisions of the courts since the judgment of Stocker J I would have felt equally constrained from finding that there was any general duty based on foreseeability. However, since the decision of Stocker J, there have been three further authorities which throw more light on the subject.

The first is *Anns v London Borough of Merton* [1977] 2 All ER 492, [1978] AC 728. The facts of that case bear no relation to the facts under consideration. However, in the course of his speech Lord Wilberforce dealt in general terms with the circumstances in which a duty of care can arise. He said ([1977] 2 All ER 492 at 498–499, [1978] AC 728 at 751):

> 'Through the trilogy of cases in this House, *Donoghue v Stevenson* [1932] AC 562, [1932] All ER Rep 1, *Hedley Byrne & Co Ltd v Heller & Partners Ltd* [1963] 2 All ER 575, [1964] AC 465 and *Home Office v Dorset Yacht Co Ltd* [1970] 2 All ER 294, [1970] AC 1004, the position has now been reached that in order to establish that a duty of care arises in a particular situation, it is not necessary to bring the facts of that situation within those of previous situations in which a duty of care has been held to exist. Rather the question has to be approached in two stages. First one has to ask whether, as between the alleged wrongdoer and the person who has suffered damage there is a sufficient relationship of proximity or neighbourhood such that, in the reasonable contemplation of the former, carelessness on his part may be likely to cause damage to the latter, in which case a prima facie duty of care arises. Secondly, if the first question is answered affirmatively, it is necessary to consider whether there are any considerations which ought to negative, or to reduce or limit the scope of the duty or the class of person to whom it is owed or the damages to which a breach of it may give rise (see the *Dorset Yacht* case [1970] 2 All ER 294 at 297–298, [1970] AC 1004 at 1027, per Lord Reid). Examples of this are *Hedley Byrne & Co Ltd v Heller & Partners Ltd* where the class of potential plaintiffs was reduced to those shown to have relied on the correctness of statements made, and *Weller & Co v Foot and Mouth Disease Research Institute* [1965] 3 All ER 560, [1966] 1 QB 569 and (I cite these merely as illustrations, without discussion) cases about 'economic loss' where, a duty having been held to exist, the nature of the recoverable damages was limited (see *SCM (United Kingdom) Ltd v W J Whittall & Son Ltd* [1970] 3 All ER 245, [1971] 1 QB 337, *Spartan Steel and Alloys Ltd v Martin & Co (Contractors) Ltd* [1972] 3 All ER 557, [1973] QB 27).'

And Lord Salmon, in the course of his speech, said ([1977] 2 All ER 492 at 512–513, [1978] AC 728 at 769):

> 'There are a wide variety of instances in which a statement is negligently made by a professional man which he knows will be relied on by many people besides his client, eg a well-known firm of accountants certifies in a prospectus the annual profits of the company issuing it and unfortunately, due to negligence on the part of the accountants, the profits are seriously overstated. Those persons who invested in the company in reliance on the accuracy of the accountants' certificate would have a claim for damages against the accountants for any money they might have lost as a result of the accountants' negligence: see the *Hedley Byrne* case.'

The second case is a decision of the New Zealand Court of Appeal, *Scott Group Ltd v McFarlane* [1978] 1 NZLR 553. As is apparent from the headnote, the facts of that case were similar to this case. Richmond P thought the maker of a statement would not owe a duty unless the maker of the statement was or ought to have been aware that his advice or information would in fact be made available to and would be relied on by a particular person or class of persons for the purpose of the particular transaction or type of transaction. I stress the reference to a particular person and a particular transaction, because on the facts in this case the plaintiffs could not comply with this requirement.

In his examination of the authorities Richmond P referred to a Canadian decision, *Haig v Bamford, Hagan, Wicken and Gibson* [1976] WWR 331. Richmond P pointed out that in that case the court held it was sufficient that the accountants were aware when they prepared the statements that they were intended to be used by a limited class of potential investors. It was unnecessary to show that they had actual knowledge of the specific plaintiff who would use and rely on the statements. Richmond P added (at 562):

> 'With this conclusion I unhesitatingly and respectfully agree. But in the *Haig* case it was not necessary to decide whether something less than actual knowledge of the

purpose for which the statement was required would be sufficient. In particular it was not necessary to decide whether it would have been sufficient if the accountants ought reasonably to have foreseen, in a general way, that the statement might be used for the purpose of attracting investors.'

The second judgment in the New Zealand case was a dissenting judgment given by Woodhouse J, who relied on the passage from the speech of Lord Wilberforce in *Anns v London Borough of Merton*, which I have cited, and stated that it was his opinion that the problem was to be approached 'by the comprehensible straightforward test of foreseeability'. With regard to Lord Wilberforce's second stage Woodhouse J stated (at 574):

'. . . a need to establish knowledge of the very identity of those proposing to act upon advice would seem not merely an extremely stringent but an almost fortuitous test of responsibility.'

Woodhouse J however, thought it unwise to endeavour to lay down in advance precise rules as to when responsibility should be waived or modified and considered the facts of individual cases are likely to provide a far more reliable and equitable guide. When he examined the case before the court he came to the conclusion that a duty of care was owed notwithstanding the fact that the auditors had no direct knowledge of the plaintiffs or that a takeover from any quarter was contemplated.

The third judge, Cooke J, expressly agreed with Woodhouse J that in the circumstances of that case a duty of care was owed. Cooke J (at 584) also relied on the speech of Lord Wilberforce in *Anns v London Borough of Merton* and took the view that the evidence disclosed 'a plain risk of a takeover and the virtual certainty that in such an event the accounts would be relied upon by an offeror'. He therefore decided that, on the facts of the case as between the alleged wrongdoer and the person who had allegedly suffered damage, there was a sufficient relationship of proximity or neighbourhood such that it should have been in the reasonable contemplation of the former that carelessness on his part would be likely to cause damage to the latter. So, prima facie, a duty of care arose.

Cooke J went on to consider whether there were any considerations which ought to negative or to reduce or limit the scope of the duty or the class of persons to whom it was owed or the damages to which a breach of it may give rise, and concluded that the class was narrowly limited; and liability to even that limited class could have been excluded by disclaimer.

It follows that, although Woodhouse J dissented, on the question which is important here both he and Cooke J were of the opinion that a duty of care could arise even though the auditor was not aware that his information would be made available to a particular person for the purpose of a particular transaction, and, on this point, it was Richmond P who was in the minority.

The third of the three cases is *Ross v Caunters* [1979] 3 All ER 580, [1980] Ch 297, a decision of Sir Robert Megarry V-C. That was a case concerning solicitors' negligence in which the Vice-Chancellor, in considering the question of whether or not a solicitor owed a duty to a named beneficiary in a will of his client, also adopted the test laid down by Lord Wilberforce in *Anns v London Borough of Merton*, and decided that a duty was owed. The issues were very different from those in this case, but having examined the authorities the Vice-Chancellor summarised his conclusions, inter alia, as follows ([1979] 3 All ER 580 at 599–600, [1980] Ch 279 at 322–323):

'The basis of the solicitor's liability to others is either an extension of the *Hedley Byrne* principle or, more probably, a direct application of the principle of *Donoghue v Stevenson* . . . A solicitor who is instructed by his client to carry out a transaction that will confer a benefit on an identified third party owes a duty of care towards that third party in carrying out that transaction, in that the third party is a person within his direct contemplation as someone who is likely to be so closely and directly affected by his acts or omissions that he can reasonably foresee that the third party is likely to be injured by those acts or omissions . . . The mere fact that the loss to such a third party caused by the negligence is purely financial, and is in no way a physical injury to person or property, is no bar to the claim against the solicitor . . . In such circumstances there are no considerations which suffice to negative or limit the scope of the solicitor's duty to the beneficiary.'

If foreseeability of risk of causing injury plays a part in establishing the liability of a solicitor, it must also play a part in establishing the liability of an accountant, and for this reason alone the judgment of Sir Robert Megarry V-C is of help. However, he said ([1979] 3 All ER 580 at 592, [1980] Ch 279 at 313–314), with regard to *Hedley Byrne*:

> '*Hedley Byrne* is important, of course, as opening the door to the recovery of damages for negligence to at least some cases where the negligence has caused purely financial loss, without any injury to person or property . . . But for present purposes its importance is that the House of Lords rejected pure *Donoghue v Stevenson* principles as forming the basis of liability for negligent mis-statements and instead based liability on the plaintiff having trusted the defendant to exercise due care in giving information on a matter in which the defendant had a special skill, and knew or ought to have known of the plaintiff's reliance on his skill and judgment. In this type of case, reliance forms part of the test of liability, as well as part of the chain of causation: and the effect of such a test of liability is to confine the extent of liability far more closely than would an application of pure *Donoghue v Stevenson* principles. If liability for negligently putting into circulation some innocent misrepresentation were to be imposed on the same basis as negligently putting into circulation some dangerous chattel, the resulting liability might be for enormous sums to a great multiplicity of plaintiffs. One way of preventing any such liability being imposed is to make the test of liability more strict: and that was the way adopted in *Hedley Byrne*. But that does not affect those cases in which the principles of *Donoghue v Stevenson* apply. If I am right in thinking that the case before me falls within those principles, then there is no need to consider questions of reliance.'

The importance of this passage is that if Sir Robert Megarry V-C is right, as with respect I think he is, the fact of reliance on the statement is sufficient limitation on liability to overcome the danger raised by Cardozo CJ. In view of Stocker J's statement that he regarded it as—

> 'paradoxical that no duty of care should be owed to those who can be foreseen as likely to sustain damage if carelessness existed, but that a duty of care should be owed to those, their clients, in respect of whom there is no foreseeable risk of damage,'

I have little doubt that if the three cases to which I have made reference were available to him, Stocker J would not have felt the same constraint. Particularly as the law in the United States appears also to have advanced as a result of *Hedley Byrne* (see the Second Restatement of the Law of Torts (1977), § 552, and *Rhode Island Hospital Trust National Bank v Swartz, Bresenoff, Yavner & Jacobs* (1972) 455 F 2d 847).

Without laying down any principle which is intended to be of general application, on the basis of the authorities which I have cited, the appropriate test for establishing whether a duty of care exists appears in this case to be whether the defendants knew or reasonably should have foreseen at the time the accounts were audited that a person might rely on those accounts for the purpose of deciding whether or not to take over the company and therefore could suffer loss if the accounts were inaccurate. Such an approach does place a limitation on those entitled to contend that there has been a breach of duty owed to them. First of all, they must have relied on the accounts and, second, they must have done so in circumstances where the auditors either knew that they would or ought to have known that they might. If the situation is one where it would not be reasonable for the accounts to be relied on, then, in the absence of express knowledge, the auditor would be under no duty. This places a limit on the circumstances in which the audited accounts can be relied on and the period for which they can be relied on. The longer the period which elapses prior to the accounts being relied on, from the date on which the auditor gave his certificate, the more difficult it will be to establish that the auditor ought to have foreseen that his certificate would, in those circumstances, be relied on.

It was argued on behalf of the defendants in this case that, if contrary to their primary contention they were under any liability to the plaintiffs, then the plaintiffs were guilty of contributory negligence. The plaintiffs contended that the Law Reform (Contributory Negligence) Act 1945 did not apply to actions founded on an allegation of negligent misrepresentation. It was submitted on behalf of the plaintiffs that there was no precedent for a defence based on contributory negligence. In support of this contention the plaintiffs relied on *Sykes v Midland Bank Executor Co* [1970] 2 All ER 471, [1971] 1 QB 113 and *Barton v Armstrong* [1975] 2 All ER 465, [1976] AC 104. In neither of those cases was the court considering the question of the application of the Law Reform (Contributory Negligence) Act 1945, and I do not consider that they are of any assistance on this issue.

It is true that in the latter case Lord Cross said ([1975] 2 All ER 465 at 474, [1976] AC 104 at 118):

> 'If on the other hand Barton relied on the misrepresentation Armstrong could not have defeated his claim to relief by showing that there were other more weighty causes which contributed to his decision to execute the deed, for in this field the court does not allow an examination into the relative importance of contributory causes.'

That statement of Lord Cross is of great assistance in deciding whether or not there liability is owed by the representor to the representee, but it does not help as to whether the representor is entitled to have his damages reduced under the provisions of the Law Reform (Contributory Negligence) Act 1945. The words of s 1(1) of that Act are in very wide terms and I can see no reason why those terms are not sufficiently wide to cover a case involving a negligent misrepresentation.

In the course of argument, counsel for the plaintiffs also referred me to 31 Halsbury's Laws (4th Edn) paras 1066–1069. I am afraid that I deterred him from citing additional authorities in support of the statements in those paragraphs. I did not consider that they would assist me because, again, in my view, they were not considering the question which I have to consider, which is the application of the 1945 Act.

I do, however, recognise that it may well be that in the case of negligent misrepresentation the scope for contributory negligence is limited since an auditor will only be liable if he should foresee that someone might rely on his accounts and, as I have sought to indicate, this involves it being reasonable for the person concerned to rely on the accounts. If it is reasonable to rely on the accounts, it is difficult to envisage circumstances where as a matter of fact it would be negligent to do so without taking further steps to protect yourself from the consequence of relying on the auditor's certificate.

Having expressed my views as to the matters of law which are in dispute, the issues between the parties can be summarised as follows.

1. The foreseeability issue: that is, ought the defendants to have realised, when auditing BG Fasteners Ltd's accounts for the year ending 31st October 1974, that those accounts could be relied on in the circumstances in which they were allegedly relied on by the plaintiffs for the purpose of taking over BG Fasteners Ltd?

2. The reliance issue: in coming to their decision to take over BG Fasteners Ltd, did the plaintiffs rely on the accounts audited by the defendants?

3. The negligence issue: were the defendants negligent in the preparation of those accounts?

4. The causation issue: that is, did the plaintiffs suffer any loss in consequence of the alleged negligence?

5. The contributory negligence issue: that is, did the plaintiffs contribute to their alleged loss by their own negligence?

6. The quantum issue: the assessment of the plaintiffs' alleged loss.

Before considering each issue in turn, it is necessary to say something more about the facts of the case. The defendants are a small firm of chartered accountants. The membership of the firm has changed from time to time but the one constant feature has been Mr Marks, who is a chartered accountant of many years' standing. He qualified before the last war and has been continuously in practice since that time.

The plaintiffs are well-established suppliers of industrial fasteners, fasteners coming in many sorts from screws upwards. The company is a family one run by the Bufton family. There were two principal directors at the times with which this case was mainly concerned, John Bufton and his brother Eric Bufton. Eric Bufton has unfortunately since died, and it is to John Bufton I will mainly refer in the course of this judgment. John Bufton has some accounting training and spent some time in Shell before becoming involved with the plaintiffs' business.

By 1974 the plaintiffs were in a position where they had finance available for the expansion of their business, and the Buftons were anxious to make use of this finance by extending the area of their operations. They became aware of another fastener business, namely, that of BG Fasteners Ltd which carried on similar activities to the plaintiffs, but in an adjacent area. The business of BG Fasteners Ltd had been initially commenced by Mr George Godridge under the name BG Fasteners. Mr Godridge had previously been employed by a large public company which, among other things, manufactured fasteners, and in about August 1972 he set up in business on his own account under the style BG Fasteners. Subsequently he was joined by Mr Wigg and in due course, on the 20th September 1973, the company BG Fasteners Ltd, was incorporated to take over the business which had previously been carried on by Mr Godridge and Mr Wigg.

On 1st November 1973 BG Fasteners Ltd started trading with Mr Godridge and Mr Wigg acting as its directors.

From the time that Mr Godridge had started trading on his own account in 1972, Mr Marks acted as his accountant, giving general financial advice. In due course the defendants became auditors of the company and ultimately they prepared the first audited accounts of the company for the year ended 31st October 1974, which were dated 14th April 1975. BG Fasteners Ltd's turnover expanded satisfactorily but, as often happens with new companies, liquidity proved a problem and from an early stage the defendants were well aware that financial support was being sought in various forms. Although Mr Marks was not very happy about this, resort was had to factoring. Loans had to be obtained from the company's bankers, and in 1974 the question arose of some sort of arrangement being come to between the plaintiffs and BG Fasteners Ltd whereby the plaintiffs would invest money in that company. At that time, however, there was no question of a take-over.

As early as 2nd August 1974, Mr Marks was writing to Mr Godridge enclosing copies of the draft trading and profit and loss account, covering the period 1st November 1973 to 17th July 1974, which he indicated the company required for their dealing with the plaintiff company. Mr Marks said that he was of the opinion that the plaintiffs would want further information and that, if he could be of any assistance, not to hesitate to let him know.

On 14th April 1975 Mr Marks, who was undoubtedly aware of the financial problems of BG Fasteners Ltd, wrote to Mr Godridge and Mr Wigg enclosing a fair copy of the accounts for the year ended 31st October 1974, indicating that he was anxious that the accounts should be received at that stage in order that those gentlemen could visit the bank manager with the figures. He also stated that he had forwarded a copy of the accounts to the bank manager although they had not been signed by him or certified. Subsequently the accounts were certified by the defendants and dated 14th April 1975.

The certificate was in these terms:

'REPORT OF THE AUDITORS TO THE MEMBERS OF B. G. FASTENERS LTD.

'In our opinion the above Balance Sheet and Trading and Profit and Loss Account gives a true and fair view of the state of the Company's affairs as at the 31st October, 1974 and of its Profit at that date and complies with the Companies Acts 1948 and 1967.'

The trading and profit and loss account showed a net profit of £11·25. The account also showed stock, as at 1st November 1973, of £5,051·96, purchases of £54,251·65, and a gross profit of £23,262·78. Sales were indicated as being £59,486·03 and stock, as at 31st October 1974, of £23,080·36. In the balance sheet under 'current assets' it was stated, 'Stock as valued at lower of cost and net realisable value £23,080·36'.

After the accounts had been certified there was first canvassed a proposal by the plaintiffs to take over BG Fasteners Ltd. Mr Marks was fully aware of the progress of the negotiations on which he advised Mr Godridge and Mr Wigg. He also supplied information to the plaintiffs at the request of Mr Bufton.

On 23rd June 1975 the plaintiffs acquired the share capital of BG Fasteners Ltd from Mr Godridge and Mr Wigg. In exchange for the 500 £1 shares in BG Fasteners Ltd, Mr Godridge and Mr Wigg each received 50 £1 ordinary shares in the plaintiffs. In addition, Mr Godridge and Mr Wigg were appointed directors of the plaintiffs and loans which they had made to BG Fasteners Ltd were repaid.

On 24th June the defendants submitted their account in connection with advising relative to the take-over, including correspondence with the plaintiffs and telephone conversations with Mr Bufton in the sum of £68·26.

On 8th July Mr Bufton wrote to the defendants asking them if they would provide a schedule giving details of debtors and creditors as at 31st October 1974, so that double entry accounts for the period 1st November 1974 to 30th June 1975, in respect of BG Fasteners Ltd, could be produced. That schedule was forwarded on 10th July 1975.

By 23rd July Mr Bufton had prepared elementary accounts relating to BG Fasteners Ltd for the period up to 30th June 1975, which showed a net loss before tax of £910 based on an estimated gross profit of 36% on sales. The figure for sales for that period shown in that account was £59,839, approximately the same figure as the sales shown in the audited accounts for the previous 12 months.

On 22nd July Mr Bufton was already unhappy about the accounts for the 12 months' period and he wrote to the defendants indicating that the accounts failed to show sales amounting to £5,040·59, that certain purchases had not been taken up in the accounts and that an error had been made in arriving at trade debtors. He also indicated that he thought there was difficulty in verifying the cash on hand and indicating his view that it would be prudent for the accounts already failed to be withdrawn. Mr Marks did not agree to this.

In the proceedings before me, Mr Godridge and Mr Wigg did not give evidence, but certain serious criticisms were made of them by Mr Bufton and it appeared that those criticisms could well have substance. As I have not heard the answer which those gentlemen may have to the allegations, I do not propose to say any more about their shortcomings in this judgment, although I should make it clear that, in my consideration of these issues, I am going to assume that the criticisms were justified. The results during the period which is relevant to these proceedings make it quite clear that Mr Godridge and Mr Wigg were a great disappointment to the plaintiffs. Mr Bufton, in the course of his evidence, made no secret of the fact that he and his brother had been influenced to take over BG Fasteners Ltd because of the high regard they had for Mr Godridge and Mr Wigg, and their belief that they would, with the plaintiffs' backing, be able to build BG Fasteners Ltd into a flourishing business.

On 3rd May 1976 Mr Godridge wrote resigning from both companies, and Mr Wigg did likewise on 5th December 1976. If by that time the plaintiffs had not advanced substantial funds to BG Fasteners Ltd it is quite clear that that company would have had

to go into liquidation owing substantial sums, and I am quite satisfied that in the short
term the plaintiffs would have been substantially better off if they had not acquired the
company. *a*

Within a relatively short time of the acquisition, the plaintiffs were well aware of the
mistake which they had made, and as early as 23rd August 1976 their solicitors were
writing to Mr Marks pointing out that they had been asked to advise the plaintiffs with
regard to the affairs of BG Fasteners Ltd, and that the plaintiffs' auditors had drawn their
attention to certain aspects of the 1974 accounts which gave rise to serious concern. The
letter set out in some detail matters which were canvassed in detail before me. *b*

Having completed an investigation, on 3rd December 1976, the plaintiffs' then
auditors, Turquands, Barton, Mayhew & Co, submitted their report as to the accounts
prepared and certified by the defendants for the year ended October 1974, and these
proceedings were commenced by a writ issued on 31st May 1978.

The majority of the eight days during which the trial lasted were taken up with the
evidence of four witnesses, Mr Bufton and Mr Morphitis on behalf of the plaintiffs and *c*
Mr Marks and Mr Bolton on behalf of the defendants. Mr Morphitis was employed at
the material time by Turquands and was responsible for carrying out the audit of the
plaintiffs' accounts and the investigation into the October 1974 accounts of BG Fasteners
Ltd, prepared by the defendants. Mr Bolton is a partner in the firm of Viney Merretts, a
well-known firm of chartered accountants now incorporated in Binder Hamlyn.

I am satisfied that all the witnesses who gave evidence before me were doing their best *d*
to assist me. So far as Mr Bufton and Mr Marks were concerned they had the difficulty
that they were dealing with what occurred as long ago as 1975. Fortunately, what had
happened is documented and the facts can be substantially ascertained from the
documents. However, in critical matters Mr Bufton's evidence was vital and it is
therefore necessary for me to indicate my assessment of him. Quite clearly he is an
honest and careful man. Perhaps because of his partial training as an accountant he has *e*
a very high regard for the professional qualification of a chartered accountant and the
certificate of an auditor who holds the qualification of chartered accountant is one which
is of significance to him. He feels very strongly indeed about what has happened in
consequence of the take-over of BG Fasteners Ltd. Indeed, at one stage in his evidence he
associated the death of his brother with the results of that take-over. Because of the
intensity of his feeling, I came to the conclusion that it was necessary to look at Mr *f*
Bufton's evidence with a degree of caution because his recollection could be coloured by
the firm belief which he has now that all the troubles which followed the take-over could
properly be put at Mr Marks's door.

So far as Mr Morphitis is concerned, I was impressed by his undoubted skill,
intelligence and ingenuity as an accountant. I did, however, feel that in certain respects,
no doubt influenced by his own very high standards, he was apt to be unduly harsh in his *g*
criticism of the standards adopted by others.

Mr Marks was an amiable witness and I have no doubt he is an accountant who in
general provides very sound service and advice to his clients. He was in the unenviable
position in this case of at times being embarrassed into seeking to defend the
undefendable. However, in general I felt his evidence was more reliable than that of Mr
Bufton's and, in so far as hereafter my conclusions are inconsistent with the evidence *h*
given by Mr Bufton, I have not accepted that evidence.

Mr Bolton is clearly a competent accountant. In giving his opinion as to the propriety
of accountants' conduct I considered that his standards were more in accord with those
which should be required of the profession as a matter of law than Mr Morphitis. I did,
however, regard Mr Morphitis as being more authoritative in respect of the calculations
which he made and in relation to the investigation which he had carried out. *j*

I will now turn to the issues I adumbrated earlier.

1. *The foreseeability issue*

As Mr Marks was aware of the financial difficulties of BG Fasteners Ltd and the fact that they were going to need financial support from outside of some sort, I am satisfied that Mr Marks, whom I can treat as being synonomous with the defendants, ought to have realised the accounts could be relied on up till the time that a further audit was carried out by the commercial concerns to whom BG Fasteners Ltd were bound to look for financial assistance. When he audited the accounts, Mr Marks would not know precisely who would provide the financial support, or what form the financial support would take, and he certainly had no reason to know that it would be by way of takeover by the plaintiffs. However, this was certainly one foreseeable method and it does not seem to me that it would be right to exclude the duty of care merely because it was not possible to say with precision what machinery would be used to achieve the necessary financial support. Clearly any form of loan would have been foreseeable including the raising of money by way of debenture, and, while some methods of raising money were more obvious than others and a take-over was not the most obvious method, it was certainly one method which was within the contemplation of Mr Marks. I have little doubt that if Mr Marks had asked himself, before the accounts were certified by him, whether those accounts would be used by BG Fasteners Ltd for the purpose of raising money during the coming year he would have answered Yes, and if he had then been asked whether one method of raising money which could be used would be a take-over he would also have answered Yes, although a take-over is not strictly speaking a method of raising finance. He would not know that the financial support would be provided by the plaintiffs, but certainly by the time the accounts were certified they were sufficiently on the scene to be a possible source of finance.

I would therefore answer the first issue in favour of the plaintiffs.

2. The reliance issue

As I have partially anticipated in outlining the facts, it is my view that the predominant motive for the plaintiffs deciding to take over BG Fasteners Ltd was the fact that they thought that Mr Godridge and Mr Wigg, in the form of BG Fasteners Ltd, would be the ideal vehicle to complement their existing business. I do not think that the plaintiffs were particularly concerned about the progress that BG Fasteners Ltd had made up to that time, as the plaintiffs, through their directors, took the view that, allied to the plaintiffs, BG Fasteners Ltd would be in a much better position to achieve sales and profits than they had been previously. In this they were right, but, as I have indicated, they were not right about the value of Mr Godridge's and Mr Wigg's services. Therefore, I do not think that the accounts up to October 1974 were of critical importance to the plaintiffs, but this does not mean that they did not rely on them. I have no doubt that they were studied by Mr Bufton with care and they would indicate to him, as he said in evidence, that if they were correct the company, during its first year, had done reasonably well and was in a position of balance where it was making neither profits nor losses. Such a picture would certainly encourage him to take over the company, and in that sense I think the plaintiffs relied on the accounts, although as will appear hereafter I think that before the take-over Mr Bufton had reservations as to the accuracy of the accounts and their limited influence would be the importance which he attached to the auditors' certificate.

3. The negligence issue

There were various allegations of negligence with which I must deal in turn.

First, because it can be easily dealt with, there was the question of sales omitted. The revised figure in respect of the value of sales omitted, set out in the report prepared by Mr Morphitis, shows the figure as being £4,667. Mr Marks did not dispute that a figure in respect of sales in that region was omitted. He took a serious view of the error and it resulted in the member of his staff who was responsible, Mr Ahmed, being dismissed. While it was quite proper to employ Mr Ahmed to extract the figures, there was no justification for the error, and this was due to negligence for which the defendants were responsible. It was, however, an error, the effect of which was to make the accounts appear less favourable rather than more favourable to BG Fasteners Ltd. It did, however, mean that the certificate was wrong. It also cancelled out two other alleged errors to which I must refer.

One is the alleged omission of purchases amounting to £2,606. On the evidence before me I find that purchases of approximately this amount were omitted. The explanation for the omission was not the failure to make a request to the bank for information. This was done in a satisfactory form, but not until 9th April 1975, so that the reply from the bank was only received on 18th April 1975, after the accounts had been certified. However, the reply, when it was received, would not have helped since it did not refer to the invoices which were being held by the bank awaiting payment, as, Mr Bolton says in his report, perhaps it should have done. This does not exonerate the defendants since I am satisfied that if the inquiry to the bank had not been delayed to the extent which it was, or if more exhaustive investigations had been made of the company's directors, these omitted purchases would have been discovered. There was, therefore, a default by the defendants which amounts to negligence in not ascertaining this.

The other alleged error relates to the expenses which are said to be understated, and which are scheduled as appendix 3 to Mr Morphitis's report. The individual items are not in themselves significant, apart from the ones which I shall deal with shortly hereafter. Their significance, the plaintiffs contend, is their number. I have reservations about this approach because there can be some small errors even in the most carefully audited accounts which will be revealed by a later investigation when the investigators often have information available to them which was not available at the time of the audit. In this respect I accept Mr Bolton's evidence that any subsequent examination of a set of accounts is likely to disclose variations from the figures set out in the accounts, some of which are dependent on estimations which have to be made at the audit date, and that the minor differences do not warrant detailed comment.

The first of the significant amounts is the £700 in respect of directors' remuneration, which it is alleged was negligently omitted. Twelve salary payments were charged for the year to October 1974, but Mr Morphitis is right in contending that cheques for salary were probably drawn before the year-end, which were omitted from the accounts because they were not debited in the bank account until after the year-end. Certain post year-end debits in the bank account were written into the expenses of the year up to October 1974 in the accounts; and so it appears cheques drawn before the year-end but debited after the year-end were investigated and a conscious decision taken not to include this £700. Such a decision would not be taken without reason and I am not satisfied, on the balance of probability, that there is not some explanation for this of which the witnesses who gave evidence before me would not be aware, such as while the cheques were drawn earlier they were not delivered to the directors until after the year-end when the salary became due. I am therefore not prepared to draw any inference of negligence in respect of the non-inclusion of this sum in the accounts.

The other significant item is interest. The amount here is £366. As the defendants were well aware that the company was overdrawn, they should have appreciated that there must be some interest referable to the year in question, and in so far as it is relevant to do so I do think that the defendants were at fault in not making some provision for this in the accounts.

Before moving on to the last item, I should emphasise that the negligence to which I have already made reference has little significance because the sums involved would be set off by the omission of sales.

Finally there is the allegation that the stock was wrongly described in the accounts. The criticism which can properly be made is not that the stock could not possibly have properly been valued at the figure shown in the accounts but that it was wrongly described as being the lower of cost and net realisable value. (It is not in dispute that that means lower of cost or net realisable value.) Quite clearly it was known by the defendants that in the figures supplied to them by the directors of BG Fasteners Ltd, there was a sum for stock included which was put at a value which was in excess of cost because it was contended that its net realisable value was higher than cost. Normally it is not proper practice to include in the accounts, as the valuation of stock, an item at a figure higher than cost. This is a matter of which Mr Marks was fully aware and in fact had commented on in the correspondence which is before me. Apparently a substantial part of the stock had been obtained at less than its normal selling price from Torrington Co Ltd; there is a letter of 11th October 1974 confirming this fact. On 17th October 1974 Mr Marks wrote to Mr Godridge and to Mr Wigg in respect of this, and the relevant parts of the letter read as follows:

'With regard to the valuation of the parcel of stock as shown on the aforementioned invoice of the Torrington Co. Ltd., as was explained to you previously it is not in accordance with good accountancy practice to bring in a value of stock other than the cost or market price whichever be the lower at the date of stock as taken and in a general way it is wrong to increase profits on an inflated stock figure. On the other hand if a separate valuation of the stock in question could be obtained to reflect the value as proposed this would be most useful and whilst I realise that the stock in question does run into a considerable number of items, you can of course appreciate the reason for having a third party valuation but in view of your agreement that the figure could be taken as £11,000 then subject to the note on any Balance Sheet as audited by myself or in any communication to a third party then I am prepared to deal with this point along these lines. I do of course appreciate your reasons for wanting this stock position to be clarified as far as H. & H. Factors are concerned and I will communicate with them along the lines of this letter but I would be much happier if sales could be made at the current prices or at a special price which would show a value of not less than 150% more than invoiced cost to you by the Torrington Co. Ltd. of any particular item as included on their invoice. This accordingly means that the minimum value of the prices to be received from the Torrington stock must exceed £11,000 after taking VAT at 8% into consideration.'

When the accounts were prepared, they included the items referred to in the letter which I have just read, at an inflated value, but there was no note to indicate that this is what had happened. The entry was clearly wrong and, furthermore, in my view there was negligence in not including a note to make the position clear in the way envisaged by Mr Marks in the letter to which I have just referred. This was, I am afraid, a case where, no doubt because of the very many pressures that were on Mr Marks, he fell short of the standards he no doubt normally adopts. To aggravate the difficulty Mr Bufton spoke to Mr Marks on about 19th June about stock and Mr Marks omitted to tell him on that occasion of what he should have been aware about the inflated value, but told him instead how the stock had been valued for the purpose of the audit in a manner which was misleading in that it stated that a figure of £29,000 had been the starting point of the valuation, from which had been deducted 20% for obsolescence and slow movers, and a further 2½% for possible errors in stock casting. (It seems that the latter figure was probably 2·8%.) On this matter I accept the evidence of Mr Bufton in preference to that of Mr Marks. I was not clear whether Mr Marks was conceding that he appreciated at the time that stock had been valued at a higher figure than cost, but if he was in any doubt about the matter he should not have been because a proper audit would have revealed what he knew previously, namely that the directors were intending to uplift the value of certain stock. The precise extent to which stock was wrongly shown, as the lower of cost or net realisable value, is difficult to ascertain with precision. It is not important for the present purposes that it should be. However, on the evidence before me, on the balance of probability, I accept the figures given by Mr Morphitis set out in appendix 3 of his report. That figure in the account is £12,097 in excess of cost, and an additional provision of £1,483 is needed to reduce cost to net realisable value, the result being that there is an overstatement of approximately £13,500 as to the figure for value of stock. This is an important matter in respect of which the defendants were negligent because, if the stock value is wrong, so is the profit figure wrong, and instead of a profit of £11 the accounts should have shown a loss in excess of £13,000.

4. The causation issue

Where a representation is made and it is relied on, there is a strong inference, in the absence of evidence to the contrary, that the results which follow were brought about by the representation. In addition, in this case, Mr Bufton gave evidence that if the accounts had shown what the defendants had represented them as showing, namely a true and fair view of the financial state of BG Fasteners Ltd, the plaintiffs would not have purchased that company. If he is right, then the loss which the plaintiffs suffered as a result of so doing came about because of a misrepresentation by the defendants. The issue is whether Mr Bufton is right.

In considering this issue, the important wrong entry is that as to the stock. The other errors in total, as I have already pointed out, approximately cancel themselves out, and, in any event, I do not accept that either individually or cumulatively they have affected the plaintiffs' decision in any way.

With regard to the stock, the plaintiffs had carried out their own stock check in June, prior to the take-over. This had thrown up a value of £13,500 which was increased to £15,000 to cover the cost of plating which the company had carried out on certain items. This figure apparently did not cover a large number of shoe heel nails at anything like the same value as had been attributed to them by BG Fasteners Ltd as the plaintiffs regarded them as being valueless. In addition, in the course of his evidence, Mr Bufton gave a picture of the stock generally which showed that it was in a very poor state indeed. Part could be described as 'slow moving', if it was at all saleable. It had not been stored in anything like ideal conditions, and I conclude from the evidence that a figure of £15,000 was well below its net realisable value.

I certainly accept Mr Bufton's view that the shoe heel nails, which were 1½ tons of stock, had a nil value. As Mr Bufton had been told by Mr Godridge that the stock was worth £25,000 at the time of the stock-taking, Mr Bufton must have been well aware that there was a very substantial difference between the view of the company as to the value of the stock and what had been found by the plaintiffs at stock-taking. Mr Bufton said (which is not surprising) that the question of stock valuation was discussed at great length with Mr Godridge and there were arguments about it. He says that Mr Godridge strongly disputed the plaintiffs' valuation and the plaintiffs' contention that lots of the stock was rubbish. However, despite what may have been said by Mr Godridge, I am sure that Mr Bufton must have appreciated it was being overvalued. Furthermore, he must also have known that if this was true in June 1975 it was also probably true in October 1974 since the condition of the stock was such that it indicated that it had been held a long time.

Mr Bufton was sufficiently knowledgeable about accounts to know that the question of the stock value was important, not only because of its significance in assessing the value of the assets of the company, but also because, if the stock value was wrong, other figures, and in particular the profit figure, in the accounts would be wrong.

It is true that, in addition to what his own stock valuation had shown, Mr Bufton had only limited information available. Mr Bufton said that the books were not made available to him and he had difficulty in getting information, and this I accept. However, he agreed that he did have figures which gave an indication as to creditors and trade debtors and was given sales figures and projections for the following six months. His recollection when he gave evidence was that the information which he was given created a picture very much in line with the previous accounts. The company was still making neither a profit nor a loss. However, in the course of his evidence the original copy of the accounts up to October 1974, with which he was supplied, was produced, and from that it could be seen that various figures had been inserted in different colours, presumably at different times. When asked about this, when initially giving evidence, Mr Bufton said that the pencilled figures were ones which he had written before the take-over.

a
Against stock appeared in pencil £12,000 in the profit and loss account, though in the balance sheet the figure £15,000 plus or minus also appeared. Looking at the pencil figures, it became reasonably apparent that, when those pencil figures were written, Mr Bufton had tried to recast the accounts working backwards from the information he had, so as to get a correct view of the company's financial position as at the end of May 1975. While doing this, the fact that the company was not breaking even must have become clearly apparent although the figures which were being used were very approximate and, to a large extent, estimated figures. If the exercise was carried out,

b
then, even though, as Mr Bufton says, he was working on the worst position which could arise, I have no doubt that that is what would have caused him to talk to Mr Marks about stock valuation. It is interesting to note that the note which Mr Bufton prepared in respect of that conversation says against stock 'not up to valuation'. Mr Bufton said that Mr Marks could have told him that he was sure that the stock was valued at cost during

c
this conversation, but I do not accept that Mr Bufton's recollection is right as to this.

Subsequently, at my invitation, Mr Bufton set out in writing the dates on which he made the various annotations on the accounts. He said that, whereas certain of the entries were before acquisition, others, the critical ones, were made after acquisition. I find that I cannot accept the pencilled figures were made in two stages, some before and some after the take-over. I find that Mr Bufton's first recollection was correct and these

d
figures were all inserted before acquisition. If part of the figures were inserted at that time, it would only be sensible to insert all the information available since the exercise was purposeless unless as much information was put in as could be put in. I have therefore come to the conclusion that before the acquisition Mr Bufton knew that there was something seriously wrong with the stock valuation. He also had worked out figures which indicated that the company's position could be much less attractive than

e
was shown by the accounts. This did not mean that Mr Bufton did not rely on the accounts, but it does satisfy me that Mr Bufton was not so concerned about the position of the company as he now believes. He did say, in evidence, something to which I have already alluded, namely, what motivated the plaintiffs to take over the company was the two men, Mr Godridge and Mr Wigg, and it is my conclusion, on the balance of probabilities, that, even if the accounts up to October 1974 had shown the position which

f
they represented to show, the plaintiffs would have still acted in exactly the same way and taken over the company. The consideration payable for the company was nominal, and it is my view that the plaintiffs would have concluded that BG Fasteners Ltd, under their umbrella, could be made financially successful, as indeed it has ultimately become after a long and painful process. There is no dispute that the plaintiffs were aware that the company had financial difficulties, as it was those financial difficulties which had

g
brought the two companies together in the first place. Even though the condition of the stock in June 1975 was not necessarily the same as it had been in October 1974, stock in that condition, when contrasted with the valuation placed on it, would have made a director as careful as Mr Bufton unwilling to proceed unless, as I think was the case, he really was prepared to acquire the company if its financial position was that which should have been shown in the accounts at October 1974, if they had shown the true position.

h
Accordingly, on this issue, I find in favour of the defendants and conclude that the negligence of the defendants was not causative of any loss which the plaintiffs may have suffered as a result of taking over this company.

At first sight my conclusion on causation may seem inconsistent with my finding that the plaintiffs relied on the accounts. The distinction, as I see it, is that you can be influenced by something even though if you had not been influenced you would have

j
acted in the same way. The plaintiffs relied on the accounts in deciding to take over BG Fasteners Ltd but they would have acted no differently even if they had known the true position as to the accounts. I therefore reject Mr Bufton's evidence on this issue. In doing so, I do not suggest that he deliberately lied. On the contrary, he gave evidence as to the position as he now believes it to be. His recollection is, however, tainted by how badly things went after the take-over.

Because of my decision on this issue it is not really necessary for me to consider the final two issues. However, in case of an appeal, I will express my views very shortly.   *a*

5. *Contributory negligence*

The picture which was revealed before the take-over was certainly one which in my view required the plaintiffs to try to make further inquiries if they thought it was critical that the company should be in the position which the accounts purported to indicate. There were however limited steps which they could take and ultimately the best they *b* could do was to ask for access to more information. This was refused to the plaintiffs and so it does not seem to me that they can be held guilty of contributory negligence. If the position of the company had been important, the plaintiffs would have had to make a choice either to not go on or to go on with the information which was available to them. If I am wrong in taking the view that they were not really concerned with the precise financial position of the company, then the decision to go on is fully *c* understandable. If I am wrong in my finding, they were still entitled to make the business decision to proceed without being held guilty of contributory negligence.

6. *Quantum*

With regard to the alleged loss suffered by the plaintiffs, the defendants first of all contended that the proper course for the plaintiffs to have adopted when they realised the *d* true position of the company was to put it in liquidation and in that way cut down the losses. I do not consider that they can be said to have acted unreasonably or to have failed to mitigate their loss because they did not take such a course. Having decided to see the company through, they were forced to incur expenditure of a substantial nature. Two written schedules of that loss have been put before me which speak for themselves. One is based on the money introduced by the plaintiffs plus interest and notional interest; the *e* other is based on the losses for the period shown. I regard those schedules as giving an indication of the upper figure for the plaintiffs' loss. From that has to be deducted some allowance for the fact that, if the plaintiffs had not taken over the company, they themselves would have had the expenses of setting up their own operation in the area where the company was carrying on operations. I can only hazard a guess as to what allowance should be made for this.   *f*

Doing the best that I can on the material before me, having taken into account the answers put forward by the defendants, both in argument and in writing, to the plaintiffs' quantification, I have come to the conclusion that an appropriate figure by way of damages if the plaintiffs had succeeded would have been £20,000.

I do not accept the major part of the defendants' criticisms of the plaintiffs' calculations because, in my view, it is not right to look at the position on the basis that this company *g* had been taken over but its financial position should have been as disclosed by the accounts. The correct initial approach is to calculate the loss on the basis that if the accounts had been correct the plaintiffs would not have acquired the company.

It only remains for me to thank counsel for the very considerable assistance they have given me in this case.

h

Judgment for the defendants.

Solicitors: *Taylor & Humbert* (for the plaintiffs); *Hewitt, Woollacott & Chown* (for the defendants).

K Mydeen Esq   Barrister.

London Borough of Lewisham v M and others

FAMILY DIVISION

HOLLINGS J

23rd, 24th, 25th, 26th FEBRUARY 1981

Ward of court – Care and control – Power to commit ward of court to care of local authority – Local authority initiating wardship proceedings – Local authority applying for care and control in wardship proceedings – Undesirable for mother to have care of children – Foster parent with whom children placed by local authority unable to afford to maintain children – Foster parent not a party to wardship proceedings – Whether statutory power to commit ward to care of local authority where wardship proceedings initiated by local authority – Whether conditions for exercise of statutory power fulfilled – Family Law Reform Act 1969, s 7(2).

In May 1978 the local authority received the five children of the mother into care. The three eldest children were placed with a long-term foster parent and the two youngest children were placed with a temporary foster parent. In July 1979 the local authority instituted wardship proceedings to make all five children wards of court because no progress had been made towards bringing the children and the mother together and the mother had lodged an objection to a resolution passed by the authority to assume parental rights over the children. The mother was the sole defendant to the wardship proceedings and the foster parents were not made parties, but subsequently the Official Solicitor agreed to act for the two youngest children, whom the local authority wished to have adopted, and those children were then made defendants also. The local authority applied in the wardship proceedings for an order under s 7(2)[a] of the Family Law Reform Act 1969 committing care and control of all the children to them. They sought an order under s 7(2) to enable them to pay for the maintenance of any of the wards placed with a foster parent who could not afford to maintain them, since the foster parent caring for the three eldest children, who in other respects was suitable, could not afford to maintain them. On the hearing of the application the judge decided that it was undesirable that the mother should have the care of any of the children and that the three eldest children should remain with the foster parent and the mother should not, for the time being, have any access to them; he also decided that adoption proceedings in regard to the two youngest children should be commenced. The question arose whether there was power in wardship proceedings commenced by a local authority to make a care order in the authority's favour under s 7(2).

Held – The power in s 7(2) of the 1969 Act to commit the care of a ward to a local authority was unrestricted and therefore applied even though the local authority itself was the plaintiff in the wardship proceedings, for there was no restriction on the exercise of the power either in s 7(2) itself or in s 43(1)[b] of the Matrimonial Causes Act 1973, which contained a similar power in divorce proceedings and of which the power in s 7(2) of the 1969 Act was an extension. On the facts, the conditions in s 7(2) for making a care order thereunder had been fulfilled since it was 'undesirable', within s 7(2), for the children to be under the mother's care, and there was no 'other individual' to whom it was 'practicable' to commit the care of them because the foster parent of the eldest

---

a   Section 7(2) is set out at p 316 *j* to p 317 *a*, post

b   Section 43(1), so far as material, provides: 'Where the court has jurisdiction by virtue of this Part of this Act to make an order for the custody of a child and it appears to the court that there are exceptional circumstances making it impracticable or undesirable for the child to be entrusted to either of the parties to the marriage or to any other individual, the court may if it thinks fit make an order committing the care of the child to the council of a [local authority] . . .'

children could not afford to maintain them and the two youngest children were only temporarily with their foster parent pending adoption, and there was therefore nobody in the longer term to care for them. Accordingly, the court was entitled to and would **a** make an order under s 7(2) committing the care and control of the children to the local authority (see p 319 *d* to *g* and p 320 *c* to *g*, post).

Dictum of Ormrod LJ in *Re C B (a minor)* [1981] 1 All ER at 24 not followed.

Per Curiam. Although a care order under s 7(2) of the 1969 Act gives the local authority the powers contained in Part II of the Children Act 1948 which include control **b** of access, nevertheless, because it is an order made in wardship proceedings, the court retains the power to make such directions as to access as it thinks fit (see p 320 *f g*, post).

Notes

For the courts' powers in respect of the care of a ward, see 24 Halsbury's Laws (4th Edn) paras 595–596, and for cases on jurisdiction of the court over wards of court, see 28(2) **c** Digest (Reissue) 911–916, 2220–2258.

For the Family Law Reform Act 1969, s 7, see 17 Halsbury's Statutes (3rd Edn) 797.

Cases referred to in judgment

C B *(a minor)*, *Re* [1981] 1 All ER 16, [1981] 1 WLR 379, 79 LGR 153, CA.

J v C [1969] 1 All ER 788, [1970] AC 668, [1969] 2 WLR 540, HL, 28(2) Digest (Reissue) **d** 800, *1230*.

Y *(a minor)* *(child in care: access)*, *Re* [1975] 3 All ER 348, [1976] Fam 125, [1975] 3 WLR 342, 140 JP 19, 73 LGR 495, CA, Digest (Cont Vol D) 531, *2441b*.

Summons

On 24th July 1979 the local authority as the plaintiffs instituted wardship proceedings in **e** respect of five illegitimate children, their mother being the defendant to the proceedings. The local authority applied in the wardship proceedings for an order committing care and control of the children to the local authority. On 16th August 1979 Mr Registrar Holloway gave interim care and control of the children to the local authority. In 1980 the Official Solicitor consented to act on behalf of the two youngest children in respect of whom the local authority was planning adoption and those **f** children were therefore parties as second defendants to the application. The foster parents respectively of the three eldest children and the two youngest children were not parties to the application. The summons was heard and judgment was given in chambers. The case is reported by permission of Hollings J. The facts are set out in the judgment.

g

Anita M Ryan for the local authority.
Judith Parker for the mother.
Mary Hogg for the Official Solicitor as guardian ad litem.

HOLLINGS J. This is an application by the local authority, the plaintiffs in wardship **h** proceedings, relating to the care and control of five children. There are two sets of twins: first, Jason and Adrian, born on 5th October 1972, now aged 8 years and 4 months; there is Twayna, who was herself a twin but sadly her twin died soon after birth, born on 5th April 1974, therefore aged 6 years and 10 months; and twin boys, Denvil and Gavin, born on 30th October 1977 and now aged 3 years and 4 months. They are all the illegitimate children of the defendant.

The defendant (the mother, as I shall call her) is now aged 27. She first came to the **j** notice of the local authority's social services department in July 1972, because she had left home at the age of 18 when she was expecting the twins, Jason and Adrian. She had, according to the social services records at that time, no fixed address and had been staying with various friends until she was admitted to a charitable hospital where the twins were

born. Jason and Adrian were kept in hospital because of certain respiratory disabilities
a and after ten weeks they were discharged and the family were accepted as homeless and
were housed by the local authority in temporary accommodation. In July 1973 the
mother became pregnant again, and in September 1973 she took the twins to visit her
parents and left them with them for them to care for. Jason and Adrian remained with
their grandparents until September 1974. During that time it appears that the mother
only made one visit to see them, in November 1973, despite indications from her parents
b that they were having difficulties in caring for the twins.

In April 1974 she gave birth to further twins, girls, Twayna being the one that
survived. She had been living in temporary accommodation, which she felt was unfit for
babies, and adoption or long-term fostering was discussed; but she then decided that she
would take them home. Two months later, the other twin died, through no fault (I
hasten to say) of the mother. Twayna was taken into hospital for observation as a
c precautionary measure. The mother was still refusing to take the other children back
because, she said, with justification, her housing was damp and unsuitable. And it is the
fact that at that early stage she was experiencing financial difficulties. She was on social
security, but nevertheless she had allowed her gas and electricity accounts to get into
arrears.

In July 1974 she was offered, and accepted, her present accommodation. She then took
d the care of Twayna who, as I say, had been in hospital for observation. Her present
accommodation in London has been described as very unsuitable accommodation: two
bedroomed accommodation, very damp, liable to condensation and lacking in many
respects proper equipment and furnishings.

In September 1974 she collected Jason and Adrian from her parents, so that from that
date she had all three children. In September 1975 Jason and Adrian joined a nursery
e class, and Twayna did so later. There is an affidavit of the headmistress of the infant
school, which refers to how the children appeared to her when they came in September
1975. She describes how the twins always appeared immature and had to be given a
great deal of adult time and attention in an attempt to sort out their problems. They had
few accomplishments, and their lack of ability was very obvious, and their other
disabilities are set out in her affidavit; but the headmistress says that Twayna has always
f appeared a more normal and average child. To conclude, the headmistress said that the
learning and living process had had such a late start with these children 'that it is difficult
to judge the exact rate of their progress. But it is certainly slower than that of their peers
and their general maturity and behaviour are below that of their age range'.

Some time in 1976 the mother started an association with P. The mother is of West
Indian origin. She herself described how she had a deprived upbringing, coming from
g Jamaica to England at the age of 11 and having a most unhappy time with her mother,
whom she first met properly (as it were) when she came to England at that age. P is a
West Indian also, and he is the father of the last two children, Denvil and Gavin. He is
not concerned in these proceedings. Nor, of course, are the fathers of the other three
children. The association between the mother and P was quite evidently a stormy one.
There were scenes of violence. The mother agrees that she would react with violence to
h P if he was violent to her. The mother agrees that she is a person who is liable to bad
moods and depression, and there is no doubt, having regard in particular to what the
three elder children said later to their foster mother, Mrs B, that they have very sad,
unhappy memories of life when their mother was associating with P.

It is said that there is more than one indication that this may be true, though it is
denied by the mother, or denied that it happened to any significant extent, that quite
j apart from the children witnessing scenes of violence such as they told their foster
mother about at a later stage, they were left alone, on one occasion for as long as five
hours and on other occasions for shorter times. The mother says that there were times
'When I left them for five or ten minutes to go shopping. Only once for longer than that
when I was let down by a neighbour.' There is a memory that the children apparently
have, too, of being left, and, as they say, locked, in a room. And there was an occasion

when a social worker called and found the children alone, and the mother has sought to give an explanation about that.

The situation caused such concern that the local authority through a different social worker from the social worker now supervising proposed that the children might be received into care under s 1 of the Children Act 1948. However, as the present social worker says in one of her affidavits, by September 1976 matters so far as they could tell were going well enough for the case to be closed or for its closing to be contemplated. It was at that time that the social worker changed.

In February 1977 the local authority received an anonymous letter, and this caused the local authority to send two social workers, and they found these three children alone; that is the occasion to which I have already referred. The mother was interviewed. She was found to be very depressed, and she agreed that the children should go into care under s 1 of the 1948 Act; that was on 2nd February 1977. Jason and Adrian were placed with a foster mother, Mrs B. She still has care of those children. She has filed two affidavits and has given evidence before me. In her first affidavit, of 1st February 1980, she described the condition in which the twins Jason and Adrian were, then aged 4 years 4 months. How they knew only about fifty words between them; they seemed to have no understanding; everything seemed new; they were clearly insecure; frightened easily by noises. There were other aspects of the emotional condition set out in the affidavit which I will not set out in detail in this judgment.

Their physical condition gave cause for concern. They were very pot-bellied with thin limbs. They had enormous appetites and they had splinters in the bottom of their feet. They developed very fast when they stayed with her. They were placed in a nursery. Twayna was placed elsewhere at that time. She always has been less disturbed and less liable to regression than the twins.

All this time the mother stayed in the same accommodation, apparently still associating with P. But the local authority, working as local authorities always do with the aim of getting children back to their parents if at all possible, returned Twayna to the mother on 21st June 1977 and Jason and Adrian on 6th August 1977. At that stage the mother was six months pregnant with the youngest twins. This was plainly a difficult time for her and one understands that. By 4th October 1977 all three of the children were back in s 1 care and this time all three children, including Twayna, went back to Mrs B. She found that Jason and Adrian had regressed, to put it shortly, once more, though Twayna was less disturbed.

In September 1977 there was a further change of social worker and the present social worker took over. On 30th October Denvil and Gavin were born. The mother again was depressed when she was seen by the social workers. Both twins were kept in hospital because of heart murmurs, and on 21st November 1977 these twins also were placed in s 1 care and placed with a short-term foster parent, Mrs D; but after seven weeks they were returned to the mother on 23rd December.

By this time P, the father of the youngest twins, who had not been living all the time in the house, one understands, had moved into the mother's home.

Jason and Adrian started school in January 1978, and though the local authority felt that P was antipathetic to the elder children, particularly Jason and Adrian, nevertheless the three elder children, Jason, Adrian and Twayna, were returned to the mother on 4th April 1978. Throughout the period up to then the mother had been receiving financial help by way of social security and extra payments from the local authority. She, indeed, had been offered home help but had refused it. It was during this period that the scenes of violence occurred to which I have referred.

In May 1978 the mother became pregnant once more. This time she went to hospital and an abortion was performed, and later she was sterilised. This led to the final reception of all five children into care on 17th May 1978. Gavin and Denvil went to Mrs D. All the children except Twayna again had regressed, to put it shortly, again; their condition is set out in the affidavits.

In spite of the assistance that the mother had been receiving, rent arrears had built up

and gas and electric bills were owing. She has said in these proceedings that she wished
a for better housing, but of course the arrears of rent and the electricity and gas arrears
made rehousing difficult. Nevertheless it is the fact, as I find, that the local authority did
(as their housing department has testified) from time to time make offers to the mother
to rehouse her. Letters were sent, appointments were sought to be made, but the mother
did not take advantage of the offers in the letters or take up the appointments which were
made. The mother says she was offered in particular some accommodation which she
b says is in a very undesirable area and to which she would not dream of going. In fact the
local authority say the offer was made of accommodation somewhere near there, but in
new accommodation that was entirely suitable. It does not appear that the mother went
to look at it.

On 7th August 1978 Gavin and Denvil were placed with Mrs C, with whom they still
are at present. The mother was offered transport to visit the young twins at Mrs C's
c house. About the same time, on 14th August, the mother was nominated by the local
authority for housing priority; but, as I have indicated already, although attempts were
made to communicate with the mother with a view to implementing this priority, no
contact could be made. By December 1978, indeed, suitable accommodation, I have
been told, was earmarked.

During the time the children had been with the mother it had been necessary in the
d case of Adrian and Jason for them to attend for speech therapy, and the evidence indicates
that the mother was not enthusiastic, to say the least, in taking the children for that
therapy. Indeed, she has told me that she did not think it was achieving the desired
results, and there was no follow-up by her. This is an indication, amongst many other
indications, of the kind of attitude the mother had towards the care and upbringing of
her children.

e Between August 1978 and April and May 1979 the mother's visits to the children were
irregular. The two youngest, Gavin and Denvil, she visited eight times, twice with their
father, P; and she visited the other three children only five times. The difficulties that
she had with the local authority continued. Letters were sent to her, which she says she
never received, in February 1979. Notice to quit was served in May 1979 (which she says
she did not receive) because her rent was so much in arrears.

f The mother last saw Jason and Adrian and Twayna on Boxing Day 1980 or on 23rd
December 1980 when she went to visit them at Mrs B's home with presents. One recalls
that they had been in s 1 care from May 1978. The mother had had by June 1979 a year
in which to make attempts to bring the family together, get herself better accommodation
and show herself motivated as a mother; and she was supported throughout this time by
the social services, in particular by the present social worker. Up to June 1979 I
g understand that the relationship, such as it was, between the mother and the social
worker was perfectly without strain and without any hostility.

The local authority became so concerned that no progress was being made towards
rehabilitation that they decided that application should be made under s 2 of the
Children Act 1948 (as substituted by s 57 of the Children Act 1975) for a resolution of the
local authority assuming parental rights, and that was done in respect of all five
h children. The mother lodged an objection notice pursuant to the Act, and that led to the
institution of these wardship proceedings on 24th July 1979.

On 16th August 1979 Mr Registrar Holloway gave interim care and control of the
children to the local authority. He ordered that there should be reasonable access to the
three elder children by the mother, and directed that the mother be at liberty to apply
to a judge for access in respect of the youngest twins. There were further orders made
j by the registrar, which I do not propose to detail, until on 21st August 1980 in particular
there was an order made that Jason and Adrian should be examined by a psychiatrist.
The Official Solicitor had been invited in January 1980 to act on behalf of the youngest
twins, in respect of whom the local authority were then planning (or thinking of
planning) adoption, or taking steps towards adoption. The Official Solicitor has consented
to act and has appeared by counsel on behalf of Denvil and Gavin. I have had the benefit

of her submissions, and the benefit also of a report from the representative of the Official Solicitor. The children then are parties to the application. None of the foster parents concerned are parties.

Mrs B, who is the foster mother looking after the three eldest children, gave evidence before me, and I must say that I was most impressed by her. She is well experienced as a foster mother; she is a qualified teacher and she has a very loving understanding (quite apparent) of all the children. What is particularly impressive is that she has gained the confidence of the mother herself, to such an extent, indeed, that, when the mother was asked why she did not visit the children as much as she had in fact been urged to do so by the social worker, she said that was because the children were so well off, meaning so well looked after by Mrs B. Indeed, the mother has said that, if the three eldest children are not to be returned to her, then she cannot think of anybody better than Mrs B to look after them. Mrs B has told me what happened during such visits as the mother made, and during the visits the mother, it is true, has not shown such interest in the children as one would expect during the length of the visit. She has not maintained her interest.

Mrs C has told me of her experience of the visits. In her affidavit she sets out the kind of visits there have been and their frequency. The mother has not sent the youngest twins any birthday cards, but the pattern of the visits shows very spasmodic regularity, or perhaps irregularity, and shows how there were times when she made arrangements to visit them and did not turn up. The mother has not had the care of the youngest twins since they were five months old, and it is accepted now by all parties that so far as the mother is concerned she is a stranger to the youngest twins, Gavin and Denvil.

One result of the s 2 resolution was to create hostility in the mother towards the social worker, so the mother has told me, because of the fact that she was instrumental, she thinks, in this s 2 resolution being passed. The mother says that is one of the reasons why she has not been so co-operative as she might otherwise have been since then. She has also told me that from what she has been told it is very rarely that a mother recovers care and control of her children once an order of that kind has been made. There again she puts that forward as an excuse for not being more persevering in her efforts to rehabilitate herself (if that is the right phrase) with her children.

Besides the psychiatrist's report which was authorised, the court has also been supplied with the report of an educational psychologist, both in respect of the elder boy twins, Jason and Adrian. I do not propose to read the report of the consultant psychiatrist, save that his recommendation is that the boys remain with their foster mother, Mrs B, on a long-term basis. It is plain that the reason why Twayna was not referred to him is that she is not considered to be so emotionally or psychiatrically affected as the two boys, though it is not urged that Twayna should be separated from her brothers. The psychologist's report is dated December 1980 and the mother's solicitor, in an affidavit of 13th February 1980, has produced a psychologist's report on Adrian and Jason based on knowing them from March 1978. That report concludes:

'I consider that their attitudes to learning and their perseverance and optimism have been substantially facilitated by the home environment they have shared for the most part since March 1978. I know that [Mrs B] has worked hard in building up their coping skills and their self-esteem. I would see it as being in the twins' best interests that this quality support should remain available.'

The mother says that P ceased to live with her in 1979. The last time, before 23rd December 1980, she had anything to do with him, she said, was some time early in 1979; on 23rd December 1980 he came with her to visit his youngest children at his insistence. She says that she has no more to do with him, that he has another girlfriend and that he has moved out of London, though he has only moved to a part of Kent quite near the edge of London. And the evidence in this case shows that P still maintains an interest in his two children; and that, in my judgment, is a threat to their security, for I see no good coming from these children seeing anything of their putative father. Nor do

I see any good coming from these children being present once more with their mother
a and P in a home setting when, as the mother herself admits, there might well be further
scenes of violence arising out of her personality, her moods of depression and P's own
violent disposition.

On behalf of the mother (and may I say that counsel has placed the mother's case
before me fully and admirably and with most sympathetic care, so that I have been
greatly assisted by the presentation of the case that she has made) it is urged by counsel
b that I must have regard to the difficult conditions which the mother has been in
throughout the period I have talked about, certainly from July 1974 through until
today. But I must look not too much at the past but at the future. Housing itself is, I
agree, something which can be cured. The housing manager has told me that he is sure
that, if the mother were given the care and control of any of these children, appropriate
accommodation would be available within a reasonable time; and so the housing in itself
c is neither here nor there and is not a bar to the mother having the return of the children.

Counsel for the mother submits that what has been lacking in the past is a capability
on the part of the mother to look after the children through her lack of knowledge of
how to do it and through the interference and presence of P. Counsel submits that she
has the motivation to be a good mother, and that that motivation should be allowed to
be tested, subject, of course, to supervision by the social services.

d There are, of course, other unfortunate features of this case which militate against my
feeling that it is safe to allow these children, or any of them, to go back into the care and
control of the mother. There is not only the past that I have referred to, the possibility
that some of the events of the past will be repeated; there are other features of the
mother's history which give cause for concern. She has been convicted of crimes of
dishonesty. She has not been imprisoned. She has been conditionally discharged or put
e on probation. The last time was on 10th January 1980 when she was put on 12 months'
probation for theft. When I asked the mother the details of these offences I found her
remarkably evasive, considering how comparatively recent those offences were.

In addition, as the mother herself reveals in one of her affidavits, there are two trials
pending in the Crown Court, at Inner London and at Knightsbridge, in which she is
charged in one case with offences under the Forgery Act 1913 and in the other with theft,
f I understand shop-lifting in conjunction with other women. She says she denies those
charges and there will be trials. She was committed for trial in respect of those earlier in
1980. It is not known yet when those trials will take place, but there is that
uncertainty. Quite apart from that, there is this record of dishonesty. And that gives
one ground for having doubts as to what she says about her intentions in the future, and
also about her suitability as a parent for these children.

g She denies that she has been unkind to them in the way of leaving them alone or
beating them up. The children themselves, according to Mrs B, have said that their
mother has beaten them with a belt. I make no findings, this is hearsay; but in matters
concerning children one must look at the whole of the case, and I am bound to say that
in the light of the history which I have touched on already I am left with a sense of unease
as to how those children were treated in the past, particularly having regard to the
h admission that she makes as to her own temper.

Counsel for the local authority submits that in the case of the first three children, the
twins Adrian and Jason and Twayna, the order required in their best interests is that they
should continue to be in the care and control of the local authority, and I use that in a
general sense because I have to refer to this at a later stage in more detail, and fostered by
Mrs B on a long-term basis. It is submitted, and the social worker has given her reasons
j for this, that there should be no access at least for the time being by the mother to the
three children, and that such access as there may be should be as Mrs B in conjunction
with the social worker then in charge would consider appropriate and beneficial at a later
stage, if she and the local authority ever think such a stage is reached.

It is also submitted by counsel for the local authority, and as I recall it supported by counsel on behalf of the Official Solicitor, that it would be beneficial for there to be contact between the three eldest children and the two youngest, wherever those two youngest are. That is something with which I respectfully agree.

One objection put forward on behalf of the mother has been in relation to the youngest children. So far as the eldest children are concerned, she approved highly of Mrs B. Ideally, she says, 'I would like my five children back, but if I can't have five then I would like my two youngest back.' But, in respect of the two youngest, it is asked on behalf of the local authority that I should make an order which would enable them to place them with persons who might become their adopters, that is take steps towards adoption. In this regard the mother has, through her counsel, made representations that if there is to be adoption then it should be with black parents, parents of similar racial and cultural background as herself. And I had the impression that if that condition were satisfied, then the mother would not be so concerned about having the children herself. The mother has shown a certain ambivalence in this way in regard to care and control in the same way as she has shown a certain ambivalence in regard to access. For, so far as the three elder children are concerned, she has said in one breath, 'I would like to see them once a year', and then she has changed and said, 'No, once a fortnight, once a month'; and one is left with an unease as to the genuineness of any feelings which this mother has for any of her children. As counsel for the Official Solicitor pointed out, when she was asked why she wanted any of the children she said words to the effect, 'Well, they are my children.' She did not say she loved them. One does not take answers out and hold them against a mother just like that, but that is just one more factor or feature in this case.

In support of the request that they may be allowed to take steps for adoption, the local authority have called the person in charge of their adoption agency. She is very expert; she has been in this position with the local authority since 1965; her qualifications are set out in her affidavit. Over that period she has been responsible for about 800 referrals to the adoption unit, and of those about one-half were placed for adoption, the other children remaining with their natural parents or parent. She says there are very excellent prospects of suitable adopters being found; and, she says, the rate of breakdown is very minimal. There were, out of those 400, some four that broke down; and three only were of significance, one due really to the ill health of the child. So, subject to the question of colour and cultural background, she is sure that there are excellent prospects of appropriate parents being found within a reasonable time, say six or seven months. I think seven or eight months is the average time.

Mrs C has indicated so far as the two youngest children are concerned that she does not wish to keep them on in the long term, though she is prepared to keep them in the interim until they are moved to wherever they are going to be moved to.

I had the assistance of a lady from Trinidad with a Chinese grandmother who was called to tell me about the relative merits of matching a coloured child with coloured parents, or placing a coloured child with white adoptive parents. Basing herself on the evidence of the person in charge of the adoption agency, while there are a number of black potential adopters, those black adopters are really looking for little black babies and not children of this age, and she accepts that the number of black potential adopters is comparatively small. She, like the person in charge of the adoption agency, stresses that the most important factor in adoption is the security, stability and the motherly skills of the adoptive parents. There has been discussion of the difficulties which are to be found, particularly in areas like that of the local authority, if the adoption takes place and if the adoption is by parents in the authority's area, which would not necessarily of course be the case. There are many imponderables about it, but of course there have been mixed adoptions in the past and there is nothing to suggest that they are more likely to break down than non-mixed adoptions, if I may so describe them.

Counsel for the Official Solicitor has not been able in conjunction with her instructing solicitor to make a submission whether the two youngest should be fostered or adopted. The Official Solicitor does submit that, broadly for the reasons that I have

sought to set out, it is not in the best interests of these young twins that they should be
a returned to the mother, a comparative stranger. Counsel points out that if these young
children are adopted the local authority would have no monitoring powers. On the
other hand the evidence of the person in charge of the adoption agency is that there is a
great difference in the breakdown rate between adoptions and long-term fostering. Her
experience, or the experience of adoption agencies generally, is that there is a 50% chance
of breakdown in long-term fostering cases. Like counsel for the Official Solicitor, I find
b the choice between those two courses a difficult one. Then there is the question of access
between the eldest and the two youngest. If adopted, the two youngest could of course
still be in contact with the eldest three, but there would be no power to monitor on
behalf of the local authority.

Counsel for the local authority and counsel for the Official Solicitor both submit that
in any event, so far as the youngest two children are concerned, it would not be in their
c interests for there to be any access by the mother. I entirely accept that that must be so,
whether it is to be a long-term fostering or otherwise.

There is the risk that the mother might take up again with P, or P might through her
wish to see his children. It is submitted by both the local authority and the Official
Solicitor that on balance it would be good for the three eldest children, who know of the
two babies, the two young ones, to keep contact, not very frequent, rather cousinly
d contact. If that occurs, of course, and there is access by the mother to the three eldest
children, there is a risk that the whereabouts of the two youngest might get known by
P. All this has to do with what kind of access there should be to the three eldest children,
as well as generally with what orders are appropriate in the case of all five children.

In the circumstances I am quite satisfied that in the case of the three eldest children
they should continue in the long-term fostering care of Mrs B, and that there should be
e no access at this stage by the mother to those children. I by no means rule out access at
a later stage, if circumstances permit and the best interests of the children dictate. I think
that by all means the mother should be allowed to send letters and should be kept
informed of the welfare of her children if she wishes to know.

At this stage the mother has understandably shown a certain upset, and I do not wish
to say more except that it demonstrates that she has a temperament of the kind which I
f have indicated already.

So far as the youngest children are concerned, because of the comparatively high rate
of breakdown in fostering, and because of the great confidence expressed by the adoption
agency to their ability to place children, albeit in all probability with white parents, I
think it is right that I should authorise the adoptive process to be commenced.

I have not fully dealt with the argument or discussion about black adopting parents.
g Suffice it to say, I do not think from what I have been told that there is any real prospect
of obtaining parents of the right cultural background. But the effort should be made to
find such parents, because if there are such parents then there is a slight advantage in
having them as parents. But even if such parents are not available I am quite satisfied
that it is better for the children to be with white adopted parents.

I now come to the form of order, and this is where counsel for the local authority in
h particular has asked me to consider a decision in the Court of Appeal and its effect on local
authorities. As I said earlier in this judgment, the foster parents, or rather Mrs B, the
foster mother, is not a party; and so far as the youngest twins are concerned there is no
relevant foster parent because Mrs C will fade out of the picture in due course. And so
all the local authority can do is ask for an order that care and control in one way or
another should be committed to them generally.

j In the past it has been quite usual, to my knowledge, where plaintiffs are local
authorities for an application to be made that the ward should be committed to their care
under s 7(2) of the Family Law Reform Act 1969; and it has been to my knowledge quite
usual for judges to make orders under that section in favour of the plaintiff local
authority. In those circumstances it has not been necessary, even if there has been a

foster parent or parents caring for or intending to care for the children, to make the foster parents themselves parties to the proceedings.

In *Re C B (a minor)* [1981] 1 All ER 16, [1981] 1 WLR 379 the Court of Appeal had to consider a decision of Bush J in relation to an illegitimate child. I think it is useful if I set out the facts more or less as they are set out in the headnote ([1981] 1 All ER 16), because I think they are important in relation to the decision which was actually made in that case:

'In October 1977 an illegitimate child then aged 8 or 9 months who had been left by her 17-year-old mother in the care of the child's grandmother was taken into voluntary care by the local authority with the mother's consent. The local authority placed the child with a short-term foster mother, Mrs R, who provided a good home for her. The mother occasionally visited the child. In April 1978 she married a man who was not the father of the child and she told the local authority that she wanted the child back. The local authority was not satisfied with the mother's proposed arrangements for the child and decided to make her a ward of court. Accordingly, the local authority, as plaintiff, took out an originating summons, dated 26th May 1978, to which the mother was the defendant, asking (i) that the child remains a ward of court during her minority and (ii) that care and control of her be committed to the local authority. An interim order was made granting care and control to the local authority and the child remained with Mrs R. The mother visited the child in June 1978 but thereafter did not see her again until January 1979, which was the last time she saw her. Consequently the child did not form any relationship with the mother, and both she and the child's father were strangers to her. In February 1979 the local authority decided that the situation at Mrs R's home was disturbing for the child and that she should be transferred to long-term foster parents. On 28th September, without referring the matter to the court, the local authority transferred the child from Mrs R to the new foster parents, who were eminently suitable and with whom the child was forming a secure relationship.'

I interpose here to say that it appears from the judgment of Ormrod LJ ([1981] 1 All ER 16 at 25, [1981] 1 WLR 379 at 389) that these new foster parents were proposed adopters. The headnote continues:

'Mrs R was distressed at the transfer. The court was informed of the change in the foster parents on 11th October. The mother, who had left her husband, went back to live with the child's father and wanted the child to be returned to Mrs R, who was therefore made second defendant to the originating summons. The local authority's view was that the child should remain in the care of the new foster parents. The judge, however, having ordered that the child should remain a ward of court, ordered that the mother should have care and control of her, since he though that the matter was governed by s 7(2) of the Family Law Reform Act 1969 and he found that there were "no exceptional circumstances making it impracticable or undesirable", within that subsection, for the child to be under the mother's care so as to justify an order under that subsection committing the child to the care of the local authority. The local authority appealed.'

Now, before I consider the judgment in particular of Ormrod LJ, I should say this. The particular concern of the local authority, and indeed of local authorities, is that if a simple order under the inherent jurisdiction is made giving care and control of a ward to the local authority, and not an order under s 7(2) of the 1969 Act, to which I have yet to refer, there may be no power in the local authority to provide for the maintenance of that ward placed in their control if that ward is placed with a foster parent or parents. Section 7(2) of the Family Law Reform Act 1969 provides as follows:

'Where it appears to the court that there are exceptional circumstances making it impracticable or undesirable for a ward of court to be, or to continue to be, under the care of either of his parents or of any other individual, the court may, if it thinks fit, make an order committing the care of the ward to a local authority; and thereupon Part II of the Children Act 1948 (which relates to the treatment of children in the care of the local authority) shall, subject to the next following subsection, apply as if the child had been received by the local authority into their care under section 1 of that Act.'

Part II of the Children Act 1948 contains provisions relating to the general duty of local authorities in care cases, and in particular s 13 provides for the provision of accommodation and maintenance for children in care. And so, if a care order is made under s 7(2) of the 1969 Act, the local authority to whom the care of the ward is committed would be enabled, without being surcharged by their district auditor, to make payments for the maintenance and other financial support of any ward placed in their care under that section. But, as I have said, it is greatly doubted that they have such power without such a care order.

Now I turn to *Re C B (a minor)* [1981] 1 All ER 16, [1981] 1 WLR 379. The decision of the Court of Appeal was that the judge at first instance erred in basing his decision on the requirements and wording of s 7(2) of the 1969 Act, the Court of Appeal holding that the proper approach in considering where the care and control of a child should be is that laid down in the Guardianship of Minors Act 1971 and in *J v C* [1969] 1 All ER 788, [1970] AC 668 in the House of Lords. That is, the court in its discretion must decide what the paramount interests of the child required, to quote Ormrod LJ's words, and that the judge was wrong in saying that the words of s 7(2) enabled him or directed him to decide whether it was impracticable or undesirable for the ward to continue to be under the care (in this case) of his mother (see [1981] 1 All ER 16 at 23, [1981] 1 WLR 379 at 387); the judge had decided that in the circumstances of the case it was right, having regard to the provisions of s 7(2), that the child in question should be with its mother rather than with either of the pairs of foster parents. As Ormrod LJ said ([1981] 1 All ER 16 at 22, [1981] 1 WLR 379 at 385):

'So the judge, in practice, had three possible alternative solutions to this problem: 'one was to leave the child where she is with the present foster parents; another to send her back to her pseudo-mother, her mother substitute, Mrs R; and the third was to hand her over to her mother.'

And he set out the pros and cons in the case of each. Then Ormrod LJ continued ([1981] 1 All ER 16 at 23, [1981] 1 WLR 379 at 386–387):

'Now the judge did not, as I see it, approach the case in the way which I have just indicated. In his judgment, having set out very fairly the facts, he said: "This decision does not turn on the relative merits of John and Margaret [the present foster parents] and the mother in the ideal parents stakes. No doubt the mother would come off second best, particularly as she has not been given a chance to show what she can do with Claire. The question turns on whether the local authority has shown that it is undesirable that the child should be or continue to be under the care of either of her parents. The court must look at the totality of the circumstances, bearing in mind that Parliament intended that children should remain with their parents if at all possible, and bearing in mind also, that the welfare of the child is the paramount consideration." With respect to the judge I think he was wrong and misdirected himself there in that passage because the decision *does* turn on what he called "the relative merits of John and Margaret and the mother in the ideal parents stakes". It may be that the judge was confused by the form of relief which was sought in the originating summons ... It seems to have got into the mind of the judge that the whole case was dominated and controlled by s 7(2) of the Family Reform Act 1969. [Having set out that subsection, he continued:] That is the section which the judge treated as controlling the whole of the case. So, instead of considering who was going to look after this child and considering, as he ought to have done, what the welfare of the child as the paramount consideration required, he was led to consider whether or not there were exceptional circumstances making it "impracticable or undesirable" for the ward to be under the care of either of her parents. He treated the matter as one of law. He felt that he had to find first that the circumstances were exceptional and second he had to decide whether it was impracticable or undesirable for the ward to continue to be in the care of either of her parents or any other individual [and I stress those words 'any other individual']. In fact, of course, s 7(2) of the 1969 Act never applied at all in this case because at all times the proposal of the local authority was that the child should remain in the care of the present foster parents, that is "another individual" within s 7(2). Nor is it at all difficult, in a case like this, to find exceptional circumstances. No one, I venture to think, would dream of making an order committing the care of a ward to a local authority unless the circumstances were exceptional. Nor would they contemplate doing it unless it was the only practical solution open to the court at the time.'

Pausing there, in Re CB (a minor), as I have stressed in reading the headnote, the parents to whom the Court of Appeal in the end gave care and control were the last foster parents, the proposed adopters. They were parties to the wardship proceedings; and ex hypothesi because they were prospective adopters they were prepared to assume full responsibility, including financial responsibility, for the child. So there was, in Re CB (a minor), 'another individual' which the ward could be under the care of; and it was not impracticable or undesirable for the ward to be in the care of that individual (or those individuals in that case). Indeed, that was never in issue.

And so, in examining the decision in Re CB (a minor) at this stage one sees two reasons given by the Court of Appeal: one, that the judge misdirected himself when saying that the decision does not turn on the relative merits of the prospective adopters and the mother in the ideal parent stakes, and misdirected himself indeed in being guided by the terms of s 7(2), and, secondly, on the ground that s 7(2) was in any event irrelevant and inapplicable and inappropriate because the conditions of s 7(2) were not fulfilled. But Ormrod LJ went on in two other passages to say something in more general terms, and it is these other passages which have given rise to concern. Continuing from the passage which I have just quoted, he said ([1981] 1 All ER 16 at 23, [1981] 1 WLR 379 at 387): 'It was a mistake to treat this case as if it was an s 7(2) case because the local authority were the plaintiffs.'

Taking those words as they are set out, they do not perhaps take the argument much further. One can understand from that that Ormrod LJ was assuming that Bush J treated it as an s 7(2) case because the local authority were the plaintiffs. Well, that may be so. Ormrod LJ went on ([1981] 1 All ER 16 at 23, [1981] 1 WLR 379 at 387):

'This is the first point to be made so far as the wardship jurisdiction is concerned. It is an unfettered jurisdiction to place the ward in the care and control of any person who can best look after him or her.'

Then he stressed the difficulties that local authorities are under and how the local authorities are not to be discouraged from making applications in wardship proceedings, and emphasised ([1981] 1 All ER 16 at 24, [1981] 1 WLR 379 at 388):

'I am most anxious to emphasise that once the child is a ward of court the major decisions relating to that child are for the court to take. That is equally the case whether the care and control is granted to either parent or to some other individual or to a local authority. The judge unfortunately did not approach the matter, I think, in the right way. He was side-tracked by considering whether he had the necessary jurisdiction under s 7(2) of the 1969 Act. But in this case the local authority were themselves the plaintiffs in the originating summons asking for "care and control", not for an order under s 7(2). Had he had the present foster parents before him as parties, I do not think that this error would have crept in. The result is that, with respect to the judge, the conclusion is inescapable that he exercised his discretion on an entirely wrong basis. He did not, at any stage, compare the mother's proposals with the present foster parents' proposals for the child. He did not weigh one against the other and make an assessment of the advantages to the child in regard to one course or the other, in the short-term or the long-term. He was almost wholly concerned with deciding whether the local authority had made out their case under s 7(2), but, as I have already said, if a local authority takes the initiative of making a child a ward I do not think that s 7(2) comes into the case at all.'

And this is the passage which particular concern is felt about:

'Section 7(2) was passed to give the court power in proceedings between parents, or between a parent and a third party, to make an order committing the child to the care of the local authority, or to make it clear that the court, in wardship proceedings, had the same powers as it has under the Matrimonial Causes Act 1973.'

That sentence, in my judgment, has to be taken in context with the immediately preceding sentence; and that is that Ormrod LJ was seeking to show how he thought that Bush J had been led into considering in the first place the terms of s 7(2), basing his decision on the wording of s 7(2). But what Ormrod LJ is saying there is much wider in its implications than the two reasons for the decision of the Court of Appeal to which I have already adverted, and it is that which has caused concern.

Section 7(2) is an extension of a valuable tool that was given to the court in divorce legislation under s 43 of the Matrimonial Causes Act 1973. I say a valuable tool; it is plainly there for the court (a judge of the court) to make use of in the interests of a child or children if he thinks it necessary to do so. There is no restriction, as counsel for the Official Solicitor has pointed out, in the section itself as to the circumstances in which use of s 7(2) may be made. Parliament has not thought fit to make any express restriction, and there is no restriction under the original s 43. And there is no restriction in a similar power which is granted under the later Act, the Guardianship Act 1973, s 2(2)(b), which has also been considered by Parliament in the Children Act 1975, where an amendment is proposed but it has not yet come into force to that section, an amendment which does not itself again make any restriction on the use of s 7(2).

Were it not, therefore, for the words of Ormrod LJ one would have, I think, no hesitation in saying that the present case is plainly one where it is desirable that there should be an order under s 7(2), whether the local authority have asked for such an order in their summons or not, because it is, as I say, a tool available to the court which has considered what is necessary in the interests of the children.

I look to the judgment of Bridge LJ to see if there is any further assistance to be found. This was a two-judge Court of Appeal. One sees that Bridge LJ referred to the words of the judge at first instance and s 7(2) and said ([1981] 1 All ER 16 at 25–26, [1981] 1 WLR 379 at 389–390):

'Now the situation with which s 7(2) is dealing is a situation where it is impracticable or undesirable for a ward of court to be under the care of either of his parents or any other individual, and I emphasise those concluding words, "or any other individual", and once that is appreciated it becomes apparent that s 7(2) had nothing whatever to do with this case. No one could possibly have suggested that it was either impracticable or undesirable in this case for Claire to continue in the custody of either the present foster parents or to be returned to the custody of Mrs R, the previous foster parent, or of the natural parents. The reason why s 7(2) seems to have loomed so large was that by what seems to have been a purely procedural accident the present foster parents were not parties before the court, so it was the local authority who, in form, were applying for an order to be made in their favour. But in substance, nobody could have been in any doubt that the issue was whether the little girl should be in the care of her natural parents, or one or other of the sets of foster parents who were "other individuals" within the meaning of s 7(2). In fact, s 7(2) indicates no parliamentary a priori preference for giving the care of a child to its natural parents as against giving it to anybody else. The paramount consideration in a simple case like this, and the sole consideration, is what will best serve the welfare of the child. Once the misapprehension derived from s 7(2) is cleared out of the way, and the case is approached on the basis of what will best serve the welfare of this little girl of now just over 3 years old, the solution to the problem to my mind stands out so as to be unmistakable.'

And he dealt thereafter with the merits. One notes that he did not make the general observation as to applicability of s 7(2) where the local authority are the plaintiffs; and he stressed that in that case there was 'another individual'.

Here, in the case of the three elder children, as I have said already, there is the foster parent who is 'another individual' who in this case, unlike Re CB (a minor) it is impracticable to give care and control to because she does not have enough money to look after the children. In the case of the young twins, Gavin and Denvil, there is nobody effectively able at the moment to have day-to-day, physical control of them for anything like a significant length of time. Their stay with Mrs C is purely temporary. So again in the case of those two there is, subject to the demands or subject to the desirability of the mother having the children, no 'other individual' to whom it is practicable to commit the care of those children. So this is a case where the conditions of s 7(2) are complied with.

I have, as I said earlier, found that it is undesirable that any of these children should go to the care of their mother. That satisfies the other aspect, the other condition in s 7(2).

I also bear in mind, as I am told by counsel for the local authority (who appeared in Re CB), that in fact no argument was addressed to the question whether s 7(2) could or could not be used if the local authority was a plaintiff in the proceedings.

In the circumstances, I think I am justified, with the greatest respect to Ormrod LJ, in assuming that when he made the references to which I have referred it was in the context of explaining how the judge at first instance had come to deal with the matter in the way in which he did. And it was for the reason only that Ormrod LJ was giving expression to that view. In any event, I think in the circumstances that it is right to consider that observation as obiter.

I add that although a care order under s 7(2) gives the local authority the powers contained in Part II of the Children Act 1948, which include control of access, nevertheless, because it is an order made in wardship proceedings, if, as here, the wardship continues, the wardship court retains the power to make such directions as to access as it thinks fit, as well, of course, as the power to discharge the care order: see Re Y (a minor) (child in care: access) [1975] 3 All ER 348, [1976] Fam 125.

For those reasons I order that there should be a care order under s 7(2) in relation to each of these five children. The order, therefore, will be on that basis with provision for care and control and access as I have already indicated.

Order accordingly.

Solicitors: *R A Joy*, Catford (for the local authority); *Gillian Butler*, Deptford (for the mother); *Official Solicitor*.

Bebe Chua   Barrister.

Reel v Holder and another

COURT OF APPEAL, CIVIL DIVISION
LORD DENNING MR, EVELEIGH AND BRANDON LJJ
26th, 29th, 30th JUNE 1981

Unincorporated association – Rules – Construction – International athletics association – Members consisting of national associations controlling athletics in their 'countries' – Rules providing that jurisdiction of member limited to political boundaries of 'country' it represented – Association controlling athletics in mainland China elected – Subsequently association controlling athletics in Taiwan elected – Taiwan not recognised as separate state under international law – Taiwan remaining member of international association for 22 years – International association resolving to recognise mainland association as sole body controlling athletics on mainland and in Taiwan – Whether resolution valid – Whether Taiwan remaining a member of international association – Whether 'country' in rules meaning a nation recognised in international law – Whether resolution purporting to expel Taiwan association ultra vires powers given by rules.

The IAAF, the international body controlling athletics, was an unincorporated association with its head office in England. The rules of the IAAF provided that (i) the 'national' governing body for athletics in each 'country' was eligible for membership of the IAAF, (ii) the membership of the IAAF should comprise duly elected national governing bodies controlling athletics in each country, and (iii) the jurisdiction of each member was limited to the political boundary of the country it represented. In 1954 the IAAF, on the application of the Chinese government in Peking, accepted the body controlling athletics on the Chinese mainland ('the mainland body') as a member, but at the same time it invited an application for membership from the body controlling athletics on the island of Formosa (subsequently Taiwan). Under international law Taiwan was not recognised as a separate state and was treated as a province of the mainland Republic of China. In 1956 the IAAF decided by a majority to elect to membership the body controlling athletics in Taiwan ('the Taiwan body'). In 1958 the mainland body withdrew from membership of the IAAF because of the election of the Taiwan body. For 22 years the Taiwan body was treated as the member of the IAAF having jurisdiction over Taiwan. In 1978 the IAAF passed a resolution accepting reaffiliation of the mainland body as a member and recognising it as the only body having jurisdiction over mainland China and Taiwan. The effect of the resolution was, therefore, to exclude Taiwan from membership of the IAAF. The plaintiff, representing the Taiwan body, brought an action in England against representatives of the IAAF seeking declarations that the Taiwan body was and remained a member of the IAAF and that the 1978 resolution, so far as it purported to deprive the Taiwan body of membership, was void and of no effect. The Taiwan body submitted that it had been validly elected to membership of the IAAF in 1956 because it was the national governing body for athletics in a 'country', within the IAAF rules, namely Taiwan. The IAAF submitted that the 'country' concerned for the purpose of the rules was 'China' which embraced both the mainland and the island of Taiwan and therefore the election in 1956 of the Taiwan body had been invalid under the rules because there was then already an elected member for the country of China, ie the mainland body. The judge ([1979] 3 All ER 1041) held that the Taiwan body had been validly elected a member of the IAAF in 1956 and wrongfully excluded from membership in 1978 and accordingly granted the plaintiff the declarations sought. The representatives of the IAAF appealed.

Held – In construing the IAAF rules the court was not concerned with international or political sovereignty, since the term 'country' was used in the rules in the sense of a territory or area where the inhabitants shared the right to live as a distinct people and where the applicant for membership had complete authority over athletics. Accordingly, eligibility for membership of the IAAF did not depend on whether the area over which the applicant had control of athletics was a state in the international or political sense but on whether the applicant exercised control over athletics in a separate and distinct territory or area. Since Taiwan was a separate and distinct territory, the Taiwan body was the governing body for athletics in the 'country' of Taiwan, within the rules, and had been validly elected as a member of the IAAF in 1956. Since the 1978 decision expelling it from membership was beyond the powers conferred on the IAAF by its rules, the expulsion was wrongful. It followed that the plaintiff was entitled to the declarations sought and that the appeal would be dismissed (see p 324 *g h*, p 325 *b* to *d* and *f* to p 326 *b* and *f* to p 327 *a*, post).

Decision of Forbes J [1979] 3 All ER 1041 affirmed.

Notes

For the territory of a state in international law, see 18 Halsbury's Laws (4th Edn) paras 1453–1472.

Case referred to in judgments

Shen Fu Chang v Stellan Mohlin (5th July 1977, unreported), QBD.

Cases also cited

Alan (W J) & Co Ltd v El Nasr Export & Import Co [1972] 2 All ER 127, [1972] 2 QB 189, CA.
Buttes Gas and Oil Co v Hammer (No 3) [1980] 3 All ER 475, [1980] 3 WLR 668, CA.
Harington v Sendall [1903] 1 Ch 921.
Kawasaki Kisen Kabushiki Kaisha of Kobe v Bantham Steamship Co Ltd [1939] 1 All ER 819, [1939] 2 KB 544, CA.
Lee v Showmen's Guild of Great Britain [1952] 1 All ER 1175, [1952] QB 329, CA.
Luigi Monta of Genoa v Cechofracht Co Ltd [1956] 2 All ER 769, [1956] QB 552.
Prenn v Simmonds [1971] 3 All ER 237, [1971] 1 WLR 1381, HL.
Tobacco Trade Benevolent Association, Re, Baron Sinclair v Finlay [1958] 3 All ER 353, [1958] 1 WLR 1113.

Appeal

By an originating summons dated 25th January 1979 the plaintiff, Cheng Chi Reel, secretary-general of the Republic of China Track and Field Association ('ROCTFA'), suing on behalf of herself and as representing the members of ROCTFA, sought as against the defendants, Frederick W Holder and Adriaan Paulen, the honorary treasurer and president respectively of the International Amateur Athletic Federation ('IAAF'), sued on behalf of themselves and as representing the members of the IAAF, declarations (1) that ROCTFA were and remained members of the IAAF, (2) that ROCTFA were and remained entitled to all the rights and privileges of membership of the IAAF, and (3) that the resolution dated 5th October 1978 of the congress of IAAF, in so far as it purported to deprive or had the effect of depriving ROCTFA of membership or alternatively of the rights and privileges of membership of the IAAF, was void and of no effect. The plaintiff also sought an injunction restraining the defendants whether by themselves, their servants, their agents or otherwise from doing any act pursuant to or in consequence of the resolution of 5th October 1978 in so far as any such act was inconsistent with ROCTFA being a member of the IAAF and entitled to all the rights and privileges of such membership. On 2nd April 1979 Forbes J ([1979] 3 All ER 1041, [1979] 1 WLR 1252) granted the declarations sought by the plaintiff and gave liberty to apply for the injunction. The defendants appealed. The facts are set out in the judgment of Lord Denning MR.

Konrad Schiemann QC and *Stephen Ruttle* for the defendants.
Robert Alexander QC and *Brian Davenport QC* for the plaintiff.

LORD DENNING MR. In 1912 there was formed the International Amateur Athletic Federation ('IAAF'). The athletic associations of many countries joined together to arrange their activities on an international scale. They took part in the Olympic Games and in competitions between countries, and so forth. For many years the president was the distinguished athlete Lord Burghley, afterwards the Marquis of Exeter.

The question which arises for decision in this case is in what circumstances a 'country' can be admitted or expelled from the federation. I use the word 'country' because it is the word used in the rules. But it is very ambiguous.

The 'China' problem has been with the world since 1949. The government of mainland China, operating from Peking, claimed to have sovereignty over the mainland and also the island of Formosa, now called Taiwan. The Taiwan government claimed to have sovereignty over the island and also over the whole of mainland China. So both governments claimed to have sovereignty over the whole of the two territories.

I put on one side any thought of international politics. In international law Taiwan's claim is not recognised. I will read the statement made by the Foreign and Commonwealth Relations Office to the solicitors in this case:

'HMG [Her Majesty's Government] do not, and have never regarded Taiwan as a State. Nor do we regard the Chinese Nationalist authorities in Taiwan as a Government and have not done so since 1950, when we ceased to recognise them as the Government of China . . . the Government of the United Kingdom acknowledge the position of the Chinese Government that Taiwan is a province of the People's Republic of China.'

That is in the international sphere of statehood and sovereignty so declared by this country as far back as 1950. We are told that in 1971 the United Nations followed suit. To my mind those considerations have no application whatever to the problem which we have to decide today under the rules of the IAAF. As long ago as 1954 an application was made by the government in Peking to become a member of the IAAF. They were accepted only as the representatives of mainland China. They were told that if Formosa wished to apply for membership, their application would be considered separately. That decision was set out quite clearly in letters which passed at that time. On 9th November 1954 the secretary-treasurer of the IAAF wrote to the president of the China National Amateur Athletic Federation in mainland China saying:

'. . . I must advise you that the application of the All China Athletic Association for membership of the I.A.A.F. was considered at the Congress in August this year and that association was accepted as a new member. At the time it was agreed that an application for membership from the controlling body of athletics in Formosa would receive consideration.'

Two years later in 1956 Formosa (now Taiwan) applied to become a member. There was objection from the Eastern bloc, from Russia, Czechoslovakia, Romania and mainland China. It is interesting to note what the president, Lord Burghley, said when Taiwan applied for membership:

'The President [that is, Lord Burghley] said that he himself wished to support this application for affiliation in the same way as he had done for other countries. The young people from a country with a population of 18,000,000 [that is the population of Taiwan] were involved and any question of politics should be left out of any discussion for the aim in view was to bring as many young athletes as possible into the family group of the Federation. It was impossible for the athletic association in Peking to organise athletic matches for the Taiwan athletes as there was no communication between the two countries and he therefore moved from the Chair that this application be accepted. [The minutes went on to say:] The delegates from the U.S.S.R., Czechoslovakia and Roumania supported the A.A. of the People's Republic of China in their opposition. On a vote being taken it was agreed, with only four dissentients, that the application of the China National Amateur Athletic Federation be accepted on the understanding that they would compete and be known as "Taiwan".'

From that time onwards Taiwan attended the meetings, paid their subscriptions, and were members of the association. But mainland China did not approve. Two years later they withdrew their own membership. That was in 1958.

I will now pass on to the critical year in this case. In 1978 there was to be a meeting of the congress of the IAAF in Puerto Rico. The agenda looked quite innocent. It simply proposed that Taiwan should remain as a member but should be referred to only by the name of 'Taiwan' in future. Then on the very morning of the meeting a circular was distributed of a proposed amendment. It was proposed that Taiwan should be excluded from membership; and that mainland China should come in as the sole representative of all the territories. I will read the resolution which was put forward. It is what is in dispute in this case:

'In connection with the request for affiliation of the Athletic Association of The People's Republic of China [that is, mainland China] and 1. having considered I.A.A.F. Rule 4 with particular reference to political boundaries; and 2. having heard from the United Nations that the political boundaries of The People's Republic of China include the Island of Taiwan; and 3. having received a guarantee that Taiwan athletes may compete in international competitons under I.A.A.F. Rules, under the jurisdiction of the Athletic Association of The People's Republic of China, the Council recommends the re-affiliation of The People's Republic of China as the only representative in the I.A.A.F. for China.'

That resolution was debated at some length. Eventually, after a long discussion, the congress proceeded to vote. The vote was in favour of mainland China by 200 to 153. The final minute said:

'The Athletic Association of The People's Republic of China was, therefore, accepted as an I.A.A.F. Member, to have jurisdiction also over the Territory where athletics was at present governed by the existing I.A.A.F. Member in Taiwan.'

It is quite plain that that amounted to the exclusion of Taiwan from the IAAF. Mainland China was to be admitted, exercising jurisdiction not only over the mainland but also over the island.

That gave rise to much perturbation as to the validity of the resolution. An action has been brought in the High Court in England to resolve the matter. The court has been asked to declare that Taiwan still remains a member of the IAAF; that they have been wrongly excluded; and that the resolution of 1978 is void and of no effect.

The court was faced with a similar problem in relation to badminton in 1977 (*Shen Fu Chang v Stellan Mohlin* (5th July 1977, unreported)). The judge, Robert Goff J, took the view, with which I agree, that we are not concerned with international law or with sovereignty. We are simply concerned with the interpretation of the rules of the IAAF. The rules are in English. The head office of the IAAF is in England. It is right that, if the rules need to be construed, the matter should come to the English courts to be decided. At the end of his judgment in the badminton case, Robert Goff J made a declaration that Taiwan could be a member of the International Badminton Federation. He made an injunction to that effect.

We now have to construe the rules of the International Amateur Athletic Federation. Firstly, we have to consider whether the application by Taiwan in 1956 was valid; whether Taiwan was eligible for membership. At that time the rules were not as full as they are now. They have been developed in the course of time. Rule 7 said: 'The National Governing Body for amateur athletics in any country shall be eligible for membership of the Federation.' 'National' is one of the words which gives rise to trouble. Rule 1(2) presents another problem: 'The jurisdiction of members of the Federation shall be limited to the political boundaries of the country they represent.' But some help is to be derived from r 9(7). It said that a 'colony' can be eligible to be affiliated as a member. That shows a departure from statehood. It shows that places such as Hong Kong and Gibraltar, even though they are under the sovereignty of the United Kingdom, can be affiliated as members.

In my opinion the membership of this international association is not confined to sovereign states in the international sense. Every athletic association in any territory is eligible for membership provided that it is the supreme athletic association for that territory and is not subject to any control by another athletic association. Take, for instance, the United Kingdom. We have the Amateur Athletic Association which governs all amateur athletics in this country, England, Scotland and Wales. So the Amateur Athletic Association is the association to represent the United Kingdom as a member of the IAAF. But if Wales formed their own independent amateur athletic association and wanted to be separately represented, it seems to me that Wales would be a 'country' eligible for membership under the rules of the IAAF.

In the rule, 'The jurisdiction of members of the Federation shall be limited to the political boundaries of the country they represent', the governing word is 'country'. One 'country' is Taiwan. Another 'country' is mainland China. The jurisdiction of the Athletic Association of Taiwan is limited to Taiwan. The jurisdiction of the Athletic Association of mainland China is limited to mainland China.

One can argue to and fro on the interpretation of these rules. The people who drew them up could not possibly have envisaged all the problems which would have to be coped with in the future in regard to them. The courts have to reconcile all the various differences as best they can. It is interesting to notice r 3 of the 1978 rules, which are certainly applicable in this case. It says:

> 'The objects of the Federation shall be: 1.—To establish friendly and loyal co-operation between all Members for the benefit of amateur athletics throughout the world. 2.—To strive to ensure that no racial, religious, political or other kind of discrimination be allowed in athletics, and to take all necessary measures to stop such discrimination.'

One would hope there would not be any racial discrimination against Taiwan. That is the point in this case. Was Taiwan eligible for membership when it applied, and was accepted, in 1956 with only four dissentients? It seems to me that the decision to accept Taiwan, by a majority, was perfectly rightly made.

We have had discussions as to how far rulings should be unanimous. There was no provision in the 1956 rules for their being altered in any way. It was a membership of a club. There was a contract between the parties. If the rules are to be altered later, that can only be done by agreement between all the parties. It has to be unanimous. But, when the rules are not to be altered, and the only question is application of the rules by a committee or a body of that kind, then the ordinary rule applies that the decision can be by a majority. In this case the decision in 1956 to admit Taiwan by a majority was perfectly valid.

If that be right, there is no need to go into the question of an estoppel. That would only arise if the admission of Taiwan were wrong. Even if it had been wrong, nevertheless there is a strong case for saying that as everyone, except the People's Republic of China, accepted them as a member for 22 years, it would be too late to say that their admission was not valid. But there is no need to go into that in view of the opinion I have expressed that on the rules they were validly admitted.

That brings me to the final point in the case. In 1978 the IAAF resolved to make mainland China the sole representative of the whole area including Taiwan. That amounted to a decision to expel Taiwan. That was beyond any power conferred on the congress by the rules. If the IAAF want to have power to expel, then the rules will have to be altered.

I would agree with Forbes J ([1979] 3 All ER 1041, [1979] 1 WLR 1252) that Taiwan was validly elected a member in 1956. It was wrongfully excluded in 1978. It is still a member. These courts can and should make a declaration in favour of Taiwan to that extent. We do not think this should give rise to any international complications. We are making a declaration on the meaning of the rules according to English law, which is the governing law. We grant no injunction. We simply state what we think the rules mean. I would therefore agree with the judge and dismiss the appeal.

EVELEIGH LJ. I agree. Rule 1 of the rules as they were in 1956 reads:

'The title shall be the International Amateur Athletic Federation. It shall comprise duly elected national governing associations or federations of countries, in control of amateur track and field athletics . . . Only one member for each country can be affiliated.'

By r 7 it is provided: 'The National Governing Body for amateur athletics in any country shall be eligible for membership of the Federation.' The question as argued in the court below ([1979] 3 All ER 1041, [1979] 1 WLR 1252) was whether Taiwan was eligible for membership in 1956.

Reading the rules, one comes clearly to the conclusion that the International Amateur Athletic Federation is an affiliation of athletic governing bodies formed to pursue certain objects. It has been contended in this court that the word 'country' in the rules means that which is internationally recognised as a state or at least that the congress of the federation is entitled so to construe it. What would that involve? It would, as I see it, involve a different meaning being attached to the rules depending on which court decided the matter. It would mean a different meaning attached to the rules depending on whether reliance was placed on recognition by this state or that state. For example, in 1950 the United Kingdom recognised Peking but other countries did not, and neither did the United Nations at that time although they now do.

Those who formed the IAAF were not concerned with international politics: they were concerned to set standards for athletics throughout the world. They were concerned to collect together people who would be in a position to exercise control over athletics in various parts of the world. Unless a governing body of some kind applies for membership, the IAAF is not concerned to determine if a given place or area is a country. It is only in connection with an application for membership by an applicant who puts himself forward as a governing body for a particular place, district or region that it becomes necessary to consider the meaning of 'country' in the rules. One thing that is clear is that there may only be one member for each country. Therefore, in entertaining an application, it has to be seen whether or not there is an existing member who has control, or a measure of control, over the same area as that for which the applicant contends. There must be no doubt who is to speak with authority as the governing body for a particular group of athletes. The word 'country' has been used in the rules in order to delineate the area of authority. They do not use the word in the sense of sovereign state. That is clear from r 9(7) which reads:

'In international competitions, members of this Federation shall be represented only by native born or naturalised subjects of the country which the affiliated member represents, except in the case of citizens of a colony, when they shall be eligible to represent the mother country if such colony is not represented by membership of the I.A.A.F.'

That rule clearly contemplates that there may be an existing member of the IAAF which is a colony and not itself a sovereign state. I think that the word is used in the rules in the sense of an area or part of the world where the applicant has authority in relation to athletics and an area to which the word 'country' is appropriate because the inhabitants share the right to live there in common as one distinct people. This is a question to be answered broadly and not on a political basis alone. Political status may have some relevance. It may perhaps help to see the inhabitants as being one people, but it is not the decisive factor.

a For those reasons I agree with the judgment delivered by Lord Denning MR.

BRANDON LJ. I agree with both the judgments which have been delivered.

Appeal dismissed. Declarations accordingly. Injunction refused. Leave to appeal to the House
b of Lords refused.

Solicitors: *Linklaters & Paines* (for the defendants); *Herbert Smith & Co* (for the plaintiff).

Sumra Green   Barrister.

c

Regent OHG Aisenstadt und Barig v Francesco of Jermyn Street Ltd

d QUEEN'S BENCH DIVISION
MUSTILL J
22nd, 23rd, 24th, 28th JANUARY 1980

Sale of goods – Delivery – Separate consignments – Short delivery – Rejection of goods – Contract
for sale of suits – Delivery by instalments at sellers' discretion – Short delivery of one suit on one
e instalment – Whether contract divisible – Whether short delivery of one suit going to root of
contract – Whether buyers entitled to treat whole contract as repudiated – Sale of Goods Act
1893, ss 30(1), 31(2).

The plaintiffs, who were manufacturers of menswear, agreed to sell 62 suits to the defendants, who owned a retail shop. Delivery was to be by instalments, the number and size of the consignments being left to the plaintiffs' discretion. The defendants
f subsequently informed the plaintiffs that they wished to cancel the order but the plaintiffs insisted on delivery of the suits, which were already in production. Because of shortage of cloth one consignment was delivered one suit short, the plaintiffs having previously informed the defendants of the fact. The defendants, consistent with their wish to cancel the entire order, rejected delivery of all the consignments. The plaintiffs
g were forced to sell the suits elsewhere at a much lower price and brought an action against the defendants claiming damages for loss occasioned by the non-acceptance. The defendants contended that short delivery on one instalment amounted to short delivery on the whole contract and, the plaintiffs having delivered a quantity of goods less than they had contracted to sell, the defendants were entitled under s 30(1)[a] of the Sale of Goods Act 1893 to reject all the goods, notwithstanding that the parties had agreed that
h for convenience delivery was to be made in instalments. The plaintiffs contended that the contract was divisible into separate instalments and accordingly, under s 31(2)[b] of the

---

a Section 30(1) provides: 'Where the seller delivers to the buyer a quantity of goods less than he contracted to sell, the buyer may reject them, but if the buyer accepts the goods so delivered he must pay for them at the contract rate.'

j *b* Section 31(2) provides: 'Where there is a contract for the sale of goods to be delivered by stated instalments, which are to be separately paid for, and the seller makes defective deliveries in respect of one or more instalments, or the buyer neglects or refuses to take delivery of or pay for one or more instalments, it is a question in each case depending on the terms of the contract and the circumstances of the case, whether the breach of contract is a repudiation of the whole contract or whether it is a severable breach giving rise to a claim for compensation but not to a right to treat the whole contract as repudiated.'

1896 Act, whether the short delivery of one suit was a repudiation of the whole contract or merely a severable breach depended on the terms of the contract and the circumstances. *a*

Held – The plaintiffs were entitled to damages for the following reasons—

(1) On its true construction the contract was a divisible contract notwithstanding that the number and size of the individual deliveries were not fixed in advance but were left to the plaintiffs' discretion. It followed that s 30(1) of the 1893 Act did not apply to the contract and accordingly the plaintiffs were not entitled to cancel the whole contract *b* under s 30(1) because of the short delivery of one suit (see p 334 g and p 335 g, post).

(2) In any event, where the nature of the misdelivery of goods was the short delivery of one instalment, so that the position was covered by the mutually inconsistent provisions of ss 30(1) and 31(2) of the 1893 Act, the more flexible provisions of s 31(2) were to be applied in preference to those of s 30(1). Applying s 31(2), the short delivery of one suit did not, in the context of the terms of the contract and the circumstances, go *c* to the root of the contract and therefore did not entitle the defendants to treat of the whole contract as repudiated (see p 334 j to p 335 c and g, post).

Notes

For short delivery of goods and misdelivery of an instalment of goods, see 34 Halsbury's Laws (3rd Edn) 97, 105, paras 144, 159, and for cases on the subjects, see 39 Digest (Repl) *d* 485–487, 694–695, 1797–1813, 1875–1886.

For the Sale of Goods Act 1893, ss 30, 31, see 30 Halsbury's Statutes (3rd Edn) 26, 27.

As from 1st January 1980 ss 30(1) and 31(2) of the 1893 Act have been replaced by ss 30(1) and 31(2) of the Sale of Goods Act 1979.

Cases referred to in judgment *e*

Braithwaite v Foreign Hardwood Co [1905] 2 KB 543, 74 LJKB 688, 92 LT 637, 10 Asp MLC 52, 10 Com Cas 189, CA, 39 Digest (Repl) 508, 523.

British & Beningtons Ltd v North Western Cachar Tea Co Ltd [1923] AC 48, [1922] All ER Rep 224, 92 LJKB 62, 128 LT 422, 28 Com Cas 265, 13 Ll L Rep 67, HL, 39 Digest (Repl) 664, 1643.

Esmail v Rosenthal & Sons Ltd [1964] 2 Lloyd's Rep 447. *f*

Jackson v Rotax Motor & Cycle Co [1910] 2 KB 937, 80 LJKB 38, 103 LT 411, CA, 39 Digest (Repl) 555, 856.

Maredelanto Compania Naviera SA v Bergbau-Handel GmbH, The Mihalis Angelos [1970] 3 All ER 125, [1971] QB 164, [1970] 3 WLR 601, [1970] 2 Lloyd's Rep 43, CA, 12 Digest (Reissue) 420, 3059.

Millar's Karri and Jarrah Co (1902) *v Weddel, Turner & Co* (1908) 100 LT 128, 11 Asp *g* MLC 184, 14 Com Cas 25, 39 Digest (Repl) 700, 1911.

Reuter, Hufeland & Co v Sala & Co (1879) 4 CPD 239, 48 LJQB 492, 40 LT 476, 4 Asp MLC 121, CA, 39 Digest (Repl) 709, 1975.

Taylor v Oakes, Roncoroni & Co (1922) 127 LT 267, 27 Com Cas 261, CA, 39 Digest (Repl) 727, 2083.

h

Action

By a writ issued on 1st March 1978 the plaintiffs, Regent OHG Aisenstadt & Barig, claimed against the defendants, Francesco of Jermyn Street Ltd, the sum of DM36,898·10 and interest, or alternatively damages for breach of contract and interest, arising out of the defendants' refusal to accept goods supplied by the plaintiffs under a contract made *j* between the plaintiffs and the defendants. The facts are set out in the judgment.

Andrew Hillier for the plaintiffs.
C J R Flint for the defendants.

Cur adv vult

28th January. **MUSTILL J** read the following judgment: At the beginning of 1977 the
plaintiffs, who are manufacturers of menswear in Germany, entered into a contract with
the defendants, who are retailers in London, for the sale of 62 suits and 48 jackets, at a
total price of DM37,312·10, for delivery during August, September and October 1977.
By this action, the plaintiffs claim damages for breach of the contract alleging that the
defendants wrongfully refused to accept any of the goods which the plaintiffs tendered
to them. The defendants agreed that the goods were rejected when tendered but deny
that this was a breach of contract. They put forward a counterclaim on the basis that the
plaintiffs had themselves repudiated the contract.

The events giving rise to the dispute were as follows. The garments which it is the
plaintiffs' business to manufacture are of high quality and are very expensive. The
market for menswear of this kind is quite narrow and is highly seasonal. Essentially
there are two seasons: spring/summer and autumn/winter. Orders are placed several
months in advance. Goods delivered late will often be of little use. The retailer is given
a wide variety of choice as regards size, cloths, dye, lapels, buttons and so on; so that,
although the total value of an order may be large, the quantity of any particular garment
purchased will often be small. Since 1975 the plaintiffs have been promoting their sales
in the United Kingdom through a selling agent, Mr Robert Rosen. Amongst the
customers of Mr Rosen were the defendants, who, by the end of 1976, had placed a
number of orders with the plaintiffs through his agency. Amongst these was an order
for about 150 suits intended for sale during the spring/summer season of 1977. I will call
this 'the spring order'.

The next transaction was the contract for the autumn/winter season 1977, under
which the present action is brought. I will call this 'the winter order'. It was negotiated
in accordance with the usual practice.

On 10th January 1977 Mr Rosen called on the defendants with his sample cloths and
pattern book. The defendants' managing director, Mr J B Goldin, selected the various
cloths and styles of the garments which he wished to order. These were recorded on a
printed order sheet which both he and Mr Rosen signed. This sheet included various
terms in the German language, one of which was to the effect that the price of certain
sizes of garment would be subject to a surcharge of 5%. As I have said, the order
consisted of 62 suits and 48 jackets.

On 15th February the plaintiffs sent to the defendants direct a brief acknowledgment
of the order incorporating a confirmation of the delivery dates, although these were not,
as it happened, in quite the same terms as the dates written on the order form.

Subsequently, on 15th March, the plaintiffs sent a detailed specification of the goods
ordered. The form on which this was written intimated that certain sizes would carry
a surcharge of 10%, not 5% as had been stated in the order form.

Meanwhile a problem had arisen concerning the spring order. The defendants found
themselves temporarily overstocked and asked Mr Rosen to arrange for the cancellation
of their order. Mr Rosen referred the matter to the plaintiffs in Germany, receiving in
due course a letter to the effect that they could accept a cancellation of only part of the
order, namely 42 suits. The letter went on to say that as a matter of principle the
plaintiffs did not accept late cancellations. Mr Rosen notified the defendants of the part
cancellation but caused them to sign a written confirmation that the winter order was a
binding contract and would not be cancelled by the defendants.

Not long afterwards, on 12th April, the defendants decided to place a repeat order,
which I will call the 'order for 22 suits', in respect of garments for the current season.
They completed the order sheet in the usual way. Since the garments were needed for
sale during that summer, a delivery of five to six weeks was stipulated and noted on the
form. There must however have been some breakdown of communication since, when
the plaintiffs sent their acknowledgment and detailed confirmation of the order, the
delivery period was stated as May/June. In due course this led to trouble. By the middle
of June the goods had not arrived in London and the defendants were complaining that
delivery was late. They were right if the delivery period was five to six weeks and
ordered on 12th April, but not if the goods were due during May and June.

On 14th June the defendants wrote cancelling the order for 22 suits on the ground of later delivery. This was embarrassing to Mr Rosen since it was through his mistake that the delivery periods failed to coincide, and his principals' previous letter indicated that another cancellation by the defendants would not be well received.

There is an issue about what happened next. Mr Rosen claims that he persuaded Mr Goldin to change his mind and withdraw the cancellation. Mr Goldin denies this. I will return to the issue later.

The next event is the arrival at the defendants' shop of the invoice for the 22 suits, an indication that the goods had been, or very shortly would be, dispatched. Mr Alan Wyatt, a director of the defendants, saw the invoice on 27th June and telephoned Mr Rosen about it. The two parties give radically different accounts of what happened. According to Mr Rosen he had already spoken to Mr Goldin on the morning of the same day and arranged an appointment for that afternoon to enable Mr Goldin to inspect samples of the plaintiffs' new collection which had just arrived at Mr Rosen's flat. Later, as Mr Rosen was sitting down to lunch with his wife, his assistant and his housekeeper, he received a telephone call from Mr Wyatt who wanted to know why the plaintiffs were delivering the 22 suits in view of the previous cancellation. Mr Rosen tried to explain that Mr Goldin had withdrawn the cancellation but Mr Wyatt would not hear of this and started to raise his voice. He made it clear that the defendants would not take delivery of the 22 suits and Mr Rosen had no choice but to accept this although he did not agree. Nothing was said about the winter order. The discussion was heated but no bad language was used. He and his wife waited for Mr Goldin to call to inspect the new samples but the appointment for that afternoon was not kept and there was no further telephone call from the defendants. The evidence as to the occurrence of a call from Mr Goldin earlier in the day was supported by the housekeeper; and both this lady and Mrs Rosen also testified to the general tenor of Mr Rosen's end of the later discussion with Mr Wyatt. For his part, Mr Goldin did not recall fixing any appointment for 27th June, although his evidence on this point was not very emphatic, nor did he recall having agreed to cancel the order for the 22 suits.

According to the defendants the first discussion resulted from a call by Mr Wyatt. The latter's evidence as to the reason for this call was confused but ultimately he settled on the view that he had telephoned because he wanted to know why the plaintiffs had tendered goods in respect of a cancelled order. Almost at once Mr Rosen completely lost his temper and started shouting. He asked who the defendants thought they were and said that he would sue the defendants and make them take the 22 suits. He went on to say more than once that he would make sure that the defendants would never be supplied by the plaintiffs again and would never get any of the plaintiffs' goods again. He then put the phone down. Mr Goldin was close to Mr Wyatt when this was happening and heard a loud voice from the other end of the line; so, after asking Mr Wyatt what had happened, he himself telephoned Mr Rosen, some ten or fifteen minutes later, in order to find out the cause of the trouble; but Mr Rosen immediately became hysterical, using bad language and saying that he never wanted to supply the defendants again or to hear from them again. This call lasted only twenty or thirty seconds and ended when Mr Rosen put down the receiver.

Whatever precisely was said during this conversation, a crucial issue to which I will return later, I am satisfied that Mr Wyatt was indignant and upset about what had happened. On his own initiative he prepared a letter dated 27th June 1977 which he sent direct to the plaintiffs in Germany. This was headed with a reference to the order for 22 suits and made three points. The first was that 11 weeks had now passed since the order and delivery could not be accepted. Second, that when the defendants' unwillingness to accept the order had been pointed out to Mr Rosen he had shouted at Mr Wyatt in a most disgusting manner. The third point read as follows:

'Because of your later delivery to us, it bothers us about our future orders that we have placed with you. Also your agent's attitude toward your clients has a lot to be said for. Therefore our business relationship must cease until you can better your position with us. You have been sent recently a cheque for all the outstanding amounts due to your company.'

This letter, as I have said, was sent directly to the plaintiffs in Germany. The defendants did not write to Mr Rosen himself nor did the latter apparently communicate about the winter order with either the defendants or his principals. He did however recognise that the 22 suits would not be accepted by the defendants and he therefore arranged for them to be redirected to other customers at a 10% discount. For their part, the defendants also began to assess the results of the telephone conversations. The evidence of Mr Goldin and Mr Wyatt, which to this extent I accept, was that after waiting for a few days for word from Mr Rosen they began to look around for alternative sources of supply and made tentative arrangements to call on foreign manufacturers, after the summer holidays, with a view to choosing replacement stock for the winter season.

Not long afterwards there arrived the plaintiffs' reply, dated 13th July 1977, to Mr Wyatt's letter of complaint. This was mainly concerned with the order for 22 suits, acceptance of which the plaintiffs agreed to forego, since Mr Rosen had been able to dispose of them elsewhere; but they went on to insist on delivery of the winter order, a large proportion of which was already in production. This produced a letter dated 18th July 1977 from Mr Goldin in which he repeated the defendants' complaint about Mr Rosen's behaviour, and he went on:

'As I have bought more merchandise from other manufacturers to replace your cancelled order, I suggest you speak to Mr Rosen before you try to reconcile the situation, as he originally cancelled our winter order on your behalf.'

The plaintiffs did not reply, but instead dispatched an invoice with the first of five consignments in purported performance of the winter order. This invoice, which covered 15 suits and 13 jackets, imposed a surcharge of 10% in respect of the outsize garments.

On receipt of the invoice Mr Goldin wrote reiterating that Mr Rosen had cancelled the order and stressing that the defendants would not accept the merchandise. Meanwhile the goods had been tendered by the carriers at the defendants' shop where they were rejected, the delivery note being marked 'Not accepted—cancelled order'. Similar deliveries met with the same treatment, the delivery notes for the third and fourth consignment being indorsed by the defendants to the effect that no deliveries from the plaintiffs would be accepted until further notice.

There is one important aspect to the attempted deliveries which it is convenient to mention at the present stage. On 27th September 1977, after three consignments had been tendered and refused, the plaintiffs wrote to the defendants to tell them that the cloth suppliers had short delivered and that accordingly they would have to cancel one suit. When the invoice for the next consignment came forward it showed that the quantity of one style delivered and charged for was indeed one fewer than had been ordered and this deficiency was not made up when the fifth and final consignment was tendered.

Thereafter the plaintiffs made a number of attempts to sell the garments elsewhere, but without success, until very shortly before the trial they were able to dispose of them at less than one-quarter of the original contract price. Meanwhile they had expended some £630 in respect of storage and insurance.

On these facts the plaintiffs put forward alternative claims for the contract price of the goods and for damages in respect of non-acceptance. The former claim, which could not have been sustained, was abandoned at the trial. The defendants counterclaimed for travelling expenses incurred in obtaining substitute goods from the Continent.

The pleadings in the action disclosed four principal issues. (1) Did the plaintiffs through their agent, Mr Rosen, wrongfully repudiate the contract, and, if so, did the defendants accept their conduct as a wrongful repudiation and bring the contract to an end, thus discharging themselves from the obligation to take delivery of the goods? (2) Did the contract provide for a 5% or a 10% surcharge in respect of outsize goods? If *a* the former, did the plaintiffs wrongfully repudiate the contract by consistently invoicing the goods on the basis of a 10% surcharge and thereby relieve the defendants from the obligation to take delivery? (3) Did the short delivery of the one suit constitute either a wrongful repudiation by the plaintiffs or a failure by them to perform a condition precedent to the defendants' obligation to take delivery? (4) Did the plaintiffs do all that was reasonable to mitigate their loss? *b*

Two of these issues may be dealt with briefly. In the course of the trial it was conceded by the plaintiffs that the contract provided for a 5% not a 10% surcharge; but the defendants for their part ceased to maintain that the inclusion of an excessive surcharge in the invoices was a repudiatory act. In my view, each of these concessions was right. In the result, the second issue disappears, although any damages recoverable by the plaintiffs would need to be reduced by the amount of the excess surcharge. The fourth *c* issue does not require elaborate discussion. The burden of proving that the plaintiffs failed to resell the goods to the best advantage was on the defendants, and nothing said on their behalf has persuaded me that this burden has been discharged.

I now return to the first issue, that of repudiation. Essentially this depends on the credibility of the witnesses, assessed in the light of the probabilities and of the contemporary correspondence. As regards the probabilities, there is obvious force in the *d* plaintiffs' comment that Mr Rosen is unlikely to have made a calculated decision to cancel the contract for the winter order without any valid excuse. This would have lost him a steady customer and left his principals with a quantity of specially manufactured goods and no buyer. Furthermore, it would have cost him his commission, and probably his agency as well. Such a course was made the more unlikely by the firm line which his principals had previously taken with regard to the cancellation of existing orders, and by *e* the fact that Mr Rosen's mistake about delivery dates had led to a dispute about the 22 suits. This does not however rule out the possibility that he cancelled the winter order in a fit of pique over the defendants' attitude about the 22 suits, having regard to the fact that he had helped them out in respect of the previous difficulty with the spring order.

The course of events after the telephone conversations also casts doubt on the defendants' version of what was said. If Mr Rosen had indeed allowed himself to be *f* carried away into committing a serious error of judgment, it is rather surprising that he made no effort to retrieve it. More important is Mr Wyatt's letter of 27th June 1977. This is not at all the letter one would expect if the defendants had just received a wholly unjustified cancellation of an order placed by them months previously. Instead, the letter was concerned with the order for the 22 suits, the defendants' justification for refusing delivery of those suits, and Mr Wyatt's indignation about Mr Rosen's attitude *g* during the telephone conversation. The winter order was mentioned only at the end of the letter with the words, 'Because of your late delivery to us it bothers us about our future orders that we have placed with you'. This is not the language of someone who, on the same day, has been told in emphatic terms that the future order is not going to be delivered at all. The letter indicated the defendants themselves proposed to bring the relationship to an end; not that the relationship had already been ended by Mr Rosen's *h* wrongful act. It was not until a later stage that the defendants first put forward an allegation that Mr Rosen had cancelled the contract.

Against this background, I turn to the oral evidence. I was not able to place complete reliance on what was said by any of the three principal witnesses, for it seems to me that the conversations were so angry that the witnesses' accounts were inspired more by what they felt than by what they actually heard. Nevertheless, having seen and heard the *j* witnesses I am able to make the following findings.

First, on the questions (very much on the periphery of the case) whether the order for the 22 suits had in fact been restored and whether there was a telephone call on the morning of 27th June, making an appointment which Mr Goldin did not keep, I prefer the evidence of Mr Rosen to that of Mr Goldin.

Second, I accept the evidence of Mr Goldin that there was a further telephone conversation, ie the third of the day, after the one which took place between Mr Rosen and Mr Wyatt. I do not believe that Mr Goldin has simply invented this conversation. On the other hand I am not prepared to find that Mr Rosen then used the bad language attributed to him or that the conversation involved any explicit repudiation by Mr Rosen of the winter order. The conversation or argument was too brief and incoherent for that.

This leads to the most important issue on the factual side of the case, what was said between Mr Rosen and Mr Wyatt. I did not form the impression that Mr Wyatt was deliberately exaggerating or embroidering his account of the conversation. I believe that Mr Rosen, who hoped that he had been extricated from his mistake about the delivery dates of the 22 suits, became so annoyed when he found that this was not the case that he expressed himself more vehemently than was wise and more vehemently than he was afterwards willing to admit. I am also prepared to accept that he did utter threats about suing the defendants and that he did say that he wanted no more to do with them. But the winter order was not one with which he would himself have had anything further to do, since the execution of it was in the hands of his principals; nor is it material whether Mr Rosen said that he would do no more business with the defendants in the future. What the defendants have to prove is that in respect of the winter order, the subject of an existing contract which the plaintiffs were preparing themselves to fulfil, Mr Rosen said something which amounted to a clear intimation on behalf of his principals that they did not intend to perform their part of the bargain. I am quite unable to find on the evidence that Mr Rosen did say anything of the sort; and I hold that the defence based on repudiation has not been made out.

This being so, it is unnecessary to consider the additional question whether, if there was a repudiation, the defendants ever elected to treat it as such before the plaintiffs made it clear by their letter of 13th July that they, for their part, were proposing to fulfil the contract and expected the defendants to do the same. It had at one time seemed to me that there was substance in the proposition that they did not. Counsel for the plaintiffs was not disposed to press this argument, and on reflection, I consider that he was right.

Having thus concluded that the plaintiffs did not, by the conduct of their agent, release the defendants from all further contractual obligations, I turn to the other half of the case, which revolves round the issue whether, as a matter of law, the short delivery of one suit entitles the defendants to say that they were excused from the consequences of what would otherwise have been a wrongful rejection of the goods. The defendants have not set out to say that the argument has any attractions from the commercial point of view. Nevertheless, as a matter of law, it cannot lightly be brushed aside. The contentions addressed by counsel for the defendants may be summarised as follows. (1) The seller must tender the entire quantity of goods contracted for. Any shortfall, unless it is so trivial as to fall within the maxim de minimis non curat lex, entitles the buyer to reject the tender in its entirety (see s 30(1) of the Sale of Goods Act 1893.) (2) The short delivery of one suit was not de minimis. The plaintiffs did not challenge this part of the argument. (3) Since the plaintiffs had elected not to treat the contract as repudiated, they were themselves obliged to fulfil it in exactly the same way as if there had never been a repudiation at all. This they failed to do since they short-delivered; and the short delivery excused the defendants from their duty to accept the tender. (4) The fact the defendants did not rely on the short delivery at the time did not disentitle them from relying on it now. Again, the plaintiffs did not dispute this proposition. (5) Alternatively, the short delivery was a repudiation of the contract by the plaintiffs themselves since the defendants' own prior repudiation had not been accepted as such by the plaintiffs. The defendants were therefore justified in refusing to perform, at least as regards the quantity yet to be delivered.

For the plaintiffs, counsel maintained that s 30(1) has no application to a case such as the present, where the contract was not entire but contemplated fulfilment by instalments. A contract of this kind is governed by s 31(2) not s 30 of the 1893 Act. Where a party to such a contract relies on a breach by the other party as a justification for refusing to go ahead with his side of the bargain, he must show either that the breach is in itself sufficient to go to the root of the contract or alternatively that it forms part of a group of acts from which it can be inferred that the person committing the breach no longer intends to be bound by the obligation to perform in the future. On this basis, the plaintiffs argued, the short delivery of one suit did not justify the defendants in refusing to go ahead with the contract. The short delivery, they said, was not a breach at all, since the amount of each consignment was not fixed in advance, and it was not until the last delivery was received (an occasion which the defendants prevented from ever taking place) that there could be said to have been one suit delivered less than had been contracted for. Moreover, even if there was a breach, the shortage of one suit was not either a repudiatory breach or an intimation that the plaintiffs no longer regarded themselves as bound by the contract. Furthermore, quite apart from this, the plaintiffs were dispensed from the need to make a perfect tender by the defendants' repeated intimation that, if a tender was made, they would not accept it.

These are the arguments which were deployed by counsel in a very clear and concise manner, and they may be conveniently approached in two stages. The first involves dealing with the problem as if there had never been a quarrel between the parties and as if all that had happened was an intimation that one suit would not be delivered, followed in due course by a failure to deliver that single suit. If the contract had been for a single undivided delivery there could be no doubt that a rejection by the defendants would have been justified. Section 30(1) of the 1893 Act may set a stricter standard than would now be applied if the subject were governed by the more recent reported cases on repudiatory breach, recognising, as they do, that there are intermediate terms, the consequences of whose breach depend on the magnitude of the breach rather than any automatic categorisation of the term as either a condition or a warranty. Nevertheless, the words of the Act are plain, any short delivery otherwise than in the nature of de minimis is sufficient to entitle the buyer to reject.

From this starting point the defendants go on to argue that the position must be the same, notwithstanding that, for the sake of convenience, it had been agreed that delivery should be effected by partial shipments. The contract was for the full quantity and if, at the end of the day, less than that quantity had been delivered the defendants could (retrospectively as it were) reject all they had previously received. In theory there is no doubt that the law recognises that there can be contracts which yield this result (see *Reuter, Hufeland & Co v Sala & Co* (1879) 4 CPD 239), but it is a question of construction in each case whether the contract is intended to be entire or divisible; and in construing the contract the court will consider whether the parties can really have intended that a breach as to one consignment will justify rejection of them all: see Farwell LJ in *Jackson v Rotax Motor & Cycle Co* [1910] 2 KB 937. I feel no doubt that in this case the contract must be construed as divisible, notwithstanding that the number and size of the individual deliveries were not fixed in advance but were left to the plaintiffs' discretion. I therefore reject this part of the defendants' argument.

The defendants have, however, an alternative contention on the following lines. Let it be assumed against us, they say, that a misdelivery of one consignment in the sense that (for example) the goods are unmerchantable does not justify rejection of the entire contract quantity unless the circumstances are such as to show that there is a repudiation of the contract as a whole. Such a case is, no doubt, covered by s 31(2). There is, however, no room for this solution where the breach consists of short delivery, for this is dealt with by s 30(1) in unqualified terms: if the quantity delivered is too small, the buyer is not obliged to accept any part of it. If under-delivery is a defence where all the goods are delivered in one single batch, there is no logic in arriving at a different conclusion where the contract is performed by instalments.

I accept the difficulty of finding a logic in this distinction. But no more is there any logic in distinguishing between cases of misdelivery and short delivery; for if a misdelivered consignment is rejected the result is to create a short delivery. Sections 30(1) and 31(2) are not, in this respect, mutually consistent. One must yield to the other;

and it seems to me that the business sense of a contract of sale requires the more flexible provisions of s 31(2) to be applied in preference to those of s 30(1) (see Benjamin on the Sale of Goods (9th Edn, 1974, para 654, note 12)).

Even when the defendants' case on the interpretation of the 1893 Act is rejected, there remains the further question, namely, whether the plaintiffs' breach as regards the one suit was founded only in damages or whether it was serious enough to amount to a repudiation of the contract as a whole. Here there can be no reason for doubt. If one looks at the short delivery as an actual breach, occurring at the very end of the delivery period, which, in my view, is the right analysis, it plainly was insufficiently serious to go to the root of the contract, nor, if one asks whether it took place or was foreshadowed by the plaintiff's warning in such circumstances as to lead to the inference that similar breaches would be committed in the future (see *Millar's Karri and Jarrah Co (1902) v Weddel, Turner & Co (1908)* 100 LT 128): the answer is equally clear that it was not. Accordingly, I conclude that the plaintiffs' defective tender did not excuse the defendants' outright refusal to accept delivery of any goods at all.

This makes it unnecessary to consider the further and much more difficult question whether in the circumstances the plaintiffs can be regarded as having been in breach at all, for they contend that, since the defendants had made it plain that any tender of the goods would be rejected, they were not obliged to go through the useless formality of making one and that, although in fact they chose to perform this formality, they cannot be worse off than if they had saved themselves the trouble. This question turns on the correct interpretation of *Braithwaite v Foreign Hardwood Co* [1905] 2 KB 543, as explained in cases such as *British & Beningtons Ltd v North Western Cachar Tea Co Ltd* [1923] AC 48, [1922] All ER Rep 224, *Taylor v Oakes, Roncoroni & Co* (1922) 127 LT 267 and *Esmail v Rosenthal & Sons Ltd* [1964] 2 Lloyd's Rep 447.

Notwithstanding the interesting arguments addressed, I believe that this controversial topic is best left for detailed discussion in a case where it is necessary to the decision. I would however just add this: that, whether or not *Braithwaite v Foreign Hardwood Co* is to be regarded as a case in which the buyer's repudiation was accepted, there seems little practical sense in saying that a seller must make a perfect tender when he has been told not to make one at all, and still less sense in distinguishing between cases where the seller offers to tender but is told that the goods will be rejected if he does so and where he actually tenders and finds that the goods are in fact rejected.

A more businesslike way of dealing with the problem of the seller who would not have been able to perform, or to perform fully, even if there had been no refusal to take delivery is to take the matter into account when assessing damages, as in *Maredelanto Compania Naviera SA v Bergbau-Handel GmbH, The Mihalis Angelos* [1970] 3 All ER 125, [1971] QB 164. As I say however, it is unnecessary to reach any conclusion on this point.

In the result, therefore, the plaintiffs' claim succeeds, but the damages must be reduced to allow for the revision of the surcharge to 5%. The defendants' counterclaim is dismissed.

Judgment for the plaintiffs. Defendants' counterclaim dismissed.

Solicitors: *Harry I Alkin & Co* (for the plaintiffs); *Herbert Oppenheimer, Nathan & Vandyk* (for the defendants).

K Mydeen Esq   Barrister.

Air Canada and others v Secretary of State for Trade and another

QUEEN'S BENCH DIVISION
PARKER J
9th, 10th, 11th, 12th, 18th FEBRUARY 1981

Aerodrome – Aerodrome open for public use – Landing and take-off – Foreign aircraft – Carriage for hire or reward – Aerodrome owned by British Airports Authority – Authority increasing landing and take-off charges – Foreign aircraft operators bringing action challenging validity of increase – Operators meanwhile paying at old rate and withholding increase – Authority seeking injunction to restrain operators from using aerodromes save on payment of full charges pending determination of validity of increase – Authority entitled to detain aircraft on default of payment of charges – Whether operating permit granted by Secretary of State conferring absolute right as against authority to use its aerodromes – Whether authority's right to detain aircraft precluding it from seeking injunction – Whether authority should be granted injunction sought – Civil Aviation Act 1968, s 14 – Airports Authority Act 1975, s 2(3) – Air Navigation Order 1976 (SI 1976 No 1783), arts 68, 72, 77, 91.

The British Airports Authority was a body constituted under the Airports Authority Act 1975 to manage certain aerodromes, including the aerodrome at Heathrow, of which it was the beneficial owner in possession and for which it held a licence granted under art 68 of the Air Navigation Order 1976, which required it at all times when its aerodromes were available for the take-off and landing of aircraft to make them so available to all persons on equal terms and conditions. The authority was entitled to charge landing fees in respect of, inter alia, the use of its aerodromes for the landing and take-off of aircraft. Under s 14 of the Civil Aviation Act 1968 the authority was empowered to detain and sell any aircraft in respect of which default was made in the payment of the fees. The plaintiffs were a number of airline operators from contracting states (ie states which were parties to the 1944 Chicago Convention) engaged in operating scheduled passenger flights using Heathrow airport and which held permits granted under art 77[a] of the 1976 order. Article 77 provided that aircraft such as those operated by the plaintiffs could not, without the permission of the Secretary of State and in accordance with any conditions to which such permission was made subject, take on board or discharge passengers or cargo in the United Kingdom when carried for hire or reward. In April 1980 the authority introduced new landing fees which were considerably higher than those previously charged. In October 1980 the plaintiffs brought an action against the authority challenging the validity of the charges being imposed, and thereafter withheld from the authority a part of the fees charged being an amount equal to the increase introduced in April 1980. The amount withheld was paid into an interest-bearing trust account to await the result of the action. The authority sought an interlocutory injunction to restrain the plaintiffs from using Heathrow airport for the landing of their aircraft save on payment of the full landing and take-off fees. The plaintiffs opposed the granting of an injunction, contending, inter alia, (i) that, by virtue of art 77 of the 1976 order and pursuant to their operating permits granted thereunder, they had an absolute right to land as against the authority whether or not they paid the charges and that therefore no injunction could be granted, and (ii) that the authority could only enforce charges in accordance with the provisions of s 14 of the 1968 Act and accordingly so long as any unpaid charges were fully secured the authority could not circumvent those provisions by obtaining an injunction in aid of its rights as owner in possession.

Held – (1) In view of the requirement of the authority's licence under art 68 of the 1976 order to make its aerodromes, at all times when they were available for the take-off and

---

a   Article 77 is set out at p 340 *f*, post

landing of aircraft, available to all persons on equal terms and conditions, and in view of
a the similar requirement imposed by art 72 of that order on the authority in respect of
aircraft registered in contracting states, both of which carried with them implied rights
to land and take off and since a right to land and take off could only be implied in a
permission granted under art 77 if such a right existed nowhere else, it followed that the
permission granted to the plaintiffs under art 77 conferred on them, as against the
authority, no absolute right to land or take off. In any event, art 91(1)[b] of the 1976 order
b provided that, subject to arts 68 and 72, nothing in the order conferred any right to land
in any place as against the owner of the land or other persons interested therein (see p 340
j and p 341 *b* to *j*, post).

(2) It did not follow from the fact that s 14(12) of the 1968 Act provided that nothing
in s 14 was to prejudice the right of an aerodrome authority to recover charges or any
part thereof by action that all other remedies, including an injunction, were excluded.
c Furthermore although the authority might not be able to prevent an aircraft from
leaving one of its aerodromes where there was a genuine dispute about fees due in respect
of it, provided the fees were properly secured, it did not follow that the authority was
without a remedy where an operator claimed, notwithstanding the conditions of use of
the aerodrome, to be able to continue landing at the aerodrome with the intention of
withholding part of the fees, even though it had not and might never be established that
d those fees were otherwise than fully exigible. In view of the Secretary of State's power
to prescribe or permit certain charges and to make or permit as a condition of use of a
public aerodrome that they should be paid on demand, it could not be supposed that
Parliament had intended that an airline operator should be able to continue to use the
aerodrome while flouting the conditions merely because it genuinely disputed the
validity of the charges (see p 342 *b* to *e* and *g h*, post).

e (3) Since it was clear that under s 2(3)[c] of the 1975 Act the authority had power to
prohibit entry onto its aerodromes so long as such a prohibition was not shown to be
unreasonable and since if deprived of the amounts withheld the authority might not be
able to fulfil its financial obligations, it was clear that there were serious questions to be
tried in addition to the issue of the validity of the charges. Furthermore because of the
complex effect of withholding the amounts which could be serious and difficult, if not
f impossible, to quantify in money, damages would not be an adequate remedy. It
followed that the balance of convenience was in favour of granting the injunction. The
injunction sought would therefore be granted (see p 342 *j* to p 343 *a* and *d* to *h*, post);
Cinnamond v British Airports Authority [1980] 2 All ER 368 applied.

Per Curiam. In view of the Secretary of State's power under art 71 of the 1976 order
with respect to charges or maximum charges for the use of aerodromes for which a
g licence for public use has been granted under art 68 of that order, the charges established
by the authority for the use of its aerodromes are, in practice, charges which the Secretary
of State permits (see p 342 *f g*, post).

Notes
For the use of public aerodromes by foreign aircraft, see 2 Halsbury's Laws (4th Edn) para
h 1000, and for the powers of an aerodrome authority to detain and sell aircraft for unpaid
airport charges, see ibid paras 1025–1026.

For the Civil Aviation Act 1968, s 14, see 40 Halsbury's Statutes (3rd Edn) 207.

For the Airports Authority Act 1975, s 2, see 45 ibid 50.

For the Air Navigation Order 1976, arts 68, 71, 72, 77, 91, see 3 Halsbury's Statutory
Instruments (Fourth Reissue) 140, 143, 146, 158.

j As from 9th February 1981 arts 68, 71, 72, 77, 91 of the 1976 order were replaced by
the Air Navigation Order 1980, SI 1980 No 1965, arts 70, 73, 74, 80, 94.

---

b Article 91(1) is set out at p 341 *g*, post

c Section 2(3) provides: 'The Authority shall have power to do anything which is calculated to
facilitate the discharge of its duties under this Act.'

Case referred to in judgment

Cinnamond v British Airports Authority [1980] 2 All ER 368, [1980] 1 WLR 582, [1980] *a*
RTR 220, 78 LGR 371, CA.

Summons

By a summons dated 10th November 1980 the British Airports Authority, the second
defendant to an action brought against the authority and the first defendant, the Secretary
of State for Trade, by the plaintiffs, Air Canada and 17 other named airlines ('the *b*
operators'), all of which used aircraft registered in states which were parties to the 1944
Chicago Convention on International Civil Aviation, sought an injunction restraining
the operators and each of them by themselves, their servants or agents or otherwise from
landing at London Heathrow Airport without paying direct to the authority in full the
landing charges set out in the authority's published conditions of use (1st April 1980
edition) at the time specified in those conditions. The summons was heard in chambers *c*
but judgment was given by Parker J in open court. The facts are set out in the judgment.

Peter Scott QC and *Timothy Walker* for the authority.
Anthony Lester QC and *Bruce Coles* for the operators.
Nicholas Phillips QC and *Christopher S C S Clarke* for the Secretary of State.

Cur adv vult *d*

18th February. **PARKER J** read the following judgment: This judgment arises out of
an application in chambers for interlocutory relief by way of injunction. It is given in
open court by reason of the serious issues which arise and with the full consent of the
parties.

The British Airports Authority is the beneficial owner in possession of Heathrow *e*
Airport which is one of several aerodromes owned by it. It has, by virtue of s 1(1) of the
Airports Authority Act 1975 under which it is presently constituted, the statutory duty
to manage such aerodromes.

It is entitled to and does charge fees in respect of, inter alia, the use of its aerodromes
for the landing and take-off of aircraft. Such fees are set out in its published conditions
of use from time to time in force. Condition 2.2 of the conditions of use provides so far *f*
as presently material as follows:

'The operator shall pay the appropriate charges for the landing, taking off, parking
or housing of aircraft as set out below . . . The charges . . . shall accrue from day to
day and, unless some other arrangement has been agreed in writing by the
Authority, shall be payable to the Authority on demand and, whether a demand has
been made or not, before the aircraft departs from the airport.' *g*

The fees currently being charged were introduced on 1st April 1980 and are
considerably higher than those in force up to that date. They are due to remain in force
until 30th March 1981. As from that date the authority intends to introduce new
charges which will almost certainly be higher than those now in force.

In October 1980 a number of airline operators ('the operators'), who regularly use *h*
Heathrow for the landing and take-off of aircraft engaged on schedule passenger flights
operated by them, joined together as plaintiffs in an action launched against the
authority. In that action they challenge the validity of the current charges on various
grounds, which for present purposes it is unnecessary to specify. It is sufficient to say
that the challenge raises issues which are fit to be tried.

From 1st April 1980 until the commencement of their action the operators had paid *j*
the current charges in full. They continued to do so for about a month thereafter but all
save one then began to withhold from the authority part of the fees charged. The
amounts withheld are intended to be broadly equal to the difference between the full
amounts charged and the amounts which would have been charged had there been no
increase in April 1980.

The operators intend to continue withholding part of the fees charged on this basis for
a so long as the current fees remain in force and also if and when new fees are introduced
in April next.

It is estimated that if judgment in their action is given in mid-summer of 1892, which
the parties accepted as a reasonable, realistic estimate of the time it will take to reach that
stage, the total amounts which will by then have been withheld by the operators will be
in the region of some £14m.

b The authority now comes to this court seeking interlocutory relief by way of an
injunction pending trial or further order to restrain the operators from using Heathrow
for the landing of their aircraft save on payment to it in full in accordance with the
conditions of use of the landing and take-off fees set out from time to time in their
conditions of use at the time specified in those conditions. It contends that unless and
until the operators establish in their action that such charges are otherwise than fully
c exigible they ought not to be allowed to continue to use Heathrow without paying them
in full.

By its counterclaim in the operators' action the authority seeks judgment for the
amounts withheld and a permanent injunction to the same effect as the interlocutory
injunction which it now seeks.

It is a curious feature of the present situation that although the operators are
d withholding part of the charges from the authority they are not themselves retaining the
amounts withheld. They are paying them, and intend to continue paying them, into an
interest-bearing account in the name of their solicitors to abide the result of their
action. Their intention in so doing is that, by such means and by a suitable trust deed or
such other steps as shall be satisfactory to the authority, the payment with interest of all
amounts withheld shall, in the event that their challenge to the validity of the charges
e fails, be fully secured to the authority. The operators have adopted and intend to
continue this course, not out of the generosity of their hearts or from any innate sense of
fair play, but because, unless any unpaid charges are genuinely disputed and sufficient
security for their payment is given to the authority, the authority is entitled to detain
their aircraft under s 14 of the Civil Aviation Act 1968. The risk of any such detention
is one which the operators are, quite naturally, not prepared to accept.

f In this situation, if an injunction is granted and the operators continue to use
Heathrow, which they will certainly do for it is commercially impracticable for them to
do otherwise, the only effect on them will be that instead of paying the withheld
amounts to their solicitors and thus depriving both themselves and the authority of their
use they will be compelled to pay them direct to the authority, which may then use
them.

g There would be a readily apparent purpose in the operators paying the money to their
solicitors rather than to the authority if there were any doubt about the authority's
obligation and ability to repay any amounts which the operators might be held by
judgment in the action to have overpaid, but it is accepted that there is no such doubt,
at all events on the basis that the operators remain, as at present, the only users of
Heathrow to withhold charges and that judgment is achieved by the summer of 1982.
h For present purposes I proceed on this basis, for an injunction, if granted, would only be
valid until trial or further order and if circumstances were to change the parties could
return to the court, as indeed they could if an injunction were now refused.

In the light of the apparent uselessness of sterilising large sums of money pending
trial, I invited the operators at an early stage of the argument to consider whether they
would not be prepared, pending trial, to pay direct to the authority as all other operators
j are doing. Having considered the matter, counsel on their behalf, stated that the
operators were not so prepared on three principal grounds: (1) that they had, under the
relevant legislation and their operating permits, an absolute right to land as against the
authority whether they paid charges or not and therefore no injunction could be granted;
(2) that the effect of s 14 of the Civil Aviation Act 1968 was that the authority's only right
to enforce charges was in accordance with that section and accordingly that as long as any

unpaid charges were fully secured the authority could not circumvent the section by obtaining an injunction in aid of its alleged rights as owner in possession or its rights *a* under s 2(3) of the Airports Authority Act 1975 to do anything calculated to facilitate the discharge of its duties under that Act; (3) that they feared that if the money withheld were paid over to the authority the authority would not co-operate in bringing the action on for trial as soon as possible.

As to the third of these grounds I am satisfied that it is without substance. The authority is as anxious as the operators to secure an early trial of the action. Moreover, *b* if the withholding of the money is intended to exert such pressure on the authority as to force it to proceed to trial faster than is reasonably required for the purpose of fairly and properly preparing for trial, it is in my judgment an abuse of their rights under s 14 and of the process of the court. If it is intended to do no more than to secure that the authority proceeds as fast as is consistent with fair and proper preparation of their case, it appears to me to be both unnecessary and a usurpation of the function of the court. *c*

The other two matters occupied most of the time in argument, for it was contended on behalf of the operators that both were fatal to the claim for an injunction, both could and should be decided at this stage and success on either would make it unnecessary to consider either the adequacy of the authority's remedy in damages or the balance of convenience.

Both the authority and the Secretary of State for Trade, who is the first defendant in *d* the action and supported the authority's application, also desired that the 'right to land' point should be determined at this stage and were prepared to have the point on s 14 also so decided if the court thought fit. I shall therefore consider these two points first.

The alleged right to land

The operators' alleged right rests entirely on the fact that they are holders of permits *e* granted under art 77 of the Air Navigation Order 1976, SI 1976 No 1783. This order has since been replaced by the Air Navigation Order 1980, SI 1980 No 1965, but without material differences and, since the 1976 order is referred to in the documents, it, rather than the current order, was for convenience referred to in argument. I shall also refer to it in this judgment.

Article 77 of the 1976 order provides as follows: *f*

'An aircraft registered in a Contracting State other than the United Kingdom, or in a foreign country, shall not take on board or discharge any passengers or cargo in the United Kingdom, being passengers or cargo carried or to be carried for hire or reward, except with the permission of the Secretary of State granted under this Article to the operator or the charterer of the aircraft or to the Government of the country in which the aircraft is registered, and in accordance with any conditions to *g* which such permission may be subject.'

By art 90 of the order a 'Contracting State' means any state (including the United Kingdom) which is a party to the Convention on International Civil Aviation signed on behalf of the government of the United Kingdom at Chicago on 7th December 1944 (Cmd 8742). I shall refer to this as the Chicago Convention. *h*

On the face of it permission granted under art 77 has nothing to do with either a right to land or a right to take off. It concerns only taking on board or discharging passengers or cargo carried or to be carried for hire or reward. Permits in fact granted under the article follow the wording of the article.

An aircraft which does not wish either to discharge or take on board passengers or cargo or, if it does, does not do so for hire or reward therefore needs no permission under *i* art 77 and, if it has such permission, does not on the particular flight need to use it.

It was submitted however that permission under art 77 included by necessary implication the right both to land and to take off. This might have some force if no right to land could be found elsewhere, although it would be strange if the only right to land could be found in a permission relating to the embarkation and disembarkation of

passengers or cargo carried or to be carried for hire or reward. It would mean that an
aircraft with no desire to do anything but carry out proving flights with non-fare-paying
complimentary passengers could not lawfully get down without obtaining a permission
which it did not at all want.

The right of an aircraft to fly in or over the United Kingdom stems from art 3 of the
order, and the operators' aircraft with which this application is concerned have such a
right under that article. This however is a right of flight only. Landing is dealt with in
Part IX of the order. It begins with a prohibition on landing save, in the case of such
aircraft, at an aerodrome licensed under the order for the take-off and landing of such
aircraft and in accordance with any condition subject to which the aerodrome may have
been licensed. The authority is the holder, under art 68 of the order, of a licence for
public use in respect of Heathrow and condition 1 of that licence is that the authority
shall, at all times when it is available for the take-off or landing of aircraft, make it so
available to all persons on equal terms and conditions. This condition is mandatory
under art 68(3) of the order. By condition 7 of the licence the authority must inform the
Civil Aviation Authority (which is the grantor of the licence) of the times during which
Heathrow is to be generally available for the take-off or landing of aircraft and must keep
it so available during those times. Condition 8 of the licence provides:

'Subject to condition 1 nothing in this licence shall be taken to confer on any
person the right to use the aerodrome without the consent of the licensee.'

There is, here, no right to land conferred in express words but there is a clear implied
right to land and take off at a licensed aerodrome on the same terms and conditions as
anyone else during the times when it is generally available for take-off and landing. To
this extent but no further there is thus a right to enter on the aerodrome without the
consent of the licensee, which consent would, in the absence of some such special
provision, be required.

The matter is taken a little further by art 72 which obliges the person in charge of any
aerodrome in the United Kingdom which is open to public use by aircraft registered in
the United Kingdom (whether or not the aerodrome is a licensed aerodrome) to be
available for use by aircraft registered in any part of the Commonwealth or in other
contracting states on the same terms and conditions as for use by aircraft registered in the
United Kingdom. Again one finds a clearly implied right of use, albeit landing and take-
off, is not, as it is in art 68, specifically mentioned.

That the right to land is intended to be conferred by arts 68 and 72 is made plain by
art 91(1) which provides:

'Subject to the provisions of Articles 68 and 72 of this Order, nothing in this
Order or the regulations made thereunder shall confer any right to land in any place
as against the owner of the land or other persons interested therein.'

There being therefore a clear right to land under arts 68 and 72 there is no room for
any implication in art 77 or any permit given thereunder of any such right, and the
operators' argument that they have, as against the authority, an absolute and independent
right, in my judgment, fails.

The operators sought to bolster their argument by reference to the Chicago Convention
and various bilateral treaties but such attempt cannot succeed. In the case of ambiguity
reference may no doubt be made to treaties which domestic legislation appears designed
to put into effect but there is no ambiguity here.

The only right against the owner is to land on the same terms and conditions as
everyone else.

I should, before passing to the next point, mention one further argument advanced for
the operators, namely that, since art 91 only saves from conferring as against an owner
a right to land the provisions of the order itself or of the regulations made under it, such
saving does not affect a permit granted under art 77. On the view I take of the order this
point does not arise, but I am in any event unable to see how it could be said to be intra

vires if the Secretary of State expressly granted a right to land in purported pursuance of art 77.   *a*

The effects of s 14 of the Civil Aviation Act 1968

This section affords the authority a draconian remedy where fees are outstanding and one of the defaulter's aircraft is on the aerodrome. It has nothing to do with the aircraft's right to be there in the first place. It is said however that, since s 14(12) provides that nothing in the section shall prejudice the right of an aerodrome authority to recover *b* charges, or any part thereof, by action, all other remedies, including the remedy by injunction, interim or otherwise, are excluded. This does not in my judgment follow. It may well be that if an aircraft has landed and there is a genuine dispute about fees due in respect of it or if an operator is in dispute about fees for other aircraft, the authority could not, provided that the fees were properly secured, prevent that or any other aircraft from leaving the aerodrome. That however appears to me to be a different situation *c* altogether from the case where, as here, an operator or operators claim, notwithstanding the conditions of use, to continue to go on landing at Heathrow with the intention of withholding part of the fees, albeit that it has not been and may never be established that those fees are otherwise than fully exigible. If the authority is without remedy in such a case it would mean that such an operator, although only entitled to land in compliance with the terms of the licence, one of which is that, subject to being afforded the same *d* conditions as everyone else, it has no right to land without the owner's consent, could land despite a prohibition and without complying with such conditions. They could then, on supplying security, take off again and repeat the process again and again and again for an unlimited period of time.

Section 14 affords no such rights in express words. Nor in my judgment does it do so by implication, necessary or otherwise.   *e*

It is to be observed that by art 71(1) of the order the Secretary of State may, in relation to any aerodrome in respect of which a licence for public use has been granted, prescribe the charges or the maximum charges which may be made for the use of the aerodrome and may further prescribe the conditions to be observed in relation to those charges. He has not done so in the case of Heathrow, but had he in fact prescribed the charges now in dispute, the authority would have been obliged under art 71(2) to make such charges *f* and not to permit any breach of the conditions. Although, in the case of Heathrow, the Secretary of State has not prescribed charges or maximum charges he nevertheless retains control, for the authority is, under art 71(3), obliged if required by him to furnish particulars of the charges established by it. If, therefore, he considers them to be excessive or otherwise in some way defective he can under art 71(1) himself prescribe charges. The charges established by the authority are therefore, in practice, charges *g* which the Secretary of State permits to be made.

If the Secretary of State prescribes or permits certain charges and makes or permits a condition of use that they shall be paid on demand I can see no reason to suppose that Parliament must have intended that airline operators should be permitted to continue to use the aerodrome whilst flouting the conditions merely because they genuinely dispute the validity of the charges.   *h*

If there be any ambiguity about the matter, so as to make reference to the treaties permissible, it is to be observed that the Chicago Convention contemplates that, in the event of dispute about charges at aerodromes open for public use, the dispute shall be subject to a review procedure and not that such aerodromes may be continued to be used notwithstanding a continuing refusal to pay the charges and notwithstanding also that such charges may be fully exigible.   *j*

It is now necessary, these two matters having been disposed of, to consider whether the authority can otherwise successfully establish its case for interim relief. In this connection the recent case of *Cinnamond v British Airports Authority* [1980] 2 All ER 368, [1980] 1 WLR 582 is of very considerable assistance. It is plain from that case that the authority's right as owner to prohibit entry, even without the restrictions placed on such right in respect of landing and take-off by its licence and by arts 68 and 72 of the order, are

a limited. It is, however, also plain that the authority may nevertheless prohibit entry in pursuit of its general power under s 2(3) of the Airports Authority Act 1975 coupled with its rights as owner unless the prohibition is shown to be an unreasonable exercise of its power. It will not be so shown if the persons whom it seeks to prohibit are abusing rights of entry which prima facie they may have. The authority contends that to exclude the operators while they pursue their present course is a perfectly reasonable use of its

b power. It is obliged under s 3(1) of the 1975 Act to conduct its business so that its revenue is not less than sufficient to meet charges properly chargeable to revenue, which include proper provision for depreciation or renewal of assets and proper allocations to a general reserve which it is obliged to keep, and it is currently engaged on an expansion programme at Heathrow. If deprived of the amounts withheld it will have, if it is to pursue its programme, to exceed the borrowing limits placed on it under the 1975 Act,

c which it cannot do without the consent of the Secretary of State. It is, it is said, at the least unfair and probably a breach of its obligations to make the aerodrome equally available to all users that these operators should be allowed to go on withholding when other users of Heathrow are complying with the current conditions of use and paying in full. Furthermore it is, they submit, an abuse by the operators of their right to land to continue to do so without paying the charges.

d Such contentions raise at the very least serious questions to be tried in addition to the issue whether the charges themselves are valid, which is also admittedly so fit. The first matter which the authority must establish in pursuit of its claim for interim relief is therefore made out.

I consider next whether if no injunction were granted damages would be an adequate remedy. It is contended for the operators that it clearly would for the dispute is simply

e about money and the payment of the money with interest will be fully secured.

This is in my judgment a fallacious approach. The effect of withholding will be complex. It may be both serious and difficult, if not impossible, to quantify in money. The authority may or may not be granted an increase in its borrowing rights and even if it is it may not, in present circumstances, be sufficient to allow it to maintain and increase the facilities which it intends and desires and is obliged to provide. Other users

f of Heathrow and the travelling public may all be affected. I have no doubt that damages would not be an adequate remedy.

With regard to balance of convenience there can in my judgment only be one answer. It is in the circumstances which I have already mentioned plain that it is in favour of granting the injunction. The effect of so doing on the operators will be merely that the moneys withheld will be paid to the authority rather than into the trust

g account. The status quo will be preserved. All users of Heathrow will be treated alike. The authority will be able to continue to fulfil its statutory duties. If and to the extent that the operators succeed they will recover the amounts overpaid from the authority rather than from their solicitors. The granting of the injunction can therefore do them no harm. Its refusal would or might have serious consequences and cause unquantifiable damage to the authority.

h The injunction sought will therefore be granted on the usual undertaking in damages. If, in addition, the operators considered that it should also be made a condition that the authority undertook to repay with interest any amount which might ultimately be held to have been overpaid I would be prepared to consider making such an undertaking also a term of the grant. It may, however, be that the operators will be content with the plain statement made in court on behalf of the authority that there

j would of course be no doubt that in such an event the amounts would be promptly repaid and with interest.

In conclusion I must repeat in open court a warning, which I gave to both parties in the course of argument, that the dispute between them is now sub judice and will be tried by the court and not in the press or other media of mass communication. There must therefore be no repetition of the resort to press releases, or even more limited statements, such as have occurred since the issue of the writ. If there are, the consequences to the offenders may be very serious. I must also urge both parties to *a* remember that however much relations between them may recently have been soured, and it is plain from the correspondence that feeling is running high, the early determination of the dispute will best be achieved by co-operation. The acrimonious scoring of debating points by correspondence reflects no credit on either side. This is a serious and important dispute between responsible parties who must be expected to behave in a responsible manner. The action is one which should clearly be tried as soon *b* as possible and I am prepared now to hear suggestions for directions from either or all parties.

Injunction granted. Leave to appeal to the Court of Appeal granted.

Solicitors: *M W T Nott* (for the authority); *Freshfields* (for the operators); *Treasury Solicitor* *c* (for the Secretary of State).

K Mydeen Esq   Barrister.

Tradax Internacional SA v Cerrahogullari TAS
The M Eregli

d

QUEEN'S BENCH DIVISION
KERR J
11th, 25th FEBRUARY 1981

e

Arbitration – Commencement – Charterparty – Time bar – Claim barred if arbitrator not appointed in time – Centrocon arbitration clause – Claimant having indisputable claim but other party not expressly admitting claim – Claim for dispatch money – Owners admitting invoices for money correct but otherwise ignoring claim – Claimant appointing arbitrator outside time limit *f* *– Claimant also bringing action to enforce claim and applying for summary judgment in action – Whether arbitration clause applicable to bar action – Whether a 'dispute' between the parties – Whether claimant required to appoint arbitrator within time limit subject to extension of time – Whether time limit should be extended – Arbitration Act 1950, s 27.*

Arbitration – Stay of court proceedings – Refusal of stay – Indisputable claim – Claimant *g* *pursuing claim by action in courts concurrently with arbitration proceedings – Application for summary judgment in action – Claimant appointing arbitrator outside time limit prescribed by arbitration clause – Centrocon clause – Claimant seeking extension of time for appointing arbitrator at same time as applying for summary judgment in action – Whether if claim indisputable claimant entitled to pursue arbitration proceedings and action concurrently – Whether existence of action precluding claim for extension of time in arbitration – Whether if* *h* *extension of time granted claimant can obtain either award in the arbitration or summary judgment in action.*

A voyage charterparty made between the plaintiffs as charterers and the defendants as owners of the chartered vessel incorporated the amended Centrocon arbitration clause which provided that 'All disputes from time to time arising out of this contract' were to *j* be referred to arbitration and that 'Any claim must be made in writing and Claimant's arbitrator appointed within nine months of final discharge and where this provision is not complied with the claim shall be deemed to be waived and absolutely barred'. Final discharge of the vessel was completed on 3rd November 1975. The plaintiffs had earned dispatch money and in May, June and July 1976 sent invoices for that money to the

defendants. The defendants admitted that the invoices were correct and did not dispute
a the claim for dispatch money but they did not expressly admit liability for the claim and
simply ignored it and all communications relating to it. The time limit for the
appointment by the plaintiffs of an arbitrator expired on 3rd August 1976 without the
plaintiffs appointing an arbitrator. On 25th August 1977, about a year out of time, the
plaintiffs appointed an arbitrator and subsequently the defendants agreed that he should
be the sole arbitrator. In November 1977 the defendants submitted to the arbitrator that
b the plaintiffs' claim was time-barred under the arbitration clause. Thereafter the
arbitrator took no further steps in the arbitration. On 9th January 1978 the plaintiffs
issued an originating summons seeking an extension, under s 27[a] of the Arbitration Act
1950, of the time for appointing an arbitrator. In July 1978 the plaintiffs issued a writ
against the defendants claiming as liquidated sums the dispatch money due to them.
The defendant served a defence disputing part of the claim on a ground they subsequently
c abandoned, made no admission as to the rest of the claim, and pleaded that in any event
the claim was time-barred under the arbitration clause. On 15th August 1980 the
plaintiffs issued a summons under RSC Ord 14 for summary judgment in the action.
That summons and the summons to extend time were heard together in February
1981. At the hearing the defendants admitted that they had no defence to the action
either on liability or on quantum but submitted (i) that the arbitration clause applied to
d bar the claim, or (ii) alternatively, that the plaintiffs could not seek relief in the
arbitration, namely an extension of the time for appointing an arbitrator, when the
subject matter of the arbitration (the claim for dispatch money) was concurrently before
the court in an action. The plaintiffs submitted (i) that they were entitled to summary
judgment in the action and that the arbitration clause did not apply to prevent them
from so doing because in effect their claim was undisputed, and if there was no 'dispute'
within the arbitration clause the time bar, which was dependent on there being a
e 'dispute', could not apply, and (ii) that if the arbitration clause was applicable, they were
entitled to an extension of time under s 27 of the 1950 Act.

Held – (1) Where a claim was made by a party to a contract containing an arbitration
clause similar to the Centrocon clause, then, even though the claim was indisputable,
f there could only be said to be no 'dispute' between the parties, so as to make the clause
inapplicable, if the other party had expressly admitted the claim and there was, therefore,
in effect, an agreement to pay and thus no further basis for a reference to arbitration.
Where, however, a claim made within the time limit prescribed by the clause for
appointing an arbitrator had been neither admitted nor disputed by the other party
within that time but had simply been ignored, a 'dispute' within the clause existed even
though the claim was indisputable and, accordingly, the claimant was obliged to appoint
g an arbitrator within the time prescribed by the clause, subject to any extension of time.
It followed that the arbitration clause applied to the plaintiffs' claim, that they were
required to appoint an arbitrator within nine months of discharge of the vessel and could
only overcome the time bar imposed by the clause by obtaining an extension of time
under s 27 of the 1950 Act (see p 350 *a* to *c* and p 351 *a* and *h j*, post); *London and North*
h *Western Railway Co v Jones* [1915] 2 KB 35 and *Bede Steam Shipping Co Ltd v Bunge y Born*
Limitada SA (1927) 27 Ll L Rep 410 applied; *Nova (Jersey) Knit Ltd v Kammgarn Spinnerei*
GmbH [1977] 2 All ER 463, *Ellis Mechanical Services Ltd v Wates Construction Ltd* [1978] 1
Lloyd's Rep 33 and *Associated Bulk Carriers Ltd v Koch Shipping Inc, The Fuohsan Maru*
[1978] 2 All ER 254 considered.

j _____

a Section 27, so far as material, provides: 'Where the terms of an agreement to refer future disputes
to arbitration provide that any claims to which the agreement applies shall be barred unless notice
to appoint an arbitrator is given or an arbitrator is appointed . . . within a time fixed by the
agreement, and a dispute arises to which the agreement applies, the High Court, if it is of opinion
that in the circumstances of the case undue hardship would otherwise be caused, and
notwithstanding that the time so fixed has expired, may, on such terms, if any, as the justice of the
case may require . . . extend the time for such period as it thinks proper.'

(2) However, an indisputable claim which was within the provisions of an arbitration clause similar to the Centrocon clause could be pursued by the claimant both in arbitration proceedings and by an action in the courts leading to summary judgment and both proceedings could be pursued concurrently. Accordingly, the existence of an action concurrently with arbitration proceedings did not preclude the claimant from applying in the arbitration proceedings for an extension of the time for appointing an arbitrator. Moreover, where a claimant succeeded in obtaining an extension of time under s 27 of the 1950 Act in the case of a claim which was indisputably due, he could either obtain an award in the arbitration or apply for summary judgment in the action, although it would be more convenient to apply for summary judgment in the action than to refer an undisputed claim back to arbitration (see p 351 *d* to *g* and *j*, post); *SL Sethia Liners Ltd v Naviagro Maritime Corpn, The Kostas Melas* [1981] 1 Lloyd's Rep 18 applied.

(3) The plaintiffs were therefore entitled to apply under s 27 of the 1950 Act for an extension of the time for appointing an arbitrator notwithstanding the existence of the action, and, in all the circumstances, were entitled to an extension of time on the grounds of undue hardship and because the defendants would not be prejudiced, since they had admitted that they had no answer to the plaintiffs' claim. The plaintiffs would accordingly be granted an extension of the time for appointing an arbitrator so as to validate the appointment made on 25th August 1977, and they would also be given summary judgment in the action for the admitted claim (see p 352 *a* to *f*, post).

Notes

For the nature of a dispute for the purpose of a reference to arbitration, see 2 Halsbury's Laws (4th Edn) para 503.

For court proceedings by a party to arbitration, see ibid para 555.

For the Arbitration Act 1950, s 27, see 2 Halsbury's Statutes (3rd Edn) 457.

Cases referred to in judgment

A/S Det Dansk-Franske Dampskibsselskab v Compagnie Financière d'Investissements Transatlantiques SA (Compafina), The Himmerland [1965] 2 Lloyd's Rep 353, 3 Digest (Reissue) 8, 11.

Associated Bulk Carriers Ltd v Koch Shipping Inc, The Fuohsan Maru [1978] 2 All ER 254, [1978] 1 Lloyd's Rep 24, CA, 3 Digest (Reissue) 76, 390.

Bede Steam Shipping Co Ltd v Bunge y Born Limitada SA (1927) 27 Ll L Rep 410, 43 TLR 374, 3 Digest (Reissue) 42, 201.

Doleman & Sons v Ossett Corpn [1912] 3 KB 257, 81 LJKB 1092, 107 LT 581, 76 JP 547, 10 LGR 915, CA, 3 Digest (Reissue) 60, 321.

Ellis Mechanical Services Ltd v Wates Construction Ltd [1978] 1 Lloyd's Rep 33.

London and North Western Railway Co v Jones [1915] 2 KB 35, 84 LJKB 1268, 113 LT 724, DC.

Nova (Jersey) Knit Ltd v Kammgarn Spinnerei GmbH [1977] 2 All ER 463, [1977] 1 WLR 713, [1977] 1 Lloyd's Rep 463, HL, 3 Digest (Reissue) 75, 389.

Richmond Shipping Ltd v Agro Co of Canada Ltd, The Simonburn (No 2) [1973] 2 Lloyd's Rep 145, 3 Digest (Reissue) 8, 12.

SL Sethia Liners Ltd v Naviagro Maritime Corpn, The Kostas Melas [1981] 1 Lloyd's Rep 18.

Originating summons and action

On 9th January the plaintiffs, Tradax Internacional SA, as the charterers under a voyage charterparty on the Baltimore Form C charterparty of a vessel, the M Eregli, owned by the defendants, Cerrahogullari TAS, applied under s 27 of the Arbitration Act 1950 for an extension of the time prescribed in the charterparty for the appointment of an arbitrator in the case of a dispute arising out of the charterparty. The summons was returnable for hearing on 12th December 1978. In the interim, by a writ dated 7th July 1978, the plaintiffs claimed from the defendants $4,765·6 and $22,004·16, alternatively $20,504·16, alternatively $12,444·79 as dispatch money due to the plaintiffs, and interest a thereon, and applied for summary judgment under RSC Ord 14.   The originating summons and the summons for summary judgment were heard together in chambers but judgment was given by Kerr J in open court.   The facts are set out in the judgment.

Roderick Cordara for the plaintiffs.
Martin Moore-Bick for the defendants.

b   *Cur adv vult*

25th February.   **KERR J** read the following judgment: These proceedings arise under a voyage charter dated 28th August 1975 between the plaintiffs, a Panamanian company, as charterers, and the defendants, a Turkish company, as owners, in which the plaintiffs' primary claim is for summary judgment under RSC Ord 14 for dispatch money admittedly earned at the loading and discharging ports in the total sum of $26,769·76. The charterparty incorporated the amended Centrocon arbitration clause which bars all claims after a time limit of nine months, as set out below.   The plaintiffs are out of time under the arbitration clause but submit that this does not matter, because the sum claimed is, in fact, indisputably due by the defendants; and the defendants admitted before me that, subject to this time limit, the claimed sum is correct and payable by them.

Against this background the plaintiffs issued two proceedings which are both before me; a writ and an application for summary judgment as already mentioned, and an application for an extension of time under s 27 of the Arbitration Act 1950, to validate the appointment of an arbitrator which was made out of time.   Their primary case, however, is that since their claim is, in effect, undisputed, the court should disregard the arbitration clause, and the time limit in it, and give summary judgment in the action. They rely on certain recent decisions, referred to below, in which the courts have effectively disregarded arbitration clauses when the claim, or a part of it, appeared to be indisputable, although in those cases the arbitration clauses did not, as here, contain any time limit.

The defendants contend that both applications must fail in limine because they are misconceived.   They submit, first, that the time limit in the arbitration clause bars all claims even though, apart from the time limit, the amount claimed is indisputably due, and that there can therefore be no judgment for the plaintiffs in the action.   Second, they submit that there can also be no extension of time under s 27, because the plaintiffs cannot at the same time apply for an extension of time to arbitrate and to seek to recover their claim by action.   Finally, they submit that in all the circumstances an extension of time should not be granted in any event.

Both parties agree that the first two of these points raise questions of principle which do not appear to have arisen before, on which it would be helpful to have judgment in open court.

I must now shortly summarise the facts, as to which there is substantially no dispute. The arbitration clause in the charterparty was in the following terms:

'All disputes from time to time arising out of this contract shall, unless the parties agree forthwith on a single Arbitrator, be referred to the final arbitrament of two Arbitrators carrying on business in London who shall be members of the Baltic and engaged in the Shipping and/or Grain Trades, one to be appointed by each of the parties, with power to such Arbitrators to appoint an Umpire.   Any claim must be made in writing and Claimant's Arbitrator appointed within nine months of final discharge and where this provision is not complied with the claim shall be deemed to be waived and absolutely barred . . .'

The M Eregli loaded at Houston and proceeded to Odessa, where she completed her discharge on 3rd November 1975, earning dispatch money at both ports.   The time limit under the arbitration clause accordingly expired on 3rd August 1976. In May, June and July 1976, the plaintiffs sent invoices to the defendants for the dispatch money due respectively at the loading port, the discharging port, and for the total amount of dispatch due. All these invoices are now admitted to have been correct. However, none of them produced any response whatever from the defendants. The time limit of 3rd August 1976 then went by without the plaintiffs having appointed an arbitrator. In January 1977, as I am satisfied on the evidence, the defendants' brokers agreed with the plaintiffs' brokers in a telephone conversation that the amount claimed was indeed due from their clients, but the defendants contend that their brokers had no authority to make any such admission, and this was treated as a disputed issue before me. The plaintiffs' brokers then asked the defendants' brokers to agree to an extension of time under the arbitration clause; this request was passed on to the defendants but again produced no response whatever. There were further 'chasers' across the line in July 1977, including a strong registered letter sent by the plaintiffs on the advice of the defendants' brokers, but again no response. On 19th August 1977, the plaintiffs then wrote that they were appointing Mr Cedric Barclay as their arbitrator, and he accepted this appointment on 25th August 1977. The appointment was therefore about a year out of time. Since the defendants again did not respond in any way, Mr Barclay was appointed as sole arbitrator and wrote to the defendants on 12th October 1977, giving directions for service of their defence and fixing a date for the hearing on 11th November 1977. This finally produced a response from the defendants: they instructed solicitors who wrote to Mr Barclay on 28th October that they were happy for him to act as sole arbitrator. He subsequently agreed to adjourn the hearing to 26th November. However, on 17th November 1977, the defendants' solicitors again wrote to him, contending for the first time that the claim was time-barred, and also taking a point on the amount claimed, which is now abandoned. Mr Barclay then first adjourned and finally vacated the date for the hearing, because it seemed to him that the plaintiffs' claim might be 'for a debt' and that they should take legal advice on how to proceed. In January 1978, he was then unfortunately taken ill before this question was resolved and took no further part in the subsequent events.

I now come to the proceedings issued by the plaintiffs which are before me. On 9th January 1978, they issued an originating summons for an extension of time under s 27 of the Arbitration Act 1950 returnable for hearing on 12th December 1978. I do not know the reason for this lengthy allowance of nearly a year for the hearing to come on, but presumably the plaintiffs' solicitors wanted to allow plenty of time for service of the summons, and the defendants raised no objection to the delay. Their position was, no doubt, that the plaintiffs might fail to get an extension, in which case they would not have to pay at all; and that, even if the plaintiffs succeeded, they would meanwhile have the use of the money. In the interim, however, the plaintiffs evidently took further legal advice, and in July 1978, they issued a writ. Their reason for doing so may have been that by that time a practice had come into vogue, as illustrated by the recent cases referred to below, to seek to recover, by summary judgment under Ord 14 in disregard of an arbitration clause, claims as to which it was clear that there was no arguable defence. Notice of the writ was duly served on the defendants in Turkey and on 29th November 1978, they served their points of defence. These disputed part of the claim on a ground which has now been abandoned, made no admission as to the rest, and pleaded that the claim was in any event time-barred under the second sentence of the arbitration clause.

At this stage, the summons for an extension of time was ready for hearing and the pleadings in the action were evidently closed; indeed, the summons was due to be heard shortly thereafter, on 12th December 1978. However, this date was vacated, apparently by consent, and nothing happened thereafter until 15th August 1980, when the plaintiffs issued the summons for summary judgment in the action. The intervening delay of over 18 months is unexplained. In effect, the matter simply went to sleep. The main reason was, no doubt, inaction on the part of the plaintiffs' solicitors which the

defendants' solicitors saw no ground to question, but of course it would have been open
to either side to have brought matters to a head by applying for a date for the hearing of
either or both proceedings. These now come before me in February 1981, and the
defendants' counsel immediately admitted that there was no defence as to liability or
quantum apart from the effect of the time limit in the arbitration clause.

I deal first with the plaintiffs' application under Ord 14 for summary judgment. Their
submission was that since the claim was in effect undisputed, the arbitration clause, as
well as the time limit in the second sentence, were irrelevant, and that the court could
and should disregard them and give judgment under Ord 14, since there was effectively
no dispute. Their submission was that the second sentence of the arbitration clause
beginning with 'Any claim . . .' must be subordinated to the first sentence which refers
to 'All disputes . . .', and that the second sentence had no effect unless there was a dispute
within the time limit of nine months. In the present case, as they submitted, there was
no dispute, since the defendants had never responded to the plaintiffs' invoices, let alone
disputed them, within the time limit. They relied, in particular, on a number of recent
cases on what constitutes a 'no dispute' situation, and therefore submitted that they were
entitled to judgment in the action and could disregard the arbitration clause, including
the time limit imposed by the second sentence.

It is necessary shortly to review a number of authorities in which attempts have been
made, successfully or unsuccessfully, to disregard an arbitration clause by applying for
summary judgment in an action in the courts when the claim, or part of it, admits of no
dispute as to either liability or quantum, and it is convenient to begin with three recent
decisions.

The first is a decision of the Court of Appeal in 1976, *Ellis Mechanical Services Ltd v
Wates Construction Ltd* [1978] 1 Lloyds Rep 33. The dispute concerned a 'domestic'
arbitration agreement (ie one to which the Arbitration Act 1975 had no application)
where both parties were in agreement that the dispute had to go to arbitration at least in
part, but where the plaintiffs claimed, and the defendants denied, that there could and
should be summary judgment for the plaintiffs for an undisputed liquidated sum and
that this should not be included in the reference to arbitration. The Court of Appeal
unanimously accepted the plaintiffs' contention and gave judgment for that part of the
claim, thus only leaving the disputed balance to go to arbitration.

Next, in *Nova (Jersey) Knit Ltd v Kammgarn Spinnerei GmbH* [1977] 2 All ER 463, [1977]
1 WLR 713, the House of Lords, in effect, reached the same conclusion in relation to an
arbitration clause which was subject to s 1 of the Arbitration Act 1975 by holding as part
of the ratio that in relation to certain unpaid bills of exchange there was 'not in fact any
dispute between the parties with regard to the matter agreed to be referred', and that the
arbitration clause had no application to claims under the bills.

Finally, there was the decision of the Court of Appeal in *Associated Bulk Carriers Ltd v
Koch Shipping Inc, The Fuohsan Maru* [1978] 2 All ER 254. It was there sought to extend
the decision in the *Ellis* case to a claim for unliquidated damages where there was no
arguable defence as to liability and (as the plaintiffs contended) also no arguable defence
to a substantial amount by way of damages for which they asked for summary
judgment. In that case, as in the *Nova Knit* case, the arbitration clause was subject to s 1
of the Arbitration Act 1975, and the plaintiffs contended that to the extent of part of
their claim for damages 'there was not in fact any dispute'. They failed in this contention
(Lord Denning MR dissenting) because their claim was for unliquidated damages and
the whole amount was effectively in dispute. However, it is clear from the majority
judgments that if the claim, or any part of it, had been 'indisputably due', the decision
would to that extent have been different and that judgment under Ord 14 would have
been given irrespective of the arbitration clause.

In the present case the plaintiffs sought to rely on these decisions and submitted that
they were in an a fortiori position, since their claim was for a liquidated sum in relation
to which there had never been any arguable defence but which was not expressly
admitted. However, they were of course faced with the difficulty of the second sentence

of the arbitration clause and the fact that in the decisions referred to above the arbitration clauses contained no time limit barring claims. Their submission was that this difficulty *a* could be overcome by treating the second sentence of the arbitration clause as subordinated to the first sentence beginning 'All disputes from time to time arising . . .' and that, since there was effectively no dispute, the whole arbitration clause, including the second sentence, could simply be disregarded.

I cannot accept this contention. Where an arbitration clause contains a time limit barring all claims unless an arbitrator is appointed within the limited time, it seems to *b* be that the time limit can only be ignored on the ground that there is no dispute between the parties if the claim has been admitted to be due and payable. Such an admission would, in effect, amount to an agreement to pay the claim, and there would then clearly be no further basis for referring it to arbitration or treating it as time-barred if no arbitrator is appointed. But if, as here, a claim is made and is neither admitted nor disputed, but simply ignored, then I think that the time limit clearly applies and that the *c* claimant is obliged (subject to any possible extension of time) to appoint an arbitrator within the limited time. The fallacy in the plaintiffs' argument can be seen at once if one considers what would have been the position if the plaintiffs had in fact purported to appoint Mr Barclay as their arbitrator within the time limit of nine months. They could clearly have done so, and indeed any commercial lawyer or businessman would say that this is what they should have done under the clause to enforce their claim. Arbitrators *d* are appointed every day by claimants who believe, rightly or wrongly, that their claim is indisputable. However, on the plaintiffs' own argument, Mr Barclay would have had no jurisdiction, since there was then, as they now say, no 'dispute' to which the arbitration clause could have applied. In my view this argument is obviously unsustainable.

The fallacy of the plaintiffs' argument is also demonstrated by a number of earlier cases. Much the same issue arose in the well-known decision of MacKinnon J in *Bede* *e* *Steam Shipping Co Ltd v Bunge y Born Limitada SA* (1927) 27 Ll L Rep 410. This was also a case under the Centrocon arbitration clause (when the time limit was only three months) which the plaintiffs had disregarded, but in that case the defendants had made an express admission of liability as to part of the claim within the limited time. MacKinnon J held that to this extent, and for this reason, the plaintiffs were entitled to judgment, because it was only to this extent that there was clearly no dispute to be referred to arbitration, *f* but that the remainder of the claim was time-barred. (It should be noted in passing that there was then no provision for any extension of time, which was only enacted by the Arbitration Act 1934.) In this context he followed the decision of the Divisional Court in *London and North Western Railway Co v Jones* [1915] 2 KB 35 at 40 where Rowlatt J said:

> 'It seems to me that we are bound to hold, firstly, that the only case in which the Court can be appealed to before arbitration is where the defendant has agreed the *g* demand and merely refuses to pay; secondly, that wherever this cannot be shown and he has not paid, the case must be treated as one in which a difference has arisen . . .'

While this was a case which arose under certain legislation concerning claims against railways which cannot impair the authority of the recent cases referred to above, I think *h* that it is helpful to show in what cases, and only in what cases, there is no dispute *capable of being referred to arbitration.*

Finally, on this point, the defendants also relied strongly on a decision of Mocatta J in *The Himmerland* [1965] 2 Lloyd's Rep 353, where he gave effect to the second sentence of the Centrocon arbitration clause in a situation where, on one view, no claim could have been put forward within the time limit because the cause of action had not arisen. The *j* judge nevertheless held that effect must be given to the second sentence to bar all claims in all cases, even if the cause of action only arose after the time had expired. Whether the effect of the second sentence should be taken as far as this may perhaps be open to question if a similar situation arises again; for present purposes, however, it is sufficient to say that the case is on any view a further authority against the plaintiffs' argument here.

In the result, therefore, both as a matter of common sense and on the authorities, it
a seems to me that this is a straightforward case of the plaintiffs having made a claim to
which the arbitration clause and the time limit in it prima facie applied, and that they
can only overcome this difficulty by 'going through the hoop' of s 27 of the Arbitration
Act 1950 and obtaining an extension of time.

However, the second issue is then whether, as the defendants contend, the plaintiffs
are now barred from doing so because they have also started an action and to this extent
b seek to pursue both proceedings concurrently. The defendants' submission was, in
effect, that the plaintiffs could not seek an extension of time for appointing an arbitrator
when the courts were also seised of their claim in an action, and they relied on the
decision of the Court of Appeal in *Doleman & Sons v Ossett Corpn* [1912] 3 KB 257, as a
basis for submitting that a party could not seek relief in relation to an arbitration when
the same subject matter is also before the courts.

c One must, I think, pay tribute to counsel for the defendants for the ingenuity of this
argument, but I think that the case is clearly distinguishable and that the argument goes
too far. All that the case decided, I think, as correctly stated in the first paragraph of the
headnote, is that, when the court is seised of a dispute in an action, an arbitrator cannot
(in effect) oust the jurisdiction of the court by purporting to make a final award in a
concurrent arbitration, and that any award so made cannot be a defence to the action
d before the court. This does not arise in the present case, since Mr Barclay (rightly) did
nothing further in the arbitration after the challenge to his jurisdiction had been raised,
let alone after the issue of the writ.

In my view the legal position is clear. The fact that arbitration proceedings are
pending between parties is clearly not in itself any ground for preventing the courts from
becoming seised of the same dispute in an action. Conversely, as it seems to me, the
e concurrent existence of an action should not preclude an application under s 27 of the
Arbitration Act 1950, to remove the time bar to a claim imposed by an arbitration
clause. The contrary conclusion would be highly inconvenient and make little sense in
practice. It would mean that a claimant or plaintiff would have to pursue his possible
remedies consecutively instead of concurrently, perhaps even to the extent of having to
discontinue his action, obtain relief under s 27, and then start a fresh action in order to
f apply for summary judgment on a claim which is then no longer barred and which may
be indisputably due. I think that the practice of this court shows that the formal
requirements of the law do not go as far as this. Claims which are covered by an
arbitration clause, but which are said to be indisputable, are nowadays frequently put
forward in an arbitration, but then also pursued concurrently by an attempt to obtain
summary judgment in the courts. In effect, a claimant can, and in my view should be
g able to, obtain an order for payment in such cases by either means, and the coexistence
of both avenues towards a speedy payment of an amount which is indisputably due was
recently referred to in this court by Robert Goff J in *The Kostas Melas* [1981] 1 Lloyd's Rep
18 at 27. It was there held that, as an alternative to an application for summary
judgment under Ord 14 in an action, there was jurisdiction to make an interim award
for an indisputable part of the claim in an arbitration; which also shows, incidentally, the
h misconception of the plaintiffs' first submission in the present case with which I have
already dealt.

In my view, the correct position is as follows. Where there is a claim which is subject
to a time limit in an arbitration clause, the claimant must operate the arbitration clause
unless there is no dispute because the other party has admitted liability. If he fails to
abide by the clause, then he can only recover if he succeeds in obtaining an extension of
j time under s 27. However, if he does, then the bar to his claim is removed, and if the
claim, or part of it, is indisputably due, he can either obtain a final or interim award in
the arbitration, as the case may be, or summary judgment under Ord 14 in an action,
even though the action and the arbitration are both concurrent. However, if both are
concurrent, as here, and the claim is indisputably due, it is obviously far more sensible
and convenient to give judgment under Ord 14 than to refer the undisputed claim back
to the arbitrator. Subject to his reliance on the *Doleman* case, as mentioned above,

counsel for the defendants did not dispute this; nor did he raise any objection to this course under s 1 of the Arbitration Act 1975, which would be applicable to the present *a* case if there were in fact any dispute to be referred to arbitration.

If this analysis is correct, then it only remains to decide whether or not the plaintiffs' application for an extension of time under s 27 is entitled to succeed. In my view it is, because a refusal would in all the circumstances cause 'undue hardship' to the plaintiffs, and an extension of time clearly cannot in itself cause any prejudice to the defendants on the extreme facts of this case. Counsel for the defendants pressed me with what I had *b* said in *The Simonburn* (No 2) [1973] 2 Lloyd's Rep 145, about the duty of claimants to apply promptly under the section. But in that case the plaintiffs deliberately delayed their application for tactical reasons, and there was also prejudice to the defendants. However, each case depends on its own facts, and it seems to me very clear where the balance of justice lies in the present one. The defendants simply ignored the plaintiffs' invoices, which were admittedly correct throughout, and all other communications, *c* including those from their own brokers concerning the plaintiffs' justified claim. Of course, the plaintiffs should have appointed Mr Barclay about a year earlier than they did, but I think that in the circumstances it was a pardonable error on their part to think that the defendants would ultimately react and discharge their clear liability without the need for proceedings. The plaintiffs should, no doubt, also have appointed Mr Barclay immediately in January 1977, when it must have become clear to them that the *d* defendants were deliberately prevaricating, instead of first asking for an extension of time and then letting a further seven months go by. But these are errors of a kind which are frequently made and which the section is designed to forgive if there are no countervailing circumstances. The delays thereafter were no doubt also primarily on the side of the plaintiffs, but the defendants always had it in their power to put an end to them. The dominant feature of this case, in my view, which incidentally does not appear to have any *e* parallel in any previous application under the section, is that it is rightly admitted that the defendants never had any answer to a straightforward debt. They have had the use of the money due to the plaintiffs for well over five years and no merits whatever other than the legal points skilfully deployed on their behalf, which in my judgment fail. In these circumstances, despite the long delay, I think that it would be an undue hardship on the plaintiffs if an extension of time were refused to enable them to recover a debt *f* which clearly should have been acknowledged and paid years ago, without the need for any proceedings.

I will hear counsel on what should be the appropriate terms of the order. As it seems to me, this should be, first, that the plaintiffs' time for the appointment of an arbitrator under the Centrocon clause is extended so as to validate the appointment of Mr Barclay which he accepted on 25th August 1977. This has the effect of removing the time bar *g* to the plaintiffs claim. Second, to give summary judgment for the plaintiffs in the action under Ord 14 for the admitted sum of $26,769·76. However, I will hear counsel on this, and on interest and costs.

Time for appointment of arbitration extended. Summary judgment for the plaintiffs under RSC Ord 14. Leave to appeal.

Solicitors: *Sinclair, Roche & Temperley* (for the plaintiffs); *Constant & Constant* (for the defendants).

K Mydeen Esq   Barrister.

Re Lowrie (a bankrupt), ex parte the trustee of the bankrupt v The bankrupt and another

CHANCERY DIVISION
GOULDING AND WALTON JJ
11th MAY 1981

Bankruptcy – Property available for distribution – Matrimonial home – Home held by husband and wife on trust for sale for themselves in equal shares – Exercise of court's discretion to execute trust for sale – Exceptional circumstances justifying postponement of trust for sale – Young children in family – Husband a bankrupt and likely to have difficulty in obtaining loan to purchase another home – Husband and wife offering to make payments to trustee out of their earnings – Payments such as might pay off husband's debt within 30 months – Judge deciding that there were exeptional circumstances and postponing sale of matrimonial home for 30 months – Whether exceptional circumstances – Whether judge properly exercising discretion – Law of Property Act 1925, s 30.

The husband and wife were married in March 1974 and in October 1974 the husband purchased the matrimonial home in his own name for £12,000, with a mortgage from the local authority of £11,500. By August 1975 the husband was insolvent. He attributed his insolvency to entering into the mortgage commitment. In October 1976 the petitioning creditor obtained judgment for £898. By May 1977 the husband had borrowed further sums from finance companies and incurred a bank overdraft and other debts. In 1977 the wife ceased working because she was expecting her first child who was born in October 1977. A second child was born in February 1980. On 13th August 1979 the husband was adjudicated bankrupt. Some £9,600 was needed to discharge his debts and the costs of the bankruptcy. His only asset was the matrimonial home which by then was worth £30,000, and after deducting £10,000 still outstanding on the mortgage there was a net equity in the house of £20,000. The husband's trustee in bankruptcy applied in the county court for an order for the sale of the house. On the hearing of the application the judge determined that, on the basis of her contributions to the household, the wife was entitled to a half interest in the house and made an order for the sale of the house. However, he ordered that the sale be postponed for 30 months (i) because he considered that there were exceptional circumstances arising out of there being young children living in the house and the facts that it would be difficult for the family to obtain another home and also for the husband to obtain a loan for another home, and that those exceptional circumstances displaced the presumption in favour of the trustee that there should be an immediate sale, and (ii) because he believed that the proposed monthly payments to the trustee by the husband and wife out of their earnings (the wife having offered to return to work) would pay off the husband's debts within 30 months. The trustee appealed.

Held – Where a husband's trustee in bankruptcy applied for an order for the sale of a matrimonial home in which the innocent wife held a half interest, the facts that there were young children living in the house and that it would be difficult for the bankrupt husband to raise a loan for another home did not amount to exceptional circumstances or exceptional hardship justifying the court in postponing the sale of the house, pursuant to its discretion under s 30[a] of the Law of Property Act 1925, since those were circumstances generally present in such cases. Having regard to the facts that the creditors would suffer hardship by the postponement of payment of their debts for any

---

[a] Section 30, so far as material, provides: 'If the trustees for sale refuse to sell . . . or any requisite consent cannot be obtained, any person interested may apply to the court for a vesting or other order for giving effect to the proposed transaction or for an order directing the trustees for sale to give effect thereto, and the court may make such order as it thinks fit.'

appreciable time, that the proposed payments by the husband and wife could not be relied on to pay off the debts within 30 months and that the immediate sale of the house *a* would leave the wife with £10,000 (her half share) to put towards the purchase of another home, the judge had been wrong to exercise his discretion by postponing the sale for 30 months. An order for an immediate sale would be made subject to completion not taking place before three months from the court's decision. The appeal would therefore be allowed (see p 356 b c g to p 357 a d and h to p 358 a and d to j and p 359 d to h, post).

Re Holliday (a bankrupt) [1980] 3 All ER 385 distinguished.

Notes
For a trustee in bankruptcy's power of sale, see 3 Halsbury's Laws (4th Edn) para 525, and for cases on the subject, see 5 Digest (Reissue) 1031-1034, 8277-8307.

For the Law of Property Act 1925, s 30, see 27 Halsbury's Statutes (3rd Edn) 385. *c*

Cases referred to in judgments
Birkett v James [1977] 2 All ER 801, [1978] AC 297, [1977] 3 WLR 38, HL, Digest (Cont Vol E) 666, 2698b.
Holliday (a bankrupt), Re, ex parte the trustee of the bankrupt v The bankrupt [1980] 3 All ER 385, [1981] 2 WLR 996, CA.

Appeal
The trustee in bankruptcy of the husband applied for an order for the sale of the matrimonial home where the husband and his wife, the respondents to the application, lived with their two young children. On 24th February 1981 Mr Timothy Ryland sitting as a deputy circuit judge in the Slough County Court in bankruptcy gave judgment ordering the sale of the house with vacant possession but suspended the sale *e* for 30 months from 24th February 1981. The trustee appealed, seeking an order for the sale of the house suspended for a period not exceeding two months or such other period as the Divisional Court might order. The wife opposed the sale. The facts are set out in the judgment of Walton J.

Simon Mortimore for the trustee. *f*
Peter Griffiths for the wife.
The husband appeared in person.

WALTON J delivered the first judgment at the invitation of Goulding J. In this matter the bankrupt and the second respondent, his wife, were married on 4th March 1974. On 4th October of that year the property which forms the subject matter of the *g* dispute in this matter, which was in Maidenhead, Berkshire, was bought in the sole name of the bankrupt, there being a mortgage from the local authority of £11,500. The bankrupt made further charges of the property in February 1975 to the local authority in the sums of £230 and £200 respectively. By August 1975 the bankrupt realised that he was in fact insolvent. And he gives the reason why he became insolvent as being that in common parlance he had, in taking on the property, bitten off more than he could *h* chew. And the evidence about that, which has not been challenged in any effective way, is that the bankrupt attributed his insolvency to entering into a mortgage commitment which was essential to the purchase of the property which he could not support from his income. Then by May 1977 the bankrupt had borrowed further sums totalling £4,300 from seven further finance companies. He had also incurred a bank overdraft of £400 and a debt due under a credit card facility of £100. On 15th June 1976 the local *j* authority obtained an order for possession of the property on the ground of non-payment of the mortgage interest but this order was duly suspended. The petitioner/creditor in the present case obtained judgment for £898 on 26th October 1976. By September 1977 the second respondent, the bankrupt's wife, ceased to work because she was expecting the birth of her first child, who was born on 25th October 1977. She went back to work in

February 1978. On 13th July 1979 the receiving order against the bankrupt was made and on 13th August 1979 he was adjudicated bankrupt. The wife ceased to work again in December 1979 and the second child was born on 3rd February 1980.

Though that is a bare outline of the history of the matter there is no doubt that the wife made a very substantial contribution to the welfare of the family. She apparently purchased all the furniture, or at any rate the bulk of the furniture, and fittings in the matrimonial home, and she also made various contributions to the paying off of mortgages and deposits and matters of that nature in respect of which the judge has awarded her a half interest in the property. And there has been no challenge to the judge's finding in that regard.

The situation is that at the present moment, in order to discharge the bankrupt's debts and the costs of the bankruptcy, something of the order of £9,600 is required, and the only asset that there is is the property which, doubtless owing to inflation since it was bought, is now worth something of the order of £30,000, and with a mortgage of approximately £10,000 on it this gives a net equity (and it is impossible to be more precise nor is it necessary so to be) of somewhere in the order of £20,000, a half share of which would be £10,000 which would be just about sufficient to pay off the bankrupt's debts and costs and possibly leave something very slightly over.

In those circumstances the trustee in bankruptcy applied in the Slough County Court before the deputy circuit judge, and by an order of 24th February 1981 it was ordered that the property should be sold with vacant possession and that the conduct of the sale should be given to the trustee in bankruptcy providing that such sale be suspended for 30 months from the date of the order of 24th February 1981. One immediately asks oneself how did the judge arrive at the very curious period of 30 months, and really there is not anything at all in his judgment which leads one to see precisely how he arrived at it. But counsel for the wife has suggested that as the result of the evidence which was then in front of the judge on his client's behalf, which was to the effect that a sum of about £6,000 would be forthcoming in two years, the judge said, 'Well that will mean £9,000 in three years and therefore if I cut the three years down to 30 months from 36 months that will be about it.' And that is the explanation of the expression which he uses in his judgment when he says when talking about the 30 months: 'I do so taking into account all the circumstances and the belief that the creditors will be paid in consideration of this spur.' That seems to me to be altogether too much of a reconstruction, and I do not accept that the judge can have arrived at the period as a result of any such complicated considerations.

What is the position when a trustee in bankruptcy asks for an order for the sale of property which is held, as the present property is held, on trust for the bankrupt husband and the innocent wife in equal part shares? I think that the deputy judge correctly appreciated the drift of what I think all the cases quite uniformly laid down to date when he said in his judgment:

> 'It is quite right to say that the effect of these cases is that there is a discretion to order a sale, and the fact that there is going to be a sale should be regarded as just and proper because the creditors should in fact be paid. The approach of the court as I understand it is that the trustee has certain presumptions in his favour except in exceptional circumstances. The presumption that there are debts outstanding, a sale should be ordered. A short period of suspension so that the bankrupt and his family should make their arrangements.'

I would not, speaking for myself, quarrel with a word of that. But of course one must always look at the whole of the circumstances of the case, and in exceptional circumstances there is no doubt that the trustee's voice will not be allowed to prevail in equity and the sale will not be ordered. A brilliant example of just such a situation is to be found in *Re Holliday (a bankrupt)* [1980] 3 All ER 385, [1981] 2 WLR 996, where the petition in bankruptcy had been presented by the husband himself as a tactical move, and quite clearly as a tactical move, to avoid a transfer of property order in favour of his

wife, or ex-wife, at a time when no creditors whatsoever were pressing and he was in a
position in the course of a year or so out of a very good income to discharge whatever *a*
debts he had. He had gone off leaving the wife in the matrimonial home, which was the
subject matter of the application, with responsibility for all the children on her own.
One can scarcely, I think, imagine a more exceptional set of facts, and the court gave
effect to those exceptional facts.

Before one looks at the conclusion of the judge, since he had rightly in the beginning
set out what the law was, I think it is desirable to step back for a moment and look at the *b*
situation which must in these cases inevitably occur, or at any rate must occur so
frequently as to be almost inevitable. The first one is of course that the whole family are
going to be rendered homeless. That is not an exceptional circumstance. It is a normal
circumstance and is the result, the all too obvious result, of a husband having conducted
the financial affairs of the family in a way which has led to bankruptcy. The second
result almost invariably is that it is going to be incredibly hard and incredibly bad luck *c*
on the co-owner, the wife, who is in most cases a totally innocent person who has done
nothing to bring about the bankruptcy. Of course, as against that, one has to realise that
she has been enjoying over whatever period it may be the fruits of the debts which the
bankrupt has contracted and which debts are not at the moment being paid. So that
although it may be very bad luck on her, she at any rate has had some enjoyment of the
fruits which led to the bankruptcy. *d*

That being so, let us now look and see what the judge said:

'I look to see all the circumstances. I of course have very much in mind in cases
of a sale the bankrupt comes along and says it is going to be a great hardship. It is
not a submission which finds much favour with me as regards [the bankrupt]
himself. However, when I look at all the circumstances of the persons who occupy
this house my judgment is that I am justified in suspending the order for sale. The *e*
position is that the wife has worked throughout the marriage and she had to give up
work to look after the children. One of the children has medical treatment and is
getting better. The two children are extremely young. It is going to be a situation
that [if the wife] were ordered to leave she is going to be in a position that is
unenviable: she is not going to be in a good position to get alternative
accommodation. She would rely on the resources of the local authority. The local *f*
authority will not be sympathetic with a husband earning an income of £9,500.
The hope of obtaining accommodation on the private market would in my view be
difficult given the fact that there are two young children.'

Pausing there, it appears to me that nothing in that circumstance is a matter which is
either unusual or of exceptional hardship. Indeed, one can very well see the case that is *g*
from time to time put up where the children are going to be interrupted at a sensitive
stage in their schooling, for example taking O levels, or more particularly, because O
levels or CSE are not in general all that important, when taking their A levels. There the
court, I think, has always hitherto been sympathetic if it can be shown that the eviction
will necessarily entail the children having to change schools. The court will always be
sympathetic to the extent of allowing a year or something of that nature before the order *h*
for sale is carried out. But here we are dealing with two young children, children who
are going to remain young for a long period and who will still be extremely young even
after the expiration of 30 months. And it does not seem to me that so far as such children
are concerned there is any grave hardship in their being evicted from a place which they
barely recognise at the moment. Then it is said in addition that the bankrupt is going to
be in a bad position with regard to raising a loan or mortgage because it is well known *j*
that bankrupts are not well regarded by mortgagees. Again, pausing there, that is a
universal circumstance. It cannot, even if it can be classified as hardship, be regarded as
exceptional hardship. Also one must take into account that the wife throughout this sad
episode has shown responsibility. She is the mainstay of this family. That I think is up
to a point true in that I think she is the one who is keeping the family together, and

indeed the bankrupt very sensibly, and it is a thousand pities that he did not do this
a before, is now placing the whole of his earnings under the wife's control so that the
family will not find themselves in this sort of situation again. But to suggest that she is
the mainstay of this family in the sense that she brings in the greater income is palpably
not true. On the latest affidavit sworn by her the bankrupt's monthly salary is £650 net
and her salary is between £200 and £250 monthly net.

Then the judge goes on:

b   'I am quite satisfied that [the bankrupt] from the date of [the trustee's] affidavit
      has accepted his responsibility to make the repayments there set out. The matter of
      the creditors has been the subject of comment by [counsel for the wife]. They are
      mostly banks. He submitted that it is not right to make this family unit homeless
      by ordering the sale. Among the creditors are judgment creditors and all creditors
      are entitled to equal consideration. I do not make any distinction between any
c   creditor. I do not accept his submissions in this regard. Therefore in considering all
      the circumstances I have to decide whether or not I have to make an order for this
      family unit to be rendered homeless. For the reasons set out I have come to the
      conclusion that there are exceptional circumstances which do not enable me to
      make the normal order.'

d Now I have been through all the circumstances on which the judge relies, and it does
not appear to me that any of those circumstances are exceptional in the kind of context
in which this jurisdiction has to operate. I think it would not be fair to cut the judge's
judgment off there. He goes on:

e   'I have looked at the history of [the wife's] work. I have had regard to [the
      bankrupt and his wife's] offer to work to make substantial contributions towards the
      debts. I attach a considerable amount of weight to the fact that the bankrupt is a
      different person from his innocent wife. [The wife's] offer stands on its merits. She
      has been the backbone of the family and working for a considerable amount of
      time. The only matter that gave me some pause was that [the bankrupt] did not
      want his wife to go out to work. That wish does not come from her. It is no more
f   than an indication of the view of [the bankrupt]. Perhaps the indication was based
      not too fairly on the facts. [The bankrupt] must pay his creditors. There is going
      to have to be a considerable amount of money paid over. She will take that job.
      Therefore it is necessary to decide for what amount of time the order should be
      suspended.'

The present situation is that, pursuant to an affidavit put in at the last moment on 7th
g May and not objected to by counsel for the trustee, the wife says:

      'We have so far made payments of £250 a month to the Trustee in Bankruptcy
      and I hope that this sum will rise to £300 when I have paid my Legal Aid
      contributions. I further hope that this sum can be increased to £350 in a further 9
      to 12 months depending on whether I get an increase in pay at my present job or a
      vacancy arises in ICI.'

h But what the judge does not appear to have appreciated and certainly does not appear
to express himself to understand is that any contribution which is here spoken of is a
payment which is being made out of the total earnings of the bankrupt and the wife,
and, in so far as any payment is made out of the bankrupt's earnings if he has anything
over, that as it were belongs to his creditors anyway, and the trustee in bankruptcy would
j be entitled on making a proper application to attach those moneys for the use of the
creditors. Therefore it does not seem to me that any contribution coming from the
bankrupt is really of any particular interest. But so be it. It still remains the fact that
even if there were these contributions and even if the contributions were to discharge the
liabilities of the bankrupt it would require a period of something of the order of 30
months for that to take place. And it seems to me, in a circumstance where there is no

special hardship or exceptional hardship, a period which is far too long. It is put this way
in the notice of appeal:

> 'That the Learned Judge failed to give any or any sufficient weight to the facts
> that: (a) the creditors of the Bankrupt have been pressing for payment since 1976,
> that several of them had obtained judgment against the Bankrupt, and that one of
> them had presented a Petition against the Bankrupt which led to these bankruptcy
> proceedings [and that] (b) the Bankrupt's indebtedness to the said creditors was
> incurred in order to pay for the maintenance of the property and the acquisition of
> its contents and in order to maintain the Respondents in a standard of living which
> they could not afford from their own incomes [and that] (c) the suspension of the
> sale would prejudice creditors by reason of the consequent delay in payment of
> dividends to them in discharge or partial discharge of their debts . . .'

The matter is indeed in some ways ironic. The only reason why either the bankrupt
or his wife has an asset of any value is because of inflation taking place steadily since the
purchase of the property in the year 1974 and continuing ever since. Apart from that the
equity, the difference between the mortgage and the worth of the property, would be
very little indeed. At the same time the money which the bankrupt owes to his creditors
year by year is steadily diminishing in value as the worth of the property increases, and
the princely rate of interest laid down under the bankruptcy legislation of 4% was a rate
laid down in times when the value of money was stable, and bears no relation to what is
happening today. So the situation undoubtedly is that there will be totally unlooked-for
and unnecessary hardship on the creditors if they are kept out of their money for any
appreciable length of time. Eighteen months has already elapsed between the date of the
order for adjudication and the order of the deputy circuit judge. Of course I suppose the
trustee in bankruptcy might have made an application earlier, but he did not do so, and
the bankrupt and his wife have had the benefit of the property during all that time.

Looking at the other side of the coin, it seems to me that if a sale is ordered the wife
will have in her hands the not inconsiderable sum of £10,000 which should go at any
rate some way towards providing for a deposit on another house even if that house has
to be obtained on her sole income without the income of her husband. The husband
informed us that he had been told that as a bankrupt there would be precious little
chance of his obtaining any mortgage. That I can undoubtedly see. But of course if, as
I confidently expect, as a result of the sale of the property the whole of his debts are
discharged and he obtains a discharge from his bankruptcy the matter may very well be
of a totally different complexion thereafter. But be that as it may this is not a case where
the family would be being thrown out in the gutter without anything. They will be
thrown out as it were with a sum of £10,000 which is, as I have already said, due not to
any merit of either of them but due to the passage of time and the rate of inflation that
we have been enjoying. But at any rate it is sufficient to ensure that they do not get
totally cast out without any resources of any description with which to rehouse
themselves.

Therefore it seems to me at the end of the day that the deputy curcuit judge went so
plainly wrong that this court is in a position to come to a different conclusion. He went
wrong because after having correctly cited the approach laid down in all the cases he then
did not so frame the remainder of his judgment as to bring himself within the law so laid
down, and he did not do so because he treated matters which are as it were, however
regrettably, of everyday incidence and occurrence in this type of jurisdiction as if they
were exceptional circumstances where none of them in fact were. Therefore for those
reasons I would be in favour of allowing the appeal.

GOULDING J. I agree with Walton J that the appeal must be allowed. For my part
I have had more difficulty in coming to that conclusion. In all cases where a home is the
subject of co-ownership between a trustee in bankruptcy for the benefit of the bankrupt's
creditors on the one hand and the wife of the bankrupt on the other, the court, in

exercising its discretionary jurisdiction to order or not to order a sale pursuant to s 30 of the Law of Property Act 1925, has to effect a comparison of merits and hardship which in its nature is very difficult, because the position of creditors on the one hand and a family on the other are in themselves hard to compare. Very often I think problems of that kind involve (I use the words of Lord Diplock in *Birkett v James* [1977] 2 All ER 801 at 804, [1978] AC 297 at 317)—

> 'balancing against one another a variety of relevant considerations on which opinions of individual judges may reasonably differ as to their relative weight in a particular case.'

Lord Diplock went on to say:

> '... an appellate court ought not [on such occasions] to substitute its own "discretion" for that of the judge merely because its members would themselves have regarded the balance as tipped against the way in which he had decided the matter.'

So in this present case I felt at one time that I might support the judgment of the deputy circuit judge on the ground that, although it did not appeal to me as a view I would myself have taken, it was such that an appellate court ought not to interfere. However, having heard the matter fully argued, I have come to a different conclusion. On the one hand the hardship to the co-owner, the bankrupt's wife, in this case is certainly no greater than in the ordinary run of such cases where early sale is ordered. On the other hand creditors invariably suffer hardship through delay in satisfying their debts, which is a source of real loss in times of high interest rates and depreciating currency. And the order as pronounced below does considerably add to the burden of delay by postponing the satisfaction of creditors' claims far beyond what might reasonably be hoped for.

What I think led to the judge's view was his conviction that the proposed monthly payments by the bankrupt and his wife out of their earnings could be relied on to secure the promised sum for the creditors within the period of two and a half years that was under discussion. The evidence, and the advocacy of counsel for the wife, presented an attractive picture of a young couple whose finances became disordered, but who have seen the disaster into which they have fallen and have reformed their affairs by the responsible wife taking over control from the insufficiently careful husband. But when one looks at the figures, at the family budget that has been put before us, it is perfectly apparent to anyone who has experience of these affairs that the completion of the scheme of payments is by no means to be relied on as limiting the burden imposed on creditors. Any unexpected misfortune or expense of any magnitude might lead to a disappointment of the proposed scheme of payments. It is a brave proposal but it is hope rather than secure promise, and if that applied, as I think it did, to what was before the judge below it applies all the more strongly to the larger payment scheme offered in this court. Thus, although I agree with Walton J that no exception can be taken to the statement of the law which the judge made in his judgment, I am convinced that in applying it to the facts of the case and making the order that he did he has gone wrong in law.

For that reason I too would allow the appeal.

Appeal allowed. Sale not to proceed to completion before three months from date of Divisional Court's judgment. Leave to appeal refused.

Solicitors: *Hewett, Pim & Dixon*, Reading (for the trustee); *D Miles Griffiths, Piercy & Co*, Maidenhead (for the wife).

Evelyn M C Budd   Barrister.

Barge v Graham Brown (Oasis Trading) Ltd   a

QUEEN'S BENCH DIVISION

DONALDSON LJ AND FORBES J

19th FEBRUARY 1981

Hallmarking – Unhallmarked articles – Exempted articles – Articles of minimum fineness –   b
Articles comprised of precious metal and other materials – Article not exempted unless it complies
with requirements relating to articles comprised of precious metal and other materials – Complies
with – Brooch consisting of less than 1 g of gold of minimum fineness and of other materials –
Brooch not hallmarked – Brooch not meeting requirements for hallmarking of articles comprised
of precious metal and other materials – Brooch described as being 'encased in a mantle of 24 carat
gold' – Whether article 'complied with' requirements relating to articles comprised of precious   c
metal and other materials – Whether 'complies with' meaning 'capable of complying with' –
Whether prohibited description – Hallmarking Act 1973 (as amended by the Hallmarking
(Exempted Articles) (Amendment) Order 1975 (SI 1975 No 1883)), s 1, Sch 1, paras 12, 14B,
Sch 2, Part III.

On three occasions a company sold or offered for sale an unhallmarked brooch which was   d
partly made of gold and was described as 'encased in a mantle of 24 carat gold'. The
brooch consisted of an orchid, covered by base metals and a layer of 24 carat gold, the
gold weighing less than 1 g. By para 12[a] of Sch 1 to the Hallmarking Act 1973 any article
containing only one precious metal, being of minimum fineness and, in the case of gold,
of weight of less than 1 g, was exempted from the requirement to be hallmarked. By
para 14B[b] of Sch 1 an article which was described in para 12 and which contained   e
materials other than precious metals did not fall within para 12 unless it complied with
Part III[c] of Sch 2 to the 1973 Act. By s 4(1)(c)[d] of the 1973 Act articles comprised of
precious metal and other materials could only be hallmarked if they complied with
certain requirements specified in Part III of Sch 2. The brooch did not qualify for
hallmarking under any of the requirements of Part III of Sch 2. The company was
charged with supplying or offering to supply in the course of a trade or business an   f
unhallmarked article to which was applied a description that it was wholly or partly
made of gold, contrary to s 1[e] of the 1973 Act. The informations were dismissed by the
justices, who found that since the brooch contained less than 1 g of gold and no other
precious metal it was exempted by para 12 of Sch 1 from the requirement of
hallmarking. The justices did not go on to consider para 14B of Sch 1 or Part III of Sch
2. The prosecutor appealed.

Held – Since the brooch did not qualify for hallmarking under any of the requirements   g
of Part III of Sch 2 to the 1973 Act the company had 'complied' with Part III in not having
it hallmarked. Accordingly, by para 14B of Sch 1 to that Act it fell within para 12 of that
schedule and was not required to be hallmarked. It followed that the justices had been
correct to dismiss the informations, and the appeal would therefore be dismissed (see
p 362 h to p 363 f, post).   h

---

a   Paragraph 12, so far as material, is set out at p 362 c, post

b   Paragraph 14B, so far as material, is set out at p 362 d, post

c   Part III, so far as material, is set out at p 362 f, post

d   Section 4(1), so far as material, provides: 'Subject to the provisions of this section and of Schedule
    2 to this Act, any article of precious metal, which is submitted to an assay office for hallmarking
    and which upon assay is found in all its parts to be of a standard of fineness not less than the   j
    minimum fineness for that precious metal, shall be struck by that assay office with the approved
    hallmarks, namely . . . (c) as respects articles comprised of precious metal and other materials and
    satisfying the conditions of Part III of the said Schedule 2, marks struck in accordance with that
    Part . . .'

e   Section 1, so far as material, is set out at p 361 j to p 362 a, post

Per Curiam. The words 'complies with Part III of Schedule 2 to [the 1973 Act]' in para
a 14B of Sch 1 to that Act cannot be read as meaning 'is capable of complying with Part III
of Sch 2 to that Act' (see p 363 *b c*, post).

Notes

For the hallmarking of precious metals, see Supplement to 38 Halsbury's Laws (3rd Edn)
para 830A.
b   For the Hallmarking Act 1973, ss 1, 4, Schs 1, 2, see 43 Halsbury's Statutes (3rd Edn)
1769, 1773, 1789, 1791.

Case stated

Leslie Albert Barge, the county trading standards officer of the Oxfordshire County
c Council, appealed by way of case stated by the justices for Oxford in respect of their
adjudication as a magistrates' court sitting at the Court House, Speedwell Street, Oxford
whereby on 11th August 1980 they dismissed three informations laid by the appellant
against the respondent, Graham Brown (Oasis Trading) Ltd, that on three occasions in
December 1979 the respondent in the course of a trade or business supplied or offered to
supply an unhallmarked article, namely an orchid brooch, to which was applied a
d description indicating that the brooch was partly made of gold, namely 'This natural
orchid from Thailand is encased in a mantle of 24 carat gold', contrary to s 1 of the
Hallmarking Act 1973. The justices were of the opinion that 24 carat gold could be
measured in fineness and therefore the definition of minimum fineness in s 22 of the
1973 Act could apply to such gold, that as the article was encased in 24 carat gold that was
in excess of the minimum fineness and as it weighed less than 1 g the article fell within
e para 12 of Sch 1 to the 1973 Act, that that could be considered in isolation and that
therefore it was not necessary to consider para 14B of Sch 1 or para 6 of Sch 2 to that
Act. The facts are set out in the judgment of Forbes J.

Anthony King for the appellant.
f The respondent was not represented.

FORBES J delivered the first judgment at the invitation of Donaldson LJ. This is an
appeal by way of case stated by the justices for Oxford in respect of their adjudication as
a magistrates' court sitting at the Court House, Speedwell Street, Oxford.
  It concerns the provisions of the Hallmarking Act 1973. What had happened was that
g on three occasions there had been a sale or offer for sale of an orchid brooch, which was
partly made of gold, and had this description attached: 'This natural orchid from Thailand
is encased in a mantle of 24 carat gold.' In fact what the justices found was that each of
the three articles had a thin outer covering of 24 carat gold, the gold in each case
weighing less than 1 g, which is a significant weight.
  Apart from gold, each article contained an organic substance, presumably the orchid
h itself, covered by base metals, copper and nickel respectively. We are told, and I do not
see any reason why we should not accept it, that in fact the article consists of an orchid
covered originally with copper and then with a much thinner layer of nickel, and then
to the outside of that is applied a layer of 24 carat gold which is no more than 0·3 micron
thick.
  The question is whether or not in describing that article as 'encased in a mantle of 24
j carat gold' the persons who were supplying or offering to sell it were committing an
offence under the Act.
  Turning to the 1973 Act, s 1, so far as is material, says this:

  '(1) Subject to the provisions of this Act, any person who, in the course of a trade
  or business . . . (*b*) supplies, or offers to supply, an unhallmarked article to which

such a description is applied [that is that it is wholly or partly made of gold, silver or platinum] shall be guilty of an offence.

'(3) Subsection (1) above shall not apply to an article within Part II of [Sch 1].'

These articles were not in fact hallmarked so that they were an unhallmarked article to which a description, that they were wholly or partly made of gold, was in fact applied. An offence would be committed therefore unless they fell within Part II of Sch 1.

Part II of Sch 1 has been amended and the amending powers are contained in Part IV of that schedule. Part II is headed 'Exempted Articles', and we can go straight to the amended para 12 which reads in this way:

'Any article containing only one precious metal, being a metal of minimum fineness and of a weight less than that specified in the following table—

gold	..	..	..	..	..	..	..	..1	gram
silver	..	..	..	..	..	..	..7·78	grams
platinum	..	..	..	..	..	..	..0·5	gram.'

The point about 'a metal of minimum fineness' need not trouble us, because minimum fineness for gold is the appropriate figure for 9 carat gold. It is not disputed that this article, as it contained only one precious metal and that was 24 carat gold, contained a metal of minimum fineness. It is not disputed that the precious metal had a weight less than 1 g. Thus the article falls within para 12 as an exempted article so long as it satisfies a new para 14B. Para 14B, so far as is material, reads:

'Where an article described in paragraph 12 ... contains materials other than precious metals the article shall not be taken as falling within that paragraph unless it complies with Part III of Schedule 2 to this Act.'

One then turns to Part III of Sch 2, and that is headed 'Articles Comprised of Precious Metal and Other Materials'. Paragraph 6 reads:

'An article comprised of precious metal and one or more other materials (in this paragraph referred to as "other materials") shall be hallmarked as if the precious metal were comprised in a separate article if, but only if, it complies with one or other of the following sub-paragraphs—(a) where the other materials include base metal, the article shall be hallmarked only if [and then there is a series of tests which the article has to pass] (b) where the other materials do not include base metal, the article shall be hallmarked only on the precious metal part thereof and only if—(i) those materials are clearly distinguishable ...'

I find it quite impossible to read any intelligible sense into the combination of the new para 14B and the form in which Part III of Sch 2 is cast.

Counsel for the appellant says that he accepts that para 14B read as it stands is incapable of an intelligible meaning; one has, he says, to read the words 'complies with Part III' as if they meant 'is capable of complying with Part III'.

This is a statute creating an offence, and nothing seems to me to be better settled than that where an offence is created by a statute it must be quite plain what the offence is and how it may be committed. It seems to me that if a trader were trying to make certain that in marketing some article he was complying with the provisions of this Act, he would go first to s 1; he would understand from that section that, if it was an unhallmarked article (as it is), he could not sell it as gold without committing an offence unless he could find that it fell within one of the exceptions in Part II; he would then look at Part II and he would find that if he were marketing these particular articles they do fall provisionally within para 12 and are therefore exempted articles.

He would then have to look at para 14B. He would say to himself: 'Now I see that this article has to comply with Part III of Sch 2. Let us look at Part III of Sch 2. What does that provide so that I have to comply with it? That provides that this article shall be hallmarked only if it complies with a number of requirements. It does not comply with any of those requirements. Therefore it cannot be hallmarked under Part III. I cannot therefore get it hallmarked, and in not hallmarking it under that Part I am complying with its provisions. Therefore it must follow, it seems to me, if one is approaching it in that way that I am safe in calling it "gold" because it falls within para 12, as the necessary mechanical matters, if I may call them that, are satisfied, and it complies with Part III because it cannot be hallmarked under that paragraph unless it complies with certain other requirements which do not apply.'

It seems to me that one cannot read in, in order to save this piece of legislation, the words 'is capable of complying with Part III' instead of the words 'complies with' for the reason I have given, namely that this is a statute creating a penal offence. It seems to me that, if the Secretary of State wants to make certain that an offence is committed and is triable, the wording of para 14B will require a certain amount of overhaul. But as it stands it seems to me that the justices were right in dismissing these informations for the reasons I have indicated.

DONALDSON LJ. I agree. Part III of Sch 2 to the Hallmarking Act 1973 applies, as it says, to articles comprising precious metal and other material, and this article is in that category.

Having followed the statutory route that Forbes J has indicated, I then come to ask myself the question: does the article comply with Part III of Sch 2? Since that article is purely concerned with requiring certain articles to be hallmarked if, but only if, they comply with the particular conditions, it seems to me that the only articles that comply with the section are those which are hallmarked in accordance with the section or those which are not hallmarked in accordance with the section.

To put it another way which may be easier to understand, the only way in which you can fail to comply with the section is if you hallmark an article which should not be hallmarked or if you fail to hallmark an article which should be hallmarked.

In this case this article did not qualify for hallmarking. It was not hallmarked. It therefore complied with Part III of Sch 2. Ergo it qualifies for para 12 of the schedule; ergo no offence is committed under s 1. I have a suspicion that that is not what the draftsman of the Act intended. But since he has taken this quite remarkable power to alter the Act by statutory instrument, the remedy lies in his own hands.

Appeal dismissed.

Solicitors: *P J Floyd*, Oxford (for the appellant).

April Weiss   Barrister.

North West Leicestershire District Council v East Midlands Housing Association Ltd

COURT OF APPEAL, CIVIL DIVISION

STEPHENSON, BRANDON LJJ AND SIR STANLEY REES

10th, 13th, 14th APRIL, 15th MAY 1981

Local authority – Contract – Accordance with standing orders – Non-compliance with standing orders – Validation of non-compliance with standing orders if contract otherwise valid – Council clerk agreeing to amend terms of contract – Clerk having no authority to agree to amendment – Contract sealed but not in accordance with council's standing orders – Whether contract 'otherwise valid' – Whether clerk's lack of authority resulting in void contract which was unable to be subsequently validated – Local Government Act 1933, s 266(2) proviso.

Shortly before local government reorganisation in 1974, an urban district council, the appellant's predecessors, entered into negotiations with the respondent housing association for the building of three blocks of flats. In December 1973 the council accepted a fixed price tender submitted by the association and a draft contract in standard form was sent to the association. On 5th March 1974, at the last committee meeting of the council, it was resolved that the chairman of the council should be authorised to deal with any matter requiring urgent attention during the period prior to reorganisation. On 18th March it was agreed between the clerk of the council and the chief executive of the association that the contract should incorporate a price fluctuation clause. The contract was later attested by the clerk and the chairman of the council. However, the contract failed to comply with the council's standing order governing the sealing of contracts, in that no resolution had been passed authorising the sealing and the two attesting witnesses were not present at the time of the sealing. After building had commenced and the council had paid out sums on interim certificates, the council brought an action claiming moneys overpaid, on the basis that the contract did not contain a price fluctuation clause. The appellants contended that the council had never intended to make or authorise the making of any contract with the association other than a fixed price contract. The association counterclaimed for sums due on its final account on the basis that the contract did contain a price fluctuation clause. The judge found that the price fluctuation clause was incorporated as a term of the contract because (i) although the clerk had exceeded his authority in agreeing to the price fluctuation clause, authority had nevertheless been conferred on the chairman by the resolution of 5th March 1974 authorising him to execute the contract, which he had done by attesting the sealing, and (ii) in any event the contract as amended was validated by the proviso to s 266(2)[d] of the Local Government Act 1933, which relieved a person entering into a contract with a local authority from any duty to inquire whether the standing orders applicable to the contract had been complied with, and further provided that a contract entered into by a local authority, 'if otherwise valid', was to have full force and effect, notwithstanding any failure to comply with the standing orders. The judge accordingly dismissed the appellants' claim and allowed the association's counterclaim. The appellants appealed to the Court of Appeal.

Held – (1) On the facts, the council's clerk had had no authority, actual or ostensible, to agree to the amendment to the proposed contract by the insertion of a price fluctuation clause. Furthermore, the terms of the resolution of 5th March 1974 giving the chairman authority to deal with urgent matters did not authorise the amendment since in signing the contract the chairman had not executed the contract but merely attested the sealing

---

a   Section 266 is set out at p 368 *j* to p 369 *b*, post

of it, and in any event it had not been established that the matter was urgent (see p 367 *j* to p 368 *a* and *g*, p 372 *j* and p 374 *f g*, post).

(2) (Brandon LJ dissenting) On the true construction of the proviso to s 266(2) of the 1933 Act, a contract was 'otherwise valid' only if it was valid otherwise than by reason of non-compliance with an applicable standing order. The proviso did not operate to validate a contract with a local authority made as a result of an agreement deliberately and knowingly entered into by an agent in contravention of the local authority's intention. Accordingly, the association could not rely on the proviso to s 266(2) to validate the council's clerk's want of authority and in the absence of such authority there was no contract between the council and the association to be validated, and the non-compliance with the council's standing order governing the sealing of contracts was irrelevant. It followed that the contract was wholly void with the consequences that the appellants could not recover any moneys paid under it and that any remedy open to the association was by way of a possible claim on a quantum meruit for work done if it had been paid less than its work was worth. The appeal would therefore be allowed and both the claim and counterclaim dismissed (see p 370 *j*, p 371 *e* to p 372 *f* and p 375 *h*, post).

Notes

For liability in contract of corporations, see 9 Halsbury's Laws (4th Edn) paras 1366–1373, and for cases on the subject, see 13 Digest (Reissue) 317–339, 2779–2907.

For the Local Government Act 1933, s 266, see 19 Halsbury's Statutes (3rd Edn) 550.

As from 1st April 1974 s 266 of the 1933 Act was replaced by s 135 of the Local Government Act 1972.

Cases referred to in judgments

Freeman & Lockyer (a firm) v Buckhurst Park Properties (Mangal) Ltd [1964] 1 All ER 630, [1964] 2 QB 480, [1964] 2 WLR 618, CA, 9 Digest (Reissue) 573, 3422.

L'Estrange v F Graucob Ltd [1934] 3 KB 394, [1934] All ER Rep 16, 103 LJKB 730, 152 LT 164, DC, 12 Digest (Reissue) 78, 415.

Wright (A R) & Son Ltd v Romford Corpn [1956] 3 All ER 785, [1957] 1 QB 431, [1956] 3 WLR 896, 121 JP 44, 54 LGR 647, 13 Digest (Reissue) 320, 2800.

Cases also cited

Bonelli's Telegraph Co, Re, Collie's Claim (1871) LR 12 Eq 246.

Reuter v Electric Telegraph Co (1856) 6 E & B 341, 119 ER 892.

Royal British Bank v Turquand (1856) 6 E & B 327, [1843–60] All ER Rep 435, Ex Ch.

Staple of England (Mayor, Constables and Co of Merchants) v Governor and Co of Bank of England (1887) 21 QBD 160, DC.

Appeal

The North West Leicestershire District Council appealed against the judgment of Swanwick J given on 23rd July 1979 whereby he dismissed the council's claim for £70,651·39 overpaid on a contract made under seal between the appellants' predecessor, the Coalville Urban District Council, and the respondent, East Midlands Housing Association Ltd, and gave judgment for the housing association on its counterclaim for £40,988·88 with £10,140·52 interest. By a respondent's notice dated 17th June 1980 the association contended that the decision of Swanwick J should be affirmed on grounds additional to those relied on by the judge. The facts are set out in the judgment of Stephenson LJ.

Harold Burnett for the council.
John Dyson for the housing association.

Cur adv vult

15th May. The following judgments were read.

STEPHENSON LJ. On 1st April 1974 the Coalville Urban District Council ceased to exist and all its rights and duties were taken over by the appellant council. During the weeks preceding the transfer life in the offices of the urban district council was, in the words of Mr Brackenbury, chief administrative assistant in the department of Mr Marson, the clerk to the urban district council, 'very, very hectic'. One matter under its consideration in its last year of life was the building of three blocks of flats for old people. On 14th August 1973 its health and housing committee had resolved that the council approved in principle the scheme submitted by the respondent housing association for the provision of this accommodation and that the council's officers hold discussions with representatives of the Department of Environment and the association.

On 4th December 1973 the clerk submitted to a meeting of the urban district council the association's fixed price tender for its consideration and the council resolved that subject to arithmetical check that tender, in the sum of £467,795·62, be accepted. On 18th December 1973 the health and housing committee resolved that the fixed price tender submitted by the association in the revised sum of £468,985·36 be accepted subject to written approval with regard to the housing costs yardstick from the Department of the Environment.

In the last hectic month before transfer Mr Marson, the clerk, was no doubt extremely busy, but only two of his actions concern us. First, on 5th March 1974 he reported to the finance and general purposes committee of the urban district council that this was the last committee meeting of the council and at his request the committee resolved 'that the Chairman of the Council be authorised to deal with any matter requiring urgent attention during the period up to 31st March, 1974'. Second, on 18th March 1974 he met Mr Elderfield, secretary and chief executive of the association, and on a date not precisely fixed by the evidence but agreed to be the same day attested the sealing of a printed contract for the building of the flats by the association. That contract was in one of the standard forms of what used to be called the RIBA contract, and it contained manuscript insertions and amendments by way of deletion, alteration and addition, of which only two are important.

First, in the margin of cl 31B(b)(ii) was written: '(iii) The Contract shall also be adjustable on the index based formula of the Department of Environment's Circular No. 158/73', subscribed with three sets of initials 'for EMHA' (the association).

Second, the date for completion was amended from 24 months from the date for possession to 'Eighteen' and the alteration was signed by Mr Marson, 'Clerk of the Council', and Mr Elderfield, 'Secretary'.

The effect of incorporating the manuscript cl 31B(b)(iii) as a term of the contract would be to turn a fixed price contract into a contract with a price fluctuation clause. The appellant council has paid out £550,999 on interim certificates of its architect. It was not until the formula referred to in the fluctuation clause was published that the architect referred to it; he did so in the sixth certificate, and in November 1976 the district auditor took the view that the contract was a fixed price contract.

Hence the council's action claiming from the association £70,651·39 overpaid as money had and received to the use of the association if the contract did not contain the fluctuation clause, and the association's counterclaim for £40,988·88 due on its final account and not paid if the contract did contain the fluctuation clause.

On 23rd July 1979 Swanwick J, in a reserved judgment, held that the fluctuation clause was incorporated as a term of the contract and so, dismissing the claim, gave judgment for the association on the counterclaim for £40,988·88 with £10,140·52 interest. From that judgment the council appeals.

The judge reached his conclusion that the fluctuation clause was a term of the contract by accepting the evidence of Mr Elderfield, supported by the evidence of Mr Brackenbury, that Mr Marson agreed the addition of the fluctuation clause and by rejecting Mr Marson's denial that he agreed it. To that finding of the judge there is no challenge.

That finding also in effect disposed of the association's claim to rectification of the contract and that claim is not pursued. But there remain two other issues which the judge had to decide and this court has to decide. (1) Did Mr Marson have authority to agree the clause on behalf of the council? (2) Even if he did not, is the council bound by the contract to which its seal is affixed?

The question of Mr Marson's authority was raised in the council's reply, which alleged that, if he did make the agreement pleaded in the defence as an agreement made at a meeting between Mr Elderfield and Mr Marson that in consideration of a reduction of the contract period from 24 to 18 months the council would accept cl 31B(b)(iii), he had no authority to do so and/or an agreement containing this clause was never authorised by the council and the council was accordingly not bound by it. That was followed by an answer to a request for particulars of the agreement pleaded, which alleged that Mr Marson made the agreement as agent for the council; but the only particulars which the association could give of the facts and matters relied on in support of his agency and the council's authorisation of the agreement were none of his actual authority at that stage, and of his ostensible authority three things which indicated that Mr Marson held himself out as the council's agent but not that the council held him out as its agent. Particulars of that holding out were not supplied until a late stage of the appeal, when we gave counsel for the association leave to add the fact that the council placed Mr Marson in a position where he could do those three things and/or acquiesced in his doing them. Those three things were (a) his correspondence with Mr Elderfield, (b) his agreement to meet him to discuss the amendment contained in the clause, and (c) his telling Mr Elderfield at the meeting that the amendment was acceptable if the contract period was reduced to 18 months.

The judge found that Mr Marson and Mr Elderfield did make the agreement pleaded in the defence at their meeting on 18th March 1974 and he said that he would have held that in striking that bargain with Mr Elderfield Mr Marson exceeded his authority, actual or ostensible, had he not found (a) that the bargain embodied in the two amendments to cl 31B(b) and the contract period was authorised by the resolution of 5th March 1974, which I have read, and (b) that the contract as amended was validated by the proviso to s 266(2) of the Local Government Act 1933, which I shall have to read later.

It is the council's case put before the judge, and before this court in counsel's notice of appeal and in his helpful submissions, that the council never intended to make or authorised the making of any contract with the association except a fixed price contract, that Mr Marson had no actual authority express or implied, from the resolution of 5th March 1974 or any other source, and no ostensible or apparent authority from the council to agree to a fluctuation clause or to make a contract containing such a clause, and that s 266 did not have the effect of validating the contract which contained such a clause. If his submissions are accepted, it would appear to follow that his first ground of appeal is also correct, namely that the judge ought to have held that the whole contract was void or there was no contract, but that his last ground, that the judge might have held that the sum of £70,051·39 was recoverable as moneys paid under a mistake of fact, would be unsustainable.

Counsel for the association seeks by equally helpful arguments to support the judge's judgment on the grounds which he gave for it, but also, by a respondent's notice, on the additional ground that on the evidence Mr Marson had 'usual and/or implied and/or ostensible authority' to agree to the insertion of a price fluctuations clause in the contract.

The conflict between the two parties has been reduced in one respect. The terms of the resolution of 5th March 1974 as analysed by counsel for the council were too clear to support the argument that they gave Mr Marson the necessary authority. They gave authority to the chairman, not to the clerk, and though Mr Simpson, the chairman, attested the sealing of the contract with Mr Marson, he did not execute the contract in any other manner; to treat his signature as any more than an attestation would be to confuse the party to a written contract who signs it with a witness to his signature. And the matter did not require such urgent attention on 18th March that it could not have been dealt with by a resolution of the council, which met for the last time, as was admitted in spite of Mr Marson's evidence that it did not, on the very next day, 19th March. These obstacles led counsel for the association to abandon the point.

He did not, however, abandon the point in his respondent's notice that Mr Marson had actual implied authority. Ostensible authority, he accepted from the judgment of Diplock LJ in *Freeman & Lockyer (a firm) v Buckhurst Park Properties (Mangal) Ltd* [1964] 1 All ER 630, [1964] 2 QB 480, had to be conferred by the council's representing that Mr Marson had authority to do something which someone in his position of clerk to a local authority would by virtue of that position have authority to do. But, though there was nothing in the constitution of the urban district council prohibiting it from giving its clerk authority to contract on its behalf, there was no evidence that clerks to such local authorities ever had that authority or that Mr Marson had authority to make other contracts like this. Counsel for the association had therefore to rely, and did rely, for Mr Marson's authority mainly if not solely on actual implied authority.

There he was confronted by Mr Marson's own emphatic evidence, supported by the equally positive opinion of Mr Simpson, the chairman, that Mr Marson had no authority to agree to a fundamental change to conditions and contents of this contract with its financial implications. And that was the basis of his denial that he ever agreed to the fluctuation clause which changed the fixed price contract approved by the council. He said in evidence:

'First of all, I had no authority to agree that fluctuating clause myself; secondly, I would have needed the authority of the council for the amendment to the contract in these terms; and, thirdly, it would have been necessary to obtain the approval of the Department of the Environment to the variation of the contract to include the fluctuation clause on the formula laid down in that circular.'

Though he retracted in cross-examination the third requirement, he stuck to the first and second; he would have had authority to shorten the contract period but not to agree the fluctuation clause.

Mr Marson had a lifetime's experience in local government and considered himself meticulous in the drafting of documents and in contractual procedures; he became the chief executive of the new council until he retired for medical reasons. He had no legal qualifications but his council relied on him for advice on contractual matters. Counsel for the association was driven to submit that the fact found by the judge of Mr Marson's agreement to the fluctuation clause spoke louder than his words denying that he agreed to it and asserting that it was so fundamental that he would not agree to it without reference to his council. I am afraid that I cannot accept that bold submission; in my opinion, the judge was clearly right in concluding that Mr Marson would have had no authority, actual or ostensible, but for the resolution of 5th March 1974, which is no longer relied on as conferring it, and for s 266 of the Local Government Act 1933, on which the whole of the association's case must now rest.

Was the judge right to regard that section, when applied to the facts of this case, as validating an agreement which Mr Marson had no authority to make and making that agreement binding on the urban district council and so on its successor? This was not the ground on which the main battle was fought below; that was the issue whether the fluctuation clause was agreed to by Mr Marson. So the judge had less argument on s 266 than has helped us in this court on what is, in my judgment, a far from easy matter.

Section 266 of the 1933 Act enacted:

'(1) A local authority may enter into contracts necessary for the discharge of any of their functions.

'(2) All contracts made by a local authority or by a committee thereof shall be made in accordance with the standing orders of the local authority, and in the case of contracts for the supply of goods or materials or for the execution of works, the standing orders shall—(a) require that, except as otherwise provided by or under the standing orders, notice of the intention of the authority or committee, as the case a   may be, to enter into the contract shall be published and tenders invited; and (b) regulate the manner in which such notice shall be published and tenders invited: Provided that a person entering into a contract with a local authority shall not be bound to inquire whether the standing orders of the authority which apply to the contract have been complied with, and all contracts entered into by a local authority, if otherwise valid, shall have full force and effect notwithstanding that the standing orders applicable thereto have not been complied with.'

b   The urban district council had a standing order relating to its contracts. It was standing order no 23, which reads:

'(1) The Common Seal of the council shall not be affixed to any document unless the sealing has been authorised by a resolution of the council or of a committee to which the council have delegated their powers in this behalf, but a resolution of the council (or of a committee where that committee has the power) authorising the c   acceptance of any tender, the purchase, sale, letting, or taking of any property, the issue of any stock, the presentation of any petition, memorial, or address, the making of any rate or contract, or the doing of any other thing, shall be a sufficient authority for sealing any document necessary to give effect to the resolution.

'(2) The seal shall be attested by one at least of the following persons present at d   the sealing, viz. the Chairman or Vice-Chairman of the Council or other member of the council, and the Clerk or Deputy Clerk of the Council and an entry of every sealing of a document shall be made and consecutively numbered in a book kept for the purpose and shall be signed by a person who has attested the seal.'

The sealing of this contract was not authorised by any resolution of the council or of a committee. It was never suggested that it was authorised except by the resolution of e   5th March 1974, and that resolution did not authorise it; and, as the only resolution authorising the acceptance of a tender or the making of a contract was the resolution of 18th December 1973 authorising the acceptance of the association's fixed price tender, it was an unauthorised sealing.

The evidence as to the sealing, both the affixing of the common seal and its attestation, was not completely clear. There was no evidence proving who actually affixed the seal. f   The judge treated the seals register as proving that the document was in fact signed and sealed on 18th March 1974. Mr Brackenbury arranged for the document, already signed by Mr Marson and Mr Elderfield, to be entered in the seals register, but he had no independent recollection of the date when the document was 'executed', presumably by affixing and attesting the seal. Nor did Mr Simpson, the chairman. But he remembered signing the document without reading it, when it was already signed by Mr Marson, in g   Mr Marson's office with several other documents. Mr Marson agreed that he himself signed it and would probably have obtained Mr Simpson's signature in his office later the same evening. There was no evidence that either Mr Simpson or Mr Marson was present at the sealing as required by the standing order, or that they signed it when it was already sealed. They probably attested the sealing by signing after it had been sealed in their absence.

h   Mr Elderfield was not asked about any seal on the document except the seal of his association. But it is a curiosity of the case that he had been in fact a member of the Coalville Urban District Council from 1971 or 1972. According to his own evidence, though he was not familiar with its standing orders, he knew that when it came to make a contract of substance it passed a resolution that contract documents should be prepared and the common seal of the council be affixed to it; and he had received the minutes of j   the meetings which contained the two resolutions of December 1973 which I have read, but had not read them and after Mr Marson had told him that the council accepted the fluctuation clause assumed that there was a minute delegating him to do so and did not question his authority.

The judge must be taken, in accepting Mr Elderfield's version of his meeting with Mr Marson on 18th March, to have accepted his evidence that he believed Mr Marson was speaking the truth and had his council's authority to incorporate the fluctuation clause, which Mr Elderfield regarded as essential to his association's agreeing to build the flats. So we must place him and his association, as the judge did, in a position to take advantage of the proviso to s 266 of the 1933 Act.

There is no doubt that standing order no 23 applied to this contract and was not complied with in two respects. (1) The sealing had not been authorised by the necessary resolution. (2) The seal had not been attested by either the chairman (or the vice-chairman or other member) of the council or the clerk (or deputy clerk) of the council being present at the sealing. But those defects, serious though the first was, did not deprive the contract of its full force and effect 'if otherwise valid'. Was it otherwise valid? Counsel for the council submits that it was not; counsel for the association that it was. The correct answer to the question would seem to turn on the standing order and whether there was more wrong with the making of this contract complete with fluctuation clause than mere non-compliance with the standing order.

Counsel for the council submits that the contract was made when the seal of the council was affixed to the document, or when Mr Marson instructed someone to affix it, but, although standing order no 23 had not been complied with, the contract containing the fluctuation clause was not 'otherwise valid'. This submission was not considered by the judge separately from analogies by which counsel sought to support it below but no longer seeks to support it in this court.

Section 266 of the 1933 Act is not perhaps as clear as s 135 of the Local Government Act 1972 which replaced it after this contract came into existence. That later section appears to make standing orders with respect to the making of contracts generally permissive, but mandatory with respect to some contracts. However that may be, I would read s 266(2) as requiring a local authority to make standing orders relating to contracts within s 266(1), including those which are also within s 266(2). I think that a local authority must make standing orders to apply to a contract for the supply of goods and materials or for the execution of work (like this contract) because the wording of s 266(2)(a) assumes that there will be standing orders applicable to all such contracts, whatever the position of other contracts within s 266(1). But standing orders regulate internal management and procedure. The power to make them was derived from s 75 of and para 4 of Part V of Sch 3 to the 1933 Act relating to 'meetings and proceedings' and 'proceedings and business' respectively. When the Act was passed, sealing was a matter which standing orders might be expected to deal with, because it was then the law that a corporation could only contract by deed under seal. So a contract made by a local authority not under seal could not be 'otherwise valid' within the proviso because it did not comply with a requirement of the common law: see *A R Wright & Son Ltd v Romford Corpn* [1956] 3 All ER 785 at 787, [1957] 1 QB 431 at 436. In that case there was a standing order authorising sealing (though its terms are not given), and a standing order which required certain contracts to be in writing which had been complied with, but there was non-compliance with the common law so that the contract was invalid. Parliament altered the law, presumably in consequence of that case, by doing away with the requirement of sealing for a corporation's contracts: see the Corporate Bodies' Contracts Act 1960. So in 1974 a local authority could make a valid contract in writing or orally. But counsel for the council submits that it must authorise a contract before it can be bound by it and an agent who has no authority to make contracts for it still cannot bind it to something it has never agreed. Such a contract is invalid not for non-compliance with a standing order authorising sealing but for non-compliance with another requirement of the common law that a party cannot be bound by a contract made by another without his authority, unless he ratifies it or is estopped from denying that it is his.

Counsel for the association submits, in my judgment correctly, that 'if otherwise valid' means 'if valid otherwise than by reason of non-compliance with an applicable standing order', which standing order no 23 certainly is, and excludes contracts which are illegal or ultra vires the local authority, or voidable, e g for misrepresentation, or which infringe a rule of law like that in *A R Wright & Son Ltd v Romford Corpn*. He goes on to submit that this contract is only capable of being invalidated on the ground that it is unauthorised, and it is only unauthorised because no resolution authorised it, and that was a breach of standing order no 23. But for non-compliance, therefore, with that standing order, the contract would be valid and the association can rely on the proviso to s 266 of the 1933 Act. The council's predecessor having elected to require authorisation of its contracts by sealing, there is no contract until its seal is affixed to a contract and it cannot rely on any want of authority, such as Mr Marson's, to make this contract, if the association wishes to enforce it; if the council wished to enforce it, it would or might be different.

I accept counsel for the council's submission in reply that all turns on this standing order and its precise terms on their true construction, including the negative form of its opening. It does not state that no contract, or rate, can be made or be valid, or any of the other acts enumerated in the standing order, unless sealed or unless sealed in pursuance of a resolution; that may be a natural but is not a necessary assumption, certainly as regards contracts since the 1960 Act; it deals only with the conditions in which the seal can be affixed, not must be affixed. It authorises not acts including contracts but the sealing of documents necessary to give effect to resolutions authorising the acceptance of certain tenders, the presentation of certain things and the making of certain other things including contracts, all things usually made in documentary form. It is, as the standing order of the Romford Corporation was described (see [1957] 1 QB 431 at 433), an order providing for the sealing of documents and how the authority for sealing was to be given, not an order authorising contracts. I suspect that it is in a common form which was in use before the 1960 Act, but it must be interpreted and applied against the background of the law as it was when this contract was made.

If Mr Marson had made this contract with the association in writing but unsealed, he would not have been in breach of the standing order because it would not have been applicable. He would not have complied with the December resolutions, but because the contract had ceased to be a fixed price contract. The association could not enforce it against the council, not because it was not authorised by the order but because it was made contrary to the resolution. Why should the council be bound by a contract made contrary to the resolution by an unauthorised agent, because it was sealed and the sealing had not been authorised? No contract, oral or written, with a fluctuation clause was ever entered into or made by this local authority. The only person who entered into or made such a contract with the association was Mr Marson. When he agreed to Mr Elderfield's unauthorised alteration of the contract authorised by his council, he and the association were ad idem, but his council and the association were no longer ad idem. There was no contract to be sealed. The sealing of the altered contract did not make the council and the association ad idem or make a contract where none was. It would be extraordinary in the absence of any plea of estoppel or ratification that sealing should have the effect of validating an invalid contract when all standing order no 23 lays down is how sealing is to be authorised and carried out and all the proviso to s 266 of the 1933 Act, as I read it, permits is that a person entering into a contract with a local authority shall not be bound to inquire into compliance with its standing orders and such a contract shall have full force and effect if non-compliance is all that is wrong with it.

I cannot read the standing order or the proviso as giving to the sealing of the amended document the effect of making a contract which the council did not make or the effect of a signature to a written contract. The proviso contains the important qualification 'if otherwise valid'. I accept the submission of counsel for the association which I have already referred to that 'otherwise valid' means 'valid otherwise than by reason of non-compliance with an applicable standing order' or, as it is better put by Brandon LJ in the judgment which he will deliver, 'valid apart from the failure to comply with the standing order or standing orders applicable'. But I regret that I am unable to regard that as meaning 'valid if the standing order or standing orders applicable had been complied with instead of not being complied with', if by that is meant an irrebuttable presumption that there had been a resolution authorising the particular contract and it is therefore a valid contract. That limits unnaturally the meaning of the qualifying words, which are, in my judgment, wide enough to cover not merely voidable or illegal contracts duly authorised by resolution complying with the standing order, but contracts never made, agreed to or authorised by any resolution or at all. I do not believe that the proviso has any application to a case where the non-compliance with a standing order is not just a failure to obtain a resolution required by the order but is merely incidental to a deliberate contravention of the will and intention of the local authority expressed in a resolution. Then more is wrong with the contract than non-compliance with a standing order; there is also non-compliance with a resolution authorising a different kind of contract and accordingly no contract. Non-compliance with a resolution is quite different from non-compliance with an order requiring a resolution by failing, perhaps by mistake, to obtain any resolution. It is the latter sort of defect in 'indoor management', a matter of form, not a departure from authorised terms of contract, a matter of substance, from which the proviso protects those who contract with a local authority.

Suppose the council had resolved to let some of its houses to tenants and its clerk, from arrogance or incompetence, had drawn up and sealed conveyances of the freeholds to them: could it be said that the sales were otherwise valid at the time when the conveyances were sealed or the clerk gave instructions to seal them, whatever difficulties there might be in avoiding the sales later? I think not.

I would accordingly hold that there is nothing in s 266 of the 1933 Act and standing order no 23 which binds the council to a contract which its predecessor never intended to make and which purported to be made by Mr Marson in circumstances which the judge was unable fully to explain or understand.

I would therefore allow the appeal and, subject to any further submissions of counsel, dismiss both claim and counterclaim. Though the council has claimed the recovery of what it has overpaid on the basis of a fixed price contract unamended to include cl 31B(b)(iii) of the standard form, it has successfully challenged the validity of the whole document with the consequence rightly described by the judge, if he had found the other way, that—

'the council cannot recover any moneys paid under it and the association are left to a possible claim on a quantum meruit if they can prove that they have been paid less than their work was worth.'

BRANDON LJ. I have had the advantage of reading in draft the judgment which Stephenson LJ has just delivered, and I gratefully adopt the account of the facts material to this appeal which is contained in it.

As he has stated there were at the end of the argument only two questions left to this court for decision.

The first question is whether Mr Marson, the clerk of the Coalville Urban District Council, had the actual or ostensible authority of that council to agree to the addition to the terms of the proposed contract as originally drawn of the new cl 31B(b)(iii) of the standard form, conveniently called the price fluctuation clause. That first question is one of fact, depending on the evidence adduced before the judge in the court below and the inferences properly to be drawn from such evidence.

The second question is whether, even if Mr Marson did not have such authority, there nevertheless came into being between the council and the association a binding contract including that additional clause as a result of the contractual document to which it had been added being subsequently sealed and delivered on behalf of the council. That second question is one of law, depending on the true meaning and effect of the proviso to s 266 of the Local Government Act 1933 and the application of that proviso to the facts of the present case.

Stephenson LJ has expressed in his judgment his conclusion that both the two questions set out above should be answered in the negative. He has expressed the further conclusion that the result of answering both questions in the negative is that no express contract between the council and the association ever came into being.

So far as the first question is concerned I agree with the conclusion reached by Stephenson LJ and with the reasons which he has given for it. So far as the second question is concerned, however, I have reached a conclusion opposite to that of

a Stephenson LJ, my opinion being that, for reasons which I shall develop, that question should be answered in the affirmative.

The manner in which it was contemplated by both parties that the council would enter into the contract here in issue was by the contractual document which had been prepared being sealed and delivered on behalf of the council.

The sealing of the contractual document on behalf of the council was governed by its

b standing order no 23. That standing order contained two requirements relevant to the present case. The first requirement was that the seal of the council should not be affixed to any document unless such sealing had been authorised by a resolution of the council, or of a committee to which the council had delegated its power to give such authorisation. The second requirement was that the seal should be attested by two persons present at the time when it was affixed, one of whom was to be the chairman,

c vice-chairman or other member of the council, and the other the clerk or deputy clerk of the council.

In the present case the seal of the council was affixed to the contractual document concerned after the new cl 31B(b)(iii), the price fluctuation clause, had been added to the terms of that document as originally drawn. The affixing of the seal further appeared on the face of the document itself to have been done in the presence of the chairman of the

d council, Mr Simpson, and its clerk, Mr Marson, in that their signatures were written alongside the seal in the spaces provided for them, with a statement that the seal had been affixed in their presence.

In fact, however, neither the affixing of the council's seal nor the attestation of the seal by the two witnesses complied with the two requirements of the council's standing order no 23 referred to above. The first requirement was not complied with in that there had

e never been any resolution of the council, or of any committee of the council with the necessary delegated power, authorising the sealing of the contractual document with the additional price fluctuation clause contained in it. The second requirement was not complied with in that, despite what appeared on the face of the document, the two attesting witnesses were not in fact present at the time when the seal was affixed.

It is a well-established principle of law that, when a person signs a document which he

f knows to be of a contractual nature, he is bound by all the terms which the document so signed contains, whether he has read, understood and approved such terms or not: see *L'Estrange v F Graucob Ltd* [1934] 2 KB 394, [1934] All ER Rep 16. This is so, moreover, even though the draft of the contract has been prepared by an agent of the person signing it, and contains terms which such agent had no authority from the latter to include in it.

The same principle applies a fortiori to a case where a person, knowing a document to

g be of a contractual nature, seals and delivers it as his deed. It is in the light of that principle that I turn to consider the true meaning and effect of the proviso to s 266 of the 1933 Act, and the application of that proviso to the present case. Section 266 provides, so far as material, as follows:

'(1) A local authority may enter into contracts necessary for the discharge of any of their functions.

h   '(2) All contracts made by a local authority or by a committee thereof shall be made in accordance with the standing orders of the local authority ... Provided that a person entering into a contract with a local authority shall not be bound to inquire whether the standing orders of the authority which apply to a contract have been complied with, and all contracts entered into by a local authority, if otherwise valid, shall have full force and effect notwithstanding that the standing orders

j   applicable thereto have not been complied with.'

The second part of the proviso deals with cases in which a local authority enters into a contract with a person without complying with one or more of the local authority's standing orders applicable to the making by it of such a contract. It provides that, in such cases, the contract will be binding on the local authority despite such non-compliance, if otherwise valid.

The question then arises as to what is meant, in the context in which it occurs, by the expression 'otherwise valid'. In my opinion, that expression means valid apart from the failure to comply with the standing order or standing orders applicable, that is to say valid if the standing order or standing orders applicable had been complied with instead of not being complied with.

On the basis that that is the meaning of the expression 'otherwise valid', what is the effect of the proviso to s 266 on the facts of the present case? The effect must be that, if the contract would have been binding on the council if the two requirements of standing order no 23 referred to above had been complied with, then it is still binding on the council even though those two requirements were not complied with.

Would the contract then have been binding on the council if the two requirements of standing order no 23 had been complied with? In my view, in accordance with the principles which I discussed earlier, it clearly would have been so binding in respect of all its terms, including the additional price fluctuation clause, even though Mr Marson, who acted as the agent of the council in preparing the contractual document, did not have the authority of the council to include that clause.

The only circumstances which would, on the hypothesis concerned, have made the contract otherwise invalid, and so not binding on the council, would in my view have been if it had been void as being ultra vires or illegal, or voidable as having been entered into in reliance on a fraudulent or innocent misrepresentation. There was no suggestion that any of these circumstances existed in the present case.

In particular it was not suggested that the council, if it had been minded to do so, could not lawfully have authorised Mr Marson to agree to the additional price fluctuation clause on its behalf, as Mr Elderfield, acting for the association, honestly believed that it had done.

In the result I agree with the view of the judge that the effect of the proviso to s 266 was to make the whole contract, including the additional price fluctuation clause, binding on the Coalville Urban District Council, and therefore on its successors in title, the North West Leicestershire District Council. It follows that I would affirm the decision of the judge and dismiss the appeal.

SIR STANLEY REES. I have had the advantage of reading in draft the judgments delivered by Stephenson and Brandon LJJ. I respectfully agree with both of them that the trial judge was fully justified on the evidence before him in holding that Mr Marson had neither actual nor ostensible authority on behalf of the Coalville Urban District Council to agree to the addition of the price fluctuation clause to the proposed contract.

The only remaining issue, and the one on which Stephenson and Brandon LJJ have expressed differing opinions, is as to the impact on the contract of the provisions of s 266 of the Local Government Act 1933, which was in force at the time when the contract was made, although it was replaced by s 135 of the Local Government Act 1972, which came into force shortly afterwards. The relevant provisions of s 266 have been read by Stephenson and Brandon LJJ and I need not repeat more than the terms of the proviso to sub-s (2), which is in these terms:

'Provided that a person entering into a contract with a local authority shall not be bound to inquire whether the standing orders of the authority which apply to the contract have been complied with, and all contracts entered into by a local authority, if otherwise valid, shall have full force and effect notwithstanding that the standing orders applicable thereto have not been complied with.'

Stephenson and Brandon LJJ have expressed differing views as to the proper construction of this proviso. Stephenson LJ's view is that the vital words 'if otherwise valid' mean 'if valid otherwise than by reason of non-compliance with an applicable standing order'. Brandon LJ's view is 'otherwise valid' means 'valid apart from the failure to comply with the standing order or standing orders applicable, that is to say valid if the

standing order or standing orders applicable had been complied with instead of not being
a complied with'.

We were referred to only one reported case in which the provisions of s 266 of the
1933 Act have been considered. This was a decision of Lord Goddard CJ in *A R Wright
& Son Ltd v Romford Corpn* [1956] 3 All ER 785, [1957] 1 QB 431.

In that case the standing orders of a local authority required that the contract of the
kind in issue in that case should be in writing but did not require it to be sealed. The
b contract was in writing but was not sealed. At the relevant time (which was prior to the
Corporate Bodies' Contracts Act 1960) the common law required that to be valid such a
contract must be sealed. So the contract complied with the applicable standing orders
but did not comply with the common law. In order to escape liability under the contract
the defendant local authority argued that the contract was not binding on it and was not
validated by the terms of the proviso to s 266 because it was not 'otherwise valid' in that
c it was invalid by the common law. Lord Goddard CJ's approach to the interpretation of
s 266 appears from this brief passage taken from his judgment ([1956] 3 All ER 785 at
787–788, [1957] 1 QB 431 at 436–437):

'Standing orders deal with the internal affairs of the body making them and, as
the proviso shows, do not affect other persons such as those who contract or desire
to contract with the corporation. Section 266 of the Act of 1933 requires that the
d standing orders shall provide for certain steps to be taken before contracts are made,
and the orders provide for the carrying out of these directions. The party
contracting or proposing to contract with the corporation is not concerned with
whether the corporation has acted in accordance with its standing orders and, if
otherwise valid, a contract will be binding though the orders may not have been
followed; but I can find no words entitling me to say that, if a corporation does
e comply with its standing orders, the seal is no longer necessary either to bind the
corporation or to confer contractual rights on it.'

I respectfully adopt this approach to the proviso, namely that regard must be paid to
the relevant provisions of the common law and statute law when the validity of a local
authority's contract is in issue. In the instant case the terms of standing order no 23 were
f not complied with in two respects: (1) the sealing had not been authorised by any
appropriate resolution, and (2) the sealing had not been attested by the chairman (or the
vice-chairman or other member) of the urban district council or its clerk or deputy clerk
being present at the sealing.

But as Stephenson LJ has pointed out, there was far more wrong with the contract than
mere non-compliance with the standing orders. It is an inescapable inference from the
g findings of the trial judge that Mr Marson entered into the oral agreement with Mr
Elderfield knowing that he had no authority of any kind to do so and that the agreement
was in direct conflict with the expressed intentions of his employers. The evidence also
established that it was the intention of Mr Marson and a direct consequence of this
wholly unauthorised oral agreement that the sealing of the contract took place.

I respectfully agree with the view expressed by Stephenson LJ that the proviso should
h not be so construed as to validate a contract made as a result of an agreement deliberately
and knowingly made by an agent in contravention of the intention of his principal in a
case in which no estoppel or ratification is or can be relied on.

Accordingly I respectfully agree with the decision of Stephenson LJ and with the
reasons he has given, and would allow the appeal.

j *Appeal allowed.*

Solicitors: *Sharpe, Pritchard & Co* (for the council); *McMorrans*, Coalville (for the housing
association).

Patricia Hargrove   Barrister.

Sony Corpn and another v Time Electronics   *a*

CHANCERY DIVISION
GOULDING J
17th MARCH 1981

Discovery – Order for discovery – Information obtained on service of order – Collateral use of   *b*
information obtained – Passing-off action – Counterfeit goods observed while serving order for
discovery and injunction in respect of another category of counterfeit goods – Test purchase of
second category of counterfeit goods made – Whether improper to seek further order for discovery
and injunction in respect of second category of goods.

The plaintiffs obtained an order granting injunctions to stop alleged dishonest trading by   *c*
the defendant in the plaintiffs' goods and ordering delivery up of the goods and disclosure
by the defendant of, inter alia, the names and addresses of the defendant's suppliers and
the production of certain documents. While serving the order, the plaintiffs' solicitor
discovered on the defendant's premises goods of a second type which were also
manufactured by the plaintiffs. He instructed one of his firm's employees to make a test
purchase of the second type of goods. The goods were easily obtainable and clearly   *d*
imitations of the plaintiffs' goods. The plaintiffs sought a further order to restrain the
defendant trading in the second type of goods, for delivery up of goods bearing the
plaintiffs' name and for disclosure in similar terms to the first order. Because the
plaintiffs had only been in a position to discover the alleged infringement of their rights
as regard the second class of goods by entering the defendant's premises in the course of
serving the earlier order the question arose whether an order could properly be made in   *e*
respect of the second type of goods.

Held – The new action was not founded on something that the court had ordered to be
disclosed in the earlier order but on the evidence which had been obtained on the test
purchase, and the observation by the solicitor of the suspect goods of the second class
when he served the earlier order was merely collateral to the execution of that order and   *f*
did not depend on that order for its justification. It would be applying too strict a rule
to say that a fresh cause of action could not be pursued because of its collateral connection
with the disclosure ordered in the earlier order. Accordingly the further order sought by
the plaintiffs would be made (see p 378 *a* to *c*, post).

Notes

For collateral use of information obtained following disclosure pursuant to an order of   *g*
the court, see 13 Halsbury's Laws (4th Edn) para 66, and for cases on the subject, see 18
Digest (Reissue) 70, 492–495.

Cases referred to in judgment

Home Office v Harman [1981] 2 All ER 349, [1981] 2 WLR 310, CA.
Riddick v Thames Board Mills Ltd [1977] 3 All ER 677, [1977] QB 881, [1977] 3 WLR 63,   *h*
    CA, Digest (Cont Vol E) 180, 495*b*.

Motion

By a notice of motion dated 11th March 1981 the plaintiffs, Sony Corpn and Sony (UK)
Ltd, applied for orders (i) restraining the defendant, Time Electronics, from selling,   *j*
buying, importing or parting with (without the plaintiffs' consent) cassette tapes,
packaging or advertising material bearing the word 'Sony', from representing that any
tape not manufactured by the plaintiffs was of the plaintiffs' manufacture, from
disclosing the subject matter of the action and the plaintiffs' interest therein and from
parting with or concealing relevant documents, (ii) that the defendant deliver up all

cassette tapes, packaging and advertising material bearing the word 'Sony' and relevant
documents, and (iii) that the defendant disclose names and addresses of suppliers and
a buyers, dates of the transactions and relevant documents, and the whereabouts of certain
tapes, packaging or advertising material with the relevant documents. The application
was heard in chambers but judgment was given by Goulding J in open court. The facts
are set out in the judgment.

b M R T Howe for the plaintiffs.
The defendant was not represented.

GOULDING J. I am giving judgment in open court, although for reasons that will
become obvious, I heard the application in camera. The reason I am giving judgment in
open court is that a point of law or practice is involved. The plaintiffs are two companies,
c one operating internationally in the manufacture and sale of goods, and the other a
subsidiary or associated company incorporated in the United Kingdom.

The intended defendant (a writ has not yet been issued) is a firm carrying on business
in this country. On 12th March 1981, on evidence of passing off on the part of the
defendant firm, I made an order which contained certain injunctions to stop the alleged
dishonest trading and ordered the defendant on service of the order forthwith to disclose
d to the person serving it the names and addresses of the firm's suppliers and to produce
certain documents and deliver up the apparently improper goods to the person serving
the order, all that being restricted by a certain proviso, which I need not read now, and
being, of course, subject to the liberty of the defendant firm to move to discharge or vary
the order on notice.

In the course of serving that order of 12th March 1981, a solicitor employed by the
solicitors for the plaintiffs visited the defendant firm's premises and found there not only
e goods of the type to which the order related but also goods of another type quite
different, also manufactured by the plaintiffs, which he thought might be counterfeit.
He knew that goods of that second type had been the subject of counterfeit production
and trade. Accordingly the solicitor to whom I have referred instructed an employee of
his firm to make a test purchase of such goods. So far as his draft affidavit goes there was
f no difficulty in getting them. When brought back they turned out to be, in the opinion
of this solicitor, who has had extensive experience of these particular goods, clearly
counterfeit. Accordingly, the plaintiffs desire to commence a fresh action against the
defendant firm and have applied in camera for an order similar to that of 12th March
1981, but referring to goods of the second class with which, so far as this defendant was
concerned, the previous order had nothing to do.

The difficulty which has very properly been brought to my attention by counsel
g results from the fact that the plaintiffs were only in a position to discover the alleged
infringement of their rights as regards the second class of goods by entering the
defendants' premises in the course of serving the order of 12th March. The order
contains, as I mentioned, obligations to make certain compulsory disclosure of facts and
documents relating to goods of the first class. It is well established that a party who
makes disclosure on discovery is entitled to the protection of the court against the facts
h or documents disclosed being used, otherwise than in the action in which disclosure took
place, without special leave of the court given on proper grounds: see *Riddick v Thames
Board Mills Ltd* [1977] 3 All ER 677, [1977] QB 881. The whole subject of the restrictions
on the use of material disclosed on discovery has of course been more recently considered
by the higher courts in *Home Office v Harman* [1981] 2 All ER 349, [1981] 2 WLR 310.
Moreover, in addition to that general principle the order of 12th March 1981 contained,
j among other undertakings, an undertaking by the plaintiffs not without the leave of the
court to use any document or information obtained 'as a result of the execution of this
order' save for the purpose of civil proceedings against the defendant firm or other parties
in connection with the subject matter of the action.

Accordingly, counsel has invited me to consider whether I can properly make an order in the form of an injunction restraining the alleged improper trade, and requiring disclosure of material facts, against the defendant firm in regard to the second class of goods, their connection with which only became apparent through the visit of the plaintiffs' solicitors to their premises for the purpose of executing the order of 12th March. In my view I ought not to refuse the plaintiffs the relief they seek. The new action is not founded on something that the court ordered to be disclosed in the earlier order. The real foundation of the present action is the evidence obtained on the test purchase. The observation by the solicitor of suspect goods, of the second class was merely a collateral matter in the execution of the order of 12th March and did not depend on that order for its justification. In other words a solicitor saw something that was there but it was not something that the court had ordered to be disclosed. He then obtained the evidence, which is sufficient in itself, by a test purchase.

Accordingly, for my part I think that it would be applying too strict a rule to say that this fresh cause of action cannot be pursued because of its collateral connection with disclosure ordered by the court in the pending action. I will therefore make the order desired by the plaintiffs, which was explained to me when the court was sitting in camera.

Order accordingly.

Solicitors: *Baker & McKenzie* (for the plaintiffs).

Evelyn M C Budd   Barrister.

West Mercia Constabulary v Wagener and others

QUEEN'S BENCH DIVISION AT BIRMINGHAM
FORBES J
10th, 14th APRIL 1981

Injunction – Interlocutory – Preservation of subject matter of cause – Preservation of proceeds of crime – Proceeds held in bank account – Police applying for injunction to freeze account – Identifiable sums resulting from alleged crime paid into bank account – Whether High Court having power to grant police an injunction restraining dealings with bank account to preserve material evidence for use in trial of offender and to enable proceeds of crime to be restored to rightful owner after offender's trial – RSC Ord 29, r 2(1).

The police alleged that on 2nd and 3rd April 1981 the first defendant had placed advertisements in local newspapers inviting the public to send cheques to the second defendant, a private company owned by the first defendant, for the purchase of certain electronic equipment at below trade prices, that neither the first nor the second defendant possessed any such equipment, and that the second defendant had a bank account which had been credited with payments of £4,280 on 7th April, £6,700 on 8th April and £1,880 on 9th April which it could be inferred had resulted from the advertisements. The first defendant was arrested on suspicion of having committed an offence under the Theft Act 1968 and was subsequently charged with fraudulently obtaining property contrary to s 20(2) of that Act. The police then applied in the High Court, pursuant to RSC Ord 29, r 2(1)[a], for, inter alia, an injunction restraining the second defendant from

---

a   Rule 2(1) provides: 'On the application of any party to a cause or matter the Court may make an order for the detention, custody or preservation of any property which is the subject-matter of the cause or matter, or as to which any question may arise therein, or for the inspection of any such property in the possession of a party to the cause or matter.'

making any withdrawals from the account. The police submitted that at common law
a they had a right to seize or preserve property which was the subject of crime and that the
High Court ought to lend its support to their doing so.

Held – Since magistrates were not empowered to issue a search warrant to deal with the
proceeds of an alleged crime held in a bank account, the High Court could fill that gap
by using the power to preserve the subject matter of a cause conferred on the court under
b RSC Ord 29, r 2 in order to preserve the proceeds of an alleged crime held in a bank
account, because that would preserve material evidence for use in the prosecution of the
offender for the crime and enable the proceeds to be restored to the rightful owner after
the offender's trial. Accordingly, as sums identifiable as resulting from the first
defendant's alleged criminal activity had been paid into the second defendant's account,
the court would make an order restraining the second defendant until further order
c from dealing with any moneys in its account which had accrued since 7th April (see
p 382 *b* to *g*, post).
    Dictum of Diplock LJ in *Chic Fashions (West Wales) Ltd v Jones* [1968] 1 All ER at 238
applied.

Notes
d For the grant of interlocutory injunctions generally, see 24 Halsbury's Laws (4th Edn)
para 953, and for cases on the subject, see 28(2) Digest (Reissue) 968–980, 67–161.

Cases referred to in judgment
Chic Fashions (West Wales) Ltd v Jones [1968] 1 All ER 229, [1968] 2 QB 299, [1968] 2 WLR
    201, 132 JP 175, CA, 14(1) Digest (Reissue) 215, 1573.
e *Cowles v Dunbar and Callow* (1827) 2 C & P 565, Mood & M 37, 172 ER 257, 14(1) Digest
    (Reissue) 196, 1401.
Dillon v O'Brien and Davis (1887) 16 Cox CC 245, 14(1) Digest (Reissue) 193, *915.

Originating summons
By a summons dated 10th April 1981 the plaintiffs, the West Mercia Constabulary,
f applied in the Worcester District Registry of the Queen's Bench Division of the High
Court for the following relief: (1) that the first defendant, Jurgen Wagener, by himself,
his servants or agents be enjoined and restrained by injunction from making or
attempting to make any withdrawals or transfers or other transactions in respect of
certain numbered bank accounts held by the third defendant, Barclays Bank Ltd; (2) that
the first defendant, by himself, his servants or agents be restrained from handling or
g processing or otherwise dealing with any bills of exchange or valuable security due to or
made payable to the second defendant, Tradette Ltd; (3) that the second defendant by
itself, its servants or agents be restrained from making or attempting to make any
withdrawals or transfers or other transactions in respect of any bank or other accounts;
and (4) that the third defendant, by itself its servants or agents be restrained from
handling or processing or otherwise dealing with any withdrawals, transfers or payments
h and any transactions in respect of the above numbered bank accounts and any accounts
held to the order of the first and/or the second defendant. The summons was heard in
chambers but judgment was given by Forbes J in open court at the request of counsel.
The facts are set out in the judgment.

Richard Gibbs for the plaintiffs.
j *Charles Durman* for the first and second defendant.
The third defendant was not represented.

FORBES J. This is an originating summons of a somewhat novel character. On Friday
last Mr Hallmark, the solicitor for the plaintiffs, the West Mercia Constabulary, made an
ex parte application to me for an injunction in this matter and I was extremely troubled

about it, particularly whether the plaintiffs could arguably be said to have any locus to move the High Court in any way for the relief which was sought; but, in view of the importance of the matter and taking the view that there was at least at that stage some arguable case, I granted an ex parte injunction to last until this morning in the hope that the defendants in the case would be represented, and, if necessary, place further evidence before me. They are represented today and I have heard argument in chambers from counsel appearing for the plaintiffs and counsel for the first and second defendants, the third defendant, Barclays Bank, having indicated that it would not wish to take part in the proceedings.

In view of the importance of the matter, both counsel have asked me to adjourn the matter into open court for judgment.

The case arises in this way. The first defendant, Jurgen Wagener, has been arrested by the plaintiffs, initially on suspicion of committing an offence under the Theft Act 1968. If I compendiously describe the offence as fraudulently causing someone else to execute a valuable security or some other fraudulent obtaining of property of that kind, I do not think I need define the matter any further. I understand that the first defendant has now in fact been charged with an offence under s 20(2) of the 1968 Act.

It would be wrong I think to go too far into the allegations made by the plaintiffs about this matter because of course the question still remains to be tried, but very broadly what is said is this. The first defendant trades under the style and title of J Wagener Television Centre. He also has a wholly-owned private limited liability company known as Tradette Ltd, the second defendant. At some time at the beginning of April 1981 it is alleged by the plaintiffs that the first defendant caused advertisements to be placed in a number of local newspapers inviting the public to send cheques to the second defendant at an address, a post office box in Worcester, for the purchase of certain electronic appliances. I need not detail them but they were either video cassette recorders or colour television sets or radio sets with cassette recorders. The affidavit evidence before me is that the prices at which those goods were advertised were well below trade prices. The advertisements, as I understand it, indicated that if the goods were not supplied within so many days, 28 days I think, the customer would have his or her money back.

There is evidence that neither the first nor the second defendant at any time material to this matter possessed any of these electronic equipments, and there is some other evidence, whether good, bad or indifferent I of course know not at this stage, that the suggestion was that the money which was coming in for the first of the equipments could be used to buy more to sell to others; or alternatively it was said, as part of the evidence, that there were not in fact going to be any of these equipments; the only object was to bank the money to get the interest and then send the money back to the customers.

Now of course it is not part of my duty to assess any of that evidence. All those questions will no doubt be ventilated at the trial of the first defendant. But the important evidence which I have on the affidavit before me is this: that the advertisements appeared on 2nd and 3rd April; that the second defendant has a bank account with the third defendant at a bank in Great Malvern; that that bank account, that is the second defendant's bank account, was credited on 7th April with payments in of £4,280, on 8th April with payments in totalling nearly £6,700, and on 9th April with a further £1,880. So those are identifiable payments in, and it is plain as a matter of inference that those payments in would be at any rate likely to have been the result of the advertisements to which I have referred. That at any rate is the inference which the Crown will no doubt be inviting any jury to draw.

The application in the originating summons is that this court should make orders in effect freezing that bank account. There was a request to freeze the first defendant's own bank account but there is no evidence before me that any moneys were asked for from the public to be paid into that account, and I think counsel for the plaintiffs accepts that the only matter he can now ask me to deal with is the bank account of the second defendant. What is being said is that this court, under the powers of RSC Ord 29, r 2, should make an order for the potential custody or preservation of any property under *a* this cause or matter, that is this originating matter, as is normal or frequently done in ordinary cases in the High Court. This involves looking, it seems to me, at two questions. Initially it was I think argued, and it may have been my fault, on the basis that perhaps the plaintiffs could be said in some ways to have a representative capacity and be bringing these proceedings on behalf of the members of the public who had sent off cheques to the second defendant, but there is no evidence about that and if that ever was a live issue it has been dropped. The way counsel for the plaintiffs now puts the case *b* quite simply is that the plaintiffs have a common law right to seize or preserve property which is the subject of crime, and that this court ought to lend its support to them in doing that.

It is unnecessary it seems to me to go into the matter in any very great detail because in *Chic Fashions (West Wales) Ltd v Jones* [1968] 1 All ER 229, [1968] 2 QB 299 the Court of Appeal dealt with the powers of police officers at common law. I will read a short *c* passage from the judgment of Diplock LJ in that case ([1968] 1 All ER 229 at 238, [1968] 2 QB 299 at 316):

> '. . . unless forced to do so by recent binding authority, I decline to accept that a police officer who is unquestionably justified at common law in arresting a person whom he has reasonable grounds to believe is guilty of receiving stolen goods, is not likewise justified in the less draconian act of seizing what he, on reasonable grounds, *d* believes to be the stolen goods in that person's possession. The purpose of the seizure in such a case is twofold: first, that the goods may be produced as material evidence on the prosecution of a criminal charge against the person from whom they were seized, and, secondly, that after the trial they may be restored to their rightful owner, and a similar justification exists for their detention so long as the detainer has reasonable grounds for believing that such a charge will lie and that the *e* goods will be material evidence on its prosecution.'

In the same case Salmon LJ had this to say ([1968] 1 All ER 229 at 239, [1968] 2 QB 299 at 318):

> 'It is a narrow question but one of great general importance, namely, whether the common law allows a policeman to seize goods which he finds in the possession or *f* custody of a person if he believes, on reasonable grounds, that that person has stolen the goods or received them knowing them to be stolen. Since undoubtedly such a person can lawfully be arrested (*Cowles v. Dunbar and Callow* ((1827) 2 C & P 565, 172 ER 257)), it is difficult to discover any sensible reason for conferring immunity from seizure on the goods found on his premises. The production of stolen goods from the possession of an accused often provides most material evidence at his trial.'

g Perhaps I should go back to the authority of *Dillon v O'Brien and Davis* (1887) 16 Cox CC 245 at 249–250 because the words of Palles CB have been quoted:

> 'I, therefore, think that it is clear, and beyond doubt, that, at least in cases of treason and felony, constables (and probably also private persons) are entitled, upon a lawful arrest by them of one charged with treason or felony, to take and detain *h* property found in his possession which will form material evidence in his prosecution for that crime . . . the interest of the State in the person charged being brought to trial in due course necessarily extends, as well to the preservation of material evidence of his guilt or innocence, as to his custody for the purpose of trial. His custody is of no value if the law is powerless to prevent the abstraction or destruction of this evidence, without which a trial would be no more than an empty *j* form.'

It will be noticed, particularly when comparing the passage I have just read from Palles CB with what fell from Diplock LJ, that Diplock LJ goes a little further than Palles CB, because Diplock LJ puts the principle on two grounds: first, the preservation of material evidence, which is the ground advanced by Palles CB, but, second, and importantly in my view, 'so that after the trial they may be restored to their rightful owner'.

In the course of argument I put to counsel for the first and second defendants the following: suppose you have a bank robber who has stolen a million pounds in easily negotiable notes from a bank, and the police know that he has deposited those notes in two large suitcases in the strong room of a bank. It seems to me quite clear, and counsel accepted, that a search warrant would be available to enter the bank's strong room and seize those notes. On the other hand, if instead of depositing them in the strong room the bank robber deposits them in his current account, counsel says no such warrant could possibly be issued. So be it; I am content to accept that that is the situation, and magistrates would be wholly unable in those circumstances to issue a search warrant to seize and preserve the moneys in the bank account. It would, it seems to me, be a strange lacuna in the armoury of the courts in their endeavour to assist in the prevention of crime that there may be no remedy available for the police in such a circumstance. I think that it may not have been done before but it seems to me that this court should, in those circumstances, take the step of doing that which the magistrates cannot do by the issue of a search warrant, namely to use the powers conferred on the courts by RSC Ord 29, r 2 to preserve the proceeds of the allegedly criminal activities in the bank account. That would be in Diplock LJ's words to ensure that after the trial those proceeds should be restored to their rightful owners, a term which potentially includes the second defendant. If of course it were open to the justices to issue search warrants to deal with bank accounts in that way, it would seem to me these proceedings would be misconceived, because the appropriate remedy would be to go to the justices for such a warrant. But while counsel accepts that a warrant could not be issued in those circumstances it seems to me, as I have indicated, that this court should be ready to fill that particular gap.

I want to make it clear that the order I am making is a limited one. It relates simply to the amounts which seem to me to be identifiably deposited in the second defendant's bank account, that is the amounts accruing to that account since 7th April 1981. When I say it is limited to those amounts, because of time I have only got an affidavit which deals with the three days of 7th, 8th and 9th April. I have no evidence from anybody that any subsequent amounts credited to that account are not the result of the advertisements to which I have referred, and it seems to me that in the circumstances I ought to make an order restraining the second defendant from dealing with any moneys in that account which have accrued since 7th April. I am conscious that in doing so this may prevent the second defendant, if it is a legitimate trading company, from trading, and as I have no affidavit from the first or the second defendant relating to these matters I want to make it clear that when I make this order, and in common with most orders of this kind I say until trial of the action or further order, the words 'further order' are not a mere formality because I can conceive situations in which the second defendant might wish to put before the court evidential material to indicate that at any rate some latitude ought to be allowed to the company to trade from its own bank account. But I have no such evidence, and on such evidence as I have it seems evident to me that this company was set up for the purpose of this particular kind of trading and it is doubtful whether any other legitimate trading activities have been undertaken by the second defendant. I say all that, as I have indicated, to enable the second defendant, should it be so advised, to apply to the court for some alteration of that injunction to allow it to trade. As at present I think I should make the orders asked for subject to the deletion of the two accounts named in the originating summons which are not the accounts of the second defendant. In other words, the relief will only be given in relation to the bank account no 50883611.

Order accordingly.

Solicitors: *Curtler & Hallmark*, Worcester (for the plaintiffs); *Parkinson, Wright*, Worcester (for the first and second defendants).

Frances Rustin   Barrister.

R v Howell

COURT OF APPEAL, CRIMINAL DIVISION
WATKINS LJ, CANTLEY AND HOLLINGS JJ
15th, 16th JANUARY, 13th APRIL 1981

Arrest – Arrest without warrant – Breach of the peace – Apprehended breach of the peace – When arrest may be made for actual breach of the peace – When arrest may be made for apprehended breach of the peace – What belief must be established where arrest is made for apprehended breach of the peace.

Criminal law – Breach of the peace – Common law offence – Necessity for act or threatened act harming person or, in his presence, his property or which puts person in fear of such harm.

Arrest – Resisting arrest – Unlawful arrest – Reasonable force to resist arrest – Whether any distinction between escaping from arrest and resisting arrest.

The appellant, together with others, had been making a disturbance on the street after a party. After complaints made by neighbours the police arrived and told the appellant and the others to leave or be arrested for breach of the peace. The appellant swore several times at two of the policemen who again warned him that he would be arrested for a breach of the peace if he did not leave. The appellant continued to swear whereupon one of the police constables took hold of the appellant, but before he could explain why he was arresting the appellant, the appellant struck him in the face and together with the others set on the two policemen. The appellant was convicted of an assault occasioning actual bodily harm on the police constable. He appealed against conviction on the grounds, inter alia, that his arrest was unlawful because no breach of the peace had been proved against him, and accordingly, on the supposition that he had, contrary to his own evidence, struck the police constable, he had been acting lawfully in escaping from a wrongful arrest in that he had used no more force than had been necessary.

Held – (1) A constable or an ordinary citizen had a power of arrest without warrant where there was a reasonable apprehension of an imminent breach of the peace even though the person arrested had not at that stage committed any breach. Accordingly, there was a power of arrest for breach of the peace where (a) a breach of the peace was committed in the presence of the person making the arrest, or (b) the arrestor reasonably believed that such a breach would be committed in the immediate future by the person arrested even though at the time of the arrest he had not committed any breach, or (c) where a breach had been committed and it was reasonably believed that a renewal of it was threatened. When such a power was exercised on the basis of a belief that a breach of the peace was imminent it had to be established not only that it was an honest, albeit possibly mistaken, belief but that it was a belief which was founded on reasonable grounds (see p 388 *d* to *h*, post); *R v Podger* [1979] Crim LR 524 overruled.

(2) There could not be a breach of the peace unless an act was done or threatened to be done which either actually harmed a person or, in his presence, his property or was likely to cause such harm or which put someone in fear of such harm being done (see p 388 *j* to p 389 *a* and *f*, post).

(3) It followed that, in all the circumstances, the appellant had been rightly convicted, and the appeal would accordingly be dismissed (see p 389 *g*, post).

Per Curiam. (1) A constable makes a valid arrest when he reasonably believes a breach of the peace is about to be committed if he says merely 'I am arresting you for a breach of the peace'. In such a case he is not to be taken as referring only to the actual commission of a breach, and is not therefore forbidden from giving evidence the effect of which would be that he had in fact carried out the arrest for an apprehended breach (see p 389 *h j*, post).

(2) In circumstances where a person is entitled to use reasonable force to resist arrest, there is no distinction to be drawn between the word 'escape' and the words 'resist the arrest' (see p 391 *b c*, post).

Notes

For arrest for breach of the peace, see 11 Halsbury's Laws (4th Edn) para 108, and for cases on breach of the peace generally, see 14(1) Digest (Reissue) 199–200, *1434–1452*.

Cases referred to in judgment

Baynes v Brewster (1841) 2 QB 375, 1 Gal & Dav 669, 11 LJMC 5, 5 JP 799, 6 Jur 392, 114 ER 149, 14(1) Digest (Reissue) 199, *1436*.

Christie v Leachinsky [1947] 1 All ER 567, [1947] AC 573, [1947] LJR 757, 176 LT 443, 111 JP 224, 45 LGR 201, HL, 14(1) Digest (Reissue) 206, *1491*.

Gelberg v Miller [1961] 1 All ER 291, [1961] 1 WLR 153, 125 JP 123, DC, 45 Digest (Repl) 6, *20*.

R v Light (1857) Dears & B 332, [1843–60] All ER Rep 934, 27 LJMC 1, 30 LTOS 137, 21 JP 758, 3 Jur NS 1130, 7 Cox CC 389, 169 ER 1029, CCR, 14(1) Digest (Reissue) 200, *1446*.

R v Podger [1979] Crim LR 524.

Timothy v Simpson (1835) 1 Cr M & R 757, 3 Nev & MMC 127, 5 Tyr 244, 4 LJMC 73, 149 ER 1285, 14(1) Digest (Reissue) 199, *1437*.

Cases also cited

Albert v Lavin [1981] 1 All ER 628, [1981] 2 WLR 1070, DC.
Anon (1593) Poph 12, 79 ER 1135.
Cohen v Huskisson (1837) 2 M & W 477, 150 ER 845.
Coupey v Henley (1797) 2 Esp 539, 170 ER 540, NP.
Grant v Moser (1843) 5 Man & G 123, 134 ER 507.
Hardy v Murphy (1795) 1 Esp 294, 170 ER 362, NP.
Howell v Jackson (1834) 6 C & P 723, 172 ER 1435, NP.
Ingle v Bell (1836) 1 M & W 516, 150 ER 539.
Pedro v Diss [1981] 2 All ER 59, DC.
Price v Seeley (1843) 10 Cl & Fin 28, 8 ER 651, HL.
R v Abraham [1973] 3 All ER 694, [1973] 1 WLR 1270, CA.
R v Bright (1830) 4 C & P 387, 172 ER 752, NP.
R v Curvan (1826) 1 Mood CC 132, 168 ER 1213, CCR.
R v Holah [1973] 1 All ER 106, [1973] 1 WLR 127, CA.
Spilsbury v Micklethwaite (1808) 1 Taunt 146, 127 ER 788.
Walker v Lovell [1975] 3 All ER 107, [1975] 1 WLR 1141, HL.
Webster v Watts (1847) 11 QB 311, 116 ER 492.
Wheeler v Whiting (1840) 9 C & P 262, 173 ER 828, NP.

Appeal

On 16th August 1979 at the Crown Court at Coventry before Mr Recorder J A D Owen QC and a jury the appellant, Errol Howell, was convicted by a majority of ten to two of assault occasioning actual bodily harm on Pc Hammersley, arising out of the appellant's resistance to his arrest for an apprehended breach of the peace. He was sentenced to three months' imprisonment suspended for two years. He appealed against conviction on the grounds, inter alia, that his arrest was unlawful because no breach of the peace had been proved against him and that, accordingly, on the supposition that he had, contrary to his own evidence, struck Pc Hammersley, he had been acting lawfully in escaping from a wrongful arrest, in that he had used no more force than had been necessary for the purpose. The facts are set in the judgment of the court.

A J Engel (assigned by the Registrar of Criminal Appeals) for the appellant.
J W H Raggatt for the Crown.

Cur adv vult

13th April. **WATKINS LJ** read the following judgment of the court: At the Crown
 a Court at Coventry on 10th August 1979 the appellant, then 28 years of age, and a young
woman, Tina McNulty, were tried on an indictment which charged each of them, in
separate counts, with an assault occasioning actual bodily harm on two police constables
named Hammersley and Lewis respectively. McNulty was acquitted altogether. The
appellant was acquitted of assaulting Pc Lewis but found guilty of the assault on Pc
Hammersley whereupon he was sentenced by Mr Recorder J A D Owen QC to three
 b months' imprisonment suspended for two years. He appeals against that conviction.
On 2nd September 1978 about seventy young people, white and coloured, attended a
party at a house called 12 Guild Street, Coventry. It was a very noisy affair. Neighbours
were disturbed and upset by the loudness of the music being played. In the early hours
of the following morning the party got out of control. Many of those attending it went
into the street outside the house and caused an uproar.
 c Someone telephoned the police in the hope that they would put an end to this unruly
and uncivil behaviour. Soon afterwards a police inspector and a number of police
constables appeared on the scene. The inspector advised the party-goers who were in the
street to either go back into 12 Guild Street or go home, and said that if they did not take
his advice they would be arrested for committing a breach of the peace. So far as is
known no violence had been used by anyone up to that time.
 d The arrival of the police was resented. The inspector's advice was ignored. There was
loud jeering, cries of 'police brutality', accusations that the police were interfering only
because it was a West Indian party and much foul language used. Some pushing and
shoving began which did not, fortunately, erupt into acts of serious violence. However,
a few people were arrested for breaches of the peace, placed in a police van and taken
away to be charged.
 e Meanwhile, Pcs Hammersley and Lewis decided to encourage the appellant, who is
coloured, McNulty, who is white, a coloured youth, a white youth and a coloured girl
who had all been to the party and who were being noisily offensive and generally making
a nuisance of themselves to go to their homes. The constables were treated to much foul
abuse from these people who slowly but unwillingly moved away from the scene
denying that they were causing the breach of the peace of which Pc Lewis said he accused
 f them.
Pcs Hammersley and Lewis followed them to ensure that they did not return in view
of their apparent reluctance to depart. As they did so the appellant and others in very
loud voices swore foul oaths as they stopped in their tracks every now and again, and one
or more of them said that they were being picked on merely because they were black.
All that was said could have been heard by local residents who had been aroused from
their beds and who were in the street where the constables were moving the group on
 g their way.
Pc Hammersley said to the appellant: 'If you swear once more you will be arrested for
disturbing public order.' The appellant said that the foul language he was using was not
disturbing public order, to which Pc Hammersley replied: 'At 4 am in the morning, and
in the middle of the street, it is. Now go home or you will be arrested.' McNulty then
 h exclaimed: 'It will take more than two of you to take him in,' and the appellant made
another foul and offensive remark about police brutality. By now this encounter had
become thoroughly unpleasant and as likely as not to become more so unless brought to
an end.
Consequently, Pc Hammersley moved forward, caught hold of the appellant's right
arm and said: 'I am arresting . . .' He had no opportunity to say anything further because
the appellant punched him very hard in the face and most of the group set on him and
 j Pc Lewis. In the course of the violent struggle which ensued, Pc Lewis drew his
truncheon before he and Pc Hammersley gained the upper hand and arrested the
appellant and McNulty. Pc Hammersley who had been jumped on by McNulty held
onto the appellant who lashed out at him again. They then exchanged several blows
before the appellant was finally subdued.
The appellant described this account of what happened as a complete fabrication by

the constables. He was, he told the jury, the innocent victim of their perjury. The truth of the matter was that he was walking away from the scene peacefully when Pc Lewis came from nowhere and said: 'You are going to get it.' He was then attacked by both constables and hit on the head with a truncheon by Pc Lewis several times before being arrested without any cause whatsoever. He did not lay so much as a finger on Pc Hammersley. His version was supported by McNulty and a woman who claimed to have witnessed from nearby what happened between the constables, the appellant and his companions.

Counsel for the Crown submitted that the jury must have believed Pc Hammersley's account of the affair to a very substantial extent, if not entirely, in convicting the appellant. We cannot tell who or what the jury believed, and whether the jury convicted on the basis that they believed the appellant was lawfully arrested or that he was using unreasonable force in a proper endeavour to escape from unlawful arrest we cannot be sure. At best we feel able to say there are indications that the verdict was founded on there having been a lawful arrest.

The appeal is based on points of law most of which were argued before the recorder at the end of the Crown's case, when counsel for the appellant submitted that the jury should be directed to acquit the appellant at that stage of the proceedings since he had no case to answer. In summary form this submission was based on the ground that the appellant's arrest was unlawful because no breach of the peace had been proved against him. Accordingly, on the supposition that the appellant had, contrary to his own account of the matter as put in cross-examination, struck Hammersley, he was acting lawfully in escaping from a wrongful arrest in that he was using no more force than was necessary for the purpose.

It is obvious from what has been said already of the actual termination of the proceedings that the recorder rejected counsel's submission and allowed the trial to proceed to the appellant's conviction by the jury.

What was the lawful excuse, if any, which caused Pc Hammersley, according to him, to arrest the appellant? It was, he said when being cross-examined, a breach of the peace committed by the appellant, with or without the assistance of his companions. This has, of course, to be put alongside what he told the appellant immediately prior to arrest, which was 'You will be arrested for disturbing public order'.

When re-examined he told the jury that he was aware there had previously been some kind of incident in the house where the party had taken place as he followed the appellant down the street. He belived that if he had not followed the appellant he would have returned to the vicinity of that house and worked the scene up again with shouting and swearing. His decision to arrest arose out of what he saw and what he feared. The appellant was obviously refusing to be quiet and to go home and there was a possibility of his returning to the vicinity of the house and causing further trouble. He saw a number of local residents in their front gardens who were clearly disturbed by what was going on.

Although Pc Hammersley at one stage of his evidence said that he was not thinking of violence as he was following the group, it seems to this court that it was open to the jury to infer from the entirety of his evidence that he had feared a breach of the peace arising from the imminent use of violence by the appellant as he was following him or, if the appellant was allowed to return to it, at the scene outside 12 Guild Street.

It is possible that Pc Hammersley was in the heat of the moment confusing his power of arrest at common law for a breach of the peace with a similar power of arrest for offensive conduct conducive to a breach of the peace contrary to s 5 of the Public Order Act 1936. However, the appellant was not charged with this statutory offence. Accordingly, and for the additional reason that the appellant was told at the police station on arrival there that he had been arrested for 'a breach of the peace', we think it was open to the jury when deciding whether there had been a lawful arrest to have regard to the constable's power at common law only. Since this was the effect of the manner in which the jury was directed on this matter by the judge we are not, strictly speaking, called on

to decide whether an arrest for a breach of the peace at common law would serve also to
a constitute a lawful arrest under s 7(3) of the 1936 Act for committing an offence under
s 5. But we feel it right to say our tentative view is that it would serve this dual purpose,
seeing that a breach of the peace is involved in both offences.

It is submitted that the recorder was wrong to refuse to direct the jury to acquit the
appellant at the close of the Crown's case. His refusal, it is said, was based on errors of law
and a failure to appreciate that there was insufficient evidence to establish that there had
b been a breach of the peace involving either the actual use of violence or a reasonable
apprehension of the use of violence which would have entitled Pc Hammersley to arrest
the appellant. The comment already made on the quality of it plainly indicates that we
do not agree that the evidence available was not sufficient to be considered by the jury for
this purpose.

The recorder's initial and fundamental error of law lay, so it is said, in his
c comprehension of the extent of the power of arrest for the offence, and in the definition
he chose to adopt, of 'breach of the peace'. Counsel for the appellant submits in respect
of the power of arrest that the recorder should have followed the ruling in *R v Podger*
[1979] Crim LR 524 of a recorder sitting in the Crown Court at Bristol which was to the
effect that the power to arrest for a breach of the peace at common law is confined to cases
in which a breach was either committed in the presence of the arrestor or where one had
d been committed and its renewal was threatened.

The recorder in the present case declared the definition to include also a power of arrest
where there is reasonable ground to suppose a person who has caused no trouble
previously is about to commit a breach of the peace. In other words he said that a
threatened breach is a valid ground of arrest.

This power, if it then did, was not acknowledged to exist in Stone's Justice's Manual
e (3rd Edn, 1845, p 15) which sets out the common law power of arrest in these terms:

'A private person may apprehend without a warrant, on view of a breach of the
peace, and before the affray is over, and deliver the offender to a constable; and he
is justified in giving in charge, and a constable in arresting without a warrant, a
party who has been guilty of a breach of the peace, if there are reasonable grounds
for apprehending its continuance or immediate renewal, but not otherwise. (*Baynes*
f   v. *Brewster* ((1841) 2 QB 375, 114 ER 149) and cases there cited.) *The general rule is*
"that, for the sake of the preservation of the peace, any individual who sees it broken may
restrain the liberty of him whom he sees breaking it, so long as his conduct shews that the
public peace is likely to be endangered by his acts" (*Timothy v. Simpson* ((1835) 1 Cr M
& R 757 at 762, 149 ER 1285 at 1288)).

'BY CONSTABLES – A constable may arrest without a warrant *on a charge made*,
g   having reasonable ground to suspect that a felony has been committed, though
none have in fact – He may also arrest in all cases in which a private individual may
(see 7 JP Jo 237). A constable may apprehend without a warrant on view of a breach
of the peace, but not after the affray is over unless there be reasonable grounds for
apprehending its continuance or immediate renewal. (*Baynes* v. *Brewster* and cases
there cited.) A constable may also apprehend any person obstructing him in the
h   execution of his duty.'

The comments and commentary on *R v Podger* [1979] Crim LR 524 which accompany
the report of it are particularly noteworthy. They suggest that the power exists now even
if it was correct to say that it did not in 1845. They are:

'If this decision be right then Smith and Hogan, Moriarty, Glanville Williams and
j   *Halsbury's Laws* 3rd and 4th Editions are wrong. It is supported (in the more used
texts) only by Stone, *Justices Manual* 1978, I 567 and II 3165. Further the statement
in *Archbold, Criminal Pleading Evidence and Practice* (39th ed., 1976) at p 2802 (that all
common law powers of arrest without warrant are now superseded by section 2,
Criminal Law Act 1967) cannot be right in any event and was disowned by both
sides. The learned Recorder approved of only the first sentence in *Halsbury's Laws*

(4th edn.), Vol. 11, para. 108: "A private person or a constable may at common law arrest without warrant anyone who, in his presence commits a breach of the peace, where the offence is continuing or, if it is not continuing, where there is reasonable ground for apprehending its renewal. A private person or a constable may also arrest without warrant anyone who there is reasonable ground to suppose is about to commit or about to renew a breach of the peace in his presence."

'*Commentary.* It is clear that where a breach of the peace has occurred but it is over and there is no ground for believing that it will be renewed, there is no power to arrest. It is also clear that where there are reasonable grounds for supposing that a breach of the peace will be renewed, an arrest in order to prevent it is lawful. This is so even where the constable did not himself witness the first breach but it has been reported to him. Clearly the fact that a breach of the peace has occurred is important evidence of the existence of reasonable grounds for apprehending a further breach. It is submitted, however, that that is all it is; it is not a condition precedent and none of the authorities referred to, including *Light* ((1857) Dears & B 332, 169 ER 1029), suggest that it is a condition precedent. It is plain that the law is here concerned not with what has happened but with what is reasonably expected to happen. It would be wrong if a constable (or any other person) had overwhelming evidence for believing that a grave breach of the peace was about to be committed in the immediate future but could do nothing to prevent it because no previous breach had occurred.'

Professor Glanville Williams in his article 'Arrest for Breach of the Peace' [1974] Crim LR 578 at 586 in which, inter alia, he makes reference to *R v Light*, stated:

'It seems clear that there may be an arrest for breach of the peace which is reasonably apprehended in the immediate future, even though the person arrested has not yet committed any breach.'

We share the opinions expressed in the foregoing quotations. We entertain no doubt that a constable has a power of arrest where there is reasonable apprehension of imminent danger of a breach of the peace; so for that matter has the ordinary citizen. *R v Podger* involved the examination, by the recorder who tried it, of a number of authorities, including *Light's* case, all of which we have perused. *R v Podger* was in our opinion wrongly decided. We hold that there is power of arrest for breach of the peace where (1) a breach of the peace is committed in the presence of the person making the arrest, or (2) the arrestor reasonably believes that such a breach will be committed in the immediate future by the person arrested although he has not yet committed any breach, or (3) where a breach has been committed and it is reasonably believed that a renewal of it is threatened.

The public expects a policeman not only to apprehend the criminal but to do his best to prevent the commission of crime, to keep the peace in other words. To deny him, therefore, the right to arrest a person who he reasonably believes is about to breach the peace would be to disable him from preventing that which might cause serious injury to someone or even to many people or to property. The common law, we believe, whilst recognising that a wrongful arrest is a serious invasion of a person's liberty, provides the police with this power in the public interest. In those instances of the exercise of this power which depend on a belief that a breach of the peace is imminent it must, we think we should emphasise, be established that it is not only an honest, albeit mistaken, belief but a belief which is founded on reasonable grounds.

A comprehensive definition of the term 'breach of the peace' has very rarely been formulated so far as we have been able, with considerable help from counsel, to discover from cases which go as far back as the eighteenth century. The older cases are of considerable interest but they are not a sure guide to what the term is understood to mean today, since keeping the peace in this country in the latter half of the twentieth century presents formidable problems which bear on the evolving process of the development of this branch of the common law. Nevertheless, even in these days when

affrays, riotous behaviour and other disturbances happen all too frequently, we cannot
accept that there can be a breach of the peace unless there has been an act done or
threatened to be done which either actually harms a person, or in his presence his
property, or is likely to cause such harm, or which puts someone in fear of such harm
being done. There is nothing more likely to arouse resentment and anger in him, and
a desire to take instant revenge, than attacks or threatened attacks on a person's body or
property.

In 11 Halsbury's Laws (4th Edn) para 108 it is stated:

'For the purpose of the common law powers of arrest without warrant, a breach
of the peace arises where there is an actual assault, or where public alarm and
excitement are caused by a person's wrongful act. Mere annoyance and disturbance
or insults to a person or abusive language, or great heat and fury without personal
violence, are not generally sufficient.'

That is an amalgam of opinions expressed in various old cases which is principally
criticised by counsel for the appellant for its failure to attach the actual commission of
violence to all acts which are said to be capable of causing a breach of the peace. He
makes a similar criticism of the crisp definition provided by the Attorney General,
referred to in *Gelberg v Miller* [1961] 1 All ER 291 at 295, [1961] 1 WLR 153 at 158 with
reference to the word disturbance. Lord Parker CJ said:

'The Attorney-General, to whom the court is grateful for his assistance, has
appeared and has told the court that he feels unable to contend that a constable is
entitled to arrest somebody for obstructing him in the course of his duty—which,
of course, is a misdemeanour under s 2 of the Prevention of Crimes Amendment
Act, 1885—unless the circumstances show that a breach of the peace or an
apprehended breach of the peace is involved, meaning by that some affray or
violence or possibly disturbance.'

The statement in Halsbury's Laws of England is in parts, we think, inaccurate because
of its failure to relate all the kinds of behaviour there mentioned to violence.
Furthermore, we think, the word 'disturbance' when used in isolation cannot constitute
a breach of the peace. We are emboldened to say that there is a breach of the peace
whenever harm is actually done or is likely to be done to a person or in his presence to
his property or a person is in fear of being so harmed through an assault, an affray, a riot,
an unlawful assembly or other disturbance. It is for this breach of the peace when done
in his presence or the reasonable apprehension of it taking place that a constable, or
anyone else, may arrest an offender without warrant.

The recorder in the present case in ruling on the submission clearly regarded violence
as of the essence of a breach of the peace. So we find that neither in that nor in any other
way did he misdirect himself on the associated matters of the power of arrest and the
definition of a breach of the peace. Furthermore, as to the appellant's knowledge of why
he was arrested he correctly applied the principles laid down in *Christie v Leachinsky*
[1947] 1 All ER 567, [1947] AC 573. The evidence at the end of the prosecution showed
plainly that either the appellant knew without being told at the moment of arrest the
reason for it or, by striking Pc Hammersley when he did, he made it impossible for that
officer to tell him why he was being arrested. In this connection we should make it clear,
since the point was argued, that a constable makes a valid arrest when he reasonably
believes a breach is about to be committed if he says merely: 'I am arresting you for a
breach of the peace.' It is ridiculous to expect him to give, in what may be for him very
trying circumstances, some such incantation as: 'I am arresting you because I reasonably
believe you are about to commit a breach of the peace.' In speaking merely of a 'breach
of the peace' on arrest the arrestor is not, as counsel for the appellant seemed to suggest,
to be taken as referring only to the actual commission of a breach and, therefore,
forbidden from giving evidence the effect of which would be that he had in fact carried
out the arrest for an apprehended breach.

In an alternative attempt to persuade the recorder that the appellant had no case to answer it was submitted that the blows allegedly struck by the appellant could not have *a* amounted to the use of excessive force in escaping from an unlawful arrest. This effort was in vain. This was an issue which on the evidence could only have been decided by the jury to whom it was rightly entrusted. Accordingly, we reject as wholly unjustified the criticism of the recorder for leaving it to them.

What about the grounds of appeal said to arise out of the summing up? The recorder directed the jury that in order for there to have been a lawful arrest it had to be proved *b* that Pc Hammersley was a witness to the shouting and swearing of the appellant and had, therefore, reasonable grounds for believing, and did believe, that the appellant's conduct, either alone or as part of a general shouting and swearing, was likely to lead to the use of violence by the appellant or somebody else in the officer's presence. We are invited to condemn that as a misdirection. We can think of no good reason why we should do so. In our view it was a clear, correct and, in the circumstances of the case, wholly appropriate *c* direction according to law.

It is said there was no evidence to warrant the giving of it. We simply cannot accept that. The evidence of Pc Hammersley, if believed, was of the kind which called for a direction on a reasonable apprehension of a breach of the peace and, as has already been stated, it was in our view sufficient to merit consideration by a jury which could surely draw the inference, if it chose to, that a lawful arrest for an apprehended breach of the *d* peace had been made.

The summing up is said to have been defective in a number of other respects. It is submitted that the factual issues involved in the question of whether or not there had been a lawful arrest were not put before the jury and, in effect, that no assistance whatsoever was given to the jury about what parts of the relevant evidence could be allied to any, and if so what, issues.

At the outset of the summing up the recorder said: *e*

'Now what about the lawful excuse. In this case, the only lawful excuse which you have to consider comes about in this way. If you strike a blow or use force to resist an unlawful arrest, then it may be that your blow is not unlawful. So you have to consider whether there was a lawful arrest. In the circumstances of this case, if there was shouting by [the appellant], for instance, and if there were obscenities *f* to which he was acceding and if all of this led Pc Hammersley to fear that [the appellant] was about to be violent in his presence, then the officer was entitled to arrest him because there was about to be or was a breach of the peace. Technical terms do not matter and I am not going to weary you with them, but that is really the situation. You have to ask yourselves: was there shouting and were there abusive obscenities of a kind which led Pc Hammersley reasonably to fear that [the *g* appellant] was about to be violent in his presence? If so, he was entitled to arrest him. You must not think that this country is such that a police officer is entitled to arrest anybody who does not do what he wants him to do. We have not got to that stage in this country, and please God we never will. A police officer has certain powers; maybe they ought to have more powers, one can see it is a difficult job that they have to do, but they have to abide by the law just as other people have to abide *h* by the law.'

This was followed later on by a satisfactory reminder in, we are glad to observe, summary form of the evidence of Pcs Hammersley and Lewis. At the end of the summing up the jury were again reminded of what had to be proved to establish a lawful arrest. No jury could have failed, we believe, to understand with this assistance how they *j* should approach and finalise the task of deciding whether the appellant had been lawfully arrested. There is no substance in this ground of appeal.

Finally, it is submitted that there was no evidence for the jury safely to consider on the issue of the use of excessive force in escaping from unlawful arrest, that the recorder failed to direct the jury that it was for the prosecution to prove that the force used by the

appellant was excessive, and finally that no direction was provided to the effect that a
a person unlawfully arrested has the right to escape.

The recorder said of the right to resist unlawful arrest:

> 'Now what is the position if it was an unlawful arrest. In those circumstances a
> person is entitled to use reasonable force to resist the arrest. You will have to ask
> yourselves: in those circumstances, if you find that the arrest was illegal, was it
> reasonable for [the appellant] to swing a punch when all that had happened to him
b > was that he had been taken on the arm? That is something which you will have to
> ask yourselves and decide whether it was a reasonable thing or not.'

In our judgment this was proper and adequate guidance on this subject. It was later
in the summing up repeated. We fail to appreciate the distinction apparently sought to
be drawn between the word 'escape' and the words 'resist the arrest'. In this context they
c amount to the same thing. With respect to what otherwise has been helpful assistance
provided by counsel for the appellant, he plays with words in this submission.

It must be acknowledged that the recorder did not anywhere say that the Crown had
to prove that the alleged force used by the appellant was excessive. In that he erred.
However, we cannot accept that injustice could have arisen from that error. The general
and correct direction on standard of proof was firmly stated early and late in the
d summing up. The summing up as a whole was impeccably balanced and fair. This one
blemish in it could not in our view have had the effect of producing an injustice by the
verdict of guilty of an assault occasioning actual bodily harm which we cannot bring
ourselves to regard as in any respect unsafe and unsatisfactory.

For these reasons the appeal is dismissed.

e *Appeal dismissed.*

Solicitors: *Ian S Manson*, Birmingham (for the Crown).

N P Metcalfe Esq   Barrister.

Blacklocks v JB Developments (Godalming) Ltd

CHANCERY DIVISION

HIS HONOUR JUDGE MERVYN DAVIES QC SITTING AS A JUDGE OF THE HIGH COURT

16th, 17th, 18th, 19th, 20th, 23rd, 24th MARCH, 2nd APRIL 1981

Land registration – Overriding interest – Rights of person in actual occupation of land – Right to rectification of title – Sale of land under common mistake as to position of boundary – Vendor having right to rectification of title – Whether right to rectification capable of enduring through different ownerships of land – Whether vendor having overriding interest as against purchaser's successors in title – Land Registration Act 1925, ss 20(1), 70(1)(g).

In 1969 the plaintiff sold land consisting of a farm to G. By a common mistake a triangle of land belonging to the plaintiff was included in the title and was registered as being in G's ownership. Neither the plaintiff nor G was aware that the triangle of land had been transferred to G and, on the basis of the actual agreement between the parties, fencing was erected along the correct boundary so that the triangle of land did not pass into G's occupation. The plaintiff built a barn on, and continued to occupy, the land. In 1972 G sold the farm to the defendant and after the sale it was discovered that the triangle of land had been wrongly included in the title to the farm. The plaintiff brought an action seeking a declaration that the defendant held the land as trustee for the plaintiff and rectification of the register, on the grounds that he had a right to rectify as against G accompanied by 'actual occupation', that accordingly at the time of the transfer to the defendant the right to rectify was an overriding interest within s 70(1)(g)[a] of the Land Registration Act 1925, and that by virtue of s 20(1)(b)[b] of that Act the defendant had received the land subject to the overriding interest

Held – The plaintiff had a right to rectification of title as against G and that right was capable of enduring through different ownerships of the land. The right was therefore an equity and ancillary interest in land that was transmissable, and as such it was a 'right' for the purposes of s 70(1)(g) of the 1925 Act, which when coupled with the plaintiff's actual occupation amounted to an 'overriding interest' binding on the land and to which the land was subject in the hands of the defendant. The defendant accordingly held the triangle of land on trust for the plaintiff and the plaintiff was entitled to rectification (see p 400 h j and p 401 a b, post).

Stump v Gaby (1852) 2 De GM & G 623, dicta of Russell LJ in National Provincial Bank Ltd v Hastings Car Mart Ltd [1964] 1 All ER at 701 and of Lord Wilberforce in Williams & Glyn's Bank Ltd v Boland [1980] 2 All ER at 412 applied.

Latec Investments Ltd v Hotel Terrigal Pty Ltd (1965) 113 CLR 265 considered.

Notes

For common mistake as to the identity of the subject matter of a transaction, see 32 Halsbury's Laws (4th Edn) paras 12, 15.

For overriding interests in land and rectification of the register, see 26 ibid paras 987, 1054, and for cases on the subjects, see 38 Digest (Repl) 891–892, 899–900, 931–933, 944–950.

---

a   Section 70, so far as material, is set out at p 399 d, post

b   Section 20(1), so far as material, provides: 'In the case of a freehold estate registered with an absolute title, a disposition of the registered land . . . for valuable consideration shall, when registered, confer on the transferee or grantee an estate in fee simple . . . together with all rights, privileges, and appurtenances belonging or appurtenant thereto . . . subject . . . (b) unless the contrary is expressed on the register, to the overriding interests, if any, affecting the estate transferred or created. . .'

For the Land Registration Act 1925, ss 20, 70, see 27 Halsbury's Statutes (3rd Edn) 801, 843.

Cases referred to in judgment

Craddock Brothers v Hunt [1923] 2 Ch 136, 92 LJ Ch 378, 129 LT 228, 40 Digest (Repl) 385, 3091.

Dickinson v Burrell, Stourton v Burrell (1866) LR 1 Eq 337, 35 Beav 257, 35 LJ Ch 371, 13 LT 660, 12 Jur NS 199, 55 ER 894, 40 Digest (Repl) 574, 787.

Gross v Lewis Hillman Ltd [1969] 3 All ER 1476, [1970] Ch 445, [1969] 3 WLR 787, CA, Digest (Cont Vol C) 872, 3150a.

Joscelyne v Nissen [1970] 1 All ER 1213, [1970] 2 QB 86, [1970] 2 WLR 509, CA, Digest (Cont Vol C) 707, 307a.

Latec Investments Ltd v Hotel Terrigal Pty Ltd (in liquidation) (1965) 113 CLR 265 (Aust HC).

Leuty v Hillas (1858) 2 De G & J 110, 27 LJ Ch 534, 22 JP 96, 4 Jur NS 1166, 44 ER 929, sub nom *Lenty v Hillas* 30 LTOS 299, LC; *subsequent proceedings* sub nom *Wild v Hillas* 28 LJ Ch 170, 40 Digest (Repl) 152, 1164.

National Provinical Bank Ltd v Ainsworth [1965] 2 All ER 472, [1965] AC 1175, [1965] 3 WLR 1, HL; *rvsg* sub nom *National Provincial Bank Ltd v Hastings Car Mart Ltd* [1964] 1 All ER 688, [1964] Ch 665, [1964] 2 WLR 751, CA, 27(1) Digest (Reissue) 92, 675.

Stump v Gaby (1852) 2 De GM & G 623, 22 LJ Ch 352, 20 LTOS 213, 17 Jur 5, 42 ER 1015, LC, 40 Digest (Repl) 394, 3149.

Williams & Glyn's Bank Ltd v Boland, Williams & Glyn's Bank Ltd v Brown [1980] 2 All ER 408, [1981] AC 487, [1980] 3 WLR 138, HL; *affg* [1979] 2 All ER 697, [1979] Ch 312, [1979] 2 WLR 550, CA.

Action

By a writ dated 18th August 1977 the plaintiff, David John Sam Blacklocks, sought as against the defendant, JB Developments (Godalming) Ltd, (i) a declaration that the defendant held part of the land in title K320824 on trust for the plaintiff absolutely, and (ii) rectification of the register of title K320824 by omission of part of the land therein from the land delineated on the registered plan or alternatively registration of the plaintiff as proprietor of part of the land. By a defence and counterclaim served on 27th October 1977 the defendant counterclaimed for an order cancelling a caution registered by the plaintiff against title K320824. The facts are set out in the judgment.

David Ritchie for the plaintiff.
John Brookes for the defendant.

Cur adv vult

2nd April. **HIS HONOUR JUDGE MERVYN DAVIES QC** read the following judgment: In this action the plaintiff is Mr David John Sam Blacklocks. He claims a declaration that the defendant, JB Developments (Godalming) Ltd, is a trustee for him of a small triangle of land. The triangle is included in title no K320824 and the defendant is the registered proprietor. The plaintiff also claims a rectification of the register pursuant to s 82 of the Land Registration Act 1925. The triangle is coloured green on the plan annexed to the statement of claim and I shall refer to it as 'the green triangle'.

The Blacklocks family have farmed over an extensive area near Lydd for many years. As well as other land, there was in 1967 in the ownership of the family partnership a derelict farmhouse and outbuildings together with nine or ten acres of land of doubtful quality. This was known as Brickwall Farm. In former years the land had been used by the War Department. In 1967 the partners were the plaintiff, his uncle, Stanley Herbert Blacklocks, and his aunt, Mrs Baxter. Of these three it was Stanley Blacklocks who was actively concerned in running the farming business. Mrs Baxter took no part in the farming and the plaintiff was at that time principally engaged in following his own poultry farm interests in the locality and in other parts of England. The partners wished to erect two Dutch barns as hay stores, one to be at Manor Farm, sometimes known as Denge Marsh Farm, and the other to be at Jacques Court. To raise money for this purpose the partners decided to sell Brickwall Farm. It was agreed that part of the Brickwall land, some three acres or more, would be sold for poultry purposes to a company, W C Blacklocks Ltd, in which the plaintiff had an interest. These three acres lie beyond the north-west boundary of the land edged red on the statement of claim plan. No difficulty has arisen respecting those three acres or their boundary with the adjoining red-edged land. With the three acres I have mentioned promised to W C Blacklocks Ltd, the partners' land that was left for sale was about five or six acres together with the derelict farmhouse and buildings.

Early in 1968 a prospective purchaser was found for those remaining acres. He was Mr Robert Godden. Mr Godden had in mind living on the land in a caravan while restoring the old farmhouse. In evidence Mr Godden explained that he first saw Brickwall Farm in 1967, and early in 1968 he met Mr Stanley Blacklocks at the farm. They discussed a price and the boundaries of the land to be sold. The price was agreed at £2,750. The boundaries were agreed in this way. Mr Godden and Mr Blacklocks sat in a motor car near to the old entrance gate to Brickwall Farm. The car was on or near the roadway coloured brown on the statement of claim plan. The old gate was at the northern end of the brown boundary. That roadway is the Denge Marsh road. Mr Godden was ready to buy the entirety of Brickwall Farm but it was explained to him that W C Blacklocks Ltd were to have about three acres for their poultry purposes. With this in mind a boundary was agreed in respect to the W C Blacklocks land. This boundary is the north-west boundary of the red-edged land on the statement of claim plan, and, as I have said, no difficulty arises over that boundary. With that line settled as one of the boundaries of the land to be bought, Mr Godden and Mr Stanley Blacklocks implicitly accepted that the front boundary of the land to be sold would run along the Denge Marsh road. This is obviously so, because the farm has a frontage to the Denge Marsh road. Mr Godden then said that the boundary went along the Denge Marsh road as far as a junction with a concrete road running off the Denge Marsh road. This junction is the most northerly point of the green triangle. The concrete road runs south along the longest side of the green triangle. From the southernmost point of the green triangle the concrete road runs on for some way in a south-westerly direction, ie along the red edging. Mr Godden said he got out of the motor car and walked along the Denge Marsh road to the concrete road. He did not walk up the concrete road. He said Mr Blacklocks told him that the concrete road was the boundary on that side, with the ditch taking over as the boundary on the curved red edging shown as the south-west boundary of the land marked on the statement of claim plan. In summary, Mr Godden said that the concrete road and the dykes or ditches were the boundary of the land he was to buy. That means that the green triangle was excluded from the area of land agreed in February 1968 between Mr Godden and Mr Stanley Blacklocks as the area of land to be sold to Mr Godden. Mr Godden explained the agreed boundary in clear terms referring to plans 1 and 2 that were before me and to four photographs. I have not the slightest hesitation in accepting Mr Godden's evidence. Mr Stanley Blacklocks was not available to give evidence. He died in 1970.

With the price and boundary settled in this way the matter was put in the hands of the solicitors. Messrs Hallet & Co acted for both sides. Mr Russell of that firm acted for the purchaser, Mr Godden. Mr Chalklen acted for the vendors. On 21st March 1968 Mr Chalklen asked the plaintiff to mark on an Ordnance Survey plan the boundaries of the land to be sold to Mr Godden. This request was made to the plaintiff rather than to Mr Stanley Blacklocks because Mr Stanley Blacklocks was not very well at that time. It is to be noted that the plan sent by the solicitors is an Ordnance Survey plan that does not show the concrete road that has been mentioned. It seems that the Ordnance Survey plan was made before the road was made. Since this Ordnance Survey plan was used in all future contracts and conveyances it follows that none of the plans in the title documents show the concrete road. The plaintiff did not get on with the marking right away because he was much taken up with his poultry activities. However in April he went to see his uncle about marking out the boundaries. The plaintiff himself did not know exactly what had been agreed between Uncle Stanley and Mr Godden. The plaintiff said he expected his uncle to mark the plan. But the uncle was ill and asked the plaintiff to mark the plan. The plaintiff said in evidence that his uncle specifically mentioned the Denge Marsh road and the concrete road as the boundaries. The plaintiff marked the plan with the boundaries as he understood them to have been agreed. He produced the plan which is shown in the agreed bundle. That plan shows the plaintiff's markings. That plan is the same plan as appears in the contract which was signed later. It will be observed that the south-east boundary runs in a straight line from the Denge Marsh road. The plaintiff stated that he supposed that that line was the line of the concrete road. That is, of course, not so because the concrete road does not run straight along its whole length. There is a distinct bend at the south point of the green triangle. What appears to have happened is that the plaintiff, not knowing or not remembering that there was a bend in the concrete road, took the line of the road as it runs straight north-east along enclosure 427 and extended that line as far as the Denge Marsh road. He should, of course, have made a left incline in the line at the south point of the green triangle. The result was that the plaintiff's marking wrongly included the green triangle within the area of land to be sold. The plaintiff was, of course, unaware of his mistake, and so was his uncle. The mistake was, I think, very understandable. The plaintiff was by no means very familiar with the land in question. It had run to waste for many years and it may be that the plaintiff did not then appreciate that there was any bend in the concrete road. However that may be, it is quite clear that both Stanley Blacklocks and the plaintiff on the one hand and Mr Godden on the other are in agreement that the plaintiff marked the boundary wrongly. The intended boundary was the concrete road.

On 25th April 1968 the plaintiff sent the wrongly marked plan to his solicitor. His letter of that date states that the vendors would fence the land. The vendors did in fact fence the land at or about the time when the sale was completed. The fencing was put up without any objection along the length of the concrete road and on its western side thus leaving the road outside the land sold and free for use by the vendors. This fact affords support, if support is necessary, for the fact that the plaintiff made a mistake in the marking of the boundaries of the land intended to be sold.

The transaction between the Blacklocks and Mr Godden went ahead slowly, chiefly because Mr Godden was seeking planning permission. However, contracts were exchanged soon after 21st November 1968. A copy of the contract documents signed by Mr Godden was before me. It is not dated but it is accepted that exchange took place soon after the date I have mentioned. By November 1968 Mrs Baxter had ceased to be a partner and so the vendors are named as Stanley Blacklocks and the plaintiff. The purchasers are named as Mr Godden, his wife and son. The price was, as I have said, £2,750, and the land was described as—

'ALL THAT Farmhouse with the buildings and land thereto containing altogether by estimation Six acres forming part of Brickwall Farm situate in the Parish of Lydd in the County of Kent and delineated for the purpose of identification only in the plan annexed hereto and thereon edged pink . . . TOGETHER WITH a right of way at all times and for all purposes so far as the Vendors can grant the same over the roadway to the north east coloured brown on the plan annexed hereto.'

Special condition K in the contract was in these terms:

'The boundaries of the property sold except where these are ditches will be fenced by the Vendors at their own expense prior to completion and the Purchaser shall in his Conveyance covenant with the Vendors that he will at all times thereafter maintain such fences in good and substantial repair.'

The plan in the contract may be taken as the same as the statement of claim plan without the green colouring. I was told that the dotted lines on the plan represented *a* roads or tracks and the unbroken double lines represented ditches. As I have said, the plan does not show the concrete road.

The contract was followed by completion on 6th January 1969. The parcels and the plan therein are for practical purposes as in the contract. At that time registration of title was already compulsory in Kent. Accordingly the Godden title was on 30th January 1969 registered under title K320824. The filed plan showed the title as comprising the *b* land edged red in the statement of claim plan, ie that the green triangle was in Godden ownership.

On 1st November 1968 Mr Stanley Blacklocks received a quotation for the Dutch barns I have mentioned. It had been intended to place one of these barns at Manor (or Denge Marsh) Farm but at some time before December 1968 it was decided that there should be a barn not at Manor Farm but near the concrete road. The barn contractors *c* produced a site plan dated 11th December 1968 showing the intended site of the barn. The site plan does not show the concrete road but reference to the statement of claim plan makes it plain that the contractors contemplated the barn as being just outside the green triangle. The barn was in fact erected in 1969. It was not erected on the site shown on the barn contractors' plan. It was erected within the green triangle. There was no objection taken by anyone to the barn being placed on this site. I gather the planning *d* authority asked Mr Godden if he had any objection. He had none. He did not regard the green triangle as being his land and it seemed he had no objection on planning grounds to the Blacklocks putting their adjoining land to barn use. Ever since its construction the barn has been in use for storing hay. By August each year the barn would be reasonably full and its contents reduced throughout the winter months. It is, of course, the Blacklocks who have used the barn: Mr Stanley Blacklocks and the plaintiff together in *e* partnership until 1970. Since 1970 the plaintiff has been the sole user, since, as I have said, his uncle and partner died in 1970. The Blacklockses' user has throughout all these years never been questioned or disturbed; at any rate until there arose the events which have given rise to this action.

After the sale of Brickwall Farm to Mr Godden in January 1969 Mr Godden and his family lived in the caravan and began the restoration of the old farmhouse. The green *f* triangle with its new barn was in the possession of the plaintiff. The new fencing along the concrete road fenced the farm away from the barn so that the plaintiff could use the road when his vehicles had to go to the barn. Neither the plaintiff nor his uncle nor Mr Godden had any idea that the green triangle was registered in the Godden name.

I have considered the events I have mentioned at some length because the plaintiff cannot assert any rights against the defendant unless he first establishes that he had a *g* right to rectify as against Mr Godden. I am satisfied that the plaintiff has shown me 'the convincing proof' (see *Joscelyne v Nissen* [1970] 1 All ER 1213 at 1222, [1970] 2 QB 86 at 98) that is necessary before a rectification will be considered. I have in mind the clear evidence given by Mr Godden and by the plaintiff, and, as well, the fencing and barn-building activity that accompanied the sale of Brickwall Farm. I am satisfied that it was by a mistake common to both the vendors and the purchasers that the green triangle was *h* included in the Godden title. Had the mistake come to light at any time before Mr Godden sold his land I am quite satisfied that the title would have been rectified by consent. Unfortunately there was no suspicion at that time of any inaccuracy in the title and so no rectification was then ever thought of. However that may be, there was after 6th January 1969 a right in Stanley Blacklocks and the plaintff, as against Mr Godden, to rectify title K320824, being a right in the plaintiff alone after Stanley's death in 1970. *j*

Mr Godden never completed the restoration of the old farmhouse. In 1972 he decided to sell. His agents prepared some sale particulars. There was of course no reference therein to the barn forming part of the land to be sold. The solicitors acting for Mr Godden were again Hallett & Co. On 18th October 1972 they submitted a contract of sale to Wood & Sons, the solicitors acting for the defendants. The draft contract had no plan because the title was registered. Wood & Sons submitted some inquiries before contract. One answer to those inquiries stated that there was 'a concrete W.D. road running along the south-east boundary'. This information was expressly confirmed in a later letter dated 17th November 1972. Thus a reference to the filed plan, on a visit to the site, would have shown clearly that the vendors were, in effect, stating that the green triangle was outside the boundary of the land being sold. As well, in the context of an inquiry about boundary fences, it was stated that the south-east fence belonged to the vendors, thus indicating that the boundary of the land being sold was the fence on the west side of the concrete road. No inquiry at all was made about the barn.

Before the solicitors began their correspondence leading to an exchange of contracts, the defendant's representatives had made a visit to Mr Godden's land. The defendant is a development company. At the material time its directors included four brothers of the name of Else. One of the brothers, Mr Henry Thomas Else, gave evidence. He said that in about September 1972 he and his three brothers went to look at the land with a view to buying. He met Mr Godden on the land. Mr Else said that when they were outside the farmhouse the barn was in view and Mr Godden volunteered the information that the barn belonged to an adjoining farmer, Mr Blacklocks, that is to say the plaintiff. Mr Godden, it was said, went on to say that had given Mr Blacklocks permission to erect the barn on the land it stood on and that that land and the roadway, ie the concrete road, were within the Godden boundary. Mr Else thought he had a plan with him. Mr Else seemed very doubtful about whether he did indeed have a plan, and did not in any way identify what plan he thought he had, save to say that it was on glossy paper. It was not put to Mr Godden that Mr Else had a plan. He said there was no further talk than that about boundaries, and that he had made no inquiries about them. He agreed a price of £18,000 with Mr Godden.

Mr Godden's evidence about what took place when Mr Else inspected the land in September or October 1972 before contract does not at all accord with the evidence of Mr Else. Mr Godden said he remembered that visit of Mr Else with his brothers. He said he stood in front of the house and pointed at his boundaries. He indicated the boundary fence and the ditches at the back. He said he was asked if the barn was his property. He said it was not. In an answer to interrogatories (which I will mention later) Mr Else said that he was told by Mr Godden that the barn would be removed before completion. Mr Godden emphatically denied that he said any such thing. He agreed that he had said that he had given permission to the plaintiff to site the barn where it was, but I am satisfied that this was, in Mr Godden's mind, a reference to the fact that he had consented as a planning matter to the barn being sited where it was. It was abundantly clear from Mr Godden's evidence that he explained to Mr Else that his boundary was the fence on his (Mr Godden's) side of the concrete road. I entirely accept Mr Godden's evidence.

Contracts were exchanged on 17th November 1972 and completion was on 5th December. The defendants became the registered proprietors on 12th January 1973. Their title extended, of course, over the green triangle because that triangle is part of title K320824. Mr Else visited the land for the second time on the day of completion. He collected such keys as were necessary and made arrangements for the securing of the property after Mr Godden should remove himself, as he did that day, or soon after. There was no discussion on this occasion about boundaries.

The defendant company has submitted various planning applications for the land. One of these led to a local inquiry held at Folkestone in January 1975. The plaintiff was given notice of the inquiry. It was at this stage that it dawned on the plaintiff that the defendant's planning application embraced not only the land that the plaintiff thought he had sold to Mr Godden but, as well, the green triangle. The source of the error was quickly established, ie that the contract and conveyance plans used on the occasion of the Blacklocks/Godden sale were inaccurate in so far as they included the green triangle. Correspondence ensued between Halletts for the plaintiff and Woods for the defendant.

No compromise proved possible. With the consent of the Chief Land Registrar under s 83(5)(c) of the Land Registration Act 1925, this action was commenced on 18th August 1977.

I need not mention the pleadings save to say that the plaintiff relies on s 70(1)(g) of the 1925 Act, and that the defendant counterclaims for the removal of a caution lodged by the plaintiff. However, certain interrogatories were allowed and I must refer to some of the answers. These answers were given to Mr H T Else. The last answer is relevant to s 70(1)(g) and is to the effect that the defendant, when acquiring its title, did not make any inquiry of the plaintiff or any other person concerning the rights of the plaintiff in the green triangle. Another answer was 'Yes' to the question whether any representative of the defendant walked the boundaries. I am satisfied that Mr Else did no such thing. There was an admission that the plaintiff was using the barn at the time of the Else inspection.

In summary, the position as I see it is as follows. In 1969 Mr Blacklocks sold Brickwall Farm to Mr Godden. By mutual mistake the green triangle was included in the land sold. But neither the Blacklockses nor Mr Godden appreciated that the green triangle had been transferred to Mr Godden. On the basis of the real agreement between the parties, new fencing was put up along the concrete road so that the green triangle did not pass into any Godden occupation. On the contrary, after the Godden completion Mr Blacklocks built the barn on the green triangle. In these circumstances Mr Blacklocks had, as against Mr Godden, a right of rectification. In 1972 Mr Godden sold to the defendant. Accepting, as I do, Mr Godden's evidence as against that of Mr Else, both Mr Godden and the defendant supposed that the land being transferred was bounded by the concrete road. The defendant accepted on the site that the concrete road was the boundary. No representative of the defendant or its solicitors had any idea that the filed plan extended the area of title K320824 beyond the concrete road. It seems to me that the same mistake took place as between Mr Godden and the defendant as had previously taken place between Mr Blacklocks and Mr Godden.

Throughout the periods of the Godden and the defendant's ownerships neither Mr Godden nor the defendant had made any use of the green triangle and such user of the land as there has been has been by Mr Blacklocks, who has had continuous use of the barn.

I now come to the plaintiff's claim. His counsel's submission was that the plaintiff had a right to rectify as against Mr Godden. I have found that he did. Counsel then said that such right was, at the time of the transfer to the defendant, an overriding interest in that the right was accompanied by actual occupation: see s 70(1)(g) of the 1925 Act. If that is so, the transfer to the defendant took effect subject to the overriding interest: see s 20(1)(b) of the 1925 Act. I must therefore consider whether or not at the time of the transfer to the defendant, dated 5th December 1972, Mr Blacklocks had an overriding interest in the land transferred. Before considering this particular problem I draw attention to the following observations of Lord Wilberforce in *Williams & Glyn's Bank Ltd v Boland* [1980] 2 All ER 408 at 412, [1981] AC 487 at 504:

'The exception just mentioned consisted of "overriding interests" listed in s 70 [of the Land Registration Act 1925]. As to these, all registered land is stated to be deemed to be subject to such of them as may be subsisting in reference to the land, unless the contrary is expressed on the register. The land is so subject regardless of notice actual or constructive. In my opinion, therefore, the law as to notice as it may affect purchasers of unregistered land, whether contained in decided cases or in a statute (eg the Conveyancing Act 1882, s 3 and the Law of Property Act 1925, s 199) has no application even by analogy to registered land. Whether a particular right is an overriding interest, and whether it affects a purchaser, is to be decided on the terms of s 70, and other relevant provisions of the Land Registration Act 1925, and on nothing else. In relation to rights connected with occupation, it has been said that the purpose and effect of s 70(1)(g) of the Land Registration Act 1925 was to make applicable to registered land the same rule as previously had been held to apply to unregistered land (see *National Provincial Bank Ltd v Ainsworth* [1964] 1 All ER 688 at 697, [1964] Ch 665 at 689 (per Lord Denning MR) and [1965] 2 All ER 472 at 501–502, [1965] AC 1175 at 1259 (in this House)). I adhere to this, but I do not accept the argument counsel for the appellant sought to draw from it. His submission was that, in applying s 70(1)(g), we should have regard to and limit the application of the paragraph in the light of the doctrine of notice. But this would run counter to the whole purpose of the Act. The purpose, in each system, is the same, namely, to safeguard the rights of persons in occupation, but the method used differs. In the case of unregistered land, the purchaser's obligation depends on what he has notice of, notice actual or constructive. In the case of registered land, it is the fact of occupation that matters. If there is actual occupation, and the occupier has rights, the purchaser takes subject to them. If not, he does not. No further element is material.'

Accordingly I must concentrate my attention on s 70 and any other relevant provisions of the 1925 Act. Overriding interests are defined in s 3(xvi) of the Act. Section 70, so far as material is as follows:

'(1) All registered land shall, unless under the provisions of this Act the contrary is expressed on the register, be deemed to be subject to such of the following overriding interests as may be for the time being subsisting in reference thereto, and such interests shall not be treated as incumbrances within the meaning of this Act, (that is to say) . . . (g) The rights of every person in actual occupation of the land or in receipt of the rents and profits thereof, save where enquiry is made of such person and the rights are not disclosed . . .'

As to the saving words at the end of para (g) it is common ground that the defendant made no inquiry of the plaintiff, so those words may be disregarded. Counsel for the defendant conceded that the plaintiff was at all material times in actual occupation of the green triangle. The question for consideration, therefore, is whether or not the plaintiff's right to rectify is a right subsisting in reference to the land within the opening words of s 70. Counsel for the defendant said not so because the right to rectify is a mere equity or personal right subsisting as between the plaintiff and Mr Godden. Such a right, he said, is not within s 70. He drew attention to these words of Russell LJ in *National Provincial Bank Ltd v Hastings Car Mart Ltd* [1964] 1 All ER 688 at 701, [1964] Ch 665 at 696:

'It seems to me that s. 70 of the Land Registration Act, 1925, in all its parts is dealing with rights in reference to land which have the quality of being capable of enduring through different ownerships of the land, acccording to normal conceptions of title to real property. If such a right as is now in question is not of this quality, I would not be prepared as a matter of construction to hold that it is embraced by the language of s. 70; the contrary would indeed involve a startling result from a statute designed as a simplification of the processes of making and investigating title to land. The statute after all uses the very phrase "overriding *interests*" subsisting in reference to land, and, when subjecting dispositions of registered land to overriding interests, it frees them from "*other* estates and interests"; see s. 20. Section 107(1), I think, points in the same direction. Nor should the mind be in any way distracted by the fact that the owner of the rights under s. 70(1)(g) is identified as a person in actual occupation. It is the rights of such a person which constitute the overriding interest and must be examined, not his occupation.' (Russell LJ's emphasis.)

Those observations were fully supported by their Lordships in the House of Lords when the *Hastings Car Mart* case went to appeal: see *National Provincial Bank Ltd v Ainsworth* [1965] 2 All ER 472 at 481, 482, 503, [1965] AC 1175 at 1226, 1228, 1262, per Lord Hodson, Lord Cohen and Lord Wilberforce.

The right to rectify is often described as a mere equity: see for example Williams on Vendor and Purchaser (4th Edn, 1936, vol 2, p 791) and Snell's Principles of Equity (27th Edn, 1973, p 53). So the question is: does this right to rectify (or mere equity) have 'the quality of being capable of enduring through different ownerships of land according to the normal conceptions of title to real property'? In *National Provincial Bank Ltd v Ainsworth* [1965] 2 All ER 472 at 488, [1965] AC 1175 at 1238 Lord Upjohn considered that a mere equity might be either 'naked and alone' or ancillary to or dependent on an equitable estate or interest in land, and in *Latec Investments Ltd v Hotel Terrigal Pty Ltd* (1965) 113 CLR 265 at 277, Kitto J made a distinction between an equity which is and an equity which is not accompanied by an equitable interest. It is plain that the wife's equity in *National Provincial Bank v Ainsworth* was naked and alone and had not the enduring quality that might render it capable of being a right under s 70. But was the mere equity possessed by Mr Blacklocks of the same kind, or was it an equity ancillary to an interest in land? If the equity was of the latter kind it may be transmissible and so have the 'quality of being capable of enduring' spoken of by Russell LJ.

The cases show that a right to set aside a deed may be assigned or devised. In *Stump v Gaby* (1852) 2 De GM & G 623 at 630, 42 ER 1015 at 1018 Lord St Leonards LC said:

'My strong impression is that this very point is concluded upon authority, but if not I am ready to make an authority on the present occasion, and to decide that, assuming the conveyance to have been voidable, the grantor had an equitable estate which he might have devised . . .'

Dickinson v Burrell (1866) LR 1 Eq 337 shows that when there is a voidable conveyance the grantor has rights which may be assigned. Referring to that case in *Gross v Lewis Hillman Ltd* [1969] 3 All ER 1476 at 1482, [1970] Ch 445 at 460–461 Cross LJ said:

'There, property had been assigned by A. to B., in circumstances which, so it was claimed, gave A. an equitable right to recover it and the equitable interest in it. A. assigned that equitable interest to C., and it was held that C. could sue B. to recover the legal estate.'

Taylor J said in the *Latec Investments* case 113 CLR 265 at 284:

'I regard these authorities as establishing that when the owner of property has been induced by fraud to convey the grant or continues to have an equitable interest therein, that interest may be devised or assigned inter vivos, and that the grantor's interest in the property does not come into existence only if and when the conveyance is set aside.'

Those words may be read as referring to mistake as well as to fraud.

The *Latec Investments* case shows that a right or equity to set aside a conveyance of Blackacre is, when in competition with other interests in Blackacre, likely to be regarded as a mere personal claim rather than as a right ancillary to an equitable interest then subsisting (see 113 CLR 265 at 280ff, 290 per Taylor and Menzies JJ). No doubt that is so when the rules as to the priority of equitable interests have to be applied. But in this case those rules do not fall to be applied. Here what one has to decide is whether or not a right to rectify is of the enduring character explained by Russell LJ. In the light of *Stump v Gaby* and the other authorities I have mentioned, I regard the right to rectify as having that character. The plaintiff had an equity that was ancillary to an interest in land, being an equity and an ancillary interest that was transmissible. It follows that he had a right within s 70(1)(g) of the Land Registration Act 1925. The right is not itself an overriding interest but it has been accompanied at all times by actual occupation. The association of the right with actual occupation constitutes an overriding interest that is binding on the land in the hands of the defendant: see *Williams & Glyn's Bank Ltd v Boland* [1980] 2 All ER 408 at 417, [1981] AC 487 at 511.

I add that my finding would be the same were the land unregistered. If that were so there would have been a contest between the Blacklockses' right to rectify and the *a* defendant's legal estate. That contest would have been decided by reference to s 199 of the Law of Property Act 1925. On the particular facts of this case the right to rectify would, in my view, be enforceable against the legal estate.

There will be a declaration as sought, together with an order of rectification of the register. I had some hesitation in deciding that the relief sought in the statement of claim was appropriate, but I think it is. For a helpful analogy in this connection, see *Leuty v Hillas* (1858) 2 De G & J 110, 44 ER 929 and *Craddock Brothers v Hunt* [1923] 2 Ch

b 136.

There will be a declaration that the defendant holds the green triangle on trust absolutely for the plaintiff, and an order that the Land Registry title K320824 be rectified by the removal therefrom of the area of land covered by the green triangle.

Declaration accordingly.

c

Solicitors: *Hallet & Co*, Ashford, Kent (for the plaintiff); *Spon-Smith & Co*, Shortlands (for the defendant).

Hazel Hartman   Barrister.

d

Re W (a minor)

COURT OF APPEAL, CIVIL DIVISION
STEPHENSON, SHAW AND BRANDON LJJ

e 21st MARCH 1979

County court – Jurisdiction – Application for custody order – Power to grant interlocutory injunction – Whether power to support custody order by injunction – Guardianship of Minors Act 1971, s 9 – County Courts Act 1959, s 74.

f When making a custody order under s 9[a] of the Guardianship of Minors Act 1971, the county court has power to grant an interlocutory injunction under s 74[b] of the County Courts Act 1959 in support of the order, for example, by restraining the other parent from removing the minor from the custody of the parent seeking the order or from assaulting, molesting, or otherwise interfering with the minor or the parent seeking the order (see p 403 *j* to p 404 *h*, post).

g

Notes

For the Guardianship of Minors Act 1971, s 9, see 41 Halsbury's Statutes (3rd Edn) 766.

For the County Courts Act 1959, s 74, see 7 Halsbury's Statutes (3rd Edn) 349.

For the Supreme Court of Judicature (Consolidation) Act 1925, s 45, see 25 Halsbury's Statutes (3rd Edn) 717.

h For jurisdiction of county courts to grant matrimonial injunctions, see Supplement to 13 Halsbury's Laws (4th Edn) para 1228.

Originating summons

On 6th March 1979 the appellant issued an originating summons which was headed 'In the Matter of the Guardianship of Minors Act 1971' and a notice of application for an

j ───

a Section 9, so far as material, provides: '(1) The court may, on the application of the mother or father of a minor (who may apply without next friend), make such order regarding—(a) the custody of the minor; and (b) the right of access to the minor of his mother or father, as the court thinks fit having regard to the welfare of the minor and to the conduct and wishes of the mother and father.'

b Section 74, so far as material, is set out at p 403 *g*, post.

interlocutory injunction against the respondent. At the Willesden County Court, on 6th March 1979 his Honour Judge Honig granted an ex parte interim injunction. The respondent was served with the documents on 8th March. On 13th March 1979 the matter came before the same judge again on notice and he discharged the order of 6th March. The appellant appealed. The facts are set out in the judgment of Brandon LJ.   a

Richard Slowe for the appellant.
The respondent was not represented.   b

BRANDON LJ delivered the first judgment at the invitation of Stephenson LJ. This is an appeal from an order of his Honour Judge Honig, made on 13th March 1979, whereby he discharged an ex parte injunction which he had granted to the appellant previously.

The facts of the matter are these. The appellant has been associating for a number of   c
years with the respondent at a council flat of which she is the tenant. When I say she has been associating with him there, I do not mean necessarily that they have been living there as man and wife. According to her affidavit, however, he has been visiting her frequently and staying frequently with her there. Whether that amounts to living together for certain purposes or not, does not have to be determined in this case.

This couple have, as a result of their association, a child, a boy born on 14th May 1976,   d
and who will therefore shortly be three years old. There seems to have been a good deal of violence between the appellant and the respondent, and more recently, in February, the respondent, according to the appellant's affidavit, made a series of assaults on her, as a result of which she sustained scratching, bruising and other injuries. He also behaved in such a way as to drive her out of the flat of which she is the tenant, and to deprive her temporarily of the care of the boy.   e

The appellant fled to the home of her parents where she has remained since, and after a certain period she got the child back and now has that child with her at her parents' home.

In that situation, the appellant applied to the Willesden County Court for protection from the behaviour of the respondent. She issued an originating application which was headed 'In the Matter of the Guardianship of Minors Act 1971–1973', and she also issued   f
a notice of application for an interlocutory injunction, and the relief which she sought was in the form of a series of injunctions restraining the respondent from removing the child from her care and control; restraining him from assaulting, molesting or otherwise interfering with her or the child; and requiring him to vacate the flat; she also asked for a power of arrest to be attached to the order.

The originating application and the notice of application for an interlocutory   g
injunction were both issued on 6th March, and they were supported by the affidavit of the appellant sworn on the same date. The matter came before the learned judge on the same day, and he made the order asked for without going into the matter at all fully. Following that, on 8th March a process server instructed by the appellant's solicitors served certain documents on the respondent, and those documents were the originating application, the notice of application for an injunction, the appellant's affidavit and the   h
ex parte injunction granted by the learned judge.

On 13th March the matter came before the learned judge again on notice. On that occasion the appellant was represented but the respondent did not appear nor was he represented.

The learned judge appears to have had second thoughts about what he had done on 6th March, and reached the conclusion that he did not have jurisdiction to make the order   j
which he had made, and that it should therefore be discharged. In dealing with the matter he said:

'The applicant's application under the Guardianship of Minors Act 1971 for an anti molestation order and against interference with the applicant's care and control of the child is misconceived. It is not appropriate to proceed under that Act in this case. The originating summons does not include a claim by the applicant for custody, and I give leave to amend the application to add such a claim. An application under the Domestic Violence and Matrimonial Proceedings Act 1976 is also inappropriate in this case, as the parties are not living together as man and wife. Now that I realise the merits of this application, I feel that the ex parte injunction granted last week was granted inadvertently and should never have been granted, and I discharge it. I make no order on the application. The applicant is not legally aided and I make no order for costs.'

It would seem that, when the learned judge there spoke of his realisation of the merits of the application, he was referring to the merits in law rather than the merits on the facts. There had been no change in the merits on the facts since he granted the ex parte injunction.

Before us it has been contended that the learned judge was in error in concluding that he did not have jurisdiction to grant the injunction asked for, and that on the facts he should have done so. So far as the question of jurisdiction is concerned, the jurisdiction of the county court in this matter is conferred on it by the Guardianship of Minors Act 1971, s 15, which provides that a county court shall be one of the courts to which applications under that Act can be made. Section 9 of the Act gives power to all courts having jurisdiction under the Act to make, on the application of the mother or father of a minor, such order regarding the custody of the minor as the court thinks fit, having regard to the welfare of the minor and to the conduct and wishes of the mother and father.

So the county court clearly had jurisdiction to entertain an application by the appellant for the custody of the minor, so soon as leave was given to amend the originating application to include an application for a custody order. I think it would be right to say that, until that was done, there was no foundation, really, for the application for the injunction. We must, I think, take it that that amendment has been made, although no formally amended application has been placed before us, and no amended application has so far been served on the respondent. If the formal amendment has not yet been made, it ought to be made forthwith. In any case, I think it is right for this court to deal with the matter on the footing that the amendment has been made.

Given that the court has power over the substantive matter under the Guardianship of Minors Act 1971, the power of the court to grant interlocutory injunctions depends on s 74 of the County Courts Act 1959 which provides:

'Every county court, as regards any cause of action for the time being within its jurisdiction, shall ... (a) grant such relief, redress or remedy or combination of remedies, either absolute or conditional; and (b) give such and the like effect to every ground of defence or counter-claim equitable or legal (subject to the provisions of section sixty-five of this Act); as ought to be granted or given in the like case by the High Court and in as full and ample a manner.'

The jurisdiction of the High Court with regard to interlocutory injunctions is governed by s 45 of the Supreme Court of Judicature (Consolidation) Act 1925, which provides:

'(1) The High Court may grant a mandamus or an injunction or appoint a receiver by an interlocutory order in all cases in which it appears to the court to be just or convenient so to do. . .'

There is no doubt in my mind that the High Court has power, in any case where it has made a custody order, to support that order as may be just and convenient by interlocutory injunction, and it follows that the county court, which has the same jurisdiction, also has power to support a custody order by injunction.

The County Court Rules themselves provide in Ord 13, r 8 for applications for interlocutory injunctions to be made and that rule extends to all kinds of proceedings including, in my view, the sort of proceedings with which we are here concerned.

For these reasons I am of opinion that the learned county court judge was in error in holding that he did not have jurisdiction to grant injunctions once he had been put in a position to make a custody order by the amendment of the proceedings which he allowed.

So far as the merits are concerned, the court is not adequately informed about the present situation. The affidavit of the appellant was sworn on 6th March, which is more than 14 days ago, and there have been changes in the situation since then. It would be more satisfactory if the court had up-to-date information about the whereabouts of the respondent and his present behaviour in relation to the appellant and her child.

Nevertheless it seems to me that the situation as it existed immediately before 6th March was of such a grave character that this court ought to do all it can by way of interlocutory relief to protect the appellant and her child. That can best be done by granting injunctions of the kind asked for but not necessarily specifically in the words asked for.

In the first place I think that there should be an order that the appellant do have the interim custody of the child until further order. Second, there should be an injunction restraining the respondent from removing the child from the custody, care or control of the appellant without the leave of the court. Third, there should be an injunction restraining the respondent from assaulting, molesting or otherwise interfering with the appellant or the child. Fourth, there should be an order that, if the respondent is in occupation of the appellant's flat, he should vacate that flat forthwith, and, if he is not at present in occupation of that flat, he should be restrained from entering it or visiting it without the leave of the court. There should further be liberty to the respondent to apply on two days' notice to the county court to vary or discharge this order. There may be something to be said in this dispute on behalf of the respondent which has not yet been said. It may be that he is entitled to be heard on such matters as access arrangements or other matters connected with the welfare of the child of whom he is also a parent. If so, it will be open to him to apply to the county court judge about those matters, and the county court judge can deal with them on their merits. The order which I am suggesting should be made is essentially an interlocutory order to give the appellant and the child protection in the present crisis which has arisen. When things have settled down, it will be for consideration whether the order should be continued or not.

SHAW LJ. I agree.

STEPHENSON LJ. I agree. The law would indeed be a poor thing if the only means available to this mother of guarding the welfare of this little boy and protecting herself and him from injury by the father was an action for damages (and an injunction) for assault, as we are told the learned judge thought. I am satisfied that the court can and should now give the mother, in these amended proceedings under the Guardianship of Minors Act 1971, the relief proposed by Brandon LJ.

Appeal allowed.

Solicitors: *Alexander & Partners* (for the appellant).

Bebe Chua   Barrister.

a

Wheeler v Copas

QUEEN'S BENCH DIVISION

CHAPMAN J

11th, 12th, 13th JUNE 1980

b *Occupier's liability – Duty to independent contractor – Moveable structure – Ladder – Contractor undertaking building work for farmer – Farmer providing farm ladder for use in building work – Whether farmer 'occupying' ladder – Occupiers' Liability Act 1957, s 1(3)(a).*

Negligence – Duty to take care – Extent of duty to contractor – Equipment provided for contractor – Duty to provide suitable equipment for work undertaken – Contractor undertaking building work for farmer – Farmer providing farm ladder for use in building work – Ladder
c *unsuitable for building work – Contractor injured when ladder collapsing – Whether farmer liable for contractor's injuries.*

Negligence – Contributory negligence – Lack of reasonable care by plaintiff for own safety – Contractor undertaking building work for farmer – Farmer providing farm ladder for use in building work – Contractor not rejecting.ladder as unsuitable – Contractor injured when ladder
d *collapsing – Whether contractor contributorily negligent.*

The plaintiff was a partner in a firm of bricklayers. The defendant was a farmer who wished to build a house on his farm, and negotiated directly with the plaintiff and his partner. A labour-only contract was agreed whereby the plaintiff and his partner were to lay bricks and erect and dismantle scaffolding. The defendant agreed to provide the
e building materials and any equipment necessary for the work. The plaintiff and his partner had begun work and needed a long ladder to erect the second lift of scaffolding. They were offered two farm ladders belonging to the defendant, and chose one to use to carry up building materials. The defendant did not ask them whether the ladder was adequate for their use, nor was he told it was unsuitable. The plaintiff fell off the ladder and was injured when the ladder gave way. Expert evidence was given at the hearing
f that the ladder was too flimsy for building work and that that was the cause of the accident. The plaintiff sued the defendant for damages for personal injuries on the grounds (i) that the defendant owed a duty of care as an occupier of the premises under the Occupiers' Liability Act 1957, or alternatively (ii) that the defendant was negligent in failing to provide suitable equipment for the work.

g **Held** – (1) Although s 1(3)(a)[d] of the 1957 Act did make provision with respect to movable structures, such as vessels, vehicles and aircraft, and could in appropriate circumstances apply to a ladder, it could not be said that, once the defendant had handed the ladder over to the plaintiff and his partner for the purpose of bricklaying, the defendant was still the occupier of the ladder for the purposes of that Act (see p 408 *c d*, post).

h (2) The defendant was, however, liable to the plaintiff in negligence, either as the bailor or lender of a chattel, or as an occupier of property who intended that others should come onto it for the purposes of work or business and use appliances owned or supplied by him. In either case the duty of care was the same, namely to take reasonable care to see that the appliance or chattel was fit and safe for the purpose for which it was to be used. Since the defendant had taken on the obligation to provide the equipment,

j _____

a   Section 1(3), so far as material, provides: 'The rules ... enacted in relation to an occupier of premises and his visitors shall also apply, in like manner and to the like extent as the principles applicable at common law to an occupier of premises and his invitees or licensees would apply, to regulate—(a) the obligations of a person occupying or having control over any fixed or moveable structure, including any vessel, vehicle or aircraft ...'

he was liable in negligence for failure to ensure that the ladder was suitable (see p 408 *d* to p 409 *d*, post); dictum of Coleridge J in *Blakemore v Bristol and Exeter Railway Co* (1858) 8 E & B at 1050–1051 and *Marney v Scott* [1899] 1 QB 986 applied.

(3) However, since the plaintiff was an experienced builder and had accepted use of the ladder in spite of its apparent inadequacy, he was therefore contributorily negligent and the damages awarded would be reduced accordingly (see p 409 *g h*, post).

Notes

For the duty of an occupier of a moveable structure, see 34 Halsbury's Laws (4th Edn) para 21, and for cases on occupation, see 36(1) Digest (Reissue) 75–79, 299–309.

For the personal duty of an employer of an independent contractor, see 16 Halsbury's Laws (4th Edn) para 757, and for cases on the subject, see 36(1) Digest (Reissue) 257–260, 1011–1025.

For the effect of contributory negligence, see 34 Halsbury's Laws (4th Edn) para 68, and for cases on the plaintiff's knowledge of danger, see 36(1) Digest (Reissue) 298–299, 1193–1201.

For the Occupiers' Liability Act 1957, s 1, see 23 Halsbury's Statutes (3rd Edn) 793.

Cases referred to in judgment

Blakemore v Bristol and Exeter Railway Co (1858) 8 E & B 1035, 31 LTOS 12, 120 ER 385, sub nom *Blackmore v Bristol and Exeter Railway Co* 27 LJQB 167, 4 Jur NS 657, 3 Digest (Reissue) 432, 2926.

Marney v Scott [1899] 1 QB 986, 68 LJQB 736, 36(1) Digest (Reissue) 82, 324.

Smith v Manchester City Council (1974) 118 Sol Jo 597, CA, Digest (Cont Vol D) 717, 1329a.

Action

By writ dated 8th August 1977 the plaintiff, George Edward Wheeler, brought an action against the defendant, G W Copas, for damages for personal injuries arising out of an accident to the plaintiff on 18th February 1976 while he was employed by the defendant and was using an unsafe ladder provided by the defendant. The facts are set out in the judgment.

Brian Leech for the plaintiff.
Raymond Croxon for the defendant.

CHAPMAN J. This case arises out of an accident which occurred on 18th February 1976, when the plaintiff had a fall because the ladder up which he was going with a hod of bricks broke. Both the stiles broke and down he came. I think the history of the matter can probably be taken quite shortly. I have had the evidence of the plaintiff and Mr Hogg, who was his partner. They were carrying on business together in partnership, the purpose of their business being bricklaying. They were acting as labour only subcontractors. Very often they would work for head contractors, and on occasions, as occurred on this occasion, they would work for a private owner.

The defendant owned a farm and he was minded towards the end of 1975 to build a house on a portion of that farm. He got the plans prepared by an architect and he then, according to his evidence, put out invitations to a number of bricklayers, including the plaintiff and his partner, to quote for the work. First contact was made by telephone. They both went round, collected the plans and then in due course, the actual date I do not think matters (they put it at some time in January 1976; the defendant says it was towards the end of 1975), Mr Hogg prepared an estimate, his wife did the writing of it, and it reads: 'For brick construction of new house and erection of scaffolding and dismantling of scaffolding. Price as follows: £1,200 for brickwork below dampcourse level at £25 per thousand.' Whether this had gone to the defendant earlier or whether they took it with them and discussed it after letting him see it, I do not think again matters. There was discussion about this document. Mr Copas had beat them down on

the price, and he said: '£1,000, not £1,200.' That is written in in the defendant's writing
a with the word after it: '(Reduced)'. He also added, and it was agreed to at the discussion:
'£1·25 per yard.' It is common ground that this was for the breeze blocks that had to be
used for a portion of the work below the brickwork. The brickwork would start at about
ground level, and from the foundations up to ground level there would be breeze blocks
laid both inside and outside. This was the figure which was agreed to cover that.

On its face, it seems to me that this is quite plainly what is in common parlance
b nowadays called 'a labour only contract'. They were to lay the bricks, erect scaffolding and
dismantle the scaffolding. Plainly the defendant's obligation was, as he accepted in his
evidence, to provide the bricks, provide the mortar, provide the cement mixer, sand and
cement for the mortar, and any other equipment which would be necessary for the
work. In effect, as he agreed with me when I put it to him, he was putting himself into
the position of a building contractor using subcontractors in order to erect the house. He
c did his own supervision. No doubt he had a number of other subcontractors from time
to time doing the drainage work and the plumbing work. Whether it was centrally
heated or not I do not know, but there would be tilers to do the tiling work. We have
pictures of the house which show, if I may say so, a very nice house indeed. One of the
facings, a material one which figures in the case, is in fact tiled, and that would be the
tilers' responsibility. The roofing contractors, carpenters and so forth would lay the joists
d for the floors, the rafters and purlins for the roof, and the tilers would do the tiling of the
roof. So there would be quite a number of subcontractors apparently employed by the
defendant, he having put himself, in effect, into the position of a building contractor. It
is an example, perhaps of a do-it-yourself effort in a field which is really not practical for
that sort of private enterprise.

Anyhow, that was the arrangement with the plaintiff and his partner. They started
e pretty well straight away. In the first instance they had a short ladder. It was a fruit-
picking ladder, like the ladder which later figured in the accident. They used that until
the scaffolding which they erected had to go up to the second lift. They used the words
'first lift' for the lower layer of the scaffold, and then they had to build the next lift of the
scaffold and work from that. For this purpose they wanted the longer ladder.

It was put to the plaintiff that in fact they went along to the farm and made their own
f pick of ladders. The defendant said in evidence that he agrees he was asked to provide
the longer ladder. He produced two ladders: one had 35 rungs, which one would have
thought for what the plaintiff wanted was pretty obviously too long, and the other one
had 25 rungs. The plaintiff, his partner, or both of them chose the 25-rung ladder as
being the appropriate height they wanted. It was, in fact, a fruit ladder.

A good deal of the equipment had, of course, necessarily been hired. The bricks no
g doubt had been bought. I have an invoice dated 27th January 1976, showing a
considerable amount of scaffolding material: clips, certain trestles and tubes, so on and so
forth, which were hired by the defendant from Lovell Plant Hire. He never apparently
asked anybody what sort of ladder would be needed for the work of building a house.
It seems he took no advice on that at all and simply assumed that the ladders he had, all
of which were fruit-picking ladders, would suit the purpose. Unfortunately, it is now
h common ground that they did not.

There is controversy as to how long this longer ladder was in use. Whether it was two
or three weeks, as the defendant thinks, or whether they merely had it for a day having
asked for it the previous day and finding it the next morning on the site, I do not think
really matters. They immediately started to use it. Mr Hogg indeed carried up it a
pretty heavy lintel. The lintel, I was told, was for the right-hand window in the tiled
j gable end which one sees in the photographs, and he had of course to carry it up fairly
slowly. He noticed as he went up this ladder that it gave a good deal under the weight
which he was carrying. He was moving slowly, and it may be he was fortunate in
succeeding in getting up all right with that heavy lintel weighing about a hundredweight.

Towards the evening the plaintiff was carrying a hod of mortar up the ladder. It was
about 4.30 pm on 18th February, and he was just approaching the second lift of the

scaffold when both stiles of the ladder simply snapped. Of course, the whole thing came down with a crash. There is some question whether the ladder was lashed at the top or whether it was not. The defendant said that he had put it in position up against the runner of the second lift of the scaffold. The plaintiff in fact said that he had tied it before they started using it. I do not think it matters, because whether it was tied or not had no bearing on the accident.

What is common ground on the expert evidence in this case is that such a ladder was too flimsy for building work. It was not a builder's ladder at all. Its stiles were about half the size of an ordinary pole ladder which is used for building work, and it is quite plain, both the experts agree, that the reason for this accident was the inadequate dimensions of the stiles. As Mr Richardson, the plaintiff's expert, said in terms in his report which was put in evidence, and Mr Wood, the defendant's expert, agreed, this sort of ladder is simply not suitable for building work, and that was the cause of the accident. It is on this basis that I have to decide where the liability arises.

The plaintiff puts his case to a considerable extent on the Occupiers' Liability Act 1957, but it seems to me that there may well be considerable difficulty in relation to that because that Act is dealing with an occupier. It is true it covers moveable structures, such as vessels, vehicles and aircraft. I do not doubt that in appropriate circumstances it could apply to a ladder, but I see considerable difficulty in saying that once the defendant had handed the ladder over to the plaintiff and his partner for the purpose of the bricklaying the defendant was still the occupier of this ladder.

The case is put alternatively in negligence, which seems to me to be the proper way in which the case ought to be put. It is clear that there are no cases really which deal with this particular aspect of liability; the nearest case that I know of in England is *Marney v Scott* [1899] 1 QB 986, which the plaintiff's counsel relied on, where Bingham J said (at 989–990):

'I think that a man who intends that others shall come upon property of which he is the occupier for purposes of work or business in which he is interested, owes a duty to those who do so come to use reasonable care to see that the property and the appliances upon it which it is intended shall be used in the work are fit for the purpose . . .'

This ladder was plainly an appliance on the defendant's property. That seems to get reasonably near the situation.

I have myself derived a considerable amount of benefit from Prosser on Tort (4th Edn, 1971, p 668) dealing in particular with the position of a bailor, and what he says is this:

'A similar duty of care rests upon other persons who deliver goods in return for a consideration. One who rents a horse or an automobile, for example, or any other bailor for hire is required not only to disclose to the bailee defects of which he has knowledge, but also to exercise affirmative care to inspect and repair the chattel so that it is safe for its intended purpose. The same obligation is imposed upon a restaurant serving food to customers and a shipper turning goods over to a carrier for transportation.'

In other words, he is saying that there is a duty on a bailor within the ambit of negligence to take reasonable care to see that what he is lending is, so far as reasonable care can secure it, made safe for the purpose.

One has the same sort of principle laid down in Paton's Bailment in the Common Law (1952). Coleridge J in *Blakemore v Bristol and Exeter Railway Co* (1858) 8 E & B 1035 at 1050–1051, 120 ER 385 at 391 makes the comment that there is very little in the books on the subject, but he then goes on to say:

'The lender must be taken to lend for the purpose of a beneficial use by the borrower; the borrower therefore is not responsible for reasonable wear and tear; but he is for negligence, for misuse, for gross want of skill in the use; above all, for anything which may be qualified as legal fraud. So, on the other hand, as the lender lends for beneficial use, he must be responsible for defects in the chattel with reference to the use for which he knows the loan is accepted, of which he is aware, and owing to which directly the borrower is injured.'

It seems to me that that does lay down a general principle which, as Coleridge J said, was consonant with reason and justice, and it cannot but be part of our law.

It is said here that the defendant was after all a farmer, but his difficulty in that respect is that he was, as he agreed with me, taking on himself in the present case the burden of a building contractor in employing subcontractors to come along and do the building work which he wanted done. His obligations under a labour only contract, such as the plaintiff and his partner had in the present case, would be, so far as reasonable care could secure that result, to see that the equipment which he provided for their work was reasonably fit for the purpose, but unfortunately he apparently took no advice from anybody. One would have thought it was absolutely obvious that these fruit-picking ladders, which as he knew were fruit-picking ladders, were not builders' ladders. They were not the sort of ladder, a pole ladder, which one sees on building sites. It seems to me that liability is established against him for supplying for this building work a ladder which was totally unsuitable for the purpose. It may be that he did not know it was unsuitable for the purpose, but at any rate he ought to have known. He ought to have taken advice, apprised himself, made inquiries to find out whether it was a suitable piece of equipment for builders to use in their building work.

The matter does not stop there, because the plaintiff himself and his partner both saw the ladder. It was either left at the site or brought to the site for them to choose whether they wanted the longer or shorter of the two which were offered. They could see that neither ladder offered was a builder's ladder. They both recognised that they were fruit-picking ladders. I do not say it had any effect on the accident, but they had a splayed base which fruit-picking ladders always have. What was a fundamental defect in the ladder was the total inadequacy of the stiles for carrying weights. Of course, as happens, the plaintiff said when he was carrying his hod up he was moving fairly fast with a certain rhythm to keep his movement going, the ladder was whipping underneath and he could feel that as he went up. It may be that on previous occasions these two men have been fortunate in not having had an accident, but at the same time they were experts. That is the way the defendant puts it: they were experts far more than the defendant in ladders. They were in the building trade and they knew builders' ladders. They worked on builders' ladders, I suppose, every working day of their lives.

They gave their evidence, if I may say so, extremely frankly, as did the defendant. I have the advantage here of having had witnesses. Although there were variations on matters which do not really matter, all of them gave their evidence, I thought, extremely well. The plaintiff said as soon as he saw the ladder, 'I had doubts about it, it looked flimsy', but he said he did not complain or reject it. There it was being provided for him, and he decided to get on with the job and use it. In that respect I think he was seriously at fault, because after all he did know a good deal more about ladders than probably he had any reason to suppose a farmer did, and yet he decided to use this ladder knowing it was flimsy. That means to some extent he must bear responsibility for this accident. In all the circumstances, I think this is a fifty–fifty case.

I think both really were equally responsible. In one sense, the bricklayers would trust their building contractor, in effect, to provide material which was suitable. On the other hand, the farmer who put himself rather rashly in the position of a building contractor was to some extent entitled to look to the experienced subcontractors he was employing to check the materials, the equipment they were provided with, and to tell him if there was anything wrong with them. Then, as we see on a later occasion, that would be immediately corrected. When the carpenter came to work in the roof he refused to use the fruit-picking ladder, and an order was put in on 2nd March 1976 for a pole ladder. That was provided by Lovell Plant Hire. If only that had been done in the first instance, and ladders as well as scaffold poles had been ordered for the job, then this accident would not have happened.

When it comes to special damage I am in a bit of difficulty, because, as is more or less now conceded, the basis on which the claim is put forward seems to me to be entirely wrong. The accountant who put in the report supporting it seems to me to have worked on an entirely wrong basis. He worked on the basis of the gross earnings of each of the partners, totally ignoring the fact that it was a partnership and that all the expenses would be continuing whether one partner was away sick or whether he was not. The way I have worked, having had the benefit now of the profit and loss account, is to try and do the calculations based on the profit and loss account which does cover the two material years. In 1976 the gross income was £5,702; the net profit after deducting the expenses was £3,902. If one divides that by 52 one gets in round figures £75 a week as the earnings of the partnership. That means that each partner was earning £37·50. From that one has to make some deductions for tax and insurance. So I take a figure of about £35 a week as being the loss which the plaintiff sustained for the 11 weeks which he was away from work. There was then, it was alleged, a continuing loss which was put at £1,080, but the profit and loss account for the year 3rd May 1976 to 3rd May 1977 shows the gross earnings at £7,100 and the net profit at £4,655. That makes weekly earnings of about £89 plus, call it £90 a week, and that makes £45 a week each.

If the plaintiff was totally unemployed during that period this would produce a figure of £810, but in fact he was not. He, with great fortitude and good sense, was back at work again fairly soon, but until about 6th September he was working shorter hours. It is on this basis that I have to make some estimate as to what the loss was for that period. It was suggested that I should look at the hourly rate for a bricklayer in 1976, which was said to be about £75 to £80 a week for a 42½-hour week, but I do not see how I can do that because that is for a person who is working for a contractor and not for a person who is working on his own account as an independent contractor, as a member of a partnership. My calculations are on the basis that he was losing about an hour or so a week, perhaps the odd day a week, and I make the estimate for the 18 weeks involved at £4 a week. So the special damage comes to £385, plus £72 for the 18 weeks. There is a £10 figure for hospital costs, fares to the hospital, which has not been disputed, and I take it that it is agreed this should be added. That gives me a figure of £467. There is to be deducted half the benefits which he was drawing at the relevant period when he was earning benefit of about £69. I think if I take a round figure of £400 that would be about right.

On general damage, he made a most remarkable recovery, largely, if I may say so, owing to his own efforts, because he was back at work in a very short time after what was undoubtedly a nasty injury. A fractured oscalcis, as one knows, in many cases is a very crippling injury indeed. With some people it goes on for years and produces a very substantial degree of physical impairment. In the case of the plaintiff he had in addition a fractured talus, but that seems to have cleared up fairly quickly. He could not go into plaster straight away. He was in plaster for quite a short period, but he is left, and on the medical reports which are agreed it will probably last for the rest of his life, with an ankle which aches pretty regularly and at times he has to sit down. It shortens his hours of work, but that may improve as things go on. He was in plaster for less than a month. It think it was on 12th March that he was put into a walking plaster below the knee, and that was removed on 2nd April. So it was a very short period in plaster. That no doubt did assist to diminish his incapacity, but there is the continual aching which the surgeon says one must now accept will probably be permanent. There is also a permanent loss of movement of the ankle in the two main movements which impedes him in walking over rough ground and climbing ladders. Whether he is now capable of climbing ladders I am not sure. The last medical report says he still finds a slight difficulty in walking over rough ground and climbing ladders. Of course, climbing ladders is very much the day-to-day occupation of a person in his trade. So one cannot treat that as a trivial injury in any way, but having regard to the degree of improvement that he has

shown it is certainly in the lower order of damages for injuries of that kind. I assess the
a appropriate figure at £1,500.

   I think this is a case, although nobody has mentioned it at all, in which I ought to
include a figure under *Smith v Manchester City Council* (1974) 118 Sol Jo 597 for potential
loss of earnings, because if a person who has this impairment were to go on to the open
labour market and seek to get employment in the ordinary way, not self-employed but
become an employed person, his difficulties in getting employment would be
b substantially impaired. At the moment and for years he has been working as an
independent contractor, and accordingly the figure that I shall award for the potential
future loss of earnings is again in the low bracket. I assess that at £1,000. That makes
a total, with the £400 special damage, of £2,900, and as I have held that he is 50% to
blame, that means he is entitled to recover half that figure, namely £1,450.

c *Judgment for the plaintiff for £1,450.*

Solicitors: *C R Thomson & Son*, Maidenhead (for the plaintiff); *Kidd, Rapient, Badge & Co*,
Maidenhead (for the defendant).

K Mydeen Esq   Barrister.

d

Weller v Akehurst and another

CHANCERY DIVISION
e FOX J
16th JULY, 23rd OCTOBER, 21st NOVEMBER 1980

*Landlord and tenant – Rent – Review – Failure to comply with time limits – Effect – Clause
providing machinery for determination of rent for specified period of term – No other provision
in lease for rent during that period – Notice to operate clause to be given by landlord within
f specified time limits before termination of preceding period of term – Lease expressly providing
that time of the essence – Landlord failing to give notice within time limits – Whether failure
precluding recourse to machinery for determination of rent – Whether proper inference that
parties intended old rent to continue.*

   Under a lease of premises for 14 years from 1st July 1972 the tenant was to pay a rent of
g £850 a year for the first seven years and for the second seven years the open market rental
value of the premises at the review date. The lease provided that the open market rental
value was to be either (i) a sum specified in a notice in writing to the tenant at any time
before the beginning of a clear period of two quarters of a year immediately preceding
the review date, or (ii) a sum agreed between the parties before the expiration of three
months immediately after the posting of such notice or (iii) a sum determined by an
h independent surveyor to be appointed jointly by the parties. Clause 1(4)(1) provided that
if such a determination of an independent surveyor was not published prior to the
review date the tenant was to pay rent at the yearly rate payable immediately before the
review date. The lease further provided that all stipulations as to time in the rent
provisions of the lease were to be of the essence of the contract and incapable of
enlargement save by agreement between the parties. By a letter dated 25th January 1979
the landlord purported to give the tenant notice specifying that the annual rent under
j the lease for the second seven-year period commencing 1st July 1979 was to be £2,500
a year. Pursuant to the terms of the lease however the clear period of two quarters of a
year commenced on 25th December 1978, and accordingly the notice was out of time.
The landlord sought the determination by the court of the rent payable under the lease
for the second seven years. The tenant contended that the rent review provisions having

become inoperative because of the landlord's failure to observe the timetable, the rent for the second seven years was, pursuant to cl 1(4)(1) of the lease, the rent payable *a* immediately before the review date.

Held – (1) Although the lease provided that the rent for the second seven years was to be the open market rental value and defined that term with sufficient precision, the lease also required the ascertainment of the open market rental value to be effected in a particular way and stipulated that time was to be of the essence of that procedure. *b* Furthermore, although in general strict adherence to timetables specified in a rent review clause was not of the essence of a lease, where the parties provided that it was of the essence the court would give effect to their expressed intention. The parties having chosen the procedure for rent review with precision and having made it plain that that procedure was only to be available on a strict timetable, it followed that the procedure was intended to be followed timeously or not at all (see p 415 *c* to *g*, post); dicta of Lord *c* Diplock in *United Scientific Holdings Ltd v Burnley Borough Council* [1977] 2 All ER at 67, 77 applied; *Kenilworth Industrial Sites Ltd v E C Little & Co Ltd* [1975] 1 All ER 53 distinguished.

(2) The tenant could not rely on the provisions of cl 1(4)(1) to deal with the position, since it was clear that that provision assumed that an independent surveyor had already been appointed pursuant to the rent review clause and did not deal with the circumstances *d* where no surveyor had been or could any longer be appointed (see p 416 *b* to *e*, post).

(3) Since the rent review provision contained strict requirements for its operation and since it did not operate because the person at whose option the rent review was to be made had not complied with those requirements, the reasonable and necessary inference was that in the circumstances the parties intended the old rent to continue. The court would accordingly make a declaration that the rent for the second seven years was to be *e* £850 a year (see p 416 *e* to *j*, post).

Notes
For agreements to review rents subject to a time limit for giving notice, see Supplement to 23 Halsbury's Laws (3rd Edn) para 1197A, and for a case on the subject, see 31(1) Digest *f* (Reissue) 481, 3952.

Cases referred to in judgment
Brown v Gould [1971] 2 All ER 1505, [1972] Ch 53, [1971] 3 WLR 334, 22 P & CR 871, 31(1) Digest (Reissue) 285, 2351.
Kenilworth Industrial Sites Ltd v E C Little & Co Ltd [1975] 1 All ER 53, [1975] 1 WLR 143, *g* 29 P & CR 141, CA, Digest (Cont Vol D) 580, 3952c.
United Scientific Holdings Ltd v Burnley Borough Council, Cheapside Land Development Co Ltd v Messels Service Co [1977] 2 All ER 62, [1978] AC 904, [1977] 2 WLR 806, 75 LGR 407, 33 P & CR 220, HL, Digest (Cont Vol E) 364, 3952ba.

h
Summons
By an originating summons dated 24th April 1980 Florence Lily Weller ('the landlord') sought (i) a declaration that a letter dated 25th January 1979 sent by the landlord to Richard Charles Akehurst and Jill Susan Akehurst ('the tenants') purportedly pursuant to cl 1(3)(a) of a lease dated 14th August 1972 and made between the landlord of the one part and Eric David Filmer (the tenants' predecessor in title) of the other part of a shop, *j* store and dwelling house at 29–29A Church Street, Willingdon, Eastbourne, East Sussex, for a term of 14 years from 1st July 1972 was a valid notice for the purposes of that clause, or (ii) alternatively, the determination of whether on the true construction of the lease and in the events which had happened the rent reserved for the residue of the term demised was (a) the open market value of the premises at the review date as defined in

the lease or (b) £850 per annum or (c) some other and if so what rent. The facts are set

a out in the judgment.

Nigel Meares for the landlord.

John Stuart Colyer QC and *Jonathan Brock* for the tenants.

Cur adv vult

b 21st November. **FOX J** read the following judgment: This case is concerned with the interpretation of a rent review clause in a lease. The lease is dated 14th August 1972 and is a lease of a shop, store and dwelling house. The term demised was 14 years from 1st July 1972.

Clause 1 of the lease makes the following provisions as to rent:

c '(a) For the first Seven Years of the said term a yearly rent of £850 (b) For the next Seven Years of the said term the open market value of the demised premises at the review date which revised rent shall remain constant during the whole period referred to in this sub-clause . . . Provided that for the purposes of sub-clause (b) hereof it is hereby agreed that the following definitions and provisions shall apply namely:—

d '(1) The expression "open market value" means the annual rental value of the demised premises on the open market which might reasonably be demanded by a willing Landlord on a lease for a term of years certain equivalent in length to the residue unexpired at the review date of the term of years hereby granted with vacant possession at the commencement of the term but upon the supposition (if not a fact) that the tenant has complied with all the obligations as to repair and decoration herein imposed on the tenant (but without prejudice to any rights or

e remedies of the lessor in regard thereto) and there being disregarded (if applicable) those matters set out in paragraphs (a) (b) and (c) of Section 34 of the Landlord and Tenant Act 1954 and there being disregarded (so far as may be permitted by law) all restrictions whatsoever relating to rent or to security of tenure contained in any statute or orders rules or regulations thereunder . . . such lease being on the same

f terms and conditions . . . as this present demise without the payment of any fine or premium . . .

'(2) The expression "review date" means the expiration of the Seventh year of the said term for the purpose of ascertainment of the open market rental value under sub-clause (b) hereof

'(3) The open market rental value shall be determined in manner following that

g is to say it shall be such annual sum as shall be (a) specified in a notice in writing signed by or on behalf of the Lessor and posted by recorded delivery post in a prepaid envelope addressed to the Tenant at the demised premises at any time before the beginning of a clear period of two quarters of a year (commencing on one of the usual quarter days hereinbefore mentioned) immediately preceding the review date . . . or (b) agreed between the parties before the expiration of three

h months immediately after the date of posting of such notice as aforesaid in substitution for the said sum or (c) determined by the election of the Tenant (to be made by counter-notice in writing served by the Tenants upon the Lessor not later than the expiration of the said three months) by an independent surveyor appointed for that purpose by the parties jointly in writing or upon their failure to agree upon such appointment within one month immediately after the date of service of the said counter-notice then by an independent surveyor appointed for that purpose on

i the application of either party alone by the President for the time being of the Royal Institution of Chartered Surveyors and in either case in accordance with the provisions of the Arbitration Act 1950

'(4) (1) In the event of the determination of such independent surveyor not having been published prior to the review date for any reason whatever then in respect of the period of time (hereinafter called the said interval) beginning with the review date and ending on the quarter day immediately following the date on which such determination shall have been published the Tenant shall pay to the Lessor in manner hereinbefore provided rent at the yearly rate payable immediately before the review date PROVIDED that at the expiration of the said interval there shall be due as a debt payable by the Tenant to the Lessor or on demand a sum of money equal to the amount whereby the yearly rent determined by such independent surveyor shall exceed the yearly rent at the yearly rate aforesaid but duly apportioned on a daily basis in respect of the said interval

'(5) All stipulations as to time in the foregoing sub-clauses numbered (1) (2) (3) and (4) shall be of the essence of the contract and shall not be capable of enlargement save as agreed in writing by the parties . . .'

By a letter to the tenants dated 25th January 1979 on behalf of the landlord, it was specified that the annual rent payable under the lease for the period of seven years commencing 1st July 1979 should be £2,500 per annum. The notice contained in that letter purported to be given under the provisions of cl 1(3)(a) of the lease. In fact, however, the clear period of two quarters of a year commencing on one of the usual quarter days and immediately preceding the review date commenced on 25th December 1978 (not on 25th January 1979). Clause 1(3)(a) requires the notice to be sent at any time before the commencement of the said clear period to which I have referred.

In these circumstances, the originating summons asks: (1) for a declaration that the letter of 25th January 1979 was a valid notice for the purposes of cl 1(3) of the lease, or (2) alternatively, that it may be determined whether on the true construction of the lease the rent reserved for the seven-year period from the review date is (a) the open market value (as defined in the lease) of the premises at the review date or (b) £850 per annum or (c) some other and if so what rent.

In the event, it was conceded by the plaintiff landlord that the letter of 25th January 1979 was *not* a good notice for the purposes of cl 1(3) of the lease as it was not given in time. The question then is what rent is payable for the seven years of the lease commencing on the review date.

It is contended on behalf of the landlord that such rent is the open market value (as defined in the lease) of the premises at the review date and that the court should now order an inquiry to determine that. It is submitted by the tenants that such rent is £850 per annum (ie the original rent).

The argument on behalf of the landlord, put shortly, is this. The lease expressly provides that for the second seven years of the term (ie the seven years from the review date) the rent payable shall be the open market value. That expression is defined in the lease in terms sufficiently certain to be capable of ascertainment. Accordingly, while it is true that the particular machinery contained in cl 1(3) of the lease for ascertaining the open market value cannot be operated (because the landlord failed to serve in due time the notice which would bring cl 1(3) into operation), nevertheless the open market value is capable of ascertainment and the court should direct an inquiry for that purpose. The rent so ascertained would then be the rent payable for the second seven years of the term.

I do not feel able to accept that argument. The open market value as defined in the lease is, it is true (as indeed is conceded by the landlord) expressed with sufficient certainty to be capable of ascertainment. But the lease expressly provides in cl 1(3) that the open market value shall be determined 'in manner following that is to say it shall be such annual sum as shall be . . .' There then follows the series of provisions, all of which hinge on the giving by the landlord of such a notice as is specified in cl 1(3)(a). The landlord failed to give such notice within the time specified in the lease. Further, cl 1(5) provides that all stipulations as to time in the relevant provisions of the lease shall be of the essence of the contract and shall not be capable of enlargement save by agreement between the parties.

The general presumption is that strict adherence to the timetables specified in the rent review clause is not of the essence of the contract: see the decision of the House of Lords in *United Scientific Holdings Ltd v Burnley Borough Council* [1977] 2 All ER 62, [1978] AC 904. But as Lord Diplock observed ([1977] 2 All ER 62 at 67, [1978] AC 904 at 923):

'It is not disputed that the parties to a lease may provide expressly that time is or time is not of the essence of the contract in respect of all or any of the steps required to be taken by the landlord to obtain the determination of an increased rent, and that if they do so the court will give effect to their expressed intention.'

Later he said ([1977] 2 All ER 62 at 77, [1978] AC 904 at 936):

'. . . the best way of eliminating all uncertainty in future rent review clauses is to state expressly whether or not stipulations as to the time by which any step provided for by the clause is to be taken shall be treated as being of the essence.'

The position therefore in the present case is that although the lease provides that the rent shall be the open market value and defines that term with sufficient precision, the lease also requires that the ascertainment of the open market value shall be effected in a particular way and stipulates that time shall be of the essence of the provisions in that procedure.

In my judgment, the parties cannot have intended that if the landlord failed to observe the time provisions she could still be free to obtain the determination of the open market value by the court. The parties chose the procedure for rent review with precision and made it plain that the procedure was only to be available on a strict timetable. The landlord having failed to observe that timetable, it seems to me that there is thereafter no room for the operation of any procedure to determine the open market value. If the open market value cannot 'be determined in manner following' (to use the language in cl 1(3)) it cannot, in my view, be determined at all. Clause 1(3) states in terms that the open market value shall be 'such annual sum as shall be . . .' There then follow paras (a), (b) and (c). That language, coupled with the direction for determination 'in manner following', excludes, I think, the possibility of it being any other sum or determined in any other way. For the court now to take on itself the determination of the open market value would, I think, be to fly in the face of the clearly expressed requirement of strict compliance with the time provisions. I think that the rent revision procedure was intended to be carried out timeously or not at all. The provision for revising the rent was in the landlord's favour; only the landlord could invoke it. But the landlord could only invoke it on strict terms. I see no reason to suppose that the parties intended that the landlord should get a rent increase in any other way.

I was referred to the decision of the Court of Appeal in *Kenilworth Industrial Sites Ltd v E C & Co Ltd* [1975] 1 All ER 53, [1975] 1 WLR 143, but I do not think that that decision assists me on any aspect of the present case since in *Kenilworth* it was held that time was not of the essence of the provisions. And, in so far as the case proceeded on the basis of a dichotomy between 'option' clauses on the one hand and 'obligation' or 'machinery' provisions on the other, it is now inconsistent with the decision of the House of Lords in *United Scientific Holdings Ltd v Burnley Borough Council* [1977] 2 All ER 62 at 77, [1978] AC 904 at 936 per Lord Diplock. I was also referred to *Brown v Gould* [1971] 2 All ER 815, [1972] Ch 53. In that case the lease contained a formula for ascertaining the rent but no machinery for working out the formula. The question was whether the provision was void for uncertainty. It was held that it was not; the court could itself work out the formula. In the present case the lease provides both a formula and a specific mode of working out the formula. The question is whether, in view of the provisions that time is of the essence, any other mode of working out the formula is permissible. For the reasons which I have given, I do not think that it is.

I should add this. If the landlord gave a bona fide notice under cl 1(3)(a) stating an amount which was in fact above the open market value and the tenants failed to give a counter-notice in due time, the tenants could not, I think, invoke the definition to redress the position. The tenants would have to accept the amount stated in the landlord's notice. It would be a curious result if the tenants, having failed to observe the timetable, are bound by the cl 1(3) procedure but if the landlord fails to serve notice in time, the landlord can still get the open market value determined by the court.

I should mention that the expression used in the opening sentence of cl 1(3) is 'open market *rental* value' not 'open market value', but that, I think, was merely a slip and the contrary was not contended.

The result in my view is that the provisions of cl 1(3) are wholly inoperative and that the provisions of the lease do not permit the open market value to be determined in any other manner than that specified in cl 1(3).

In those circumstances, the tenants assert that the rent for the second seven years is £850 per annum. Two arguments are advanced in support of that. First, it is contended that the position is expressly dealt with by cl 1(4). It is said that the language of that provision is very wide. It begins: 'In the event of the determination of such independent surveyor not having been published prior to the review date for any reason whatever ...' While I agree that that language is indeed wide, it seems to me that cl 1(4) is assuming that an independent surveyor has been duly appointed under cl 1(3). The provision, I think, is simply dealing with the period which elapsed after the review date until the quarter day after the determination of the rent by the surveyor. The whole provision, I think, assumes that the surveyor will issue a determination, but that there will be an interval before he does so. Thus the proviso begins: 'PROVIDED that at the expiration of the said interval ...' I do not think that cl 1(4) is dealing at all with the present circumstances where no surveyor has been or can now be appointed.

In my view, therefore, the lease contains no express provisions to deal with the present case.

What then is the position? That the parties should, in the circumstances, have contemplated that no rent at all should be payable for the residue of the term, I reject altogether. The lease grants a term for 14 years and it is inconceivable that the parties contemplated that no rent might be payable during the second period of seven years.

A liability on the part of the tenant to pay rent must have been intended. The question is how much. In my opinion, if the parties had been asked at the time of the grant of the lease what was to happen if the lessor chose not to serve a notice under cl 1(3), or failed to serve such notice in time, it is wholly reasonable to suppose that they would have said that the old rent of £850 per annum was to continue. Thus, I do not think that the parties could have been contemplating any reduction of the rent at all. The lease was granted during a period of inflation, and it is clear that only the landlord could set the cl 1(3) procedure in motion. It was a provision for the landlord's benefit.

On the other hand, I see no reason to suppose that they would have contemplated that the rent should be increased in the event of no valid notice being given under cl 1(3) by the landlord. The landlord was adequately protected by cl 1(3) if he wished to increase the rent in line with the market. But, it having been agreed that time was of the essence of those provisions, it cannot, in my view, have been contemplated that, having failed to operate cl 1(3), the landlord should still be free to get the rent increased by a quite different machinery not expressed in the lease at all. Clause 1(3) was in general for the benefit of the landlord but the time provisions in cl 1(3)(a) were for the protection of the tenant.

What I am dealing with is a rent review provision containing strict requirements for its operation. It did not operate because the person at whose option the rent review was to be made did not comply with the requirements. I think that in those circumstances the reasonable and necessary inference is that the old rent continues. I will so declare.

Declaration accordingly.

Solicitors: *Mayo & Perkins*, Eastbourne (for the landlord); *Burton & Ramsden* (for the tenants).

Azza M Abdallah   Barrister.

a # R v Crown Court at Knightsbridge, ex parte International Sporting Club (London) Ltd and another

QUEEN'S BENCH DIVISION

b GRIFFITHS LJ AND MAY J

12th, 13th, 14th, 15th MAY, 5th JUNE 1981

Certiorari – Error of law on face of record – Form of record – Inferior court – Decision of court embodied in formal order – Judge giving reasons for decision in oral judgment – Whether judge's oral judgment forming part of record.

c

Between 1974 and 1979 the licences to run three London casinos were held by limited companies all of which were subsidiaries of a large gaming group. The clubs were operated in a manner which seriously contravened the Gaming Act 1968 and in 1979 the police and the gaming board applied to the licensing justices to cancel the companies' licences. The justices having heard evidence of serious breaches of the 1968 Act cancelled *d* the licences on the ground that the companies were not fit and proper persons to hold a gaming licence. The companies gave notice of appeal to the Crown Court and, as they were entitled to do pending the outcome of the appeal, continued to operate the casinos. Prior to the hearing of the appeal, however, the gaming group sold their entire interests in the three clubs and their shares in the companies to new owners. At the hearing of the appeal before the Crown Court, which was by way of a rehearing, the new *e* owners contended that regardless of the companies' past misconduct, they had been completely restructured with new shareholders and management and were fit and proper persons to hold a licence. At the end of the hearing the Crown Court dismissed the companies' appeals and a formal order to that effect was drawn up. The judge also delivered an oral judgment in which he gave the reasons for the dismissal of the appeals. The judge stated that the question whether the companies were fit and proper *f* persons could only be judged by their past conduct and in effect disregarded the restructuring in deciding that point. The new owners applied to the Divisional Court for orders of certiorari to quash the Crown Court's decision, on the ground that the judge's oral judgment disclosed an error on the face of the record in that it showed that the court had not taken the restructuring into account when deciding whether there were grounds for cancelling the licences. At the hearing of the application the police and the gaming *g* board contended, inter alia, that the 'record' was confined to the formal order and did not include the oral reasons given by the judge for the decision.

Held – Orders of certiorari to quash the Crown Court's decision would be granted for the following reasons—

(1) For the purposes of granting certiorari for error on the face of the record, the *h* 'record' was not restricted to the formal order but extended to the reasons given by the judge in his oral judgment and set out in the official transcript thereof (see p 421 *j* to p 422 *b*, p 423 *a b* and p 424 *b c*, post); *R v Northumberland Compensation Appeal Tribunal, ex parte Shaw* [1952] 1 All ER 122 applied; *Walsall Overseers v London and North Western Railway Co* (1878) 4 App Cas 30 not followed.

(2) When considering whether grounds for the cancellation of the companies' licences *j* had been established and in particular whether the companies were at the time of the hearing fit and proper persons to hold a gaming licence, the Crown Court ought to have taken into account the restructuring of the companies. If the court found that, as a result of the restructuring, the companies were fit and proper persons but that there were other grounds for cancelling the licences, eg because the premises had been used for an unlawful purpose, then it should have gone on to consider whether to exercise its

discretion to cancel the licences, at which stage it was entitled to take into account the companies' past misconduct. Since the judge's oral reasons showed that the court had *a* taken past misconduct into account at the stage of considering whether the companies were fit and proper persons rather than at the later stage of deciding whether to exercise its discretion and had thereby ignored the restructuring of the companies, the record disclosed an error on its face (see p 424 *j* to p 425 *b* and p 426 *d* to *j*, post).

Per Curiam. It is the function of professional judges to give reasons for their decisions and the court will look askance at a refusal by an inferior judge to do so, particularly if *b* a party has requested that reasons be given. It may be that in such a case the court has power to order the judge to give reasons for his decision (see p 423 *d e*, post).

Notes

For error on the face of the record, see 1 Halsbury's Laws (4th Edn) para 84, and for cases on the subject, see 16 Digest (Reissue) 425–427, 4683–4701.

For the remedy of certiorari, see 1 Halsbury's Laws (4th Edn) paras 147–167, and for *c* cases on the subject, see 16 Digest (Reissue) 388–435, 4237–4797.

Cases referred to in judgment

Baldwin & Francis Ltd v Patents Appeal Tribunal [1959] 2 All ER 433, [1959] AC 663, [1959] 2 WLR 826, [1959] RPC 221, HL, 16 Digest (Reissue) 394, 4355.

Gilmore's Application, Re [1957] 1 All ER 796, [1957] 1 QB 574, [1957] 2 WLR 498, CA, *d* 16 Digest (Reissue) 427, 4700.

Inland Revenue Comrs v National Federation of Self-Employed and Small Businesses Ltd [1981] 2 All ER 93, [1981] 2 WLR 722, HL.

R v Chertsey Justices, ex parte Franks [1961] 1 All ER 825, [1961] 2 QB 152, [1961] 2 WLR 442, 125 JP 305, 59 LGR 260, 12 P & CR 278, DC, 16 Digest (Reissue) 416, 4578.

R v Crown Court at Knightsbridge, ex parte Ladup Ltd (18th March 1980, unreported). *e*

R v Crown Court at Leeds, ex parte City of Bradford Chief Constable [1975] 1 All ER 133, [1975] QB 314, [1974] 3 WLR 715, 139 JP 156, DC.

R v Justices for Court of Quarter Sessions for the County of Leicester, ex parte Gilks [1966] Crim LR 613, DC.

R v Northumberland Compensation Appeal Tribunal, ex parte Shaw [1952] 1 All ER 122, [1952] 1 KB 338, 116 JP 54, 50 LGR 193, 2 P & CR 361, CA; *affg* [1951] 1 All ER 268, *f* [1951] 1 KB 711, DC, 16 Digest (Reissue) 425, 4686.

R v Preston Supplementary Benefits Appeal Tribunal, ex parte Moore [1975] 2 All ER 807, [1975] 1 WLR 624, CA, Digest (Cont Vol D) 711, 94Ac.

R v Supplementary Benefits Commission, ex parte Singer [1973] 2 All ER 931, [1973] 1 WLR 713, [1973] RA 97, DC, Digest (Cont Vol D) 1052, 1710a.

Racecourse Betting Control Board v Secretary of State for Air [1944] 1 All ER 60, [1944] Ch *g* 114, 113 LJ Ch 129, 170 LT 29, CA, 17 Digest (Reissue) 498, 157.

South East Asia Fire Bricks Sdn Bhd v Non-Metallic Mineral Products Manufacturing Employees Union [1980] 2 All ER 689, [1981] AC 363, [1980] 3 WLR 318, PC.

Walsall Overseers v London and North Western Railway Co (1878) 4 App Cas 30, 48 LJMC 65, 39 LT 453, 43 JP 108, HL, 16 Digest (Reissue) 244, 2384.

Cases also cited *h*

Anisminic Ltd v Foreign Compensation Commission [1969] 1 All ER 208, [1969] 2 AC 147, HL.

Attorney General v British Broadcasting Corpn [1980] 3 All ER 161, [1981] AC 303, HL.

Boulter v Kent Justices [1897] AC 556, HL.

Company, Re a [1980] 2 All ER 634, [1981] AC 374, HL.

Hanks v Minister of Housing and Local Government [1963] 1 All ER 47, [1963] 1 QB 999. *j*

Pearlman v Keepers and Governors of Harrow School [1979] 1 All ER 365, [1979] QB 56, CA.

R v Midhurst Justices, ex parte Thompson [1973] 3 All ER 1164, [1974] QB 137, DC.

R v Patents Appeal Tribunal, ex parte Swift & Co [1962] 1 All ER 610, [1962] 2 QB 647.

Applications for judicial review

The International Sporting Club (London) Ltd and Palm Beach Club Ltd applied, with

the leave of the Divisional Court granted on 9th April 1981, for orders of certiorari
a quashing the decision of the Crown Court at Knightsbridge (his Honour Judge Friend
and four licensing magistrates) given on 9th March 1981 dismissing the applicants'
appeals against an order of the Gaming Licensing Committee for the South Westminster
Division of Inner London made on 24th September 1980 cancelling the gaming licences
held by the applicants under the Gaming Act 1968 in respect of the International
Sporting Club and Palm Beach Club casinos in London.   The facts are set out in the
b judgment of the court.

Gavin Lightman QC and *D W Tudor Price* for International Sporting Club Ltd.
Mark Cran for Palm Beach Club Ltd.
John Marriage QC and *Timothy Cassel* for the Commissioner of Police of the Metropolis.
Simon Ruckey QC for the Gaming Board.

c
Cur adv vult

5th June.   **GRIFFITHS LJ** read the following judgment of the court: Between 1974 and
1979 Coral Leisure Group Ltd controlled and managed three London gaming clubs: they
were the International Sporting Club, the Curzon House Club and the Palm Beach
d Club.   The clubs were very badly run and with scant regard to the provisions of the
Gaming Act 1968.   Eventually they were all raided by the police in November 1979 and
thereafter the Metropolitan Police Commissioner and the Gaming Board of Great Britain
joined in applications to the Gaming Licensing Committee for the South Westminster
division to cancel the gaming licences of the three clubs.
In each case the gaming licence was held by a limited company.   They were
e International Sporting Club (London) Ltd, Curzon House Club Ltd and Palm Beach Club
Ltd.   Coral Casinos (UK) Ltd, a wholly-owned subsidiary of Coral Leisure Group Ltd,
owned the whole of the share capital of the International Sporting Club Ltd and Curzon
House Club Ltd, and Coral Leisure Group Ltd itself owned two-thirds of the share capital
of Palm Beach Club Ltd, the remaining one-third being owned by Gordon Hotels Ltd.
Coral Casinos (UK) Ltd were responsible for the management of each of the clubs.
f The applications to cancel the licences were made on three grounds: first, that the
companies were not fit and proper persons to hold a gaming licence; second, that Coral
Casinos (UK) Ltd, for whose benefit the clubs were operated, were not fit and proper
persons to hold a licence and third that the clubs had been used for unlawful purposes.
The evidence took many days to hear and revealed a whole catalogue of wrongdoing.
It is not necessary to enumerate all the various breaches of the 1968 Act that the
companies had been committing; it will suffice to say that they were numerous, serious
g and extended over a number of years.   The licensing committee on 24th September 1980
cancelled the licences on the ground that the companies were not fit and proper persons
to hold gaming licences.   It is conceded that that was a proper finding and a correct
exercise of their discretion by the licensing committee on the material then before them.
The committee did not make any specific finding on whether the clubs had been used
for an unlawful purpose or purport to cancel the licence on that ground.   No doubt it
h seemed to them unnecessary to do so.   But had they wished to do so it appears that there
was ample material on which they could have acted.   Nevertheless, although the
committee invited submissions on the point, it did not exercise its discretion to disqualify
the premises under para 49 of Sch 2 to the 1968 Act.
On 9th October the companies entered notices of appeal.   That meant that despite the
fact that their licences had been cancelled the clubs could continue operating until their
j appeals were determined by the Crown Court: see Sch 2, para 44.
Before the hearing of the appeal there was much business activity.   The two Coral
companies sold out their entire interests in the three clubs, and handed over their
management to the new owners.   They sold the shares of the International Sporting Club
(London) Ltd to AVP Ltd, a wholly-owned subsidiary of Lonrho Ltd.   They sold the
shares of the Curzon House Club Ltd to the Aspinal organisation.   They sold the two-

thirds share-holding in Palm Beach Club Ltd to Mecca Sportsman Ltd. By the time the appeal commenced on 17th February 1981 Coral Casinos (UK) Ltd had ceased to have any *a* interest in the ownership or management of any of the clubs, and the appeals were pursued by the new owners.

An appeal to the Crown Court is by way of rehearing. Counsel for the Metropolitan Police Commissioner opened the facts to the court but he was not required to call any evidence because the transgressions of the three companies that had been proved before the licensing authority were admitted, and it was also conceded that at the date of the *b* hearing in September the companies were not fit and proper persons to hold a licence. Nevertheless we are told it took counsel a day to open the facts which gives some idea of the scale of the past wrongdoing.

The new owners of the clubs called a great deal of evidence in an attempt to satisfy the Crown Court that, whatever their past sins, the casino companies were completely reformed characters and were now fit and proper persons to hold gaming licences. Their *c* argument was that, whereas it might be difficult for an individual with a bad record to persuade a court that he had completely reformed, a company was in a different position for it was as good or as bad as the people who controlled and managed it and, where there had been a complete change of share holding and management, there should be no impediment to holding that the company was now a fit and proper person to hold a gaming licence if the shareholders and managements were now respectable and capable *d* of the proper management of a gaming club. But their argument did not prevail and the appeals were dismissed.

The hearing in the Crown Court was before a circuit judge sitting with four licensing magistrates. At the end of the hearing the judge gave a judgment in which he gave the reasons why the appeals were dismissed. He ended his judgment by saying:

'For those reasons, I think it is right that I should express our reasons and the *e* appeal is dismissed. I could have said simply, "The appeals are dismissed", but I thought it right and proper that you should all know precisely why they are dismissed.'

In these proceedings the International Sporting Club (London) Ltd and the Palm Beach Club Ltd apply for orders of certiorari to quash the orders of the Crown Court dismissing *f* their appeals on the grounds that the reasons stated in the judgment show errors of law on the face of the record; alternatively that the Crown Court exceeded their jurisdiction or, in the further alternative, that the Crown Court failed to determine the question referred.

Counsel for the Gaming Board, with the somewhat reluctant support of counsel for the Metropolitan Police, has submitted that the judgment forms no part of the 'record' *g* and that this court is entitled to look only at the formal order of the court and not at the reasons that the court gave for making the order.

If this submission is well founded, the supervisory power of this court to review the decisions of inferior courts for errors of law will be drastically curtailed. The 'order' of the court rarely, if ever, contains the reasons that led to the making of the order. The order merely recites the decision of the court, not its reasons. In the case of an appeal the *h* order will normally say no more than 'it is ordered that the appeal be dismissed' and then record any order as to costs. So, if it is only the order that constitutes the record, there will be scarcely any occasion when it will be possible to obtain an order for certiorari on the ground of error of law on the face of the record. In fact in the present case the order was drawn in a somewhat curious form; it is dated 9th March 1981 and reads:

'In the appeals of Curzon House Club Ltd., International Sporting Club (London) *j* Ltd. and Palm Beach Casino Club Ltd. On the 9th March 1981 when the appeals were dismissed. The above-named appellants were ordered to pay one third of the taxed or agreed costs of the respondents: (1) The Commissioner of Police for the Metropolis; (2) The Gaming Board; and (3) Licensing Justices.'

a Counsel for International Sporting Club (London) Ltd has argued that the order does not record the dismissal of the appeals but by the use of the word 'when' refers to it only as a matter of history and that accordingly the only record of the dismissal of the appeal is to be found in the judgment which, whatever the general rule, must in this particular case form a part of the record. We cannot accept this submission; we read the order as recording the dismissal of the appeal; if the general rule is found to be that the reasons contained in a judgment do not form part of the record they should not be admitted b because of some slightly unusual wording used by a clerk in drawing up the order of the court.

The historical review of the use of certiorari by the Court of King's Bench to exercise a supervisory jurisdiction over inferior courts and tribunals contained in the judgments of Lord Goddard CJ and Denning LJ in *R v Northumberland Compensation Appeal Tribunal, ex parte Shaw* [1951] 1 All ER 268, [1951] 1 KB 711; [1952] 1 All ER 122, [1952] 1 KB c 338 show how for over a hundred years the use of certiorari to quash a decision for error of law on the face of the record fell into disuse. So far as criminal jurisdiction was concerned, it flowed from the decision of Parliament to put a stop to the over-formalistic approach of the lawyers which allowed the conviction by the lower court to be quashed for any defect in form in any of the documents that in the seventeenth and eighteenth centuries the Court of King's Bench required to be kept as part of the record of the d inferior court. These included the charge, the evidence and the reasons for the conviction.

The result was that many convictions were quashed for want of form rather than merit. This unsatisfactory state of affairs was put an end to by the Summary Jurisdiction Act 1848 which prescribed a standard form in which convictions were to be recorded but which omitted any mention of the evidence or the reasons for the decision. Therefore, e as the record no longer disclosed the reasons of the justices, there was nothing at which the court could look to see if they had made an error of law and certiorari fell into disuse save in those cases in which it was alleged that the court or tribunal had exceeded or abused its jurisdiction. In so far as civil matters were concerned the Summary Jurisdiction Act 1857 enabled justices to state a case for the opinion of the court and this enabled the parties to have points of law decided without resort to certiorari.

f So far had the jurisdiction to quash for error of law on the face of the record been forgotten that its very existence was denied by the Court of Appeal in *Racecourse Betting Control Board v Secretary of State for Air* [1944] 1 All ER 60, [1944] Ch 114. But that case was decided without full citation of authority and was disapproved in *R v Northumberland Compensation Appeal Tribunal, ex parte Shaw*, particularly by Lord Goddard CJ, who had been a party to the earlier decision of the Court of Appeal in the *Racecourse Betting Control Board* case.

g Once reborn, the jurisdiction has proved to be a most valuable development in our system of administrative law. In the ever increasing complexity of a modern society there has inevitably been a great increase in the number of tribunals required to regulate their affairs. Trained lawyers play their part in manning these bodies but it is neither possible, because there are not enough lawyers, nor desirable, because lawyers may lack h the special expertise of people from other walks of life, that they should all be in the hands of the lawyers. Laymen play their part and will often outnumber and be able to outvote any lawyer among them when it comes to making a decision. The citizen affected by these decisions is entitled to expect that they will be given in accordance with the law and, if the rule of law is to mean anything, a court manned by trained lawyers is required to speak with authority to correct the decision where it appears that it is j founded on error of law. This function is now performed in many cases by the Divisional Court of the Queen's Bench Division by the use of an order of certiorari to quash an erroneous decision; in other cases Parliament may often give a right of appeal to the High Court.

But before the Divisional Court can exercise its supervisory jurisdiction it must be able to see what the error of law is said to be. A document to which anyone would naturally expect it to look must surely be that which records the reasons given by the court or tribunal for its decision, in this case the transcript of Judge Friend's judgment.

In the collective experience of the members of this court and the very experienced counsel appearing before us it has been the practice of the Divisional Court under the presidency of successive Lord Chief Justices over the last four decades to receive the reasons given by a court or tribunal for its decision and if they show error of law to allow certiorari to go to quash the decision. The court has regarded the reasons as part of the record. They are sometimes referred to as a 'speaking order'. Many of the cases are of course unreported but examples of the court acting on such reasons are to be found in *R v Chertsey Justices, ex parte Franks* [1961] 1 All ER 825, [1961] 2 QB 152 (an oral judgment of magistrates), *R v Justices for Court of Quarter Sessions for the County of Leicester, ex parte Gilks* (1966) Crim LR 613 (an oral judgment of quarter sessions), *R v Crown Court at Leeds, ex parte City of Bradford Chief Constable* [1975] 1 All ER 133, [1975] 1 QB 314 (an oral judgment of the Crown Court in a liquor licensing appeal). *R v Supplementary Benefits Commission, ex parte Singer* [1973] 2 All ER 931, [1973] 1 WLR 713 shows how far the modern practice has extended to include the reasons for a decision as part of the record. The applicant was aggrieved by a refusal of a grant of legal aid on the ground that the Supplementary Benefits Commission had determined his disposable income at greater than £950 pa. Bridge J, giving the reserved judgment of the Divisional Court, said ([1973] 2 All ER 931 at 932, [1973] 1 WLR 713 at 715):

'There is no document before the court embodying the commission's determination, although that is the order sought to be quashed, because it was not communicated directly to the applicant but only to the Law Society. But on hearing of it the applicant wrote to the Department of Health and Social Security, as representing the commission, on 15th June 1972 expressing himself as "completely mystified" by the decision, setting out his financial circumstances, and asking that the matter might receive further consideration. The department replied on 29th June 1972 on behalf of the commission: "A thorough re-examination", the writer says, "has been made of the basis of the determination already issued to the Law Society". The letter proceeds to set out that basis, in other words, to disclose the reasons for the earlier determination, and concludes: "I must confirm that the determination was correct." Counsel for the commission has taken the point that the letter of 29th June is not part of the record relating to the determination which is questioned; indeed, that there is no such record available for the court to consider. We cannot accept this submission. It seems to us that whenever a statutory body, having made a decision of a kind which can be questioned in proceedings for an order of certiorari, has subsequently chosen to disclose the reasons for the decision, whether it could have been compelled to do so or not, and however informal the document embodying the reasons, the decision with the added reasons becomes a "speaking order" and if an error of law appears in the reasons certiorari will lie to quash the decision.'

In order to do justice the court has, in addition to regarding the reasons for a decision as part of the record, been prepared to regard other documents as part of the record where if read with the decision they will show that the tribunal has erred in law. In *Baldwin & Francis Ltd v Patents Appeal Tribunal* [1959] 2 All ER 433, [1959] AC 663 Lord Denning held that the decision of the superintending examiner and two patent specifications formed part of the record of the proceedings before the Patents Appeal Tribunal. In *Re Gilmore's Application* [1957] 1 All ER 796, [1957] 1 QB 574 the Court of Appeal held that the report of a medical specialist constituted part of the record. As Lord Denning MR said in *R v Preston Supplementary Benefits Appeal Tribunal, ex parte Moore* [1975] 2 All ER 807 at 810, [1975] 1 WLR 624 at 628: 'The "record" is generously interpreted so as to cover all the documents in the case.'

Parliament has set its seal of approval on this practice of the court in the case of all those bodies to which the Tribunals and Inquiries Acts 1958 and 1971 apply. They are required to state their reasons, and it is provided that the reasons constitute part of the record and that certiorari will lie: see ss 12 and 14 of the 1971 Act.

We can see no sensible reason why the court should adopt a different approach to a decision of an inferior court or other quasi-administrative body such as licensing justices from that which it is required to adopt in the cases to which the 1971 Act applies. If we were now to hold that the practice of the Divisional Court over the past forty years was wrong and that the court could look only at the order dismissing the appeal, we should be putting the clock back to the days when archaic formalism too often triumphed over justice.

The argument for the Gaming Board is that it is only if the inferior court chooses to embody its reasons in its order that it becomes part of the record, for only then does it exist as a document for which the Divisional Court can call and examine. So if at the end of the judgment giving the reasons the judge or chairman adds the words 'and I direct that this judgment be made part of the order', the court may look at it but not otherwise. It seems to us that it would be a scandalous state of affairs that, if having given a manifestly erroneous judgment, a judge could defeat any review by this court by the simple expedient of refusing a request to make his judgment part of the order. That would indeed be formalism triumphant.

It may be said that the same end can be achieved by the court refusing to give any reasons, as the judge said he was entitled to do, in this case. However, it is the function of professional judges to give reasons for their decisions and the decisions to which they are a party. This court would look askance at the refusal by a judge to give his reasons for a decision, particularly if requested to do so by one of the parties. It does not fall for decision in this case but it may well be that, if such a case should arise, this court would find that it had power to order the judge to give his reasons for his decision.

The Metropolitan Police Commissioner took the same point on the scope of the record in *R v Crown Court at Knightsbridge, ex parte Ladup Ltd* (18th March 1980, unreported). In his judgment Lord Widgery CJ quoted extensively from some of the earlier authorities and expressed the view that they gave some support to the commissioner's submission; he then contrasted this to the modern practice of the court over which he had presided but in the event found it unnecessary to express any concluded view as he held that the Crown Court's reasons did not in fact disclose an error of law.

There are undoubtedly passages in the older authorities that support the Gaming Board's arguments. It would appear that at the time when those cases were decided in the last century the Court of Queen's Bench would not look at the reasons of quarter sessions unless they had been formally recorded in their order: see in particular the speech of Lord Cairns LC in *Walsall Overseers v London and North Western Railway Co* (1878) 4 App Cas 30.

But the courts must adapt their procedures to modern conditions. In the last century the facilities available for recording spoken reasons were not comparable to those which exist today. Shorthand had only recently been invented and there was no electronic recording apparatus with which many courts are now equipped. This court can now rely with confidence on a transcript of the oral judgment given by a lower court or tribunal as accurately setting out its reasons which may not have been the case a hundred years ago. Furthermore the recent decision of the House of Lords in *Inland Revenue Comrs v National Federation of Self-Employed and Small Businesses Ltd* [1981] 2 All ER 93, [1981] 2 WLR 722 concerned with the remedy of mandamus shows that administrative law is in a phase of active development and that the judges will adapt the rules applying to the issue of the prerogative orders to protect the rule of law in a changing society. As Lord Diplock said: 'Any judicial statements on matters of public law if made before 1950 are likely to be a misleading guide to what the law is today', and Lord Roskill said:

'... in the last thirty years, no doubt because of the growth of central local government intervention in the affairs of the ordinary citizen since the 1939–45 war, and the consequent increase in the number of administrative bodies charged by Parliament with the performance of public duties, the use of prerogative orders to check a usurpation of power by such bodies to the disadvantage of the ordinary citizen, or to insist on due performance by such bodies of their statutory duties and to maintain due adherence to the laws enacted by Parliament, has greatly increased. The former and stricter rules determining when such orders, or formerly the prerogative writs, might or might not issue, have been greatly relaxed.'

(See [1981] 2 All ER 93 at 103, 115–116, [1981] 2 WLR 722 at 736, 751.)

Although the old authorities do show a stricter approach to what constituted the 'record', the modern authorities show that the judges have relaxed the strictness of that rule and taken a broader view of the 'record' in order that certiorari may give relief to those against whom a decision has been given which is based on a manifest error of law. We therefore hold that the reasons contained in the transcript of the oral judgment of the Crown Court constitute part of the record for the purposes of certiorari and we are entitled to look at it to see if they contain errors of law.

The statutory provisions governing applications to licensing justices for cancellation of a gaming licence and appeals from the decision of the licensing justices are contained in Sch 2 to the 1968 Act. Paragraph 42 provides that the licensing justices may cancel the licence on any of the grounds specified in para 20 or para 21. The grounds relevant to this application are those in para 20(1)(b), namely that the applicant is not a fit and proper person to be the holder of a licence under this Act, and in para 21(1)(e), namely that, while the licence has been in force, the relevant premises have been used for an unlawful purpose or as a resort of criminals or prostitutes. In addition to cancelling the licence there is also a power to make a disqualification order prohibiting a licence being held in respect of the premises for a period not exceeding five years: see para 49. Paragraphs 45 and 29 provide for an appeal to the Crown Court to be by way of a rehearing with a power to make any order that might have been made by the licensing justices, and provides that the judgment of the Crown Court shall be final. In passing we observe that the fact that the appeal is said to be final is no ground for refusing certiorari if error is found on the face of the record: see Re Gilmore's Application [1957] 1 All ER 796, [1957] 2 WLR 498 and South East Asia Fire Bricks Sdn Bhd v Non-Metallic Mineral Products Manufacturing Employees Union [1980] 2 All ER 689, [1981] AC 363.

We turn now to the judgment of the Crown Court. We would have expected the judge's judgment to have followed this basic outline: first a consideration of and decisions on whether it had been shown that the appellants were not fit and proper persons to hold a licence (Sch 2, para 20(1)(b)) or that while the licences had been in force the relevant premises had been used for an unlawful purpose (para 21(1)(e)); and second, assuming findings against the appellants on either or both of these grounds, whether the court should exercise its discretion to cancel the licences.

At this point we should observe that, if the court concludes that the appellants are not fit and proper persons to hold gaming licences, it is difficult to conceive of any grounds on which it would be right to exercise a discretion not to cancel the licence. The judgment, after apparently holding that the appellant companies because of past misconduct are not fit and proper persons to hold a gaming licence, then devotes pages to the consideration of discretion; this suggests a confusion of thought in the approach of the court.

The court made no finding whether or not the premises had been used for an unlawful purpose, though, subject to any argument that counsel for International Sporting Club (London) Ltd may hereafter wish to address on the subject, we should have thought that they clearly had been so used, as counsel for Palm Beach Club Ltd conceded in the course of his argument.

On the question of whether or not the appellants are fit and proper persons to hold the licence it is conceded that this question must be determined in the light of the circumstances existing at the time of the appeal. Past conduct will of course be relevant as we shall discuss more fully hereafter. There are, however, other considerations which should be taken into account, particularly when the licence holder is a limited company;

a for instance, whether the shareholding or management of the company remains the same at the date of the material hearing as they were when the past misconduct occurred; the general character and reputation of the shareholders and directors of the company at the date of the hearing should be taken into account. So should any evidence that the 'restructured' licence holder has the capacity and intention to run the casino on different lines, or indeed that it may have already started to do so. It is conceded by the respondents that a failure to take these very material matters relating to the restructuring of the

b companies into account when considering an application to cancel a licence would amount to an error of law.

This had already been decided in the *Ladup* case which we are told was cited to the Crown Court. Furthermore it was apparently on the basis of the 'restructuring' of the licence holder company that the judge and the magistrates allowed the earlier appeal of the Victoria Sporting Club against the cancellation of their gaming licence. This makes

c it all the more difficult to understand why in the present case the Crown Court refused to consider the restructuring to be a relevant consideration. That they did not do so is, we think, clearly demonstrated by the repeated assertion in the judgment that because of their past misconduct the companies were not fit and proper persons, coupled with the refusal to make any findings on the board's submission that even in their restructured form the companies were not fit and proper persons to hold a gaming licence. We cite

d two passages which clearly demonstrate the approach of the Crown Court:

'The respondents, and indeed the Gaming Board have submitted to us that what is a fit and proper person can only be judged by past conduct because every person is a fit and proper person at one moment, and you have to look and see what they have done in the past to judge whether they are fit and proper persons, and it is on the evidence given before the justices that the Gaming Board and the respondents

e both submit to us that by reason of their past conduct they must be judged not to be fit and proper persons to hold a licence. Well, there it is. We have come to the conclusion and we are quite satisfied that that is the only proper way to approach this matter. There had been considerable confusion in the hearing of this appeal between International Sporting Club, which is now Lonrho, but that is not so; it is still International Sporting Club Ltd, Curzon House is still Curzon House Club Ltd

f and, likewise, the Palm Beach is still Palm Beach Club Ltd; each of these three companies is tainted, each of them has misconducted its affairs in the past and it is only by past conduct that we can judge them; accordingly we have come to the conclusion that they are not fit and proper persons to hold a licence because of the past misconduct.'

g Later the following passage appears:

'The Gaming Board also put forward various reasons why the three purchasers should not be allowed to hold the shares, Lonrho because they are, as I put it, thin on the ground in directive personnel, Aspinal because of the warning in the past and the manner in which the Aspinal club has been run, and Mecca because they had two directors on the board who ought to have moved off and done what they could

h to stop, or make inquiry into what was happening; and they were met with a blunt refusal to be of any assistance from the other directors appointed by Corals, got a firm no answer and were obstructed in every way. It may be that one or other or all of those matters have good foundation but we are not going to make any finding upon them. Our finding simply is this, that each of those casino limited liability companies has transgressed in the past, the present situation must be judged by the

j manner in which they have conducted themselves and, as I say, we find that they are not fit and proper persons.'

Counsel for International Sporting Club (London) Ltd conceded that past misconduct was a relevant consideration but submitted it was of marginal weight in a case such as this. Counsel for Palm Beach Club Ltd went further and submitted that it was irrelevant. We have no hesitation in saying that past misconduct by the licence holder will in every case be a relevant consideration to take into account when considering whether to cancel a licence. The weight to be accorded to it will vary according to the circumstances of the case. There may well be cases in which the wrongdoing of the company licence holder has been so flagrant and so well publicised that no amount of restructuring can restore confidence in it as a fit and proper person to hold a licence; it will stand condemned in the public mind as a person unfit to hold a licence and public confidence in the licensing justices would be gravely shaken by allowing it to continue to run the casino. Other less serious breaches may be capable of being cured by restructuring.

It is also right that the licensing justices or the Crown Court on an appeal should have regard to the fact that it is in the public interest that the sanction of the cancellation of a licence should not be devalued. It is obvious that the possibility of the loss of the licence must be a powerful incentive to casino operators to observe the gaming laws and to run their premises properly. If persons carrying on gaming through a limited company can run their establishment disgracefully, make a great deal of money and then when the licence is cancelled sell the company to someone who, because he is a fit and proper person must be entitled to continue to hold the licence through the company, it will seriously devalue the sanction of cancellation. But logically this is a consideration that falls to be taken into account when deciding whether or not to exercise the discretion to cancel and not at the point at which the court is considering whether or not one of the grounds for cancellation has been established. As we have already said, if the court concludes that even at the date of the rehearing and taking into account the restructuring the company is not a fit and proper person to hold a gaming licence, it is difficult to see how they could exercise their discretion otherwise than by cancelling the licence. On the other hand if because of the restructuring the court considers that the company is now a fit and proper person, but it also found that in the past the company has used the premises for an unlawful purpose, it would certainly be open to the court in the exercise of its discretion to cancel the licence. A licensing authority is fully entitled to use the sanction of cancellation in the public interest to encourage other operators or would-be operators of gaming establishments to observe the law in the area of their jurisdiction.

It is clear from the judgment that these considerations weighed heavily with the Crown Court. It may be that, even if the court had been prepared to take the restructuring into account, they would either have found that the companies were not fit and proper persons or, alternatively, even if they were, that by reason of the part use of the premises for unlawful purposes the licence should be cancelled. Certiorari is a discretionary remedy and we have thought long about the question whether, even if the court had taken the restructuring into account, it would inevitably have ordered the cancellation of the licence. We think that it might have done so. But, taking into account that in the Victoria Sporting Club case the same court allowed an appeal against cancellation after taking into account the restructuring of the company and the fact that neither the licensing justices nor the court saw fit to make an order pursuant to para 49 of Sch 2 to the 1968 Act disqualifying the premises, we have decided that it would not be right to deny these applicants a rehearing. If we did so we should be substituting our discretion for that of the Crown Court and that we are not permitted to do on an application for an order for certiorari. Therefore somewhat reluctantly, because we do not look on these applicants as good Samaritans coming to the rescue of the gaming public as at one stage in the argument we were invited to do, but because as counsel for International Sporting Club (London) Ltd said, everyone, including gaming companies, is entitled to fair treatment under the law, we grant the applications and orders will go to quash the decisions of the Crown Court at Knightsbridge. This means that the orders of the licensing justices cancelling the licences still stand. If the applicants wish to pursue their appeals, they should be expedited and heard by another judge sitting with a different panel of licensing justices.

As we are of the view that the judgment forms part of the record and discloses error of law, it is not necessary for us to express our opinion on the alternative ground that the

court exceeded its jurisdiction. To some extent the two points are interrelated because
a if the judgment is part of the record it is not necessary for this court to seek by subtle
reasoning to find excess or abuse of jurisdiction in order to enable it to do justice by
quashing a decision founded on error of law. On this difficult question of jurisdiction
we are at the moment divided. But as the point is not necessary to our decision we shall
not set out on the necessary lengthy analysis to defend our respective positions. It is
sufficient to say that if our decision on the scope of the record is challenged it will be open
b to the applicants to seek to uphold the decision of this court on the ground that the
Crown Court exceeded their jurisdiction.

Applications allowed. Orders of certiorari granted.

Solicitors: *Cameron Markby* (for International Sporting Club (London) Ltd); *M J Kusel &*
c *Co* (for Palm Beach Club Ltd); *R E T Birch* (for the Commissioner of Police of the
Metropolis); *Gregory, Rowcliffe & Co* (for the Gaming Board).

Sepala Munasinghe Esq   Barrister.

d # Gaskill v Preston

QUEEN'S BENCH DIVISION
STOCKER J
17th DECEMBER 1980, 30th JANUARY 1981

e *Damages – Personal injury – Loss of earnings – Deduction of family income supplement – Return*
after injury to less well paid work – Whether family income supplement deductible from special
damages awarded for plaintiff's loss of earnings – Whether deductible from damages awarded
for future loss of earnings – Whether if deductible in principle possible to evaluate future benefit
for purpose of making deduction.

f The plaintiff, a married man with children, was injured in a road accident caused by the
defendant's admitted negligence. At the time of the accident the plaintiff was in
employment as a packer. As a result of his injuries he had to take another job where his
wages were less than those he received as a packer, and because of his reduced income he
became entitled to and was paid a family income supplement under the Family Income
Supplements Act 1970. On the issue of quantum at the trial the defendant contended
g that payments of family income supplement were deductible both from the plaintiff's
special damages for loss of earnings to the date of trial and from the damages awarded for
loss of future earnings. The plaintiff contended that family income supplement was paid
in respect of insufficiency of means and was not directly related to loss of earnings and
therefore was not deductible from the damages for loss of future earnings. He appeared
to concede that the benefit was deductible from the special damages.

h **Held** – (1) Since the effect of the scheme of state-financed benefit was that unemployment
benefit paid to an employee injured by a defendant's negligence (which was deductible
from the special damages payable for his loss of earnings) was, after the expiry of a
prescribed period, replaced by supplementary benefit (which was also deductible from
the special damages for loss of earnings) if the employee did not return to full-time
j employment and that after the employee's return to full-time employment any shortfall
of income below the limits prescribed in the 1970 Act was supplemented by the payment
of a family income supplement, each of those three forms of benefit achieved the same
object of replacing all or part of the employee's earnings lost by the defendant's
negligence. To that extent, therefore, there was no distinction between the three kinds
of benefit. Accordingly, since unemployment and supplementary benefit were

deductible from special damages for loss of earnings, so was family income supplement, and the payments of that benefit which had already been made were therefore deductible from the plaintiff's special damages (see p 432 a to c, post); *Nabi v British Leyland (UK) Ltd* [1980] 1 All ER 667 and *Plummer v P W Wilkins & Son Ltd* [1981] 1 All ER 91 applied.

(2) Since for the purpose of deducting family income supplement from damages for loss of earnings no distinction could be drawn between past lost earnings and future lost earnings, the supplement was deductible from damages for the loss of future earnings where future payments of the supplement could be calculated with certainty. Moreover, even where the existence or amount of future payments of the supplement was unclear, if there was a reasonable expectation of the continuance of the benefit a deduction for it could be made from the damages for loss of future earnings. In the particular circumstances, however, any assessment of the plaintiff's future prospects of receiving a family income supplement were so speculative as to amount to mere guesswork, since the amount of the supplement might be reduced or might cease to be payable at all, and accordingly no deduction from the damages for loss of future earnings could be made on the basis of his reasonable expectation of future receipts of the supplement since no value could be put on that expectation. It followed that no deduction for family income supplement could be made from the damages for loss of future earnings (see p 430 e and p 432 a to j, post); *Baker v Dalgleish Steam Shipping Co Ltd* [1922] 1 KB 361 applied.

Notes

For deduction for benefits received or receivable in assessing damages in tort, see 12 Halsbury's Laws (4th Edn) para 1152, and for cases on the subject, see 17 Digest (Reissue) 87–90, 32–46.

Cases referred to in judgment

Baker v Dalgleish Steam Shipping Co Ltd [1922] 1 KB 361, 91 LJKB 392, 126 LT 482, CA, 36(1) Digest (Reissue) 370, *1493*.

Foxley v Olton [1964] 3 All ER 248n, [1965] 2 QB 306, [1964] 3 WLR 1155, 36(1) Digest (Reissue) 325, *1323*.

Nabi v British Leyland (UK) Ltd [1980] 1 All ER 667, [1980] 1 WLR 529, CA.

Parry v Cleaver [1969] 1 All ER 555, [1970] AC 1, [1969] 2 WLR 821, [1969] 1 Lloyd's Rep 183, HL, 36(1) Digest (Reissue) 320, *1295*.

Parsons v BNM Laboratories Ltd [1963] 2 All ER 658, [1964] 1 QB 95, [1963] 2 WLR 1273, [1963] TR 183, 42 ATC 200, CA, 17 Digest (Reissue) 90, *45*.

Plummer v P W Wilkins & Son Ltd [1981] 1 All ER 91, [1981] 1 WLR 831.

Shaw v Cape Insulation Co Ltd (18th July 1977, unreported), QBD at Manchester.

Action

By a writ dated 1st October 1980 the plaintiff, Henry Gaskill, claimed against the defendant, James William Charles Preston, damages for personal injuries and pecuniary loss caused by the defendant's negligence in driving a motor car on 13th December 1974. The defendant admitted liability. In assessing the damages the question arose whether payments to the plaintiff of a family income supplement under the Family Income Supplements Act 1970 were deductible from the special damages for loss of earnings to the date of trial of the action and from any award of damages for loss of earnings in the future. The facts are set out in the judgment.

Andrew Massey for the plaintiff.
A W Stevenson for the defendant.

Cur adv vult

30th January. **STOCKER J** read the following judgment: In this action the plaintiff claims damages for personal injuries and consequential losses resulting from a road

accident which occurred on 13th December 1974. On that date a motor car driven by
a the defendant collided with a moped ridden by the plaintiff at crossroads in Totton in
Hampshire. Liability had been admitted on the pleadings and the sole issue before me
is the proper amount of damages to be awarded.

The main injuries were a Potts fracture, dislocation of the right ankle and a sprain of
the right knee. The medical evidence has been agreed, and consists of five reports or
letters from Mr Fitzgerald and a report from Mr John Wilkinson. As these are agreed
b reports it seems unnecessary to burden this judgment with lengthy extracts from
them. As appears from the first report from Mr Fitzgerald, dated 13th March 1975, the
fractured ankle was reduced and fixed under general anaesthetic at the Southampton
General Hospital. Unfortunately, discharge developed from the wound and continued
to do so despite antibiotic therapy. This is described as causing a virtual destruction of
the ankle joint. A plaster cast was applied to the ankle joint to achieve bony fusion, since
c it was apparent that no useful movement of the ankle could be regained. [His Lordship
then referred to the medical reports and assessed the damages for pain, suffering and loss
of amenity at the sum of £12,500 to include the plaintiff's lost prospects of return to his
trade as a stonemason. His Lordship continued:] I now turn to consider the award to be
made for pecuniary losses. These fall to be considered under the following heads: (1)
special damages, including loss of earnings to date; (2) future loss of earnings; (3) loss of
d earning capacity in so far as this arises is a matter additional to item (2). At the time of
the accident the plaintiff was employed as a packer by Giltspur Packaging Ltd at an
agreed net weekly wage of £60. His present net average wage as a cleaner in a hospital
is £37·42 a week. In this case an assessment of past and future losses based simply on the
arithmetical difference between these figures cannot be made. In the first place his job
as a packer with Giltspur was not really the job of his choice. Between 1959 and 1964 he
e carried out a five year apprenticeship as a stonemason, and for several years thereafter was
employed as such by various employers.

In 1968 he moved with his family to Southampton but found that employment as a
stonemason involved so much travelling away from home that it upset his family life.
He has three children aged 14¾, 12½ and 8½. His intention was to return to stonemasoning
as soon as his children, and in particular his eldest child, reached an age to appreciate the
cause of his absences. His evidence was that he hoped to return to work as a stonemason
f in about two years or at the latest eight years, when all his children would have reached
the age of 16. As a stonemason his earnings would be of the order of £77 a week net.

In the second place payments have been made to the plaintiff pursuant to the
provisions of the Family Income Supplements Act 1970. It is contended on behalf of the
defendant that payments under this Act should be deducted from that part of the special
g damages which relates to loss of earnings to the date of trial, and that payments likely to
be made in the future should be deducted from any award for the loss of earnings in the
future.

So far as special damages for losses to date of trial are concerned, figures have been
agreed as representing the sum to be awarded with and without deduction of payments
made under the Act. If the payments are not deductible then the loss of earnings to date
h of trial is £3,901·86 plus £1,239·60 in interest. If the payments are deductible, the
agreed figures are £2,059·46 plus £650 interest.

I have therefore to decide as a matter of law whether or not payments under the 1970
Act are deductible from an award of damages for loss of earnings. In summary the
scheme of the Act is as follows. By s 1 a supplement is to be paid to families as defined
where the resources of such family fall short of the amount described by s 2 and the
j breadwinner is in wholetime employment. By s 3 the weekly rate of the payment is
normally half of the difference between the family income and the amount prescribed.
The supplement is payable only where there is a child in the family, and it is increased
by £2 a week for each additional child. The resources to be taken into account are, by s 4,
to be the aggregate of the normal gross income of the family calculated as provided in
regulations made under the Act. The relevant regulations are the Family Income

Supplements (General Regulations) 1971, SI 1971 No 226. By s 5(2) of the Act where the family includes both a man and a woman the claim is to be made jointly, and any sums payable shall be receivable by either of them. Any question as to the right or the amount of the family income supplement shall be decided by the Supplementary Benefits Commission. Payment of benefit under this Act is a non-contributory social security benefit.

At present the plaintiff's family is receiving the sum of £19 a week family income supplement. When the eldest child of the family reaches the age of 16 this will be reduced by £2 a week, and a further reduction of £2 a week will take place in four years' time when the second child reaches the age of 16. After eight years the supplementary payments, when the third child becomes 16 years of age, must cease. That is by s 2 of the Act. This is, of course, on the assumption that payments are made at all after this case is ended.

Counsel for the defendant contends that as a matter of law payments under this Act should be deducted both from the special damages in respect of the lost earnings to date and for that period thereafter in respect of future loss of earnings for such period as the family income supplement continues to be payable. Counsel for the plaintiff drew an apparent distinction between the special damages already accrued and prospective future losses. He appeared to concede that the benefits under the Act should be deducted from the special damages for losses already accrued, on the basis that the Court of Appeal decision in *Nabi v British Leyland (UK) Ltd* [1980] 1 All ER 667, [1980] 1 WLR 529, if not distinguishable, was binding on me. In the event of such a finding he wished to reserve his position to argue his contentions in a higher court. He argued that the position in the future was different but that there should be no deduction against the sum awarded for future losses. If future receipt of benefit under the Act can be regarded as calculable with certainty I cannot see how, as a matter of principle, there can be any distinction between earnings lost in the past forming part of the special damage and future loss of earnings. The argument of counsel for the defendant proceeded on the basis that there was no such distinction.

I therefore consider the question as a matter of principle in the light of the authorities. I do not propose to consider all the cases in which various forms of benefit, insurance, public or private benefits or state-funded benefits have been considered in the context of their deductibility from awards of lost earnings caused by negligence. As far as I am aware the question whether or not payments under the Family Income Supplements Act 1970 fall to be deducted from the damages in respect of lost earnings has not been considered by any court, although the situation with regard to supplementary benefits payable under the Supplementary Benefit Act 1976 and earlier legislation has been considered by courts at first instance with apparently conflicting consequences.

It seems to me I must first, therefore, shortly consider the various forms of state benefit which fall to be considered when an award is made in respect of loss of earnings in order to decide whether or not each involve some degree of common factor as a matter of principle. The first of these is unemployment benefit. This is payable as of right to a person qualified to receive it for a period of 312 working days pursuant to the provisions of the Social Security Act 1975. Thereafter, payment ceases until the claimant has requalified by making contributions on return to work. Instances occur where the claimant does not return to work. He is then eligible to receive other benefits. Under the National Insurance Act 1948 a claimant might thereafter receive national assistance, which has been described as a modern successor to the poor law relief. Payments of national assistance were to some extent discretionary. National assistance has been replaced by supplementary benefits, now payable pursuant to the provisions of the Supplementary Benefits Act 1976. These payments are non-contributory, and are payable as of right in cases where the claimant's resources are insufficient to meet his requirements. This is by s 1(1) of the 1976 Act. By s 6 of that Act benefits are not payable to a person engaged in wholetime remunerative work. In practice, therefore, a person receives supplementary benefit in place of unemployment pay, where the unemployment continues beyond the period of 312 days. The Family Income

Supplements Act 1970 provides for payments to be made for any family if the weekly
a amount of its resources falls short of the prescribed amount where the breadwinner is in
wholetime employment, thus covering the situation excluded by the Supplementary
Benefits Act 1976 where the recipient is in whole-time remunerative work. It is
unnecessary to consider those other forms of state funded benefit, the deductibility of
which is regulated by statute, such as sickness benefit.

I have summarised the basic provisions of the various types of state-financed post-
b accident receipts because it is clear that the Court of Appeal has recently confirmed that
unemployment benefit is deductible. That was in *Nabi v British Leyland*. If, therefore,
the basis of that decision applies equally to the other forms of post-accident receipts such
as supplementary benefits, then, in this instance of family income supplement, I regard
myself as bound to apply the rule for that form of benefit also, even if not technically
bound to do so.

c I therefore turn to consider the various forms of state-financed post-accident receipts
in the light of the decisions affecting them. In *Parsons v B N M Laboratories Ltd* [1963] 2
All ER 658, [1964] 1 QB 95 the Court of Appeal held that unemployment benefit was
deductible from an award of damages for loss of earnings in the context of a claim for
wrongful dismissal. On this point the decision of the court was unanimous although the
reasons of the members of the court were not expressed in precisely similar terms, Sellers
d and Harman LJJ putting it on the basis that the employer was a contributor to the
funding of the scheme. Pearson LJ agreed with this view and said ([1963] 2 All ER 658
at 684, [1964] 1 QB 95 at 143–144):

> 'The dismissal caused the plaintiff to become unemployed, and therefore entitled
> as a matter of general right under the system of state insurance and not by virtue of
> any private insurance policy of his own, to receive unemployment benefit. The
e effect of the dismissal was not to deprive him of all income but to reduce his income
> by substituting unemployment benefit for his salary. It would be unrealistic to
> disregard the unemployment benefit because to do so would confer on the plaintiff,
> to the extent of £59 2s. 6d., a fortuitous windfall in addition to compensation.'

This decision was followed by Stephenson J in *Foxley v Olton* [1964] 3 All ER 248n,
f [1965] 2 QB 306 in the context of a personal injury claim for loss of earnings. The judge
found himself bound by *Parsons*. He refused to deduct national assistance benefits either
from the special damages for loss of earnings to date or from future continuing loss, his
reasons for declining being the discretionary nature of the payments. A number of cases
at first instance then followed. *Parsons* and *Foxley v Olton* were considered in the House
of Lords in *Parry v Cleaver* [1969] 1 All ER 555, [1970] AC 1. In that case the basis for
g the deductibility or otherwise of various forms of state post-accident receipts were
considered by their Lordships, though the decision itself related to a police pension.
Several cases at first instance then followed, most of them unreported. Hollings J in *Shaw
v Cape Insulation Co Ltd* (18th July 1977, unreported) in extracts cited in the report of
Nabi, deducted unemployment benefit on the basis that he was bound by *Parsons*, but
declined to deduct supplementary benefit. The detailed reasons for his distinction do not
h clearly emerge from the extract cited, but seem to me to have been that whereas
unemployment benefit is paid in lieu of wages, supplementary benefit is payable by
reference to the inadequacy of his resources and is not specifically a replacement for lost
earnings. The effect of *Parry v Cleaver* on the earlier decisions of the Court of Appeal in
Parsons and in the *Foxley* case were considered by the Court of Appeal in *Nabi v British
Leyland (UK) Ltd*. The court rejected the submission that these two cases must be
i considered as overruled and decided to follow the earlier decision of the Court of Appeal
in *Parsons*. There therefore can be no doubt that unless and until *Parsons* is reviewed by
the House of Lords the law is established that unemployment benefit is deductible.

The question I have to answer is whether this decision, based as it is on *Parsons*,
constrains me to apply the same approach to family income benefit. Since supplementary
benefit and family income benefit are paid in respect of insufficiency of means, either of
the claimant or his family, and these are not directly related to the loss of earnings, the

plaintiff submits they should not be deducted. In practice, however, this is the effect of all these benefits whatever the basis of assessment. National assistance, which no longer *a* exists, might be a different category due to its partly discretionary nature. In fact, the scheme of state-financed benefit has the effect that unemployment benefit, which has to be deducted, is replaced, inter alia, by supplementary benefit after the expiration of the relevant period, where the claimant is not in full-time gainful employment, and after his return all or part of any shortfall can be claimed as of right up to the prescribed limits under the Family Income Supplements Act 1970. Thus in practice each form of benefit *b* achieves the same object, the replacement of all or part of the earnings lost by the defendant's breach of duty. To this extent and to this purpose there seems no distinction between unemployment benefit and supplementary benefit or family income supplement.

In a recent case, *Plummer v P W Wilkins & Son Ltd* [1981] 1 All ER 91, [1981] 1 WLR 831, Latey J held that supplementary benefit was deductible from damages for lost *c* earnings on the basis that such payments were indistinguishable from unemployment benefit. If practical effect is the correct criterion this seems to me to be correct. I refer to the dicta of Lord Reid in *Parry v Cleaver*, that he found it difficult to distinguish for this purpose between unemployment benefit and national assistance, although he was not deciding this point without further consideration.

I am therefore of the opinion that payments which are actually made under the Family *d* Income Supplements Act 1970 are deductible. As I have already said, to a very large extent this was conceded on behalf of the plaintiff. I have considered this matter at some length despite this apparent concession, since I can see no distinction in principle between past and future losses in the light of the submissions that the payments under the 1970 Act should not be deductible from future losses.

The question therefore is whether I should attempt to evaluate future payments under *e* the 1970 Act. It seems to me clear (see *Baker v Dalgleish Shipping Co Ltd* [1922] 1 KB 361) that where the existence of any future payments under the Act or the amount of them, if made, is unclear, that the proper approach is to take into account in assessing the sum to be awarded for lost earnings, the reasonable expectation of the continuance of the benefits. Accepting that this is the correct approach, how is it to be applied? Section 4(1) of the 1970 Act states that the resources of the family shall be the aggregate of the gross *f* income of its members, and by s 4(2) that such income should be calculated or estimated as regulations may provide, and by s 4(2)(c) that regulations may provide for the assessment of capital resources or the income therefrom. Regulations made under the 1970 Act for the calculation of the gross income are the Family Income Supplements (General Regulations) 1971. By reg 2(4) it is provided:

'In so far as a person's normal gross income does not consist of earnings from a *g* gainful occupation, the weekly amount thereof shall be calculated or estimated on such basis as appears to the Commission or the Appeal Tribunal to be appropriate in the circumstances of the particular case.'

It seems to me, therefore, that whether or not the same payments will continue in the future, or, the amount of such payments if made, is wholly unascertainable. At present *h* interest rates it may be, after payment of damages for his injuries, that the plaintiff's gross family income may be assessed at a figure which exceeds the figures below which the supplement is payable. Any assessment of the future prospects of receipt of benefit in the future seems to me to be so speculative as to amount to no more than a pure guess; that payments will be reduced seems to me probable; perhaps the reduction will be to nil. It therefore seems to me that it is impossible to apply the general principle of *j* making an allowance for the reasonable expectation of future receipts, and to fix a figure purely as a guess is not, it seems to me, a proper method of assessing damages. For these reasons I made no deduction from future loss of earnings, not as a matter of principle, but because in practice no value can be put on the expectation of future benefits under the Act.

I therefore find that there falls to be deducted from the damages the benefits already

paid or already assessed as payable, and thus this head of damage results in an award of
£2,059·46 plus £650 interest, equalling £2,709·46. The future loss is agreed to be the
difference between £60, the pre-accident earnings, and £37·42, the current earnings, or
£1,200 per annum in round figures. I would apply a multiplier of 12, giving a total of
£14,000. If the plaintiff were to return to work as a stonemason his earnings, it is agreed,
would increase to £76·46 a week net. From the plaintiff's evidence I do not think he
would have attempted to return to this form of work until his youngest child was at least
16, that is to say, in about eight years from now. He might well have not done so then,
as many years will have passed since he was last employed as a stonemason. What he has
lost is the chance of so returning at a date well into the future, and I value that lost chance
at £1,000. He has also lost earning capacity and will be at a disadvantage on the labour
market should he lose his present job. I value this aspect of the matter at £1,000 since
there is no reason to suppose that he will lose that job within the immediate or foreseeable
future. That award in total for future loss of earnings and earning capacity is therefore
£16,400.

Accordingly, I award the plaintiff £31,609·46 made up of £12,500 general damages,
£16,400 future loss of earnings and £2,709·46 special damages. Accordingly, there will
be judgment for the plaintiff for the sum of £31,609·46.

Judgment accordingly.

Solicitors: *Jasper & Vincent*, Southampton (for the plaintiff); *B A Wrigley* (for the
defendant).

K Mydeen Esq   Barrister.

Practice Direction

Crown Court – Distribution of court business – Bail – Applications – Notice required – Hearing of applications.

Directions given by the Lord Chief Justice with the concurrence of the Lord Chancellor
under ss 4(5) and 5(4) of and Sch 10 to the Courts Act 1971.

The following paragraph shall be substituted for para 15 of the practice directions on
the distribution of Crown Court Business given by the Lord Chief Justice on 14th
October 1971 ([1971] 3 All ER 829, [1971] 1 WLR 1535):

'*Applications to the Crown Court for bail*
'15. (1) (a) Notice of intention to apply for bail shall be given to the appropriate
officer at the location of the Crown Court where the proceedings in which the
application for bail arises took place or are pending. (b) Where a person gives notice
in writing that he wishes to apply for bail and requests that the Official Solicitor
shall act for him in the application, the application shall be heard by a judge of the
Crown Court in London. (c) In any other case, the application shall be heard at the
location of the Crown Court where the proceedings in respect of which it arises took
place or are pending, or at any other location which the court may direct.

'(2) Subject to such directions as may be given in any case by or on behalf of the
Lord Chief Justice with the concurrence of the Lord Chancellor, any application for
bail (a) by a person charged with a class 1 offence, or in any case where a presiding
judge so directs, shall be heard by a High Court judge or by a circuit judge
nominated by a presiding judge for this purpose; (b) by a person charged with a class
2 offence may be heard by a High Court judge or by a circuit judge or (on the
authority of a presiding judge) by a recorder; (c) in any other case may be heard by
any judge of the Crown Court.'

16th October 1981   LANE CJ

R v Rochdale Justices, ex parte Allwork

QUEEN'S BENCH DIVISION

LORD LANE CJ AND MICHAEL DAVIES J

26th JUNE 1981

Crown Court – Appeal to Crown Court – Power of court on appeal – Defendant pleading guilty before magistrates – Defendant appealing against sentence – Defendant wishing on appeal to change plea to not guilty because plea of guilty was equivocal – Duty of Crown Court in determining issue of equivocality – Whether case should be remitted to magistrates.

Where a defendant enters a plea of guilty in a magistrates' court and then on appeal to the Crown Court against sentence wishes to change his plea to not guilty on the ground that his plea of guilty was equivocal, the Crown Court should first hear evidence from or on behalf of the defendant as to the basis on which the assertion of equivocality is made. Where there is produced to the Crown Court credible prima facie evidence tending to show that the plea of guilty was a qualified plea, ie a plea of 'guilty but . . .', the Crown Court should then inquire from the magistrates what in fact happened before them and, on such an inquiry being made, the chairman of the bench or the magistrates' clerk, or both, should swear an affidavit as to what happened, and only after considering the affidavit should the Crown Court come to a conclusion on the issue of equivocality. Furthermore, it is only in exceptional circumstances that it will be proper for the Crown Court to remit a case to the magistrates' court; in most cases where an issue of equivocality is raised, the proper forum to determine the matter will be the Divisional Court. Where no credible prima facie evidence tending to show that the defendant's plea in the magistrates' court was equivocal is produced to the Crown Court, the question of equivocality ceases to be in issue and the Crown Court should proceed to decide the appeal against sentence (see p 437 *b* to *h* and p 428 *b c*, post).

Dictum of Lord Parker CJ in *R v Marylebone Justices, ex parte Westminster City Council* [1971] 1 All ER at 1026 applied.

Notes

For change of plea in summary proceedings, see 29 Halsbury's Laws (4th Edn) para 360.

For appeals to the Crown Court, see ibid para 472.

Cases referred to in judgment

R v Durham Quarter Sessions, ex parte Virgo [1952] 1 All ER 466, [1952] 2 QB 1, 116 JP 157, DC, 33 Digest (Repl) 304, 1289.

R v Marylebone Justices, ex parte Westminster City Council, R v Inner London Quarter Sessions, ex parte Westminster City Council [1971] 1 All ER 1025, [1971] 1 WLR 567, 135 JP 239, DC, Digest (Cont Vol D) 636, 1289c.

R v Tottenham Justices, ex parte Rubens, R v Middlesex Quarter Sessions [1970] 1 All ER 879, [1970] 1 WLR 800, 134 JP 285, 54 Cr App R 183, DC, Digest (Cont Vol C) 650, 361ea.

Application for judicial review

Linda Elizabeth Allwork applied, with leave of the Divisional Court granted on 10th October 1980 and 18th March 1981, for an order of mandamus directed to the Rochdale magistrates requiring them to allow her to enter a plea of not guilty to a charge of theft and to hear and determine the case against her. The ground of the application was that although she pleaded guilty before the magistrates her plea was equivocal because she did not fully appreciate the effect and meaning of the plea. The facts are set out in the judgment of Lord Lane CJ.

Mukhtar Hussain for the applicant.

The respondents did not appear.

LORD LANE CJ. The applicant applies for judicial review directed to the Rochdale
a justices pursuant to leave granted by the single judge.

The applicant is aged 18, or was at the time of these events, and is of good character.
She was employed as a cashier at a shop in Rochdale operating the till, one imagines at the
exit point of the shop. The prosecution case, in the upshot, was very simple. They
alleged that on 10th December 1979, when this girl was acting as a cashier in the way
described, there was a customer in the shop who was a friend of the applicant's. The case
b against the applicant was that the friend took from the shelf an item priced at £3·29 and
took it to the till, ostensibly for the purpose of paying £3·29 and, having done so, to take
the article home. But that is not what happened because the applicant, instead of ringing
up £3·29, rang up 29p only. When she realised that the actions had been observed, she
tried to hide the article between two of the tills of the check-out point.

She was seen by the police, they having been called to the shop. Pc Wright was the
c officer summoned. The circumstances which I have described were outlined to him by
the manageress of the shop in the presence of the applicant. She was then cautioned by
the police constable and told that she was being arrested. She said 'Yes, it is correct, she
hadn't enough money to buy it'.

In due course before the justices on 3rd January 1980 she was charged with the theft
of property valued at £3·29. She pleaded guilty and was fined £50 with £5 towards the
d prosecution costs. She was unrepresented. She was offered legal aid, but declined the
offer. So the matter apparently ended.

However, on 19th February 1980, having instructed solicitors, she appealed to the
Crown Court at Manchester not only against sentence (ie the fine), but also against the
conviction. Her appeal against conviction was on the basis that her plea below had been
equivocal. What she says in her affidavit before this court is as follows:

e   '3. On the 3rd day of January 1980 I appeared before the Rochdale Justices
      charged with theft of property valued at £3·29 the property being that of Kays
      Cosmetics Ltd. 4. I was not legally represented and hitherto have been a person of
      good character. 5. I purported to plead guilty to the said charge, although not fully
      appreciating the true effect and meaning of the said plea. 6. The Prosecution
      Solicitor opened the case and read brief circumstances of the case from the
f   prosecution file . . . 7. I did not say anything other than merely utter the words
      "guilty". 8. I was sentenced by the said Justices to a fine of £50 and £5 costs towards
      the prosecution costs.'

The Crown Court, apparently having heard evidence from the applicant herself and
also from the solicitor who had prosecuted the case, remitted the case to the justices with
g a view to a fresh plea being taken, and presumably for the matter to be tried as a plea of
not guilty.

The matter came back to the justices on 3rd April 1980 and they having been present
when the plea of guilty had been entered in the first instance, took the view that there
was nothing in the slightest equivocal about what had happened on that first occasion.
They accordingly took the view that their court was functus officio and that there was
h nothing they could properly do. So one gets the unseemly situation of the Crown Court
sending the matter back to the justices and the justices declining to try it. So the
applicant, so to speak, is in limbo.

What this court is now asked to do is to issue an order of mandamus requiring the
justices to allow the applicant to enter a plea of not guilty and to hear and determine the
case.

j But in the meantime there are now before us three affidavits apart from that filed by
the applicant. The first is from the prosecuting solicitor, that is to say the gentleman
who prosecuted in the magistrates' court. He sets out what happened. He says in para
4 that the clerk to the justices asked the applicant, 'Is there anything you would like to
say to the Magistrates about the offence?', to which the applicant replied, 'Only that I'm
sorry'. In para 7 he says: 'I respectfully express my opinion, namely, that there was no
equivocality in the face of the Court in respect of the [applicant's] plea of guilty.' If that

is the evidence which he gave before the Crown Court, as presumably it was, it is difficult
to see how the Crown Court came to the conclusion that they did.

Apart from that affidavit there is one from Mr Arthur William Marcroft, who is a
justice of the peace and indeed was the chairman of the court of three justices who on 3rd
January heard the original plea made by the applicant. He says:

'3. The [applicant] was not legally represented and refused an opportunity given
to her of applying for legal aid. 4. Our Clerk read the charge to the [applicant] who
indicated that she understood it and entered a plea of guilty. 5. After we had heard
the brief circumstances of the case from the prosecuting solicitor representing the
Chief Constable for Greater Manchester and further that the [applicant] had no
previous convictions our Clerk asked the [applicant] if she agreed with the account
given of the circumstances and whether she had anything which she wished to say
to us. 6. The [applicant] agreed with the account given to us but said only that she
was sorry. 7. Nothing was said before us which led us to believe that the [applicant's]
plea of guilty was in any way equivocal and we proceeded after a brief retirement
to order a fine of £50·00 to be paid by the [applicant], together with a contribution
towards central funds costs of £5·00.'

In para 13, which is the only other paragraph I need read, he says:

'During my fourteen years on the Bench I have been always aware of the need to
ensure that pleas of guilty to criminal charges are unequivocal especially when
entered by defendants who are not legally represented and who are young persons.'

Counsel on behalf of the applicant submits to us that there was evidence of equivocality
in that the applicant said, as already reported, in answer to the policeman's caution and
question in the shop, 'Yes, it is correct, she hadn't enough money to buy it'. Speaking for
myself, I cannot see how that could possibly amount to equivocality, coupled as it was
with a plea of guilty.

The problem posed by this case has been the subject matter of debate in this court on
a surprising number of occasions. Counsel for the applicant has referred us to two of
those cases: *R v Tottenham Justices, ex parte Rubens* [1970] 1 All ER 879 esp at 882, [1970]
1 WLR 800 esp at 803, and *R v Marylebone Justices, ex parte Westminster City Council* [1971]
1 All ER 1025 at 1026, [1971] 1 WLR 567 at 570. It is a passage from the latter that I
desire to read because it is a helpful guide to the approach which should be made to this
problem. It is a judgment of this court and the leading judgment was given by Lord
Parker CJ. He said:

'For myself, I am quite satisfied that in considering whether a plea is an equivocal
or an unequivocal plea, one looks solely to what happened before the justices. A
typical case was that of *R v Durham Quarter Sessions, ex parte Virgo* [1952] 1 All ER
466, [1952] 2 QB 1. That was a case in which an apparently unequivocal plea of
guilty was entered to stealing a bicycle, but before sentence was imposed and before
there ever was a conviction, it was revealed that the defendant was saying "But I
took it by mistake", a typical case of "guilty but". In that case quarter sessions,
having come to that conclusion, sent it back to the justices for re-trial. The enquiry
in each case is as to what took place before the magistrates' court to see whether the
court acted properly in accepting an apparent plea of guilty as an unequivocal
plea. As I understand this case, quarter sessions never went into that aspect of the
matter at all. If they had, they would have found not only was the greatest care
taken by the magistrate to see that [the defendant] understood fully what she was
pleading to, but that nothing emerged in the statement of the police, in any
mitigation, indeed in any part of the case to show that there was any suspicion of it
being a "guilty but" case. In those circumstances once it is shown that nothing that
took place before the magistrate cast any doubt on the plea, it is too late not merely
to entertain a change of plea but also to send the case back to the magistrate on the
basis that, although the plea was unequivocal, [the defendant], if believed, did not
intend to do what she did do.'

a Where a defendant before the justices pleads guilty to an offence, the justices, if there is any doubt about the matter, will always take steps to ensure that the defendant, particularly if he is young or under any sort of disability, fully understands the charge levelled against him and the nature and effect of the plea before they pass to sentencing him. It is plain from the affidavit of the chairman of the justices in this case that that is exactly the view taken by him and no doubt by every chairman of justices up and down the country.

b If the defendant, after a plea of guilty, on appeal against sentence to the Crown Court wishes to change his plea to one of not guilty, asserting that his plea of guilty was equivocal, what should the Crown Court do? The answer to that, in my view, is this. First of all they should hear evidence from, or on behalf of, the defendant (the appellant as he will be by then) as to the basis on which the allegation of equivocality is founded. In the great majority of cases the evidence will fall far short of demonstrating any *c* equivocality at all. It is the plea which must be equivocal: in other words the equivocality must be shown by what went on before the magistrates' court, as Lord Parker CJ pointed out in the *Marylebone Justices Case*. The fact that the defendant has subsequently thought better of the plea or has in some way changed his mind, is not sufficient on its own. It must be apparent to the justices that the defendant is saying, 'I am guilty but': for instance, 'I plead guilty to stealing, but I thought the article was mine', that type of *d* situation. If there is no such evidence, then that is the end of the matter. The issue of equivocality has gone, and the Crown Court will proceed to deal with the appeal against sentence.

In my judgment that is exactly what should have happened here. The only point which counsel for the applicant makes on equivocality seems to me, if I may say so respectfully, to be no evidence of equivocality at all, and if that was the evidence before *e* the Crown Court, they should not have entertained any further argument. They should have proceeded immediately to hear the appeal against sentence, having rejected the application for the case to be sent back.

But there may be the very rare case when the appellant in the Crown Court does produce some prima facie evidence, and credible evidence, tending to show that the plea before the justices was equivocal. If the Crown Court then, without further ado, sends *f* the case back to the justices for retrial, the justices, who will be aware of the true facts which took place at the original hearing, are likely to say, 'There was nothing equivocal about this plea. This court is functus officio. We decline to act.' And so arises an unseemly dispute between the two courts.

It is essential that in those rare cases, when there is some prima facie and credible evidence, that the Crown Court should seek help from the magistrates' court as to what *g* in fact happened at the original hearing. The chairman of the bench or the clerk, whichever may be more convenient, or possibly both, should swear an affidavit as to what happened in the magistrates' court for the benefit of the Crown Court, and only after considering such an affidavit should the Crown Court come to a conclusion about the equivocality or otherwise. They must not remit the case to the justices without asking for such evidence. It is apparent that the circumstances in which it will be proper *h* to remit a case to the justices are likely to be out of the ordinary, to say the least, and it may well be that in most such cases the proper forum would be this court rather than the Crown Court to determine that particular issue.

In the present case, as I have already indicated, there is no suggestion that I am able to find that the Crown Court had any credible, prima facie evidence on the equivocal nature of the plea before it at all. They should not have entertained the plea. They should have *j* proceeded to hear the appeal against sentence. But if, contrary to that view, there was some prima facie evidence before them, though we have not been told what it could have been, then the answer is to be found in the two affidavits which I have read. If the Crown Court had inquired at the magistrates court what had gone on there, which they did not, they would have had two affidavits, one from the prosecuting solicitor and one from the chairman of the justices, which would have put the matter beyond doubt. In that case they would have determined that there was nothing equivocal here at all and this unhappy situation would not have arisen at all.

We are not concerned in this case with considering the slightly different situation which arises when there has been a committal for sentence by the justices to the Crown Court, and I do not propose to embark on an examination of that particular situation which does in some respects differ slightly from the present events. But, so far as this matter is concerned, I would refuse the application for mandamus directed to the justices and remit the case to the Crown Court to hear the appeal against sentence for the reasons which I have endeavoured to explain.

MICHAEL DAVIES J. I entirely agree.

Application refused. Case remitted to Crown Court to hear appeal against sentence.

Solicitors: *Lickfolds, Wiley & Powles,* agents for *Freer & Co,* Rochdale (for the applicant).

N P Metcalfe Esq   Barrister.

London Borough of Hackney v Ezedinma

QUEEN'S BENCH DIVISION

GRIFFITHS LJ AND MAY J

11th, 15th MAY 1981

Housing – House in multiple occupation – House occupied by persons who do not form single household – Household – Shared amenities – Separate rooms in three-storey house let to individual tenants – One kitchen on each floor – Tenants on each floor sharing use of kitchen – Whether tenants on each floor constituting a 'household' – Whether each room in house let to individual tenant constituting a 'household' – Whether estate agent authorised to let rooms 'the occupier for the time being' – Housing Act 1961, s 19(2)(10) – Housing Act 1964, s 67(5).

A house comprising a basement and ground, first and second floors contained single rooms which were let to students. There were three kitchens in the house; one was used by the occupants of the basement and ground floor, one by the occupants of the first floor and one by the occupants of the second floor. The local authority gave a direction, pursuant to s 19(1)[d] of the Housing Act 1961, restricting the maximum number of 'households' permitted to occupy the house in its existing condition to three. By s 19(2) the direction imposed a duty on 'the occupier for the time being' of the house not to permit the number of households to be increased above that limit. The owner authorised the respondent, an estate agent, to let out rooms in the house. Five rooms were already let and the respondent let three more to students, thus increasing the number of tenants occupying rooms in the house to eight. Informations were laid against the respondent alleging that he knowingly failed to comply with the requirements imposed on him by the direction, because the lettings made by him increased the number of households in the house to eight, contrary to s 19(10) of the 1961 Act. The prosecutor contended that each room let to a student constituted a household. The magistrates dismissed the informations on the ground that the prosecutor had not proved (i) that the respondent was 'the occupier for the time being' of the house, for the purpose of s 19(2) of the 1961 Act, or (ii) that there were more than three households in the house, since the evidence showed that the occupants lived in three groups, ie the group occupying the basement and ground floor, the group occupying the first floor and the group occupying the second floor, each group using a separate kitchen, and in the magistrates' opinion each group constituted a household. The prosecutor appealed.

---

a   Section 19, so far as material, is set out at p 440 *d* to *f, post*

Held – (1) The respondent was 'the occupier for the time being' of the house within
_a_ s 19(2) of the 1961 Act, since s 67(5)[b] of the Housing Act 1964 extended the definition of
the occupier for the time being to include any person who was for the time being
entitled or authorised to permit individuals to take up residence in a house or part of a
house, and the respondent was a person who had such authority (see p 441 _d_ to _f_ and
p 442 _e_ to _g_, post).

(2) Although it would have been open to the magistrates to hold that each room in the
_b_ house which was let constituted a 'household' within s 19 of the 1961 Act, what
constituted a 'household' for the purpose of s 19 was a question of fact and degree and
there was just sufficient evidence before the magistrates to entitle them to conclude that
the prosecutor had not proved beyond reasonable doubt that there were more than three
households in the house. It followed that the magistrates had been right to acquit the
respondent (see p 441 _g h_ and p 442 _b_ to _j_, post); dictum of Lord Hailsham in _Simmons v_
_c_ _Pizzey_ [1977] 2 All ER at 441 applied.

Notes
For a direction fixing the number of households in a house to prevent overcrowding and
for the offence of failing to comply with such a direction, see 22 Halsbury's Laws (4th
Edn) paras 687–688.
_d_   For the Housing Act 1961, s 19, see 16 Halsbury's Statutes (3rd Edn) 342.
For the Housing Act 1964, s 67, see ibid 409.

Case referred to in judgments
Simmons v Pizzey [1977] 2 All ER 432, [1979] AC 37, [1977] 3 WLR 10, 141 JP 414, 75
LGR 583, 36 P & CR 36, HL, Digest (Cont Vol E) 251, _112Aba_.

Case stated
The London Borough of Hackney appealed by way of case stated by the justices for the
petty sessional division of Thames in respect of their adjudication as a magistrates' court
on 21st October 1980 whereby they dismissed three informations laid by Ronald Alfred
Benge, the solicitor for the appellants, against the respondent, Emeka Ezedinma, alleging
_f_ that on 16th, 19th and 25th January 1980 the respondent knowingly failed to comply
with the requirements imposed on him by s 19(2) of the Housing Act 1961 in that he
permitted Adeniji Oduwole, Emmanuel Chukura and Kenneth Igwenagu to take up
residence in the house at 69 Sandringham Road, London E8 thereby increasing the
number of households living therein to eight, contrary to a direction given by the
appellants on 5th August 1970 fixing eleven persons or three households as the
_g_ maximum number of individuals or households permitted to live in the house in its
existing condition, contrary to s 19(10) of the 1961 Act. The facts are set out in the
judgment of May J.

David Altaras for the appellants.
The respondent appeared in person.

_h_

Cur adv vult

15th May. The following judgments were read:

MAY J (delivering the first judgment at the invitation of Griffiths LJ). This is a
_j_ prosecutor's appeal by way of case stated against the dismissal by justices sitting in the
Thames Magistrates' Court on 21st October 1980 of three informations preferred by the
appellants against the respondent alleging offences under s 19(10) of the Housing Act
1961.

_b_   Section 67(5), so far as material, is set out at p 440 _f g_, post

The relevant provisions of the 1961 Act are contained in Part II which is expressly stated to comprise amendments of the Housing Act 1957. There is, thereunder, a sub- *a* title: 'Houses in multiple occupation'. By s 12(1) of the 1961 Act, if it appears to a local authority that a house which is occupied by persons who do not form a single household is in an unsatisfactory state in consequence of failure to maintain proper standards of management, then the local authority may, by order, direct that management directions made by it under provisions of the Act shall apply to that house.

Similarly, by s 15(1), if the condition of a house which is occupied by persons who do *b* not form a single household is, in the opinion of the local authority, so far defective with respect to such matters as ventilation, water supply, drainage and sanitary conveniences or facilities for the storage, preparation and cooking of food and for the disposal of waste water, having regard to the number of individuals or households, or both, accommodated on the premises, as not to be reasonably suitable for occupation by those individuals or households, then the local authority may serve on the appropriate person a notice *c* specifying the works which, in the opinion of the local authority, are required for rendering the premises reasonably suitable for such occupation and requiring the person on whom the notice is served to execute those works.

Then, in so far as is material for present purposes, s 19 of the 1961 Act, as amended by the Housing Act 1969, s 62(1), provides as follows:

'(1) A local authority may, for the purpose of preventing the occurrence of, or *d* remedying, a state of affairs calling for the service of a notice or a further notice, under section fifteen of this Act, fix as a limit for the house what is in their opinion the highest number of individuals or households or both who should, having regard to the considerations set out in subsection (1) of that section, occupy the house in its existing condition, and give a direction applying that limit to the house.

'(2) A direction under the foregoing subsection shall have effect so as to make it *e* the duty of the occupier for the time being of the house not to permit the number of individuals or households occupying the house to increase to a number above the limit specified in the direction and, if it is for the time being above that number, not to permit it to increase further . . .

'(10) If any person knowingly fails to comply with the requirements imposed upon him by subsection (2) of this section, he shall be guilty of an offence under this *f* subsection . . .'

Finally, s 67(5) of the Housing Act 1964 provides:

'In section 19(2) of the Act of 1961 . . . the reference to the occupier for the time being of the house shall include a reference to any person who is for the time being entitled or authorised to permit individuals to take up residence in the house or any *g* part of the house.'

The premises with which this case is concerned are a house at 69 Sandringham Road, London E8. On 5th August 1970 the local authority gave a direction under s 19(1) of the 1961 Act fixing eleven persons or three households as the highest number of individuals or households who should occupy the house in its then existing condition. That direction *h* remained unchanged at all material times.

The house comprised a basement, ground and two other floors containing single rooms which were generally let to students. It also contained three kitchens, one which was used by the occupants of the basement and ground floor and the other two by the occupants of the first and second floors respectively.

The justices found as a fact that the respondent, who was an estate agent, was authorised *j* by the owners of the house to let out rooms when they became vacant and to collect rents, and that he did this from about July 1979 to February 1980. It was not in dispute that in this capacity he let one room which fell vacant to a student on 16th January 1980 as the result of which the number of individuals in occupation of the house at that time became six; that on 19th January 1980, he let another vacant room to another man so that the number of individuals in occupation rose to seven; and that on 25th January a 1980 he let yet another vacant room to another student which increased the occupation of the house to a total of eight individuals. These three lettings formed respectively the subject matter of the three informations which the justices heard.

It was never the appellants' contention, either before the justices or before us, that there had been a failure to comply with the direction which had been made in respect of the material house in so far as this placed a limit on the number of individuals who were permitted to occupy it. Their contention has throughout been that each of the rooms in

b the house, let as I have described, constituted a household in itself and, consequently, the stipulated limit of three was certainly exceeded by the respective lettings to which I have referred.

The respondent's contentions were, first, that the appellants had not made out their case that the households exceeded three in number; these tenants were not living as separate households but either as individuals or, at most, as three households comprising

c students on the respective floors who used the separate kitchens. The respondent secondly contended that he was not 'the occupier for the time being' of the premises within the meaning of s 19(2) of the 1961 Act and, therefore, could not be liable for the alleged offences in any event.

The justices found that the appellants had not proved beyond a reasonable doubt, either that there were more than three households in the premises on the dates in

d question, or that the respondent was 'the occupier for the time being' of the premises for the purposes of the relevant statutory provisions. They accordingly dismissed the informations. The questions stated in the case for our opinion effectively ask whether they were correct in so finding.

I can deal with the second question, namely whether the respondent was 'the occupier for the time being' of the premises, quickly. In my opinion, he was clearly a person who

e was for the time being entitled to authorise to permit individuals to take up residence in the house or any part of it and, consequently, was clearly within the extended definition of the material phrase set out in s 67(5) of the 1964 Act. In my opinion, the justices were wrong in failing to hold that the appellants had proved that the respondent was the person guilty of the offences created by s 19(10) of the 1961 Act if the relevant lettings did breach the limits in the relevant direction in so far as the number of households in

f the premises was concerned.

I therefore turn to consider the question of the number of households that there could be said to have been in the relevant house on the material dates. The 1961 Act itself contains no definition of what is a 'household' in relation to the provisions which it enacts. However, it is clear that premises comprising a number of separate rooms let singly, as was the situation in the present case, cannot be said to form a single household.

g If it did, then although it would clearly be a house in multiple occupation, it would not be subject to the code relating to such houses contained in Part II of the 1961 Act, having regard to the opening words of ss 12 and 15. It will be remembered that a local authority is only entitled to act under the sections with which we are concerned if the material house is occupied by persons who do not form a single household. In my opinion, therefore, it would have been open to the justices in the present case, had they been so

h minded, to hold that each of the separate rooms, singly let, constituted a household on its own and that, accordingly, the direction had been breached by the three specific lettings, the subject matter of the informations.

We were, however, referred to Simmons v Pizzey [1977] 2 All ER 432, [1979] AC 37. In that case the question which arose was whether the substantial, but fluctuating number of battered wives for whom the appellant had provided refuge in her dwelling

j house could properly be described as a single household. The material issue, in so far as we are concerned, before the House of Lords was whether, on the facts proved, any reasonable bench of magistrates, properly directing themselves, could have come to the conclusion that the prosecution in that case had failed to prove that the residents at the material time did not form a single household.

Asking himself what was meant by the expression in the Housing Acts, Lord Hailsham referred to the definition of 'household' in the Oxford English Dictionary and also to certain views expressed in cases referred to in Words and Phrases Legally Defined (2nd Edn, 1974, vol 2, pp 379, 380), and then continued ([1977] 2 All ER 432 at 441–442, [1979] AC 37 at 59):

> 'I do not find any of these references particularly helpful except to make clear to me what I would have supposed in any case, that both the expression "household" and membership of it is a question of fact and degree, there being no certain indicia the presence or absence of any of which is by itself conclusive.'

With respect, I think that this is the only possible approach to the problem. In the result the substantial question which we have to consider in the present case, bearing in mind that the material house was certainly in multiple occupation, is whether there was any evidence on which justices, properly directing themselves on the facts and the law, could have come to the conclusion that this house contained any less than six, seven or eight single households at the relevant times.

The only evidence on which the justices could so have acted was, in my opinion, that to the effect that the single tenants in this house lived in groups, at least to this extent, that each group occupied a separate floor or, in the case of the basement and ground floors, two floors forming a single unit, and each such group shared only one particular kitchen of the three that there were in the house.

I do not find this altogether compelling evidence that the tenants of the rooms in this house comprised three 'households' in the way I have indicated. Nevertheless, if, as I think it is, the question is a matter of fact and degree for the justices, I think that this evidence was just sufficient for them to conclude, as they did, that the appellants had not proved beyond a reasonable doubt that there were more than three households in the premises on the dates in question.

In the result, therefore, I answer the questions asked by the justices in this way. On the evidence before them they were entitled to conclude that at the material time the premises were not occupied by more than three households. However, I do not think that they were right in concluding that on the evidence before them the respondent was not 'the occupier for the time being' of the premises within the meaning of s 19(2) of the 1961 Act. In my judgment he clearly was such a person. Nevertheless, having regard to the answer to the first question posed by the justices, I think that one must go on to answer the third one in this way, that in my opinion they were in all the circumstances right in acquitting the respondent on the three summonses.

For these reasons, in my opinion, this appeal must be dismissed.

GRIFFITHS LJ. I agree. During the course of the argument I had considerable doubt whether the word 'household' could be construed so as to include a student lodging in a single room. It certainly is not the meaning that is normally attached to the word 'household' which generally envisages a number of people living together rather than a single occupant in a single room. However, on reflection, I have been persuaded that it must be so construed in the context in which it is used in the Housing Act 1961, for unless it includes a person lodging in a single room, it means that lodging houses would be taken out of the code which is applied by the Act for houses in multiple occupation. This, I am satisfied, cannot have been the intention of Parliament.

For myself, I am very doubtful if, on the material before the justices, I would have concluded that these students were living as three households. I believe that I would have concluded they were living as six, seven or eight separate households. However, I feel unable to say that there was no evidence on which any bench could reasonably have come to the conclusion that these magistrates did and, accordingly, I agree that this appeal should be dismissed.

Appeal dismissed.

Solicitors: *R A Benge*, Hackney (for the appellants).

N P Metcalfe Esq   Barrister.

R v Olugboja

COURT OF APPEAL, CRIMINAL DIVISION
DUNN LJ, MILMO AND MAY JJ
21st MAY, 17th JUNE 1981

Criminal law – Rape – Consent – Force – Relevance – Whether prosecution must prove consent vitiated by force or fear of force – Whether sufficient to prove merely that victim did not consent – Sexual Offences (Amendment) Act 1976, s 1(1).

Section 1(1)[a] of the Sexual Offences (Amendment) Act 1976, which defines rape as being unlawful sexual intercourse with a woman who at the time of the intercourse does not consent to it, is merely declaratory of the common law. Accordingly, in proving a charge of rape, it is not necessary for the prosecution to prove that the consent of the victim of the sexual intercourse was vitiated by force, the fear of force or fraud, but merely that the victim did not in fact consent (see p 448 *f*, post).

Observations on the directions to be given to the jury concerning the issue of consent in cases of rape (see p 448 *h* to p 449 *c*, post).

Notes

For rape and consent in relation to rape, see 11 Halsbury's Laws (4th Edn) paras 1226, 1229, and for cases on the subject, see 15 Digest (Reissue) 1209, 1212–1214, *10,373– 10,378, 10,395–10,425.*

For the Sexual Offences (Amendment) Act 1976, s 1, see 46 Halsbury's Statutes (3rd Edn) 322.

Cases referred to in judgment

Director of Public Prosecutions v Morgan [1975] 2 All ER 347, [1976] AC 182, [1975] 2 WLR 913, 139 JP 476, 61 Cr App R 136, HL; *affg* sub nom *R v Morgan* [1975] 1 All ER 8, CA, 15 Digest (Reissue) 1212, *10,398.*
Latter v Braddell (1881) 50 LJQB 448, 44 LT 369, 45 JP 520, CA, 15 Digest (Reissue) 1177, *10,027.*
R v Day (1841) 9 C & P 722, 173 ER 1026, 15 Digest (Reissue) 1186, *10,143.*
R v Galbraith [1981] 2 All ER 1060, [1981] 1 WLR 1039, CA.
R v Hallett (1841) 9 C & P 748, 173 ER 1036, 15 Digest (Reissue) 1213, *10,403.*
R v Howard [1965] 3 All ER 684, [1966] 1 WLR 13, 130 JP 61, 50 Cr App R 56, CCA, 15 Digest (Reissue) 1222, *10,457.*
R v Lang (1975) 62 Cr App R 50, CA, 15 Digest (Reissue) 1213, *10,414.*
R v Mayers (1872) 12 Cox CC 311, 15 Digest (Reissue) 1213, *10,409.*
R v Wright (1866) 4 F & F 967, 176 ER 869, 15 Digest (Reissue) 1209, *10,378.*

Application for leave to appeal

Stephen Olubunmi Olugboja applied for leave to appeal against his conviction, on 18th October 1979 in the Crown Court at Oxford before his Honour Judge Leo Clark QC and a jury, of rape contrary to s 1 of the Sexual Offences Act 1956. The Court of Appeal granted leave and treated the hearing of the application as the hearing of the appeal. The facts are set out in the judgment of the court.

Daryl R Trewella for the appellant.
Michael Brent for the Crown.

Cur adv vult

---

a   Section 1(1) is set out at p 444 *c*, post

17th June. **DUNN LJ** read the following judgment of the court: In this case we grant leave to appeal against conviction and we treat the hearing of the application as the hearing of the appeal.

The question of law raised by this appeal is whether to constitute the offence of rape it is necessary for the consent of the victim of sexual intercourse to be vitiated by force, the fear of force or fraud, or whether it is sufficient to prove that in fact the victim did not consent.

The offence of rape was defined for the first time by statute in 1976. Section 1(1) of the Sexual Offences (Amendment) Act 1976 amended s 1 of the Sexual Offences Act 1956 by providing as follows:

'For the purposes of section 1 of the Sexual Offences Act 1956 (which relates to rape) a man commits rape if—(a) he has unlawful sexual intercourse with a woman who at the time of the intercourse does not consent to it; and (b) at that time he knows that she does not consent to the intercourse or he is reckless as to whether she consents to it; and references to rape in other enactments (including the following provisions of this Act) shall be construed accordingly.'

In this appeal it is not disputed that the appellant had sexual intercourse with Jayne. The only questions for the jury were whether she had consented, and if she had not whether the appellant knew she had not or was reckless whether she consented or not. In this appeal we are only concerned with the actus reus and not with the mens rea of the appellant.

The appellant, who is a Nigerian, aged 20 at the time and studying at Oxford, had sexual intercourse with Jayne, then aged 16, on 8th March 1979 at the bungalow of his co-accused Lawal. She had been taken there with her friend Karen (aged 17) with Lawal in a car driven by the appellant from a discotheque in Oxford where they had all been dancing. Lawal had offered the girls a lift home, but the appellant had driven them to the bungalow which was virtually in the opposite direction from where they lived. This was a deliberate trick to get them to the bungalow. When they got there both girls refused to go in, and started walking away. They did not know where they were. Lawal followed them in the car, and after some argument they got in. After a further argument Karen again got out, and, as she was trying to get Jayne out, Lawal drove off, stopped in a lane, and raped Jayne.

Lawal then drove back to the bungalow, picking Karen up on the way, and the three of them went inside. The appellant was there lying on the sofa asleep, and saw them arrive. Jayne was the last to come in. She was either crying or obviously had been. Music was put on. Jayne declined to dance. She went to the lavatory and returned to find Lawal dragging Karen into the bedroom. The appellant switched the sitting room lights off and told Jayne that he was going to fuck her. She told him that Lawal had had her in the car and asked why could the appellant not leave her alone. He told her to take her trousers off and she did because she said she was frightened. She was still crying and the room was in darkness. The appellant pushed her on the settee and had intercourse with her. It did not last long. She did not struggle; she made no resistance; she did not scream or cry for help. She did struggle when she thought after penetration that the appellant was going to ejaculate inside her, and he withdrew. She put her clothes on and the other two emerged from the bedroom, where Lawal had raped Karen. The appellant and Jayne then went into the bedroom. She told him she was going to call the police. He said that if she opened her big mouth he would not take her home. He later did.

Once home Jayne made a complaint to her mother about Lawal but not about the appellant. She said later she did not know why she did not complain to her mother about the appellant. She supposed that she was more upset 'about the first one', meaning Lawal.

After she had made her complaint to her mother about Lawal she saw the police and a doctor, with whom she spent a total of eight hours. She made no complaint against the appellant; indeed she said he had not touched her.

The police initially saw the appellant as a witness to the complaints by both Jayne and Karen with regard to the rapes on each of them by Lawal. In the course of the interview the police said to the appellant that Lawal had said that he, the appellant, had had sexual intercourse with Jayne. When they put that to him, Jayne had made no complaint against him. The appellant at once admitted he had had sexual intercourse with Jayne and in answer to the question 'Did she consent?' he replied: 'Well not at first but I persuaded her.' At the end of the interview the appellant made a written statement. The police then saw Jayne who said that the appellant had indeed had intercourse with her against her will. The police then went back to see the appellant and put to him what Jayne had said. There followed a further long and detailed interview.

At the trial a submission was made at the conclusion of the case for the Crown on behalf of the appellant that there was no case to answer. The judge ruled that the case should go to the jury. The appellant did not give evidence, and relied on his statement to the police as constituting his defence.

The judge dealt with the question of consent in his summing up in a number of passages. He said:

> 'The question of consent is a question of fact for you to decide, approaching it in a commonsense way. You are concerned, are you not, with the field of human sexual behaviour and in particular in this case teenage sexual behaviour? You have to consider it in a commonsense way applying your own experience or knowledge of human nature and your knowledge of the ways of the world.'

Later he said: 'Sometimes a woman gives in and submits out of fear or constraint or duress.'

These directions were quite general in relation to both girls.

In relation to Jayne the judge said:

> 'You will consider her evidence very carefully and decide whether or not there were any constraints operating on her will, so that you are satisfied that in taking her trousers down, and letting him have sexual intercourse with her, she was not, in fact, consenting to it.'

Then the judge said:

> 'Members of the jury, you are concerned with what was the reason. Was it circumstances in which she was consenting, or was it circumstances in which there was constraint operating on her mind, fear or constraint, so that in doing that, she was doing it without her consent?'

Finally the judge said:

> 'Let me remind you finally that the defence point out that it is not a case where the girl was struggling or screaming. Unless what was said about intercourse and then going home contained any implied threat in it, no threats were uttered, certainly no threats of force or violence, or anything of that sort. The defence say this girl removed her own trousers and that was in itself an open invitation to sex. That of course depends on why and in what circumstances she removed her trousers. Was it because she was consenting, or was it because she was giving in out of fear or constraint, so that she was removing her own trousers without consent? It is a matter for you to decide.'

The appellant was convicted of rape by a majority of eleven to one and sentenced to 30 months' imprisonment.

Counsel for the appellant, in a series of very able submissions, said that these statements by the judge constituted a misdirection. She submitted that the statutory definition of rape introduced by the 1976 amendment into s 1 of the Sexual Offences Act 1956 was declaratory only, and had not changed the common law whereby the type of threat that vitiates consent is limited to threats of violence either to the victim or as in duress to some close or near relative. She relied in support of that submission on a number of cases going back to the middle of the last century, *R v Hallett* (1841) 9 C & P 748, 173 ER 1036, *R v Day* (1841) 9 C & P 722, 173 ER 1026, *R v Wright* (1866) 4 F & F 967, 176 ER 869 and *R v Mayers* (1872) 12 Cox CC 311, and by analogy *Latter v Braddell* (1881) 50 LJQB 448, where a domestic servant whose mistress had insisted that she be examined for pregnancy by a doctor was held to have no cause of action in assault because, although she was tearful and did not wish to be examined, no force or violence or threat had been used to persuade her to undergo the examination.

Counsel for the appellant also relied on two more recent cases, *R v Howard* [1965] 3 All ER 684, [1966] 1 WLR 13 and *R v Lang* (1975) 62 Cr App R 50, where it was held that sexual intercourse after submission induced by force or the threat of force was the classic example of rape. She also relied on a case decided by Winn J, reported in The Times newspaper as a news item on 19th December 1961, where the judge appears to have withdrawn from the jury a case where a police constable was charged with rape on the basis that he had threatened the victim that he would report her for an offence unless she had sexual intercourse with him, which she did. Counsel submitted that in that case there was certainly a constraint on the will of the victim but she did not submit by reason of force or the threat of force.

Counsel for the appellant accepted that submission by the victim did not necessarily involve consent, but contended that the submission must be induced because of fear of violence: see *R v Day* (1841) 9 C & P 722, 173 ER 1026. She submitted that moral or economic pressure or even blackmail causing a woman to submit to sexual intercourse could never be enough to found a charge of rape. Otherwise, she said, the film producer who induced an actress to have sexual intercourse by telling her she would not get a part in his new film if she did not, or the man who induced a woman to have sexual intercourse by telling her that if she did not he would tell her fiancé that she had been a prostitute, would be guilty of rape.

She submitted that those classes of case would constitute offences under s 2 of the 1956 Act. That section provides:

'(1) It is an offence for a person to procure a woman, by threats of intimidation, to have unlawful sexual intercourse in any part of the world . . .'

Although the section was first enacted in the Criminal Law Amendment Act 1885 and was probably intended to deal with a person who procured a woman to have sexual intercourse with a third party, it also applies to a man who causes a woman to have sexual intercourse with himself. Although the section is little used, counsel for the appellant said that it is apt to cover cases of threats and intimidation falling short of threats of death or violence. The maximum penalty under the section is two years' imprisonment as compared with life imprisonment for rape. It is right that the law should confine rape to the most serious cases and that lesser offences should be dealt with under s 2.

Counsel for the appellant submitted that just as the law limits the circumstances in which any person may say he has acted involuntarily to duress, which involves threats of death or violence to that person or a close relative, so it is consistent that the common law has limited the circumstances in which a woman who has had sexual intercourse may say that the act was not consensual.

Counsel submitted finally that to say, as the judge did, that any constraint on Jayne's will could negative consent constituted a misdirection. The word 'constraint' includes moral as well as physical pressure and moral pressure is not enough. Even to tell a girl that she would not be taken home until she had sexual intercourse, in the absence of any threat of violence expressed or implied, would not vitiate her consent.

The definition of rape imported into the 1956 Act by the 1976 amending Act makes no mention of force, fear or fraud. It simply defines rape as being unlawful sexual intercourse with a woman who at the time of the intercourse does not consent to it. The 1976 Act by its long title is described as 'An Act to amend the law relating to rape'. Is it a true amending Act or is it merely declaratory of the common law? To answer that question it is necessary to look at the history of the legislation.

Director of Public Prosecutions v Morgan [1975] 2 All ER 347, [1976] AC 182 stated the law of rape as it then stood. Their Lordships were primarily concerned with the necessary mens rea of the offence. They were not concerned with, nor did they consider, the actus reus. But there is a passage in the speech of Lord Hailsham which appears to indicate that he was accepting the common law definition of rape, that is to say sexual intercourse by force, fear or fraud (see [1975] 2 All ER 347 at 358, [1976] AC 182 at 210).

Following the decision in *Morgan* an advisory group on the law of rape was set up under Heilbron J. The group reported to the Home Secretary on 14th November 1975 (Cmnd 6352). Like the House of Lords in *Morgan* they were principally concerned in the material part of the report with the mens rea of the offence. However in a section headed 'The Crime of Rape' there appear the following paragraphs:

'18. There is no modern definition of the crime of rape and although it is an offence under s. 1 of the Sexual Offences Act 1956, the statute contains no attempt at a definition. The traditional common law definition, derived from a 17th Century writer (1 Hale 627 ff. 1 East PC 434) and still in use, is that rape consists in having unlawful sexual intercourse with a woman without her consent, by force, fear or fraud.

'19. This definition can be misleading, since the essence of the crime consists in having sexual intercourse with a woman without her consent and it is, therefore, rape to have intercourse with a woman who is asleep or with one who unwillingly submits without a struggle.

'20. As Smith and Hogan point out in their text book on the Criminal Law (3rd Edn, 1973, p 326): "Earlier authorities emphasised the use of force; but it is now clear that lack of consent is the crux of the matter and this may exist though no force is used. The test is not 'was the act against her will?' but 'was it without her consent?'"

'21. It is, therefore, wrong to assume that the woman must show signs of injury or that she must always physically resist before there can be a conviction for rape. We have found this erroneous assumption held by some and therefore hope that our recommendations will go some way to dispel it.

'22. The *actus reus* in rape, which the prosecution must establish for a conviction consists of (a) unlawful sexual intercourse and (b) absence of the woman's consent.'

Paragraph 84 of the report is in these terms:

'Finally, as rape is a crime which is still without statutory definition, the lack of which has caused certain difficulties, we think that this legislation should contain a comprehensive definition of the offence which would emphasise that lack of consent (and not violence) is the crux of the matter.'

That paragraph was incorporated into a recommendation for what was described as 'declaratory legislation'.

In its working paper on sexual offences of October 1980, the Criminal Law Revision Committee, under the heading 'Consent in Rape' stated:

'20. Until the second half of the nineteenth century, the courts seem to have had no problems about what amounted to consent. If a woman was made by the use of force to have sexual intercourse, or submitted in fear under a threat of force, she was adjudged to have been raped. She had not consented to the intercourse. This is still the law and, in our opinion, should continue to be the law. In the ordinary case of rape there has been force or the threat of force. Where sexual intercourse is procured by fraud, there is under section 3 of the Act of 1956 a special offence which we propose should continue. The judges and Parliament have intervened, in a few situations, to interpret the notion of absence of consent so as to extend the law of rape to what are basically cases of fraud. In paragraphs 21 to 25 we consider whether the law in this respect should be altered . . .

'24. A majority of us are of the opinion that the offence of rape should not apply when a woman has knowingly consented to the defendant putting his penis into her vagina. Mistake as to his identity, whether as a husband or otherwise, or as to the purpose for which the penetration has been made should be irrelevant. Nor should the use of threats or other intimidation short of threats of force amount to rape. Most of us are of the opinion that the distinctions drawn in the cases cannot bear the weight they have been made to carry, and we doubt whether many laymen would regard the examples we have given as cases of rape. In particular, we consider that the distress which the victim of such frauds or threats may suffer is, though a serious matter, not really comparable with the fear and shock that often accompanies true rape. Most of us therefore take the view that inducing sexual intercourse by fraud or threats (other than threats of force) or other intimidation should be criminal and attract heavy penalties but should not be forms of rape.

'25. A minority of our members consider that the present is not the right time in which to narrow the law of rape. For over 100 years now the crucial question to be asked in rape cases has been not whether the act was against the woman's will but whether it was without her consent . . .'

Those paragraphs indicate that the committee were of the opinion that under the law as it now stands consent may not only be vitiated by force or threats of force but that inducing sexual intercourse by fraud or threats (other than threats of force) or other intimidation may be sufficient to negative consent and constitute rape.

We have not been persuaded by counsel for the appellant that the position at common law before 1976 was different from that stated in the report of the advisory group, but whatever it may have been we think that Parliament must have accepted the group's recommendation in para 84 of their report and incorporated it in the 1976 Act. Accordingly in so far as the actus reus is concerned, the question now is simply: at the time of the sexual intercourse did the woman consent to it? It is not necessary for the prosecution to prove that what might otherwise appear to have been consent was in reality merely submission induced by force, fear or fraud, although one or more of these factors will no doubt be present in the majority of cases of rape.

We do not agree, as was suggested by counsel for the appellant, that once this is fully realised there will be a large increase in prosecutions for rape. Nor, on the other hand, do we agree with the submission of counsel for the Crown that it is sufficient for a trial judge merely to leave the issue of consent to a jury in a similar way to that in which the issue of dishonesty is left in trials for offences under the Theft Act 1968. In such cases it is sufficient to direct the jury that 'dishonest' is an easily understood English word and it is for them to say whether a particular transaction is properly so described or not. Although 'consent' is an equally common word, it covers a wide range of states of mind in the context of intercourse between a man and a woman, ranging from actual desire on the one hand to reluctant acquiescence on the other. We do not think that the issue of consent should be left to a jury without some further direction. What this should be will depend on the circumstances of each case. The jury will have been reminded of the burden and standard of proof required to establish each ingredient, including lack of consent, of the offence. They should be directed that consent, or the absence of it, is to be given its ordinary meaning and if need be, by way of example, that there is a difference between consent and submission; every consent involves a submission, but it by no means follows that a mere submission involves consent: see R v Day (1841) 9 C & P 722 at 724, 173 ER 1026 at 1027 per Coleridge J. In the majority of cases, where the allegation is that the intercourse was had by force or the fear of force, such a direction coupled with specific references to and comments on the evidence relevant to the absence of real consent will clearly suffice. In the less common type of case where intercourse a   takes place after threats not involving violence or the fear of it, as in the examples given by counsel for the appellant, to which we have referred earlier in this judgment, we think that an appropriate direction to a jury will have to be fuller. They should be directed to concentrate on the state of mind of the victim immediately before the act of sexual intercourse, having regard to all the relevant circumstances, and in particular the events leading up to the act, and her reaction to them showing their impact on her mind. Apparent acquiescence after penetration does not necessarily involve consent, b   which must have occurred before the act takes place. In addition to the general direction about consent which we have outlined, the jury will probably be helped in such cases by being reminded that in this context consent does comprehend the wide spectrum of states of mind to which we earlier referred, and that the dividing line in such circumstances between real consent on the one hand and mere submission on the other may not be easy to draw. Where it is to be drawn in a given case is for the jury to decide, c   applying their combined good sense, experience and knowledge of human nature and modern behaviour to all the relevant facts of that case.

Looked at in this way we find no misdirection by the judge in this case. We think it would have been better not to have used the word 'constraint' in explaining the offence, but whenever he used it the judge linked it with the word 'fear', so that in the context the word seems to us to be unexceptional.

d   Finally it was submitted by counsel for the appellant that the judge should have upheld the submission that there was no case to go to the jury, and that the verdict was unsafe and unsatisfactory. As to the first submission, we refer to *R v Galbraith* [1981] 2 All ER 1060, [1981] 1 WLR 1039. There was in the instant case evidence of rape sufficient to be left to the jury, but it depended entirely on the jury's view of the reliability of the witnesses. These were essentially matters for the jury and the judge was e   plainly right in exercising his discretion to rule against the submission.

As to the second submission, counsel for the Crown pointed to a number of matters which fully justified the verdict. Jayne was tricked into going to the bungalow in the first place. She had already been raped by Lawal. She was crying and frightened. She saw Lawal dragging Karen into the bedroom. The appellant was determined to have sexual intercourse with her. She was kept at the bungalow against her will until she f   submitted, although no force was used or threatened. In those circumstances the jury were fully justified in coming to the conclusion that she did not consent.

The appeal is accordingly dismissed.

Appeal dismissed. Leave to appeal against sentence refused.

The court refused leave to appeal to the House of Lords but certifed, under s 33(2) of the Criminal Appeal Act 1968, that the following point of law of general public importance was involved in the decision: whether to constitute the offence of rape it is necessary for the consent of the victim of sexual intercourse to be vitiated by force, the fear of force or fraud, or whether it is sufficient to prove that in fact the victim did not consent.

26th October. The Appeal Committee of the House of Lords (Lord Diplock, Lord Keith of Kinkel and Lord Bridge of Harwich) dismissed a petition by the appellant for leave to appeal.

Solicitors: *Cole & Cole*, Oxford (for the appellant); *C S Hoad*, Kidlington (for the Crown).

April Weiss   Barrister.

Hayward v Thompson and others   a

COURT OF APPEAL, CIVIL DIVISION
LORD DENNING MR, SIR GEORGE BAKER AND SIR STANLEY REES
2nd, 3rd, 4th, 5th, 22nd JUNE 1981

Libel and slander – Defamatory words – Words capable of defamatory meaning – Accusation of
being involved in murder plot – Newspaper reports that name of person 'connected with' plot **b**
given to police – Plaintiff identified as person whose name was given to police – Whether words
capable of bearing defamatory meaning.

Libel and slander – Identification of plaintiff as person defamed – Separate publications – First
publication bearing defamatory meaning but not identifying plaintiff – Second publication
identifying plaintiff as being person referred to in first publication – Whether jury entitled to look **c**
at second publication in order to identify person referred to in first publication.

Libel and slander – Verdict – Separate libels – Defamatory words published on separate occasions
– Single verdict – Validity – Defendant's counsel at trial asking for separate verdicts – Judge
directing jury to make single award of damages if they found in favour of plaintiff – Whether
judge having discretion to direct jury to give single verdict – Whether judge exercising discretion **d**
correctly.

Libel and slander – Damages – Assessment – Aggravated damages – Libel in newspaper –
Whether in awarding damages distinction should be drawn between publisher, editor and
journalist.
                                                                                  e
The plaintiff was well known for his support of many charitable causes in Great
Britain. Between 1970 and 1975 the plaintiff contributed over £200,000 to the Liberal
Party. On 9th April 1978 an article appeared in a national newspaper, stating that the
names of two more people 'connected with' an alleged murder plot had been given to the
police, one of them being 'a wealthy benefactor of the Liberal Party'. The article did not
name the plaintiff, but on 16th April the newspaper published a second article which **f**
named the plaintiff in connection with the investigations. The plaintiff brought an
action for libel against the editor and the proprietors of the newspaper and the journalist
responsible for the articles. The plaintiff contended that the words in the articles meant
and were understood to mean that the plaintiff was guilty or reasonably suspected of
participating in or condoning the murder plot and that the second article identified the
plaintiff as the person referred to in the first article. The plaintiff did not identify any **g**
particular persons who understood the articles as referring to him, but the defendant
raised no objection to that failure. At the trial of the action the judge directed that the
words complained of in the two articles were capable of meaning that the plaintiff was
guilty as well as being reasonably suspected of participating in or condoning the murder
plot, that the jury could look at the second article to identify the plaintiff as 'the wealthy
benefactor', and that if they found in favour of the plaintiff they could make one award **h**
of damages in respect of both articles. The jury found in favour of the plaintiff and
awarded £50,000 against the defendants. The defendants appealed.

Held – The appeal would be dismissed for the following reasons—
    (1) The words used and the details given in the first article were clearly capable of
bearing the meaning that the plaintiff was guilty of participating in or condoning the **j**
murder plot and that he was reasonably suspected of such guilt. Accordingly the judge
had properly directed the jury that it was open to them to decide whether the words used
did bear those meanings without giving separate verdicts on guilt and suspicion of guilt
(see p 458 *b* to *d*, p 460 *b c h*, p 461 *a* and p 465 *j*, post); dicta of Lord Reid and of Lord
Devlin in *Lewis v Daily Telegraph Ltd* [1963] 2 All ER at 155, 173–174 applied.

(2) Where words in a publication were not on the face of them capable of bearing a
a defamatory meaning it was not permissible to bring in a subsequent publication so as to
make them defamatory. However that did not apply where the words used in the first
publication were defamatory and the only question was one of identification. Since the
words used in the first article were clearly defamatory and the mention of 'a wealthy
benefactor of the Liberal Party' was intended to refer, and was understood by a number
of people to refer, to the plaintiff, the judge had rightly directed the jury that they were
b entitled to look at the second article in order to identify the person referred to in the first
article (see p 456 *g* to *j*, p 457 *c* to *e*, p 464 *c d* and p 466 *f g*, post); *Grappelli v Derek Block
(Holdings) Ltd* [1981] 2 All ER 272 distinguished.

(3) Although the plaintiff should have specified in the pleadings the particular persons
to whom the words complained of had been published and the special circumstances
known to those persons, it was open to the plaintiff at the trial to expand his case and
c draw attention to other persons who had read the article as referring to the plaintiff.
However, since the defendants had raised no objection to the plaintiff's failure to give
such particulars, the jury were entitled to take into account all the evidence and give it
such weight as they thought fit and they might well have inferred that many people on
reading the first article understood it to refer to the plaintiff (see p 457 *g* to *j*, p 462 *j*,
p 463 *c* to *f*, p 464 *f g* and p 466 *f g*, post); *Fullam v Newcastle Chronicle and Journal Ltd*
d [1977] 3 All ER 32 distinguished.

(4) The question whether one or more causes of action were to be included in one
verdict or judgment was at the trial judge's discretion. Accordingly, in the circumstances
the judge was justified in directing the jury to make a single award of damages in respect
of both publications if they found in favour of the plaintiff (see p 458 *e* to *g*, p 464 *j* and
p 467 *d* to *h*, post); dicta of Scott LJ in *Barber v Pigden* [1937] 1 All ER at 129 and of Lord
e Denning MR in *Pedley v Cambridge Newspapers Ltd* [1964] 2 All ER at 797 applied.

(5) (Per Lord Denning MR and Sir George Baker) In libel actions against newspapers
it was impossible to draw a distinction between one defendant and another either as to
exemplary damages or as to aggravated damages. The assessment of damages was for the
jury in a libel action and they were entitled to fix whatever sum they thought fit in
aggravation of damages without distinguishing between the defendants (see p 459 *a* to
f *e* and p 465 *a*, post).

Per Lord Denning MR. (1) In an action for libel an appeal court should pay no regard
to any supposed misdirection by the judge on law or on fact, unless it was plainly such
as to lead to a miscarriage of justice (see p 459 *f g*, post).

(2) It is of the essence of the law of libel that the words should be defamatory and
untrue and should be published 'of and concerning' the plaintiff. If the defendant
g intended to refer to the plaintiff, he cannot escape liability simply by not giving his
name. Even if he does not aim at the plaintiff or intend to refer to him, nevertheless if
he names the plaintiff in such a way that other persons will read it as intended to refer to
the plaintiff, then the defendant is liable (see p 456 *j* to p 457 *b*, post); *E Hulton & Co v
Jones* [1908–10] All ER Rep 29 applied.

(3) The meaning of the words in a libel action is not to be treated as a matter of
h construction in the way a lawyer construes a contract but is a matter of impression such
as an ordinary person gets on a first reading of the publication (see p 458 *c*, post).

Notes
For particulars required in support of an innuendo, see 28 Halsbury's Laws (4th Edn)
paras 175–178, and for cases on the subject, see 32 Digest (Reissue) 166–171, 1460–1491.
j For pleadings in defamation actions, see 28 Halsbury's Laws (4th Edn) paras 171–172,
179–180, and for cases on the subject, see 32 Digest (Reissue) 158–161, 1394–1414.

Cases referred to in judgments
Barber v Pigden [1937] 1 All ER 115, [1937] 1 KB 664, 106 LJKB 858, 156 LT 245, CA, 27
Digest (Reissue) 243, 1774.

Broome v Cassell & Co Ltd [1971] 2 All ER 187, [1971] 2 QB 354, [1971] 2 WLR 853, CA;
on appeal [1972] 1 All ER 801, [1972] AC 1027, [1972] 2 WLR 645, HL, 17 Digest
(Reissue) 197, 697.

Bruce v Odhams Press Ltd [1936] 1 All ER 287, [1936] 1 KB 697, 105 LJKB 318, 154 LT
423, CA, 32 Digest (Reissue) 331, 2759.

Chubb v Westley (1934) 6 C & P 436, 172 ER 1309, NP, 32 Digest (Reissue) 299, 2439.

Egger v Viscount Chelmsford [1964] 3 All ER 406, [1965] 1 QB 248, [1964] 3 WLR 714, CA,
32 Digest (Reissue) 291, 2360.

Fullam v Newcastle Chronicle and Journal Ltd [1977] 3 All ER 32, [1977] 1 WLR 651, CA,
32 Digest (Reissue) 161, 1414.

Grappelli v Derek Block (Holdings) Ltd [1981] 2 All ER 272, [1981] 1 WLR 822, CA.

Hulton (E) & Co v Jones [1909] 2 KB 444, [1908–10] All ER Rep 29, 78 LJKB 937, 101 LT
330, CA; affd [1910] AC 20, [1908–10] All ER Rep 29, 79 LJKB 198, 101 LT 831, HL,
32 Digest (Reissue) 301, 2462.

Lewis v Daily Telegraph Ltd, Lewis v Associated Newspapers Ltd [1963] 2 All ER 151, sub
nom *Rubber Improvement Ltd v Daily Telegraph Ltd, Rubber Improvement v Associated
Newspapers Ltd* [1964] AC 234, [1963] 2 WLR 1063, HL, 32 Digest (Reissue) 1, 1550.

Pedley v Cambridge Newspapers Ltd [1964] 2 All ER 794, [1964] 1 WLR 988, CA, 32 Digest
(Reissue) 329, 2736.

Rookes v Barnard [1964] 1 All ER 367, [1964] AC 1129, [1964] 2 WLR 269, [1964] 1
Lloyd's Rep 28, HL, 17 Digest (Reissue) 81, 14.

Russell v Kelly (1872) 13 Amer 169, 44 Col 641.

Sadgrove v Hole [1901] 2 KB 1, 70 LJKB 455, 84 LT 647, CA, 32 Digest (Reissue) 235,
1977.

Simon's Pty Ltd v Riddell [1941] NZLR 913.

Weber v Birkett [1925] 1 KB 720; affd [1925] 2 KB 152, [1925] All ER Rep 244, 94 LJKB
767, 133 LT 598, CA, 32 Digest (Reissue) 318, 2640.

Appeal

The defendants, John William McWean Thompson, Christopher House and Sunday
Telegraph Ltd, appealed against the verdict given and judgment entered for the plaintiff,
Jack Arnold Hayward, in the sum of £50,000 as damages for libel on the trial of the
action on 9th November 1979 before O'Connor J and a jury, the action arising out of
articles in the Sunday Telegraph on 9th and 16th April 1978. The facts are set out in the
judgment of Lord Denning MR.

Andrew Bateson QC and *Patrick Milmo* for the defendants.
Lord Rawlinson QC, Lord Campbell QC and *David Eady* for the plaintiff.

Cur adv vult

22nd June. The following judgments were read.

LORD DENNING MR. This libel action is an aftermath of the tragic story of Mr
Jeremy Thorpe, a man of great charm, a politician of much skill, who was in his day the
leader of the Liberal Party in Parliament.

It is a tragic story because it all flows from an allegation made by a Mr Norman
Scott. That man alleged that he had had a homosexual relationship with Mr Thorpe. If
there was ever such a relationship it was many years ago. It should have been erased and
forgotten long since. But even so, one can well see that, if it became public knowledge,
Mr Thorpe's political career would be ruined and much harm done to the Liberal Party.

In 1975 this man Mr Scott was walking with his dog on Exmoor. An airline pilot, Mr
Andrew Newton, came in close. He shot the dog, but not Mr Norman Scott. Mr
Newton was charged with unlawful possession of a firearm. He was convicted and sent

to prison. In the court Mr Scott made an outburst. He alleged that he had had a
homosexual relationship with Mr Thorpe.

a

This allegation excited the attention of the journalists of Fleet Street. Their excitement
was enhanced when Mr Newton came out of prison. He alleged that he had been hired
as an assassin to murder Mr Scott. He had been paid, he said, £5,000 to do it, but instead
of shooting Mr Scott, he shot the dog. At once speculation in Fleet Street was rife. Who
were the 'conspirators'? Where did the money come from?

b

The journalists soon discovered that an investigation had been ordered by the Director
of Public Prosecutions, that the police were making inquiries and were interviewing
people connected with it. Further information was obtained surreptitiously from
someone or other. As a result some journalists tried to interview Mr Jack Hayward. I
must say something about him. He is a man of the highest character and reputation. In
1978 he was only 54. He was born in Wolverhampton in 1923. At the age of 18 in 1941

c

he joined the Royal Air Force. He became a pilot and was on active service in South-East
Asia, being awarded the Burma Star. After the war he went into his father's business;
and at the age of 28 he went to the United States to start its operations there. He
succeeded well. He saw great potentialities in the Bahama Islands, then British. He
developed the Grand Bahama. By his own abilities and enterprise, he accumulated great
wealth. But he remained intensely loyal to this country. In Who's Who his recreations

d

are recorded as 'Promoting British endeavours, mainly in sport; watching cricket;
amateur dramatics; preserving the British landscape, keeping all things bright, beautiful
and British'. His home here was at Lyndhurst, Warninglid, Sussex; and in the Grand
Bahama at Freeport.

He used his money to support many good causes. They included the bringing back of
the ss Great Britain from the Falkland Islands to Bristol; the acquisition of Lundy Island

e

and its transfer to the National Trust; and support of the Wildfowl Trust.

It was in connection with Lundy Island that Jack Hayward first met Jeremy Thorpe.
They became great friends. Their wives too. Their correspondence is in the papers.
Fulsome letters from Jeremy Thorpe, telling of his meetings with the great, of the
political scene, and asking for money for the Liberal Party to fight election after
election. Jack Hayward gave £150,000 for the 1970 election, and £40,000 and £10,000

f

for the 1974 election. Then £10,000 in 1975. Jeremy Thorpe asked for those two
cheques of £10,000 to be made payable to a friend of his called Nadir Dinshaw in
Jersey. He called it an external account which was to be used so as to avoid difficulties
raised by the law as to financing parliamentary elections. Jack Hayward did not know
Nadir Dinshaw from Adam. He trusted Jeremy Thorpe completely: that it was a
legitimate way of contributing towards election expenses.

g

On Thursday or Friday, 6th or 7th April 1978 Jack Hayward left his home at
Lyndhurst, Warninglid, for the Bahamas. His wife drove him to the airport. When she
got back, she found that this had happened (I quote from a contemporary letter of Mr
Hayward to Mr Thorpe):

> 'The day I left England for Freeport, four men appeared at Lyndhurst asking my
> whereabouts and refusing to give their names. They arrived in two separate cars.

h

> That afternoon, a small private plane ominously circled the house six times and then
> flew off southwards, presumably towards Shoreham.'

Mr Hayward added this in evidence about that day: 'My wife was puzzled. My wife
phoned me, in great distress, wondering who they were.'

j

Mr Christopher House

Now one who was interested was Mr Christopher House, the crime correspondent of
the Sunday Telegraph. On 7th April he got hold of a good deal of information about the
police inquiries. He was told it by 'an informant'. He decided to make a story of it for
the issue of the Sunday Telegraph of 9th April 1978. He wrote an article which in its
original form he says, accurately represented what his 'informant' told him. But the sub-

editor, he says, altered it in some material particulars and in so doing changed the
meaning of it. It would have been very illuminating if the court could have seen Mr *a*
House's notebook. It would contain, I presume, the note of his conversation with the
'informant', and the article as he originally wrote it before it went to the sub-editor. But
it has not been produced. This was his evidence about it:

'Q So we have an alteration after you had written your story? A Yes, sir.
'Q And you were unable to produce here the original piece of writing you did in
the offices of the Sunday Telegraph, so that we could see what you had actually *b*
written? A Yes, sir.
'Q That has got lost, too, has it? A Well, the original story—I don't know what's
happened to it. I assume that's got lost.'

Sunday, 9th April 1978   *c*
On Sunday, 9th April 1978 the article appeared in the Sunday Telegraph. It was
published on the front page. The editor so decided. The important thing to notice is
that it did not mention Mr Hayward by name. It was headed in large letters:

'TWO MORE IN SCOTT AFFAIR
'By CHRISTOPHER HOUSE, Crime Correspondent
'The names of two more people connected with the Norman Scott affair have *d*
been given to the police. One is a wealthy benefactor of the Liberal party and the
other is a businessman from the Channel Islands. Both men, police have been told,
arranged for a leading Liberal supporter to be "reimbursed" £5,000, the same
amount Mr Andrew Newton alleges he was paid to murder Mr. Scott. Mr. Scott, a
former male model, once claimed he had a homosexual relationship with Mr.
Jeremy Thorpe, the former Liberal leader. Mr. Thorpe has repeatedly denied the *e*
claim. The new names were made known to police only during the past two
weeks. Inquiries are being made and it may be some time before they are
interviewed.

'VISIT TO ISLANDS
'Police have been told that some time last year the benefactor flew to the Channel *f*
Islands where he had a meeting, arranged several days before, with a business friend
living there. During the meeting he was allegedly handed £5,000. He then
returned and later paid the money to a leading Liberal supporter, either directly or
through another source. Last night the officers investigating the Scott affair, Det.
Chief Supt. Michael Challes and Det. Supt. David Greenhough, were not available
for comment. Both officers, based at Bristol police headquarters, have continued a
policy of not making statements since the investigation was ordered seven months *g*
ago by Mr. Thomas Hetherington, the Director of Public Prosecutions . . .'

You will notice there the name of Chief Supt Michael Challes. He gave evidence: he
said that he was possessed of information on similar lines to that in the article, but that
the article was not entirely accurate. He said: 'I am not happy with the word "connected",
and what that portrays in my mind, there. I did not know about the "reimbursement".' *h*
Seeing that the information was so largely accurate, it must have been obtained by the
'informant' surreptitiously from someone closely in touch with the police. The
'informant' passed it to Christopher House. He made it into a story for the Sunday
Telegraph. The sub-editor altered it in such a way as to change its meaning. Later we
will consider what its meaning was.

j

The impact of that article of 9th April 1978
Many read the article. In England Sir Peter Scott did so. He said that the words 'One
is a wealthy benefactor of the Liberal party' conveyed to him Mr Jack Hayward. They
did likewise to a Mrs Cowper who gave evidence. In the Bahamas Mr Hayward's
daughter and son-in-law read it and thought it referred to him. But the most telling

evidence came from Mr Hayward himself. He said that in the Bahamas, after the article, the telephone never stopped ringing, day or night, either at home or at the office. He set it out in a contemporary letter from the Bahamas: 'The telephone has hardly stopped ringing since I returned and reporters from virtually every newspaper have been on the line.' The most striking incident was that:

> 'The USA based representative of ITV (Norman Rees) arrived on this island unannounced, with a camera crew, to interview me! The main point of his questioning was based on the report in the Sunday Telegraph of the 9th April which no doubt you have seen, mentioning a wealthy Liberal Party benefactor and a Channel Island courier, etc.'

There follows a sentence which shows that Norman Rees, the ITV man, had other information too which must have been obtained from some other 'informant':

> 'Norman Rees asked me if the name Nadir Dinshaw meant anything to me, or his daughter Nali or Nari ... I could not fathom why he kept mentioning the daughter. Eventually he said that by "sheer coincidence" the daughter worked in David Steel's office!'

(Note that at that time David Steel was the leader of the Liberal Party.)

Friday, 14th April 1978

Mr House said that he did not know the identity of Mr Hayward until Friday, 14th April 1978. He said that it 'was by pure chance that I met another person who knew him'. No doubt this person was another 'informant' whose identity is not disclosed. Mr House said that he then telephoned Mr Hayward in the Bahamas. He took a note of the conversation in his notebook. This notebook was not produced. Nor was the original note itself. But he produced what was said to be a photograph of it. The significance of it is that there is a direct conflict of evidence about the telephone conversation. According to Mr House's note Mr Hayward said:

> 'I have been informed that the police would like to interview me about the Scott affair, but so far no one has contacted me officially.'

But according to Mr Hayward's contemporary letter it was quite different:

> 'Christopher House of the Sunday Telegraph telephoned me in the middle of last week to ask if the police had tried to interview me, to which I replied that they had not and that I had no knowledge that they wanted to, but IF they wanted to, I would obviously help them all I could.'

I expect that the jury accepted Mr Hayward's version and not Mr House's. But Mr House made his version the leading feature in his second article.

Sunday, 16th April 1978

On Sunday, 16th April 1978 the second article appeared. It named Mr Hayward and said that the police wanted to interview him:

'NEW NAME IN SCOTT AFFAIR
'By CHRISTOPHER HOUSE

'Mr Jack Hayward, the Bahamas-based millionaire, who once gave the Liberal party £150,000 to help to pay its overdraft and boost its election fighting fund, said last night that police want to interview him about the Norman Scott affair. At his home in Freeport, Bahamas, Mr. Hayward, 54, who was once known as "Union Jack" because of his many Back Britain campaigns, told me: "I have been informed that the police would like to interview me about the Scott affair, but so far no one has contacted me officially. Obviously I will help them if I can. But I have no knowledge of the Scott affair other than what I have read in the newspapers."

'TWO PEOPLE NAMED

'Last week I revealed exclusively in "The Sunday Telegraph" that the names of *a*
two people, a wealthy Liberal party benefactor and a Channel Island businessman,
had been given to police. Both, it has been alleged to police, arranged for a leading
Liberal supporter to be "reimbursed" £5,000, the same amount of money airline
pilot Mr. Andrew Newton alleges he was paid to murder Mr. Scott . . .'

The writ   *b*
On 26th April 1978 Mr Hayward issued a writ claiming damages for libel in the two
issues. On 27th April 1978 his solicitors wrote a letter asking for an apology and a
statement in open court. They were not forthcoming. So the action went for trial. The
jury awarded Mr Hayward £50,000 damages. The Sunday Telegraph appeal to this
court.

The facts   *c*
In view of the verdict of the jury, I would think that they accepted Mr Hayward's
evidence and rejected Mr House's. I take the facts to be therefore that in the beginning
of April 1978 the 'informant' surreptitiously got access to much information which was
in the possession of the police about the Scott affair. The 'informant' passed on this
information to various journalists. These included Mr House. They were all agog with *d*
it. The 'informant' must have named Mr Hayward. That information led to the private
plane on Friday, 7th April, circling ominously six times round Mr Hayward's house in
Sussex, and to Norman Rees of the ITV going on about Wednesday, 12th April 1978 with
a camera crew to his house in the Bahamas to interview him.

Some of that information got to Mr House. How much we do not know. But as he
did not disclose the name of his 'informant' and had lost his notebook, the jury may well *e*
have thought that he knew Mr Hayward's name, just as the other journalists did, but
deliberately concealed it in the first article by referring only to a 'wealthy benefactor of
the Liberal party'. The jury may not have believed him when he said that it was 'by pure
chance' that he got to know the name in the next week.

So much for the facts. I will now turn to the legal points raised by counsel for the
defendants.   *f*

Identity in first article
The first article did not mention Jack Hayward by name. It said only of him 'a wealthy
benefactor of the Liberal party'. The judge ruled that it was permissible for the jury to
look at the second article so as to see to whom the first article referred. Counsel for the
defendants submitted that this ruling was erroneous. He cited the recent decision of this *g*
court in *Grappelli v Derek Block (Holdings) Ltd* [1981] 2 All ER 272, [1981] 1 WLR 822. It
was there held that, where words in a publication were not on the face of them capable
of a defamatory meaning, it was not permissible to bring in a subsequent publication so
as to make them defamatory. I there said ([1981] 2 All ER 272 at 274, [1981] 1 WLR 822
at 825):

'I prefer to go by the principle that in defamation a cause of action arises (and a *h*
writ can be issued) as soon as the words are published to a person *then* knowing all
the material facts. If there are extrinsic facts, he must know them *then*, at the time
of publication. That is when a cause of action arises. It cannot be made into a cause
of action by reason of facts subsequently coming to the knowledge of the reader or
hearer.'

                                                                                        j
Counsel for the plaintiff submitted that that case did not apply where the words were
defamatory on the face of them, and the only question was one of identification. Did
they refer to the plaintiff? Or would they be understood as referring to the plaintiff?

I readily accept counsel's submission. One thing is of the essence in the law of libel.
It is that the words should be defamatory and untrue and should be published 'of and

concerning the plaintiff'. That is, the plaintiff should be aimed at or intended by the
a defendant. If the defendant intended to refer to the plaintiff, he cannot escape liability
simply by not giving his name. He may use asterisks or blanks. He may use initials or
words with a hidden meaning. He may use any other device. But still, if he intended to
refer to the plaintiff, he is liable. He is to be given credit for hitting the person whom he
intended to hit. The law goes further. Even if he did not aim at the plaintiff or intend
to refer to him, nevertheless if he names the plaintiff in such a way that other persons will
b read it as intended to refer to the plaintiff, then the defendant is liable. This is settled by
E Hulton & Co v Jones [1910] AC 20, [1908–10] All ER Rep 29, in which the House of
Lords expressly approved the judgment of Farwell LJ in the Court of Appeal when he
said ([1909] 2 KB 444 at 482, [1908–10] All ER 29 at 46):

> 'If a man chooses to make statements of fact about persons whom he names, as in
> this case, I see no reason why he should not be liable to every one whom he injures
c > who can convince a jury that *he is reasonably intended* by the words used.' (My
> emphasis.)

Applied to this case it is quite clear that, when Mr House in the first article of 9th April
1978 spoke of 'a wealthy benefactor of the Liberal party', he intended to refer to Mr Jack
Hayward. Mr House says he did not know Mr Hayward's name at that time. I do not
d suppose that the jury believed Mr House for one moment. Other journalists knew the
name before that Sunday. Witness the aeroplane which flew over Mr Hayward's house
in Sussex on the Friday before. And in the next week's issue Mr House explicitly named
Mr Jack Hayward. The jury, no doubt, inferred that Mr House knew the name all the
time, and simply used the phrase about 'a wealthy benefactor' as a cover-up, hoping that
it would give him an answer to an action for libel. It gives him no answer. The second
e article was admissible in evidence so as to show that in the first article Mr House aimed
at Mr Jack Hayward and intended to refer to him, and therefore that the first article was
published 'of and concerning' Mr Hayward.

Extrinsic evidence
    Apart from the second article, there was much evidence that many people read the
f article as intended to refer to Mr Hayward. Counsel for the defendants quite correctly
told us that the plaintiff ought to have given particulars of those persons. As I said in
Fullam v Newcastle Chronicle and Journal Ltd [1977] 3 All ER 32 at 35, [1977] 1 WLR 651
at 655:

> '. . . he must in his statement of claim specify the particular person or persons to
> whom they were published and the special circumstances known to that person or
g > persons . . . there is no exception in the case of a newspaper . . .'

That is correct on the pleadings at that stage. But when it comes to the trial, then it is
open to the plaintiff to expand his case and draw attention to other persons who read the
article as referring to the plaintiff. The defendant may object that it is not pleaded, and
the judge may, if he thinks right, disallow it on that ground or grant an adjournment.
h But if no objection is raised at the trial, then the jury can take into account all the
evidence and give it such weight as they think fit.
    In our present case the jury could well infer that many people, on reading the first
article, would understand it to refer to Mr Hayward; not only Sir Peter Scott and Mrs
Cowper, who gave evidence, but also Mr Hayward's son-in-law and daughter, and other
people in the Bahamas. Also people in the Liberal hierarchy. And innumerable
j journalists working for newspapers and television, such as Mr Norman Rees from New
York. So I can see no misdirection on that score.

Meaning
    Counsel for the defendants next questioned the judge's ruling on the meaning of the
articles. He suggested that they were not capable of a defamatory meaning at all.

Alternatively, they were at most only capable of meaning that Mr Jack Hayward was *suspected* of complicity in a plot to kill Mr Scott. He asserted vigorously that they were *a* not capable of meaning that Mr Jack Hayward was *guilty* of complicity in the plot. He relied much on the decision in *Lewis v Daily Telegraph Ltd* [1963] 2 All ER 151, [1964] AC 234 where the House of Lords held that the judge (Salmon J) had misdirected the jury in leaving the meaning of 'guilt' to them. At most the words there about an inquiry were capable of 'suspicion', not of 'guilt'.

Lewis v Daily Telegraph Ltd was a ruling on the particular words of the article there. In *b* my opinion it has no bearing on the words in these articles. These articles do not stop at there being an inquiry. The headings are significant: the first on 9th April, 'Two more in Scott affair'; and the second on 16th April, 'New name in Scott affair'; and the articles go on into some detail. Especially the words 'connected with', the inverted commas around '"reimbursed" £5,000', and that 'the police want to interview Mr. Jack Hayward'. As Lord Reid said, the meaning of the words in a libel case is not a matter of *c* construction as a lawyer construes a contract. It is a matter of impression as an ordinary person gets on a first reading, not on a later analysis. It seems to me that on a first reading any ordinary person might well think that Jack Hayward was an accomplice in the plot to assassinate Mr Scott, if not beforehand at any rate afterwards, by providing money for the purpose.

d

Leave and licence

Counsel for the defendants suggested that Mr Hayward, by speaking to the journalist Mr House, gave him permission to publish the words as they appeared in the second article, but Mr Hayward gave a different version. I feel sure the jury believed Mr Hayward. So that point goes.

Separate verdicts   *e*

Counsel for the defendants submitted that the judge should have asked the jury to find two separate verdicts. Each article was, he said, a separate cause of action and should have been kept separately, citing *Weber v Birkett* [1925] 2 KB 152, [1925] All ER Rep 224 and Gatley on Libel (7th Edn, 1974, para 1369). But I prefer the judgment of Scott LJ in *Barber v Pigden* [1937] 1 All ER 115 at 129, [1937] 1 KB 664 at 684:   *f*

'... the question whether one or more causes of action are to be included in one verdict or judgment will depend upon the exercise of the trial judge's discretion upon all the circumstances of the case.'

The present was clearly a case for one verdict.

Aggravated damages   *g*

The plaintiff relied in aggravation of damages on the failure of the Sunday Telegraph to apologise and on their omission to publish the disclaimers. That arose because in the prosecution of Mr Thorpe and others Sir David Napley and Mr Carman QC stated that there was no suggestion that Mr Hayward had any knowledge of the plot or had been guilty of any impropriety. Yet the Sunday Telegraph, in its report of the proceedings, omitted to publish those disclaimers. Counsel for the defendants submitted that that *h* piece of aggravation was available only against the Sunday Telegraph, but not against Mr House; that the judge ought to have told the jury so. He cited *Egger v Viscount Chelmsford* [1964] 3 All ER 406, [1965] 1 QB 248, but that was concerned with qualified privilege, not with aggravated damages. It has no bearing here.

More to the point would have been the observations of Lord Hailsham LC in *Broome v Cassell & Co Ltd* [1972] 1 All ER 801 at 817, [1972] AC 1027 at 1063 when he said that *j* both in exemplary damages and in aggravated damages, the jury must award 'the *lowest* sum for which any of the defendants can be held liable on this score' (Lord Hailsham LC's emphasis). I do not think that this is at all satisfactory. Suppose there are some circumstances of aggravation available against the Sunday Telegraph. There may be be other circumstances of aggravation against Mr House. Likewise there may be

mitigating circumstances in the one and not in the other. No one can say what is the
a 'lowest' sum.

Assessment of damages
The problem arises, of course, because of the settled rule that there can only be one
judgment for one sum against all the defendants. I must say that I think that, in
newspaper cases, it is impossible to draw a distinction between one defendant and
b another, either as to exemplary damages or aggravated damages or any damages. Suppose
the unknown 'informant' had been a defendant, he might have been a wicked inventor
of lies. Or he might have been paid money for his story by a more wicked journalist.
Again, the journalist may have written a comparatively innocuous story but it was
'doctored' by the sub-editor, just as Mr House says his story was. So long as journalists
insist on keeping secret their sources of information (for which they are now to get
c statutory authority in cl 11 of the Contempt of Court Bill now passing through
Parliament[1]) I think they must take the rough of it together with the smooth. They
cannot expect the jury to believe that they got their information from a trustworthy
informant on whom they were entitled to rely, when they refuse to give his name. They
cannot expect the jury to believe that it was not solicited or not paid for or rewarded by
them when they will not disclose how they got it. They cannot expect the jury to be
d sympathetic to them when they 'lose' their notebooks, so that they cannot be disclosed
to the court. The assessment of damages is peculiarly the province of the jury in an
action of libel. If they take a poor view of the conduct of any of the defendants, be it
journalist, sub-editor, editor or proprietor, they are entitled to fix whatever sum they
think fit in aggravation of damages without distinguishing between them, so long as
they do not wander off into the forbidden territory of exemplary damages. That was
e made plain by Lord Devlin in *Rookes v Barnard* [1964] 1 All ER 367, [1964] AC 1129.

Allegation of misdirection
As the argument of counsel for the defendants proceeded, I could not help feeling how
unfortunate it is that our law of libel has become so technical and so complicated. He
submitted that the judge ruled wrongly on this point or on that, misdirected the jury on
f this point or that, or failed to direct them on this distinction or that, and that there
should be a new trial on one or other of those grounds.
To my mind in an action for libel a court of appeal should pay no regard to any
supposed misdirection by the judge, on law or on fact, unless it was plainly such as to lead
to a substantial miscarriage of justice. In *Lewis v Daily Telegraph Ltd* there was such a
misdirection. It did lead to a substantial miscarriage of justice in that it gave rise to an
g altogether excessive assessment of damages. There was no such misdirection here.

Conclusion
Counsel for the plaintiff submitted that this was a vicious and unjustifiable libel on Mr
Jack Hayward and that the jury were fully entitled to condemn it by the award of
£50,000 damages. I would myself accept the submission. It seems to me a case where
h in the search for a sensational story the Sunday Telegraph published these articles which
carried the implication that Mr Jack Hayward, a man of the highest reputation, was
implicated in a plot to murder. No such story should have been published. I would
dismiss the appeal.

SIR GEORGE BAKER.
j *The meanings*
'IN' means 'In'. The article of 9th April 1978 is headed 'Two More *In* Scott Affair'.
What, asks the uninformed reader, is the 'Scott affair'? On reading further he will
discover that it is an allegation by a Mr Andrew Newton that he had been paid £5,000

---

1   See now in s 10 of the Contempt of Court Act 1981

to murder a Mr Scott, who had once claimed he had a homosexual relationship with Mr
Thorpe, the former Liberal leader. He will also discover that 'police have been told' that   *a*
'a wealthy benefactor of the Liberal party' and the other man had 'arranged for a leading
Liberal supporter to be "reimbursed" £5,000' and that the names of the two men had
been given to the police, who must have already taken into custody a Mr Le Mesurier
described as 'on police bail'. The article is 'By Christopher House, Crime Correspondent'.
So the reader can now expand the heading to 'a wealthy benefactor of the Liberal Party
is involved in this payment of £5,000 to Newton to murder Scott and one man has   *b*
already been arrested and bailed'.

On this analysis it seems to me impossible to contend that the opening sentence of the
article, 'The names of two more people connected with the Norman Scott affair have
been given to the police' means no more than that there is an investigation which may
result in the wealthy Liberal benefactor being eliminated from the inquiry or even, as
happened, being a prosecution witness as was suggested to Chief Supt Challes in cross-   *c*
examination.

If the article as a whole said no more than that the police were going to see this wealthy
Liberal benefactor and that 'connected with' in its context meant suspicion of being
concerned in a conspiracy to murder and not participating in or condoning the plot
described, then guilt should not have been left to the jury (*Lewis v Daily Telegraph Ltd*
[1963] 2 All ER 151, [1964] AC 234). The judge in his summing up referred to para 4   *d*
of the statement of claim, which reads:

> 'The said words meant and were understood to mean that the plaintiff was guilty
> or reasonably suspected of participating in or condoning a plot to murder Norman
> Scott and of paying £5,000 in order to achieve that purpose.'

He then said: *e*

> 'The sting of the libel is that he was a participating member of a plot to murder
> Norman Scott and was putting up the money for it. That is the sting which is
> contended for. As I have said, I rule that the words are capable of meaning both
> those things. Whether they mean one or other is entirely for you to say.'

Counsel for the defendants has criticised this direction. He says there was nothing said   *f*
about suspicion; that there should have been separate verdicts on guilt and on suspicion;
that the judge should have drawn a distinction between guilt and suspicion for the
purposes of damages. Towards the conclusion of the summing up the judge said:

> 'So, do the words mean that Mr Hayward was a party to the plot to murder Scott
> or that he was suspected of that? Because he never was suspected of it. There is no
> suggestion that if the words mean that they are true. If they do mean either of those   *g*
> things, you may come to the conclusion that they are plainly defamatory and in that
> case it is a question of how much.'

Then he reminded the jury of the defendants' suggestion that the meaning was no more
than that 'two more names have come forward who may have something useful to say   *h*
about this investigation or to the police'.

This seems to me to be clear, simple and completely accurate both in fact and in law.
Of course there are cases in which to report a police or other inquiry into accounts and
so on is not defamatory of the individual responsible for such accounts. But, as Lord
Devlin said in his speech in *Lewis v Daily Telegraph Ltd* [1963] 2 All ER 151 at 173–174,
[1964] AC 234 at 284–285:   *j*

> 'It must depend on whether the impression conveyed by the speaker is one of
> frankness or one of insinuation . . . A man who wants to talk at large about smoke
> may have to pick his words very carefully, if he wants to exclude the suggestion that·
> there is also a fire; but it can be done. One always gets back to the fundamental
> question: what is the meaning that the words convey to the ordinary man; a rule

cannot be made about that. They can convey a meaning of suspicion short of guilt; but loose talk about suspicion can very easily convey the impression that it is a suspicion that is well founded.'

The judge ruled that the article of 9th April could be defamatory (for the moment I assume the identification of the wealthy benefactor). He was right. The jury said after proper direction that it was defamatory. It is suggested that the damages of £50,000 show they must have decided the words meant 'guilty'. I think this is an unprofitable speculation. The crime correspondent put the wealthy benefactor 'In' the Scott affair and he never got him out. Ultimately of course only the jury can pronounce that a man is guilty of crime. To the purist who would say that until verdict a man is presumed innocent and there can be no more than suspicion, counsel for the plaintiff's reply is that this was journalistic sensationalism resulting in a very bad libel accusing the wealthy benefactor of being 'the paymaster of blood money' is compelling. If this was suspicion it was so malignant, so virulent, as to be equivalent to a categorical statement of participation in the plot.

The interrelation of the two articles

That the article of 9th April was not 'innocent' is I think of importance when one comes to consider the other arguments for the defendants. Counsel for the defendants says that the article of 16th April cannot be admitted to throw light on the article of 9th April and that the judge was wrong in refusing to order that sub-para (ii) of the particulars of innuendo under para 5 of the statement of claim be struck out. That sub-paragraph reads:

'The words above complained of from the article in the edition of 16th April 1978 identified the plaintiff as the wealthy benefactor referred to in the article of 9th April 1978.'

Particulars were requested of the facts and matters relied on in support of the allegations that the words of 9th April referred to the plaintiff.

The reply was that such particulars had already been pleaded in para 5 of the statement of claim.

The judge gave his reasons for ruling against counsel for the defendant's submission. He referred to *Sadgrove v Hole* [1901] 2 KB 1 at 6, in which Collins LJ said:

'The case is analogous to the one that was put during the argument—of publication of a libellous statement as to someone whose name is expressed by a cipher intelligible only to the person addressed.'

He referred to *Chubb v Westley* (1834) 6 C & P 436, 172 ER 1309 and to a Californian decision, *Russell v Kelly* (1872) 13 Amer 169, in which a subsequent publication by the defendant naming the plaintiff as the person previously referred to was admitted. He did not find these cases conclusive but expressed his conclusion thus:

'It seems to me, if you publish words of the nature which were published on 9th April and then on 16th April identify the plaintiff as the person, that a grave injustice would occur if the plaintiff were not entitled to show that his identity had been established as the subject of the defamatory statement.'

We have been referred to further authorities: *Bruce v Odhams Press Ltd* [1936] 1 All ER 287, [1936] 1 KB 697, where particulars were ordered of facts on matters relied on from which it was to be inferred that words 'an enterprising Englishwoman' who had been smuggling aeroplanes abroad for conversion to warplanes referred to the plaintiff, for otherwise it was impossible for the defendants to know how to plead. *Simons Pty Ltd v Riddell* [1941] NZLR 913, where the company published in a newspaper on 6th June an advertisement that H and R 'are no longer in our employ and are not authorised to canvass or collect cash or empties on our behalf'. It was held that such words were not per se capable of a defamatory meaning *and* that a news item in the issue of 13th June that H had been convicted of issuing a worthless cheque with intent to defraud was inadmissible to prove the advertisement was defamatory. *Fullam v Newcastle Chronicle and Journal Ltd* [1977] 3 All ER 32, [1977] 1 WLR 651, which was 'straight within the general rule of pleading contained in RSC Ord 18, r 7, and also within the particular rule in libel actions contained in RSC Ord 82, r 3'. And finally *Grappelli v Derek Block (Holdings) Ltd* [1981] 2 All ER 272, [1981] 1 WLR 822, where the defendants on 21st September 1976 cancelled concerts which they had purported to arrange for the plaintiff on the false ground that Mr Grappelli was seriously ill in Paris and unlikely ever to tour again. Later, in November advertisements and a press release in Manchester and on 28th November by advertisement in the Sunday Times, concerts to be given by the plaintiffs were announced (presumably by the defendants) for 2nd and 6th December. In addition to a claim for damages for injurious falsehood the plaintiffs claimed for defamation, saying that—

'when people read in November 1976 in the Sunday Times that these other new engagements had been made for him, they would read an innuendo into the statement made in September 1976. They would say to themselves, "That was a put-up job. He was not really ill. He gave a reason which he knew to be false".'

(See [1981] 2 All ER 272 at 274, [1981] 1 WLR 822 at 824 per Lord Denning MR.)

But there the court was dealing with an attempt to make an innocent statement defamatory by facts which came into existence subsequent to its publication. That is clear from the adoption by Lord Denning MR of a passage from the judgment of Blair J in *Simons Pty Ltd v Riddell* [1941] NZLR 913 at 932 which he summarises thus ([1981] 2 All ER 272 at 275, [1981] 1 WLR 822 at 825):

'That principle seems to me to be applicable here. The inferences which were put on the statements *after* the publication (by facts subsequently learned) do not render them defamatory in the beginning.'

And from the words of Dunn LJ ([1981] 2 All ER 272 at 279, [1981] 1 WLR 822 at 831):

'. . . there is no room for the doctrine that the cause of action can, so to speak, be allowed to be inchoate or lie dormant until such time as some fact emerges which would transform an otherwise innocent statement into a defamatory one.'

In the present case there was nothing innocent about the publication of 9th April. It could have left out the references to the wealthy benefactor, to his visit to the Channel Islands last year, which was in any event untrue, and to the handing over to him of £5,000 which he later paid to a leading Liberal supporter which seems to have been a sub-editor's garbled account of the untruths House had originally written.

But a statement that two more names of persons connected with the Scott affair had been given to the police would have been dull stuff; interest had to be titillated by introducing the wealthy benefactor and the businessman from the Channel Islands. It seems to me to have been a kind of crossword puzzle or colloquially a 'whodunit' on page one, with an invitation to solve the identity from the clue 'a wealthy benefactor of the Liberal party'. Why else was it written? Mr House said that the wealthy benefactor and businessman had not been identified by his informant in any way. He was not cross-examined about this. But it is obvious that Mr House and every crime reporter and indeed every reporter worth his salt who had read or heard of the article of 9th April would be trying to identify this generous benefactor and get a story from him. This is exactly what happened to cause Mr Hayward to use in his evidence the words, 'I think this started the holocaust'. So too every reader with a liking for puzzles was being invited to guess the identity, and to search his memory or elsewhere for the answer. This may be one of the exceptions to the rule requiring identification of persons with knowledge of the special circumstances to whom publication is alleged where the publication is in a national newspaper with a very wide circulation and the only reasonable inference is that some readers must know the special facts: per Dunn LJ in *Grappelli v Derek Block Ltd* a [1981] 2 All ER 272 at 278, [1981] 1 WLR 822 at 830 (adopting Scarman LJ's views in *Fullam v Newcastle Chronicle and Journal Ltd* [1977] 3 All ER 32 at 39, [1977] 1 WLR 651 at 659).

Then in his article on Sunday, 16th April Mr House named the plaintiff, thus revealing the answer to his conundrum of the previous week. Having given an account of a telephone conversation with Mr Hayward (I need not dwell on the conflict over what was said which was for the jury, who obviously accepted Mr Hayward's version) Mr House
b wrote:

'Last week I revealed exclusively in the Sunday Telegraph that the names of two people, a wealthy Liberal party benefactor and . . . had been given to police.'

Counsel for the plaintiff says it was a saga or series. Counsel for the defendants says even so it should have been pleaded as an extrinsic fact. I am unimpressed by pleas that the form of the statement of claim and particulars prejudiced the defendants here so that
c they did not know what case they had to meet and that counsel for the defence would have had to indulge in a form of judicial telepathy to produce an adequate defence.

The plaintiff's case was very simple, that he was and was understood to be the generous benefactor defamed on 9th April and named on 16th April. He was a generous benefactor, having given £219,000 for the Liberal Party between 8th May 1970 and 15th
d November 1975. He was defamed in both articles, and in my judgment the judge was entirely justified in refusing to strike out the particulars on the ground that to do so would cause a grave injustice to the plaintiff.

Identification of the plaintiff and publication

Many complaints are made about the evidence or, more accurately, suggested lack of evidence of identification. Two witnesses were called, Sir Peter Scott and Mrs Cowper.
e It is said their names were never given in the pleadings, although counsel for the defendants accepts he did not object to them at the trial. In any event, the defendants never asked for names; only for 'facts and matters relied on'. It is suggested that Sir Peter Scott's evidence should not have been left to the jury. On rereading it, I still fail to see why not.

Then it is said that the judge should not have referred to the hierarchy of the Liberal
f Party who had not featured in the trial or to the press and ITV who certainly had featured in the evidence of Mr Hayward and in his letters.

What did the judge say in his summing up?

'But there are a number of people about who have got special knowledge and if it is published to them then they do identify the person. That is this case, because
g what is said is that there were a number of people about who knew that the plaintiff was a wealthy benefactor of the Liberal Party and that if they read the words would put two and two together and say: "That is the person who is being referred to." If you come to the conclusion that there were a number of people about, and we have seen two, who had got that special knowledge, then it is for you to say whether, as ordinary people with that special knowledge, it was reasonable to say that the article
h meant the plaintiff . . . The question is: first of all, are you satisfied on the evidence that there were people about to whom the Sunday Telegraph was published who had that knowledge? You have seen two of them and you may think, and you are entitled to draw inferences from the evidence, that the fact that he was a handsome contributor to the Liberal Party would have been known to quite a lot of people. For example, all the people in the hierarchy of the Liberal Party, you may think, would have known those facts. As I say, it has got to be proved that it was published
j to such people. Again it is not for the plaintiff to bring hundreds of people here and say: "I read the Sunday Telegraph." It is sufficient for him to bring some people who did so to establish that there are such people about . . . On that topic you have heard the evidence of two people who said they read the Sunday Telegraph and at once connected Mr Hayward. The fact that they connected him does not matter; it is whether they proved that there were such people, you may think (it is for you)

and if there were such people then with that knowledge would they clearly point to Mr Hayward?.... But you may think more important, if you accept his evidence *a* [that is, Mr Hayward's], that during that week he was getting telephone calls from a lot of people in London, journalists, on this topic. If it was an exclusive article in the Sunday Telegraph the inference which you may think it right to draw, though it is entirely for you, is to say there are a lot of people about in Fleet Street who put two and two together, but why were they ringing up Mr Hayward? What is ITV doing sending their United States unit across to the Bahamas? It is said that the very *b* same source of information that gave it to House may have given it to other people. That is what is being suggested. It is entirely a matter for you. Or do you think that it stems from the exclusive disclosure about these two men?'

There are few civil actions in which nothing new emerges in the course of the hearing. If there is no objection, what is the judge to do? Ignore it? Tell the jury to disregard it? Had he told them to ignore what had been said about the press, there *c* would be a cross-appeal here. The judge's references were accurate and fair and it is impossible to sustain the arguments that there should be a new trial on the grounds that he should have withdrawn from the jury the issue whether the words published on 9th April referred to the plaintiff and that he erred in holding that there was evidence or sufficient evidence for the jury that there were readers of the Sunday Telegraph who knew he had contributed £150,000 (at least) to the Liberal Party.   *d*

Separate verdicts

Counsel for the defendants asked the judge for separate verdicts on each publication. The judge ruled against him leaving three questions to the jury. (1) Do you find for the plaintiff or the defendants? (2) If you find for the plaintiff what sum do you award him? (3) If you have awarded damages have you included the period 9th to 16th *e* April? He said:

'... the reason for the third question is a way of getting your answer whether reasonable people with the knowledge contained in para 5(1) [that he had paid £150,000 to the Liberal Party] that he was a wealthy benefactor could reasonably have come to the conclusion that the words pointed to the plaintiff because for that *f* period he cannot rely on the fact that he was named on 16th April ... The answer will tell us whether you have come to the conclusion that he was sufficiently identified through the limited number of people who knew that he was a wealthy benefactor ...'

The jury answered: 'Both dates are included.' I myself think that the direction erred if at all in being over-favourable to the defendants, but counsel for the defendants says *g* that the decision of the House of Lords in *Lewis v Daily Telegraph Ltd* [1963] 2 All ER 151, [1964] AC 234 entitles him to separate verdicts. (See also Gatley on Libel (7th Edn, 1974, para 1369).) Most of the cases have been concerned with payment into court (see *Weber v Birkett* [1925] 1 KB 720). I prefer to adopt the reasoning of Lord Denning MR in *Pedley v Cambridge Newspapers Ltd* [1964] 2 All ER 794 at 796–797, [1964] 1 WLR 988 at 981– 982 in which *Lewis* was cited: *h*

'If you look at the substance of the claim, apart from any technicality, it seems to me that it is but one cause of action for libel. Technically, we must treat it as three causes of action. But that is a technicality which is of dubious value ...'

In *Pedley* there were two separate letters to the editor in one edition of the paper. The plaintiff relied on the natural meaning and on two innuendoes. The defendants asked *j* and were granted leave to make one payment into court. It would, said Lord Denning MR, 'be absurd to ask the jury to split up the damages into three separate heads one for each innuendo'. Here Mr Hayward claims damages for libel; not damages for each libel. The statement of claim treats the libel as one. I fail to see how the defence was prejudiced. If they thought they were they could have made an application before trial. The judge had a discretion. I am unable to see that he exercised it wrongly.

Aggravated damages

a   I agree with all that Lord Denning MR has said, and would add only that the failure to publish the disclaimers was by neglect born of indifference: an attitude of 'We don't care'. Mr House, the crime correspondent, knew that his account of the telephone conversation mentioned in his article of 16th April was challenged as 'wholly misleading and inaccurate'; he had failed even to inquire how or why sub-editing of his article of 9th April had produced a complete distortion of what he said he wrote, and he lost his

b notebook despite a request for its production. He can hardly be described as having been assiduous in trying to right the wrong done to the man of whom the solicitors for all three defendants had written on 4th May 1978: 'We would like to repeat on behalf of our clients that they have the greatest respect for Mr Haywood [sic] as a patriot and public benefactor.'

If his co-defendants with whom he is a joint tortfeasor accept what counsel for the

c defendants said for Mr House, to the extent of believing that he will suffer any financial injustice, then the remedy is in their hands.

In conclusion I agree with counsel for the plaintiff's comment that it would be a sad reflection on the state of the law of defamation if a new trial is necessary in this case. One sometimes forgets that what is said to a jury has to be understood by them. I consider the summing up here was lucid and fair. The jury was entitled to give the answers they

d gave, and I too would dismiss the appeal.

SIR STANLEY REES. In view of the judgments which have been delivered by Lord Denning MR and Sir George Baker, I can express my views shortly on the three major

e issues which arise for our decision in this interesting and important case.

1. *Meaning of the words in the publication on 9th April 1978*

It was strongly argued by counsel for the defendants that the words complained of were incapable of bearing the meaning that the plaintiff was guilty of participating in or condoning a plot to murder Norman Scott and of paying £5,000 in order to achieve that

f purpose. There is no doubt but that the judge did direct the jury that the words were capable of bearing the meaning that the plaintiff was guilty, as well as being reasonably suspected, of acting in the manner alleged. Having so ruled, he then properly directed the jury that it was a matter for them to decide whether the words did bear either of the two meanings alleged. The first question for this court is therefore whether the words are capable of bearing the meaning that the plaintiff was guilty in the manner alleged.

g I need not repeat the words of the article published in the Sunday Telegraph on 9th April 1978. Counsel for the plaintiff relied on the following aspects of the articles in support of his argument that the words were capable of bearing a meaning that the plaintiff was 'guilty' in the respects alleged. The heading in large type stated 'Two more *in* Scott affair—By Christopher House, Crime Correspondent'; in the text it was stated that 'the names of two more people *connected with* the Norman Scott affair have been given to the

h police' (emphasis mine); there is the allegation that both men 'arranged for a leading Liberal supporter to be "reimbursed" [which is placed within inverted commas] £5,000, the same amount Mr. Andrew Newton alleges he was paid to murder Mr. Scott'; it is stated that the Liberal benefactor flew to the Channel Islands where he was allegedly handed £5,000 and then returned and later paid the money to a leading Liberal supporter either directly or through another source; and finally there is a passage which indicates

j that the police want to interview the two 'new names'.

In my judgment, approaching the matter on the lines laid down by Lord Reid in his speech in *Lewis v Daily Telegraph Ltd* [1963] 2 All ER 151 at 155, [1964] AC 234 at 259–260, the article published on 9th April 1978 is plainly capable of bearing the meaning of imputation of 'guilt' as well as of 'suspicion' of guilt. Accordingly I would therefore hold that the judge properly directed the jury that it was open to them to say whether they did bear these meanings.

2. *Reliance on the publication of 16th April 1978 to provide evidence of*
   identification of the plaintiff referred to in the publication of 9th April 1978

The judge directed the jury that they were entitled to look at the second article dated 16th April 1978 in order to identify the plaintiff as from 16th April as being the wealthy benefactor referred to in the article of 9th April. Counsel for the defendants strongly argued that it is not open in law in any circumstances to rely on a subsequent publication in order to provide evidence of a defamatory meaning or of identification. A number of cases were relied on in support of this submission. They included the New Zealand case of *Simons Pty Ltd v Riddell* [1941] NZLR 913, *Fullam v Newcastle Chronicle and Journal Ltd* [1977] 3 All ER 32, [1977] 1 WLR 651, and *Grappelli v Block* [1981] 2 All ER 272, [1981] 1 WLR 822, all of which have been referred to by Lord Denning MR and Sir George Baker. In each of these cases the original publication was of innocent material which only became defamatory on the publication of subsequent material. The principle derived from these cases is that a writer of innocent matter cannot by reason of facts which came into existence subsequent to the original innocent publication become liable in damages for libel because the subsequent material attributes a defamatory meaning to the innocent publication. The question we have to consider is whether that well-established principle applies to a case such as the instant one when (1) the original publication is defamatory, (2) the second publication relied on explicitly identifies the person defamed and (3) it is published by the same party who published the original libel. In the course of argument it was put to counsel for the defendant that if the principle were to apply in such circumstances then it would be open to a newspaper to publish a virulent libel without identifying the person defamed but adding a statement that the victim would be identified in a week's time. The newspaper could then a week later publish the name of the person defamed without attracting liability for libel. Counsel for the defendants' reply to this was that the second publication should be pleaded as the libel and reliance placed on the original article as a legal innuendo.

Counsel for the plaintiff argued that there was a clear distinction between the instant case and the line of cases in which the original publication was innocent and only became defamatory of the plaintiff by reason of the later publication. He relied on the American decision in *Russell v Kelly* (1872) 13 Amer 169, in which it was held that a subsequent publication by the defendant identifying the plaintiff as the person defamed by the first publication was admissible in evidence.

In my judgment it was open to the judge to rule as he did that the jury were entitled to find that the publication of 9th April 1978 was defamatory and was understood by a limited number of people to relate to the plaintiff and that as from the publication on 16th April they would be justified in awarding damages on the basis that he was publicly named as the person referred to in the article on 9th April.

3. *Separate verdicts*

Counsel for the defendants also strongly argued before us that the jury should have been directed to return separate verdicts in respect of the publications of 9th April 1978 and the 16th April 1978. He submitted that it was a clear case for separate verdicts since there were two publications each of which was a separate cause of action and there were also two innuendoes pleaded each of which should have been the subject of a separate verdict. He had specifically raised the matter at the trial and the judge ruled against him. The judge directed the jury to answer three questions of which the third was: 'If you have awarded damages have you included the period 9th to 16th April?' To this question the jury's reply was: 'Both dates are included.' He relied on a number of reported cases to which I must briefly refer. The first was *Weber v Birkett* [1925] 2 KB 152, [1925] All ER Rep 244, in which the plaintiff relied on a publication of a slander and of a libel. The jury returned a single verdict for a lump sum of damages. The defendant had pleaded an apology and paid two sums of money into court, one in respect of slander and one in respect of libel. The trial judge held that no judgment could be entered for either party because the two causes of action were of different genus, namely one of slander and the other of libel. The Court of Appeal upheld this decision.

The next case relied on was *Barber v Pigden* [1937] 1 All ER 115, [1937] 1 KB 664, in
a which the plaintiffs claimed damages for three similar slanders uttered by one defendant
on different occasions during the years 1934 and 1935. It was not suggested on behalf of
the defendants that the jury should be directed to enter separate verdicts of damages in
respect of each publication of slander and the judge did not so direct. Accordingly the
jury returned a single verdict for damages. The Court of Appeal upheld the judgment
entered for the single lump sum of damages on the ground that the defendant was
b disentitled to take the point that there was no verdict given (it had not been taken in the
court below). Scott LJ made two observations which are of importance for the present
purpose. In relation to the observations of Bankes LJ in *Weber v Birkett*, Scott LJ said
([1937] 1 All ER 115 at 129, [1937] 1 KB 664 at 683):

> c '. . . a single verdict may validly dispose of an action in which several causes of
> action are alleged, unless the parties by their pleadings or their conduct of the action
> have rendered it essential that there should be more than one verdict in order that
> justice between the parties may be done.'

He stated his conclusion on the question whether in every case in which there is more
than one cause of action there must always be separate verdicts, in these words ([1937] 1
All ER 115 at 129, [1937] 1 KB 664 at 684):

> d 'The result is that the question whether one or more causes of action are to be
> included in one verdict or judgment will depend upon the exercise of the trial
> judge's judicial discretion upon all the circumstances of the case.'

Lord Denning MR approved these views of Scott LJ in his judgment in *Pedley v
Cambridge Newspapers Ltd* [1964] 2 All ER 794 at 797, [1964] 1 WLR 988 at 992. I
e respectfully accept that statement as an accurate exposition of the law. Counsel for the
defendants accordingly conceded that he would have to establish that there were
circumstances which justified interference with the judge's exercise of his discretion. He
emphasised that there were important points of difference between the publication of
9th April 1978 and that of 16th April 1978 in the following respects. Reference to the
plaintiff; the issue whether 'leave and licence' to publish could be relied on in relation to
f the 16th April 1978 publication and as to the meaning of the words respectively
published on the two occasions. Counsel further impressed on us the difficulties facing
practitioners in the field of defamation unless the technical rules governing the practice
are strictly enforced and this plea deserves an appropriate degree of support.

In my judgment the circumstances of the present case fully justified the decision of the
trial judge in the exercise of his discretion to direct the jury to make a single award of
g damages in respect of both publications if they found in favour of the plaintiff. A single
claim for damages was made in the statement of claim, the publication on 9th April was
defamatory and contained some degree of identification of the plaintiff, the second
publication on 16th April was deliberately published by the defendants to name and to
identify the plaintiff as the person referred to in their earlier publication and could be
treated as a 'republication' of the former article, the time span between the two articles
h was only one week, the judge properly directed the jury that any damages awarded in
respect of the first publication should be small and no issue as to payment into court
arose.

Accordingly, I would dismiss the appeal.

Appeal dismissed. Leave to appeal to the House of Lords refused.

Solicitors: *Simmons & Simmons* (for the defendants); *Oswald Hickson, Collier & Co* (for the
plaintiff).

Henrietta Steinberg   Barrister.

Faulkner v Talbot   *a*

QUEEN'S BENCH DIVISION
LORD LANE CJ, BOREHAM AND DRAKE JJ
2nd APRIL 1981

Criminal law – Indecent assault – Assault by woman on boy under 16 – Consent of victim –
Woman touching boy's penis during intercourse – Whether woman committing an indecent *b*
assault – Sexual Offences Act 1956, s 15(1)(2).

Where a woman touches the penis of a boy under the age of 16 during or preliminary to
sexual intercourse with the boy, the woman commits an indecent assault contrary to
s 15(1)[a] of the Sexual Offences Act 1956, notwithstanding that sexual intercourse between
a woman and a boy under the age of 16 is not itself illegal, or that the boy may be willing *c*
and co-operative, since by virtue of s 15(2) the boy's consent does not prevent the act
being an assault (see p 471 *g* to *j* and p 472 *a* to *c* and *j* to p 473 *b*, post).

Dictum of Fenton Atkinson LJ in *R v McCormack* [1969] 3 All ER at 373 applied.

R v Mason (1968) 53 Cr App R 12 overruled.

Notes   *d*

For indecent assault on a boy under 16 years of age, see 11 Halsbury's Laws (4th Edn) para
1036, and for cases on the subject, see 15 Digest (Reissue) 1051, 9052–9058.

For the Sexual Offences Act 1956, s 15, see 8 Halsbury's Statutes (3rd Edn) 425.

Cases referred to in judgments

Director of Public Prosecutions v Rogers [1953] 2 All ER 644, [1953] 1 WLR 1017, 117 JP *e*
424, 37 Cr App R 137, DC, 15 Digest (Reissue) 1233, *10, 525.*

Fairclough v Whipp [1951] 2 All ER 834, 115 JP 612, 35 Cr App R 138, 49 LGR 36, DC,
15 Digest (Reissue) 1233, *10, 522.*

R v Hare [1934] 1 KB 354, [1933] All ER Rep 550, 103 LJKB 96, 150 LT 279, 98 JP 49,
24 Cr App R 108, 32 LGR 14, 30 Cox CC 64, CCA, 15 Digest (Reissue) 1051, 9057.

R v Mason (1968) 53 Cr App R 12, 15 Digest (Reissue) 1051, 9058.   *f*

R v McCormack [1969] 3 All ER 371, [1969] 2 QB 442, [1969] 3 WLR 175, 133 JP 630, 53
Cr App R 514, CA, 14(1) Digest (Reissue) 416, *3525.*

R v Sutton [1977] 3 All ER 476, [1977] 1 WLR 1086, 141 JP 683, 66 Cr App R 21, CA,
Digest (Cont Vol E) 153, *9054a.*

R v Upward (7th October 1976, unreported).

Case stated   *g*

Patricia Ann Faulkner appealed by way of case stated by the Crown Court at Stafford (Mr
Recorder Weizman) in respect of its adjudication on 18th July 1980 whereby it dismissed
her appeal against her conviction by the justices for the County of Stafford on 5th
February 1980 on a charge of indecent assault on a male, contrary to s 15(1) of the Sexual
Offences Act 1956. The facts are set out in the judgment of Lord Lane CJ.   *h*

Malcolm Lee for the appellant.
Anthony Barker for the respondent.

LORD LANE CJ. This is an appeal by way of case stated from the Crown Court at
Stafford in respect of an adjudication of that court sitting then on appeal from the justices *j*
for the County of Stafford.

The way in which the case arises is this. The appellant was convicted by the justices
on 5th February 1980 of indecent assault on a boy, who was then aged 14 years, contrary

---

a   Section 15, so far as material, is set out at p 469 *b c*, post

to s 15(1) of the Sexual Offences Act 1956. The events happened at the appellant's home,
a   and there is no dispute as to the material facts. The 14-year-old boy was living in the
appellant's home, having left his parents. The appellant and the boy watched a horror
film on the television; the boy was scared, or said he was scared, by the film. As a result
of that the appellant told the boy that he could sleep with her if he wished. That he chose
to do.

Once they were in bed together, the appellant invited the boy to have sexual
b   intercourse with her. The boy's account, in so far as it was material, was this: the
appellant tried to put her hand on his penis, but he would not let her. She then pulled
the boy on top of her; she took hold of his penis and put it inside her vagina. On those
facts the charge was laid.

It is a well-known fact that there is no statutory provision specifically forbidding a
woman to have sexual intercourse with a boy of 14. But what s 15 of the Sexual Offences
c   Act 1956, under which this case was brought, says is as follows:

'(1) It is an offence for a person to make an indecent assault on a man.
'(2) A boy under the age of sixteen cannot in law give any consent which would
prevent an act being an assault for the purposes of this section . . .'

The way in which counsel for the appellant, in his attractive argument to this court,
d   has put the matter is as follows. He submits that, since the act of sexual intercourse in
these circumstances is not an offence on the part of the woman, therefore that touching
of the boy as a prelude to, or as part of, or as postlude to, the act of sexual intercourse
cannot in logic itself be an offence.

He submits, secondly, if, for example, in an act of sexual intercourse, in the way
described by Wien J in *R v Upward* (7th October 1976, unreported), to which reference
e   will be made later, a woman lies passively and does nothing at all except let the boy have
sexual intercourse, that, suggests counsel, would be no offence; whereas if she took any
part in the act, by touching the boy for instance on the buttock during the act of sexual
intercourse, it would be an offence. That, counsel submits, is contrary to common sense
and contrary to logic and therefore, he goes on to argue, it cannot be right that the act of
sexual intercourse under any circumstances can amount to indecent assault by the
f   woman on the boy.

We have been referred to a number of authorities and it is right, both for the purpose
of clarity and in deference to the arguments addressed to us, that I should refer to
them. The first case we were referred to was *R v Hare* [1934] 1 KB 354, [1933] All ER
Rep 550. The appellant was a woman who had been convicted under s 62 of the
Offences against the Person Act 1861 (which was a precursor of the 1956 Act) of indecent
assault on a boy of 12. In so far as it was material, that section of the 1861 Act read:
g   'Whosoever . . . shall be guilty . . . of any indecent Assault upon any Male Person shall be
guilty of a misdemeanour . . .'

The judgment of the court was delivered by Avory J. Having stated the facts, he went
on as follows ([1934] 1 KB 354 at 355–356, [1933] All ER Rep 550 at 551–552):

'We are asked in this case to hold that it was not competent to the Recorder to
h   leave the case to the jury or for the jury to convict the appellant. The argument put
forward on behalf of the appellant is that the charge being laid under s. 62 of the
Offences against the Person Act, 1861, no woman can be convicted of the offences
charged. The boy, being under the age of sixteen, was by law incompetent to
consent to any such conduct as took place between him and the appellant. There is
no question that the nature of that which took place between them was indecent.
j   The whole question is, as has been concisely put by counsel for the appellant,
whether the offence under s. 62 is to be limited to an indecent assault of a
sodomitical character . . . there is no reason for saying that the phrase: "Whosoever
. . . shall be guilty . . . of any indecent assault" does not include a woman.'

That case provides a formidable hurdle for counsel for the appellant to clear.

The next case to which we were referred was *Director of Public Prosecutions v Rogers* [1953] 2 All ER 644, [1953] 1 WLR 1017. That was a case where the facts were somewhat special, as will be observed. The headnote reads (37 Cr App R 137):

'On two occasions, the respondent, when alone in the house with his daughter aged 11, put his arm round her and led her upstairs, and when they were upstairs exposed his person and invited her to masturbate him, which she did. No compulsion or force was used by the defendant, and the child neither objected nor resisted, but submitted to the defendant's request. Justices dismissed informations charging the defendant with indecent assault on the child.'

The Divisional Court held, on those facts, 'that as the defendant had not used compulsion or force, or acted in a hostile manner towards the child, there had been no assault, and consequently no indecent assault on her, and that the decision of the justices was, therefore, right'. The facts were that the father, being alone in the house with the little daughter, put his arms round her and said 'come upstairs'. She made no objection or resistance and no force was used on either of the two occasions. That was the basis for the decision of the court, namely that the justices were right and the appeal was dismissed.

It seems to me that the circumstances there were exceptional. There was no reason why the father should not put his arm round the shoulder of his daughter; there was a lawful excuse for doing that, because he was the father. There was no touching of the child in an indecent way.

The next case was *R v Mason* (1968) 53 Cr App R 12. The headnote reads as follows:

'The defendant, a married woman, was arraigned on a number of counts, each alleging indecent assault against one of six different boys, all between the ages of fourteen and sixteen years. Over a substantial period of time she had been visited by the boys, sometimes singly, sometimes more than one at a time, and had had sexual intercourse with them. There was no suggestion that she had used any force or committed any hostile act against any of the boys. Intercourse had taken place sometimes at her suggestion, sometimes at the suggestion of the boys themselves. *Held*, that as there was no evidence of the use of any force or of any hostile act by the defendant, there had been no assault, and consequently no indecent assault, so that the counts must be quashed.'

I read one passage from the judgment of Veale J, which was really the high spot of counsel's argument (at 18):

'I am further prepared to hold that acts of touching readily submitted to and enjoyed during or preliminary to intercourse in such circumstances should be regarded as part of the intercourse and are equally not an assault by the woman on the boy.'

Those words were echoed in a different form in a case to which we have been referred, *R v Upward* (7th October 1976, unreported) which was heard at Caernarvon before Wien J and a jury. Wien J was there, in the passage to which we have been referred, informing the jury of the reason why he was directing them to acquit the woman in similar circumstances to those which I have described in *Mason*. Wien J, as I say, echoed and expanded the words used by Veale J in *Mason*.

One turns now to consider whether those two passages correctly reflect the law as it stands at the moment and in order to reach that decision it is necessary to look at two more recent decisions. The first is *R v McCormack* [1969] 3 All ER 371, [1969] 2 QB 442. That was a decision of the Court of Appeal, Criminal Division, before Fenton Atkinson LJ, Melford Stevenson and James JJ. The headnote reads as follows (53 Cr App R 514):

'A charge of unlawful sexual intercourse with a girl under sixteen necessarily includes an allegation of indecent assault on the same girl and, where there is clear a   evidence of indecent assault, the judge should leave this lesser offence also to the jury, even though the prosecution have not relied on it. When a man inserts his finger into the vagina of a girl under sixteen, this is an indecent assault, however willing and co-operative the girl may be.'

I read a passage from the judgment of the court delivered by Fenton Atkinson LJ ([1969] 3 All ER 371 at 373, [1969] 2 QB 442 at 445);

b   'Then there followed an argument by counsel for the appellant, which he has repeated to this court and put very attractively before us, whether in view of the girl's consent, there could be a conviction of indecent assault, there being here a willing girl and no evidence of any compulsion or hostility; and he referred to a line of authorities such as *Fairclough* v. *Whipp* ([1951] 2 All ER 834) and *Director of Public Prosecutions* v. *Rogers* ([1953] 2 All ER 644, [1953] 1 WLR 1017), cases which have

c   shown that where the accused adult invites a child, for example, to touch his private parts, but exercises no sort of compulsion and there is no hostile act, the charge of indecent assault is not appropriate. But, in our view, that line of authorities has no application here, and, in the view of the members of this court, it is plain beyond argument that if a man inserts a finger into the vagina of a girl under sixteen that is an indecent assault, in view of her age, and it is an indecent assault however

d   willing and co-operative she may in fact be.'

Finally, so far as authorities are concerned, I turn to *R v Sutton* [1977] 3 All ER 476, [1977] 1 WLR 1086. In that case the facts were that the appellant took three boys, all under the age of 14, to his home and photographed them partially clothed and in the nude. He remained fully clothed. He neither touched or fondled the boys, except touch them on the hands and legs and bodies in order to arrange their poses for the purpose of

e   photography. The boys consented to these acts.

The appellant was charged with indecently assaulting the boys contrary to s 15(1) of the 1956 Act. The jury were directed that any touching without consent was an assault and the law did not permit persons under 16 to consent to the touching, if it was accompanied by circumstances of indecency. The jury convicted. On appeal it was held by the Court of Appeal, Criminal Division, that they had been misdirected.

f   The holding was (66 Cr App R 21)—

'that whereas section 15(2) of the Sexual Offences Act 1956 bars consent from preventing an act with a boy under 16 from being an indecent assault—i.e. if the act alleged to constitute the assault is itself an indecent act—and thus the defence of consent will not avail a defendant; in the present case the touching of the boys by the appellant, which was merely to indicate a pose, was not of itself indecent, was

g   consented to and was not hostile or threatening, the consent of the boys to the acts complained of prevented such acts being an assault, and, therefore, an indecent assault; thus the question of indecency did not arise; accordingly, the jury had been misdirected and the appeal would be allowed and the conviction quashed.'

One turns, in the light of those authorities, to the present case. First of all what is an

h   assault? An assault is any intentional touching of another person without the consent of that person and without lawful excuse. It need not necessarily be hostile or rude or aggressive, as some of the cases seem to indicate. If the touching is an indecent touching, as in this case it plainly was because the appellant took hold of the boy's penis, then the provisions of s 15(2) of the Sexual Offences Act 1956 come into play: 'A boy under the age of sixteen cannot in law give any consent which would prevent an act being an

j   assault for the purposes of this section.' Consequently, the touching undoubtedly being indecent, the boy in this case, being aged 14, could not consent to it. It was intentional touching; it was touching without lawful excuse, and in view of s 15(2) it was a touching to which the boy could not in law consent and therefore did not consent. Accordingly, as I see it, one has all the necessary ingredients of the offence of indecent assault, and the consequence is that the recorder was correct in the conclusion to which he came.

The question which is asked by the case is as follows:

'... whether the acts of the appellant to which the complainant consented in *a*
pulling him on top of her and touching his penis immediately before sexual
intercourse by him with her were an indecent assault by the appellant on the
complainant contrary to s. 15(1) of the Sexual Offences Act, 1956?'

The answer I would give to that is Yes, it was an indecent assault. In my judgment the
decision of Veale J in *Mason* was wrong, and in so far as it is necessary to refer to the
matter, where Wien J was making explanation to the jury, he was likewise in error.   *b*
For these reasons I would dismiss this appeal.

BOREHAM J. I agree for the reasons given by Lord Lane CJ. I add only a few words
of my own out of deference for the argument of counsel for the appellant.

Without going into detail, there is, in my judgment, now ample authority for this   *c*
general proposition: where, in a charge of indecent assault on a person under the age of
16, the act complained of is indecent that act would, if it were done without consent, be
an assault, then the offence is made out. The authority for that is to be found in a
number of decisions from *Fairclough v Whipp* [1951] 2 All ER 834, to which Lord Lane
CJ has made reference, to *R v Sutton* [1977] 3 All ER 476, [1977] 1 WLR 1086. That
being so, s 15(2) of the Sexual Offences Act 1956 provides that the consent of the   *d*
complainant or the victim does not prevent it from constituting an offence.

In my judgment *Director of Public Prosecutions v Rogers* [1953] 2 All ER 644, [1953] 1
WLR 1017 is entirely consistent with that proposition. Indeed the court there, through
the words of Lord Goddard CJ, expressly confirmed the principle which had been laid
down in *Fairclough v Whipp*. In my judgment the problem which faced the prosecutor
in *Rogers* was this, that the act which might have constituted an assault was not an   *e*
indecent act. The defendant was the father who simply put his arm round the shoulder
of his little daughter. The act which was indecent, namely her touching of his private
parts at his behest, was not capable in the circumstances, for the reasons given in
Fairclough v Whipp, of constituting an assault. As Lord Goddard LJ pointed out in
Rogers's case, the picture might have looked very different indeed if there had been
evidence that that act by the little girl had been induced by threats or compulsion or by   *f*
any hostile act. That was no more than a repetition of what was said in *Fairclough v
Whipp*.

In my judgment the reference to aggression, hostility, compulsion or the like has been
misapplied in later decisions. It is unnecessary to go into detail. It is sufficient to say
that, in so far as Veale J decided that it was necessary in cases of this kind that there should
be evidence of aggression or hostility, then I would respectfully disagree with him for the   *g*
reasons given by Lord Lane CJ. The same applies to the observations made by Wien J
when explaining to a jury why he had decided to direct them to return verdicts of not
guilty. I suspect, as Lord Lane CJ said in the course of argument, that Wien J would be
very surprised to know that his words to the jury by way of explanation were likely to
be quoted in argument in later cases.

I agree with the way the matter was put in *R v McCormack* [1969] 3 All ER 371, [1969]   *h*
2 QB 442. The headnote has already been read by Lord Lane CJ; repetition of it would
therefore be unhelpful. It is sufficient to quote one small passage of the judgment given
by Fenton Atkinson LJ. He had referred to the case of *Rogers* and suggested that that line
of authority had no application to the case with which the court was then dealing. He
concluded ([1969] 3 All ER 371 at 373, [1969] 2 QB 442 at 445): '... it is plain beyond
argument that if a man inserts a finger into the vagina of a girl under sixteen that is an   *j*
indecent assault ... however willing and co-operative she may in fact be.'

If that is right, and if I may say so it clearly is right, why then it seems to me that where
the roles of the sexes are reversed, where it is the woman who deliberately gets hold of
the penis of a young boy, then she too is equally, and beyond dispute, guilty of indecent

assault (and I quote the words again) 'however willing and co-operative [the young boy]
a may be'.

I have said enough I trust to do justice to the argument so attractively put before us.
I respectfully agree with Lord Lane CJ's decision and with the reasons for that decision.
In my judgment the answer to the question posed by the recorder here is an unqualified
Yes.

b **DRAKE J.** I also agree. I agree with everything that has been said by Lord Lane CJ and
Boreham J and I would answer the question in the same way.

I would just add that the decision of Veale J in *R v Mason* (1968) 53 Cr App R 12 and
the view expressed by Wien J in *R v Upward* (7th October 1976, unreported) are in fact
both referred to in well-known textbooks, although they were not referred to in
argument, that is to say Professor Smith and Professor Glanville Williams in their
c textbooks on criminal law. Both of these learned writers came to the conclusion that the
decision in *Mason* of Veale J and the views expressed by Wien J are plainly wrong in law
and unable to stand against the other authorities, particularly that of *McCormack*. The
decision of this court confirms those views.

Appeal dismissed.

d Solicitors: *Gregory, Rowcliffe & Co* (for the appellant); *Kenneth Wainwright & Co* (for the
respondent).

April Weiss   Barrister.

e

R v de Vere

COURT OF APPEAL, CRIMINAL DIVISION
LORD LANE CJ, WATKINS LJ AND STOCKER J
16th JUNE 1981

f *Criminal evidence – Character of accused – Imputation on character of prosecutor or witness –*
Witness for prosecution – Accused not called to give evidence – Evidence of bad character not
admissible merely because he has attacked character of prosecution witnesses.

Criminal evidence – Character of accused – Previous convictions – Cross-examination as to
previous conviction – Imputation on character of prosecutor or witness – Imputation made in
statement from dock – Statutory provision allowing cross-examination as to previous convictions
g *not applying – Criminal Evidence Act 1898, s 1(f)(ii).*

Criminal evidence – Character of accused – Good character – Accused asserting his good
character in statement from dock – Whether accused thereby putting his character in issue –
Whether prosecution entitled to call evidence of accused's bad character.

h Where an accused person attacks witnesses for the prosecution and suggests that they are
not reliable, he is not thereby putting his character in issue, since he is not stating,
directly or indirectly, anything about his own character, and accordingly there is nothing,
so far as his character is concerned, which the prosecution is called on or entitled to rebut
either by cross-examination or by independent testimony. That rule is not relaxed by
s 1(f)(ii)[a] of the Criminal Evidence Act 1898 where the accused person's attack is made
j in a statement from the dock since s 1(f)(ii) only applies where the accused person is
himself called as a witness. However, where an accused person states from the dock that
he is of good character he is putting his character in issue, and at common law the judge

_____

a   Section 1, so far as material, is set out at p 476 *a* to *c*, post may in the exercise of his discretion allow the prosecution to call evidence to the contrary (see p 476 c to j, p 477 j and p 478 g h, post).

R v Gadbury (1838) 8 C & P 676 and *R v Butterwasser* [1947] 2 All ER 415 followed.

Dicta of Wanstall J and of Stable J in *R v Macecek* [1960] Qd R at 258–259, 271 and of Bridge LJ in *R v Campbell* (1979) 69 Cr App R at 226 applied.

Notes

For evidence of character of an accused person and for cross-examination as to his character, see 11 Halsbury's Laws (4th Edn) paras 368–369, 388, and for cases on the subject, see 14(2) Digest (Reissue) 499–503, 4074–4125.

For the Criminal Evidence Act 1898, s 1, see 12 Halsbury's Statutes (3rd Edn) 865.

Cases referred to in judgment

Brown v R (1913) 17 CLR 570, 14(1) Digest (Reissue) 370, *2053.

R v Butterwasser [1947] 2 All ER 415, [1948] 1 KB 4, 111 JP 527, 32 Cr App R 81, 45 LGR 570, CCA, 14(2) Digest (Reissue) 502, 4112.

R v Campbell (1979) 69 Cr App R 221, [1979] Crim LR 173, CA.

R v Chantler (1891) 12 NSWLR 116, 14(1) Digest (Reissue) 375, *2078,

R v Gadbury (1838) 8 C & P 676, 173 ER 669, 14(2) Digest (Reissue) 499, 4080.

R v Macecek [1960] Qd R 247 (Qld CCA).

R v McKenna [1951] QSR 299 (Qld CCA).

Selvey v Director of Public Prosecutions [1968] 2 All ER 497, [1970] AC 304, [1968] 2 WLR 1494, 132 JP 430, 52 Cr App R 443, HL, 14(2) Digest (Reissue) 642, 5203.

Cases also cited

R v Coughlan (1977) 64 Cr App R 11, CA.

R v George (1978) 68 Cr App R 210, CA.

Appeal and application

On 6th March 1980 in the Crown Court at Gravesend before his Honour Judge John Finlay QC and a jury the appellant, Raymond John Charles Moncrieffe de Vere, was convicted of obtaining services by deception (counts 1 and 2), procuring the execution of a valuable security (count 3) and obtaining property by deception (counts 4 to 8). He was sentenced to a total term of imprisonment of seven years. He appealed against conviction and applied for leave to appeal against sentence. The facts are set out in the judgment of the court.

William Geldart (assigned by the Registrar of Criminal Appeals) for the appellant.
Seddon Cripps for the Crown.

LORD LANE CJ delivered the following judgment of the court: This is an appeal which has had a somewhat chequered career. It starts off with a conviction and sentence on the appellant on 6th March 1980 at the Crown Court at Gravesend before his Honour Judge John Finlay QC and a jury. There were a number of offences of which he was found guilty: counts 1 and 2, obtaining services by deception, for which he was sentenced to two years' imprisonment on each; count 3, procuring the execution of a valuable security, for which he received four years' imprisonment; and then counts 4 to 8 inclusive, obtaining property by deception, each of the counts carrying a concurrent sentence, the greater sentence being that on count 5 of seven years' imprisonment. So the total term of imprisonment was one of seven years' imprisonment. It is not immaterial to notice that he represented himself during the trial, although he did have the advantage of legal advice short of advocacy on his behalf.

He now appeals against his conviction and sentence by leave of the full court. This is the second time on which the full court has considered the matter. The reason for that is this: the first occasion was on 6th April 1981, when the applications were refused by *a* the full court, but it transpired that the notice of hearing on that particular occasion was sent to the appellant at the wrong prison and he never received it; consequently, when that matter was brought to the attention of the court, it was thought proper that the case should be relisted before a differently constituted court, and that is how it comes about here.

The facts of the case can be dealt with with comparative brevity, because nothing now turns directly on them. This was in fact a highly sophisticated and complicated swindle *b* operated by the appellant in order to obtain for himself property in the shape of a dwelling house and a service station for something like £250,000 when he had absolutely no assets at all. There were a series of fraudulent transactions, as the number of counts in the indictment indicates. He was passing off cheques in order to give the appearance of being a man of means. There was an occasion on which he tricked a bank clerk into believing the same thing. He used a false name to create a bogus lease, and so on. It was, *c* as I say, a well-thought out, sophisticated and cunning fraud.

It was the subject of overwhelming evidence on behalf of the prosecution, and on the face of it there could have been little doubt about this man's guilt. He did not give evidence himself from the witness box but instead made a long statement from the dock, and this is yet again an occasion when this court has had to consider the effect of such a statement which, we are bound to say, is an anomaly and is continually giving rise to *d* difficulties, not only to trial judges who have a difficult task trying to explain to the jury the precise position of a statement from the dock, but also this court, as will be illustrated in just a moment.

During the course of that statement from the dock, portions of which we have read and need not be repeated, this man attacked two prosecution witnesses, alleging that they were persons of bad character who had behaved dishonestly. Secondly, it is plain from *e* what we have seen that he set himself up in that statement from the dock to be a man of considerable wealth, setting out in terms for the benefit of the jury the sums to which, he said, by reason of a bequest, he had become entitled in America or Canada, giving the precise number of dollars, namely $7,317,941. He not only set himself up as a man of substance well able to afford the total transaction, the subject of inquiry before the jury, but also represented quite plainly that he 'was a man of good character and good *f* background.

At the conclusion of that statement from the dock, prosecuting counsel made a submission to the judge that in all those circumstances he should be entitled to call rebutting evidence to show first of all that this man was not a man of substance as he had made out and, secondly, not only was he not a man of good character but had in fact in the past sustained a number of convictions involving fraudulent behaviour.

g The judge dealt with that matter in a brief judgment with great clarity. It must be said on behalf of the judge that he was suffering under some difficulty because the defendant was not represented by counsel and the relevant authorities on these matters were not cited to the judge. The judge came to these two conclusions: first, that the defendant had not given evidence of his own good character because statements from the dock are not evidence. The way he put it, if I may cite his words, was this:

h 'The other instances where the defendant has put forward his character as a man of substance are all instances founded on what he has said in his unsworn statement from the dock. They cannot, in my judgment, be subsumed under the words of s 1(*f*)(ii) [of the Criminal Evidence Act 1898] as giving evidence of his good character because, whatever the nature of the statement from the dock is, I do not regard it as constituting evidence of good character.'

j The second finding which he made was this, that the nature or conduct of the defence was such as to involve imputations on the prosecution witnesses, that is the words of the statement from the dock being part of the conduct of the defence. Therefore he held the words of s 1(*f*)(ii) of the 1898 Act were fulfilled, and therefore the prosecution was entitled to prove previous convictions.

The wording of s 1 of the 1898 Act is as follows:

'Every person charged with an offence, and the wife or husband, as the case may be, of the person so charged, shall be a competent witness for the defence at every stage of the proceedings, whether the person so charged is charged solely or jointly with any other person. Provided as follows . . . (*f*) A person charged and called as a witness in pursuance of this Act shall not be asked, and if asked shall not be required to answer, any question tending to show that he has committed or been convicted of or been charged with any offence other than that wherewith he is then charged, or is of bad character, unless . . . (ii) he has personally or by his advocate asked questions of the witnesses for the prosecution with a view to establish his own good character, or has given evidence of his good character, or the nature or conduct of the defence is such as to involve imputations on the character of the prosecutor or the witnesses for the prosecution . . .'

We have come to the conclusion, for reasons which will emerge in a moment, that the judge was wrong in both those conclusions at which he arrived.

The situation is this. If the defendant puts his character in issue, that is to say adduces evidence of his own good character, whether by cross-examination on his behalf or by means of giving evidence himself or by means of calling witnesses as to character, the prosecution may rebut that evidence either by cross-examination or by independent testimony, and that right has existed at common law for very many years going back, as found expressed, in *R v Gadbury* (1838) 8 C & P 676, 173 ER 669. It is repeated more recently in *R v Butterwasser* [1947] 2 All ER 415, [1948] 1 KB 4.

However, Lord Goddard CJ also said in that case ([1947] 2 All ER 415 at 416, [1948] 1 KB 4 at 6):

'However that may be, there is no authority for the proposition—and it is certainly contrary to what all the present members of the court have understood during the whole of the time they have been in the profession—that, where the prisoner does not put his character in issue, but has merely attacked the witnesses for the prosecution, evidence can be called by the prosecution to prove that the prisoner is a man of bad character.'

The reason for that is this, that, by attacking the witnesses for the prosecution and suggesting that they are not reliable, he is not putting his character in issue. He is putting their character in issue, that is to say he is not stating, directly or indirectly, anything about his own character at all. Accordingly there is nothing, so far as his character is concerned, which the prosecution are called on or are entitled to rebut. Such confusion as exists has perhaps been caused by the loose use of the expression 'puts his character in issue'. It is sometimes used incorrectly to cover cases where the defendant has subjected himself to cross-examination as to character by attacking the character of the prosecution witnesses. That is, strictly speaking, not putting his character in issue.

The exception has already been dealt with, that is to say, where he gives evidence and subjects himself to cross-examination under the terms of s 1(*f*)(ii) of the 1898 Act. If he is not called as a witness, then that section does not apply at all, and one is cast back on the ordinary rules of evidence. These do not permit, as a general rule, proof of a defendant's bad character as part of the prosecution case. In general it is not of course permissible, in order to prove a defendant's guilt, to adduce evidence as part of the prosecution case that the defendant has a bad reputation or a disposition to commit, or indeed has committed, crimes in the past. Nor is there any relaxation of that rule on the ground, so to speak, of tit for tat if the defence attacks the character of the prosecution witnesses. The rule is only relaxed by virtue of s 1(*f*)(ii). That only applies when the defendant is being cross-examined and he himself is giving evidence. If he does not give evidence it does not apply and *R v Butterwasser* is binding authority to that effect.

The result of that is that the judge was wrong in coming to the conclusion that the calling of rebutting evidence as to this man's character was admissible because he had made imputations on the character of prosecution witnesses.

a Therefore one has to turn to the question of whether, that being a material irregularity, it is right or proper that the proviso to s 2(1) of the Criminal Appeal Act 1968 should be applied and that the conviction should nevertheless stand. In order to determine this question, one has to ask oneself whether the judge was right in excluding evidence of bad character of the defendant because a statement from the dock was not evidence strictly so called, because that is what the judge did.

b We have been referred to authority on this matter and the first, and possibly the most important, is *R v Campbell* (1979) 69 Cr App R 221, a judgment of this court. It is necessary for me to read a passage from the judgment of the court, which was delivered by Bridge LJ (at 226):

c 'How far is it permissible, when an unsworn statement from the dock has been made, for the Crown in rebuttal to lead evidence to controvert a matter which has been raised for the first time in the course of the statement from the dock and so may be said to arise *ex improviso* and not to have been foreseeable by those presenting the prosecution case in the first instance? A statement from the dock is not, of course, evidence. It is, as many think—the fact that a defendant is still at liberty to make a statement of fact from the dock, invite a jury to consider his version of the facts without taking the oath and without subjecting himself to cross-examination—
d an anomalous historical survival from the days before the Criminal Evidence Act 1898 when a person could not give evidence on his own behalf. There it is, anomaly or not; the courts have to grapple with it and a statement from the dock unsworn now seems to have taken on in current practice a somewhat shadowy character half-way in value and weight between sworn evidence and mere hearsay. A jury cannot be told to disregard it altogether. They must be told to give it such weight as they
e think fit, but it can be properly pointed out to them that it cannot have the same value as sworn evidence which has been tested by cross-examination. The first question one asks is whether, as a matter of law, if a statement of fact relevant to the issues in the trial is made in the course of an unsworn statement from the dock which would, if given in evidence by the defendant or witnesses called on his behalf, give rise to an opportunity to call rebutting evidence, the same opportunity arises
f in a case where the evidence is unsworn. There is no authority on this point in this country. The current edition of Archbold (40th Edn, 1979, para 583a), observes: "In principle there can be no objection to the Crown being allowed to call evidence in rebuttal of an assertion made during the course of a statement from the dock where, had such a statement been made during the course of sworn evidence, rebuttal evidence would properly be admissible." Reliance is placed for that
g proposition on certain Australian cases which have said that if the law were otherwise it would be a manifest absurdity. We are urged in this case to say that that is a correct principle which ought to be applied in English law and for present purposes we are content to assume that this is correct . . . Let it then be assumed on those authorities that evidence to rebut relevant statements of fact arising *ex improviso*, or evidence of good character introduced for the first time in an unsworn
h statement from the dock, can in appropriate cases be rebutted by the Crown.'

We respectfully agree with those suggestions. It would be indeed an extraordinary state of affairs if a defendant were to be allowed in an unsworn statement from the dock to set himself up as a man of good character, of unblemished record, who has had no trouble with the police, a man of substance, highly thought of by his friends and neighbours, immune from any contradiction, if the fact were that he was a man with a
j long string of convictions, whom nobody trusted. It cannot be right that such a state of affairs should exist and we agree whole-heartedly and respectfully with what Bridge LJ said on that occasion. The simple question is whether the defendant has made his character an issue in the case. If he states from the dock that he is of good character it seems to us that he clearly does make that an issue, whether the statement is classified as evidence or as a mere averment.

We are reinforced in that view by an Australian judgment to which we have been referred, namely *R v Macecek* [1960] Qd R 247, a decision of the Court of Criminal Appeal of Queensland. It was a majority judgment to the effect of what Bridge LJ was saying, but there are certain passages which are so striking that they can be read and incorporated in this judgment to the benefit of all.

The first passage is in the judgment of Wanstall J, one of the majority. He said (at 258):

'I think that the drawing of analogies and comparisons on the procedural level cannot assist to elucidate this matter. The difficulty arises because the position is anomalous and it must be treated as an anomaly. It would be fallacious to argue that because statements of facts from the dock "are not evidence of the facts stated" (*R. v. McKenna* ([1951] QSR 299 at 307)) there is no evidence to be rebutted, and therefore such statements may not be contradicted by evidence in reply. It is true that both in form and in timing such a statement is an address or speech, but it nevertheless adds factual matter to the material for consideration by the jury, and in that sense has an evidentiary character and effect.'

It seems to this court that that last sentence at any rate precisely encapsulates the effect, or the possible effect, of the statement from the dock and is a very happy exposition of the difficulty. Wanstall J then said (at 259):

'In *Brown* v *The King* ((1913) 17 CLR 570 at 588) Issacs J. and Powers J. quoted the remark of Windeyer J. in *R. v. Chantler* ((1891) 12 NSWLR 116) that the object of the provision which allowed a prisoner to make an unsworn statement from the dock "was not to enable a guilty man to escape from justice but to enable the court to discover the true facts of the case", and went on to say: "And so the court held in that case that the prisoner's statements might be contradicted by ordinary testimony in reply. If not, said Innes J. it would encourage fabrication".'

The final passage is from Stable J, the other judge in the majority (at 271):

'So, even though the unsworn statement may be less than "evidence", its factual content—apart from argumentative content—may have a profound effect upon the mind of the jury. It may well provide that upon which a reasonable doubt is founded so that a guilty man may go free, perhaps through his skill in lying fortified by the knowledge that his lie will not be tested, or perhaps even questioned beyond a direction to the jury as to the weight to be given it.'

These pronouncements are weighty support for the view which this court has taken, namely that in a proper case where, as here, the defendant in a statement from the dock puts his character in issue, in the sense of setting himself up as being a man of good repute, that evidence may, on the judge exercising his discretion, be rebutted by the prosecution calling evidence to the contrary. So up to that point the judge having been wrong in his exclusion of rebutting evidence on that ground, the foundation is laid for the application of the proviso, because, quite plainly, if the judge had acted in the way which we think is correct, the evidence which was admitted wrongly would have been properly admitted on the other ground.

The only question that remains is the final point raised by counsel for the appellant in his argument, which was clear, succinct and, if we may say so, admirably presented, and that was that in any event the convictions which the prosecution proved before the jury in rebuttal were not properly proved. He relied for his submission on this point again on *R v Butterwasser* [1947] 2 All ER 415 at 416–417, [1948] 1 KB 4 at 8. It was the third aspect of that case to which this court had to pay attention. Lord Goddard CJ said:

'The second ground of appeal is that, even assuming the evidence of bad character was admissible, it could not be proved in the way in which it was proved in this case, *viz.*, by calling a police officer, who did not pretend that he knew the appellant, to say that, according to the records at Scotland Yard, the appellant had certain convictions recorded against him. That evidence would be properly admissible after verdict, but what happens after verdict is very different from what happens before verdict. After verdict, there is no longer an issue between the Crown and the prisoner.'

He was saying that it was an improper method of proving convictions in these particular circumstances.

But the facts here are very different. First of all the officer who proved the convictions was an officer involved in the case and knew the defendant. Secondly it is to be observed that in *Selvey v Director of Public Prosecutions* [1968] 2 All ER 497, [1970] AC 304 a similar sort of situation arose and it is dealt with in the headnote as follows ([1970] AC 304 at 305):

> 'That the failure to prove the previous record formally or to warn the jury that it had not been proved was not a ground for allowing the appeal, for in the circumstances the jury were entitled to treat the appellant's attitude as tantamount to an admission of the record.'

Finally on this point one only has to turn to the transcript to see that this man in fact admitted the convictions. First, he did not cross-examine the officer who was giving the evidence about previous convictions, and, second, he said this in the presence of the jury: 'Since these convictions, which were in 1971, other than the lottery, of which I was only a promoter, I have since married a young lady . . .' So he was there admitting that the convictions which the officer proved were in fact true.

In those circumstances, although, I will repeat, understandably the judge was mistaken in allowing the evidence to be adduced on the basis which he did, he was nevertheless wrong in excluding the very same evidence on another ground. From what we have said, it is apparent that there was nothing unsafe or unsatisfactory about the conviction. If everything has gone right, all this evidence would have been given in any event. For these reasons, despite counsel's able arguments for the appellant, this appeal is dismissed.

[After hearing submissions on sentence his Lordship continued:] We turn now to consider the question of sentence, the submission to us being that in view of the circumstances, despite the extent of the offences and this man's criminality, seven years' imprisonment was too long.

The circumstances are these. The man is now 51. He has a wife and four children. He was not altogether forthcoming in regard to the details of his employment but he told the police that he had an average weekly income of some £147. The depressing feature is his criminal record. Having seen that, one is driven to the conclusion that this man is a persistent confidence trickster, the size of whose tricks has been increasing as the years have gone by. Indeed the instant offences were committed at a time when he was awaiting the outcome of his appeal with regard to a fraudulent lottery. The judge described him as a man of imagination, ingenuity and also unbridled dishonesty. With those remarks we would agree. The fine in respect of the lottery was an act of great mercy which gave him the opportunity to change his style of life. He is obviously determined not to. The size of the present fraud or attempted fraud was so great that a long term of imprisonment was absolutely necessary.

In those circumstances we are driven to the conclusion that there is nothing wrong in these sentences. Accordingly the application for leave to appeal against sentence is refused.

Appeal dismissed. Application for leave to appeal against sentence refused.

Solicitors: *R A Crabb*, Maidstone (for the Crown).

April Weiss Barrister.

Practice Direction

SUPREME COURT TAXING OFFICE

Practice – Queen's Bench Division – Counsel's fees – Interlocutory fees – Accident cases – Scale of fees to be allowed on taxation.

The list of counsel's fees which was last increased in December 1979 has been the subject of discussion between the Chief Taxing Master and the Senate of the Inns of Court and the Bar. New fees relating to such cases will come into operation in respect of instructions and briefs delivered on or after 1st December 1981. The new list is set out below. The masters of the Supreme Court Taxing Office have said that the fees in the new list would be proper to be allowed on taxation in the normal run of such cases where the item has been dealt with fully. Each fee is intended to cover any necessary perusal of papers in connection with the item. A lower fee may however be appropriate where the item has not been dealt with comprehensively, was unusually simple, or where more than one item has been dealt with simultaneously. If a higher fee has been agreed it will need to be justified on taxation, as indeed will any fee which is claimed whether included in the list or not.

	Personal injury cases	Running down cases
Statement of claim	£30	£20
Defence without counterclaim	£25	£18
Defence (plain admission)	£10	£10
Particulars—request	£13	£13
answers	£15	£15
Reply with or without defence to counterclaim	£18	£15
Third party notice (not to stand as statement of claim)	£18	£18
Interrogatories and answers	£25	£25
Advice on evidence	£35	£35
Opinion (including opinion on appeal)	£25	£25
Opinion on liability	£32	£32
Opinion on quantum	£32	£32
Opinion on liability and quantum	£45	£45
Notice of appeal to Court of Appeal and counter-notice	£30	£30
Brief on summons before master	£25	£25

Conference fees
    Queen's Counsel   £25 first half hour, £15 each succeeding half hour
    Junior counsel   £12·50 first half hour, £10 each succeeding half hour

1st October 1981

E J T MATTHEWS
Chief Master.

Alan Estates Ltd v WG Stores Ltd and another

COURT OF APPEAL, CIVIL DIVISION

LORD DENNING MR, ACKNER LJ AND SIR DENYS BUCKLEY

15th, 18th, 19th MAY, 1st JULY 1981

Deed – Escrow – Condition – Operation of deed – Delivery as an escrow – Deed signed, sealed and delivered as an escrow – Date left blank – Deed subsequently becoming effective on fulfilment of conditions of escrow – Whether deed operative from date of delivery as an escrow or date when conditions of escrow fulfilled.

Under the terms of an undated lease, the tenants were to rent certain premises from the landlords. On 1st November 1976 the lease and counterpart were duly executed, exchanged and delivered subject to the fulfilment of certain conditions. The lease provided that rent was to be paid from 'the date hereof' but no date was inserted in the lease. The tenants subsequently attempted to repudiate the agreement but, by an action brought by the landlords, it was held that the lease was delivered as an escrow and that the lease would become binding on fulfilment of the last of the conditions. That condition was satisfied on 18th November 1977. The landlords brought a second action to ascertain the date from which rent was payable under the lease. The landlords contended that rent was payable from 1st November 1976, the date of the delivery of the escrow. The trial judge held that the lease commenced on the fulfilment of the last condition, ie on 18th November 1977, and that rent was payable from that date, being 'the date hereof' for the purposes of the lease. The landlords appealed.

Held (Ackner LJ dissenting) – The appeal would be allowed for the following reasons—

(1) The date properly to be inserted in a deed delivered as an escrow subject to the fulfilment of a condition was the date on which it was delivered and not the date when the condition was fulfilled. Thus, where the deed delivered as an escrow was a lease, then, although it could not vest a legal term in the tenant until the conditions attached to the escrow were fully satisfied, when those conditions were in fact satisfied so that it became an immediately operative deed that effect related back to the date of its delivery as an escrow for the purpose of giving effect to the lease. Accordingly, since the lease was delivered as an escrow on 1st November 1976, the lease had legal effect from that date when the outstanding condition was subsequently satisfied, and the rent which was expressed in the lease to run from 'the date hereof' therefore ran from 1st November 1976 and not from 18th November 1977 (see p 486 *b c g h*, p 487 *b* to *e* and p 492 *f* to *j*, post); dictum of Vaisey J in *Re Duke of Devonshire's Settlement* (1952) 31 ATC at 405 applied; dictum of Walton J in *Terrapin International Ltd v Inland Revenue Comrs* [1976] 2 All ER at 465–467 not followed.

(2) (Per Lord Denning MR) Since the tenants' repudiation of the contract had prevented a date from being inserted in the lease and since the lease would have been dated 1st November 1976 had the tenants not repudiated the contract, they could not take advantage of their own repudiation so as to postpone the date of the deed or the term from which rent should run (see p 485 *e* to *h*, post).

Per Sir Denys Buckley. The difference between a deed and an escrow lies not in the binding quality of the instrument but in the time at and the circumstances in which the obligation can be enforced. An instrument delivered as an escrow is as much a deed as a precisely similar instrument delivered unconditionally in the first instance save that the operative effects of the instrument are suspended while it remains an escrow (see p 491 *e f*, post).

Notes

For delivery of a deed as an escrow, see 12 Halsbury's Laws (4th Edn) paras 1332–1334, *a*
and for cases on the subject, see 17 Digest (Reissue) 256–258, 200–230.

For the formalities of execution of a deed, see 12 Halsbury's Laws (4th Edn) paras
1325–1331, and for cases on the subject, see 17 Digest (Reissue) 246–255, 104–199.

Cases referred to in judgments

Beesly v Hallwood Estates Ltd [1961] 1 All ER 90, [1961] Ch 105, [1961] 2 WLR 36, CA, 17 *b*
Digest (Reissue) 259, 244.

Butler and Baker's Case (1591) 3 Co Rep 25a, 1 And 348, 3 Leon 271, Moore KB 254, 76
ER 684, 17 Digest (Reissue) 253, 173.

Cory (Wm) & Son Ltd v Inland Revenue Comrs [1965] 1 All ER 917, [1965] AC 1088, [1965]
2 WLR 924, [1965] 1 Lloyd's Rep 313, [1965] TR 77, 44 ATC 61, HL; *rvsg* [1964] 3 All
ER 66, [1964] 1 WLR 1332, CA, 9 Digest (Reissue) 422, 2495.   *c*

Devonshire (Duke) Settlement, Re (1952) 31 ATC 399, [1952] TR 375, 45 R & IT 753.

Eccles v Bryant [1947] 2 All ER 865, [1948] 1 Ch 93, [1948] LJR 418, CA, 12 Digest
(Reissue) 78, 416.

Foundling Hospital (Governors and Guardians) v Crane [1911] 2 KB 367, 80 LJKB 853, 105
LT 187, CA, 17 Digest (Reissue) 252, 170.

Harrison v Battye [1974] 3 All ER 830, [1975] 1 WLR 58, CA, Digest (Cont Vol D) 114, *d*
417a.

Kingston v Ambrian Investment Co Ltd [1975] 1 All ER 120, [1975] 1 WLR 161, CA, Digest
(Cont Vol D) 274, 209a.

Perryman's Case (1599) 5 Co Rep 84a, 77 ER 181, 17 Digest (Reissue) 260, 251.

Security Trust Co v Royal Bank of Canada [1976] 1 All ER 381, [1976] AC 503, [1976] 2
WLR 437, PC, Digest (Cont Vol E) 60, 2412Aa.   *e*

Terrapin International Ltd v Inland Revenue Comrs [1976] 2 All ER 461, [1976] 1 WLR 665,
[1976] STC 197, [1976] TR 57, Digest (Cont Vol E) 508, 401a.

Thompson v McCullough [1947] 1 All ER 265, [1947] KB 447, [1947] LJR 498, 176 LT 493,
CA, 17 Digest (Reissue) 259, 243.

Tupper v Foulkes (1861) 9 CBNS 797, 30 LJCP 214, 3 LT 741, 7 Jur NS 709, 142 ER 314, *f*
17 Digest (Reissue) 248, 121.

Vincent v Premo Enterprises (Voucher Sales) Ltd [1969] 2 All ER 941, [1969] 2 QB 609,
[1969] 2 WLR 1256, 20 P & CR 591, CA, 17 Digest (Reissue) 256, 205.

Xenos v Wickham (1867) LR 2 HL 296, 36 LJCP 313, 16 LT 800, 2 Mar LC 537, HL; *rvsg*
(1863) 14 CBNS 435, 143 ER 515, Ex Ch, 17 Digest (Reissue) 251, 153.

Cases also cited   *g*

Bradshaw v Pawley [1979] 3 All ER 273, [1980] 1 WLR 10.

Coare v Giblett (1803) 4 East 85, 102 ER 763.

Edmunds v Edmunds [1904] P 362.

Glessing v Green [1975] 2 All ER 696, [1975] 1 WLR 863, CA.

Graham v Graham (1791) 1 Ves 272, 30 ER 339.

Hooper v Ramsbottom (1815) 6 Taunt 12, 128 ER 936.   *h*

Styles v Wardle (1825) 4 B & C 908, 107 ER 1297.

Appeal

The plaintiffs, Alan Estates Ltd ('the landlords'), appealed against the judgment of his
Honour Judge Rubin sitting as a judge of the High Court, given on 1st February 1980 in
favour of the first defendants, WG Stores Ltd ('the tenants'), and the second defendant, *j*
Derek Desmond Solomons ('the surety'), whereby he ordered that the landlords'
originating summons be dismissed and that the tenants were liable to pay rent in respect
of premises at 32 Goldhawk Road, Hammersmith, London W12 from 18th November
1977. In their originating summons the landlords sought the following relief: (1) a
declaration that the obligations of the tenants under the lease commenced or alternatively

should be deemed to have commenced on 1st November 1976; (2) further or alternatively, a declaration that the tenants became liable, or alternatively should be deemed to have become liable, to pay sums due by way of rent and/or apportioned insurance premiums pursuant to the terms of the lease with effect from 1st November 1976. The facts are set out in the judgment of Lord Denning MR.

Gordon Nurse for the landlords.
Lawrence Cohen for the tenants and the surety.

Cur adv vult

1st July. The following judgments were read.

LORD DENNING MR. In this case we have to consider the medieval law about an 'escrow' and to put it into its modern setting.

The facts
There is a lock-up shop at 32 Goldhaw Road, London W12. In September 1976 it was empty. WG Stores Ltd were keen to take a lease of it from the landlords, Alan Estates Ltd. They wanted to occupy it as soon as possible. In anticipation of the lease, the landlords allowed the tenants to have they key, so as to measure up for shop fittings. The tenants paid a quarter's rent to the landlords' solicitors, asking them to hold it as stakeholders pending completion of the lease. Inquiries were made as to title and so forth. But no preliminary contract was entered into. The solicitors got on straight away with preparing the lease, and getting it engrossed and executed. Then on Monday, 1st November 1976, the solicitors exchanged the lease and counterpart duly executed. But this is to be noted. Both lease and counterpart were undated. Each started off:

> 'THIS LEASE is made the   day of   One thousand nine hundred and seventy-six BETWEEN ALAN ESTATES LIMITED . . . [and] W. G. STORES LIMITED . . .'

The tenants' solicitors wrote this letter to the landlords' solicitors:

> '. . . we now enclose the Lease duly executed by our Client . . . As agreed on the telephone you will hold this document to our order pending receipt by us of satisfactory final searches [and various other conditions] . . . Pending clarification of all the above points by way of confirmation you will hold the executed Lease to our order and also continue to hold the sum of £937·50 [the first quarter's rent].
> 'Yours faithfully,
> 'PAUL WOOLF & CO. [Tenants' solicitors.]
> 'PS. Our Company Agents advise us that there is an undischarged charge in favour of Northern Commercial Trust Ltd. and we shall also require your undertaking in respect of this.'

The landlords' solicitors replied on the same day:

> 'We thank you for your letter of today's date enclosing the Lease, duly executed . . . We presume it is acceptable that we date the Lease today [that is, 1st November 1976]? We enclose herewith our Clients' part of the Lease duly executed by way of exchange . . .
> 'Yours faithfully,
> 'MARTIN BOSTON & CO. [Landlords' solicitors.]'

Those letters were written on Monday, 1st November 1976. On the following Monday, 8th November 1976, the tenants' solicitors wrote to the landlords' solicitors. They took no objection to the date being inserted, 1st November 1976. They simply said:

> 'Thank you for your letter of the 1st November with enclosures as therein stated. Unfortunately there still appears to be a problem regarding the mortgage to

Northern Commercial Trust Ltd. . . . Our Client is anxious to complete this matter and indeed we did try to telephone your Mr. Boston on Friday without success.' *a*

That was Monday, 8th November. On the next day, Tuesday, 9th November, the tenants decided to call off the whole thing. Their solicitors telephoned to the landlords' solicitors. They replied that they regarded the transaction as binding. The tenants' solicitors wrote this letter on Tuesday, 9th November 1976:

'As explained on the telephone today our Client has decided to withdraw from *b* the transaction and we should be obliged if you would return our Client's cheque in the sum of £937·50 which, under the terms of our letter dated 1st November, you are still holding to this firm's order. As explained on the telephone we very much regret the lateness of our Client's decision and we must confess we were surprised to hear from you that you considered the transaction to have been completed . . .'

So there it was. The landlord's solicitors considered that the transaction was binding. *c* The tenants' solicitors said it was not binding. Two days later, on Thursday, 11th November 1976, the landlords' solicitors issued a writ claiming a declaration that the lease and counterpart were binding; alternatively, that it was an escrow. The defendants denied it.

The decision of Whitford J *d*

The action took a year to come on. Then on 14th and 15th November 1977 it was tried by Whitford J. At the end of the day it was accepted by both sides that the lease was delivered as an escrow on the terms set out in the tenants' solicitors' letter of 1st November 1976. The only question was whether the various conditions had been fulfilled. It was accepted that all had been fulfilled save for the postscript requiring an undertaking about the 'undischarged charge in favour of Northern Commercial Trust *e* Ltd'. It would have been quite easy to fulfil this but the landlords' solicitors had not done it. The tenants' solicitors submitted that it was too late for them to do it. But Whitford J held otherwise. He said:

'I reject the conclusion that is urged on me by counsel on behalf of the [the tenants] that it is now too late for [the landlords] to satisfy the outstanding *f* condition. They ought to have had a reasonable time after 8th November 1976 to meet this last condition contained in that letter then outstanding, and I am prepared to give them a reasonable time to satisfy that condition and accordingly to make the transaction binding to date.'

The landlords did satisfy the condition on 18th November 1977 so the lease became *g* binding.

At the end of the hearing before Whitford J, counsel then raised the question of rent. From what date was it payable? Whitford J said: 'There is nothing about this in the pleadings in this connection at all. I am not prepared to deal with it.'

These proceedings *h*

So these proceedings were commenced to ascertain the date from which rent was payable. Was it from 1st November 1976 (when the lease and counterpart were exchanged)? Or from 18th November 1977 (when the last condition was fulfilled)? The landlords took out an originating summons to determine it.

His Honour Judge Rubin held that the rent is only payable from 18th November 1977. The landlords appeal. *j*

The blank in the lease

The difficulty has arisen because of the blank in the lease. No date was inserted. But the rent was to run 'from the date hereof'. So we have the problem. From what date is the rent to run?

Something may turn on the wording of the document. So I will set it out. The lease was in this form:

'THIS LEASE is made the   day of   One thousand nine hundred and seventy-six BETWEEN ALAN ESTATES LIMITED . . . [and] W. G. STORES LIMITED . . . the Landlord HEREBY DEMISES unto the Tenant ALL THAT property . . . TO HOLD the demised premises unto the Tenant for a term of TWENTY FOUR YEARS from the Twenty-ninth day of September One thousand nine hundred and seventy-six (determinable as hereinafter provided) PAYING THEREFOR unto the Landlord from the date hereof and throughout the said term hereby granted yearly and proportionately for any fraction of a year the several rents hereinafter referred to: A. Until the Twenty-ninth day of September One Thousand nine hundred and eighty the yearly rent of THREE THOUSAND TWO HUNDRED AND FIFTY POUNDS (£3,250) . . . IN WITNESS whereof the parties hereto have hereunto set their respective common seals and hands and seals as appropriate the day and year first before written . . .

THE COMMON SEAL OF
W. G. STORES LIMITED
was hereunto affixed in the   }   Seal
presence of:—

B. Solomons   Director.
B. Solomons   Secretary.'

If there had been no repudiation
In order to solve the problem, I would ask this question: 'Suppose the tenants had not repudiated their obligations. What date would have been inserted in the lease?' I feel sure that the solicitors would have inserted 1st November 1976. I say this because of the letter of the landlords' solicitors of 1st November 1976 in which they said: 'We presume it is acceptable that we date the Lease today?', to which the tenants' solicitors took no objection. In addition, both lease and counterpart were exchanged on 1st November 1976; and, by analogy with contract and conveyances of land, the effective date when the parties are bound is the date of exchange: see *Eccles v Bryant* [1947] 2 All ER 865, [1948] 1 Ch 93 and *Harrison v Battye* [1974] 3 All ER 830, [1975] 1 WLR 58.

However, no date was inserted. It remained blank. The reason was because the tenants repudiated the transaction altogether. They denied that the tenants were bound. I cannot think that they can take advantage of their own repudiation, so as to postpone the date of the deed, or the term from which rent should run. No one can take advantage of his own wrong. We should insert the date which would have been inserted had they not repudiated. That is 1st November 1976. The rent should run from that date.

In case this simple solution be erroneous, I must go on to deal with the law about escrow.

When does an escrow take effect?
Another way of approaching the problem is to ask: at what date does an escrow take effect? On the date when the deed is delivered? Or on the date when the conditions are fulfilled? Judge Rubin held that—

'a deed, delivered as an escrow, takes effect from the satisfaction of the condition and not from the date of its delivery as an escrow. Applied to the present case, in my judgment both lease and counterpart took effect together on the satisfaction of the condition on 18th November 1977 and, accordingly, such date is "the date hereof", and the rent ought to be calculated from and become payable from that date.'

In coming to this conclusion Judge Rubin felt that he had the clearest possible authority in the judgment of Walton J in *Terrapin International Ltd v Inland Revenue Comrs* [1976] 2 All ER 461 at 465–466, [1976] 1 WLR 665 at 669–670, who said of an escrow: **a**

> '. . . although of course it contains within itself the possibility of becoming an effective deed, a deed rising phoenix-like from the ashes of the escrow, at the stage before the condition is fulfilled it is of no effect whatsoever.'
> **b**

To the contrary, however, is the dictum of Vaisey J in *Re Duke of Devonshire's Settlement* (1952) 31 ATC 399 at 405:

> '. . . as a rule the date properly to be inserted in a deed delivered as an escrow is the date at which it was so delivered and not the date when the condition of the delivery has been fulfilled.'
> **c**

The doctrine of escrow

The doctrine of 'escrow' is a relic of medieval times. It dates from the time when conveyances were made by feoffment and livery of seisin. It has survived to the present day and often operates in regard to conveyances of land or the creation or disposition of estates and interests in land such as a term of years. It has changed its features much since the days of Sheppard's Touchstone (1st Edn, 1641; 7th Edn, 1820) and Preston's Abstracts **d** of Title (1st Edn, 1818–19; 2nd Edn, 1823–24). We no longer speak of a first delivery or a second delivery. But it does predicate a document which is executed and delivered. The accustomed formula is 'signed, sealed and delivered'. When that formula is used in the document and it is signed by the party (or in the case of a company its seal is affixed) and attested by a witness with intent by the maker that it should be binding on him, it is conclusively presumed to be 'signed, sealed and delivered'. If it is handed over to **e** another unconditionally, it is delivered as a deed. If it is handed over to another conditionally, it is delivered as an escrow. It only becomes a deed when the conditions are fulfilled.

Thus far there can be no dispute. The question in this case is: what is the effect of an escrow before the conditions are fulfilled? One thing is clear. Whilst the conditions are in suspense, the maker of the escrow cannot recall it. He cannot dispose of the land or **f** mortgage it in derogation of the grant which he has made. He is bound to adhere to the grant for a reasonable time so as to see whether the conditions are to be fulfilled or not. If the conditions are not fulfilled at all, or not fulfilled within a reasonable time, he can renounce it. On his doing so, the transaction fails altogether. It has no effect at all. But if the conditions are fulfilled within reasonable time, then the conveyance or other disposition is binding on him absolutely. It becomes effective to pass the title to the land **g** or other interest in the land from the grantor to the grantee. The title is then said to 'relate back' to the time when the document was executed and delivered as an escrow. But this only means that no further deed or act is necessary in order to perfect the title of the grantee. As between grantor and grantee, it must be regarded as a valid transaction which was effective to pass the title to the grantee as at the date of the escrow: see *Perryman's Case* (1599) 5 Co Rep 84a at 84b, 77 ER 181 at 182–183. But this doctrine of **h** 'relation back' does not operate so as to affect dealings with third parties: see *Butler and Baker's Case* (1591) 3 Co Rep 25a, 76 ER 684. So far as the grantee is concerned, whilst the conditions are in suspense, he gets no title such as to validate his dealings with third persons. He cannot collect rents from the tenants. Nor can he give the tenants notice to quit. He cannot validly mortgage the land, though, if he purports to do so, the mortgage might be 'fed' later when he acquires the title. **j**

Such are the principles which I deduce from the very learned work of Williams on Real Property (19th Edn, 1901, p 151, note (*k*)) and the authorities cited therein, and from the judgment of Farwell LJ in *Governors and Guardians of Foundling Hospital v Crane* [1911] 2 KB 367 at 377 and of Lord Cross in *Security Trust Co v Royal Bank of Canada* [1976] 1 All ER 381 at 390, [1976] AC 503 at 517. I said likewise in *Wm Cory & Sons Ltd*

v Inland Revenue Comrs [1964] 3 All ER 66 at 70–71, [1964] 1 WLR 1332 at 1341. I realise
a that both Diplock LJ and Lord Reid said otherwise (see [1964] 3 All ER 66 at 74, [1964]
1 WLR 1332 at 1346 and [1965] 1 All ER 917 at 921, [1966] AC 1088 at 1107–1108).
But they had not the benefit of having cited to them the earlier authorities, and their
observations are said in the latest textbook to be erroneous: see Emmet on Title (17th
Edn, 1978, p 650).

b *What date is to be inserted?*
    The question in this case is as between grantor and grantee. The counterpart lease was
executed (a day or two beforehand) and delivered in escrow on 1st November 1976. In
exchange the lease was executed (a day or two beforehand) and delivered in escrow on 1st
November 1976. The date of delivery in escrow was therefore 1st November 1976. The
conditions were fulfilled on 18th November 1977. Thereupon the title related back to
c the delivery on 1st November 1976. That is the date to be inserted in the lease as 'the
date hereof'. For this purpose we go back to Co Lit 46b:

> 'If the *habendum* be for the terme of twenty-one years, without mentioning when
> it shall begin, it shall begin from the deliverie, for there the words take effect, as is
> aforesaid. If an indenture of lease beare date which is void or impossible, as the
> thirtieth day of *Februarie*, or the fortieth of *March*, if in this case the terme be
d > limited to begin from the date, it shall begin from the deliverie, as if there had been
> no date at all.'

Conclusion
    This case has taken us back to the language and thought of the medieval lawyers. The
result is that the lessees must pay the rent of the lock-up shop from 1st November 1976
e and not from 18th November 1977. This seems to me the just result. It would not be
right that the lessees, by repudiating their obligations on 9th November 1976, should
thereby get out of paying any rent for a whole year, whilst the issue was being litigated,
in which they were found to be wrong.
    I would therefore allow the appeal.

f **ACKNER LJ.** The habendum in the lease, the subject matter of this dispute, provides
for 'a term of TWENTY FOUR YEARS from the Twenty-ninth day of September One thousand
nine hundred and seventy-six (determinable as hereinafter provided) PAYING THEREFOR
unto the Landlord from the date hereof ... the several rents hereinafter referred to'.
'The date hereof' is a reference back to the date of the execution of the lease. But the lease
is not dated. The question which we have to decide is from what date did the obligation
g to pay rent begin. Was it 1st November 1976, the date when the lease was executed by
the appellant landlord in escrow, the condition being the unconditional delivery by the
tenant of the counterpart, or 18th November 1977 when for the first time the only
outstanding term (the production of a certified copy of the transfer of the mortgage)
under which the counterpart had been delivered was first satisfied?
    This appeal thus raises the short but by no means simple question: from what date
h does an escrow become operative? From the date it was delivered as an escrow or from
the date when the conditions subject to which it was delivered have all been satisfied?
At first instance the judge found in favour of the second alternative. He held that the
execution of a lease only occurred when it was signed, sealed and unconditionally
delivered.

j *The nature of an escrow*
    If an instrument be delivered to take effect on the happening of a specified event, or
on condition that it is not to be operative until some condition is performed, then
pending the happening of the event or the performance of the condition the instrument
is called an escrow: see Norton on Deeds (2nd Edn, 1928, p 18) citing Lord Cranworth LC
in *Xenos v Wickham* (1867) LR 2 HL 296 at 323:

'The maker [of a deed] may so deliver it as to suspend or qualify its binding effect. He may declare that it shall have no effect until a certain time has arrived, or *a* until some condition has been performed, but when the time has arrived, or the condition has been performed, the delivery becomes absolute, and the maker of the deed is absolutely bound by it, whether he has parted with possession or not. Until the specified time has arrived, or the condition has been performed, the instrument is not a deed. It is a mere escrow.'

This view of the nature of an escrow was accepted by Diplock LJ in *Wm Cory & Sons* *b* *Ltd v Inland Revenue Comrs* [1964] 3 All ER 66 at 74, [1964] 1 WLR 1332 at 1346. He said:

'So long as it remains an escrow it is not yet executed as a deed; for delivery again as a deed is required before it becomes one. While an escrow it conveys nothing, it transfers nothing.'
c

However, a party who executes a deed of transfer as an escrow has no locus poenitentiae. It is well established that during the intervening time between the execution of the escrow and the satisfaction of the condition subject to which it was so delivered, the maker of the escrow cannot withdraw. He cannot recall it or repudiate it. He must await the event to see whether or not the condition is fulfilled: see *Beesly v Hallwood Estates Ltd* [1961] 1 All ER 890, [1961] Ch 105, *Vincent v Premo Enterprises (Voucher Sales)* *d* *Ltd* [1969] 2 All ER 941, [1969] 2 QB 609 and *Kingston v Ambrian Investment Co Ltd* [1975] 1 All ER 120 at 125, [1975] 1 WLR 161 at 166. The dicta to the contrary by Lord Reid in *Cory's case* [1965] 1 All ER 917 at 921, [1965] AC 1088 at 1107–1108 is generally accepted as being per incuriam: see Emmet on Title (17th Edn, 1978, p 650) referring to the decision of Walton J in *Terrapin International Ltd v Inland Revenue Comrs* [1976] 2 All ER 461 at 465–466, [1976] 1 WLR 665 at 669–670, a case to which I shall make a more *e* detailed reference hereafter. While this is clearly an important characteristic of an escrow, it does not seem to me to relate to the problem we have to solve. It is, of course, common ground that all the conditions subject to which the escrow was delivered have now been satisfied. This escrow had therefore ceased, so to speak, to be in suspended animation and we are not therefore concerned with what might have been the position during the interregnum between the execution of the escrow and the satisfaction of the *f* conditions.

The doctrine of relation back
In Preston's Abstracts of Title (2nd Edn, 1823–1824, vol 3, p 65), the law is stated as follows:

'The rules respecting *escrows* are, 1st, The writing will not operate as a deed till the *g* second delivery. 2dly, The party deputed to make the second delivery, cannot give effect to the writing by delivering the same before the conditions are performed. 3rdly, On the second delivery of the writing, it will have relation, for the purposes of title, and not for the purpose of giving a right to the intermediate rents, &c., from the delivery. 4thly, So as the conditions be peformed, and the deed delivered a second time, the deed will be good, notwithstanding the death of either or both of *h* the parties before the second delivery.'

These observations have frequently been cited with approval: see in particular *Governors and Guardians of Foundling Hospital v Crane* [1911] 2 KB 367 at 377 per Farwell LJ. The reference to a second delivery was because under the old law an escrow had to be delivered to a third party, not to the person intended to take thereunder since *j* otherwise there would have been a technical delivery. On the fulfillment of the condition the third party would then deliver it to the person intended to take thereunder. The limited nature of this doctrine is apparent from the following observations of Lord Cross giving the opinion of the Board in *Security Trust Co v Royal Bank of Canada* [1976] 1 All ER 381 at 390, [1976] AC 503 at 517:

> 'On fulfilment of the condition subject to which it was delivered as an escrow a
> deed is not taken to relate back to the date of its delivery for all purposes but only
> for such purposes as are necessary to given efficacy to the transaction, ut res magis
> valeat quam pereat (see *Butler and Baker's Case* (1591) 3 Co Rep 25a, 76 ER 684).
> Thus the fact that the grantor has died before the condition of an escrow is fulfilled
> does not entail the consequence that the disposition fails. If and when the condition
> is fulfilled the doctrine of relation back will save it—but notwithstanding the
> relation back for that limited purpose the grantee is not entitled to the rents of the
> property during the period of suspense or to lease it or to serve notices to quit (see
> Sheppard's Touchstone (7th Edn, 1820, p 60); *Thompson v McCullough* [1947] 1 All
> ER 265, [1947] KB 447).'

This doctrine does not seem to me to advance the landlord's case.

I return now to *Terrapin International Ltd v Inland Revenue Comrs* [1976] 2 All ER 461,
[1976] 1 WLR 665, which raised for decision the correct rate of stamp duty payable on
a document originally delivered as an escrow. Walton J, to decide this question,
considered that he had to go back to first principles as to the nature of escrows. Having
cited from Preston's Abstracts of Title, in the terms referred to above, he went on to say
([1976] 2 All ER 461 at 465–466, [1976] 1 WLR 665 at 669):

> 'A document which is intended to take effect as a deed when conditions have been
> fulfilled may be executed as an escrow; that is to say, with all the formalities of a
> deed save that the vital unconditional delivery, which is essential for the proper
> execution of a true deed, is missing; it is replaced by a conditional delivery, usually
> express, but capable of being assumed. At this stage, the document is not a deed;
> and although of course it contains within it the possibility of becoming an effective
> deed, a deed rising phoenix-like from the ashes of the escrow, at the stage before the
> condition is fulfilled it is of no effect whatsoever.'

Having quoted that part of the judgment of Diplock LJ in *Wm Cory & Sons Ltd v Inland
Revenue Comrs* to which I have made reference above, he continued ([1976] 2 All ER 461
at 467, [1976] 1 WLR 665 at 670–671):

> 'If I may repeat the crucial passage: "So long as it remains an escrow it is not yet
> executed as a deed; for delivery again as a deed is required before it becomes one."
> It follows in my judgment that . . . the first date on which the deed of exchange
> which is the subject-matter of the present appeal was "executed" was on the day on
> which the conditions were fulfilled and it was in the eye of the law for the first time
> delivered unconditionally, and thus for the first time delivered as a deed . . .'

After anxious hesitation, having had the advantage of reading in draft the judgments
of Lord Denning MR and Sir Denys Buckley, I agree with Walton J, as did the judge. A
deed delivered as an escrow takes effect from the satisfaction of the conditions and not
from the date of its delivery as an escrow.

I am conscious that in reaching this decision I am not following the dicta of Vaisey J
in *Re Duke of Devonshire's Settlement* (1952) 31 ATC 399 at 405. The learned judge was
not, however, dealing with an escrow, nor was this point apparently the subject matter
of argument, and it certainly did not arise for his decision. Moreover, it is clear from the
observations made by counsel at the conclusion of the judgment that for the special
reasons referred to the case had been taken out of its turn and dealt with with special
expedition.

Thus, with all proper diffidence, I also would decide that both lease and counterpart
took effect together on the satisfaction of the condition on 18th November 1977, and
accordingly such date is 'the date hereof'.

SIR DENYS BUCKLEY. It was common ground between the parties in the 1976
action that the counterpart lease was executed in escrow by the tenants. Whitford J's

judgment proceeded explicitly on that basis and that judgment is undisturbed. It is common ground before us that the conditions of that escrow were fully satisfied on 18th **a** November 1977. The question for decision in the present proceedings is how in the circumstances set out in the judgment of Lord Denning MR the expression 'from the date hereof' should be interpreted. The plaintiffs say that it signifies 1st November 1976; the defendants say it signifies 18th November 1977. The plaintiffs as landlords naturally contend that the former is correct; the defendants as tenants equally naturally contend that the latter is correct. The determination of the question depends in my view **b** on the true effect of the delivery of a deed in escrow.

The law in this respect is ancient but has not become anachronistic. Deeds are not uncommonly delivered in escrow today.

The tenants' argument is to the effect that a document delivered as an escrow does not acquire any of the characteristics of a deed until the conditions of the escrow have been fulfilled. Thereupon unconditional delivery of the document as the deed of the maker **c** takes place, and the document is then for the first time effective as a deed. Since the essential characteristics of a deed are that it is a written instrument which has been signed, sealed and delivered, an escrow cannot rank as a deed until there has been unconditional delivery.

The landlords' argument on the other hand is to the effect that as soon as the instrument is delivered in escrow it has all the characteristics of a deed save in one respect **d** which is that, although the instrument is binding on the maker from the moment when it has been signed, sealed and delivered in escrow, so that he cannot resile from it, it has otherwise no operative power or effect until the condition of the escrow has been fulfilled. It is consequently a deed ab initio, but subject to a temporary restriction on its operative effect. It is a deed the operative effect of which, but not its binding quality, has been suspended by the maker until a certain event or time by the manner in which he **e** has delivered it.

Over the ages the books contain many authoritative statements of what constitutes an escrow. It is not easy to reconcile all of them. They can be found collected in Norton on Deeds, itself a work of great authority (2nd Edn, 1928, pp 18ff). The difficulty in reconciling some of these statements derives, I think, from a difficulty in being sure in precisely what sense the various writers use the word 'deed'. Norton starts his work with **f** a discussion of how difficult it is to give a satisfactory definition of a deed. His own definition is at p 3 of the second edition. Three of its essential requirements are (1) writing, (2) sealing and (3) delivery. Since 1st January 1926, an individual executing a deed must sign it or put his mark on it (see the Law of Property Act 1925, s 73). It is universally accepted that to constitute a deed a written instrument must have been 'delivered' by the maker of it.

'Delivery' for this purpose is not to be confused with any form of exchange of **g** documents or of physical delivery of the instrument to someone other than the maker:

> '. . . no particular technical form of words or acts is necessary to render an instrument the deed of the party sealing it. The mere affixing of the seal does not render it a deed; but as soon as there are acts or words sufficient to shew that it is **h** intended by the party to be executed as his deed presently binding on him, it is sufficient.' (Per Blackburn J in *Xenos v Wickham* (1867) LR 2 HL 296 at 312.)

It is a question of intention and fact to be tried by the jurors (see LR 2 HL 296 at 309 per Pigott B). The maker of the deed may retain it physically in his own possession and yet 'deliver' it so long as he makes clear that he intends it as his deed presently binding on him. Anything which shows that he treats the instrument as his deed will suffice see **j** (*Tupper v Foulkes* (1861) 9 CBNS 797 at 809 per Williams J). If, however, an instrument intended to take effect as a deed be delivered with the intention that it shall operate only at some future time or on the happening of a specified event, or on condition that it shall not be operative until some condition is performed, it is said to be delivered as an escrow:

'The maker may so deliver [the instrument] as to suspend or qualify its binding effect. He may declare that it shall have no effect until a certain time has arrived, or till some condition has been performed, but when the time has arrived, or the condition has been performed, the delivery becomes absolute, and the maker of the deed is absolutely bound by it, whether he has parted with the possession or not. Until the specified time has arrived, or the condition has been performed, the instrument is not a deed. It is a mere escrow.' (Per Lord Cranworth LC in *Xenos v Wickham* LR 2 HL 296 at 323.)

Again no special form of words is necessary to constitute a delivery of an instrument delivery as an escrow: it is a question of intention, however that intention may be displayed.

After the happening of the event or the performance of the condition on which delivery of an escrow was made, the instrument operates as a deed without any further delivery.

It has been accepted as common ground by the parties in this case that, once the maker of an instrument has delivered it as an escrow, he cannot by any means withdraw from it or alter it (see *Beesly v Hallwood Estates Ltd* [1961] 1 All ER 890, [1961] Ch 105 and *Kingston v Ambrian Investment Co Ltd* [1975] 1 All ER 120 at 125, [1975] 1 WLR 161 at 166). It may perchance never take effect because the condition or event on which the instrument is intended to become operative never occurs, but otherwise it will certainly take effect on the satisfaction of that condition or the occurrence of that event. The maker, having delivered the instrument, has lost all control and dominion over it. It is as binding on him as if he had delivered it unconditionally.

I am much disposed to think that the effect of delivery on a deed is the same as the effect of delivery on an escrow. Each renders the delivered instrument inescapably binding on the deliverer. The difference between a deed and an escrow lies not in the binding quality of the instrument but in the time at and circumstances in which the obligation can be enforced. For my part I should be prepared to hold that an instrument delivered in escrow is as much a deed as is a precisely similar instrument delivered unconditionally in the first instance save that the operative effects of the instrument are suspended while it remains in escrow. In *Xenos v Wickham*, in the passage I have already cited, Lord Cranworth LC used language suggesting that, until the time specified for the maturity of the escrow has arrived or the condition of the escrow has been satisfied, the instrument is not a deed: it is a mere escrow. And in *Governors and Guardians of Foundling Hospital v Crane* [1911] 2 KB 367 at 377 Farwell LJ said:

'Now an escrow or script is not a deed at all; it is a document delivered upon a condition on the performance of which it will become a deed, and will take effect as from the delivery, but until such performance it conveys no estate at all.'

Lord Cranworth LC it seems to me was clearly using the term 'deed' to describe an instrument binding on the grantor and immediately enforceable against him. Farwell LJ was considering whether the instrument in question in his case was capable of having conveyed a legal estate, ie was a deed in the full sense. In the event, however, the document was held not to have been delivered at all. Norton does not deal with the point, but more modern writers seem to favour the view that an escrow, while it remains in escrow, is not a deed (see, for example, 12 Halsbury's Laws (4th Edn) para 1334). It is perhaps merely a matter of semantics whether an instrument which is delivered as an escrow should properly be described as a deed, the operative effect and so the enforceability of which are temporarily suspended, or as a document delivered on a condition on the performance of which (and not before) it will become a deed. The substantial point, I think, for the purposes of this question of construction, is that the maker cannot resile from the terms and effect of the document which he has 'delivered', notwithstanding that he may have delivered it in circumstances which for the time being deprive it of operative effect and enforceability.

I have laboured this point perhaps at undue length because it seems to me to have an important bearing on the meaning to be attributed to the words 'the date hereof' in the present case. The date was left blank in both the lease and the counterpart; the dates which are now to be found there were inserted later and not by agreement. So we are left to discover the date of the lease from extrinsic evidence. We must surely look for the date when the lease first had some legal effect. That was when the lease and counterpart were delivered in escrow, ie 1st November 1976. True, it cannot then have vested a legal term in the tenants but it created a state of affairs in which the landlords could do nothing with the property inconsistent with their ability to implement their grant on the instant of the fulfilment of the conditions attached to the escrow. On the facts the lease and counterpart were both in my opinion delivered in escrow on 1st November 1976.

I agree with Lord Denning MR that if the tenants had not repudiated the bargain, it is likely that the solicitors would have inserted the date 1st November 1976 in both the lease and the counterpart; but for my part I prefer to base my decision on the reasons contained in the last preceding paragraph of this judgment rather than on the first ground adopted by Lord Denning MR.

When the conditions of an escrow are fully satisfied, so that it becomes an immediately operative deed, that effect relates to the date of its delivery in escrow, but not for all purposes: only for such purposes as are necessary to give effect to the transaction (see *Security Trust Co v Royal Bank of Canada* [1976] 1 All ER 381 at 390, [1976] AC 503 at 517 per Lord Cross), which I take to mean all the terms and provisions of the instrument which remain capable of being given effect to implement the bargain between the parties. A grant in escrow of a lease, or an assignment in escrow of the reversion to a lease, falling within the Law of Property Act 1925, s 52(1), cannot while it remains in escrow convey or create any legal estate which did not previously exist. It cannot, accordingly, while the instrument remains in escrow create the legal relationship of reversioner and tenant. So during the subsistence of the escrow the intended reversioner is not at law the reversioner on a term vested at law in the tenant. Accordingly the grant or assignment, while it remains in escrow, will not entitle the intended reversioner to demand the rents or to serve notices to quit (see *Security Trust Co v Royal Bank of Canada* [1976] 1 All ER 381 at 390, [1976] AC 503 at 517). But if the intention of the parties was that, on the escrow ceasing to be such, the rights and liabilities of the parties shall be treated as being those which would have arisen if the instrument had been delivered absolutely, and not as an escrow, in the first place the lease, when it ceases to be an escrow and becomes an effective deed, is, it seems, to be given effect as between the parties so far as practicable as though the term had vested in the tenant and the reversion in the reversioner when that would have occurred if the instrument had been originally delivered unconditionally. Certainly for the purpose of ascertaining the date when the term will expire it must be calculated from the date, if any, specified in the lease. Where no such date is specified, see Co Lit 46b. In this case that period is specified as '24 years from 29th September 1976'. The term will expire on 29th September 1996. Similarly the periods by reference to which instalments of rent are to be calculated must, I think, be ascertained as though the lease had not been delivered in escrow but unconditionally. In this case that period runs *'from the date hereof* and throughout the said term hereby granted'. It is of course perfectly possible that a lease should reserve a rent to be calculated as from a date anterior to the date on which the lease takes effect. There is nothing here to make 1st November 1976 an inappropriate date to treat as 'the date hereof' when construing the reddendum of the lease.

As a matter of construction there can, in my opinion, be only one 'date hereof'. If the lease dates back for any purpose to the original delivery, that date must in my judgment be the 'date hereof' within the meaning of the lease.

For these reasons I am of opinion that, according to the true construction of the lease in the events which have happened, 'the date hereof' means 1st November 1976. I would accordingly allow this appeal.

Appeal allowed. Order for payment of amount due from 1st November 1976 with interest to be
a agreed (liberty to apply). Leave to appeal to the House of Lords refused.

Solicitors: *Martin Boston & Co* (for the landlords); *Woolf, Seddon* (for the tenants and the surety).

Sumra Green   Barrister.

b

McGovern and others v Attorney General and another

CHANCERY DIVISION

c SLADE J

20th, 21st, 22nd, 23rd, 26th JANUARY, 13th MARCH 1981

Charity – Public benefit – Political purposes – Trust to secure release of prisoners of conscience and procure abolition of torture or inhuman or degrading treatment or punishment – Purpose of trust to be achieved by seeking changes in foreign legislation and reversal of administrative d decisions of foreign governments – Whether a trust for political purposes – Whether trust charitable.

Charity – Public benefit – Research – Trust for research into maintenance and observance of human rights – Trust for dissemination of results of such research – Whether trust for such research charitable.

e

The Amnesty International Trust was set up in 1977 to administer those purposes of Amnesty International that were thought to be charitable. Amnesty International itself was an unincorporated, non-profit making body formed with the object of securing throughout the world that prisoners of conscience (ie persons who were imprisoned, detained or restricted because of their political, religious or conscientious beliefs, or their *f* ethnic origin, sex, colour or language) were treated in accordance with the United Nations Universal Declaration of Human Rights, and to that end Amnesty International provided assistance to, and worked to secure the release of, prisoners of conscience by exposing and publicising the plight of such prisoners, mobilising public opinion and applying persuasion and pressure on imprisoning authorities. Amnesty International worked independently of any particular government, political faction or religious creed, *g* and, although philanthropic, was admittedly non-charitable. The objects of the trust as set out in the trust deed were (i) the relief of needy persons within the categories of prisoners of conscience or who were or were likely to become prisoners of conscience or their relatives (cl 2A), (ii) attempting to secure the release of prisoners of conscience (cl 2B), (iii) procuring the abolition of torture or inhuman or degrading treatment or punishment (cl 2C), (iv) research into the maintenance and observance of human rights *h* (cl 2D), (v) disseminating the results of such research (cl 2E) and (vi) doing all such other things as would promote the specific objects. The trust deed further provided that the objects of the trust were 'restricted to those which [were] charitable according to the law of the United Kingdom but subject thereto they may be carried out in all parts of the world'. The trustees of the trust applied to the Charity Commissioners for registration of the trust as a charity under s 4 of the Charities Act 1960. The commissioners refused *j* to register the trust and the trustees appealed to the court under s 5(3) of the 1960 Act by way of an originating summons seeking a declaration that the trust ought to be registered as a charity.

Held – (1) Although a trust for the relief of human suffering and distress was capable of being of a charitable nature, within the spirit and intendment of the preamble to the

Charitable Uses Act 1601, as being a charity of compassion, nevertheless, if the means of achieving that relief was by securing a change in the laws of a foreign country and that was a direct and main object of the trust, then the trust had a political purpose and was not capable of being charitable under English law, because the court had no means of judging whether the proposed change in the law of the foreign country would or would not be for the public benefit, either locally or internationally. Similarly, if a direct and principal purpose of the trust was to procure a reversal of government policy or a particular governmental decision in a foreign country, it was not capable of being charitable under English law. On the other hand, if the main objects of the trust were exclusively charitable, the mere fact that the trustees had incidental powers under the trust to employ political means to further the non-political purposes of the trust would not deprive the trust of its charitable status, provided the political means were not the designated means of carrying out the trust but merely consequential to carrying it out (see p 503 *j* to p 504 *b*, p 505 *b*, p 506 *e f* and *j* to p 507 *d* and *f* to p 508 *c* and *e* to p 509 *g*, p 510 *a* and p 511 *b c*, post); dicta of Lord Herschell and of Lord Macnaghten in *Income Tax Special Purposes Comrs v Pemsel* [1891–4] All ER Rep at 50, 55, of Lord Parker in *Bowman v Secular Society Ltd* [1916–17] All ER Rep at 18, of Lord Wright and of Lord Simonds in *National Anti-Vivisection Society v Inland Revenue Comrs* [1947] 2 All ER 224–225, 231–232 and of Lord Wilberforce in *Scottish Burial Reform and Cremation Society Ltd v Glasgow City Corpn* [1967] 3 All ER at 223 applied; dictum of Evershed MR in *Camille and Henry Dreyfus Foundation Inc v Inland Revenue Comrs* [1954] 2 All ER at 471 considered.

(2) Applying those principles, the trust set out in cl 2B, namely attempting to secure the release of prisoners of conscience, was a trust for political purposes, and not simply a trust for the redemption and relief of captives, since it contemplated, as the primary means of achieving the purpose of the trust, the application of moral pressure on foreign governments or authorities to persuade them to change their decisions to imprison prisoners of conscience. The trust was therefore not for the public benefit and not charitable (see p 513 *j* to p 514 *c f* to *h* and p 515 *b* to *d*, post); dictum of Lord Parker in *Bowman v Secular Society Ltd* [1916–17] All ER Rep at 18 applied; *Jackson v Phillips* (1867) 96 Mass 539 distinguished.

(3) Similarly, the trust set out in cl 2C, namely procuring the abolition of torture or inhuman or degrading treatment or punishment, was a trust for political purposes, and not simply a trust for the relief of suffering and distress, since the phrase 'inhuman or degrading treatment or punishment' included capital and corporal punishment by process of law and the abolition of such punishment necessarily included procuring reforming legislation, whether in the United Kingdom or elsewhere. The trust set out in cl 2C was accordingly not charitable (see p 516 *e* to *h* and p 517 *f* to p 518 *c*, post).

(4) The trusts set out in cll 2D and 2E, namely promoting research into the maintenance and observance of human rights and the dissemination of such research, would, if the trusts had stood alone, have been charitable, since the subject matter of the research was a useful subject of study and the research would have been for the benefit of the public (see p 518 *j* to p 519 *c*, post).

(5) Since the trusts set out in cll 2B and 2C were non-charitable, the purposes of the trust deed generally were not wholly and exclusively charitable and therefore none of the trusts contained in the deed could be regarded as charitable. The proviso in the trust deed to the effect that the objects of the trust were restricted to those which were charitable according to the law of the United Kingdom did not operate to exclude from the trust purposes which were not charitable, but merely made it clear that the trustees should, even when operating outside the United Kingdom, be restricted to purposes which were charitable under United Kingdom law. The declaration would accordingly be refused (see p 511 *j* to p 512 *b* and p 519 *c d* and *g h*, post).

Notes

For the requirement that a charity be for the public benefit, see 5 Halsbury's Laws (4th Edn) para 505, for trusts for political purposes, see ibid para 558, and for cases on the subject, see 8(1) Digest (Reissue) 301–302, 425–428.

Cases referred to in judgment

a *Attorney General v Gibson* (1835) 2 Beav 317, 48 ER 1208, 8(1) Digest (Reissue) 406, *1391*.

Attorney General v Ironmongers' Co (1834) 2 My & K 576, [1824–34] All ER Rep 620, 3 LJ Ch 11, 39 ER 1064, LC; *affd* 10 Cl & Fin 908, 8 ER 983, HL, 8(1) Digest (Reissue) 457, *2093*.

Barralet v Attorney General [1980] 3 All ER 918, sub nom *Re South Place Ethical Society* [1980] 1 WLR 1565.

b *Besterman's Will Trusts, Re* (21st January 1980, unreported).

Bonar Law Memorial Trust v Inland Revenue Comrs (1933) 17 Tax Cas 508, 28(1) Digest (Reissue) 478, *1724*.

Bowman v Secular Society Ltd [1917] AC 406, [1916–17] All ER Rep 1, 86 LJ Ch 568, 117 LT 161, HL, 8(1) Digest (Reissue) 302, *427*.

Bushnell (deceased), Re, Lloyds Bank Ltd v Murray [1975] 1 All ER 721, [1975] 1 WLR 1596,
c Digest (Cont Vol D) 91, *142a*.

Camille and Henry Dreyfus Foundation Inc v Inland Revenue Comrs [1954] 2 All ER 466, [1954] Ch 672, [1954] 3 WLR 167, [1954] TR 211, 33 ATC 209, 47 R & IT 476, CA, 22 Digest (Reissue) 680, *7272*.

De Themmines v De Bonneval (1828) 5 Russ 288, 7 LJOS Ch 35, 38 ER 1035, 8(1) Digest (Reissue) 301, *425*.

d *Duport Steels Ltd v Sirs* [1980] 1 All ER 529, [1980] 1 WLR 142, [1980] ICR 161, QBD, CA and HL.

Habershon v Vardon (1851) 4 De G & Sm 467, 20 LJ Ch 549, 17 LTOS 196, 15 Jur 961, 64 ER 916, 8(1) Digest (Reissue) 302, *428*.

Hobourn Aero Components Ltd's Air-raid Distress Fund Trusts, Re, Ryan v Forrest [1946] 1 All ER 501, [1946] Ch 194, 115 LJ Ch 158, 174 LT 428, CA, 8(1) Digest (Reissue) 250, *72*.

e *Hood, Re, Public Trustee v Hood* [1931] 1 Ch 240, [1930] All ER Rep 215, 100 LJ Ch 115, 143 LT 691, CA, 8(1) Digest (Reissue) 259, *133*.

Hopkin's Will Trusts, Re, Naish v Francis Bacon Society Inc [1964] 3 All ER 46, [1965] Ch 669, [1964] 3 WLR 840, 8(1) Digest (Reissue) 257, *120*.

Hopkinson (deceased), Re, Lloyds Bank Ltd v Baker [1949] 1 All ER 346, 8(1) Digest (Reissue) 261, *142*.

f *Income Tax Special Purposes Comrs v Pemsel* [1891] AC 531, [1891–4] All ER Rep 28, 61 LJQB 265, 65 LT 621, 55 JP 805, 3 Tax Cas 53, HL, 8(1) Digest (Reissue) 237, *1*.

Incorporated Council of Law Reporting for England and Wales v Attorney General [1971] 3 All ER 1029, [1972] Ch 73, [1971] 3 WLR 853, 47 Tax Cas 321, CA, 8(1) Digest (Reissue) 260, *137*.

Inland Revenue Comrs v City of Glasgow Police Athletic Association [1953] 1 All ER 747,
g [1953] AC 380, [1953] 2 WLR 625, 117 JP 201, 34 Tax Cas 76, [1953] TR 49, 32 ATC 62, 46 R & IT 207, 1953 SC (HL) 13, 1953 SLT 105, HL, 28(1) Digest (Reissue) 481, *1734*.

Inland Revenue Comrs v McMullen [1980] 1 All ER 884, [1981] AC 1, [1980] 2 WLR 416, HL.

Inland Revenue Comrs v Yorkshire Agricultural Society [1928] 1 KB 611, [1927] All ER Rep
h 536, 97 LJKB 100, 138 LT 192, 44 TLR 59, 13 Tax Cas 58, CA, 28(1) Digest (Reissue) 475, *1705*.

Ironmongers Co v Attorney General (1844) 10 Cl & Fin 908, 8 ER 983, HL, 8(1) Digest (Reissue) 408, *1407*.

Jackson v Phillips (1867) 96 Mass 539.

Lewis (deceased), Re, Public Trustee v Allen [1954] 3 All ER 257, [1955] Ch 104, [1954] 3
j WLR 610, 8(1) Digest (Reissue) 245, *46*.

National Anti-Vivisection Society v Inland Revenue Comrs [1947] 2 All ER 217, [1948] AC 31, [1947] LJR 1112, 177 LT 226, 28 Tax Cas 311, HL, 8(1) Digest (Reissue) 238, *3*.

Prison Charities, Re (1873) LR 16 Eq 129, 42 LJ Ch 748, 37 JP 420, 8(1) Digest (Reissue) 400, *1348*.

Robinson (deceased), Re, Davis v Robinson [1950] 2 All ER 1148, [1951] Ch 198, 8(1) Digest (Reissue) 244, *41*.

Scottish Burial Reform and Cremation Society Ltd v Glasgow City Corpn [1967] 3 All ER 215,
[1968] AC 138, [1967] 3 WLR 1132, 132 JP 30, [1967] RA 272, 1967 SC (HL) 116, HL,
8(1) Digest (Reissue) 301, 424.

Shaw (deceased), Re, Public Trustee v Day [1957] 1 All ER 745, [1957] 1 WLR 729; *on appeal*
[1958] 1 All ER 245n, CA, 8(1) Digest (Reissue) 266, 157.

Thornton v Howe (1862) 31 Beav 14, 31 LJ Ch 767, 6 LT 525, 26 JP 774, 8 Jur NS 663, 54
ER 1042, 8(1) Digest (Reissue) 270, 191.

Thrupp v Collett (No 1) (1858) 26 Beav 125, 32 LTOS 365, 5 Jur NS 111, 53 ER 844, 8(1)
Digest (Reissue) 302, 429.

Wallis v Solicitor General for New Zealand [1903] AC 173, 72 LJPC 37, 88 LT 65, PC, 8(1)
Digest (Reissue) 269, 183.

Cases also cited

Anglo-Swedish Society v Inland Revenue Comrs (1931) 16 Tax Cas 34.

Armstrong v Reeves (1890) LR 25 Ir 325.

Baldry v Feintuck [1972] 2 All ER 81, [1972] 1 WLR 552.

Buxton v Public Trustee (1962) 41 Tax Cas 235.

Cole, Re [1958] 3 All ER 102, [1958] Ch 877.

D'Aguiar v Guyana Inland Revenue Comrs [1970] TR 31, PC.

Gouriet v Union of Post Office Workers [1977] 3 All ER 70, [1978] AC 435, HL.

Inland Revenue Comrs v Temperance Council of Christian Churches of England and Wales
(1926) 10 Tax Cas 748.

Jackson, Re, Bell v Adlam (1910) Times, 11th June.

Jenkins' Will Trusts, Re [1966] 1 All ER 926, [1966] Ch 249.

Jones, Re, Public Trustee v Earl of Clarendon (1929) 45 TLR 259.

Keren Kayemeth Le Jisroel Ltd v Inland Revenue Comrs [1931] 2 KB 465, CA.

Marsh v Means (1857) 3 Jur NS 790.

McDougall (Arthur) Fund, Re [1956] 3 All ER 867, [1957] 1 WLR 81.

Mercers (Mystery) v Attorney General (1828) 2 Bli NS 165, 4 ER 1094.

Moss (deceased), Re, Hobrough v Harvey [1949] 1 All ER 495.

R v Chief Immigration Officer, Heathrow Airport, ex parte Salamat Bibi [1976] 3 All ER 843,
[1976] 1 WLR 979, CA.

Strakosch, Re, Temperley v Attorney General [1949] 2 All ER 6, [1949] Ch 529, CA.

Wedgwood, Re, Allen v Wedgwood [1915] 1 Ch 113, [1914–15] All ER Rep 322, CA.

Williams' (Sir Howell Jones) Trustees v Inland Revenue Comrs [1947] 1 All ER 513, [1947] AC
447, HL.

Originating summons

By an originating summons dated 11th September 1978, the plaintiffs, Edmund
McGovern, Nicholas Harding, Lord Avebury, Paul Oestreicher, Alec Bristow, David Ive
and Sir Osmond Williams, applied by way of appeal against a decision of the Charity
Commissioners for England and Wales on 14th August 1978 for a declaration that the
Amnesty International Trust constituted by a declaration of trust dated 2nd November
1977 ought to be registered as a charity under s 4 of the Charities Act 1960 on the ground
that the purposes of the trust consisted exclusively of either: (1) purposes beneficial to the
community namely, (a) the relief and rehabilitation of distressed persons, or (b) the
promotion of health by means of the procurement of the abolition of torture, or (c) the
promotion of the moral welfare of the community by the repression of brutality and
inhuman or degrading treatment or punishment, or (d) by attempting to secure the
release from imprisonment, restriction, physical coercion or restraint of persons who in
violation of the rights laid down by and contained in the Universal Declaration of
Human Rights were imprisoned, detained, restricted or otherwise subjected to physical
coercion or restraint by reason of their political, religious or other conscientiously held
beliefs or by reason of ethnic origin or colour (not being persons who were party to or
privy to or who advocated or approved the use of violence or persons lawfully imprisoned

or detained within the United Kingdom); or (2) the advancement of education by the
a undertaking, promotion and commission of research into the maintenance and
observance of human rights and by the dissemination of the results of such research; or
(3) the relief of poverty. The defendants were Her Majesty's Attorney General and the
Inland Revenue Commissioners. The facts are set out in the judgment.

Leonard Hoffmann QC and *Hubert Picarda* for the plaintiffs.
b *John Mummery* for the Attorney General.
John Knox QC and *C H McCall* for the Inland Revenue Commissioners.

Cur adv vult

13th March. **SLADE J** read the following judgment: This is an appeal under s 5(3) of
c the Charities Act 1960 against a decision of the Charity Commissioners that a declaration
of trust dated 2nd November 1977 is not a charitable trust and should not be entered in
the central register of charities under s 4 of the Charities Act 1960. The trust established
by this deed is thereby given the name 'Amnesty International Trust'. The seven persons
who executed it and are its present trustees are the plaintiffs in these proceedings. The
defendants are Her Majesty's Attorney General and the Inland Revenue Commission-
d ers. Entry of the trust was refused on the grounds that its objects are not exclusively
charitable.

On 10th December 1948 the General Assembly of the United Nations proclaimed the
Universal Declaration of Human Rights (Cmnd 3220 (1967)) as 'a common standard of
achievement for all peoples and all nations'. This declaration included the following
articles:

e '(3) Everyone has the right to life, liberty and security of person . . .
'(5) No one shall be subjected to torture or to cruel, inhuman or degrading
treatment or punishment . . .
'(9) No one shall be subjected to arbitrary arrest, detention or exile.
'(10) Everyone is entitled in full equality to a fair and public hearing by an
independent and impartial tribunal, in the determination of his rights and
f obligations and of any criminal charge against him . . .
'(18) Everyone has the right to freedom of thought, conscience and religion; this
right includes freedom to change his religion or belief, and freedom, either alone or
in community with others and in public or private, to manifest his religion or belief
in teaching, practice, worship and observance.
'(19) Everyone has the right to freedom of opinion and expression; this right
g includes freedom to hold opinions without interference and to seek, receive and
impart information and ideas through any media and regardless of frontiers.'

The Universal Declaration of Human Rights is not binding on the United Kingdom
as a treaty obligation and does not form part of its law. It has, however, strongly
influenced the form of the subsequent European Convention for the Protection of
h Human Rights and Fundamental Freedoms (TS 71 (1953); Cmd 8969), to which the
United Kingdom in 1963 subscribed as a matter of treaty, though the treaty is not part
of the law of the United Kingdom. Article 1 of this convention provides that 'the High
Contracting Parties', of whom the United Kingdom is one, shall secure to everyone
within their jurisdiction the rights and freedoms defined in s 1 of the convention.
Section 1 includes among others the following articles. Article 3 provides: 'No one shall
j be subjected to torture or to inhuman or degrading treatment or punishment.' Subject
to the omission of the word 'cruel', it is thus in the same form as art 5 of the Universal
Declaration of Human Rights. Article 5 of the European Convention is a much more
elaborate version of art 10 of the Universal Declaration. Articles 9 and 10 of the European
Convention, though in much fuller form, are more developed versions of arts 18 and 19
of the Universal Declaration.

The first chapter of the Amnesty International Handbook of March 1977 begins with the following words: *a*

> 'In recent years, people throughout the world have become more and more aware of the urgent need for effective international protection of fundamental human rights. Reports have steadily documented the increasing imprisonment of large numbers of political prisoners (many detained without trial for more than five years), the escalating use of torture as an instrument of routine government administration, disappearances and summary executions of political "undesirables" *b* carried out by semi-official death squads—taking place in countries of diverse cultures, economies and ideologies. Despite efforts at the United Nations and in the field of international law, the world is still without efficient machinery to prevent these and other violations of human rights or to protect the victims.'

The substantial, lamentable truth of these words has not been questioned in these *c* proceedings. Nor has there been any dispute over the proposition stated in the same handbook that—

> 'Perhaps the only alternative which has proven at all effective has been the force of awakened world opinion which has become a potent instrument of international intervention in human rights crises.'
>   *d*

Based on this belief and experience, an unincorporated, non-profitmaking organisation named Amnesty International was founded in 1961, effectively with the object of securing throughout the world observance of the provisions of the Universal Declaration of Human Rights in regard to the categories of persons referred to in its constitution, who are principally, though not exclusively, the persons therein defined as 'prisoners of conscience'. Article 1 of this constitution, which is known as the Statute of Amnesty *e* International (as amended in September 1979), defines its object as being:

> '... to secure throughout the world the observance of the provisions of the Universal Declaration of Human Rights, by: (a) irrespective of political considerations working towards the release of and providing assistance to persons who in violation of the aforesaid provisions are imprisoned, detained or otherwise physically *f* restricted by reason of their political, religious or other conscientiously held beliefs or by reason of their ethnic origin, sex, colour or language, provided that they have not used or advocated violence (hereinafter referred to as "Prisoners of Conscience"); (b) opposing by all appropriate means the detention of any Prisoners of Conscience or any political prisoners without trial within a reasonable time or any trial procedures relating to such prisoners that do not conform to internationally recognized norms; (c) opposing by all appropriate means the imposition and *g* infliction of death penalties and torture or other cruel, inhuman or degrading treatment or punishment of prisoners or other detained or restricted persons whether or not they have used or advocated violence.'

Article 2 of the statute sets out the methods which Amnesty International 'shall' (not 'may') adopt to achieve its object. It states: *h*

> 'In order to achieve the aforesaid object, AMNESTY INTERNATIONAL shall: (a) at all times maintain an overall balance between its activities in relation to countries adhering to the different world political ideologies and groupings; (b) promote as appears appropriate the adoption of constitutions, conventions, treaties and other measures which guarantee the rights contained in the provisions referred to in *j* article 1 hereof; (c) support and publicize the activities of and cooperate with international organizations and agencies which work for the implementation of the aforesaid provisions; (d) take all necessary steps to establish an effective organization of national sections, affiliated groups and individual members; (e) secure the adoption by groups of members or supporters of individual Prisoners of Conscience

or entrust to such groups other tasks in support of the object set out in article 1; (f)

a   provide financial and other relief to Prisoners of Conscience and their dependants and to persons who have lately been Prisoners of Conscience or who might reasonably be expected to be Prisoners of Conscience or to become Prisoners of Conscience if convicted or if they were to return to their own countries, and to the dependants of such persons; (g) work for the improvement of conditions for Prisoners of Conscience and political prisoners; (h) provide legal aid, where necessary

b   and possible, to Prisoners of Conscience and to persons who might reasonably be expected to be Prisoners of Conscience or to become Prisoners of Conscience if convicted or if they were to return to their own countries, and where desirable, send observers to attend the trials of such persons; (i) publicize the cases of Prisoners of Conscience or persons who have otherwise been subjected to disabilities in violation of the aforesaid provisions; (j) send investigators, where appropriate, to investigate

c   allegations that the rights of individuals under the aforesaid provisions have been violated or threatened; (k) make representations to international organizations and to governments whenever it appears that an individual is a Prisoner of Conscience or has otherwise been subjected to disabilities in violation of the aforesaid provisions; (l) promote and support the granting of general amnesties of which the beneficiaries will include Prisoners of Conscience; (m) adopt any other appropriate methods for

d   the securing of its object.'

The organisation of Amnesty International consists of national sections which embrace affiliated groups and individual members. I am told that it now has affiliated sections in 39 countries, individual supporters in another 95 countries and about 250,000 members. All the plaintiffs are members of the British section. In addition, the first plaintiff is the former treasurer of this section and the second and fourth plaintiffs are

e   members of its council. The British section has a formal constitution under which it adopts the objects and methods of Amnesty International.

The authority for the conduct of the affairs of Amnesty International is vested in its international council. The international executive committee, elected by the international council, is responsible for the conduct of the affairs of the organisation and for the implementation of the council's decisions. The day-to-day affairs of the organisation are

f   conducted by the international secretariat under the direction of the international executive committee. The international secretariat and the British section both have their offices in the same premises in London, so that in this sense the organisation is based in England.

I think that a fair, though necessarily incomplete, summary of the manner in which Amnesty International conducts its activities is to be found in the following passage from

g   its handbook of 1977 (pp 7–8):

'Through the network of members and supporters, Amnesty International mobilises public opinion, works for the release of prisoners of conscience, protects their families from hardship and seeks improved international standards in the treatment of prisoners and detainees. Amnesty International's work is based on

h   detailed research into specific cases of individual prisoners as well as mass violations of human rights. To do this, the International Secretariat in London maintains a Research Department comprised of expert staff who study allegations of torture and detention from all parts of the world. The Research Department receives information from many sources including the international press, transcriptions of radio announcements, reports from legal experts, letters from prisoners' colleagues

j   and a wide network of Amnesty International contacts in numerous countries. It also dispatches official fact-finding missions to assess situations on-the-spot, to meet prisoners and interview government authorities. The detailed reports of the Research Department are then sent to the members of the organization with specific requests and instructions for action. In addition to general activities in defence of human rights Amnesty International is the foremost non-governmental organization handling specific casework in this field. When the detention of a prisoner of conscience has been verified, the International Secretariat assigns the case *a* to one of Amnesty International's adoption groups. It is each of these small groups which then undertakes the vital work of demonstrating international concern for the protection of the basic human rights violated in each case. The relevant government and prison officials are faced with an insistent, continuous and informed appeal urging a reconsideration of the case and the release of the prisoner. Letters are dispatched not only to government ministers, embassies, *b* leading newspapers and to international organizations, but to the prisoner and to his or her relatives and friends. If possible, money will be raised to meet relief needs. Influential persons are asked to add their names to the petitions and protests. In emergencies, distinguished jurists may be sent to controversial trials or to plead for the life of a sentenced victim. In many cases, individual prisoners are released after sustained effort by an Amnesty International group. Others may benefit from a *c* general or partial amnesty following a general Amnesty International campaign.'

Article 2(a) of the statute of Amnesty International imposes on it an overriding obligation to maintain an overall balance between its activities in relation to countries adhering to the different world ideologies and groupings. The defendants, who have filed no evidence in these proceedings, have not suggested in argument that Amnesty International has failed in any way to comply with this obligation. So far as the evidence *d* shows, it works independently of any particular government, political faction or religious creed. It operates instead through persuasion and pressure and the public exposure of violations of human rights, though the very nature of its purposes is such that the relevant persuasion or pressure must normally be applied to governmental authorities if it is to be effective. Its humanitarian work received conspicuous recognition by the award to it of the Nobel Peace Prize in December 1977. *e*

However, the mere fact that an organisation may have philanthropic purposes of an excellent character does not by itself entitle it to acceptance as a charity in law. The unincorporated association, Amnesty International, has never been regarded as a charity, and itself makes no claim to be regarded as such in these proceedings. In or before 1977, however, the plaintiffs were advised that at least some of its objects were charitable. Accordingly, on 2nd November 1977 they executed the declaration of trust, with which *f* this case is concerned, with the intention that there should be hived off into a trust those purposes which they had been advised were charitable.

The declaration of trust (which I will hereafter call 'the trust deed') recites that the trustees were in possession of a sum of £100 on the trusts thereinafter named and that it was apprehended that further sums or assets might be paid or transferred to the trustees to be held on the like trusts. Clause 1(a) names the trust thereby created *g* 'Amnesty International Trust'. Clause 1(b) defines 'human rights' as meaning 'the rights laid down by and contained in the Universal Declaration of Human Rights'. Clause 1(c) defines 'prisoner of conscience' as meaning—

> 'any person who in violation of human rights is imprisoned detained restricted or otherwise subjected to physical coercion or restraint by reason of his or her political *h* religious or other conscientiously held beliefs or by reason of his or her ethnic origin colour or language but does not include—(i) any person who has been party or privy to or has advocated or approved the use of violence (ii) any person who is lawfully imprisoned or detained within the United Kingdom.'

Clause 2 provides:

j

> 'THE Trustees shall hold the said sum of £100 and any further sums or assets transferred to them hereafter upon trust for the following purposes (hereinafter called "the Trust Purposes") that is to say
>
> 'A The relief of needy persons within any of the following categories: (i) Prisoners of Conscience (ii) persons who have recently been Prisoners of Conscience (iii)

persons who would in the opinion of the Trustees be likely to become Prisoners of
Conscience if they returned to their country of ordinary residence (iv) relatives or
dependants of the foregoing persons; by the provision of appropriate charitable (and
in particular financial educational or rehabilitational) assistance
   'B Attempting to secure the release of Prisoners of Conscience
   'C Procuring the abolition of torture or inhuman or degrading treatment or
punishment
   'D The undertaking promotion and commission of research into the maintenance
and observance of human rights
   'E The dissemination of the results of such research by (a) the preparation and
publication of the results of such research (b) the institution and maintenance of a
library accessible to the public for the study of matters connected with the objects
of this Trust and of the results of research already conducted into such matters (c)
the production and distribution of documentary films showing the results of such
research
   'F The doing of all such other things as shall further the charitable purposes set
out above PROVIDED ALWAYS that the foregoing objects shall be restricted to those
which are charitable according to the law of the United Kingdom but subject
thereto they may be carried out in all parts of the world.'

Clauses 3 to 14 contain a number of administrative powers and provisions. These
include cl 9(b), which provides that the power of appointing new trustees of the trust
deed shall be vested in the council of Amnesty International's British section.
   Clause 15 provides:

'The Trustees shall have power at any time if they so resolve by a majority of
three-quarters of those attending and voting by deed to revoke the trusts herein
declared or some of them and in lieu thereof to declare new trusts for charitable
purposes as near as possible to the trusts herein declared such powers to be exercised
with the consent of the Charity Commission if the trust is a registered charity or
without such consent if any of the trusts herein declared requires to be revoked or
amended to ensure the charitable status of the Trusts.'

Clause 16 begins with the following words:

'In the exercise of their powers and discretions the Trustees shall so far as is
consistent with the objects of the Trust act in accordance with any resolutions of the
Council of Amnesty International British Section . . .'

Counsel for the plaintiffs explained that the purpose of the trust deed was effectively
to constitute a pilot trust which could be brought before the Charity Commission and,
if necessary, the court for the purpose of testing whether the objects are in law charitable
or not. On 4th November 1977 copies of the executed trust deed were sent by the
trustees' solicitors to the Charity Commission, and formal application was made for the
trust to be registered as a charity. After some intermediate correspondence the Charity
Commission replied on 14th August 1978 saying that the commissioners had concluded
that the objects of the trust were not exclusively charitable and that it could not be
registered under s 4 of the Charities Act 1960. On 11th September 1978 the plaintiffs
issued the originating summons initiating the appeal which is now before the court.
   On the hearing of the summons counsel for the Attorney General neither supported
nor opposed the claim of the plaintiffs to charitable status, but helpfully placed before the
court a number of considerations of law and fact which he considered should be drawn
to its attention. Counsel for the Inland Revenue Commissioners accepted that the trusts
declared by cl 2A of the trust deed, if they stood alone, would themselves be charitable as
being for the relief of poverty. He submitted, in effect, that none of the trusts declared
by cll 2B, 2C, 2D and 2E were charitable, one principal feature of his attack being the
submission that those trusts were of a political, rather than charitable, nature. Though

I have had the benefit of exceptionally full, clear and interesting argument, the case raises some very difficult and to some extent novel questions of principle relating to the law of charities, especially in regard to so-called 'political' trusts.

Relevant principles of the law of charities

With a view to making clear the reasons for my ultimate decision I think that, before turning to the particular provisions of the trust deed, I should attempt to state what I conceive to be a few of the relevant basic principles of the law of charities.

Trusts for charitable purposes in this country enjoy a number of special privileges which are not enjoyed by trusts for purposes of a non-charitable nature. Thus, if a trust deed shows a clear intention to devote the trust assets to charity, the trust purposes will not fail for uncertainty merely because they are inadequately defined. Charitable trusts are in most respects exempt from the rule against perpetuities. They are capable of being varied by way of scheme. Finally, they are enforceable at the suit of the Crown:

> 'It is the province of the Crown as parens patriae to enforce the execution of charitable trusts, and it has always been recognised as the duty of the law officers of the Crown to intervene for the purpose of protecting charities and affording advice and assistance to the Court in the administration of charitable trusts.'

(See *Wallis v Solicitor General for New Zealand* [1903] AC 173 at 181–182 per Lord Macnaghten.)

In the circumstances it is not surprising that the law requires a number of conditions to be fulfilled before trusts can be accepted as being charitable. The general rule is that in order to achieve charitable status a trust, however philanthropic, must satisfy each of the following three requirements: (1) it must be of a charitable nature, within the spirit and intendment of the preamble to the Statute of Elizabeth I (the Charitable Uses Act 1601, 43 Eliz I c 4), as interpreted by the courts and extended by statute; (2) it must promote a public benefit of a nature recognised by the courts as a public benefit; (3) the purposes of the trust must be wholly and exclusively charitable: see generally Snell's Principles of Equity (27th Edn, 1973, pp 143ff). I will make some observations on each of these three requirements in turn.

The requirement of a charitable nature

A recent authoritative statement of the legal test to be applied in considering whether purposes are of a charitable nature is to be found in the speech of Lord Wilberforce in *Scottish Burial Reform and Cremation Society Ltd v Glasgow Corpn* [1967] 3 All ER 215 at 223, [1968] AC 138 at 154:

> 'On this subject, the law of England, though no doubt not very satisfactory and in need of rationalisation, is tolerably clear. The purposes in question, to be charitable, must be shown to be for the benefit of the public, or the community, in a sense or manner within the intendment of the preamble to the statute 43 Eliz. I c. 4. The latter requirement does not mean quite what it says: for it is now accepted that what must be regarded is not the wording of the preamble itself, but the effect of decisions given by the courts as to its scope, decisions which have endeavoured to keep the law as to charities moving according as new social needs arise or old ones become obsolete or satisfied.'

The preamble to the Statute of Elizabeth contained the following list of charitable objects:

> 'The relief of aged, impotent, and poor people; the maintenance of sick and maimed soldiers and mariners, schools of learning, free schools, and scholars in universities; the repair of bridges, ports, havens, causeways, churches, seabanks, and highways; the education and preferment of orphans; the relief, stock, or maintenance of houses of correction; marriage of poor maids; supportation, aid, and

a help of young tradesmen, handicraftsmen, and persons decayed; the relief or redemption of prisoners or captives; and the aid or ease of any poor inhabitants concerning payment of fifteens, setting out of soldiers, and other taxes.'

It is at first sight difficult to detect any common thread running through this list of diverse objects. Lord Macnaghten, however, in *Income Tax Special Purposes Comrs v Pemsel* [1891] AC 531 at 583, [1891–4] All ER Rep 28 at 55 categorised charity in its legal

b sense as comprising four principal divisions, namely:

  '. . . trusts for the relief of poverty; trusts for the advancement of education; trusts for the advancement of religion; and trusts for other purposes beneficial to the community, not falling under any of the preceding heads.'

This grouping of the heads of recognised charity has proved to be of great value, as is

c indicated by its frequent subsequent citation. Nevertheless, Lord Wilberforce in *Scottish Burial Reform and Cremation Society Ltd v Glasgow City Corpn* [1967] 3 All ER 215 at 223, [1968] AC 138 at 154 gave three warnings in this context:

  '. . . first that, since it is a classification of convenience, there may well be purposes which do not fit neatly into one or other of the headings: secondly, that the words used must not be given the force of a statute to be construed, and thirdly, that the

d law of charity is a moving subject which may well have evolved even since 1891.'

As counsel pointed out on behalf of the plaintiffs, a number of the specific objects mentioned in the preamble to the Statute of Elizabeth and recognised by decided cases as charitable do not fall neatly within any of the first three of the categories mentioned by Lord Macnaghten. Examples of such are the relief of aged and impotent people. The

e words 'aged, impotent and poor people' fall to be read disjunctively: see *Re Robinson (deceased)* [1950] 2 All ER 1148 at 1150, [1951] Ch 198 at 201 and *Re Lewis (deceased)* [1954] 3 All ER 257 at 259, [1955] Ch 104 at 108. Aged and impotent persons may thus qualify as objects of charity without necessarily being poor. A similar comment may be made in relation to some other objects referred to in the statute, such as 'the education and preferment of orphans', 'the supportation, aid and help of young tradesmen' and 'the

f relief or redemption of prisoners or captives'. Persons falling within any of these categories are not necessarily suffering from poverty. All persons included within any of these categories, however, have this much in common, namely that they are suffering from some form of human suffering or distress. Thus, counsel for the plaintiffs submitted, it is possible to detect in the preamble to the statute a genus or division of charity not mentioned by Lord Macnaghten, of which poverty is merely a species; this

g genus includes the relief of human suffering and distress in all the various forms enumerated. In general terms I accept this analysis, which derives some support from what Lord Herschell said in *Pemsel's* case [1891] AC 531 at 572, [1891–4] All ER Rep 28 at 50:

  'I think, then, that the popular conception of a charitable purpose covers the relief of any form of necessity, destitution, or helplessness which excites the compassion

h or sympathy of men, and so appeals to their benevolence for relief.'

Adopting a similar approach, Lord Greene MR in *Re Hobourn Aero Components Ltd's Air-raid Distress Fund Trusts* [1946] 1 All ER 501 at 506, [1946] Ch 194 at 200–201 said this:

  'I am not concerned for one moment to dispute the proposition that a fund put

j up for air-raid distress in Coventry generally would be a good charitable gift. I have very little doubt that it would be.'

As a broad proposition, I would thus accept that a trust for the relief of human suffering and distress would prima facie be capable of being of a charitable nature, within the spirit and intendment of the preamble to the Statute of Elizabeth, as being what

counsel for the plaintiffs termed a 'charity of compassion'. It does not, however, follow
that a trust established for good compassionate purposes will necessarily qualify as a   *a*
charity according to English law, any more than it necessarily follows that such a
qualification will attach to a trust for the relief of poverty or for the advancement of
education or for the advancement of religion. There are other requirements which it
must still satisfy if it is to enjoy charitable status. I now turn to the requirement of public
benefit.

b

The requirement of public benefit
  Save in the case of gifts to classes of poor persons, a trust must always be shown to
promote a public benefit of a nature recognised by the courts as being such, if it is to
qualify as being charitable. The question whether a purpose will or may operate for the
public benefit is to be answered by the court forming an opinion on the evidence before
it: see *National Anti-Vivisection Society v Inland Revenue Comrs* [1947] 2 All ER 217 at 221,   *c*
[1948] AC 31 at 44 per Lord Wright. No doubt in some cases a purpose may be so
manifestly beneficial to the public that it would be absurd to call evidence on this
point. In many other instances, however, the element of public benefit may be much
more debatable. Indeed, in some cases the court will regard this element of being
incapable of proof one way or the other and thus will inevitably decline to recognise the
trust as being of a charitable nature.   *d*
  Trusts to promote changes in the law of England are generally regarded as falling into
the latter category and as being non-charitable for this reason. Thus Lord Parker said in
Bowman v Secular Society Ltd [1917] AC 406 at 442, [1916–17] All ER Rep 1 at 18:

  'The abolition of religious tests, the disestablishment of the Church, the
  secularization of education, the alteration of the law touching religion or marriage,
  or the observation of the Sabbath, are purely political objects. Equity has always   *e*
  refused to recognize such objects as charitable. It is true that a gift to an association
  formed for their attainment may, if the association be unincorporated, be upheld as
  an absolute gift to its members, or, if the association be incorporated, as an absolute
  gift to the corporate body; but a trust for the attainment of political objects has
  always been held invalid, not because it is illegal, for everyone is at liberty to
  advocate or promote by any lawful means a change in the law, but because the   *f*
  Court has no means of judging whether a proposed change in the law will or will
  not be for the public benefit, and therefore cannot say that a gift to secure the
  change is a charitable gift. The same considerations apply when there is a trust for
  the publication of a book. The Court will examine the book, and if its objects be
  charitable in the legal sense it will give effect to the trust as a good charity: *Thornton
  v. Howe* ((1862) 31 Beav 14, 54 ER 1042); but if its objects be political it will refuse   *g*
  to enforce the trust: *De Themmines v. De Bonneval* ((1828) 5 Russ 288, 38 ER 1035).'

  In the latter case a gift of some stock in trust to apply the dividends in printing and
promoting the circulation of a treatise written in French and Latin, which inculcated the
doctrine of absolute supremacy of the Pope in eccleslastical matters, was held void. As
was said in the judgment (5 Russ 288 at 292, 38 ER 1035 at 1037):   *h*

  'It is against the policy of the country to encourage, by the establishment of a
  charity, the publication of any work which asserts the absolute supremacy of the
  Pope in ecclesiastical matters over the sovereignty of the state.'

  The passage from Lord Parker's speech in the *Bowman* case which I have read is often
cited as authority for the broad proposition that trusts for 'political objects' can never be   *j*
supported as legal charities. However, before this proposition is accepted, it is necessary
to consider what is meant by political objects in this context. It would appear that Lord
Parker himself in using the phrase was referring primarily to objects which involved
changes in the existing laws of England. The implementation of any item in the list of
examples of political objects given by him (beginning with the words 'The abolition of

religious tests') would have involved changes in the law of this country.   The object of the
trust in *De Themmines v De Bonneval* would likewise have involved the advocacy of a
change in English law, because this would have been the only means of giving the Pope
the absolute supremacy in ecclesiastical matters over the sovereignty of the state which
the donor desired to secure.

There is now no doubt whatever that a trust of which a principal object is to alter the
law of this country cannot be regarded as charitable.   In *National Anti-Vivisection Society v
Inland Revenue Comrs* [1948] AC 31, [1947] 2 All ER 217 a society which had as its object
the total suppression of vivisection was held not to be 'a body of persons . . . established
for charitable purposes only', within s 37(1)(b) of the Income Tax Act 1918 on two
separate grounds.   The first was that any assumed public benefit in the advancement of
morals would be far outweighed by the detriment to medical science and research and
consequently to public health.   This was a finding on the evidence.   The second ground
was that a main object of the society was the promotion of legislation.   As Lord Wright
said ([1947] 2 All ER 217 at 224, [1948] AC 31 at 49–50):

> 'But there is another and essentially different ground on which, in my opinion,
> it must fail.   That is because its object is to secure legislation to give legal effect to
> it.   It is, in my opinion, a political purpose within the meaning of LORD PARKER's
> pronouncement in *Bowman* v. *Secular Society, Ltd.* ([1917] AC 406 at 442, [1916–17]
> All ER Rep 1 at 18).'

Similarly, Lord Simonds, in a very significant passage in his speech, said ([1947] 2 All
ER 217 at 232, [1948] AC 31 at 62–63):

> 'My Lords, I see no reason for supposing that LORD PARKER, in the cited passage,
> used the expression "political objects" in any narrow sense or was confining it to
> objects of acute political controversy.   On the contrary, he was, I think, propounding
> familiar doctrine, nowhere better stated than in a text book, which has long been
> regarded as of high authority, but appears not to have been cited for this purpose to
> the courts below (as it certainly was not to your Lordships), TYSSEN ON CHARITABLE
> BEQUESTS.   The passage which is at p. 176 [in the original 1898 Edn] is worth
> repeating at length: "It is a common practice for a number of individuals amongst
> us to form an association for promoting some change in the law, and it is worth our
> while to consider the effect of a gift to such an association.   It is clear that such an
> association is not of a charitable nature.   However desirable the change may really
> be, the law could not stultify itself by holding that it was for the public benefit that
> the law itself should be changed.   Each court in deciding on the validity of a gift
> must decide on the principle that the law is right as it stands.   On the other hand,
> such a gift could not be held void for illegality."   LORD PARKER uses slightly different
> language, but means the same thing, when he says that the court has no means of
> judging whether a proposed change in the law will or will not be for the public
> benefit.   It is not for the court to judge and the court has no means of judging.   The
> same question may be looked at from a slightly different angle.   One of the tests,
> and a crucial test, whether a trust is charitable, lies in the competence of the court
> to control and reform it.   I would remind your Lordships that it is the King as *parens
> patriae* who is the guardian of charity, and that it is the right and duty of his
> Attorney-General to intervene and inform the court, if the trustees of a charitable
> trust falls short of their duty.   So too is his duty to assist the court, if need be, in
> the formulation of a scheme for the execution of a charitable trust.   But, my Lords,
> is it for a moment to be supposed that it is the function of the Attorney-General, on
> behalf of the Crown, to intervene and demand that a trust shall be established and
> administered by the court, the object of which is to alter the law in a manner highly
> prejudicial, as he and His Majesty's Government may think, to the welfare of the
> State?   This very case would serve as an example, if upon the footing that it was a
> charitable trust it became the duty of the Attorney-General on account of its
> maladministration to intervene.'

The House of Lords in *National Anti-Vivisection Society v Inland Revenue Comrs*, like Lord Parker in *Bowman v Secular Society Ltd*, was directing its attention primarily, if not exclusively, to one particular form of political trust, namely a trust of which it was a main object to obtain an alteration of the law of England. Lord Simonds and Lord Wright clearly felt some difficulty about the generality of the words which had been used by Lord Parker in saying that 'the court has no means of judging whether a proposed change in the law would or would not be for the public benefit'. In most cases the court would not have the means to judge this question. On the particular facts of *National Anti-Vivisection v Inland Revenue Comrs*, however, their Lordships clearly did regard themselves as having such means, because one ground of their decision was that the proposed change in the law would be detrimental to the public. The explanation and justification for Lord Parker's opinion was expressed by Lord Wright. After having referred to the passage from Tyssen on Charitable Bequests cited by Lord Simonds, he said ([1947] 2 All ER 217 at 224–225, [1948] AC at 31 at 50):

> 'It is, I think, a very important contribution to this question. It appears to me to go to explain and justify LORD PARKER's opinion. I refer especially to TYSSEN's words: "the law could not stultify itself by holding that it was for the public benefit that the law itself should be changed" and again: "Each court . . . must decide on the principle that the law is right as it stands." I am reminded of the words of a great common law judge who warned the courts against usurping the functions of the legislature. I regard the statements of LORD PARKER and TYSSEN not as inconsistent, but as complementary.'

From the passages from the speeches of Lord Parker, Lord Wright and Lord Simonds which I have read, I extract the principle that the court will not regard as charitable a trust of which a main object is to procure an alteration of the law of the United Kingdom for one or both of two reasons. First, the court will ordinarily have no sufficient means of judging, as a matter of evidence, whether the proposed change will or will not be for the public benefit. Second, even if the evidence suffices to enable it to form a prima facie opinion that a change in the law is desirable, it must still decide the case on the principle that the law is right as it stands, since to do otherwise would be to usurp the functions of the legislature. I interpret the point made by Lord Simonds concerning the position of the Attorney General as merely illustrating some of the anomalies and undesirable consequences that might ensue if the courts began to encroach on the functions of the legislature by ascribing charitable status to trusts of which a main object is to procure a change in the law of the United Kingdom, as being for the public benefit.

A further warning to the courts against usurping the functions of the legislature has recently been given by the House of Lords in *Duport Steels Ltd v Sirs* [1980] 1 All ER 529 at 542, [1980] 1 WLR 142 at 157. Lord Diplock pointed out that certain trade union legislation might in actual operation have turned out to have injurious consequences that Parliament had not anticipated at the time when the statutes were passed. However, he said: 'But if this be the case it is for Parliament, not for the judiciary, to decide whether any changes should be made to the law as stated in the Acts.' And he referred to 'public confidence in the political impartiality of the judiciary, which is essential to the continuance of the rule of law . . .'

Thus far, the only types of political trust to which I have directed specific attention have been those of which a main object is to procure a change in the law of this country. The principles established by *Bowman's* case and the *National Anti-Vivisection Society* case will render such trusts non-charitable, whether or not they are of a party political nature. Conversely, however, several cases cited to me illustrate that trusts of which a main object is to promote the interests of a particular political party in this country fail to achieve charitable status, even though they are not directed towards any particular change in English law: see, for example, *Bonar Law Memorial Trust v Inland Revenue Comrs* (1933) 17 Tax Cases 508 and *Re Hopkinson (deceased), Lloyds Bank Ltd v Baker* [1949] 1 All ER 346. In my judgment any such trusts are plainly 'political trusts' within

the spirit, if not the letter, of Lord Parker's pronouncement, and the same reasons for the
a court's refusing to enforce them would apply, but a fortiori. Since their nature would ex
hypothesi be very controversial, the court could be faced with even greater difficulties in
determining whether the objects of the trust would be for the public benefit;
correspondingly, it would be at even greater risk of encroaching on the functions of the
legislature and prejudicing its reputation for political impartiality, if it were to promote
such objects by enforcing the trust.

b   I now turn to consider the status of a trust of which a main object is to secure the
alteration of the laws of a *foreign* country. The mere fact that the trust was intended to
be carried out abroad would not by itself necessarily deprive it of charitable status. A
number of trusts to be executed outside this country have been upheld as charities,
though the judgment of Evershed MR in *Camille and Henry Dreyfus Foundation Inc v
Inland Revenue Comrs* [1954] 2 All ER 466 at 471–472, [1954] Ch 672 at 684–685
c illustrates that certain types of trust, for example trusts for the setting out of soldiers or
the repair of bridges or causeways, might be acceptable as charities only if they were to
be executed in the United Kingdom. The point with which I am at present concerned
is whether a trust of which a direct and main object is to secure a change in the laws of
a foreign country can *ever* be regarded as charitable under English law. Though I do not
think that any authority cited to me precisely covers the point, I have come to the clear
d conclusion that it cannot.

I accept that the dangers of the court encroaching on the functions of the legislature
or of subjecting its political impartiality to question would not be nearly so great as when
similar trusts are to be executed in this country. I also accept that on occasions the court
will examine and express an opinion on the quality of a foreign law. Thus, for example,
it has declined to enforce or recognise rights conferred or duties imposed by a foreign
e law, in certain cases where it has considered that, on the particular facts, enforcement or
recognition would be contrary to justice or morality. I therefore accept that the
particular point made by Mr Tyssen (about the law stultifying itself) has no application
in this context. There is no obligation on the court to decide on the principle that any
foreign law is ex hypothesi right as it stands; it is not obliged for all purposes to blind
itself to what it may regard as the injustice of a particular foreign law.

f   In my judgment, however, there remain overwhelming reasons why such a trust still
cannot be regarded as charitable. All the reasoning of Lord Parker in *Bowman v Secular
Society Ltd* seems to me to apply a fortiori in such a case. A fortiori the court will have no
adequate means of judging whether a proposed change in the law of a foreign country
will or will not be for the public benefit. Evershed MR in *Camille and Henry Dreyfus
Foundation Inc v Inland Revenue Comrs* [1954] 2 All ER 466 at 471, [1954] Ch 672 at 684
g expressed the prima facie view that the community which has to be considered in this
context, even in the case of a trust to be executed abroad, is the community of the United
Kingdom. Assuming that this is the right test, the court in applying it would still be
bound to take account of the probable effects of attempts to procure the proposed
legislation, or of its actual enactment, on the inhabitants of the country concerned, which
would doubtless have a history and social structure quite different from that of the
h United Kingdom. Whatever might be its view as to the content of the relevant law from
the standpoint of an English lawyer, it would, I think, have no satisfactory means of
judging such probable effects on the local community.

Furthermore, before ascribing charitable status to an English trust of which a main
object was to secure the alteration of a foreign law, the court would also, I conceive, be
bound to consider the consequences for this country as a matter of public policy. In a
j number of such cases there would arise a substantial prima facie risk that such a trust, if
enforced, could prejudice the relations of this country with the foreign country
concerned (cf *Habershon v Vardon* (1851) 4 De G & Sm 467, 64 ER 916). The court would
have no satisfactory means of assessing the extent of such risk, which would not be
capable of being readily dealt with by evidence and would be a matter more for political
than for legal judgment. For all these reasons, I conclude that a trust of which a main

purpose is to procure a change in the laws of a foreign country is a trust for the attainment of political objects within the spirit of Lord Parker's pronouncement and, as *a* such, is non-charitable.

Thus far, I have been considering trusts of which a main purpose is to achieve changes in the law itself or which are of a party political nature. Under any legal system, however, the government and its various authorities, administrative and judicial, will have wide discretionary powers vested in them, within the framework of the existing law. If a principal purpose of a trust is to procure a reversal of government policy or of *b* particular administrative decisions of governmental authorities, does it constitute a trust for political purposes falling within the spirit of Lord Parker's pronouncement? In my judgment it does. If a trust of this nature is to be executed in England, the court will ordinarily have no sufficient means of determining whether the desired reversal would be beneficial to the public, and in any event could not properly encroach on the functions of the executive, acting intra vires, by holding that it should be acting in some other *c* manner. If it is a trust which is to be executed abroad, the court will not have sufficient means of satisfactorily judging, as a matter of evidence, whether the proposed reversal would be beneficial to the community in the relevant sense, after all its consequences, local and international, had been taken into account.

It may be added that Lord Normand, in the *National Anti-Vivisection Society* case ([1947] 2 All ER 217 at 240, [1948] AC 31 at 77) specifically equated legislative change and *d* changes by way of government administration in the present context. As he said:

> 'The society seems to me to proclaim that its purpose is a legislative change of policy toward scientific experiments on animals, the consummation of which will be an Act prohibiting all such experiments. I regard it as clear that a society professing these purposes is a political association and not a charity. If for legislative changes a change by means of government administration was substituted the *e* result would be the same.'

If the crucial test whether a trust is charitable formulated by Lord Simonds (see [1947] 2 All ER 217 at 232, [1948] AC 31 at 62), namely the competence of the court to control and reform it, is applied, I think one is again driven to the conclusion that trusts of the nature now under discussion, which are to be executed abroad, cannot qualify as charities *f* any more that if they are to be executed in this country. The court, in considering whether particular methods of carrying out or reforming them would be for the public benefit would be faced with an inescapable dilemma, of which a hypothetical example may be given. It appears from the Amnesty International Report (1978, p 270) that Islamic law sanctions the death penalty for certain well-defined offences, namely murder, adultery and brigandage. Let it be supposed that a trust were created of which the object *g* was to secure the abolition of the death penalty for adultery in those countries where Islamic law applies and to secure a reprieve for those persons who have been sentenced to death for this offence. The court, when invited to enforce or to reform such a trust, would either have to apply English standards as to public benefit, which would not necessarily be at all appropriate in the local conditions, or it would have to attempt to apply local standards of which it knew little or nothing. An English court would not, it *h* seems to me, be competent either to control or reform a trust of this nature and it would not be appropriate that it should attempt to do so.

Summary of conclusions relating to trusts for political purposes

Founding them principally on the House of Lords decisions in the *Bowman* and *National Anti-Vivisection Society* cases, I therefore summarise my conclusions in relation to *j* trusts for political purposes as follows. (1) Even if it otherwise appears to fall within the spirit and intendment of the preamble to the Statute of Elizabeth, a trust for political purposes falling within the spirit of Lord Parker's pronouncement in *Bowman*'s case can never be regarded as being for the public benefit in the manner which the law regards as charitable. (2) Trusts for political purposes falling within the spirit of this

pronouncement include (inter alia) trusts of which a direct and principal purpose is
either—

    (i) to further the interests of a particular political party, or
    (ii) to procure changes in the laws of this country, or
    (iii) to procure changes in the laws of a foreign country, or
    (iv) to procure a reversal of government policy or of particular decisions of
governmental authorities in this country, or
    (v) to procure a reversal of government policy or of particular decisions of
governmental authorities in a foreign country.

This categorisation is not intended to be an exhaustive one, but I think it will suffice
for the purposes of this judgment. I would further emphasise that it is directed to trusts
of which the *purposes* are political. As will appear later, the mere fact that trustees may
be at liberty to employ political *means* in furthering the non-political purposes of a trust
does not necessarily render it non-charitable.

The requirement that trust purposes must be wholly and exclusively charitable
The third requirement for a valid charitable trust is that each and every object or
purpose designated must be of a charitable nature. Otherwise, there are no means of
discriminating what part of the trust property is intended for charitable purposes and
what part for non-charitable purposes and the uncertainty in this respect invalidates the
whole trust.

Nevertheless, in any case where it is asserted that a trust is non-charitable on the
grounds that it introduces non-charitable as well as charitable purposes, a distinction of
critical importance has to be drawn between (a) the designated purposes of the trust, (b)
the designated means of carrying out these purposes and (c) the consequences of carrying
them out. Trust purposes of an otherwise charitable nature do not lose it merely because,
as an incidental consequence of the trustees' activities, there may enure to private
individuals benefits of a non-charitable nature. Thus, for example, in *Incorporated Council
of Law Reporting for England and Wales v Attorney General* [1971] 3 All ER 1029 at 1035,
[1972] Ch 73 at 87 per Russell LJ, the Court of Appeal rejected contentions that the
Council of Law Reporting was a non-charitable body merely because publication of the
law reports supplied members of the legal profession with the tools of their trade.

Similarly, trust purposes of an otherwise charitable nature do not lose it merely
because the trustees, by way of furtherance of such purposes, have incidental powers to
carry on activities which are not themselves charitable. In *Re Hood, Public Trustee v Hood*
[1931] 1 Ch 240 at 241, [1930] All ER Rep 215 at 216 a testator by his will, after certain
recitals, directed that his residuary estate should be applied 'in spreading the Christian
principles before mentioned and in aiding all active steps to minimise and extinguish the
drink traffic'. If regard had been paid solely to the grammatical form of the gift, it might
therefore have been held that the reference to minimising and extinguishing the drink
traffic was an independent additional object in itself. Having regard to the recitals to the
gift, however, the Court of Appeal found that, on its true construction, the main object
of the bequest was the application of Christian principles to all human relationships, and
thereby to spread such principles, and that the reference to the drink traffic was not an
independent additional object but was merely introduced by the testator as pointing out
one of the ways by which his main object could be obtained (see [1931] 1 Ch 240 at 251–
253, [1930] All ER Rep 215 at 220–221 per Lawrence and Romer LJJ). On this basis, as
one of the two alternative grounds for the decision, the court held that the main purpose
was a valid charitable purpose. As Lawrence LJ said:

> 'That main purpose being charitable, it seems to me that it is none the less good
> because the testator has pointed out one of the means by which in his opinion that
> main object could best be obtained, which in itself might not have been charitable
> if it had stood alone.'

The distinction is thus one between (a) those non-charitable activities authorised by the trust instrument which are merely subsidiary or incidental to a charitable purpose, *a* and (b) those non-charitable activities so authorised which in themselves form part of the trust purpose. In the latter but not the former case, the reference to non-charitable activities will deprive the trust of its charitable status.

The distinction is perhaps easier to state than to apply in practice. It was actively canvassed in the *National Anti-Vivisection Society* case. The society's counsel submitted ([1948] AC 31 at 36–37): 'So far as the society is seeking to alter the law its object is to *b* secure the abolition of vivisection; the ultimate object is charitable and the incidental political means to be adopted do not vitiate it.' The House of Lords seems to have accepted that the object of the society could have been a charitable one if, on a true analysis, this was to secure the abolition of vivisection and if legislation was merely to be regarded as ancillary to the attainment of this object (see, for example, [1947] 2 All ER 217 at 231, 240, [1948] AC 31 at 61, 77 per Lord Simonds and Lord Normand). *c*

The difference of opinion between the majority of the House and Lord Porter who dissented, centred on the question whether an alteration in the law should itself be regarded as being a main object of the trust. Lord Porter thought it should not. He referred to the illustration given by Lord Parker in *Bowman's* case of the political matters which he had in mind. Lord Porter continued ([1947] 2 All ER 217 at 227, [1948] AC 31 at 54–55): *d*

> 'The object in each case is to do away with a positive injunction to which an end can only be put by repealing the law; an Act of Parliament is required in order to do so. An example may be taken from the first illustration given by LORD PARKER. No agreement come to by individuals or groups could dispense with the obligation of complying with the provisions of the Test Acts, whereas slavery or vivisection could be put an end to without disobedience to the law if all members of the community *e* could be induced to desist from these practices. It is in the narrower sense in which I think the phrase "purely political objects" is rightly used, i.e., as applicable to objects whose only means of attainment is a change in the law ... Their primary object, as I see it, is to prevent animal suffering caused by vivisection, though a main method of effecting that end is to repeal the present Act and such repeal is in that *f* sense a main object of the society.'

The rest of their Lordships took a view different from that of Lord Porter on this point. Lord Simonds dealt with it thus ([1947] 2 All ER 217 at 231, [1948] AC 31 at 61–62):

> '... I cannot agree that in this case an alteration in the law is merely ancillary to the attainment of a good charitable object. In a sense, no doubt, since legislation is *g* not an end in itself, every law may be regarded as ancillary to the object which its provisions are intended to achieve. But that is not the sense in which it is said that a society has a political object. Here the finding of the commissioners is itself conclusive. "We are satisfied," they say, "that the main object of the society is the total abolition of vivisection ... and (for that purpose) the repeal of the Cruelty to Animals Act, 1876, and the substitution of a new enactment prohibiting vivisection *h* altogether." This is a finding that the main purpose of the society is the compulsory abolition of vivisection by Act of Parliament. What else can it mean? And how else can it be supposed that vivisection is to be abolished? Abolition and suppression are words that connote some form of compulsion. It can only be by Act of Parliament that that element can be supplied ... [I come] to the conclusion that it is a main object, if not the main object, of the society, to obtain an alteration of the law ...' *j*

Lord Normand formulated the question thus ([1947] 2 All ER 217 at 239, [1948] AC 31 at 76–77):

> 'The problem is, therefore, to discover the general purposes of the society and whether they are in the main political or in the main charitable. It is a question of degree of a sort well known to the courts.'

In *Re Bushnell (deceased), Lloyds Bank Ltd v Murray* [1975] 1 All ER 721 at 728, [1975] 1 WLR 1596 at 1604 Goulding J observed that a test propounded in such general terms is easier to state than to apply. Earlier in his judgment he had pointed out that the existence of some political motive is not necessarily fatal to a good charitable trust. In that case the trust in question was, in effect, one to further knowledge of the application of socialised medicine to public and personal health in a socialised state. Ultimately, applying Lord Normand's test, Goulding J concluded that its main or dominant or essential object was a political one and that it did not constitute a valid charitable trust (see [1975] 1 All ER 721 at 728, 729, [1975] 1 WLR 1596 at 1603, 1605).

From all these authorities, I think that two propositions follow in the present case. First, if any one of the main objects of the trusts declared by the trust deed is to be regarded as 'political' in the relevant sense, then, subject to the effect of the proviso to cl 2, the trusts of the trust deed cannot qualify as being charitable. Second, however, if all the main objects of the trust are exclusively charitable, the mere fact that the trustees may have incidental powers to employ political means for their furtherance will not deprive them of their charitable status.

After this introduction I now turn to examine these trusts themselves. A convenient starting point is the proviso to cl 2 of the trust deed.

The proviso to cl 2 of the trust deed

The definition of 'prisoner of conscience' contained in cl 1(c) of the trust deed is capable of including all persons who are imprisoned outside the United Kingdom, provided that they otherwise fall within the definition. Even if the trust deed had stopped at cl 2B, it would thus have been clear, by necessary implication, that it was intended that the purposes set out in cll 2A and 2B might be carried out outside, as well as inside, the United Kingdom. Without further express provision, however, there might perhaps have been doubt whether the purposes set out in cll 2C, 2D, 2E and 2F could be carried out outside the United Kingdom. Any such doubt is removed by the closing words of the proviso to cl 2, 'but subject thereto they may be carried out in all parts of the world'. The manifest object of these words is to declare that, subject to the other restrictions imposed by the trust deed, the trustees shall be subjected to no territorial limitations in furthering the trust purposes.

The opening limb of the proviso to cl 2, 'PROVIDED ALWAYS that the foregoing objects shall be restricted to those which are charitable according to the law of the United Kingdom . . .', gives rise to greater difficulties. Three possible constructions of these words have been suggested in argument. First, it has been suggested that they merely express the intention of the parties that a benignant construction should be given to the deed (in particular the description of the trust purposes in cl 2) in accordance with the general principle expressed by Lord Hailsham LC in *Inland Revenue Comrs v McMullen* [1980] 1 All ER 884 at 890, [1981] AC 1 at 14 in the following terms: '. . . in construing trust deeds the intention of which is to set up a charitable trust, and in others too, where it can be claimed that there is an ambiguity, a benignant construction should be given if possible.' Second, it has been suggested that the opening limb of the proviso was intended to have what was described as a 'blue-pencil' operation, so that the trust deed should be construed as if all references to any of the particular purposes set out in cll 2A to 2F which are not legally charitable had been expunged from the deed ab initio. Third, it has been suggested that the opening limb was merely intended to make it clear that the trustees, though entitled to carry out the trust purposes in any part of the world, should, even when operating outside the United Kingdom, be restricted to purposes which are charitable according to the law of the United Kingdom.

The wording of the proviso to cl 2 is not very clear or satisfactory. I think it fair to say that of these three suggested constructions none has been urged on me by counsel with any great force or conviction. On balance, however, I prefer the third of them. It is readily intelligible that the draftsman should have wished to include a provision making it clear that the trustees should be restricted to objects which are charitable according to United Kingdom law, even though they might in fact be operating in foreign countries (for example, the United States) which have their own laws relating to charities. Furthermore, this third construction seems to me the only one which gives adequate force to the words 'but subject thereto', which seem to suggest that he regarded the generality of the second limb of the proviso as being restricted by the first. a

It thus follows that if any one of the trust purposes set out in cl 2 of the trust deed is of a non-charitable nature, the proviso to cl 2 cannot enable the trusts declared by the deed to escape total invalidity.

It will not be necessary to consider the trusts declared by cl 2A, since it is common ground that, if read in isolation, these trusts are of a charitable nature. Of the remaining subclauses, I shall begin by considering the construction and legal effect of cl 2B. b

Clause 2B of the trust deed

The trust purpose declared by cl 2B of the trust deed, 'Attempting to secure the release of Prisoners of Conscience', as I read it, is one that by its very nature would be executed almost exclusively outside the United Kingdom. This follows from the exclusion from the definition of 'prisoner of conscience' of 'any person who is lawfully imprisoned or detained within the United Kingdom'. Strictly, I suppose, a person who was unlawfully imprisoned in the United Kingdom (for example, by kidnappers or a terrorist gang) would fall within the definition, but I attach little importance to this point. It does not appear to me that the release of persons imprisoned by terrorists, kidnappers or the like, whether in this country or abroad, is what the parties to the trust deed had primarily in mind. Principally, I do not doubt, they envisaged attempts to secure the release of prisoners of conscience, within the definition, who are detained by governments or governmental authorities in foreign countries, with or without the sanction of the local law. According to the Amnesty International Handbook (1977, p 9): 'Well over ninety governments today are holding their own citizens in prison either on political, religious or racial grounds or else without trial or charge altogether.' c d e

Counsel for the plaintiffs cited a number of cases in which the scope of the reference to the redemption and relief of captives in the Statute of Elizabeth has been considered: for example, *Attorney General v Gibson* (1835) 2 Beav 317, 48 ER 1208, *Attorney General v Ironmongers' Co* (1834) 2 My & K 576, [1824–34] All ER Rep 620, *Ironmongers Co v Attorney General* (1844) 10 Cl & Fin 908, 8 ER 983, *Re Prison Charities* (1873) LR 16 Eq 129 and *Thrupp v Collett (No 1)* (1858) 26 Beav 125, 53 ER 844. Perhaps the strongest case in his favour was a United States decision, *Jackson v Phillips* (1867) 96 Mass 539 at 540. In the latter case Gray J, sitting in the Supreme Court of Massachusetts, held that a bequest to trustees which had been made at a time before slavery had been abolished in the United States and was to be expended 'for the preparation and circulation of books, newspapers, the delivery of speeches, lectures and such other means as in their judgment will create a public sentiment that will put an end to negro slavery in this country' was a legal charity. f g

In the course of a learned and powerful judgment, Gray J expressed the opinion (at 567): 'To deliver men from a bondage which the law regards as contrary to natural right, humanity, justice and sound policy is surely not less charitable than to lessen the sufferings of animals'. He said (at 568): h

'The authorities already cited show that the peaceable redemption or manumission of slaves in any manner not prohibited by law is a charitable object. It falls indeed within the spirit, and almost within the letter, of many clauses in the Statute of Elizabeth. It would be an anomaly in a system of law, which recognised as charitable uses the relief of the poor, the education and preferment of orphans, marriages of poor maids, the assistance of young tradesmen, handicraftsmen and persons decayed, the relief of prisoners and the redemption of captives, to exclude the deliverance of an indefinite number of human beings from a condition in which they were so poor as not even to own themselves, in which their children could not be educated, in which marriages had no sanction of law or security of duration, in which all their earnings belonged to another, and they were subject, against the law of nature, and j

without any crime of their own, to such an arbitrary dominion as the modern usages of nations will not countenance over captives taken from the most barbarous enemy.'

A little earlier in his judgment Gray J had dealt with an argument based on public policy as follows (at 565):

'We fully concur with the learned counsel for the heirs at law that if this trust could not be executed according to the intention of the testator without tending to excite servile insurrections in other states of the Union, it would have been unlawful; and that a trust which looked solely to political agitation and to attempts to alter existing laws could not be recognized by this court as charitable. But such does not appear to us to be the necessary or the reasonable interpretation of this bequest. The manner stated of putting an end to slavery is not by legislation or political action, but by creating a public sentiment, which rather points to moral influence and voluntary manumission. The means specified are the usual means of public instruction, by books and newspapers, speeches and lectures. Other means are left to the discretion of the trustees, but there is nothing to indicate that they are not designed to be of a kindred nature. Giving to the bequest that favourable construction to which all charitable gifts are entitled, the just inference is that lawful means only are to be selected, and that they are to be used in a lawful manner.'

It is to be presumed that the creators of the trust in the present case would not have intended the trustees to carry out the trust imposed on them by cl 2B by means that were unlawful according to the law of the foreign country concerned (for example, by the use of violence to secure the desired release). Nor do I accept the submission of counsel for the Inland Revenue Commissioners that the wording of cl 2B by its terms suggests the procurement of the repeal of any municipal law which provides for the detention of prisoners of conscience. It may be that on occasions the trustees would consider attempts to secure the repeal of such laws to be the best method of securing the release of prisoners of conscience lawfully detained in a particular foreign country. On a fair reading of the wording of cl 2B, however, I do not think it can properly be said that an attempt to secure changes in municipal laws can be treated as being itself an object of the trust falling within cl 2B, or as being suggested by its very wording.

Counsel for the plaintiffs pointed out that one of the underlying principles of the purposes set out in the preamble to the Statute of Elizabeth is the relief of human suffering and distress. This proposition I have already accepted in general terms. He submitted, in effect, that the line of cases relating to captives shows that a trust to secure the release of prisoners of conscience would be well within the spirit and intendment of the statute, provided only that its particular terms were not such as to offend against public policy. He pointed out that the definition of prisoners of conscience specifically excludes persons lawfully imprisoned in the United Kingdom and that, so far as it may relate to persons unlawfully imprisoned there, it can be regarded as a trust to enforce the existing law. (Cases such as *Inland Revenue Comrs v City of Glasgow Police Athletic Association* [1953] 1 All ER 747, [1953] AC 380 illustrate that trusts connected with the enforcement of the existing law of this country may well qualify as charitable trusts.) Counsel for the plaintiffs submitted that, just as Gray J gave a beneficent construction to the trust in *Jackson v Phillips*, inferring that only lawful means were to be selected by the trustees, so in the present case it should be inferred that the trustees are only to use means appropriate to the trustees of a charity, such as moral influence and the creation of public sentiment. He referred me to the decision of Dillon J in *Barralet v Attorney General* [1980] 3 All ER 918, [1980] 1 WLR 1565 as illustrating that the cultivation of a certain attitude of mind can be a good charitable object.

Even giving the wording of cl 2B the beneficent construction to which it is entitled, I cannot construe it in the manner suggested. If in construing the sub-clause one rejects, as I have done, the possibility that the activities of the trustees thereunder may be unlawful or may consist of attempts to procure changes in the local laws, it is obvious *a* that the primary activity contemplated by cl 2B is the imposition of moral pressure on governments or governmental authorities. The crucial difference between the nature of the trust of cl 2B and the relevant trust in *Jackson v Phillips* is that in the latter case the pressure was to be directed by the trustees against individual persons, rather than governments, with a view to obtaining the 'voluntary manumission' of the slaves belonging to such individuals. In the present case, the persons who are effecting the *b* imprisonment or detention of prisoners of conscience in a foreign country will, ex hypothesi, normally be the governments or governmental authorities concerned exercising a judicial, penal or administrative function, or in some cases acting quite outside the law. I do not think that the trust can be construed as being one of which the main purpose is merely to influence public opinion in the country where the imprisonment is taking place. Its very terms suggest the direction of moral pressure or *c* persuasion against governmental authorities.

As Buckley LJ said in *Incorporated Council of Law Reporting for England and Wales v Attorney General* [1971] 3 All ER 1029 at 1043, [1972] Ch 73 at 99:

> '. . . in order to determine whether an object, the scope of which has been ascertained by due processes of construction, is a charitable purpose it may be necessary to have regard to evidence to discover the consequences of pursuing that *d* object.'

Examples of forms of pressure which would specifically fall within the wording of cl 2B, and were no doubt contemplated by the parties to the trust deed, are to be found in the following extract from the Amnesty International Handbook of 1977 (p 29):

> 'Pressure to free prisoners of conscience can mean all of the following: thousands *e* of postcards and letters to the foreign government; distributing leaflets at trade fairs; special appeals signed by prominent individuals; trade union embargoes against goods from the foreign government; continuous international news reports on the human rights violations by the governments concerned.'

Expressed in one sentence, the main object of the broadly-defined trust contained in *f* cl 2B must in my judgment be regarded as being the procurement of the reversal of the relevant decisions of governments and governmental authorities in those countries where such authorities have decided to detain prisoners of conscience, whether or not in accordance with the local law. The procurement of the reversal of such decisions cannot, I think, be regarded merely as one possible method of giving effect to the purposes of cl 2B, any more than in the *National Anti-Vivisection Society* case the alteration of the law *g* could be regarded as merely one method of giving effect to the purpose of abolishing vivisection. On the construction which I place on cl 2B, it is the principal purpose itself. On this view of the matter, the trust declared by cl 2B cannot in my judgment qualify as a charitable trust. It is a trust for political purposes within the fifth of the categories listed above (see p 509, ante).

In conclusion in this context, I would merely add the following observations. Counsel *h* for the Inland Revenue Commissioners drew my attention to a number of examples, drawn from the Amnesty International Report of 1978, showing what Amnesty International had been doing in practice towards securing the release of prisoners of conscience during the period from July 1977 to June 1978. I mention only three of them. During this period Amnesty International had been working on a number of cases of persons who had been imprisoned in France, in accordance with French law, *j* because of conscientious objection to military service (see pp 210–211 of the report). It also wrote to the Minister of Justice in the Netherlands giving its views on the conditions of detention of three Red Army Faction prisoners in the Netherlands, who had been held in solitary confinement since their arrest on murder charges and had been on hunger strike for improved conditions (see pp 222–223). The report also refers to a large

number of missions to foreign countries to observe trials of persons on whose behalf
a Amnesty International was concerned (see pp 278–279).

All these activities, so far as I can see, would fall fairly and squarely within the wording
of cl 2B, and indeed would be the very sort of activity which cl 2B would suggest. No
criticism whatever of these activities was expressed at the hearing before me, and I intend
no such criticism; so far as the evidence shows, they were perfectly proper and
legitimate. However, they do in my judgment well illustrate the difficulty, indeed the
b impossibility, of treating as charitable a trust such as that of cl 2B. The reasoning which
led Lord Parker to conclude in *Bowman v Secular Society Ltd* [1917] AC 406, [1916–17] All
ER Rep 1, that a trust for political purposes, of the nature referred to by him, is invalid
applies in full force to a trust of the nature of cl 2B; if it were asked to execute it, the court
would have no adequate means of judging as a matter of evidence whether it would be
for the public benefit after all the possible consequences, local and international, had
c been taken into account.

For these reasons it must in my judgment follow that the trusts of cl 2B are not
charitable. Unlike those of cl 2A, they cannot be regarded as purely eleemosynary. It
must also follow from this that the trusts of the trust deed as a whole are invalid as not
being for exclusively charitable purposes. Nevertheless, having heard full argument as
to cll 2C, 2D and 2E, I will express my conclusions in relation to them, in case this may be
d of assistance either to the parties or to a higher court.

Clause 2c of the trust deed

It is common ground that in the light of the proviso to cl 2 of the trust deed the trust
purpose declared by cl 2C must, as a matter of language, cover 'procuring the abolition of
torture or inhuman or degrading treatment or punishment' in the United Kingdom or
e any other part of the world. The first problem caused by cl 2C concerns the meaning of
the phrase 'inhuman or degrading treatment or punishment', which does not define
what particular treatments or punishments are or are not to be regarded as inhuman or
degrading within its meaning. I have not been invited and shall not attempt to give a
comprehensive answer to this question. There is, however, one particular point with
which I must deal, since it has constituted an important feature in the argument of
f counsel for the Inland Revenue Commissioners. He has submitted that, in its context,
the phrase 'inhuman or degrading treatment or punishment' manifestly includes capital
and corporal punishment.

It is common ground that, in construing the ambiguous wording of cl 2C and, indeed,
any other ambiguous wording contained in the trust deed, the court is at liberty, so far
as it can, to derive assistance from the statute of the unincorporated association, Amnesty
g International. Not only does the trust deed borrow the name 'Amnesty International' as
the name of the trust; it specifically refers to Amnesty International in cll 9(b) and 16.
The statute of this association is manifestly part of the factual matrix accompanying the
execution of the trust deed.

The wording of art 1(c) of the statute refers to 'death penalties and torture or other
cruel, inhuman or degrading treatment or punishment'. The use of the word 'other' in
h this context makes it clear that the association regards the death penalty as one form of
cruel or inhuman or degrading treatment or punishment; and, indeed, this is borne out
by the other evidence as to the principles according to which it carries on its activities in
practice.

Is there, then, any reason why the relevant phrase in cl 2C of the trust deed should be
construed in any different sense? Counsel for the plaintiffs submitted that there is. He
j pointed out that cl 2C closely echoes the wording of art 3 of the European Convention for
the Protection of Human Rights and Fundamental Freedoms which provides: 'No one
shall be subjected to torture or to inhuman or degrading treatment or punishment.' He
pointed out that, in the context of that convention, the phrase 'inhuman or degrading
treatment or punishment' appears not to include capital punishment because art 2
provides, inter alia: 'No one shall be deprived of his life intentionally save in the

execution of a sentence of a court following his conviction of a crime for which this penalty is provided by law.' It thus apparently contemplates that the infliction of capital *a* punishment will not necessarily constitute an infringement of the convention.

In this context it is to be observed that the Universal Declaration of Human Rights provides in art 3: 'Everyone has the right to life, liberty and security of person.' Article 5 provides: 'No one shall be subjected to torture or to cruel, inhuman or degrading treatment or punishment.' But it contains no specific reference to capital punishment.

Counsel for the plaintiffs submitted, in effect, that the plaintiffs, in executing the trust *b* deed containing cl 2c in the form which that sub-clause took, must be deemed to have had in mind the very similar wording of art 3 of the European Convention and to have used the phrase 'inhuman or degrading treatment or punishment' in a corresponding sense. While I feel no doubt that, for the purpose of construing cl 2c of the trust deed, the court is entitled to look at the statute of Amnesty International and also at the Universal Declaration of Human Rights, which is specifically referred to in the trust *c* deed, I feel rather more doubt whether it can properly look at the European Convention, which is not referred to. However, even assuming in favour of the plaintiffs that it can properly do so, I still do not think that the introduction of this evidence leads to the conclusion for which counsel for the plaintiffs contends. It is still necessary to consider whether art 1(c) of the statute of Amnesty International or the European Convention is to be regarded as the more reliable source for ascertaining the true meaning and intent *d* of the phrase 'inhuman or degrading treatment or punishment', as used in this particular trust deed.

I feel no doubt that the statute should be regarded as the more reliable source. It is true that, as counsel for the plaintiffs pointed out, the trust deed, unlike the statute, makes no express reference to capital punishment. In my judgment, however, one important feature of the factual background against which the trust deed must be *e* construed is that, as is stated in the handbook of Amnesty International (1977 Edn, p 7), Amnesty International opposes the death penalty 'in all cases and without reservation'. For its own part, it clearly regards the death penalty as an inhuman and degrading punishment, as cl 1(c) of its statute illustrates. In these circumstances, I think it must be assumed that, if the phrase 'inhuman or degrading punishment' in the context of the trust deed had not been intended to include capital punishment, the deed would have *f* expressly so provided. It may well be that the draftsman considered that any express reference to the abolition of capital punishment would render more difficult the achievement of charitable status for the trust and thus preferred to leave a deliberate ambiguity. In my judgment, however, it cannot be inferred that, by the omission of any such reference, he or the plaintiffs, who executed the deed, intended to exclude the abolition of capital punishment from the trust purposes.

I think that the statute of Amnesty International gives no specific guidance as to *g* whether corporal punishment is to be regarded as an 'inhuman or degrading punishment' within the meaning of cl 2c of the trust deed. In my judgment, however, the expression 'inhuman or degrading treatment or punishment' in the context of cl 2c would include any form of corporal punishment when inflicted by process of law. I am fortified in this conclusion by reading in the Amnesty International Report (1978, p 187) of Amnesty *h* International's opposition to caning as a punishment for certain criminal offences, an opposition which I do not doubt would extend to other forms of corporal punishment when so inflicted.

The next question of construction which arises in relation to cl 2c of the trust deed concerns the meaning of the phrase 'procuring the abolition of'. On the footing that cl 2c had no application to capital punishment, counsel for the plaintiffs submitted that *j* there was no evidence that 'torture or inhuman or degrading treatment or punishment' was lawful in any country and that it was highly unlikely that any country's legal system specifically permits any such treatment or punishment. More customarily, he suggested, such treatment or punishment or torture would be administered in practice by the executive agencies of the government without any express authority conferred on them

by the law of the country concerned. In these circumstances he suggested that the phrase
a 'procuring the abolition of' should not be construed as specifically referring to the
procurement of changes in the law, either of this country or of any foreign state. In his
submission it should be construed rather as referring to the elimination of these practices
in a much more general sense, and thus as a trust of compassion, for the purpose of
protecting human beings in any part of the world from the suffering and distress which
would otherwise be inflicted on them by these practices.
b   He accepted, I think, that the procurement of changes in the laws of some foreign
countries might be one method of carrying out this general purpose. He suggested,
however, that more important methods would comprise those which are regularly used
by Amnesty International itself, namely the exercise of moral pressure, persuasion and
influence on the states concerned and their governmental agencies, public exposure and
influencing public sentiment and changing opinion. The mere fact that the trustees
c might on occasions see fit to use political means in this country or abroad to achieve their
main compassionate purpose would not, in his submission, render this purpose non-
charitable. The initiation or support of legislative steps for the purpose of eliminating
torture or cruel or degrading punishment cannot, he submitted, be regarded as expressly
comprehended within the phrase 'procuring the abolition of'.
        Though this summary of counsel's submissions for the plaintiffs does not reproduce
d the words used by him, I think it fairly represents the substance of his submissions as to
the construction of this phrase. On the basis of this construction, he submitted that cl 2C
embodied a trust which falls within the spirit and intendment of the Statute of Elizabeth
as interpreted by the court, that this trust promotes a public benefit and that, as being for
the relief of suffering and distress, it is wholly and exclusively charitable. The trust, it
was submitted, could not be said to be of a political nature within the decided cases,
e because any involvement of the trustees with legislation would be merely ancillary to the
attainment of good charitable purposes: compare, for example, *National Anti-Vivisection
Society v Inland Revenue Comrs* [1947] 2 All ER 217 at 240, [1948] AC 31 at 77 per Lord
Normand, *Inland Revenue Comrs v Yorkshire Agricultural Society* [1928] 1 KB 611 at 632,
[1927] All ER Rep 536 at 543 per Atkin LJ, and *Re Hood* [1931] 1 Ch 240 at 247–248,
[1930] All ER Rep 215 at 218–219 per Lord Hanworth MR.
f   I find myself unable to accept this suggested construction of cl 2C. If it had stopped
with the word 'torture', there would have been much to be said for the view that the
phrase 'procuring the abolition of' should not be construed as referring specifically to the
procurement of changes in the law. However, I think the subsequent reference to the
word 'punishment' really puts the matter beyond doubt. In its context, this word, to my
mind, primarily connotes punishment by process of law and, as I have indicated, is wide
g enough to include capital and corporal punishment by such process. Correspondingly,
the phrase 'procuring the abolition of' necessarily includes the procurement of
appropriate reforming legislation, which is the first and most obvious way to put an end
to such forms of punishment. As Lord Simonds said in the *National Anti-Vivisection
Society* case [1947] 2 All ER 217 at 231, [1948] AC 31 at 61: 'Abolition and suppression
are words that connote some form of compulsion.' I accept that the phrase does not refer
h exclusively to the procurement of legislation, because the phrase 'torture or inhuman or
degrading treatment or punishment' is, in my judgment, wide enough to cover illegal,
as well as legal, activities of this nature, and the procurement of legislation would not be
necessary for the purpose of procuring the elimination of illegal activities. Nevertheless,
I think it inevitably suggests (inter alia) the initiation or support of appropriate legislation
in those countries where 'inhuman or degrading punishment' is authorised by law. In
j this respect the construction which I place on cl 2C differs materially from the
construction which I place on cl 2B.
        If this be the correct construction of cl 2C, the trust thereby declared must be regarded
as a trust of which a main object is to attempt to procure the passing of the appropriate
reforming legislation for the purpose of abolishing inhuman or degrading punishments
by process of law, including capital and corporal punishment, in any countries in the

world where such punishments are for the time being lawful. As counsel for the Inland
Revenue Commissioners pointed out, the death sentence can still be passed even in the   *a*
United Kingdom for treason and certain forms of piracy: see 11 Halsbury's Laws (4th
Edn) para 493. The initiation of a campaign to procure the final and complete abolition
of the death sentence in the United Kingdom would, therefore, in my judgment, fall
within the ambit of the purposes contained in cl 2c. This point alone, in my judgment,
must render the trusts of cl 2c non-charitable, as constituting a trust, inter alia, to procure
a change in the law of this country and thus as constituting a trust for political purposes,   *b*
within the second of the five heads of political trust categorised earlier in this judgment
(see p 509, ante). However, I prefer to base my conclusion in relation to the trusts of cl 2c
on the wider grounds that they include the procurement not only of changes in the law
of the United Kingdom but also of changes in the laws of foreign countries and the
reversal of particular decisions of governmental authorities in foreign countries. They
are therefore political trusts within the second, third and fifth of the heads categorised   *c*
above (see p 509, ante). For these reasons, it must follow that, in my judgment, the trusts
of cl 2c are not charitable.

Clauses 2D and 2E of the trust deed
    Having already decided that the trusts of cll 2B and 2c are non-charitable, I shall
express my views on cll 2D and 2E more shortly. Over the past 25 years the courts have   *d*
considered a number of trusts for research, in the context of the law of charities: see, for
example, *Re Shaw (deceased), Public Trustee v Day* [1957] 1 All ER 745, [1957] 1 WLR 729,
Re Hopkin's Will Trusts, Naish v Francis Bacon Society Inc [1964 3 All ER 46, [1965] Ch 669
and *Incorporated Council of Law Reporting for England and Wales v Attorney General* [1971]
3 All ER 1029, [1972] Ch 73.
    In *Re Besterman's Will Trusts* (21st January 1980, unreported) I attempted to summarise   *e*
certain principles to be deduced from the earlier authorities in the following passage,
which I venture to repeat:

    '(1) A trust for research will ordinarily qualify as a charitable trust if, but only if
    (a) the subject-matter of the proposed research is a useful subject of study; and (b) it
    is contemplated that knowledge acquired as a result of the research will be
    disseminated to others; and (c) the trust is for the benefit of the public, or a   *f*
    sufficiently important section of the public. (2) In the absence of a contrary context,
    however, the court will be readily inclined to construe a trust for research as
    importing subsequent dissemination of the results thereof. (3) Furthermore, if a
    trust for research is to constitute a valid trust for the advancement of education, it
    is not necessary either (a) that a teacher/pupil relationship should be in contemplation
    or (b) that the persons to benefit from the knowledge to be acquired should be   *g*
    persons who are already in the course of receiving 'education' in the conventional
    sense. (4) In any case where the court has to determine whether a bequest for the
    purposes of research is or is not of a charitable nature, it must pay due regard to any
    admissible extrinsic evidence which is available to explain the wording of the will
    in question or the circumstances in which it was made.'
                                                                                    h
The correctness of this summary of the law, so far as it goes, was not challenged in the
present case.
    As counsel for the Inland Revenue Commissioners has pointed out, cll 2D and 2E
cannot be read in isolation from the sub-clauses which precede them. He has submitted
that the purposes of these sub-clauses, read in their context, are merely adjuncts to the
political purposes declared by cll 2B and 2c.   *j*
    If cll 2D and 2E had been the only trust purposes contained in the trust deed, I would
have held them to be of a charitable nature. The subject matter of the proposed research
seems to me manifestly a subject of study which is capable of adding usefully to the store
of human knowledge. And, indeed, this is borne out by the evidence contained in an
affidavit sworn on behalf of the plaintiffs by Mr David Simpson, who was the director of

Amnesty International from 1974 to 1979. From this affidavit and the exhibits thereto
a it appears that the study of human rights has become an accepted academic discipline;
the subject is taught in many universities, and is part of the curriculum in departments
of many schools. I think that cll 2D and 2E when read together make it clear that it is
contemplated that the knowledge acquired as a result of the research would be
disseminated to others. Furthermore, if these two sub-clauses had stood in isolation, I
would have felt little difficulty in holding that the trusts thereby declared were for the
b benefit of the public. The mere theoretical possibility that the trustees might have
implemented them in a political manner would not have rendered them non-charitable;
the two sub-clauses would have been entitled to a benignant construction and to the
presumption, referred to by Gray J in *Jackson v Phillips* (1867) 96 Mass 539, that the
trustees would only act in a lawful and proper manner appropriate to the trustees of a
charity and not, for example, by the propagation of tendentious political opinions.

c   As things are, the trusts of cll 2D and 2E, just as much as the trusts of cll 2A and 2F, must
in my judgment fail along with cll 2B and 2C. None of the trusts of this trust deed can
be regarded as being charitable. The proviso to cl 2 does not, in my judgment, save
them. Nor has any attempt been made to submit that the trusts can be rescued from
invalidity by an exercise of the trustees' powers under cl 15, which, on the footing that
the earlier trusts of the trust deed are non-charitable, are of a perpetuitous nature.

d
Conclusion
     In eloquent passages at the end of their addresses counsel for the Inland Revenue
Commissioners and counsel for the plaintiffs made reference to the classic problem
facing Antigone, who believed that there are certain laws of men which a higher law
may require them to disregard. Counsel for the plaintiffs, by reference to the various
e international conventions to which this country has been a party, submitted that it is
committed to the elimination of unjust laws and actions wherever these may exist or
occur throughout the world.

     Indisputably, laws do exist, both in this country and in many foreign countries, which
many reasonable persons consider unjust. No less indisputably, laws themselves will
from time to time be administered by governmental authorities in a manner which
f many reasonable persons consider unjust, inhuman or degrading. Amnesty International,
in striving to remedy what it considers to be such injustices, is performing a function
which many will regard as being of great value to humanity. Fortunately, the laws of
this country place very few restrictions on the rights of philanthropic organisations such
as this, or of individuals, to strive for the remedy of what they regard as instances of
injustice, whether occurring here or abroad. However, for reasons which I think
g adequately appear from Lord Parker's pronouncement in *Bowman's* case, the elimination
of injustice has not as such ever been held to be a trust purpose which qualifies for the
privileges afforded to charities by English law. I cannot hold it to be a charitable purpose
now.

     For all these reasons, I must decline to make the declaration sought by the originating
summons, namely, that the trust constituted by the trust deed ought to be registered as
h a charity.

Appeal dismissed.

Solicitors: *Goodman, Derrick & Co* (for the plaintiffs); *Treasury Solicitor; Solicitor of Inland
Revenue.*

Jacqueline Metcalfe   Barrister.

Trendtex Trading Corporation and another v Crédit Suisse

HOUSE OF LORDS

LORD WILBERFORCE, LORD EDMUND-DAVIES, LORD FRASER OF TULLYBELTON, LORD KEITH OF KINKEL AND LORD ROSKILL

20th, 21st, 22nd, 23rd JULY, 22nd OCTOBER 1981

Maintenance of action – Common interest – Commercial and financial interest – Cause of action – Assignment – Bank financing corporation in commercial transaction – Corporation bringing action against third party in respect of that transaction – Bank guaranteeing corporation's legal costs – Corporation assigning to bank its rights of action against third party – Whether assignment valid – Whether bank having sufficient interest in subject matter of action.

Practice – Stay of proceedings – Foreign jurisdiction clause – Agreement made in Switzerland containing purported assignment by Swiss corporation to Swiss bank of its rights of action in England against another – Agreement providing that all disputes regarding it to be determined by Swiss court – Bank selling rights of action to third party for large sum – Corporation bringing action in England against bank claiming assignment void – Application for stay of proceedings – Whether Switzerland appropriate forum for dispute – Whether application should be granted.

In 1975 the first plaintiff, a Swiss corporation ('Trendtex'), contracted to sell to an English company 240,000 tonnes of cement c i f Lagos. Under a letter of credit to be issued by the Central Bank of Nigeria ('CBN') and payable in London the English company agreed to pay the purchase price and demurrage. CBN issued the letter of credit but subsequently failed to honour it, with the result that Trendtex was left heavily indebted to the defendants, a Swiss bank ('Crédit Suisse'), which had from the outset provided finance to Trendtex to enable it to fulfil its contractual obligations to the English company and which anticipated recoupment from the letter of credit later repudiated by CBN. Trendtex issued a writ in England against CBN claiming $US14m by way of damages. Crédit Suisse, whose only substantial prospect of payment lay in the litigation succeeding, agreed to guarantee all the legal fees and costs incurred by Trendtex in the proceedings. CBN successfully pleaded sovereign immunity in the action and the writ was set aside by the High Court. Trendtex appealed to the Court of Appeal which allowed the appeal but gave CBN leave to appeal to the House of Lords, so that the matter was then still unresolved. From the autumn of 1976 Crédit Suisse, who were not Trendtex's only creditors, had been anxious to secure their advances to Trendtex and by a series of agreements made between September and November 1976 Trendtex purported to assign to Crédit Suisse by way of security its cause of action against CBN. On 4th January 1978 an agreement was signed in Geneva which recited that Trendtex was indebted to Crédit Suisse for $US1,500,000 and that Crédit Suisse had received an offer from a third party to buy Trendtex's rights against CBN for $US800,000, such rights having previously been assigned by Trendtex to Crédit Suisse in guarantee of Crédit Suisse's claim. The agreement stated that Trendtex did not oppose the sale to the third party, released to Crédit Suisse its residual rights of action against CBN, acknowledged that it had no further interest in the action and that Trendtex would deposit 90% of its shares, which were owned by the second plaintiff, a Liechtenstein corporation ('Temo'), with P, Crédit Suisse's Swiss lawyer, in return for which Crédit Suisse agreed to pay off all Trendtex's other creditors. The agreement expressly stated that it was to be governed by Swiss law and that 'Any dispute regarding its conclusion, interpretation or fulfilment shall be judged by the Court of Geneva, exclusive of any other jurisdiction'. On 9th January P, on behalf of Crédit Suisse, assigned to a third party (whose identity P never disclosed) all the rights of action against CBN for $US1,100,000. On 20th January Trendtex gave P full *a* power of attorney enabling him, inter alia, to settle its action against CBN. On 12th February P negotiated a settlement in Nigeria of the action against CBN for $US8m. In March Trendtex and Temo brought an action in England against Crédit Suisse claiming, inter alia, that the agreements of the autumn of 1976 and 4th January 1978 were void as constituting an assignment of a bare cause of action and therefore the cause of action against CBN should be declared to remain vested in Trendtex. Crédit Suisse applied for a stay of the proceedings under the inherent jurisdiction of the court and/or on the *b* ground that Trendtex's claim constituted a dispute within the exclusive jurisdiction clause in the agreement of 4th January 1978. The plaintiffs argued (i) that by English law the assignment was illegal and unenforceable because, as an assignment of a bare cause of action, it savoured of maintenance and champerty and that accordingly, whatever the proper law of the agreement of 4th January 1978 was, English law would not enforce the agreement by giving effect to the exclusive jurisdiction clause, (ii) that *c* even if the assignment was valid the proceedings should continue in England because discovery of documents could be had there but not in Switzerland. The judge ([1980] 3 All ER 721) granted the stay on the grounds that the plaintiffs had failed to show sufficient cause why effect should not be given to the exclusive jurisdiction clause, that everything pointed to Switzerland as the more appropriate forum and that the advantages of a trial in England were not such as to outweigh the Swiss connection. The Court of *d* Appeal ([1980] 3 All ER 721) dismissed an appeal by the plaintiffs on the grounds that the purported assignment was valid because Crédit Suisse had a sufficiently genuine and legitimate interest in the subject matter of Trendtex's action against CBN to justify them in maintaining a suit and taking a charge on the proceeds of it, that even if the contemplated transaction with the third party was in fact one to which English law would not give effect and which therefore would equally be treated as ineffective by the *e* Swiss court, it did not follow that the agreement as a whole was void by Swiss law, and that the question whether the agreement gave rise to enforceable rights and duties was 'a dispute regarding [the] conclusion, interpretation or fulfilment' of the agreement within the exclusive jurisdiction clause and therefore fell to be determined by Swiss law. The plaintiffs appealed to the House of Lords.

f **Held** – (1) In determining the validity of an assignment of a cause of action it was the totality of the transaction that was to be looked at and if the assignment was of a property right or interest and the cause of action was ancillary to that right or interest, or if the assignee had a genuine commercial interest in taking the assignment and enforcing it for his own benefit, the assignment would not be struck down as an assignment of a bare cause of action or as savouring of maintenance. Accordingly, if no parties other than *g* Trendtex and Crédit Suisse had been involved, the agreement of 4th January 1978 would have been valid even though it involved an assignment of Trendtex's residual interest in the CBN litigation, because Crédit Suisse had a genuine and substantial interest in the success of that litigation. However, the introduction of the third party rendered the agreement void under English law because the agreement clearly showed on its face that *h* its purpose was to enable the cause of action against CBN to be sold to an anonymous third party with the likelihood of that third party, which had no genuine commercial interest in the claim, making a profit out of the assignment. Such an agreement was a step towards the sale of a bare cause of action and savoured of champerty since it involved trafficking in litigation which was contrary to public policy under English law (see p 524 *e* to p 525 *d* and *j*, p 526 *e*, p 531 *c* to *j* and p 532 *h*, post) Re Trepca Mines Ltd [1962] 3 All *j* ER 351 and Laurent v Sale & Co (a firm) [1963] 2 All ER 63 applied.

(2) However, the proper law of the agreement was Swiss law and it did not follow that because the assignment of the English cause of action was void under English law the agreement as a whole, including the exclusive jurisdiction clause, was void by Swiss law. The effect of the invalidity of the assignment on the agreement as a whole was a matter to be considered by the Swiss court and the judge had correctly exercised his

discretion to grant Crédit Suisse a stay of proceedings in England. The appeal would accordingly be dismissed (see p 525 d to h, p 526 a to e and p 531 j to p 532 f and h, post). a
Decision of the Court of Appeal [1980] 3 All ER 721 affirmed.

Notes

For assignment of rights of action, see 6 Halsbury's Laws (4th Edn) paras 15, 86, 87, and for cases on the subject, see 8(2) Digest (Reissue) 504–507, 100–122.

For maintenance and champerty in relation to assignment of fruits of litigation, see 9 b Halsbury's Laws (4th Edn) paras 400–401, 404.

Cases referred to in opinions

Compania Colombiana de Seguros v Pacific Steam Navigation Co, Empressa de Telefona de Bogota v Pacific Steam Navigation Co [1964] 1 All ER 216, [1965] 1 QB 101, [1964] 2 WLR 484, [1963] 2 Lloyd's Rep 479, 8(2) Digest (Reissue) 506, 110. c

Ellis v Torrington [1920] 1 KB 399, [1918–19] All ER Rep 1132, 89 LJKB 369, 122 LT 361, CA, 8(2) Digest (Reissue) 506, 108.

Glegg v Bromley [1912] 3 KB 474, [1911–13] All ER Rep 1138, 81 LJKB 1081, 106 LT 825, CA, 8(2) Digest (Reissue) 507, 118.

Guy v Churchill (1888) 40 Ch D 481, 58 LJ Ch 345, 60 LT 473, 5 Digest (Reissue) 1077, 8630. d

Henry v Geopresco International Ltd [1975] 2 All ER 702, [1976] QB 726, [1975] 3 WLR 620, [1975] 2 Lloyd's Rep 148, CA, Digest (Cont Vol D) 108, 1413a.

Heyman v Darwins Ltd [1942] 1 All ER 337, [1942] AC 356, 111 LJKB 241, 166 LT 306, HL, 3 Digest (Reissue) 88, 453.

Laurent v Sale & Co (a firm) [1963] 2 All ER 63, [1963] 1 WLR 829, [1963] 1 Lloyd's Rep 157, Digest (Cont Vol A) 3, 823a. e

Mackender v Feldia AG [1966] 3 All ER 847, [1967] 2 QB 590, [1967] 2 WLR 119, CA, 50 Digest (Repl) 341, 689.

Martell v Consett Iron Co Ltd [1955] 1 All ER 481, [1955] Ch 363, [1955] 2 WLR 463, CA; affg [1954] 3 All ER 339, [1955] Ch 363, [1954] 3 WLR 648, 8(2) Digest (Reissue) 632, 115.

Trendtex Trading Corpn v Central Bank of Nigeria [1977] 1 All ER 881, [1977] QB 529, f [1977] 2 WLR 356, [1977] 1 Lloyd's Rep 581, [1977] 2 CMLR 465, CA; rvsg [1976] 3 All ER 437, [1976] 1 WLR 868, [1976] 2 CMLR 668, 1(1) Digest (Reissue) 59, 382.

Trepca Mines Ltd, Re (Application of Radomir Nicola Pachitch (Pasic)) [1962] 3 All ER 351, [1963] Ch 199, [1962] 3 WLR 955, CA, Digest (Cont Vol A) 3, 777a.

Interlocutory appeal   g

The first plaintiffs, Trendtex Trading Corpn ('Trendtex'), a company incorporated in accordance with the laws of Switzerland, and the second plaintiffs, Temo Anstalt ('Temo'), a corporation established in accordance with the laws of the Principality of Liechenstein, appealed by leave of the Court of Appeal against the judgment of the Court of Appeal (Lord Denning MR, Bridge and Oliver LJJ) ([1980] 3 All ER 721, [1980] QB 629) given on 2nd May 1980 affirming the judgment of Robert Goff J ([1980] 3 All ER 721) given h on 30th March 1979 in which he ordered that the plaintiffs' action, commenced by writ issued on 29th March 1978, against the defendants, Crédit Suisse, a company incorporated in accordance with the laws of Switzerland, be stayed. The facts are set out in the opinion of Lord Roskill.

Stanley Brodie QC and Stephen Nathan for the appellants.   j
Richard Yorke QC and David Hunt for the respondents.

Their Lordships took time for consideration.

22nd October. The following opinions were delivered.

LORD WILBERFORCE. My Lords, this is a further episode in the worldwide
a litigation which followed from the Nigerian cement débâcle. Its history has been told
with characteristic lucidity by Lord Denning MR in *Trendtex Trading Corpn v Central
Bank of Nigeria* [1977] 1 All ER 88, [1977] QB 529 ('the CBN case') and in his judgment
in the present case ([1980] 3 All ER 721, [1980] QB 629).

The situation which gave rise to this particular action was that Trendtex, having a
claim situated in England against the Central Bank of Nigeria ('CBN') for damages, put
b at $US14m, had difficulty in financing the litigation necessary to recover it. It therefore
sought and obtained assistance from the respondents, Crédit Suisse, which guaranteed its
costs in the CBN case. This was perfectly legitimate since Trendtex, in respect of the
relevant trading in cement, owed Crédit Suisse a large sum of money which Crédit Suisse
had no hope of recovering unless Trendtex succeeded in its claim against CBN.

Trendtex failed at first instance in the CBN case on the ground that CBN had state
c immunity (see [1976] 3 All ER 437, [1976] 1 WLR 868), but succeeded (in January 1977)
in the Court of Appeal ([1977] 1 All ER 881, [1977] QB 529). Leave was given to appeal
to this House and a petition of appeal was lodged (in April 1977). So the position at that
stage was that Trendtex had a cause of action in this country of uncertain value; Trendtex
might fail in the House of Lords and even if it succeeded there might be subsequent
obstacles to be overcome before it recovered any money.

d   The present case arises out of a series of transactions between Trendtex and Crédit
Suisse, the third of which was designed to make room for a settlement of Trendtex's
claim against CBN. A Swiss lawyer, Maître Patry, was engaged to act for Crédit Suisse.
On Trendtex's side, the main representative was Dr Hauser, its Swiss director, Trendtex
itself, as was also Crédit Suisse, being a Swiss company. There were three critical
documents. 1. On 6th September 1976 Trendtex assigned to Crédit Suisse all its claims
e arising out of the cement contracts 'until the claims of the Assignee are covered'. Crédit
Suisse was given power to bring actions in its own name or that of Trendtex. (The CBN
litigation had started in November 1975.) 2. On 26th November 1976 Trendtex
surrendered to Crédit Suisse all its claims (which must have included claims against CBN)
arising from the cement contracts and from a specified letter of credit issued by CBN 'to
the full extent of the indebtedness to the transferee'. I do not think that, whatever is the
f governing law of these documents, there can be much doubt that they were normal
assignments by way of security from a debtor to its creditor bank. 3. A further agreement
appears to have been reached at a meeting held on 14th November 1977 but the terms
of this are the subject of dispute. However, on 4th January 1978 a formal and fairly
elaborate agreement was entered into between Trendtex (acting by Dr Hauser), Dr
Hauser personally, and Crédit Suisse (acting by Maître Patry). It commenced by some
g recitals, the third of which stated that Trendtex was indebted to Crédit Suisse for
$US1·5m, and the fourth of which recited an agreement that Crédit Suisse would
attempt to recover its claim against Trendtex by negotiating with CBN. The fifth recital
was that Crédit Suisse had received an offer from a third party to buy Trendtex's claim
against CBN for $US800,000. The agreement then provided (in art 1) that Trendtex did
not oppose the sale by Crédit Suisse to a purchaser of its choice of all Trendtex's claims
h against CBN and recognised that it had no further interest in the CBN case. Subsequent
articles contained some elaborate arrangements for the satisfaction, out of money to be
provided by Crédit Suisse, of Trendtex's other creditors, authorisations to Maître Patry to
conduct the CBN case on behalf of Trendtex or to settle it by negotiation, and security for
Crédit Suisse through transfer to Maître Patry of the controlling shares of Trendtex (then
owned by the second appellant Temo Anstalt) and resignation of Dr Hauser as director
j of Trendtex. Article 6 was as follows:

> 'This Agreement is governed by Swiss Law. Any dispute regarding its conclusion,
> interpretation or fulfilment shall be judged by the Court of Geneva, exclusive of any
> other jurisdiction.'

Soon after this, in February 1978, it is alleged that Maître Patry went to Nigeria and

settled the CBN case for a payment of $US8m. No part of this has been paid to
Trendtex. The greater part of it, so it is said, has been paid to a third party who *a*
negotiated the settlement, whose identity Maître Patry refuses to disclose.

Thereupon two persons claiming to be able to issue instructions for Trendtex,
commenced this action in Trendtex's name, with Trendtex's parent company, Temo
Anstalt, as joint plaintiff, claiming that the agreement of 4th January 1978 is void as
contrary to public policy and offending against the law of champerty and maintenance.
It is further asserted that Trendtex was induced to enter into the agreement by undue *b*
influence and economic duress, that Maître Patry acted in breach of fiduciary duty and
that Crédit Suisse was vicariously liable for the loss thereby caused. The claim is for
appropriate declarations, accounts and damages, and Temo Anstalt claims the return of
the controlling shares in Trendtex. On this Crédit Suisse applied to the court for the
action to be stayed on the ground (inter alia, but this alone is relevant at the present stage)
that the parties had agreed to the exclusive jurisdiction of the Swiss court. This depends, *c*
as I see it, on two questions: (1) whether the agreement of 4th January 1978, and so the
exclusive jurisdiction clause, is void as offending the law against champerty and
maintenance; (2) whether the court in its discretion should stay the action on the ground
that the issues raised ought properly to be tried in Switzerland.

In the courts below an examination in some depth was conducted into the English law
of maintenance and champerty and in this House learned arguments in these matters *d*
were deployed. I wish to acknowledge indebtedness to the treatment in the judgments
of the Court of Appeal and to the submissions of counsel. However, I do not think it
necessary to pronounce on such areas of this still obscure subject as remain in dispute, for
in my opinion the appeal can and should be decided on fairly simple grounds, essentially
those which appealed to Robert Goff J and, in part, to Oliver LJ, and on the basis of the
law laid down so clearly by Danckwerts J and the Court of Appeal in *Martell v Consett Iron* *e*
Co Ltd [1954] 3 All ER 339, [1955] Ch 363; [1955] 1 All ER 481, [1955] Ch 363.

If no party had been involved in the agreement of 4th January 1978 but Trendtex and
Crédit Suisse, I think that it would have been difficult to contend that the agreement,
even if it involved (as I think it did) an assignment of Trendtex's residual interest in the
CBN case, offended against the law of maintenance or champerty. As I have already
shown, Crédit Suisse had a genuine and substantial interest in the success of the CBN *f*
litigation. It had, and I do not think that the legitimacy of its action was challenged,
guaranteed the previous costs. It had by the documents of 6th September and 26th
November 1976 taken a security interest in the litigation or its proceeds. To carry this
a stage further by a surrender of Trendtex's residual interest (if this was the effect of the
agreement of 4th January 1978) would, in my view, have been lawful, though a question
might have arisen (and indeed may arise) whether, after Crédit Suisse had been satisfied *g*
as creditors, Trendtex could claim the return to it of any surplus. The possibility of this
could not invalidate the agreement, it would arise under it, and clearly fall within the
exclusive jurisdiction clause.

The vice, if any, of the agreement lies in the introduction of the third party. It appears
from the face of the agreement not as an obligation, but as a contemplated possibility,
that the cause of action against CBN might be sold by Crédit Suisse to a third party, for *h*
a sum of $800,000. This manifestly involved the possibility, and indeed the likelihood
of a profit being made, either by the third party or possibly also by Crédit Suisse, out of
the cause of action. In my opinion this manifestly 'savours of champerty', since it
involves trafficking in litigation, a type of transaction which, under English law, is
contrary to public policy. I take the definition of 'champerty' (etymologically derived
from 'campi partito') from 9 Halsbury's Laws (4th Edn) para 400: *j*

> 'Champerty is a particular kind of maintenance, namely maintenance of an action
> in consideration of a promise to give the maintainer a share in the proceeds or
> subject matter of the action.'

Although ancient in origin, and so no doubt encrusted with disposable obsolescencies, it

has been given statutory recognition by the Criminal Law Act 1967, ss 13 and 14, which,
a while abolishing criminal and tortious liability for champerty, expressly preserves any
rule of law as to the cases in which a contract involving champerty is to be treated as
contrary to public policy and/or otherwise illegal.

Two modern cases in which agreements have been held void for champerty are *Re
Trepca Mines Ltd* [1962] 3 All ER 351, [1963] Ch 199 and *Laurent v Sale & Co (a firm)*
[1963] 2 All ER 63, [1963] 1 WLR 829. *Re Trepca Mines Ltd* was concerned with an
b agreement governed by French law which contained provisions remarkably similar to
those of the agreement of 4th January 1978: it involved the participation by a third
party, M Teyssou, in contemplated litigation to the extent of 25%, and M Teyssou was
given power to conduct the litigation. The Court of Appeal held this agreement to be
champertous.

In *Laurent v Sale & Co (a firm)* there was an assignment to Laurent of debts due from
c a finance house, which it was known would have to be sued for, in consideration of the
payment by Laurent of a proportion of the amount recovered, the litigation to be
conducted by Laurent. It was held that this agreement and the assignment of the debts
were champertous and unenforceable. I think that these decisions are sound in law and
that the principle of them should be applied in the present case. In my opinion
accordingly any such assignment of the English cause of action (in the CBN case) as was
d purported to be made by the agreement of 4th January 1978 for the purpose stated, was,
under English law, void.

However this does not conclude the matter. It remains to be decided what effect this
has on the agreement as a whole. The proper law of the agreement is Swiss and it is for
the Swiss court to decide that question. In fact the agreement contains other provisions,
of some of which Trendtex has had the benefit, on which art 6 can certainly operate.
e Moreover other, and serious, questions are in issue between the parties as to the position
of Maître Patry which, I say with all proper reserve since the matter will have to be tried,
appears equivocal. These latter questions may not fall within the exclusive jurisdiction
clause but they must, in any event, be tried under Swiss law, as the law governing Maître
Patry's duties to Trendtex and his professional responsibilities. They are closely connected
with the questions which arise strictly under the agreement of 4th January 1978.

f There is therefore room for the operation of art 6 in spite of the champertous element
in the agreement so far as concerns any assignment of the claim against CBN. In these
circumstances, while it is a matter of discretion whether a stay should be granted, some
strong reason must be shown by Trendtex why the article should not be given effect in
accordance with the parties' contractual intentions. All the relevant factors, including
the procedural benefit to Trendtex of obtaining discovery under English law, were
g meticulously examined and balanced by Robert Goff J who decided to grant a stay. After
a further examination in the Court of Appeal, the same result was reached. Concurrent
decisions of this character in any event carry great weight, but I am satisfied, after my
own balancing of the arguments, that the decision to stay was right, and that this
litigation ought to be tried in Switzerland. I would accordingly dismiss the appeal.

h **LORD EDMUND-DAVIES.** My Lords, I am in respectful agreement with the
speeches prepared by my noble and learned friends Lord Wilberforce and Lord Roskill,
which I have had the advantage of reading in draft. I therefore concur in holding that
this appeal should be dismissed.

LORD FRASER OF TULLYBELTON. My Lords, my noble and learned friends
j Lord Wilberforce and Lord Roskill, whose speeches I have had the privilege of reading
in advance, have explained the issues in this appeal and I respectfully agree with them
that the assignment by Trendtex of its cause of action against CBN, purported to be made
by the agreement of 4th January 1978, was, under English law, void.

What is the result so far as the present proceedings are concerned? The respondents,
Crédit Suisse, seek to have them stayed in order that effect may be given to the provision

in art 6 of the agreement of 4th January 1978 that 'Any dispute regarding its conclusion, interpretation or fulfilment shall be judged by the Court of Geneva, exclusive of any other jurisdiction'. Robert Goff J decided that the proceedings ought to be stayed, and the Court of Appeal affirmed his judgment. I have reached the same conclusion and I can state my reasons quite shortly as follows.

The agreement contains provisions about several other matters besides the assignment or conveyance of Trendtex's right against CBN to Crédit Suisse. I respectfully agree with Oliver LJ in the Court of Appeal that, even if the assignment was invalid, it is possible that the parts of the agreement relating to other matters ought to receive effect. The agreement being governed by Swiss law, it would in my opinion be appropriate that the effect of the invalidity of the assignment on the agreement as a whole should be considered by a Swiss court rather than by an English court. It is also relevant that both parties to the appeal are Swiss corporations and that the natural persons principally concerned in the negotiations that led up to the agreement, Maître Patry and Dr Hauser, are both Swiss nationals. This appeal is an interlocutory stage in an action which raises other questions, including questions whether a fiduciary duty was owed by Maître Patry, a Swiss avocat, to Trendtex, a Swiss corporation, and if so as to the standard of legal duty (and perhaps of professional ethics) incumbent on such an avocat. These are matters on which the Swiss courts are evidently better qualified to decide than the English courts. The whole agreement and the circumstances which led up to it are closely associated with Switzerland, and, the parties having agreed that the Court of Geneva was to have exclusive jurisdiction in all matters arising out of the agreement, I am of opinion that no sufficient reason has been shown for departing from the decisions of the judge and the Court of Appeal in favour of giving effect to that provision of the agreement.

For these reasons I would dismiss the appeal.

LORD KEITH OF KINKEL. My Lords, I have had the benefit of reading in draft the speeches of my noble and learned friends Lord Wilberforce and Lord Roskill. I agree that, for the reasons which they give, the appeal should be dismissed.

LORD ROSKILL. My Lords, this appeal arises out of an application by the respondents ('Crédit Suisse') to stay an action brought against them by the two appellants, Trendtex Trading Corpn ('Trendtex'), a corporation incorporated in Switzerland and carrying on business in Zurich, and Temo Anstalt ('Temo'), a corporation incorporated in Liechenstein, which was the beneficial owner of the entire share capital (100 bearer shares) of Trendtex. Temo was at all material times controlled by a Mr London who was and still claims to be one of the two joint general managers of Trendtex, the other being a Dr Kennedy. Temo has no separate interest in this appeal from that of Trendtex and for convenience I shall treat Trendtex as the sole appellants, as indeed they were treated in argument before your Lordships' House. Though other grounds for seeking the stay were advanced in the summons, the sole ground relied on in these proceedings was the presence of an exclusive jurisdiction clause in an agreement dated 4th January 1978, between Trendtex and Crédit Suisse, which by art 6 provided:

'This agreement is governed by Swiss law. Any dispute regarding its conclusion, interpretation or fulfilment shall be judged by the Court of Geneva, exclusive of any other jurisdiction.'

My Lords, on 30th March 1979 Robert Goff J granted Crédit Suisse's application and stayed the action (see [1980] 3 All ER 721 at 726–737). With the leave of the learned judge Trendtex appealed to the Court of Appeal (Lord Denning MR, Bridge and Oliver LJJ) who on 2nd May 1980 dismissed the appeal but gave leave to appeal to your Lordships' House (see [1980] 3 All ER 721 at 738–759, [1980] QB 629). Though the Court of Appeal was unanimous in dismissing the appeal, the reasons given in the judgment of Oliver LJ, with whom Bridge LJ agreed, differ from certain of the reasons given by the learned Master of the Rolls.

My Lords, the factual background to this appeal is extremely complex. It is fully set
a out in the judgment of Robert Goff J and I shall do no more than gratefully borrow from
his judgment so much of his statement of the facts as is necessary for the understanding
of the principal issues involved in this appeal.

On 24th July 1975 Trendtex sold 240,000 metric tons of cement to Pan-African Export
and Import Co, cif Lagos/Apapa. Pan-African Export and Import Co, as buyers, were to
be responsible for discharging port demurrage. Payment of the purchase price and that
b demurrage was to be made under a letter of credit to be opened by the Central Bank of
Nigeria ('CBN'). The letter of credit was duly opened. Trendtex was notified of that fact
by the Midland Bank in London. The Midland Bank was the corresponding bank of
CBN but it did not confirm the letter of credit. The first four shipments of cement were
made and duly paid for. But there was great congestion at Lagos and large sums became
payable in respect of those four shipments for demurrage. Trendtex made two more
c shipments. CBN refused to accept the documents presented for the fifth shipment or
liability for any of the demurrage claimed on two of the earlier shipments. Trendtex
thereupon treated CBN as having repudiated the contract contained in the letter of
credit, and on 4th November 1975 began proceedings in England claiming some
$14m. On 16th December 1975 CBN issued a summons to set aside those proceedings
on the ground of sovereign immunity. On 26th March 1976 Donaldson J upheld that
d claim to immunity (see [1976] 3 All ER 437, [1976] 1 WLR 868). But on 13th January
1977 the Court of Appeal reversed that decision (see [1977] 1 All ER 88, [1977] QB 529),
at the same time granting CBN leave to appeal to your Lordships' House.

My Lords, this repudiation of the letter of credit by CBN gave rise to grave financial
problems for Trendtex, for Crédit Suisse had financed Trendtex's purchases of the cement
from German suppliers. As a result Trendtex became heavily indebted to Crédit Suisse
e who had anticipated recoupment from the letter of credit which CBN had repudiated.
Crédit Suisse in November 1975 agreed to guarantee the costs incurred by Trendtex in
the action against CBN which I have already mentioned. It was in this connection that
on 6th September 1976 Trendtex executed in favour of Crédit Suisse a document in
German of which your Lordships have both a translation and a copy of the original,
headed (in translation) 'Assignment'. The 'Assignment' provides, inter alia, that Trendtex
f hereby 'assigns all its claims from the contracts which it has made with Pan-African . . .
to the Crédit Suisse; this until the claims ·of the assignee are covered . . .' On 26th
November 1976 a further document was executed in favour of Crédit Suisse, also in
German, of which your Lordships have both a translation and a copy of the original,
headed (in translation) 'Declaration of Surrender'. This provides, inter alia, that
Trendtex—

g   'in fulfilment of its declaration of surrender of 6th September 1976 . . . surrenders
all its claims arising from the said contract and from the letter of credit issued by the
Central Bank of Nigeria . . . to the full extent of the indebtedness to the transferee . . .'

My Lords, it will be convenient to observe at this juncture that the letter of credit on
which CBN defaulted was payable in London. Trendtex's cause of action against CBN
h was thus situate in London and was governed by English law. This has been common
ground throughout all these proceedings.

My Lords, following on the grant to CBN of leave to appeal against the reversal of
Donaldson J's judgment upholding their claim to immunity, CBN on 20th April 1977
presented a petition to your Lordships' House. But around this time, Theodore Goddard
& Co, who were then on the record as solicitors for Trendtex, received an indication that
CBN wished to enter into negotiations for the settlement of this claim. At this juncture
j Crédit Suisse appointed a Swiss lawyer, Maître Patry, to act on their behalf. This
gentleman, who plays a prominent part in the remainder of the story, thereupon took a
very strong line on behalf of Crédit Suisse vis-à-vis Trendtex, making it plain that the
purpose of Crédit Suisse was to recover the sum owing by Trendtex to Crédit Suisse. The
details of what followed will be found in the judgment of Robert Goff J and I do not

repeat it. Clearly, Crédit Suisse and Maître Patry on their behalf were in an extremely strong negotiating position vis-à-vis Trendtex. On 21st December 1977 Maître Patry in *a* a telex (the original was in French but your Lordships have a copy both of the original and of a translation) to Trendtex mentioned that he had informed them several times that 'Crédit Suisse has a possibility of realising Trendtex's rights with regard to the Central Bank of Nigeria for a substantial sum. The sum in question is $US800,000'.

On 4th January 1978 the all-important agreement, out of which the present litigation arises, was concluded between Trendtex acting by Dr Hauser, its sole director in *b* Switzerland, and Crédit Suisse acting by Maître Patry. I quote only from the third and fifth recitals, noting as respects the third that in the letter of 7th November 1977 there referred to, that debt had been described as 'reduced' to $1,500,000:

> 'WHEREAS as a result TTC [that is Trendtex] became indebted to CS [that is Crédit Suisse] and the amount of such indebtedness has been agreed upon by TTC and CS as being US dollars 1·5 million as per a letter Agreement dated November 7th, 1977, *c* and . . .
> 'WHEREAS CS has received an offer from a third party to buy TTC's rights against the CENTRAL BANK OF NIGERIA—such rights having been assigned by TTC to CS on the 26th of November 1976 in guarantee of CS's claim—for an amount of US dollars 800,000 . . .'
d

Article 1 provided as follows:

> 'Subject to the terms and conditions of this Agreement, TTC is not opposed to the sale by CS, to a purchaser of CS's choice, of all rights and claims of any sort originally held by TTC against CENTRAL BANK OF NIGERIA and/or against the PERMANENT SECRETARY, MINISTRY OF DEFENCE OF THE FEDERAL REPUBLIC OF NIGERIA and/or PAN AFRICAN IMPORT EXPORT company Ltd of London, (Great Britain), for a consideration *e* and terms of payment to be determined only by CS. Consequently TTC hereby irrevocably recognizes that it has no further interest of whatsoever nature in the legal action conducted in London in its sole name but for the sole and exclusive benefit of CS (or the above mentioned purchaser) against CENTRAL BANK OF NIGERIA, in which claim TTC is represented by the Lawfirm Theodore Goddard & Co., Solicitors, in London and which claim is now pending before the House of Lords.' *f*

Robert Goff J summarised the remaining provisions of this agreement in his judgment as follows ([1980] 3 All ER 721 at 729):

> 'Crédit Suisse were to pay $388,000 to Trendtex on (i) a statement by Dr Hauser to Crédit Suisse that, by collecting that sum, he had been able to obtain a release from Trendtex's creditors and (ii) releases from Trendtex's creditors. In addition, *g* Crédit Suisse committed themselves to pay a further $72,000 to a certain Nigerian company . . . if it established a valid claim against Trendtex. To give Crédit Suisse "proper control of the good fulfilment by [Trendtex] of its obligations and undertakings hereunder", Dr Hauser undertook three things: (i) to deposit 90% of the shares of Trendtex with Dr Patry, to be kept by Dr Patry "in escrow until such time that Dr Patry thinks he can return the shares to Dr Hauser"; (ii) to complete the *h* formalities necessary to enable Dr Patry, as long as he held the shares in escrow, to exercise the voting rights appertaining to them, as he deemed fit; (iii) to hand over to Dr Patry his resignation as director of Trendtex to be used by Dr Patry at the time of Dr Patry's sole choice. Apparently the remaining 10% of the shares in Trendtex had already been pledged to Temo as security for a loan.'
j

I have already quoted art 6, the exclusive jurisdiction clause.

My Lords, on 20th January 1978 Trendtex, acting by Dr Hauser, gave Maître Patry a full power of attorney. Maître Patry then pursued negotiations with the Nigerian authorities. In a letter dated 14th February 1978 to their negotiating committee, Maître Patry asserted that Trendtex's total claim in the House of Lords and in other proceedings was $24,913,460·38 and was increasing. Whence this figure emanated is not made plain

in any document before your Lordships' House. On 24th February 1978 Trendtex,
a acting by Maître Patry, settled with CBN and the Nigerian authorities for $8m which
your Lordships were told was paid to the Midland Bank, New York.

When Mr London and Dr Kennedy became aware of what had happened they were,
perhaps understandably, suspicious of what had occurred. Further correspondence
followed to which it is not necessary to refer in detail beyond observing that in a telex
dated 30th March 1978 from Maître Patry to Dr Hauser, the former stated that the claim
b against CBN had been assigned to a third party on 9th January 1978 for $1,100,000.
Who the fortunate third party was, who seemingly made a profit of $6,900,000 (ie $8m
less $1,100,000) within a few weeks, is not known. Crédit Suisse have not revealed it and
Maître Patry, claiming that it is not relevant, has also declined to reveal it. In an affidavit
sworn by Maître Patry on 22nd October 1979 he deposes as follows:

> *c* '2. I am informed by Messrs. Theodore Goddard & Co., and I verily believe, that
> the non-disclosure of the identity of the purchaser of Trendtex's claim was the
> subject of adverse comment by Counsel for the Plaintiffs during the hearing before
> the Honourable Mr. Justice Goff. I regret that this non-disclosure may have
> conveyed a wrong impression. Accordingly, and despite my continuing belief that
> in the circumstances of the present action and in particular in the light of the
> Agreement of 4th January, 1978 the identity of the purchaser is not relevant, I
> *d* consider that in the interests of the Defendants I should explain the circumstances
> in which Trendtex's claim was sold to the unidentified purchaser and why I continue
> to be unable to disclose the purchaser's identity.
> '3. The sale was to a subsidiary of a Swiss trading corporation, not a bank or
> finance house. The subsidiary concerned is not a subsidiary or associated or affiliated
> company of Credit Suisse. I was convinced at the time of the sale that it was the best
> *e* commercial settlement possible for the Defendants. I was entirely satisfied from
> my general experience in other matters of attempting to negotiate with the Nigerian
> authorities that no higher figure than the sale price could have been obtained before
> or in early January, 1978 nor, in my view, was there any prospect of the Defendants
> themselves negotiating any settlement direct with the Nigerian authorities . . .
> '6 . . . I was entirely satisfied that there was no other potential purchaser either in
> *f* Switzerland or elsewhere. Nor could I have obtained a higher price, if I could have,
> I would have been under a duty to have done so and I would have done so. Of
> course, I appreciated that the purchasers expected to make a profit on the transaction,
> otherwise they would not have agreed to pay $1·1m. But the amount which they
> did make, and the speed with which they made it, I did not and had no grounds to
> foresee.'

g Beyond this sparse information your Lordships have no knowledge of the terms on
which the benefit of Trendtex's claim against CBN which, on 4th January 1978 Trendtex
had assigned to Crédit Suisse, was sold to this anonymous third party, save that a large
profit was apparently made by that third party. But your Lordships may think it obvious
that one object, and indeed the principal object, of the agreement of 4th January 1978
h was to enable Crédit Suisse to resell the benefit of the assignment which they had that day
obtained from Trendtex, their purchaser entering into the transaction with the avowed
object of making a profit on it if he possibly could from his purchase.

My Lords, it is Trendtex's purpose in these proceedings brought in this country to seek
to set aside these transactions and if possible to obtain the benefit of this $8m for
themselves. Crédit Suisse having issued the summons to stay the action on the ground,
j inter alia, of the existence of the exclusive jurisdiction clause, Trendtex's first task must,
in the circumstances, be to show that the English courts should entertain these
proceedings and not insist on whatever proceedings may be appropriate being heard and
determined in accordance with art 6 by the court sitting in Geneva. Trendtex seeks to
displace art 6 by contending that English law, which is already stated as the proper law
of the chose in action which was the subject of the assignment to and reassignment by
Crédit Suisse, does not permit assignment of what is sometimes called a bare cause of

action. This assignment and reassignment were not merely assignments of a bare cause of action against CBN but also were void for maintenance and champerty and were thus *a* illegal and this illegality extended to the exclusive jurisdiction clause itself: see the decision of your Lordships' House in *Heyman v Darwins Ltd* [1942] 1 All ER 337, [1942] AC 356. Alternatively, it was argued that as a matter of discretion this action should be allowed to proceed here for the several reasons considered by Robert Goff J in his judgment.

My Lords, learned counsel for Trendtex put in the forefront of his attack on the *b* judgment of Oliver LJ, with which, as already stated, Bridge LJ agreed, the contention that the learned Lord Justice had failed to distinguish between the different nature of the interest required to support an assignment of a cause of action and an interest which would justify the maintenance of the cause of action by a third party and had considered that if there were a sufficient interest to support the one it was, without more, sufficient to support the other. Further, he contended that no interest could justify a champertous *c* agreement save in the specific case of a sale by a trustee in bankruptcy to a creditor of a cause of action on the basis of a division of any proceeds, this being authorised by statute: see *Guy v Churchill* (1888) 40 Ch D 481.

My Lords, before considering these submissions in any detail it is necessary to recall that the Criminal Law Act 1967 by s 13(1) abolished the crimes of maintenance and champerty and by s 14(1) provided that neither should any longer be actionable as a *d* tort. But s 14(2) further provided that these provisions should not affect any rule of law as to the cases in which a contract was to be treated as contrary to public policy or otherwise illegal. It therefore seems plain that Parliament intended to leave the law as to the effect of maintenance and champerty on contracts unaffected by the abolition of them as crimes and torts.

My Lords, it is clear, when one looks at the cases on maintenance in this century and *e* indeed towards the end of the last, that the courts have adopted an infinitely more liberal attitude towards the supporting of litigation by a third party than had previously been the case. One has only to read the classic judgment of Danckwerts J, affirmed by the Court of Appeal, in *Martell v Consett Iron Company Ltd* [1954] 3 All ER 339, [1955] Ch 363; [1955] 1 All ER 481, [1955] Ch 363 to see how this branch of the law has developed and how the modern view of sufficiency of interest has come about. My Lords, learned *f* counsel cited to your Lordships many of the cases on maintenance which are there discussed. For my part I think no further review of them is necessary today. I would only emphasise the importance when reading them of distinguishing between the use of the word maintenance to denote *lawful* maintenance and the use of that word to denote what was then both a crime and a tort.

My Lords, one of the reasons why equity would not permit the assignment of what *g* became known as a bare cause of action, whether legal or equitable, was because it savoured of maintenance. If one reads the well-known judgment of Parker J in *Glegg v Bromley* [1912] 3 KB 474 at 490, [1911-13] All ER Rep 1138 at 1146, one can see how the relevant law has developed. Though in general choses in action were assignable, yet causes of action which were essentially personal in their character, such as claims for defamation or personal injury, were incapable of assignment for the reason already *h* given. But even so, no objection was raised to assignments of the proceeds of an action for defamation as in *Glegg v Bromley*, for such an assignment would in no way give the assignee the right to intervene in the action and so be contrary to public policy (see [1912] 3 KB 474 at 488-489, [1911-13] All ER Rep 1138 at 1145-1146 per Fletcher Moulton LJ).

My Lords, just as the law became more liberal in its approach to what was *lawful* *j* maintenance, so it became more liberal in its approach to the circumstances in which it would recognise the validity of an assignment of a cause of action and not strike down such an assignment as one only of a bare cause of action. Where the assignee has by the assignment acquired a property right and the cause of action was incidental to that right, the assignment was held effective; *Ellis v Torrington* [1920] 1 KB 399, [1918-19] All ER Rep 1132 is an example of such a case. Scrutton LJ stated ([1920] 1 KB 399 at 412-413,

[1918–19] All ER Rep 1132 at 1138–1139) that the assignee was not guilty of
a maintenance or champerty by reason of the assignment he took because he was not
buying in order to obtain a cause of action but in order to protect the property which he
had bought. But, my Lords, as I read the cases it was not necessary for the assignee always
to show a property right to support his assignment. He could take an assignment to
support and enlarge that which he had already acquired as, for example, an underwriter
by subrogation: see *Compania Colombiana de Seguros v Pacific Steam Navigation Co* [1964] 1
b All ER 216, [1965] 1 QB 101. My Lords, I am afraid that, with respect, I cannot agree
with Lord Denning MR when he said in the instant case ([1980] 3 All ER 721 at 744,
[1980] 1 QB 629 at 657) that 'The old saying that you cannot assign a "bare right to
litigate" is gone'. I venture to think that still remains a fundamental principle of our
law. But it is today true to say that in English law an assignee who can show that he has
a genuine commercial interest in the enforcement of the claim of another and to that
c extent takes an assignment of that claim to himself is entitled to enforce that assignment
unless by the terms of that assignment he falls foul of our law of champerty, which as has
often been said, is a branch of our law of maintenance. For my part I can see no reason
in English law why Crédit Suisse should not have taken an assignment to themselves of
Trendtex's claim against CBN for the purpose of recouping themselves for their own
substantial losses arising out of CBN's repudiation of the letter of credit on which Crédit
d Suisse were relying to refinance their financing of the purchases by Trendtex of this
cement from their German suppliers.

My Lords, I do not therefore think that counsel for the appellants is correct in
criticising the judgment of Oliver LJ on the ground that the learned Lord Justice failed
to distinguish between the interest necessary to support an assignment of a cause of
action and the interest which would justify the maintenance of an action by a third
e party. I think, with respect, this submission involves over-analysis of the position. The
court should look at the totality of the transaction. If the assignment is of a property
right or interest and the cause of action is ancillary to that right or interest, or if the
assignee had a genuine commercial interest in taking the assignment and in enforcing it
for his own benefit, I see no reason why the assignment should be struck down as an
assignment of a bare cause of action or as savouring of maintenance.

f But, my Lords, to reach that conclusion and thus to reject a substantial part of the
argument of counsel for the appellants for substantially the same reasons as did Oliver LJ
does not mean that at least art 1 of the agreement of 4th January 1978 is not objectionable
as being champertous, for it is not an assignment designed to enable Crédit Suisse to
recoup their own losses by enforcing Trendtex's claim against CBN to the maximum
amount recoverable. Though your Lordships do not have the agreement between Crédit
g Suisse and the anonymous third party, it seems to me obvious, as already stated, that the
purpose of art 1 of the agreement of 4th January 1978 was to enable the claim against
CBN to be sold on to the anonymous third party for that anonymous third party to
obtain what profit he could from it, apart from paying to Crédit Suisse the purchase price
of $1,100,000. In other words, the 'spoils', whatever they might be, to be got from CBN
were in effect being divided, the first $1,100,000 going to Crédit Suisse and the balance,
h whatever it might ultimately prove to be, to the anonymous third party. Such an
agreement, in my opinion, offends, for it was a step towards the sale of a bare cause of
action to a third party who had no genuine commercial interest in the claim in return for
a division of the spoils, Crédit Suisse taking the fixed amount which I have already
mentioned. To this extent I find myself in respectful disagreement with Oliver LJ.

My Lords, in English law, at least as I think, contrary to the submission of counsel for
j the respondents which Oliver LJ accepted (see [1980] 3 All ER 721 at 758, [1980] QB 629
at 675), the agreement of 4th January 1974 does assign the cause of action. By English
law I doubt if the two earlier documents do have that effect. The language of those
documents is that of security rather than of out-and-out assignment. But however this
may be, if my view as to the effect in English law of art 1 is correct, I nevertheless
respectfully agree with Oliver LJ that it by no means follows that the whole agreement,
including the exclusive jurisdiction clause, is void by Swiss law. I agree with the

following passage in his judgment ([1980] 3 All ER 721 at 758, [1980] QB 629 at 675–676):

'I agree with Robert Goff J that, assuming that the contemplated transaction with the third party was in fact one to which English law does not give effect and which therefore would be treated equally as ineffective by the Swiss court, it does not follow that the agreement as a whole is void by Swiss law. There was nothing ex facie necessarily illegal in the agreement. Whether any assignment under it fell foul of the English rules with regard to maintenance or champerty would depend on the identity and interest of the unidentified third party, and in my judgment the judge was right in applying to the exclusive jurisdiction clause the reasoning of Diplock LJ in *Mackender v Feldia AG* [1966] 3 All ER 847 at 851–853, [1967] 2 QB 590 at 601–604 and in holding that the question whether the agreement gave rise to enforceable rights and duties was a dispute regarding the conclusion, interpretation or fulfilment of the agreement, was within the clause, and fell to be determined according to the proper law of the agreement. Once that was determined, it was a matter for the judge's discretion whether or not to give effect to the exclusive jurisdiction clause by granting the stay sought by Crédit Suisse . . .'

In reaching this conclusion I have not lost sight of the two affidavits of Monsieur Bächi; but this evidence, in my judgment, affords far too insecure a foundation on which to reach the conclusion that the whole agreement, including the jurisdiction clause, is void by Swiss law.

On this view it became a matter for the discretion of the learned judge whether or not this action should be stayed. He dealt with this matter fully and at considerable length in his judgment. The Court of Appeal agreed with his reasoning. Like Oliver LJ, I see no reason for your Lordships' House to interfere with the learned judge's exercise of his discretion which seems to me, if I may respectfully say so, to have been entirely correct in principle. I would only add that I do not think that the obvious advantages to Trendtex of obtaining an order for discovery which would not be available to them in Switzerland can be allowed to outweigh the other reasons for leaving the parties to the forum of their own choosing, especially those mentioned by my noble and learned friend Lord Fraser in his speech, which I have had the advantage of reading in draft.

It remains only to deal with one short point which counsel for the appellants took at the outset of his submissions to your Lordships' House. This was founded on the report of the argument of counsel for the respondents in the Court of Appeal ([1980] 1 QB 629 at 640 and 647), when he invited that court to decide the question of maintenance and champerty. From this, counsel for the appellants argued that counsel for the respondents had submitted the whole question to the jurisdiction of the English courts within the principle enunciated by the Court of Appeal in *Henry v Geopresco International Ltd* [1975] 2 All ER 702 at 720–721, [1976] QB 726 at 749. It is a striking fact that no such submission was made to the Court of Appeal. My Lords, in my view this submission is untenable. Counsel for the respondents was simply inviting the Court of Appeal to express their view as to the effect of English law of maintenance and champerty on the assignment for such help as it might be to any Swiss court thereafter dealing with the matter. In the result I would dismiss this appeal.

I would add that since preparing this speech I have had the advantage of reading in draft the speech of my noble and learned friend Lord Wilberforce, with which I find myself in respectful agreement.

Appeal dismissed.

Solicitors: *Herbert Oppenheimer, Nathan & Vandyk* (for the appellants); *Theodore Goddard & Co* (for the respondents).

Mary Rose Plummer   Barrister.

Cerealmangimi SpA v Alfred C Toepfer
The Eurometal

QUEEN'S BENCH DIVISION (COMMERCIAL COURT)

LLOYD J

12th, 13th, 25th NOVEMBER 1980

Sale of goods – Cif contract – Documents to be tendered – Alternative documents – Seller to provide alternative documents to buyer if shipping documents not sighted on vessel's arrival – Shipping documents not sighted on vessel's arrival – Seller not providing alternative documents – Whether seller's failure to provide alternative documents a breach of condition entitling buyer to refuse to take delivery of goods – GAFTA form 61, cl 13.

Estoppel – Conduct – Sale of goods – Seller led to believe buyer would not rely on his rights – Cif contract – Documents to be tendered – Documents not sighted on vessel's arrival – Buyer refusing to accept delivery of cargo on ground that it was infested – Documents tendered after arrival of vessel – Buyer rejecting documents but not on ground of late tender – Whether buyer estopped from relying on late tender at subsequent arbitration for damages.

Contract – Damages for breach – Sale of goods – Loss of profit on resale – Liability for demurrage – Whether seller able to recover amount of demurrage in addition to loss of profit on resale – Whether additional loss on resale only available to buyer in event of breach by seller – GAFTA form 61, cl 26.

Under a contract which incorporated GAFTA form 61 the buyers agreed to purchase 10,000 tonnes of Spanish barley at $132 per tonne for delivery cif one safe port west coast Italy. Clause 13[a] of GAFTA form 61 provided, inter alia, for payment in cash in exchange for shipping documents and that if the shipping documents were not sighted at the time of the vessel's arrival at the port of discharge the sellers were to provide alternative documents (countersigned by a recognised bank if the buyers so required) which would entitle the buyers to obtain delivery of the goods. Clause 26[b] of GAFTA form 61 provided, inter alia, that, in default of fulfilment of the contract by either party, the other had the right to sell or purchase, as the case might be, against the defaulter, who was to make good the loss, if any, on the sale or purchase, and that in special circumstances the buyer might be awarded a sum in respect of loss of profit on any sub-contract. Pursuant to the contract 6,139 tonnes of barley were shipped in Spain on 28th May 1976. The vessel arrived at La Spezia in Italy on 30th May, but the shipping documents had not come forward by that date. Although the buyers did not need the documents to obtain delivery, they declined to accept delivery on the ground that the barley was infested with live weevils. The buyers insisted on the barley being fumigated before they would accept delivery. There was a dispute about who would pay for the fumigation, which would have cost about $10,000, and in the meantime the vessel was waiting at La Spezia incurring demurrage. On 23rd June the sellers tendered the shipping documents, but the buyers rejected them the next day, on the ground that the barley was infested. At no stage did they seek to reject the documents on the ground that they had been forwarded late. On 28th June the sellers declared the buyers in default under cl 26. The sellers promptly asked for bids. The highest bid, which was accepted, came from S, who offered $116 per tonne. S also agreed to pay $63,839 demurrage out of an accrued total of $87,267. The effective cost to S, taking demurrage into account, was thus $126 per tonne. At no time did the buyers express dissatisfaction with the resale price. The sellers sought to recover their loss on the resale, which they claimed

---

a   Clause 13 is set out at p 536 g to p 537 a, post

b   Clause 26, so far as material, is set out at p 541 c to f, post

amounted to the difference between the contract price and the resale price to S, ie $16 per tonne, plus the amount of the demurrage not paid by S, ie $23,428. The buyers refused to pay, and the dispute was referred to arbitration. The buyers were dissatisfied with the umpire's award and appealed to the board of appeal of GAFTA, which found, inter alia, that the fair market value of the barley at La Spezia on the date of default was $126 per tonne. On an application by the buyers, the board of appeal was ordered by the High Court to state its award in the form of a special case. The questions for the opinion of the High Court were whether the sellers had been entitled to payment of the price on the presentation of the documents, and whether, if the sellers were entitled to damages from the buyers, the amount thereof was restricted by cl 26, and if so what the maximum entitlement permitted by cl 26 was. The buyers contended that the sellers had been obliged by cl 13 to tender either the shipping documents or other documents entitling the buyers to obtain delivery on the arrival of the vessel, that the failure to tender any documents at all until 23rd June was a breach of condition entitling the buyers to reject the documents and that it was irrelevant that the buyers had not relied on that ground of rejection at the time. On the question of damages, the sellers contended that, since the buyers had never expressed dissatisfaction with the price at which the barley was sold to S, the restriction in cl 26 on the amount of damages which could be awarded did not apply, and that accordingly the sellers were entitled to recover their actual loss on resale.

Held – (1) Notwithstanding that cl 13 of GAFTA form 61 made no express provision that cash was to be paid against documents on the arrival of the vessel, it was clear that, on the true construction of that clause, if the shipping documents were not sighted at the time of the vessel's arrival, the alternative documents referred to in that clause were to be provided forthwith, since otherwise the buyers would or might not be able to take immediate delivery of the goods, which was plainly one of the main objects of the clause. Had the buyers required the alternative documents to be countersigned by the bank, any delay that might have resulted would have been brought about at the buyers' own request and could not, accordingly, have justified the buyers rejecting them (see p 537 c f to h and p 538 b, post); *Toepfer v Lenersan-Poortman NV* [1980] 1 Lloyd's Rep 143 applied.

(2) However, if a buyer who had the right to reject goods or documents so conducted himself as to lead the seller reasonably to believe that he would not rely on that right, whether he knew of it or not, he could not afterwards assert that right when it would be unfair or unjust to allow him to do so. The sole reason for the buyers' refusal to take delivery of the cargo was its infestation with weevils, and, by making and maintaining a request that the cargo be fumigated at the sellers' expense, the buyers conducted themselves in a way which was wholly inconsistent with an intention to exercise any present right to reject the shipping documents. Notwithstanding that the sellers did not have the cargo fumigated, it was to be inferred that the sellers had incurred liability for demurrage in the belief, reasonably induced by the buyers, that the buyers would not insist on the immediate provision of alternative documents. It was irrelevant that the buyers may have asked for the cargo to be fumigated in ignorance of their right to insist on the production of alternative documents or to treat the non-production of those documents on arrival of the vessel as a breach of condition, since such ignorance was ignorance of law; the fact that the alternative documents had not been provided on arrival had been obvious to all. It followed that the buyers had waived their right to treat the non-production of the alternative documents on the arrival of the vessel as a breach of condition, and the buyers could not justify their rejection of the shipping documents on that ground. The sellers had accordingly been entitled to payment of the price on the presentation of the shipping documents on 23rd June 1976 (see p 539 d to j and p 540 e f, post); *Bremer Handelsgesellschaft mbH v Vanden Avenne-Izegem PVBA* [1978] 2 Lloyd's Rep 109 and *Bremer Handelsgesellschaft mbH v C Mackprang Jr* [1979] 1 Lloyd's Rep 221 applied.

(3) On the true construction of cl 26 of GAFTA form 61, although in special

circumstances the buyer could recover loss of profit under a sub-contract, there was no
a power to award the seller any loss in excess of the ordinary measure of damages. The
buyer was only obliged to make good the seller's loss on resale, ie loss which was not too
remote in law, which in most cases was the difference between the contract price and the
resale price. Since the sellers could not have recovered the demurrage as part of the loss
on resale, it followed that they could not increase their recoverable loss by transferring
the liability for demurrage to S and reducing the resale price pro tanto. It followed that
b the maximum loss recoverable by the sellers was the difference between the contract
price and the market price for the cargo as it lay at La Spezia (see p 542 *b* to *g*, post);
Toprak Mahsulleri Ofisi v Finagrain Compagnie Commerciale Agricole et Financière SA [1979]
2 Lloyd's Rep 98 followed.

Notes
c For the tender of documents in cif contracts, see 34 Halsbury's Laws (3rd Edn) 171, para
291, and for cases on the subject, see 39 Digest (Repl) 639–641, 1476–1490.
For estoppel by conduct, see 16 Halsbury's Laws (4th Edn) para 1609, and for cases on
the subject, see 21 Digest (Reissue) 198, 1430–1438.
For the measure of damages for the seller in breach of contract, see 34 Halsbury's Laws
(3rd Edn) 145–148, paras 242–245, and for cases on the subject, see 39 Digest (Repl) 795–
d 797, 2661–2678.

Cases referred to in judgment
Bremer Handelsgesellschaft mbH v C Mackprang Jr [1979] 1 Lloyd's Rep 221, CA.
Bremer Handelsgesellschaft mbH v Vanden Avenne-Izegem PVBA [1978] 2 Lloyd's Rep 109,
HL.
e *Central London Property Trust Ltd v High Trees House Ltd* (1946) [1956] 1 All ER 256,
[1947] KB 130, [1947] LJR 77, 175 LT 332, 31(1) Digest (Reissue) 477, *3933*.
Cerealmangimi SpA v Toepfer, The Eurometal [1979] 2 Lloyd's Rep 72.
Heisler v Anglo-Dal Ltd [1954] 2 All ER 770, [1954] 1 WLR 1273, [1954] 2 Lloyd's Rep 5,
CA, 26 Digest (Repl) 11, *17*.
Panchaud Frères SA v Etablissments General Grain Co [1970] 1 Lloyd's Rep 53, CA.
f *Toepfer v Lenersan Poortman NV* [1978] 2 Lloyd's Rep 555, affd [1980] 1 Lloyd's Rep 143,
CA.
Toprak Mahsulleri Ofisi v Finagrain Compagnie Commerciale Agricole et Financière SA [1979]
2 Lloyd's Rep 98, CA.

Special case
g Cerealmangimi SpA of Rome ('the buyers') appealed against the award of the board of
appeal of the Grain and Feed Trade Association Ltd ('GAFTA') stated in the form of a
special case dated 3rd August 1979 pursuant to the order of Lloyd J dated 19th January
1979 whereby, on a reference to the board of a dispute between the buyers and the
respondents, Alfred C Toepfer of Hamburg ('the sellers'), arising out of a contract dated
30th April 1976 incorporating GAFTA contract form no 61 entered into by the buyers
h and the sellers for the sale of 10,000 tonnes of Spanish barley for delivery cif one safe port
west coast Italy for payment, cash in exchange for shipping documents, the board
referred to the High Court of Justice the following questions of law: on the facts found
by the board and on the true construction of the contract, (i) whether the sellers were
entitled to payment of the price on the presentation of the shipping documents and (ii)
in the event that the sellers were entitled to damages from the buyers, whether the
j damages payable were restricted in amount by cl 26 of GAFTA contract form no 61 and,
if so, what was the maximum entitlement of sellers permitted by that clause. The facts
are set out in the judgment.

Michael Dean for the buyers.
Bernard Rix for the sellers.

Cur adv vult

25th November. **LLOYD J** read the following judgment: This is a special case stated
by the board of appeal of the Grain and Feed Trade Association Ltd ('GAFTA'). The *a*
dispute between the parties arises out of a contract dated 30th April 1976 for the sale by
the respondents of 10,000 metric tons of Spanish barley to the appellants. The contract
was for delivery cif one safe port west coast Italy. The buyers declined to accept the
goods or the documents, whereupon the sellers claimed arbitration.

The dispute first came before the court on an application by the buyers that the board
of appeal state their award in the form of a special case. I granted the application on the *b*
grounds that substantial and clear-cut questions of law were likely to arise: see *The
Eurometal* [1979] 2 Lloyd's Rep 72. Those questions have now been fully argued. Before
stating my conclusion, I must first give a brief account of the facts.

A cargo of 6,139 metric tons of barley was shipped in pursuance of a sale contract at
Tarragona in Spain on 28th May 1976 on a vessel called the Eurometal. She arrived at La
Spezia on 30th May. The shipping documents had not by then come forward. But there *c*
is a finding that the buyers did not need the documents in order to obtain delivery of the
goods from the ship. The buyers declined to accept delivery of the goods on the ground
that they were infested with live weevils. They insisted on the goods being fumigated
before they would accept delivery. This could have been done at a cost of about
$10,000. It would have been money well spent. But there was a dispute as to who
should pay, for the contract contained a clause whereby the quality and condition of the *d*
goods was to be 'final at shipment'. I shall have to return to consider the meaning of that
clause later on. Meanwhile the vessel was waiting at La Spezia incurring demurrage.
From mid-June onwards, the buyers were expressing reluctance to take the goods unless
the contract was varied, so that the quality and condition of the goods at loading could
be determined by reference to samples on out-turn. But the sellers would not agree.

As for the documents, there is a finding that the sellers acted with reasonable dispatch *e*
once the documents came under their control. They were eventually tendered on 23rd
June. They were rejected by the buyers the next day. The buyers gave all sorts of
technical reasons for rejecting the documents. None of these reasons have any validity,
and they are no longer relied on. On 25th June the sellers offered a guarantee to cover
any shortcomings in the documents. But the buyers maintained their rejection, on the
ground that the goods were infested. At no stage did they seek to reject the documents *f*
on the ground that they had come forward late.

On 28th June the sellers declared the buyers in default. In due course the goods were
sold to a company called SIAT at the best available price. I shall have to return to the
circumstances of that sale when I come to the question of damages.

I consider first the question of liability. Counsel for the buyers takes two points. The
first point turns on cl 13 of the contract which reads:

g

> 'PAYMENT—Payment, cash in ... in exchange for Shipping Documents ... If
> Shipping Documents have not been sighted at time of vessel's arrival at port of
> discharge, Sellers shall provide other documents (such documents to be counter-
> signed if required by Buyers by a recognised Bank) entitling Buyers to obtain
> delivery of the goods, and, without prejudice to Buyers' rights under the contract,
> payment must be made in exchange for same, provided that if such payment be *h*
> made, proved additional expenses, if any, incurred by reason of such non-sighting
> of Shipping Documents shall be borne by Sellers and allowed for in final invoice.
> When payment is due on a Non-Business Day, Buyers shall have the option of taking
> up the Shipping Documents on the previous business day—payment to be made
> not later than 12 noon. Should Shipping Documents be presented with an
> incomplete set of Bill(s) of Lading or should other Shipping Documents be missing, *j*
> payment shall be made provided that delivery of such missing documents be
> guaranteed, such guarantee to be counter-signed, if required by Buyers, by a
> recognised Bank. No obviously clerical error in the documents shall entitle the
> Buyer to reject them or delay payment, but Seller shall be responsible for all loss or

expense caused to Buyer by reason of such error and Seller shall on request of Buyer furnish an approved guarantee in respect thereto.'

Counsel submits that the sellers were obliged under cl 13 to tender either the shipping documents or some other document entitling the buyers to obtain delivery, on arrival of the vessel; that the failure of the sellers to tender any documents at all until 23rd June was a breach of condition which entitled the buyers to reject the documents, and that it was no answer in law that the buyers did not rely on that ground of rejection at the time.

Counsel for the sellers submits that the clause does not require the sellers to tender the alternative documents until a reasonable time after the arrival of the vessel. There is no finding in the award that a reasonable time had expired before the 23rd June when they tendered the shipping documents; and in any event any breach by the sellers in relation to time for delivery of the documents was not a breach of condition.

In my judgment the arguments on this part of the case are concluded in favour of the buyers by the decision of the Court of Appeal in *Toepfer v Lenersan-Poortman NV* [1980] 1 Lloyd's Rep 143. In that case there were contracts for the sale of rapeseed cif Rotterdam. A quantity of 1,000 tons was shipped on the Grand Justice at Thunder Bay in Canada. The bills of lading were dated 11th December 1974. Unfortunately the vessel grounded in the St Lawrence on 20th December, and the cargo had to be transhipped. The substitute vessel did not arrive until April 1975. Meanwhile the documents had been tendered on 7th February 1975. The buyers rejected the documents. They said that they were tendered too late. The contract in that case provided: 'Payment: net cash against documents and/or delivery order on arrival of the vessel at port of discharge but not later than 20 days after date of Bill of Lading . . .' It was held by Donaldson J and the Court of Appeal that the sellers were obliged to tender documents under the contract not later than 20 days from the bill of lading date, which expired on 31st December 1974, and that their failure to do so was a breach of condition: see [1978] 2 Lloyd's Rep 555 at 559, [1980] 1 Lloyd's Rep 143 at 148.

Counsel for the sellers sought to distinguish *Toepfer v Lenersan-Poortman NV* on the ground that there was, as he put it, in that case a timetable based on the bill of lading date. The contract provided specifically that cash was to be paid against documents not later than 20 days after the date of the bill of lading. There is, submitted counsel, no equivalent provision in the present contract.

I would accept that there is no express provision that cash was to be paid against documents on arrival of the vessel. But that that is the true construction of cl 13 is not, to my mind, in doubt. If one asks oneself the question, when are the alternative documents to be furnished, if the shipping documents have not been sighted at the time of the vessel's arrival, the answer could only be that they must be provided forthwith. Otherwise the buyers would or might not be able to take immediate delivery of the goods, which is plainly one of the main objects of the clause. It is true that there might be some delay if the buyers required the documents to be countersigned by the bank. But in that case any delay would have been brought about by the buyers' own request. In *Toepfer v Lenersan-Poortman NV* it was held that the time for tendering documents was the earlier of two events, namely the arrival of the vessel or 20 days after the date of the bill of lading. In the present case there is only one event, not two, namely the arrival of the vessel. In all other respects the contracts appear to be indistinguishable.

I would only add two points by way of postscript. First, if counsel's argument for the sellers were correct, that there is no fixed time for payment under the clause, and therefore no fixed time for tendering the shipping documents, it is difficult to see how the documents could ever be said to have arrived before payment is due. Yet the second sentence of the clause plainly confers on the buyers the option to take up the documents *before* payment is due. The obvious inference is that the parties were providing for payment to become due when the vessel arrived.

Second, there is the proviso to the first sentence, on which counsel placed much reliance. The fact that the proviso is introduced by the words 'if such payment be made' does not, I think, mean that the buyers have a choice whether to pay or not to pay against the alternative documents, any more than it gives the sellers a choice whether to tender *a* such documents. The 'if' merely refers back to the 'if' in the first line of the clause ie if shipping documents have not been sighted at the time of the vessel's arrival. Nor can counsel for the sellers find comfort in the buyers' right to recover additional expenses for the non-sighting of the documents. Whatever lies behind that proviso, it would not be right to infer from it that the alternative documents were only to be provided at some interval of time after the arrival of the vessel.   *b*

For the above reasons I would reject the main argument under this head of counsel for the sellers. That means I must go on to consider what is to my mind a much more difficult question, namely that of waiver. Assuming I am right that the sellers were obliged to tender the alternative documents on arrival of the vessel, did the buyers by their conduct waive strict compliance with that obligation?

One of the difficulties in dealing with that question is that there are no findings *c* directed specifically to the question of waiver in the award. I was assured, however, that the question had been strongly argued; I must therefore do my best on such material as there is.

I take the law from what I believe to be the most recent authority in the Court of Appeal on this topic, namely *Bremer Handelsgesellschaft mbH v C Mackprang Jr* [1979] 1 Lloyd's Rep 221. Lord Denning MR reviewed a number of cases including the decision *d* of the House of Lords in *Bremer Handelsgesellschaft mbH v Vanden Avenne-Izegem PVBA* [1978] 2 Lloyd's Rep 109. He quoted a passage from Lord Salmon's speech as follows (at 225):

> 'To make an unequivocal representation or waiver, it is not necessary for the buyers to say, "We hereby waive it". It is quite enough if they behave or write in such a way that reasonable sellers would be led to believe that the buyers were *e* waiving any defect there might be in the notice and were accepting it as effectively extending the date for delivery ... If the buyers, by their telexes or by their conduct lead the sellers to believe that they accepted the notice as a good notice, they necessarily waived any defect it might contain, whether they were aware of it or not.'

Lord Denning MR went on to state the principle thus (at 226):   *f*

> 'I regard the decision of the House in *Bremer v. Vanden* as a most important decision on waiver. As [counsel for the sellers] said, it is the final step in the series [starting with] *Central London Property Trust Ltd. v. High Trees House* ([1956] 1 All ER 256, [1947] KB 130) ... Applied to cases of waiver in GAFTA cases, it may be stated thus: If a buyer, who is entitled to reject goods or documents on the ground of a *g* defect in the notices or the timing of them, so conducts himself as to lead the seller reasonably to believe that he is not going to rely on any such defect—whether he knows of it or not—then he cannot afterwards set up the defect as a ground for rejecting the goods or documents when it would be unfair or unjust to allow him to do so.'

Shaw LJ expressed himself in complete agreement with views stated by Lord Denning *h* MR. He said (at 230):

> '[Conduct] need not be such as to amount virtually to an express declaration that this or that right is waived or surrendered. If in the prevailing conditions affecting the position of the parties to a contract the conduct of one of them affords a reasonable foundation for the inference that he is prepared to forgo any right or *j* rights he may have in a certain regard and the other contracting party does draw that inference and persists in the residual contractual relationship upon that basis, then whether it be regarded as waiver or estoppel the forgoing of those rights cannot thereafter be gainsaid. This seems to me the effect of the observations of Lord

Salmon in *Bremer v. Vanden . . .* [Counsel for the buyers] sought to reinforce his
argument against the implication of waiver by laying emphasis on the buyers'
ignorance as to whether, on the facts if and when they became known, the sellers
could claim to be exonerated from liability for failing to deliver as required by their
contract. I see no reason, however, to limit the effect of waiver to rights known to
exist. It may be embracing enough, and so intended, as to forgo rights which *might*
exist in regard to a particular contract or in a particular context.' (Shaw LJ's
emphasis.)

Stephenson LJ dissented. In his view the majority in *Bremer Handelsgesellschaft mbH v
C Mackprang Jr* were carrying the doctrine of waiver further than it had been carried by
the House of Lords in *Bremer Handelsgesellschaft mbH v Vanden Avenne-Izegem PVBA*. But
Stephenson LJ's judgment contains this important paragraph (at 229):

'I do not understand Lord Salmon's reference to the buyers waiving any defect in
the notice under cl. 22 "whether aware of it or not" as laying down any principle
that there can be waiver or equitable estoppel on the part of someone who does not
know that his rights have been infringed or has not, at the least, such obvious means
of knowing that his rights have been infringed that the other party can reasonably
assume that the party waiving or estopped is acting with knowledge of their
infringement. Lord Salmon was, I think, referring to a patent defect which could
only be missed by not reading the notice or not knowing the law.'

Have the sellers succeeded in bringing the present case within the principles stated in
Bremer Handelsgesellschaft mbH v C Mackprang Jr? In my judgment they have.

In the award it is found that the sole reason for the buyers' refusal to take delivery of
the cargo was infestation with weevils. They asked for the cargo to be fumigated at the
sellers' expense. By making and maintaining that request, the buyers were conducting
themselves in a way which was wholly inconsistent with an intention to exercise any
present right to reject the documents. If the sellers had complied with the buyers'
request, it would have been clear beyond argument that the buyers could not
subsequently reject the documents on the ground that they ought to have been tendered
on arrival. Does it make any difference that the cargo was not in fact fumigated? I do
not think it does, provided always that the sellers can show that they relied on the buyers'
request in some other respect. Fair dealing in commerce, though not in cards, requires
that if a party has a trump in his hand he should play it. In the present case the sellers
incurred liability to demurrage in the belief, reasonably induced by the buyers, that the
buyers were not insisting on the immediate provision of alternative documents. In so
doing they relied on a representation to be inferred from the buyers' conduct. There is
no express finding to that effect in the award. The 'causal link', as counsel for the buyers
described it, is not spelt out. But the inference to my mind is irresistible.

Counsel made the point that at the time the buyers were asking for the cargo to be
fumigated they may not have been aware of their right to insist on the production of
alternative documents, or to treat the non-production of those documents on arrival of
the vessel as a breach of condition. In other words they may not have known that they
had a trump in their hand. But their ignorance in that respect was ignorance of law.
The fact that the alternative documents had not been provided on arrival was obvious to
all. So regarded, it seems to me that this case falls not only within the principles stated
by the majority in *Bremer Handelsgesellschaft mbH v C Mackprang Jr* but also within the
principle as stated by Stephenson LJ.

Accordingly I would hold on the facts of this case, as set out in the award, that the
buyers waived their right to treat the non-production of the alternative documents on
the arrival of the vessel as a breach of condition. Nothing happened to affect the position
between the date of the waiver and the date when the documents were rejected. I would
hold that the buyers cannot now justify their rejection on that ground.

Lest there be any misunderstanding, I would emphasise that the buyers' conduct on arrival of the vessel would not have affected any *future* right to reject the documents, as, for example, if the documents had turned out to be defective. But that is not this case. The buyers are not relying on a future right but on a right which existed and could have been exercised at the time they asked the sellers to pay for the fumigation.

Before leaving the waiver point I should mention two other authorities relied on by counsel for the sellers. The first is *Heisler v Anglo-Dal Ltd* [1954] 2 All ER 770, [1954] 1 WLR 1273. That was a case in which it was sought to take a point as to the sufficiency of certain documents which had not been taken at the time. To some extent there is therefore a similarity between that case and the present. But in that case the point, if taken earlier, could have been put right. In the present case, if counsel for the buyers is right on his main argument, as I have held that he is, the alternative documents had to be provided forthwith. There was no time to put the matter right later. I doubt therefore, whether *Heisler v Anglo-Dal Ltd* is as helpful to counsel for the sellers as it seems at first sight.

The second case is *Panchaud Frères SA v Etablissements General Grain Co* [1970] 1 Lloyd's Rep 53. Here counsel is on safer ground. Counsel for the buyers seeks to distinguish *Panchaud* on the ground that in that case the defective documents were at least tendered. Here there was no tender at all. There was nothing, save the passage of time. I do not accept that analysis. It ignores what is, to my mind, the crucial finding as to the request for fumigation of the cargo. That finding makes the case, if anything, stronger than *Panchaud*, for in *Panchaud* the only conduct which could be relied on was the purely passive failure to reject the documents from which it was apparent that the goods had been shipped late. But in the present case there was not merely the passive failure of the buyers to exercise their right to reject on the ground that the alternative documents were not tendered on arrival of the vessel, there was also the active steps taken by the buyers to get the sellers to fumigate the cargo at their expense.

For the above reasons I would hold that, though the buyers were entitled to treat the sellers' failure to provide alternative documents on arrival of the vessel as a breach of condition, they had waived that right before they rejected the documents on 24th June 1976 and can no longer rely on that ground to justify their rejection.

I can deal with the second argument of counsel for the buyers much more shortly. He submits that, on the true construction of the contract, the certificate of quality submitted by the sellers was not final as to condition. The umpire and the board of appeal decided that point against the buyers; and so do I. The quality clause in the contract provided: 'Quality and condition final at shipment as per tender-terms "por Sociedad de Control solvente" for seller's account'. 'Tender-terms' is a reference to a contract dated 28th April 1976 under which the sellers bought 50,000 tons of Spanish barley from Servicio Nacional de Productos Agrarios. I shall refer to that contract as the 'supply contract'. 'Por Sociedad de Control solvente' means 'by reliable quality control company'.

On 2nd June 1976 Supercontrol issued a certificate of quality as a result of an analysis which they carried out on samples of the cargo. There was an annex to the certificate, also dated 2nd June, as follows:

> 'It is hereby DECLARED: That no deficiency was found in the above cargo when samples were taken, the merchandise to the best of our knowledge and understanding appearing: sound, fit and merchantable. And shipped in good condition.'

There is a finding in the award that Supercontrol is an established superintendence company. It is the quality control company named in the supply contract. Counsel for the buyers accepts that a certificate as to condition, which the certificate of 2nd June purports to be, would cover such matters as the presence of live weevils. Why then should it not be regarded as conclusive?

The argument is that the supply contract does not make the certificate conclusive as to condition. Indeed under the supply contract the certificate does not cover condition at all. It covers such matters as the percentage of moisture, and the presence of impurities

(which would not include weevils) and split or damaged grains. Since under the sale
a contract the certificate was to be 'as per tender-terms', it is submitted that the finality of
the certificate is confined to such matters, ie to the matters set out in the supply contract.
I cannot accept that submission. It seems to me that it gives no meaning at all to the
word 'condition' in the phrase 'quality and condition final at shipment'. In my judgment
the reference to 'tender-terms' is a reference to the provision in the supply contract
whereby weight and quality certificates were to be issued by Supercontrol in accordance
b with the usual procedure at Spanish ports. There is an express finding in the award that
the documents, including the certificate of quality and condition, are in the form usual
in the trade. It would be impossible for this court, even if it were so minded, to interfere
with that finding. Counsel for the buyers submits that conclusive evidence clauses must
be strictly construed. Even if that is so, I am satisfied that the board of appeal reached the
right result. On the true construction of the contract, the certificate of quality was final
c as to condition as well as quality. I would reject counsel's second main argument.
    That leaves only the question of damages. Clause 26 of the contract provides:

    'DEFAULT—(a) In Default of fulfilment of contract by either party, the other, at his
    discretion, shall, after giving notice in writing, have the right to sell or purchase, as
    the case may be, against the defaulter, who shall make good the loss, if any, on such
    sale or purchase. If the party liable to pay shall be dissatisfied with the price of such
d   sale or purchase, or if the above right is not exercised, the damages, if any, payable
    by the party in default shall be settled by arbitration and such damages in the
    absence of special circumstances shall not exceed the difference between the contract
    price and the market price (or its equivalent as found by the Arbitrators or the Court
    of Appeal) on the day of default, and nothing contained in or implied under this
    contract shall entitle the Buyer to any damages in respect of any loss of profit
e   suffered or liability incurred by him upon any sub-contract. Where, however, any
    special circumstances, in the opinion of the Arbitrators or Court of Appeal, exist, the
    latter may, in their or its sole and absolute discretion, award to the Buyer such sum
    in respect of loss of profit so suffered or liability so incurred as they or it shall think
    fit. In the event of default in shipment or delivery, any damages shall be computed
    upon the mean contract quantity. . .'

f As already mentioned, the sellers declared the buyers in default under cl 26 on 28th June
1976. They promptly asked for bids. The highest bid came from SIAT. They offered
$114 per metric ton, free out La Spezia. There was an option in the contract between the
sellers and SIAT, which SIAT exercised, to take delivery of the cargo at Venice instead of
La Spezia for an additional $2 per metric ton. There was a further term that SIAT should
g pay accrued demurrage amounting to $55,066 plus any further demurrage accruing at
Venice, amounting in all to $63,838. There is a finding in the award that taking
demurrage into account, the effective cost to SIAT was the equivalent of $126 per metric
ton, compared with a contract price of $132 per metric ton. There is a further important
finding that $126 represents the fair market value of the cargo at La Spezia on the date
of default.
h   The sellers claimed damages based on the difference between $116 and $132 per
metric ton, together with certain additional expenses, namely the balance of demurrage
not recovered from SIAT, for expenses at La Spezia, for bunkers, etc. The board of appeal
has allowed the claim in full. The question is whether they were right to do so. That
question turns on the true construction of cl 26.
    The effect of an identical clause was considered by Robert Goff J and the Court of
j Appeal in *Toprak Mahsulleri Ofisi v Finagrain Compagnie Commerciale Agricole et Financière
SA* [1979] 2 Lloyd's Rep 98. One of the questions in that case was whether the sellers
could recover the loss which they suffered by reason of the cancellation of a charterparty
over and above the normal measure of damages based on the difference between contract
and market price. It was held that they could not. Clause 26 provides that the *buyer* can
recover loss of profit under a sub-contract, in special circumstances, if the board of appeal

in its discretion should so decide. Nothing in cl 26 entitles the board of appeal to award the *seller* any loss in excess of the ordinary measure of damages.

Counsel for the sellers sought to distinguish *Toprak v Finagrain*. He submitted that the difference between contract and market price would only have applied if the buyers had expressed dissatisfaction with the price at which the sellers sold to SIAT. Here there is a finding that the buyers never expressed any such dissatisfaction. Accordingly the sellers can recover their actual loss on resale as found by the board of appeal. This is essentially the same argument as was accepted by the board of appeal.

Although I have every sympathy with the board of appeal's approach to the question of damages, I regret that I cannot agree with it. It seems to me that this case is on all fours with *Toprak v Finagrain*. In the first place the clause does not require the buyer, or seller, as the case may be, to express dissatisfaction *before* the sale or purchase. They can express their dissatisfaction at any time. But putting that on one side, the buyers were still only obliged to make good the sellers' loss on resale. What is meant by 'loss'? It means loss which is not too remote in law. In most cases such loss would be represented by the difference between the contract price and the resale price. But here the resale price contained hidden elements. First, there was the option to take delivery in Venice. In arriving at the 'loss' on resale it is essential to compare like with like. Second, and much more important, there was the obligation on the part of SIAT to pay the demurrage. But for that obligation, the price would have been $126. If the sellers had remained liable for demurrage, could they have recovered the demurrage as part of their 'loss' on resale? Plainly not. It would have been exactly the same as the cancellation charges which the sellers sought, and failed, to recover in *Toprak v Finagrain*. That being so, can the sellers increase their recoverable loss by transferring the liability for demurrage to SIAT, and reducing the price pro tanto? The answer must, I think, be no. The sellers can recover the difference between the contract and market price, but no more,

I could understand an argument that the market price for this barley must take account of the liability for accrued demurrage, that is to say for the $55,066. But no such argument was advanced by counsel for the sellers, no doubt because of the express finding that the market value of the barley where it lay at La Spezia was $126. It seems to me to follow that the difference between $126 and $132 represents the maximum loss recoverable under this contract.

The same also applies to the other items of loss such as port expenses etc which the Board of Appeal have included in their award.

I would therefore answer the questions of law in the award as follows: (1) yes; (2) the maximum entitlement of the sellers to damages is the difference between contract and market price for the cargo as it lay at La Spezia. On the findings I take this to be the difference between $126 and $132, but I leave the calculation of the precise amount, together with interest, to the board of appeal, unless this can be agreed by the parties.

Finally, there is before the court a motion to remit the award to the board of appeal for further findings of fact. In view of my conclusion that the certificates are conclusive as to the condition of the barley on shipment, that motion no longer serves any purpose.

Order accordingly.

Solicitors: *William A Crump & Son* (for the buyers); *Richards, Butler & Co* (for the sellers).

K Mydeen Esq   Barrister.

Edwards (Inspector of Taxes) v Clinch

HOUSE OF LORDS

LORD WILBERFORCE, LORD SALMON, LORD EDMUND-DAVIES, LORD LOWRY AND LORD BRIDGE OF HARWICH

16th, 17th, 18th JUNE, 22nd OCTOBER 1981

Income tax – Emoluments from office or employment – Office – Inspector appointed to hold a public local inquiry – Whether inspector holding an 'office' – Whether inspector's remuneration taxable under Sch E, Case I – Income and Corporation Taxes Act 1970, s 181(1).

The taxpayer was one of a panel of persons invited by the Department of the Environment from time to time to act as inspectors at public local inquiries for the Secretary of State for the Environment. The taxpayer would be contacted by an official of the department, informed of the location and date of the inquiry and the daily fee payable, and invited to undertake the inquiry. The taxpayer could then either accept or refuse the invitation. If he accepted, the taxpayer was sent the relevant papers together with an authority in writing, signed on behalf of the Secretary of State, appointing him to hold the particular inquiry. The taxpayer was solely responsible for the conduct and procedure at the inquiry, subject to the rules governing tribunals and inquiries. The taxpayer was remunerated by daily fees according to the length of the inquiry and received no retainer or salary. The Revenue claimed that the taxpayer's position was a public office capable of being held by persons in succession and therefore an 'office' within s 181(1)[a] of the Income and Corporation Taxes Act 1970, and accordingly the fees received by him were chargeable to tax under Case I of Sch E. The taxpayer appealed to the General Commissioners, contending that his appointment was not an office within s 181(1) because the holding of each inquiry was an ad hoc appointment of indeterminate length which he was free to accept or refuse. The General Commissioners allowed the appeal but their decision was reversed by the judge ([1979] 1 All ER 648), who held that for the purposes of s 181(1) an inspector at a public local inquiry held a series of offices to which he was appointed from time to time by the person having the power of appointment to such offices. The Court of Appeal ([1980] 3 All ER 278) allowed an appeal by the taxpayer, holding that an office was a post which existed independently of the identity of the person who occupied it for the time being and which had a sufficient degree of continuance and permanence to enable it to be held by successive incumbents. The Crown appealed, contending that the term 'office' ought to be given its ordinary and natural meaning without reference to previous authority.

Held (Lord Edmund-Davies and Lord Bridge dissenting) – For the purposes of the assessment of tax under Sch E in the 1970 Act, an 'office' was a post involving a degree of continuance (although not necessarily continuity) and independent existence, and to which a person could be appointed, which he could vacate and to which a successor could be appointed. Since each appointment of the taxpayer to conduct a public local inquiry was temporary, ad hoc and personal to the taxpayer, such appointments lacked the characteristics of an 'office' within s 181(1) of the 1970 Act and the taxpayer was not assessable to tax under Sch E in respect of fees received by him for conducting such inquiries. The Crown's appeal would therefore be dismissed (see p 546 b to d g h, p 547 d, p 548 e f, p 549 h, p 550 c d, p 551 d, p 553 a d to h, p 555 a h, p 556 f, p 557 j to p 558 b, p 559 g h and p 560 h j, post).

Dictum of Rowlatt J in *Great Western Railway Co v Bater (Surveyor of Taxes)* [1920] 3 KB at 274 approved.

---

a   Section 181(1) so far as material, provides: 'The Schedule referred to as Schedule E is as follows:—
     SCHEDULE E 1. Tax under this Schedule shall be charged in respect of any office or employment on
     emoluments therefrom . . .'

McMillan v Guest (Inspector of Taxes) [1942] 1 All ER 606 and *Inland Revenue Comrs v Brander & Cruickshank* [1971] 1 All ER 36 applied.

Decision of the Court of Appeal [1980] 3 All ER 278 affirmed.

Notes

For the meaning of 'office' and 'employment', see 23 Halsbury's Laws (4th Edn) paras 647–648, and for cases on the subject, see 28(1) Digest (Reissue) 320–323, *1130–1147*.

For the Income and Corporation Taxes Act 1970, s 181, see 33 Halsbury's Statutes (3rd Edn) 255.

For 1974–75 and subsequent years of assessment, s 181(1) of the 1970 Act has been amended by s 21(1) of the Finance Act 1974.

Cases referred to in opinions

Dale v Inland Revenue Comrs [1953] 2 All ER 671, [1954] AC 11, [1953] 3 WLR 448, 34 Tax Cas 468, 32 ATC 294, [1953] TR 269, 46 R & IT 513, HL, 28(1) Digest (Reissue) 583, *2163*.

Davies (Inspector of Taxes) v Braithwaite [1931] 2 KB 628, [1931] All ER Rep 792, 18 Tax Cas 198, 100 LJKB 619, 145 LT 693, 28(1) Digest (Reissue) 241, *746*.

Farrell v Alexander [1976] 2 All ER 721, [1977] AC 59, [1976] 3 WLR 145, 32 P & CR 292, HL, Digest (Cont Vol E) 382, *8375b*.

Graham v White (Inspector of Taxes) [1972] 1 All ER 1159, [1972] 1 WLR 874, 48 Tax Cas 163, 50 ATC 481, [1971] TR 477, Digest (Cont Vol D) 462, *1143a*.

Great Western Railway Co v Bater (Surveyor of Taxes) [1920] 3 KB 266, 90 LJKB 41, 124 LT 92, 8 Tax Cas 231; *affd* [1921] 2 KB 128, 90 LJKB 550, 125 LT 321, 8 Tax Cas 231, CA; *rvsd* [1922] 2 AC 1, 91 LJKB 472, 127 LT 170, 8 Tax Cas 231, HL, 28(1) Digest (Reissue) 321, *1132*.

Inland Revenue Comrs v Brander & Cruickshank [1971] 1 All ER 36, [1971] 1 WLR 212, 46 Tax Cas 574, [1970] TR 353, HL; *affg* 1970 SC 116, 1970 SLT 159, 46 Tax Cas 574, Ct of Sess, 28(1) Digest (Reissue) 46, *193*.

McMillan v Guest (Inspector of Taxes) [1942] 1 All ER 606, [1942] AC 561, 24 Tax Cas 190, 111 LJKB 398, 167 LT 329, HL; *affg* [1940] 4 All ER 452, [1941] 1 KB 258, 24 Tax Cas 190, 110 LJKB 125, CA, 28(1) Digest (Reissue) 337, *1219*.

Mitchell (Inspector of Taxes) v Ross [1961] 3 All ER 49, [1962] AC 813, [1961] 3 WLR 411, 40 Tax Cas 11, 40 ATC 199, [1961] TR 191, HL; *rvsg* [1960] 2 All ER 218, [1960] Ch 498, [1960] 2 WLR 766, 40 Tax Cas 11, 39 ATC 52, [1960] TR 79, CA; *affg* [1959] 3 All ER 341, [1960] Ch 145, [1959] 3 WLR 550, 40 Tax Cas 11, 38 ATC 422, [1959] TR 225, 28(1) Digest (Reissue) 321, *1138*.

Ryall (Inspector of Taxes) v Hoare, Ryall (Inspector of Taxes) v Honeywill [1923] 2 KB 447, [1923] All ER Rep 528, 92 LJKB 1010, 129 LT 505, 8 Tax Cas 521, 28(1) Digest (Reissue) 313, *1087*.

St Aubyn (L M) v Attorney General (No 2) [1951] 2 All ER 473, [1952] AC 15, 30 ATC 193, HL.

Taylor v Provan (Inspector of Taxes) [1974] 1 All ER 1201, [1975] AC 194, [1974] 2 WLR 394, [1974] STC 168, 49 Tax Cas 579, 53 ATC 40, [1974] TR 45, HL, Digest (Cont Vol D) 465, *1226e*.

Appeal

The Crown appealed against the decision of the Court of Appeal (Buckley, Ackner and Oliver LJJ) ([1980] 3 All ER 278, [1981] Ch 1) given on 9th May 1980 allowing the appeal of Frank Howard Clinch ('the taxpayer') against the judgment of Walton J ([1979] 1 All ER 648, [1979] 1 WLR 338) given on 29th November 1978 whereby he allowed an appeal by the Crown from the decision of the Commissioners for the General Purposes of the Income Tax that he was not assessable to income tax under Sch E for the years 1973–74 and 1974–75 in respect of payments for conducting public local inquiries as the

holder of an office within s 181(1) of the Income and Corporation Taxes Act 1970. The
a facts are set out in the judgment of Lord Bridge.

The Solicitor General (Sir Ian Percival QC), Brian Davenport QC and *Robert Carnwath* for the
Crown.
Michael Nolan QC and *John Gardiner* for the taxpayer.

b Their Lordships took time for consideration.

22nd October. The following opinions were delivered.

LORD WILBERFORCE. My Lords, this appeal is concerned with the taxation of fees
received by the taxpayer, a civil engineer by profession, in respect of public inquiries
c which he was asked to carry out by the Secretary of State for the Environment. Should
they be taxed under Sch E or under Sch D? The Revenue seeks to tax him under Sch E
as the holder of an office. The existence of two separate schedules under which the
citizen may be assessed, with different results, for income tax has over the 140 years in
which it has survived, with minor changes, created perplexity. This is none the less so
because apparently minor changes are made in the schedules from time to time as to
d which it is not disclosed whether any change in principle or substance has been intended.
     The word 'office' has been in the income tax legislation all along: the Income Tax Act
1842 referred to 'Every public office'. Since 1922 the qualification 'public' has
disappeared, so all offices are now taxed under Sch E. At no time has any definition of
'office' been provided, so the judges have been left to work out what the word included.
     In performing this task, they naturally looked for a context. They found one in r 1 of
e Sch (E) to the 1842 Act (quoted by my noble and learned friend Lord Bridge) which
contemplated that the tax would be levied on the office as such over a whole year.
     This it was, I think, which led to the well-known Rowlatt definition of office, or, as it
has later been called, a generally sufficient statement of the meaning of the word as used
in the 1842 Act. An office was something 'which was a subsisting, permanent,
substantive position, which had an existence independent of the person who filled it, and
f which went on and was filled in succession by successive holders' (see *Great Western
Railway Co v Bater (Surveyor of Taxes)* [1920] 3 KB 266 at 274), a definition or statement,
which was, I dare to say, bred into the bones of every practitioner in income tax matters,
and, more importantly, was known to the legislature, and its drafting agents, on the
many occasions when revisions of the schedules were made or considered.
     Because this was the origin of the income tax meaning of 'office', I have doubts as to
g the value, or indeed legitimacy, of now resorting to a dictionary for a definition. Of
course it would be desirable in an ideal world for expressions in tax legislation to bear
ordinary meanings, such as the citizen could find out by consulting the Oxford English
Dictionary. But it is a fact that many words of ordinary meaning acquire a signification
coloured over the years by legal construction in a technical context such that return to
the pure source of common parlance is no longer possible. I think that 'office' is such a
h word.
     Lord Bridge has rendered us a service by designating as the critical question whether
the Rowlatt definition should be considered as still retaining all its ingredients through
successive legislative changes which have, inter alia, led to the disappearance of r 1. I do
not, for myself, regard the disappearance of r 1, and its successor para 2 of Sch 9 to the
Income Tax Act 1952, rules concerned with the machinery of assessment, as indicating
any legislative intention to change the meaning of the word 'office'. For the same reason
j I would reject the taxpayer's counterpart argument based on the (assessment) provision
now contained in s 204 of the Income and Corporation Taxes Act 1970. But I would
agree that, in the natural course of development, it is open to the courts, and right, to
consider whether the ingredients of the Rowlatt definition are still appropriate, at least

in their full force. It would seem to me that the legislature, by continuing to use the
word in the taxing words of Sch E without any corrective definition, showed a general *a*
intention to adopt the judicial interpretation of it which, though uncritically, has been
consistent and continuous. For myself I would accept that a rigid requirement of
permanence is no longer appropriate, nor is vouched by any decided case, and continuity
need not be regarded as an absolute qualification. But still, if any meaning is to be given
to 'office' in this legislation, as distinguished from 'employment' or 'profession' or 'trade'
or 'vocation' (these are the various words used in order to tax people on their earnings), *b*
the word must involve a degree of continuance (not necessarily continuity) and of
independent existence: it must connote a post to which a person can be appointed, which
he can vacate and to which a successor can be appointed. This is the concept which was
accepted by all three of the members of the Court of Appeal, who all desired, in my
opinion rightly, to combine some degree of consistency with what had become accepted
notions in the law of income tax, with practical common-sense requirements, and *c*
without 'treating as authoritative decisions which were reached for reasons which may
no longer be appropriate' (see [1980] 3 All ER 278 at 280, [1981] Ch 1 at 5 per Buckley
LJ). Thus Buckley LJ accepted that to constitute an office a post need not be capable of
permanent or prolonged or indefinite existence, a development of the law with which I
agree.

Acceptance of the admittedly somewhat indefinite guidelines suggested above does *d*
not, of course, solve the instant, or any similar, problem. It is necessary to appraise the
characteristics of the taxpayer's 'appointment'. There is in this task an element of
common-sense evaluation of fact, a task which is committed in the first place to the
General Commissioners. Their finding was for the taxpayer, and though this is far from
sacrosanct, indeed I think that they applied the Rowlatt definition too literally,
nevertheless it is not in my opinion wholly to be disregarded. They described it as *e*
'merely a transient, indeterminate, once-only execution of a task for which [the taxpayer]
was peculiarly qualified' (see [1979] 1 All ER 648 at 650), adding an analogy which I do
not find appropriate.

The Crown does not contend that the taxpayer, who was a member of a panel, and was
called on to conduct a number of inquiries, held one office. Its contention, which would
seem an odd one to an ordinary man, is that he held a series of offices; so did, I suppose, *f*
each of the other 60 members of the panel who were called on to act. So each
'appointment' has to be judged separately.

The relevant facts concerning a typical appointment are detailed in other opinions. I
am happy to take those presented by Lord Bridge. But with very great hesitation, I have
formed the opposite view, on this matter of impression, to his. I agree, on the other
hand, with the conclusions of the members of the Court of Appeal: *g*

> '. . . each appointment was personal to the taxpayer; it lacked the characteristic of
> independent existence and continuance which, in my judgment, is one of the
> essential characteristics of an "office".'

(See [1980] 3 All ER 278 at 286, [1981] Ch 1 at 12 per Buckley LJ.)

> 'It was a temporary ad hoc appointment confined to the taxpayer. He was not *h*
> appointed to a position which had an existence of its own. It had no quality of
> permanency about it.'

(See [1980] 3 All ER 278 at 289, [1981] Ch 1 at 17 per Ackner LJ.)

> 'There is no office of "inquirer" or "inspector" created by the Act, but merely a
> provision authorising the Minister to "cause to be held" the appropriate inquiries.' *j*

(See [1980] 3 All ER 278 at 290, [1981] Ch 1 at 19 per Oliver LJ; surely an effective point.)
And again:

> 'This [the concept of continuance apart from the individual holder] . . . is
> something entirely lacking in the instant case. The duty of making the inquiry is

one which is offered to and accepted by the individual ad hoc. If he is unable to complete it and to make his report for any reason, there is no question of appointing a successor to the office of conducting that inquiry. There has to be a new inquiry by another individual equally appointed ad hoc, and on terms which fall to be separately negotiated with him.'

(See [1980] 3 All ER 278 at 293, [1981] Ch 1 at 23 per Oliver LJ.)

There is no doubt that the factual ingredients detected by their Lordships are correctly stated; I agree with their estimation of their weight.

Each of the Lords Justices moreover carefully examined and, in my opinion effectively, answered the four points on which Walton J relied in order to decide for the Crown, and disposed of the argument that the public nature of the taxpayer's duties and their statutory background were significant elements (see [1979] 1 All ER 648 at 654, [1979] 1 WLR 338 at 344). I would add that I do not find that any decisive argument can be based on analogy with such cases as recorders or deputy judges or on the relative convenience of taxing the taxpayer under one or other of Sch D or Sch E. The latter provides for bringing temporary employment within the PAYE system, and, though perhaps some element of estimation would have to be used, the taxpayer's fees could be dealt with in a similar way. Assessment under Sch D, on the other hand, assuming that this is the right method (we are not called on so to decide), would present no difficulty at all.

I would dismiss the appeal.

LORD SALMON. My Lords, from time to time prior to 1973 and during the fiscal years 1973–74 and 1974–75 the Secretary of State for the Environment invited the taxpayer to hold a public local inquiry for the purposes of hearing objections and representations in respect of compulsory purchase orders and other like matters for which the Secretary of State was responsible. Neither the Secretary of State nor any subordinate or representative of his could hold such an inquiry.

The taxpayer was a most experienced and distinguished civil engineer, and no doubt it was for this reason that he was invited to hold the public local inquiries to which I have referred. The taxpayer accepted a number of these invitations. He received no retainer or salary. His fees, professional fees, as Walton J pointed out, were paid only in response to the fee accounts which he submitted. It is agreed that he was not employed by the Secretary of State or by anyone else.

When an invitation to hold a public local inquiry was accepted, the taxpayer received a written authority signed by the Secretary of State appointing him to hold that inquiry. He then held the inquiry entirely as he thought best, without any direction or guidance from the Secretary of State. Indeed he always announced the independence of his status at the commencement of each inquiry.

The taxpayer held a number of public local inquiries of various kinds. The parties have however agreed that the inquiries were all alike, but separate from each other, and therefore that the inquiry relating to a proposed compulsory purchase order for the land required for a trunk road should be regarded as typical of all the other inquiries held by the taxpayer.

At the conclusion of an inquiry, the taxpayer made a report to the Secretary of State. This report set out the taxpayer's findings of fact and recommendations, or his reasons for not making any recommendations. In spite of his power to compel witnesses to attend the inquiry to give evidence and produce documents, he had no power to make any decision. He could only report his findings of fact and his recommendations to the Secretary of State, which the Secretary was entitled to reject. The taxpayer's function was only to inform and advise but never to decide. Accordingly, his function, in my view, was in no way judicial or even quasi-judicial.

Prior to 1973 the Revenue clearly considered (and I think rightly) that the taxpayer and others like him who did the kind of work to which I have referred were earning their income arising or accruing from their profession or vocation, and were therefore taxable only under Case II of Sch D (see ss 108(1)(a)(ii) and 109(2) of the Income and Corporation Taxes Act 1970), which relates only to tax in respect of 'profits or gains arising or accruing ... from ... any profession or vocation not contained in any other Schedule'. And this was the way in which the taxpayer always had been taxed prior to 1973.

It seems never to have occurred to the Revenue prior to that year that the taxpayer or anyone of his profession doing his kind of work could be regarded as holding 'an office'; and therefore it was concluded that they could not be taxed under Case I of Sch E (s 181 of the 1970 Act) which relates only to tax charged 'in respect of any office or employment on emoluments therefrom ...' During 1973, however, the Revenue appears to have changed its mind. It assessed the taxpayer, and those like him, for tax under Case I of Sch E without giving the taxpayers any warning. Walton J states that the Revenue had behaved in 'an extremely insensitive manner, and are to be censured accordingly' (see [1979] 1 All ER 648 at 652, [1979] 1 WLR 338 at 342). I agree, and might have been tempted to use even stronger language.

To be taxed under Case I of Sch E instead of under Case II of Sch D usually results in the taxpayers such as the taxpayer paying substantially more tax than they had previously paid. For example, the assessment for tax under Case I of Sch E in the years 1973–74 amounted to £6,678 and in the year 1974–75 to £11,579. Had the assessment of tax for those two years been made under Case II of Sch D it would, as the commissioners found, have amounted only to £4,871 and £4,651 respectively.

The commissioners found in favour of the taxpayer, that he should be taxed just as he always had been under Case II of Sch D. Walton J reversed the commissioners' findings and the Court of Appeal allowed the appeal from Walton J's judgment. My Lords, the question on which this appeal to your Lordships turns is whether the Revenue was right in asserting that the Secretary of State for the Environment had appointed the taxpayer and his like taxpayers to 'an office'. The Revenue prior to 1973 had never made any such assertion and indeed for very many years had acted on the basis that such an assertion was impossible.

My Lords, there is no shortage of authorities in which most distinguished lawyers clearly support the taxpayer's case. They state clearly what facts are necessary to exist in order to enable anyone to be appointed an officer holder. In my opinion, no such facts exist in the present case; and I certainly find nothing to justify any dissent from what was said by Lord Atkin, Lord Wright, Lord Porter, Lord Morris and a number of others to whom I am about to refer.

In *McMillan v Guest (Inspector of Taxes)* [1942] 1 All ER 606, [1942] AC 561 the point arose whether a non-executive director of a private limited company was assessable under Sch E for his remuneration as a director on the ground that he held an 'office'. Lord Atkin said ([1942] 1 All ER 606 at 607, [1942] AC 561 at 564):

'It is necessary to consider whether the appellant (i) held an office ... On the first point there was no dispute. There is no statutory definition of "office". Without adopting the sentence as a complete definition one may treat the following expression of ROWLATT, J., in *Great Western Ry Co.* v. *Bater* ([1920] 3 KB 266 at 274) as a generally sufficient statement of the meaning of the word: "... an office or employment which was a subsisting, permanent, substantive position, which had an existence independent of the person who filled it, which went on and was filled in succession by successive holders ..." This statement was adopted by LORD ATKINSON in his judgment in the same case in the House of Lords ([1922] 2 AC 1 at 15). There can be no doubt that the director of a company holds such an office as is described.'

Lord Roche agreed with Lord Atkin. Lord Wright said ([1942] 1 All ER 606 at 608, [1942] AC 561 at 566):

'The word "office" is of indefinite content. Its various meanings cover four columns of the NEW ENGLISH DICTIONARY ...'

He then went on to say that he imagined that the words in *Bater's* case were deliberately
left vague and that the words should be applied 'according to the ordinary use of
language and the dictates of common sense, with due regard to the requirement that
there must be some degree of permanence and publicity in the office' (see [1942] 1 All ER
606 at 609, [1942] AC 561 at 567). I shall later return to Lord Wright's speech.

It has not been disputed that each inquiry by the taxpayer came to an end if he did not
finish it, or, if when he did finish it, he reported it to the Minister. Thus all the inquiries
were disconnected from each other.

The last authority to which I need refer is *Inland Revenue Comrs v Brander & Cruickshank*
[1971] 1 All ER 36, [1971] 1 WLR 212 on the termination of the taxpayers' appointments
as registrars of two companies which had been taken over. They were paid £2,500 by
those companies. The Inland Revenue claimed that that payment should have been
treated as profits assessable under Case II of Sch D. The First Division of the Court of
Session and (on appeal) your Lordships' House held that the payment could not be taxed
under Case II of Sch D and that it could not be taxed under Sch E since it amounted to not
more than £5,000 (see s 38(3) of the Finance Act 1960); and but for s 38(3) the taxpayers
would have been liable to be taxed under Sch E because they held an 'office'.

In the Court of Session Lord Guthrie and Lord Migdale, respectively, treated the words
of Rowlatt J in *Bater's* case as a generally sufficient statement of the meaning of the word
'office'. Lord Guthrie said (46 Tax Cas 574 at 584):

'What the Special Commissioners had to decide was whether in the particular
cases of the two companies the Respondents were holders of substantive positions to
which duties were attached, *and which had the quality of permanency irrespective of the
particular holder's tenure*, or whether they merely did some work of a particular kind
for the companies.' (The emphasis is mine.)

Lord Migdale said (at 587):

'This work of keeping the registers entailed a position which had an existence of
its own. If one holder gave it up someone else had to be appointed to carry it on.'

Lord Morris said ([1971] 1 All ER 36 at 41, [1971] 1 WLR 212 at 215):

'Even though the Companies Act 1948 does not require that there should be an
appointment as registrar, a company must arrange that some person or persons
should on its behalf perform the statutory duties of maintaining its register. In
doing so, it may establish a position which successively will be held by different
persons. If it does so the company may have created what could rationally for
income tax purposes be called an office. In *McMillan v Guest* [1942] 1 All ER 606 at
607, [1942] AC 561 at 564 Lord Atkin, while pointing out that there is no statutory
definition of "office" was prepared to accept what Rowlatt J had said in *Great
Western Ry Co v Bater* [1920] 3 KB 266 at 274 (as adopted by Lord Atkinson ([1922]
2 AC 1 at 15)) as being a generally sufficient statement of meaning.'

The highly respected authorities to which I have referred have all agreed as to the
meaning of the word 'office' in Sch E, namely 'a subsisting, permanent, substantive
position which has an existence independent of the person who fills it'. Accordingly, if
that meaning is missing, as it is in the present case, the person concerned could not be
taxed under Sch E as an office holder.

The meaning of 'employment' cannot, in my view, by any means, always have the
same meaning as that of 'office' in Sch E. This, in my opinion, is because the meaning
of 'employment' in Sch E obviously refers very often to the host of persons being
employed to work for no more than a salary or wage which will be taxed under that
schedule. In *McMillan v Guest (Inspector of Taxes)* [1942] 1 All ER 606 at 608, [1942] AC
561 at 566 Lord Wright said:

'To hold that the director of a company . . . does not have an office within the meaning of the schedule would ... be an abuse of language ... The word "employment" ... has to be construed with and takes its colour from the word "office".'   *a*

In a contract of employment between a company and a person, the contract of employment sometimes in the commercial field has a clause which gives the person employed an office as a director. This may be what Lord Wright had in mind when he said 'The word "employment," in my opinion, has to be construed with and takes its colour from the word "office".'   *b*

Unlike the word 'employment', the word 'office' is fairly difficult to understand in its context; and it has no statutory definition.

The taxpayer (who it is agreed was not employed) held a number of separate public local inquiries over the years. These inquiries did not constitute one continuing office; nor did the Revenue suggest that they did. The Revenue, however, argued that each local public inquiry from the moment it commenced to the moment that it finished made the taxpayer the holder of an office under Sch E. I do not agree with that argument. I should like to adopt the words of Ackner LJ ([1980] 3 All ER 278 at 289, [1981] Ch 1 at 17–18):   *c*

> 'It was a temporary ad hoc appointment confined to the taxpayer. He was not appointed to a position which had an existence of its own. It had no quality of permanency about it ... It was, as the General Commissioners correctly observed, a transient, indeterminate, once-only execution of a task for which the taxpayer was peculiarly qualified.'   *d*

I cannot agree that the dictionary meaning of the word 'office' can or was intended to be of any real help in construing the word 'office' in Sch E, particularly having regard to the authorities to which I have referred.   *e*

I have had the advantage of reading the speech of my noble and learned friend Lord Bridge, which I admire but with which I respectfully cannot agree. He relies on one of the many definitions in the Oxford English Dictionary of the word 'office' which reads as follows:

> 'A position or place to which certain duties are attached, esp. one of a more or less public character; a position of trust, authority, or service under constituted authority; a place in the administration of government, the public service, the direction of a corporation, company, society, etc.'   *f*

The taxpayer, no doubt, occupied a position to which duties of a public character are attached. So does a dustman. The taxpayer was in a position of authority. So is a foreman. But neither the dustman nor the foreman can be the holder of an 'office'. I do not think that the taxpayer holds a place in the administration of government. In any event, there are some people who do but do *not* hold an 'office'. The taxpayer certainly has no employer; nor has a doctor or a solicitor. I do not understand however how the lack of an employer prevents these characters from earning a fee for exercising their professional skill and experience unless they occupy an 'office' which they rarely do. I do not agree that the taxpayer was not acting in a personal capacity 'but in a capacity which derives its existence wholly from ... his statutory appointment'. I agree with Ackner LJ that—   *g*

        h

> 'the person who conducts the inquiry is the taxpayer considered as a person. He owes his appointment to the particular skill and/or experience which he has. Of course he would have no locus standi without the formal appointment first being made, but then the same would equally apply to an arbitrator, who counsel for the Crown concedes is not appointed to an "office".'   *j*

(See [1980] 3 All ER 278 at 288, [1981] Ch 1 at 15.)

I also agree with Ackner LJ that the phrase 'That the duty placed on the inspector was one placed by statute' means—

> 'that, once having accepted the appointment, the taxpayer's conduct of the public local inquiry was, to some extent, controlled and circumscribed by the [relevant] statutes . . . The obligation to observe statutory requirements cannot in itself create an office.'

(See [1980] 3 All ER 278 at 288, [1981] Ch 1 at 15–16.)

Naturally, the taxpayer will have to be taxed in respect of the fees he has received for holding national local inquiries for the years 1973–74 and 1974–75. Although, for the reasons I have given, he cannot, in my view, be taxed under Case I of Sch E, the fees he has earned are taxable as part of his professional earnings. After all, when the holder of the inquiry has to listen to the evidence and inspect the land, his professional skill and experience will enable him to make recommendations whether or not it ought to be compulsorily purchased for the purpose of making a trunk road. It seems plain to me that a distinguished civil engineer, because of his particular expertise on this subject, would be the most likely person to be asked, as a part of his professional activities, to make those recommendations. And I would consider it reasonable and right to describe the fees he received as professional receipts under Sch D, just as they had always been prior to 1973.

My Lords, for the reasons I have stated, I would dismiss the appeal.

LORD EDMUND-DAVIES. My Lords, the question raised in this appeal is whether fees paid by the Department of the Environment to the taxpayer, a civil engineer, for services rendered by him in conducting from time to time, during the years 1973–74 and 1974–75, public inquiries into such matters as highway construction and improvements and the compulsory acquisition of land were assessable to tax under Sch E in s 181(1) of the Income and Corporation Taxes Act 1970. The answer is clearly of considerable importance both to the public and to many self-employed people who periodically accept the invitations of government departments to conduct such inquiries on a fee basis calculated mainly on their duration. Were it not for the fact that others more experienced than I in matters of taxation have hitherto forcefully differed from each other, I would, with the utmost respect, have thought and said that the question did not present great difficulty. Yet the Revenue assessed the taxpayer under Sch E, the General Commissioners under Sch D, Walton J under Sch E, and the Court of Appeal unanimously held that his fees fell to be assessed under Sch D. And the Solicitor General has now appealed to your Lordships' House to secure restoration of the order made three years ago by Walton J.

The question at the heart of the appeal is: when conducting such an inquiry was the taxpayer the holder of an 'office' falling within Case I of Sch E in s 181(1)? The Solicitor General contends that he was and should therefore be taxed pursuant to that schedule. For the taxpayer, on the other hand, it is contended that the correct schedule is Sch D, Case II.

My Lords, I have already had the advantage of reading in draft what I venture to describe as the admirable speech prepared by my noble and learned friend Lord Bridge and, had I been left in any doubt at the conclusion of counsel's submissions, his speech would doubtless have completely convinced me that the appeal should be allowed. But in reality I was from the outset impressed by the clarity and cogency of the judgment of Walton J, and in those circumstances I have been particularly vigilant to detect any grounds on which his approach and conclusion could be faulted. At the end of the day, I have discovered none.

I am fully alive to the veneration which over the years has attached to the decision of Rowlatt J in *Great Western Railway Co v Bater (Surveyor of Taxes)* [1920] 3 KB 266, and particularly to his adoption (at 274) of the submission that—

'what those who used the language of the [Income Tax Act 1842] meant when they spoke of an office or an employment of profit was an office or employment which was a subsisting, permanent, substantive position, which had an existence independent of the person who filled it, and which went on and was filled in succession by successive holders . . .'

The indicia enumerated by the learned judge are doubtless useful pointers to the existence of an 'office'. It would probably prove difficult to conclude that the occupant of a position having all those characteristics was nevertheless not the holder of an 'office', and it may well be that it is in that sense that Rowlatt J's words have received over the years exalted judicial acceptance in cases considered in the lower courts during the progress of this appeal and again in your Lordships' House. But I respectfully find it well-nigh startling to have those words invoked as providing the definitive test of the existence of an 'office', so that no post lacking all or any of Rowlatt J's indicia can possibly deserve the term. The word is not a term of art, but a wide-ranging noun of ordinary usage, as the dictionary definitions demonstrate. And during the expansive submissions of counsel a substantial number of posts were considered which in my judgment completely fitted within the everyday understanding of the term, notwithstanding that they were transient in their very nature and not simply in the duration of tenure of office of a particular person, and furthermore that they were 'tailor-made' for people possessing particular talents to discharge tasks of a non-recurring type. My noble and learned friend Lord Bridge has dealt with some such posts, but he has by no means exhausted the list. Walton J rightly said ([1979] 1 All ER 648 at 655, [1979] 1 WLR 338 at 345):

'. . . whilst the permanency of the duties to be discharged may well, in a suitable case, form an apt guide as to whether the person discharging them is or is not holding an office, this test is wholly inapplicable to a case where the office is confined to the discharge of one (or a few) specific duties which, in the very nature of such duties, will be discharged within a finite space of time.'

My Lords, learned counsel for the taxpayer submitted that the provisions of s 204 of the 1970 Act themselves indicate that 'office' must be given a meaning severely restricted on the lines indicated by Rowlatt J. He said that sub-s (3) thereof demonstrates such a necessity, and he indicated certain practical difficulties which would arise in relation to PAYE coding were the holder of an 'office' in receipt of emoluments episodic and irregular in their payment and unpredictable in their amounts. But for my part I reprehend giving an everyday word a special meaning simply because it would be more convenient to do so owing to the nature of the currently adopted machinery for the assessment and recovery of taxes. If it was desired to give 'office' a meaning tailored to the PAYE system why did the relevant legislation not provide its own dictionary by defining in a special sense a word of such everyday use?

My Lords, no case similar in its facts to those of the present appeal has been cited or has apparently arisen hitherto. I believe, with the Solicitor General, that the proper test to be applied is to consider *the nature of the function* performed by the taxpayer. Applying that test to the fact of this case, and notwithstanding the impermanence of the duties discharged from time to time by the taxpayer, whenever the taxpayer accepted an appointment to conduct a public inquiry of the kind under consideration he became, in my judgment, the holder of an 'office' and he continued to hold it until he completed his task by submitting his report. For these reasons, I concur in holding that the appeal of the Solicitor General should be allowed.

LORD LOWRY. My Lords, I gratefully adopt the summary of the facts contained in the speech of my noble and learned friend Lord Bridge, which I have had the opportunity of reading in draft. I find, too, that I respectfully agree with nearly all of what he is about to say and also with most of what has already been said by my noble and learned friend *a*   Lord Edmund-Davies. Nevertheless, with regret and inevitably with some diffidence, I have reached a different conclusion on the point at issue.

I consider that the taxpayer was not the holder of an office (and therefore was not assessable under Sch E) because, in my opinion, the mere appointment to perform a function (in this case the statutory function of holding a public local inquiry) does not by itself mean that the person appointed holds an office within the meaning of Sch E.

b   To say that the alleged office has no name, since the word 'inspector' is merely a convenient description, may put the matter too simply, but it is the base from which I set out. There is no statutory definition of 'office', but everyone has been content with the following definition from the Oxford English Dictionary:

> 'A position or place to which certain duties are attached, esp. one of a more or less public character; a position of trust, authority, or service under constituted authority; a place in the administration of government, the public service, the
> *c*   direction of a corporation, company, society, etc.'

The word 'position' here is ambiguous, since by itself it may either denote a situation in which someone is placed or a specific post to which he is appointed. The latter meaning seems to apply more naturally to an office, particularly in this case, when one looks at such statutory provisions as para 7 of Sch 9 to the Income Tax Act 1952 and now *d*   s 181(1) and Sch E, Case I, of the 1970 Act, which refer to the holder 'of any office or employment' and 'the duties of the office or employment'. It is also permissible to consider the words 'office or employment' elsewhere in Part VIII of the 1970 Act: see ss 182, 187 and 188 and Sch 8. Accordingly, I consider that the ordinary meaning of 'office' in this context involves the notion of a specific post to which a person can be appointed, which he can hold and which he can vacate. I concede that this is not the only sense in which the word can be understood, but I feel satisfied that it is the primary sense and that *e*   the words 'position or place' in the dictionary definition ordinarily have a similar meaning.

It would seem to follow that, when we describe the taxpayer as the holder of an office, we are using the word 'office' not in its ordinary meaning but with a special meaning which the ordinary use of English would not readily recognise. Much less, I suggest, *f*   would he be likely to think that, after carrying out a number of inquiries, the taxpayer had held a series of offices. The taxpayer has argued for a limited meaning of the word 'office', but I consider that the ordinary meaning would serve his purpose, but not the purpose of the Revenue.

There is a subtler but perhaps more cogent argument in the taxpayer's favour than the mere absence of a name. The 'office' comes into being with the act of appointment and automatically ceases to exist when the person appointed concludes his task. I think that *g*   to regard this as the holding of an office by the appointed person confuses his function with his so-called office. The taxpayer here was in one sense 'in an official position', but not, in my opinion, in an official post (or office). A genuine office does not lapse because the holder dies, retires or completes his assignment. To be in a position of authority is not necessarily to hold an office, and when you appoint somebody to *do* something you do not thereby appoint him to *be* something (in other words to hold an office), unless the *h*   Act or other relevant instrument says so.

It is unnecessary for me to review at length the history of the legislation or the earlier decisions. In both respects my work has again been done for me by my noble and learned friend Lord Bridge, and I have no trouble in accepting his illuminating comments on the cases. One can fairly say that the true ratio decidendi of this House in *Great Western Railway Co v Bater (Surveyor of Taxes)* [1922] 2 AC 1 was that Mr Hall held *j*   no office and that his employment was not public and that, in so far as other reasons were advanced, their Lordships were strongly influenced by r 1 of Sch (E) in the 1842 Act.

The decisions in all the cases reviewed are easily justified by reference to what I have called the ordinary meaning of 'office'. They also satisfy the full *Bater* test and we have no examples so far of a court's refusal to apply Sch E on the ground that *Bater* was not satisfied. Therefore the test has not been relevantly considered. Lord Bridge also rightly points out that the discussion embraces employment as well as office, and now the private as well as the public domain. It is therefore impossible to accept that employment (or, by the same token, office) must be 'permanent'; if so, Sch E could not apply to temporary employment or to an office created by name for the performance and completion of a specific task. On this branch of the argument it would be no answer for the taxpayer to fall back on Sch D, Case VI, when one thinks of the formerly different consequences of being taxed under this heading.

The reason for the decision of the General Commissioners must be deduced from para 8 of the case stated (see [1979] 1 All ER 648 at 650) where they said that the taxpayer's discharge of the duties of an inspector did not amount to the holding of an office—

'as the appointment was merely a transient, indeterminate, once-only execution of a task for which [the taxpayer] was peculiarly qualified, the nearest analogy to which was a barrister or solicitor conducting a case for a client.'

The commissioners' analogy with a barrister or solicitor is, in my view, misconceived, and I cannot find a meaning for 'indeterminate' which advances the argument. It is, however, clear that the commissioners found as they did on the ground that the taxpayer did not hold an office because his appointment was (or involved) merely a transient and once-only execution of a task.

Is that, speaking generally, a good reason in law for holding that Sch E did not apply? I think not, because a decision against Sch E based on complete acceptance of the *Bater* test is unsound in law, and the commissioners' decision appears to be so based. Where the Crown's argument goes astray, in my estimation, is in submitting, in effect, 'The *Bater* test is wrong and was accepted by the commissioners. Therefore we are right.'

I wish now to examine the judgment of Walton J, which was at the commencement of this appeal the only pronouncement in favour of the Crown. The learned judge set out four considerations which strongly appealed to him as showing that a person appointed to conduct an inquiry under the Acquisition of Land (Authorisation Procedure) Act 1946 was the holder of an office (see [1979] 1 All ER 648 at 654, [1979] 1 WLR 338 at 344). I would, by way of answer, draw attention to the observations critical of his arguments which were made by the learned judges of the Court of Appeal, Buckley, Ackner and Oliver LJJ (see [1980] 3 All ER 278 at 284–285, 288, 293–294, [1981] Ch 1 at 10–12, 15–16, 23–24). I consider, with due respect, that these comments entirely dispose of the case as it found favour with the learned judge at first instance. The first point, 'That the inspector has no employer', can only be based on a misapplication of what Lord Normand said in *Dale v Inland Revenue Comrs* [1953] 2 All ER 671 at 673, [1954] 1 1 at 26, which Walton J cited (see [1979] 1 All ER 648 at 653–654, [1979] 1 WLR 338 at 343–344). I note that he again mentions trustees and reverts to the fallacy of 'not employed, therefore holding office' (see [1979] 1 All ER 648 at 656, [1979] 1 WLR 338 at 346–347). (This reasoning resembles the Crown's argument that the absence of control over the inspector spells the holding of office rather than employment, which is equally a non sequitur since the real choice is between the holding of office and being engaged on an independent basis.) As to Walton J's second point, Ackner LJ shrewdly points out that the same could be said of an arbitrator. The judge's third point, although relevant, would also apply to an arbitrator. As for the last point, a second person appointed would not be a 'successor in office' in the ordinary way. To sum up, the four points do not in any way persuade me that the word 'office' and the phrase 'holder of an office' ought to receive the meaning which the Crown is compelled to give them in preference to what I have ventured to call the ordinary meaning.

It should also be remembered by those who would place emphasis on the public nature of the office, the statutory background and the public source of the remuneration that, since 1922, Sch E is capable of applying, in the right type of case, to private offices.

a
I respectfully agree with Walton J that the temporary nature of the 'office' is not by itself fatal to the Crown's argument nor is the method of payment.

The learned judge was rightly wary of accepting the Crown's point based on asking what profession the taxpayer was carrying on if he was not the holder of an office (see [1979] 1 All ER 648 at 655, [1979] 1 WLR 338 at 346). The words 'profession or vocation' can be given a wide meaning without strain. This point tends to dispose of the learned judge's further observations at [1979] 1 All ER 648 at 655–656, [1979] 1 WLR

b
338 at 346. After all, both businessmen and professional men (whether their main source of income is taxed under Sch D or Sch E) may undertake engagements of many kinds which do not involve their holding office or being employed. And yet the remuneration from such engagements can be taxed quite easily under Sch D.

If the course of the appeal in your Lordships' House was remarkable for one thing, it was the avoidance of detailed reference to the judgments delivered by a unanimous and

c
distinguished Court of Appeal, as if to say that all one had to consider was the rightness or wrongness of the *Bater* test. If I may indulge in a metaphor from the occupation of gold-mining, I would say (without any disrespect, I hope) that the *Bater* test is the crude ore which has now by a series of processes, most recently in the Court of Appeal, been refined into something of superior quality. Let me try to illustrate the point.

In *Great Western Railway Co v Bater (Surveyor of Taxes)* [1920] 3 KB 266 at 274 Rowlatt

d
J, whose opinion was indorsed by Lord Atkinson ([1922] 2 AC 1 at 15), thought that Sch E required 'a subsisting, permanent, substantive position, which had an existence independent of the person who filled it . . .' and (no doubt under the influence of r 1 of Sch (E) in the 1842 Act) went on to speak of an office or employment 'which went on and was filled in succession by successive holders'. I would digress to say that, if one could have overlooked the fatal absence of a public element, Mr Hall (as an employee) seems to me to have been capable of satisfying the exacting test which Rowlatt J laid down.

e
In the same case Lord Atkinson said ([1922] 2 AC 1 at 14):

'Again, the word "successor" is very significant. It seems to indicate continuity of the office or employment, and also to indicate the existence of something external to the person who may hold the one or exercise the other.'

f
(Rule 1 continues to have a strong influence here.)

Bater was followed by a series of cases which satisfied the *Bater* test, and therefore further refinement was unlikely in the meantime, but, like my noble and learned friend Lord Bridge, I do not forget the words of Harman LJ in *Mitchell (Inspector of Taxes) v Ross* [1960] 2 All ER 218 at 230, [1960] Ch 498 at 530:

g
'An office is a position or post which goes on without regard to the identity of the holder of it from time to time, as was said, in effect, by ROWLATT, J., in *Great Western Ry. Co. v. Bater* ([1920] 3 KB 266 at 274) and approved by LORD ATKIN in *McMillan v. Guest* ([1942] 1 All ER 606, [1942] AC 561).'

Thus, when the present case came to be decided, some refining had already been done. The emphasis on permanence and continuity had lessened and the possibility of

h
a once-only appointment had been recognised. But the concept of an office which exists independently of its holder still held sway.

Let me now consider what the Court of Appeal has said, starting with Buckley LJ ([1980] 3 All ER 278 at 280, [1981] Ch 1 at 5):

j
'In the present case we are faced with the problem of putting a meaning on an ordinary word in the English language, which has been used over a long period in income tax legislation. The courts have from time to time had to consider the proper meaning to be attributed to that ordinary English word in that legislation. It is not, in my judgment, in conflict with the principle enunciated by Lord Wilberforce to look at past decisions to discover what the courts in the past have

thought to be the appropriate meaning to attribute to that ordinary English word. In doing so, however, we should guard ourselves against treating as authoritative decisions which were reached for reasons which may no longer be appropriate.'

The learned Lord Justice carried this idea forward to his discussion of *Bater*: 'I would consequently accept that that decision should be regarded as coloured by the form of the legislation then in force' (see [1980] 3 All ER 278 at 282, [1981] Ch 1 at 7.) He adverted to the Oxford English Dictionary definition saying ([1980] 3 All ER 278 at 281, [1981] Ch 1 at 5):

'This appears to me to indicate, if any such clarification were necessary, that the office is something which is distinct from the holder of the office.'

It is fair comment to say that this view does not appear to have been dictated by the *Bater* test or the now repealed r 1 of the 1842 Sch E.

I also consider helpful the reflections of Buckley LJ that ([1980] 3 All ER 278 at 281, [1981] Ch 1 at 6):

'Before considering the authorities which bear on this question, I may perhaps be allowed to say in what sense, unguided by authority and without attempting to formulate a precise definition, I should be inclined to understand the word "office" as used in Sch E. An "office" in this context is, in my opinion, a post which can be recognised as existing, whether it be occupied for the time being or vacant, and which, if occupied, does not owe its existence in any way to the identity of the incumbent or his appointment to the post. It follows, I think, that the office must owe its existence to some constituent instrument, whether it be a charter, statute, declaration of trust, contract (other than a contract of personal service) or instrument of some other kind. It also follows, in my view, that the office must have a sufficient degree of continuance to admit of its being held by successive incumbents; it need not be capable of permanent or prolonged or indefinite existence, but it cannot be limited to the tenure of one man, for if it were so it would lack that independent existence which to my mind the word "office" imports.'

He then ([1980] 3 All ER 278 at 283, [1981] Ch 1 at 8) takes note of Lord Porter's observation about the position of the non-executive director in *McMillan v Guest (Inspector of Taxes)* [1942] 1 All ER 606 at 611, [1942] AC 561 at 570: 'That it is an office is, I think, plain. *It has permanency apart from the temporary holder* and is held in one of the specified corporations' (my emphasis).

Again ([1980] 3 All ER 278 at 284, [1981] Ch 1 at 9–10), he has neatly extracted from the speech of Lord Morris an important view of *Inland Revenue Comrs v Brander & Cruickshank* [1971] 1 All ER 36 at 41, [1971] 1 WLR 212 at 215:

'Even though the Companies Act 1948 does not require that there should be an appointment as registrar, a company must arrange that some person or persons should on its behalf perform the statutory duties of maintaining its register. In doing so, it may establish a position which successively will be held by different persons. If it does so the company may have created what could rationally for income tax purposes be called an office.'

After a review of the cases Buckley LJ said ([1980] 3 All ER 278 at 284, [1981] Ch 1 at 10): 'In particular I would draw attention to the frequent references to the characteristic of continuance.'

Dealing with what seems also in this House to be one of the Crown's main points, Buckley LJ said ([1980] 3 All ER 278 at 285–286, [1981] Ch 1 at 12):

'That the duties are statutory . . . cannot be denied. Nevertheless I for my part cannot regard these characteristics alone as sufficient to constitute the appointment an appointment to an "office".'

He concluded:

a
> 'So each appointment was personal to the taxpayer; it lacked the characteristic of independent existence and continuance which, in my judgment, is one of the essential characteristics of an "office".'

Ackner LJ ([1980] 3 All ER 278 at 286, [1981] Ch 1 at 13) reminds us of what Lord Wright said in *McMillan's* case [1942] 1 All ER 606 at 609, [1942] AC 561 at 567 that the
b word 'office' has to be construed in relation to the facts of the particular case—

> 'according to the ordinary use of language and the dictates of common sense, with due regard to the requirement that there must be *some degree* of permanence and publicity in the office.' (My emphasis.)

(The reference to publicity was made because s 18 of the Finance Act 1922 did not
c apply.)

Ackner LJ also drew attention ([1980] 3 All ER 278 at 286–287, [1981] Ch 1 at 13) to Lord Guthrie's observation in the Court of Session in *Inland Revenue Comrs v Brander & Cruickshank* (1969) 46 Tax Cas 574 at 584:

d
> 'What the Special Commissioners had to decide was whether in the particular cases of the two companies the Respondents were holders of substantive positions to which duties were attached, and which had the quality of permanency irrespective of the particular holder's tenure, or whether they merely did some work of a particular kind for the companies.'

Lord Migdale's similar observation (at 587) is noted. It is also useful to meditate on the passages from *Davies (Inspector of Taxes) v Braithwaite* [1931] 2 KB 628, [1931] All ER Rep
e 792 which Ackner LJ quoted and also his gloss on these passages ([1980] 3 All ER 278 at 289, [1981] Ch 1 at 17–18):

> 'I return to the character of the appointment by the Minister of the taxpayer. It was a temporary ad hoc appointment confined to the taxpayer. He was not appointed to a position which had an existence of its own. It had no quality of
f permanency about it. It was conceded that it subsisted only from the date when he was appointed to the date when the report of the inquiry was delivered to the Secretary of State.'

I respectfully associate myself with Ackner LJ's final paragraph ([1980] 3 All ER 278 at 289–290, [1981] Ch 1 at 18).

Oliver LJ strikes a first blow for the taxpayer by saying ([1980] 3 All ER 278 at 290,
g [1981] Ch 1 at 19):

> 'It is however worth noting that there is nothing in the 1946 Act itself to indicate the machinery by which inquiries are to be made. There is no office of "inquirer" or "inspector" created by the Act but merely a provision authorising the Minister to "cause to be held" the appropriate inquiries.'

h
He also had criticisms to make of the Crown's heavy reliance on the public character of the duties (see [1980] 3 All ER 278 at 291, [1981] Ch 1 at 20).

Oliver LJ then gives us his point of view on the characteristics of independence and permanence. After reviewing the authorities and having recognised the drafting changes, he adverts to *Inland Revenue Comrs v Brander & Cruickshank* [1971] 1 All ER 36,
j [1971] 1 WLR 212 and says ([1980] 3 All ER 278 at 293, [1981] Ch 1 at 23): 'So here, once again, emphasis is laid on the concept of continuance apart from the individual holder.'

I think I can fairly summarise the Court of Appeal's attitude by saying that all the judges recognised the changes since *Bater* and accepted the principle in *Farrell v Alexander* [1976] 2 All ER 721, [1977] AC 59, but still considered that a degree of permanence and continuity was essential and were unwilling to disregard a clear thread of supporting opinion which ran through a long line of cases.

The characteristic of permanence need only amount to the independent existence of an office, as opposed to its incidental creation and automatic demise with the beginning and the end respectively of the appointment of an individual to perform a task. And the continuity required need have no magic beyond the existence of the post (subject always to its abolition ab extra) after the holder left it, with the *possibility* of a successor being appointed.

The Crown's argument in your Lordships' House was well and faithfully outlined in advance in its printed case to which I shall now address myself.

Paragraph 7 embodies the Crown's primary submission, that the words 'office or employment' are ordinary English words and should be given their 'ordinary and natural meaning in modern English'. I accept the proposition, but at the same time believe that it would lead us away from, and not towards, the conclusion advocated by the Crown. I also note the reference to the Chambers Twentieth Century Dictionary definition, 'a function or duty: a position imposing certain duties, etc.' It must be obvious that the 'meaning of function or duty', however it might suit the Crown's case, is not the meaning to be ascribed in this context. I might also note at this point the Crown's chapter from Bacon's Abridgment which treats of the nature of an office, if only to observe that the definition which was most helpful to the Crown was too wide to have applied and therefore was not relied on by it; see also, for a similar result, *Graham v White (Inspector of Taxes)* [1972] 1 All ER 1159, [1972] 1 WLR 874.

Paragraphs 12 and 13 of the Crown's case highlights the courts' reliance in *Bater's* case on r 2 as a guide. That is a fair point, but it does not explain why the cases decided since the repeal of r 2 by the Finance Act 1956 still lay stress on independent existence, a degree of permanence and a certain continuity. A better point for the Crown, I freely admit, is that made by my noble and learned friend Lord Bridge that subsequent cases have not until now called for a critical approach to Rowlatt J's definition.

Paragraph 15 discusses in detail the role of para 2 of Sch 9 to the 1952 Act; it strikes me (because it simply dealt with the *procedure* of assessment) that its later repeal ought not to affect the construction of the words 'office or employment'.

The assumption in para 17 of the case that the requirement of independent existence is derived from r 1 in the 1842 Act is not, in my opinion, justified. I refer in support to the judgment of the members of the Court of Appeal, who freely acknowledged the passing of r 1 and its successor, para 2.

With regard to para 17(b), Lord Greene MR was in *McMillan v Guest (Inspector of Taxes)* [1940] 4 All ER 452, [1941] 1 KB 258 specifically referring to 'the office of director'.

Paragraph 17(d) mentions *Dale v Inland Revenue Comrs* [1953] 2 All ER 671, [1954] AC 11, where there was an office of trustee; Lord Normand's speech does not help the Crown.

With regard to para 17(e), I would point out that the quotation from *Inland Revenue Comrs v Brander & Cruickshank* as reported in both 1970 SC 116 at 121–122 and 46 Tax Cas 574 at 581 ends with the words 'a particular task', not 'a particular piece of work'. In any event, the selected person is 'appointed to a position' and I do not see where the point takes the Crown.

Paragraph 18, where the concept of continuity is discounted, is an important part of the Crown's argument. My observations are as follows: (1) an office can be created for an occasion but that, in my view involves creating an office, which can be filled by the appointing authority, and (2) if the person to be appointed refuses or resigns or dies before or after taking office, one must appoint a successor or an alternative or else leave the office vacant or abolish it. That is an example of a degree of permanence or continuity, although not necessarily of long duration. The situation is not typical of the present case where the 'office' can be created only by appointing someone to *do* something and where the 'office' does not have to remain vacant or be abolished after the holder has gone.

The position of judge's marshal is an office, but at least a successor in this short-lived office can, if necessary, be contemplated: the office exists independently of the holder. The same is true of a presiding officer at an election.

In *Taylor v Provan (Inspector of Taxes)* [1974] 1 All ER 1201, [1975] AC 194 the motive for the appointment was personal to the appointee, but there was an *office* of director to which he was appointed, which he could vacate and to which others had been appointed in the past and must be appointed in the future while the company existed and the law continued as it was.

Paragraph 19 of the case seeks to say that because certain tenures of office involve no contract and some contracts do not involve holding an office, therefore the taxpayer's engagement (because not contractual) involved his holding an office. The argument is fallacious because: (1) there was an oral contract in *Inland Revenue Comrs v Brander & Cruickshank*, and yet the taxpayers held an office; (2) the example accordingly fails to illustrate why a judge holds an office; (3) if an arbitrator does not hold an office, this is not because he is appointed by virtue of a contract between the parties and a further contract between them and the arbitrator; (4) the consultants in *Mitchell (Inspector of Taxes) v Ross* [1961] 3 All ER 49, [1962] AC 813 had contracts but were also holding offices or employments; (5) all employments the emoluments of which fall to be assessed under Sch E (like the emoluments of offices) arise from contracts between employer and employee; and (6) the taxpayer in this case had a contract by virtue of the offer and acceptance of an engagement on agreed pecuniary and other terms; this is a neutral factor, but not according to para 19.

Paragraph 21 kept open an alternative argument that the taxpayer was employed, but the Crown did not pursue this line. The fact that he could not have hoped to succeed on this point has some relevance, because most offices, other than that of a judge, can credibly be presented as a form of employment.

It is tempting to seek a logical solution, but this is not always reliable in tax cases. The contrast now, however, is not between public and private occupations but between trade, profession or vocation on the one hand and office or employment on the other. We might therefore look for logical links between office and employment and should not be too ready to equate an independent contractor with an office holder, since the latter has a deemed employer and his holding of an office has much in common with employment.

The Crown conceded that a private arbitrator does not hold an office within Sch E, but, in my opinion, such an arbitrator would hold at least a private office if the Crown's main submission were correct. The mere fact that two parties agree to appoint an arbitrator in certain eventualities instead of going to court does not, in my view, make the slightest difference to the question whether the person appointed to hold the arbitration holds an office by virtue of this appointment while he is seised of the task. He has at least a familiar name (of 'arbitrator'). This, however, emphasises the importance of my second point, that a person does *not* hold a so-called office if it comes into being only as the inevitable accompaniment of the fact of the alleged holder's appointment to perform a task: the 'office' has no independent existence and is 'distinct from the holder'. This, I consider, is important, quite independently of the *Bater* view of permanence and continuity. Nor do I omit to emphasise that an arbitrator under the Arbitration Act 1950 (or the corresponding legislation outside England and Wales) exercises a judicial jurisdiction which for interlocutory, enforcement and appellate purposes is tied by statute to our public court system.

I respectfully agree that it would be unsound to deny the existence of an office or employment in every case where a post did not exhibit all the indicia postulated by Rowlatt J but I would not regard *Taylor v Provan (Inspector of Taxes)* as providing support for the Crown. There the office was that of a director and its occupant clearly a Sch E taxpayer. This was due to the nature of the office, and its temporary occupation by a person of particular talents for a specific, limited purpose did not provide a precedent helpful to the Crown. I do not overlook Lord Reid's words (see [1974] 1 All ER 1201 at 1204–1205, [1975] AC 194 at 205–206); neither do I forget what Lord Wilberforce said

([1974] 1 All ER 1202 at 1213, [1975] AC 194 at 215): 'A director with a special assignment is nonetheless a director . . .'

The taxpayer's case is not helped by reliance on s 204 of the 1970 Act or by reference to the practical difficulty, which is quite common, of assessing a taxpayer under Schs D and E. On this point I entirely agree with my noble and learned friends. I think, however, that consideration of the position of recorders and deputy judges does not advance the Crown's cause since, as deputy holders of an office, they are in a class of their own, sharing much of the character of a locum tenens which was notice by Upjohn J in *Mitchell (Inspector of Taxes) v Ross* [1959] 3 All ER 341 at 350, [1960] Ch 145 at 169:

'The phrase "locum tenens" is in fact a most apt and appropriate expression to describe the work. The specialist in doing such work is in fact holding the post of another. He is for the time being exercising the functions and holding the public office of another.'

I might just point out that the Crown strongly relied on *Mitchell (Inspector of Taxes) v Ross* and contended that the present case was a fortiori. This could never be so except in the limited sense that Dr Ross and his colleagues were rightly taxed under two different schedules although they were at all times doing their usual work of treating the sick. But that is not significant when one remembers that a person could be taxed under Sch D in respect of two different trades or professions or under Sch E in respect of different offices or employments. Dr Ross was clearly occupying a part-time but permanent post in the health service which satisfied every criterion of the *Bater* test (see [1960] 2 All ER 218 at 225–226, [1960] Ch 488 at 522 per Lord Evershed MR). It was quite unnecessary for the Crown in that case to advance any of the submissions which are essential to the Crown's present case.

Schedule D speaks of 'annual profits or gains', but Rowlatt J in *Ryall (Inspector of Taxes) v Hoare* [1923] 2 KB 447 at 455, [1923] All ER Rep 528 at 530 explains the meaning of 'annual' as being appropriate to occasional earnings or even a single venture.

In approaching this problem of statutory interpretation I have kept in mind two further points. One is that the onus is on the Crown which asserts that Sch E applies. As Lord Sterndale MR said in *Great Western Railway Co v Bater (Surveyor of Taxes)* [1921] 2 KB 128 at 136: '. . . where a question of taxation arises, the subject should be able to know clearly whether he is taxable or not.'

The other is what was said by Lord Simonds in *St Aubyn (L M) v Attorney General* [1951] 2 All ER 473 at 485, [1952] AC 15 at 32 and adopted by Pearce LJ in *Mitchell (Inspector of Taxes) v Ross* [1960] 2 All ER 218 at 228, [1960] Ch 498 at 526:

'The question is not at what transaction the section is according to some alleged general purpose aimed, but what transaction its language according to its natural meaning fairly and squarely hits.'

Following the example of Lord Westbury in *Bater's* case [1922] 2 AC 1 at 30–31 and respectfully sharing his view of the difficulties of the tax legislation, I consider that my only safe course is to decide the individual case before us without showing too much concern for supposed analogies and contradictions, but remembering that the case, if decided in favour of the Crown, would provide the first example of 'innominate office' under Sch E.

I consider that the General Commissioners, in so far as they accepted the full *Bater* formula as their guide, misdirected themselves in law, but, on the view which I take of the interpretation of the phrase 'office or employment' (which is a question of law), there is only one correct answer on the facts: the taxpayer was not holding an office. The decision of the court below should therefore be affirmed and the appeal dismissed.

Since preparing this speech I have had the opportunity of reading in draft the speeches of my noble and learned friends Lord Wilberforce and Lord Salmon, with which I most respectfully concur.

LORD BRIDGE OF HARWICH. My Lords, the important question raised by this
appeal, which we are told is a test case, is what is: the correct basis of assessment to
income tax of the remuneration of persons appointed under statutory powers to hold
public local inquiries of a kind which have become a familiar feature of the contemporary
social scene and an important part of the machinery of administrative law regulating
relationships between the executive and the citizen? The question depends on the
construction of the relevant provisions of the Income and Corporation Taxes Act 1970.
The Crown contends that such remuneration falls to be charged in respect of 'any office
or employment on emoluments therefrom' under Case I of Sch E (s 181). The taxpayer
contends that the tax is to be charged in respect of 'profits or gains arising or accruing
. . . from . . . any profession or vocation not contained in any other Schedule' under Case
II of Sch D (ss 108 and 109).

The taxpayer is a civil engineer. During the years of assessment in question (1973–74
and 1974–75) he was one of a panel of some 60 persons who were invited from time to
time by the Secretary of State for the Environment to hold public local inquiries. He was
free to accept or refuse any such invitation. If he accepted he was paid daily fees
according to the length of the inquiry with notional time added for preparatory reading,
travelling time, site visits and writing his report. In respect of these earnings he was
assessed to tax under Sch E. He appealed against the assessments to the General
Commissioners, who concluded that his—

> 'discharge of the duties of an inspector holding a public local inquiry did not
> amount to the holding of an office within the meaning of Case I of Sch E as the
> appointment was merely a transient, indeterminate, once-only execution of a task
> for which he was peculiarly qualified, the nearest analogy to which was a barrister
> or solicitor conducting a case for a client.'

(See [1979] 1 All ER 648 at 650.)

They accordingly allowed the appeal. On appeal by case stated to the High Court,
Walton J reversed the decision of the commissioners and restored the Sch E assessments
(see [1979] 1 All ER 648, [1979] 1 WLR 338). The Court of Appeal (Buckley, Ackner and
Oliver LJJ) in turn allowed the taxpayer's appeal (see [1980] 3 All ER 278, [1981] Ch 1).
From that decision the Crown now appeals to your Lordships' House.

The Crown does not and could not say that the taxpayer held a continuing office in the
exercise of which he held successive inquiries. On the contrary, the essence of the
Crown's case is that each separate appointment of the taxpayer to hold a public local
inquiry constituted him the holder of an office created ad hoc by the appointment itself
and which subsisted only from the time of the appointment until the duties of the office
were completed by the submission to the Secretary of State of the taxpayer's report.
Herein lies the essence of the controversy, for it is argued by the Crown and accepted in
the decision of Walton J that the term 'office' as used in Sch E in the 1970 Act is capable
of embracing such a temporary ad hoc appointment, whereas the Court of Appeal, on the
other hand, giving more precise and explicit expression to the view which no doubt
underlies the General Commissioners' decision, have held it to be an essential attribute
of an 'office' in this context that it should, in the language of Buckley LJ, 'have a sufficient
degree of continuance to 'admit of its being held by successive incumbents' (see [1980]
3 All ER 278 at 281, [1981] Ch 1 at 6).

It seems probable that during the two years in question the taxpayer held inquiries of
various kinds under the provisions of different statutes. But your Lordships must
perforce proceed on the assumption that nothing turns on any differences in the statutory
provisions under which he was from time to time appointed, since both parties invite
your Lordships to accept as typical and to treat as decisive of the appeal a particular
appointment of the taxpayer, made in June 1975, under s 5 of para 4(2) of Sch 1 to the
Acquisition of Land (Authorisation Procedure) Act 1946 to hold a public local inquiry for
the purpose of hearing objections and representations with regard to a proposed

compulsory purchase of land required for a trunk road, such inquiry being governed by
the Compulsory Purchase by Ministers (Inquiries Procedure) Rules 1967, SI 1967 No   *a*
720. It is important to consider the powers and duties of a person so appointed. He can
compel witnesses to attend, to give evidence and to produce documents. If they refuse
they are subject to penalties. In the conduct of the inquiry and in making his report he
is under a duty to act independently, impartially and fairly. Subject to the express
provisions of the 1967 rules, the procedure at the inquiry is in his discretion. After the
inquiry he is under a duty to make his report to the Secretary of State, which is to include   *b*
his findings of fact and his recommendations, if any, or his reasons for not making any
recommendations. In short, his function is clearly, if not judicial, at least quasi-judicial
in character. It should be added that under the relevant statutory provisions the person
appointed to hold the public local inquiry has no designation or title and under the 1967
rules he is simply referred to as the 'appointed person'. The commonly used appellation
'inspector' finds no place in this statutory code. I mention this, but I do not myself attach   *c*
any significance to the innominate character of the office, if office it be.

The relevant definition of the word 'office' in the Oxford English Dictionary is:

> 'A position or place to which certain duties are attached, esp. one of a more or less
> public character; a position of trust, authority, or service under constituted
> authority; a place in the administration of government, the public service, the
> direction of a corporation, company, society, etc.'   *d*

At first blush, it seems to me that the appointed person holding a public local inquiry
under the provisions to which I have referred occupies an 'office' which falls fairly and
squarely within each of the three limbs of this definition. He occupies a position to
which duties of a public character are attached. He is in a position of authority. He
holds a place in the administration of government. To this I would add, as reinforcing   *e*
my view that he holds an 'office' in the ordinary sense of the word, three of the four
factors which weighed with Walton J. First, the 'appointed person' has no employer in
any ordinary sense; he exercises his functions quite independently. Second, he is not
acting in any personal capacity, but in a capacity which derives its existence wholly from,
and is clothed with powers and duties by, his statutory appointment; this embraces
under a single head the factors listed as (2) and (3) in Walton J's enumeration (see [1979]   *f*
1 All ER 648 at 654, [1979] 1 WLR 338 at 344).

I confess that, with all respect, I do not share Buckley's LJ's expressed inclination,
'unguided by authority', to understand the word 'office' in the context of Sch E as
connoting—

> 'a post which can be recognised as existing, whether it be occupied for the time
> being or vacant, and which, if occupied, does not owe its existence in any way to the   *g*
> identity of the incumbent or his appointment to the post.'

(See [1980] 3 All ER 278 at 281, [1981] Ch 1 at 6.)

If 'office' is given its ordinary meaning, then, in my opinion, the taxpayer held an
office whenever he was appointed to hold a public local inquiry and the fees paid to him
were the emoluments of that office. Conversely, when holding such inquiries, he was   *h*
certainly not practising his profession as a civil engineer and the fees could only be
brought within the ambit of Sch D, Case II on the footing that the holding of statutory
inquiries is itself a separate 'vocation', which involves, to my mind, an unacceptable
straining of language.

However, it is not for the taxpayer to establish the basis on which he is properly
assessable. If he can successfully impugn the Sch E assessments, he is entitled to have the   *j*
decision of the Court of Appeal in his favour upheld. It remains, therefore, to consider
whether either the authorities on which the Court of Appeal relied or anything in the
provisions governing assessments under Sch E, as now embodied in the 1970 Act, lead to
the conclusion that the word 'office' in Sch E is to be construed as having some more
restricted meaning than that which it ordinarily bears.

To understand the authorities it is necessary to bear in mind certain aspects of the relevant history of income tax legislation. Under the Income Tax Act 1842 tax was charged under Sch (D) on 'the annual Profits or Gains arising or accruing ... from any Profession, Trade, *Employment*, or Vocation'; it was charged under Sch (E) on 'every *public* Office or Employment of Profit'. The added emphasis in each case is mine. These charging words and the distinction they drew between the two schedules survived unaltered in the consolidating Income Tax Act 1918. The Finance Act 1922 made the important change of transferring from Sch D to Sch E, with exceptions which are immaterial for present purposes, the charge to tax on the profits of any 'office or employment'. Hence the public element in Sch E ceased to be of importance and ever since 1922 it is again sufficient for present purposes to say that, although the form of Sch E was recast by the Finance Act 1956, the basis of charge under the schedule has remained in substance unaltered.

The first of the 'Rules for charging the said Duties' under Sch (E) in the 1842 Act is of crucial importance. It provides, so far as material:

'The said Duties shall be annually charged on the Persons respectively having, using, or exercising the Offices or Employments of Profit mentioned in the said Schedule (E.) ... and each Assessment in respect of such Offices or Employments shall be in force for One whole Year, and shall be levied for such Year without any new Assessment, notwithstanding a Change may have taken place in any such Office or Employment, on the Person for the Time having or exercising the same; provided that the Person quitting such Office or Employment, or dying within the Year, or his Executors or Administrators, shall be liable for the Arrears due before or at the Time of his so quitting such Office or Employment, or dying, and for such further Portion of Time as shall then have elapsed, to be settled by the respective Commissioners, and his Successor shall be repaid such Sums as he shall have paid on account of such Portion of the Year as aforesaid ...'

The substance of this rule reappeared in the 1918 and 1952 consolidating Acts, but was finally repealed, save in so far as it preserves the liability of personal representatives for unpaid tax, by the Finance Act 1956.

In *Great Western Railway Co v Bater (Surveyor of Taxes)* [1920] 3 KB 266 (Rowlatt J); [1921] 2 KB 128 (CA); [1922] 2 AC 1 (HL) the railway company had been assessed to tax in respect of the salary of a clerk in the company's employ. The Income Tax Act 1860, s 6 made the employing company liable for 'the Duties payable under Schedule (E.) in respect of all Offices and Employments of Profit held in or under any Railway Company'. As your Lordships' House eventually held, Lord Buckmaster dissenting this provision, on its true construction, only applied to offices and employments having the necessary public character to bring them within Sch (E) of the 1842 Act and the ratio of the decision was that the employment of the clerk in question lacked that attribute. But the importance of the case for present purposes is in the observations of Rowlatt J at first instance and of Lord Atkinson in this House. To appreciate their true significance it is necessary to cite the relevant passages at some length. Rowlatt J said ([1920] 3 KB 266 at 273–274):

'But it is contended, and this is the real point in the case, that this man Hall is not the holder of an office or employment of profit at all. It is said that he is just one of a number of clerks. I gather that is the point, although it is not specifically so stated in the case before me. It is said that the position which he holds is not the sort of office that is referred to in this Schedule, and it is pointed out that under rule 1 of Sch (E) in the Act of 1842 the assessment is to be made for a year in respect of the office, and that it shall be in force for a whole year and levied without any new assessment, notwithstanding a change has taken place in the office or employment, on the person having or exercising the same. In this case that would not have effect, because the assessment would be on the railway company. Then it is pointed out that in the case of a man dying or leaving the office he is responsible for the proportion of arrears and the proportionate part of the current year. It is argued, and to my mind argued most forcibly, that that shows that what those who used the language of the Act of 1842 meant when they spoke of an office or an employment of profit was an office or employment which was a subsisting, permanent, substantive position, which had an existence independent of the person who filled it, and which went on and was filled in succession by successive holders, and that if a man was engaged to do any duties which might be assigned to him, whatever the terms on which he was engaged, his employment to do those duties did not create an office to which those duties were attached; he was merely employed to do certain things, and the so-called office or employment was merely the aggregate of the activities of the particular man for the time being. I myself think that that contention is sound, but having regard to the state of the authorities I do not think I ought to give effect to that contention. My own view is that Parliament in using this language in 1842 meant by an office a substantive thing that existed apart from the holder of the office.'

Lord Atkinson, quoting the important provisions of r 1 under Sch (E) in the 1842 Act, comments on them as follows ([1922] 2 AC 1 at 14–15):

'That is, the tax for the year shall be assessed upon the person holding the office or exercising the employment at the time the assessment is made. A proviso is then introduced adjusting, when the change contemplated has taken place, the burden of the tax between the persons who together have filled the office or exercised the employment during the entire year of assessment ... Thus the entire year of assessment seems to be treated as a unit of service, and the salary as a unit of recompense, not an aggregate of a number of smaller sums payable at different times, and each recompensing the service rendered during an independent fraction of the year. Again, the word "successor" is very significant. It seems to indicate continuity of the office or employment, and also to indicate the existence of something external to the person who may hold the one or exercise the other. Employment of profit, if it be not identical with office, is thus treated as something closely akin to it. I fully concur in the opinion happily expressed by Rowlatt J. in the following passage of his judgment.'

And he quotes from the passage I have already cited, beginning at the words 'It is argued ...'

It is especially to be noted that the opinion of Rowlatt J indorsed by Lord Atkinson, that what was required under Sch (E) in the 1842 Act was 'a subsisting, permanent, substantive position, which had an existence independent of the person who filled it', applied alike to an office *or* an employment. It is also clear, to my mind, that they were constrained to this opinion solely by the language of the rule on which they expressly relied.

In *McMillan v Guest (Inspector of Taxes)* [1942] 1 All ER 606 at 607, 608, 611, [1942] AC 561 at 564, 566, 570 there are observations in the speeches of Lord Atkin, Lord Wright and Lord Porter which in effect adopt, expressly or by implication, the view of what constitutes an office under Sch E derived from Rowlatt J and Lord Atkinson in *Bater's* case. But since it was there undisputed that the taxpayer held an office in what I may call the *Bater* sense and the point presently at issue for your Lordships' decision was, therefore, never argued, I cannot see that these dicta add any independent weight to what was said in *Bater's* case.

Similar considerations apply to the dictum of Harman LJ in *Mitchell (Inspector of Taxes) v Ross* [1960] 2 All ER 218 at 230, [1960] Ch 488 at 530, where he observed:

'An office is a position or post which goes on without regard to the identity of the holder of it from time to time, as was said, in effect, by ROWLATT, J., in *Great Western*

Ry. Co. v. Bater ([1920] 3 KB 266 at 274) and approved by LORD ATKIN in *McMillan v. Guest* ([1942] 1 All ER 606, [1942] AC 561).'

Finally, in *Inland Revenue Comrs v Brander & Cruickshank* [1971] 1 All ER 36 at 41, [1971] 1 WLR 212 at 215, where your Lordships' House affirmed the Special Commissioners and the Court of Session in holding that a firm of advocates employed as registrars of a number of companies were, as such, the holders of offices whose emoluments were assessable under Sch E, Lord Morris said:

'A duty is imposed on a company to keep a register of members (Companies Act 1948, s 110). Even though the Companies Act 1948 does not require that there should be an appointment as registrar, a company must arrange that some person or persons should on its behalf perform the statutory duties of maintaining its register. In doing so, it may establish a position which successively will be held by different persons. If its does so the company may have created what could rationally for income tax purposes be called an office. In *McMillan v Guest* [1942] 1 All ER 606 at 607, [1942] AC 561 at 564 Lord Atkin, while pointing out that there is no statutory definition of "office" was prepared to accept what Rowlatt J had said in *Great Western Ry Co v Bater* [1920] 3 KB 266 at 274 (as adopted by Lord Atkinson ([1922] 2 AC 1 at 15)) as being a generally sufficient statement of meaning. Rowlatt J had referred to ([1920] 3 KB 266 at 274): ". . . a subsisting, permanent, substantive position, which had an existence independent of the person who filled it, and which went on and was filled in succession by successive holders . . .".'

It will thus be seen that all the relevant authorities hark back to *Bater's* case. Your Lordships have no need to quarrel with any decision that the holder of an office which *does* exhibit the *Bater* criteria of a Sch E office is properly assessable under Sch E. But there is certainly no case which establishes the converse of that proposition. I hope I can say without any disrespect that the indorsement of the opinion of Rowlatt J and Lord Atkinson in all the cases following *Bater's* case has been quite uncritical, since there has been, so far as I can discover from any report we have looked at, no occasion before the instant case when any court or your Lordships' House has been invited to criticise that opinion, still less to re-examine the foundation on which it rests to see if it is still valid as applied to the phrase 'office or employment' in Sch E in the form it assumed in 1956, which reappears in the 1970 consolidating Act.

It is precisely such a re-examination that your Lordships now have to undertake. It leads, in my opinion, inevitably to the conclusion that the opinion is no longer good law. The rule on which both Rowlatt J and Lord Atkinson based their interpretation has gone. Moreover, now that Sch E embraces all employments, it surely would be absurd to suggest that 'employment' under the schedule can be limited to 'a subsisting, permanent, substantive position which has an existence independent of the person who fills it'. If that construction no longer applies to 'employment' in Sch E, I can see no logic whatever in continuing to apply it to 'office'. So far as authority is concerned, therefore, your Lordships are, in my opinion, wholly unconstrained and free to give the word 'office' its ordinary dictionary meaning.

Counsel for the taxpayer sought to support the restricted interpretation of 'office' in Sch E, independently of authority, by reference to its context in the 1970 Act. He referred to s 204. It is pursuant to regulations made under this section that the familiar tax tables are prepared which govern the deduction of tax under the PAYE system from emoluments assessable under Sch E. He relied in particular on s 204(3) which provides;

'The said tax tables shall be constructed with a view to securing that, so far as possible—(a) the total income tax payable in respect of any income assessable under Schedule E for any year of assessment is deducted from such income paid during that year, and (b) the income tax deductible or repayable on the occasion of any payment of, or on net account of, any such income is such that the total net income

tax deducted since the beginning of the year of assessment bears to the total income
tax payable for the year the same proportion that the part of the year which ends   *a*
with the date of the payment bears to the whole year.'

He pointed out, rightly, that there would be great practical difficulty in determining
accurately in advance the appropriate PAYE coding to regulate deductions from the
emoluments of an office holder if those emoluments were irregular and unpredictable,
especially when other relevant factors, eg the office holder's tax liability in respect of
other income assessable under Sch D, were unknown at the time when the deductions   *b*
had to be made. It is argued that the necessity to avoid this practical difficulty should
lead us to the conclusion that a person in the position of the taxpayer in this case cannot
be the holder of a series of offices under Sch E.

The argument, in my opinion, loses most, if not all, of its force if the Crown can point
to other undoubted holders of offices under Sch E whose position is such as to give rise
to the same practical difficulty in relation to PAYE deductions. This leads me to consider   *c*
the position of recorders. No one could doubt that the recorder of a borough before the
Courts Act 1971 was the holder of an office under Sch E. Recorders appointed under the
Courts Act 1971 are in a somewhat different position. Their appointment is for a specific
term: see s 21(3). Their jurisidiction is not, like that of the old recorder, confined to any
one place. They assume an obligation to be available to sit in the Crown Court for a
minimum number of days in a year (normally 20) though in practice they may not be   *d*
called on to sit, or may be excused from sitting, for this minimum, or conversely may sit
for many more days. Though the point was not formally conceded, it was not seriously
argued that these latter-day recorders are not the holders of offices under Sch E, as, in my
opinion, they clearly are. The practical difficulty of determining the appropriate PAYE
coding of recorders must be no less acute than it would be in the case of persons in the
position of the taxpayer. Hence I remain unimpressed by counsel's argument based on   *e*
s 204 of the 1970 Act.

In considering, in the course of argument, the position of recorders, your Lordships
were naturally also invited to consider the position of deputy High Court and circuit
judges. These are appointed under s 24 of the Courts Act 1971 by the Lord Chancellor
and the appointment may be 'during such period or on such occasions as he thinks fit'.
It is clear that an occasional appointment may be, and sometimes is, made ad hoc for the   *f*
trial of a single case. Under r 12 of Sch 9 to the Income Tax Act 1952 the deputy holder
of an office was expressly brought within Sch E. But this provision has since disappeared
from the code. I am not sure what, if any, significance to attach to this. But I cannot
doubt that a deputy High Court or circuit judge, whether appointed for a period, or ad
hoc to conduct a particular trial, is the holder of an office under Sch E. I appreciate, of
course, that this conclusion may be justified on the footing that the deputy judge   *g*
occupies for the time being what is essentially the same office as the regular judge and
thus is by no means decisive of the issue in this appeal.

I do not think any real assistance is to be gained by considering examples of various
statutory referees or arbitrators whose appointment is necessarily ad hoc. They may
provide more or less apt analogies with 'appointed persons' under the code your Lordships
are considering, but they are analogies of a kind calculated to beg, rather than to answer,   *h*
the question. Nor do I think that the taxpayer can take much comfort from the
concession made by the Crown, rightly in my view, that a private arbitrator does not
hold an office under Sch E. The conduct of private arbitrations may be largely regulated
by statute, but the arbitrator derives his jurisdiction to decide the dispute referred to him
exclusively from the consent of the parties and herein lies the critical distinction between
his position and that of a person exercising a judicial or quasi-judicial jurisdiction which   *j*
derives from a statutory appointment.

Looking at the matter broadly and considering, in so far as one may properly do so
when construing a taxing statute, the policy of the Act, I can certainly see no sensible
reason which would make it appropriate to differentiate the basis of assessment to

income tax of persons remunerated out of public funds for performing public, statutory,
a judicial or quasi-judicial functions on an occasional basis, according to whether they hold
a continuing nominal appointment in which they act from time to time or whether their
names are on a panel from which they are chosen from time to time and appointed ad
hoc to act on each occasion.

All these considerations have led me to the conclusion that there is no reason to
construe the word 'office' in Sch E under the 1970 Act otherwise than in its ordinary,
b dictionary meaning and for the reasons I have earlier expressed I am of opinion that that
meaning is apt to describe the position of the taxpayer on appointment to hold a public
local inquiry under the statutory provisions in question. I would accordingly allow the
appeal and restore the order of Walton J.

Appeal dismissed.

c
Solicitors: *Solicitor of Inland Revenue*; *Lovell, White & King* (for the taxpayer).

Mary Rose Plummer   Barrister.

d
Cummins Engine Co Ltd v Davis Freight Forwarding (Hull) Ltd and others

COURT OF APPEAL, CIVIL DIVISION
EVELEIGH, BRANDON AND O'CONNOR LJJ
e 16th, 17th, 20th JULY 1981

*Carriers – Loss or damage to goods – Successive carriage – Contributions to compensation by
successive carriers – Carriers concerned – Goods carried from Scotland to Holland by English
carrier and three successive Dutch carriers – Goods damaged while being carried by last carrier
in Holland – Owner of goods claiming against English carrier in England – English carrier*
f *wishing to join three Dutch carriers as third parties – Whether English carrier entitled to
indemnity from all three successive carriers – Whether English carrier's right of indemnity
restricted to carrier in whose care goods were damaged – Whether English carrier claiming
contribution 'one of the carriers concerned' – Whether English carrier required to bring action for
indemnity in court where the 'carrier concerned' has his residence or principal place of business
– Carriage of Goods by Road Act 1965, Sch, arts 37, 39(2).*

g
By a contract made in May 1977 the first defendants ('Davis'), an English company,
agreed to carry or arrange for the carriage of the plaintiffs' diesel engines from their
factory in Scotland to Amsterdam in Holland. The contract was subject to the
Convention on the Contract for the International Carriage of Goods by Road, as set out
in the schedule to the Carriage of Goods by Road Act 1965. The engines were
h subsequently collected at the plaintiffs' factory on Davis's trailer and were conveyed
under arrangements made by them to Europoort at the Dutch port of Rotterdam where
they arrived undamaged on 13th June 1977. There Davis asked the second defendants
('Charterway') to arrange for the further on-carriage of the engines in the trailer to
Amsterdam. Charterway asked the third defendant ('Graaf') to undertake the carriage
and Graaf in turn asked the fourth defendants ('Boers') to do it. Charterway, Graaf and
j Boers were all engaged either in the forwarding or the carriage of goods by road in the
Netherlands. Boers sent a tractor unit to Europoort and collected the trailer and the
accompanying documents which included the invoices and a consignment note in which
the plaintiffs were shown as the sender and Davis as the carrier. While en route for
Amsterdam the tractor and trailer crashed over the side of a bridge and the trailer and the

goods were severely damaged. By art 34 of the convention if carriage governed by a single contract was performed by successive road carriers each of them became a party to the contract of carriage. By art 36 legal proceedings in respect of liability for loss, damage or delay could only be brought against the first carrier, the last carrier or the carrier who was performing that portion of the carriage during which the event causing the loss, damage or delay occurred, provided however that an action could be brought at the same time against several such carriers. By art 37[a] a carrier who paid compensation to the owner of the goods was entitled to recover such compensation from the other carriers who had taken part in the carriage in proportion to their liability, provided however that the carrier responsible for the loss was solely liable for the compensation. Article 39(2)[b] provided that a carrier who wished to take proceedings to enforce his right to recovery 'may' make his claim before the competent court or tribunal of the country 'in which one of the carriers concerned' was ordinarily resident or had his principal place of business. The plaintiffs issued a writ in England against all four defendants claiming damages in respect of their loss but the writ was served only on Davis, who obtained leave to serve third party notices on the other defendants in Holland under RSC Ord 11, r 1(1)(l), as applied to third party proceedings by Ord 16, r 3(4). On the application of Charterway, Graaf and Boers service of the third party notices on them was set aside on the grounds that (i) with respect to Charterway and Graaf, assuming that they were consecutive carriers neither of them was responsible for the loss of or damage to the goods so as to entitle Davis to sue them for an indemnity under art 37, and (ii) with respect to all three defendants, Davis were not entitled to bring proceedings under art 39(2) for an indemnity against them in an English court. Davis appealed, contending that in a secondary claim under art 39 for compensation between carriers it was sufficient to claim in the country where 'one of the carriers concerned', including the carrier wishing to enforce his right of recovery, had his residence or principal place of business, and that Davis as 'one of the carriers concerned' was therefore entitled to claim in England.

Held – The appeal would be dismissed and the setting aside of the third party notices affirmed for the following reasons—

(1) (Per Brandon and O'Connor LJJ) With respect to Charterway and Graaf, even if they were to be treated as successive carriers, since the damage to the goods occurred during the carriage by Boers it followed that under art 37 of the convention Boers were the only successive carriers from whom Davis were entitled to recover any compensation which they were held liable to pay the plaintiffs, and, accordingly, the third party proceedings against Charterway or Graaf must fail (see p 574 b to d, p 575 g h and p 576 e, post).

(2) The expression 'one of the carriers concerned' in art 39(2) of the convention referred, having regard to the context in which it was used, to the carrier who would be required to make contribution (ie Charterway, Graaf or Boers) and did not include the carrier claiming contribution (ie Davis). Furthermore (Eveleigh LJ dubitante), a carrier wishing to enforce his claim under art 39(2) against the other carriers taking part in the carriage was required to take proceedings against them in a country where one of the carriers from whom contribution was claimed had his residence or principal place of business, and did not merely have the option of doing so. Since Charterway, Graaf and Boers all had their principal places of residence in Holland, Davis were not entitled to bring proceedings for an indemnity against any of them in an English court, whether by way of third party proceedings or separate action (see p 574 e to j, p 575 g h and p 576 d to h, post).

Notes

For proceedings and contribution between successive international carriers by road, see 5 Halsbury's Laws (4th Edn) para 441.

---

a　Article 37 is set out at p 572 f to h, post
b　Article 39 is set out at p 572 j to p 573 c, post

a   For the Carriage of Goods by Road Act 1965, Sch, arts 31, 34, 36, 37, 39, see 28 Halsbury's Statutes (3rd Edn) 454–457.

Case referred to in judgments
Ulster-Swift Ltd v Taunton Meat Haulage Ltd [1977] 3 All ER 641, [1977] 1 WLR 625, [1977] 1 Lloyd's Rep 346, [1977] RTR 475, CA, Digest (Cont Vol E) 36, *1435*.

b   **Cases also cited**
County and District Properties Ltd v C Jenner & Son Ltd [1976] 2 Lloyd's Rep 728.
Buchanan (James) & Co Ltd v Babco Forwarding and Shipping (UK) Ltd [1977] 1 All ER 518, [1977] QB 208, CA.
Fatton (William) & Co Ltd v Ferrymaster Ltd (1973) 9 European Transport Law 167.
Fothergill v Monarch Airlines Ltd [1980] 2 All ER 696, [1981] AC 251, HL.
c   *Green (R H) & Silley Weir Ltd v British Railways Board* (1980) Times, 8th October.

Interlocutory appeal
By a writ issued on 7th June 1978 the plaintiffs, Cummins Engine Co Ltd, brought an action against the defendants, Davis Freight Forwarding (Hull) Ltd, Charterway Shipping BV, R C A Van der Graaf and D Boers BV, claiming damages for breach of contract and
d   negligence arising out of the carriage of the plaintiffs' goods from the plaintiffs' premises at Shotts, Lanarkshire, Scotland to Amsterdam, Holland in or about June 1977. The plaintiffs served the writ on the first named defendants only. The first named defendants served third party notices on the second, third and fourth named defendants in Holland pursuant to an order of Robert Goff J dated 25th February 1980 made ex parte under RSC Ord 11, r 1, as applied to third party proceedings by RSC Ord 16, r 3(4), claiming to be
e   indemnified by each of those defendants against the plaintiffs' claim and the costs of the action. On 6th March 1981 Mocatta J set aside the order of Robert Goff J and the service of the third party notices on the second, third and fourth defendants. The first defendants appealed. The respondents to the appeal were the second, third and fourth defendants. The facts are set out in the judgment of Brandon LJ.

f   *Murray Pickering* for the appellants.
G D Kinley for the second defendants.
Gavin Kealey for the third defendants.
Richard Aikens for the fourth defendants.
The plaintiffs were not represented.

g   **BRANDON LJ** delivered the first judgment at the invitation of Eveleigh LJ. This appeal arises in an action in the Commercial Court in which Cummins Engine Co Ltd are the plaintiffs, Davis Freight Forwarding (Hull) Ltd are the first defendants, Charterway Shipping BV are the second defendants, R C A Van der Graaf is the third defendant, and D Boers BV are the fourth defendants. I shall refer to these five parties as
h   Cummins, Davis, Charterway, Graaf and Boers respectively.
Cummins are an English company which manufacture and export diesel engines. Davis are another English company engaged in, among other things, the carriage and forwarding of goods from the United Kingdom to the Continent. Charterway and Boers are Dutch companies and Graaf is a Dutch trader, all engaged in either the forwarding or the carriage of goods by road in the Netherlands.
j   The appeal raises questions with regard to the true meaning and effect of certain provisions of the Convention on the Contract for the International Carriage of Goods by Road (Geneva, 19th May 1956; TS 90 (1967); Cmnd 3455), which has been part of English law since October 1967. The convention is commonly known as CMR and I shall refer to it by those initials.
The facts giving rise to the action are these. At about the end of May 1977 Cummins and Davis entered into a contract under which Davis were to carry, or arrange the

carriage of, 14 diesel engines from Shotts in Lanarkshire to Amsterdam. The goods were
subsequently loaded by Davis at Shotts into a road trailer belonging to them. They were   **a**
accompanied by various documents, including invoices and a consignment note of the
kind prescribed by arts 4 to 6 of CMR. In that consignment note Cummins were shown
as the sender, NV Nederlandsche Ford of Amsterdam as the consignee, and Davis as the
carrier. After the goods have been loaded into the trailer by Davis, a tractor unit
belonging to them hauled the trailer by road to Hull. There Davis arranged for the on-
carriage of the trailer by sea to Europoort at Rotterdam, where the trailer, and the 14   **b**
diesel engines contained in it, arrived safely on 13th June 1977.

There remained the further on-carriage of the goods in the trailer to Amsterdam.
Davis asked Charterway to arrange this. Charterway asked Graaf to do the job. Graaf in
turn asked Boers to do it. In the result, Boers sent a tractor unit to Europoort and
collected the trailer and the accompanying documents from there. Boers' tractor unit,
with the trailer in tow, set out for Amsterdam. Unfortunately, at about 3 am on the   **c**
morning of 14th June 1977, the tractor and trailer crashed over the side of a bridge at
Leiden. As a result of the crash the trailer and the goods contained in it were severely
damaged by fire. The accompanying documents, however, were recovered, although
they too had been partly damaged by fire. Those documents included the CMR
consignment note.

On 7th June 1978, very shortly before the expiry of the one-year time limit for claims   **d**
prescribed by art 32 of CMR, Cummins began the action against Davis, Charterway,
Graaf and Boers in the Commercial Court to which I referred earlier. The writ was
subsequently served on Davis, the only defendants within the jurisdiction, but no
attempt appears to have been made to obtain leave to serve notice of the writ on the other
three defendants outside the jurisdiction in the Netherlands. Points of claim, points of
defence and further and better particulars of either pleading were served between 18th   **e**
May 1979 and 3rd July 1980. The amount claimed by Cummins against Davis for the
damage to the diesel engines was £41,452·89 with interest.

Meanwhile, on 25th February 1980, Davis had made an ex parte application supported
by affidavit for leave to serve out of the jurisdiction, in the Netherlands, third party
notices on Charterway, Graaf and Boers, in which Davis claimed in each case an
indemnity in respect of any liability to Cummins which might be found against them   **f**
in the main action. The ex parte application was heard by Robert Goff J, who acceded to
it and made an order giving Davis the leave for which they had asked. Third party
notices were subsequently served on Charterway, Graaf and Boers at their respective
addresses in the Netherlands.

On 8th August 1980 Boers, on 25th September 1980 Graaf and on 29th January 1981
Charterway issued summonses supported by affidavits in which they asked that the ex   **g**
parte order of Robert Goff J made on 25th February 1980, and the service of the third
party notices issued and served pursuant to that order, should be set aside. The three
summonses came on for hearing together before Mocatta J on 6th March 1981. Because
they involved questions on the meaning and effect of an international convention, the
learned judge decided to give judgment in open court. He found against Davis on all
three summonses, and made orders setting aside the order of Robert Goff J of 25th   **h**
February 1980 and the service of the three third party notices issued and served pursuant
to that order. He gave Davis leave to appeal against his orders and it is with that appeal
that we are now concerned.

The Carriage of Goods by Road Act 1965 was passed on 5th August 1965 and came
into force on 19th October 1967. It provides, so far as material, as follows:

> '**1.** Subject to the following provisions of this Act, the provisions of the   **j**
> Convention on the Contract for the International Carriage of Goods by Road (in this
> Act referred to as "the Convention"), as set out in the Schedule to this Act, shall have
> the force of law in the United Kingdom so far as they relate to the rights and
> liabilities of persons concerned in the carriage of goods by road under a contract to
> which the Convention applies . . .

'**5.**—(1) Where a carrier under a contract to which the Convention applies is liable in respect of any loss or damage for which compensation is payable under the Convention, nothing in section 6(1)(c) of the Law Reform (Married Women and Tortfeasors) Act 1935, section 16(1)(c) of the Law Reform (Miscellaneous Provisions) Act (Northern Ireland) 1937, or section 3(2) of the Law Reform (Miscellaneous Provisions) (Scotland) Act 1940 shall confer on him any right to recover contribution in respect of that loss or damage from any other carrier who, in accordance with article 34 in the Schedule to this Act, is a party to the contract of carriage.

'(2) The preceding subsection shall be without prejudice to the operation of article 37 in the Schedule to this Act . . .

'**14.** . . . (2) The persons who, for the purposes of this Act, are persons concerned in the carriage of goods by road under a contract to which the Convention applies are—(a) the sender, (b) the consignee, (c) any carrier who, in accordance with article 34 in the Schedule to this Act or otherwise, is a party to the contract of carriage, (d) any person for whom such a carrier is responsible by virtue of article 3 in the Schedule to this Act, (e) any person to whom the rights and liabilities of any of the persons referred to in paragraphs (a) to (d) of this subsection have passed (whether by assignment or assignation or by operation of law) . . .'

The effect of s 5(1) and (2) of the Act is to exclude the statutory provisions relating to contribution and indemnity between persons jointly or concurrently liable for the same loss or damage in force in the three parts of the United Kingdom, so leaving the way clear for the operation of the special provisions of CMR relating to those matters to which I shall be referring later. The reference in s 5 to s 6(1)(c) of the Law Reform (Married Women and Tortfeasors) Act 1935 must be taken today to be a reference to the corresponding provisions of the Civil Liability (Contribution) Act 1978. This Act, however, did not come into force until 1st January 1979, well after the casualty here concerned.

CMR, as scheduled to the 1965 Act, is divided into seven chapters. Chapter I, containing arts 1 and 2, is entitled 'Scope of Application'. Article 1, para 1 provides:

'This Convention shall apply to every contract for the carriage of goods by road in vehicles for reward, when the place of taking over of the goods and the place designated for delivery, as specified in the contract, are situated in two different countries, of which at least one is a Contracting country, irrespective of the place of residence and the nationality of the parties.'

Both the United Kingdom and the Netherlands are contracting parties, and it is not in dispute that CMR applied to the carriage of diesel engines from Shotts to Amsterdam with which this case is concerned.

Chapter II of CMR, containing art 3, is entitled 'Persons for whom the Carrier is Responsible'. Article 3 provides:

'For the purposes of this Convention the carrier shall be responsible for the acts and omissions of his agents and servants and of any other persons of whose services he makes use for the performance of the carriage, when such agents, servants or other persons are acting within the scope of their employment, as if such acts or omissions were his own.'

Chapter III of CMR, containing arts 4 to 16, is entitled 'Conclusion and Performance of the Contract of Carriage'. It is only necessary to refer to art 4, which provides:

'The contract of carriage shall be confirmed by the making out of a consignment note. The absence, irregularity or loss of the consignment note shall not affect the existence or the validity of the contract of carriage which shall remain subject to the provisions of this Convention.'

Chapter IV of CMR, containing arts 17 to 29, is entitled 'Liability of the Carrier'. Article 17, para 1 provides that the carrier shall be liable for the total or partial loss of the goods or for damage thereto occurring between the time when he takes over the goods and the time of delivery, as well as for any delay in delivery, subject to various defences set out in art 17, paras 2 and 4, and art 18. Article 27 provides for interest on any compensation payable.

Chapter V of CMR, containing arts 30 to 33, is entitled 'Claims and Actions'. Article 31 provides:

> 'In legal proceedings arising out of carriage under this Convention, the plaintiff may bring an action in any court or tribunal of a contracting country designated by agreement between the parties and, in addition, in the courts or tribunals of a country within whose territory (a) the defendant is ordinarily resident, or has his principal place of business, or the branch or agency through which the contract of carriage was made, or (b) the place where the goods were taken over by the carrier or the place designated for delivery is situated, and in no other courts or tribunals.'

Chapter VI of CMR, containing arts 34 to 40, is entitled 'Provisions Relating to Carriage Performed by Successive Carriers'. Article 34 provides:

> 'If carriage governed by a single contract is performed by successive road carriers, each of them shall be responsible for the performance of the whole operation, the second carrier and each succeeding carrier becoming a party to the contract of carriage, under the terms of the consignment note, by reason of his acceptance of the goods and the consignment note.'

Article 36 provides:

> 'Except in the case of a counter-claim or a set-off raised in an action concerning a claim based on the same contract of carriage, legal proceedings in respect of liability for loss, damage or delay may only be brought against the first carrier, the last carrier or the carrier who was performing that portion of the carriage during which the event causing the loss, damage or delay occurred; an action may be brought at the same time against several of these carriers.'

Article 37 provides:

> 'A carrier who has paid compensation in compliance with the provisions of this Convention, shall be entitled to recover such compensation, together with interest thereon and all costs and expenses incurred by reason of the claim, from the other carriers who have taken part in the carriage, subject to the following provisions: (a) the carrier responsible for the loss or damage shall be solely liable for the compensation whether paid by himself or by another carrier; (b) when the loss or damage has been caused by the action of two or more carriers, each of them shall pay an amount proportionate to his share of liability; should it be impossible to apportion the liability, each carrier shall be liable in proportion to the share of the payment for the carriage which is due to him; (c) if it cannot be ascertained to which carriers liability is attributable for the loss or damage, the amount of the compensation shall be apportioned between all the carriers as laid down in (b) above.'

Article 38 provides:

> 'If one of the carriers is insolvent, the share of the compensation due from him and unpaid by him shall be divided among the other carriers in proportion to the share of the payment for the carriage due to them.'

Article 39 provides:

> '1. No carrier against whom a claim is made under articles 37 and 38 shall be entitled to dispute the validity of the payment made by the carrier making the claim if the amount of the compensation was determined by judicial authority after

the first mentioned carrier had been given due notice of the proceedings and afforded an opportunity of entering an appearance.

'2. A carrier wishing to take proceedings to enforce his right of recovery may make his claim before the competent court or tribunal of the country in which one of the carriers concerned is ordinarily resident, or has his principal place of business or the branch or agency through which the contract of carriage was made. All the carriers concerned may be made defendants in the same action.

'3. The provisions of article 31, paragraphs 3 and 4, shall apply to judgments entered in the proceedings referred to in articles 37 and 38.

'4. The provisions of articles 32 shall apply to claims between carriers. The period of limitation shall, however, begin to run either on the date of the final judicial decision fixing the amount of compensation payable under the provisions of this Convention, or, if there is no such judicial decision, from the actual date of payment.'

Article 40 provides: 'Carriers shall be free to agree among themselves on provisions other than those laid down in articles 37 and 38.'

Chapter VII of CMR, containing art 41, is entitled 'Nullity of Stipulations Contrary to the Convention'. The effect of art 41 is to render void any term of a contract of carriage which is inconsistent with the provisions of CMR except as specially permitted by art 40.

It is clear from the provisions of CMR contained in Chapters V and VI that it contemplates two kinds of legal proceedings arising out of a contract of carriage. The first kind of legal proceedings which it contemplates are actions brought by a sender or consignee of goods against one or more carriers. Where successive carriers are involved, the effect of art 31, para 1 combined with art 34, is that the plaintiff can bring a single action against one, more than one, or all the carriers concerned. Article 31, para 1 further requires him to bring his action in certain courts only. These courts are: first, any court of a contracting state which has been agreed between the parties; second, the courts of the country where any of the carriers sued is ordinarily resident, or has his principal place of business, or the branch or agency through which the contract of carriage was made; and, third, the courts of the place where the goods were taken over for the carriage or the place where they were to be delivered.

It is on the basis of these provisions that, in the present case, Cummins issued a writ against four parties, Davis, Charterway, Graaf and Boers, although they have only served such writ on Davis.

The second kind of legal proceedings which CMR contemplates are actions in which one carrier, who has been compelled to pay compensation to a sender or consignee, seeks to recover an indemnity or contribution from one or more other carriers involved in the carriage.

CMR appears to contemplate that these two kinds of legal proceedings will be separate from each other, the first and main action being followed by a second and consequential action. I say this because the opening words of art 37 are: 'A carrier who *has* paid compensation in compliance with the provisions of this Convention, shall be entitled to recover . . .' It seems to me, however, that, where the procedure of the court in which the first and main action is brought allows claims by a defendant for contribution or indemnity to be added to the main action by way of third party proceedings, as is the situation in the present case, there is no good reason in principle why what is contemplated by CMR as the second and consequential action should not be brought by way of such third party proceedings. It is only right to add that none of the defendants who are respondents to this appeal have sought to contend otherwise.

The application for leave to serve third party notices out of the jurisdiction was made by Davis under RSC Ord 11, r 1(1)(*l*), as made applicable to third party proceedings by RSC Ord 16, r 3(4). Order 11, r 1(1)(*l*) provides for service out of the jurisdiction 'if the action begun by the writ is brought under the Carriage by Air Act 1961, the Carriage by Air (Supplementary Provisions) Act 1962, the Carriage of Goods by Road Act 1965, the Nuclear Installations Act 1965, or the Protection of Trading Interests Act 1980'.

The grounds on which Charterway, Graaf and Boers succeeded before Mocatta J in
having the earlier order of Robert Goff J and the service of the third party notices on each   *a*
of them set aside were as follows: first, so far as Charterway and Graaf are concerned, that,
even assuming that they are to be regarded as consecutive carriers at all, as the decision
in *Ulster-Swift Ltd v Taunton Meat Haulage Ltd* [1977] 3 All ER 641, [1977] 1 WLR 625
appears to indicate that they should be, neither was the carrier responsible for the loss or
damage to the goods, so as to entitle Davis to sue them for an indemnity under art 37;
second, so far as all three respondents are concerned, that, under art 39, para 2, Davis   *b*
were not entitled to bring proceedings for an indemnity against them, whether by way
of third party proceedings or separate action, in an English court.

So far as the first ground relied on by Charterway and Graaf is concerned, I do not see
any answer to it. On the footing that they were successive carriers, the evidence
establishes clearly that the damage to the goods took place while they were being carried
by Boers, with the result that, under art 37, Boers are the only successive carrier from   *c*
whom Davis are entitled to recover over any compensation which they are held liable to
pay to Cummins. It follows that third party proceedings by Davis against Charterway or
Graaf must fail, and on that ground alone the order of Robert Goff J giving leave to Davis
to serve third party notices on Charterway and Graaf out of the jurisdiction in the
Netherlands, and the subsequent service of such notices, must be set aside. It was
suggested that, if Boers became insolvent, Davis would then be entitled to recourse   *d*
against Charterway and Graaf under art 38. There was, however, no evidence to suggest
that Boers were, or were likely to be, insolvent, and, in the absence of such evidence, I
think that the possibility should be disregarded.

I turn to the second ground relied on by all three respondents, namely that, under art
39, para 2, Davis were not entitled to bring proceedings for an indemnity against them
in an English court. The validity of this ground depends on the meaning to be given to   *e*
the expression 'the carriers concerned' where that expression first occurs in art 39, para
2. For the respondents it was contended that the expression means, and means only, the
carriers from whom the carrier primarily liable to a sender or consignee is seeking to
recover the compensation which he has had to pay. I shall call that the first meaning.
For the appellants it was contended that the expression includes not only the carriers
from whom compensation is being sought to be recovered, but also the carrier who is   *f*
seeking to recover it. I shall call that the second meaning.

If the first meaning is correct Davis would have to sue Charterway, Graaf and Boers in
a court in the Netherlands and would not be entitled to proceed against them in a court
in England. If the second meaning is correct Davis would be entitled to sue the three
other carriers either in a court in the Netherlands or in a court in England.

In my view, it is necessary to interpret the expression 'the carriers concerned' where   *g*
first occurring in art 39, para 2 in the context in which it is used. That context is a
situation in which one carrier, who has been made primarily liable to a sender or
consignee, is seeking to recover over against one or more other carriers. That being the
context in which the expression is used, I have no doubt at all that it should be given the
first meaning contended for by the respondents, rather than the second meaning
contended for by the appellants.   *h*

I should reach that conclusion even without considering the rest of art 39, para 2
where the expression 'the carriers concerned' is used a second time. It is used in the last
sentence of art 39, para 2, which reads: 'All the carriers concerned may be made
defendants in the same action.' Counsel for the appellants conceded, as he was bound to
do, that in this last sentence the expression 'the carriers concerned' has, and can only have,
the first meaning, and he was therefore compelled to argue that the expression when first   *j*
used had a different meaning from the same expression when used a second time.

In my view it is highly improbable that those who drafted CMR intended that the
same expression, used twice in the same paragraph and in the same context, should be
given one meaning when used the first time and another meaning when used the second
time. This consideration strongly reinforces the view which I should in any case form

about the meaning of the expression when first occurring, quite independently of its
further use a second time.

a   Counsel for the appellants put forward various arguments against our holding that
Davis could not sue Charterway, Graaf or Boers for an indemnity in England. One
argument was that art 31, para 1 applied not only to primary actions brought by a sender
or consignee against one or more carriers, but also to secondary actions for an indemnity
brought by one carrier against other carriers. That argument is, in my view, quite
untenable for two reasons. First, it is inconsistent with the whole way in which the

b   various subject matters in CMR are dealt with successively. Second, when those who
drafted CMR wished to incorporate parts of art 31 into art 39, they said so expressly, as
in para 3 of the latter article.

A second argument was that art 39, para 2 only provides that a carrier may make his
claim in certain countries, not that he must do so. I do not think there is anything in this

c   argument either, again for two reasons. The first reason is that I think, having regard to
the context, that this is one of those cases where the word 'may' must be interpreted, in
effect, as meaning 'must'. The second reason is that, if the word is interpreted as
permissive only, then there is nothing anywhere else in art 39, or any other part of CMR,
which permits actions by one carrier against other carriers for an indemnity to be
brought in the courts of any countries other than those specified in art 39, para 2.

d   A third argument was that it was very inconvenient if, in a case like the present one,
both the primary and the secondary proceedings arising out of the same event could not
be dealt with by the same court. I agree that it is inconvenient, but that consideration
cannot be allowed to distort what I regard as the clear meaning of art 39, para 2. It may
also be observed that the difficulty would have been avoided if Cummins had sued all
four defendants in the Netherlands, although I recognise that it is unlikely that they

e   would have chosen to do so.

A fourth argument was that, if Davis were not allowed to serve third party proceedings
on Charterway, Graaf and Boers out of the jurisdiction in the Netherlands, there would
be no way in which those three parties could be bound by the result of the main action
in the manner contemplated by art 39, para 1. I do not agree with that argument. There
is no reason why Davis, instead of seeking to institute third party proceedings against

f   Charterway, Graaf and Boers, should not have given them notice by letter of the action
brought against them by Cummins. If they had done so, those notified, since they were
named as defendants in the writ, would have been entitled to enter appearances
voluntarily under RSC Ord 10, r 1(3). Or, supposing a different case, where those
notified were not already named as defendants, they could, following notice, apply to be
joined as further defendants under RSC Ord 15, r 6(2)(b)(ii).

g   The conclusions at which I have arrived about this case accord with those expressed in
the clear and impressive judgment of Mocatta J. Those conclusions mean that this
appeal, strenuously as it has been argued by counsel for the appellants, fails and must be
dismissed.

h   **O'CONNOR LJ**. I agree that the appeal must be dismissed. Brandon LJ has set out all
the relevant facts and the relevant articles of the CMR convention and I need not repeat
them. During the course of the case it seemed to me that, if possible, art 39, para 2
should be construed in such a fashion as to limit the number of places in which litigation
arising out of a single casualty had to be heard. So, as Cummins were entitled to, and did,
commence proceedings in England, that meant that, if possible, the claims for

j   contribution by one carrier against another, if disputed, should also be heard in
England. But, as Brandon LJ has pointed out, the provisions of the Law Reform (Married
Women and Tortfeasors) Act 1935 in England had been expressly excluded by the
Carriage of Goods by Road Act 1965, and the sole provision for dealing with claims over
by one carrier against another has to be found in art 39. In order to achieve the result
which, to my mind, would be desirable, it would be necessary to construe art 39, para 2

in the way contended for by the appellants, namely that Davis were themselves a 'carrier concerned' and, therefore, the suit could be entertained in England.

At first it seemed to me that that might be a viable argument, but in the end I have been driven to the conclusion that it will not do. It will be seen that the scheme of the convention, starting in art 31, is that normally, unless the parties otherwise agree, any legal proceedings are to be originated in the jurisdiction of 'the defendant' (see art 31, para 1(*a*)), and I am content, under the ordinary rules of interpretation, to read 'defendant' for 'defendants'. The only alternative there given is the place where the goods were taken over or the place designated for delivery. The place where the goods were taken over by the carrier, in my judgment, refers to the place where the contract of carriage commenced (see art 1 of the convention) and cannot be repeated down the line where successive carriers have participated in the carriage at various stages. That in the present case was Scotland and the place of delivery was Holland. Therefore, Cummins were limited to bringing the action, as far as the jurisdiction of the defendant was concerned, either in England (Davis) or in Holland (the other three).

Starting from that and turning back to art 39, which is providing the machinery for a carrier defined in art 37 as 'A carrier who has paid compensation in compliance with the provisions of this Convention', there it will be seen that 'A carrier wishing to take proceedings to enforce his right of recovery may make his claim before the competent court or tribunal of the country in which one of the carriers concerned is ordinarily resident'. In my judgment, the 'carrier concerned' there is the carrier concerned with *making* contribution and not *claiming* contribution. Read in that way, it fits comfortably with the last sentence of that paragraph of art 39: 'All the carriers concerned may be made defendants in the same action.' That being so, unfortunate as I regard it, it is not possible to construe art 39, para 2 to give effect to what I would regard as a desirable result.

For those reasons and for the reasons given by Brandon LJ, with which I agree, the appeal should be dismissed.

EVELEIGH LJ. I am not prepared to go so far as to say that the word 'may' in art 39, para 2 is the equivalent of 'must'. That article does not contain the words which we read in art 31, 'and in no other courts or tribunals'. Thus I would leave open the question whether a defendant can claim indemnity or contribution in this country against a carrier who has entered an appearance for the purpose of disputing the validity of a payment after receiving notice under art 39. However, I regard RSC Ord 11, r 1(1)(*l*) as envisaging only a claim which could be made according to the procedure specifically permitted or envisaged by art 39, para 2. For the reasons given by Brandon LJ, I do not think that the present claim by Davis can be covered by art 39, para 2. If I am wrong, as a matter of construction as to the effect of Ord 11, r 1(1)(*l*), then I would say that, in exercising its jurisdiction, the court should act in such a way as to comply with the procedure specifically permitted by the convention.

In the result then, I too come to the conclusion that this appeal should be dismissed.

Appeal dismissed. Leave to appeal to the House of Lords in relation to D Boers BV refused.

Solicitors: *Clyde & Co*, Guildford (for the appellants); *Wm A Merrick & Co* (for the second defendants); *Sinclair, Roche & Temperley* (for the third defendants); *Ince & Co* (for the fourth defendants).

Mary Rose Plummer   Barrister.

Amalgamated Investment & Property Co Ltd (in liquidation) v Texas Commerce International Bank Ltd

COURT OF APPEAL, CIVIL DIVISION

LORD DENNING MR, EVELEIGH AND BRANDON LJJ

30th JUNE, 1st, 2nd, 3rd, 6th, 7th, 31st JULY 1981

Guarantee – Construction – Surrounding circumstances – Guarantor requesting bank to make loan to guarantor's subsidiary – Loan made by off-the-peg company set up by bank – Guarantee not including advances made by off-the-peg company – Whether guarantee to be construed in isolation or in context of surrounding circumstances – Whether guarantee extending to advances made by off-the-peg company.

Estoppel – Convention – Parties adopting conventional basis for their relations – Parties agreeing and assuming certain facts to be true – Parties assuming that loan made by bank to company's subsidiary would be repaid by company – Company guaranteeing loan – Loan made by off-the-peg company set up by bank – Guarantee not including advances made by off-the-peg company – Whether state of affairs assumed by bank and company to be true giving rise to estoppel by convention – Whether company estopped from denying liability to repay loan.

An English property company arranged with an English merchant bank that the bank should lend it $3m on the security of properties in England owned by the company and should also lend $3,250,000 ('the Nassau loan') to a wholly-owned Bahamian subsidiary of the company on the security of an office building in Nassau owned by the subsidiary and a guarantee provided by the English company. On 23rd September 1970, in a letter to the subsidiary, the bank confirmed the arrangements made and expressly referred to the security of the guarantee. Under the guarantee, which was signed on 28th September 1970, in consideration of the bank from time to time making loans or advances or giving credit to its Bahamian subsidiary, the English company covenanted to pay the bank on demand all moneys at any time owing or payable to the bank by the subsidiary. On the same date, by a letter to the bank, the English company acknowledged the completed guarantee, the letter being expressed to be in relation to the proposed loan of $3,250,000 secured on the Nassau building by the company's Bahamian subsidiary. In order to circumvent Bahamian restrictions on foreign banks trading in the Bahamas, the bank purchased an 'off the shelf' Bahamian subsidiary ('the Bahamian bank') and on 31st December 1970 the Nassau loan was effected by the bank making a loan to the Bahamian bank which in turn advanced the same sum to the company's Bahamian subsidiary. The mortgage of the Nassau building was executed between the Bahamian bank and the subsidiary, but the guarantee was never amended and remained a guarantee by the English company in respect of money owing to the bank rather than to the Bahamian bank. In the course of dealings between the parties, however, it was apparent that both the bank and the English company believed the guarantee to be binding and effective and to cover the liability of the English company in respect of the Nassau loan. Some time later the English company got into financial difficulties and was ordered to be compulsorily wound up. Both the bank and Bahamian bank exercised their respective powers as mortgagees and sold the Nassau building and the English properties owned by the English company. That left some $750,000 outstanding on the Nassau loan while the bank held a credit balance of about the same amount after the sale of the English properties. The bank thereupon applied the credit balance to discharge the amount owing on the Nassau loan claiming that under the guarantee it was entitled to do so. The liquidator of the English company issued a writ seeking a declaration that the English company was under no liability to the bank under the guarantee in respect of the amount still owing on the Nassau loan. The bank contended (i) that the Bahamian bank was no more than a nominee of the bank and the relationship between the two was so *a* close that the guarantee ought to apply to the Nassau loan made by the Bahamian bank, and (ii) that the English company was estopped from contending that the guarantee did not cover its subsidiary's liability to the Bahamian bank, because the English company had actively acquiesced in and encouraged the bank's assumption that it had certain legal rights against the company and it would be unjust or unconscionable for the company subsequently to deny the existence of those rights. The judge ([1981] 1 All ER 923) *b* dismissed the claim for a declaration, holding that the English company's conduct estopped it from denying that it had given an effective guarantee to the bank in respect of money owed by the company's Bahamian subsidiary to the Bahamian bank, even though on the natural and ordinary construction of the guarantee it applied only to the money owing to the bank and not to the money owing to the Bahamian bank. The English company appealed. *c*

Held – The appeal would be dismissed for the following reasons—

(1) The guarantee was to be construed in the general context of the parties' transaction, rather than as a separate document in isolation, and it was clear from the context of the transaction as a whole (a) that, as evidenced by the correspondence, the English company was not merely a guarantor brought in after the formation of the principal contract but *d* had initially requested the English bank to make the loan, had negotiated the terms, and was itself financially interested in the transaction, (b) that the parties always intended that the English company would be responsible for seeing that the Nassau loan was repaid, and (c) that the Bahamian bank through which the loan was effected was entirely the creature of its parent company, the English bank, and was no more than a conduit through which the loan was channelled. Accordingly, the English company was *e* contractually bound to the English bank, on the basis of the guarantee, to discharge any moneys owing by the company's Bahamian subsidiary to the Bahamian bank (see p 582 *c* to *g*, p 585 *b*, p 586 *e* to *j*, p 588 *b*, p 590 *a* and p 592 *a*, post).

(2) In any event, the conduct of the parties took place on the basis of a state of affairs, namely that the guarantee given by the English company would cover repayment of the Nassau loan by the company's Bahamian subsidiary, which was agreed and assumed by *f* both parties to be true and on the basis of which they had entered into the loan transaction and the guarantee. That gave rise to an estoppel by convention which estopped each party as against the other from questioning the truth of the facts assumed by them to be true. The English company was therefore estopped from denying that by the contract relating to the Nassau loan it had undertaken to repay the loan (see p 582 *h* *j*, p 583 *c d*, p 584 *a* to p 585 *b*, p 587 *h* to p 588 *b*, p 591 *c* to *e* and *j* to p 592 *a*, post). *g*

Per Brandon LJ. Although a party cannot in terms use an estoppel as a sword or found a cause of action on an estoppel, he may, as a result of being able to rely on an estoppel, succeed on a cause of action in which but for being able to rely on the estoppel he would necessarily have failed (see p 591 *h*, post).

Decision of Robert Goff J [1981] 1 All ER 923 affirmed on other grounds.

Notes *h*

For guarantees, see 20 Halsbury's Laws (4th Edn) paras 101–148, and for cases on the subject, see 26 Digest (Repl) 370–395, *127–139*.

For estoppel by conduct, see 16 Halsbury's Laws (4th Edn) paras 1609–1639, and for cases on the subject, see 21 Digest (Repl) 411–461, *1310–1601*.

Cases referred to in judgments *j*

Brogden v Metropolitan Railway Co (1877) 2 App Cas 666, HL, 12 Digest (Reissue) 60, *313*.
Crabb v Arun District Council [1975] 3 All ER 865, [1976] Ch 179, [1975] 3 WLR 847, CA, 21 Digest (Reissue) 6, *48*.
DHN Food Distributors Ltd v London Borough of Tower Hamlets [1976] 3 All ER 462, [1976]

1 WLR 852, 74 LGR 506, 32 P & CR 240, [1976] RVR 269, CA, Digest (Cont Vol E)
a   84, *165a*.
Grundt v Great Boulder Pty Gold Mines Ltd (1937) 59 CLR 641.
Hollier v Rambler Motors (AMC) Ltd [1972] 1 All ER 399, [1972] 2 QB 71, [1972] 2 WLR
     401, [1972] RTR 190, CA, 3 Digest (Reissue) 439, *2971*.
Kendall (Henry) & Sons (a firm) v William Lillico & Sons Ltd [1968] 2 All ER 444, [1969] 2
     AC 31, [1968] 3 WLR 110, sub nom *Hardwick Game Farm v Suffolk Agricultural &*
b   *Poultry Producers Association Ltd* [1968] 1 Lloyd's Rep 547, HL, 2 Digest (Reissue) 163,
     993.
McCutcheon v David MacBrayne Ltd [1964] 1 All ER 430, [1964] 1 WLR 125, [1964] 1
     Lloyd's Rep 16, 1964 SC (HL) 28, HL, 8(1) Digest (Reissue) 46, *265*.
Miller (James) and Partners Ltd v Whitworth Street Estates (Manchester) Ltd [1970] 1 All ER
     796, [1970] AC 583, [1970] 2 WLR 728, [1970] 1 Lloyd's Rep 269, HL, 11 Digest
c   (Reissue) 462, *776*.
Spurling (J) Ltd v Bradshaw [1956] 2 All ER 121, [1956] 1 WLR 461, [1956] 1 Lloyd's Rep
     392, CA, 3 Digest (Reissue) 447, *3007*.
Sutton & Co v Grey [1894] 1 QB 285, 63 LJQB 633, 69 LT 673, 9 R 106, CA, 26 Digest
     (Reissue) 100, *564*.
Wallersteiner v Moir [1974] 3 All ER 217, [1974] 1 WLR 991, CA, 16 Digest (Reissue) 24,
d   *223*.
Watcham v Attorney General of East African Protectorate [1919] AC 533, [1918–19] All ER
     Rep 455, 87 LJPC 150, 120 LT 258, PC, 17 Digest (Reissue) 50, *564*.

Cases also cited
Balkis Consolidated Co Ltd v Tomkinson [1893] AC 396, HL.
e   *Bolsom (Sidney) Investment Trust Ltd v E Karmios & Co (London)* [1956] 1 All ER 536, [1956]
     1 QB 529, CA.
Calgary Milling Co v American Surety Co of New York [1919] 3 WWR 98, PC.
Canadian Superior Oil Ltd v Paddon-Hughes Development Co Ltd (1970) 12 DLR (3d) 247.
Central Newbury Car Auctions Ltd v Unity Finance Ltd [1956] 3 All ER 905, [1957] 1 QB
     371, CA.
f   *Combe v Combe* [1951] 1 All ER 767, [1951] 2 KB 215, CA.
De Tchihatchef v Salerni Coupling Ltd [1932] 1 Ch 330, [1931] All ER Rep 233.
Eaves, Re, Eaves v Eaves [1939] 3 All ER 260, [1940] Ch 109, CA.
Edgington v Fitzmaurice (1885) 29 Ch D 459, [1881–5] All ER Rep 856, CA.
Habib Bank Ltd v Habib Bank AG Zurich [1981] 2 All ER 650, [1981] 1 WLR 1265, CA.
Hopgood v Brown [1955] 1 All ER 550, [1955] 1 WLR 213, CA.
g   *M'Cance v London & North Western Railway Co* (1864) 3 H & C 343, 159 ER 563.
McCathie v McCathie [1971] NZLR 58.
Moorgate Mercantile Co v Twitchings [1976] 2 All ER 641, [1977] AC 890, HL.
Ramsden v Dyson (1866) LR 1 HL 129, HL.
Ruben v Great Fingall Consolidated [1906] AC 439, [1904–7] All ER Rep 460, HL.
Sarat Chunder Dey v Gopal Chunder Laha (1892) LR 19 Ind App 203, PC.
h   *Simm v Anglo-American Telegraph Co* (1879) 5 QBD 188, CA.
Sohio Petroleum Co v Weyburn Security Co Ltd (1970) 13 DLR (3d) 340.
Spiro v Lintern [1973] 3 All ER 319, [1973] 1 WLR 1002, CA.
Syros Shipping Co SA v Elaghill Trading Co, The Proodos C [1981] 3 All ER 189.
Taylor Fashions Ltd v Liverpool Victoria Trustees Co Ltd, Old & Campbell Ltd v Liverpool
     Victoria Trustees Co Ltd [1981] 1 All ER 897, [1981] 2 WLR 576.
Western Fish Products Ltd v Penwith District Council [1981] 2 All ER 204, CA.
j   *Willmott v Barber* (1880) 15 Ch D 96.

Appeal
The plaintiff, Amalgamated Investment & Property Co Ltd (in liquidation), appealed
from the judgment of Robert Goff J ([1981] 1 All ER 923, [1981] 2 WLR 554) given on

16th May 1980 whereby he dismissed the plaintiff's claim for declaratory relief against the defendant, Texas Commerce International Bank Ltd. The facts are set out in the judgment of Lord Denning MR.

Andrew Morritt QC and *Paul Walker* for the plaintiff.
Anthony Colman QC and *Mark Hapgood* for the defendant.

Cur adv vult

31st July. The following judgments were read.

LORD DENNING MR. This case is complicated beyond measure by the existence of wholly-owned subsidiaries. These are the dramatis personae: a property company registered in England called Amalgamated Investment & Property Co Ltd (now in liquidation). I will call it 'Amalgamated'. It had a wholly-owned subsidiary registered in the Bahamas called Amalgamated (New Providence) Property Ltd. I will call it 'ANPP'. Also a merchant bank registered in England called Texas Commerce International Bank Ltd. I will call it the 'bank'. It had a wholly-owned subsidiary registered in the Bahamas called Portsoken Properties Ltd; I will call it 'Portsoken'.

Treating the wholly-owned subsidiaries as one with their parent companies, the facts in broad outline are these. There was a building site in the centre of Nassau in the Bahamas. It was ripe for development. Amalgamated wanted to raise $US3,250,000 in order to erect a building on the site. They borrowed it from the bank. Amalgamated mortgaged the property to the bank to secure the loan. As further security Amalgamated also gave a guarantee to the bank. It is on that guarantee that the whole case depends. I will call it the 'guarantee'. The loan was not repaid. The property was sold. It realised $2,500,000, leaving a deficit of $750,000 unpaid, for which the guarantee was the only security.

Amalgamated also owned properties in England which they had mortgaged to the bank. These were 'all money' mortgages covering all moneys owing to the bank by Amalgamated on any account whatever. These mortgages covered, not only the moneys advanced by the bank on the English properties, but also the moneys owing by Amalgamated on the guarantee in the Bahamas.

Amalgamated defaulted on the English loan. The English properties were realised. These more than covered the English loan. There was a surplus of $750,000 in the hand of the bank. The bank claimed to apply that surplus to wipe out the $750,000 unpaid on the guarantee.

A year later Amalgamated went into liquidation. The liquidator looked into the papers. He contended that the guarantee did not cover the deficit of $750,000 on the Nassau loan. He said that Amalgamated were entitled to the surplus of $750,000 which was realised on the sale of the English properties. The liquidator claimed that it should be paid over to him.

The liquidator bases his case on the introduction into the story of wholly-owned subsidiaries. He says that the guarantee only covered the sums which Amalgamated owed to the bank: and that it did not cover the sums which were owed by their wholly-owned subsidiary, ANPP, to the bank. The bank say that it *did* cover them: or alternatively that Amalgamated were *estopped* from saying that it did not cover them. The full facts are set out by Robert Goff J ([1981] 1 All ER 923, [1981] 2 WLR 554). I will only set out such details as are necessary for the points of law.

The execution of the guarantee

The guarantee was signed on 28th September 1970. It is to be construed together with these two letters. On 23rd September 1970 the bank wrote to ANPP:

'We confirm that we will be pleased to make available to A.N.P.P. a facility of U.S. $3,250,000 for a period of five years from the date that the borrowing is taken . . .

The borrowing will be secured by a legal mortgage in respect of the freehold property, The Harrison Building, Marlborough Street, Nassau, Bahamas, together with a guarantee for US $3,250,000 from Amalgamated Investment & Property Co. Ltd.'

On 28th September 1970 Amalgamated replied:

'Proposed Eurodollar Loan—US $3,250,000—Harrison Building—Amalgamated (New Providence) Property Ltd. Thank you for your letter of the 23rd instant wherein you enclose a guarantee which has been completed and is returned herewith.'

The guarantee was on a printed form. It was addressed to the bank with blanks filled in in type (here shown in capitals):

'We, AMALGAMATED INVESTMENT & PROPERTY CO. LTD. 9–10 GRAFTON STREET, LONDON, W1X 4DA, (hereinafter called "the Guarantor"), in consideration of your from time to time making or contributing loans or advances to or otherwise giving credit or affording banking accommodation or facilities to AMALGAMATED (NEW PROVIDENCE) PROPERTY LTD. of P.O. BOX 868, NASSAU, BAHAMAS (hereinafter called "the Principal"), hereby unconditionally guarantee to and agree with you as follows:

'1. The Guarantor will pay to you on demand all moneys which now are or shall at any time or times hereafter be due or owing or payable to you on any account whatsoever by the Principal, either solely or jointly with any other person, firm or company, together with all . . . banking charges and expenses which you may in the course of your business as bankers charge against the Principal . . . provided nevertheless that the total amount recoverable from the Guarantor hereunder shall not exceed U.S. $3,250,000 . . .

'10. For all purposes including any legal proceedings a copy of the account of the Principal in your books signed by any of your officers shall be accepted by the Guarantor as conclusive evidence of the state of such account . . .

'17. This Guarantee is to be governed by and construed according to English Law and the Guarantor submits to the jurisdiction of the English Courts.

'Dated this 28TH day of SEPTEMBER 1970.'

At that date, 28th September, 1970 as the covering letters show, the facilities were to be made available by the bank to ANPP.

The interposition of a subsidiary

The judge describes the introduction of a wholly-owned subsidiary of the bank ([1981] 1 All ER 923 at 927, [1981] 2 WLR 554 at 559). It was a Bahamian company called Portsoken Properties Ltd ('Portsoken'). This was done for exchange control purposes. It was a channel through which money passed. The position was well stated in a letter by the bank's solicitors to the Controller of Exchange in the Bahamas on the 15th December 1970. The wholly-owned subsidiary (Portsoken) was to—

'1. Receive the U.S. dollar funds from its parent company and lend them to A.N.P.P. in U.S. dollars without conversion into Bahamian dollars or sterling. 2. Take a Mortgage from A.N.P.P. expressed in U.S. dollars. 3. Maintain a U.S. dollar bank account for the purpose of handling payments of principal and interest in connection with this back-to-back loan.'

The transaction of 31st December 1970

On 31st December 1970 ANPP executed a mortgage on the Harrison Building in favour of Portsoken for securing $3,250,000. That sum was entered in the books as a loan by the bank to Portsoken and then as a loan by Portsoken to ANPP. And likewise with interest paid by ANPP to Portsoken: and by Portsoken to the bank. On many occasions, however, the interest was paid direct by ANPP to the bank.

Note the important point. The guarantee was not touched. It still remained dated 28th September 1970. It still remained a guarantee of moneys owing to the 'Principal', *a* that is, to the bank. The judge considered this to be 'a crucial defect'. He said ([1981] 1 All ER 923 at 928, [1981] 2 WLR 554 at 560).

> '... there was a crucial defect in these arrangements; the guarantee furnished by [Amalgamated] to the bank was not amended; it remained a guarantee in respect of money due or owing or payable *to the bank*, not to Portsoken.'

b

Was it a crucial defect?

I take a different view from the judge. He has construed the guarantee in its strict literal sense, all by itself without regard to the letters which accompanied it and without regard to the surrounding circumstances or the 'factual matrix' to use the modern equivalent.

The guarantee of 28th September 1970 was of no effect by itself. It only took effect on *c* 31st December 1970 when the sum of $3,250,000 was advanced. That sum of $3,250,000 is the connecting link which joins everything together. It was the 'facility' which the bank promised on 23rd September 1970 to make available to ANPP and which was to be supported by a mortgage on the Harrison Building; and by a guarantee from Amalgamated to the bank. It was the 'banking facilities' contained in the guarantee itself. It was the 'facility' which was in fact granted on 31st December 1970 and *d* supported by a mortgage. The words of the printed form must, in my opinion, be subordinated to the express provisions of the correspondence which brought it into being. That correspondence shows, beyond doubt, that the guarantee was intended to cover the $3,250,000 lent by the bank to ANPP, even though it was done through the channel of its wholly-owned subsidiary, Portsoken.

Apart from this, I think that this is one of those cases where a wholly-owned subsidiary *e* is to be regarded as the alter ego of the parent company. We have often lifted the corporate veil so as to show forth the realities of company life. This wholly-owned subsidiary was the creature of the parent company. It did exactly what the parent company told it to do. It was nothing more nor less than a conduit pipe through which payments were made and received. It received no fees. It made no profits. It sustained no losses. Its transactions were all paper transactions, all book entries, recording the sums *f* in and out. It was a puppet which danced to the bidding of the parent company just as Dr Wallersteiner's companies did (see *Wallersteiner v Moir* [1974] 3 All ER 217 at 238, [1974] 1 WLR 991 at 1013), and as the 'three in one' companies did in *DHN Food Distributors Ltd v London Borough of Tower Hamlets* [1976] 3 All ER 462, [1976] 1 WLR 852. If we regard Portsoken as the alter ego of the bank, the moneys owing by ANPP to Portsoken (a wholly-owned subsidiary) are moneys owing to the bank. They are *g* therefore covered by the guarantee.

Then again there is the conduct of the parties at the time of the transaction. This may be very relevant (see *Miller (James) and Partners Ltd v Whitworth Street Estates (Manchester) Ltd* [1970] 1 All ER 796 at 805, [1970] AC 583 at 611). In this case just look at the time when the $3,250,000 was advanced by Portsoken to ANPP. The parties must have thought that the guarantee covered the loan. Otherwise they would surely have *h* amended the guarantee so as to cover it.

In my opinion, therefore, the guarantee given by Amalgamated covered the moneys owing by ANPP to Portsoken which was the wholly-owned subsidiary of the bank. If this be correct, it is the end of the case. But as the judge thought the guarantee did not cover the loan, I shall go on to consider subsequent conduct.

Subsequent conduct

j

For many years I thought that when the meaning of a contract was uncertain you could look at the subsequent conduct of the parties so as to ascertain it. That seemed to me sensible enough. The parties themselves should know what they meant by their words better than anyone else. In this I was supported by *Watcham v Attorney General of*

East African Protectorate [1919] AC 533, [1918–19] All ER Rep 455, a Privy Council case
a which was applied repeatedly in my early days in the common law courts. But it was
always repudiated by the more logical minds in Chancery. Eventually the logicians
prevailed. In *James Miller (James) and Partners Ltd v Whitworth Street Estates (Manchester)
Ltd* [1970] 1 All ER 796 at 798, [1970] AC 583 at 603 Lord Reid said:

> '. . . it is not legitimate to use as an aid in the construction of the contract anything
> which the parties said or did after it was made. Otherwise one might have the result
b > that a contract meant one thing the day it was signed, but by reason of subsequent
> events meant something different a month or a year later.'

I can understand the logic of it when the construction is clear; but not when it is
unclear. Still, we must accept it. Nevertheless a way of escape was left open by Viscount
Dilhorne in that very case when he said ([1970] 1 All ER 796 at 805, [1970] AC 583 at
c 611): '. . . subsequent conduct by one party may give rise to an estoppel.'
So here we have available to us, in point of practice if not in law, evidence of
subsequent conduct to come to our aid. It is available, not so as to construe the contract,
but to see how they themselves acted on it. Under the guise of estoppel we can prevent
either party from going back on the interpretation they themselves gave to it.

d *The conduct here*
The evidence is overwhelming to show that, from the very moment when the
$3,250,000 was advanced to ANPP, all the parties thought that it was secured not only by
the mortgage of the Harrison Building but also by the guarantee of Amalgamated. In
pursuance of that belief the bank embarked on a course of conduct, rearranging their
portfolio of investments, releasing properties and moneys to Amalgamated which they
e would not have done except on the basis that the guarantee of Amalgamated covered the
loan to ANPP. The judge tells the story ([1981] 1 All ER 923 at 929–934, [1981] 2 WLR
554 at 562–568).
Now assuming that this belief was mistaken (and the judge thought it was but I do
not) a question arises about the law of estoppel. The mistake by the bank was self-
induced. They had overlooked the wording of the guarantee. They thought it applied
f to moneys owing to Portsoken as well as moneys owing to the bank. This was the bank's
own mistake. It was not induced by Amalgamated. Nor did Amalgamated do anything
to contribute to it or to reinforce it, except this: they did not contradict it. They did not
tell the bank that it was mistaken. But then, it is said, how could Amalgamated be
expected to contradict it, when they were under the same mistake? So runs the argument
on behalf of Amalgamated. The bank made a mistake of its own; everything it did
g followed from its own mistake. So it should put up with the consequences.
The judge put this telling point: suppose that Amalgamated knew that the bank were
under a mistake, and did not tell the bank but took advantage of it for their own
benefit. Could Amalgamated then take advantage of it? Clearly not. Then what
difference does it make that Amalgamated were under the same mistake?

h *Course of dealing*
Although subsequent conduct cannot be used for the purpose of interpreting a contract
retrospectively, yet it is often convincing evidence of a course of dealing after it. There
are many cases to show that a course of dealing may give rise to legal obligations. It may
be used to complete a contract which would otherwise be incomplete: see *Brogden v
Metropolitan Railway* (1877) 2 App Cas 666 at 682 per Lord Hatherley. It may be used so
j as to introduce terms and conditions into a contract which would not otherwise be there:
see *J Spurling Ltd v Bradshaw* [1956] 2 All ER 121, [1956] 1 WLR 461, and *Henry Kendall
& Sons (a firm) v William Lillico & Sons Ltd* [1966] 1 All ER 309 at 322, 327–329, [1966] 1
WLR 287 at 308, 316, CA; [1968] 2 All ER 444 at 462, 474–475, 481, [1969] 2 AC 31 at
90, 104, 113 (per Lord Morris, Lord Guest and Lord Pearce in the House of Lords all
disapproving the dictum of Lord Devlin in *McCutcheon v David Macbrayne Ltd* [1964] 1

All ER 430 at 437, [1964] 1 WLR 125 at 134) and *Hollier v Rambler Motors Ltd* [1972] 1 All ER 399 at 403–404, [1972] 2 QB 71 at 77–78 per Salmon LJ. If it can be used to introduce terms which were not already there, it must also be available to add to, or vary, terms which are there already, or to interpret them. If parties to a contract, by their course of dealing, put a particular interpretation on the terms of it, on the faith of which each of them to the knowledge of the other acts and conducts their mutual affairs, they are bound by that interpretation just as if they had written it down as being a variation of the contract. There is no need to inquire whether their particular interpretation is correct or not, or whether they were mistaken or not, or whether they had in mind the original terms or not. Suffice it that they have, by the course of dealing, put their own interpretation on their contract, and cannot be allowed to go back on it.

To use the phrase of Latham CJ and Dixon J in the Australian High Court in *Grundt v Great Boulder Pty Gold Mines Ltd* (1937) 59 CLR 641 the parties by their course of dealing adopted a 'conventional basis' for the governance of the relations between them, and are bound by it. I care not whether this is put as an agreed variation of the contract or as a species of estoppel. They are bound by the 'conventional basis' on which they conducted their affairs. The reason is because it would be altogether unjust to allow either party to insist on the strict interpretation of the original terms of the contract when it would be inequitable to do so, having regard to dealings which have taken place between the parties. That is the principle on which we acted in *Crabb v Arun District Council* [1975] 3 All ER 865, [1976] Ch 179. It is particularly appropriate here where the judges differ as to what is the correct interpretation of the terms of the guarantee. The trial judge interpreted it one way. We interpret it in another way. It is only fair and just that the difference should be solved by the course of dealing, by the interpretation which the parties themselves put on it and on which they have conducted their affairs for years.

So I come to this conclusion: when the parties to a contract are both under a common mistake as to the meaning or effect of it and thereafter embark on a course of dealing on the footing of that mistake, thereby replacing the original terms of the contract by a conventional basis on which they both conduct their affairs, then the original contract is replaced by the conventional basis. The parties are bound by the conventional basis. Either party can sue or be sued upon it just as if it had been expressly agreed between them.

Conclusion

The doctrine of estoppel is one of the most flexible and useful in the armoury of the law. But it has become overloaded with cases. That is why I have not gone through them all in this judgment. It has evolved during the last 150 years in a sequence of separate developments: proprietory estoppel, estoppel by representation of fact, estoppel by acquiescence and promissory estoppel. At the same time it has been sought to be limited by a series of maxims: estoppel is only a rule of evidence; estoppel cannot give rise to a cause of action; estoppel cannot do away with the need for consideration, and so forth. All these can now be seen to merge into one general principle shorn of limitations. When the parties to a transaction proceed on the basis of an underlying assumption (either of fact or of law, and whether due to misrepresentation or mistake, makes no difference), on which they have conducted the dealings between them, neither of them will be allowed to go back on that assumption when it would be unfair or unjust to allow him to do so. If one of them does seek to go back on it, the courts will give the other such remedy as the equity of the case demands.

That general principle applies to this case. Both Amalgamated and the bank proceeded for years on the basis of the underlying assumption that the guarantee of Amalgamated applied to the $3,250,000 advanced by the bank for the Nassau building. Their dealings in rearranging the portfolio, in releasing properties and moneys, were all conducted on that basis. On that basis the bank applied the surplus of $750,000 (on the English properties) in discharge of the obligations of Amalgamated under the guarantee. It would be most unfair and unjust to allow the liquidator to depart from that basis and to

claim back the $750,000 now. That was ultimately the paramount reason why the judge
a rejected the liquidator's claim. He summed up his view in this one sentence ([1981] 1
All ER 923 at 938–939, [1981] 2 WLR 554 at 574):

> '... I am satisfied that [Amalgamated's] conduct, though of course completely
> innocent, so influenced [the bank's] conduct, as to render it unconscionable on the
> part of [Amalgamated] now to take advantage of the bank's error.'

b And the judge speaks of it as being 'unconscionable' for the representor to go back on his
representation. In those phrases the judge is applying the general principle of estoppel
which I have stated. I agree with his analysis of the cases and with his conclusion. I
would dismiss the appeal.

EVELEIGH LJ. The obligations assumed by Amalgamated, the plaintiffs, and the
c bank, the defendant, in my opinion clearly emerge from the correspondence between
the parties. There would have been no problem had there not been injected into their
agreement a standard banking form which has been treated in argument as being the
guarantee. The phrase 'being the guarantee' would be more appropriate in the case
where the guarantor has no other interest in the transaction than to guarantee the
obligations of another. In such a case the document alone is treated as the agreement
d between the parties. As in all written contracts, however, it can embody terms previously
agreed by other means. But to satisfy the Statute of Frauds (1677) it is put into writing
as a written note or memorandum necessary for the enforcement of a contract of
guarantee.

Where the guarantee does not stand alone but is part of a larger transaction, even an
oral promise of guarantee is enforceable (see *Sutton & Co v Grey* [1894] 1 QB 285). Not
e unnaturally, however, businessmen like to have written evidence of their agreements
whether the Statute of Frauds requires it or not.

I make these preliminary remarks because at times it seemed that we were in danger
of treating the bank's printed form as though it stood alone and was to be construed in
isolation as if it required the strictness of construction appropriate to commercial
documents such as bills of lading which have a universally recognised character which is
f of importance to a number of people other than those concerned in the original contract.

Amalgamated did not come into this matter simply as guarantors after the formation
of a principal contract. They and the bank were the principal negotiators in reaching an
agreement whereby the bank at the request of Amalgamated agreed to provide money
to be used in connection with property development in the Bahamas in which
Amalgamated had a great financial interest. The Harrison Building was charged to
g Barclays Bank. At the request of Amalgamated the bank offered on 11th July 1969 to
make available a facility of $3,000,000 for a period of five years to Gleniston Gardens
Estate Ltd, a subsidiary of Amalgamated. They wrote:

> 'The borrowing would be secured by a legal mortgage in respect of the freehold
> property, the Harrison Building, now in the course of erection at Marlborough
> Street, Nassau, Bahamas, together with a guarantee for the full amount of the
h > facility from Amalgamated Investment Property Co. Ltd. ... Your company would
> be responsible for the bank's legal fees, stamp duty, etc.'

It is not clear who actually owned the Harrison Building at that stage. It does not
matter. The building was charged to Barclays Bank to secure a loan and the intention
was that the defendant bank should provide facilities for Barclays to be paid off and for
j the balance of the agreed sum to be made available to Gleniston who would be the
owners of the Harrison Building. Amalgamated accepted the offer 'on behalf of
Amalgamated and the Gleniston Gardens Estate Ltd'. They signed a standard guarantee,
the printed terms of which were clearly appropriate.

Amalgamated themselves were asking for the money. The bank was agreeing to
provide it and to allocate it as Amalgamated requested. Amalgamated were clearly
undertaking to see that the defendants were repaid.

Subsequently Amalgamated asked for ANPP to be substituted for Gleniston and for the loan to be increased to $3,250,000. Amalgamated wrote to the bank on 12th May 1970: 'As discussed, I confirm that Mr Harrison wishes to transfer the Harrison Building from the Gleniston Gardens Estate Ltd to another wholly owned subsidiary of ours in the Bahamas, Amalgamated (New Providence) Property Ltd.' On 23rd September 1970 the bank wrote confirming their agreement to the variation. In setting out the terms that had been agreed they stated that the borrowing would be secured by a legal mortgage in respect of the Harrison Building together with a guarantee from Amalgamated. They stated that the guarantee completed in relation to Gleniston Gardens Estate Ltd had been cancelled. Amalgamated signed another standard guarantee form which, in so far as is material, read as follows:

'We, AMALGAMATED INVESTMENT & PROPERTY CO. LTD. 9–10 GRAFTON STREET, LONDON, WIX 4DA, (hereinafter called "the Guarantor"), in consideration of your from time to time making or contributing loans or advances to or otherwise giving credit or affording banking accommodation or facilities to AMALGAMATED (NEW PROVIDENCE) PROPERTY LTD. of PO BOX 868, NASSAU, BAHAMAS (hereinafter called "the Principal"), hereby unconditionally guarantee to and agree with you as follows:
    '1. The Guarantor will pay to you on demand all moneys which now are or shall at any time or times hereafter be due or owing or payable to you on any account whatsoever by the Principal . . .'

Then, for exchange control reasons and as the judge explains in detail, the bank, to use its own solicitor's word, 'channelled' the loan through Portsoken Ltd, a paper company brought into action solely for the purpose. No new standard form guarantee was signed.

Ignoring the existence of the guarantee form, in my opinion the agreement reached between the parties orally and evidenced by or contained in (it matters not) the correspondence was clearly to the effect that Amalgamated would be responsible for seeing that the bank was repaid. The subsequent negotiations between Amalgamated and the bank after the money was made available on 31st December 1970 and up to 1976 in which Amalgamated clearly recognised this obligation provides admissible and strong evidence of this. Are we driven to arrive at a different conclusion because of the existence of the standard guarantee form containing the name of ANPP?

It might have been possible to have approached this case on the basis that the form was not introduced into the final contract. In that case the position would be as I have stated above. However, this case has been argued on the basis that it formed part of the final agreement. In that case the undertaking by the guarantor must be construed in the general setting of the transaction. It was a document that had been used by the bank to secure its own position in relation to the facilities it was affording. I think that the reference to 'all monies . . . payable to you . . . by the Principal' (ie ANPP) can only refer to the facility which the bank was affording. In the context of the whole transaction, it can in my opinion have no other meaning. The fact that the money could be legally demanded in the first instance by Portsoken does not rob it of its character of moneys payable to the bank, and the fact that Portsoken would first receive it and hand it over to the bank does not rob it of the description of moneys payable by ANPP. To deny this result by an analytical examination of the different legal liabilities engendered by the form which the transaction ultimately took is to deprive the words of the guarantee of a wider meaning which they are fully capable of bearing. It runs counter to all principles of construction to give the words a meaning that would defeat the clear intention of the parties as revealed by the rest of the relevant evidence of the agreement. I too am of the opinion that Amalgamated's claim fails on this ground.

As the question of estoppel has been argued before this court, I think I should say a few words on that matter on the assumption that the guarantee was so worded as not to cover the transaction. After 31st December 1970 changes were made in the arrangements by which a number of properties had been charged to secure to the bank two separate loans, namely one of $US3,000,000 (called the UK loan) and one of $3,250,000 (the Nassau

loan). These loans were quite independently secured, the UK loan by a number of
a properties and the Nassau loan by the Harrison Building. It seems probable that the
bank at all times thought that the charges were related in that they supported an all
moneys guarantee covering both loans. The negotiations which took place and the
subsequent agreements arrived at were clearly based upon the common understanding
that the guarantee in relation to ANPP made them liable to the bank in respect of the
Nassau loan. In so far as it is said that the bank acted to its detriment in relying on that
b assumption, I find it difficult to say that Amalgamated were responsible, therefore,
simply on the basis that their mistake might be said to have strengthened the bank's
assumption. Furthermore, I find it difficult to see how the substitution of properties in
the list of those charged to the bank and their revaluation was detrimental to the bank's
interests. The only property charged to secure the Nassau loan was the Harrison
Building. The revaluation showed that that building would no longer realise an amount
c sufficient to cover the loan. The bank required a 150% cover on the joint value of the
two loans. A variation in the list of properties was designed not only to release some at
the request of Amalgamated but also, on the bank's insistence, to provide that 150%
overall cover. Ex hypothesi, the ANPP guarantee being worthless, the only guarantee
which the bank was entitled to enforce, namely in respect of the UK loan, now became
more firmly secured. Therefore the guarantee position was more favourable to the bank
d than it had been. However, in the later stages of the negotiations the bank refrained
from calling in the loan, and in particular the Nassau loan, at a time which might have
been more favourable from its point of view and also extended the time for repayment
so that increased interest charges were incurred. In this respect it can be said that the
bank acted to its detriment. With some hesitation, I think it may be right to conclude
that when Amalgamated asked for further time they were asserting that they themselves
were ultimately liable for the Nassau loan and can be said to have induced the bank to act
e to their detriment partly as a result of their assertion, and therefore a case of estoppel in
pais can be made out. However, I would prefer to treat this case as one of estoppel by
convention.
    Counsel for the bank referred us to a passage in Spencer Bower and Turner on Estoppel
by Representation (3rd Edn, 1977, p 157):

f   'When the parties have acted in their transaction upon the agreed assumption
    that a given state of facts is to be accepted between them as true, then as regards that
    transaction each will be estopped against the other from questioning the truth of the
    statement of facts so assumed.'

It is clear that the parties negotiated on the agreed assumption that Amalgamated
g guaranteed the Nassau loan. The detailed negotiations are set out in the judgment of the
judge. Suffice it to say that there came a time when the parties agreed that all the
properties should be available to secure both the liability of Amalgamated in respect of
the UK loan and also their liability in respect of the Nassau loan, which latter liability was
assumed to exist. The bank sold the properties. They claimed the right to appropriate
the proceeds of both loans. As I have said, the proceeds of the Harrison Building would
h not satisfy the Nassau loan. Amalgamated challenge this, saying that the properties were
charged to secure their liability and that they were not liable under the guarantee for
ANPP. In my opinion, they cannot be allowed to say this. The bank had been given the
right to sell the properties and satisfy both loans on the agreed assumption that
Amalgamated were liable for the Nassau loan. The bank sold and appropriated the
proceeds on that assumption. Amalgamated cannot deny the truth of it.
    It is important to appreciate that the transaction with which we are concerned is the
j realisation of the securities by the bank. We are not concerned to decide whether
Amalgamated would have had a defence to an action on the ANPP guarantee itself if the
security had proved insufficient. For myself I do not think that the bank could have
succeeded in a claim on the guarantee itself. Estoppel operates so as to prevent a party
from denying a representation or an assumed state of facts in relation to the transaction

supported by that representation or assumed state of facts. The estoppel does not go beyond the transaction in which it arose. The representation or assumed state of facts are not to be held irrefutable beyond the purpose for which the representation or assumption was made. In the present context the representation is not made for the purpose of establishing its own truth but as a part of the whole transaction. An assumption is not to be treated as having the effect of an assumpsit.

However, I too would dismiss this appeal.

BRANDON LJ. In this judgment I shall refer to the various parties concerned by the same abbreviations as those used by Robert Goff J in his judgment. That is to say, I shall refer to Amalgamated Investment and Property Co Ltd as 'AIP'; to Gleniston Garden Estates Ltd as 'Gleniston'; to Amalgamated (New Providence) Property Ltd as 'ANPP'; to Burston and Texas Commerce Bank Ltd (later renamed Texas Commerce International Bank Limited) as 'the bank'; and to Portsoken Properties Ltd as 'Portsoken'. I shall also, like the judge, refer to the two loans made by the bank as 'the Nassau loan' and 'the UK loan' respectively.

The nature of the action, and the circumstances out of which it arises, are set out in detail in the full and comprehensive judgment of the judge, and no useful purpose would be served by my repeating his account of these matters in my own judgment. The important thing which I consider that it is necessary to do, in order to consider the appeal which is before us, is to formulate with as much precision as is possible the two questions which arise for decision in it.

Those two questions should, in my view, be formulated as follows. First, did AIP, by the contract which it made with the bank in relation to the Nassau loan, undertake to the bank that it would discharge any indebtedness of ANPP to Portsoken? Second, if AIP did not so undertake, is it nevertheless estopped from denying that it did so by reason of the basis, accepted by both the bank and AIP, on which the transactions between them were later conducted during the period from 1974 to 1976?

The first question is raised by the respondent's notice dated 16th September 1980. The second question is raised by the appellant's notice of appeal dated 26th August 1980. It is, however, logical to examine the two questions in the order in which I have stated them.

The making of the contract between AIP and the bank in relation to the Nassau loan took place in four stages. At the first stage, which occurred in July 1969, it was agreed, first, that the amount of the loan should be $US3,000,000; second, that the loan should be made directly by the bank to Gleniston, one of AIP's wholly-owned subsidiaries in the Bahamas; third, that the full amount of the loan should be taken up by 30th June 1970; and, fourth, that the loan should be secured in two ways, first by a mortgage on a property in Nassau known as the Harrison Building, and, secondly, by a guarantee to be given by AIP.

At the second stage, which occurred in April 1970, it was agreed that the date for taking up the loan in full should be postponed from 30th June 1970 to 31st December 1970.

At the third stage, which occurred between May and September 1970, it was agreed that the contract should be varied in two respects. The first variation was that there should be substituted for Gleniston as the borrower another wholly-owned subsidiary of AIP in the Bahamas, namely ANPP. The second variation was that the amount of the loan should be increased from $3,000,000 to $3,250,000. At this third stage, on 28th September 1970 there was signed on behalf of AIP, by way of security for any indebtedness of ANPP to the bank, a standard printed form of the bank entitled 'GUARANTEE'.

At the fourth stage, which occurred in December 1970, it was agreed that, instead of the loan being made directly by the bank to ANPP, it should be channelled by the bank through Portsoken, a wholly-owned subsidiary of the bank in the Bahamas. The effect a of so channelling the loan through Portsoken was that the bank first lent the money to Portsoken and Portsoken then re-lent it to ANPP. The sole reason for this change was that, if the bank had made the loan directly to ANPP as previously arranged, it would under Bahamian law have been obliged to register itself as trading in the Bahamas, and this would have involved it in complications in which it was not willing to be involved. There was no other purpose whatever for the change.

b When the fourth stage in the making of the contract just described occurred, it would have been sensible for the bank to have required AIP to have signed on its behalf a fresh guarantee, the express terms of which would have covered beyond doubt the indebtedness of ANPP to Portsoken instead of its indebtedness to the bank. It is quite clear that, if the bank had required AIP to do this, AIP would willingly have complied with such requirement. In fact, however, the matter was overlooked by the bank, and the original document entitled 'GUARANTEE', which had been signed on behalf of AIP at the third stage

c on 28th September 1970, and which I shall call 'the guarantee', remained, ostensibly at any rate, unchanged.

Following the fourth stage, the bank (by certain indirect methods which are not material) lent the sum of $3,250,000 to Portsoken and Portsoken immediately re-lent it to ANPP. At the same time, by way of security for the loan made by Portsoken to ANPP, ANPP mortgaged the Harrison Building, of which it had by that time become the

d freehold owner, to Portsoken. All these transactions took place on 30th and 31st December 1970.

The guarantee, which is addressed to the bank, provides so far as material as follows:

'We, AMALGAMATED INVESTMENT & PROPERTY CO. LTD. . . . (hereinafter called "the Guarantor"), in consideration of your from time to time making or contributing loans or advances or otherwise affording banking accommodation or facilities to

e AMALGAMATED (NEW PROVIDENCE) PROPERTY LTD . . . (hereinafter called "the Principal"), hereby unconditionally guarantee to and agree with you as follows:

'1. The Guarantor will pay to you on demand all moneys which are now or shall at any time or times hereafter be due or owing or payable to you on any account whatsoever by the Principal . . .'

f It was contended on behalf of the liquidator of AIP in the court below that, having regard to the terms of the guarantee as set out above, AIP never became contractually bound to the bank to discharge the indebtedness of ANPP to Portsoken, but only the indebtedness of ANPP to the bank. Robert Goff J accepted this contention as correct. In my opinion, for reasons which I shall develop, the judge was in error in the conclusion which he reached on this matter.

g The contract between the bank and AIP did not reach its final form until the fourth stage in the negotiations in December 1970, when it was agreed that the loan should be channelled from the bank to ANPP through Portsoken. It follows from this that the guarantee, which formed part of the contract, falls to be interpreted by reference to the situation which then existed, rather than the situation which existed earlier when the guarantee was signed on behalf of AIP at the third stage on 28th September 1970.

h What then was the situation which existed when the contract between the bank and AIP relating to the Nassau loan was at last finalised in December 1970? It was that it had been decided that the bank should not make the loan available directly to ANPP as originally arranged, but indirectly through the medium of its wholly-owned subsidiary Portsoken, in such a manner that any indebtedness of ANPP to Portsoken was accompanied by an exactly corresponding indebtedness of Portsoken to the bank. It is by reference to that situation that the words in para 1 of the guarantee, 'moneys due or

j owing or payable to you on any count whatsoever by the Principal', fall to be construed. In my opinion, when those words are construed by reference to the situation which I have just described, they are wide enough to include moneys due or owing or payable by ANPP to Portsoken, which Portsoken are then immediately required to pass on, without deduction of any kind, to the bank.

On that ground it is my view that AIP did become contractually bound to the bank, on the basis of the guarantee, to discharge any indebtedness of ANPP to Portsoken. I would, therefore, answer the first of the two questions which I formulated earlier in the affirmative.

I turn now to examine the second of the two questions which I formulated earlier. That question is whether, supposing my answer to the first question is wrong, and AIP did not, by the contract which it made with the bank in relation to the Nassau loan, undertake to the bank to discharge any indebtedness of ANPP to Portsoken, AIP is nevertheless estopped from denying having done so by reason of the basis, accepted by both AIP and the bank, on which the transactions between them were conducted during the period from 1974 to 1976.

The judge answered this question in the affirmative and dismissed the claim of AIP in liquidation on that account. He based his decision on the question of estoppel on three matters. The first matter was that, from 1974 to 1976, both the bank and AIP conducted the transactions which took place between them in what must for present purposes be regarded as the mistaken belief that the guarantee relating to the Nassau loan effectively bound AIP to discharge any indebtedness of ANPP to Portsoken in respect of that loan. The second matter was that, although it had originally been due to the bank's own error that it came to hold its mistaken belief, AIP, being under the same mistaken belief itself, by its conduct encouraged and reinforced the mistaken belief held by the bank. The third matter was that the bank, in reliance on the mistaken belief concerned, accorded various indulgences to, and refrained from exercising various rights against, AIP in a way which, but for the bank's mistaken belief, it would never have done.

The judge has set out in detail in his judgment all the primary facts relevant to the question of estoppel. In what follows I shall adopt his account of those facts in its entirety, without doing more than is absolutely necessary by way of repeating or summarising such account.

The Nassau loan was not the only loan made by the bank at the request of AIP. Following negotiations between AIP and the bank which took place during January, February and March 1970 the bank made a loan to AIP in England of $US3,000,000 for a period of five years (the UK loan). That loan was secured by mortgages or sub-mortgages on a large number of properties in England, the value of which was thought to be such as to comply with the general practice of the bank to require 150% security for any loans which it made.

Nothing significant with regard to the UK loan occurred until June 1974, when a series of developments relating to it began and continued until 1976. These developments are set out in detail by the judge ([1981] 1 All ER 923 at 929–932, [1981] 2 WLR 554 at 562–566). The account there given fully substantiates the judge's finding that from 1974 to 1976 the bank and AIP conducted transactions between them in relation to the overall liabilty of AIP in respect of the UK and Nassau loans in the mistaken belief, common to both of them, that the guarantee relating to the Nassau loan bound AIP to discharge any indebtedness of ANPP to Portsoken in respect of that loan. It further fully substantiates his finding that the bank, in reliance on that mistaken belief, granted various indulgences to, and refrained from exercising various rights against, AIP in a manner which, but for such belief, it would never have done.

Two main arguments against the existence of an estoppel were advanced on behalf of AIP both before Robert Goff J and before us. The first argument was that, since the bank came to hold its mistaken belief in the first place as a result of its own error alone, and AIP had at most innocently acquiesced in that belief which it also held, there was no representation by AIP to the bank on which an estoppel could be founded. The second argument was that, in the present case, the bank was seeking to use estoppel not as a shield, but as a sword, and that that was something which the law of estoppel did not permit.

I consider first the argument based on the origin of the bank's mistaken belief. In my opinion this argument is founded on an erroneous view of the kind of estoppel which is *a* relevant in this case. The kind of estoppel which is relevant in this case is not the usual kind of estoppel in pais based on a representation made by A to B and acted on by B to his detriment. It is rather the kind of estoppel which is described in Spencer Bower and Turner on Estoppel by Representation (3rd Edn, 1977, pp 157–160) as estoppel by convention:

b 'This form of estoppel is founded, not on a representation of fact made by a representor and believed by a representee, but on an agreed statement of facts the truth of which has been assumed, by the convention of the parties, as the basis of a transaction into which they are about to enter. When the parties have acted in their transaction upon the agreed assumption that a given state of facts is to be accepted between them as true, then as regards that transaction each will be estopped as against the other from questioning the truth of the statement of facts so assumed.'

c Applying that description of estoppel by convention to the present case, the situation as I see it is this. First, the relevant transactions entered into by AIP and the bank were the making of new arrangements with regard to the overall security held by the bank in relation to both the UK and Nassau loans. Second, for the purposes of those transactions, both the bank and AIP assumed the truth of a certain state of affairs, namely that the guarantee given in relation to the Nassau loan effectively bound AIP to discharge any *d* indebtedness of ANPP to Portsoken. The transactions took place on the basis of that assumption, and their course was influenced by it in the sense that, if the assumption had not been made, the course of the transactions would without doubt have been different.

Those facts produce, in my opinion, a classic example of the kind of estoppel called estoppel by convention as described in the passage from Spencer Bower and Turner on Estoppel by Representation and so deprive the first argument advanced on behalf of AIP of any validity which, if the case were an ordinary one of estoppel by representation, it *e* might otherwise have.

I turn to the second argument advanced on behalf of AIP, that the bank is here seeking to use estoppel as a sword rather than a shield, and that that is something which the law of estoppel does not permit. Another way in which the argument is put is that a party cannot found a cause of action on an estoppel.

f In my view much of the language used in connection with these concepts is no more than a matter of semantics. Let me consider the present case and suppose that the bank had brought an action against AIP before it went into liquidation to recover moneys owed by ANPP to Portsoken. In the statement of claim in such an action the bank would have pleaded the contract of loan incorporating the guarantee, and averred that, on the true construction of the guarantee, AIP was bound to discharge the debt owed by ANPP *g* to Portsoken. By their defence AIP would have pleaded that, on the true construction of the guarantee, AIP was only bound to discharge debts owed by ANPP to the bank, and not debts owed by ANPP to Portsoken. Then in their reply the bank would have pleaded that, by reason of an estoppel arising from the matters discussed above, AIP were precluded from questioning the interpretation of the guarantee which both parties had, for the purpose of the transactions between them, assumed to be true.

h In this way the bank, while still in form using the estoppel as a shield, would in substance be founding a cause of action on it. This illustrates what I would regard as the true proposition of law, that, while a party cannot in terms found a cause of action on an estoppel, he may, as a result of being able to rely on an estoppel, succeed on a cause of action on which, without being able to rely on that estoppel, he would necessarily have failed. That, in my view, is, in substance, the situation of the bank in the present case.

j It follows from what I have said above that I would reject the second argument against the existence of an estoppel put forward on behalf of AIP as well as the first. It further follows, from my rejection of both arguments against the existence of an estoppel, that I would answer the second of the two questions which I formulated earlier by holding that, if AIP did not, by the contract relating to the Nassau loan, undertake to the bank to discharge any indebtedness of ANPP to Portsoken, it is nevertheless estopped from denying that it did so by reason of the basis, accepted by both the bank and AIP, on which the transactions between them were later conducted during the period from 1974 to 1976. *a*

Since I have, for the reasons which I have given, answered both the questions which I formulated earlier in my judgment in the affirmative, it follows that, in my opinion, the appeal of AIP in liquidation fails and must be dismissed.

Appeal dismissed. Leave to appeal to the House of Lords refused. *b*

Solicitors: *Allen & Overy* (for the plaintiff); *Nabarro Nathanson* (for the defendant bank).

Henrietta Steinberg   Barrister.

c

Yianni and another v Edwin Evans & Sons (a firm)

QUEEN'S BENCH DIVISION
PARK J   *d*
7th, 8th, 28th JULY 1981

Negligence – Information or advice – Knowledge third party might rely on information – Surveyor and valuer – Valuation report to building society – Surveyor's report stating that property adequate security for amount of loan sought by purchaser of property – Building society offering to lend that amount to purchaser in reliance on report – Surveyor negligent in failing to *e* *discover defects in foundations of property – Property inadequate security for loan – Purchaser accepting building society's offer and purchasing property – Whether surveyor liable to purchaser for negligent statement in report to building society – Whether relationship between surveyor and purchaser sufficiently proximate for duty of care to arise.*

In October 1974 the owners of a house discovered serious defects in it stemming from *f* subsidence and distortion in the foundations. Without remedying the defects the owners sold the house to P in about April 1975. P carried out extensive repairs and redecoration to the house but did not remedy the defects in the foundations. Later in 1975 P offered to sell the house to the plaintiffs, who were of modest means and were looking for an inexpensive house. The plaintiffs decided to buy the house at P's asking price of £15,000 if they could obtain a loan of £12,000 from a building society. Accordingly they applied *g* to a building society for a loan of £12,000 and paid to the society a survey fee for the valuation of the property which, under s 25[a] of the Building Societies Act 1962, the society was required to carry out. The building society instructed the defendants, a well-established firm of valuers and surveyors who regularly carried out valuations for the society, to inspect the house and value it. The society's instructions to the defendants named the plaintiffs as the purchasers of the house, the purchase price of the house and *h* the loan required by the plaintiffs. The defendants' representative inspected the house and following his inspection the defendants made a report to the building society in which they stated that the house was adequate security for a loan of £12,000. The building society accepted the report and notified the plaintiffs that it was willing to lend them £12,000 and also sent them a copy of the society's booklet on mortgages, which in a paragraph headed 'Valuation' stated that the society did not accept responsibility for the *j* condition of the property offered as security, that it did not warrant that the purchase price was reasonable, that the valuer's report was confidential to the society and for its exclusive use, and that if a borrower required a survey of the property for his own

---

a   Section 25, so far as material, is set out at p 596 *e, post*

information and protection he should instruct an independent surveyor. The society
a also sent the plaintiffs a notice under s 30^b of the 1962 Act stating that the making of an
advance would not imply any warranty by the building society that the purchase price
was reasonable. It was common knowledge among building societies and known to the
defendants that 90% of applicants for mortgages to purchase lower-priced houses relied
on the building society's valuation of the property and did not instruct an independent
surveyor, despite the guidance given to applicants in building society literature and the
b service of s 30 notices. The plaintiffs accepted the building society's offer without having
the house independently surveyed. In January 1976 they completed the purchase of the
house and in October discovered cracks in the foundations. The cost of repairing the
foundations was estimated at £18,000. The plaintiffs brought an action against the
defendants for damages for negligence, alleging that the defendants' statement in their
report to the building society that the house was adequate security for a loan of £12,000
c meant that the house was worth at least that sum, that that was a negligent statement,
that the defendants ought reasonably to have contemplated that the building society
would pass on the contents of that statement to the plaintiffs, and that the plaintiffs
would rely on it and be induced to purchase the house for £15,000 and to mortgage it.
The plaintiffs claimed that having done so they had in consequence suffered damage.
The defendants admitted that they were negligent in their inspection of the house and
d in failing to notice the defects in the foundations and were consequently negligent in
stating in their report that the house was adequate security for a loan of £12,000 when
in fact it was worth little more than its site value, but they contended, however, that they
owed no duty of care to the plaintiffs, that any duty of care was owed only to the building
society, and that, in failing to have an independent survey, in making no inquiries about
what had been done to the house before they bought it and in failing to have regard to
e the building society's literature, the plaintiffs had been contributorily negligent.

Held – The defendants were liable in negligence to the plaintiffs for the following
reasons—
    (1) The defendants owed the plaintiffs a duty of care because the relationship between
them was sufficiently proximate to establish that it was within the defendants' reasonable
f contemplation that carelessness on their part might be likely to cause the plaintiffs
damage, because (a) the defendants knew that the building society would rely on their
valuation report in assessing the adequacy of the house as security for a loan and the
amount of the loan, (b) they therefore knew that because of their report the building
society would offer to lend the plaintiffs £12,000 and by virtue of that offer would pass
on to the plaintiffs the defendants' valuation of the house, and (c) having regard to the
g common practice, known to the defendants, of borrowers who were purchasing lower
priced houses relying on a building society's valuation of the property and not having an
independent survey, the defendants also knew that the plaintiffs, in deciding to purchase
the house for £15,000 and to mortgage it would rely on the defendants' valuation which
was communicated to them in the building society's offer to lend £12,000 (see p 600 b,
p 604 c to p 605 g and p 606 h, post); dicta of Denning LJ in *Candler v Crane, Christmas*
h *& Co* [1951] 1 All ER at 433–436, of Lord Morris, of Lord Hodson, of Lord Devlin and
of Lord Pearce in *Hedley Byrne & Co Ltd v Heller & Partners Ltd* [1963] 2 All ER at 594,
597, 611, 617–618 and of Lord Wilberforce in *Anns v London Borough of Merton* [1977] 2
All ER at 498 applied.
    (2) There were no policy considerations which required that the defendants' duty to
the plaintiffs should be negatived, since (a) to hold that the defendants were liable to the
i plaintiffs would not result in a valuer to a building society having unlimited liability to
third parties, since his liability would be limited to liability to the purchaser named in
the building society's instructions to value a property, and (b) it would not be
objectionable if the consequence of holding that the defendants were liable to the
plaintiffs was that applicants for building society mortgages would always rely on the

---

    b   Section 30 is set out at p 596 f, post

building society's valuation and would not have the property they wished to purchase independently surveyed, since there was nothing objectionable in having a property surveyed once only, namely by the building society's surveyor (see p 605 *g h* and p 606 *a* to *c* and *h*, post).

(3) The plaintiffs had not been guilty of contributory negligence in failing to have the house independently surveyed or in failing in general to take steps to discover the condition of the house because it was reasonable for the plaintiffs to rely on the defendants' valuation (see p 606 *f* to *h*, post).

Notes

For the duty to take care generally, see 34 Halsbury's Laws (4th Edn) para 5 and for negligence in relation to statements, see ibid para 53.

For cases on the duty to take care, see 36(1) Digest (Reissue) 17–32, 34–103.

Cases referred to judgment

Anns v London Borough of Merton [1977] 2 All ER 492, [1978] AC 728, [1977] 2 WLR 1024, 141 JP 526, 75 LGR 555, HL, Digest (Cont Vol E) 449, 99*b*.

Candler v Crane, Christmas & Co [1951] 1 All ER 426, [1951] 2 KB 164, CA, 36(1) Digest (Reissue) 22, 75.

Donoghue v Stevenson [1932] AC 562, [1932] All ER Rep 1, 101 LJPC 119, 147 LT 281, 37 Com Cas 350, 1932 SC(HL) 31, 1932 SLT 317, HL, 36(1) Digest (Reissue) 144, 562.

Hedley Byrne & Co Ltd v Heller & Partners Ltd [1963] 2 All ER 575, [1964] AC 465, [1963] 3 WLR 101, [1963] 1 Lloyd's Rep 485, HL, 36(1) Digest (Reissue) 24, 84.

Home Office v Dorset Yacht Co Ltd [1970] 2 All ER 294, [1970] AC 1004, [1970] 2 WLR 1140, [1970] 1 Lloyd's Rep 453, HL, 36(1) Digest (Reissue) 27, 93.

Le Lievre v Gould [1893] 1 QB 491, 62 LJQB 353, 68 LT 626, 57 JP 484, 4 R 274, CA, 36(1) Digest (Reissue) 9, 27.

Nocton v Lord Ashburton [1914] AC 932, [1914–15] All ER Rep 45, 83 LJ Ch 784, 111 LT 641, HL, 43 Digest (Repl) 115, 1038.

Robinson v National Bank of Scotland 1916 SC (HL) 154, 25 Digest (Reissue) 89, 459.

Ross v Caunters [1979] 3 All ER 580, [1980] Ch 297, [1979] 3 WLR 605.

Action

By a writ issued on 19th November 1979 the plaintiffs, George Yianni and Anna Yianni, claimed against the defendants, Edwin Evans & Sons, a firm of surveyors and valuers, damages for negligence in regard to a representation in their report to the Halifax Building Society on the value of a house at 1 Seymour Road, Hornsey, London N8, in regard to the purchase of which the plaintiffs were seeking a loan from the building society. The facts are set out in the judgment.

Robert Johnson QC and *Malcolm Stitcher* for the plaintiffs.
Richard Fernyhough for the defendants.

Cur adv vult

28th July. **PARK J** read the following judgment: In this case the question to be decided is, in broad terms, whether surveyors who in a valuation report on a dwelling house for a building society negligently misrepresent its value are liable to purchasers who, in reliance on the statement as to its value, purchase the house and in consequence suffer damage.

1 Seymour Road, Hornsey, London N8 is a two-storey end of terrace house. It was built about the turn of the century and was of standard construction for the period. On the ground floor there is now an entrance hall, living room and kitchen, and on the first floor two double and two single bedrooms, bath and lavatory. It is a suitable house for a person of modest means with a small family.

Between 1960 and 1975 it was owned by the Mountmorres Property Co Ltd. The company used to let the house unfurnished. In August 1974 the tenants advised the company that cracks had appeared. The company called in a surveyor. As a result of his report the company obtained two quotations from local builders as to the cost of remedial works. One estimate was £6,600 and the other £8,550. Neither estimate

included the cost of underpinning works which would have had to be carried out by a
a specialist firm. The company thereupon made a claim on their insurers. The insurers
instructed a firm of chartered loss adjusters and surveyors, Thomas Howell, Selfe & Co,
to investigate the claim and report on it. Their report is by a Mr Kilbey and is dated 17th
October 1974. Of the nature and extent of damage Mr Kilbey reported—

> 'There is scarcely a wall which is free from signs of settlement and distortion. On
> the front elevation there are signs of historic settlement of the party wall, the front
> **b** door having obviously been adapted from time to time to enable it to close. The bay
> window shows signs of a separate subsidence, tending to crack away from the main
> wall and incline outwards. The arch over the entrance is fractured and has at some
> time previously been reinforced with a steel semi-circular arch bar. Clear signs of
> brickwork fractures extend from above this arch to the window above, which is
> **c** distorted. The flank wall shows numerous bulges and distortions, as indeed do the
> rear walls. Internally, most of the floors appear to slope in one direction or
> another. The corniced ceilings show numerous cracks, some having previously
> been made good, and it would appear that the flank wall has moved outwards. Few
> doors or windows function owing to distortion.'

As to the cause of that state of affairs Mr Kilbey reported—

> **d** 'For the most part, all damage seen was of long standing and obviously various
> attempts have been made in the past to make good cracks and defects. There is little
> doubt that the situation was exacerbated by a succession of dry years, causing the
> clay subsoil to dry out under foundations which were probably shallow and
> movement to take place. The fruit trees in the adjoining property have probably
> contributed to this.'

e The report recommended that as the inception date of the policy was July 1974 and as the
movement which caused the damage had occurred long before that date the insurers
should not accept liability. The report also said that to carry out repairs of the kind
described in the builders' quotations would be uneconomic.

At some time thereafter, and certainly before April 1975 the company sold the
f property to Mr Andreas Protopapas for £7,250. Mr Protopapas caused extensive repairs
and redecoration to be carried out, no doubt at considerable cost. It is not necessary to
refer to them in detail. It is sufficient to say that they included the following: new
plasterboard ceilings to bedrooms, landing and front part of the house. Doors and
frames were renewed. An opening was cut in the partition to unite two sitting rooms
into one through lounge. That opening was spanned by an RSJ extending from the party
wall to the flank wall, and at the end of the RSJ was a large restraining plate fixed to the
g outside. The flank wall chimney breast on both floors and the stacks had been taken
away. The windows throughout the house had been modernised with fixed glass and
louvre vents. The whole of the external brickwork had been stuccoed; the exterior had
been repainted and the interior redecorated throughout. Central heating had been
installed.

h Mr Protopapas is Mrs Yianni's brother. Mr and Mrs Yianni (the plaintiffs), Mr
Protopapas and a solicitor, Mr Nicolaou, all come from the same village near Famagusta
in Cyprus. Mr Yianni came to this country in 1961. He married some 15 years ago. He
has two children who in 1975 were aged nine and eight. He was then and still is
employed as a salesman in a furniture company owned by one of his wife's relatives. In
1975 he and his wife and children were living in a flat in East London, of which Mr
Protopapas was the landlord. In or about November 1975 Mr Protopapas told Mr Yianni
j that he had a house for sale, and that the keys were kept by Mr Nicolaou. Mr Yianni and
his wife, who does not speak English, paid two visits to 1 Seymour Road. They walked
around it. No doubt, because it had been recently redecorated, it looked in good
condition. It appeared to them to be a suitable home for themselves and their young
family. It also happened to be about five minutes' walk from Mr Yianni's place of work,
and was not far from the shops. For these reasons the plaintiffs decided that they would
like to buy the house. Mr Protopapas's price was £15,000. Mr Yianni didn't ask him

what he had paid for the house, nor about the extent or cost of the repairs and redecoration that had been carried out. Mr Protopapas volunteered no information on the subjects. The plaintiffs probably trusted him and assumed that the price he asked was fair. Mr Yianni was then earning £90 per week. He had savings of just over £3,000, so he needed £12,000 in order to be able to buy the house.

On or about 29th November 1975 the plaintiffs consulted Mr Nicolaou. He was also Mr Protopapas's solicitor and an agent for the Halifax Building Society. The plaintiffs had never previously bought a house or engaged in a mortgage transaction. Mr Nicolaou at some stage told the plaintiffs that he thought £15,000 was a reasonable price. He used the expression that it was a 'good buy'. He evidently told them that they could apply to the Halifax for an advance of £12,000 to enable them to buy the house. Mr Yianni said in evidence that he and his wife decided that if the Halifax agreed to provide £12,000 they would buy the house. If the Halifax did not agree to do so they would, as he put it, 'let the house go', as they had no money apart from the £3,000. Accordingly, they completed, apparently in Mr Nicolaou's office, a form of application for a loan to the Halifax, dated 1st December 1975.

By s 25 of the Building Societies Act 1962 the directors of a building society have imposed on them the duty to make arrangements for the valuation of properties offered as security for advances. Those arrangements have to be such as may reasonably be expected to ensure (inter alia) that there will be made available to every person in the society who has to assess the adequacy of any security an appropriate report as to the value of any freehold estate comprised in the security, and as to any matter likely to affect the value thereof. Section 25(2) also says this:

'. . . the reference to an appropriate report, in relation to any freehold or leasehold estate, is a reference to a written report prepared and signed by a competent and prudent person who—(a) is experienced in the matters relevant to the determination of the value of the estate . . .'

I need read no more words in that subsection.

By s 30 of the 1962 Act it is provided:

'Where a building society makes to a member an advance for the purpose of its being used in defraying the purchase price of freehold or leasehold estate, the society shall be deemed to warrant to the member that the purchase price is reasonable, unless, before any contract requiring a member to repay the advance is entered into, the society gives to the member a notice in writing in the prescribed form stating that the making of the advance implies no such warranty.'

On the application form the second paragraph forewarns the applicant that the making of an advance does not imply any warranty as to the reasonableness of the purchase price. Mr Yianni read that paragraph. He was also informed by Mr Nicolaou that he would, to use Mr Yianni's words, have to pay money for the house to be looked at. The fee was £33·30. Mr Yianni borrowed that sum from Mr Protopapas. He handed it over to Mr Nicolaou and subsequently repaid his brother-in-law that money.

On 1st December 1975 Mr Nicolaou spoke to the building society's branch manager at Finsbury Pavement and by arrangement sent him the form completed by the plaintiffs, together with a letter to which I need not refer.

On 8th December 1975 the branch manager sent to the defendants, a firm of surveyors and valuers, a printed document headed 'Instructions to valuer'. There is a reference in the document to s 25 of the 1962 Act. It can safely be assumed therefore that the defendants were aware of the provisions of s 25 and therefore of the purpose for which the report was required by the building society. This document also informed them of the purchase price of 1 Seymour Road, namely £15,000, and the advance required, £12,000. It would also appear from the document that the defendants had carried out valuations for the building society prior to 8th December 1975 because they were advised to include the charge for their valuation of 1 Seymour Road in their next

quarterly account to the building society's Finsbury Pavement office. Mr Yianni,
a remembering that the form that he had signed suggested that applicants who desired a
survey for their own information and protection should consult a surveyor on their own
account, made inquiries about the cost of employing a surveyor to make a report to him
on 1 Seymour Road. He discovered that the fee would be between £60 and £100, the
difference in amount being attributable probably to the difference in the standing of the
surveyor consulted and the kind of report which was sought. In any event, that was
b more than Mr Yianni could afford, so he decided not to have a report of any kind on the
house.

Was Mr Yianni's decision not to obtain a surveyor's report for his own information in
any respect unusual? On this question an important witness was Mr Hunter, the chief
surveyor to the Abbey National Building Society and a person with very high
qualifications in this field, who gave evidence in his private capacity. He told me how
c members of the public usually act when seeking to purchase house property with the aid
of an advance from a building society. He spoke from experience gained from the fact
that about 200,000 mortgage applications passed through his society each year. The
Abbey National and the Halifax are not the only building societies in business. According
to Wurtzburg and Mills on Building Society Law (14th Edn, 1976), in 1975 there were
about 447 of them. Out of that number it is probable that few handle mortgage
d applications on the same scale as the Abbey National and the Halifax but, whether that
is right or not, it is clear that in every year many thousands of people make mortgage
applications to building societies.

Since 1975, or thereabouts, the subject of the frequency with which independent
surveys are sought by intending mortgagors has been one of increasing interest both to
the building societies and to the Royal Institute of Chartered Surveyors. Mr Hunter has
e been taking spot checks over this period, and he has found that out of the total
applications received by his society the proportion of mortgagors who have their own
independent survey is less than 10%. The Royal Institute of Chartered Surveyors also
conducted a spot check and found the proportion to be between 10% and 15%. From his
experience Mr Hunter was able to advance a number of reasons for the failure to take the
building society's advice to employ an independent surveyor. In the first place, intending
f mortgagors trust the building societies. This trust is no doubt in part engendered by
successful advertising. There was put in evidence an attractive brochure issued by the
Halifax Building Society. On the front there is a picture in colour of a young man and
a young woman with two children in a garden, a modern house in the background and
the words prominently printed 'The Halifax guide to a home of your own'. Inside there
are ten pages containing the questions which an intending mortgagor would probably
g ask and the building society's answers. At the end of the book under the heading
'Personal service at over 380 branches and 1,300 agencies' is set the address of each
branch. Another reason, said Mr Hunter, is that each intending mortgagor knows that
he has paid a fee for someone on behalf of the building society to look at the house.
Many of them are not sufficiently informed to be able to distinguish between a surveyor's
report on valuation and a surveyor's report on condition because the usual intending
h mortgagor is, as Mr Hunter said, a lay person, not a professional. 'They have to have their
hands held a little bit', he said. In addition the intending mortgagor feels that the
building society, whom he trusts, must employ for the valuation and survey competent
qualified surveyors; and, if the building society acts on its surveyor's report, then there
can be no good reason why he should not also himself act on it. The consequence is that
if, after inspection by the building society's surveyor, an offer to make an advance is
j made, the applicant assumes that the building society has satisfied itself that the house is
valuable enough to provide suitable security for a loan and decides to proceed by
accepting the society's offer. So, if Mr Yianni had had an independent survey, he would
have been exceptional in the experience of the building societies and of those employed
to carry out surveys and valuations for them.

I come back now to the narrative. In compliance with the instructions from the building society, dated 8th December 1975, the defendants' representative, on 12th December 1975, surveyed 1 Seymour Road. The defendants' report and valuation is *a* dated 15th December 1975. At the foot of it there is a further reference to s 25 of the 1962 Act. Their valuation of the house was £15,000. Their confidential observations for the information of the building society's directors to enable those directors to assess the adequacy of 1 Seymour Road as security for an advance was that it was suitable for maximum lending. That meant that it was suitable security for an advance of 80% of the value of the house, which was £12,000. The directors did not take long to arrive at their *b* decision to accept the defendants' recommendation. By a notice dated 19th December 1975, to which I will refer in a moment, the plaintiffs were informed that the building society was willing to make an advance of £12,000.

But the defendants' report and valuation was the result of a grossly incompetent and negligent survey. None of the serious faults in the foundations discovered by Mr Kilbey in October 1974 and never remedied were disclosed in it. Those faults gravely affected *c* the value of the house. The report was referred to with scorn by Mr Hunter. 'I speak as a surveyor', he said, 'I don't look with any pride at a document such as this'. In truth, notwithstanding the extensive repairs and redecoration carried out by Mr Protopapas, the house at this time was worth little more than its site value.

By their solicitors' letter dated 16th October 1980 the defendants admitted that in inspecting the house they were negligent in the following respects: that they failed to *d* notice that the property had been the subject of subsidence, failed to take proper steps to ascertain whether the property had been the subject of subsidence and reported to the Halifax Building Society that the property was suitable for maximum lending.

Months after the survey, and after the true condition and value of the house had been discovered, the building society, on 1st March 1978 wrote to the defendants. The second paragraph of the letter says:
e

'Had the subsidence in the property or in the adjacent property been made known to the Society, the situation would have been investigated before an offer of advance was made and the application would subsequently have been declined.'

In that paragraph the building society makes it abundantly plain that, but for the defendants' negligent report, no offer to advance money on the security of the house *f* would ever have been made to the plaintiffs.

I return again to the narrative. A few days after receiving the defendants' report and valuation the building society's Finsbury Pavement branch sent out three forms, all dated 19th December 1975. Two were sent to the plaintiffs and one to Mr Nicolaou. One of the forms sent to the plaintiffs says, among other things:

'In response to your application, the Society is willing to make an advance as *g* detailed below provided that the title to the property and to any additional security is acceptable to the Society and you execute a mortgage deed in the form prescribed by the Society and lodge it, together with any necessary documents of title, with the Society until the mortgage is discharged. A copy of the Society's explanatory booklet "MORTGAGES: INFORMATION FOR MEMBERS", is enclosed. You will be required to pay any costs of the Society's solicitors arising from investigation of title and the *h* preparation of the mortgage deed and any other documents, whether or not the advance is made. By receiving the advance you will become a member of the Society and subject to its rules.'

Below those words is a panel which states the advance to be £12,000.

The building society's explanatory booklet was enclosed. There is a copy in *j* evidence. Mr Yianni did not read it. If he had done so he would have read on page 2 the following paragraph under the heading 'Valuation':

'The Society does not accept responsibility for the construction or condition of the property offered as security, nor does it warrant that the purchase price is reasonable. The valuer's report is confidential to the Society and is exclusively for the use of the directors and officers in determining whether a loan should be made and if so, for what amount. The Society may bring to your notice any defects which the valuer mentions but it should not be assumed that no other defects exist. If you require a survey for your own information and protection, you should instruct a surveyor independently. You are recommended to do this.'

Mr Hunter, in reply to questions from counsel for the defendants about building society literature, said that the Abbey National's literature, like the Halifax's, included words to the effect that the society recommended the applicant to obtain independent advice. Mr Hunter was then asked if he would expect applicants to read the literature. He replied that he would not expect all of them to read the literature like this handbook; or if they did, to understand it and follow the advice given, because, he said, the majority of people who buy in the lower income groups just do not have the understanding. Later on he said of applicants generally:

'They are not all fools. Lots of them understand the situation and read all the literature. But they have paid the survey fee, so they rely on the building society and on the building societies' surveyors. They therefore have confidence in the survey report.'

The form received by Mr Nicolaou, among other things, says:

'The applicant has been notified that the Society is willing to make an advance as detailed below. Will you please act for the Society in investigating the title and completing the mortgage, submitting your report on title together with the enclosed surveyor's report when you requisition the cheque.'

The enclosed surveyor's report was presumably the defendants' report. If it was there is no evidence that Mr Nicolaou ever showed it to the plaintiffs, and indeed Mr Yianni says in terms that he never saw it.

The other form received by the plaintiffs was for use if the plaintiffs decided to accept the offer contained in the form dated 19th December 1975. It says:

'To the Chief General Manager, Halifax Building Society. We wish to proceed with the advance as detailed in your letter under the above reference number. We acknowledge receipt of a statutory notice under the Building Societies Act, 1962, Section 30, and a copy of the explanatory booklet "Mortgages: Information for Members".'

The statutory notice is not with the documents in the bundle but it is not disputed that such a notice was received by the plaintiffs. It was a notice in the prescribed form, that is form 3 in Part I of Sch I to the Building Societies Rules 1962, SI 1962 No 1936. The notice informed the plaintiffs that in the event of the building society making an advance to assist them in the purchase of 1 Seymour Road the making of the advance would not imply any warranty by the building society that the purchase price of the property was reasonable. Mr Yianni was in fact already aware of this and had been aware of it since he completed the application form.

The plaintiffs evidently consulted Mr Nicolaou on or about 29th December 1975. They then completed the form whereby they informed the building society that they wished to accept the society's offer.

Counsel for the defendants submitted that when the plaintiffs decided to accept the building society's offer they placed no reliance on any statement in this document, save for the statement that the building society was willing to advance £12,000 on the security of 1 Seymour Road. Accordingly, says counsel, all the plaintiffs did was to accept, as he put it, the offer of the mechanics or means whereby they could acquire the house they had already made up their minds to buy, subject to the building society agreeing to make available to them the necessary funds. It could not have been easy for Mr Yianni over five years after making the decision to accept the building society's offer to describe precisely what matters influenced his mind and his wife's mind at the time that decision was made. Undoubtedly they liked the house and, for the reasons he mentioned, wanted to buy it. Were it not for those matters they would not have applied to the building society for a loan in the first place. Having made that application it is clear that, unless in response to it the building society had stated that it was willing to advance the whole £12,000, the plaintiffs would not have proceeded further. But in addition there is also evidence by Mr Yianni that at the time the offer to advance £12,000 was made he made some remark to his wife to the effect that the house must be good. I am satisfied that the statement that the building society was willing to advance £12,000 served in the minds of the plaintiffs to confirm the fact that the house was worth at least £12,000 and that undoubtedly was a factor which they took into account when their decision to buy was made.

The correspondence shows that, after the acceptance of the offer, Mr Nicolaou proceeded to make the necessary searches. He also requested the building society to provide full insurance cover against all risks in the sum of £15,000. Eventually completion took place on 6th January 1976 and the plaintiffs and their family went into occupation of the house.

In or about October 1976 Mr Yianni's attention was drawn to cracks in the house by his next door neighbour, at no 3, who complained that there were cracks in no 3 caused by the fact that no 1 was tilting away from it. Mr Yianni therefore instructed a chartered surveyor, Mr Hurrell, to inspect the house. Mr Hurrell found extensive damage caused by fractures. These were due to the leaning out of the main structural walls owing to subsidence of the foundations which had been built on clay. He considered that the end wall would have to be rebuilt and all the remaining walls underpinned at an approximate cost of £8,000. On Mr Yianni's behalf Mr Hurrell made a claim on the insurers who, quite by chance, appointed Thomas Howell, Selfe & Co to investigate the matter. Their representative, Mr Kilbey, at once recollected that he had investigated the claim for subsidence damage to the house in October 1974. On inspecting it again in January 1977 Mr Kilbey noticed that, while a certain amount of redecoration had been done, none of the extensive underpinning work he had envisaged in his report of 17th October 1974 had been carried out. In those circumstances the insurers declined to accept responsibility for the damage. Mr Hurrell, however, on Mr Yianni's behalf persisted in his efforts to get the insurers to change their minds, but without success. Over this period the building society had informed the defendants of the allegations being made against them, and eventually the building society wrote the letter dated 1st March 1978 to which I earlier referred. By that time the cost of repairing 1 Seymour Road was estimated to be £18,000. That concludes my summary of the facts.

On that evidence the case for the plaintiffs is that the defendants' statement to the building society that 1 Seymour Road was suitable as security for a loan of £12,000 meant that the property was worth at least £12,000, that that was a negligent statement, that the defendants ought reasonably to have contemplated that the statement would be passed on by the building society to the plaintiffs, that the defendants knew or ought to have known that the plaintiffs would rely on it and would be induced by it to buy the property and mortgage it to the building society, and that the plaintiffs in fact did so and in consequence suffered damage.

The defendants called no evidence. They contend that, although they were negligent, they owed no duty of care to the plaintiffs and, in consequence, are not liable for the plaintiffs' grievous loss. The building society has taken no steps to sue the defendants. Counsel for the defendants suggests that the building society was not able to do so because it had suffered no damage as a result of the defendants' negligence. In these circumstances I respectfully adopt and repeat a sentence from the judgment of Sir Robert Megarry V-C in *Ross v Caunters* [1979] 3 All ER 580 at 583, [1980] 1 Ch 297 at 303: 'If this is right, the result is striking. The only person who has a valid claim has suffered no loss, and the only person who has suffered a loss has no valid claim.'

Thus, the first question to be decided is whether, on the facts, the defendants owed a duty of care to the plaintiffs. On this question, there can be no doubt that the dissenting judgment of Denning LJ in *Candler v Crane, Christmas & Co* [1951] 1 All ER 426, [1951] 2 KB 164 is very much in point. The headnote ([1951] 2 KB 164) summarises the facts of that case in this way:

'The plaintiff was considering the possibility of his investing 2,000l. in a limited liability company, but, before deciding to do so, desired to see the accounts of the company. The managing director of the company accordingly instructed the defendants, the accountants of the company, who were getting out the accounts, to press on and complete them, informing a clerk of the accountants, who had been requested by them to prepare the accounts, that they were required to be shown to the plaintiff who to his knowledge was a potential investor in the company. The clerk accordingly prepared the accounts and at the request of the managing director showed them to and discussed them with the plaintiff who took a copy of them and submitted them to his own accountant for advice. As a result the plaintiff invested his money in the company. The accounts were carelessly prepared, contained numerous false statements and gave a wholly misleading picture of the state of the company, which was wound up within a year, the plaintiff losing the whole of his investment.'

In his judgment Denning LJ said ([1951] 1 All ER 426 at 433–436, [1951] 2 KB 164 at 179–184):

'Let me now be constructive and suggest the circumstances in which I say that a duty to use care in making a statement does exist apart from a contract in that behalf. First, what persons are under such duty? My answer is those persons, such as accountants, surveyors, valuers and analysts, whose profession and occupation it is to examine books, accounts, and other things, and to make reports on which other people—other than their clients—rely in the ordinary course of business. Their duty is not merely a duty to use care in their reports. They have also a duty to use care in their work which results in their reports ... Secondly, to whom do these professional people owe this duty? I will take accountants, but the same reasoning applies to the others. They owe the duty, of course, to their employer or client, and also, I think to any third person to whom they themselves show the accounts, or to whom they know their employer is going to show the accounts so as to induce him to invest money or take some other action on them. I do not think, however, the duty can be extended still further so as to include strangers of whom they have heard nothing and to whom their employer without their knowledge may choose to show their accounts. Once the accountants have handed their accounts to their employer, they are not, as a rule, responsible for what he does with them without their knowledge or consent. [After referring to *Le Lievre v Gould* [1893] 1 QB 491 he continued:] Excluding such cases as those, however, there are some cases—of which the present is one—where the accountants know all the time, even before they present their accounts, that their employer requires the accounts to show to a third person so as to induce him to act on them, and then they themselves, or their employers, present the accounts to him for the purpose. In such cases I am of opinion that the accountants owe a duty of care to the third person ... Thirdly, to what transactions does the duty of care extend? It extends, I think, only to those transactions for which the accountants knew their accounts were required ... [He then drew certain distinctions:] Thus, a doctor, who negligently certifies a man to be a lunatic when he is not, is liable to him, although there is no contract in the matter, because the doctor knows that his certificate is required for the very purpose of deciding whether the man should be detained or not, but an insurance company's doctor owes no duty to the insured person, because he makes his examination only for the purposes of the insurance company ... So, also, a Lloyd's surveyor who, in surveying for classification purposes, negligently passes a mast as sound when it is not, is not liable to the owner for damage caused by it breaking, because the

surveyor makes his survey only for the purpose of classifying the ship for the Yacht
Register and not otherwise . . . My conclusion is that a duty to use care in statement   **a**
is recognised by English law, and that its recognition does not create any dangerous
precedent when it is remembered that it is limited in respect of the persons by
whom and to whom it is owed and the transactions to which it applies.'

Denning LJ's judgment was referred to in all the speeches in *Hedley Byrne & Co Ltd v
Heller & Partners Ltd* [1963] 2 All ER 575, [1964] AC 465 to which I now turn. The
headnote ([1964] AC 465) reads: **b**

'The appellants were advertising agents, who had placed substantial forward
advertising orders for a company on terms by which they, the appellants, were
personally liable for the cost of the orders. They asked their bankers to inquire into
the company's financial stability and their bankers made inquiries of the respondents,
who were the company's bankers. The respondents gave favourable references but   **c**
stipulated that these were "without responsibility". In reliance on these references
the appellants placed orders which resulted in a loss of £17,000. They brought an
action against the respondents for damages for negligence:—*Held*, that a negligent,
though honest, misrepresentation, spoken or written, may give rise to an action for
damages for financial loss caused thereby, apart from any contract or fiduciary
relationship, since the law will imply a duty of care when a party seeking   **d**
information from a party possessed of a special skill trusts him to exercise due care,
and that party knew or ought to have known that reliance was being placed on his
skill and judgment . . . However, since here there was an express disclaimer of
responsibility, no such duty was in any event, implied . . . *Candler* v. *Crane,
Christmas & Co.* overruled.'

Lord Reid, after saying that *Candler v Crane, Christmas & Co* was wrongly decided, said   **e**
([1963] 2 All ER 575 at 583, [1964] AC 465 at 487):

'The majority of the Court of Appeal held that they were bound by *Le Lievre* v.
Gould ([1893] 1 QB 491) and that *Donoghue* v. *Stevenson* ([1932] AC 562, [1932] All
ER Rep 1) had no application. In so holding I think that they were right. The
Court of Appeal have bound themselves to follow all rationes decidendi of previous   **f**
Court of Appeal decisions, and, in face of that rule, it would have been very difficult
to say that the ratio in *Le Lievre* v. *Gould* did not cover *Candler's* case. LORD DENNING,
who dissented, distinguished *Le Lievre* v. *Gould* on its facts . . .'

Lord Morris referred briefly to *Candler's* case, observing only that there the Court of
Appeal had followed *Le Lievre v Gould*. But he said ([1963] 2 All ER 575 at 590, 594,
[1964] AC 465 at 496–497, 502–503):   **g**

'It seems to me, therefore, that if A claims that he has suffered injury or loss as a
result of acting upon some mis-statement made by B who is not in any contractual
or fiduciary relationship with him the inquiry that is first raised is whether B owed
any duty to A: if he did the further inquiry is raised as to the nature of the duty.
There may be circumstances under which the only duty owed by B to A is the duty   **h**
of being honest: there may be circumstances under which B owes to A the duty not
only of being honest but also a duty of taking reasonable care. The issue in the
present case is whether the bank owed any duty to Hedleys and if so what the duty
was. Leaving aside cases where there is some contractual or fiduciary relationship
there may be many situations in which one person voluntarily or gratuitously
undertakes to do something for another person and becomes under a duty to   **j**
exercise reasonable care. I have given illustrations. Apart from cases where there
is some direct dealing, there may be cases where one person issues a document
which should be the result of an exercise of the skill and judgment required by him
in his calling and where he knows and intends that its accuracy will be relied on by
another . . . My Lords, I consider that it follows and that it should now be regarded
as settled that if someone possessed of a special skill undertakes, quite irrespective of

a contract, to apply that skill for the assistance of another person who relies on such skill, a duty of care will arise. The fact that the service is to be given by means of, or by the instrumentality of, words can make no difference. Furthermore if, in a sphere in which a person is so placed that others could reasonably rely on his judgment or his skill or on his ability to make careful inquiry, a person takes it on himself to give information or advice to, or allows his information or advice to be passed on to, another person who, as he knows or should know, will place reliance **b** on it, then a duty of care will arise.'

Lord Hodson ([1963] 2 All ER 575 at 597, [1964] AC 465 at 509) said:

'So far I have done no more than summarise the argument addressed to the Court of Appeal in *Candler's* case to which effect was given in the dissenting judgment of DENNING, L.J., with which I respectfully agree in so far as it dealt with the facts of **c** that case. I am, therefore, of opinion that his judgment is to be preferred to that of the majority, although the opinion of the majority is undoubtedly supported by the ratio decidendi of *Le Lievre* v. *Gould*, which they cannot be criticised for following.'

He agreed with passages from Lord Morris's speech which I have already read.

Lord Devlin, after declaring that he did not think it possible to formulate with exactitude all the conditions under which the law would in a specific case imply voluntary **d** undertakings to accept responsibility for an act, then said ([1963] 2 All ER 575 at 611, [1974] AC 465 at 530):

'But in so far as your lordships describe the circumstances in which an implication will ordinarily be drawn, I am prepared to adopt any one of your lordships' statements as showing the general rule; and I pay the same respect to the statement by DENNING, L.J., in his dissenting judgment in *Candler* v. *Crane, Christmas & Co* **e** about the circumstances in which he says a duty to use care in making a statement exists.'

Lord Pearce quoted from the report of Denning LJ's judgment the passages I have already read and said ([1963] 2 All ER 575 at 617–618, [1964] AC 465 at 538–539):

f 'I agree with those words. In my opinion, they are consonant with the earlier cases and with the observations of LORD HALDANE [in *Nocton v Lord Ashburton* [1914] AC 932 at 947, [1914–15] All ER Rep 45 at 49 and in *Robinson v National Bank of Scotland* 1916 SC (HL) 154 at 157] ... Was there such a special relationship in the present case as to impose on the respondents a duty of care to the appellants as the undisclosed principals for whom the National Provincial Bank, Ltd. was making the **g** inquiry? The answer to that question depends on the circumstances of the transaction. If, for instance, they disclosed a casual social approach to the inquiry no such special relationship or duty of care would be assumed ... To import such a duty the representation must normally, I think, concern a business or professional transaction whose nature makes clear the gravity of the inquiry and the importance and influence attached to the answer ... A most important circumstance is the **h** form of the inquiry and of the answer.'

Finally I was referred to *Anns v London Borough of Merton* [1977] 2 All ER 492 at 498–499, [1978] AC 728 at 751, a case which was not in any way concerned with negligent statements. However, Lord Wilberforce said this:

'Through the trilogy of cases in this House, *Donoghue v Stevenson* [1932] AC 562, **j** [1932] All ER Rep 1, *Hedley Byrne & Co Ltd v Heller & Partners Ltd* [1963] 2 All ER 575, [1964] AC 465 and *Home Office v Dorset Yacht Co Ltd* [1970] 2 All ER 294, [1970] AC 1004, the position has now been reached that in order to establish that a duty of care arises in a particular situation, it is not necessary to bring the facts of that situation within those of previous situations in which a duty of care has been held to exist. Rather the question has to be approached in two stages. First one has to ask whether, as between the alleged wrongdoer and the person who has suffered damage there is a sufficient relationship of proximity or neighbourhood such that, in the reasonable contemplation of the former, carelessness on his part may be likely to cause damage to the latter, in which case a prima facie duty of care arises. Secondly, if the first question is answered affirmatively, it is necessary to consider whether there are any considerations which ought to negative, or to reduce or limit the scope of the duty or the class of person to whom it is owed or the damages to which a breach of it may give rise ... Examples of this are *Hedley Byrne & Co Ltd v Heller & Partners Ltd* where the class of potential plaintiffs was reduced to those shown to have relied on the correctness of statements made ...'

I do not think that cases cited in argument which were decided before *Hedley Byrne* are of assistance in the present case.

Accordingly, guided by the passages in the judgment of Denning LJ in *Candler's* case and by the speeches in the House of Lords cases, I conclude that, in this case, the duty of care would arise if, on the evidence, I am satisfied that the defendants knew that their valuation of 1 Seymour Road, in so far as it stated that the property provided adequate security for an advance of £12,000, would be passed on to the plaintiffs who, notwithstanding the building society's literature and the service of the notice under s 30 of the 1962 Act, in the defendants' reasonable contemplation would place reliance on its correctness in making their decision to buy the house and mortgage it to the building society. What therefore does the evidence establish?

These defendants are surveyors and valuers. It is their profession and occupation to survey and make valuations of houses and other property. They make reports about the condition of property they have surveyed. Their duty is not merely to use care in their reports, they also have a duty to use care in their work which results in their reports. On the instructions of the building society, the defendants sent a representative to 1 Seymour Road to make a survey and valuation of that property. He knew that the object of the survey was to enable the defendants, his employers, to submit a report to the building society for the use of the directors in discharging their duty under s 25 of the Act. The report, therefore, had to be directed to the value of the property and to any matter likely to affect its value. The defendants knew, therefore, that the director or other officer in the building society who considered their report would use it for the purpose of assessing the adequacy of 1 Seymour Road as security for an advance. There is no evidence that the building society had access to any other reports or information for this purpose or that the defendants believed or assumed that the building society would have any information beyond that contained in their report. Accordingly, the defendants knew that the director or other officer of the building society who dealt with the plaintiffs' application would rely on the correctness of this report in making on behalf of the Society the offer of a loan on the security of 1 Seymour Road. The defendants therefore knew that the plaintiffs would receive from the building society an offer to lend £12,000, which sum, as the defendants also knew, the plaintiffs desired to borrow. It was argued that, as the information contained in the defendants' report was confidential to the directors, the defendants could not have foreseen that the contents of their report would be passed on to the plaintiffs. But the contents of the report never were passed on. This case is not about the contents of the entire report, it is about that part of the report which said that 1 Seymour Road was suitable as security for a loan of £12,000. The defendants knew that that part would have to be passed on to the plaintiffs, since the reason for the plaintiffs' application was to obtain a loan of £12,000. Accordingly, the building society's offer of £12,000, when passed on to the plaintiffs, confirmed to them that 1 Seymour Road was sufficiently valuable to cause the building society to advance on its security 80% of the purchase price. Since that was also the building society's view the plaintiffs' belief was not unreasonable.

It was argued that there was no reasonable likelihood that the plaintiffs would rely on the fact that the defendants had made a valuation report to the building society or, alternatively, that the defendants could not reasonably have foreseen or contemplated

first, that the plaintiffs would rely on the valuation in the report or, second, that they
would act unreasonably in failing to obtain an independent surveyor's report for their
own guidance. These submissions were founded on the fact that the defendants would
know that the plaintiffs would have been provided with the building society's literature
and that the building society, for its own protection, would have served with their offer
the statutory notice pursuant to s 30 of the 1962 Act. Now these defendants, plainly, are
in a substantial way of business in London as surveyors and valuers. The documents
show that they have an address at Down Street, Mayfair, and another in Lavender Hill,
London SW11. They must have on their staff some members of the Royal Institute of
Chartered Surveyors. The terms of the building society's request to them to value 1
Seymour Road indicated that they had regularly carried out valuations for the Halifax,
and no doubt for other building societies. Mr Hunter's evidence is that for some six years
over 90% of applicants for a building society mortgage have relied on the building
society's valuation, as represented by the building society's offer of an advance, as a
statement that the house in question is worth at least that sum. These applicants, and in
particular applicants seeking to buy houses at the lower end of the property market, do
not read building society literature, or, if they do, they ignore the advice to have an
independent survey and also the terms of the statutory notice. Mr Hunter's evidence was
unchallenged. No witness was called to suggest that he had in any way misrepresented
the beliefs, conduct and practice of the typical applicant. I think that Mr Hunter was
telling me what was common knowledge in the professional world of building societies
and of surveyors and valuers employed or instructed by them. I am satisfied that the
defendants were fully aware of all these matters.

The defendants' representative who surveyed and valued 1 Seymour Road noted the
type of dwelling house it was, its age, its price and the locality in which it was situated.
It was plainly a house at the lower end of the property market. The applicant for a loan
would therefore almost certainly be a person of modest means who, for one reason or
another, would not be expected to obtain an independent valuation, and who would be
certain to rely, as the plaintiffs in fact did, on the defendants' valuation as communicated
to him in the building society's offer. I am sure that the defendants knew that their
valuation would be passed on to the plaintiffs and that the defendants knew that the
plaintiffs would rely on it when they decided to accept the building society's offer.

For these reasons I have come to the conclusion that the defendants owed a duty of care
to the plaintiffs because, to use the words of Lord Wilberforce in *Anns v London Borough
of Merton*, there was a sufficient relationship of proximity such that in the reasonable
contemplation of the defendants carelessness on their part might be likely to cause
damage to the plaintiffs.

I turn now to consider whether there are any considerations which ought to negative
or to reduce or limit the scope of the duty or the class of person to whom it is owed.
Counsel for the defendants submitted that for a number of reasons of policy the plaintiffs
should have no remedy against the defendants. First he said a decision in favour of the
plaintiffs would encourage applicants for a mortgage to have no independent survey of
the house they wished to buy. I can see nothing objectionable in a practice which would
result in a house being surveyed once by one surveyor. In my view, the Abbey National,
since September 1980, have adopted a sensible procedure for dealing with the survey
problem, if it is a problem. Mr Hunter said that as a matter of courtesy the Abbey
National now disclose their valuation report to applicants. He also said: 'We felt that we
had information which had been obtained by qualified and experienced people and it
was of benefit to give that information to the applicant.' In addition, the Abbey National
are about to introduce a report on condition and valuation so that, as Mr Hunter put it,
the applicant has the choice of either the standard building society mortgage valuation
report or the report on condition and valuation which covers the popular conception of
structural survey, market valuation and mortgage valuation.

Counsel also submitted that if the defendants were held liable to the plaintiffs no
professional man would be able to limit his liability to a third party, even if he could do

so to his own client. He would be at the mercy of a client who might pass on his report to a third party and, as defects in the property he had surveyed might not manifest themselves for many years, he would be likely to remain under a liability for those defects he ought to have detected for a very long period, and at the end of the period, for an unlimited amount by way of damages. In my view, the only person to whom the surveyor is liable is the party named in the building society's 'Instructions to Valuer' addressed to him. That party, as well as the building society, has to be regarded as his client. That does not seem to me to be unreasonable, since, to his knowledge, his fee for the valuation is paid by that party to the building society which hands it over to him. On this submission, it can also be said that the surveyor's report is concerned with the valuation of a dwelling house, the condition of which is important only in so far as it affects its value at that time. It is common knowledge that in the ordinary way, the market value of a dwelling house is not static. Consequently, a valuation made at one time for the purpose of assessing its suitability as security for a loan would be of limited use.

Counsel for the defendants also argued that the plaintiffs do not need to establish any remedy against the defendants since they have a good claim for damages against Mr Protopapas either at common law or under the Defective Premises Act 1972 for his failure properly to carry out the repairs at 1 Seymour Road. Nowhere in the defence to the plaintiffs' claim, nor in any document before me, is there any suggestion that the plaintiffs have such a claim. In consequence, no evidence has been led by the plaintiffs to deal with the allegation.

Counsel also contended that the plaintiffs have a good claim for damages against Mr Nicolaou, who negligently failed, among other things, to advise the plaintiffs to have an independent survey. Again, this suggestion has never previously been advanced and no evidence has been called to deal with it. It is not clear to me whether these last two arguments were addressed to me as part of what counsel called his policy argument, but whether they were or not I reject them and all the arguments directed to establishing that there are considerations which ought to negative or reduce or limit the scope of the duty to the plaintiffs to the extent that they should have no remedy against the defendants.

Finally counsel said that the plaintiffs should be held guilty of contributory negligence because they failed to have an independent survey, made no inquiries with the object of discovering what had been done to the house before they decided to buy it, failed to read the literature provided by the building society and generally took no steps to discover the true condition of the house. It is true that the plaintiffs failed in all these respects, but that failure was due to the fact that they relied on the defendants to make a competent valuation of the house. I have been given no reason why they were unwise to do so. I have earlier read the paragraph under the heading 'Valuation' in the building society's handbook which Mr Yianni did not read. No doubt if the paragraph had been in stronger terms, and had included a warning that it would be dangerous to rely on the valuer's report, then I think that the plaintiffs might well have been held to be negligent. But, in my judgment, on the evidence the allegation of contributory negligence fails.

In my judgment for these reasons the defendants are liable to pay damages to the plaintiffs for the grievous loss they have suffered by the defendants' negligence.

Judgment for the plaintiffs.

Solicitors: *Michael Votsis & Co* (for the plaintiffs); *Reynolds, Porter, Chamberlain* (for the defendants).

K Mydeen Esq　Barrister.

a # Power Curber International Ltd v National Bank of Kuwait SAK

COURT OF APPEAL, CIVIL DIVISION
LORD DENNING MR, GRIFFITHS LJ AND WATERHOUSE J
15th, 16th, 17th JUNE, 3rd JULY 1981

b

Bank – Documentary credit – Irrevocable credit – Kuwaiti buyers instructing Kuwaiti bank to issue letter of credit in favour of US sellers – Bank issuing irrevocable letter of credit payable in North Carolina – Kuwaiti court granting buyers order of 'provisional attachment' against sums payable under letter of credit – Order preventing bank from honouring letter of credit – Whether bank required to honour obligation to pay despite order of Kuwaiti court.

c

Conflict of laws – Contract – Proper law – Commercial credit – No express provision as to law governing credit – Law with which transaction has closest and most real connection – Kuwaiti bank issuing letter of credit in favour of US company – Letter of credit payable in US dollars in North Carolina – Whether lex situs of debt arising out of letter of credit Kuwait or North Carolina – Whether proper law of letter of credit law of Kuwait or of North Carolina.

d

On 6th July 1979 the plaintiff, a United States exporting company based in North Carolina, contracted to sell machinery on c i f terms to buyers in Kuwait. Payment was to be made as to 25% on presentation of documents and as to 75% one year after the date of shipment. The buyers agreed to give a letter of credit in respect of the 75% of the price that would remain outstanding and instructed the defendant, which was their bank in *e* Kuwait, to issue a letter of credit to a bank in North Carolina in favour of the plaintiff. On 6th September the defendant bank issued an 'irrevocable' letter of credit for up to $US300,000 to a North Carolina bank in favour of the plaintiff. The credit was stated to be subject to the Uniform Customs and Practice for Documentary Credits (1974 Revision). On 26th December 1979 machinery to the value of over $US100,000 was shipped by the plaintiff to the buyers who paid 25% of the price against presentation of *f* the documents and drew a bill of exchange on the defendant bank for the 75% balance, being some $US75,000. The bill of exchange was due to mature on 26th December 1980. In November 1980 the buyers obtained an order of 'provisional attachment' in a Kuwaiti court against the plaintiff in respect of an unrelated claim. The order, which was later upheld by the Kuwait Court of Appeal, attached the amount due to the plaintiff under the letter of credit and prevented the defendant bank from making further *g* payments to the plaintiff under it. The plaintiff brought an action in England against the defendant bank claiming the $US75,000 due under the letter of credit. The defendant bank, although incorporated in Kuwait, traded and had a registered office in London. The judge gave summary judgment for the plaintiff but stayed execution of the judgment until further order. The plaintiff appealed against the stay of execution. The defendant bank cross-appealed against the judgment itself, contending that the proper *h* law of the letter of credit was Kuwaiti law which forbade payment under the letter of credit, or alternatively that the lex situs of the debt arising out of the letter of credit was Kuwait and the effect of the attachment order was therefore governed by Kuwaiti law.

Held – (1) The proper law of the letter of credit was that with which it had the closest and most real connection, which was the law of North Carolina because that was where the *j* defendant bank was required by the letter of credit to perform its obligation to pay. Furthermore (Waterhouse J dubitante), the lex situs of the debt was also North Carolina, because a debt under a letter of credit was situated in the place where it was payable against documents, unlike an ordinary debt which could be situated where the debtor was resident. Accordingly, since under the proper law and the lex situs neither Kuwaiti law nor the order of provisional attachment made under it had any effect on the existence or validity of the debt owed by the defendant bank under the letter of credit, it followed that the defendant bank had no ground for resisting summary judgment and its cross-appeal would therefore be dismissed (see p 612 c to e, p 613 h, p 614 b c and p 615 a to c, post); *Offshore International SA v Banco Central SA* [1976] 3 All ER 749 approved.

(2) Because letters of credit were established as a universally acceptable means of payment, equivalent to cash, in international trade and commerce on the basis that the promise of the issuing bank to pay was wholly independent of the contract between the buyer and the seller and that therefore the issuing bank would honour its obligation to pay regardless of any dispute between the buyer and the seller, and because the order of the Kuwaiti court ran counter to those internationally accepted principles, the court would not recognise the order of the Kuwaiti court as being a ground for granting a stay of execution of the summary judgment obtained by the plaintiff. The plaintiff's appeal against the stay of execution would therefore be allowed and the stay removed (see p 612 g to p 613 d f to h and p 614 e to p 615 a and g to j, post); *Nova (Jersey) Knit Ltd v Kammgarn Spinnerei GmbH* [1977] 2 All ER 463 and *R D Harbottle (Mercantile) Ltd v National Westminster Bank Ltd* [1977] 2 All ER 862 applied.

Notes

For commercial letters of credit, see 3 Halsbury's Laws (4th Edn) paras 131–137, and for cases on the subject, see 3 Digest (Reissue) 665–670, 4114–4137.

For the proper law of a contract, see 8 Halsbury's Laws (4th Edn) paras 587–588, and for cases on the subject, see 11 Digest (Reissue) 458–462, 760–776.

Case referred to in judgments

Discount Records Ltd v Barclays Bank Ltd [1975] 1 All ER 1071, [1975] 1 WLR 315, [1975] 1 Lloyd's Rep 444, 3 Digest (Reissue) 668, 4133.

Harbottle (R D) (Mercantile) Ltd v National Westminster Bank Ltd [1977] 2 All ER 862, [1978] 1 QB 146, [1977] 3 WLR 752, 3 Digest (Reissue) 669, 4134.

Intraco v Notis Shipping Corpn of Liberia (1981) Times, 7th July, CA.

MacShannon v Rockware Glass Ltd [1978] 1 All ER 625, [1978] AC 795, [1978] 2 WLR 362, HL, Digest (Cont Vol E) 100, 1691a.

Malas (trading as Hamzeh Malas and Sons) v British Imex Industries Ltd [1958] 1 All ER 262, [1958] 2 QB 127, [1958] 2 WLR 100, [1957] 2 Lloyd's Rep 549, CA, 3 Digest (Reissue) 667, 4129.

Nova (Jersey) Knit Ltd v Kammgarn Spinnerei GmbH [1977] 2 All ER 463, [1977] 1 WLR 713, [1977] 1 Lloyd's Rep 463, HL, 3 Digest (Reissue) 76, 389.

Offshore International SA v Banco Central SA [1976] 3 All ER 749, [1977] 1 WLR 399, [1976] 2 Lloyd's Rep 402, Digest (Cont Vol E) 92, 776b.

Owen (Edward) Engineering Ltd v Barclays Bank International Ltd [1978] 1 All ER 976, [1978] QB 159, [1977] 3 WLR 764, [1978] 1 Lloyd's Rep 166, CA, Digest (Cont Vol E) 18, 4136a.

R v Grossman [1981] Crim LR 396, CA.

Cases also cited

Arab Bank Ltd v Barclays Bank (Dominion, Colonial and Overseas) [1954] 2 All ER 226, [1954] AC 495, HL.

Helbert Wagg & Co Ltd, Re, Prudential Assurance Co, Re [1956] 1 All ER 129, [1956] Ch 323.

Martin v Nadel [1906] 2 KB 26, CA.

Montecchi v Shimco (UK) Ltd [1979] 1 WLR 1180, CA.

Naval, Military & Civil Service Co-op Society of South Africa Ltd v Services Ltd (1906) 51 Sol Jo 13.

Rossano v Manufacturers' Life Assurance Co [1962] 2 All ER 214, [1963] 2 QB 352.

Swiss Bank Corpn v Boehmische Industrial Bank [1923] 1 KB 673, CA.

Trendtex Trading Corpn v Crédit Suisse [1980] 3 All ER 721, [1980] QB 629, QBD and CA.

Appeal

a This was an appeal by the plaintiff, Power Curber International Ltd, against that part of the order of Parker J made on 27th March 1981 whereby he imposed a stay of execution in respect of a judgment by the judge in favour of the plaintiff under RSC Ord 14 for the sum of $US75,794·46 plus interest claimed by them against the defendant, the National Bank of Kuwait. By a cross-appeal the defendant appealed from the judgment of Parker J. The facts are set out in the judgment of Lord Denning MR.

b *Peter Cresswell* for the plaintiff.
Andrew Longmore for the defendant.

Cur adv vult

3rd July. The following judgments were read.

c **LORD DENNING MR.** This case raises an important point in international trade. It has nothing to do with England except that an action has been brought here. It is brought by United States sellers who exported goods from the United States to buyers in Kuwait. They were to be paid by a letter of credit issued by the National Bank of Kuwait, the defendant. The bank wish to honour their obligations. They wish to pay the sums due under the letter of credit. But the courts in Kuwait have forbidden the bank to *d* pay. What is the bank to do?

The plaintiff company's name is Power Curber International Ltd. You might think that it was an English company seeing that its name ends with 'Ltd'. But it is in fact a United States corporation which carries on business at Salisbury in North Carolina. I will call it 'Power Curber'. It exports machinery to countries in the Middle East. It operates through a firm of distributors in Kuwait called Hammoudeh & Al Fulaij General Trading & Contracting Co WLL. I will call the firm 'Hammoudeh'. The directors have *e* close contacts with the United States and spend their time between that country and the Middle East. They are the 'distributors' for Power Curber in the Middle East. By which I take it they buy goods on their own account from Power Curber and resell them on a commission or other basis in the Middle East.

In about July 1979 Power Curber agreed to supply machinery to Hammoudeh to be *f* shipped from the United States not later than the 1st March 1980 on cif terms and paid as to 25% on presentation of documents and the remaining 75% one year after date of shipment. The buyers (Hammoudeh) were to give usance drafts (that is, bills of exchange payable at a later date) for this remaining 75%.

In order to be sure of payment Power Curber required Hammoudeh to open a letter of credit in their favour. Hammoudeh went to their bank, the National Bank of Kuwait, *g* ('the bank') and asked them to issue a letter of credit. No doubt Hammoudeh put the bank in funds or otherwise secured the bank so that the bank would be indemnified against their liability under the letter of credit.

The letter of credit

The letter of credit is dated 'Kuwait 6th Sept. 1979'. It was issued by the National Bank *h* of Kuwait (the issuing bank) to the Bank of America, Florida, Miami, United States of America (the advising bank) through the North Carolina National Bank in Charlotte, North Carolina. It was an irrevocable credit but not a confirmed credit. It is so important that I will set out most of it:

'[To] BANK OF AMERICA,   Kuwait 6th Sept. 1979.
j 'FLORIDA, MIAMI, USA.
'OUR IRREVOCABLE CREDIT NO. A02/164018/7 . . .

'Dear Sirs,
    'At the request of Hammoudeh & Al Fulaij General Trading & Contracting Company WLL, (A/c 49554-9), please advise our irrevocable credit through North

Carolina National Bank in Charlotte, North Carolina in favour of Power Curber International Ltd, P.O. Box 1639, Salisbury, North Carolina, 28144, USA (A/c No. 411003742) . . . irrevocably valid in U.S.A. until 1st March 1980 and available by draft(s) without recourse as shown below drawn on the opener for 100% of the invoice value and accompanied by the documents marked (X) below [Here were set out invoices, bills of lading, etc] evidencing current shipment not later than 1st March 1980 . . . from U.S.A. to Kuwait of:—EQUIPMENTS AND SPARE PARTS . . .

'The value of the usance drafts will be remitted by us at relative maturity dates provided all credit terms should have been fully complied with.

'PAYMENT TERMS: 25% of the Ex-Works value . . . to be paid against presentation of documents called for in order as per credit terms. Remaining 75% of the Ex-Works value after one year of the date of shipment . . .

'All drafts drawn under this credit must contain the clause:—"DRAWN UNDER L/C NO. (as above) OF THE NATIONAL BANK OF KUWAIT S.A.K. DATED (date of this advice,)".

'In reimbursement of your negotiations under this credit, please . . . draw on our account with Bank of America (International), New York, in respect of sight payment provided you certify to us that all terms of the credit have been complied with, and forward the original documents direct to us by first Registered Airmail, duplicates by following Airmail.

'This credit is irrevocable on our part and we hereby undertake that all drafts drawn in compliance with the terms hereof will be duly honoured.

'Except as otherwise stated herein, this Credit is Subject to the Uniform Customs and Practice for Documentary Credits (1974 Revision) International Chamber of Commerce Publication No. 290.

'Yours faithfully,
'For THE NATIONAL BANK OF KUWAIT S.A.K.'

The goods are shipped

On 26th December 1979 the goods were duly shipped from the United States. The shipment value was $101,059·28, of which 25% was paid against presentation of documents. Hammoudeh drew a usance draft on the National Bank of Kuwait for the remaining 75%, which was $75,794·46, maturing on 26th December 1980. It was accepted by the National Bank of Kuwait who wrote on 4th March 1980 to the North Carolina National Bank:

'Our Letter of Credit No. A02/164018/7.

'. . . please note that the relative usance draft for U.S. $75,794·46 maturing on 26th December 1980 has been accepted by our principals. We shall not fail to remit to you the above mentioned amount through Morgan Guaranty Trust Co. New York at maturity on 26th December 1980.'

The effect of the letter of credit

The law on the point is clear. I take it first from what I said in *Edward Owen Ltd v Barclays Bank International Ltd* [1978] 1 All ER 976 at 981, [1978] QB 159 at 169:

'It has been long established that when a letter of credit is issued and confirmed by a bank, the bank must pay it if the documents are in order and the terms of the credit are satisfied. Any dispute between buyer and seller must be settled between themselves. The bank must honour the credit. That was clearly stated in *Malas (trading as Hamzeh Mallas & Sons) v British Imex Industries Ltd* [1958] 1 All ER 262 at 263, [1958] 2 QB 127 at 129. Jenkins LJ, giving the judgment of this court, said: "... It seems to be plain enough that the opening of a confirmed letter of credit constitutes a bargain between the banker and the vendor of the goods, which imposes upon the banker an absolute obligation to pay, irrespective of any dispute which there may be between the parties on the question whether the goods are up to contract or not. An elaborate commercial system has been built up on the footing that bankers' confirmed credits are of that character, and, in my judgment, it would be wrong for this court in the present case to interfere with that established practice." To this general principle there is an exception in the case of what is called established or obvious fraud to the knowledge of the bank.'

Those words apply not only to confirmed credits but also to irrevocable credits. To which I would add these provisions of the Uniform Customs and Practice for Documentary Credits (1974 Revision) which I take from Gutteridge and Megrah on the Law of Commercial Credits (6th Edn, 1979, p 221–222):

'... (c) Credits, by their nature, are separate transactions from the sales or other contracts on which they may be based and banks are in no way concerned with or bound by such contracts ...

'A. *Form and notification of credits*

'ARTICLE 3

'(a) An irrevocable credit constitutes a definite undertaking to the issuing bank, provided that the terms and conditions of the credit are complied with: (i) to pay, or that payment will be made, if the credit provides for payment, whether against a draft or not; (ii) to accept drafts if the credit provides for acceptance by the issuing bank or to be responsible for their acceptance and payment at maturity ...'

The order made in Kuwait

It appears that early in November 1980 Hammoudeh filed a claim in the courts of Kuwait against Power Curber for 50,000 Kuwaiti dinars. That is about $180,000. We do not know the nature of the claim but it is thought it may be a claim for commission. Following on that claim, Hammoudeh applied to the court in Kuwait for an order for 'provisional attachment' of the sums payable by the National Bank of Kuwait under the letter of credit to Power Curber. On 5th November 1980 the court in Kuwait ordered the 'provisional attachment'. This order prevented the bank from making any further payment under the letter of credit in Kuwait or outside Kuwait, and made the bank accountable to the court for the amount involved. The bank lodged a protest against the attachment, and applied to the court in Kuwait to set aside the order for provisional attachment. But the court refused to set it aside. And its refusal has been upheld by the Court of Appeal in Kuwait.

The steps taken by Power Curber

As Power Curber did not receive payment, they sent a telex to the bank in January 1982, saying:

'We have not received the payment in the amount of US Dlrs 75,794·46 which matured for payment on Dec. 26, 1980. You had agreed to honor the draft upon maturity under the Rules and Regulations of the Uniform Customs and Practices for Documentary Credits (1974 Revision) International Chamber of Commerce Publication No. 290. Unless we receive this payment immediately, we will begin legal proceedings against you for failure to pay the balance legally due us.'

Power Curber started proceedings in North Carolina, but afterwards discontinued them and started proceedings in England.

On 27th January 1981 Power Curber issued a writ in the High Court in England against the National Bank of Kuwait (which was trading here and had a registered address in London). They claimed $75,794·46 and applied for judgment under RSC Ord 14. On 27th March 1981 Parker J gave judgment in favour of Power Curber against the National Bank of Kuwait for that amount but stayed execution on it until further order. There is now an appeal by Power Curber against the stay and by the bank against the judgment.

The questions debated before us were these. (1) Should Power Curber be granted summary judgment? (2) Even if summary judgment is granted, should execution be stayed? By English law a plaintiff is entitled to have summary judgment given for him if the defendant has no arguable defence to the claim. Parker J gave summary judgment for the plaintiffs. But he stayed execution on it until further order. Each side appeals. I will deal first with summary judgment.

Summary judgment

On the face of it, the National Bank of Kuwait are in default. They promised to pay the sums due under the letter of credit at maturity. They have not paid those sums.

Counsel for the bank submits, however, that the 'provisional attachment' gives the bank an arguable defence. He says that the proper law of the contract was Kuwaiti law and that, by that law, the payment of the sums was unlawful. Alternatively, he says that the lex situs of the debt was Kuwait, and it is that law which governs the effect of the attachment. If the attachment was lawful by Kuwaiti law, he says that all other countries should give effect to it.

I cannot accept counsel's submissions. The proper law of the contract is to be found by asking: with what law has the contract its closest and most real connection? In my opinion it was the law of North Carolina where payment was to be made (on behalf of the issuing bank) against presentation of documents. Counsel for the bank sought to say that the case of *Offshore International SA v Banco Central SA* [1976] 3 All ER 749, [1977] 1 WLR 399 decided by Ackner J was either wrongly decided or was distinguishable on grounds parallel to those canvassed in Gutteridge and Megrah on the Law of Commercial Credits (6th Edn, 1979, pp 213–214). But I think the case was rightly decided and cannot be distinguished on any valid grounds. The letter of credit, and the payments under it, were certainly valid by its proper law.

Nor can I agree that the lex situs of the debt was Kuwait. It was in North Carolina. A debt under a letter of credit is different from ordinary debts. They may be situate where the debtor is resident. But a debt under a letter of credit is situate in the place where it is in fact payable against documents.

I would hold therefore that Parker J was right in giving summary judgment against the bank for the sums due.

If it were a case where leave to defend should be given, I would hold that the action should be tried in England. By bringing the action in England, Power Curber have a legitimate juridical advantage of which it would not be right to deprive them (see *MacShannon v Rockware Glass Ltd* [1978] 1 All ER 625, [1978] AC 812).

Stay of execution

In considering the 'provisional attachment' order, it must be remembered that the orders of a foreign court fall into three categories. First, those which are enforceable in England by our English courts. Second, those which are recognised in England by virtue of the comity of nations, so that we will do nothing contrary to them. Third, those which will not be recognised here in England because they do not accord with the public policy of our law.

On this question of recognition, I must draw attention to the importance of letters of credit in international trade. They are the means by which goods are supplied all the world over. It is vital that every bank which issues a letter of credit should honour its obligations. The bank is in no way concerned with any dispute that the buyer may have with the seller. The buyer may say that the goods are not up to contract. Nevertheless the bank must honour its obligations. The buyer may say that he has a cross-claim in a large amount. Still the bank must honour its obligations. A letter of credit is like a bill of exchange given for the price of goods. It ranks as cash and must be honoured. No set-off or counterclaim is allowed to detract from it (see *Nova (Jersey) Knit Ltd v Kammgarn Spinnerei GmbH* [1977] 2 All ER 463, [1977] 1 WLR 713). All the more so with a letter of credit. Whereas a bill of exchange is given by buyer to seller, a letter of credit is given by a bank to the seller with the very intention of avoiding anything in the nature of a set-off or counterclaim. This is borne out by the Uniform Customs and Practice for Documentary Credits which have been adopted by the banks in all, or practically all, the countries of the world, from China to Andorra, from Cuba to Nauru. All subscribe to

the Uniform Customs and Practice which declare in the general provisions and
a declarations '. . . (c) Credits, by their nature, are separate transactions from the sales or
other contracts on which they may be based and banks are in no way concerned with or
bound by such contracts . . .'

If the court of any of the countries should interfere with the obligations of one of its
banks (by ordering it not to pay under a letter of credit), it would strike at the very heart
of that country's international trade. No foreign seller would supply goods to that
b country on letters of credit because he could no longer be confident of being paid. No
trader would accept a letter of credit issued by a bank of that country if it might be
ordered by its courts not to pay. So it is part of the law of international trade that letters
of credit should be honoured and not nullified by an attachment order at the suit of the
buyer.

Added to this, it seems to me that the buyer himself by his conduct has precluded
c himself from asking for an attachment order. By opening the letter of credit in favour
of the seller, he has implicitly agreed that he will not raise any set-off or counterclaim,
such as to delay or resist payment. He has contracted under the terms of the Uniform
Customs and Practice by which he promises that the bank will pay without regard to any
set-off or counterclaim, and implicitly that he will not seek an attachment order. I gather
that, if the court in Kuwait had looked at the case in this way, they would not have
d granted the 'provisional attachment'. To my mind it is implicit in the Uniform Customs
and Practice that such an attachment is precluded.

Yet another consideration occurs to me. Many banks now have branches in many
foreign countries. Each branch has to be licensed by the country in which it operates.
Each branch is treated in that country as independent of its parent body. The branch is
subject to the orders of the courts of the country in which it operates: but not to the
e orders of the courts where its head office is situate. We so decided in the recent case
about bankers' books in the Isle of Man (see *R v Grossman* [1981] Crim LR 396). In this
case I think that the order for 'provisional attachment' operates against the head office in
Kuwait, but not against the branch office in London. That branch is subject to the orders
of the English courts. Only the other day this court held that a Mareva injunction should
not be granted to stop payment of a bank guarantee outside the jurisdiction (see *Intraco*
f *v Notis Shipping Corpn of Liberia* (1981) Times , 7th July).

It is my opinion that the courts of England are not bound by the comity of nations to
recognise the 'provisional attachment' issued by the courts in Kuwait. We should not
grant a stay of execution. The judgment here should operate against the branch in
London so as to require it to pay the sums due under the letter of credit.

g ### Conclusion

The striking fact is that the courts here in London are asked to enforce a letter of credit
opened by buyers in Kuwait in favour of sellers in the United States for payment in the
United States. But this is because London is an important centre of international trade.
Merchants from all the world come here to settle their disputes. Banks from all the
world over have branches here to receive and make payments. So far as we can be of
h service to international trade, we will accept the task and fulfil it to the best of our ability.

I would approve the judgment of Parker J in favour of the sellers. I would not grant
a stay of execution.

GRIFFITHS LJ. I will deal first with the cross-appeal. The bank submit that the judge
should give leave to defend because payment of the sums due under the letter of credit
j is unlawful according to the proper law of the contract. This submission depends on the
proper law of the letter of credit being Kuwaiti law. In my view the proper law of the
letter of credit was the law of the state of North Carolina. Under the letter of credit the
bank accepted the obligation of paying or arranging the payment of the sums due in
United States dollars against presentation of documents at the sellers' bank in North
Carolina. The bank could not have discharged its obligation by offering payment in

Kuwait. Furthermore the bank undertook to remiburse the advising bank if they paid on their behalf in dollars in America. In *Offshore International v Banco Central* [1976] 3 All ER 749, [1977] 1 WLR 399 Ackner J held that the place at which the bank must perform its obligation under a letter of credit determines the proper law to be applied to the letter of credit. In my view that case was correctly decided.

Secondly, it was submitted that payment was unlawful according to the lex situs of the debt which it is said is Kuwait. But this is a debt that is owed in United States dollars in North Carolina; I do not regard the fact that the bank that owes the debt has a residence in Kuwait as any reason for regarding Kuwait as the lex situs of the debt. The lex situs of the debt is North Carolina, and this ground for giving leave to defend cannot be supported.

No other grounds were advanced for resisting judgment under RSC Ord 14 and I agree that the cross-appeal should be dismissed.

Now as to the appeal; should the judge have granted a stay of the judgment? At the time the case was before Parker J the order of the Kuwait court was under appeal to the Kuwait Court of Appeal. In those circumstances I think I should have been very tempted to grant a short stay to await the outcome of the decision of the Court of Appeal because I fear that I should have thought it highly unlikely that the Court of Appeal would uphold an order that interfered so seriously with the well-recognised international obligation of a bank under an irrevocable letter of credit. By granting the stay I should have been relieved of the disagreeable obligation to refuse to recognise the order of a court of a friendly state.

But now we know the result of the Court of Appeal hearing in Kuwait and must face the choice between enforcing the obligation on the bank to pay under its irrevocable letter of credit or recognising the order of the Kuwait court.

I have no doubt that we should uphold the obligation to pay under the irrevocable letter of credit and remove the stay. Letters of credit have become established as a universally acceptable means of payment in international transactions. They are regarded by merchants the world over as equivalent to cash; they have been rightly described by that most distinguished commercial lawyer, Kerr J, as the life-blood of international commerce (see *R D Harbottle Mercantile Ltd v National Westminster Bank Ltd* [1977] 2 All ER 862, [1978] QB 146). The banker's promise to pay the seller is wholly independent of the underlying contract of sale between the seller and the buyer, or of any other contractual dispute that may arise between them. The whole purpose of this form of payment is that a seller should not be kept out of his money by litigation against him at the suit of the buyer. In the absence of fraud the seller is entitled to be paid on presentation of genuine documents.

In the present case we do not even know with certainty the nature of the buyers' claim in Kuwait because they obtained their provisional attachment order at an ex parte hearing and have never served the United States seller with any documents specifying the claim. It may be in respect of commission, or it may arise in respect of the goods in respect of which the letter of credit was issued. There is no suggestion of fraud and, in the absence of fraud, an English court would not have interfered with the banker's obligation to pay under the letter of credit (see *Discount Records Ltd v Barclays Bank Ltd* [1975] 1 All ER 1071, [1975] 1 WLR 315, *R D Harbottle (Mercantile) Ltd v National Westminster Bank Ltd* [1977] 2 All ER 862, [1978] QB 159 and *Edward Owen Engineering Ltd v Barclays Bank International Ltd* [1978] 1 All ER 976, [1978] QB 159).

We should do the bank a grave disservice if we were not to remove this stay for it would undoubtedly seriously damage their credibility as an international bank if it was thought that their paper was not worth holding because an ex parte application to their domestic courts could prevent payment under an expressedly irrevocable obligation.

There is no recognised rule of international law that compels this court to recognise this ex parte order of the Kuwaiti court. It is of course entitled to be treated with respect and wherever possible this court will, in the interests of comity, seek to recognise and uphold the order of the court of a friendly state. But unhappily in this case the approach of the Kuwait court appears to be so out of step with that of our own courts and the courts of other trading nations that I fear we cannot recognise it. The choice lies between upholding the world-wide practices of international commerce or the order of the Kuwaiti court. I choose the first option and would remove the stay.

WATERHOUSE J (read by Griffiths LJ). I agree that this appeal should be allowed and that the cross-appeal should be dismissed. Despite the forceful argument of counsel for the bank, I am unable to accept that leave to defend the action should have been granted. On the issue as to the proper law of the letter of credit, I respectfully agree with what has been said by Lord Denning MR and Griffiths LJ about the correctness and application to the instant case of the reasoning of Ackner J in *Offshore International SA v Banco Central SA* [1976] 3 All ER 749, [1977] 1 WLR 399. The more difficult issue for me has been that relating to the lex situs of the debt.

A debt is generally to be looked on as situate in the country where it is properly recoverable or can be enforced, and it is noteworthy that the sellers here submitted voluntarily to the dismissal of their earlier proceedings against the bank in North Carolina. We have been told that they did so because of doubts about the jurisdiction of the North Carolina court, which was alleged in the pleadings to be based on the transaction of business by the bank there, acting by itself or through another named bank as its agent. As for the question of residence, the bank has been silent about any residence that it may have within the United States. In the absence of any previous binding authority, I have not been persuaded that this debt due under an unconfirmed letter of credit can be regarded as situate in North Carolina merely because there was provision for payment at a branch of a bank used by the sellers in Charlotte; and I do not regard the analogy of a bill of exchange or a security transferable by delivery as helpful.

Nevertheless Parker J was right, in my judgment, to refuse the bank leave to defend because the Kuwaiti provisional order of attachment did not affect the existence of the debt. Counsel for the bank has submitted that the effect of that order was to alter the debt from one due to the sellers to a debt due to the court or held to the order of the court awaiting a decision as to whom it should be paid. I agree with Parker J that this submission is based on a single sentence in an affidavit and that it does not bear that weight. There is no acceptable evidence that, according to the law of Kuwait, the debt has ceased to be due to the sellers. There is no ground, therefore, for granting leave to defend and counsel for the bank has not sought to argue that a stay of proceedings is justified if leave to defend was properly refused. If there had been an arguable defence, I would have held that the action should be tried in England because there is a legitimate juridicial advantage to the sellers in proceeding here, which outweighs any disadvantage to the bank.

The sellers' appeal against the stay of execution granted by Parker J has to be considered in the changed circumstances that the bank's appeal to the Court of Appeal in Kuwait against the provisional order of attachment has failed. Although a further appeal to the Cour de Cassation there is proceeding, we have been told that it will not be heard until the end of the year. I agree, therefore, that the overwhelming balance of the argument now is in favour of removal of the stay of execution. Part of the argument for the bank on this issue has been that it is inexpedient for the court to permit execution to proceed pending resolution of the dispute between Hammoudeh and the sellers; it is suggested that the bank may be exposed to the risk of proceedings for contempt in Kuwait or of double payment. One has sympathy with the bank in its dilemma, and its good faith is not in doubt, not least because it has already paid to the plaintiffs $US82,546·89 due earlier on 7th November 1980 in respect of the same letter of credit, despite the provisional attachment order. However, the action of Hammoudeh, and the reasoning of the Kuwait Court of Appeal appear to me to strike at the essential foundations of the international acceptability of letters of credit so that the stay ought not to continue.

Appeal allowed. Cross-appeal dismissed. Leave to appeal to the House of Lords refused.

Solicitors: *Jaques & Co* (for the plaintiff); *Allen & Overy* (for the defendant).

Henrietta Steinberg   Barrister.

Buttes Gas and Oil Co v Hammer and another (Nos 2 & 3)
Occidental Petroleum Corpn and another v Buttes Gas and Oil Co and another (Nos 1 & 2)

HOUSE OF LORDS

LORD WILBERFORCE, LORD FRASER OF TULLYBELTON, LORD RUSSELL OF KILLOWEN, LORD KEITH
OF KINKEL AND LORD BRIDGE OF HARWICH

22nd, 23rd, 25th, 29th, 30th JUNE, 1st, 2nd, 6th, 7th, 8th, 9th JULY, 29th OCTOBER 1981

*Constitutional law – Act of state – Acts of foreign government – Justiciability in English courts
– Exercise of judicial restraint – Action claiming damages for slander – Defence pleading
justification – Counterclaim alleging fraudulent conspiracy with foreign ruler – Object of
conspiracy to procure ruler to make decree so as to benefit plaintiffs at defendants' expense –
Validity of decree not challenged – Whether counterclaim should be struck out and action allowed
to continue – Whether action and counterclaim raising non-justiciable issues on which court should
abstain from adjudicating.*

Sharjah and Umm al Qaiwan ('UAQ') were adjacent independent sovereign states in the
Arabian Gulf whose foreign relations were controlled by the United Kingdom
government under treaty. Until 1970 3 miles was the width of territorial waters in the
Gulf recognised by the United Kingdom government and those states in treaty with it.
Forty miles from the mainland of the two states was an island, Abu Musa, which at all
material times was recognised by the United Kingdom government and by UAQ as
belonging to Sharjah, although it had been claimed by Iran since the nineteenth
century. In November 1969 the ruler of UAQ with the approval of the United Kingdom
government granted an exclusive concession to an American corporation ('Occidental')
giving it the right to exploit oil in UAQ's territorial and offshore waters and the sea bed
and subsoil underlying such waters. A map attached showed the concession area as
extending up to the 3-mile limit of Abu Musa's waters. In December the ruler of Sharjah
granted an oil concession to another American corporation ('Buttes') over its territorial
waters including all islands within its jurisdiction and the territorial waters of the islands,
including Abu Musa. That agreement was approved by the United Kingdom
government in the belief that Sharjah had sovereignty over Abu Musa and that its
territorial waters were limited to 3 miles. In February 1970 Occidental discovered a
promising area for exploration 9 miles from Abu Musa. In April 1970 the ruler of
Sharjah published a decree, dated 10th September 1969 and thus ante-dating the two
concession agreements, extending the limits of its territorial waters to 12 miles from the
baseline around its coasts and the islands, including Abu Musa. The ruler of UAQ
protested but after intervention by the governments of the United Kingdom and Iran he
accepted the decree and instructed Occidental not to operate within 12 miles from Abu
Musa. Thereafter Buttes found oil in the area discovered by Occidental and exploited it
to the exclusion of Occidental. Meanwhile in July 1970 Buttes issued a circular to
shareholders commenting on Occidental's activities. In October Occidental's chairman,
at a press conference in London, accused Buttes of using improper methods and colluding
with the then ruler of Sharjah to back date the decree of 10th September 1969 so as to
obtain for itself the benefit of the oil-bearing deposit, which he claimed was discovered
by and belonged to Occidental. Buttes issued a writ against Occidental and its chairman
claiming damages for slander. Occidental served a defence in which it pleaded
justification and counterclaimed for damages for fraudulent conspiracy by Buttes with
the ruler of Sharjah and libel by Buttes in its shareholders' circular. Buttes applied for an
order that the particulars in support of the plea of justification and fair comment and the
counterclaim for conspiracy should be struck out in that they raised matters which were

'acts of state' of the governments of Sharjah, UAQ, Iran and the United Kingdom and
a which were not therefore justiciable in the English courts. On 5th December 1974 the
Court of Appeal ([1975] 2 All ER 51) refused to strike out the conspiracy counterclaim
or parts of the plea of justification or the libel counterclaim. Thereafter further pleadings
were exchanged. In May 1978 Buttes, in compliance with RSC Ord 26, r 2, served a list
of documents on Occidental but claimed that particular documents were protected from
production because of either legal professional privilege or 'foreign state privilege', ie
b that production was contrary to the public interest because it would be injurious to the
interest of foreign sovereign states. Occidental's claim for discovery of the disputed
documents was upheld by the master but on appeal by Buttes the judge varied the order,
holding that some of the documents should be produced. Occidental appealed while
Buttes cross-appealed in respect of documents which had been ordered to be produced.
The Court of Appeal ([1980] 3 All ER 745) dismissed Occidental's appeal and allowed
c Buttes's cross-appeal, holding that all the disputed documents were protected from
production on the ground (per Lord Denning MR) that the court's powers as to discovery
were discretionary and the case was one for the exercise of judicial restraint since it would
be contrary to the comity of nations to order discovery without the consent of the foreign
sovereign concerned, ie the ruler of Sharjah, and (per Donaldson and Brightman LJJ) that
the courts should recognise a category of United Kingdom public interest immunity
d relating to copies of confidential documents of a foreign sovereign (ie the ruler of
Sharjah) in the possession of a third party (ie Buttes). Occidental appealed against that
decision and Buttes appealed against the earlier decision whereby the court refused to
strike out Occidental's counterclaim.

Held – There was a general principle, wider than the well-defined rules of act of state, of
judicial abstention from adjudicating directly on the transactions of foreign sovereign
e states. That principle was not one of discretion but was inherent in the very nature of the
judicial process. Accordingly, the court would refuse to recognise as justiciable the acts
of a foreign sovereign state not only within its own territory but also vis-à-vis other
governments, since there were no judicial or manageable standards by which a municipal
court could judge issues arising between one state and another. It followed therefore
f that, since Occidental could not succeed either in its counterclaim for conspiracy and
libel or in the slander action without bringing to trial non-justiciable issues involving
examination of a series of transactions between Sharjah, UAQ, Iran and the United
Kingdom government during the period from 1969 to 1973, the court would not
entertain the counterclaim. Buttes's appeal would therefore be allowed, and its action for
damages for slander and Occidental's counterclaim for conspiracy and libel would be
stayed. The staying of the counterclaim would necessarily also require that Occidental's
g application for discovery be similarly stayed (see p 625 *b* to *e*, p 627 *h j*, p 628 *g* to *j*, p 629
c d h j and p 633 *d* to p 634 *d*, post).
Decision of the Court of Appeal [1975] 2 All ER 51 reversed.
Application the subject of Court of Appeal decision [1980] 3 All ER 475 stayed.

Notes
h For acts of foreign governments as acts of state, see 7 Halsbury's Laws (3rd Edn) 282, para
599, and for cases on the subject, see 11 Digest (Reissue) 727–732, 480–494.
For public interest and Crown privilege, see 13 Halsbury's Laws (4th Edn) paras 86–91,
and for cases on the subject, see 18 Digest (Reissue) 154–160, 1265–1301.

Cases referred to in opinions
j *Aksionairnoye Obschestvo A M Luther v James Sagor & Co* [1921] 3 KB 532, [1921] All ER
Rep 138, 90 LJKB 1202, 125 LT 705, CA, 11 Digest (Reissue) 344, 23.
Banco Nacional de Cuba v Sabbatino (1964) 376 US 398.
Blad's Case (1673) 3 Swan 603, 36 ER 991, PC; subsequent proceedings sub nom *Blad v
Bamfield* (1674) 3 Swan 604, 36 ER 992, sub nom *Badtolph v Bamfeild* Cas *temp* Finch
186, 11 Digest (Reissue) 727, 480.
British South Africa Co v Companhia de Moçambique [1893] AC 602, [1891–4] All ER Rep
640, 63 LJQB 70, 69 LT 694, 6 R1, HL, 11 Digest (Reissue) 398, 388.

Brunswick (Duke) v King of Hanover (1844) 6 Beav 1, 6 State Tr NS 33, 13 LJ Ch 107, 2 LTOS
306, 8 Jur 253, 49 ER 724; *affd* (1848) 2 HL Cas 1, 9 ER 993, HL, 11 Digest (Reissue) *a*
727, *483.*

Buron v Denman (1848) 2 Exch 167, 3 New Pract Cas 62, 6 State Tr NS 525, 10 LTOS 523,
154 ER 450, 11 Digest (Reissue) 726, *470.*

Carr v Fracis, Times & Co [1902] AC 176, 71 LJKB 361, 85 LT 144, HL, 11 Digest
(Reissue) 728, *487.*

Compania Naviera Vascongada v Steamship Cristina [1938] 1 All ER 719, [1938] AC 485, *b*
107 LJP 1, 159 LT 394, 19 Asp MLC 159, HL, 1(1) Digest (Reissue) 228, *1297.*

Cook v Sprigg [1899] AC 572, [1895–9] All ER Rep 773, 68 LJPC 144, 81 LT 281, PC, 11
Digest (Reissue) 732, *495.*

Duff Development Co Ltd v Kelantan Government [1924] AC 797, [1924] All ER Rep 1, 93 LJ
Ch 343, 131 LT 676, HL, 11 Digest (Reissue) 721, *430.*

Foster v Globe Venture Syndicate Ltd [1900] 1 Ch 811, 69 LJ Ch 375, 82 LT 253, 1(1) Digest *c*
(Reissue) 62, *397.*

Hesperides Hotels Ltd v Muftizade [1978] 2 All ER 1168, [1979] AC 508, [1978] 3 WLR
378, 142 JP 541, HL, Digest (Cont Vol E) 90, *389a.*

Oetjen v Central Leather Co (1918) 246 US 297.

Princess Paley Olga v Weisz [1929] 1 KB 718, [1929] All ER Rep 513, 98 LJKB 465, 141 LT
207, CA, 11 Digest (Reissue) 728, *488.*   *d*

Secretary of State in Council of India v Kamachee Boye Sahaba (1859) 13 Moo PCC 22, 7 Moo
Ind App 476, 15 ER 9, PC, 11 Digest (Reissue) 721, *433.*

Tito v Waddell (No 2), Tito v Attorney General [1977] 3 All ER 129, [1977] Ch 106, [1977]
2 WLR 496, Digest (Cont Vol E) 634, *15a.*

Underhill v Hernandez (1893) 65 F 577; *affd* (1897) 168 US 250.

United States of America v Dollfus Mieg et Compagnie SA [1952] 1 All ER 572, [1952] AC *e*
582, HL, 1(1) Digest (Reissue) 60, *388.*

Wagg (Helbert) & Co Ltd, Re, Re Prudential Assurance Co Ltd [1956] 1 All ER 129, [1956]
Ch 323, [1956] 2 WLR 183, 11 Digest (Reissue) 345, *25.*

Appeals

Buttes Gas and Oil Co v Hammer and another (No 2) *f*
Occidental Petroleum Corpn and another v Buttes Gas and Oil Co and another

By a writ dated 15th October 1970 the plaintiff, Buttes Gas and Oil Co ('Buttes'), an
American corporation, brought an action against the defendants, Armand Hammer and
Occidental Petroleum Corpn ('Occidental'), another American corporation, claiming
damages for slander published by Dr Hammer (chairman and chief executive of
Occidental) and Occidental at the Great Eastern Hotel, London, on 5th October 1970 and
an injunction restraining the defendants from further publishing the slander or any *g*
similar words defamatory of Buttes. By their defence dated 7th April 1972 Dr Hammer
and Occidental pleaded that the words complained of were true in substance and in fact
and furthermore were fair and bona fide comment on a matter of public interest. Dr
Hammer and Occidental gave detailed particulars of the matters relied on in support of
the pleas of justification and fair comment. By a counterclaim served with the defence *h*
Occidental claimed damages against Buttes for conspiracy and also claimed damages
against Buttes and John Boreta for libel in respect of a letter dated 14th July 1970 written
by Mr Boreta as president of Buttes and addressed to the shareholders of Buttes. By a
summons dated 7th July 1972 Buttes applied for an order (1) that the court should not
exercise jurisdiction in respect of certain matters referred to in the defence and
counterclaim being acts of state of the governments of Sharjah, Umm al Qaiwain, Iran *j*
and the United Kingdom, (2) further or alternatively that certain parts of the defence and
counterclaim be struck out and/or all proceedings be stayed as to any issue arising
therefrom. By a summons dated 16th November 1972 Mr Boreta also sought an order
that the counterclaim, the service thereof and all subsequent proceedings be set aside.
On 11th June 1973 Master Warren in chambers ordered that the court 'should not
exercise jurisdiction in respect of the following matter being an Act of State of the
Governments of Sharjah, Umm al Qaywayn, Iran and the United Kingdom, namely the

conspiracy alleged in the Counterclaim'. Dr Hammer and Occidental appealed against
that order, seeking to have it set aside. Buttes appealed against so much of the order as
refused to make the orders sought in its summons. Mr Boreta appealed against the
refusal to make any order on his summons. On 31st July 1974 May J, having heard
argument in chambers, gave judgment in open court and varied the order of Master
Warren by ordering that part of the counterclaim be struck out. Occidental appealed
against that order. Buttes and Mr Boreta cross-appealed. On 5th December 1974 the
Court of Appeal (Lord Denning MR, Roskill LJ and Sir John Pennycuick) ([1975] 2 All
ER 51, [1975] QB 557) allowed Occidental's appeal and dismissed Buttes's and Mr
Boreta's cross-appeal. Leave to appeal to the House of Lords was refused. On 27th
February 1975 the Appeal Committee of the House of Lords refused leave to appeal. By
a further summons dated 11th July 1980 Buttes and Mr Boreta applied for an order that
all further proceedings on the counterclaim be stayed on Buttes undertaking to consent,
on application by Occidental and Dr Hammer, to a stay of its claims for damages for
slander. On 11th November 1980 an Appeal Committee of the House of Lords gave
leave to Buttes and Mr Boreta to appeal out of time against the decision and discharged
its previous order and ordered that the fresh summons issued by Buttes and Mr Boreta
on 11th July 1980 should be dealt with on the hearing of the appeal.

Buttes Gas and Oil Co v Hammer and another (No 3)
Occidental Petroleum Corpn and another v Buttes Gas and Oil Co and another (No 2)
Occidental and Dr Hammer appealed with leave of an Appeal Committee of the House
of Lords granted on 11th November 1980 from an interlocutory order of the Court of
Appeal (Lord Denning MR, Donaldson and Brightman LJJ) dated 20th June 1980 ([1980]
3 All ER 475, [1980] 3 WLR 668) dismissing their appeals from an order of McNeill J
dated 31st July 1979 and allowing a cross-appeal by Buttes and Mr Boreta from an order
of Master Warren dated 8th January 1979 on two summonses issued by Occidental and
Dr Hammer seeking production of certain documents referred to in Buttes's reply and
defence to counterclaim in the action brought by Buttes against Occidental and Dr
Hammer for slander. The Court of Appeal held that all the disputed documents were
protected from production.

The two appeals were heard together. The facts are set out in the opinion of Lord
Wilberforce.

Maurice Bathurst QC, Anthony Evans QC, Robert Y Jennings QC and John Previté for Buttes
and Mr Boreta.
Colin Ross-Munro QC, Murray Rosen and David Lloyd Jones for Dr Hammer.
Mark Littman QC, Elihu Lauterpacht QC, Murray Rosen and Andrzej J Kolodziej for
Occidental.

Their Lordships took time for consideration.

29th October. The following opinions were delivered.

LORD WILBERFORCE. My Lords, this action and counterclaim arise from the
discovery of oil in a 'location' (hereafter referred to as 'the location') in the sea bed of the
Arabian Gulf. This lies about 9 miles from an island called Abu Musa. This island is
about 40 miles distant from the southern shore. On that southern shore are two
neighbouring Arab emirates, Sharjah and Umm al Qaiwain ('UAQ'). The island of Abu
Musa is, and at material times was, recognised by both emirates and by Her Majesty's
government in the United Kingdom to belong to Sharjah. As a result of various events
occurring in 1969 to 1973 Buttes Gas and Oil Co ('Buttes') emerged as concessionaire
entitled to exploit the location, to the exclusion of Occidental Petroleum Corpn
('Occidental'); out of this situation, which was unwelcome to Occidental, the present
litigation arose. Both companies are incorporated in California, USA. (References
hereafter to Occidental include reference where appropriate to its local subsidiary in the

Gulf, and include, if necessary or relevant, Dr Armand Hammer, its chairman and co-appellant/respondent.)

It is necessary to describe the history of the litigation. It was triggered by a press conference given in London on 5th October 1970 by Dr Hammer. At this conference he accused Buttes, inter alios, of using improper methods and colluding with the then ruler of Sharjah to backdate a decree by the ruler extending the territorial waters of Sharjah, in respect of Abu Musa, from 3 miles from the coast of the island to 12 miles so as to obtain for themselves the benefit of the oil-bearing deposit at the location which he claimed was discovered by and belonged to Occidental.

On 15th October 1970 Buttes issued a writ against Occidental and Dr Hammer claiming damages for slander, and obtained leave to serve it out of the jurisdiction under RSC Ord 11. On 21st July 1971 the Court of Appeal ([1971] 3 All ER 1025) (the 'first decision') dismissed an application by the defendants to have this order set aside. Leave to appeal to the House of Lords was refused both by the Court of Appeal and by this House.

On 7th April 1972 the defendants delivered their defence and counterclaim. The defence contained a full and elaborate justification of the slander, alleging the backdating of the decree of the ruler of Sharjah at the request or on the advice of Buttes and setting out a whole sequence of events which, it was said, resulted in operating limits, excluding the location, being imposed on Occidental.

The counterclaim repeated the factual allegations in the defence and then alleged that, in or about December 1969 and onwards, the plaintiffs, the then ruler of Sharjah and others whom Occidental could not then particularise—

'wrongfully and fraudulently conspired . . . to cheat and defraud [Occidental], and further or alternatively to cause and procure Her Majesty's Government and others to act unlawfully to the injury of [Occidental]'.

A number of overt acts (as pleaded in the defence) were alleged as a result of which Occidental and its local subsidiary or associate were 'permanently deprived of their rights' to exploit the location. They claimed damages amounting to more than $US4m.

The counterclaim also alleged that Mr John Boreta, president of Buttes (joined as defendant to the counterclaim), had libelled Occidental on 14th July 1970 in a report to the shareholders of Buttes in which he said that certain United States proceedings brought by Occidental against Buttes were, in the opinion of Buttes's attorneys, 'wholly without merit'.

On 7th July 1972 a summons was issued by Buttes seeking an order that the court should not exercise jurisdiction in respect of certain specified acts being acts of state of the governments of Sharjah, UAQ, Iran and the United Kingdom, or, alternatively, that certain specified parts of the defence and counterclaim should be struck out or all proceedings stayed as to any issue arising therefrom on the ground that they raised matters which are acts of state. A further summons, dated 16th November 1972, requested that service of the counterclaim on Mr Boreta should be set aside. After proceedings before Master Warren and, on appeal, May J (who acceded in part to Buttes's application), the summonses came before the Court of Appeal.

The decision of the Court of Appeal was given on 5th December 1974 (see [1975] 2 All ER 51, [1975] QB 557) (the 'second decision'). The court refused to strike out the conspiracy counterclaim or parts of the plea of justification, or the libel counterclaim. Lord Denning MR based his decision in the main on his conclusion that the scope of 'act of state' was ill-defined in English law but that it did not extend as widely as in the United States, where the courts had refused to entertain an action by Occidental against Buttes in respect of the same issues as those raised in these proceedings. Roskill LJ held that the power to strike out should be used sparingly and only in a clear case; the present action was not such a case since it involved difficult questions of general importance and the grounds of defence or causes of action were far from obviously bad and unarguable.

Against this decision, Buttes and Mr Boreta sought leave to appeal to this House, but their application was refused by an Appeal Committee on 27th February 1975.

a   After the second decision of the Court of Appeal a number of further pleadings have been exchanged. On 2nd May 1975 Buttes served a reply to the defence, and Buttes and Mr Boreta a defence to the counterclaim of Occidental. These pleadings referred to a number of specific documents. While other documents may be material (and indeed are requested to be produced on discovery), those now available enable the issues raised by the action and counterclaim to be analysed far more clearly than was possible in 1975.

b   At various dates further and better particulars of the defence and counterclaim of Occidental have been requested and delivered. A rejoinder has been delivered on 19th January 1979, and an amended reply and defence and counterclaim on 8th May 1980. Moreover, since the second decision there have been important decisions in the USA on similar issues.

    Apart from these proceedings on the substance of the case, issues have arisen as regards discovery of documents. On 11th April 1976 Occidental applied for an order for
c   inspection of 23 documents referred to in Buttes's reply and defence to counterclaim; Buttes declined to allow inspection of a number of these documents. Occidental persisted in its application for inspection of these and other documents, and after production had, on 8th January 1979, been ordered by Master Warren, McNeill J in chambers (31st July 1979) partly allowed Buttes's appeal, holding that most of the documents were privileged. Both sides thereupon appealed to the Court of Appeal. On 20th June 1980
d   the Court of Appeal ([1980] 3 All ER 475, [1980] 3 WLR 668) (the 'third decision') dismissed the appeal of Occidental and allowed that of Buttes, and refused leave to appeal to this House. The grounds given by the Court of Appeal were: (i) by Lord Denning MR, that the court's powers as to discovery were discretionary, that the case was one for the exercise of judicial restraint since it would be contrary to the comity of nations to order discovery without the consent of the foreign sovereign concerned, in casu the ruler of Sharjah; (ii) by Donaldson and Brightman LJJ, that the courts should recognise a category
e   of United Kingdom public interest immunity relating to copies of confidential documents of a foreign sovereign (the ruler of Sharjah) in the possession of a third party (Buttes).

    These judgments clearly gave rise to novel and important questions. Moreover it was said by Occidental to be illogical and unfair in that, while the counterclaim was, by the
f   second decision, permitted to go on, the result of the third decision was to deny to Occidental the means necessary for its prosecution.

    On 11th November 1980 an Appeal Committee of this House (i) gave leave to Occidental to appeal against the third decision (1980) of the Court of Appeal, (ii) gave leave to Buttes and Mr Boreta to appeal out of time against the second decision (1974) of the Court of Appeal and discharged the previous order (1975) refusing leave to appeal, (iii) ordered that a fresh summons issued by Buttes and Mr Boreta on 11th July 1980
g   should be dealt with on the hearing of the appeal. This fresh summons sought an order that, on Buttes undertaking to consent on application by Occidental and Dr Hammer (if so advised) to a stay of the slander claim, the counterclaims of Occidental and Dr Hammer be stayed on the grounds, inter alia, that the said counterclaims raised issues which are non-justiciable by the court and/or which it is contrary to the public interest
h   for the court to adjudicate on.

    This narrative has been necessary to show two things: first, that this House is now in a position to adjudicate on the entirety of the issues raised by the parties at the various stages between 1971 and 1980; second, that since the last substantive decision of the Court of Appeal (the second decision of 1974) the issues have been more clearly defined and crystallised. This House is now in as good a position as any court is likely to be to
j   form an opinion as to the justiciability of the claims of either side, and the decision has to be made whether the proceedings should be allowed to continue to trial with appropriate discovery or should be terminated by stay or striking out.

    Only two final preliminary observations. First, though at times some of the arguments addressed seemed to lose sight of this, we are not now trying the merits of the cases or any part of them. We must deal with the applications on the basis of facts alleged in the pleadings and of such documents as have emerged, resisting, in the latter case, the temptation to try to interpret the documents (many of which are not governed by English law) beyond the parties' allegations. Second, it is convenient, and was agreed by the parties, to consider first the general issue of justiciability, decision on which may make the discovery issues unnecessary to consider. However, the fact that, if the action is allowed to proceed, discovery of certain classes of documents may have to be given may have implications for the prior question whether the action should be allowed to proceed. To that extent argument heard on the discovery issue (other than that of legal professional privilege) has been enlightening.

I shall now attempt a summarised account of the relevant facts.

I have already mentioned that we are here concerned with the territories of three states, the emirates of Sharjah and UAQ, and the state of Iran. Sharjah and UAQ are neighbours lying on the south side of the Arabian Gulf; they were, at the relevant times, sovereign states in separate treaty relations with the United Kingdom which was responsible for their foreign relations. At all material times Sharjah has claimed title to Abu Musa, and this has been recognised by Her Majesty's government and by UAQ. Since the nineteenth century the island has been claimed by Iran.

The waters of the Arabian Gulf are less than 200 metres in depth, and so potentially have continental shelf status of some coastal state or states. It is obvious that there may be conflicting claims, and that the position of median or other boundary lines may be a matter of controversy. The Gulf contains a number of islands. Although islands are mentioned in art 4, para 1 of the Convention on the Territorial Sea and the Contiguous Zone (Geneva, 29th April 1958; TS 3 (1965); Cmnd 2511), there is no universal rule as to when, and for what distance, islands can generate a continental shelf for themselves. Further, there are differences as regards the width of territorial waters. Many of the adjoining states, including Iran, claim a width of 12 miles, but 3 miles was the distance recognised by the United Kingdom and claimed, until the events in question, by Sharjah, as also by other states in treaty relations with the United Kingdom.

Following the Truman Declaration of 1945, proclamations were made in 1949 by the rulers of Sharjah and UAQ, in identical form, that the sea bed and subsoil contiguous to the territorial waters of Sharjah/UAQ and extending seaward to boundaries to be determined more precisely, as occasion arises, on equitable principles, by each ruler after consultation with the neighbouring states, appertain to the land of Sharjah/UAQ and are subject to its exclusive jurisdiction and control. These proclamations were approved by Her Majesty's government. It is apparent that, while in principle staking the emirates' claims to continental shelf rights, they left a number of vital questions to be settled by agreement or adjudication on equitable or other appropriate principles.

In 1964 the rulers of Sharjah and of UAQ, again with the approval of Her Majesty's government, issued 'parallel instruments'. They were in slightly different form, that of Sharjah taking into account the existence of another small territory, Ajman, which lies partly within the territory of Sharjah. Each was, however, headed, in the English version, 'Sea-bed boundary—agreement by the Ruler of [Sharjah or UAQ]', and continued:

'I agree that the sea-bed boundary between Sharjah and UAQ [or UAQ and Sharjah] shall be a line starting from a point on the coast near the site of the dead well Mirdar bu Salaf and going out to sea on a bearing of 312°.'

It is said to be disputable whether the word 'sea-bed' is a correct translation from the Arabic; apart from this, it does not appear how far out to sea the lateral line referred to is intended to go, or what, if any, frontal boundary is contemplated. No map was attached to either declaration, but, later, various maps were produced. One Admiralty chart in HM Foreign and Commonwealth Office showed the lateral boundary line skirting Abu Musa at a distance of 3 nautical miles.

In 1968 Her Majesty's government announced its intention to terminate its special treaty relationship with the emirates and to withdraw British forces from the area within three years.

In 1969 the rulers of Sharjah and UAQ invited bids for oil concessions in their offshore sea bed. On 10th November Occidental obtained from the ruler of UAQ, with the

approval of the Foreign and Commonwealth Office, an exclusive concession to explore
and exploit the territorial and offshore waters of UAQ and the sea bed and subsoil
underlying such waters. It is said by Occidental that the concession area was outlined on
an attached map based on the above-mentioned Admiralty chart and shown as including
the disputed location, where oil deposits were later discovered some 9 miles from Abu
Musa, but Buttes contends that no such map was shown to Buttes or the ruler of Sharjah
at the time and was never agreed by them. It made no allowance for any continental
shelf round Abu Musa. On 29th December 1969 Buttes obtained from the ruler of
Sharjah the exclusive right to explore and exploit—

'the territorial waters of the main land of Sharjah . . . all islands within the
jurisdiction of the Ruler and the territorial waters of the said islands and all the area
of the sea bed and subsoil lying beneath the waters of the Arabian Gulf contiguous
to the said territorial waters over which the Ruler exercises jurisdiction and control.'

No map was, it appears, attached to the grant.

Buttes contends that this grant included the location by virtue of a decree of the ruler
of Sharjah dated 10th September 1969 whereby he declared the territorial sea of his
emirate as of a width of 12 nautical miles from the baselines around its coasts *and islands*,
and also by virtue of Sharjah's rights over the continental shelf.

Occidental alleges that the decree was in fact made in March or April 1970, that it was
backdated to September 1969, and that this was unlawful and fraudulent. This allegation
is central both to the defence of justification of the slander and to Occidental's
counterclaim for conspiracy.

This being the situation between Sharjah and UAQ, both Iran and Her Majesty's
government became involved. Iran had already, in 1959, claimed a 12-mile belt of
territorial waters for its mainland and islands, and at various dates between 1949 and
1966, issued continental shelf proclamations which in terms extended to islands owned
by it in the Arabian Gulf. In May 1970 Iran reiterated her claim to Abu Musa and
demanded that no exploration or other activities take place in the disputed area.

In May 1970 Her Majesty's government intervened. It recommended to the ruler of
UAQ that he should not permit operations of any kind by Occidental in the area claimed
by the ruler of Sharjah for a period of three months. It was indicated that Her Majesty's
government hoped for a 'third-party settlement'. Occidental, however, sent a drilling
platform towards the location, but this was turned back by HMS Yarnton of the Royal
Navy. After what is described as a show of force by Her Majesty's government, the ruler
of UAQ on 2nd June 1970 ordered Occidental not to operate within 12 miles from Abu
Musa.

There followed proposals for arbitration and an attempt at mediation, but these came
to nothing. In November 1971, shortly before the intended British withdrawal from the
Arabian Gulf, an understanding was reached between Sharjah and Iran whereby: (a)
neither Iran nor Sharjah ceded its claim to sovereignty over Abu Musa; (b) Iranian troops
were permitted to occupy a part of Abu Musa; (c) all parties accepted the existence of a
12-mile territorial sea round Abu Musa, with Buttes as the concessionaire for the area on
the terms of its agreement with Sharjah; (d) the revenues resulting from such exploitation
were to be shared between Sharjah and Iran, and it appears that Sharjah, in turn, agreed
to share its royalties with UAQ. This understanding appears to have been approved by
Her Majesty's government.

In January 1972 the ruler of Sharjah was assassinated, an event which, it is suggested,
was connected with his participation in the 1971 understanding.

Later, in June 1973, Occidental's concession was terminated by the ruler of UAQ
acting under a clause in the concession agreement.

It is obvious that even these skeleton facts, and many more may be or become relevant,
raise far-reaching issues. Before reaching a conclusion whether these admit of
adjudication by an English court, I shall summarise the legal arguments.

In support of their contention that the proceedings necessarily involved non-justiciable
issues, the appellants, Buttes and Mr Boreta, relied on a number of distinct arguments.

First, they contended that the English courts will not try an action which would

require them to pronounce, directly or indirectly, on rights in immovable property
situated abroad. They appealed to the decisions of this House in *British South Africa Co v*
Companhia de Moçambique [1893] AC 602, [1891–4] All ER Rep 640 and *Hesperides Hotels*
Ltd v Muftizade [1978] 2 All ER 1168, [1979] AC 508.

Second, they invoked the doctrine of sovereign immunity, in so far as this excludes
actions concerning property which is in the ownership, possession or control of a foreign
sovereign state, or in which a foreign state claims an interest: see *Compania Naviera*
Vascongada v Steamship Cristina [1938] 1 All ER 719, [1938] AC 485 and *United States of*
America v Dollfus Mieg et Cie SA [1952] 1 All ER 572, [1952] AC 582.

Third, they argued that the English courts will not entertain actions either: (a)
requiring the interpretation of, or the ascertainment of the precise nature of obligations
arising under, transactions between foreign sovereign states: see *Cook v Sprigg* [1899] AC
572, [1895–9] All ER Rep 773; or (b) questioning the validity of effectiveness of foreign
legislation; or (c) examining the validity of, or motives for, acts of foreign sovereign
states in their international relations; or (d) challenging the legality of acts of Her
Majesty's government outside the United Kingdom and not relating to British subjects.

In answer to these, the contentions of Occidental can be summarised as follows. (1).
There is no absolute rule forbidding English courts from entertaining questions relating
to foreign land. Such questions have, in fact, been considered (see *Foster v Globe Venture*
Syndicate Ltd [1900] 1 Ch 811, more fully 82 LT 253, and *Duff Development Co Ltd v*
Kelantan Government [1924] AC 797, [1924] All ER Rep 1). Such questions may be, and
are, decided by English courts where decision on them is incidental to other questions,
such as domicile, or is collateral to the main question (see *Tito v Waddell (No 2)*, *Tito v*
Attorney General [1977] 3 All ER 129 at 259, 266, [1977] 1 Ch 106 at 262, 271). In the
present case a decision on the title to the location (a) is not necessary in the conspiracy
claim; Occidental in fact does not dispute the validity of the decree of 1969 under the law
of Sharjah, (b) is rendered unnecessary or is precluded by the attitude taken by Her
Majesty's government, (c) alternatively can be decided on evidence. (2) There is no
absolute or general rule forbidding English courts from 'sitting in judgment on' or
'inquiring into' the validity or nature of a foreign law. In particular the courts may do
so when that law either is not confined in operation to the territory of the enacting state
or is contrary to public policy, or to international law. (3) There is in English law no
general doctrine of 'act of state' which can be applied to the facts of the present case. Nor
is there any rule of judicial restraint such as is found in some United States cases. (4) The
doctrine of sovereign immunity has no application.

These respective arguments cover a wide area but I think that in the end they leave for
decision a limited number of, admittedly difficult, points.

The doctrine of sovereign immunity does not in my opinion apply since there is no
attack direct or indirect on any property of any of the relevant sovereigns, nor are any of
them impleaded directly or indirectly.

I will deal first with the 'territorial argument' and the contention that we are here
concerned with a non-justiciable dispute as to the title to foreign land. As to this I am
prepared to accept much of the respondents' argument. I would agree, in the first place,
that this is not just a question arising between private individuals as to the title to, or
possession of, foreign land so as to come directly within the rule laid down in the
Moçambique and *Hesperides* cases; we do not have once more to examine that much
criticised rule. The present case is more nearly within the category of boundary disputes
between states. As to these it would be too broad a proposition to say that the mere
emergence in an action here of a dispute as to the boundaries of states is sufficient to
preclude the jurisdiction of the court. The main authorities cited by the respondents'
counsel, *Foster v Globe Venture Syndicate Ltd* and *Duff Development Co Ltd v Kelantan*,
though as I read them depending essentially on recognition, are at least instances where
the court has without difficulty decided questions depending on the ascertainment of
boundaries, and I would agree that there may be other cases where a question relating to
foreign land, even to the title to foreign land, may either be capable of determination as
a matter of fact (see per Lord Sumner in *Duff Development*, whom I do not understand as

arguing for justiciability in all cases) or may arise incidentally or collaterally to some other question, and may be decided. I need only quote Lord Herschell LC's words in the *Moçambique* case [1893] AC 602 at 626, [1891–4] All ER Rep 640 at 648:

> 'It is quite true that in the exercise of the undoubted jurisdiction of the Courts it may become necessary incidentally to investigate and determine the title to foreign lands . . .'

words applied by Sir Robert Megarry V-C in the great case of the Banaban Islands, *Tito v Waddell (No 2), Tito v Attorney General* [1977] 3 All ER 129 at 259, 266, 299, [1977] Ch 106 at 262, 271, 311 ('incidentally' or 'as a collateral incident').

But here the question of title to the location does not arise incidentally or collaterally: it is at the heart of the case. It is essential to Occidental's claim (both in its counterclaim and in its defence of justification) to establish that before the intervention of Buttes and Sharjah it had a right with some degree of legal validity over the sea bed at the location, ie 9 miles from Abu Musa (see the words in its counterclaim, quoted above, 'permanently deprived of their rights' to exploit the location). Occidental does not contend, it is true, that the action of Sharjah in extending its territorial waters so as to include the location was unlawful under Sharjah law; and, in so far as this is so, the dispute avoids the area of municipal law, or of conflict of (private) law. But that very fact makes it, not more, but less justiciable by a municipal court, either, as counsel for Buttes and Mr Boreta argued, as an a fortiori case to, or as an extension of *Hesperides*, or, as I would rather see it, as an issue in a different, and international, dimension. This cannot be decided simply as an issue of fact on evidence: it calls, on the contrary, for adjudication on the validity, meaning and effect of transactions of sovereign states. While, therefore, I agree with the respondents that the *Moçambique* rule is not of itself decisive of this case, we have still to consider whether a wider principle of judicial abstention has to be applied. I reserve this point for discussion later.

At this point it is convenient to deal with the argument of counsel for Occidental mentioned above under (1)(b); this is special to this case. The contention was that might otherwise have been a non-justiciable question (as concerning transactions between states) became justiciable through the actions of Her Majesty's government. It, so counsel for Occidental claimed, had set its seal of approval on all the relevant dispositions by Sharjah and by UAQ up to 1971, so that there would be no evidential difficulty, or potential breach of comity, or possibility of embarrassing the United Kingdom in its foreign relations if the court were to pass on them.

In order to appraise this argument, which I found the most formidable of his submissions, it is necessary to state some additional facts.

1. On 29th March 1973, in response to an inquiry from the chambers of Master Warren, made in the course of this action, the Foreign and Commonwealth Office supplied a certificate signed by the Foreign Secretary. I must set out the most relevant portions:

> 'Between the 9th September 1969 and the 1st December 1971 Her Majesty's Government recognised the State of Sharjah as an independent sovereign State in special treaty relations with the United Kingdom. By virtue of the special treaty relations, Her Majesty's Government were generally responsible for the conduct of the international relations of Sharjah and for its defence . . .
>
> 'Between the 9th September 1969 and the 1st December 1971 Her Majesty's Government recognised His Highness Shaikh Khalid bin Muhammed al Qasimi as the sovereign Ruler of the State of Sharjah. Thereafter, between the 2nd and the 30th December 1971 His Highness continued to be the sovereign Ruler of the State of Sharjah as a member Emirate of the United Arab Emirates.
>
> 'Her Majesty's Government did not during any part of the period between the 9th September 1969 and the 30th December 1971 exercise or claim any rights of sovereignty over or in relation to the affairs of Sharjah. However, as indicated [above], Her Majesty's Government had, until the 1st December 1971, general

responsibility for the conduct of the international relations of Sharjah. During the
period between the 9th September 1969 and the 30th December 1971, Her Majesty
the Queen also had jurisdiction within the State of Sharjah, including the territorial
waters thereof and all other areas over which the Ruler had jurisdiction, over certain
persons and matters, the extent and exercise of which were regulated by the Foreign
Jurisdiction Acts 1890 and 1913, by the Trucial States Orders 1959 to 1969 made
under those Acts, and by Queen's Regulations made under those Orders . . .'

On this it was found by May J, in my view correctly, that at the relevant time Sharjah was
an independent sovereign state and the ruler the sovereign ruler of that state. On the
other hand, Her Majesty's government had and retained until 1971 control over Sharjah's
foreign relations.

There is no certificate with regard to UAQ or its ruler, but I think we must assume
that, if one had been applied for, a certificate to a similar effect would have been given.
The later actions of Her Majesty's government must be viewed in the light of this
certificate. There were a number of interventions, including, as I have mentioned, the
approval of the concessions to Buttes and to Occidental. In February 1970 an informal
note was given by a Foreign Office official to Buttes stating that 'the seaward boundaries
of all the offshore areas have never been defined, in the absence of an agreed median
line'. At various dates, the Foreign and Commonwealth Office prepared maps and
provided them, and information about them, to one or other of the parties but I need
not, and in the interest of brevity, ought not to describe them since the whole attitude
of Her Majesty's government is set out most fully and clearly in two letters. The first is
a letter to Occidental's solicitors of 8th May 1970. In it the Foreign and Commonwealth
Office referred to 'unilateral action on the part of Sharjah', to 'problems raised by an
extension of the breadth of Sharjah's territorial waters', to 'a claim by Sharjah to
jurisdiction over the same area' (viz the 'location'). It is clear from this letter that Her
Majesty's government did not authorise, or approve, the extension, by decree, of Sharjah's
territorial waters to 12 miles from Abu Musa.

The letter explains the position of Her Majesty's government vis-à-vis the 1969 (1970)
decree at considerable length. It is clear that Her Majesty's government did not approve
of the extension, considered that there were international law questions as to its validity,
and expressed its own opinion that there was an agreed sea (sic) boundary based on a
3-mile limit of territorial waters around Abu Musa. There was, it states, a whole series
of problems in relation to other states in the area, which had to be faced before it was safe
to regard the territorial waters of Sharjah as having been effectively extended. The letter
continued:

> 'At the same time, it must be recognised that a claim exists, made on the basis of
> legal advice, to part of the area of seabed which has been regarded as under the
> jurisdiction of the Ruler of Umm al Qaiwain. Whatever may be the merits of this
> claim, the fact that it has been made must be faced and . . . a means for resolving the
> problems which it raises must be found . . . We do not ourselves wish to propose
> any particular means of resolving the problem but we remain fully prepared to
> assist in any way we can.'

This paragraph may be read as referring not or not only to an extension of territorial
waters but to a continental shelf in respect of Abu Musa.

The second letter was written on 16th May 1970 to the ruler of Sharjah by Her
Majesty's political agent at Dubai. This letter explained that the concession agreement
with Buttes, and the agreement between UAQ and Occidental, proceeded and were
approved by Her Majesty's government on the basis that the breadth of the territorial
waters of Sharjah was 3 miles. I quote the next paragraph:

> 'Having said this, I must at once go on to say that the extent of a state's territorial
> waters is to be determined in accordance with international law and a state may
> treat as its territorial waters those waters adjacent to its shores which international
> law permits it to treat as territorial waters. It is not necessary for a state to make a
> declaration claiming its territorial waters or stating the breadth of those waters.

But, if it chooses to do so, a state may declare the extent of its territorial waters. Many states (including the United Kingdom, the United States and the Persian Gulf States in special treaty relations with the United Kingdom) have territorial waters of 3 miles. Many states (including most of the other states in the Persian Gulf, that is the States other than those in special treaty relations with the United Kingdom) claim territorial waters of 12 miles . . .'

It continued by pointing out that there was another aspect of the problem:

'As a matter of international law, it is not right for a state simply to extend its territorial waters regardless of the consequences on its neighbours. If there are agreements or settled legal situations with its neighbours, or if vested rights have been acquired in the area, account must be taken of these agreements, situations and rights. In the case of Sharjah for example, there is a particular problem arising in relation to Umm al Qaiwain, where there is an agreed sea boundary of 1964 between Sharjah and Umm al Qaiwain and where a Concession Agreement was concluded by the Ruler of Umm al Qaiwain and approved by Her Majesty's Government on the basis of that sea boundary. It is not right simply to ignore the existence of the sea boundary and the Concession Area of Occidental of Umm al Qaiwain. But there is a whole series of further problems stemming from an extension of Sharjah's territorial waters. There are potential problems with Ras al Khaimah (the Tunbs), Ajman, Dubai and Abu Dhabi (in connection with Sir Abu Nu'Air). All these problems would have to be faced and sorted out before it would be safe to regard the territorial waters of Sharjah as having been effectively extended.'

It concluded by expressing hope of a solution by agreement, and, as stated above, attempts were made to dispose of the matter by mediation.

These letters show beyond any doubt that Her Majesty's government regarded the issues between Sharjah and UAQ, and between their respective concessionaires, as issues of international law, and involving difficult problems as to the width of territorial waters, and by implication of the continental shelf, in the light, not merely of geographical considerations, but of existing arrangements between Sharjah and UAQ, and of the interests of other states, amongst which Iran must have been in mind. Even if they can be read as expressing, or implying, an acceptance by Her Majesty's government of a 3-mile width of territorial waters, they do not, and in view of the claims of Iran could not, involve any recognition, or non-recognition, of continental shelf rights in respect of Abu Musa, or of Sharjah or of UAQ. On these questions, Her Majesty's government was willing, up to a point, to express its own opinion, but it regarded the matter as one to be solved by diplomacy, or 'third-party settlement'. Ultimately, as we know, it was solved temporarily at least, after the use of force, by agreement.

These considerations make it impossible to accept counsel for Occidental's contention. The issues as to the extent and nature of Occidental's rights cannot either be said to have been solved in advance for the courts by Her Majesty's government through its attitude to the various relevant transactions, or be said to be capable of being solved by a request to Her Majesty's government for an executive certificate or statement. Her Majesty's government regarded the whole matter as lying in the international sphere, subject at most to such influence as Her Majesty's government could bring to bear, but not susceptible of decision by Her Majesty's government. The issues are, as Her Majesty's government saw them, international issues, and it is in that character that their justiciability by a municipal court must be considered. I take up this question, with others, at the end of this opinion.

I pass now to the second branch of the argument which is described, broadly, as the 'act of state' argument. As to this the submissions of the respondents have brought some much needed clarification to a generally confused topic. Not the least of its difficulty has lain in the indiscriminating use of 'act of state' to cover situations which are quite distinct, and different in law.

In the first place we can segregate that version of 'act of state' which concerns action by an officer of the Crown taken outside this country against foreigners otherwise than under colour of legal right; the classic example of this is provided by *Buron v Denman* (1848) 2 Exch 167, 154 ER 450. The action taken by officers of Her Majesty's government, by means of HMS Yarnton, and in bringing pressure to bear on the ruler of UAQ, might fall into this category. They are not directly attacked in these proceedings, but it is part of Occidental's case that they were unlawful. However, the question whether these actions can be described as 'acts of state' within this doctrine does not lie at the heart of the dispute and I do not propose to pursue it.

A second version of 'act of state' consists of those cases which are concerned with the applicability of foreign municipal legislation within its own territory, and with the examinability of such legislation, often, but not invariably, arising in cases of confiscation of property. Counsel for Occidental gave us a valuable analysis of such cases as *Carr v Fracis, Times & Co* [1902] AC 176, *Aksionairnoye Obschestvo A M Luther v James Sagor & Co* [1921] 3 KB 532, [1921] All ER Rep 138, *Princess Paley Olga v Weisz* [1929] 1 KB 718, [1929] All ER Rep 513, suggesting that these are cases within the area of the conflict of laws, concerned essentially with the choice of the proper law to be applied.

Two points were taken as regards the applicability of this line of authority. First, it was said that foreign legislation can be called in question where it is seen to be contrary to international law or to public policy; the decree of 1969–70 was so contrary. Second, it was contended that foreign legislation is only recognised territorially, ie within the limits of the authority of the state concerned.

In my opinion these arguments do not help the appellants. As to the first it is true, as I have pointed out, that the attack on Sharjah's decree of 1969–70 is not on its validity under the law of Sharjah, but on its efficacy in international law. But this brings it at once into the area of international dispute. It is one thing to assert that effect will not be given to a foreign municipal law or executive act if it is contrary to public policy, or to international law (cf *Re Helbert Wagg & Co Ltd* [1956] 1 All ER 129, [1956] Ch 323) and quite another to claim that the courts may examine the validity, under international law, or some doctrine of public policy, of an act or acts operating in the area of transactions between states.

The second argument seems to me to be no more valid. To attack the decree of 1969–70 extending Sharjah's territorial waters, ie its territory, on the ground that the decree is extra-territorial seems to me to be circular or at least question begging.

However, though I reject these particular arguments relied on by way of exception to the rule derived from the authorities mentioned above, I do not regard the case against justiciability of the instant disputes as validated by the rule itself. If it is to be made good it must be on some wider principle.

So I think that the essential question is whether, apart from such particular rules as I have discussed, viz those established by (a) the *Moçambique* and *Hesperides* cases and by (b) *Aksionairnoye Obschestvo A M Luther v James Sagor & Co* and *Princess Paley Olga v Weisz*, there exists in English law a more general principle that the courts will not adjudicate on the transactions of foreign sovereign states. Though I would prefer to avoid argument on terminology, it seems desirable to consider this principle, if existing, not as a variety of 'act of state' but one for judicial restraint or abstention. The respondents' argument was that although there may have been traces of such a general principle, it has now been crystallised into particular rules (such as those I have mentioned) within one of which the appellants must bring the case, or fail. The Nile, once separated into a multi-channel delta, cannot be reconstituted.

In my opinion there is, and for long has been, such a general principle, starting in English law, adopted and generalised in the law of the USA, which is effective and compelling in English courts. This principle is not one of discretion, but is inherent in the very nature of the judicial process.

The first trace of it is in the seventeenth century in *Blad's Case* (1673) 3 Swan 603, 36 ER 991; (1674) 3 Swan 604, 36 ER 992. The record of the decision from Lord Nottingham's manuscript contains this passage (3 Swan 604 at 607, 36 ER 992 at 993):

'. . . the Plaintiff hath proved letters patent from the King of *Denmark* for the sole

trade of *Iceland*; a seizure by virtue of that patent; a sentence upon that seizure; a
confirmation of that sentence by the Chancellor of *Denmark*; an execution of that
sentence after confirmation; and a payment of two-thirds to the King of *Denmark*
after that execution. Now, after all this, to send it to a trial at law, where either the
Court must pretend to judge of the validity of the king's letters patent in *Denmark*,
or of the exposition and meaning of the articles of peace; or that a common jury
should try whether the *English* have a right to trade in *Iceland*, is monstrous and
absurd.'

Lord Nottingham records that 'I thought fit to put an end to [the case]', and he decreed
that the plaintiff should have a perpetual injunction to stay the defendant's suit at law, a
decision clearly on justiciability, and not merely on defence.

More clearly as a recognition of a general principle is *Duke of Brunswick v King of
Hanover* (1844) 6 Beav 1, 49 ER 724; *affd* (1848) 2 HL Cas 1, 9 ER 993, a case in this House
which is still authoritative and which has influenced the law both here and overseas.
There are two elements in the case, not always clearly separated, that of sovereign
immunity ratione personae, and that of immunity from jurisdiction ratione materiae;
it is the second that is relevant. I find the principle clearly stated that the courts in
England will not adjudicate on acts done abroad by virtue of sovereign authority. Thus
Lord Cottenham LC states the question, quite apart from any personal immunity, as
being whether the courts of this country can 'sit in judgment' on the act of a sovereign,
effected by virtue of his sovereign authority abroad. His decision is conveyed in the
words (2 HL Cas 1 at 21, 9 ER 993 at 1000):

'It is true, the bill states that the instrument was contrary to the laws of Hanover
and Brunswick, but, notwithstanding that it is so stated, still if it is a sovereign act,
then, whether it be according to law or not according to law, we cannot inquire into
it.'

And he continues by distinguishing cases of private rights (cf *Aksionairnoye Obschestvo
A M Luther v James Sagor & Co*):

'If it were a private transaction ... then the law upon which the rights of
individuals may depend, might have been a matter of fact to have been inquired
into ... But ... if it be a matter of sovereign authority, we cannot try the fact
whether it be right or wrong.'

(See 2 HL Cas 1 at 22, 9 ER 993 at 1000.)

Lord Campbell is still more definite. The question he says is 'as to the validity of an act
of sovereignty', and he expresses the view that even if the Duke of Cambridge (ie not the
sovereign) had been sued, 'it would equally have been a matter of state'.

It is justly said of this case, and of their Lordships' observations, that they are directed
to the question whether a sovereign can be brought to account in this country in respect
of sovereign acts, and that such general phrases as 'sitting in judgment on', 'inquiring
into', 'entertaining questions' must be read in their context. I agree that these phrases are
not to be used without circumspection; the nature of the judgment or inquiry or
entertainment must be carefully analysed. It is also to be noted that the acts in question
were performed within the territory of the sovereign concerned (reliance is placed on
this in some passages); an argument on this I have already dealt with. These qualifications
accepted, the case is nevertheless support, no doubt by reference to the issue in dispute,
for a principle of non-justiciability by the English courts of a certain class of sovereign
acts.

The discussion now shifts to the United States. The *Duke of Brunswick* case was
followed in *Underhill v Hernandez* (1893) 65 F 577 (Second Circuit Court of Appeals). In
the Supreme Court ((1897) 168 US 250 at 252) Fuller CJ used the much-quoted words:

'Every sovereign State is bound to respect the independence of every other
sovereign State, and the courts of one country will not sit in judgment on the acts

of the government of another done within its own territory. Redress of grievances
by reason of such acts must be obtained through the means open to be availed of by   *a*
sovereign powers as between themselves.'

Again it is a just observation that the words 'sit in judgment' must be related primarily
to the issue under discussion, viz whether a remedy could be obtained in the United
States for an alleged wrong committed by a foreign government in its own territory. But
a principle is nevertheless stated.

A few years later the Earl of Halsbury LC uttered the well-known sentence: *b*

'It is a well-established principle of law that the transactions of independent States
between each other are governed by other laws than those which municipal courts
administer.'

See *Cook v Sprigg* [1899] AC 572 at 578, [1895–9] All ER Rep 773 at 776, a case in which
lines of argument similar to those in the present case can be found. An earlier   *c*
recognition, in an appropriate circumstance, of non-justiciability had been given by Lord
Kingsdown in *Secretary of State in Council of India v Kamachee Boye Sahaba* (1859) 13 Moo
PCC 22 at 86, 15 ER 9 at 32–33. These authorities carry the doctrine of non-justiciability
into a wider area of transactions in the international field.

Fuller CJ's principle was taken up and again applied by the Supreme Court in *Oetjen v
Central Leather Co* (1918) 246 US 297 at 304 and applied to a case involving the title to   *d*
property brought within the custody of a United States court:

'To permit the validity of the acts of one sovereign State to be re-examined and
perhaps condemned by the courts of another would very certainly "imperil the
amicable relations between governments and vex the peace of nations".'

It is worth noting that this case and that of *Underhill* were referred to in the judgments   *e*
in *Aksionairnoye Obschestvo A M Luther v James Sagor & Co* and *Princess Paley Olga v Weisz*,
Scrutton LJ in the latter stating that English law on the point was the same as American
law.

On the much-commented case of *Banco Nacional de Cuba v Sabbatino* (1964) 376 US 398
no extended discussion is here appropriate or necessary. The case was one of 'act of state'
in the normal meaning, viz action taken by a foreign sovereign state within its own   *f*
territory. It affirms the doctrine of *Underhill* and *Oetjen*. It states (and for this was relied
on by the respondents) that international law does not *require* application of the doctrine
of 'act of state'. Granted this, and granted also, as the respondents argue, that United
States courts have moved towards a 'flexible' use of the doctrine on a case to case basis,
there is room for a principle, in suitable cases, of judicial restraint or abstention. Let us
see where this has led, in the United States, in relation to the very same situation as that   *g*
before us. Their courts have given two important decisions.

In 1970 Occidental brought two suits in California on allegations closely similar to
allegations made in this action: that the ruler of Sharjah had been induced by Buttes to
back date the decree enlarging the territorial sea to 12 miles to September 1969, that
Buttes had induced and procured illegal acts by the United Kingdom and by the ruler of
Sharjah, that Buttes had induced Iran to make a claim to the 'location'. These were   *h*
claimed to be common law torts as well as violations of the Sherman Act.

The United States District Court (Pregerson J, 17th March 1971) granted Buttes's
motion to dismiss the federal suit. It found that the essence of Occidental's case was to
prove a conspiracy and that characterisation of the case as a boundary dispute clouded the
issue. However, it found that Occidental—

'necessarily ask this court to "sit in judgment" upon the sovereign acts pleaded,   *j*
whether or not the countries involved are considered co-conspirators. That is, to
establish their claim as pleaded plaintiffs must prove, inter alia, that Sharjah issued
a fraudulent territorial waters decree, and that Iran laid claim to the island of Abu
Musa at the behest of the defendants. Plaintiffs say they stand ready to prove the
former allegation by use of "internal documents". But such inquiries by this court

into the authenticity and motivation of the acts of foreign sovereigns would be the very sources of diplomatic friction and complication that the act of state doctrine aims to avert.'

It concluded that Buttes's motion to dismiss should be granted for failure to state a claim on which relief may be granted. This judgment was affirmed by the Ninth Circuit Court of Appeals (23rd June 1971).

In 1974 Occidental brought numerous actions directed towards cargoes of oil shipped from the location, based on similar allegations.

The United States District Court in Louisiana (Hunter, Chief Judge, 8th July 1975) granted Buttes's motion for summary judgment against Occidental. The court gave attention to the boundary aspects of the dispute, which it considered were 'intricately interwoven with the "act of state" doctrine'. I quote two passages from the judgment:

'The entire fabric of [Occidental's] complaint is woven out of attacks on the validity of, or questioning the reasons for, the acts of Sharjah, Iran and [UAQ], with respect to the precise rights which [Occidental] asserts. It traces a series of wrongs of foreign states to reveal why the lease agreement cancellation by [UAQ] was invalid and why neither Sharjah nor Iran had a right to honour the lease contract (concession) by Buttes and its joint venturers . . .'

It listed ten 'acts of state' as appearing in Occidental's claim and continued:

'Practical considerations underlying a specific situation must be precisely examined to avoid conclusions making for eventual confusion and conflict. The instant case presents one of those problems for the rational solution of which it became necessary to take soundings. The case before us is this: Sharjah and Iran recognise the Buttes concession. [UAQ] cancelled the Occidental concession, but participates in the rentals received from Buttes. In the light of this history and what we perceive to be the purpose of Hickenlooper [the Hickenlooper amendment of 2nd October 1964 which restricted application of the act of state doctrine], I just cannot bring myself to believe that Congress intended to permit United States courts to tell these three foreign countries: "You are wrong and we are right as to the ownership of your offshore waters".'

On appeal by Occidental to the Fifth Circuit Court of Appeals the United States filed an amicus curiae brief (May 1978) to which was attached a letter from the legal adviser to the Department of State to the Attorney General. I quote a passage from that letter, without apology for its length, because of its obvious pertinence and rationality:

'It is our understanding that the disposition of this case would require a determination of the disputed boundary between Umm al Qaiwain on the one hand and Sharjah and Iran on the other at the time Umm al Qaiwain granted the concession in issue to Occidental. It is our view that it would be contrary to the foreign relations interests of the United States if our domestic courts were to adjudicate boundary controversies between third countries and in particular that controversy involved here. The extent of territorial sovereignty is a highly sensitive issue to foreign governments. Territorial disputes are generally considered of national significance and politically delicate. Even arrangements for the peaceful settlement of territorial differences are often a matter of continued sensitivity. These conditions are applicable to the question of Umm al Qaiwain's sovereignty over the continental shelf surrounding Abu Musa at the time of the concession to Occidental and to the subsequent arrangements worked out among the affected states. For these reasons, the Department of State considers that it would be potentially harmful to the conduct of our foreign relations were a United States court to rule on the territorial issue involved in this case. We believe that the political sensitivity of territorial issues, the need for unquestionable U.S. neutrality and the harm to our foreign relations which may otherwise ensue, as well as the evidentiary and jurisprudential difficulties for a U.S. court to determine such issues, are compelling grounds for judicial abstention. We do not believe that this judicial self-restraint should turn on such analytical questions as whether the so-called act of state doctrine which is traditionally limited to governmental actions within the territory of the respective state can apply to an exercise of disputed territorial jurisdiction. It rather follows from the general notion that national courts should not assume the function of arbiters of territorial conflicts between third powers even in the context of a dispute between private parties. As a result, we are of the view that the court should be encouraged to refrain from settling the extent of Umm al Qaiwain's sovereign rights in the continental shelf between its coast and Abu Musa at the time of its grant of the concession to Occidental.'

The Court of Appeals dismissed Occidental's appeal (9th August 1978) and held:

'The issue of sovereignty is political not only for its impact on the executive branch, but also because judicial or manageable standards are lacking for its determination. To decide the ownership of the concession area it would be necessary to decide (1) the sovereignty of Abu Musa, (2) the proper territorial water limit and (3) the proper allocation of continental shelf. A judicial resolution of the dispute over Abu Musa between Iran and Sharjah is clearly impossible.'

Occidental applied to the Supreme Court of the United States for certiorari and extensive briefs were filed, including again an elaborate amicus brief for the United States. On 11th June 1979 the Supreme Court denied the petition.

The constitutional position and the relationship between the executive and the judiciary in the United States is neither identical with our own nor in itself constant. Moreover the passages which I have cited lay emphasis on the 'foreign relations' aspect of the matter which appeared important to the United States at the time. These matters I have no wish to overlook or minimise. I appreciate also the argument of counsel for Occidental that no indication has been given that Her Majesty's government would be embarrassed by the court entering on these issues. But, the ultimate question what issues are capable, and what are incapable, of judicial determination must be answered in closely similar terms in whatever country they arise, depending, as they must, on an appreciation of the nature and limits of the judicial function. This has clearly received the consideration of the United States courts. When the judicial approach to an identical problem between the same parties has been spelt out with such articulation in a country, one not only so closely akin to ours in legal approach, the fabric of whose legal doctrine in this area is so closely interwoven with ours, but that to which all the parties before us belong, spelt out moreover in convincing language and reasoning, we should be unwise not to take the benefit of it.

The proceedings, if they are to go on, inevitably would involve determination of the following issues, and here I pick up the strands left over in the preceding discussion.

(1) Whether Occidental acquired in 1969 a vested right to explore the sea bed at the location within 12 miles from the coast of Abu Musa. This involves consideration of the questions (a) which state had sovereignty over Abu Musa, (b) what was the width of the territorial waters of Abu Musa, (c) what was the boundary of the continental shelf between (i) Sharjah and UAQ, (ii) Abu Musa and UAQ, (iii) Iran and both emirates?

These questions in turn involve consideration of the meaning and effect of the parallel declarations of 1964. Did they amount to an interstate agreement? Are they to be interpreted in the light of maps and how are the maps to be interpreted? Was the agreement (if any) superseded or modified by later conduct? Was it really the intention of the ruler of Sharjah at that time to give up any continental shelf in respect of Abu Musa? How is any bilateral agreement between Sharjah and UAQ to be fitted in with the claims of other states to the continental shelf in the Arabian Gulf? And how can any dispute as to the continental shelf be decided in the absence of Iran which has asserted claims to the relevant part of the continental shelf? Even if question (1)(b) is justiciable (in view of the attitude of Her Majesty's government or otherwise), insuperable difficulties arise as regards question (1)(c).

(2) If Occidental did acquire any vested rights as above, how and why was it deprived

of those rights? Directly, it was deprived of them by actions of sovereign states, viz
Sharjah, Iran, Her Majesty's government and UAQ. Consideration of these involves
examination of a series of interstate transactions from 1969 to 1973. If Occidental is to
succeed either in its counterclaim for conspiracy or in the slander action, it is necessary
to show that these actions were brought about by Buttes, more exactly by a fraudulent
conspiracy between Buttes and Sharjah. This certainly involves an examination of the
motives (exclusive or dominant?) for the action of Sharjah in making and, if proved, back
dating the decree of 1969–70. It involves establishing that the actions at least of Sharjah,
and it appears also of Iran and of Her Majesty's government, were at some point
unlawful. 'Unlawful' in this context cannot mean unlawful under any municipal law
(I remind that Occidental does not contend that the Sharjah decree was unlawful under
the law of Sharjah), but under international law. As Mr Lauterpacht QC put it, it
involves deciding whether the Sharjah decree was inefficacious, at least for a time, in
international law. If, in the absence of unlawful means, it is alleged that the action taken
by Sharjah and the co-conspirators was predominantly to injure Occidental (I am not
convinced that Occidental makes this case but I will assume it), this involves an inquiry
into the motives of the then ruler of Sharjah in making the decree, and a suggestion that
he invited Iran to enter into an arrangement about Abu Musa predominantly in order to
injure Occidental.

It would not be difficult to elaborate on these considerations, or to perceive other
important interstate issues and/or issues of international law which would face the
court. They have only to be stated to compel the conclusion that these are not issues on
which a municipal court can pass. Leaving aside all possibility of embarrassment in our
foreign relations (which it can be said have not been drawn to the attention of the court
by the executive), there are, to follow the Fifth Circuit Court of Appeals, no judicial or
manageable standards by which to judge these issues, or, to adopt another phrase (from
a passage not quoted), the court would be in a judicial no man's land: the court would be
asked to review transactions in which four foreign states were involved, which they had
brought to a precarious settlement, after diplomacy and the use of force, and to say that
at least part of these were 'unlawful' under international law. I would just add, in answer
to one of the respondents' arguments, that it is not to be assumed that these matters have
now passed into history, so that they now can be examined with safe detachment.

It remains to consider the practical effect of the above conclusions.

There is no doubt that, as found by May J in his judgment of 1974, the counterclaim
in conspiracy is 'really the kernel of this litigation'. For the reasons I have just given, this
counterclaim cannot succeed without bringing to trial non-justiciable issues. The court
cannot entertain it.

As regards the libel counterclaim, the innuendo pleaded, that Occidental had
attempted to seize part of or to interfere with Buttes's oil concession granted by Sharjah
knowing that it had no right to do so, involves consideration of the same issues as arise
in relation to the rest of the counterclaim and for the same reason cannot be entertained.

The plea of justification made by Occidental in the slander action raises the same issues
as the conspiracy counterclaim and is for the same reason not capable of being entertained
by the court. In these circumstances a problem might arise if Buttes was to insist on the
action proceeding: to allow it to proceed but deny Occidental the opportunity to justify
would seem unjust, although Buttes suggests that there are precedents for such a situation
being accepted by the court. However, in the event, Buttes has, in its summons of 11th
July 1980, offered to submit to a stay on the claim, if the counterclaims are stayed. Buttes
should be held to this offer.

I suggest that Buttes's appeal against the order of the Court of Appeal dated 5th
December 1974 be allowed, that that order be set aside and that an order be made on
Buttes's summons of 11th July 1980 that, on Buttes by their counsel consenting to all
proceedings on the claim herein being stayed, the counterclaim of the first and second
defendants, Armand Hammer and Occidental Petroleum Corpn, be stayed.

The stay of the counterclaim would necessarily involve that the pending application
of the defendants for discovery and/or production of documents be similarly stayed.

LORD FRASER OF TULLYBELTON. My Lords, I have had the privilege of reading in draft the speech of my noble and learned friend Lord Wilberforce and I agree with it. For the reasons given by him I would dispose of the appeal in the way that he has suggested.

LORD RUSSELL OF KILLOWEN. My Lords, I also have had the advantage of reading in draft the illuminating speech of my noble and learned friend Lord Wilberforce. I agree with his reasons and conclusions.

LORD KEITH OF KINKEL. My Lords, I have had the benefit of reading in draft the speech of my noble and learned friend Lord Wilberforce and agree entirely with his reasoning and conclusions. I would accordingly dispose of the appeal in the manner which he has proposed.

LORD BRIDGE OF HARWICH. My Lords, I have had the advantage of reading in draft the speech of my noble and learned friend Lord Wilberforce. I entirely agree with it and with the order he proposes.

Appeal by Buttes and Mr Boreta allowed; action and counterclaim stayed on Buttes consenting to all proceedings on their claim being stayed.

Action for discovery of documents stayed.

Solicitors: *Coward Chance* (for Buttes and Mr Boreta); *Herbert Smith & Co* (for Dr Hammer and Occidental).

Mary Rose Plummer   Barrister.

The Jogoo

QUEEN'S BENCH DIVISION (ADMIRALTY COURT)
SHEEN J
14th, 15th, 16th, 30th JANUARY 1981

Admiralty – Appraisement and sale – Payment out of proceeds of sale – Priorities – Cost of discharging cargo from arrested ship before order for sale – Whether first charge on proceeds as part of administrative costs of sale.

The shipowners purchased a ship and mortgaged it to the mortgagees as security for the outstanding balance of the purchase price. While the ship was in port, in the course of a voyage carrying a mixed cargo under contracts of carriage under which the freight had been pre-paid, the mortgagees issued a writ against the shipowners, who had defaulted on the mortgage repayments, claiming the principal sum due under the mortgage and interest thereon and later arrested the ship in the port. The court ordered the Admiralty Marshal to permit the cargo owners to discharge their cargo on their undertaking to pay the costs of discharge. The cargo was discharged and the costs of the discharge borne by the cargo owners. Subsequently the mortgagees obtained judgment against the shipowners for the principal sum due under the mortgage and interest thereon and, since the shipowners (who were insolvent and unable to complete the voyage) had failed to provide security to obtain release of the ship from arrest, the court ordered that the ship be appraised and sold by the marshal but reserved all questions of the priority of claims against the proceeds of the sale. The ship was sold pursuant to the order for a sum less than the amount of the mortgagees' judgment against the shipowners. By a notice of motion the cargo owners, who had been anxious to have the cargo discharged from the

ship for their own benefit, intervened in the mortgagees' action seeking (i) a declaration
a that the costs of discharging the cargo which they had borne should rank equally with
the marshal's charges and expenses in executing the commission of appraisement and
sale, and should therefore, like the marshal's charges and expenses, be a first charge on the
proceeds of the sale of the ship and take priority over the mortgagees' judgment against
the shipowners, and (ii) an order that the cargo owners be paid £148,540 plus interest out
of the proceeds of the sale as representing the proved costs of discharging the cargo. That
b sum appeared to include items not solely incurred in freeing the ship of her cargo and the
mortgagees asserted that only some £30,000 was attributable to the costs of discharging
the cargo. The cargo owners submitted (i) that the costs of discharging the cargo borne
by them should take priority over the mortgagees' judgment, because where a vessel had
been arrested in proceedings in rem any expense reasonably incurred which conferred a
benefit on the res by enhancing its value should be reimbursed out of the proceeds of sale
c of the vessel as part of the costs of the sale, and (ii) that since the discharge of the cargo had
conferred such a benefit by enabling the ship to be sold, or sold at a higher price than
would have been the case if the cargo had still been on board. The mortgagees submitted
that as the cargo owners had claims against the shipowners for breach of contract of
carriage and those claims would include a claim for reimbursement of the costs incurred
in discharging the cargo, the claim for reimbursement of those costs could not be
d elevated to the position of a secured claim having priority over the mortgagees' claim.

Held – The costs of discharging the cargo were not a first charge on the proceeds of the
sale of the ship, and the motion would therefore be dismissed, for the following reasons—
(1) The principle applicable under English Admiralty law was that, where a shipowner
failed to complete a contract for the carriage of cargo by, for example, causing the ship
e to be arrested for failure to pay his creditors or failure to put up security to obtain release
from arrest of the ship, the cargo owner had to pay for the removal of the cargo from the
ship and could then make a claim against the shipowner for the damage he had suffered
by the failure to complete the contract. The practice in the United States of treating the
costs of discharging cargo from an arrested ship as an expense incurred in administering
a common fund available for distribution constituted by the arrested ship, and therefore
f as an administrative cost of realising the ship and payable as such out of the proceeds of
sale, was incompatible with English law and inapplicable in England (see p 638 *j* and
p 640 *e f*, post); dictum of Roskill LJ in *The Myrto* [1978] 1 Lloyds' Rep at 13–14 applied;
The Poznan (1927) 274 US 117 and *The Emilia* [1963] AMC 1447 not followed.
(2) Furthermore, even assuming that the discharge of the cargo resulted in a higher
price being fetched for the ship when it was subsequently sold by order of the court, the
g effect of acceding to the cargo owners' application would be that the costs of the discharge
would in the end have to be borne by the mortgagees, despite the fact that the cargo
owners had no claim against the mortgagees because of the absence of any principle
requiring a person to contribute to an outlay merely because he had derived a material
benefit from it (see p 639 *e* to *g*, post); *Ruabon Steamship Co Ltd v London Assurance Co*
[1895–9] All ER Rep 677 applied.
h Per Curiam. If the cost of discharging the cargo is to be held to be a first charge on the
proceeds of the sale of a ship, the amount so charged should be the cost of discharging the
cargo onto the quay and no more (see p 640 *f*, post).

Notes
j For the determination of priorities of claims against a vessel, see 1 Halsbury's Laws (4th
Edn) para 456, and for cases on the subject, see 42 Digest (Repl) 655–660, 4075–4128.

Cases referred to in judgment
Brave Enterprise, The (14th April 1975, unreported).
Carl Hendric, The (1903) Fo 468.

Dharamdas & Co (Nigeria) Ltd v Owners of the ship or vessel Mingren Development [1979]
     Hong Kong LR 159.
Emilia, The [1963] AMC 1447.
Myrto, The [1978] 1 Lloyd's Rep 11, CA.
Poznan, The (1927) 274 US 117, [1927] AMC 723.
Ruabon Steamship Co Ltd v London Assurance Co [1900] AC 6, [1895–9] All ER Rep 677, 69
     LJQB 86, 81 LT 585, 9 Asp MLC 2, 5 Com Cas 71, HL, 29 Digest (Repl) 287, 2167.
Selina Stanford, The (1908) Times, 17th November, 1(1) Digest (Reissue) 295, 1766.
Unity, The (1909) Shipping Gazette, 3rd May.

Cases also cited

Fothergill v Monarch Airlines Ltd [1980] 2 All ER 696, [1981] AC 251, HL.
Gettysburg, The (1885) 52 LT 60.
Helmville Ltd v Yorkshire Insurance Co Ltd, The Medina Princess [1965] 1 Lloyd's Rep 361.
Orion, The (1932) 66 Ll L Rep 33.
Smith v SS Zigurds (owners) and E A Casper, Edgar & Co Ltd [1934] AC 209, [1933] All ER
     Rep 717, HL.

Motion

In an action commenced by the mortgagees of the ship Jogoo, Marmondo Compania
Naviera SA, against the shipowners, Eastern Africa National Shipping Line Co Ltd, the
cargo owners of cargo now or lately laden on board the Jogoo intervened in the action
and claimed by a notice of motion issued on 23rd December 1980 (1) a declaration that
the costs of discharging the Jogoo's cargo at the Port of Newport, Gwent, between 23rd
April and 2nd June 1980 which were borne by the cargo owners should be ranked pari
passu with the charges and expenses incurred by the Admiralty Marshal in executing the
commission of appraisement and sale of the Jogoo and should thus become a first charge
on the proceeds of the sale of the Jogoo; (2) an order that the cargo owners should be paid
the sum of £148,540·83 plus accumulated interest out of the proceeds of the sale as
representing the proved costs of discharging the ship. The facts are set out in the
judgment.

Geoffrey Kinley for the cargo owners.
Jonathan Mance for the mortgagees.
The shipowners were not represented.

Cur adv vult

30th January. **SHEEN J** read the following judgment. On 16th April 1980 I gave leave
to the owners of cargo lately laden on board the ship Jogoo to intervene in the action
commenced by mortgagees of that vessel against her owners. The court now has before
it a motion by the cargo owners, which will be more readily understood when I have set
out the relevant facts leading up to this motion.

By a memorandum of agreement dated 28th April 1978 the shipowners, Eastern
Africa National Shipping Line Ltd (a company incorporated in Dar Es Salaam, Tanzania),
agreed to purchase the Jogoo from her previous owners for the sum of DM12,250,000.
The shipowners paid 10% of the price in cash on delivery while the balance of 90% was
payable over seven years. As security for the outstanding balance the shipowners
provided a first and second mortgage on the vessel. In February 1980 the Jogoo was
engaged in a voyage from Dar Es Salaam to Newport and certain ports on the continent
of Europe. On 27th February 1980 when the Jogoo was in Newport she was arrested at
the suit of Harding Brothers, who claimed that the shipowners were indebted to them

for various goods supplied to the vessel for her maintenance and upkeep. The Jogoo was
a still in Newport under arrest on 27th March 1980 when the writ in this action was issued
by the mortgagees. The shipowners had failed to make payments due under the
mortgage deeds. It soon became apparent to Harding Brothers that their claim would be
postponed to the rights of the mortgagees and that there was no point in pursuing their
claim against the vessel. The Jogoo was arrested by the mortgagees on 27th March
1980. On 16th April 1980 I heard a motion by the cargo owners and, after hearing the
b arguments of counsel and of the Admiralty Marshal in person, I made the following
order:

'(1) The Admiralty Marshal shall permit the discharge of all the cargo presently
laden aboard the ship JOGOO and deliver to the [cargo owners] such portions of the
cargo as to which they do produce to him reasonable evidence of title on their
Solicitors having undertaken to the Court to pay the Admiralty Marshal's costs in
c relation to the [cargo owners'] cargo.

'(2) The balance of the said cargo to be stored and the owners thereof notified as
to its storage.

'(3) The Admiralty Marshal to be at liberty to apply as to the storage of cargo and
disposal of any cargo unclaimed within 30 days after completion of discharge.

'(4) The costs of this application to be reserved.'

d
The Jogoo was laden with 5,500 tons of mixed cargo, about half of which was copper
destined for Antwerp. There were over 100 different cargo owners. All except six of
them instructed Ince & Co to act on their behalf. Only those cargo owners who have
given such instructions to Ince & Co have intervened in this action. The cargo was
discharged from the Jogoo at the port of Newport between 23rd April and 2nd June
e 1980. At that time I had not made an order that the Jogoo be appraised and sold.

On 9th June 1980 I gave judgment for the mortgagees in the sum of DM11,025,000
in respect of the principal sum due under both the mortgages and in the sum of
DM419,311·46 in respect of interest due thereon. I further ordered that the Jogoo be
appraised and sold by the Admiralty Marshal by private treaty and reserved all questions
as to priorities. Pursuant to that order the Jogoo was sold on 6th August 1980 for the
f sum of $US4,500,000. Therefore the mortgagees cannot recover out of the proceeds of
sale the full amount for which they have judgment.

The motion now before the court is a motion by the interveners, the cargo owners, for
a declaration that the cost of discharging the cargo at Newport, which was borne by
them, should rank pari passu with the charges and expenses incurred by the Admiralty
Marshal in executing the commission of appraisement and sale of the vessel, and that that
g cost should thus become a first charge on the proceeds of sale of the Jogoo; and for an
order that the cargo owners should be paid a sum of £148,540·83 and interest thereon
out of the proceeds of sale. It is contended by the cargo owners that this sum was the cost
incurred by them in discharging the cargo.

The financial collapse of the shipowners made it impossible for that company (1) to
pay its debt to Harding Brothers, (2) to meet its commitments under the mortgage deeds,
h and (3) to finance the completion of the voyage on which the Jogoo was engaged and its
obligations to discharge the cargo as set out in the bills of lading. Harding Brothers, the
mortgagees and the cargo owners have money claims against the shipowners. The first
two of them took the opportunity provided by the presence of the Jogoo within the
jurisdiction of this court to try to make some financial recovery. Harding Brothers have
now recognised that the mortgagees will be paid in priority to them and accordingly
j they have not pursued their claim. I must now decide the order of priority as between
the judgment in favour of the mortgagees and the expense incurred by the cargo owners
in discharging the cargo.

The rival contentions are these. The cargo owners say that the Jogoo could not have
been sold (or could only have been sold for a lower price) while she remained laden with
cargo. Therefore the cargo had to be discharged and therefore the cost of discharging the

cargo is part of the cost of selling the ship. They contend that as they have borne the cost
of discharging the cargo and as they have, to that extent, conferred a benefit on the
mortgagees they are entitled to be reimbursed out of the proceeds of sale in priority to a
the claim of the mortgagees. On the other hand, the mortgagees say that the cargo
owners have a claim against the shipowners for damages for breach of the contract of
carriage and that part of the cargo owners' claim is for reimbursement of the expense
incurred by them in discharging the cargo. The mortgagees contend that no part of the
cargo owners' claim can be elevated into the position of a secured claim having priority b
over the claim of the mortgagees.

Counsel for the cargo owners submitted that when a vessel has been arrested in
proceedings in rem any expense reasonably incurred which confers a benefit on the res
by enhancing its value should be reimbursed out of the proceeds of sale. He submitted
that this is in conformity with a decision of the United States Supreme Court and not
contrary to any English decision. It was submitted that any plaintiff who arrests a vessel c
in order to obtain security for his claim takes the vessel as she is. If she is laden with cargo
then the cost of discharging the cargo is part of the cost of realising the security.

Counsel was unable to find any decision of this court which supported his motion. He
drew my attention to a decision of the Supreme Court of the United States in *The Poznan*
(1927) 274 US 117 and to the decision of the United States Court of Appeals Second
Circuit in *The Emilia* [1963] AMC 1447. In the latter case Jacob Mishler DJ in the United d
States District Court (Eastern District of New York) said ([1963] AMC 1447 at 1449):

'. . . the Court finds that the presence of cargo aboard has an adverse effect on the
sale to the detriment of all parties who have an interest, claim or lien in the vessel.
The propriety of charging the cost of discharging the cargo against the proceeds of
sale as an administrative expense again arises. The Court, at the time of the issuance
of the order of May 21, 1963, informally expressed its reasons for considering the e
cost of discharging the cargo as an administrative expense and takes this opportunity
to formally set them forth. The cargo is lawfully and rightfully aboard ship. The
owner of the vessel did not have the right to direct removal of the cargo at the
expense of the owners of the cargo . . . The sale of the owner's interest in the vessel
cannot serve to vest a greater right than the owner had, nor can it impose an
additional liability on the cargo owners. Discharge of the cargo is a service furnished f
on authority of the Court and should be paid out of the proceeds of sale as an
"expense of justice". *The Poznan* ((1927) 274 US 117 at 121). Since the vessel is in
custodia legis the charge against the fund is not a lien. The right of the Court to
direct payment of such charges before pre-custodial liens is stated in Gilmore and
Black, the Law of Admiralty (p 497) as follows: ". . . if equity and good conscience
require that they be paid in priority to pre-custodial claimants who do have liens, g
the Admiralty court may properly decree the prior payment".'

This decision was affirmed by the United States Court of Appeals, Second Circuit, with
the words ([1963] AMC 1447 at 1448):

'Service rendered to the ship after arrest, in aid of the discharge of cargo, and h
afterwards pending the sale, necessarily inured to their [the lienor's] benefit, for it
contributed to the creation of the fund [now] available to them. The district court
has jurisdiction to "require that expenses which have contributed either to the
preservation or creation of the fund in its custody shall be paid before a general
distribution among those entitled to receive it".'

Counsel for the cargo owners sought to persuade me to give new heart to English j
Admiralty law and practice by transplanting those decisions from the United States. It
seems to me, however, that those decisions are incompatible with the sound body of
English case law and must be rejected.

In *The Myrto* [1978] 1 Lloyd's Rep 11 the question which I now have to decide came
before the Court of Appeal on an interlocutory appeal against an order of Brandon J. The

Court of Appeal made an order which left the point open for decision at a later date,
a when it could be fully argued, because of the urgency of the matter and the pressure of
time. Roskill LJ said in the course of his judgment (at 13–14):

> 'I would only add this with regard to the United States authorities to which we
> were referred. It is well known that United States Admiralty law on priorities is not
> always the same as English law, and therefore while giving the utmost weight to
> any decision of the United States Courts, and particularly to the decision of the
b > Supreme Court in *The Poznan* in 1927, I do not think that that affords a certain guide
> as to the course we should follow in the present case, where we are concerned with
> priorities to be determined in accordance with the law prevailing in this country.'

Counsel on behalf of the mortgagees, at the forefront of his submissions, invited me
to consider the contractual relationship between the cargo owners and the shipowners.
c The cargo was carried in the Jogoo under a contract of carriage, one of the terms of which
was that freight was pre-paid at Mombasa. When freight is paid in advance the cargo
owners accept the commercial risk that the voyage will not be completed for whatever
reason. If the contract is frustrated the cargo owners bear the loss because the Law
Reform (Frustrated Contracts) Act 1943 does not apply to contracts for the carriage of
goods by sea (see s 2(5)(*a*)). The shipowners repudiated the contract of carriage by failing
d to pay their creditors or put up security in order to obtain the release from arrest of their
vessel, with the result that the cargo owners now have claims for damages against
them. The cargo owners have a right to remove their cargo from the ship, or they may
abandon it.

Counsel for the mortgagees pointed out that the cargo owners applied to intervene in
this action because they were anxious to have the cargo discharged for their own benefit
e and primarily with their own interests in mind. Furthermore, I did not order the cargo
to be discharged. My order was that the Admiralty Marshal should permit the cargo
owners to remove their cargo. At the time when the cargo owners arranged for the
discharge of the cargo the mortgagees had not obtained judgment and I had not ordered
that the Jogoo be sold.

I will assume that one result of the discharge of the cargo was that when the Jogoo was
f subsequently sold by order of the court, the price paid was higher than it would have
been if the cargo had still been on board. Even on that assumption the cargo owners
have no claim against the mortgagees, because there is no principle of law which requires
a person to contribute to an outlay merely because he has derived a material benefit from
it (see *Ruabon Steamship Co Ltd v London Assurance Co* [1900] AC 6, [1895–9] All ER Rep
677). Counsel for the cargo owners did not submit that the cargo owners had any direct
g claim for reimbursement against the mortgagees, but the effect of acceding to his
application would be that the expense of discharging the cargo would come out of the
pockets of the mortgagees.

The practice of this court is stated in Roscoe's Admiralty Practice (5th Edn, 1931, p
287) in these words:

> 'When the marshal has in his custody a vessel with a cargo on board, and he is
h > ordered to sell the vessel only, the cargo-owners will be given a reasonable time by
> the Court wherein to effect the unlivery of the cargo, but if the unlivery is not
> effected in the time fixed, the cargo-owners will thereafter be ordered to pay the cost
> of the detention of the vessel for which they may be responsible (see *The Carl Hendric*
> ((1903) Fo 468); *The Selina Stanford* ((1908) Times, 17th November)).'

In *The Selina Stanford* Barnes P said that he was informed by the marshal that—
j
> 'it was very desirable the cargo should be transhipped, because if it were landed
> at Portland under his directions it would be worthless, *and* the cost of landing would
> probably have to come out of the proceeds of the vessel.'

The sense of the report of this case suggests that the word 'and' (which I have
emphasised) should be read as 'and therefore'. In *The Unity* (1909) Shipping Gazette, 3rd

May, Bargrave Deane J made an order permitting the marshal to discharge and sell the cargo, recouping himself out of the proceeds and paying the balance into court unless the cargo owners took the cargo from the vessel. In *The Brave Enterprise* (14th April 1975 unreported) the Admiralty Registrar made an order that the Admiralty Marshal be at liberty to discharge and sell or if necessary destroy the cargo and his expenses incurred in discharge, sale or destruction be paid out of the proceeds of such sale, any expenses not so recovered to form part of the Admiralty Marshal's expenses in that action.

This same question has recently arisen in Hong Kong in *Dharamdas & Co (Nigeria) Ltd v Owners of the ship or vessel Mingren Development* [1979] Hong Kong LR 159 when Cons J decided that the expenses of off-loading and storage of the cargo were to be taken first from the securities lodged by the cargo claimants. In the course of his judgment (with which I entirely agree) Cons J said (at 163):

> 'It seems to me that the English position derives from the old common law doctrine of frustration. American courts have approached from a different direction. They appear to look at it this way, that from the moment of its arrest a ship is a common fund administered by the court for the common benefit of all those interested in the fund and that any expenses incurred in the administration of that fund should be borne by the fund itself as an "expense of justice". [The judge then referred to *The Poznan* and *The Emilia* and continued:] The present position is of long standing. As I see it the position was confirmed in 1943 when contracts for the carriage of goods by sea were deliberately excluded from the operation of the Law Reform (Frustrated Contracts) Act. I am not persuaded that the American approach is so much more just or that conditions now are so different from those in 1943 that I should take it on myself to make a general change.'

Such few cases as have been reported show that in England the Admiralty Court has consistently taken the view that the cargo owners must pay for removal of their own cargo in the event of the contract of carriage not being completed by the shipowners, and then make a claim against the shipowners for the damage which they have suffered. It seems to me that this is correct in principle. For these reasons this motion by the cargo owners must fail.

In case my decision should be reversed on appeal I must say something further about the amount claimed. If it should be held hereafter that the cost of discharging the cargo should be a first charge on the proceeds of sale of the Jogoo, then the amount so charged should be the cost of discharging the cargo onto the quay and no more. The cargo owners allege that the cost of discharging cargo amounted to £148,540·83. That sum appears to include many items which were of benefit to the cargo owners but were not incurred solely for the purpose of freeing the vessel of her cargo. The mortgagees contend that the amount attributable to discharging alone is less than £30,000. It was agreed between the parties that the assessment of the true discharging costs should be deferred until the question as to who should bear these costs had been decided.

Motion dismissed.

Solicitors: *Ince & Co* (for the cargo owners); *Richards, Butler & Co* (for the mortgagees).

N P Metcalfe Esq   Barrister.

R v Heron and others

COURT OF APPEAL, CRIMINAL DIVISION
SHAW LJ, MAIS AND TUDOR EVANS JJ
14th APRIL, 31st JULY 1981

Criminal law – Coinage offence – Making counterfeit coins resembling current coinage – Intent – Whether intent to defraud by uttering counterfeit coins necessary ingredient of offence – Whether mere act of producing counterfeit coins an offence – Coinage Offences Act 1936, s 1(1).

Because the object of s 1(1)[a] of the Coinage Offences Act 1936 is to preserve the purity of current coinage and therefore to obviate even a latent threat to the purity of the coinage, the very act of producing counterfeit coins with intent to produce such coins is an offence under s 1(1), and it is not necessary to prove a dishonest intent to utter the counterfeit coins to establish the offence. Although s 8[b] of the 1936 Act makes it an offence to make an article resembling current coinage but which is not counterfeit coinage, that does not displace the purpose of s 1(1), namely the protection of the purity of the coinage, or mean that the offence under s 1(1) is confined to producing counterfeit coins with an intent to pass them off as genuine, since the effect of s 8 is merely to extend s 1(1) (see p 643 *e*, p 644 *f* to *h* and p 645 *a b*, post).

Notes

For making counterfeit coins, see 11 Halsbury's Laws (4th Edn) para 978, and for cases on the subject, see 15 Digest (Reissue) 1001–1002, 8656–8663.

For the Coinage Offences Act 1936, ss 1, 8, see 8 Halsbury's Statutes (3rd Edn) 317, 322.

As from 27th October 1981 the Coinage Offences Act 1936 was repealed by the Forgery and Counterfeiting Act 1981, which makes fresh provision with respect to, inter alia, counterfeiting of coins and kindred offences.

Cases referred to in judgment

R v Sutton (1841) 5 JP 195, 15 Digest (Reissue) 1002, 8662.
Selby v Director of Public Prosecutions [1971] 3 All ER 810, [1972] AC 515, [1971] 3 WLR 647, 135 JP 619, 56 Cr App R 72, HL, 15 Digest (Reissue) 1004, 8692.

Cases also cited

R v Hermann (1879) 4 QBD 284, CCR.
R v Hollingberry (1825) 4 B & C 329, 107 ER 1081.
R v McMahon (1894) 15 NSWLR 131.
R v Phekoo [1981] 3 All ER 84, [1981] 1 WLR 1117, CA.
R v Sheppard [1980] 3 All ER 899, [1981] AC 394, CA.
R v Vickers [1975] 2 All ER 945, [1975] 1 WLR 811, CA.
Sweet v Parsley [1969] 1 All ER 347, [1970] AC 132, HL.
United States v King (1851) 5 McLean 208, US Circuit Ct, Seventh Circuit.
Warner v Metropolitan Police Comr [1968] 2 All ER 356, [1969] 2 AC 256, HL.

Appeals

At the trial of the appellants, David Heron, Peter Edwin Storey, Christopher Robin Thomas and George Santi, in September 1980 at the Central Criminal Court before his

---

a Section 1(1), so far as material, is set out at p 643 *d*, post
b Section 8, so far as material, provides: 'Every person who, without lawful authority or excuse (the proof whereof shall lie on the person accused), makes, sells, offers for sale or has in his possession for sale, any medal, cast, coin . . . (a) resembling in size, figure and colour any current gold or silver coin . . . shall be guilty of [an offence] . . .'

Honour Judge Abdela QC and a jury, on two counts of an indictment charging them with conspiring together to falsely make or counterfeit coins resembling current coins, namely half-sovereigns (count 1), and conspiring to defraud such persons as might be induced to purchase false or counterfeit half-sovereigns by false representations that they were genuine (count 2), Santi pleaded guilty and the other appellants pleaded not guilty to count 1, and all appellants pleaded not guilty to count 2. On 12th September 1980, at the end of the Crown's case, the trial judge ruled that the voluntary pursuance of the operation of counterfeiting was all that was necessary to import the necessary mental element in the substantive offence under s 1(1) of the Coinage Offences Act 1936 on which count 1 was based, and that count 1 should therefore be left to the jury. Heron, Storey and Thomas then changed their pleas on count 1 to guilty and verdicts of guilty on count 1 in respect of all the appellants were returned by the jury. The jury were discharged from returning a verdict on count 2. Heron was sentenced to 3½ years imprisonment, Storey to 3 years' imprisonment and Thomas and Santi each to 2¼ years' imprisonment. Storey, Heron and Thomas appealed against conviction on the ground that the trial judge erred in ruling that the substantive offence under s 1(1) of the 1936 Act was an absolute offence. All the appellants appealed against sentence. The facts are set out in the judgment of the court.

Louis Blom-Cooper QC and *Paul Dodgson* for the apellants Heron, Storey and Thomas.
Spencer Robert Bernard (assigned by the Registrar of Criminal Appeals) for the appellant Santi.
Michael Sayers and *Andrew Macrea* for the Crown.

At the conclusion of the arguments Shaw LJ announced that the appeals against conviction would be dismissed for reasons to be given later, and that the appeals against sentences would be allowed and the sentences varied.

31st July. **SHAW LJ** read the following judgment of the court: The appellants appeared at the Central Criminal Court in September 1980 to answer an indictment which charged them on two counts. The first count alleged that between 1st January and 22nd September 1978 they conspired together 'falsely to make or counterfeit coins resembling current gold coins, namely half sovereigns'. The second count charged them with having conspired together between those dates 'to defraud such persons as might be induced to purchase false or counterfeit half sovereigns by false representations that the same were genuine'.

The circumstances which brought them before the court were stark and telling. At some time in 1978 Heron procured the use of premises at 60 Southgate Road in North London. With the help of Thomas and a man named Barry he conveyed a die-stamping machine from Santi's address to those premises. Thereafter all the appellants as well as other persons were seen in July, August and September 1978 going to and coming from no 60.

On 21st September 1978 the police made concerted raids at that address as well as at the Jolly Farmers public house in the same road, where Storey was the licensee, and at an address in East London where Santi was then living. At 60 Southgate Road they found a hydraulic press, a number of dies and a quantity of copper discs. There were also some antique coins, a metal-cutting machine and about a thousand copper coins, o which half that number had been plated with gold. In addition there were a number of counterfeit half-sovereigns. Thomas was in the premises at the time. Asked about the various items there, he said: 'You know Heron organised it', and in reply to a question about how many coins had been made he said: 'Only those you found. We'd only just started.' He later amended this to 'about a thousand plus what's on the premises'.

Heron was arrested outside the Jolly Farmers. At first he denied any involvement with the activities at no 60. When told that he had been seen assisting in the taking of the die-stamping machine to that address he was more forthcoming and said: 'I gave them the chance to make a lot of money and they do this to me.'

Storey was seen inside the Jolly Farmers. He told the police that Heron owed him money and that he hoped to get his money back by taking part in a scheme for making (counterfeit) half-sovereigns. He also admitted that he had arranged for the use of 60 Southgate Road. When Santi was seen he admitted his connection with the enterprise described by Storey, but said that he had played only a minor part in the matter.

The account of the police observation, supplemented and augmented by the admissions attributed to the respective appellants, left little room for the defendants (as they were at the Central Criminal Court) to manoeuvre. On their arraignment Santi pleaded guilty to count 1. The others pleaded not guilty. At the close of the Crown case it was submitted on behalf of Heron that count 2 ought not to be left to the jury as the evidence did not demonstrate that the defendants intended to use the counterfeit half-sovereigns for the purpose of defrauding anyone. A further submission was developed to the effect that, in the absence of any intention to commit the fraud envisaged by count 2, the substantive offence on which count 1 was founded was not intended or envisaged, and that accordingly that count was not supported by the evidence before the jury.

The judge ruled against these submissions, holding that the substantive offence to which count 1 related required no specific intent beyond an intention 'to falsely make or counterfeit any current coin.' That substantive offence is concisely defined in s 1(1) of the Coinage Offences Act 1936 in these terms:

> 'Every person who falsely makes or counterfeits any coin resembling any current coin shall be guilty of [an offence] . . .'

No particular intent is required as a constituent element of the offence by the terms of the subsection; but it is inherent in the nature of the activity described that there should be an intent to produce coin which simulates current coin. It is hardly conceivable that a person could produce coins which were imitations of current coins otherwise than purposefully, that is to say with the intention of making his products resemble current coin.

Counsel for the appellants contended that in order to give rise to an offence under s 1(1) there must also exist a dishonest intention to utter the spurious coins so as to pass them off as genuine. The only authority advanced in support of this proposition was *R v Sutton* (1841) 5 JP 195. The recital of the facts reads thus:

> 'The prisoner who had every appearance of being a most respectable person, was a native of Canada, and along with many others was engaged in the fur trade with the native Indians, inhabiting the rocky mountains and the banks of the Colombia river. The persons engaged in this traffic with the Indians do not pay them for those commodities in money, but give in exchange for the furs, beads, knives, or other articles of a similar description. The prisoner was sent over to this country for the purpose of procuring articles to traffic with the native Indians, and amongst other things he was directed to procure a quantity of medals. The prisoner sent to a tradesman in Sheffield, and showed him a medal with a ring through the upper part of the medal, and requested to have a number made similar to the one he exhibited. The tradesman consented to make the medals, and the prisoner gave him an order for 2500 of these medals. It appeared that the medals could not be struck from the die with a hole through the top as the prisoner desired, and therefore the medals were struck in a perfect state. After a number of the medals had been made, but before the order was completed, the person at Sheffield from some information he received, discovered that the medals he was making were an exact representation of a Mexican dollar; he therefore refused to proceed with his work, and caused the prisoner to be apprehended. There are certain signs and letters upon the Mexican dollars denoting the value of the coin and the mint at which it is coined, these were all faithfully represented upon the medals that had been struck.'

The indictment was laid under the statute 37 Geo 3 c 126 (1797), which is entitled:

> 'An Act to prevent the counterfeiting of any copper coin in this Realm . . . or any *a* foreign gold or silver coin; and to prevent the bringing into this Realm or uttering any counterfeit foreign gold or silver coin.'

The report concludes with the ruling of Rolfe B, which was in these terms:

> '. . . the facts and circumstances of the case, together with the conduct of the prisoner, proved to his mind that there was no intention on the part of the prisoner *b* to use these medals as coin, but merely as ornaments to gratify the taste of the Indians, and to be given in exchange for their furs. He was also of opinion that upon his construction of the statute on which the prisoner had been indicted, the jury must be satisfied that the intention of the prisoner in procuring these medals to be made, was to defraud and cheat the people of this country.'

c

This direction had the immediate result of a verdict of acquittal.

Counsel for the appellants, while acknowledging that the statutory context was different from the present case, urged that by analogy a corresponding construction should be put on the provisions of s 1(1) of the 1936 Act. Section 2 of the 1797 Act renacted:

> '. . . that if any person or persons shall from and after the passing of this Act make, *d* coin or counterfeit any kind of coin not the proper coin of this realm nor permitted to be current within the same but resembling or made with intent to resemble or look like any gold or silver coin of any foreign . . . country or to pass as such foreign coin, such person or persons shall be . . . guilty of felony . . .'

Section 3 went on to make uttering such counterfeit coin an offence if the utterer knew *e* it to be 'fake or counterfeit'.

The interpretation of Rolfe B of those provisions may have been influenced by the reputation and standing of the accused, who had wanted the reproduction Mexican dollars made with a hole punched through them so that they could be used as medals. However that may be, the case is not one which affords any real guidance in the construction of the modern statute. *f*

Two considerations are important. The first is that s 1 of the 1936 Act is concerned with the preservation of the integrity of current coin of the realm. It is manifest that this is put at risk as soon as spurious coins are brought into existence, for they may, whether by accident or design, pass into circulation. There is an immediate threat to the purity of the coinage, and it seems clear that the object of s 1(1) is to obviate even the latent threat by making the very act of counterfeiting an offence in itself. If reinforcement for *g* this view were necessary it is to be found in s 1(2), which in effect provides that an offence under s 1(1) shall have been committed although the coin made or counterfeited has not been finished or perfected. This subsection contemplates a situation in which the counterfeited coin may not be in a fit state to be uttered with any confident prospect of passing it off as genuine. Thus the intent so to pass it off is clearly not an ingredient of the offence of counterfeiting per se. *h*

Counsel for the appellants placed some reliance on the phrase 'falsely makes' in s 1(1). He submitted that 'falsely' imported a fraudulent intent. This does not appear to this court to be a valid argument. It may be that those words were necessary to cover the situation where an employee at the Mint goes beyond his authority to mint coins of the realm.

A further argument was that, so far as the protection of the purity of the currency was *j* concerned (in contradistinction to actually putting counterfeit coin into circulation), it was s 8 of the 1936 Act that made provision in that regard, so that it was superfluous to look to s 1, which dealt with a more advanced activity, namely a prospective uttering with intent to defraud.

This is a misconception of the object and design of s 8. What is there enacted is that selling or having in possession articles in the form of 'any medal, cast, coin . . . made wholly or partially of metal' which have some element of resemblance to current coin shall be an offence. Under this section an offence is committed even though the article cannot be said to counterfeit current coin inasmuch as there is only one or some remote factor or factors of resemblance. Section 8 extends the net cast by s 1; it does not displace it. Furthermore, s 8 affords to a person charged under it a possible defence of lawful authority or excuse. No such defence is available to a charge under s 1.

Reliance was also placed on the decision of the House of Lords in *Selby v Director of Public Prosecutions* [1971] 3 All ER 810, [1972] AC 515. That case was however concerned with the construction and operation of s 5 of the 1936 Act. The question which there fell to be decided was whether the offence of uttering counterfeit coin involved not only knowledge of its character but also an intent to pass it off as genuine. The opinion of the majority was that such an intent was a necessary ingredient of the offence defined by s 5. The objective of that section was to discourage not the making of counterfeit coin but its circulation. Section 1 seeks to strike at the mischief at source and condemns the first stage in despoiling the currency of the realm.

For those reasons we dismiss the appeals against conviction.

[After hearing submissions by counsel in connection with the appeals against sentence, the court considered that the sentences of imprisonment that had been imposed for what was a very serious offence were fully justified. However, the court felt there were exceptional circumstances in that the single judge had granted the appellants bail on the basis that if the appeal were successful they would be wrongly incarcerated pending the hearing of the appeal and some ten months had elapsed between the time when they were sentenced and the time when they were released on bail. The court felt that in those circumstances and not because of any merit or claim of right in the appellants the sentences ought to be quashed and in their place sentences of 2½ years' imprisonment in the case of the appellant Heron, 2 years' imprisonment in the case of the appellant Storey and 15 months' imprisonment in the cases of Thomas and Santi would be substituted.]

Appeals against conviction dismissed. Appeals against sentences allowed and sentences varied.

The court refused leave to appeal to the House of Lords but certified, under s 33(2) of the Criminal Appeal Act 1968, that the following point of law of general public importance was involved in the decision: whether the offence of counterfeiting under s 1(1)(a) of the Coinage Offences Act 1936 is an absolute offence which requires no element of dishonest intent.

12th November. The Appeal Committee of the House of Lords granted leave to appeal.

Solicitors: *Hepburns*, Peckham (for the appellants Heron, Storey and Thomas); *Director of Public Prosecutions.*

N P Metcalfe Esq   Barrister.

Re Savoy Hotel Ltd

a

CHANCERY DIVISION
NOURSE J
9th, 10th, 14th, 15th APRIL 1981

Company – Scheme of arrangement – Jurisdiction to sanction – Scheme to acquire control of
company by transfer of two classes of members' shares to applicant – Applicant seeking order   *b*
giving it liberty to hold separate meetings of classes for purpose of obtaining shareholders'
approval of scheme – Company's board not approving and unlikely to approve of scheme – Scheme
not providing for company's approval to be obtained in general meeting – Scheme requiring
company to register transfer of members' shares to applicant – Whether a scheme 'between'
company and its members – Whether jurisdiction to sanction scheme of arrangement in regard to
members of a company where company not approving scheme – Whether if no jurisdiction without   *c*
company's approval court having power to order meetings to be convened – Whether court should
in the exercise of its discretion refuse to order meetings to be convened – Companies Act 1948,
s 206(1)(2).

The issued ordinary share capital of a company was divided into A and B shares. The A
and B shares ranked equally in all respects except in regard to voting rights, in respect of   *d*
which the B shares carried 40 times as many votes as A shares of an equivalent nominal
value. Accordingly, the holders of the A shares, who together owned 97·7% of the
equity, were entitled to only 51·45% of the votes whilst the holders of the B shares, who
together owned only 2·3% of the equity, were entitled to 48·55% of the votes.
Moreoever, some 65% of the B shares (carrying about 31·68% of the votes) were held by
members of the company's board either beneficially or as trustees. In practice, therefore,   *e*
the B shareholders controlled the company in general meeting and could block an
outside offer to acquire the company's share capital. The applicant, another company,
was the beneficial owner of 88,000 A shares, of which 44,000 were registered in its
name. The applicant did not own or hold any B shares. The applicant wished to acquire
control of the company and proposed to the company a transfer scheme of arrangement
to be sanctioned by the court under s 206[d] of the Companies Act 1948, whereby the   *f*
applicant was to acquire all the company's A and B shares (other than those it already
held) in exchange for shares in the applicant or cash sums. The applicant applied to the
court under s 206(1) for an order giving it liberty to convene separate meetings of the A
and B shareholders to implement the scheme. The applicant's purpose in convening
separate meetings was to obtain at the meeting of the A shareholders a 75% majority in
favour of the scheme and thereby to make the scheme binding on the company, under   *g*
s 206(2). The scheme did not provide for the company's approval to be obtained in
general meeting and was disapproved of by the board of the company. The only
provision in the scheme which in terms involved the company's participation was a
clause conferring power on the applicant, in order to give effect to the transfer of the
shares, to appoint a third party to execute a transfer of the shares in its favour in place of
the existing shareholder and requiring the company to register a transfer of shares in   *h*
favour of the applicant provided certain conditions were satisfied. The company opposed
the application to convene separate meetings of the A and B shareholders on the ground
that the court had no jurisdiction to sanction the proposed scheme, and submitted (i) that
the scheme was not one 'between' the company and its members or any class of them,
within s 206(1), since it did not sufficiently materially affect the rights and obligations
between them, (ii) that, even if it were such a scheme, there was no jurisdiction to   *j*
sanction it in the absence of the company's approval, and (iii) that therefore the court
either had no power to convene the meetings or, in the exercise of its discretion, ought
not to convene them in all the circumstances.

---

a   Section 206, so far as material is set out at p 650 *j* to p 651 *b*, post

Held – (1) The word 'arrangement' in s 206 of the 1948 Act was to be interpreted widely,
a and, since the scheme would affect the contractual relationship subsisting between the
company and its members by requiring the company to register the applicant in place of
existing members as the holders of the company's shares, the rights and obligations
between the company and its members were sufficiently affected for the proposed
scheme to be an 'arrangement . . . between' them within s 206(1) (see p 652 *f* to *h* and p
654 *c d*, post); *Re Guardian Assurance Co* [1917] 1 Ch 431, dictum of Plowman J in *Re*
b *National Bank Ltd* [1966] 1 All ER at 1012, *Singer Manufacturing Co v Robinow* 1971 SC 11,
and dictum of Megarry J in *Re Calgary and Edmonton Land Co Ltd* [1975] 1 All ER at 1054
applied.

(2) However, since s 206(1) of the 1948 Act referred to an arrangement 'proposed
between' a company and, inter alios, its members, that assumed consent by the company,
as a legal personality separate from its members, to the arrangement. Accordingly, the
c court had no jurisdiction under s 206 to sanction an arrangement regarding the members
of a company which did not have the company's approval, either through its board or by
a majority of the members in general meeting. It followed that the court had no
jurisdiction to sanction the applicant's scheme (see p 656 *e* to p 657 *d*, post); *Re*
International Contract Co, Hankey's Case (1872) 26 LT 358 and *Re Oceanic Steam Navigation*
Co Ltd [1938] 3 All ER 740 applied.

d (3) Furthermore, although the court had power under s 206(1) of the 1948 Act to
order that separate meetings of the A and B shareholders be convened, in all the
circumstances the court would exercise its discretion to refuse to exercise that power
because the company's board had withheld approval of the scheme, the scheme did not
provide for approval to be obtained in general meeting, the board was unlikely to
reconsider its attitude or to approve the scheme and accordingly the meetings would not
e serve any useful purpose. The application would therefore be dismissed (see p 657 *g h*,
post).

Notes

For schemes of arrangement, see 7 Halsbury's Laws (4th Edn) paras 1526, 1533, 1534,
and for cases on the subject, see 10 Digest (Reissue) 1218–1223, 7659–7686.
f   For the Companies Act 1948, s 206, see 5 Halsbury's Statutes (3rd Edn) 274.

Cases referred to in judgment

Alabama, New Orleans, Texas and Pacific Junction Railway Co, Re [1891] 1 Ch 213, 60 LJ Ch
    221, 64 LT 127, 2 Meg 377, CA, 10 Digest (Reissue) 849, 4906.
Calgary and Edmonton Land Co Ltd, Re [1975] 1 All ER 1046, [1975] 1 WLR 355, 10 Digest
g   (Reissue) 1167, 7260.
Dailuaine-Talisker Distilleries Ltd v Mackenzie 1910 SC 193, 47 Sc LR 717, 10 Digest
    (Reissue) 1220, *3483.
Dominion of Canada Freehold Estate and Timber Co Ltd, Re (1886) 55 LT 347, 10 Digest
    (Reissue) 849, 4905.
Dorman Long & Co Ltd, Re, Re South Durham Steel and Iron Co Ltd [1934] Ch 635, [1933] All
h   ER Rep 460, 103 LJ Ch 316, 151 LT 347, 10 Digest (Reissue) 1221, 7675.
East of England Banking Co, Re, Pearson's Case (1872) 7 Ch App 309, 41 LJ Ch 524, 27 LT
    379, LJJ, 10 Digest (Reissue) 1232, 7752.
English, Scottish and Australian Chartered Bank, Re [1893] 3 Ch 385, [1891–4] All ER Rep
    775, 62 LJ Ch 825, 69 LT 268, 2 R 574, CA, 9 Digest (Reissue) 634, 3787.
Guardian Assurance Co, Re [1917] 1 Ch 431, 86 LJ Ch 214, 116 LT 193, [1917] HBR 113,
j   CA, 9 Digest (Reissue) 735, 4374.
Hartland, Re, Banks v Hartland [1911] 1 Ch 459, sub nom *Re Dixon Hartland, Banks v*
    Hartland 80 LJ Ch 305, 104 LT 490, 30 Digest (Reissue) 281, 894.
Hector & Sons Ltd, Re 1947 SC 641, 10 Digest (Reissue) 1220, *3485.
International Contract Co, Re, Hankey's Case (1872) 41 LJ Ch 385, 26 LT 358, 20 WR 506,
    [1872] WN 63, 10 Digest (Reissue) 1232, 7753.

NFU Development Trust Ltd, Re [1973] 1 All ER 135, [1972] 1 WLR 1548, 10 Digest
   (Reissue) 1219, 7663.   *a*
National Bank Ltd, Re [1966] 1 All ER 1006, [1966] 1 WLR 819, 9 Digest (Reissue) 735,
   4376.
Oceanic Steam Navigation Co Ltd, Re [1938] 3 All ER 740, [1939] Ch 41, 108 LJ Ch 74, 159
   LT 457, 10 Digest (Reissue) 1223, 7684.
Peebles (Bruce) & Co Ltd v William Bain & Co Ltd 1918 SC 781, 10 Digest (Reissue) 1220,
   *3484.   *b*
Singer Manufacturing Co v Robinow 1971 SC 11, Digest (Cont Vol D) 99, *3477a.

Cases also cited
Albert Life Assurance Co, Re (1871) LR 6 Ch App 381.
Anglo-Continental Supply Co Ltd, Re [1922] 2 Ch 723.
Dynevor, Dyffryn and Neath Abbey Collieries Co, Re (1879) 11 Ch D 605, CA.   *c*
Garner's Motors Ltd, Re [1937] 1 All ER 671, [1937] Ch 594.
Odhams Press Ltd, Re [1925] WN 10.
Shaw v Royce Ltd [1911] 1 Ch 138.

Originating summons
By a summons dated 27th March 1981 the applicant, Trust House Forte Ltd, sought an   *d*
order against the respondent, Savoy Hotel Ltd, that the applicant be at liberty to convene
separate meetings of the holders of the respondent's A ordinary shares and B ordinary
shares respectively for the purpose of considering and, if thought fit, approving, with or
without modification, a scheme of arrangement between the respondent and the holders
of its A and B shares, and that directions be given as to the method of convening the
meetings and the place where they were to be held, for appointing a chairman of each   *e*
meeting and for ordering them to report the results of the meetings to the court. The
summons was heard in chambers but judgment was given by Nourse J in open court.
The facts are set out in the judgment.

Andrew Morritt QC, Richard Sykes and *David Unwin* for the applicant.
Donald Nicholls QC and *Mary Arden* for the respondent.   *f*

NOURSE J. This application is the first step in an attempt by Trust House Forte Ltd
('THF') to acquire control of the Savoy Hotel Ltd ('the Savoy') by means of a scheme of
arrangement sanctioned by the court under s 206 of the Companies Act 1948.
    THF seeks an order under sub-s (1) of s 206 that it be at liberty to convene separate
meetings of the holders of the A and B ordinary shares in the Savoy for the purpose of   *g*
approving the proposed scheme. The application is opposed by the Savoy. It is very
unusual, if not unknown, for an application under sub-s (1) to be opposed, but that is
because the application is usually made by the company itself. Shortly stated, the Savoy's
contention in this case is that there is no jurisdiction to sanction the scheme, at all events
without its approval. That approval has been withheld by the board and the scheme does
not provide for it to be obtained from the company in general meeting. Therefore, says   *h*
the Savoy, and whatever the outcome of the meetings, the court can see now that the
scheme will not be sanctioned under sub-s (2) and it ought not to convene meetings
which will not serve any useful purpose.
    In 1953 and 1954 there were two unsuccessful attempts to take over the Savoy. In
April 1955, in order to protect itself against future attempts of the same kind and in
recognition of the support which it had received during the struggle of 1953 to 1954, the   *j*
Savoy reorganised its ordinary share capital in such a way as to give to all its shareholders
at that time a means of possessing substantially increased voting rights in the long
term. Its present issued ordinary share capital, which is fully paid up, consists of
27,687,825 A shares of 10p each and 1,306,267 B shares of 5p each. Voting rights apart,
the A and B shares rank pari passu in all respects in proportion to the amounts paid up
thereon respectively. But on a poll the B shares carry 40 times as many votes as A shares

of an equivalent nominal value. That means that the holders of the A shares, who
a together own 97·7% of the equity, are entitled to only 51·45% of the votes, while the
holders of the B shares, who together own 2·3% of the equity, are entitled to no less than
48·55% of the votes. Moreover, about 65·26% of the B shares (with about 31·68% of the
votes) are held, either beneficially or as trustees, by members of the board. The result is
that the control of the Savoy by the A shareholders exists only in theory. In practice the
B shareholders can control the company in general meeting and can, if they choose, block
b any general offer from outside.

All this has been well recognised for many years, and until recently it allowed the
Savoy to wear the appearance of impregnability. But if the route which THF now
proposes to take is open, and if a three-fourths majority of the A shareholders voting at
the separate meeting of that class approves a scheme which is later sanctioned by the
court, THF will have been able to acquire 51·45% of the voting rights on what could well
c be a considerably smaller percentage of the votes. For example, even if all the A
shareholders voted at the class meeting it would only need a three-fourths majority, or
about 38·6% of the votes as a whole, for the scheme to be approved. That has led THF's
proposals to be variously described on the Savoy side as a take-over by sleight of hand or
by the back door. Assertions of that sort, although no doubt valuable in the forum of
public debate as a justification for the stance which has been adopted by the Savoy, play
d no part in legal argument. Indeed they have not been put forward as such. If the door
is there you will not close it by papering it over with coloured labels. On the other hand,
the Savoy is perfectly entitled to contend in this court that the door is an illusion in the
first place, and that course is not something which needs to be justified. All this is
familiar ground. An emphasis of it is desirable when a case which has aroused public and
financial interest passes, at least temporarily, into the courtroom. It is especially desirable
e when the outcome of the case depends on questions of jurisdiction whose resolution may
affect other cases long after the echoes of this have ceased to sound.

THF's proposals were publicly announced on 12th March 1981. I will refer to them
in greater detail shortly. THF's stated intention was that the separate proposals for each
class would be effected by means of a scheme of arrangement under s 206 of the 1948
Act, but it reserved the right to make general offers to acquire the whole of the share
f capital of the Savoy on the same financial terms, within overall time limits imposed by
the City Code on Take-overs and Mergers. On the same day Sir Charles Forte, the
executive chairman of THF, wrote to Sir Hugh Wontner, the chairman of the Savoy,
informing him of the proposals and the intended method of their implementation. He
asked him to confirm that he was prepared to take appropriate steps to convene the
statutory meetings and, if appropriate, thereafter to take the necessary steps to obtain the
g sanction of the court. Sir Charles ended by saying that THF would be prepared to call the
meetings to implement its offers in the event of the Savoy's indicating its unwillingness
to do so. That letter was answered on 18th March, when Sir Hugh informed Sir Charles
that the board of the Savoy regarded THF's proposal as unacceptable. He added that the
board further believed that it would be inappropriate to try to put the proposal into effect
by way of a s 206 scheme of arrangement. Sir Hugh has confirmed in evidence that,
h other considerations apart, the board of the Savoy does not approve of the terms of the
proposed scheme.

The result of Sir Hugh's letter was that on 27th March THF issued the summons which
is now before the court. In addition to seeking liberty to convene separate meetings of
the A and B shareholders it asks for consequential directions as to the method of
convening them and so forth. Argument was heard in chambers on Thursday and
j Friday of last week and yesterday, when I said that I would give judgment in open court
today on the question whether the meetings should be convened or not. I will try to
state the arguments as fully as is reasonably possible.

THF is the beneficial owner of 88,000 A shares in the Savoy, of which 44,000 are
registered in its name. It does not own and does not hold any B shares. The scheme
proposed by THF is what is sometimes known as a transfer scheme. Shortly stated, it
provides for the acquisition by THF of the whole of the issued share capital of the Savoy

(other than the shares already beneficially owned by it) on terms that the holder of every
100 A shares should receive a specified number of THF ordinary shares or (at his election) *a*
£165 in cash, and that the holder of each B share should receive either a specified number
of THF ordinary shares or (at the like election) £9·75 in cash, and so on in proportion for
any greater or lesser number of A shares or B shares as the case may be, with provisions
for adjustment.

The only provision of the scheme which in terms involves the participation of the
Savoy is cl 1. Sub-clause (a) provides for the acquisition by THF of the A and B shares and *b*
confers power on it to appoint any person to transfer any of the shares in the place of the
existing holders. Sub-clause (b) reads as follows:

> 'Savoy shall, subject to being satisfied that THF has made delivery, pursuant to
> sub-clause (b) of Clause 7 of this Scheme, of the documents of title and cheques
> required to be delivered by THF pursuant to sub-clause (a) of such Clause 7 forthwith
> upon receipt thereof register any transfer of any Scheme Shares in favour of THF or *c*
> its nominees which is executed in manner provided by sub-clause (a) of this Clause
> and is duly stamped and issue to the transferee a certificate in respect of the Scheme
> Shares comprised in such transfer and Savoy shall effect such registration
> notwithstanding that the transfer is not accompanied by the certificate for the
> Scheme Shares comprised therein. Savoy shall not suspend the registration of
> transfers or close its register of members at any time in the period of 42 days after *d*
> the Effective Date.'

Clause 9 provides that the existing share certificates shall cease to be of value and shall
at the request of THF be surrendered to it. The only other provision of the scheme to
which I need refer is cl 13 which is headed 'Partial operation of this scheme'. That is in
these terms: *e*

> 'Notwithstanding anything hereinbefore contained, if this Scheme shall not have
> been agreed to by the statutory majority required by Section 206 of the Companies
> Act 1948 at the meeting of the holders of the Scheme "A" Shares or the Scheme "B"
> Shares, summoned in accordance with such Section to consider and, if thought fit,
> to approve this Scheme, or if this Scheme shall not be sanctioned by the Court in
> respect of either such class this Scheme shall be capable of being modified, at the *f*
> option of THF, by the exclusion from the operation of this Scheme of that class of
> shares in respect of which this Scheme shall not have been so approved or sanctioned
> and by making such modifications to this Scheme as may be approved by the Court
> as necessary or desirable having regard to such exclusion.'

That clause is of crucial importance to THF since, in the event of the scheme being *g*
approved by the A shareholders but not by the B shareholders, it would enable THF to
proceed with the further stages of the scheme in relation to the A shares alone.

I should say at this stage that many transfer schemes have in the past been approved by
the court under s 206. There is another variant which is sometimes known as the
cancellation and reduction scheme. Shortly stated, that type of scheme operates by way,
first, of the cancellation of existing shares in exchange for a consideration (often in cash) *h*
received by the shareholders and, secondly, a consequential reduction of the company's
capital. The court has not only to sanction the scheme but also to confirm the
reduction. That type of scheme is generally more popular, because the cancellation of
shares for a consideration in cash does not, like many transfer schemes, attract stamp
duty. However, it cannot be carried out without the approval of the company, because
a reduction of a company's capital can only be effected by special resolution.   *j*

I must now refer to the material provisions of s 206:

> '(1) Where a compromise or arrangement is proposed between a company and its
> creditors or any class of them or between the company and its members or any class
> of them, the court may, on the application in a summary way of the company or of

any creditor or member of the company, or, in the case of a company being wound up, of the liquidator, order a meeting of the creditors or class of creditors, or of the members of the company or class of members, as the case may be, to be summoned in such manner as the court directs.

'(2) If a majority in number representing three fourths in value of the creditors or class of creditors or members or class of members, as the case may be, present and voting either in person or by proxy at the meeting, agree to any compromise or arrangement, the compromise or arrangement shall, if sanctioned by the court, be binding on all the creditors or the class of creditors, or on the members or class of members, as the case may be, and also on the company or, in the case of a company in the course of being wound up, on the liquidator and contributories of the company . . .'

Subsection (3) provides inter alia that an order made under sub-s (2) shall have no effect until an office copy has been delivered to the Registrar of Companies. Subsection (4) provides for the imposition of a fine on the company and every officer of the company in a case where it makes default in complying with sub-s (3). I need not refer to sub-s (5). Subsection (6) provides inter alia that the expression 'arrangement' includes a reorganisation of the share capital of the company by the consolidation of the shares of different classes or by the division of shares into shares of different classes or by both those methods.

The arguments of counsel for the Savoy were to the following effect. First, while accepting that THF as a member of the company can propose an arrangement under s 206, he submitted that the scheme proposed in this case falls outside the section altogether, on the ground that it is not one 'between' the Savoy and its members or any class of them. He said that the court has no jurisdiction to sanction an arrangement of this kind and that that is an end of the case. Second, and in the alternative, he said that even if the scheme is properly to be regarded as one 'between' the Savoy and its members or any class of them, the court has no jurisdiction to sanction an arrangement which does not have the approval of the company. He then submitted that, if that be right, the court either has no power, or if it has, ought not to convene the proposed meetings in the circumstances of the present case. Third, and in the further alternative, he submitted that the court has no jurisdiction to sanction a scheme affecting the B shares on the application of a member who holds only A shares.

Before dealing with these arguments in turn, it will be convenient for me to refer to the statutory predecessors of s 206, of which counsel for the Savoy conducted a helpful and comprehensive review.

The Companies Act 1862 did not provide for compromises or arrangements to be sanctioned by the court on behalf of either creditors or members of a company. Section 136 provided for an arrangement entered into between a company about to be, or in the course of being, wound up voluntarily and its creditors to be binding on a company if sanctioned by an extraordinary resolution, and on its creditors if acceded to by three-fourths of their number and value. Section 137 gave any creditor or contributory a right of appeal to the court against any such arrangement and the court had power to amend, vary or confirm it. Sections 159 and 160 empowered a liquidator, with the sanction of the court, where a company was being wound up compulsorily or subject to supervision, and with the sanction of an extraordinary resolution of the company where it was being wound up voluntarily, to enter into compromises with creditors and contributories respectively. That was as far as the 1862 Act went. But s 2 of the Joint Stock Companies Arrangement Act 1870 introduced for the first time a rudimentary ancestor of s 206 of the 1948 Act, limited to compromises or arrangements proposed between a company which was in the course of being wound up, either voluntarily or compulsorily or under supervision, and its creditors or any class of them. The compromise or arrangement had to be approved by a three-fourths majority in value, but not in number, of the creditors, and the section provided that if that happened the arrangement or compromise should—

'if sanctioned by an order of the court, be binding on all such creditors or class of
creditors, as the case may be, and also on the liquidator and contributories of the said
company.'

The power was expressed to be in addition to any other power of the court.

That remained the position until 1900, when s 24 of the Companies Act 1900 applied
the provisions of s 2 of the 1870 Act—

'not only as between the company and the creditors, or any class thereof, but as
between the company and the members, or any class thereof.'

It was still necessary at that stage that the company should be in the course of being
wound up, but s 38 of the Companies Act 1907 provided that the 1870 Act should apply
in like manner to a company which was not in the course of being wound up. Section
39 of the 1907 Act gave a company power by special resolution confirmed by an order
of the court to modify its memorandum of association so as to reorganise its capital
'whether by the consolidation of shares of different classes, or by the division of its shares
into shares of different classes . . .' In the following year the Companies (Consolidation)
Act 1908 was passed and in s 120 there appeared for the first time a readily recognisable
predecessor of sub-ss (1) and (2) of s 206 of the 1948 Act, the only difference being that
the words 'and voting' did not at that stage appear in sub-s (2) after the word 'present'.
In other words, as I understand it, at that stage an abstention was still effectively a vote
against. However, that and other amendments were made by s 53 of the Companies Act
1928. Of the other amendments, I should mention that s 45 of the 1908 Act (which had
re-enacted s 39 of the 1907 Act) ceased to have effect. It was in effect replaced by the
extension of the definition of 'arrangement' which is now found in s 206(6). That brings
me to s 153 of the Companies Act 1929, another consolidating Act, which was in a form
identical to that of s 206, except that sub-s (5), which is immaterial to this case, had not
yet been included.

I now consider the first argument of counsel for the Savoy. He accepts that the
proposed scheme constitutes an arrangement, but he says that it is not one 'between' the
Savoy and its members or any class of them. Although this does not seem to have been
the view universally held during the period immediately following the enactment of
s 38 of the 1907 Act (see, for example, *Re Guardian Assurance Co* [1917] 1 Ch 431 per
Younger J), there can be no doubt that the word 'arrangement' in s 206 has for many
years been treated as being one of very wide import. Statements to that effect can be
found in the judgments of Plowman J in *Re National Bank Ltd* [1966] 1 All ER 1006 at
1012, [1966] 1 WLR 819 at 829, and of Megarry J in *Re Calgary and Edmonton Land Co Ltd*
[1975] 1 All ER 1046 at 1054, [1975] 1 WLR 355 at 363. That is indeed a proposition for
which any judge who has sat in this court in recent years would not require authority,
and its validity is by no means diminished by what was said by Brightman J in *Re NFU
Development Trust Ltd* [1973] 1 All ER 135, [1972] 1 WLR 1548. All that that case shows
is that there must be some element of give and take. Beyond that it is neither necessary
nor desirable to attempt a definition of 'arrangement'.

Counsel for the Savoy professes not to quarrel with that proposition. He says that in
order for an arrangement to be one 'between' the company and its members it must
materially affect the rights and obligations existing between the two. Both he and
counsel for THF subjected certain provisions of the scheme to a close scrutiny, in
particular cl 1(b). Counsel for the Savoy said that that was the only provision which
involved the participation of the Savoy and he said that it would not and could not
materially affect the rights and obligations existing between it and the members.
Counsel for THF, on the other hand, said that not only cl 1(b), but also the power in cl 1(a)
for THF to appoint a third party to transfer the shares, and cl 9, would affect the
contractual relationship subsisting between the Savoy and its members under its
memorandum and articles. In this connection he referred in particular to arts 30, 31 and
34. He also said, amongst other things, that the artificiality of counsel for the Savoy's
arguments on this point was demonstrated by the latter's acceptance that a cancellation

and reduction scheme having exactly the same result for the shareholders would be an
a arrangement between the company and its members.

I was referred to a number of authorities on this question, but the only one which is
directly in point is the Scottish case of *Singer Manufacturing Co v Robinow* 1971 SC 11,
where the same point was taken on another transfer scheme of the same general nature
as the present. In that case the scheme was proposed by the company. It was argued on
behalf of an opposing shareholder that the scheme was not one between the company
b and its members, but a sale between two members in which the company had no
interest. With regard to that argument the Lord President (Clyde), in delivering the
opinion of the court, said (at 13–14):

> 'This contention, however, is unwarranted. The petitioning company is in fact
> the first party to the scheme of arrangement. Moreover, the company had a very
> direct interest in the arrangement. If the arrangement were sanctioned by the
c > Court, they came under obligation (see clause 5 of the arrangement), on being
> satisfied that the consideration of 85s. per share had been paid by the Morgan
> Guaranty Trust Company of New York to the 145,670 shareholders, forthwith to
> register, in place of the existing holders, the Singer Company of New York as holder
> of the shares in respect of which the consideration had been so paid. The Courts
> have always interpreted section 206 and its statutory predecessors broadly, so as to
d > enable a wide variety of different types of arrangement to be put forward, and it
> seems to us clear that the present scheme falls within what is competent to achieve
> under that section. The arrangement is an arrangement between the petitioning
> company and "its members or any class of them" within the meaning of section
> 206.'

e That shows, I think, that there were three grounds for the decision. It also appears that
cl 5 of the arrangement in that case was to much the same effect as cl 1(b) of the present
scheme. Counsel for THF did not seek to support the first ground of the decision, but he
relied strongly on the second and third. He said that the case was not only strong
persuasive authority in this court but one which I should follow without expressing a
view of my own. For that he relied on the judgment of Swinfen Eady J in *Re Hartland,*
Banks v Hartland [1911] 1 Ch 459. That was a case on the Finance Act 1894, another
enactment which, like the Companies Acts, applies to Scotland as well as to England.
There had been an earlier decision of the Court of Session on precisely the same point.
Swinfen Eady J said (at 466):

> 'Where the exact point has been raised by a special case, and fully argued, and
> decided by an unanimous judgment of the Court of Session, and where the question
f > is simply one that turns upon the construction of a statute which extends to Scotland
> as well as to England, I think my duty as a judge of first instance is to follow that
> decision, leaving the parties, if so advised, to have it reviewed elsewhere.'

Counsel for THF also relied on the judgments in the Court of Appeal in *Re Guardian*
Assurance Co [1917] 1 Ch 431, and in particular on a passage in the judgment of
g Warrington LJ. The same passage appears to have been referred to in the argument for
the opposing shareholder in the *Singer* case. The part of the transaction in the *Guardian*
case which required the sanction of the court under s 120 of the 1908 Act was the transfer
of a proportionate part of the shares in the Guardian to another company with which it
had entered into a conditional contract. With regard to that transfer Warrington LJ said
(at 449–450):

> 'Now if it were possible in a large undertaking to obtain the consent of each
> shareholder to such a proposal there is no doubt it could be carried out, because
> there would be nothing to prevent any shareholder, if he pleased, transferring his
> shares, or a certain number of his shares, to anybody to whom he chooses to transfer
> them; but of course it is difficult to obtain in a large undertaking like this the actual
> consent of the individual shareholders. But, assume that such an agreement has

been made between all the shareholders in the company, it seems to me to be quite obvious that that would be an arrangement made between the shareholders and the company. I fail to see how it could be otherwise; and that is exactly what is done, because although the arrangement is not made with the individual shareholders the arrangement is one which, when sanctioned by the Court under s. 120, will bind all the shareholders concerned. In my view this is an arrangement between the members of the company and the company and as such is capable of being sanctioned under the 120th section.'

I think that, although the particular point was not argued and did not need to be argued (it not having been taken by Younger J at first instance), that passage does support the argument of counsel for THF on this question and I infer that the Court of Session may well have taken the same view.

I do not think that it would be right for me to decide this question without expressing a view of my own. I can do so quite shortly. In my judgment the arguments of counsel for THF, supported by the two authorities on which he has relied, are correct. In spite of counsel for the Savoy's professions to the contrary, it seems to me that his argument could well have a restrictive effect on the meaning of 'arrangement'. I do not think that it is necessary that the rights and obligations existing between the company and its members should be materially affected, if by that it is meant that there should be something more material or more substantial than there is in the present case. In my judgment the decision of the Court of Session in the *Singer* case was correct and there is therefore no question but that I should follow and apply it. That means that the first argument of counsel for the Savoy fails.

I now turn to the second argument of counsel for the Savoy. It was divided into two parts, of which the first raises the question whether the court has jurisdiction to sanction an arrangement which does not have the approval of the company. That is an interesting and difficult question on which there is not much authority.

The case which comes nearest to deciding the point is almost the earliest. That is *Re International Contract Co, Hankey's Case* (1872) 26 LT 358, 20 WR 506. I was told that there are also shorter reports in the Weekly Notes and the Law Journal Reports. That was a case where it was sought to obtain the sanction of the court to certain compromises with two creditors of a company which was in the course of being wound up. However, the liquidator opposed the petition on the ground that the proposed compromises were not beneficial to the company. He also argued that as they were not supported by him they could not be sanctioned by the court under the 1862 and 1870 Acts. In dismissing the application, Wickens V-C expressed himself to be of the opinion that the case was 'virtually' (the report in the Weekly Notes says 'completely', but that is in a minority of two to one, the Law Journal Reports being silent on the point) governed by that of *Re East of England Banking Co, Pearson's Case* (1872) 7 Ch App 309, which had been decided in the Court of Appeal some three weeks earlier. He went on to say that, independently of that authority, he considered that he ought not to make any order on the petition, on the ground that the evidence showed that it was for the personal benefit of the principal petitioner. Counsel for THF submitted that it is not clear that the statutory meeting required by s 2 of the 1870 Act had been held, but after a consideration of the two longer reports and on grounds of common sense I reject that argument. There was further debate as to what was the real ground of the decision, but for my part I think it clear that the primary ground at any rate was that the court had no jursidiction, under s 2 of the 1870 Act, to sanction an arrangement which did not have the approval of the liquidator. That could not have been based entirely on *Re East of England Banking Co*, because that case proceeded only on s 160 of the 1862 Act. However, if (as I think he must) Wickens V-C is taken to have been correctly reported in the Law Times and the Weekly Reporter as saying that the case before him was 'virtually' governed by the earlier one, that would suggest that he had made an independent consideration of s 2 of the 1870 Act. And I think that I must assume that the arguments of the distinguished leading counsel who appeared before him would have made it necessary for him to do so.

The importance to counsel for the Savoy's argument of this view of *Re International Contract Co* is this. Counsel for THF relied most strongly on that part of s 206(2) which provides that the arrangement shall be binding on the members 'and also on the company' as showing that the section embraced an arrangement which did not have the approval of the company. Counsel for THF said that those words are entirely unnecessary if the company's consent is a prerequisite to the sanctioning of an arrangement.

However, counsel for the Savoy pointed to the original wording of s 2 of the 1870 Act which expressly provided that the arrangement or compromise should be binding on the creditors 'and also on the liquidator and contributories of the said company'. Counsel for the Savoy said that the decision in *Re International Contract Co* was arrived at in the face of those words and that neither they nor their successors can have, or for that matter need have, the significance for which counsel for THF contends. Counsel for THF replied by relying on s 136 of the 1862 Act. He said that that section clearly provided for the approval of the company to be obtained. He said that there, if it had been intended that s 2 should operate in the same way, was a precedent readily to hand.

Counsel for the Savoy then examined a large body of authority on s 2 and its successors, with the object of showing that their purpose was to prevent a dissentient minority of a class of first creditors and then members from holding the majority to ransom and, conversely, that the court had never concerned itself with the interests of the company. That shows, argued counsel for the Savoy, that the status of the company on an application under s 206 is that of an independent party whose approval is necessary and whose interests cannot be overridden.

As to the purpose of s 2, counsel for the Savoy referred me to a number of statements made by eminent judges of the late Victorian period all of which, as they appeared to me, were to very much the same effect. A representative example can be taken from the judgment of Chitty J in *Re Dominion of Canada Freehold Estate and Timber Co Ltd* (1886) 55 LT 347 at 351, where, having referred to the difficulty, which often arose when a company got into trouble, of dealing with debenture-holders as a class, he said:

> 'That is a difficulty which the legislature itself felt when it passed the Act of 1870, allowing a majority and a sufficient majority—that is to say, not a mere absolute majority but a majority much larger than that—to bind the minority. Then it was known that before the legislation of 1870 any particular individual could hold out against a scheme, however meritorious and however beneficial it might be, in order that he might get generally speaking some special advantage for himself, or because he was a person who did not even take a fair view of the advantages to be gained. It was for the purpose of preventing that obstruction that the legislature passed the Joint Stock Companies Arrangement Act of 1870 . . .'

Counsel for the Savoy says that the way in which s 206 and its predecessors evolved requires an assumption that when the original provisions were extended to members the legislature had the same purpose in mind, that is to say that a dissentient minority of members should not be allowed to hold the majority to ransom.

As to the converse, that is to say that the court has never concerned itself with the interests of the company, counsel for the Savoy was in the position of having to prove a negative. For that purpose he referred me to a number of authorities, including the well known decisions of the Court of Appeal in *Re Alabama, New Orleans, Texas and Pacific Junction Railway Co* [1891] 1 Ch 213 and *Re English, Scottish and Australian Chartered Bank* [1893] 3 Ch 385, [1891-4] All ER Rep 775 and also of Maugham J in *Re Dorman Long & Co Ltd* [1934] Ch 635, [1933] All ER Rep 460. Those cases are usually cited for the purpose of demonstrating what is the function of the court on an application under s 206. And I think that counsel for THF was right in saying that neither they nor most of the other cases on which counsel for the Savoy relied are really of value on a question which did not have to be decided in any of them. I should add that I think that in all of them the petition was presented either by the company or by the liquidator.

There is a small residue of cases which show that it has sometimes been assumed that there is no jurisdiction to sanction an arrangement which does not have the approval of the company. There is certainly one dictum in England which comes from a source which I cannot lightly disregard. In *Re Oceanic Steam Navigation Co Ltd* [1938] 3 All ER 740 at 742, [1939] Ch 41 at 46, which decided that there is no jurisdiction to sanction a scheme which is ultra vires the company, Simonds J said:

> 'It is indeed rightly pointed out that, without the assistance of the company, the creditors alone could not avail themselves of sect. 153. They could at any moment put the company into liquidation, but, since they have chosen the path of sect. 153 without a previous liquidation, it is to be assumed that they would pay something to be allowed to take that path, and accordingly the directors should not have assisted them without exacting a price.'

In that case the petition was again presented by the company. Counsel for THF argued that when Simonds J referred to s 153 of the 1929 Act he meant s 154, or at least ss 153 and 154 together. I do not think that that can be right. Counsel for the Savoy relied strongly on that passage. He also relied on three other cases in the Court of Session: *Dailuaine-Talisker Distilleries Ltd v Mackenzie* 1910 SC 193, *Bruce Peebles & Co Ltd v William Blaine & Co Ltd* 1918 SC 781 and *Re Hector & Sons Ltd* 1947 SC 641. In each of those cases the petition was presented by the company and in none of them did the particular point arise for decision. In the first two the question was whether the company could present the petition on the authority of the board or only with the approval of the members in general meeting. In the third it was held that the company's approval had been validly given by means of a special resolution, which, although normally inappropriate to the approval of a scheme of arrangement, was in the circumstances unobjectionable because it had been passed unanimously. Nevertheless, it does seem to me that in all three cases it was to a greater or lesser extent assumed by one or more of the judges that there was no jurisdiction to sanction an arrangement which did not have the approval of the company.

The position on this question can, as it seems to me, be summarised as follows. There is one decision, *Re International Contract Co*, which is in point. That decision is in favour of the view that there is no jurisdiction to sanction any arrangement with creditors of a company in the course of being wound up which does not have the approval of the liquidator. The decision is one which I ought normally to follow. The legislative history is such that there is no ground for saying that a different view is to be taken of the position of a going company in relation to a members' scheme. There has sometimes been an assumption to the same effect, that having been most clearly expressed by Simonds J in the *Oceanic Steam Navigation* case.

In my judgment both the decision and the assumption are correct. The question turns in the end on the true construction of s 2 of the 1870 Act. Everything else follows from that. If you were to find an Act of Parliament which referred to an arrangement 'proposed between' a person who was adult and sui juris and his creditors, you would assume, first, that that person would have to be a party to the arrangement and, second, that he would have to consent to it. And you would not think that there was any the less need to obtain his consent if you found that it was expressly provided that the arrangement should be binding on the creditors 'and also on that person'. You might think that the last words had been inserted to make the position clear on both sides or you might think that they were not really necessary. But, whatever you thought, you would not think that they could disturb the assumptions which had been forced on you by the words 'proposed between' and the fact that the person concerned was adult and sui juris. Nor would you think that those assumptions were any the less valid because there was no express provision for the consent to be obtained. Next, one of the essential features of the 1862 Act, without which its cardinal objective of limited liability could not have been achieved, was that a company should have a legal personality distinct from that of its members and for most purposes capable of acting on its own. I therefore start from the position that the rights of a company cannot be overridden in the absence of a *a* provision, express or implied, to that effect. The undoubted purpose of s 2 of the 1870 Act having been that which eminent judges of the time consistently said that it was, I cannot read that section or its successors as having been a provision to that wider effect. To do so would, I think, offend the general principle in our law that the rights of a person whom it regards as having the status to deal with them on his own behalf will not (save in special circumstances, such as those for which provision is made by RSC Ord 15, r 13) be overridden.

b There remains the argument of counsel for THF based on s 136 of the 1862 Act. In my judgment that is not enough to carry him home. The effect of that section, so far as material, was that the arrangement could not be entered into by the directors, but required the sanction of an extraordinary resolution. It must be remembered that that section, unlike s 2 of the 1870 Act, applied also to companies about to be wound up. The correct view may well be that s 2, by omitting a requirement which was inappropriate,

c intended to emphasise, rather than to dispense with, the need for the liquidator's consent. In any event, it is notorious that the legislation of that period was not drafted with the insight and exactitude which we expect today. I think that I must do the best I can with s 2 as I find it.

In the result I conclude that the court has no jurisdiction to sanction an arrangement under s 206 which does not have the approval of the company either through the board

d or, if appropriate, by means of a simple majority of the members in general meeting.

The second part of counsel for the Savoy's second argument was that the court either has no power, or, if it has, ought not to convene meetings in the circumstances of the present case. I reject the argument that there is no power to do so. As to whether I ought or ought not to do so in exercise of the court's discretion, I have no doubt that I ought not to do so in the circumstances of the present case. I say that for these reasons. The board

e have withheld their approval and the scheme does not provide for approval to be obtained from the company in general meeting. It is possible, in theory at any rate, that the board might have second thoughts before the stage is reached at which the scheme would normally come back to be sanctioned by the court. However, it is most improbable that that will happen. Counsel for THF said that it might if a sufficient majority of the B shareholders approved the scheme. But since over 65% of the B shares

f are held by members of the board I cannot see that happening without the board themselves changing their minds. And if they did that, it is clear that there would be other, much more satisfactory, methods of putting the proposals into effect. Counsel for THF also suggested the possibility of there being sufficient aggregate votes in favour at the A and B meetings to constitute more than 50% of the whole. But that would still not amount to the approval of the company in general meeting and that is something which THF has made it abundantly clear that it will not seek. In all the circumstances, there

g being no reasonable probability that the meetings would serve any useful purpose, it would in my judgment be quite wrong to convene them, particularly when the attendant expense of money, time and spirit (all of which would probably be wasted) is borne in mind.

That makes it, strictly speaking, unnecessary for me to consider the third argument of

h counsel for the Savoy, which was that the court has no jurisdiction to sanction a scheme affecting the B shares on the application of a member who holds only A shares. That argument was dealt with very shortly by both sides and I propose to do the same. In my judgment it could not succeed.

The application must be dismissed.

Application dismissed. Leave to appeal.

Solicitors: *Linklaters & Paines* (for THF); *Slaughter & May* (for the Savoy).

Hazel Hartman   Barrister.

Alex Lawrie Factors Ltd v Modern Injection *a*
Moulds Ltd

QUEEN'S BENCH DIVISION
DRAKE J
19th MARCH, 12th MAY 1981

b

Interest – Debt – Jurisdiction to include interest in default judgment – Judgment in default of appearance – Whether proceedings ending with entry of judgment in default 'tried' in court – Whether court having jurisdiction to award interest up to the entry of judgment – Law Reform (Miscellaneous Provisions) Act 1934, s 3(1).

Practice – Interest – Discretion of court to award – Inherent equitable jurisdiction – Whether *c*
jurisdiction to award interest in simple action for debt.

The plaintiff brought an action against the defendant claiming a liquidated sum for goods sold and delivered and also claiming interest pursuant to s 3(1)[a] of the Law Reform (Miscellaneous Provisions) Act 1934. The defendant failed to enter an appearance to the writ and the plaintiff obtained final judgment against him for a liquidated amount in *d* default of appearance which was entered in the court records by the appropriate court official. The plaintiff claimed that he was entitled to interest under s 3(1) of the 1934 Act from the date the debt became payable to the date of the default judgment, while the defendant claimed that there was no jurisdiction under s 3(1) to award interest prior to the date of the judgment. The matter was referred to a master, who upheld the plaintiff's claim and awarded interest accordingly. The defendant appealed, contending *e* that where judgment for a debt was entered in default of appearance there was no jurisdiction to award interest under s 3(1) because proceedings ending with the entry of a default judgment were not 'proceedings tried in any court of record' within s 3(1). The plaintiff submitted that the court had jurisdiction to award interest up to the entry of a default judgment both under s 3(1) and under the court's inherent equitable jurisdiction. *f*

Held – The word 'tried' in s 3(1) of the 1934 Act meant 'determined' and covered any situation in which proceedings in a court of record had been commenced by writ or other originating process and had been ended by a judgment, irrespective of how the judgment had been arrived at, and therefore, although a court official's act in entering a judgment in default was merely an administrative act and not a judicial act in the proceedings, proceedings which were ended by the entry of a default judgment were *g* 'proceedings' which had been 'tried' within s 3(1). The court accordingly had jurisdiction under s 3(1) to award interest for the period between the date when the principal sum recovered by the plaintiff became due and the date of the default judgment. It followed that the appeal would be dismissed (see p 663 a to e and j, post).

Dictum of Ormrod LJ in *Gardner Steel Ltd v Sheffield Brothers (Profiles) Ltd* [1978] 3 All
ER at 402 applied. *h*

Per Curiam. The inherent equitable jurisdiction of the court to award interest does not include jurisdiction to award interest in the case of a simple contract debt, in the absence of a fiduciary or other special relationship (see p 663 h, post).

Notes *j*
For the court's jurisdiction under statute to award interest in actions for debt, see 32
Halsbury's Laws (4th Edn) para 110.

For the court's equitable jurisdiction to award interest, see ibid para 109.

---

a   Section 3(1), so far as material, is set out at p 660 d, post

a   For the Law Reform (Miscellaneous Provisions) Act 1934, s 3, see 25 Halsbury's Statutes (3rd Edn) 752.

Cases referred to in judgment

Cousins (H) & Co Ltd v D & C Carriers Ltd [1971] 1 All ER 55, [1971] 2 QB 230, [1971] 2 WLR 85, [1970] 2 Lloyd's Rep 397, CA, Digest (Cont Vol D) 549, 2592a.

b   *Gardner Steel Ltd v Sheffield Brothers (Profiles) Ltd* [1978] 3 All ER 399, [1978] 1 WLR 916, Digest (Cont Vol E) 172, 108Ab.

London, Chatham and Dover Railway Co v South Eastern Railway Co [1893] AC 429, HL, 50 Digest (Repl) 157, 1356.

Ozalid Group (Export) Ltd v African Continental Bank Ltd [1979] 2 Lloyd's Rep 231.

Tehno-Impex v Gebr van Weelde Scheepvaartkantoor BV [1981] 2 All ER 669, [1981] 2 WLR 821, CA.

c   *Wallersteiner v Moir (No 2), Moir v Wallersteiner (No 2)* [1975] 1 All ER 849, [1975] QB 373, [1975] 2 WLR 389, CA, Digest (Cont Vol D) 570, 518a.

Appeal from master

d   By a writ indorsed with a statement of claim issued on 5th August 1980 and served on 6th August 1980, the plaintiff, Alex Lawrie Factors Ltd, claimed against the defendant, Modern Injection Moulds Ltd, £23,946·45 as the balance of the price of goods sold and delivered to the defendant and interest pursuant to the Law Reform (Miscellaneous Provisions) Act 1934. The defendant failed to enter an appearance to the writ and on 26th August 1980 the plaintiff obtained final judgment in default of appearance for £18,946·45. The plaintiff's claim for interest on that sum from the date the sum became due to the date of the default judgment was referred to a master. The defendant

e   contended that the master had no jurisdiction to award interest prior to the date of the judgment in default. On 24th October 1980 Master Elton gave judgment for the plaintiff and assessed the interest due up to the date of the default judgment at £1,425·87. The defendant appealed from the master's order. The appeal was heard in chambers but judgment was given by Drake J in open court. The facts are set out in the

f   judgment.

P J Susman for the defendant.
Paul Norris for the plaintiff.

Cur adv vult

g   12th May. **DRAKE J** read the following judgment: This is an appeal against a decision of Master Elton given on 24th October 1980 whereby he ordered the defendant to pay interest, which he assessed, on a sum of £18,946·45, the balance of moneys due to the plaintiff.

    On 26th August 1980 the plaintiff had obtained final judgment in default of

h   appearance to the writ. The statement of claim indorsed on the writ had claimed interest 'pursuant to the Law Reform (Miscellaneous Provisions) Act 1934', and at the time when final judgment in default was entered the claim for interest on the debt, from the date on which the sum had become due up to the date of the judgment, had been referred to the master for the interest to be assessed.

    On the hearing before the master the defendant appeared by counsel and argued that

j   the court had no jurisdiction to award any interest prior to the date of final judgment in default. This was a novel point to be taken by any defendant, and one of very widespread general importance in view of the fact that masters have been assessing and awarding interest in similar cases with great frequency for at least the last 15 years.

    As it was quite clear that, whatever his decision, the matter would be appealed to the judge in chambers the master did not in fact hear any argument. He gave judgment for the plaintiff, assessed the interest due up to the date of the default judgment and expressed the hope that the judge in chambers would give his judgment in open court. *a* I now do so.

I should add, to complete the picture, that the plaintiff also claimed interest under the Judgments Act 1838, on the judgment debt from the date of the judgment until the date of the master's order. The plaintiff's right to this interest was not disputed and does not concern me on this appeal.

In argument before me, counsel for the plaintiff submitted that the court had *b* jurisdiction to award interest prior to judgment (1) under the provisions of the Law Reform (Miscellaneous Provisions) Act 1934 and/or (2) under its inherent equitable jurisdiction.

The defendant, by his counsel, submitted (1) that it is well settled law that interest is not recoverable as damages for failure to pay a debt: see *London, Chatham and Dover Railway Co v South Eastern Railway Co* [1893] AC 429; (2) that this was not one of the *c* recognised cases in which the court would exercise its inherent equitable jurisdiction to award interest; and (3) that the Law Reform (Miscellaneous Provisions) Act 1934 does not cover a case where judgment is entered in default of appearance. As my decision on the construction of the 1934 Act is sufficient to dispose of this appeal I shall deal with it first.

Section 3 of the 1934 Act provides, so far as is relevant to this appeal, as follows: *d*

> '(1) In any proceedings tried in any court of record for the recovery of any debt or damages, the court may ... order that there shall be included in the sum for which judgment is given interest ... on the whole or any part of the debt ... for the whole or any part of the period between the date when the cause of action arose and the date of judgment ...'

e

The submission made by counsel for the appellant defendant is that in the case of a judgment entered in default of appearance there have been no proceedings 'tried in any court of record', and therefore the proceedings ending with the default judgment do not fall within the provisions of s 3. In order to consider this submission it is necessary to consider precisely what takes place in the proceedings prior to judgment in default being *f* entered. I confess that before this appeal I was aware of only the bare outline of what happens when a plaintiff applies for judgment in default of appearance; and my inquiry to counsel revealed that they, too, lacked detailed knowledge of the procedure. This is not surprising since counsel are rarely concerned with such procedure, and probably never attend to ask for judgment to be entered in default of appearance.

However, after help from their respective instructing solicitors, counsel were able to *g* give me a detailed account of what happens, which is as follows:

The claim for a liquidated sum starts with the issue of the writ claiming the sum due. This is served on the defendant who, if the writ is served within the jurisdiction, has 14 days in which to enter appearance; if service is outside the jurisdiction he is given a longer period. If the defendant does not enter appearance within the time allowed the plaintiff may enter final judgment for the sum claimed and for costs. The requirements *h* of what must be done are set out in the Supreme Court Practice 1979 (vol 2, p 222, para 952). What happens is that the plaintiff, usually acting by a solicitor's clerk, attends at the appropriate office of the court and produces to the official on duty (1) the original writ, (2) an affidavit of service and (3) the draft judgment being asked for. The court official then searches the court files to satisfy himself that no appearance has been entered and, if so satisfied, he stamps the draft judgment and enters it by writing it into an *j* official ledger. The judgment may then be enforced and the sum recovered. Interest on the judgment debt runs from that moment until the judgment is satisfied, under the provisions of the Judgments Act 1838.

If the contract under which the debt has arisen provided for an agreed rate of interest to be payable on the debt becoming due then, of course, the interest may be calculated and included as a liquidated sum in the total sum claimed in the writ. It is in cases in

which interest is *not* expressly or impliedly provided for in the contract that the problem
a with which I am now concerned arises. The practice which has arisen is that the plaintiff
frequently includes in the draft final judgment a claim for interest from the date the debt
became due up to the date on which final judgment is entered. Since the rate and hence
the amount of interest has not at that stage been determined the draft final judgment
claims 'interest to be assessed'; and on being satisfied that final judgment may be entered
the court official enters judgment (1) for the liquidated sum claimed and (2) interest, to
b be assessed by the master.

What happens next is that an appointment is made for the plaintiff to go before the
master; and the plaintiff, when he knows the date of that appointment prepares and
serves on the defendant a schedule showing the interest claimed and how the total sum
is arrived at. This procedure was followed in the present case and it was on the
appointment before the master that the defendant appeared by counsel and contested the
c jurisdiction of the court to award any interest at all prior to judgment having been
entered.

I should add that I have been informed and gathered from published statistics that the
number of such judgments in default which are entered is in the order of between 2,000
and 3,000 each month in the Central Office at the Royal Courts of Justice alone, with
approximately the same number entered at district registries, ie a total of about 60,000
d per year, of which the large majority are in respect of simple claims for a liquidated sum
of money due, usually, for services or goods sold and delivered. During the first three
months of this year masters were assessing and awarding interest in about 50 cases each
month which were referred to them on judgment being entered in default of appearance.

Can it be said that such proceedings, culminating in the entry of judgment in default
have been 'tried' in any court of record? Counsel for the defendant say they have not
e been 'tried' because there has been no trial at all. He says that all that has taken place is
a clerical act performed by a court official. Counsel for the plaintiff submits (1) that the
actions of the court official in checking the documents, ascertaining that no appearance
has been entered and then entering final judgment does amount to a trial; alternatively
(2) that in the context of the 1934 Act 'tried' merely means 'determined', so that the High
Court does have jurisdiction to award interest in any case started by a writ and concluded,
f ie determined by a judgment.

The construction of s 3 of the 1934 Act has been considered by the courts on a number
of occasions, although never in the context of interest awarded on a liquidated sum for
a period prior to judgment in default of appearance.

In *Gardner Steel Ltd v Sheffield Brothers (Profiles) Ltd* [1978] 3 All ER 399, [1978] 1 WLR
916 the plaintiffs had obtained judgment under RSC Ord 14 in default of any arguable
defence. O'Connor J had decided on an appeal from the master that there was no
g arguable defence and had given the plaintiff leave to sign final judgment; but at the same
time he refused to award interest under s 3 of the 1934 Act. Unfortunately the parties
were not at all clear whether O'Connor J ruled that he had no jurisdiction to grant
interest on the grounds that the proceedings before him were not proceedings 'tried in
any court of record', or whether he held that he did have jurisdiction but declined to
h exercise his discretion to award interest. However, the Court of Appeal appears to have
acted on the assumption that O'Connor J had decided that he lacked jurisdiction and held
that he was wrong if he had so decided. The Court of Appeal held that an order that the
plaintiff was entitled to summary judgment under Ord 14 was the determination of an
issue and, as such, was a trial and therefore a proceeding 'tried in' a court of record for the
purposes of s 3 of the Law Reform (Miscellaneous Provisions) Act 1934.

j Stephenson LJ referred to a note which appeared in the then current (1976) and earlier
editions of the Supreme Court Practice under RSC Ord 6, r 2 (vol 2, p 40, para 6/2/7A).
This suggested that proceedings concluded by a summary judgment under Ord 14 were
not a trial and that interest under s 3 of the 1934 Act could not therefore be awarded; but
that the court could direct an issue to be tried whether the plaintiff ought to be awarded
interest and if so, at what rate, and for what period. The issue would then become a 'trial'
so that s 3 would become operative. Stephenson LJ referred to the decision of the Court

of Appeal in *Wallersteiner v Moir (No 2)* [1975] 1 All ER 849 at 855, [1975] QB 373 at
387–388 in which Lord Denning MR referring to the note on Ord 6, r 2 in the Supreme   *a*
Court Practice 1973 said:

> '"... interest under this section can only be awarded in proceedings that are
> 'tried', and therefore cannot be awarded on a judgment obtained in default of
> appearance or defence or failure to comply with an order or the rules, nor
> presumably in proceedings under O. 14, but in such cases the plaintiff may ask for
> final judgment for the principal sum, and for interlocutory judgment for the   *b*
> interest to be assessed, by analogy with an assessment of damages." I think that that
> note may be putting too narrow a construction on the word "tried". It seems to me
> that, after all the evidence and arguments which were heard in this case, it could
> well be said that those were proceedings "tried" in a court of record. Similarly with
> proceedings under RSC Ord 14. But it is unnecessary to go into this for this simple
> reason: we did not order interest to be paid under the 1934 Act, but under the   *c*
> equitable jurisdiction of the court.'

Stephenson LJ said that, whilst those remarks of Lord Denning MR were clearly
obiter:

> '... it commends itself to me as, if I may respectfully say so, sensible, likely to save
> costs and in accordance with the ordinary use of language. Summary trial is of
> course different from a full trial, and summary proceedings in chambers are   *d*
> different from proceedings in open court. I feel the force of those considerations
> which no doubt led to the existing practice in regarding summary judgment under
> RSC Ord 14 as judgment not given in proceedings which have been tried. But
> counsel for the plaintiffs has called our attention to a definition in the current
> edition of Stroud's Judicial Dictionary (4th Edn, 1974, vol 5, p 2827): "TRIAL;
> TRIED. (1) A 'trial' is the conclusion, by a competent tribunal, of questions in issue   *e*
> in legal proceedings, whether civil or criminal." That seems to me to be a natural
> interpretation of the words "trial" and "tried". Counsel for the defendants has
> submitted that all that was tried was an issue, and there was no trial of proceedings.
> I prefer the wider view indicated by Lord Denning MR, and now, it is to be noted,
> adopted in the supplement to the Supreme Court Practice (Fifth Cumulative
> Supplement, 1976, paras 6/2/7A, 14/3–4/19). I see no good reason why interest   *f*
> should not be awarded in accordance with s 3 of the 1934 Act in summary
> proceedings under RSC Ord 14 concluded by a competent tribunal, a judge in
> chambers, or, in some circumstances of course, a master. In those circumstances I
> would hold that O'Connor J had jurisdiction to award interest.'

(See [1978] 3 All ER 399 at 401, [1978] 1 WLR 916 at 918–919.)
Ormrod LJ, agreeing with Stephenson LJ and with the observation of Lord Denning   *g*
MR referred to above, went on ([1978] 3 All ER 399 at 402, [1978] 1 WLR 916 at 920):

> 'But I would base my judgment simply on the construction of s 3 of the 1934
> Act. "Tried" must mean "determined" in that context, and here the court has
> decided that there is no defence. It seems extraordinary that where there is a
> defence and the court has decided that the defence fails it can order interest; but   *h*
> where it has decided that there is no defence it cannot award interest. I think it is
> wholly illogical. So the opportunity having now arisen, it seems to me a convenient
> case for saying that in appropriate cases the judge can order interest on an RSC Ord
> 14 summary judgment.'

It seems to me that the effect of those judgments is that Stephenson LJ held that for the   *j*
purposes of that case it was sufficient to say that beyond any doubt the determination of
an issue under RSC Ord 14 by a judge or master was a 'trial' and therefore on any view
fell within the provisions of s 3 of the 1934 Act; whilst Ormrod LJ went somewhat
further by holding that in the context of s 3 'tried' must mean 'determined'. The word
'tried' is defined in the current edition of Stroud's Judicial Dictionary (4th Edn, 1974, vol

5, p 2827) as 'TRIAL; TRIED. (1) A "trial" is the conclusion, by a competent tribunal, of
a questions in issue in legal proceedings, whether civil or criminal'. This definition was
considered by Stephenson LJ in *Gardner Steel Ltd v Sheffield Brothers (Profiles) Ltd* to cover
an adjudication by a master or a judge in Ord 14 proceedings.

In my judgment the proceedings which culminate in the entry of judgment by the
court official who deals with the application for judgment in default of appearance to the
the writ do not amount to a 'trial', and are no more than an administrative act carried out
b in the course of proceedings. I do not think it can be said, despite the submissions of
counsel for the plaintiff to the contrary, that the actions of the court official culminating
in entry of judgment are in any way judicial actions; and I reject the plaintiff's arguments
on that point.

But I respectfully adopt and agree with the construction of s 3 of the 1934 Act given
by Ormrod LJ in the *Gardner Steel* case. In my judgment the word 'tried' in that section
c simply means 'determined' and s 3 covers any situation in which proceedings in a court
of record have been started by a writ or other originating process and ended by a
judgment, irrespective of how the judgment is arrived at.

This construction of the 1934 Act seems to me to accord with commercial sense. If a
creditor is wrongly kept out of his money he ought in fairness to be able to obtain
interest on the sum owing unless there are special circumstances which should disentitle
d him to interest. The Judgments Act 1838 provided that interest may be awarded to the
creditor after judgment; the 1934 Act undoubtedly provided that interest may be
awarded after a debtor has appeared but had his defence dismissed or disallowed as
unarguable under the Ord 14 procedure. Why then, in logic, should a debtor who
appears but unsuccessfully argues his case be in a worse position as regards having to pay
interest than a debtor who does not enter any appearance to the writ?

e I therefore hold that the master was right to award interest under the provisions of s 3
of the Law Reform (Miscellaneous Provisions) Act 1934. It follows that it is unnecessary
for me to deal with the alternative ground on which counsel for the plaintiff contended
that interest might be awarded, namely under the inherent equitable jurisdiction of the
court. Both counsel addressed full and able argument to me and cited several authorities
on this point. Counsel for the plaintiff relied, inter alia, on dicta of Lord Denning MR
f in *Wallersteiner v Moir (No 2)* [1975] 1 All ER 849, [1975] 1 QB 373 and in *Tehno-Impex
v Gebr van Weelde Scheepvaartkantoor BV* [1981] 2 All ER 669, [1981] 2 WLR 821. He also
relied on the awards of interest by the Court of Appeal in *H Cousins & Co Ltd v D C
Carriers Ltd* [1971] 1 All ER 55, [1971] 2 QB 230 and by Donaldson J in *Ozalid Group
(Export) Ltd v African Continental Bank Ltd* [1979] 2 Lloyd's Rep 231 in circumstances
which he says must have meant that the court was in each case exercising its inherent
g jurisdiction to award interest.

Counsel for the defendant in reply submits that (1) the dicta of Lord Denning MR in
Wallersteiner v Moir (No 2) were clearly obiter and the case turned on complex facts well
removed from a case of simple debt; (2) *H Cousins & Co Ltd v D C Carriers Ltd* may well
have been argued and decided on the basis that both parties wanted a 'test case' decision
on the main issues arising and deliberately ignored the basis on which interest could be
h claimed, whilst (3) the decision of Donaldson J in the *Ozalid* case was simply wrong.

In my judgment the equitable jurisdiction of the court to award interest is exercised
in a number of well-recognised cases conveniently summarised in 32 Halsbury's Laws
(4th Edn) para 109; and these categories do *not* include the case of a simple contract debt
in the absence of any fiduciary or other special relationship. Although I have given full
and careful consideration to the respective arguments of counsel, I do not think any
j useful purpose would be served by greatly lengthening this judgment, as would be
necessary if I were to set out or deal fully with those arguments and all of the many
authorities cited on this point.

For the reasons I have already given I hold that the court has jurisdiction in this case
to award interest under the provisions of s 3 of the 1934 Act and that the master was
therefore entitled to make the decision he did. Accordingly, this appeal is dismissed.

Appeal dismissed ; master's order affirmed. Leave to appeal to the Court of Appeal ; application for a certificate under s 12 of the Administration of Justice Act 1969 to appeal to the House of **a** *Lords adjourned.*

Solicitors: *Ambrose Appelbe Associates* (for the plaintiff); *Wedlake Bell*, agents for *Gartside, Harding & Davies*, Newport, Gwent (for the defendant).

b

K Mydeen Esq   Barrister.

c

Clipper Maritime Co Ltd v Mineralimportexport
The Marie Leonhardt

d

QUEEN'S BENCH DIVISION (COMMERCIAL COURT)
ROBERT GOFF J
17th, 19th, 23rd, 29th JUNE 1981

e

Injunction – Interlocutory – Danger that defendant may transfer assets out of jurisdiction – Injunction restraining removal of assets out of or disposal within jurisdiction – Protection of interests of innocent third parties – Imposition of terms to protect interests of third parties – Port authority – Injunction affecting movements of ship within port and thereby having adverse affect on port authority – Terms court will impose as condition of granting injunction to protect interests **f** *of port authority – Mode of representations to Commercial Court by third parties adversely affected by Mareva injunctions.*

Because third parties who are unrepresented when a Mareva injunction is initially granted ex parte may be affected by the injunction, the Commercial Court will, where possible, implement the Mareva jurisdiction in a manner which takes account of **g** innocent third parties' interests. Thus, where a Mareva injunction may affect the movements of a ship within a port and thereby have an adverse affect on the port authority, for example by restraining the defendant from disposing or dealing with cargo or bunkers loaded on a ship berthed in a port and thus detaining the ship in the berth, the court will, as a condition of granting the injunction and subject to the **h** circumstances of each case, impose terms to protect the port authority by, for example, requiring the plaintiff to give an undertaking to pay income lost to and administrative costs incurred by the port authority as a consequence of granting the injunction, and making the injunction subject to a proviso that the port authority shall have a discretion to move the ship within the jurisdiction or, in the event of danger, to move it outside the jurisdiction, and by giving the defendant liberty to comply with an order by the port **j** authority to move the ship (see p 665 j to p 666 g, post).

Searose Ltd v Seatrain (UK) Ltd [1981] 1 All ER 806 applied.

The Commercial Court wishes to be kept informed of the adverse effect of Mareva injunctions on third parties, such as port authorities and clearing banks, so that steps can be taken to protect their interests. Bodies wishing to make representations on the matter *a* should address them to the Secretary of the Commercial Court Committee at the Royal Courts of Justice (see p 666 *g h*, post).

Notes

b For an injunction restraining the disposition of property, see 24 Halsbury's Laws (4th Edn) para 1018, and for cases on the subject, see 28(2) Digest (Reissue) 1091–1094, 918–960.

Case referred to in judgment

Searose Ltd v Seatrain (UK) Ltd [1981] 1 All ER 806, [1981] 1 WLR 894, [1981] Lloyd's Rep 533.

c **Application**

On 17th June 1981 Robert Goff J, in chambers, gave a judgment granting the plaintiffs, Clipper Maritime Co Ltd of Monrovia, on their ex parte application, a Mareva injunction restraining the defendants, Mineralimportexport, a Romanian company, from disposing of or dealing with their assets within the jurisdiction or from removing such assets from the jurisdiction, in particular cargo or bunkers being the defendants' property loaded on *d* board the vessel Marie Leonhardt (which was in the port of Barry, South Wales), so as to reduce the value of those assets below the sum of $US123,026.40, until after the hearing of a summons returnable on 19th June 1981, on the plaintiffs' undertaking to pay the actual income lost to the port authority controlling the port of Barry and the administrative costs incurred by the port authority as a consequence of the granting of the injunction and provided that the port authority should always have a discretion for *e* operational reasons to move or order the movement of the vessel within the area of the High Court's jurisdiction, or, in the event of danger, to move or order the movement of the vessel outside the High Court's jurisdiction if a place within the jurisdiction was not available and provided that the defendants should have liberty to comply with such an order. With the plaintiffs' consent part of the judgment was repeated by the judge in open court. The facts are set out in the judgment.

f

Christopher C Russell for the plaintiffs.
The defendants were not represented.

ROBERT GOFF J. On 17th June 1981, I made an order in this case for a Mareva *g* injunction on the ex parte application of the plaintiffs. Since, however, the case raises one point which is of some importance in this developing jurisdiction, I propose, with the consent of the plaintiffs, to repeat part of my judgment in open court.

The injunction which I granted restrained, on certain undertakings and other terms, the defendants from disposing of or dealing with their assets within the jurisdiction or from removing such assets from the jurisdiction, and in particular cargo or bunkers *h* being the property of the defendants loaded on board a vessel called the Marie Leonhardt, so as to reduce the value of those assets below the sum of $US123,026.40. The evidence before the court at the time of the application was that the Marie Leonhardt was on time charter to the defendants, and that the defendants were likely to be loading her at the port of Barry in Wales with a cargo of coke for discharge at Constanza. In these circumstances, there was a danger that the injunction might have some effect on the port *j* authority of Barry, which is of course a third party having no interest in the dispute between the plaintiffs and the defendants.

In these circumstances, consistent with the recent decision of this court in *Searose Ltd v Seatrain (UK) Ltd* [1981] 1 All ER 806, [1981] 1 WLR 894, I imposed certain conditions on the grant of the injunction with a view to preventing it bearing harshly on the port authority. The particular matters I had in mind were as follows. (1) The vessel may be docked at a heavily used and high income producing berth; and, until the port authority can make satisfactory arrangements to move the vessel without infringing the terms of the injunction, income from that berth may be lost. (2) The port authority may in any event incur administrative costs as a consequence of the granting of the injunction. (3) It may be necessary for the port authority to move the vessel in the ordinary course of good administration of the port; and in cases of danger it may be necessary for the port authority to move her outside the confines of the port, and possibly even outside the jurisdiction of the court.

To take account of these contingencies I required, as a condition of granting the injunction, an undertaking by the plaintiffs to pay the actual income lost to the port authority controlling the port of Barry in South Wales and the administrative costs incurred by that port authority as a consequence of the granting of the injunction; and I also qualified the injunction by making it subject to the proviso that the port authority should always have a discretion for operational reasons to move or order the movement of the vessel within the area of the jurisdiction of the High Court or, in the event of danger, to move or order the movement of the vessel outside the jurisdiction of the High Court if a place within the jurisdiction was not available, and that the defendants should have liberty to comply with such an order.

It is right that I should record that the plaintiffs have made no objection to the imposition of these terms, and further that when, on an application by the plaintiffs to continue the injunction on 19th June, a representative of the port authority was present in court, it was accepted by the port authority that such terms were satisfactory to them.

This court will in future, on other ex parte applications for Mareva injunctions which may affect ships in port, impose similar terms, subject always of course to the particular circumstances of the case. Indeed I have imposed the same terms, again without opposition from the plaintiffs, on the grant of a Mareva injunction on another ex parte application last week.

I wish it to be known that the court has taken this course as a result of representations made to it by solicitors acting for the British Ports Association; and that the undertaking imposed in *Searose Ltd v Seatrain (UK) Ltd* was imposed as a result of representations made to the Commercial Court Committee on behalf of the clearing banks. The Commercial Court is very anxious to provide a service to the commercial community which is sensitive to its needs; and in particular it is anxious that the Mareva jurisdiction, in the administration of which the Commercial Court plays so substantial a part, should be implemented in a manner which takes account of the interests of innocent third parties. Since initially Mareva injunctions are almost invariably granted on ex parte applications, orders may be made which affect third parties who are unrepresented at the hearing of the initial application. It is therefore of great assistance if the court can be kept informed of any adverse effect which these injunctions are having on third parties, as in the case of the clearing banks and port authorities, so that steps can be taken, where possible, to protect their interests. If any other bodies wish to make representations on this point, it would be most appropriate for them to address their representations to the Secretary of the Commercial Court Committee at the Royal Courts of Justice, in which event they will immediately be drawn to the attention of the judge in charge of the Commercial List.

Injunction granted subject to terms.

Solicitors: *William A Crump & Son* (for the plaintiffs).

K Mydeen Esq   Barrister.

Oakacre Ltd v Claire Cleaners (Holdings) Ltd

CHANCERY DIVISION
HIS HONOUR JUDGE MERVYN DAVIES QC SITTING AS A HIGH COURT JUDGE
12th, 20th MAY 1981

Sale of land – Damages for breach of contract – Damages in addition to specific performance – Damages for delay in completing contract – Cause of action in damages accruing after issue of writ seeking specific performance and damages in addition thereto – Claim for specific performance not pursued at hearing because by then land conveyed to plaintiff – Plaintiff continuing claim for damages for delay in completion – Completion date occurring after date of writ – Whether damages for delay in completion recoverable in action for specific performance although cause of action accruing after issue of writ.

The plaintiffs brought an action against the defendants seeking specific performance of a contract for the sale of land and 'damages in addition to or in lieu of specific performance'. By the date of the hearing the land had been conveyed to the plaintiffs and the claim for specific performance no longer fell to be considered, but the plaintiffs nevertheless wished to pursue the claim for damages for the defendants' delay in completing the contract. The contractual date for completion did not occur until after the date of the writ and therefore at the date of the writ there was no cause of action in regard to the claim for damages. The question arose whether damages in addition to specific performance claimed in an action for specific performance were recoverable where the cause of action in regard to the claim for damages had not accrued when the writ in the action was issued, so that if the action for damages was one at law the damages would not be recoverable.

Held – Since the action had been commenced as a properly constituted action for specific performance, and not solely as a claim for damages, and the court when dealing with an action for specific performance was required to consider the whole case, that is any claim for damages for breach of the contract as well as the equitable relief properly so called (ie specific performance), the court was not obliged to consider the plaintiffs' claim for damages as being a claim at law for breach of contract separate from the equitable claim, and thus was not obliged to dismiss the claim on the ground that the cause of action in regard to it had not accrued at the date of the writ. In an action for specific performance, therefore, the court had power to award damages for delay in completion even though the action had been instituted before the occurrence of the completion date and thus before the cause of action in damages had accrued. Accordingly, the plaintiffs were entitled to claim damages in the action for the delay in completion, and an inquiry as to the damages would be ordered (see p 670 d to j, post).

Dicta of Turner LJ in *Phelps v Prothero* (1855) 7 De GM & G at 733, 735 applied.

Notes

For the principle of relief in equity, see 16 Halsbury's Laws (4th Edn) para 1297.

For damages in addition to specific performance, see 36 Halsbury's Laws (3rd Edn) 350, para 521.

Cases referred to in judgment

Chapman, Morsons & Co v Auckland Union Guardians (1889) 23 QBD 294, 58 LJQB 504, 61 LT 446, 53 JP 820, CA, 44 Digest (Repl) 363, 2008.

Hasham v Zenab [1960] AC 316, [1960] 2 WLR 374, PC, 44 Digest (Repl) 91, 741.

Phelps v Prothero (1849) 2 De G & Sm 274, 64 ER 123; *subsequent proceedings* (1855) 16 CB 370, 24 LJCP 225, 1 Jus NS 1170, 3 CLR 906, 139 ER 801; *subsequent proceedings* (1855) 7 De GM & G 722, 25 LJ Ch 105, 44 ER 280, LJJ, 1(2) Digest (Reissue) 779, 5092.

Raineri v Miles [1979] 3 All ER 763, [1980] 2 WLR 189, CA; *affd* [1980] 2 All ER 145, [1980] 2 WLR 847, HL, Digest (Cont Vol E) 530, *909d*.

Slack v Leeds Industrial Co-operative Society Ltd [1924] AC 851, [1924] All ER Rep 259, 93 LJ Ch 436, 131 LT 710, HL, 28(2) Digest (Reissue) 1017, *436*.

Action

By a writ dated 29th February 1980 the plaintiffs, Oakacre Ltd, sought as against the defendants, Claire Cleaners (Holdings) Ltd, inter alia, (1) specific performance of a written agreement dated 19th April 1978 for the sale by the defendants to the plaintiffs of certain property in Crawley, Sussex, and (2) damages in addition to or in lieu of specific performance. At the hearing of the action the claim for specific performance no longer fell to be considered because after the issue of the writ the property in question was conveyed to the plaintiffs. His Honour Judge Mervyn Davies QC sitting as a High Court judge, adjourned the action for argument on whether the plaintiffs were entitled to claim damages for delay in completing the contract although the issue of the writ had preceded the completion date. The facts are set out in the judgment.

Leonard Hoffmann QC and *Alan Boyle* for the plaintiffs.
Judith Jackson, Jeremiah Harman QC with her, for the defendants.

Cur adv vult

20th May. **HIS HONOUR JUDGE MERVYN DAVIES QC** read the following judgment: I gave judgment in this action on 10th April 1981. I had before me a contract for the sale of land dated 19th April 1978. By a writ dated 29th February 1980 the plaintiff purchasers claimed as well as alternative relief (1) specific performance and (2) damages in addition to or in lieu of specific performance. As appears from the judgment, the land was conveyed to the plaintiffs after the issue of the writ so that the specific performance claim did not fall to be considered, but the action was continued because the plaintiffs maintained a claim for damages. The damages were said to arise from the defendants' delay in failing to complete on the contractual date of completion: see *Raineri v Miles* [1980] 2 All ER 145, [1980] 2 WLR 847. In these circumstances it became material to ascertain the contractual date of completion.

Before me, the plaintiffs contended that the contractual completion date was 29th February 1980. The defendants said not so. Their view was that on that date no completion date was in being in that it was at all material times for the defendant to fix the completion date by giving a notice under cl 6 of the contract and no such notice had been given on 29th February 1980. In fact, the defendants, in May 1980, gave a cl 6 notice which they said made 6th June 1980 the contractual date of completion. I have found, on a true construction of the contract and in the events which have happened, that the contractual date was 4th March 1980. In these circumstances it would appear that the plaintiffs' claim for damages for delay in completing ought to be dismissed because the writ was issued, as I have said, on 29th February 1980, that is to say before the contractual date for completion as now found.

At the conclusion of my judgment I informed counsel that I was minded to dismiss the action but that it ought perhaps to be argued before me that the plaintiffs were entitled to damages for delay despite the fact that the writ preceded the completion date. I had in mind that a writ for specific performance may sometimes be issued before the arrival of the contractual completion date. This point was not taken at the trial. Counsel for the plaintiffs said that he wished to consider the matter and it was agreed that the action should be restored to me for argument.

At the resumed hearing counsel for the defendants accepted that the issue of the writ was not premature in so far as it claims specific performance: see *Hasham v Zenab* [1960] AC 316. Accordingly, there was before me no consideration of the question whether or

not the writ was properly issued as respects the specific performance claim. Counsel for
a the defendants then founded herself on the proposition that the claim as considered by
the court was a claim at law for breach of contract in that the defendants did not
complete in due time in accordance with the terms of the contract. The completion date
had not arrived when the writ was issued. The writ was five days premature. Thus no
cause of action had accrued as respects damages when the writ was issued. I think that
is plainly right when damages for breach of contract and nothing more are claimed.
b Counsel went on to say that the cases do not establish that the Court of Chancery has any
more power than a common law court to award damages in such a case as this, ie where
there was no accrued cause of action before the date of the writ. Counsel for the plaintiffs
accepted that had his only claim in the action been for damages at law, then damages
would not have been recoverable in that the writ was premature. Without referring to
para 4 of the writ, which is a claim in the alternative for 'damages for breach of contract',
c counsel for the plaintiffs drew attention to the fact that the writ has the two claims I have
mentioned, ie (1) specific performance and (2) damages in addition to or in lieu of
specific performance. Those claims were made, he said, in good faith when the writ was
issued. I accept that they were so made. Having got into the court on a writ that was
valid, having regard to those claims, the plaintiffs were, he said, entitled to have resolved
the whole of the issues as they existed between the parties at the time of the trial. It could
d not be right, he said, to allow the plaintiffs a specific performance writ and oblige them
to issue a second writ for damages for delay.

In essence, the argument was, as I understand, as follows. (1) The court, when dealing
with a specific performance action, has jurisdiction in equity to award damages in
addition to specific performance, the jurisdiction arising under the inherent jurisdiction
or under Lord Cairns's Act (the Chancery Amendment Act 1858). (2) The equitable
e jurisdiction is not limited to damages accrued at the date of the writ; the court looks at
the matter as at the date of the trial. (3) The damages claimed in this case may be
regarded not only as a claim at law but also as a claim in equity. (4) Regarding this claim
as a claim in equity, the claim is ancillary to the claim for specific performance, ie for
'damages in addition to specific performance' so that if a specific performance order fell
to be made, an order respecting damages for delay would also be made in respect of the
f ascertained period of delay. (5) The order for specific performance is in fact not necessary
in this case (because the land has been conveyed); nevertheless the 'damages in addition'
may still be ordered as if a specific performance order were included in the order. Thus
counsel for the plaintiffs contends he is not claiming damages at law, he is claiming
damages 'in addition to specific performance' pursuant to Lord Cairns's Act. No doubt
he is entitled to do that. The question then is whether such 'damages in addition' may
g be recovered in a situation such as this where the breach of contract which founds the
damages claim occurred after the date of the writ, it being admitted that in this situation
the damages would not be recoverable in an action at law. I was not referred to any
authority which bears clearly on this question. *Chapman, Morsons & Co v Auckland Union
Guardians* (1889) 23 QBD 294 is a case where damages were awarded in lieu of an
injunction, the damage in question being damage which had not accrued when the writ
h was issued. That is to say, damage was prospective when the writ was issued. In *Slack v
Leeds Industrial Co-operative Society Ltd* [1924] AC 851, [1924] All ER Rep 259 damages
were again awarded in lieu of an injunction despite the fact that, at the time when the
writ was issued and, indeed, at the time of the trial, no damage had accrued. However,
those instances of damages being awarded in circumstances where no damage had been
sustained when the writ was issued are of little guidance in the situation before me.
j Those were cases where an injunction was sought and, the court being able to choose
between an injunction or damages in lieu, decided for damages in lieu. There was no
question in those cases of the damages being recoverable at law.

I next refer to *Phelps v Prothero* (1855) 7 De GM & G 722, 44 ER 280. This was one of
a series of cases between the same parties: see 16 CB 370, 139 ER 801 and 2 De G & Sm
274, 64 ER 123. The facts and events are complicated. Phelps were seeking to sue at law

after having commenced proceedings for specific performance. Prothero sought to restrain the proceedings at law. The application was before the Lords Justices on appeal. Turner LJ said (7 De GM & G 722 at 733, 44 ER 280 at 285: a

> 'The first question is, whether the Defendant [that was Phelps] was at all entitled to commence the action now sought to be restrained. I am of opinion that he was not. The Defendant had originally the right to proceed, either at law, for breach of the agreement, or in this Court, for the specific performance of it. He adopted the latter remedy. I think that a Plaintiff, who has legal rights, and comes to this Court b for its aid, is bound to put his legal rights under the control of the Court, and that that principle reaches the present case. The Plaintiff, therefore, having sued in equity for specific performance, was bound, in my opinion, to submit his claim for damages to the judgment of this Court, and was not entitled to proceed at law otherwise than by leave of this Court. That it was competent to this Court to have ascertained the damages, I feel no doubt. It is the constant course of the Court, in c cases between vendor and purchaser, upon a sufficient case being made for the purpose, to direct an inquiry as to the deterioration of the estate pending the contract, and in so doing the Court is in truth giving damages to the purchaser for the loss which he has sustained by the contract not having been literally performed. This Court, when it entertains jurisdiction, deals as far as it can with the whole case, and not with part of it only; and it is well settled by authority that a d Defendant cannot be allowed, without the leave of the Court, to proceed at law on the subject-matter of the suit, whilst proceedings in this Court are pending . . .'

Those words show that even before Lord Cairns's Act the Court of Equity, when dealing with a specific performance action, dealt with 'the whole case', concerning itself not only with the equitable relief properly so called but also with damages sustained by e reason of the contract not having been performed. In dealing with 'the whole case' in this way, the court appears to have been willing to take account of damages arising after the institution of the specific performance claim, for Turner LJ said (7 De GM & G 722 at 735, 44 ER 280 at 285):

> 'It was urged, on the part of the Defendant, that the damages for which he is suing at law, in part, at least, arose after the institution of the suit; and this, no f doubt, is true, but it is unimportant, for the Defendant had ample opportunity of bringing them under the consideration of the Court.'

In the light of these observations, it seems to me that I am not obliged to consider the damages claimed in this case as a claim at law isolated and apart from the specific performance claim. Since the action before me was originally properly constituted as a specific performance action, I may now deal with the whole case as it now stands between g the parties. If I am to deal with the whole case, one must deal with the plaintiffs' claim for damages. Is the court debarred from dealing with that claim by reason of the fact that, so far as a claim at law is concerned, the writ was premature? I do not think so. This action was started in good faith as a specific performance action with a claim for damages in addition or in lieu. It was not started as a claim for damages and nothing h more. Within the framework of a specific performance action the court may, in my view, award damages for delay in completion despite the fact that the action was instituted before the contractual date of completion. I think it is satisfactory to be able to come to this conclusion. Otherwise, to my way of thinking, the situation would be unjust. Despite the fact that the specific performance writ was properly issued, the plaintiffs would find themselves deprived, in this action anyway, from part of the relief j to which they are, in my view, entitled.

There will be an inquiry as to the damages suffered by the delay in the defendants' not completing on 4th March 1980. The period of delay is 4th March to 6th June 1980. I say 6th June because there was no evidence of delay on the part of the defendants after 6th June 1980.

Judgment for the plaintiffs for damages to be assessed.

a

Solicitors: *Denton Hall & Burgin* (for the plaintiffs); *Simmons & Simmons* agents for *Wheatley, Hughes and Luscombe*, Crawley (for the defendants).

Hazel Hartman   Barrister.

b

Suedeclub Co Ltd v Occasions Textiles Ltd

c

CHANCERY DIVISION

NOURSE J

18th MAY, 2nd, 19th JUNE 1981

Judgment – Default of defence – Lapse of one year or more since last proceeding in action – Notice of intention to proceed – Notice to proceed served shortly before expiry of one year from last

d *proceeding – Judgment in default of defence entered after expiry of one year from last proceeding – Whether notice to proceed can be served only after expiry of one year from last proceeding – Whether judgment would be set aside as irregularly entered – RSC Ord 3, r 6.*

The statement of claim in an action by the plaintiff was served on the defendant on 29th February 1980. The defendant did not serve a defence. There were no further proceedings in the action. On 18th February 1981, ie ten days before the expiry of one *e* year from the last proceeding in the action, namely service of the statement of claim, the plaintiff served on the defendant notice of intention to proceed with the action, pursuant to RSC Ord 3, r 6[a], and on 3rd April 1981 entered judgment in default of defence. The defendant applied to have the judgment set aside for irregularity on the ground that a notice to proceed under Ord 3, r 6 could be given only after one year or more had elapsed *f* since the last proceeding in the action.

Held – RSC Ord 3, r 6 was to be construed literally and contemplated that a notice to proceed could be served only after one year had elapsed since the last proceeding in the action, because it was only when that year had elapsed that the plaintiff was to be assumed to have intended to abandon the action and that he was in consequence required, before entering judgment in default, to give the defendant notice to proceed. *g* Until that year elapsed it was to be assumed that the plaintiff intended to proceed with the action, and a notice to proceed was unnecessary. Accordingly, however late in the year the plaintiff might give notice to proceed, if he had not in fact proceeded with the action before the year had elapsed he was thereafter to be taken as having intended to abandon the action and had therefore to serve a further notice to proceed before he could *h* enter judgment in default of defence. It followed that the notice to proceed served on 18th February 1981 was not a valid notice under Ord 3, r 6 and that the judgment entered would be set aside (see p 673 *d* to *g*, post).

Dictum of Lindley LJ in *Webster v Myer* (1884) 14 QBD at 234 applied.

Notes

For notice of intention to proceed, see 30 Halsbury's Laws (3rd Edn) 411, paras 772–773, *j* and for cases on the subject, see 50 Digest (Repl) 259–260, 117–125.

For judgment in default of defence, see 26 Halsbury's Laws (4th Edn) para 512.

For setting aside a judgment in default, see ibid para 559, and for cases on the subject, see 50 Digest (Repl) 399–402, 1095–1119.

---

a   Rule 6 is set out at p 672 *h j*, post

Case referred to in judgment

Webster v Myer (1884) 14 QBD 231, 54 LJQB 101, 51 LT 560, CA, 50 Digest (Repl) 259, *a*
118.

Summons

By a summons dated 8th April 1981 the defendants, Suedeclub Co Ltd, applied for an
order that the judgment entered in default of defence on 3rd April 1981 by the plaintiffs,
Occasions Textiles Ltd, in a copyright action brought by them against the defendants be *b*
set aside and that the defendants have leave to defend the action. The facts are set out in
the judgment.

Christopher Floyd for the defendants.
Edward Bragiel for the plaintiffs.

Cur adv vult *c*

19th June. **NOURSE J** read the following judgment: This is an application to set aside
a judgment entered in default of defence in a copyright action. It has given rise to a short
but difficult question on RSC Ord 3, r 6. That is the well-known rule which requires
notice of intention to proceed to be given after a year's delay in the proceedings. *d*
The question arises in this way. The writ in the action was issued on 27th February
1979. In March 1979 there were interlocutory proceedings which led to certain
undertakings by the defendants pending trial. There was then a period of inactivity
which lasted for nearly a year. The statement of claim was served on 29th February
1980, that being the last proceeding in the action for the purposes of Ord 3, r 6.
In March and April 1980 there were inconclusive negotiations between the two sides *e*
and the matter then went to sleep. No defence was served. On 18th February 1981 the
plaintiffs' solicitors wrote to the defendants' solicitors in these terms: 'We hereby give
you notice of intention to proceed in this matter as we have not received your clients'
defence.' That was certainly a notice of intention to proceed, but it was given some ten
days before the expiry of one year after the service of the statement of claim. In fact the
letter never arrived, but the defendants now accept that it was properly served by post *f*
under RSC Ord 65, r 5. On 3rd April the plaintiffs entered judgment in default of
defence for damages and interest to be assessed, and costs, under Ord 19, r 3, the other
claims in the action having been abandoned.
The defendants' application to set the judgment aside was originally based solely on
the ground that it was irregular by reason of the plaintiffs' alleged failure to give a valid
notice pursuant to Ord 3, r 6. In case the judgment should be held to have been regular *g*
the application has now been amended to raise an alternative claim for leave to defend
based on the ground that the defendants have shown that they have a defence to the
action which ought to be tried. It is agreed on both sides that the defendants' alternative
claim is a good one, but that if they are forced to rely on that they will have to pay the
costs of this application. Therefore the defendants have argued that their original claim
is a good one in order, if they can, to better their position with regard to costs.
Order 3, r 6, which is headed 'Notice of intention to proceed after year's delay', is in *h*
these terms:

'Where a year or more has elapsed since the last proceeding in a cause or matter,
the party who desires to proceed must give to every other party not less than one
month's notice of his intention to proceed. A summons on which no order was
made is not a proceeding for the purpose of this rule.' *j*

Counsel for the defendants argued that the letter of 18th February 1981 was not a
notice pursuant to the rule on the ground that it was given less than a year after the
service of the statement of claim. He said that the wording of the rule, 'Where a year or
more *has* elapsed . . . the party who *desires* to proceed *must give* . . . etc', contemplates, and

a   contemplates only, the giving of a notice after the year has elapsed. He said that if it was intended that a notice could be given before the year had elapsed the rule would have read '... the party ... *must give or have given* ... etc'.

On a literal construction of the rule counsel for the defendants' argument must be correct, but it was said that it would lead to an anomalous result. On counsel's argument the plaintiffs could have entered judgment at any time up and and including 28th February 1981 without notice and at any time on or after 1st April 1981 with notice, but *b*   they could not have entered judgment at any time between 1st and 31st March, either with or without notice.

I was at one time impressed by that argument, but counsel for the defendants referred me to the judgment of Lindley LJ in *Webster v Myer* (1884) 14 QBD 231 at 234 where he said:

c   'The fact of more than a year having elapsed since the last proceedings, seems to shew that the plaintiff had intended to abandon the prosecution of the action, and it might be very unjust to allow him to sign judgment without giving the defendant an opportunity of establishing to the satisfaction of the Court that the plaintiff is not entitled to proceed further.'

That shows that the lapse of a year since the last proceeding is taken to demonstrate *d*   that the plaintiff intends to abandon the action. Conversely, until the year is up his assumed intention is to proceed. If during the year he gives notice of his intention to proceed, he does so unnecessarily. If he gives notice, however late in the year, but does not then proceed within it, he must still be taken to intend to abandon the action. That was the position in the present case and it seems to me that counsel for the defendants is right in saying that before the plaintiffs could enter judgment on 3rd April they ought, *e*   after 28th February, to have given the defendants not less than one month's notice of their intention to proceed.

I should add that the suggested anomaly caused by this construction of the rule is at the least balanced, if not outweighed, by another anomaly which would flow from the contrary construction. Counsel for the defendants contends that if a notice can be given before the year has expired, the plaintiffs in this case could have given it on 1st March *f*   1980, the day after the service of the statement of claim, and could still have relied on that notice to secure their judgment on 3rd April 1981. It seems to me that there is no answer to that contention and that its consequences are more startling than those which flow from counsel for the defendants' construction of the rule.

In all the circumstances it seems to me that the only safe course is for me to apply the literal construction of the rule and to hold that the letter of 18th February 1981 was not *g*   a notice pursuant to it. That means that the defendants' claim that the judgment was irregular was a good one and that the judgment must be set aside on that ground.

Application allowed; judgment in default of defence set aside.

Solicitors: *Whitelock & Storr* (for the defendants); *E D C Lord & Co*, Southall (for the plaintiffs).

Hazel Hartman   Barrister.

Crossley v Rawlinson

QUEEN'S BENCH DIVISION

RICHARD H TUCKER QC SITTING AS A DEPUTY JUDGE OF THE HIGH COURT

13th, 14th JULY 1981

Negligence – Duty to take care – Rescuer – Rescuer injured while attempting to reach scene of danger – Whether reasonably foreseeable that rescuer would be injured while attempting to reach scene of danger.

The defendant was driving his lorry along a main road when a tarpaulin on the lorry caught fire. He pulled in and stopped the lorry at the side of the road about 100 yards away from an AA post where the plaintiff, an AA patrolman, was on duty. The plaintiff saw the fire, grabbed a fire extinguisher and ran along a rough path alongside the road towards the lorry intending to put out the fire. As he was running he tripped in a hole, which was just off the path and obscured by grass, and was injured. He brought an action against the defendant for damages for personal injuries, contending (i) that the fire was a result of the defendant's negligence, (ii) that the defendant's negligence had caused the plaintiff's accident, and (iii) that the defendant was liable to a rescuer in the plaintiff's position even though the rescuer was injured not while actually engaged in the rescue at the scene of the danger but while attempting to reach the scene.

Held – Although it was reasonably foreseeable that a person such as the plaintiff might attempt to come to the defendant's aid and might run along the path towards the fire, it was not reasonably foreseeable that such a rescuer would suffer any injury while running along the path towards the scene of danger, and accordingly, even though the defendant's negligence had caused the fire, it had not caused the plaintiff's injuries. The plaintiff's action would therefore be dismissed (see p 678 b c f and j to p 679 b, post).

Haynes v Harwood [1934] All ER Rep 103, *Hyett v Great Western Railway Co* [1947] 2 All ER 264, *Chapman v Hearse* (1961) 106 CLR 112, *Videan v British Transport Commission* [1963] 2 All ER 860, *Corothers v Slobodian* (1975) 51 DLR (3d) 1 and *Lamb v London Borough of Camden* [1981] 2 All ER 408 considered.

Notes

For the duty of care owed to a rescuer, see 34 Halsbury's Laws (4th Edn) para 5, and for cases on the subject, see 36(1) Digest (Reissue) 301–302, 1211–1214.

Cases referred to in judgment

Chapman v Hearse (1961) 106 CLR 112.

Corothers v Slobodian (1975) 51 DLR (3d) 1.

Haynes v Harwood [1935] 1 KB 146, [1934] All ER Rep 103, 104 LJKB 63, 152 LT 121, CA, 36(1) Digest (Reissue) 246, 953.

Hughes v Lord Advocate [1963] 1 All ER 705, [1963] AC 837, [1963] 2 WLR 779, 1963 SC 31, 1963 SLT 150, HL, 36(1) Digest (Reissue) 65, 234.

Hyett v Great Western Railway Co [1947] 2 All ER 264, [1948] 1 KB 345, [1947] LJR 1243, 177 LT 178, CA, 36(1) Digest (Reissue) 75, 298.

Lamb v London Borough of Camden [1981] 1 All ER 408, [1981] 2 WLR 1038, CA.

Videan v British Transport Commission [1963] 2 All ER 860, [1963] 2 QB 650, [1963] 3 WLR 374, CA, 36(1) Digest (Reissue) 120, 461.

Action

By a writ issued on 18th May 1979 the plaintiff, Peter Crossley, claimed against the a defendant, William John Rawlinson, damages for personal injury suffered as a result of an accident on 28th September 1976. The facts are set out in the judgment.

J Crowley for the plaintiff.
G Pulman for the defendant.

b **RICHARD H TUCKER QC.** In this action the plaintiff sues the defendant for damages in respect of personal injuries sustained by the plaintiff on 28th September 1976 while he was on duty as an AA patrolman. The defendant is the owner, and was the driver of, a lorry. At about 9.15 in the morning, as the defendant was driving the lorry along the A12 road which is a dual carriageway at Romford in Essex, a tarpaulin covering the body of the lorry caught fire. The defendant accordingly stopped his lorry, partly on c the carriageway and partly on the grass verge. The place where he stopped is about 300 feet from the AA service centre at Gallows Corner where the plaintiff worked. The plaintiff saw what happened; he grabbed a fire extinguisher and ran towards the lorry intending to put out the fire. He ran along a trodden pathway on the grass verge but unfortunately his foot went into a hole and he fell and injured his back. He managed to get to the lorry and thought he had succeeded in dealing with the fire.

d The scene is illustrated in a sketch plan forming part of the further and better particulars of the statement of claim, and in six agreed photographs which were taken on the first anniversary of the accident and at about the same time of day. It can be seen from the plan and from photographs 1 and 2 that there is a lay-by alongside the AA post. There was room on it for the defendant to park his lorry there, but he had not got that far along the road and did not do so. In photograph 1 the plaintiff is shown standing in about the position where the lorry stopped. There is a verge and a rough path between e that position and the AA post. In photograph 2 the plaintiff is shown standing at about the point where he fell, and that point can be seen in close-up in photographs 3, 4 and 5. It was about 128 feet from the AA post. The road itself is a busy one, as photographs 1 and 2 reveal. It runs between London and Southend. In photographs 1 and 2 the camera is pointing towards London.

f The plaintiff is now aged 36; he is married with three children; he has been employed by the AA as a patrolman since 1974 and is still so employed. He moved to Gallows Corner in July 1976, that is to say, two or three months prior to the accident. He had previously been employed as a fitter and then as a heavy goods vehicle driver.

The plaintiff described the path. There was no paved footpath alongside the road but there was a rough path which had been made by people walking to and from work, and by an occasional horserider. He said it was bumpy and that there were a few potholes g either side of the verge, otherwise it was a normal footpath such as you find in the country. He had been on the path himself many times. In particular he had gone along it to recapture horses which had escaped from nearby riding stables, from a position beyond the dark bushes shown in photographs 1 and 2. That was something which had happened more than once before the accident. Although the plaintiff said that the grass h on the verge is normally six to eight inches high, about the length shown in photograph 3, he said the path itself was a pretty well worn track and that other emergencies had involved him going along it. He had run along it before, certainly some way towards the horses, possibly so far as the point where the hole was, or even to the bushes, depending on where the horses were. There is no suggestion that he had ever tripped or fallen before when going along the path, and he said, 'I did not think it was going to be j dangerous to run along there. I would not expect to fall or trip'. He agreed that he was one of the best people to say, having used it regularly, although he later qualified that to a great extent when he said, 'I would not have run along that path for a menial task. It was uneven and dangerous.'

I find that the plaintiff had used that path regularly, had run along it occasionally and did not regard it as dangerous to do so. It was, in my judgment, an ordinary country footpath with nothing about it which ought to lead anyone to suspect that it would be dangerous to run along it if necessary.

The plaintiff told me how the accident happened. He saw the lorry from the window of the AA post. He saw it stop about 100 yards away. The tarpaulin was ablaze. Instinctively he grabbed a fire extinguisher and ran very fast towards the lorry. It was in his mind that the fire might cause an injury, that the lorry might explode or that smoke might go across the road and cause accidents. He ran along the path, but as he got about one-third of the way towards the lorry his foot went down a pothole of some description. He said it felt like stepping off a kerb which you did not realise was there. He fell down. He felt a searing pain in his leg. He managed to get up and get to the lorry. Photograph 3 shows the hole with the plaintiff's right foot in it. He thought it had in fact been made by a lorry standing there overnight. He could not see it at the time; it was covered by grass. He said his foot was just off the pathway and he would not have known what was off the pathway.

I find that the hole was off the beaten track and was invisible. Although the plaintiff realised that there might be small holes about, he had not appreciated that there was a hole big enough to get his foot in. He made his way to the lorry. He found that the body of the lorry had been partly tipped. There are illustrations of a somewhat similar lorry. He found the blazing tarpaulin was half in the body of the lorry and half between the body and the cab, that is to say, close to the engine and the fuel tank. The plaintiff extinguished that fire with the fire extinguisher, an extinguisher of a normal type, about 15 inches long, weighing 3 lb and easily carried. In appearance it looks like a thin and elongated soda siphon.

The plaintiff hobbled back to the AA post. His leg was painful. He went straight to his general practitioner after work. It is not suggested that he did not injure himself in the way he described, and I find that he did. I thought the plaintiff was perfectly genuine in his description of his symptoms, which I find to be wholly attributable to the injury which he sustained in the accident. Had there been any doubt about the circumstances of the accident the remaining evidence called by the plaintiff would have dispelled it. A fireman who attended the scene confirmed that the tarpaulin had caught fire and produced an extract from the fire report, which gave as the supposed cause of the fire, 'Tarpaulin inadvertently placed too close to the engine exhaust, overheated and ignited.' The plaintiff also called his fellow AA patrolman who saw the fire and later saw the plaintiff limping back to the post. The defendant called no evidence.

The issues are these. (1) Was the fire due to the defendant's negligence? (2) If so, was that negligence causative of the plaintiff's accident? As to the first matter no explanation came from the defendant about the cause of the fire, but there is no difficulty about finding that it was due to his negligence because counsel for the defendant has accepted that the defendant must be found guilty of negligence, and I have no difficulty in finding that the fire was caused by some negligence on the part of the defendant. As to the second issue, counsel also conceded that it was reasonably foreseeable that the plaintiff would take a fire extinguisher and run along a path towards the fire. He abandoned the allegation that the plaintiff had voluntarily accepted the risk of injury, but counsel argued that that was not the end of the matter. He submitted that the plaintiff had not at the time of his accident brought himself within the protection afforded to a rescuer and that there was no breach of any duty owed to him by the defendant. He further submitted that a tortfeasor was not the guarantor of the safety of a victim. What was required, he submitted, was reasonable foreseeability by a reasonable man, and here there was none.

The plaintiff's counsel, on the other hand, cited a number of the rescue cases and argued that the test was whether the rescuer exposed himself to a real risk of injury and that the precise nature of the injury does not have to be foreseen. He submitted that the defendant would be liable even if injury resulted not from the danger itself but from the plaintiff attempting to deal with the danger. He cited three English cases, a Scottish case, an Australian case and a Canadian case. The English cases were *Haynes v Harwood* [1935]

1 KB 146, [1934] All ER Rep 103, *Hyett v Great Western Railway Co* [1947] 2 All ER 264,
a [1948] 1 KB 345 and *Videan v British Transport Commission* [1963] 2 All ER 860, [1963] 2
QB 650.

Haynes was the case of the police constable who was injured while stopping runaway
horses. Greer LJ in the course of his judgment said ([1935] 1 KB 146 at 156, [1934] All
ER Rep 103 at 107):

> 'There can be no doubt in this case that the damage was the result of a wrongful
b act in the sense of being one of the natural and probable consequences of the
> wrongful act. It is not necessary to show that this particular accident and this
> particular damage were probable; it is sufficient if the accident is of a class that
> might well be anticipated as one of the reasonable and probable results of the
> wrongful act.'

c Roche LJ said ([1935] 1 KB 146 at 166, [1934] All ER Rep 103 at 112):

> 'My answer is this: that the learned judge rightly arrived at an affirmative
> conclusion, because the negligence of the defendants' servant was the cause, and not
> merely the occasion, both of the horses running away and of the necessity arising for
> the very proper intervention of the plaintiff.'

In *Hyett's* case the plaintiff was injured while removing drums of paraffin from a
d blazing wagon. Tucker LJ said ([1947] 2 All ER 264 at 266, [1948] 1 KB 345 at 348):

> '... if a man is going to act at all in the case of fire, he must act swiftly, and
> applying the tests laid down in the two cases to which I have referred, the conclusion
> I have reached is that the act of the plaintiff was not *novus actus interveniens* breaking
> the chain of causation, but was the kind of act which the defendants might
e reasonably have anticipated as likely to follow from their act of negligence in
> leaving the leaking paraffin on this siding.'

In *Videan's* case a stationmaster was killed while attempting to rescue his son from the
path of an oncoming trolley. Lord Denning MR in the course of his judgment, said
([1963] 2 All ER 860 at 868, [1963] 2 QB 650 at 669):

> f 'Foreseeability is necessary, but not foreseeability of the particular emergency that
> arose. Suffice it that he ought reasonably to foresee that, if he did not take care,
> some emergency or other might arise, and that someone or other might be impelled
> to expose himself to danger in order to effect a rescue. Such is the case here ...
> Whoever comes to the rescue, the law should see that he does not suffer for it. It
> seems to me that, if a person by his fault creates a situation of peril, he must answer
g for it to any person who attempts to rescue the person who is in danger. He owes
> a duty to such a person above all others. The rescuer may act instinctively out of
> humanity or deliberately out of courage. But whichever it is, so long as it is not
> wanton interference, if the rescuer is killed or injured in the attempt, he can recover
> damages from the one whose fault has been the cause of it.'

That must be read subject to a later judgment of Lord Denning MR in the case of *Lamb*
h *v London Borough of Camden* [1981] 2 All ER 408, [1981] 2 WLR 1038, to which I shall
refer in due course. But referring back to *Videan's* case, in the judgment of Pearson LJ he
said ([1963] 2 All ER 860 at 876, [1963] 2 QB 650 at 682):

> 'It was foreseeable by Souness that, if he drove his trolley carelessly into the
> station, he might imperil the stationmaster, as the stationmaster might well have
> some proper occasion for going on to the track in the performance of his duties. For
j this purpose, it is not necessary that the particular accident which happened should
> have been foreseeable. It is enough that it was foreseeable that some situation
> requiring the stationmaster to go on the line might arise, and, if any such situation
> did arise, a careless approach to the station by Souness with his vehicle would be
> dangerous to the stationmaster.'

In all these cases the accident was caused by the original negligence itself. In all of them the victim was actually engaged in a rescue operation at the scene of the danger. The police constable was not injured because he fell over a protruding flagstone while running to stop the horses. The stationmaster's death was not caused because he fell off the platform.

Counsel for the plaintiff also cited *Hughes v Lord Advocate* [1963] 1 All ER 705, [1963] AC 837, where again the accident was caused directly by the negligence and not by something extraneous to it.

In all four cases, it seems to me, it was held that it ought to have been foreseen that injury might result from the negligence and that people might attempt to rescue those imperilled by the negligent act. It also seems to me that in all those cases it was held that a reasonable man ought reasonably to have foreseen that the accident which did befall the plaintiff, or the deceased, might well have befallen him.

Counsel for the plaintiff went on to cite two Commonwealth cases which he agreed were not binding, although of course they are of considerable persuasive authority. Both concern rescuers who were injured and in the one case killed while at or close to the scene of road accidents because they were struck by other motor vehicles than those originally involved. Thus in the Australian case of *Chapman v Hearse* (1961) 106 CLR 112 a doctor who was attending an injured driver in the middle of the road was run down and killed by another car. It was held that his widow was entitled to recover against the driver responsible for the original accident on the grounds that subsequent injury by passing traffic to those rendering aid after a collision on the highway would be by no means unlikely.

In the Canadian case of *Corothers v Slobodian* (1975) 51 DLR (3d) 1 the plaintiff assisted at the scene of a road accident, and then ran along the side of the road to seek aid for the injured victims. She was struck by another vehicle. It was held that she could recover against the driver responsible for the original accident on the grounds that her action was a reasonably foreseeable consequence of his negligence.

Although those two cases appear at first sight to extend the scope to which protection is afforded to a rescuer, in fact the basis of liability in my view remains the same: the test is foreseeability. Before applying that test to the facts of the present case I have very much in mind the decision of the Court of Appeal in the case to which I have already referred, *Lamb v London Borough of Camden* [1981] 2 All ER 408 at 414, [1981] 2 WLR 1038 at 1045, where Lord Denning MR said that the problem of limiting the range of liability for negligence 'ultimately is a question of policy for the judges to decide', and I particularly have in mind also the words of Watkins LJ ([1981] 2 All ER 408 at 421, [1981] 2 WLR 1038 at 1054):

'A robust and sensible approach to this very important area of the study of remoteness will more often than not produce, I think, an instinctive feeling that the event or act being weighed in the balance is too remote to sound in damages for the plaintiff. I do not pretend that in all cases the answer will come easily to the inquirer. But that the question must be asked and answered in all these cases I have no doubt. To return to the present case, I have the instinctive feeling that the squatters' damage is too remote. I could not possibly come to any other conclusion, although on the primary facts I, too, would regard that damage or something like it as reasonably foreseeable in these times.'

Thus if I were answering the question whether in the present case the plaintiff's damage is too remote, my instinctive feeling would be that it is. If I were answering the question, as in my judgment I have to, whether it ought reasonably to have been foreseen that the plaintiff would suffer this or any other injury while running along the path, I would say, and do say, that no reasonable man could reasonably have foreseen it. I reach this conclusion with reluctance because on any view the plaintiff acted with great presence of mind and with the best possible motives. I think it unfortunate that such a man should not recover damages for an injury which was not his fault. I dismiss the allegation that he brought it about by his own carelessness, but it was an accident in the true sense of the word, which neither party could reasonably have foreseen. Accordingly I am obliged to hold that the defendant is not liable for that injury and that no damages are recoverable. If I had awarded damages I would have awarded the plaintiff £3,500 for pain and suffering and loss of amenities. I accept that his complaints are genuine. I find that there is no real prospect of his ever being put out of employment with the AA but there is a chance that he may have to take work with them which is slightly less remunerative and I would have added a further £250 for that. As I have indicated, it is with regret that I have decided that he cannot recover those damages in this action and there must be judgment for the defendant.

Judgment for the defendant.

Solicitors: *Amery-Parkes & Co* (for the plaintiff); *Greenwoods* (for the defendant).

K Mydeen Esq   Barrister.

Harrison v British Railways Board and others

QUEEN'S BENCH DIVISION
BOREHAM J
1st, 2nd, 21st MAY, 31st JULY 1980

Negligence – Duty to take care – Rescuer – Person being rescued creating danger – Passenger attempting to board train while it was moving – Rescuer attempting to assist passenger aboard – Both passenger and rescuer falling off train – Rescuer injured – Whether person being rescued owing duty of care to rescuer.

Negligence – Contributory negligence – Emergency act – Rescue – Rescuer injured while attempting rescue – Rescuer failing to reduce danger to himself and contributing to own injuries – Whether rescuer contributorily negligent.

The plaintiff was a guard on a passenger train which the defendant attempted to board while it was moving out of the station. Under the rules regulating the conduct of train guards the plaintiff was required, in the event of an emergency, to signal the driver to stop or to apply the emergency brakes himself or both. The plaintiff attempted to signal the driver to stop but gave an incorrect signal and the train continued to accelerate away from the station. The plaintiff then tried to grab hold of the defendant who fell off the train, pulling the plaintiff with him. The plaintiff was injured. He brought an action against the defendant claiming damages for personal injuries. The defendant contended that he was not liable on the ground that a person being rescued owed no duty to his rescuer, and that, if he did owe such a duty, the plaintiff had been contributorily negligent in giving the wrong signal to the driver to stop and in not applying the emergency brake himself.

Held – (1) A person who, through lack of care for his own safety, put himself into a situation of danger, and who ought, as a reasonable person, to have foreseen that another might endanger himself by attempting to rescue him, was liable to his rescuer for injuries sustained by the rescuer in the course of the rescue or attempted rescue. Accordingly, since the defendant had created a situation of danger for himself through lack of reasonable care for his own safety and ought reasonably to have foreseen that the plaintiff might come to his aid, he was liable for the injuries sustained by the plaintiff (see p 684 b to j and p 685 a b and g h, post); *Videan v British Transport Commission* [1963] 2 All ER 860 and *Horsley v MacLaren, The Ogopogo* [1971] 2 Lloyd's Rep 410 applied.

(2) Since, however, the plaintiff had failed to apply the brakes in the emergency as required by the rules regulating the conduct of train guards and since if he had properly applied the brakes it was probable that both the possibility of his being injured and the severity of any injuries received would have been reduced, he was contributorily negligent in failing to reduce the danger to himself and the damages payable by the defendant would in the circumstances be reduced by 20% (see p 686 d to f, post).

Notes

For the duty of care owed to a rescuer, see 34 Halsbury's Laws (4th Edn) para 5, and for cases on the subject, see 36(1) Digest (Reissue) 301–302, *1211–1214*.

Cases referred to in judgment

Dupuis v New Regina Trading Co Ltd [1943] 4 DLR 275.
Haynes v Harwood [1935] 1 KB 146, [1934] All ER Rep 103, 104 LJKB 63, 152 LT 121, 36(1) Digest (Reissue) 246, *953*.
Horsley v MacLaren, The Ogopogo [1971] 2 Lloyd's Rep 410.
Videan v British Transport Commission [1963] 2 All ER 860, [1963] 2 QB 650, [1963] 3 WLR 374, CA, 36(1) Digest (Reissue) 120, *461*.
Ward v T E Hopkins & Son Ltd, Baker v T E Hopkins & Son Ltd [1958] 3 All ER 147, [1958] 1 WLR 993; *affd* [1959] 3 All ER 225, [1959] 1 WLR 966, 36(1) Digest (Reissue) 302, *1214*.

Action

By a writ issued on 5th April 1981 the plaintiff, Robin Patrick Harrison, claimed against the defendants, the British Railways Board, Patrick Howard and John Dean, damages for personal injury and consequential loss suffered as a result of an accident on 30th November 1974. The facts are set out in the judgment.

Ian Rich for the plaintiff.
Christopher Carling for the first and third defendants.
Peter Leighton for the second defendant.

Cur adv vult

31st July. **BOREHAM J** read the following judgment: This action arises out of events which occurred on the afternoon of Saturday, 30th November 1974, at Weybridge station on the Southern Region of British Rail. As a result of these events the plaintiff sustained severe and permanent injury in the course of his employment by the first defendants, as a passenger train guard. The plaintiff was then aged 34. He had joined British Rail in the previous June. His ambition was to become a train ticket inspector and, as a step in that direction, in August and September he had undergone a course of instruction as a train guard. He completed the course in September, and qualified as a guard with good marks. Thus by 30th November he had comparatively short experience as a guard but he had the advantage of having the lessons of his recent training still fresh in his mind.

On the day in question the plaintiff was the guard on the 1352 hrs passenger train from Waterloo to Portsmouth. It was a stopping train comprising two 4-coach electric units, eight coaches in all. There was a guard's van in the second coach and another in the sixth. The plaintiff used the latter. The driver of the train was Mr John Dean, the third defendant, a driver of some twelve years' experience. He and the plaintiff had worked together on a few occasions prior to 30th November.

The respective duties of guard and driver, so far as they are relevant to this action, were as follows. The driver's duty was to observe and obey the signals along his road and to

stop at the appropriate stations; it was also his duty to observe and obey the guard's
a proper signals. The safety of the train and its passengers was to a substantial extent the
guard's responsibility. In particular it was his duty to ensure that it was safe to start from
a station and then to give the driver the ready-to-start signal. It was also his duty to give
the driver the signal to stop in an emergency and/or to apply the emergency air-brake,
the lever control for which was in his van. On some trains, particularly suburban trains,
the guard's ready-to-start signal was given by hand, a flag during ordinary daylight, a
b hand-held light during the hours of darkness or in foggy conditions. The emergency
stop signal was given by applying the emergency air-brake. On the longer-distance
Southern Region trains, such as the 1352 hrs Waterloo to Portsmouth, the signals from
guard to driver were given by electric bell: two rings to start, one ring to stop. Whatever
the bell signal given by the guard, it was the driver's duty to acknowledge it by repeating
it on the Loudaphone call button (see r 4.3.2 of the rules for drivers and guards on the
c Southern Region).

The Loudaphone is an intercommunication system which enables the driver and the
guard to converse or to communicate by audible signals. The rules expressly forbade its
use (a) for speech when the train was in motion, except in an emergency, and (b) for
starting passenger trains from stations. If the starting-bell apparatus was unserviceable
the guard's ready-to-start signal had to be given by hand (see r 4.3.3). In such
d circumstances the emergency stop signal would be given by the application of the
emergency air-brake in order to attract the driver's attention. The driver's duty then was
to shut off the power and bring the train to a stop with the brakes. I am satisfied that at
the material time the plaintiff and Mr Dean were familiar with the equipment to which
reference has been made and with the rules relating to its use.

When the time came to leave Waterloo on 30th November it became apparent that the
e starting-bell apparatus was unserviceable, and so the plaintiff and Mr Dean took counsel
together over the Loudaphone. There is an important dispute as to what occurred. They
both accept that they agreed (a) that at stations where the driver was on the platform side
the plaintiff would give the ready-to-start signal by hand, in accordance with the rules
and (b) that at other stations, where the driver was not on the platform side, the plaintiff
would give the ready-to-start signal by two buzzes on the Loudaphone call button. They
f both acknowledge that this was in breach of the rules. It was agreed in order to save time
because they were already several minutes late. The plaintiff's case is that they also
agreed that the signal for an emergency stop should be one buzz on the Loudaphone,
again in breach of the rules. Mr Dean denies that there was any discussion or agreement
as to the use of the Loudaphone in an emergency. The difference is of prime importance.

I should say at once that I found the plaintiff an unreliable witness. Moreover, two
g important facets of his evidence to the court (one of them the matter of the agreement
reached with Mr Dean) were omitted from the statement he made to Pc Nicholls on 17th
December 1974, and from his evidence to the official inquiry held early in 1975. His
explanation for his omissions from his statement is that he was not given the opportunity
to read it and he never signed it. Had he been given the opportunity to read his
statement, he would have repaired the omission. I have heard Pc Nicholls, who took the
h statement, and I accept his evidence that the statement contained all that the plaintiff told
him, that the plaintiff had the opportunity to read it and that he signed it in three places.
I find that there was an agreement between the plaintiff and Mr Dean before the
departure from Waterloo to give the ready-to-start signal by means of the Loudaphone
call button when the driver was not on the platform side. This was agreed, as I have said,
to save, and hopefully to make up, time. I am satisfied that there was no mention of, and
j thus no agreement as to, the use of the Loudaphone call button in an emergency.

The train left Waterloo some ten or eleven minutes late. There were three stops before
Weybridge and the ready-to-start signal was given according to the agreement between
the guard and the driver. At Walton-on-Thames, the last stop before Weybridge, Mr
Foxon, a senior railwayman, boarded one of the front coaches of the train. He was due
to start work at Weybridge at 1430 hrs. The train arrived at Weybridge no more than
about four minutes late; six or seven minutes had already been made up. It stopped with

the doors of the plaintiff's van more or less opposite the destination board, a little forward of the exit and the access to the footbridge. A number of passengers left the train, including Mr Foxon who was the only member of the station staff on the platform. The plaintiff unloaded some mail from his van, and Mr Foxon walked from the front of the train towards the exit and arrived opposite the plaintiff's van when the train was ready to depart. He checked that all was clear and told the plaintiff that he could go. The plaintiff gave the driver the hand signal to start and the train departed. The driver had passed the platform signal at the end of the platform when he received one buzz on the Loudaphone. He, thinking that the plaintiff wished to speak to him, pressed his call button to speak, and did speak but received no reply. He concluded that the Loudaphone, like the bell, was unserviceable and continued on his way to the next station. He was entirely oblivious of the desperate situation which he had left behind at Weybridge.

What happened at Weybridge is in dispute. There were four eye witnesses. First, the plaintiff; his case is that, having given the signal to start, he entered the door of his van and was immediately distracted by an ill-mannered passenger who insisted on pushing himself and his baggage past the plaintiff. This person was not mentioned in the plaintiff's statement to Pc Nicholls, or to the official inquiry. The plaintiff then heard screaming, looked out and saw a man he recognised as the station foreman at Weybridge, Mr Howard, the second defendant, hanging onto a door handle on the seventh coach. The plaintiff says that his first reaction was to use the emergency brake, but he desisted because he thought that the effect of the deceleration might be to throw Mr Howard between the platform and the train, so he gave one buzz on the Loudaphone button as a signal to the driver to stop. He thought he heard and felt the brakes being applied and he jumped onto the platform in the hope of being able to support Mr Howard. He assessed the speed of the train at this moment at about 25 to 30 miles an hour. He says that he was thrown across the platform and sustained serious injuries which rendered him unconscious.

The accounts given by Mr Foxon and by Mr Howard differed substantially from that of the plaintiff and from each other. These three accounts were given in evidence on 1st and 2nd May 1980, when the trial was adjourned in the hope that a missing witness required by the first defendants, the British Railways Board, might subsequently be available. At the adjournment I was left with the uncomfortable feeling that none of the three eye witnesses had been entirely truthful, probably because each knew that he had been a party to or had encouraged a thoroughly irresponsible act on the part of the second defendant, an act which would have been condemned by them all had it been attempted by a member of the ordinary travelling public. Even at that time I had no doubt that none of the three had given a substantially accurate picture, though Mr Foxon had come nearer to it than had his colleagues.

When the trial was resumed on 21st May the first defendants were able to call Mr Michael Massey. He, with his family, had left the train at Weybridge and he witnessed much of what occurred. He did not see every move, for he quickly realised that a serious accident might occur and for a brief moment or two he concentrated on preventing his little daughter from witnessing it. Although he made one curious error, in identifying the guard as a coloured man, I found him an impressive and reliable witness. Where there are differences I prefer his evidence to that of the other three eye witnesses.

I find that what happened was this. When the plaintiff's train arrived at Weybridge the station foreman on duty was Mr Howard, the second defendant, who had been employed by British Rail since about 1935. For 22 years from 1949 he had been a passenger train guard and since 1971 he had been station foreman at Weybridge. On Saturday, 30th November, he was on early turn, that is from 7 am until 3 pm. For some time, however, there had been an arrangement between himself and the late-turn foreman, Mr Butler, that the latter would relieve him at 1415 hrs instead of 1500 hrs. This arrangement was entirely unofficial. On Saturday, 30th November, Mr Howard had a particularly pressing personal reason for catching the 1423 hrs down train, the plaintiff's train. Unhappily Mr Butler was late, and, although the train was running four minutes late, it was already in the station at the down platform when Mr Butler arrived

in the car park. Mr Howard was in his office on the up side of the station waiting to
a leave. On seeing Mr Butler he ran across the footbridge, his raincoat over his left arm
and his food bag in his left hand. When he reached the down platform the train had just
started to move. He was determined to catch it if he possibly could. His approach had
been observed by Mr Foxon, who shouted to the plaintiff, 'Stop the train for my mate.'
At this moment the plaintiff was still in the doorway of his van. I have no doubt that he
heard Mr Foxon shout and that he saw Mr Howard. The plaintiff then went into the van,
b gave one buzz on the Loudaphone and returned to the doorway of the van. In the
plaintiff's absence from the doorway Mr Howard, the second defendant, had managed to
grasp the rearmost vertical rail at the side of the guard's door. His intention was to board
the train. The train quickly gathered speed and by the time the plaintiff returned to the
doorway Mr Howard could no longer keep his feet. He was in grave danger and the
plaintiff realised it. He, the plaintiff, therefore reached out to take hold of Mr Howard,
c whose ability to hang on with one hand without support from his feet was nearly at an
end. His feet then went between the platform and the train, he was compelled to release
his handhold and fell into what is called the cess, and was very badly injured. His fall
pulled the plaintiff from the doorway. He, too, fell between the train and the platform,
and the train went on. The plaintiff was unconscious for a short time only. Soon after
the train had gone he was seen by Mr Massey to climb up onto the platform. It was a
d commendable effort by the plaintiff to try to save Mr Howard. He paid dearly for it.

In these circumstances the plaintiff contends that the first defendant, his employers,
are liable for failing to ensure that the platform was properly supervised and controlled
by platform staff, so as to prevent persons from attempting to board a moving train.
There was supervising staff in the person of Mr Foxon, who, instead of trying to
discourage Mr Howard, actually encouraged him to the extent of shouting to the guard
e to stop the train. But I am left in no doubt that even if Mr Foxon had tried to discourage
Mr Howard he would not have succeeded. Mr Howard was a senior employee. He was
determined to board that train if he possibly could. Nothing short of successful physical
intervention would have deterred him. He would not have responded to any request, or
obeyed any order to stand back. If there was any breach of duty in having insufficient
platform staff (and I am by no means satisfied that there was) I am satisfied that it did not
f contribute to this accident.

Next, it is alleged that the third defendant, Mr Dean, was negligent in the course of his
employment, and thus the first defendants are vicariously liable. First, it is said that Mr
Dean was negligent in not stopping when he received one buzz on the Loudaphone.
This, of course, is based on the plaintiff's evidence that it was the agreed signal for an
emergency stop. On the facts as I find them, it is an allegation without substance. Mr
g Dean did not regard it as a signal to stop and there was no reason why he should. Second,
it is contended that if Mr Dean was uncertain as to the meaning of the single buzz he
should still have stopped. This might be an argument of substance if there were
evidence that he was uncertain, but there is not. Mr Dean had worked with the plaintiff
on a few previous occasions. On one or more of those occasions the plaintiff had given
one buzz when he wanted to speak to the driver. This, of course, was contrary to the
h rules. Nevertheless, it happened. Mr Dean thought that this was the purpose of the
signal on 30th November; hence his attempt to reply. I accept his explanation and acquit
him of negligence on that account. Finally, it is said that the driver, Mr Dean, was in
breach of the rules and negligent in not looking back to ensure that the train was
following in a safe and proper manner. Rule 3(4)(ii) of section H of the British Rail Rule
Book (1972) provides:

j
'When starting the driver must take the earliest opportunity of looking back
when this can be done without detriment to his view of signals and the line ahead,
to see whether the whole of the train is following in a safe and proper manner.'

The purpose of the rule is clear. Moreover it makes clear that the duty to look back is
subordinated to the duty to observe signals and the line ahead. Thus it seems to me that

Mr Dean's duty was to observe the station signal to see that it did not change before he passed it. Very soon after he had passed it he was distracted by the signal on the Loudaphone. By the time that he realised there was no response to his own call it would have been too late for him to take any action which might have prevented the accident or reduced the chances of injury even if he had looked back and seen what was happening to Mr Howard. It is possible that he could have looked back after passing the platform signal and before he received the Loudaphone signal, but, although possible, the interval of time was so short that it would be wrong to say that he was in breach of duty, or negligent, in not doing so. I find no negligence on the part of Mr Dean, the third defendant.

I turn now to the case against the second defendant. It is unnecessary to repeat the facts. They leave me in no doubt that the second defendant was negligent to the extent that he acted with a reckless disregard for his own safety. As a very experienced railwayman, and in particular as an ex-train guard, he was well aware of the rule against attempting to board a moving train, and he was well aware of the reasons for making that rule. With all his experience he knew that by grasping a hand rail in order to board a moving train, particularly an electric train which has rapid acceleration, he was likely to find himself in grave danger. Had he expected the train to stop, he would not have been so determined to grab at the hand rail. He hoped to board the train whilst it was in motion and he knew that the only hope of doing so was to aim for the guard's door. It was the only door that was open and it was the only door which opened inwards. It would have been hopeless to attempt to board via an outward-opening passenger door. Moreover, he knew that the guard, the plaintiff, had seen him and he ought to have anticipated, indeed I think he probably expected, that if he got into trouble the guard would do his best to help him. He ought to have foreseen that by intervening in such circumstances the guard would probably endanger himself.

One might perhaps be forgiven for thinking that in those circumstances Mr Howard, the second defendant, must be liable to the plaintiff. Counsel for Mr Howard says, 'Not so', though in the end he said it somewhat tentatively. Much of his argument was based on the plaintiff's evidence that he deliberately jumped from the moving train to go to Mr Howard's assistance. That account I have been unable to accept. But he also argued that even on the facts as I have found them Mr Howard is not liable because he, being the person rescued, owed no duty to the plaintiff. In presenting this argument counsel has helpfully and responsibly referred me to the relevant authorities. It was this review, indeed, that, in the end, sapped some of his confidence in the argument.

By refraining from a detailed review of the relevant authorities, I intend no disrespect for counsel's careful argument. The question that has to be considered is this: is a man who, through lack of care for his own safety, puts himself into a situation of danger, and who ought, as a reasonable person, to have foreseen that another might endanger himself by attempting to rescue him, liable to his rescuer for injuries sustained in the course of the rescue, or attempted rescue? In the absence of authority I should have answered Yes. It has long been established that a duty of care arises whenever a reasonable person would foresee that if he did not take care he would put another in danger. That duty is owed to all who are within the sphere of the danger thus created. It is also owed to a rescuer, provided that the defendant ought, as a reasonable man, to have foreseen that someone would, or might, come to the rescue of the person imperilled by the defendant's negligence: see *Haynes v Harwood* [1935] 1 KB 146, [1934] All ER Rep 103. For some time there appeared to be room for the argument that the duty owed to the rescuer was what was called a derivative, or secondary, duty, namely a duty which arose only when the defendant owed a duty to the person being rescued: see *Dupuis v New Regina Trading Co* [1943] 4 DLR 275. There was, however, another school of thought; see, for instance, *Baker v Hopkins* [1958] 3 All ER 147, [1958] 1 WLR 993, per Barry J.

So far as this court is concerned, the principle has now been established that a duty will be owed to the rescuer if his intervention is reasonably foreseeable, albeit that the defendant owes no duty to the person being rescued: see *Videan v British Transport Commission* [1963] 2 All ER 860, [1963] 2 QB 650. The remaining question, namely whether or not a duty is owed to the rescuer when the person being rescued is he who created the dangerous situation, has, so far as I am aware, not previously been decided in this country. If however, as was decided in *Videan v British Transport Commission*, the duty may be owed to the rescuer, although no duty is owed to the person in danger, I see no reason in principle why it should not be owed to the rescuer when the person being rescued is the person who created the peril. Why should the defendant, who, by lack of reasonable care for his own safety, creates a dangerous situation which invites rescue, be in a better position than he who creates a similar situation by lack of reasonable care for another's safety? I can think of no reason, nor has any been suggested to me. In each case, of course, liability will attach only if the defendant ought, as a reasonable man, to have foreseen the likelihood of intervention by a rescuer. I am comforted by the thought that this approach is in line with the most recent decision of the Supreme Court of Canada in *Horsley v MacLaren, The Ogopogo* [1971] 2 Lloyd's Rep 410. Laskin J had this to say (at 418):

'Moreover, the liability to the rescuer, although founded on the concept of duty, is now seen as stemming from an independent and not a derivative duty of the negligent person. As Fleming on Torts (3rd Edn, 1965, p 166) has put it, the cause of action of the rescuer, in arising out of the defendant's negligence, is based ". . . not in its tendency to imperil the person rescued but in its tendency to induce the rescuer to encounter the danger. Thus viewed, the duty to the rescuer is clearly independent . . ." This explanation of principle was put forward as early as 1924 by Professor Bohlen (Studies in the Law of Torts, p 569) in recognition of the difficulty of straining the notion of foreseeability to embrace the rescuer of a person imperilled by another's negligence. Under this explanation of the basis of liability, it is immaterial that the imperilled person does not in fact suffer any injury, or that, as it turns out, the negligent person was under no liability to him either because the injury was not caused by the negligence or the damage was outside the foreseeable risk of harm to him: cf. *Videan v. British Transport Commission*. It is a further consequence of the recognition of independent duty that a person who imperils himself by his carelessness may be as fully liable to a rescuer as a third person would be who imperils another. In my opinion, therefore, *Dupuis v. New Regina Trading Company Ltd.* ([1943] 4 DLR 275) ought no longer to be taken as a statement of the common law in Canada in so far as it denies recovery because the rescuer was injured in going to the aid of a person who imperilled himself.'

This seems to me to follow almost inevitably the decision in *Videan v British Transport Commission*. It is the law of Canada. It is, in my judgment, the law of England.

Thus, two questions arise: had the second defendant, Mr Howard, by a lack of reasonable care for his own safety, created a situation of danger? I have no doubt that he had. The second question: ought he, as a reasonable man, to have foreseen that the plaintiff might very well come to his aid? I have said enough already to indicate that in my view he should have foreseen, and he probably did foresee, the probability of the plaintiff's intervention. In these circumstances I hold that the second defendant is liable in negligence to the plaintiff.

On this finding counsel for the plaintiff, pursuant to a very late amendment of the statement of claim, argued that at the material time the second defendant was acting in the course of his employment, so that the first defendants are vicariously liable for his negligence. As I understand it, his argument is this: it was by reason of his employment that the second defendant, Mr Howard, was authorised to board the train. Thus he was doing something which he was authorised to do, albeit that he was doing it in an unauthorised manner. Even assuming this to be acceptable, it is by no means conclusive of the question whether or not he was at the material time acting in the course of his employment. Counsel for the first defendants submits that the crucial question is this: at the material time was Mr Howard doing his work, or had he finished for the day? I agree that that is the essential question and I think the answer is clear. Mr Howard was no longer at work. He should have been, but he was not. That is why he was running for the train. It follows that what he did was not done in the course of his employment. In my judgment, the first defendants are not liable to the plaintiff for the second defendant's negligence.

Finally, so far as liability is concerned, the second defendant contends that the plaintiff was guilty of contributory negligence. Counsel for the second defendant argues that the plaintiff failed to observe the rules by failing to apply the emergency brake. The plaintiff's case is that he considered applying the brake but refrained from doing so because he was afraid that the sudden deceleration of the train would make matters worse for the second defendant, Mr Howard, in that it would almost inevitably have made him lose his grip and fall between the train and the platform. The difficulty I have in accepting this explanation is that I am satisfied that Mr Howard was not hanging onto the train when the plaintiff went into the guard's van to try and bring the train to a stop. Had Mr Howard by then grabbed the rail I am sure the plaintiff would have tried to help him aboard. On the other hand, Mr Howard's intentions must have been clear to the plaintiff and I am prepared to accept that he assumed at the time he was in the van that Mr Howard had, or might well have, grasped and hung onto some part of the train. But the fact remains that if he had wished to stop the train (and I accept that he did) the only proper means of doing so was by the emergency brake. I accept the evidence of Mr Girling that the brake may be applied slowly and thus a too-sudden deceleration would be avoided. Indeed, that is the proper way to apply it. It was the plaintiff's duty, according to the rules, to apply the brake in an emergency; he knew it and I think he was negligent in not doing so. Had he done so, the speed of the train would have been reduced. He should have known it was his duty, and I believe he did know it. As it was, he gave (no doubt in the heat of the moment) a meaningless signal and the train continued to accelerate. In these circumstances, I have come to the conclusion that had he acted as he should have done it is probable, though not certain, that both the chance of his being injured at all and the severity of his injuries would have been reduced. He should, therefore, bear some of the blame for those injuries.

One has a feeling of distaste about finding a rescuer guilty of contributory negligence. It can rarely be appropriate to do so, in my judgment. Here, however, the contributory negligence which is alleged does not relate to anything done in the course of the actual rescue. What is alleged is the failure by the man in authority to reduce the danger by doing what he was duty-bound to do. The major responsibility must, of course, be borne by the second defendant. I assess the plaintiff's share at 20%.

There remains the question of quantum. The plaintiff sustained a linear fracture of the left temporal bone of the skull. He was detained in hospital for six days during which time he suffered persistent headaches. The hospital staff thought that he was exaggerating his symptoms. On 20th January 1975 the plaintiff considered himself reasonably fit and returned to work, though not to guard duties. On 15th February 1975 he was seen by Dr Patten, a consultant neurologist. He was found to have lost his senses of taste and smell, but Dr Platten found no other physical abnormality. The plaintiff was then suffering at night from what Dr Patten diagnosed as depressive headaches, attributable to pressure caused by the now imminent public inquiry and his wife's nervous reaction to the accident. Mrs Harrison accepts that the accident had affected her nerves, though no doubt she did her best to keep this from her husband. Dr Patten prescribed an anti-depressant drug. He saw the plaintiff again on 7th March 1975. The plaintiff now claimed to be completely well. He told the doctor that after taking the drug for three days his headaches vanished, though he continued with and completed the course of medication. Dr Patten was surprised and delighted. So far as he, the doctor, is aware, the depressive headaches have not recurred. The plaintiff agrees that he gave this encouraging information to the doctor, but says that it was untrue. He says the truth is that he took the tablets for about three days, that they made him feel bad and so he threw the rest away. I do not accept this.

Within a short time the plaintiff resumed his duties as a passenger train guard. In about July 1975 he became involved in another incident, when a driver overshot the platform at Godalming station, and then, without a signal or permission from the plaintiff, 'backed up', as it is said, to the platform. This was not the fault of the plaintiff. The plaintiff should have reported the incident, but he refrained from doing so. The whole thing clearly upset him deeply. He lost his voice for several days and he completely lost his nerve for trains. He experienced nightmares and what he described as 'enormous headaches'. In August 1975, unhappily, he was pronounced medically unfit for guard duties. He was offered alternative employment on the railway but declined it. He then worked for about eighteen months in a circus, during which time he spent a short period in hospital with a state of severe anxiety. In March 1976 he was given another appointment to see Dr Patten. He was unable to keep the appointment but he wrote informing Dr Patten that nothing had changed since they last met. He claimed that he was still getting bad headaches and nightmares and his eyesight had deteriorated again. This was the first complaint of defective eyesight. When last seen by Dr Patten in May 1978 he was found to be much more relaxed. The only long-standing result of the injury was a complete loss of the senses of taste and smell. He was complaining of headaches which had some features of migraine. Dr Patten found it difficult to say whether these headaches were caused by the head injury. They could have been. The final medical examination was carried out by Dr Goody, another consultant neurologist, who considered it fair to accept that the plaintiff had mild headaches of a migraine pattern which might be attributable to the accident. Dr Goody concluded his report thus:

'The rest of his case, the nervous features, the dislike of trains, the difficulty in settling down, seem to me to be purely of an emotional nature. These features I do think are closely related to compensation, and, although there may be a depressive element to them I think the proportion of real depression is a very small one. As to the future, I must repeat that the sense of smell and flavour have gone for good. As to the other symptoms I think they will remain very much the same as they are now for a prolonged period. A major factor in abolishing the symptoms, and in setting Mr Harrison forth on an improved way of life would be a settlement of his claim for compensation which Mr Harrison feels was a reasonable one. I am not at all sure that he is particularly concerned in obtaining a large amount. I think he is a man with a special background for whom the notion of justice is more important than finite gain.'

There is much in those two paragraphs which redounds to the plaintiff's credit, and that is why I have read them. This is one of the agreed reports and I accept Dr Goody's opinion.

Thus, apart from the permanent loss of the senses of taste and smell, the plaintiff had by March 1975 made a good recovery from a nasty accident. It seems probable, and I accept, that the experience had left him more prone to anxiety and this aggravated the effect of the incident in July 1975. I also accept that the plaintiff was interested in a career on the railways and that the cumulative effect of the two incidents has been to deprive him of the realisation of that ambition. There is, however, no continuing loss of earnings or loss of earning capacity. In these circumstances I assess the general damages for pain, suffering and loss of amenity at £6,500. To this must be added the special damages of £150, making a total of £6,650. The plaintiff is entitled to judgment for 80% of that sum, which I calculate to be £5,320, against the second defendant. His claims against the first and third defendants are dismissed.

Judgment accordingly for the plaintiff against the second defendant for £5,320. Claims against the first and third defendants dismissed.

Solicitors: *Cripps & Shone*, Marlow (for the plaintiff); *Evan Harding* (for the first and the third defendants); *John L Williams* (for the second defendant).

K Mydeen Esq   Barrister.

China Pacific SA v Food Corpn of India
The Winson

HOUSE OF LORDS

LORD DIPLOCK, LORD SIMON OF GLAISDALE, LORD KEITH OF KINKEL, LORD ROSKILL AND LORD
BRANDON OF OAKBROOK

5th, 6th, 7th, 8th OCTOBER, 12th NOVEMBER 1981

*Shipping – Salvage – Cargo – Storage expenses – Agreement – Construction – Vessel stranding
– Master signing Lloyd's standard salvage agreement on behalf of shipowner and cargo owner
– Arrangements made by salvors for storage of cargo ashore – Voyage abandoned by shipowner
Whether shipowner or cargo owner liable for storage expenses ashore – Whether salvors'
authority limited to salving cargo – Whether cargo owner entitled to benefit of storage without
paying for it.*

In October 1974 the cargo owner chartered a vessel from the shipowner to carry a cargo
of wheat from the United States of America to India under a voyage charterparty. On
21st January 1975, in the course of the voyage to India, the vessel stranded on a reef in the
South China Sea, some 420 miles from Manila. The following day the ship's managing
agents in Hong Kong signed a salvage agreement with the salvors in Lloyd's open form
expressed to be made by the master 'as Agent for the vessel, her cargo and freight and the
respective owners thereof'. Under the agreement the salvors agreed to use their best
endeavours to salve the vessel and/or cargo and deliver them to a safe port. Between 10th
February and 20th April the salvors performed salvage services which resulted in the
saving of 15,429 tonnes of wheat, in six parcels. The parcels were taken by the salvors
from the vessel, put into barges which they had provided and taken to Manila. On
arrival of each parcel of wheat at Manila, where the salvors had no premises of their own,
it became necessary for it to be stored under cover in order to preserve it from
deterioration. All the arrangements for stevedoring and the storage in Manila were
made by the salvors. The cargo owner was kept informed of the proposals for the storage
of the wheat on its arrival at Manila and made no alternative proposals for the storage and
made no request to the salvors for delivery of any of the wheat. In making the
arrangements for storage the salvors incurred expenses for which they became personally
liable. On 24th April the shipowner abandoned the voyage and notified the cargo owner
accordingly. On 20th May the salvors gave formal notice of termination of their salvage
services. On 5th August the cargo owner, which had given a guarantee in respect of its
proportion of the salvage award, took possession of the salved cargo at Manila. The cargo
owner refused to pay the salvors the expenses they incurred in off-loading and storing the
salved cargo after its arrival in Manila and before 24th April, when the voyage was
abandoned. The salvors brought an action against the cargo owner in respect of those
expenses. The cargo owner denied liability, contending, inter alia, that the shipowner
was liable to pay those expenses because the cargo was deliverable to the shipowner and
not to the cargo owner on its arrival in Manila by virtue of the contract of carriage created
by the charterparty. The trial judge ([1979] 2 All ER 35) held that the cargo owner was
liable for those expenses, but his decision was reversed by the Court of Appeal ([1980] 3
All ER 556). The salvors appealed to the House of Lords.

Held – Although the contract of carriage created by the charterparty vested the
immediate right to possession in the shipowner as against the cargo owner so long as the
contract remained in being, it did not necessarily follow that it was to the shipowner and
not the cargo owner that the salvors were under a duty to deliver each parcel of cargo on
arrival in Manila. Where in the course of salvage operations cargo was off-loaded from
the vessel by which the contract of carriage was being performed and was carried

a separately from that vessel to a place of safety by means provided by the salvor, the relationship which arose between the salvors and the cargo owner was that of bailor and bailee. That bailment arose as soon as the cargo was loaded onto lightening vessels provided by the salvor, and on parting with possession of the cargo to the salvor the shipowner lost any possessory lien he might have had over it. Under the salvage agreement the salvors' remuneration in respect of salvage services to the cargo was a liability of the cargo owner, not the shipowner, because the salvage form had been signed

b by the master as the agent of, inter alios, the owner of the cargo, and it was the cargo owner, not the shipowner, who was responsible for paying the salvors for salvage services rendered to the cargo. When those services were completed and the cargo owner failed to give any instructions when apprised of the salvors' proposals for the storage of the cargo in Manila the salvors then held the salvaged cargo under a gratuitous bailment which required them to take such measures to preserve the cargo from deterioration by

c exposure to the elements as a prudent man would take to preserve his own property. In return for carrying out those measures the salvors had the right as bailees to be reimbursed by the cargo owner for expenses reasonably incurred by them in preserving the cargo. The appeal would therefore be allowed (see p 692 e f, p 693 e to p 694 a and d to h, p 695 c to h, p 696 g to j, p 697 a b and f to h and p 698 g to j, post).

d Per Curiam. (1) Where a Lloyd's open form of salvage agreement is signed by the master on behalf of a single owner of the whole of a bulk cargo and the salvage services involve unloading it in whole or in part and taking it to a place or places of safety separately from the carrying ship, it does not necessarily follow that, in the absence of subsequent variation either express or to be implied from the conduct of the parties, there is a 'termination' of the salvage services within the meaning of Lloyd's open form until either the whole of the cargo has been brought to places of safety or further attempts to salve cargo that has not yet been brought to any place of safety have been

e justifiably abandoned by the salvor (see p 691 j to p 692 a, p 696 g h and p 698 g to j, post).

(2) The expression 'agent of necessity' should be confined to contexts in which the question to be determined is whether circumstances exist which in law have the effect of conferring on a person authority to create contractual rights and obligations between another person and a third party that are directly enforceable by each against the other

f and should not be extended to cases where the only relevant question is whether a person who, without obtaining instructions from the owner of goods, incurs expenses in taking steps that are reasonably necessary for their preservation is in law entitled to recover from the owner of the goods the reasonable expenses incurred by him in taking those steps (see p 693 a to c, p 696 g h and p 698 g to j, post).

Decision of the Court of Appeal [1980] 3 All ER 556 reversed.

g **Notes**

For the salvor's right to a reward, see 35 Halsbury's Laws (3rd Edn) 733, para 1112, and for cases on the subject, see 42 Digest (Repl) 1040–1041, 8565–8577.

Cases referred to in opinions

Garriock v Walker (1873) 1 R (Ct of Sess) 100, 11 Sc LR 16, 41 Digest (Repl) 393, *368.

h *Gaudet v Brown, Brown v Gaudet, Geipel v Carnforth, Cargo ex Argos, The Hewsons* (1873) LR 5 PC 134, 42 LJ Adm 1, 28 LT 77, 1 Asp MLC 519, PC, 41 Digest (Repl) 391, 1782.

Great Northern Railway Co v Swaffield (1874) LR 9 Exch 132, [1874–80] All ER Rep 1065, 43 LJ Ex 89, 30 LT 562, 8(1) Digest (Reissue) 41, 225.

Morris v C W Martin & Sons Ltd [1965] 2 All ER 725, [1966] 1 QB 716, [1965] 3 WLR 276, [1965] 2 Lloyd's Rep 63, CA, 3 Digest (Reissue) 436, 2958.

j *Notara v Henderson* (1872) LR 7 QB 225, 41 LJQB 158, 26 LT 442, 1 Asp MLC 278, Ex Ch, 41 Digest (Repl) 391, 1783.

Petrinovic & Co Ltd v Mission Française des Transports Maritimes (1941) 71 Ll L Rep 208.

Prager v Blatspiel, Stamp and Heacock Ltd [1924] 1 KB 566, [1924] All ER Rep 524, 93 LJKB 410, 130 LT 672, 1(1) Digest (Reissue) 426, 2993.

Somes v British Empire Shipping Co (1860) 8 HL Cas 338, [1843–60] All ER Rep 844, 30 LJQB 229, 2 LT 547, 6 Jur NS 761, 11 ER 459, 42 Digest (Repl) 1101, 9153.

Appeals

The plaintiffs, China Pacific SA ('the salvors'), appealed by leave of the Appeal Committee
of the House of Lords granted on 23rd July 1980 against the decision of the Court of
Appeal (Megaw, Bridge and Cumming-Bruce LJJ) ([1980] 3 All ER 556, [1980] 3 WLR
891) on 30th April 1980 allowing an appeal by the defendants, the Food Corpn of India
('the cargo owner'), from the judgment of Lloyd J ([1979] 2 All ER 35) given on 28th July
1978 whereby he ordered that the cargo owner should pay the salvors a quantum meruit
payment of $US110,982·25 plus interest of $US29,177·68 at 8% per annum to date of
judgment for services rendered by the salvors to a cargo of wheat belonging to the cargo
owner from the wreck of the steam tanker Winson. The Court of Appeal held that the
salvors were not entitled to be reimbursed for their services. The facts are set out in the
opinion of Lord Diplock.

Anthony Clarke QC and *Jeremy Russell* for the salvors.
Gordon Pollock QC and *Simon Crookenden* for the cargo owner.

Their Lordships took time for consideration.

12th November. The following opinions were delivered.

LORD DIPLOCK. My Lords, the Winson, a bulk carrier owned by a one-ship
Panamanian company ('the shipowner'), was chartered by the Food Corpn of India ('the
cargo owner') to carry a full cargo of wheat from United States Gulf ports to ports in India
under a voyage charterparty in the Baltimore Berth Grain Charter form with numerous
special conditions. The cargo owner is a nationalised enterprise possessing separate legal
personality which the government of India uses for purchasing imports of foodstuffs
needed for that country.

The cargo was loaded in December 1974 and on 21st January 1975, in the course of the
voyage to India, the Winson stranded on the North Danger reef in the South China Sea.
China Pacific SA ('the salvors'), who are professional salvors, were quickly on the scene
and on the following day a salvage agreement with the salvors in Lloyd's open form was
entered into on behalf of the shipowner and the cargo owner. In the course of carrying
out the salvage services to both the shipowner and the cargo owner that the salvors by
that agreement had undertaken with each separately to use their best endeavours to
render, it was necessary to lighten the stranded vessel by off-loading part of the cargo into
barges provided by the salvors and carrying it to a place of safety. This was done, and
some 15,429 tonnes of wheat were off-loaded and carried to Manila which, it is not
disputed, was a proper place of safety. The carriage was in six separate parcels which
arrived in Manila at various dates between 10th February and 20th April 1975. The
salvage operations at the site of the stranding were temporarily suspended on 15th April
1975, owing to fighting in the vicinity having broken out between the forces of North
Vietnam and South Vietnam. It is not disputed that it never became practicable
thereafter to resume the salvage operations, and on 20th May 1975 the salvors gave
formal notice of termination of their salvage services. The Winson with the remainder
of the cargo of wheat still on board her eventually became a total loss.

On arrival of each parcel of salvaged wheat at Manila, where the salvors had no storage
premises of their own, it became necessary for it to be stored in suitable accommodation
under cover, if it were not to deteriorate rapidly from exposure to the elements during
the period before a decision as to what was to be done with it was reached by whoever at
the time that such decision was in fact made was legally entitled to require its removal
from the accommodation in which it was stored. The salvors arranged for the storage of
the salvaged wheat as to part in a vessel, the Maori, lying in Manila Harbour, and as to the
remainder in a bonded warehouse ashore. In doing so they incurred expenses for
stevedoring and charter hire of the Maori and warehouse charges ashore, and the stored
wheat was held to their order by those in whose vessel and warehouse it was stored ('the
depositaries'). These expenses, which the salvors became personally liable to pay under

the contracts that they made as principals with the depositaries, continued to be incurred
a by them until the cargo owner had completed taking possession of the salved wheat,
which it did not do until 5th August 1975.

It is not disputed that storage under cover of the salvaged wheat on its arrival at Manila
was necessary to prevent its rapid deterioration; nor is it disputed that the storage
obtained by the salvors at Manila was reasonably suitable for that purpose or that the
charges paid for it by the salvors to the depositaries were also reasonable.

b The cargo owner has accepted liability for and paid the expenses incurred by the
salvors for the storage of the wheat in Manila after the date on which the shipowner gave
notice to the cargo owner on 24th April 1975 that he had abandoned the chartered
voyage. By that date it was obvious that the completion of the carriage of the cargo in
the Winson to its destination under the charterparty, even if it were to become physically
possible (which, in the event, it did not), would involve such long delay as would
c frustrate the adventure for which the charterparty provided. Assuming that this
stranding was caused by an excepted peril (as to which I understand there may be doubt)
the shipowner had in law an option either to abandon the chartered voyage or to on-carry
the salvaged wheat from Manila to its contractual destination on other bottoms. By
giving formal notice of abandonment of the voyage the shipowner was divested of this
latter option and it is undisputed that the contract voyage terminated on 24th April
d 1975. For some reason, which is not clear, the cargo owners paid the expenses incurred
by the salvors for the storage of the wheat in Manila from 15th April instead of 24th
April, from which later date alone it acknowledges that it was under any legal liability to
do so; but, so far as concerns any issue that your Lordships have to determine in this
appeal, the relevant period for which the cargo owner disclaims liability to reimburse the
salvors for the expenses that they incurred in providing covered storage for the salvaged
e wheat is from 10th February, when the first barge-load of salvaged wheat arrived in
Manila Harbour, until 24th April 1975 when, on receipt by the cargo owner of the
shipowner's notice of abandonment, the contract voyage terminated. The action was
brought by the salvors against the cargo owner to obtain reimbursement of the expenses
incurred by them during this period, and the amount at stake is agreed at $110,982.

I hope that I do no injustice to the detailed and at times elaborate arguments addressed
f to your Lordships in this interesting and novel case if I say that, put in a nutshell, the
main propositions on which the cargo owner's case was based were (1) that, since by
virtue of the contract of carriage created by the charterparty the immediate right to
possession *as between shipowner and cargo owner* vested in the shipowner for so long as that
contract of carriage had not been terminated by performance or otherwise, it was the
shipowner and not the cargo owner to whom the salvors were under a duty to deliver
each separate parcel of the cargo on its arrival at Manila (subject to the provision to the
g Committee of Lloyd's of security for salvage remuneration if this were demanded by the
salvors), and (2) that, accordingly, it was the shipowner, and not the cargo owner, who
was liable to reimburse the salvors for any expenses reasonably incurred by them in
preserving the cargo from deterioration during the period while the contract of carriage
remained unterminated, if they were entitled to be reimbursed by anyone at all.

h My Lords, the way in which I have ventured to summarise the cargo owner's main
propositions, which were rejected by Lloyd J in the Commercial Court ([1979] 2 All ER
35) but appear to have been accepted by the Court of Appeal ([1980] 3 All ER 556, [1980]
3 WLR 891), reflects an assumption that the salvage services rendered to the cargo owner
under Lloyd's open salvage agreement came to an end separately in respect of each
individual parcel on arrival of the barge on which it was being carried at a place of safety
j in Manila Harbour. In each of the three courts through which it has progressed the case
has throughout been argued on that basis and, in the result, nothing that your Lordships
have to decide in the instant appeal turns on whether this assumption was correct or not.
I should not, however, wish to be taken as necessarily accepting that, in the absence of
subsequent variation either express or to be implied from the conduct of the parties,
where a Lloyd's open form of agreement is signed by the master on behalf of a single
owner of the whole of a bulk cargo and the salvage services involve unloading it in whole

or part and taking it to a place or places of safety separately from the carrying ship, there is a 'termination' of the salvage services within the meaning of Lloyd's open form until either the whole of the cargo has been brought to places of safety or further attempts to salve cargo that has not yet been brought to any place of safety have been justifiably abandoned by the salvor.

The instant case came on for trial before Lloyd J in July 1978. No oral evidence was tendered and the details as to what occurred between the time of stranding of the Winson and the completion of delivery to the cargo owner of the salved wheat from the depositaries have to be gleaned in the main from a series of contemporaneous telexes from persons on or near the spot reporting to the shipowner and the cargo owner through their respective agents what was going on. The learned judge's findings of fact based on this material are set out in his judgment, including citations of those passages in various telexes which he regarded as important to his decision. I do not find it necessary to repeat them here or to add to the brief summary that I have already given of them, except to add that, throughout the relevant period from the arrival of the first parcel of salved wheat at Manila Harbour on 10th February 1975 until notice by the shipowner of abandonment of the charter voyage was received by the cargo owner on 24th April 1975, both shipowner and cargo owner were well aware that the cargo on its arrival in Manila Harbour had been put in store by the salvors to preserve it from deterioration and that neither shipowner nor cargo owner had made any request to the salvors for the delivery of the salved cargo or any part of it to either of them.

My Lords, it is not suggested that there is any direct authority on the question of law that is posed in this appeal. In my opinion the answer is to be found by applying to the unusual circumstances of the instant case well-known and basic principles of the common law of salvage, of bailment and of lien.

In part (1) of the cargo owner's main proposition, the statement about the contractual rights *as between shipowner and cargo owner* to possession of the cargo so long as the contract of affreightment remained afoot is unexceptionable; to use a convenient Americanism, it is hornbook law for which no citation of authority is needed. But it does not in my view follow that *as between salvors and shipowner* or *as between salvors and cargo owner* it was to the former and not to the latter or to their order that the salvors would have been under a legal obligation to deliver up possession of the salved wheat on its arrival in Manila Harbour if such delivery had been demanded. (I leave aside for subsequent consideration the parenthetical reference to provision of security; for that relates to a separate and subsidiary argument which has been referred to as 'the lien point' on which the cargo owner would only seek to rely if its main propositions fail.)

Part (2) of the cargo owner's main propositions is predicated on the correctness of part (1). The Court of Appeal regarded the crucial question in the case as being whether part (1) was correct in law. If it were correct (as it held it was), it regarded part (2) as doing no more than state a necessary legal consequence of part (1). For my part, however, even if, contrary to my own view, part (1) of the main propositions were correct, I would not accept that it followed that part (2) also was correct. A person who holds possession of goods as sub-bailee of an original direct bailee of the owner of goods also owes some duty of care towards the owner: see *Morris v C W Martin & Sons Ltd* [1965] 2 All ER 725, [1966] 1 QB 716.

My Lords, with modern methods of communication and the presence of professional salvors within rapid reach of most parts of the principal maritime trade routes of the world, nearly all salvage of merchant ships and their cargoes nowadays is undertaken under a salvage contract in Lloyd's open form. The contract is one for the rendering of services; the services to be rendered are of the legal nature of salvage and this imports into the contractual relationship between the parties to the contract by necessary implication a number of mutual rights and obligations attaching to salvage of vessels and their cargo under common law, except in so far as such rights and obligations are inconsistent with express terms of the contract.

Lloyd's open form is expressed by cl 16 to be signed by the master 'as Agent for the vessel, her cargo and freight and the respective owners thereof and binds each (but not the one for the other or himself personally) to the due performance thereof'. The legal

a nature of the relationship between the master and the owner of the cargo aboard the vessel in signing the agreement on the latter's behalf is often, though not invariably, an agency of necessity. It arises only when salvage services by a third party are necessary for the preservation of the cargo. Whether one person is entitled to act as agent of necessity for another person is relevant to the question whether circumstances exist which in law have the effect of conferring on him authority to create contractual rights and obligations

b between that other person and a third party that are directly enforceable by each against the other. It would, I think, be an aid to clarity of legal thinking if the use of the expression 'agent of necessity' were confined to contexts in which this was the question to be determined and not extended, as it oftens is, to cases where the only relevant question is whether a person who, without obtaining instructions from the owner of goods, incurs expense in taking steps that are reasonably necessary for their preservation

c is in law entitled to recover from the owner of the goods the reasonable expenses incurred by him in taking those steps. Its use in this wider sense may, I think, have led to some confusion in the instant case, since where reimbursement is the only relevant question all of those conditions that must be fulfilled in order to entitle one person to act on behalf of another in creating direct contractual relationships between that other person and a third party may not necessarily apply.

d In the instant case it is not disputed that when the Lloyd's open form was signed on 22nd January 1975 the circumstances that existed at that time were such as entitled the master to enter into the agreement on the cargo owner's behalf as its agent of necessity. The rendering of salvage services under the Lloyd's open agreement does not usually involve the salvor's taking possession of the vessel or its cargo from the shipowner: the shipowner remains in possession of both ship and cargo while salvage services are being

e carried out by the salvors on the ship. But salvage services may involve the transfer of possession of cargo from the shipowner to the salvors, and will do so in a case of stranding as respects part of the cargo if it becomes necessary to lighten the vessel in order to refloat her. Where in the course of salvage operations cargo is off-loaded from the vessel by which the contract of carriage is being performed and conveyed separately from that vessel to a place of safey by means (in the instant case, barges) provided by the salvor, the

f direct relationship of bailor and bailee is created between cargo owner and salvor as soon as the cargo is loaded on vessels provided by the salvor to convey it to a place of safety, and all the mutual rights and duties attaching to that relationship at common law apply, save in so far as any of them are inconsistent with the express terms of the Lloyd's open agreement.

On parting with possession of cargo to the salvor the shipowner loses any possessory

g lien over it to which he may have been entitled for unpaid freight, demurrage or general average. Whether the lien in respect of liabilities of the cargo owner that had already accrued due at the time of parting with possession would revive on the shipowner's recovering possession of the cargo for on-carriage to its contractual destination is a question on which there appears to be no direct authority; but it does not arise for decision by your Lordships in the instant case. The shipowners neither obtained nor

h even sought repossession of any part of the salved wheat after it had been off-loaded from the Winson into the barges provided by the salvors on and before 24th April 1975.

My Lords, in the courts below and in argument before your Lordships there has been some discussion whether, on their obtaining possession of the cargo from the shipowner, the relationship of the salvors to the cargo owner was that of bailee or sub-bailee. A sub-bailee is one to whom actual possession of goods is transferred by someone who is not himself the owner of the goods but has a present right to possession of them as bailee of

j the owner. In the instant case Lloyd J and the Court of Appeal were of the view that the salvors were bailees of the cargo owner, and this was, in my view also, plainly right. They would only be sub-bailees of the cargo owner if the contract to render salvage services to the cargo under Lloyd's open form had been signed by the master as agent for the shipowner only. This was plainly not the case. The contract was one under which the salvors' remuneration in respect of salvage services to the cargo was a liability of the

cargo owner not of the shipowner, and security for such remuneration could be required
by the salvors to be given by the cargo owner alone; so the only consideration for salvage
services rendered to the cargo by the salvors under Lloyd's open form came from the
cargo owner. The only sub-bailments involved in the instant case were those effected by
the salvors themselves with the depositaries when they deposited the salved wheat for
safekeeping at Manila.

It follows from the existence of the legal relationship of bailor and bailee as a matter
of general principle of the law of bailment, which may also be described as hornbook
law, that as between the cargo owner and the salvors the latter as bailees were estopped
from denying the title to the goods of the former as their bailor, including as an incident
of that title its right to possession. Subject to the lien point, which I am deferring until
later, the salvors could not resist a demand for possession of the salved wheat made by the
cargo owner on its arrival at a place of safety by relying on jus tertii, viz the shipowner's
right to possession as against the cargo owner, at any rate until an adverse claim to
possession had been made on them by the shipowner. If demand for possession of the
salved wheat had been made on the salvors by the shipowner (which it never was), the
salvors would have complied with it at their peril. Their only safe course would have
been to interplead, whereas, in returning possession to the cargo owner or in accordance
with its directions before any demand for possession was made by the shipowner, they
would have run no risk of liability to the latter. So I agree with Lloyd J that (at any rate
when, as in the instant case, a salvage contract in Lloyd's open form is entered into on
behalf of a sole owner of a bulk cargo) salvors are under a duty at the conclusion of the
salvage services to deliver up possession of the salved cargo to the cargo owner or in
accordance with his directions. I thus differ in this respect from the Court of Appeal,
but, unlike it, I do not think that the point is crucial to the salvors' claim.

On the assumption, whether correct or not, to which I have already referred as being
that on which this case has been argued throughout, that the salvage services which the
salvors had contracted to render to the cargo owner came to an end as respects each parcel
of salved wheat when it arrived at a place of safety in Manila Harbour, the legal
relationship of bailor and bailee between cargo owner and salvors nevertheless continued
to subsist until possession of the wheat was accepted by the cargo owner from the
depositaries who had been the salvors' sub-bailees. Subject always to the question of the
salvors' right to the provision of security before removal of the salved wheat from
Manila, with which I shall deal separately later, the bailment, which up to the conclusion
of the salvage services had been a bailment for valuable consideration, became a
gratuitous bailment; and so long as that relationship of bailor and bailee continued to
subsist the salvors, under the ordinary principles of the law of bailment too well known
and too well established to call for any citation of authority, owed a duty of care to the
cargo owner to take such measures to preserve the salved wheat from deterioration by
exposure to the elements as a man of ordinary prudence would take for the preservation
of his own property. For any breach of such duty the bailee is liable to his bailor in
damages for any diminution in value of the goods consequent on his failure to take such
measures; and if he fulfils that duty he has, in my view, a correlative right to charge the
owner of the goods with the expenses reasonably incurred in doing so.

My Lords, as I have already said, there is not any direct authority as to the existence of
this correlative right to reimbursement of expenses in the specific case of a salvor who
retains possession of cargo after the salvage services rendered by him to that cargo have
ended; but Lloyd J discerned what he considered to be helpful analogous applications of
the principle of the bailee's right to reimbursement in *Gaudet v Brown, Cargo ex Argos*
(1873) LR 5 PC 134, from which I have taken the expression 'correlative right' and in
Great Northern Railway Co v Swaffield (1874) LR 9 Exch 132, [1874–80] All ER Rep
1065. Both these were cases of carriage of goods in which the carrier/bailee was left in
possession of the goods after the carriage contracted for had terminated. Steps necessary
for the preservation of the goods were taken by the bailee in default of any instructions
from owner/bailor to do otherwise. To these authorities I would add *Notara v Henderson*
(1872) LR 7 QB 225, in which the bailee was held liable in damages for breach of his duty
to take steps necessary for the preservation of the goods, and the Scots case of *Garriock v*

Walker (1873) 1 R (Ct of Sess) 100, in which the bailee recovered the expenses incurred
a by him in taking such steps. Although in both these cases, which involved carriage of
goods by sea, the steps for the prevention of deterioration of the cargo needed to be taken
before the contract voyage was completed, the significance of the Scots case is that the
cargo owner was on the spot when the steps were taken by the carrier/bailee and did not
acquiesce in them. Nevertheless, he took the benefit of them by taking delivery of the
cargo thus preserved at the conclusion of the voyage.

b   In the instant case the cargo owner was kept informed of the salvors' intention as to the
storage of the salved wheat on its arrival in Manila; it made no alternative proposals; it
made no request to the salvors for delivery of any of the wheat after its arrival at Manila;
and a request made by the salvors to the cargo owner through their solicitors on 25th
February 1975, after the arrival of the second of the six parcels, to take delivery of the
parcels of salved wheat on arrival at Manila remained unanswered and uncomplied with
c until after notice of abandonment of the charter voyage had been received by the cargo
owner from the shipowner.

       The failure of the cargo owner as bailor to give any instructions to the salvors as its
bailee, although it was fully apprised of the need to store the salved wheat under cover
on arrival at Manila if it was to be preserved from rapid deterioration, was, in the view
of Lloyd J, sufficient to attract the application of the principle to which I have referred
d above and to entitle the salvors to recover from the cargo owner their expenses in taking
measures necessary for its preservation. For my part I think that in this he was right and
the Court of Appeal, which took the contrary view, was wrong. It is, of course, true that
in English law a mere stranger cannot compel an owner of goods to pay for a benefit
bestowed on him against his will; but this latter principle does not apply where there is
a pre-existing legal relationship between the owner of the goods and the bestower of the
e benefit, such as that of bailor and bailee, which imposes on the bestower of the benefit a
legal duty of care in respect of the preservation of the goods that is owed by him to their
owner.

       In the Court of Appeal Megaw LJ, as I understand his judgment, with which Bridge
and Cumming-Bruce LJJ expressed agreement, was of opinion that, in order to entitle
the salvors to reimbursement of the expenses incurred by them in storing the salvaged
f wheat at Manila up to 24th April 1975, they would have to show not only that, looked
at objectively, the measures that they took were necessary to preserve it from rapid
deterioration but, in addition, that it was impossible for them to communicate with the
cargo owner to obtain from it such instructions (if any) as it might want to give. My
Lords, it may be that this would have been so if the question in the instant case had been
whether the depositaries could have sued the cargo owner directly for their contractual
g storage charges on the ground that the cargo owner was party as principal to the contracts
of storage made on its behalf by the salvors as its agent of necessity; for English law is
economical in recognising situations that give rise to agency of necessity. In my view,
inability to communicate with the owner of the goods is not a condition precedent to the
bailee's own right to reimbursement of his expenses. The bailor's failure to give any
instructions when apprised of the situation is sufficient.

h   So, on the cargo owner's main propositions of law in this appeal I think it fails and that
on these points the Court of Appeal was wrong in reversing Lloyd J.

       Finally, I turn to the lien point. This point does not appear to have been developed
before Lloyd J; it was developed before the Court of Appeal, which found it unnecessary
to deal with it as it was in favour of the cargo owner on its main propositions with which
I have so far been dealing. It was developed fully before your Lordships. The way in
j which it was put, if I have succeeded in following it aright, starts with the proposition
that, in addition to the maritime lien that is expressly conferred on the salvor (or, it may
be, confirmed) by cl 5 of Lloyd's open form and which remains inchoate unless and until
it is crystallised by arrest of the salved property in proceedings brought in a court
exercising Admiralty jurisdiction, a salvor who, after termination of salvage services,
retains actual possession of the property either directly or through his sub-bailee is also
entitled, either under cl 5 or independently of that clause, to a right, partaking of the
legal nature of a possessory lien at common law, to refuse a demand by the owner for

delivery up of possession of his salvaged property until the salvor's salvage remuneration has been secured or paid.

My Lords, the extent to which any possessory lien that a salvor would be entitled to exercise at common law is capable of surviving, or is modified by, the provisions of cll 4 and 5 of Lloyd's open form raises difficult and hitherto undecided questions of law into which, in my view, it is not necessary for this House to enter in the instant case, and it would be unwise for your Lordships to attempt to do so. The only reason why the cargo owner on the failure of its main propositions sought, by this subsidiary proposition, to reach some tabula in naufragio juridiciabile was in order to avail itself of the principle, which it contended was laid down by this House in *Somes v British Empire Shipping Co* (1860) 8 HL Cas 338, [1843–60] All ER Rep 844, to the effect that, where a person entitled to a possessory lien over goods incurs expenses in maintaining possession of them in the exercise of his right of lien and preserving in the meantime their value as security for the owner's indebtedness to him, he cannot recover such expenses from the owner. That case is, in my view, authority for the proposition that, where a lienee remains in possession of goods in the exercise of his right of lien only (ie one who has refused a demand by the lienor for redelivery of the goods with which, in the absence of the lien, the lienee would be under a legal obligation to comply), he cannot recover from the lienor loss or expenses incurred by him exclusively for his own benefit in maintaining his security as lienee and from which the lienor derives no benefit as owner of the goods. I would not seek to suggest that this authority has become outdated for the proposition that was then laid down; but I would deny that it is authority for anything more and, in particular, for the further proposition that expenditure necessary for the preservation of the goods from deterioration from which the owner *does* derive benefit is irrecoverable, where such expenditure is made by a bailee at a time *before* possession of the goods has been demanded of him by the owner and his only right to retain lawful possession of them thereafter rests on his own election to continue in possession, after such demand, in the exercise of the rights of a lienee.

However that may be, the short answer to the lien point in the instant case is that on the facts it never arose. The salvors retained possession of the wheat throughout the relevant period in the capacity only of gratuitous bailees of the cargo owner; they never had occasion to decide whether or not to exercise any possessory or maritime lien they might have had against the cargo owner or to retain possession adverse to the cargo owner in reliance on their rights as lienees; for no demand for delivery of any of the salved wheat to it or its order was made on the salvors by the cargo owners until after security had been provided on 22nd April 1975 by the Indian High Commissioner, and all requests for delivery of possession made thereafter were complied with by the salvors and the depositaries as their sub-bailees.

I would allow the appeal and restore the judgment of Lloyd J.

LORD SIMON OF GLAISDALE. My Lords, I have had the privilege of reading in draft the speech delivered by my noble and learned friend on the Woolsack. Since I am in general agreement with it, and particularly with its argument and conclusion that the salvors are entitled to succeed by reason of their bailment, what follows is by way of marginal comment.

The Lloyd's open form I would myself, like Lloyd J, also come to the same conclusion by implication from the salvage contract, the argument running closely parallel to that on bailment. It was common ground that the contract is incomplete without implication of a term stipulating to whom delivery should be tendered when cargo salved separately from its carrying vessel is brought to a place of safety. I agree with my noble and learned friend that, in the case of bulk cargo the owner of which is known to the salvors, the person entitled to delivery is the cargo owner. The shipowner, by becoming party to and implementing the salvage contract, gives up his possessory lien; and I know of no principle entitling him to repossession merely to reassert a possessory lien. As for his option to on-carry, he can exercise it merely by communication with the cargo owner.

But there is a further matter requiring provision which is not covered by the express terms of the Lloyd's open form, namely what is the duty of a salvor in respect of the cargo after it, or part of it, has been brought to a place of safety but before delivery to whoever

a is entitled to receive it? In my view, if cargo, or part of it, is salved separately from the carrying vessel, it is the duty of the salvor, owed to the cargo owner, to take reasonable steps on its arrival at the place of safety to prevent its deterioration. It is also, in my view, a necessary implication that, if the salvor incurs expense in fulfilling that duty, he is entitled to be reimbursed by the cargo owner. What I venture to submit hereafter, under the heading of 'Bailment', about the correlation of the performance of the duty to

b safeguard the goods on the one hand and the entitlement to reimbursement of expenses incurred thereby on the other, is relevant here; but it would be particularly unreasonable not to imply such correlationship in the context of the commercial nexus constituted by the Lloyd's open form.

Counsel for the cargo owner, in oral argument, urged that, as a matter of pleading, it was not open to the salvors to rely on this implied term in the Lloyd's open form. But

c the case has throughout proceeded on the basis that the salvors could argue that a term providing for reimbursement could be implied from the salvage contract. In my view, it is far too late to raise any pleading point against it.

Bailment Counsel for the cargo owner contended that even if the salvors as bailees owed a duty to the cargo owner as bailor to take reasonable steps to safeguard its goods, there was no correlative right to claim reimbursement of reasonable expenses in so

d acting: neither a bailee for reward nor a gratuitous bailee has any such general right to indemnity. Counsel for the cargo owner adopted the view of the Court of Appeal (see [1980] 3 All ER 556 at 562–563, [1980] 3 WLR 891 at 901) that, apart from specific contractual obligation, a bailee's right to reimbursement 'depends on there being something which can properly be called an element of necessity that the bailee should so act in order to preserve the goods'.

e I agree that there is no general right of a bailee to be reimbursed expenses incurred in fulfilling his duty to safeguard bailed goods; and I agree that there was an element of necessity in the cases relied on by the salvor under this head. But I think that it puts it too narrowly to say that such are the only circumstances in which the law will import an obligation to reimburse, unless, indeed, one is prepared to go further and argue that only a bailee who is an agent of necessity is entitled to reimbursement. No authority so

f stipulates. The relevance of necessity in the cases relied on by the salvors is, in my view, that justice calls for reimbursement in such circumstances: the emergency imposes obligations on the bailee beyond what will generally be contemplated on a bailment.

But such are not the only circumstances in which justice demands indemnity. In my view, the following circumstances in the instant appeal import a correlative obligation to reimburse expenses: (1) the contract of bailment was a commercial one; (2) it came to

g an end when the salved goods were brought to a place of safety, which, it has been the common assumption, was the entry into the port of Manila (though I must not be taken as necessarily indorsing this view); (3) the bailee then continued in possession as a gratuitous bailee; (4) he incurred reasonable expenses in safeguarding and preserving the goods, to the benefit of the bailor; (5) the bailor stood by, knowing that the bailee was so acting to his (the bailor's) benefit.

h *Agency of necessity* Lloyd J decided in favour of the salvors on the further ground that they were the cargo owner's agents of necessity and as such entitled to reimbursement of the expenses in issue. The Court of Appeal held that there was no agency of necessity.

One of the ways in which an agency of necessity can arise is where A is in possession of goods the property of B, and an emergency arises which places those goods in imminent jeopardy. If A cannot obtain instructions from B as to how he should act in

j such circumstances, A is bound to take without authority such action in relation to the goods as B, as a prudent owner, would himself have taken in the circumstances. The relationship between A and B is then known as an 'agency of necessity', A being the agent and B the principal. This was the situation descried by Lloyd J and denied by the Court of Appeal.

Issues as to agency of necessity generally arise forensically when A enters into a contract with C in relation to the goods, the question being whether B is bound by that contract. The purely terminological suggestion that, in order to avoid confusion, 'agent of necessity' should be confined to such contractual situations does not involve that other relevant general incidents of agency are excluded from the relationship between A and *a* B. In particular, if A incurs reasonable expenses in safeguarding B's goods in a situation of emergency, A is entitled to be reimbursed by B: see Bowstead on Agency (14th Edn, 1976, art 67, p 201), Chitty on Contracts (23rd Edn, 1968, vol 2, para 119, p 118) and *Petrinovic & Co Ltd v Mission Française des Transports Maritimes* (1941) 71 Ll L Rep 208 at 220.

To confine 'agent of necessity' terminologically to the contractual situations is justified *b* by the fact that the law of bailment will often resolve any issue between alleged principal and agent of necessity, as it has here. But sometimes the law of agency will be more useful; for example, if available here it would obviate any problem about the correlation of performance of a duty of care with a claim for reimbursement, since an agent is undoubtedly entitled to an indemnity for expenses incurred reasonably to benefit his principal. *c*

However, I respectfully agree with the Court of Appeal ([1980] 3 All ER 556 at 563, [1980] 3 WLR 891 at 902) that—

> 'the relevant time, for the purpose of considering whether there was a necessity, or an emergency . . . is . . . the time when the existence of the supposed emergency became apparent. The emergency would be the arrival, or expected arrival, of salved cargo at Manila, with no arrangements for its off-loading or for its preservation *d* in proper storage having been made or put in hand. There never was, so far as one can ascertain from the evidential matter here, such an emergency.'

In addition to the factual difficulty in treating the case as one of agency of necessity, there are legal difficulties in the way of the salvors. For an agency of necessity to arise, the action taken must be necessary for the protection of the interests of the alleged *e* principal, not of the agent; the alleged agent must have acted bona fide of the interests of the alleged principal: see Bowstead on Agency (14th Edn, 1976, art 21, p 68) and *Prager v Blatspiel, Stamp and Heacock Ltd* [1924] 1 KB 566 at 571–573, [1924] All ER Rep 524 at 528. The Court of Appeal held that the salvors' purpose in storing the salved cargo was to maintain their lien on it (see [1980] 3 All ER 556 at 563, [1980] 3 WLR 891 at 902). This was assuredly at least in part the salvors' purpose. The law does not seem to *f* have determined in this context what ensues where interests are manifold or motives mixed; it may well be that the court will look to the interest mainly served or to the dominant motive. In view of the opinion I have formed on the rights arising by implication from the Lloyd's open form and from the common law bailment, it is unnecessary to come to any conclusion on these issues.

Nor is it necessary to express any view on the arguments based on quasi-contract or *g* estoppel.

LORD KEITH OF KINKEL. My Lords, I have had the benefit of reading in draft the speech of my noble and learned friend Lord Diplock. I agree that, for the reasons which he gives, the appeal should be allowed.

LORD ROSKILL. My Lords, I have had the advantage of reading in draft the speech *h* of my noble and learned friend Lord Diplock. For reasons therein contained I agree that this appeal should be allowed and the judgment of Lloyd J restored.

LORD BRANDON OF OAKBROOK. My Lords, I have had the advantage of reading in draft the speech of my noble and learned friend Lord Diplock. I agree with it and would allow the appeal accordingly. *i*

Appeal allowed. Order of Lloyd J restored.

Solicitors: *Constant & Constant* (for the salvors); *Stocken & Lambert* (for the cargo owner).

Mary Rose Plummer   Barrister.

a   # Ashcroft v Cambro Waste Products Ltd

QUEEN'S BENCH DIVISION
LORD LANE CJ, BOREHAM AND WOOLF JJ
30th MARCH 1981

b   *Public health – Waste disposal – Prohibition of unlicensed disposal of waste – Deposit of waste in breach of conditions of waste disposal licence – Whether necessary to prove knowledge of breach of condition or merely knowledge of deposit – Control of Pollution Act 1974, s 3(1).*

On an information laid under s 3(1)[a] of the Control of Pollution Act 1974 of knowingly permitting the deposit of controlled waste in contravention of a condition of a waste disposal licence, it is not necessary for the prosecution to prove that the defendant
c   knowingly permitted the alleged breach of the condition in addition to proving that he knowingly permitted the deposit of controlled waste (see p 702 *a b* and *h j* and p 703 *a*, post).

Notes
For waste disposal and prohibition of unlicensed disposal of waste, see Supplement to 31
d   Halsbury's Laws (3rd Edn) para 183A.2.
    For the Control of Pollution Act 1974, s 3, see 44 Halsbury's Statutes (3rd Edn) 1200.

Case referred to in judgments
Tesco Supermarkets Ltd v Nattrass [1971] 2 All ER 127, [1972] AC 153, [1971] 2 WLR
    1166, 135 JP 289, 69 LGR 403, HL, Digest (Cont Vol D) 991, 1142a.
e
Case stated
Neil Ashcroft, an officer of the Derbyshire County Council, appealed by way of case stated by the justices acting in and for the petty sessional division of Chesterfield in the County of Derby in respect of their adjudication on 9th December 1980 whereby they dismissed two informations laid by the appellant against the respondent, Cambro Waste
f   Products Ltd, alleging that on 2nd and 4th August 1980 the respondents contravened certain conditions of waste disposal licence LS44 contrary to s 3(1) of the Control of Pollution Act 1974. The facts are set out in the judgment of Boreham J.

Konrad Schiemann QC and Jeremy Sullivan for the appellant.
J Fox-Andrews QC for the respondents.
g
BOREHAM J delivered the first judgment at the invitation of Lord Lane CJ. This is an appeal by way of case stated from a decision of the justices sitting in and for the petty sessional division of Chesterfield in the County of Derby in respect of an adjudication made by them on 9th December 1980.
    On 5th November and 9th December 1980 those justices heard two informations laid
h   against the respondents. Those two informations charged, first, that on 2nd August 1980 at Stretton they knowingly permitted controlled waste to be deposited in contravention of condition 19 of waste disposal licence LS44 by failing to cover solid waste material, namely oil residues, with overburden to a depth of not less than 15 centimetres.
    The second information charged a similar offence committed on 4th August 1980,
j   again at Stretton, again in breach of the conditions of the same licence, this time in respect of particularly dangerous material, namely blue asbestos.
    The primary facts found by the justices in the course of their hearing are set out in the case stated and can be shortly referred to. They found that the respondents operated a

---

a   Section 3(1), so far as material, is set out at p 700 *d*, post

waste disposal site at Morton Road, Stretton under a waste disposal licence, LS44, granted by the Derbyshire County Council on 10th August 1978; secondly, that on 2nd August *a* 1980 oil waste was deposited on that site and was not covered in accordance with condition 19 of the licence (the oil waste was solid waste within the terms of that condition); thirdly, that on 4th August 1980 bags of blue asbestos deposited on that site were not and never had been covered in accordance with condition 28 of the waste disposal licence; finally, that the deposits of oil waste and the bags of blue asbestos were permitted by the respondents. *b*

They went on to make findings that the director, who had overall responsibility for the site, had no knowledge, either actual or constructive, of the contravention of the conditions of the waste disposal licence, though the site foreman had. They found that the practical operation of the site was left to the site foreman, but there had not been delegated to him any of the functions of management. They dismissed both informations. *c*

The statutory provisions which gave rise to these informations are to be found in s 3 of the Control of Pollution Act 1974. Section 3(1), so far as it is relevant to these proceedings, reads thus:

'Except in prescribed cases [and I interpose to say that this is not a prescribed case], a person shall not—(a) deposit controlled waste on any land or cause or knowingly *d* permit controlled waste to be deposited on any land . . . unless the land on which the waste is deposited . . . is occupied by the holder of a licence issued in pursuance of section 5 of this Act . . . which authorises the deposit . . . and the deposit . . . is in accordance with the conditions . . . specified in the licence.'

Before the justices it was contended on behalf of the appellant, who is the prosecutor, first, that it was necessary only for the appellant to prove that the respondents had *e* knowingly permitted the deposit of controlled waste. It was then for the respondents to show that they had a waste disposal licence and that they had complied with the conditions of that licence. In any event it was not for the appellant (the prosecutor) to prove that the respondents had knowledge of the breach of the waste disposal licence.

Second, it was contended that, if the first argument was unacceptable and if knowledge of the breach of the conditions of the disposal licence had to be proved by the prosecutor, *f* the knowledge of the site foreman was sufficient for that purpose. In other words, the knowledge of the site foreman was, in the circumstances here, to be taken to be the knowledge of the respondent company.

Before the justices the respondents took a number of points, but it is clear from the argument put forward here by counsel on their behalf that only one of those points is now relied on. That is, in essence, that it was necessary for the prosecutor to prove not *g* only that the respondents had knowingly permitted the deposit of the waste in question but also that they had knowingly permitted a breach of the conditions of the licence. It is contended that, if that basic contention is correct, it had not been proved in current circumstances that any person concerned with the management of the respondent company had knowingly permitted a breach of the conditions of the licence. Thus the justices came to a correct determination. *h*

In the course of the argument in this court a number of authorities have been cited to the court. In my judgment, it is necessary to refer to but one of them; that is the case of *Tesco Supermarkets Ltd v Nattrass* [1971] 2 All ER 127 at 151, [1972] AC 153 at 193–194 per Lord Diplock:

'Nowadays most business transactions for the supply of goods or services are not *i* actually conducted by the person who in civil law is regarded as the party to any contracts made in the course of the business, but by servants or agents acting on his behalf. Thus, in the majority of cases the physical acts or omissions which constitute or result in an offence under the statute will be those of servants or agents of an employer or principal on whose behalf the business is carried on. That employer or principal is likely to be very often a corporate person, as in the instant appeal.

Consumer protection, which is the purpose of statutes of this kind, is achieved only
a   if the occurrence of the prohibited acts or omissions is prevented. It is the deterrent
effect of penal provisions which protects the consumer from the loss he would
sustain if the offence were committed. If it is committed he does not receive the
amount of any fine. As a taxpayer he will bear part of the expense of maintaining
a convicted offender in prison. The loss to the consumer is the same whether the
acts or omissions which result in his being given inaccurate or inadequate
b   information are intended to mislead him, or are due to carelessness or inadvertence.
So is the corresponding gain to the other party to the business transaction with the
consumer in the course of which those acts or omissions occur. Where, in the way
that business is now conducted, they are likely to be acts or omissions of employees
of that party and subject to his orders, the most effective method of deterrence is to
place on the employer the responsibility of doing everything which lies within his
c   power to prevent his employees from doing anything which will result in the
commission of an offence.'

Then comes perhaps the most important part for present purposes:

'This, I apprehend, is the rational and moral justification for creating in the field
of consumer protection, as also in the field of public health and safety, offences of
d   "strict liability" for which an employer or principal, in the course of whose business
the offences were committed, is criminally liable, notwithstanding that they are due
to acts or omissions of his servants or agents which were done without his knowledge
or consent or even were contrary to his orders. But this rational and moral
justification does not extend to penalising an employer or principal who has done
everything that he can reasonably be expected to do by supervision or inspection, by
e   improvement of his business methods or by exhorting those whom he may be
expected to control or influence, to prevent the commission of the offence ...
What the employer or principal can reasonably be expected to do to prevent the
commission of an offence will depend on the gravity of the injury which it is sought
to prevent and the nature of the business in the course of which such offences are
committed.'
f

It is unnecessary to read further. As I understand it, counsel on behalf of the appellant
relies on that as an approach to the construction of the 1974 Act in this particular case and
urges this court in effect not to be surprised to find that the Act provides an absolute
offence so far as these respondents are concerned.
The contention on behalf of the appellant here is, as I have indicated, that s 3(1) lays
g   down an absolute prohibition to this extent, that any person who himself deposits
controlled waste or causes such a deposit or knowingly permits such a deposit is guilty of
an offence unless it can be shown that that deposit was in fact on land which was the
subject of a licence and that the licence itself authorised the deposit; in other words, it
was a deposit within and in accordance with a condition of any licence. As I have
indicated, counsel's contention is that the burden of proving that the licence applied to
h   and covered the particular deposit in question is on the respondents.
On behalf of the respondents counsel relies on a number of matters in support of his
contention that it lies on the prosecution to prove that there was here a permission to
breach the terms of the licence. He points first to the wording of the informations
themselves. I have read those and repetition is unnecessary.
Second, he contends that s 3(1) is capable of being read in the same sense and to the
j   same effect as the informations themselves; in other words, he says that the words
'knowingly permit' in sub-s(1)(a) must in effect be imported into or control that which
for convenience I call the exception clause, namely that part of the subsection which
follows the word 'unless'. If that is right, then the justices certainly, so far as the first
point is concerned, came to a correct conclusion.
Another way of putting it, as I understand it, is that s 3(1) is in effect properly and

accurately paraphrased in sub-s (4)(c); I will turn to that in a moment. In other words, this is not the absolute offence for which the appellant prosecutor contends.

For my part, I find little assistance, save by way of general approach, from authorities or decisions which relate to other statutory provisions. It seems to me that the meaning of s 3(1) is clear. Both the structure of the section itself and the words themselves impel me to the conclusion that they mean what the appellant in this case contends that they mean, namely that it is prohibited to deposit or cause to be deposited or knowingly permit the deposit of controlled waste on any land unless in fact such deposit is in accordance with the conditions of a valid licence. I do not see how, as a matter of ordinary English, the words 'knowingly permit' or their effect can be imported into the exception clause in the present form.

Subsection (4)(c), on which counsel for the respondents relies heavily, is in these terms:

'It shall be a defence for a person charged with an offence under this section to prove . . . (c) in the case of an offence of making, causing or permitting a deposit or use otherwise than in accordance with conditions specified in a disposal licence, that he took all such steps as were reasonably open to him to ensure that the conditions were complied with . . .'

Two things are to be observed. First, that paragraph only becomes relevant when an offence has been prima facie made out, namely when it has been established that there has been a permitting of a deposit of controlled waste and when it has been shown that the land on which it was deposited was either not the subject of a licence or that the deposit was not in accordance with a condition of that licence, the sort of situation referred to by Lord Diplock in the paragraph from the *Tesco* case quoted above.

Second, I find it very difficult to understand what could be the purpose or effect of sub-s (4)(c) if sub-s (1) were to have the effect or were to be read in the way for which counsel contends. In any event it would be wrong to import into sub-s (1) the sort of paraphrase, if that is the correct word, which appears in sub-s (4)(c) unless perhaps there was some ambiguity or difficulty in construing sub-s (1), an ambiguity and a difficulty which I personally do not find. For these reasons I prefer to construe sub-s (1) as it stands and not by reference to sub-s (4)(c).

There has been before us, in addition to the argument as to the proper construction of this subsection, an interesting argument as to where the burden of proof lies in respect of those matters which appear in what I have called the exception clause in sub-s (1). In view of the decision that I have reached so far as the meaning to that subsection is concerned, it is unnecessary in present circumstances to decide that interesting question, and I prefer to leave it for another day. I say that for this reason. Wherever the burden lies, in this case the justices have found as facts that the deposits of oil waste and blue asbestos were made in breach of conditions of the licence. No question therefore arises at this stage of the proceedings as to the burden of proof; thus I prefer to leave that matter until it arises for decision.

In these circumstances it follows that I have come to the conclusion that the justices were wrong. I would not wish to leave this case without adding that my conclusion implies no criticism of the justices. I have no doubt that they found it a difficult point and, as is clear from the case itself, they applied their minds to the problem carefully and at some length. In those circumstances, whilst I disagree with the result, I wish to pay tribute to the care they have taken.

It only remains to say that, in my judgment, of the three questions set out in the case only one question requires an answer, that is question 1. It reads:

'Whether upon an information laid under Section 3(1) of the Control of Pollution Act 1974 of knowingly permitting the deposit of controlled waste in contravention of a condition of a waste disposal licence it is necessary for the prosecution to prove that the defendant had knowingly permitted the alleged breach of the condition as well as having knowingly permitted the deposit of controlled waste.'

My answer to that question is No.

WOOLF J. I agree.

LORD LANE CJ. I also agree. I too would like to make mention of the care and clarity with which this case has been prepared by the justices and to pay tribute to that method of presentation which is much to be encouraged.

The matter therefore will have to be sent back to the justices with a direction to convict and the appeal is accordingly allowed.

Appeal allowed.

The court refused leave to appeal to the House of Lords but certified, under s 1(2) of the Administration of Justice Act 1960, that the following point of law of general public importance was involved in the decision: whether on an information laid under s 3(1) of the Control of Pollution Act 1974 of knowingly permitting the deposit of controlled waste in contravention of a condition of a waste disposal licence it is necessary for the prosecution to prove that the defendant had knowingly permitted the alleged breach of the condition as well as having knowingly permitted the deposit of controlled waste.

Solicitors: *M W Ingham*, Matlock (for the appellant); *Bradley & Clarke*, Chesterfield (for the respondents).

Dilys Tausz   Barrister.

Practice Direction

Criminal law – Costs – Acquittal – Discretion – Costs of successful defendant – Costs out of central funds unless positive reasons for making different order – Reasons for making different order – Indictments Act 1915, s 5 – Costs in Criminal Cases Act 1973, ss 3, 4.

The Practice Direction issued on 5th June 1973 ([1973] 2 All ER 592, [1973] 1 WLR 718) is withdrawn and the following Practice Direction substituted.

1. The principal power of the Crown Court to order the payment of the costs of an acquitted defendant either out of central funds under s 3 of the Costs in Criminal Cases Act 1973 or by the prosecutor under s 4 of that Act is limited to those cases in which the accused is acquitted on all counts in the indictment.

2. There is a subsidiary and unrestricted power under s 5 of the Indictments Act 1915 to order the prosecutor or the defendant to pay any costs incurred as a result of an amendment to or the severance of an indictment.

3. The exercise of those powers is in the unfettered discretion of the court in the light of the circumstances of each particular case.

4. It should be accepted as normal practice that an order should normally be made for the payment of the costs of an acquitted defendant out of central funds under s 3 of the 1973 Act unless there are positive reasons for making a different order. Examples of such reasons are: (a) where the prosecution has acted spitefully or has instituted or continued proceedings without reasonable cause, the defendant's costs should be paid by the prosecutor under s 4 of the 1973 Act; (b) where the defendant's own conduct has brought suspicion on himself and has misled the prosecution into thinking that the case against him is stronger than it is, the defendant can be left to pay his own costs; (c) where

there is ample evidence to support a conviction but the defendant is acquitted on a technicality which has no merit, here again the defendant can be left to pay his own costs.

5. This Practice Direction is to take effect from 16th November 1981.

5th November 1981

LANE CJ

The following explanatory note was issued with the above direction.

The principal change from the 1973 Practice Direction referred to is that the power to award costs to an acquitted defendant is limited to cases in which the accused is acquitted on *all* counts in the indictment.

The Practice Direction also refers to the court's powers under the Indictments Act 1915. That Act empowers the court to make orders for costs under both s 5 and s 6.

Section 5 provides that the court may make such order for costs as it thinks fit where, either before or at the trial, it orders (i) that a defective indictment be amended under sub-s (1), (ii) that the indictment be severed under sub-s (3), (iii) that the trial be postponed as a result of (i) and (ii) above. The power is expressed in sub-s (6) of the section as being in addition to and not in derogation of any other power.

Section 6 empowers the court to make such orders as to the payment of that part of the costs of the prosecution which has been incurred by reasons of the indictment containing unnecessary matter, being of unnecessary length or materially defective in any respect.

There is a dearth of authority establishing the principles to be followed in implementing these two sections. It appears, however, that (1) under s 5 the court may (a) order the prosecution to pay the relevant costs of a defendant whether he is eventually acquitted or convicted, (b) order the defence to pay the relevant costs of the prosecution where severance is ordered, eg following a late application by the defence which has unnecessarily increased costs, (c) direct the taxing officer to disallow the relevant costs either out of central funds or inter partes either to the prosecution or to the defendant on a taxation carried out under any order made under s 3 or s 4 of the Costs in Criminal Cases Act 1973, (d) make observations for the attention of the taxing officer in respect of legal aid costs, and (2) under s 6 the court may (i) direct the taxing officer to disallow the relevant costs of the prosecution on the taxation of his costs out of central funds under s 3 of the 1973 Act, (ii) direct the taxing officer to disallow the relevant costs inter partes on any taxation of the prosecutor as against the defendant under s 4 of the 1973 Act.

It is suggested that the court should not make any order, give any directions or make any observations without giving the party or parties concerned an opportunity to show cause, if appropriate, after following the procedure set out in the relevant Practice Direction of 7th February 1977 concerning allowance and disallowance of costs out of central funds in criminal cases in the Crown Court ([1977] 1 All ER 540, [1977] 1 WLR 181) and allowance and disallowance by the taxing authority of fees and expenses under legal aid in criminal cases in the Crown Court ([1977] 1 All ER 542, [1977] 1 WLR 182).

Latchford v Beirne

QUEEN'S BENCH DIVISION
MILMO J
27th, 30th MARCH, 19th MAY 1981

Company – Receiver – Duty – Duty to creditors of company – Sale of company's assets – Receiver appointed by debenture-holder selling company's assets to repay debts – Whether receiver owing duty to all creditors to take reasonable care when realising company's assets – Whether duty owed only to debenture-holder.

The plaintiff ('the guarantor') guaranteed loans made to a company by a bank, which took a debenture over the assets of the company. When the company failed to repay moneys due, the bank, in exercise of its powers under the debenture, appointed a receiver of the company, who sold its assets to satisfy the debt owed to the bank. Subsequently the guarantor issued a writ against the receiver claiming damages for negligence and breach of duty in selling the company's assets at what was alleged to be less than their proper value. The guarantor contended that the receiver owed him, as guarantor, a duty to take reasonable care in ensuring that the company's assets were properly accounted for and to obtain a proper price when selling the assets.

Held – The receiver owed no duty of care to the guarantor, for the following reasons—
(1) Any duty of care owed by a receiver to the company to take reasonable care when realising the assets of the company could not, assuming such a duty of care to exist, be extended to each and every creditor of the company, including its guarantors, because of the considerable and possibly insoluble complexity of assessing the damage suffered by each individual (see p 709 *d* to *f*, post); dictum of Lord Wilberforce in *Anns v London Borough of Merton* [1977] 2 All ER at 498 applied.
(2) In any event, since the guarantee gave the bank certain rights without giving the guarantor the benefit of any security held by it or the right to complain about the disposal of that security, the guarantor would have had no redress against the bank if the bank itself had exercised the power of sale, and since the receiver, who was exercising the power of sale on behalf of the bank, could not be in any weaker position than the bank, it followed that the guarantor had no right of redress against the receiver (see p 710 *c d*, post); *Barclays Bank Ltd v Thienel* (1978) 247 Estates Gazette 385 applied; *Cuckmere Brick Co Ltd v Mutual Finance Ltd* [1971] 2 All ER 633 considered.

Notes
For the liability of a receiver appointed by a debenture-holder, see 7 Halsbury's Laws (4th Edn) para 886, and for cases on the subject, see 10 Digest (Reissue) 881–882, 5098–5106.

Cases referred to in judgment
Anns v London Borough of Merton [1977] 2 All ER 492, [1978] AC 728, [1977] 2 WLR 1024, 75 LGR 555, HL, Digest (Cont Vol E) 449, 99b.
Barclays Bank Ltd v Thienel (1978) 247 Estates Gazette 385.
Cuckmere Brick Co Ltd v Mutual Finance Ltd [1971] 2 All ER 633, [1971] Ch 949, [1971] 2 WLR 1207, 22 P & CR 624, [1971] RVR 126, CA, 1(2) Digest (Reissue) 914, 5941.
Donoghue (or M'Alister) v Stevenson [1932] AC 562, [1932] All ER Rep 1, 101 LJPC 119, 147 LT 281, 37 Com Cas 350, 1932 SC(HL) 31, 1932 SLT 317, HL, 36(1) Digest (Reissue) 144, 562.
Home Office v Dorset Yacht Co Ltd [1970] 2 All ER 294, [1970] AC 1004, [1970] 2 WLR 1140, [1970] 1 Lloyd's Rep 453, HL, 36(1) Digest (Reissue) 27, 93.

Preliminary issue

The plaintiff, David Francis Latchford, a director of Van (Self Drive) Hire Co Ltd ('the company'), and the guarantor under deeds of guarantee dated 17th March 1972 and 18th March 1974 of certain advances made to the company by Barclays Bank Ltd ('the bank'), brought an action by writ dated 26th April 1979 in the Brighton District Registry of the Queen's Bench Division against the defendant, Peter Joseph Beirne, who was appointed by the bank under a debenture dated 24th May 1972 to be the receiver and manager of the company. The plaintiff claimed damages for the defendant's alleged negligence when selling the company's assets. On 30th June 1980 Mr District Registrar Penny ordered a preliminary issue of law to be tried, which, as amended with the leave of Milmo J granted on 27th March 1981, was whether the defendant, as receiver and manager appointed under the debenture dated 24th May 1972, owed to the plaintiff as a guarantor of the money secured by the debenture a duty to take reasonable care in ensuring that the assets of the company were properly accounted for and that a proper price was obtained for the assets which were sold by the defendant. The facts are set out in the judgment.

David Unwin for the plaintiff.
David G M Marks for the defendant.

Cur adv vult

19th May. **MILMO J** read the following judgment: This matter comes before the court pursuant to an order made on 30th June 1980 by the district registrar of the Brighton District Registry under RSC Ord 33, r 3 directing that a preliminary issue of law raised in the statement of claim be determined before the trial of this action. At the commencement of the hearing the parties informed me that they had agreed that the issue as stated in the registrar's order should be amended in toto to read as follows:

'Whether the Defendant (as Receiver and Manager appointed under the debenture mentioned in the Statement of Claim) owed to the Plaintiff (as guarantor of the monies secured by the said debenture) a duty to take reasonable care in ensuring that the assets of Van (Self Drive) Hire Company Limited were properly accounted for and that the proper price was obtained for the assets which were sold.'

I agree to this course.

I have to decide this issue on the hypothesis that the allegations of fact contained in the statement of claim, and on which the plaintiff contends that the duty which he alleges on the part of the defendant arises, are true. I am entitled to look at the documents referred to in the statement of claim in so far as they may be relevant to the existence or otherwise of the alleged duty. I am not concerned with the decision whether the allegations in the statement of claim, if proved, would constitute a breach of the alleged duty.

Accordingly, for the determination of the issue before the court, the relevant facts as at 18th February 1980 (the date of the delivery of the statement of claim) are as follows. At all material times the plaintiff was a director and the controlling shareholder of Van (Self Drive) Hire Co Ltd (to which I shall refer as 'the company'). On 17th March 1972 the plaintiff gave to the company's bankers, Barclays Bank Ltd (to which I will refer as 'the bank'), a guarantee of the company's banking account up to £30,000, together with charges, costs, expenses and interest. On 18th March 1974 the plaintiff gave to the bank a second guarantee in identical terms increasing the figure of £30,000 to £40,000. The following terms of these guarantees were referred to by counsel in the course of argument:

'(3) This Guarantee is to be a continuing security to you notwithstanding any settlement of account or other matter or thing whatsoever but may and shall be

determined (save as below provided) and the liability hereunder crystallised (except
as regards unascertained or contingent liabilities and the interest charges costs and
expenses hereinbefore referred to) at the expiration of three months after the receipt
by you from the undersigned of notice in writing to determine it but
notwithstanding determination as to one or more of the undersigned this Guarantee
is to remain a continuing security as to the other or others.

'(4) A demand for payment or any other demand or notice under this Guarantee
may be made or given by any manager officer or agent of yours or of any branch of
yours by letter addressed to the undersigned and sent by post to or left at the last
known place of business or abode of the undersigned or at your option in the case
of a company its registered office and if sent by post shall be deemed to have been
made or given at noon on the day following the day the letter was posted . . .

'(7) This Guarantee is to be applicable to the ultimate balance that may become
due to you from the Principal and until payment of such balance the undersigned
shall not be entitled to participate in any security held or money received by you on
account of such balance or to stand in your place in respect of any such security or
money . . .

'(11) You are to be at liberty without thereby affecting your rights hereunder at
any time and from time to time (whether before or after any demand for payment
made by you under or any notice of determination of this Guarantee or receipt by
you of any notice of any disability or incapacity of the undersigned) to refuse or
grant (as the case may be) further credit to the Principal to renew any bills of
exchange or promissory notes for any period and to compound with give time for
payment or grant other indulgence to the Principal or to any obligant on bills of
exchange or promissory notes or otherwise or to accept compositions from and
make any other arrangements with the Principal or any persons liable to you in
respect of securities held or to be held by you to give up modify exchange or abstain
from perfecting or taking advantage of or enforcing any securities guarantees or
other contracts or the proceeds of any of the foregoing and to discharge any parties
thereto and to realise any securities in such manner as you think expedient . . .'

By a debenture dated 24th May 1972, and made by the company in favour of the bank,
the company granted a fixed and floating charge over all its undertakings and assets to
secure payment on demand of all moneys from time to time due and owing to the
bank.   By cl 6 of this debenture the bank was entitled at any time after demanding
payment to appoint a receiver and manager of all or any of the property thereby
charged.   This clause also provided that the receiver should have power, inter alia, to sell
all or any of the property charged by the debenture in such manner and generally on
such terms and conditions as he should think fit.   Clause 8 set out the order of priority
in which the receiver was to pay out any moneys which he received, namely:

'(a) in satisfaction of costs and expenses of the receivership; (b) in or towards
satisfaction of the monies outstanding and secured by the debenture; (c) the surplus
(if any) to the person or persons entitled thereto.

On 27th July 1976 the bank demanded the payment of all sums due on the company's
current account and loan account, including accrued interest and banking charges (which
sums on that date amounted to £43,830·51) and interest.   On the following day the bank
appointed the defendant to be the receiver and manager of all the property comprised in
and charged by the debenture.

On 26th April 1979 the plaintiff issued a writ against the defendant claiming:

'(1) a declaration that the Defendant as Receiver of the Company negligently and
in breach of duty sold the assets of the Company in or about August 1976 for less
than their proper value (2) damages for negligence and breach of duty (3) all
necessary accounts and enquiries (4) further or other profits (5) costs.'

The statement of claim delivered on 18th January 1980 claimed relief differing somewhat from that claimed in the indorsement on the writ. These read:

'(1) an order that the Defendant indemnify the Plaintiff against any liability under the guarantees; (2) alternatively, damages with statutory interest thereon at such rate or rates and for such period or periods which may be just; (3) such accounts and enquiries as may be just and necessary; (4) further and other relief; (5) costs.'

It is now well settled that a mortgagee exercising his power of sale, in the absence of contractual provision to the contrary, owes a duty to the mortgagor to take reasonable care to get the true market value of the security at the moment when he (the mortgagee) chooses to sell. He is not a trustee of the power of sale for the mortgagor and, if his interests conflict with those of the mortgagor, he can give preference to his own interests (see *Cuckmere Brick Co v Mutual Finance Ltd* [1971] 2 All ER 633 at 643, [1971] Ch 949 at 965–966 per Salmon LJ). I think it necessarily follows that a receiver appointed by a mortgagee to realise the mortgagee's security, although for certain purposes he is the agent of the mortgagor, has a primary duty to protect the interests of the mortgagee who has appointed him and cannot owe a higher duty to the mortgagor than is owed to the mortgagor by the mortgagee himself.

The issue which the court has to decide in the present proceedings is not what duty is owed by the receiver to the mortgagee or the mortgagor, but what duty (if any) the receiver owes to the guarantor of the mortgagor with whom he has no contractual relationship whatsoever. The guarantor of the mortgagor, if and when he discharges his guarantee, may become the creditor of the mortgagor but, until this happens, it was submitted to me by counsel for the defendant that he (the guarantor) is not a creditor of the mortgagor and can, at the highest, only be described as 'a contingent creditor' of the mortgagor. I think that this is a correct analysis of the relationship.

The issue to be decided in this proceeding turns on the tort of negligence and, in the course of argument, I have had a considerable number of authorities cited to me. It is unnecessary for me to refer to all of them and I think that for the present purpose it would suffice if I confine myself to two comparatively recent cases in the House of Lords turning on *Donoghue v Stevenson* [1932] AC 562, [1932] All ER Rep 1.

The first of these is *Home Office v Dorset Yacht Co Ltd* [1970] 2 All ER 294 at 297, [1970] AC 1005 at 1027. Lord Reid said:

'In later years there has been a steady trend towards regarding the law of negligence as depending on principle so that, when a new point emerges, one should ask not whether it is covered by authority but whether recognised principles apply to it. *Donoghue v Stevenson* may be regarded as a milestone, and the well-known passage in Lord Atkin's speech (see [1932] AC 562 at 580, [1932] All ER Rep 1 at 11) should I think be regarded as a statement of principle. It is not to be treated as if it were a statutory definition. It will require qualification in new circumstances. But I think that the time has come when we can and should say that it ought to apply unless there is some justification or valid explanation for its exclusion.'

The second is *Anns v London Borough of Merton* [1977] 2 All ER 492 at 498, [1978] AC 728 at 751–752. Lord Wilberforce, in a speech which commanded the approval of all the other members of the House, said:

'... the position has now been reached that in order to establish that a duty of care arises in a particular situation, it is not necessary to bring the facts of that situation within those of previous situations in which a duty of care has been held to exist. Rather the question has to be approached in two stages. First one has to ask whether, as between the alleged wrongdoer and the person who has suffered damage there is a sufficient relationship of proximity or neighbourhood such that, in the reasonable contemplation of the former, carelessness on his part may be likely to

cause damage to the latter, in which case a prima facie duty of care arises. Secondly,
a if the first question is answered affirmatively, it is necessary to consider whether
there are any considerations which ought to negative, or to reduce or limit the scope
of the duty or the class of person to whom it is owed or the damages to which a
breach of it may give rise (see the *Dorset Yacht* case, per Lord Reid).'

My attention has not been drawn to, nor have I been able to find, any case in which it
has been held that a receiver appointed under a debenture for the purpose of realising the
b security owes any duty to the creditors or shareholders of the company giving the
debenture, or to a guarantor of a debtor company in similar circumstances. Palmer's
Company Law (22nd Edn, 1976, vol 1, p 443) contains the following passage:

> 'The Receiver is entitled to exercise the power to sell in the best interests of the
> debenture holder. It does not matter that the moment of sale may be unpropitious
c > and that he might obtain a higher price by postponing the sale. But it is thought
> that the Receiver is liable to the company if, when carrying out the sale, he acts in
> bad faith or omits to take reasonable care, e.g. if he negligently fails to make public
> important particulars of the property to be sold and consequently the price obtained
> for it is lower than it otherwise would have been.'

With this proposition I would not be disposed to disagree, but it is unnecessary for me to
d make any decision on it in the present case. It is to be noted, however, that the learned
authors of Palmer are dealing only with an obligation by the receiver to 'the company',
that is to say the owner of the security which he is realising. There is no suggestion that
his duty extends to the creditors of such owner. It seems to me that there are no good
grounds for extending any duty which exists beyond the principal debtor and there are
compelling reasons against doing so. It may well be that, in the absence of any
e contractual obligation to the contrary, the defendant in the present case owed to the
bank's customer, that is to say the company, a similar duty to that owed to the customer
by the bank; but if the defendant owes the duty alleged to the plaintiff I fail to see how,
in principle or logically, it can be said that he does not owe a similar duty to each and
every creditor of the debtor company. If each of the individual creditors, as distinct from
the company itself, has a cause of action in negligence against the defendant, the
f assessment of the damage suffered by each individual would present problems of very
considerable, if not insoluble, complexity. For the foregoing reasons, I find that the
defendant did not owe to the plaintiff the duty alleged.

If I am wrong in so holding, I have to deal with a decision of Thesiger J in *Barclays Bank
Ltd v Thienel* (1978) 247 Estates Gazette 385, in which he gave a judgment on an issue
involving the construction to be put on a guarantee containing a clause in identical terms
g to cl 11 in the forms of guarantee in the instant case. I was supplied with a transcript of
Thesiger J's judgment. The case was one in which the defendants were sued by the
plaintiff bank on a guarantee which they had given to the bank of the indebtedness of
one of its customers. Clause 10 of the guarantee given by the defendant to the plaintiff
bank was identical with cl 11 of the guarantee in the present case. Paragraph 5 of the
defence read as follows:

h
> 'It was the Plaintiff's duty to the First and Second Defendants as guarantors as a
> matter of law and/or by necessary implication into the guarantee admitted in
> paragraph 1 of the defence by themselves or servants and agents to exercise
> reasonable skill, care and judgment to obtain the best price reasonably obtainable
> upon any exercise of any such power of sale as the Plaintiff Bank purported to
> exercise in respect of Thienel Shipping leasehold interests.'

j
The plaintiff denied the existence of any such duty. Thesiger J decided the issue in
favour of the plaintiff bank in the following terms (and I read from the transcript):

> 'I do not consider that any such duty is implied in the guarantee ... Clause 10
> read carefully makes it quite clear that far from implying any such duty it expressly

gives the plaintiffs, the bank, certain rights and does not in any way give the
guarantor or surety, that is to say the defendants, the benefit of any security held by   *a*
the principal creditor, the bank, or any right to complain about the disposal of that
security having taken place without due care, skill and judgment. There is no
allegation of any breach of duty to the principal debtor, and there is no authority at
present for imposing on the creditor such a duty to a surety. To extend the
principle laid down in the *Cuckmere Brick* case to this or any case of a principal
creditor and a surety would I understand admittedly be novel. I do not consider it   *b*
would be justified as a development and extension of the *Cuckmere Brick* case, nor
indeed would it be justified by way of any analogy with the cases in which there was
(I emphasise the word "was") prima facie a duty of care where the courts had then
chosen to interpret ambiguous exemption clauses very strictly.'

It is to be noted that in *Thienel's* case the bank itself exercised the power of sale and did
not appoint a receiver. In my judgment a receiver, exercising a power of sale on behalf   *c*
of a creditor, cannot be in any weaker position than the creditor would have been in had
he chosen to exercise the power himself. Following the decision of Thesiger J in *Thienel's*
case, I would hold that, if the bank in the present case had itself acted in exactly the same
way as the defendant is alleged to have done, by reason of cl 11 in the form of guarantee
the plaintiff would not have had any redress against it. I would accordingly have decided
the issue in favour of the defendant on this ground had it been necessary for me to do so.   *d*

Judgment for the defendant.

Solicitors: *Rooks, Rider & Co* (for the plaintiff); *James B Bennett & Co*, Burgess Hill (for the
defendant).

e

K Mydeen Esq   Barrister.

Sampson v Hodson-Pressinger and another

f

COURT OF APPEAL, CIVIL DIVISION,
EVELEIGH, BRANDON AND O'CONNOR LJJ
14th, 15th, 31st JULY 1981

*Nuisance – Noise – Flats – Building converted into flats – Roof terrace constructed above
plaintiff's flat – Roof terrace so constructed as to allow noise to penetrate to flat below – Tenant*   *g*
*in occupation of terrace using it in normal way and for purpose contemplated by lease – Tenant's
use of terrace interfering with use and enjoyment by plaintiff of his flat – Roof terrace constructed
by landlord's predecessor in title – Landlord taking assignment of reversion with knowledge of
disturbance created by use of roof terrace – Plaintiff's lease containing covenant for quiet
enjoyment – Whether landlord liable for nuisance – Whether appropriate case for award of
damages in lieu of injunction.*

h

The plaintiff was the tenant of a flat in a converted house under a 99-year lease granted
on 31st March 1978, which he had previously occupied as a statutory tenant. The lease
contained the usual covenant for quiet enjoyment. Between 1974 and 1978 the flat
above the plaintiff's flat, flat 7, was empty while conversion work was being carried
out. In particular the flat roof situated immediately above the plaintiff's sitting room,   *j*
kitchen and bathroom was converted into an attractive tiled terrace of some 30 feet by
19 feet and french windows were put in the wall of the sitting room of flat 7 so that it
opened onto the terrace. On 11th August 1978 the first defendant moved into flat 7
under a lease in similar terms to that of the plaintiff granted by the same landlord.
Thereafter the first defendant used the terrace in a normal way; she invited friends onto

a   it and occasionally gave a party there. However, because the tiles had been improperly laid, whenever anyone walked on the roof terrace the noise of treading feet penetrated to the plaintiff's flat below and in particular his sitting room and the plaintiff could hear conversations to such an extent that it interfered with his use and enjoyment of his premises. The plaintiff complained to the first defendant and to the landlord. In May 1979 the second defendant showed an interest in buying the freehold of the entire house. The plaintiff told him about the noise from the terrace and showed him an

b   architect's report in which the noise was described as excessive and in which remedies were advocated. The second defendant nevertheless bought the property from the landlord and thereafter denied any responsibility for the noise resulting from the use of the terrace. The plaintiff brought an action against the defendants claiming damages against the second defendant in nuisance and seeking an injunction against both defendants to restrain them from causing or permitting the terrace to be used in such a

c   manner as to cause a nuisance to the plaintiff. The judge in the county court held that the disturbance to the plaintiff from the use by the first defendant of her roof terrace amounted to a nuisance for which the second defendant was liable. The judge awarded the plaintiff £2,000 damages against the second defendant, but he refused an injunction. The second defendant appealed contending, inter alia, that he could not be liable in nuisance because the first defendant was using residential property in a normal

d   way and that, even though the original landlord might be liable, he was not because he was not responsible for the construction of the roof terrace and was unable to control the use of it by the first defendant.

Held – (1) Although the second defendant was not responsible for the construction of the roof terrace, he was liable for the nuisance created by its use because by taking the

e   assignment of the reversion from the original landlord with the knowledge that the terrace was so constructed that its use would cause a disturbance to the plaintiff he took over the original landlord's responsibility for the condition of the premises and their use and, since he was in receipt of rent which was payable to him on the basis that the first defendant was allowed by him to occupy and use the premises in the same way as she was permitted so to do by the original landlord, he was himself authorising the nuisance and

f   was therefore in breach of the covenant for quiet enjoyment. Moreover, he was liable in nuisance notwithstanding that the first defendant was using residential property in a normal way because the property itself was not fit to be used in a normal way so far as the terrace was concerned without interfering with the reasonable enjoyment by the plaintiff of his flat. Accordingly, the second defendant was liable in nuisance and for breach of the covenant for quiet enjoyment (see p 713 *h j*, p 714 *e* to *j* and p 716 *c*, post).

g   (2) In all the circumstances it was an appropriate case in which to award damages in lieu of an injunction, since an award of damages would produce a satisfactory result and achieve finality and was not against the will of the plaintiff. The award of damages against the second defendant would accordingly stand and the appeal would be dismissed (see p 715 *e* to *j* and p 716 *b c*, post); dicta of Buckley J in *Cowper v Laidler* [1903] 2 Ch at 341 and of Viscount Finlay in *Leeds Industrial Co-operative Society Ltd v Slack* [1924] All ER

h   Rep at 264 distinguished.

Notes

For actions for private nuisance, see 34 Halsbury's Laws (4th Edn) paras 359–365, and for cases on the subject, see 36(1) Digest (Reissue) 488–490, 646–662.

    For the grant of an injunction to restrain a nuisance, see 34 Halsbury's Laws (4th Edn)

j   paras 385–400, and for cases on the subject, see 36(1) Digest (Reissue) 499–504, 725–772.

Cases referred to in judgments

Cowper v Laidler [1903] 2 Ch 337, 72 LJ Ch 578, 89 LT 469, 28(2) Digest (Reissue) 1017, 437.

Harris v James (1876) 45 LJQB 545, [1874–80] All ER Rep 1142, 35 LT 240, 40 JP 663, 36(1) Digest (Reissue) 490, 659.

Leeds Industrial Co-operative Society Ltd v Slack [1924] AC 851, [1924] All ER Rep 259, 93 LJ Ch 436, 131 LT 710, HL, 28(2) Digest (Reissue) 1012, 396.

Rich v Basterfield (1847) 4 CB 783, 16 LJCP 273, 9 LTOS 77, 356, 11 Jur 696, 136 ER 715, 36(1) Digest (Reissue) 489, 651.

Wilchick v Marks and Silverstone [1934] 2 KB 56, [1934] All ER Rep 73, 103 LJKB 372, 151 LT 60, 31(2) Digest (Reissue) 647, 5256.

Cases also cited

Brew Brothers Ltd v Snax (Ross) Ltd [1970] 1 All ER 587, [1970] 1 QB 612, CA.

British Office Supplies (Auckland) Ltd v Auckland Masonic Institute and Club [1957] NZLR 512.

Gwinnell v Eamer (1875) LR 10 CP 658.

Hall v Duke of Norfolk [1900] 2 Ch 493.

Hilton v James Smith & Sons (Norwood) Ltd (1979) 251 Estates Gazette 1063, CA.

Kennaway v Thompson [1980] 3 All ER 329, [1981] QB 88, CA.

Metropolitan Properties Ltd v Jones [1939] 2 All ER 202.

Pretty v Bickmore (1873) LR 8 CP 401.

R v Pedly (1834) 1 Ad & El 822, 110 ER 1422.

Sedleigh-Denfield v O'Callagan [1940] 3 All ER 349, [1940] AC 887, HL.

Smith v Scott [1972] 3 All ER 645, [1973] Ch 314.

Wringe v Cohen [1939] 4 All ER 241, [1940] 1 KB 229, CA.

Appeal

By particulars of claim dated 29th April 1980 the plaintiff, Robert Hamilton Sampson, the tenant under a lease of flat 6, 4 Lyall St, London SW1, sought as against the first defendant, Anne Frances Mary Hodson-Pressinger, the tenant under a lease of flat 7, 4 Lyall St, London SW1, and the second defendant, Mr D M Betts, the landlord and freeholder of 4 Lyall St, London SW1, (i) an injunction to restrain the defendants by their servants or agents or otherwise howsoever from causing or permitting the roof garden at flat 7 to be used in such manner as to cause or permit a nuisance to the plaintiff or the occupier of the plaintiff's flat, and (ii) damages against both defendants, limited to £2,000. On 19th June 1980 the first defendant served a contribution notice on the second defendant seeking to be indemnified against the plaintiff's claim. On 3rd July 1980 the plaintiff withdrew his claim for damages against the first defendant. On 1st August 1980 Mr Edward Raw sitting as a deputy circuit judge in the West London County Court held that the plaintiff was entitled to damages of £2,000 against the second defendant but he refused the plaintiff an injunction. The second defendant appealed. The plaintiff served a cross-notice on the defendants seeking a variation of the judgment contending that the judge should have adjudged the plaintiff entitled to a perpetual injunction against the first defendant or/and the second defendant. The facts are set out in the judgment of Eveleigh LJ.

Robert Lamb for the second defendant.
Roderick Cordara for the plaintiff.
James Meston for the first defendant.

Cur adv vult

31st July. The following judgments were read.

EVELEIGH LJ. The plaintiff is the tenant of flat 6 situated at 4 Lyall St, London SW1, which he holds for a term of 99 years from 24th June 1977 granted by a lease dated 31st March 1978. He had previously been a statutory tenant of the flat. At one time

immediately above the plaintiff's sitting room, inner hall, kitchen and bathroom there
a was a flat roof which gave access to a fire escape and two water tanks.

The flat above the plaintiff's, no 7, was empty from 1974 until 11th August 1978,
when the first defendant moved in under a 99-year lease in similar terms to that of the
plaintiff. It was granted by the same landlords. Between 1974 and 1978 conversion
work was done to flat 7. French windows were put in the wall of the sitting room so that
it opened onto the flat roof which I have referred to. That roof was tiled and a decorative
b wall was built using Californian bricks, so that flat 7 had an attractive tiled terrace of
some 30 feet by 19 feet.

Unhappily for the plaintiff, whenever anyone walked on the terrace, the noise of
treading feet penetrated the plaintiff's flat and in particular his sitting room. The first
defendant regarded the terrace as a most desirable feature of her flat. As one would
expect, she invited friends onto the terrace. She occasionally gave a party there. She was
c a thoroughly desirable neighbour, on good terms with the plaintiff, but she insisted on
the right to use the terrace in the way that any reasonable person would who was
ignorant of any particular detrimental effect on the occupier of the flat below. When she
learned that the plaintiff was disturbed by the noise from the terrace she still took the
view none the less that she should not be obliged to modify her use of the terrace or to
put any insulating covering on it. The plaintiff complained to the first defendant and to
d the landlords.

In about March 1979 the second defendant showed an interest in acquiring the
building 4 Lyall Street. The plaintiff had told him about the noise from the terrace and
had shown him an architect's report in which the noise was described as excessive and in
which remedies were advocated. The second defendant, however, bought the property
in April or May 1979 from the landlords. Thereafter he denied any responsibility for the
e noise resulting from the use of the terrace.

The noise complained of is that of people using the terrace, particularly when treading
on the roof. The county court judge visited the premises and heard the noise for
himself. He said that, however 'pleasantly' the terrace was used by the first defendant,
the plaintiff could hear what was going on. He could hear conversations as a result of the
tiles being improperly laid. He said that the noise was a nagging noise and interfered
f with the plaintiff's use and enjoyment of his premises, particularly the sitting room.
However, he held that the first defendant was not liable because she had nothing to do
with the construction of the terrace. He regarded her as an innocent party in nuisance
proceedings. He found the second defendant liable for the nuisance. He refused an
injunction but ordered the second defendant to pay to the plaintiff £2,000 damages.
These he assessed on the basis of the diminution in value of the plaintiff's flat as a result
g of being exposed to noise from above.

The second defendant contended that the noise from flat 7 was not sufficient to
amount to a nuisance. I find this an impossible contention. The learned judge visited
the premises and concluded that the noise did in fact interfere with the reasonable
enjoyment of the plaintiff's flat. The contention of the second defendant was largely
based on the number of decibels recorded when readings were taken of the noise by an
h expert witness; but volume is not the sole test. The judge found the noise to be
aggravating and irritating and was, in my opinion, entitled, on the evidence he heard, to
reach the opinion he did.

It was also contended that the second defendant could not be guilty of a nuisance,
because the first defendant was using residential property in a normal way. The flaw in
this argument, in my opinion, is that the property itself was not fit to be used in a normal
j way in so far as the terrace was concerned. It could not so be used without interfering
with the reasonable enjoyment by the plaintiff of his flat. The use of the terrace put a
strain on the plaintiff that normal use in a normal building would not have done.

The first landlord is not a party to these proceedings. However, it is helpful to
consider what his position would have been had he continued to be the landlord. He
clearly would have been liable in nuisance to the plaintiff. He let the premises to be used

for residential purposes and those purposes, in my opinion, included the use of the
terrace in the way in which the first defendant used it.   It must have been contemplated   _a_
by the landlord that the tenant of flat 7 would walk on the terrace wearing ordinary
footwear and that she would invite others to do so and to converse while there.   He had
himself been responsible for the condition of the premises, which were not in fact
suitable for use in the manner contemplated without causing a nuisance.   It seems to me
that the position of the first landlord falls within the principle in _Harris v James_ (1876) 45
LJQB 545, [1874–80] All ER Rep 1142.   He had let the premises to a tenant for the   _b_
purpose of doing an act likely to cause a nuisance.   In that case the premises were let for
burning lime.   Any hestitation that might be felt in applying the principle to the present
case lies in the fact that burning lime very plainly carries with it the risk of causing a
nuisance and using a flat for residential purposes does not, at least not to the same
extent.   Nevertheless, the possibility of nuisance caused by treading on the floor is readily
appreciated and indeed the lease in the present case contained a provision requiring the   _c_
tenant to carpet the floor boards.   By way of contrast, however, it was clearly envisaged
that the tiles would not be covered.
    The second defendant relied on _Rich v Basterfield_ (1847) 4 CB 783, 136 ER 715.   I do not
think that that case assists the second defendant for the reasons stated by Goddard J in
Wilchick v Marks and Silverstone [1934] 2 KB 56 at 65, [1934] All ER Rep 73 at 76:

> '_Rich_ v. _Basterfield_ was a case of a tenant himself creating a nuisance (in that case   _d_
> by smoke) by the manner in which he used the premises, which could have been
> used without creating a nuisance.   The landlord therefore had done nothing wrong.'

The tenant in that case could have burned coke.   He had not been authorised specifically
to use the fuel he in fact used.   In the present case it is clear that the use made of the
terrace was the very use contemplated by the landlord and the tenant when the lease was   _e_
granted and not a use for which the tenant was solely responsible.
    Apart from the question of common law nuisance, the plaintiff's lease contains the
usual covenant for quiet enjoyment, that is that the tenant may use the premises without
interference by the landlord or those claiming under him.   The contemplated use for
which the original landlord let flat 7 to the first defendant was one which interfered with
the reasonable enjoyment of the plaintiff's flat.   Consequently that landlord was, in my   _f_
opinion, in breach of the covenant for quiet enjoyment.   The plaintiff's enjoyment of the
demised premises was unlawfully interrupted by the first defendant, a person lawfully
claiming under the lessor.   The plaintiff has not pleaded the case on this basis, but it is a
relevant consideration when I later come to consider contribution.
    It has been argued on behalf of the second defendant that even though the original
landlord might be liable the second defendant is not because, it is said, he was not   _g_
responsible for the construction of the roof terrace and he is unable to control the use of
the first defendant's flat.   I cannot accept this contention.   The second defendant knew
that the terrace was so constructed that its use would cause a disturbance to the plaintiff.
It is a disturbance which the judge has held to amount to a nuisance.   With that
knowledge the second defendant has taken an assignment of the reversion and therefore
taken over the role of the original landlord.   He took over that landlord's responsibility   _h_
for the condition of the premises and their use.   I have expressed my view as to the
liability of the original landlord.   I cannot see that the second defendant is in any
different position.   He is in receipt of rent which is payable to him on the basis that the
first defendant, his tenant, is allowed by him to occupy and use the premises in the same
way as she was permitted so to do by the original landlord.   The second defendant is
himself authorising the nuisance.   He too is in breach of the covenant of quiet   _j_
enjoyment.   He is liable in nuisance and for breach of covenant.
    Having reached this conclusion, I find it unnecessary to consider the effect of other
terms in the two leases which have been referred to in argument.   They were by no
means in the forefront of the plaintiff's case.
    In these circumstances, what remedies are available?   There could be an injunction

against the first and second defendants. Alternatively, it is possible to award damages for

a prospective nuisance in exercise of the court's power first introduced by Lord Cairns's Act (the Chancery Amendment Act 1858). In addition, damages could be granted to cover the period up to the date of trial. It is not clear on what precise legal basis the learned judge awarded the sum of £2,000. I do not think it matters for the purpose of this appeal provided this court is satisfied that the award can be justified in law.

To grant an injunction against both defendants is likely to produce a situation which

b will be very unsatisfactory from the first defendant's point of view and probably unfair to her. If the court were to grant an injunction against her an injunction against the landlord would be unnecessary. However, the first defendant would then no doubt consider whether or not she had any remedy against the second defendant or against the original landlord. She did serve a notice in the present case claiming contribution against the second defendant in respect of any damages and costs which she might be ordered to

c pay to the plaintiff and in respect of her own costs of defending the action. In the event the plaintiff withdrew his claim for damages against the first defendant hoping to remain on good terms with her, but the judge did grant her an indemnity in respect of her costs of defending the action. As drafted, the contribution notice is not in such terms as would enable the court to determine issues which might arise under the terms of the first defendant's lease if the court were to grant an injunction against the first

d defendant. For example, there might be a contention that, as the injunction resulted from the act of a person claiming under the landlord (ie the plaintiff himself), the landlord was in breach of his covenant with the first defendant for quiet enjoyment. Moreover, the court has been told that the plaintiff would prefer to uphold the judgment which he has obtained rather than to seek injunctions. The figure of £2,000 may not be enough to carry out the necessary remedial works, but, while the court has not been

e given any details, it does appear that, at least as between the plaintiff and the first defendant, something can be done to remedy the situation. As we are told that, it seems to me that this really is a case where an award of damages would produce a satisfactory result and achieve finality. However, on behalf of the landlord, it was contended that the court should not make such an award. It was said that the court should only grant damages for a prospective nuisance in exceptional circumstances and in very simple

f cases, which it was said this case was not.

A common argument against the award of damages as opposed to an injunction is that to do so would legalise or license the commission of future torts. In my opinion, while this argument may have merit when submitted by the plaintiff, it has much less strength when invoked by a defendant. In *Leeds Industrial Co-operative Society Ltd v Slack* [1924] AC 851 at 861, [1924] All ER Rep 259 at 264 Viscount Finlay quoted from the judgment

g of Buckley J in *Cowper v Laidler* [1903] 2 Ch 337 at 341:

> " 'The court has affirmed over and over again that the jurisdiction to give damages where it exists is not so to be used as in fact to enable the defendant to purchase from the plaintiff against his will his legal right to the easement.'

In the present case we would not be granting damages against the will of the plaintiff.

h That is an important consideration. In the above case the House of Lords held that it was right to grant damages as opposed to an injunction where the plaintiff's right to light was threatened by the construction of a building which had not yet reached such a height as to deprive the plaintiff's premises of light. That case also established that the power to award damages was available although Lord Cairns's Act had been repealed. I for my part then would regard the present case as an appropriate one in which to award damages

j in lieu of an injunction. It is unnecessary to state a specific figure in respect of the nuisance for the period preceding the trial and to give detailed reasons to justify any particular figure in respect of prospective nuisance. This is because the evidence establishes, as the learned judge himself thought, that an appropriate figure would exceed that which could be awarded in the county court.

Strictly speaking, there could be an award in damages against both defendants. Had the plaintiff not withdrawn his claim against the first defendant I would have made an award against her. However, I regard this as a case in which she would have been entitled to a complete indemnity from the original landlord. The original landlord had let to her premises which could not be used in the manner contemplated by the lease. These are matters which are relevant, in my opinion, when considering a claim for contribution between tortfeasors when the court in its discretion is deciding what is just as between the parties. As between these defendants I regard the first defendant as an innocent party in spite of her liablity to the plaintiff.

As I would uphold an award of damages against the second defendant it follows that it would be inappropriate to grant an injunction against the first defendant. The plaintiff is accepting damages in lieu of his right to complain of nuisance in the future. There is, therefore, no basis on which an injunction can be granted against the first defendant. I would dismiss this appeal.

BRANDON LJ. I agree.

O'CONNOR LJ. I agree.

Appeal dismissed.

Solicitors: *Franks, Charlesly & Co* (for the second defendant); *Stoneham, Langton & Passmore* (for the plaintiff); *Joynson-Hicks & Co* (for the first defendant).

Mary Rose Plummer   Barrister.

Tate & Lyle Food and Distribution Ltd v Greater London Council and another

QUEEN'S BENCH DIVISION
FORBES J
28th, 29th, 30th APRIL, 1st, 22nd MAY 1981

Damages – Tort – Special damage – Proof of damage – Plaintiff engaged in trade – Plaintiff expending managerial time in remedying wrong – Defendant negligent in failing to dredge away siltation over river bed – Plaintiff expending managerial time on remedying siltation – Whether expenditure of managerial time on remedying defendant's negligence recoverable as head of special damage – Whether plaintiff required to adduce direct evidence of time expended in remedying wrong.

Interest – Damages – Commercial cases – Appropriate rate of interest on damages – Method of assessing appropriate rate – Period over which interest allowed – Damages awarded to plaintiff for dredging costs incurred when defendant wrongfully failed to dredge away siltation in river bed – Dredging costs incurred in 7 out of 14 years after negligence occurring – Plaintiff deducting dredging costs from gross income for purposes of corporation tax – Whether plaintiff entitled to commercial rate of interest or rate of interest on short-term investment account awarded in personal injury claims – Whether tax saving made by plaintiff deductible from damages in awarding interest.

The first defendant's construction of ferry terminals on the bank of the River Thames, carried out with the consent and approval of the second defendant, the river authority, caused siltation over the bed of the river which diminished the depth of the water up river from the terminals. When the first defendant failed to dredge it away, the plaintiffs, who carried on business up river as sugar refiners and lightermen respectively at premises *a*   which included wharves, jetties and berths, incurred over a period of seven years from 1967 to 1974 dredging costs amounting to £550,000 in removing the siltation. The plaintiffs deducted the dredging costs from their gross income for the purpose of assessing liability to corporation tax and thereby made a saving in tax of £239,153. The plaintiffs brought an action against the defendants claiming, inter alia, damages for negligence and they included a claim for special damages for (i) the dredging costs and (ii) managerial and supervisory resources expended in remedying the siltation which they quantified at

b   2·5% of their total loss and damage. At the trial of the action in 1980 the judge held, inter alia, that the defendants were liable in negligence to the plaintiffs for their failure to dredge away the siltation. The quantum of the damages was adjourned for further hearing. The parties then reached agreement on quantum, namely that the plaintiffs should recover £550,000 for their expenditure on dredging costs, but the defendants disputed the plaintiffs' claim for damages for managerial and supervisory resources

c   expended in remedying the siltation, on the ground that that was not a recoverable head of damage. At a further hearing at which that disputed head of damage and the appropriate award of interest on the damages recovered were considered, the plaintiffs contended (i) that, although they had not adduced direct evidence of the managerial time they had deployed on remedying the siltation, by analogy with the Admiralty practice of allowing a shipowner in a collision case to claim damages for expenses incurred and

d   work done in his office due to the collision at the rate of 1% of the total collision damage, the plaintiffs should be allowed to claim 2·5% of their total damages for the managerial time expended on remedying the siltation, and (ii) that, in regard to the interest to be awarded on the damages recovered, it should be calculated at a commercial rate of interest but disregarding the particular position of the plaintiffs and should be calculated at that rate over the whole period up to the date of the trial, and, further, that the

e   £239,153 saving in tax effected by the plaintiffs should not be deducted from the damages when it came to awarding interest. The plaintiffs submitted that under the principle that the particular position of the plaintiff was not to be looked at in awarding interest the way in which the plaintiffs had ordered their affairs in regard to taxation was irrelevant, that the plaintiffs would have to pay tax on the award of damages and the current rate of corporation tax was higher than the rate prevailing when they claimed

f   relief for the dredging costs, and that the incidence of inflation was to be taken into account. There was evidence that the plaintiffs had in fact expended managerial time in taking measures to remedy the siltation which otherwise might have been spent on their trading activities but, although it would have been possible for them to keep office records of the time so spent, they had not done so.

g   **Held** – (1) The expenditure of managerial time in remedying an actionable wrong done to a trading concern could properly form the subject matter of special damage which could be claimed by the concern. However, by failing to record the managerial time spent on remedying the siltation, the plaintiffs had failed to prove the special damage under that head, and in the absence of proof the court would not speculate on quantum by awarding as the damages under that head a percentage of the plaintiffs' total

h   damages. Accordingly, the claim for damages for the expenditure of managerial time in remedying the siltation failed (see p 721 *a* to *f*, post).

(2) Under the recognised principle that the award of interest on damages was part of the attempt to achieve restitutio in integrum the award of interest in commercial cases was intended to reflect the rate at which the plaintiff would have had to borrow money in place of the money which had been wrongfully withheld from him by the defendant,

j   but disregarding any special position of the plaintiff, as, for example, where because of his personal position he could borrow only at a very high rate of interest or, conversely, could borrow at especially favourable rates. The guide to interest in commercial cases was, therefore, the rate at which a plaintiff with the general attributes of the actual plaintiff could have borrowed the money wrongfully withheld, and not the earning capacity of the money if the plaintiff had invested it during the time he was kept out of

it, and, accordingly was not the uncommercial rate of interest on short-term investment
account awarded on damages in personal injury cases or on judgment debts. In the *a*
circumstances, interest on the total damages would be calculated at 1% over minimum
lending rate since that rate formed the background to the financial arrangements of
commercial men and there was evidence that public companies of the size and prestige
of the plaintiffs could expect to borrow at that rate. The period over which that rate of
interest would be allowed was that adopted by the plaintiffs in their computation,
namely that dredging invoices paid during any calendar year were to be aggregated year *b*
by year, and interest at the appropriate rate of 1% above minimum lending rate was to
be calculated on the accumulating total of the dredging costs year by year until the date
of trial. However, the plaintiffs were required to bring into account in the interest
computation the amount of corporation tax they had saved by claiming relief for the
dredging costs, since the particular borrowing position of the plaintiffs could not be
disregarded and the saving ignored in awarding interest; nor could that saving be *c*
ignored because of inflation since the incidence of inflation could not be taken into
account in assessing damages. Accordingly a sum to take account of the plaintiffs' tax
saving would be deducted from the award of interest (see p 722 *d* to *h*, p 723 *b* to *d* and
h j and p 724 *b* to p 725 *b*, post).

Per Curiam. Where a sum of money accrues week by week over a period and interest
on it has to be calculated, the total interest is in effect a product of the amount, the *d*
interest rate and the period. The mathematical short cut available to solve the problem
is to halve any one of those parameters (see p 723 *e f*, post); dictum of Lord Denning MR
in *Jefford v Gee* [1970] 1 All ER at 1208 applied.

Notes

For special damage, see 12 Halsbury's Laws (4th Edn) para 1113.
    For proof of special damage, see ibid paras 1197–1198. *e*
    For general principles governing the measure of damages, see ibid paras 1127–1129,
and for cases on the subject, see 17 Digest (Reissue) 87–90, 32–46.
    For interest on damages, see 12 Halsbury's Laws (4th Edn) para 1204.

Cases referred to in judgment

BP Exploration Co (Libya) Ltd v Hunt (No 2) [1979] 1 WLR 783. *f*
British Transport Commission v Gourley [1955] 3 All ER 796, [1956] AC 185, [1956] 2 WLR
    41, 220 LT 354, [1955] 2 Lloyd's Rep 475, [1955] TR 303, 34 ATC 305, 49 R & IT 11,
    HL, 17 Digest (Reissue) 88, 35.
Cremer v General Carriers SA [1974] 1 All ER 1, [1974] 1 WLR 341, [1973] 2 Lloyd's Rep
    366, Digest (Cont Vol D) 694, 243a.
FMC (Meat) Ltd v Fairfield Cold Stores Ltd [1971] 2 Lloyd's Rep 221. *g*
Helmsing v Malta Drydocks Corpn [1977] 2 Lloyd's Rep 444.
Jefford v Gee [1970] 1 All ER 1202, [1970] 2 QB 130, [1970] 2 WLR 702, [1970] 1 Lloyd's
    Rep 107, CA, Digest (Cont Vol C) 709, 182a.
Liesbosch (Dredger) (Owners) v Owners of Steamship Edison, The Liesbosch [1933] AC 449,
    [1933] All ER Rep 144, 102 LJP 73, 149 LT 49, 38 Com Cas 267, 18 Asp MLC 380, 45
    Ll L Rep 123, HL, 17 Digest (Reissue) 103, 113. *h*
London, Chatham and Dover Railway Co v South Eastern Railway Co [1893] AC 429, 63 LJ Ch
    93, 69 LT 637, 58 JP 36, 1 R 275, HL, 25 Digest (Repl) 209, 159.
Miliangos v George Frank (Textiles) Ltd [1975] 3 All ER 801, [1976] AC 443, [1975] 3 WLR
    758, [1976] 1 Lloyd's Rep 201, HL, Digest (Cont Vol D) 691, 64c.

Action

By a writ issued on 25th March 1971, amended and reamended on 15th February and *j*
27th March 1980, and a reamended statement of claim served on 29th April 1981, the
plaintiffs, Tate & Lyle Food and Distribution Ltd, the owner and occupier of a sugar
refinery, the Thames Refinery, on the north bank of the River Thames in Woolwich
Reach, together with adjoining wharves, jetties and berths, and Silvertown Services
Lighterage, the occupier of part of the Thames Refinery and the owner and occupier of

barge moorings known as no 7 Silvertown Barge Roads, Silvertown Services Barge Pier
and North Woolwich Barge Roads from which it carried on business as lightermen,
alleged that works carried out by the first defendant, the Greater London Council ('the
GLC'), in constructing two piers about 3,000 feet down river of the plaintiffs' premises
for the use of the Woolwich Ferry, which were commenced in 1964 and executed with
the knowledge, consent, approval and permission of the second defendant, the Port of
London Authority ('the PLA'), caused, from January 1965, changes in the rate of siltation

b over the river bed and thus diminished the depth of the waters on the north side of
Woolwich Reach and thereby infringed the plaintiffs' rights and caused them loss and
damage in that access to their land and buildings by vessels including barges was
seriously restricted, previously safe berths became unsafe, barges were damaged, delay
was caused to loading and unloading operations, the intakes to pumps at the first
plaintiff's jetties were blocked by silt and the supply of river water to the condensers at

c its refinery was diminished. The plaintiffs claimed that those infringements constituted
nuisance and negligence on the part of the GLC and the PLA and sought as against them
(i) injunctions to remedy and abate the nuisance and to restore the river bed in the area
of the plaintiffs' premises, (ii) damages including special damages for surveying and
dredging costs incurred and also for managerial and supervisory resources expended by
the plaintiffs in remedying the siltation which they quantified at 2·5% of their total loss

d and damage, and (iii) interest on the damages recovered. On 15th May 1980 Forbes J
gave judgment on liability and held, inter alia, that the GLC and the PLA were liable in
negligence to the plaintiffs because they failed to dredge away the siltation caused in
constructing the piers. The quantum of damages was left for further hearing. The
parties reached agreement on quantum save for the plaintiffs' claim for managerial and
supervisory resources expended on remedying the siltation which the defendant

e submitted was not a recoverable head of damage. There also remained for determination
the appropriate award of interest on the damages recovered. The following judgment
deals with the disputed head of damage and the award of interest. The facts are set out
in the judgment.

Anthony Clarke QC and Charles Haddon-Cave for the plaintiffs.
f John Davies QC and Charles Gibson for the GLC.
Graeme Hamilton QC and Christopher Purchas for the PLA.

                                                                    Cur adv vult

22nd May. **FORBES J** read the following judgment: On 15th May 1980, after a long
g trial, I gave judgment on the question of liability in this case. The quantum of damages
was left for a further hearing. Now the parties, very sensibly, have agreed the quantum
of damages, subject to one point, and there has been consequent argument on the
question of the appropriate award of interest on the agreed damages. If I may take the
agreement on damages first.
It has been agreed that the second plaintiff should recover damages amounting to
h £200 with costs on the High Court scale on terms that neither defendant will contend
hereafter that the second plaintiff should not be entitled to costs on the issue of liability
merely on the ground that they only recovered so small a sum.
It has been agreed that the first plaintiff should recover £10,000 as representing
additional dredging survey costs and £540,000 representing the cost of additional
dredging caused by the siltation for which both defendants are liable. This agreement
j is on the express basis that (a) the defendants are liable for all the dredging carried out by
the first plaintiff at Silvertown save only for the cost of dredging 40,500 cubic yards per
annum at the Raw Sugar Jetty and 1,000 cubic yards per annum at the Refined Sugar
Jetty, and (b) the agreement is subject to, and pending, the defendants' appeal to the
Court of Appeal on liability and is subject to such order as the Court of Appeal may
make.
There remains, as I indicated, one point in relation to damages. The first plaintiff

claims that it has 'expended managerial and supervisory resources in attending to the
problems created by the infringement of [its] rights'. Originally, the first plaintiff a
asserted that such expenditure could not be quantified, but by a reamendment it now
claims such expenditure at 2·5% of the total loss and damage. Counsel for the plaintiffs
accepts that there is no direct evidence, other than passing references, of the fact that such
managerial and supervisory resources were expended or of the extent to which
managerial time was deployed on attending to the problems involved. He takes his
stand on established practice in the Admiralty Court (this case was started as an Admiralty b
case) and he has referred me to standard textbooks on Admiralty practice. Apparently,
it is usual in Admiralty collision cases for the judge to decide the issue of liability and for
all questions of damage to be subsequently referred to the arbitrament of the registrar
sitting with 'merchants'. One of the items usually allowed, without proof, is known as
'Agency'. I quote from Marsden on Collisions at Sea (11th Edn, 1971, para 520):

> 'In cases of damage to vessels, the most usual causes of loss to the claimant (apart c
> from detention which will be considered later) are out of pocket expenses. These
> may be recovered as damages from the wrongdoer. They may be classified as
> follows . . . (6) Agency, that is to say certain miscellaneous expenses and work based
> on the disturbance and extra work which a collision causes in the shipowner's office
> and those of his agents in ports, e.g. making fresh arrangements for the use of the
> vessel, paying accounts, etc. Agency is allowed as a single sum without strict proof, d
> and is assessed as far as possible on the probable expense incurred and work done
> which would not have been necessary if there had been no collision. Underwriters'
> agency is not, however, recoverable in so far as differing from owners' agency.
> Superintendence may also be recovered.'

Counsel for the plaintiffs tells me that the usual figure is taken as 1% of the collision e
damage because any exact computation of the expense due to the 'disturbance and extra
work which a collision causes in the shipowner's office' is almost impossible. He also
referred me to a passage in *Owners of Dredger Liesbosch v Owners of Steamship Edison* [1933]
AC 449 at 468, [1933] All ER Rep 144 at 162 per Lord Wright:

> '. . . compensation for disturbance and loss . . . including in that loss such items as
> overhead charges, expenses of staff and equipment, and so forth thrown away . . .' f

I do not think, however, that the *Edison* case helps counsel. I think Lord Wright in the
passage quoted was dealing with the expenses of retaining staff and hired equipment for
the period for which they could not usefully be employed because there was no dredger
available to carry on with the dredging contract, and not with the cost of staff time
involved in remedying the injury.
Counsel for both the GLC and the PLA suggest that an item of damages under this g
head and calculated in this way is unknown in a Queen's Bench action; in addition,
counsel for the GLC maintains that managerial expenses could only be recovered as loss
of profit, and counsel for the PLA that they might be recovered if quantified by acceptable
evidence, but that there is no such evidence here.
The problem, it seems to me, resolves itself into two constituents. (a) Is there any h
warrant for suggesting that managerial time, which otherwise might have been engaged
on the trading activities of the company, had to be deployed on the initiation and
supervision of remedial work (excluding anything which might properly be regarded as
preparation for litigation)? (b) If so, could this reasonably have been the subject of
evidence, or is it so difficult to quantify that the application of some suitable rule of
thumb is justified?
I think there is evidence that managerial time was in fact expended on dealing with j
remedial measures. There were a whole series of meetings, in which the first plaintiff's
top managerial people took a leading role, the object of which was to find out what could
be done to remedy the situation and to persuade the defendants to do something about
it. In addition, while there is no evidence about the extent of the disruption caused, it is

clear that there must have been a great deal of managerial time involved in dealing with
a the dredging required and in rearranging berthing schedules and so on at the Raw Sugar
Jetty to enable the delivery of material to the refinery to proceed without interruption.
I have no doubt that the expenditure of managerial time in remedying an actionable
wrong done to a trading concern can properly form the subject matter of a head of special
damage. In a case such as this it would be wholly unrealistic to assume that no such
additional managerial time was in fact expended. I would also accept that it must be
b extremely difficult to quantify. But modern office arrangements permit of the recording
of the time spent by managerial staff on particular projects. I do not believe that it would
have been impossible for the plaintiffs in this case to have kept some record to show the
extent to which their trading routine was disturbed by the necessity for continual
dredging sessions. In the absence of any evidence about the extent to which this
occurred the only suggestion counsel for the plaintiffs can make is that I should follow
c Admiralty practice and award a percentage on the total damages. But what
percentage? Counsel for the plaintiffs claims 2·5% but tells me that the usual Admiralty
figure is 1%, and this appears to cover the work of port agents as well as that in the
shipowner's office. While I am satisfied that this head of damage can properly be
claimed, I am not prepared to advance into an area of pure speculation when it comes to
quantum. I feel bound to hold that the plaintiffs have failed to prove that any sum is due
d under this head.
   There is an additional complication. The plaintiffs have succeeded not because the
defendants caused siltation at Silvertown (a great deal of the siltation which occurred was
the inevitable result of the exercise of statutory powers) but because the defendants failed
to dredge away the silt which was deposited. Now, on the hypothesis that the defendants
ought to have dredged, such dredging operations would themselves be the inevitable
e result (at least pro tanto) of the exercise of parliamentary powers, so that the plaintiffs
could not claim for disruption caused to their trading operations by all the work of
dredging, and the cost of the managerial time involved in overcoming such disruption
would thus not be wholly recoverable. As it might be necessary to analyse the disruption
and to attribute so much to dredging away the 40% siltation inevitably caused by the
adoption of the best design for the terminals, the computation becomes much too
f complicated to be solved with justice to all sides by any rule of thumb application of any
percentage.
   The main issue which remains is that of the interest to be awarded on the sum
recovered. There are three points which must be decided: (a) what is the appropriate rate
of interest, (b) over what period should it be allowed (though these points can
conveniently be taken together), and (c) what relevance, if any, has the fact that the
g plaintiffs treated all dredging costs as trading expenses and deducted them from their
gross income for corporation tax purposes?
   Broadly, counsel for the plaintiffs contends that the rate should be that at which a
commercial borrower could ordinarily borrow money in the relevant period, disregarding
the particular position of the plaintiffs themselves. As for the period, counsel for the
plaintiffs maintains that interest is payable over the whole period at the appropriate rate
h then current on the running total of the amount of the dredging costs (including survey
costs) actually incurred by the plaintiffs.
   Counsel for the GLC makes a number of submissions. The first is the rather
extraordinary one, for which no authority was quoted, that in assessing damages 'one
takes them at their lowest ebb against the plaintiff'. If this means any more than the
proposition that the plaintiff must prove his damage in the same way as he must prove
j any other essential ingredient of his case, then I can see no warrant for favouring the
defendant at the expense of the plaintiff. The second point of counsel for the GLC is that,
in considering interest, one must look to see whether there is any evidence that the
plaintiff would have made such good use of the money if he had had it as would have
given him as good a return as the interest rate; and this he says would involve an
investigation of the profitability of the business. Finally, he says that the appropriate

computation would be to average the short-term interest rate for the first six years (a figure of 7·41%) and then halve that; and award 8% as a sensible figure from 1975, that being the year after which (for the purposes of this action) it has been accepted that no further dredging costs were incurred by the plaintiffs, and the year, therefore, from which the full amount of the damages became due to the plaintiffs.

Counsel for the second plaintiff does not, I think, challenge the proposition that a commercial rate of interest is appropriate in this case. He says that bank rate (or MLR), short-term interest rates and the rate of interest on judgment debts are now virtually all in line, that it would be anomalous to have different rates of interest awarded by the courts in personal injury cases (where short-term investment rates are usually taken) and commercial cases. In addition, he made passing reference to the length of time over which the interest would be payable (14 years) and to the fact that it is the plaintiff who controls the pace of litigation. This last point I can deal with at once: there is nothing here to indicate that the plaintiffs were in any way to blame for the long period it has taken to get this case to trial. I was referred during the argument to *Jefford v Gee* [1970] 1 All ER 1202, [1970] 2 QB 130, *FMC (Meat) Ltd v Fairfield Cold Stores Ltd* [1971] 2 Lloyd's Rep 221, *Cremer v General Carriers SA* [1974] 1 All ER 1, [1974] 1 WLR 341, *Miliangos v George Frank (Textiles) Ltd* [1975] 3 All ER 801, [1976] AC 443, *Helmsing v Malta Drydocks Corpn* [1977] 2 Lloyd's Rep 444 and *BP Exploration Co (Libya) Ltd v Hunt (No 2)* [1979] 1 WLR 783.

Despite the way in which Lord Herschell LC in *London, Chatham and Dover Railway Co v South Eastern Railway Co* [1893] AC 429 at 437 stated the principle governing the award of interest on damages, I do not think the modern law is that interest is awarded against the defendant as a punitive measure for having kept the plaintiff out of his money. I think the principle now recognised is that it is all part of the attempt to achieve restitutio in integrum. One looks, therefore, not at the profit which the defendant wrongfully made out of the money he withheld (this would indeed involve a scrutiny of the defendant's financial position) but at the cost to the plaintiff of being deprived of the money which he should have had. I feel satisfied that in commercial cases the interest is intended to reflect the rate at which the plaintiff would have had to borrow money to supply the place of that which was withheld. I am also satisfied that one should not look at any special position in which the plaintiff may have been; one should disregard, for instance, the fact that a particular plaintiff, because of his personal situation, could only borrow money at a very high rate or, on the other hand, was able to borrow at specially favourable rates. The correct thing to do is to take the rate at which plaintiffs in general could borrow money. This does not, however, to my mind, mean that you exclude entirely all attributes of the plaintiff other than that he is a plaintiff. There is evidence here that large public companies of the size and prestige of these plaintiffs could expect to borrow at 1% over MLR, while for smaller and less prestigious concerns the rate might be as high as 3% over MLR. I think it would always be right to look at the rate at which plaintiffs with the general attributes of the actual plaintiff in the case (though not, of course, with any special or peculiar attribute) could borrow money as a guide to the appropriate interest rate. If commercial rates are appropriate I would take 1% over MLR as the proper figure for interest in this case.

But should a commercial rate be taken? It is usual to take the short term investment rate in personal injury cases, and there is much to be said for using the same rate in all cases. But, to my mind, there are considerable differences between personal injury cases and cases involving injury to business concerns. The award of damages in personal injury cases, or at any rate that part of them consisting of general damages, is an attempt to do one's poor best to compensate in money for the intangibles of pain, suffering and loss of amenity. The concept is widely different from the commercial scene. Disregarding any claim for loss of wages, no suggestion could be made that one should envisage the plaintiff in a personal injury case having to borrow money to take the place of the general damages which he should have been paid. While acknowledging the desirability of assimilating commercial and personal injury cases, I do not find the

argument compelling. The disadvantage is that both the short-term investment rate and
the rate of interest on judgment debts change too slowly. Due, no doubt, to the necessity
to make statutory instruments to effect necessary changes in the rates there is a
considerable time lag not only between these two rates and MLR but even between the
two rates themselves. The average MLR for 1980 was 16·3%; it changed from 16% to
14% on 24th November 1980 and from 14% to 12% on 10th March 1981. The short-
term investment rate was 12½% from 1st March 1979, 15% from 1st January 1980 and
12½% from 1st January 1981. The rate on judgment debts was 12½% from 3rd December
1979 and has stood at 15% from 9th June 1980. Today, therefore, MLR stands at 12%,
short-term investment rate at 12½% and judgment debts collect 15%. For commercial
men MLR forms a very real background to their financial arrangements because the
leading banks' base rates are normally the same as MLR. The unreality of the other two
rates is acceptable in personal injury cases, where there is a certain degree of unreality in
the award of damages for pain and suffering, and it would be impractical to have two
different rates of interest in the same case, one for general and one for special damages.
But in commercial cases it seems to me that the rate at which a commercial borrower can
borrow money would be the safest guide. I should add, perhaps, that the proper
question is: at what rate could the plaintiff borrow the required sum and not what return
could the plaintiff have expected if he had invested it? It is immaterial, therefore, to
consider, as counsel for the GLC suggested, whether the plaintiff could have used the
money profitably in his own business or what rate of profit he could have expected to
achieve by so doing. I think, therefore, interest should be calculated at 1% over MLR (or
bank rate).

So far as the period is concerned, I think the argument of counsel for the GLC springs
from a misunderstanding of *Jefford v Gee*. In that case the loss of wages was continuing
to the date of trial. Lord Denning MR awarded interest on the special damages at half
the appropriate rate (see [1970] 1 All ER 1202 at 1212, [1970] 2 QB 130 at 151). Where
a sum of money accrues week by week over a period and interest on it has to be
calculated, the total is effectively a product of the amount, the interest rate and the
period. The mathematical short cut available to solve the problem is to halve any one of
these parameters, as Lord Denning MR himself noted (see [1970] 1 All ER 1202 at 1208,
[1970] 2 QB 130 at 146). In *Jefford v Gee* it did not matter which was done as the period
over which the money was accruing stretched from the accident to the date of trial, a
period of about 2½ years. But, if the loss of wages had ceased after, say, six months, a
considerable injustice would occur to the plaintiff if the interest rate were halved over the
whole period. The appropriate calculation would be to identify the mid-point of the
period, in this hypothetical case three months after the accident, and award the full rate
of interest from that date until trial. As there were varying amounts paid for dredging
costs during the years 1967 to 1974 inclusive it would be possible to perform that
mathematical exercise here. The exercise in fact performed by the plaintiffs in the paper
they have put forward (P4) is not unduly complicated and, rather than start a new basis
for computation, I am content to accept this as the base from which the appropriate
figures can be worked out.

What has been done by the plaintiffs is to assume that all the dredging invoices which
were paid during any one calendar year were in fact paid halfway through that year,
namely on 1st July. These costs have then been aggregated year by year and interest has
been calculated year by year on the accumulating total based on the average bank rate or
MLR. Their paper shows interest calculated at 2% or 3% above MLR and a fresh
calculation for 1% above MLR will have to be done, but the basic figures stand, and I
accept them.

There remains the interesting question of what to do about the fact that the plaintiffs
deducted their costs from their gross income for the purposes of corporation tax. The
total 'saved' by this, perfectly legitimate, expedient was £239,153. Both defendants say
that, in view of this, it cannot be argued that the plaintiffs have been kept out of their
money and they suggest that it should be deducted from the amount of the damages

when it comes to awarding interest. Counsel for the plaintiffs, on the other hand, maintains that it is a principle of the award of interest that the particular position of the plaintiffs is not looked at and that, therefore, the way in which these plaintiffs ordered their affairs is irrelevant. He also points out that the plaintiffs will have to pay tax on the award of damages in the year in which the damages are paid and that, at present, corporation tax stands at 52% whereas for considerable periods while the plaintiffs were claiming relief it stood as low as 40%. It is accepted by all parties that this is a case where the damages will in fact be taxable in the plaintiffs' hands, so that the principles in *British Transport Commission v Gourley* [1955] 3 All ER 796, [1956] AC 185 do not apply, and it would, therefore, be inappropriate to deduct the tax saving from the award of damages itself. Counsel for the plaintiffs also prays in aid the incidence of inflation, but I feel confident that the law is that this should not be taken into account in considering damages. In looking at old awards in general damages in personal injury cases by way of comparison it will be necessary to take into account the drop in the purchasing power of the pound but otherwise inflation is not a matter to be considered. One is tempted to add that, if the plaintiffs have notionally had to borrow money from the bank to take the place of that which the defendants had not paid them, they are now in the happy position of notionally paying off their debt in devalued pounds rather than in the inflated equivalent of the original debt.

The award of interest in these cases is a discretionary matter and, in approaching the task of deciding on such an award, I think judges are entitled to and do adopt a very broad approach. Attempting to do so I would look at this matter in this way. The plaintiffs' accounting year runs from 1st October to 30th September. For tax purposes, therefore, in order to arrive at an average, it must be assumed that all the invoices were paid half way through the accounting year, ie on 1st April. But the plaintiffs' corporation tax liability did not have to be paid until 1st January, not of the next year but of the year after. As an example, the invoices for the year ending September 1967 would have been notionally paid on 1st March 1967 and those expenses would have been set against the gross income on which the corporation tax would have to be paid on 1st January 1969. There was thus a period of 21 months relating successively to each year's invoices. The plaintiffs have thus been kept out of the whole sum of damages for only part of the time (the precise period I shall have to look at later). For the remaining period they have been kept out of £550,000 less £239,000. It seems to me that one cannot ignore this on the principle that one does not look at the particular borrowing position of a plaintiff; and the fact the plaintiffs may have to pay more in corporation tax (because it is at a higher rate) when they are paid the damages than they saved by charging the dredging costs as an expense is unfortunate but, as Lord Denning MR said in *Jefford v Gee* [1970] 1 All ER 1202 at 1211, [1970] 2 QB 130 at 149, '... that cannot be helped. The tax man must collect all he can.' The plaintiffs must, in some way, bring into account in the interest computation the amount of corporation tax they saved. The problem is how. The answer is, I am sure, to look at the problem broadly and avoid a lot of complicated mathematics.

Now, as the total of £239,153 in tax saved is the result of aggregating sums accruing year by year over a period of 7½ years, the most appropriate mathematical short cut available is to assume that the whole sum accrued at the mid-point of that period, or after three years and nine months. But this would be the assumed date on which the plaintiffs paid the total; they would only receive the tax benefit 21 months later, or after 5½ years, ie on 1st January 1973 in this case. But interest is to continue until today, approximately eight years and four months later, so that this is the period over which the plaintiffs have enjoyed their tax benefit. As they have been notionally paying interest from a date 21 months earlier than 1st January 1973, to apply the average rate of MLR plus 1% for the period from 1st April 1971 to date would seem appropriate. If one takes the figures for the relevant years shown in the plaintiffs' paper P4, the average MLR for the whole of this period from 1st April 1971 amounts to 10·3%.

The figures for interest claimed in P4 do not, in fact, include a computation for 1% over MLR. But this figure is quickly arrived at by subtracting from the total of the 2%

column the difference between that figure and the total of the 3% column. The result is

a £668,912. The mathematics then become simple and look like this:

	£
Interest on total damages at 1% over MLR	668,912
Less £239,153 at 11·3% for 8·39 years	226,734
	442,178

b

and this is the amount of interest to which the plaintiffs are entitled.

Having disposed of the matters remaining between the plaintiffs and the defendants I am also asked to deal with contribution between the defendants. Again, it seems to me that, in deciding this question, it is essential to look at it very broadly and to avoid

c considering detail. I accept the premise of counsel for the GLC that contribution depends on the respective defendants' responsibility for the damage and that 'responsibility' here contains a mixture of both causation and culpability. Counsel goes on to say that the cause of the siltation at Silvertown was twofold. It was due to the cessation of dredging in Barking Reach by the PLA and the redistribution of the resulting waterborne silt by the ferry terminals due to design faults. Those design faults, he says,

d were themselves divisible into two: the failure to provide a more open design and the insistence of the PLA on the provision of fender piles. He adds that the PLA was statutory guardian of the river and was forearmed with the knowledge of the plaintiffs' proposals when it approved the design of the ferry terminals. Counsel for the PLA points to the serious effect of the method of constructing the coffer dams and suggests that this was out of the control of the PLA, a suggestion which I do not think can survive a reading of s 50(4) of the London County Council (Improvements) Act 1962. He adds

e that the real question is: what chance had either defendant of putting things right?

Now, in the view I took of liability, it was the failure to dredge away the siltation which was caused by the ferry terminals which made both defendants liable for the whole of the siltation which occurred. (I am disregarding, of course, all siltation which would have been caused had there been no new terminals, because this siltation is not the subject of any award of damages.) It was the ability of the defendants to dredge away the

f consequences of the construction of the terminals which, in my view, made it impossible for either defendant to rely on the defence of statutory authority. If the defence of statutory authority had succeeded, different damages would have been awarded and different considerations would have applied; in particular, on that hypothesis, it would have been necessary to examine the respective culpability of the two defendants for the design faults. But, as the failure of the defendants which led to the damages awarded was

g simply a failure to dredge, it seems to me that one must approach the problem of culpability as between the defendants on the basis of their approach to the question of remedying the effects which the terminals had created rather than their initial approach to the design which caused those effects. Looked at in this way I have no doubt where the greater blame lay. Fairly early on, and I need not refer to the documents, the PLA

h recognised that, in all probability, the cause of the siltation was the ferry terminals. It was prepared to carry out dredging to remedy the situation and would undoubtedly have done so if the GLC had been prepared to acknowledge that the siltation was due to the terminals, and that therefore, under s 50(9) of the 1962 Act, it should be liable for the cost. The GLC and its consultant engineers, on the other hand, consistently refused to acknowledge even the possibility that the terminals could in any way have been

j responsible. It was this intransigent attitude, persisted in up to and throughout the trial, which not only made it very difficult for the PLA to take the decision to undertake the dredging itself but was also responsible in large measure for the length of time which it took to get this case to trial; I need not go again into the history, for instance, of the successive model tests and the attempt by the GLC to prevent the damaging results of the first tests being disclosed to the plaintiffs' advisers, a wrangle which alone delayed the progress to trial by some two years.

On the other hand, the PLA could, and should, itself have dredged. It is only fair to say, however, that, had it done so and thus avoided damaging the plaintiffs, it would, *a* when it tried to recover any part of the cost of dredging, have found itself facing the same intransigent attitude from the GLC and its consultant engineers as has faced the plaintiffs in this case.

Counsel for the GLC has mentioned the causative effect of the decision by the PLA to cease dredging in Barking Reach. But, although this decision may have had some causative effect on the deposition of silt at Silvertown, such deposition, as I have found, *b* could not form the subject of any legitimate complaint by the plaintiffs, because the decision itself was one which the PLA was entitled to take and in respect of which no action can lie. The agreed damages in this case already exclude the costs of dredging away the deposition which the PLA's decision by itself caused. The decision cannot thus be considered as in any way causative of the injury to the plaintiffs for which damages have been recovered.

c

In my view, having regard to the general attitude of the GLC to the question of dredging to clear this siltation, I would apportion blame as to 70% to the GLC and 30% to the PLA.

Had it been necessary to consider their respective positions in relation to the design faults, I do not think that my percentages would have differed markedly. The position is analogous to that of the architect and the local authority's building surveyor. Of *d* course, each has a duty to the building owner who relies on each; but there seems to me to be a difference in principle between the culpability of the expert who initiates a faulty design and that of the person charged with some statutory duty of approving designs once submitted for inspection. If a fault is a design fault the greater culpability lies on the designer.

But, in this case, counsel for the GLC urges that there is an additional reason why the *e* PLA should be regarded as more blameworthy than the GLC: it, and it alone, insisted on the provision of fender piles. Without delving back into the mass of evidence which I heard a year ago, I am unable to say whether I had any sufficient evidence to enable me to determine the extent to which the fender piles contributed to the siltation actually caused by the Husband design. I do not recall it and I certainly made no finding about this. I had enough to enable me to make findings of fact about their effect on the *f* Mouchel design, if they were ever necessary. That they must have had some additional effect I have no doubt, but, in view of the generally obstructive nature of the Husband design, I would think it must have been very small. I decline to embark on a search through the evidence to consider this point of detail. As I have indicated earlier, on this canvas one works with a broad brush. There is enough in the point to make me revise my percentages (if looking at contribution in relation to design faults) from 70/30 to *g* ⅔/⅓. But, as I indicated earlier, I am not looking at design faults but at failure to dredge away the deposited silt, so that the contribution remains at 70/30.

Counsel for the PLA made some suggestion that perhaps the PLA could be excused from liability to pay interest to the extent that the period was prolonged by the actions of the GLC. It is clear to me that no blame can be laid at either the plaintiffs' door or that of the PLA for any undue delay in bringing this matter to trial, while it can certainly be *h* said that the attitude of the GLC was responsible for a delay of about two years. But I do not think I should go into detail of this kind when considering contribution, and the division I have made should not be further widened in favour of the PLA.

The result is that, in my view, the GLC should be responsible for 70% of the damages and interest and the PLA for 30%.

Judgment for the plaintiffs.   *j*

Solicitors: *Ingledew, Brown, Bennison Garrett* (for the plaintiffs); *Rex A Lanham* (for the GLC); *Brian Golds* (for the PLA).

K Mydeen Esq   Barrister.

Hunter v Chief Constable of West Midlands and another

HOUSE OF LORDS

LORD DIPLOCK, LORD RUSSELL OF KILLOWEN, LORD KEITH OF KINKEL, LORD ROSKILL AND LORD BRANDON OF OAKBROOK

19th, 20th, 21st OCTOBER, 19th NOVEMBER 1981

Action – Dismissal – Abuse of process of court – Civil action relating to same issue as earlier action – Accused alleging in criminal trial that he was assaulted by police officers to procure confession – Assault not proved and accused convicted – Accused commencing civil proceedings against police claiming damages for assault – Purpose of civil proceedings to prove that confession on which accused convicted was procured by force – Whether civil action abuse of process of court.

Estoppel – Issue estoppel – Criminal proceedings followed by civil proceedings – Accused alleging in criminal proceedings that he was assaulted by police officers to procure confession whilst in custody – Assault not proved and accused convicted – Civil proceedings by accused against police claiming damages for assault by police officers – Whether issue estoppel arising.

The police arrested the plaintiff together with five others on 21st November 1974 following the death of 21 people in bomb explosions in two Birmingham public houses. On 23rd November the plaintiff and the other accused confessed to the bombings and were charged with murder. On 25th November they were brought before a magistrate who ordered them to be remanded in custody. They were admitted to prison. When the accused were again brought before a magistrate, on 28th November, their faces were badly bruised. At their trial for murder the accused claimed that they had been beaten up by the police to make them confess and that therefore their confessions of 23rd November, on which the Crown heavily relied, were inadmissible. At a lengthy trial within a trial the judge heard evidence from the accused and the police officers concerned (who denied that there had been any threats or violence). However no prison officers were called despite the fact that statements taken from prison officers at a Home Office inquiry had been made available to the accused. The judge accepted the evidence of the police officers, and ruled that the confessions were admissible. The allegations and the evidence were then repeated to the jury to enable them to assess the weight to be given to the confessions. The accused were found guilty, and an appeal to the Criminal Division of the Court of Appeal, at which no complaint was made of the trial judge's ruling that the confessions were admissible, was dismissed. Subsequently the prison officers were charged with assaulting the accused but were acquitted. The accused then brought an action against the chief constable in charge of the police officers claiming damages for assault by the police. The chief constable applied to have the action struck out on the ground that it raised an issue identical to that which had been finally determined at the accused's murder trial. At the hearing of the chief constable's application the accused adduced new evidence consisting of statements by the prison officers, and expert evidence from a forensic specialist who considered that at least some of the accused's injuries had been inflicted before they left police custody. The judge held that the new evidence prevented him from striking out the civil action, because it was reasonably conceivable that another tribunal acting judicially might accept at least part of the accused's case. On appeal by the chief constable, the Court of Appeal ([1980] 2 All ER 227) held that the accused's civil action should be struck out because it would be an abuse of the process of the court to allow the accused to litigate again the identical issue that had been decided against them in the criminal trial and because they were barred by issue estoppel from raising the issue of whether they had been assaulted by the police. The plaintiff appealed to the House of Lords.

Held – The initiation of proceedings in a court of justice for the purpose of mounting a collateral attack on a final decision adverse to the intending plaintiff reached by a court of competent jurisdiction in previous proceedings in which the plaintiff had a full opportunity of contesting the matter was, as a matter of public policy, an abuse of the process of the court. The fact that the collateral attack was by means of a civil action raising an identical issue decided against the plaintiff in a competent court of criminal jurisdiction was immaterial, since if the issue had been proved against the plaintiff beyond all reasonable doubt in the criminal court it would be wholly inconsistent if it were not decided against him on the balance of probabilities in the civil action. The proper method of attacking the trial judge's decision that the plaintiff had not been assaulted by the police before his oral confession was obtained would have been to make the contention that the judge's ruling that the confession was admissible a ground of his appeal to the Criminal Division of the Court of Appeal. However, where fresh evidence was obtained since the criminal trial which entirely changed the aspect of the case, the intending plaintiff might be allowed to proceed with his civil action. Since it was clear that the purpose of the plaintiff's civil proceedings was not to obtain damages from the police but to prove that the confession on which he was convicted had been obtained by force, those proceedings were a collateral attack on the ruling of the trial judge and the verdict of the jury at the murder trial that the plaintiff's confession had not been obtained by the police by force. Furthermore, the fresh evidence sought to be adduced by the plaintiff had been available or could have been obtained at the time of the trial and did not come within the fresh evidence exception. The plaintiff's civil action had therefore properly been struck out as an abuse of the process of the court. The plaintiff's appeal would accordingly be dismissed (see p 733 b to g, p 734 b to h, p 735 d e and p 736 a to h, post).

Dicta of Lord Halsbury LC in *Reichel v Magrath* (1889) 14 App Cas at 668, of A L Smith LJ in *Stephenson v Garnett* [1898] 1 QB at 681 and of Lord Cairns LC in *Phosphate Sewage Co Ltd v Molleson* (1879) 4 App Cas at 814 applied.

Hollington v F Hewthorn & Co Ltd [1943] 2 All ER 35 and dictum of Denning LJ in *Ladd v Marshall* [1954] 3 All ER at 748 considered.

Per Curiam. The term 'issue estoppel' should for the purposes of English law be restricted to that species of estoppel per rem judicatam that may arise in civil actions between the same parties or their privies (see p 733 a and p 736 f to h, post).

Dictum of Diplock LJ in *Mills v Cooper* [1967] 2 All ER at 104 approved.

Decision of the Court of Appeal sub nom *McIlkenny v Chief Constable of West Midlands Police Force* [1980] 2 All ER 227 affirmed.

Notes

For striking out proceedings for abuse of process, see 30 Halsbury's Laws (3rd Edn) 407–409, paras 766–768, and for cases on the subject, see 51 Digest (Repl) 741–743, 3278–3300.

Cases referred to in opinions

Director of Public Prosecutions v Humphrys [1976] 2 All ER 497, [1977] AC 1, [1976] 2 WLR 857, 140 JP 386, 63 Cr App R 95, [1976] RTR 339, HL, 21 Digest (Reissue) 81, 531.

Hollington v F Hewthorn & Co Ltd [1943] 2 All ER 35, [1943] KB 587, 112 LJKB 463, 169 LT 21, CA, 22 Digest (Reissue) 270, 2470.

Ladd v Marshall [1954] 3 All ER 745, [1954] 1 WLR 1489, CA, 51 Digest (Repl) 827, 3826.

McIlkenny v Chief Constable of West Midlands Police Force [1980] 2 All ER 227, [1980] QB 283, [1980] 2 WLR 689, CA, 21 Digest (Reissue) 103, 727.

Mills v Cooper [1967] 2 All ER 100, [1967] 2 QB 459, [1967] 2 WLR 1343, 131 JP 349, 65 LGR 275, DC, 21 Digest (Reissue) 80, 530.

Phosphate Sewage Co Ltd v Molleson (1879) 4 App Cas 801, HL, 21 Digest (Reissue) 92, 642.

R v Watson [1980] 2 All ER 293, [1980] 1 WLR 991, 144 JP 350, 71 Cr App R 273, CA.

Reichel v Magrath (1889) 14 App Cas 665, HL, 21 Digest (Reissue) 73, 483.

Stephenson v Garnett [1898] 1 QB 677, 67 LJQB 447, 78 LT 371, CA, 13 Digest (Reissue) 478, 3960.

Interlocutory appeal

a Robert Gerard Hunter appealed against the decision of the Court of Appeal (Lord Denning MR, Goff LJ and Sir George Baker) (reported sub nom *McIlkenny v Chief Constable of West Midlands Police Force* [1980] 2 All ER 227, [1980] QB 283) on 17th January 1980 allowing the appeal of the Chief Constables of the West Midlands and the Lancashire Police against the decision of Cantley J given on 22nd November 1977 and ordering that an action commenced by writ dated 17th November 1977 by Mr Hunter
b against the chief constables and the Home Office be struck out. The facts are set out in the opinion of Lord Diplock.

After hearing counsel for Mr Hunter, the Appellate Committee indicated at the commencement of the hearing on the second day that it wished to hear submissions on behalf of the Home Office. The committee then heard submissions from counsel for the Home Office as amicus curiae and counsel for Mr Hunter in reply. Counsel as amicus
c curiae then withdrew and the committee heard further submissions from counsel for Mr Hunter. At the commencement of the hearing on the third day, the chairman of the committee, Lord Diplock, informed the parties that their Lordships wished to hear no further argument and that they thought that the action should be stayed as an abuse of the process of the court.

d *David Turner-Samuels QC* and *Stephen Sedley* for Mr Hunter.
Hugh Carlisle QC for the Home Office as amicus curiae.
Michael Turner QC and *Patrick Twigg* for the chief constables.

Their Lordships took time for consideration.

e 19th November. The following opinions were delivered.

LORD DIPLOCK. My Lords, this is a case about abuse of the process of the High Court. It concerns the inherent power which any court of justice must possess to prevent
f misuse of its procedure in a way which, although not inconsistent with the literal application of its procedural rules, would nevertheless be manifestly unfair to a party to litigation before it, or would otherwise bring the administration of justice into disrepute among right-thinking people. The circumstances in which abuse of process can arise are very varied; those which give rise to the instant appeal must surely be unique. It would, in my view, be most unwise if this House were to use this occasion to say anything that might be taken as limiting to fixed categories the kinds of circumstances in which the
g court has a duty (I disavow the word discretion) to exercise this salutary power.

The matter comes before your Lordships by way of an interlocutory appeal in a civil action in the High Court in which the appellant Hunter seeks damages for assaults causing him physical injuries which he alleges were inflicted on him by police officers while he was in their custody between 22nd and 24th November 1974. The respondent
h chief constables, who are the first and second defendants to the action, are sued under s 48 of the Police Act 1964 as vicariously liable for the tortious acts of the individual police officers (whom I shall call collectively 'the police') who were members of the West Midlands and Lancashire police forces respectively.

The Home Office is a third defendant to the action as vicariously liable in damages for other assaults causing him additional physical injuries which Hunter alleges were
j inflicted on him by prison officers at Winson Green prison between 25th and 27th November 1974 while he was detained there on remand. Your Lordships are not, however, concerned directly with these later injuries in respect of which the civil action against the Home Office is still continuing. The only question with which your Lordships are concerned is whether Hunter's action *against the police* ought to be struck out as an abuse of the process of the court. Cantley J, before whom the application to strike out was made, declined to do so. On appeal from his refusal, the Court of Appeal (Lord Denning MR, Goff LJ and Sir George Baker) were unanimously of opinion that the

action was an abuse of the process of the court and that the statement of claim against the first and second defendants ought to be struck out (see *McIlkenny v Chief Constable of West Midlands Police Force* [1980] 2 All ER 227, [1980] QB 283).

Hunter is one of six murderers ('the Birmingham bombers'), members or supporters of the IRA, the Irish Republican Army, who were responsible for planting and exploding two bombs in public houses in the centre of Birmingham on 21st November 1974; as a result 21 people were killed and eight score of other innocent victims injured. For a detailed account of what happened in relation to Hunter and the other Birmingham bombers after the holocaust until the launching of this action by Hunter and similar actions by those others on November 1977, reference should be made to the judgment of Lord Denning MR in *McIlkenny v Chief Constable of West Midlands* [1980] 2 All ER 227 at 231–234, [1980] QB 283 at 312–316. To paraphrase it would only be to spoil it, to improve on it I should find impossible. So I shall limit myself to as brief a summary as possible of those salient features in Lord Denning MR's account to which I find it necessary to refer in order to explain my own reasons for dismissing this appeal.

Hunter and four other of the Birmingham bombers were arrested on the night of 21st November 1974 at Heysham where they were en route to Belfast. They remained in custody of the police initially at Morecambe and subsequently at Birmingham until the morning of 25th November when they were brought before the magistrate and committed by him to Winson Green prison on remand until their next appearance before him on 27th November. Photographs of all six Birmingham bombers, including one of Hunter, were taken before the men left the police station at Birmingham. No facial injury to Hunter was apparent on inspection of these photographs, at any rate by an uninstructed eye; nor (except for a black eye in the case of one defendant which, it was accepted, had been caused accidentally) was any facial injury to any of the Birmingham bombers observed by any of the many keen observers who were present when they appeared in court on the morning of 25th November, or by the duty solicitors who were allotted to them on that occasion and who interviewed them in their cells. On their next appearance in court on 27th November, however, it was apparent to even the most casual glance that all six men, including Hunter, had sustained severe and painful facial injuries. It is not disputed, and was not disputed at their trial for murder, that by this time there were present on other parts of their bodies also physical injuries which could not have been self-inflicted; but, for reasons which will become apparent later in connection with Hunter's claim that 'fresh evidence' has become available since the date of his conviction on 15th August 1975 on 21 counts of murder, it is only facial injuries that call for specific mention here.

The trial of all six Birmingham bombers for murder took place jointly before Bridge J and a jury. The principal evidence against each one of them consisted of confessions made to the police either in writing or in the case of Hunter orally only. Against some, but not against Hunter, there was forensic evidence of faint traces of nitro-glycerine being perceptible on their hands or clothing and against the five of them, including Hunter, who were arrested at Heysham there was evidence of conduct after the time at which the bomb must have been planted that, in the absence of any other credible explanation, was capable of arousing suspicion that they had some knowledge of the plot. But all this amounted to suspicion only; unless the confessions were admissible and, if admitted, were accepted by the jury in the case of each defendant as being true then no reasonable jury could be satisfied that the prosecution's case against that defendant was proved beyond a reasonable doubt and it would be their duty to acquit him.

If it were voluntary, Hunter's oral confession, like the confessions of each of his co-defendants, bore the ring of truth, as the jury must have found when they convicted him. (That they must also have rejected his denial that he ever made it is not germane to the only matters that fall to be decided by your Lordships in this appeal.) So it became of crucial importance to Hunter and to each of the defendants to obtain a ruling from the judge on a voir dire that the confessions were not voluntary and so prevent their being admitted in evidence. This they set out to do by claiming in the 'trial within a trial' before the learned judge in the absence of the jury that the confessions were forced out a of them by the infliction of severe physical violence on them by the police and by threats of calamitous consequences of what would happen to them or to their families if they did not make confessions of their guilt in the terms that the police demanded of them. The physical injuries in respect of which Hunter claims damages in the present civil action for assaults by the police are identical with those of which he gave evidence at the trial within a trial as having been inflicted on him by the police in order to extract from him a confession.

b At the trial within a trial the issue which Bridge J had to determine was whether the prosecution had satisfied him beyond reasonable doubt that the confessions were voluntary; and that involved his being satisfied to this high standard of proof that in the case of each defendant there had been no assault on him by the police before or in the course of obtaining his confession. Assaults on any of the defendants by prison officers at Winson Green prison after the confessions had been made could not affect admissibility; but the fact that all the defendants had unquestionably been subjected to severe physical violence by the time of their second appearance in the magistrates' court on 27th November 1974 provided an added complication to the investigation of the issue that the judge had to determine on the voire dire.

So it is not surprising that the trial within a trial lasted eight days. Each of the police officers who it was claimed had participated in or was present at any of the alleged assaults gave evidence, so did each of the defendants; in addition other witnesses were called and the photographs of the defendants taken on 24th November 1974, to which I have referred, were put in evidence. At the conclusion of this evidence the judge ruled that each of the confessions was admissible. Unusually, but very helpfully for the purpose of the instant appeal to your Lordships' House, he gave full and detailed reasons for his ruling. He made it clear that he accepted the evidence of the police as establishing beyond all reasonable doubt that there had been no physical violence or threats by them to the defendants and that in his opinion the evidence taken as a whole showed that there had been what he described as 'gross perjury' on the part of each of the defendants.

The confessions were accordingly admitted and the trial resumed. The same allegations as to physical violence and threats by the police that had been made on the voire dire were repeated before the jury as relevant to the weight which they should attach to the confessions and the whole ground was gone over again in evidence given before them. In the course of what I can only describe as a model and meticulous summing up, of which no criticism has been made by counsel for Hunter in the instant appeal, Bridge J gave to the jury a firm direction that if they inclined to the view that the account by any defendant of the circumstances in which his confession was obtained might be true they should reject the confession as worthless and acquit the defendant, since the other evidence against each of them did no more than raise suspicion and was insufficient to satisfy the burden of proof beyond reasonable doubt that lay on the prosecution.

Despite this direction the jury convicted Hunter and each of the other Birmingham bombers on 21 counts of murder. The appellants appealed to the Criminal Division of the Court of Appeal against the convictions. No complaint about the judge's ruling on the voire dire that the confessions were admissible was made in this appeal on behalf of any of the appellants and their appeals were dismissed on 30th March 1976.

To complete the history of the matter, it may be added in parenthesis that, later in 1976, 14 prison officers from Winson Green prison were tried before Swanwick J and a jury on charges of assaulting the Birmingham bombers. All 14 made unsworn statements from the dock, each denying that he himself was implicated in any violence inflicted on the Birmingham bombers between 25th and 27th November 1974; and all 14 were acquitted. In the instant civil action by Hunter, however, it is admitted by the Home Office that *some* violence was inflicted on him by prison officers employed at Winson Green. For this the Home Office accepts civil liability in damages but puts Hunter to proof of the extent and severity of the resulting injuries.

The statement of claim in the present civil action alleging against the police the identical assaults that had been canvassed for eight days before Bridge J on the voire dire and again before the jury on Hunter's trial for murder was delivered in January 1978.

Prompt steps were taken by the police to have the statement of claim against them struck out and the action against them stayed or dismissed under RSC Ord 18, r 19 or else under the inherent jurisdiction of the court, on the grounds, inter alia, that it was an abuse of the process of the court.

The summons claiming this relief in the instant case together with summonses claiming similar relief in parallel actions in which the other five Birmingham bombers were plaintiffs came on for hearing before Cantley J in November 1978.

At that hearing there were put in evidence statements from prison officers that had not been used although they had been made available to the plaintiffs at their trial for murder and a report from an expert, Dr Paul, on inferences which he felt able to draw from the photographs of the plaintiffs taken on 24th November 1974, and used at the murder trial, to which reference has already been made. It would appear that in the argument on the summonses counsel for the police sought in the first place to persuade the learned judge that what had happened at the murder trial gave rise to an estoppel per rem judicatam of a kind which in recent years it had been found convenient to describe as 'issue estoppel'. The fact that, even if what had happened did not create as against the plaintiffs in favour of the police what could be strictly classified as 'issue estoppel', it nevertheless made the initiation of the present civil action against the police an abuse of the process of the court took second place in counsel's argument both chronologically and in plenitude of citation of authority.

Cantley J in a fully reasoned judgment dismissed the summonses both on the narrow ground that there was no 'issue estoppel' in the strict sense of that term and on the broader ground that he ought not to dismiss the action as an abuse of the process of the court if, in the light of evidence that was not called at the murder trial, even though it had been available then, but which the plaintiffs intended to adduce in the civil action, it was 'reasonably conceivable that another tribunal acting judicially might accept at least part of the plaintiffs' case'; and this he, hesitantly, thought was 'reasonably conceivable' if the expert evidence of Dr Paul (which could have been available to the plaintiffs at the murder trial if they had chosen to call it) were admitted at the hearing of the civil action.

Much the same course was taken in the argument in the Court of Appeal on the appeal by the police against the dismissal of the summonses. The hearing there took 12 days and involved the citation of 77 authorities, including a number of American decisions. All three members of the court were of opinion that Cantley J was wrong on the broader ground; he had applied the wrong tests as to the previous availability and the degree of cogency of evidence unadduced at the murder trial but proposed to be adduced in the civil action that the plaintiffs would need in order to prevent its being an abuse of the process of the court for them to initiate civil proceedings to mount a collateral attack on the finding of Bridge J at the murder trial that they had *not* been assaulted by the police.

Lord Denning MR and Sir George Baker were also in favour of extending the description 'issue estoppel' to cover the particular example of abuse of process of the court presented by the instant case, a question to which much of the judgment of Lord Denning MR is addressed. Goff LJ, on the other hand, expressed his own view, which had been shared by Cantley J, that such extension would involve a misuse of that expression. But if what Hunter is seeking to do in initiating this civil action is an abuse of the process of the court, as I understand all your Lordships are satisfied that it is, the question whether it also qualifies to bear the label 'issue estoppel' is a matter not of substance but of semantics. Counsel for Hunter was therefore invited to address this House first on the broader question of abuse of process and to deal in particular with the reasoning contained in the judgment of Goff LJ who dealt with the matter more closely than the other members of the court and based his decision solely on that ground. In the result, counsel for Hunter, who argued the case with their accustomed ability and diligence, were quite unable to persuade any of us that there was any error in the reasoning of Goff LJ in what proved to be the last judgment that he prepared before his much lamented and untimely death. In the result it became unnecessary to call on counsel for the police. So the debate on semantics did not take place. It could not possibly affect the outcome of the appeal or justify the public expense that would have been involved in prolonging the hearing any further.

a

Nevertheless it is my own view, which I understand is shared by all your Lordships, that it would be best, in order to avoid confusion, if the use of the description 'issue estoppel' *in English law, at any rate* (it does not appear to have been adopted in the United States), were restricted to that species of estoppel per rem judicatam that may arise in civil actions between the same parties or their privies, of which the characteristics are stated in a judgment of my own in *Mills v Cooper* [1967] 2 All ER 100 at 104, [1967] 2 QB 459 at 468–469 that was adopted and approved by this House in *Director of Public Prosecutions*

b

v Humphrys [1976] 2 All ER 497, [1977] AC 1, the case in which it was also held that 'issue estoppel' had no place in English criminal law.

The abuse of process which the instant case exemplifies is the initiation of proceedings in a court of justice for the purpose of mounting a collateral attack on a final decision against the intending plaintiff which has been made by another court of competent jurisdiction in previous proceedings in which the intending plaintiff had a full opportunity of contesting the decision in the court by which it was made.

c

The proper method of attacking the decision by Bridge J in the murder trial that Hunter was not assaulted by the police before his oral confession was obtained would have been to make the contention that the judge's ruling that the confession was admissible had been erroneous a ground of his appeal against his conviction to the Criminal Division of the Court of Appeal. This Hunter did not do. Had he or any of his

d

fellow murderers done so, application could have been made on that appeal to tender to the court as 'fresh evidence' all material on which Hunter would now seek to rely in his civil action against the police for damages for assault, if it were allowed to continue. But since, quite apart from the tenuous character of such evidence, it is not now seriously disputed that it was available to the defendants at the time of the murder trial itself and could have been adduced then had those who were acting for him or any of the other Birmingham bombers at the trial thought that to do so would help their case, any

e

application for its admission on the appeal to the Court of Appeal, Criminal Division, would have been doomed to failure.

It would call for a degree of credulity too extreme to be expected even from judicial members of your Lordships' House to fail to recognise that the dominant purpose of this action, and the parallel actions brought by the other Birmingham bombers so far as they

f

are brought against the police, has not been to recover damages but is brought in an endeavour to establish, long after the event when memories have faded and witnesses other than the Birmingham bombers themselves may be difficult to trace, that the confessions on the evidence of which they were convicted were induced by police violence, with a view to putting pressure on the Home Secretary to release them from the life sentences that they are otherwise likely to continue to serve for many years to come. A significant indication that the recovery of monetary damages is not the principal object

g

of the civil action may be discerned in the manner in which the action has been conducted as against the Home Office. Despite the fact that ever since August 1979, when the Home Office amended their defence by admitting liability for assaults by the prison officers, Hunter has been in a position to obtain judgment against the Home Office on liability and proceed to an assessment of damages, no step has yet been taken on his behalf to do so.

h

My Lords, collateral attack on a final decision of a court of competent jurisdiction may take a variety of forms. It is not surprising that no reported case is to be found in which the facts present a precise parallel with those of the instant case. But the principle applicable is, in my view, simply and clearly stated in those passages from the judgment of A L Smith LJ in *Stephenson v Garnett* [1898] 1 QB 677 and the speech of Lord Halsbury LC in *Reichel v Magrath* (1889) 14 App Cas 665 which are cited by Goff LJ in his judgment

j

in the instant case. I need only repeat an extract from the passage which he cited from the judgment of A L Smith LJ in *Stephenson v Garnett* [1898] 1 QB 677 at 680–681:

'. . . the Court ought to be slow to strike out a statement of claim or defence, and to dismiss an action as frivolous and vexatious, yet it ought to do so when, as here, it has been shewn that the identical question sought to be raised has been already decided by a competent court.'

The passage from Lord Halsbury LC's speech in *Reichel v Magrath* 14 App Cas 665 at 668 deserves repetition here in full:

> '. . . I think it would be a scandal to the administration of justice if, the same question having been disposed of by one case, the litigant were to be permitted by changing the form of the proceedings to set up the same case again.'

In the instant case the relevant final decision by a competent court in which the identical question sought to be raised has been already decided is the ruling of Bridge J, on the voire dire in the murder trial, that Hunter's confession was admissible. Initially his ruling may have been provisional in the limited sense that up to the time that the jury brought in their verdict he had power to reconsider it in the light of any further evidence that might emerge when the whole question of the circumstances in which the confession was obtained was gone into again before the jury on the question of the weight to be attached to it: see *R v Watson* [1980] 2 All ER 293, [1980] 1 WLR 991. But his ruling became final when the trial ended with the return of the jury's verdict of guilty and the pronouncement by the judge of the mandatory sentence of life imprisonment. Bridge J thereupon became functus officio. His ruling that the confession was not obtained by the use of violence by the police, as Hunter had alleged, could thereafter only be upset on appeal to the Court of Appeal.

The fact that the whole matter of the circumstances in which the confession was obtained was gone into a second time before the jury and that the jury, in view of the judge's direction to them, must clearly also have been satisfied beyond reasonable doubt that Hunter's account of the assaults on him by the police was a fabrication does not affect the finality of the judge's ruling, though it would exacerbate the public scandal to the administration of justice that would be involved if Hunter, by changing the form of the proceedings to a civil action, were to be permitted to set up in that action the same case that must have been decided against him not only once but twice, even though technically it was only the first of those decisions that eventually qualified as the final decision against him by a competent court on the very question that he seeks now to raise.

My Lords, this is the first case to be reported in which the final decision against which it is sought to initiate a collateral attack by means of a civil action has been a final decision reached by a court of criminal jurisdiction. This raises a possible complication that the onus of proof of facts that lies on the prosecution in criminal proceedings is higher than that required of parties to civil proceedings who seek in those proceedings to prove facts on which they rely. Thus a decision in a criminal case on a particular question *in favour* of a defendant, whether by way of acquittal or a ruling on a voire dire, is not inconsistent with the fact that the decision would have been *against* him if all that were required were the civil standard of proof on the balance of probabilities. This is why acquittals were not made admissible in evidence in civil actions by the Civil Evidence Act 1968. In contrast to this a decision on a particular question *against* a defendant in a criminal case, such as Bridge J's ruling on the voire dire in the murder trial, is reached on the higher criminal standard of proof beyond all reasonable doubt and is wholly inconsistent with any possibility that the decision would *not* have been *against* him if the same question had fallen to be decided in civil proceedings instead of criminal. That is why convictions were made admissible in evidence in civil proceedings by the Civil Evidence Act 1968.

That Act and the case of *Hollington v F Hewthorn & Co Ltd* [1943] 2 All ER 35, [1943] KB 587, which ss 11 and 13 of the Act were passed to overrule, call for some examination at this point. Despite the eminence of those who constituted the members of the Court of Appeal that decided it (Lord Greene MR, Goddard and du Parcq LJJ), *Hollington v Hewthorn* is generally considered to have been wrongly decided, even in the context of running-down cases brought before the Law Reform (Contributory Negligence) Act 1945 was passed and contributory negligence ceased to be a complete defence; for that is what *Hollington v Hewthorn* was about. The judgment of the court delivered by Goddard LJ concentrates on the great variety of additional issues that would arise in a civil action for damages for negligent driving but which it would not have been necessary to decide

in a prosecution for a traffic offence based on the same incident, and on the consequence
that it would still be necessary to call in the civil action all the witnesses whose evidence
had previously been given in a successful prosecution of the defendant, or a driver for
whose tortious acts he was vicariously liable, for careless or dangerous driving, even if
evidence of that conviction were admitted. So no question arose in *Hollington v Hewthorn*
of raising in a civil action the identical question that had already been decided in a
criminal court of competent jurisdiction, and the case does not purport to be an authority
on that matter.

The occasion for the reference of the decision in *Hollington v Hewthorn* that evidence of
criminal convictions was not admissible in civil actions to the Lord Chancellor's Law
Reform Committee was a notorious libel case in which despite a defence of justification
a criminal who had been convicted of serious offences was awarded damages by a jury in
a civil action against a newspaper for stating that he had committed the identical offences
of which he had been found guilty on his trial. So here, unlike the case of *Hollington v
Hewthorn*, the civil action did raise the identical question that had already been decided
against the plaintiff by a competent court; yet under the rule in *Hollington v Hewthorn*
even the fact of his conviction was inadmissible in evidence on the plea of justification
in the civil action. This is the mischief, the initiation of civil proceedings in a court of
justice for the purpose of mounting a collateral attack on a final decision against the
intending plaintiff which has been reached by a competent court of criminal jurisdiction,
that s 13 of the Civil Evidence Act 1968 was designed to cure. It is to be observed that
it makes the conviction not merely prima facie evidence of the plaintiff's guilt but
conclusive evidence. The provisions of s 13 are thus consistent with and give statutory
recognition to the public policy of prohibiting the use of civil actions to initiate a
collateral attack on a final decision *against the intending plaintiff* which has been made by
a criminal court of competent jurisdiction.

Section 13 is to be contrasted with s 11. Although s 11 is not in express terms confined
to convictions of *defendants* to civil actions or persons for whose tortious acts defendants
are vicariously liable, this must in practice inevitably be the case. It is the plaintiff who
will want to rely on a conviction of the defendant, or a person for whose tortious acts he
is vicariously liable, for a criminal offence which also constitutes the tort for which the
plaintiff sues. It is scarcely possible to conceive of a civil action in which a plaintiff could
assist his cause by relying on his own conviction for a criminal offence. So s 11 is not
dealing with the use of civil actions by plaintiffs to initiate collateral attacks on final
decisions against them which have been made by a criminal court of competent
jurisdiction; and the public policy that treats the use of civil actions for this purpose as an
abuse of the process of the court is not involved.

Section 11 makes the conviction prima facie evidence that the person convicted did
commit the offence of which he was found guilty, but does not make it conclusive
evidence: the defendant is permitted by the Act to prove the contrary if he can. The
section covers a wide variety of circumstances: the relevant conviction may be of someone
who has not been made a defendant to the civil action and the actual defendant may have
had no opportunity of determining what evidence should be called on the occasion of the
criminal trial; the conviction, particularly of a traffic offence, may have been entered on
a plea of guilty accompanied by a written explanation in mitigation; fresh evidence, not
called on the occasion of his conviction, may have been obtained by the defendant's
insurers who were not responsible for the conduct of his defence in the criminal trial, or
may only have become available to the defendant himself since the criminal trial. This
wide variety of circumstances in which s 11 may be applicable includes some in which
justice would require that no fetters should be imposed on the means by which a
defendant may rebut the statutory presumption that a person committed the offence of
which he has been convicted by a court of competent jurisdiction. In particular I
respectfully find myself unable to agree with Lord Denning MR that the only way in
which a defendant can do so is by showing that the conviction was obtained by fraud or
collusion, or by adducing fresh evidence (which he could not have obtained by reasonable
diligence before) which is conclusive of his innocence. The burden of proof of 'the
contrary' that lies on a defendant under s 11 is the ordinary burden in a civil action, ie

proof on a balance of probabilities, although in the face of a conviction after a full hearing this is likely to be an uphill task.

There remains to be considered the circumstances in which the existence at the commencement of the civil action of 'fresh evidence' obtained since the criminal trial and the probative weight of such evidence justify making an exception to the general rule of public policy that the use of civil actions to initiate collateral attacks on final decisions against the intending plaintiff by criminal courts of competent jurisdiction should be treated as an abuse of the process of the court.

I can deal with this very shortly, for I find myself in full agreement with the judgment of Goff LJ. He points out that on this aspect of the case Hunter and the other Birmingham bombers fail in limine because the so-called 'fresh evidence' on which they seek to rely in the civil action was available at the trial or could by reasonable diligence have been obtained then. He examines also the two suggested tests as to the character of fresh evidence which would justify departing from the general policy by permitting the plaintiff to challenge a previous final decision against him by a court of competent jurisdiction, and he adopts as the proper test that laid down by Lord Cairns LC in *Phosphate Sewage Co Ltd v Molleson* (1879) 4 App Cas 801 at 814, namely that the new evidence must be such as 'entirely changes the aspect of the case'. This is perhaps a little stronger than that suggested by Denning LJ in *Ladd v Marshall* [1954] 3 All ER 745 at 748, [1954] 1 WLR 1489 at 1491 as justifying the reception of fresh evidence by the Court of Appeal in a civil action, viz that the evidence 'would probably have an important influence on the result of the case, although it need not be decisive'.

The latter test, however, is applicable where the proper course to upset the decision of a court of first instance is being taken, that is to say by appealing to a court with jurisdiction to hear appeals from the first instance court and whose procedure, like that of the Court of Appeal, Civil Division, is by way of a rehearing. I agree with Goff LJ that in the case of collateral attack in a court of co-ordinate jurisdiction the more rigorous test laid down by Lord Cairns LC is appropriate.

I need not repeat Goff LJ's critical examination of the 'fresh evidence' which Hunter sought to adduce in his civil action for assault. It fell far short of satisfying either test.

I would dismiss this appeal.

LORD RUSSELL OF KILLOWEN. My Lords, I concur with the speech of my noble and learned friend Lord Diplock, and therefore would dismiss this appeal.

LORD KEITH OF KINKEL. My Lords, I agree entirely with the speech of my noble and learned friend Lord Diplock, which I have had the benefit of reading in draft, and would accordingly dismiss the appeal.

LORD ROSKILL. My Lords, I have had the advantage of reading in draft the speech of my noble and learned friend Lord Diplock. For the reasons therein contained I am clearly of the opinion that to allow this action to proceed would indeed be an abuse of the process of the court. I therefore agree that this appeal fails and should be dismissed.

LORD BRANDON OF OAKBROOK. My Lords, I have had the advantage of reading in draft the speech of my noble and learned friend Lord Diplock. I agree with it and would dismiss the appeal accordingly.

Appeal dismissed.

Solicitors: *Saunders & Co*, agents for *Geffen & Co*, Walsall (for Mr Hunter); *Barlow, Lyde & Gilbert* (for the Chief Constable of the West Midlands); *Brian Hill*, Preston (for the Chief Constable of the Lancashire Police).

Mary Rose Plummer   Barrister.

Nereide SpA di Navigazione v Bulk Oil International Ltd
The Laura Prima

HOUSE OF LORDS

LORD DIPLOCK, LORD FRASER OF TULLYBELTON, LORD SCARMAN, LORD ROSKILL AND LORD BRANDON OF OAKBROOK

2nd, 19th NOVEMBER 1981

Shipping – Charterparty – Tanker voyage charterparty – Charterers' duty to designate and procure berth reachable on arrival of vessel – Delay after arrival of vessel at port – Delay due to all berths being occupied – Charterers not responsible for delay – Charterparty providing that delay in getting into berth for any reason outside charterers' control not to count as used laytime – Vessel detained for over nine days before getting a berth – Whether delay over which charterers had no control – Whether charterers in breach of warranty to designate and procure berth reachable on arrival of vessel – Whether charterers exempted from liability for demurrage for delay – Exxonvoy 1969 charterparty, cll 6, 8, 9.

By an Exxonvoy 1969 form of tanker voyage charterparty dated 22nd November 1978 the shipowners chartered their tanker to the charterers for a voyage to carry a cargo from one safe berth in Libya to discharge at an Italian port. The charterparty provided for laydays to commence on 27th November 1978 and for laytime to run for 72 hours thereafter. Demurrage was agreed at $33,247·50 per day. Clause 6 of the charterparty provided: 'Upon arrival at customary anchorage at each port of loading or discharge, the Master . . . shall give the Charterer . . . notice . . . that the Vessel is ready to load or discharge cargo, berth or no berth, and laytime . . . shall commence upon the expiration of six (6) hours after receipt of such notice, or upon the Vessel's arrival in berth . . . whichever first occurs. However, where delay is caused to vessel getting into berth after giving notice of readiness for any reason over which Charterer has no control, such delay shall not count as used laytime.' Clause 8 made provision for payment of demurrage 'for all time that loading and discharging and used laytime . . . exceeds the allowed laytime . . .' Clause 9 provided: 'The vessel shall load and discharge at any safe place or wharf, or alongside vessels or lighters reachable on her arrival, which shall be designated and procured by the Charterer . . .' On arrival at the loading port in Libya at 0140 hrs on 27th November 1978 the master gave six hours' notice of readiness as provided by cl 6 but could not get into a berth because none was available, a situation for which the charterers were not responsible and which was beyond their control. The vessel was detained for a period of 9 days 8 hours 50 minutes before getting into berth on 6th December at 1630 hrs and she completed loading at 1900 hrs on 8th December. The shipowners claimed that the charterers were liable for the detention of the vessel from 1740 hrs on 27th November until 1900 hrs on 6th December and they claimed to be entitled to either demurrage or alternatively damages for breach of cl 9 in respect of that period. The charterers claimed to be relieved from any liability for delay before 1630 hrs on 6th December by cl 6 of the charterparty because it was caused by reasons over which they had no control. The dispute was referred to arbitration in London. The umpire rejected the shipowners' claim stating his decision in the form of a special case. His decision was reversed by the judge who upheld the alternative award for demurrage on the ground that cl 6 only applied to protect the charterers and prevent laytime running if the charterers, pursuant to their obligations under cl 9, had designated and procured a safe place or wharf or vessels or lighters reachable on the vessel's arrival, and if some intervening event then occurred causing delay over which the charterers had no control. Since no berth reachable on the vessel's arrival had been procured, cl 6 did not apply and the charterers were in breach of cl 9. The Court of Appeal allowed an appeal by the charterers and restored the umpire's award. The shipowners appealed to the House of Lords.

Held – Clauses in charterparties, as in other contracts, were to be construed as a whole, and accordingly cl 6 was not to be construed in isolation but in conjunction with cl 9. It followed therefore that the 'berth' referred to in the last sentence in cl 6 was a berth which had already been 'designated and procured' by the charterers in accordance with their obligations under cl 9 and which was reachable on arrival of the vessel. Since the charterers had not procured a berth within the six hours specified in cl 6 after the vessel's arrival, there had been no berth which could have been 'reached on arrival' within cl 9. Accordingly the warranty in cl 9 had been broken and cl 6 did not apply to protect the charterers. It followed that the appeal would be allowed and the decision of the judge restored (see p 739 *c* to *e*, p 742 *j* and p 743 *b* to *d* and *f* to *j*, post).

Notes

For a charterer's right to demurrage days, see 35 Halsbury's Laws (3rd Edn) 311, para 451, for when time begins to run against the charterer, see ibid 314, para 455, and for cases on the subject of liability for demurrage, see 41 Digest (Repl) 464–474, 2414–2496.

Cases referred to in opinions

Aldebaran Compania Maritima SA Panama v Aussenhandel AG Zurich, The Darrah [1976] 2 All ER 963, [1977] AC 157, [1976] 3 WLR 320, [1976] 2 Lloyd's Rep 359, HL, Digest (Cont Vol E) 554, 2483*b*.

North River Freighters Ltd v President of India, The Radnor [1956] 1 All ER 50, [1956] 1 QB 333, [1956] 2 WLR 117, [1955] 2 Lloyd's Rep 668, CA, 41 Digest (Repl) 337, *1330.*

Johanna Oldendorff, The, E L Oldendorff & Co GmbH v Tradax Export SA [1973] 3 All ER 148, [1974] AC 479, [1973] 3 WLR 382, [1973] 2 Lloyd's Rep 285, HL, Digest (Cont Vol D) 828, *2543a.*

Appeal

Nereide SpA di Navigazione, the owners of the oil tanker Laura Prima, appealed with the leave of the Appeal Committee of the House of Lords granted on 2nd May 1981 against the decision of the Court of Appeal (Lawton, O'Connor and Fox LJJ) on 2nd April 1981 allowing an appeal by Bulk Oil International Ltd, the charterers of the Laura Prima under an Exxonvoy 1969 tanker voyage charterparty dated 22nd November 1978, against the judgment of Mocatta J given on 12th December 1979 on the hearing of an award in the form of a special case stated under s 21 of the Arbitration Act 1950 at the request of the charterers whereby the judge ordered that the award of the umpire (Bruce Harris Esq) dated 24th September 1979 in favour of the charterers on a claim by the shipowners for demurrage, or alternatively damages for detention of the vessel, be set aside. The umpire held that the time spent waiting for a berth, after arrival and the giving of notice of readiness, due to ordinary congestion beyond the charterers' control, was exempted under the charterparty's laytime provisions and was therefore at the shipowner's risk. The question of law set out in the special case was whether on the facts found and on the true construction of the charterparty (a) laytime was to count from 0740 hrs on 27th November and demurrage therefore from 0740 hrs on 30th November 1978 until 1630 hrs on 6th December or (b) although laytime and therefore demurrage were not to count during the said period, the shipowners were entitled to damages for detention in respect of it. By para 18(a) of the award, if the answer of the court to question (a) was Yes, the umpire awarded and adjudged that the charterers should pay the shipowners the sum of $193,292·86 together with interest thereon at 8% per annum from 22nd December 1978 until date of payment; by para 18(b), if the answer of the court to question (b) was Yes, the umpire awarded and adjudged that the charterers should pay to the shipowners the sum of $145,754·83 together with interest thereon as

_a_ above; by para 18(c), in either of the events (a) and (b) he awarded and adjudged that the charterers should pay to the shipowners costs; and by para 19 of the award, if the answer of the court to both questions (a) and (b) was No, he awarded and adjudged that the shipowners should pay the charterers the sum of $161,816·44 in respect of a counterclaim by the charterers for a 'without prejudice' payment on account in respect of demurrage made to avoid the exercise of a lien on the cargo. The facts are set out in the opinion of Lord Roskill.

_b_ _Kenneth Rokison QC_ and _Bernard Rix_ for the shipowners.
Anthony Evans QC and _Stephen Tomlinson_ for the charterers.

At the conclusion of the argument their Lordships allowed the appeal stating that their reasons for doing so would be given at a later date.

_c_ 19th November. The following opinions were delivered.

LORD DIPLOCK. My Lords, I have had the advantage of reading in draft the speech prepared by my noble and learned friend Lord Roskill and for the reasons he has given I too would allow the appeal.

_d_ **LORD FRASER OF TULLYBELTON.** My Lords, I have had the benefit of reading in draft the speech prepared by my noble and learned friend Lord Roskill. I agree with it, and for the reasons stated therein I too would allow this appeal.

LORD SCARMAN. My Lords, I have had the advantage of reading in draft the speech
_e_ to be delivered by my noble and learned friend Lord Roskill. For the reasons he gives I would allow the appeal.

LORD ROSKILL. My Lords, once again your Lordships' House is invited to determine the incidence of liability as between shipowners and charterers under a voyage charterparty for delay in loading and discharging ports caused by congestion. In _The_
_f_ _Joanna Oldendorff, E L Oldendorff & Co GmbH v Tradax Export SA_ [1973] 3 All ER 148, [1974] AC 479 your Lordships' House considered at length the principles on which that incidence should be determined with particular reference to the question when and where a ship becomes an 'arrived ship' under a port charter so as to enable notice of readiness to be given and the laytime allowed for loading or discharging to start to count against the charterers. The analysis of the adventure contemplated by a voyage
_g_ charterparty and its four successive stages made by Lord Diplock ([1973] 3 All ER 148 at 174–179, [1974] AC 479 at 556–561) relieves your Lordships' House from traversing once again the same ground for the determination of the instant appeal which, in my opinion, turns on the answer to be given to a short question of construction of two clauses, cll 6 and 9, in the now well-known Exxonvoy 1969 standard tanker voyage charterparty. In the subsequent case of _Aldebaran Compania Maritima SA Panama v_
_h_ _Aussenhandel AG Zurich, The Darrah_ [1976] 2 All ER 963 at 964, [1977] AC 157 at 162–163 Lord Diplock emphasised that in this context, as indeed in others, time is money and that it is therefore of commercial importance to the parties to provide how the resultant financial loss caused by delay in loading and discharging is to be borne, such delay by congestion being in recent years one of the most common causes of delay.

My Lords, the determination of the incidence of that financial loss must turn, as in the
_j_ instant appeal, on the true construction of the particular charterparty into which the parties have entered. Perusal of the long line of decisions both in the last and in the present century suggests a tendency to determine that true construction by reference to whether the particular charterparty under consideration can be designated a port or a berth charter. In cases where the parties have made no special provision that approach may still be valid. But today many charterparties contain either as part of some standard

form or as a special addition some express provision as to the incidence of financial loss if time which would otherwise be available for loading or discharging is wasted because the ship is obliged to await a vacant berth.

In those cases, of which *North River Freighters Ltd v President of India, The Radnor* [1956] 1 All ER 50, [1956] 1 QB 33 is the first in modern times, the well-known dichotomy between port and berth charters is likely to be irrelevant. As Viscount Dilhorne pointed out in his speech in *The Darrah* [1976] 2 All ER 963 at 971, [1977] AC 157 at 171, the decision in *The Radnor* did not turn on any such distinction. In such cases where there is an express provision regarding the incidence of financial loss caused by the ship awaiting a vacant berth, it is difficult to see why the question whether the voyage charter under consideration is a port or a berth charter or whether, as in *The Radnor*, fine legalistic distinctions can be drawn between 'To one safe berth Dairen' which was the wording there in question and 'to Dairen, one safe berth' should in any way assist in ascertaining on what incidence of financial loss the parties must be taken to have agreed in any particular case. If it be relevant I would regard the charterparty presently under consideration as a port charter rather than a berth charter but I do not think that this is any way determinative of the issue your Lordships have to consider.

My Lords, it is against the background of these preliminary observations that I turn to the present case. The dispute as I have already said arises under a standard tanker voyage charterparty in the Exxonvoy 1969 form. Your Lordships were invited to examine the lineage of this form and other forms, some in the line of descent others not in that line, were placed before your Lordships. My Lords, sometimes it is possible to detect from an alteration of clauses in standard forms an obvious intention to depart from a particular judicial decision the practical effect of which the parties wish to avoid. But I do not find any assistance towards solving the instant problem in tracing the lineage of the Exxonvoy 1969 form. Its construction must be determined by reference to its own provisions and not to those of some of its predecessors.

The form is in three parts consisting of a preamble, Part I and Part II. The preamble and Part I are blank forms leaving the details to be filled in as appropriate. Part II contains the standard clauses, 26 in number, with a form of bill of lading attached. The present charterparty, which was concluded in Hamburg on 22nd November 1978, is remarkable in that unlike so many standard forms, the standard clauses have been wholly unamended, five special provisions being added in para M of Part I. That part was duly completed and of its lettered provisions the following are now relevant:

'C. Loading Port(s) one safe berth Marsa El Hariga . . . D. Discharging Port(s) 1/2 safe port(s) West Coast Italy including Islands . . . H. Total Laytime in Running Hours seventy-two sh inc [that is to say, Sundays and holidays included]. I. Demurrage per day US$33,247·50 . . . K. The place of . . . arbitration proceedings to be London. English Law to apply.'

Of the standard clauses, cll 6, 7, 8 and 9 alone are relevant. As already stated, the all-important clauses are cll 6 and 9, but for ease of reference I set all four clauses out in full:

'6. NOTICE OF READINESS. Upon arrival at customary anchorage at each port of loading or discharge, the Master or his agent shall give the Charterer or his agent notice by letter, telegraph, wireless or telephone that the Vessel is ready to load or discharge cargo, berth or no berth, and laytime, as hereinafter provided, shall commence upon the expiration of six (6) hours after receipt of such notice, or upon the Vessel's arrival in berth (i.e., finished mooring when at a sealoading or discharging terminal and all fast when loading or discharging alongside a wharf), whichever first occurs. However, where delay is caused to vessel getting into berth after giving notice of readiness for any reason over which Charterer has no control, such delay shall not count as used laytime.

'7. HOURS FOR LOADING AND DISCHARGING. The number of running hours specified as laytime in Part I shall be permitted the Charterer as laytime for loading and

discharging cargo; but any delay due to the Vessel's condition or breakdown or
inability of the Vessel's facilities to load or discharge cargo within the time allowed
shall not count as used laytime. If regulations of the Owner or port authorities
prohibit loading or discharging of the cargo at night, time so lost shall not count as
used laytime; if the Charterer, shipper or consignee prohibits loading or discharging
at night, time so lost shall count as used laytime. Time consumed by the vessel on
moving from loading or discharge port anchorage to her loading or discharge berth,
discharging ballast water or slops, will not count as used laytime.
          '8. DEMURRAGE. Charterer shall pay demurrage per running hour and pro rata for
a part thereof at the rate specified in Part I for all time that loading and discharging
and used laytime as elsewhere herein provided exceeds the allowed laytime
elsewhere herein specified. If, however, demurrage shall be incurred at ports of
loading and/or discharge by reason of fire, explosion, storm or by a strike, lockout,
stoppage or restraint of labor or by breakdown of machinery or equipment in or
about the plant of the Charterer, supplier, shipper or consignee of the cargo, the rate
of demurrage shall be reduced one-half of the amount stated in Part I per running
hour or pro rata for part of an hour for demurrage so incurred. The Charterer shall
not be liable for any demurrage for delay caused by strike, lockout, stoppage or
restraint of labor for Master, officers and crew of the Vessel or tugboat or pilots.
          '9. SAFE BERTHING-SHIFTING. The vessel shall load and discharge at any safe place
or wharf, or alongside vessels or lighters reachable on her arrival, which shall be
designated and procured by the Charterer, provided the Vessel can proceed thereto,
lie at, and depart therefrom always safely afloat, any lighterage being at the expense,
risk and peril of the Charterer. The Charterer shall have the right of shifting the
Vessel at ports of loading and/or discharge from one safe berth to another on
payment of all towage and pilotage shifting to next berth, charges for running lines
on arrival at and leaving that berth, additional agency charges and expense, customs
overtime and fees, and any other extra port charges or port expenses incurred by
reason of using more than one berth. Time consumed on account of shifting shall
count as used laytime except as otherwise provided in Clause 15.'

The simple facts which give rise to the present dispute were as follows. The Laura
Prima arrived at her Libyan loading port at 0140 hrs on 27th November 1978. She gave
the six hours' notice of readiness for which provision was made by cl 6. That notice
expired at 0740 hrs on the same day. She could not, however, proceed to a loading berth
at once since all possible loading berths were occupied by other vessels. This remained
the position until 1630 hrs on 6th December 1978, some nine days later. The shipowners
claimed that the Laura Prima came on demurrage at 0740 hrs on 30th November 1978,
this being 72 hours after the expiry of the notice of readiness, and remained on
demurrage until 1900 hrs on 8th December 1978 when loading was completed, the
relevant period on demurrage at the loading port being 8 days 11 hours 20 minutes. On
this basis the Laura Prima was on demurrage when she reached Sarroch, her Sardinian
discharging port. There was a further claim for demurrage for 2 days 8 hours 30
minutes there making a total demurrage claim of 10 days 19 hours 50 minutes which
when quantified amount gross to $US59,950·46 and net to $US355,451·08, the amount
of the shipowners' actual demurrage claim. In the alternative the shipowners advanced
a slightly smaller claim for damages for detention for breach of cl 9 totalling
$US307,913·05. The charterers claimed to be protected against these claims by the last
sentence of cl 6, contending that all the loading port delay was caused by congestion over
which they had no control.
          The resulting dispute was referred to arbitration in London. The two arbitrators
disagreed. Mr Bruce Harris as umpire rejected the shipowners' claim in its entirety. He
stated his award in the form of a special case and most helpfully, in paras 13, 14 and 15
of that special case, gave his reasons. I hope I do their clear expression no injustice if I
summarise them by saying that he was of the opinion that the last sentence of cl 6 was

very clear and protected the charterers against the demurrage claim since he had found
as a fact, in para 8 of the special case, that:

> 'The sole cause of the delay to the ship getting into berth until [1630 hrs on 6th
> December 1978] was the unavailability of a berth due to the presence of other ships.
> [The charterers] were not responsible for this situation, nor was it in any way within
> their control.'

As regards the alternative claim for damages, Mr Harris held that, though the charterers
were in breach of cl 9, they could offset against any resultant claim for damages the time
lost during any periods which, by reason of cl 6, were exempted from counting as
laytime.

The umpire made alternative awards in favour of the shipowners according to whether
it was ultimately held that they were entitled to demurrage or damages.

The special case was argued before Mocatta J. On 12th December 1979 the learned
judge upheld the alternative award for demurrage and, rightly in my opinion, did not
deal with the alternative claim for damages. The charterers appealed to the Court of
Appeal (Lawton, O'Connor and Fox LJJ), which, in a judgment delivered by Lawton LJ
on 2nd April 1981, reversed the learned judge's decision and restored the umpire's
award, essentially for the same reasons as the umpire had given, namely that cl 6
protected directly against the demurrage claim and in effect against a claim for damages
for breach of cl 9. Your Lordships' House subsequently gave leave to appeal against that
decision.

My Lords, both parties have lodged elaborate printed cases. The shipowners' case
occupies no less than 16 printed pages and 21 paragraphs. The charterers' case occupies
no less than 19 printed pages and 31 paragraphs. But the matter for decision is very short
and might perhaps be thought hardly worthy of such industrious productivity. Since,
as was indicated after the conclusion of the submissions before your Lordships' House, all
your Lordships were of the opinion that the shipowners' claim for demurrage succeeded,
that the judgment of Mocatta J was entirely correct and that accordingly the appeal
should be allowed, your Lordships did not invite argument from counsel on the
alternative claim for breach of cl 9 which could only arise if the claim for demurrage
failed because the charterers were protected against that claim by the last sentence of
cl 6. I therefore express no view on the question whether, had the demurrage claim
failed, the damages claim would have succeeded. That question must await decision if
and when it arises.

My Lords, in his judgment Mocatta J summarised the argument for the shipowners
which he accepted as being that cl 6 only applied and protected the charterers and
prevented laytime from running if the charterers, pursuant to their obligations under
cl 9, had designated and procured a safe place or wharf or vessels or lighters reachable on
arrival. Then if some intervening event occurred causing delay over which the charterers
had no control the last sentence of cl 6 applied to protect them.

Counsel for the shipowners in effect adopted this submission and put it in the forefront
of his argument. The same point may perhaps be expressed in slightly different
language. Does 'berth' in the last sentence of cl 6 mean a berth which has already been
designated and procured by the charterers in accordance with the charterers' obligations
under cl 9? If it does, then the reasoning of the Court of Appeal is, with profound
respect, wrong and the appeal must succeed. The charterers' argument involved reading
'berth' in the last sentence of cl 6 as 'any berth' and not the 'designated and procured
berth' required under cl 9. But, my Lords, it is axiomatic that clauses in charterparties
as in other contracts must be construed as a whole, and I find it impossible to ignore the
opening words of cl 9 in construing the last sentence of cl 6; and the construction which
I favour is, I think, strongly supported by the last sentence of cl 7 where the reference to
loading or discharging berth must surely mean the 'designated and procured berth' for
it is that berth to which the ship will then be moving, the time occupied by which
movement being excluded from the laytime calculation. Counsel for the charterers
sought to escape from this construction by arguing that the berth did not have to be

immediately reachable on arrival. It was enough, he said, if it could be reached after
a arrival, provided the delay in reaching that berth was not such as would frustrate the
charterparty. He sought to reinforce this argument by pointing to the fact that the
relevant berth had also to be safe. A berth was not unsafe, he continued, if it could be
made safe after the vessel arrived without frustrating delay. By parity of reasoning he
contended that a berth did not cease to be reachable on arrival if it became reachable after
arrival without frustrating delay.

b   My Lords, in my opinion this argument fails on two grounds. 'Reachable on arrival'
is a well-known phrase and means precisely what it says. If a berth cannot be reached on
arrival, the warranty is broken unless there is some relevant protecting exception. The
analogy from the requirement of safety does not assist. The berth is required to have two
characteristics: it has to be safe and it has also to be reachable on arrival.

Counsel for the charterers naturally relied on the finding of fact in para 8 of the special
c case to which I have already referred. He claimed that the finding was unequivocal. It
is unequivocal, but that fact does not avail the charterers unless the berth which the ship
is prevented from reaching by reasons over which they have no control is one which has
already been designated and procured by the charterers in accordance with their
obligations under cl 9.

Counsel for the charterers also sought to support the construction of the last sentence
d of cl 6 for which he contended by asserting that, if this form were used by any of the
major oil companies as charterers, that sentence could rarely, if ever, protect the
charterers since such companies would be likely to control all loading and discharging
berths and it could not, therefore, be claimed that any delay in reaching such berths was
due to reasons over which they had no control. The present charterers, he said, were in
a relatively small way of business without any monopoly position but operating in the
e spot market and therefore should be more readily entitled to the protection of this
sentence. My Lords, it is, at least to me, a novel proposition that the construction of a
clause such as cl 6 can be legitimately made to depend on the identity of one of the
parties.

My Lords, I would only add that the case seems to have proceeded in the courts below
on the footing that there was a conflict between cll 6 and 9 which required
f reconciliation. With respect, I am unable to see any such conflict. Properly construed,
in the manner which I have suggested, these clauses are in no way in conflict. I would
regard them on this construction as complementary one to the other.

Counsel for the charterers also faintly advanced what had become known in the lo·
courts as the 'comma' point, the submission being that because of the commas either si·
of the phrase 'or alongside vessels or lighters reachable on her arrival' in cl 9, those last
g words applied only to 'vessels or lighters' and not to 'any safe place or wharf'. This point
found no favour below and did not noticeably attract favour during the argument before
your Lordships' House. Ultimately counsel for the charterers felt able only to use this
submission to support his main arguments. Since I see no force in the 'comma' point
when one looks at cl 9 as a whole, I am unable to extend the point even that degree of life.

My Lords, for the reasons I have endeavoured to give I would allow this appeal, restore
h the decision of Mocatta J and, like that learned judge, uphold the alternative awards in
paras 18(a) and (c) of the special case.

LORD BRANDON OF OAKBROOK. My Lords, I have had the advantage of
reading in draft the speech of my noble and learned friend Lord Roskill. I agree with it
and would allow the appeal accordingly.

j   *Appeal allowed. Order of Mocatta J of 12th December 1979 restored.*

Solicitors: *Richards, Butler & Co* (for the shipowners); *Norton, Rose, Botterell & Roche* (for
the charterers).

Mary Rose Plummer   Barrister.

Midland Bank Trust Co Ltd and another v   *a*
Green and others (No 3)

COURT OF APPEAL, CIVIL DIVISION
LORD DENNING MR, FOX LJ AND SIR GEORGE BAKER
8th, 9th, 10th JUNE 1981   *b*

Tort – Conspiracy – Conspirators husband and wife – Whether conspiracy between husband and wife capable of giving rise to tortious liability – Whether immunity of husband and wife from indictment for crime of conspiracy conferring immunity from tortious liability – Whether public policy requiring immunity from tortious liability.

In 1961 a father granted his son an option to purchase a farm then owned by the father, *c*
the option to remain effective for ten years. The solicitors failed to register the option as
an estate contract and in 1967 the father conveyed the farm to his wife for considerably
less than its market value, thereby defeating the option. The son commenced an action
in 1970 against his father and the executor of his mother's estate seeking a declaration
that the option was binding on his mother's estate and also specific performance or, *d*
alternatively, damages for conspiracy. The statement of claim alleged, inter alia, that the
land was conveyed by the father to his wife pursuant to an agreement or arrangement
between them whereby they conspired together by means of the conveyance to defraud
and injure the son by depriving him of the benefit of the option. Both the father and the
son died before the action came to trial, and the action was carried on by the plaintiffs,
as executors of the son's estate, against the executrix of the father's estate ('the applicant')
and the executor of the mother's estate. The applicant adopted the defence of the *e*
mother's executor but failed to comply with an order for discovery made against her and
her defence was ordered to be struck out in her absence. On 21st October 1977 judgment
in default of defence was entered against the applicant for damages for conspiracy in
accordance with the case pleaded against her and an inquiry as to damages was ordered
(see [1978] 3 All ER 555). The applicant applied by motion under RSC Ord 35, r 2 to set *f*
aside the judgment on the ground that the facts pleaded in the statement of claim could
not support a claim for damages for conspiracy against the father or his estate because at
all material times throughout the conspiracy he was married to the other party to the
conspiracy, namely his wife, and in law a husband and wife were incapable of conspiring
together. The judge indicated that if the applicant succeeded in establishing that the
judgment entered against her could not be supported in law, the court would exercise its
discretion to set it aside. However he held ([1979] 2 All ER 193) that a husband and wife *g*
were not immune from tortious liability for conspiracy and accordingly that the facts
pleaded in the statement of claim supported the plaintiffs' claim and judgment had been
properly entered against the applicant. He therefore dismissed the motion. The
applicant appealed.

Held – Having regard to the changes in the legal position of wives over the past hundred *h*
years, there was no place in the modern law for the medieval fiction of unity between
husband and wife, and, except in so far as the doctrine of unity was retained by statute
or judicial decision, a husband and wife were to be treated in law as separate and equal
parties. Accordingly, there was no rule that for the purposes of the law of tort a husband
and wife could not conspire together. It followed that a husband and wife could be liable
in damages for the tort of conspiracy even though they were the only parties to the *j*
conspiracy. The appeal would accordingly be dismissed (see p 748 *a* to *e*, p 749 *b* to *e*,
p 750 *e* and p 751 *b* and *e f*, post).

Per Curiam. The common law rule (now contained in s 2(2)(*a*) of the Criminal Law
Act 1977) that a husband and wife cannot be convicted of the crime of conspiracy if they

a are the only parties is not applicable to the tort of conspiracy because the ambit of the two forms of conspiracy is different, the gist of the crime being an agreement to do an unlawful act without more, while the tort requires not only an agreement to injure but also an intention to injure which results in actual injury. Furthermore, the basis of the continued existence of the rule in respect of the crime of conspiracy rests not on the supposed inability of spouses to agree arising out of the doctrine of physical unity but on public policy concerning the marriage relationship (see p 748 *g* to p 749 *b* and *f* and p 750

b *a* to p 751 *f*, post).

Decision of Oliver J [1979] 2 All ER 193 affirmed.

Notes

c For the crime of conspiracy where the only parties to the agreement are husband and wife, see 11 Halsbury's Laws (4th Edn) para 59, and for cases on the subject, see 14(1) Digest (Reissue) 124–125, 825–838.

For the tort of conspiracy, see 37 Halsbury's Laws (3rd Edn) 127–129, paras 221–222, and for cases on the subject, see 45 Digest (Repl) 299–302, 162–191.

Cases referred to in judgments

Allen v Flood [1898] AC 1, [1895–9] All ER Rep 52, 67 LJQB 119, 77 LT 717, 62 JP 595,
d   HL, 45 Digest (Repl) 280, 38.

Bradford Corpn v Pickles [1895] AC 587, [1895–9] All ER Rep 984, 64 LJ Ch 759, 73 LT 353, 60 JP 3, HL, 45 Digest (Repl) 280, 37.

Broom v Morgan [1953] 1 All ER 849, [1953] 1 QB 597, [1953] 2 WLR 737, CA, 34 Digest (Repl) 172, 1218.

Crofter Hand Woven Harris Tweed Co Ltd v Veitch [1942] 1 All ER 142, [1942] AC 435, 111
e   LJPC 17, 166 LT 172, HL, 45 Digest (Repl) 534, 1175.

Gottliffe v Edelston [1930] 2 KB 378, 99 LJKB 547, 143 LT 595, 27(1) Digest (Reissue) 303, 2262.

Lonrho Ltd v Shell Petroleum Co Ltd [1981] 2 All ER 456, [1981] 3 WLR 33, HL.

Mogul Steamship Co Ltd v McGregor Gow & Co (1888) 21 QBD 544, 57 LJQB 541, 59 LT 514; *affd* (1889) 23 QBD 598, 58 LJQB 465, 61 LT 820, CA; *affd* [1892] AC 25,
f   [1891–4] All ER Rep 263, 61 LJQB 295, 66 LT 1, 56 JP 101, 7 Asp MLC 120, HL, 45 Digest (Repl) 301, 183.

Phillips v Barnet (1876) 1 QBD 436, 45 LJQB 277, 34 LT 177, 40 JP 564, 27(1) Digest (Reissue) 302, 2258.

Quinn v Leathem [1901] AC 495, [1900–3] All ER Rep 1, 70 LJPC 76, 85 LT 289, 65 JP 708, HL, 45 Digest (Repl) 280, 33.

g ### Cases also cited

Anon (1345) YB 19 Edw 3 (Rolls Series) 346.
Anon (1364) YB 38 Edw 3 fo 3.
Anon (1366) YB 40 Edw 3 fo 19 pl 10.
Anon (1367) YB 41 Edw 3 fo 29 pl 30.
h *Anon* (1444) YB 22 Hen 6 fo 38a pl 6.
Auten v Rayner (1960) Times, 15th March.
Director of Public Prosecutions v Blady [1912] 2 KB 89.
Director of Public Prosecutions v Withers [1974] 3 All ER 984, [1975] AC 842, HL.
Hoskyn v Comr of Police for the Metropolis [1978] 2 All ER 136, [1979] AC 474, HL.
Jones v Monson (1909) 119 NW 179.
i *Kamara v Director of Public Prosecutions* [1973] 2 All ER 1242, [1974] AC 104, HL.
j *Knuller (Publishing and Promotions) Ltd v Director of Public Prosecutions* [1972] 2 All ER 898, [1973] AC 435, HL.
Manby v Scott (1663) 1 Mod 124, [1558–1774] All ER Rep 274, Ex Ch.
Mawji v R [1957] 1 All ER 385, [1957] AC 126, PC.
Price v Crofts (1657) T Raym 180, 83 ER 95.

R v Cope (1719) 1 Str 144, 93 ER 438.
R v Kowbel [1953] 3 DLR 809; *rvsd* [1954] 4 DLR 337, [1954] SCR 498.   *a*
R v McKechie [1926] NZLR 1.
R v Peel (1922) Times, 8th March.
R v Robinson and Taylor (1746) 1 Leach 37, 168 ER 121.
R v Whitehouse (1852) 6 Cox CC 38.
Ralston v Ralston [1930] 2 KB 238, [1930] All ER Rep 336.
Savile v Roberts (1698) 1 Ld Raym 374, 91 ER 1147.   *b*
Subley v Mott (1747) 1 Wils KB 210, 95 ER 578.
United States v Dege (1960) 364 US 51.
Wennhak v Morgan (1888) 20 QBD 635, [1886–90] All ER Rep 572, DC.
Williams & Glyn's Bank Ltd v Boland [1979] 2 All ER 697, [1979] Ch 312, CA; *affd* [1980]
      2 All ER 408, [1980] AC 487, HL.
Worthy v Birk (1922) 224 Ill App 574.   *c*

Appeal

The applicant, Beryl Rosalie Kemp, who was the executrix of Walter Stanley Green deceased, against whom, together with the estate of his wife, Evelyne Green, the plaintiffs, the Midland Bank Trust Co Ltd and Margaret Ann Green, as executors of Thomas Geoffrey Green deceased, had brought an action claiming, inter alia, damages for *d* conspiracy arising out of an alleged conspiracy between Walter Stanley Green and Evelyne Green to defeat an option to purchase certain land granted by Walter Stanley Green to Thomas Geoffrey Green, appealed against the decision of Oliver J ([1979] 2 All ER 193, [1979] Ch 496) given on 21st December 1978 dismissing a motion dated 6th July 1978 in which the applicant applied, inter alia, to have set aside pursuant to RSC Ord 35, r 2(1) an order of Oliver J dated 21st October 1977 (see [1978] 3 All ER 555, [1980] *e* Ch 590; reversed [1979] 3 All ER 28, [1980] Ch 590, CA; but restored [1981] 1 All ER 153, [1981] AC 513, HL) entering judgment against her for damages for conspiracy, on the ground that the claim for conspiracy in the plaintiffs' amended statement of claim disclosed no reasonable cause of action against Walter Stanley Green and thus the applicant and/or that Walter Stanley Green and the applicant had a good defence to the claim in that Walter Stanley Green and Evelyne Green were at all material times *f* throughout the pleaded conspiracy lawfully married and therefore incapable in law of conspiring together. Mrs Kemp also appealed by leave of the Court of Appeal (Buckley and Shaw LJJ) given on 22nd January 1979 against the order of Oliver J dated 21st October 1977 in so far as it related to the claim by the plaintiffs against Walter Stanley Green and Mrs Kemp for damages for conspiracy. The facts are set out in the judgment of Lord Denning MR.   *g*

James Munby for Mrs Kemp.
Jonathan Parker QC and *Malcolm Waters* for the plaintiffs.

LORD DENNING MR. This is another chapter in the long story of the Green family *h* of Lincolnshire. I told the first part in *Midland Bank Trust Co Ltd v Green* [1979] 3 All ER 28, [1980] Ch 590. So many years have passed that several of the principal actors have died and are now represented by executors of their estates.

The story started over twenty years ago. In March 1961 Walter Green agreed to grant his son Geoffrey an option to purchase Gravel Hill Farm, the option to remain effective for ten years. But the solicitors failed to register the option as an estate contract, so *j* Walter Green was enabled to sell the farm and give a good title to a purchaser, even though the purchaser had full notice of the option. Walter took advantage of their failure to register the option. On 17th August 1967 he defeated the option by conveying the farm to his wife Evelyne for £500 although it was worth £50,000. In 1968 Geoffrey, the son who had been defeated in this way, brought an action ('the 1968 action'). He

brought it against Walter for breach of contract. Walter was afraid he would lose the
a action, so he got rid of most of his assets so as to defeat any judgment which might be
recovered against him. That action started in 1968. Because of the lapse and chances of
time it has not even yet come up for decision.

In 1970 Geoffrey, the son, brought an action ('the 1970 action') against his father and
mother, Walter and Evelyne's estate claiming that the option had not been defeated, that
it had been validly exercised by him, and that he was entitled to specific performance of
b the agreement to sell him the farm. Alternatively Geoffrey claimed damages against
Walter and Evelyne for conspiracy. It is the claim which we have to consider in this
appeal. I will read out the way it is formulated in the claim:

c
> 'Further, or in the further alternative, the said Conveyance was executed pursuant
> to an agreement or arrangement made between the said Walter Stanley Green and
> the said Evelyne Green whereby they conspired together to defraud and injure the
> Plaintiff by completing a sale or what purported to be a sale of Gravel Hill Farm by
> the said Walter Stanley Green to the said Evelyne Green and to deprive the Plaintiff
> of the benefit of the said option.'

And then amongst the prayers are damages for conspiracy.

In 1972 Geoffrey, the son, sued the solicitors for negligence in failing to register the
d option. Five years later Oliver J held the solicitors liable (see *Midland Bank Trust Co Ltd
v Hett, Stubbs & Kemp (a firm)* [1978] 3 All ER 571, [1979] Ch 384). The solicitors
appealed. The case was settled for much less than the damage suffered by Geoffrey.

Meanwhile Walter died, and his daughter, Mrs Kemp, was granted probate of his
estate. As executrix she was in the course of time made a defendant in both the 1968 and
the 1970 actions. Eventually, after appeals in the 1970 action, the House of Lords held
e that the option had been validly exercised and that the conveyance to Evelyne was a valid
conveyance of the farm to her (see *Midland Bank Trust Co v Green* [1981] 1 All ER 153,
[1981] AC 513).

This left outstanding Geoffrey's claim in the 1968 action for damages for breach of
contract and his claim in the 1970 action for damages for conspiracy. In each case against
the executrix Mrs Kemp. Owing to the negligence of someone or other she failed to
f plead plene administravit in either action. But after many procedural wrangles she was
allowed to plead it in the 1968 action for damages for breach of contract, but not in the
1970 action for damages for conspiracy. That is in *Midland Bank Trust Co v Green (No 2)*
[1979] 1 All ER 726, [1979] 1 WLR 460. As Walter had stripped himself of his assets, his
estate is so small that Mrs Kemp is not worried about the 1968 action. She is protected
by the plea of plene administravit there. But she is worried about the 1970 action for
g damages for conspiracy because she has not been allowed to plead plene administravit
there. If she is held liable, she will have to pay all the damages for loss of the option less
anything recovered against the solicitors who failed to register. So as a last resort to
protect herself she applied to strike out the claim for conspiracy on the ground that
there is no such tort as a conspiracy between husband and wife.

Meanwhile she has issued a writ against the lawyers who failed to plead plene
h administravit in the 1970 action. That action is being held up pending our decision in
this present case about conspiracy, because if there is no claim available against her for
conspiracy she has nothing to worry about and the 1970 action will fail. But if there is a
claim against her for conspiracy she will then look to the lawyers who she says failed to
plead plene administravit. So they are much interested in the outcome of these
proceedings.

j   After that introduction we come to the one point of law in this case. If a husband and
wife agree with one another to injure a third person and by their concerted action do
injure him, are they liable in damages for the tort of conspiracy? Or are they immune
from liability by reason of the doctrine that husband and wife are one and cannot
conspire together?

I would like to thank counsel for Mrs Kemp for his most able discourse. He has brought before us all the learning on the subject from the Book of Genesis down to the present day. I trust he will forgive us if we do not discuss it in detail. That was done by *a* Oliver J in the court below ([1979] 2 All ER 193 at 206–218, [1979] Ch 496 at 511–526). The point of principle raised by counsel for Mrs Kemp is this. He says that the doctrine of unity between husband and wife is an established doctrine in English law. So well established that the doctrine and its ramifications are still part of our law today and must still be applied by the courts except in so far as it has been altered by statute. One of the ramifications of the doctrine (that husband and wife are one) is that they *b* cannot be guilty as conspirators together. So they cannot be made liable in damages for a conspiracy.

The authorities cited by counsel for Mrs Kemp show clearly enough that medieval lawyers held that husband and wife were one person in law, and that the husband was that one. It was a fiction then. It is a fiction now. It has been eroded by the judges who have created exception after exception to it. It has been cut down by statute after statute *c* until little of it remains. It has been so much eroded and cut down in law, it has so long ceased to be true in fact, that I would reject counsel's principle.

I would put it in this way. Nowadays, both in law and in fact, husband and wife are two persons, not one. They are partners, equal partners, in a joint enterprise, the enterprise of maintaining a home and bringing up children. Outside that joint enterprise they live their own lives and go their own ways, always, we hope, in consultation one *d* with the other, in complete loyalty one with the other, each maintaining and deserving the trust and confidence of the other. They can and do own property jointly or severally or jointly and severally, with all the consequences that ownership entails. They can and do enter into contracts with others jointly or severally or jointly and severally, and can be made liable for breaches just as any other contractors can be. They can and do commit crimes jointly or severally and can be punished severally for them. They can and do *e* commit wrongs jointly or severally and can be made liable jointly or severally just as any other wrongdoers. The severance in all respects is so complete that I would say that the doctrine of unity and its ramifications should be discarded altogether, except in so far as it is retained by judicial decision or by Act of Parliament.

I turn now to our particular case, conspiracy.

So far as criminal conspiracy is concerned, a husband and wife cannot be found guilty *f* of conspiring with one another. That is now statutory in s 2(2)(a) of the Criminal Law Act 1977. But they can be found guilty if the two of them jointly conspire with a third person.

Counsel for Mrs Kemp says that the tort of conspiracy should be treated in the same way as the crime of conspiracy. He says that husband and wife cannot be made liable in tort for conspiracy with one another. But they can, he admits, be made liable if the two *g* of them jointly conspire with a third person. For instance, he agrees that if the conspiracy charged in this case was between Walter and Evelyne and their son Derek, and it was found that all three conspired together, all could be made liable in damages. But as the only conspiracy charged is against Walter and Evelyne alone, they cannot be made liable at all. That seems to me a most illogical and unreasonable state of the law, not to be accepted unless covered by authority, and there is none to cover it, no decision and really *h* no statement of authority as far as I can discover.

Next I would reject altogether the suggestion of counsel for Mrs Kemp that the tort of conspiracy should be treated in the same way as the crime of conspiracy. The crime of conspiracy is still based on an agreement to do an unlawful act without more. The tort of conspiracy is a modern invention altogether. It is entirely different from the old tort of conspiracy. That old tort lapsed into disuse. It became the action for malicious *j* prosecution. The modern law of conspiracy dates from the judgment of Lord Coleridge CJ in *Mogul Steamship Co Ltd v McGregor, Gow & Co* (1888) 21 QBD 544. It is to be found now in the decision of the House of Lords in *Crofter Hand Woven Harris Tweed Co Ltd v Veitch* [1942] 1 All ER 142, [1942] AC 435, and in *Lonrho Ltd v Shell*

Petroleum Co Ltd [1981] 2 All ER 456, [1981] 3 WLR 33, decided only last week. It

a consists of concerted action taken by two or more persons pursuant to agreement between them with the dominant purpose of damaging another and actually damaging him. It is of use primarily when the act which causes damage would not be actionable if done by one alone (as in *Bradford Corpn v Pickles* [1895] AC 587, [1895–9] All ER Rep 984 and *Allen v Flood* [1898] AC 1, [1895–9] All ER Rep 52), because it is then the only way in which the injured person can recover damages for the wrong done to him. But

b it can be used in other cases, such as the present, where the act done was a breach of contract by Walter and is actionable accordingly; but, for some reason or other, that remedy is inadequate and the only way of getting a just result and a full remedy is by an action in conspiracy.

I see no good reason for applying the doctrine of unity to the modern tort of conspiracy. It is clear that in a like case father and son could be made liable in conspiracy;

c so mother and daughter; so man and mistress. Why then should not husband and wife be made liable? If the allegations against Walter and Evelyne are correct, they did a grievous wrong to Geoffrey. Together with their son Derek they deprived Geoffrey of his birthright, just as Jacob deprived Esau. Both are now dead, but their estate can be made liable in conspiracy, or at any rate Walter's estate which is the only one now before the court. It seems to me that Mrs Kemp would be liable in full if the conspiracy were

d established which is alleged. And if she were held liable for the conspiracy and the damages which flow from it after giving any credit from the solicitor's action she would be liable for it, and then her only recourse would be against the lawyers who failed on her behalf to plead plene administravit, if she could prove that they were in any way at fault.

For these reasons I agree with the decision of Oliver J and would dismiss the appeal.

e **FOX LJ.** Counsel for Mrs Kemp in his very thorough and helpful argument has led us through some seven centuries of authorities. At the end of that journey it is evident that there is no English case which directly determines that a husband and wife cannot, by themselves, conspire together so as to be liable in tort for conspiracy. The matter is, therefore, as it seems to me at large before us, and the court has to decide, on principle, whether a husband and wife can be so liable.

f It is clear that a husband and wife cannot be convicted of the crime of conspiracy if they are the only parties to the conspiracy alleged. That has long been the law. It was confirmed by the Criminal Law Act 1977. The question is whether the same rule should be applied to the tort. The crime and the tort shared the same definition: an agreement by two or more persons to do an unlawful act or to do a lawful act by unlawful means. That suggests some considerable affinity between the two. As I will mention later, the

g affinity is not, I think, in fact very close at all.

But, before coming to that, it is necessary to consider the basis of the rule of the criminal law. The rule probably derived simply from Biblical ideas about husband and wife being one flesh. That became the principle that in law husband and wife were one person. Before the reforms which have taken place over the last one hundred years or so, the principle extended into various fields. In *Phillips v Barnet* (1876) 1 QBD 436

h Blackburn J said that a wife could not sue her husband for assault because they were one and the same person. Lush J gave as further examples of the same principle the fact that a husband could not covenant with or make a grant to his wife and she could not in law be convicted of stealing his property. But as pointed out by Professor Glanville Williams in his article 'The Legal Unity of Husband and Wife' ((1946) 10 MLR 16), to which we were referred, the rule was never applied with full rigour. It was applied very patchily.

j The common law in many respects always recognised the wife as a separate person.

The case law in this century has, not surprisingly, moved sharply away from the idea of 'unity' as between husband and wife. In *Gottliffe v Edelston* [1930] 2 KB 378 at 384 McCardie J said: 'I find it difficult to see how the old and conventional doctrine of unity can be said to operate at the present day.' He went on, however, to recognise the identity

of social and other interests between husband and wife, and said (at 385) 'that in certain
respects there should be a presumption of modified unity between husband and wife'.   *a*

In *Broom v Morgan* [1953] 1 All ER 849 at 854, [1953] 1 QB 597 at 609 Denning LJ
expressed the view that the notion that husband and wife are one 'no longer has any place
in our law'. Hodson LJ referred to *Phillips v Barnet* and said ([1953] 1 All ER 849 at 855,
[1953] 1 QB 597 at 611):

> 'It is true that the reason given for the decision in that case was that husband and
> wife were taken to be one, although no one would, I imagine, question the validity   *b*
> of the decision, it might be justified on broader grounds of public policy, such as
> those indicated in the judgment of McCARDIE, J., in *Gottliffe v. Edelston . . .*'

There have been very great changes over the past century in the legal position of a wife
and I agree entirely with the conclusion of the judge that the continued existence of the
rule in relation to conspiracy as a crime rests not on the supposed inability of the spouses   *c*
to agree as a result of a doctrine of physical unity but on public policy concerning the
marriage relationship. I do not think that the unity principle can simply be applied
mechanically to the tort of conspiracy. A wider approach is, I think, necessary.

I come then to the comparison of the crime and the tort at common law. No doubt
they have to some extent a common origin. But the definition suggests a closeness
which in fact does not exist. The essence of the crime is agreement; execution of that   *d*
agreement is not necessary. The position is quite different in the law of tort. There must
not merely be an agreement (which must be with the intention of damaging the
plaintiff, as the decision of the House of Lords in the *Lonrho* case [1981] 2 All ER 456,
[1981] 3 WLR 33 now establishes) but damage to the plaintiff must in addition be
sustained.

The ambit of the two forms of conspiracy is therefore very different. In the criminal   *e*
law the gist of the offence is the agreement. In tort, on the other hand, although the
agreement is necessary, intention to injure and actual injury are also both necessary. It
seems to me therefore that the two forms of conspiracy are so different that there is no
logical reason for asserting that the immunity given in the one case of crime ought as a
matter of principle to be extended to the tort. Nor, I should add, is the historical
development of the two forms of conspiracy so close that constituents of the one should   *f*
be regarded as being likely to be applicable to the other. The civil wrong in its present
form is really of fairly modern origin. It was largely established in three cases about the
end of the last century, the *Mogul* case (1888) 21 QBD 544; *affd* (1889) 23 QBD 598; *affd*
[1892] AC 25, [1891–4] All ER Rep 263, *Allen v Flood* [1898] AC 1, [1895–9] All ER Rep
52 and *Quinn v Leathem* [1901] AC 495, [1900–3] All ER Rep 1 followed in 1942 by the
Crofter case [1942] 1 All ER 142, [1942] AC 435. So late an origin does not suggest the   *g*
likely absorption into the tort of the, by then, archaic notion of complete unity in law
between husband and wife.

Are there then any general considerations of public policy which should lead us to
decide that, for the purposes of the law of tort, husband and wife cannot conspire
together? I can see none. One must assume that a husband and wife have agreed
together to injure a certain person and have actually done so. Short of that there is no   *h*
tort. But why should they be relieved of liability for injuring a person whom they set
out to injure? Nobody else is so relieved, be they brother and sister or parent and child.
In the criminal law itself there is no protection for husband and wife who conspire and
actually carry their design into effect; and conspiracy as a crime will exist if the husband
and the wife conspire with a third party.

I cannot see that the preservation of marriage or domestic harmony really has anything   *j*
to do with the case. The relationship, if there be any, between liability in tort and
marital discord does not seem to me to have any sensible bearing, as a matter of public
policy, on the question of whether husband and wife should be made liable to persons
whom they intended to injure and did injure.

The crime of conspiracy is not, I think, a safe analogy. Criminal responsibility follows

from the mere fact of the agreement. There may well be considerations of public policy,
a based on the marriage relationship, which justify giving protection to a husband and wife because the existence of the marriage may expose one or other of them to the risk of criminal liability from a mere agreement which the closeness of the marriage relationship might, in practice, make it very difficult for him or her to resist. The Law Commission pointed out in its Report on Conspiracy and Criminal Law Reform (Law Com no 76 (1976), p 20, para 6(a)) that to change the criminal law might offer scope for
b improper pressure to be applied to a spouse; for example, a husband who refuses to confess to the commission of a crime might be open to threat that his wife would be charged with conspiracy.

The result, in my view, is that there is nothing in the authorities or on principle which justifies the conclusion sought by Mrs Kemp. I agree with the judgment of Oliver J and I would dismiss the appeal.

c
SIR GEORGE BAKER. The law is a living thing; it adapts and develops to fulfil the needs of living people whom it both governs and serves. Like clothes it should be made to fit people. It must never be strangled by the dead hand of long discarded custom, belief, doctrine or principle.

The legal doctrine, in so far as there ever was one, of unity of husband and wife,
d whether founded originally on unity of flesh from Genesis 2:24 (and it is to be remembered that the medieval lawyers and writers were clerics) or on the subjugation of woman to man resulting in the submersion of the wife in the husband, he being the head, 'the two are one and that one is the husband', survives in the very limited rule now to be found in the exemptions from liability for conspiracy: see the sidenote to s 2(2) of the Criminal Law Act 1977. To extend this rule or exemption to the tort of conspiracy
e because of the legal fiction of ancient times that husband and wife being one person could not agree or combine with each other would to my mind be akin to basing a judgment on the proposition that the Earth is flat, because many believed that centuries ago. We now know that the Earth is not flat. We now know that husband and wife in the eyes of the law and in fact are equal.

I am content to adopt the erudite and so felicitously expressed judgment of Oliver J in
f the court below, and for the reasons there given, together with those given by Lord Denning MR and Fox LJ, to reject counsel's arguments for Mrs Kemp which he has put so skilfully and attractively. I too would dismiss this appeal.

Appeals dismissed. Leave to appeal to the House of Lords refused.

Solicitors: *Lee, Bolton & Lee* (for Mrs Kemp); *Sidney Torrance & Co*, agents for *J Levi & Co*, Leeds (for the plaintiffs).

Mary Rose Plummer   Barrister.

Routhan v Arun District Council   *a*

COURT OF APPEAL, CIVIL DIVISION
LORD DENNING MR, EVELEIGH AND BRANDON LJJ
22nd, 23rd JUNE, 24th JULY 1981

Rates – Rateable occupation – Occupation by relatives – Husband and wife – Former matrimonial   *b*
home – Husband divorced from wife – Wife and children remaining in matrimonial home – Wife
having equitable half share in house by virtue of court order – Whether husband deriving beneficial
use and occupation of it by virtue of obligation to maintain – Whether husband liable for rates
after decreee absolute.

The parties were married in 1962 and had three children. The matrimonial home was in   *c*
the sole name of the husband. In 1976 the marriage broke up and on 29th November
1976 the wife obtained a decree nisi of divorce based on the husband's behaviour, and
was granted custody of the three children. During the pendency of those proceedings
the husband remained in the house living separately from his wife and children. On
21st December 1978 an order was made that within 28 days from decree absolute the
house be transferred into the joint names of the husband and wife, to be held on trust for
sale in equal shares, the sale to be postponed until the youngest child attained the age of   *d*
17. The wife was to be responsible for the mortgage repayments on the house and the
husband was ordered to pay her £5 a week and £10 a week for each child as periodical
payments. On 22nd December 1978 the decree was made absolute. The husband did
not comply with the order for the transfer of the house until 1981 and at all material
times the house remained in his sole name. Until the decree absolute the local authority
treated the husband as the sole rateable occupier of the house and demanded the rates   *e*
from him but thereafter they decided to treat the wife as the sole rateable occupier and
assessed her for rates. The wife refused to pay and an application by the local authority
to magistrates for a distress warrant against her was granted. An appeal by the wife to
the Divisional Court of the Queen's Bench Division was dismissed. The wife appealed to
the Court of Appeal, contending (i) that there could not be joint occupation for rating   *f*
purposes except in the case of partnerships and that, therefore, if the husband was
assessable, the wife was not, and (ii) that the husband was assessable because he had a legal
interest in the house and kept the wife and children (then aged 17, 14 and 12) there in
part discharge of his obligations to maintain them and was therefore deriving sufficient
beneficial use and occupation of it to be held to be the sole rateable occupier for the
purposes of s 16[a] of the General Rate Act 1967.   *g*

Held – When a husband and wife were living together in the matrimonial home,
whether (per Lord Denning MR and Brandon LJ) the title to it was joint or (Eveleigh LJ
dubitante) single, they could properly be held to be joint occupiers of it for rating
purposes, and accordingly the departure of the husband on a permanent basis, leaving
the wife and any children still residing in it, did not result in the wife ceasing to be in   *h*
rateable occupation of it, whatever the husband's liability for rates might be, since
rateability depended on occupation and not on title. Whether the husband was also
liable for rates in such circumstances was a question of fact in each case, and the existence
of an obligation to maintain was not conclusive of occupation. Since, on the facts, the
separation between the parties had become complete after the decree nisi had been made
absolute, the husband ceased thereafter to be in rateable occupation of the house, and the   *i*
wife, as the person in actual occupation of it and having an equitable half share by virtue
of the property transfer order, became the sole rateable occupier and was alone liable for
the rates. The appeal would therefore be dismissed (see p 757 *a b* and *g* to p 758 *a*, p 759

---

a   Section 16, so far as material, is set out at p 758 *h*, post

b to *d* and *g*, p 760 *g* to *j*, p 761 *d*, p 762 *c* to *e*, p 763 *g* to *j*, p 764 *h* to p 765 *a* and p 768
a *b* to *d* and *f* to *h*, post).

Observations on the liability of husbands and wives to pay rates, both during the subsistence of a marriage and after its final dissolution (see p 756 *d* to *g*, p 757 *b* to *f*, p 760 *c d*, p 764 *g h* and p 765 *d e*, post).

Notes

b For rateable occupation by a spouse, see 32 Halsbury's Laws (3rd Edn) 20, para 23, and for cases on the subject, see 38 Digest (Repl) 482, 509, 52, 219.

For the General Rate Act 1967, s 16, see 27 Halsbury's Statutes (3rd Edn) 92.

Cases referred to in judgments

Beckwith v Barnet Urban District Council (Collector) (1950) 43 R & IT 346, DC.

Bromley London Borough Council v Brooks [1973] RA 137, 227 Estates Gazette 659, DC.

c *Cardiff Corpn v Robinson* [1956] 3 All ER 56, [1957] 1 QB 39, 120 JP 500, 54 LGR 506, 38 Digest (Repl) 482, 52.

Charnwood Borough Council v Garner [1979] RA 49, DC.

Chelmsford District Council v Carroll [1979] RA 45, DC.

Des Salles d'Epinoix v Royal Borough of Kensington and Chelsea [1970] 1 All ER 18, [1970] 1 WLR 179, 134 JP 104, 68 LGR 52, [1969] RA 691, DC, Digest (Cont Vol C) 818, 52b.

d *Earby's Case* (1633) 2 Bulst 354, 80 ER 1180, 38 Digest (Repl) 469, 1.

Electric Telegraph Co v Salford Overseers (1855) 11 Exch 181, 3 CLR 973, 24 LJMC 146, 25 LTOS 166, 19 JP 375, 1 Jur NS 733, 156 ER 795, 45 Digest (Repl) 185, 79.

Enfield London Borough Council v Woolls [1979] RA 399, 253 Estates Gazette 149, DC.

Griffiths v Gower Rural District Council (1972) 17 RRC 69.

Harrow London Borough Council v Brady [1980] RA 168.

e *Holywell Union Assessment Committee v Halkyn District Mines Drainage Co* [1895] AC 117, [1891–4] All ER Rep 159, 64 LJMC 113, 71 LT 818, 59 JP 566, 11 R 98, HL, 38 Digest (Repl) 470, 7.

Hounslow London Borough v Peake [1974] 1 All ER 688, [1974] 1 WLR 26, 138 JP 210, 71 LGR 109, [1973] RA 468, DC, Digest (Cont Vol D) 744, 52d.

Laing (John) & Son Ltd v Kingswood Assessment Committee [1949] 1 All ER 224, [1949] 1 KB
f 344, 113 JP 111, 47 LGR 64, CA, 38 Digest (Repl) 496, 147.

Lister v Reigate Borough Council [1970] RA 1, DC, Digest (Cont Vol D) 743, 8a.

Malden and Coombe Corpn v Bennett [1963] 2 All ER 527, [1963] 1 WLR 652, 127 JP 411, 61 LGR 361, [1963] RVR 328, DC, Digest (Cont Vol A) 1278, 52a.

Midland Bank Trust Co Ltd v Green (No 3) [1981] 3 All ER 744, CA.

Mourton v London Borough of Hounslow [1970] 2 All ER 564, [1970] 2 QB 362, [1970] 2
g WLR 1299, 134 JP 562, [1970] RA 295, DC, Digest (Cont Vol C) 818, 52c.

National Provincial Bank Ltd v Ainsworth [1965] 2 All ER 472, [1965] AC 1175, [1965] 3 WLR 1, HL, 27(1) Digest (Reissue) 93, 675.

Newcastle City Council v Royal Newcastle Hospital [1959] 1 All ER 734, [1959] AC 248, [1959] 2 WLR 476, 52 R & IT 293, 4 RRC 371, PC, 38 Digest (Repl) 539, *372.

Northern Ireland Comr of Valuation v Fermanagh Protestant Board of Education [1969] 3 All
h ER 352, [1969] 1 WLR 1708, 133 JP 637, [1969] RA 475, Digest (Cont Vol C) 818, 321a.

Paynter v R (1847) 10 QB 908, 16 LJMC 136, 13 JP 457, 11 Jur 973, 116 ER 344, Ex Ch; *affg* (1845) 7 QB 255, 14 LJMC 179, 9 JP 31, 38 Digest (Repl) 509, 216.

R v St Pancras Assessment Committee (1877) 2 QBD 581, 40 LJMC 243, sub nom *Willing v St Pancras Assessment Committee* 37 LT 126, 41 JP 662, Ryde Rat App (1871–85) 188, 38
j Digest (Repl) 469, 5.

Thurrock Urban District Council v Curtiss [1970] RA 359, DC, Digest (Cont Vol D) 744, 52ba.

Westminster City Council v Southern Railway Co [1936] 2 All ER 322, [1936] AC 511, 105 LJKB 537, 155 LT 33, 100 JP 327, 34 LGR 313, 24 Ry & Can Tr Cas 189, HL, 38 Digest (Repl) 634, 969.

Williams & Glyn's Bank Ltd v Boland, Williams & Glyn's Bank Ltd v Brown [1979] 2 All ER
697, [1979] Ch 312, [1979] 2 WLR 550, CA; *affd* [1980] 2 All ER 408, [1981] AC 487,   *a*
[1980] 3 WLR 138, HL.

Cases also cited

Brown v Oxford City Council [1978] 3 All ER 1113, [1979] QB 607, DC.
London County Council v Wilkins [1956] 3 All ER 38, [1957] AC 362, HL.
Robinson v Taylor [1948] 1 All ER 291, [1948] 1 KB 562, DC.   *b*

Appeal

Sonia Patricia Routhan ('the wife') appealed with leave of the Court of Appeal granted on
6th May 1980 against the judgment of the Divisional Court of the Queen's Bench
Division (Donaldson LJ and Bristow J) given on 30th April 1980 dismissing her appeal by
special case stated from the decision of the justices of the petty sessional division of   *c*
Arundel, West Sussex, dated 29th May 1979, to issue a distress warrant against her for
rates for the sum of £77·24 on the application of Arun District Council ('the local
authority') in respect of a house known as 3 Lansdowne Way, Lansdowne Road,
Angmering, Nr Littlehampton, West Sussex, in which the wife lived with her three
minor children, her marriage to the husband, Peter Arthur Routhan, having been
dissolved by decree absolute dated 22nd December 1978. The facts are set out in the   *d*
judgment of Lord Denning MR.

Roger Gray QC and *Francis Phillimore* for the wife.
Anthony Porten for the local authority.

Cur adv vult

  e

24th July. The following judgments were read.

LORD DENNING MR. Once again we have to consider the doctrine of unity. It says
that in law 'husband and wife are one and the husband is that one'. I remember well that
it was invoked when I used to prosecute in the magistrates' courts. A wife was travelling
on the railway using her husband's ticket. When she put forward the excuse: 'We are   *f*
one in the eyes of the law', the collector replied: 'But not in the eyes of the Southern
Railway.'

Now we have to consider that doctrine in the law of rating. It has embarrassed us for
years. It has long been held that, when husband and wife are living together in the
matrimonial home, they do not occupy it jointly for rating purposes. There is only one
occupier, and the husband is that one. So also when they separate. The husband deserts   *g*
her and moves elsewhere. The husband remains the occupier for rating purposes. The
wife does not become the occupier so as to be liable for the rates.

Does that remain the law today? Especially as I said in *Midland Bank Trust Co Ltd v
Green (No 3)* [1981] 3 All ER 744 at 748:

> '. . . the doctrine of unity and its ramifications should be discarded altogether,   *h*
> except in so far as it is retained by judicial decision or by Act of Parliament.'

The facts

Now for the facts of this case. The parties married in 1962 in the parish church at
Lancing. The husband was a civil engineer. He was often overseas on his work. They
made their home in a house at Angmering. It was in the name of the husband only.   *j*
They had three children, now aged 17, 14 and 12. In 1976, whilst they were still under
the same roof, the marriage broke up. On 29th November 1976 the wife obtained a
decree nisi of divorce on the ground that the marriage had broken down irretrievably.
The wife was given custody of the three children. The husband remained in the house,
living separately from the others.

In December 1978 the decree was made absolute. The husband left for good or for
worse. On 21st December 1978 an order was made that the house be transferred within
28 days into the joint names of husband and wife, to be held on trust for sale in equal
shares, the sale to be postponed till the youngest child attained the age of 17. The wife
was to be responsible for the mortgage repayments on the house. The husband was to
pay £5 a week for the wife and £10 a week for each child as periodical payments.
Nothing was said about the rates on the house.

The husband did not transfer the house into joint names during 1979 or 1980, but he
is said recently to have done so. The house remained in his name at all times material to
this case.

Until decree absolute the local authority treated the husband as liable for the rates, and
not the wife. But since decree absolute the local authority say the wife is liable. They
assessed her in the sum of £77·24 for the period from 22nd December 1978 to 31st
March 1979. She refused to pay. She said that the husband was liable and she was not.
The local authority applied for a distress warrant against her. The magistrates granted
it. But at her request they stated a case for the opinion of the High Court. The
Divisional Court upheld the decision of the magistrates. They refused leave to appeal
but, as the case involved general questions of importance in the law of rating, this court
gave leave to appeal.

Rateable occupation

Ever since the Poor Relief Act 1601 the person liable to pay the rates is the *occupier*, not
the owner. So in 1633 the tenant was held liable, not the landlord: *Earby's Case* 2 Bulst
354, 80 ER 1180. It is still the law under the General Rate Act 1967. Section 16 says that
'every occupier of property . . . shall be liable to be assessed to rates in respect of the
hereditament'. In the classic definition of rateable occupation the first ·necessary
ingredient is 'actual occupation': see *John Laing & Son Ltd v Kingswood Assessment Committee*
[1949] 1 All ER 224 at 228, [1949] 1 KB 344 at 350. In Ryde on Rating (13th Edn, 1976,
p 28) the principal heading is 'Actual Occupation'. Occupation is a matter of fact. As I
said in *Newcastle City Council v Royal Newcastle Hospital* [1959] 1 All ER 734 at 736, [1959]
AC 248 at 255:

> 'But legal possession is not the same as occupation. Occupation is a matter of fact
> and only exists where there is sufficient measures of control to prevent strangers
> from interfering . . .'

The title to the land is irrelevant save where the fact of occupation is ambiguous. Then
the title may be looked at so as to determine who is the occupier.

Husband and wife

How then do husband and wife stand as regards 'actual occupation'? So long as the law
was dominated by the doctrine of unity, it was the husband who was regarded as the
rateable occupier. He was the only one in rateable occupation, not the wife. It was the
same in other branches of the law, notably in the law of vendor and purchaser. Quite
recently Templeman J said that 'actual occupation for the purposes of s 70(1)(g) [of the
Land Registration Act 1925] does not include the position of the wife of the legal owner
who is in occupation': see *Williams & Glyn's Bank Ltd v Boland* [1979] 2 All ER 697 at 705,
[1979] Ch 312 at 332. The doctrine of unity was always a fiction. It is now rapidly being
dispelled. It has been dispelled in the law of conspiracy in *Midland Bank Trust Co Ltd v
Green (No 3)* [1981] 3 All ER 744. In the law of vendor and purchaser it was dispelled by
the decision of this court and the House of Lords in *Williams & Glyn's Bank Ltd v Boland*
[1979] 2 All ER 697, [1979] Ch 312; [1980] 2 All ER 408, [1981] AC 487. It is, to use
Lord Wilberforce's words, 'heavily obsolete' (see [1980] 2 All ER 408 at 413, [1981] AC
487 at 505). It is now established that, when husband and wife are living together in the
matrimonial home, they are joint occupiers of it just as partners are. I venture to quote
what I said in that case ([1979] 2 All ER 697 at 705–706, [1979] Ch 312 at 332):

'Most wives now are joint owners of the matrimonial home, in law or in equity, with their husbands. They go out to work just as their husbands do. Their earnings go to build up the home just as much as their husband's earnings. Visit the home and you will find that she is in personal occupation of it just as much as he is. She eats there and sleeps there just as he does. She is in control of all that goes on there, just as much as he. In no respect whatever does the nature of her occupation differ from his. If he is a sailor away for months at a time, she is in actual occupation. If he deserts her, she is in actual occupation. These instances all show that 'actual occupation' is matter of fact, not matter of law. It need not be single. Two partners in a business can be in actual occupation. It does not depend on title. A squatter is often in actual occupation. Taking it simply as matter of fact, I would conclude that in the cases before us the wife is in actual occupation . . .'

Joint ownership

Just as the fiction has been dispelled in the law of vendor and purchaser, I feel the time has now come for it to be dispelled in the law of rating. Nowadays husband and wife are usually joint owners of the matrimonial home. Often joint owners of the legal title as well as the beneficial interest. Even if the legal title is in one or the other, they both have a share in the beneficial interest: see the discussion in *Williams & Glyn's Bank Ltd v Boland* [1979] 2 All ER 697 at 702–703, [1979] Ch 312 at 328–329. In all such cases where they are living together in the house, they are jointly in actual occupation of it. Neither occupancy is 'paramount' to the other to use the word of Lord Russell in *Westminster City Council v Southern Railway Co* [1936] 2 All ER 322 at 326, [1936] AC 511 at 529. There is no competition between them so far as occupation is concerned. Be their shares in ownership equal or unequal, nevertheless their occupation is joint. Rateability does not depend on who has the title, be it legal or equitable, but on actual occupation. The actual occupation by husband and wife is joint in fact. It is, therefore, joint for rating purposes.

Single ownership

Now take the case where the husband and wife are living together in the house but they are not joint owners, either in law or in equity, only one of them is the owner without the other having any interest in it at all. Clearly that one is in rateable occupation. But I think the other may also be, because he or she may be in joint occupation, and rateable therefore as a joint occupier. Rateability depends on occupation, not on title.

Joint occupation, both living there

It was at one time supposed that in rating law you could not have a joint occupation: cf *Malden and Coombe Corpn v Bennett* [1963] 2 All ER 527, [1963] 1 WLR 652. But that is shown to be erroneous by the words of Lord Diplock in *Northern Ireland Comr of Valuation v Fermanagh Protestant Board of Education* [1969] 3 All ER 352 at 364, [1969] 1 WLR 1708 at 1728. Furthermore, there is direct authority in *R v Paynter* (1845) 7 QB 255. Putney Bridge was built by moneys provided by many shareholders. They became jointly entitled to the tolls. These were collected by one of their number who resided in the toll-house. The shareholders were held to be rateable occupiers of the tolls and to be liable for the rates. Lord Denman LJ said (at 271):

'I do not think it was necessary that a summons should have been served upon all who are actually interested. One of those parties appears: he is liable in the first instance for the whole: and he must get contribution from the others as he can.'

The decision was affirmed by the Exchequer Chamber (see (1847) 10 QB 908, 116 ER 344), when it was held that 'any one of several joint occupiers is liable for the whole amount of their joint assessment to a poor rate; and a warrant of distress against any one alone is good'.

There is a modern case, too, on the point. In *Griffiths v Gower Rural District Council*

(1972) 17 RRC 69 the joint owners of a holiday flat were held to be in joint occupation
of it. Each was liable for the rates.

In my opinion, when husband and wife are living together in the matrimonial home
(whatever the title to the house, be it joint or single), they can properly be rated as joint
occupiers of it. The observations in *Malden and Coombe Corpn v Bennett* to the contrary are
erroneous. Each is liable for the whole amount of the rates; and a warrant of distress
against either of them is good. The rating authority is not concerned with the title to the
house. It may belong to one or other or both. But that is neither here nor there.
Rateability depends on occupation, not on title.

Breakdown of the marriage, only one living there

Next is the question: what happens when the marriage breaks up, when one or other
leaves the house for good with no intention of returning ever? If it is the wife who leaves
and goes off to live with another man, no one can doubt that the husband is alone in
actual occupation of the house. He is the rateable occupier of it. She is not. The
converse is also true. If it is the husband who goes off with another woman, leaving his
wife in the house, then the wife is in rateable occupation. This is very important from
a practical point of view. Quite often the husband disappears altogether. His
whereabouts are unknown. The local authority must be able to hold the wife liable for
the rates. She is clearly in actual occupation of the house.

But the husband does not escape liability for the rates by going off with another
woman or by deserting his wife and living elsewhere. It would be deplorable if he were
able to do so. So by a series of decisions it has been held that, even though a husband has
left, he may still be liable.

The leading case is *Cardiff Corpn v Robinson* [1956] 3 All ER 56, [1957] 1 QB 39, where
the house was owned by the husband's father. The husband left the house but was held
liable for the rates because it was his obligation to keep a roof over the heads of his wife
and children. Lord Goddard CJ said ([1957] 1 QB 39 at 44; cf [1956] 3 All ER 56 at 57):

> 'It seems to me obvious, therefore, that the husband has made this provision for
> his wife as part of the obligation he is under to maintain her. Therefore, he is using
> this house, which his father has allowed him to occupy, in the most beneficial way
> he can by housing his wife and children in respect of whom he is liable to provide
> a home.'

That case was followed in these and other cases: see *Malden and Coombe Corpn v Bennett*
[1963] 2 All ER 527, [1963] 1 WLR 652, *Des Salles d'Epinoix v Royal Borough of Kensington
and Chelsea* [1970] 1 All ER 18, [1970] 1 WLR 179, *Lister v Reigate Borough Council* [1970]
RA 1, *Thurrock Urban District Council v Curtiss* [1970] RA 359, *Bromley London Borough
Council v Brooks* [1973] RA 137 and *Harrow London Borough Council v Brady* [1980]
RA 168.

None of those cases reached the Court of Appeal. We have considered them all.
Eveleigh LJ considers them to be decided on their own facts. Brandon LJ has analysed
them and shows how difficult it is to reconcile them. I will not take up time over
them. Sufficient to say that, when a husband quits the house, leaving his wife there, the
court can often regard him as continuing to be in actual occupation, just as when a sailor
leaves on a long cruise or a soldier goes on service abroad, whether he sends her an
allowance or not. I would go so far as to say that a rating authority can continue to regard
the husband as being in rateable occupation unless he proves that the separation is so
complete that he no longer has any responsibility for her. That has been the practice of
rating authorities up till now. I see no reason why it should not continue. But the wife
is also liable because undoubtedly, after he has left, she also is in actual occupation.

The present case

To return to our present case. I think that, so long as the husband was in the house,
both husband and wife were in joint occupation. Both were liable for the rates. Even

after decree nisi, whilst he remained in the house, both were in joint occupation. Both
were liable for the rates. The separation was not complete until decree absolute.
Thereafter the wife alone was liable for the rates because she was the only one in actual
occupation.

I would dismiss the appeal accordingly.

EVELEIGH LJ. On 21st December 1978, the day before the decree absolute, the court
ordered the respondent (the husband) to transfer the house, 3 Lansdowne Way, within
28 days into the joint names of himself and the petitioner to whom custody of the two
children had already been granted. The property was ordered to be held by them on
trust for sale in equal shares. No order was made as to the right to occupy the house
pending the transfer or thereafter. Mr Routhan did not effect the transfer at any time
material to the decision we have to make. However, the children and their mother have
resided in the house ever since the divorce and the father has lived elsewhere. I think it
was implicit in the court order that Mrs Routhan should have the right to occupy the
home. Moreover, the parties clearly acted on that basis. Had there been a dispute on the
matter Mrs Routhan would undoubtedly have obtained a court order. The justices held
that Mrs Routhan was liable for rates. The Divisional Court upheld that finding. She
now appeals to this court.

In the grounds of appeal we read that the Divisional Court failed to recognise and hold
that, where a former wife after decree absolute of divorce occupying the former
matrimonial home in which the former husband still retains a legal interest with the
minor children of the family, the former husband is thereby in part discharging his
obligation to maintain his former wife and children to the same extent as a separated
husband and is, therefore, deriving beneficial use and occupation of the former
matrimonial home and is to be held the sole rateable occupier as in *Cardiff Corpn v
Robinson* [1956] 3 All ER 56, [1957] 1 QB 39. It is also said that the Divisional Court
wrongly failed to follow and be bound by the decisions in *Charnwood Borough Council v
Garner* [1979] RA 49 and *Enfield London Borough Council v Woolls* [1979] RA 399.

In this court the argument has been developed in the following way. It is submitted
that there can be no joint occupation except in the case of partnership. Therefore, if Mr
Routhan was assessable to rates, Mrs Routhan was not. Mr Routhan was assessable, it is
said, because he had a legal interest in the house and kept his wife and children there in
discharge of his obligation to maintain them, or at least to maintain the children, and,
therefore, he was using the house beneficially so that he was the occupier for the purpose
of the General Rate Act 1967, s 16. *Cardiff Corpn v Robinson* is said to govern the case. It
was claimed that further support was to be found in a number of other cases between
husband and wife to which I shall refer later. The decisions in a number of those cases
have been cited to this court as though they laid down rules of law. I propose to look at
the 1967 Act itself and then to consider what principles have been laid down in deciding
how to apply the Act.

Section 16 of the 1967 Act reads:

> 'Subject to the provisions of this Act, every occupier of property of any of the
> following descriptions . . . shall be liable to be assessed to rates in respect of the
> hereditament or hereditaments comprising that property . . .'

To be an occupier a person must have possession, not legal possession but in fact. That
possession must be exclusive for the particular purposes of the possessor. The possession
must involve actual user of the property which is of benefit to the possessor and
possession must not be for too transient a period. These are the ingredients of rateable
occupation and whether or not they exist in a given case is a question of fact.

The above propositions emerge from a number of decided cases: see *R v St Pancras
Assessment Committee* (1877) 2 QBD 581 at 588, in which Lush J said: 'Occupation includes
possession as its primary element . . .', and also *John Laing & Son Ltd v Kingswood Assessment
Committee* [1949] 1 All ER 224, [1949] 1 KB 344, where the four ingredients of occupation

or possession, exclusivity, benefit and substantial duration were first laid down. Further,
the importance of the use of the premises is clearly seen in the words of Lord Diplock in
Northern Ireland Comr of Valuation v Fermanagh Protestant Board of Education [1969] 3 All
ER 352 at 365, [1969] 1 WLR 1708 at 1729: 'In the ordinary meaning of the word a
person is in "occupation" of premises if he in fact uses them and is able to control the day-
to-day use of them by other persons.'

In my opinion, Mrs Routhan fulfils all the necessary conditions. She lives in the house
with the children. She has the power to exclude others, including Mr Routhan, the
husband, from living there. While there is no court order excluding him Mrs Routhan
could obtain one should the need arise. She therefore has exclusive use for the purpose
for which she is in possession. The facts of the case do not support an argument that she
resides in the house in order to look after the children for the benefit of Mr Routhan. She
is not his licensee or his agent. She was part owner of the house in equity and, indeed,
since these proceedings have started we have been told that she is now joint owner in law
because the transfer has been completed. In my opinion she clearly falls within s 16 of
the Act.

It is argued, however, that the husband is also an occupier, that there cannot be joint
occupancy in these cases and, because of his obligation to maintain, he must be regarded
as the occupier. I accept that there may be cases of what has been called rival occupancy.
In such cases, where it is shown that one person's occupancy is paramount, he is the
occupier for the purposes of the Act. The existence of a paramount obligation shows that
the condition of exclusiveness does not exist in the other.

The submission that there could be no joint occupancy rested on words of Lord Parker
CJ in *Malden and Coombe Corpn v Bennett* [1963] 2 All ER 527 at 529, [1963] 1 WLR 654
at 656:

> 'Counsel have been unable to refer to any case of joint occupation other than, of
> course, that of partners. For my part, I see very great difficulties in any such
> relationship. It is quite clear that there is no joint rateable occupation when husband
> and wife are living together. It is also, I think, clear that there is no joint rateable
> occupation when husband and wife are living in the same house, albeit not
> cohabiting: see *Beckwith v. Barnet U.D.C. (Collector)* ((1950) 43 R & ITR 346). It
> would, accordingly, be extraordinary if the position changed, and when the husband
> and wife were not occupying the same premises at all, yet they became joint rateable
> occupiers.'

With respect I cannot accept that that passage correctly states the law. Section 16 itself
refers to every occupier, not to *the* occupier. I can understand that cases of joint occupancy
will be comparatively rare whether the occupiers are husband and wife or not. There
will usually be a person whose position is paramount. As Lord Russell said in *Westminster
City Council v Southern Railway Co* [1936] 2 All ER 322 at 326, [1936] AC 511 at 529:

> 'Where there is no rival claimant to the occupancy, no difficulty can arise; but in
> certain cases there may be a rival occupancy in some person who, to some extent,
> may have occupancy rights over the premises. The question in every such case
> must be one of fact, viz., whose position in relation to occupation is paramount, and
> whose position in relation to occupation is subordinate; but, in my opinion, the
> question must be considered and answered in regard to the position and rights of
> the parties in the premises in question, and in regard to the purpose of the
> occupation of those premises.'

(We are, of course, dealing with the case of rival occupants allegedly occupying for the
same purpose and not of separate occupations in respect of the same land where the
occupiers have different purposes: see, for example, *Electric Telegraph Co v Salford
Overseers* (1885) 11 Exch 181, 156 ER 795 and *Holywell Union Assessment Committee v
Halkyn District Mines Drainage Co* [1895] AC 117 at 126, [1891–4] All ER Rep 159 at 163–
164, per Lord Herschell LC.)

In *Northern Ireland Comr of Valuation v Fermanagh Protestant Board of Education* [1969] 3 All ER 352 at 364, [1969] 1 WLR 1708 at 1728, Lord Diplock clearly recognised the possibility of joint occupation. He said:

'Under the Northern Irish legislation, as under the English, the liability to pay rates is imposed on the occupier. Parliament cannot have intended to impose separate and independent liabilities to pay the rate for the same hereditament on more than one person except where their legal right of occupation is a joint right, as in the case of joint tenants. In English law, therefore, although there may be joint occupation of a single hereditament there cannot be rateable occupation by more than one occupier whose use of the premises is made under separate and several legal (or equitable) rights.'

It seems to me that Lord Parker CJ's remark was governed by an assumption that the husband had the only legal right in the house. In such a case his position could be paramount by virtue of that right.

When husband and wife are living together and the husband holds the legal interest in the house I find it very difficult indeed, if not impossible, to envisage a case where there could be said to be joint occupation for the purpose of rating. Title will usually show that his use is paramount. He has control. Where the property is jointly owned, particularly if husband and wife are sharing the cost of running the home, it may be very difficult to establish that the occupation of one is paramount and the conclusion will almost inevitably be that they occupy jointly and are jointly liable to be assessed to rates. In *Griffiths v Gower Rural District Council* (1972) 17 RRC 69 at 71 Lord Widgery CJ said:

'The first question raised by counsel for the appellant is the, to me, rather startling proposition, that you cannot have a joint occupation for rating purposes by two or more people. There are certain authorities dealing with occupation by husband and wife which discuss the rather special situation which then arises, but there is no authority which has been shown to us to suggest that if one leaves aside the relationship of husband and wife, there is any difficulty in the conception of two or more people being rateable occupiers if they do have similar and concurrent rights to the use of the property, and that is exactly the position here.'

Lord Widgery CJ was not saying that husband and wife were an exception, but that the solution of husband and wife cases introduced difficulties which were not found in other cases.

At this stage of the argument then it seems to me, on the facts of the present case, that Mr Routhan can only be said to be the occupier to the exclusion of Mrs Routhan if his occupation is to be treated as paramount because his is under a duty to maintain and if he was in fact discharging that duty by housing his children and his former wife. On behalf of Mrs Routhan, however, it has been submitted that, at least in so far as the children are concerned, the common law duty to maintain requires the court as a matter of law to conclude that Mr Routhan was discharging that obligation and was, therefore, the paramount occupier. In my opinion, this argument falls to the ground when it is appreciated that *Cardiff Corpn v Robinson*, the foundation of Mrs Routhan's argument, was decided as a question of fact. It is quite clear from the judgment of Lord Goddard CJ ([1957] 1 QB 39 at 44; cf [1956] 3 All ER 56 at 57) that he treated the husband as intentionally housing the family as part of his responsibility to them. He said:

'He came to an arrangement with his wife that he was to pay her for the maintenance of herself and the children £6 per week, and she was to live in this house, which he had a licence to occupy, on certain terms which he dictated to her.'

The factual position was summarised by Lord Goddard CJ in these words ([1956] 3 All ER 56 at 57, [1957] 1 QB 39 at 45): 'He has put his wife and family in the house, he being liable to maintain them and that is part of the maintenance for which he is liable.' He went on to say:

'Here there is an agreement, and the agreement seems to me to show that the husband was using this house for the purpose of maintaining his wife and, therefore, had a beneficial occupation of the house.'

On the facts, therefore, the husband was clearly established as the occupier. Not only did the husband use the house in order to provide for his family, his position was clearly paramount for, as Lord Goddard CJ said ([1957] 1 QB 39 at 45; cf [1956] 3 All ER 56 at 57):

'Here the wife is not staying in the house by virtue of a right given by statute, but under an agreement with her husband. It is agreed that part of her maintenance should be residence in this house; therefore, he is making a most beneficial use of the right which he has to occupy that house.'

Beckwith v Barnet Urban District Council (Collector) (1950) 43 R & IT 346 has also been relied on. There the marriage was still existing and the absent husband was the freeholder. The council abandoned their claim against the wife and did not appear at the hearing before the Divisional Court.

The above cases did not lay down any such principle as has been advanced in this appeal. The question of occupation is one of fact. This has frequently been asserted. It has been submitted, however, that in *Charnwood Borough Council v Garner* [1979] RA 49 Lord Widgery CJ treated *Cardiff Corpn v Robinson* as laying down a principle. It is not clear from the report whether that marriage, that is to say in *Charnwood Borough Council v Garner*, had been dissolved at any or at all material times. It seems to me that, for most of the relevant period at any rate, the marriage existed, and I noticed that there was a concession that no obligation attached after 21st October 1976, although the demand ran until 31st March 1977. I do not regard Lord Widgery CJ's judgment as saying that the *Cardiff Corpn* case lays down a principle that, where there is a duty to maintain an ex-wife or children, then the former husband must be taken to be housing them when they live together in property in which he has an interest. In so far as Lord Widgery CJ referred to that case he saw it as establishing that the housing of dependants could provide the beneficial interest which is a necessary ingredient of occupation. He said ([1979] RA 49 at 51):

'*If* the wife was enjoying the use of the matrimonial home, and *if* to that extent the husband was using the matrimonial home as a means of paying the amount due to his wife, then the husband was enjoying a beneficial interest perhaps from the house, and that was sufficient to amount to rateable occupation.'

I would emphasise the word 'if'. He went on to say:

'It was held in that case [the *Cardiff Corpn* case] that the husband had got a beneficial occupation simply because he was using the house as a means of paying some part of his obligation in common law to maintain his wife and children.'

Lord Widgery CJ does not say: 'Because he was *deemed* to be using the house.' The fact that there was an agreement that the wife (and she is consistently referred to in the judgment as the *wife*) should pay the rates was held not to prevent the husband from being the occupier. Lord Widgery CJ said (at 52): 'I see no good reason why the rating authority should not enforce its rights without regard to the personal private interests created by the agreement between the parties.' I respectfully agree with that. The husband, on the facts, might well be in occupation and yet, for convenience, give to his wife a sum of money to pay on his behalf in respect of the rates. I regard the *Charnwood* case as a decision on the facts in which it was found as a fact that the husband was using the house to provide a home for his family.

Enfield London Borough Council v Woolls [1979] RA 399 was relied on. That, however, was a case decided on its own facts. There the rating authority contended that the question of occupation was dominated by the fact that the court had ordered that the former husband should transfer the house to his former wife, and that her occupation, after the making of such an order, was not only in her own right but ruled out any question of the husband being in occupation. However, the wife's rights to a transfer of the property were conditional on her paying by three instalments a total sum of £10,500. She did not do so on the dates contemplated by the order. There were negotiations between the parties themselves relating to the transfer between the date of the order and the date when the £10,500 was paid, namely 24th June 1976. It was never contended that the husband was in rateable occupation after that date, that is 24th June 1976. Morevoer, after the order was made, the husband continued to occupy the garage part of the premises for storing a considerable amount of industrial equipment and he actually used the garage as a workshop from time to time. He had done this since leaving the home in 1972 and had paid the rates up to March 1974. The Divisional Court, therefore, took the view that the making of the order for the transfer of the property had not changed the situation significantly from what it was when the husband paid the rates in March 1974. In the present case, for the purpose of considering the position of the husband, we should treat the court order as effective in transferring the joint ownership of the property to the wife as from the date when the order was made.

I do not think it necessary to deal individually with the very large number of cases referred to in this court. It is sufficient to say that there is no authority which compels this court to hold that the existence of an obligation to maintain leads to a conclusion in law that the husband or former husband is the occupier of the matrimonial home when the wife or former wife, even with the children, are living there. The question is one of fact in every case. The existence of an obligation to maintain may be a relevant fact. It may be of assistance in interpreting other established facts. It is not conclusive of occupation. In my opinion, the test is as I have set out at the beginning of this judgment. Having said that, one may hope that, in future, the court may be spared the necessity of considering other cases which can only be regarded as decisions on their own facts. I, too, would dismiss this appeal.

BRANDON LJ. This is an appeal by leave of this court from a judgment of a Divisional Court of the Queen's Bench Division (Donaldson LJ and Bristow J) given on 30th April 1980. By that judgment the Divisional Court dismissed an appeal by way of case stated brought by Mrs Sonia Patricia Routhan against a decision of the Arundel magistrates to issue a distress warrant against her for rates amounting to £77·24 in respect of a house known as 3 Lansdowne Way, Lansdowne Road, Angmering, Nr Littlehampton, Sussex.

The appeal raises difficult questions with regard to the effect, so far as liability for rates is concerned, of three situations in which a husband and wife, or an ex-husband and ex-wife, may commonly find themselves. The first situation is where a husband and a wife live together normally in a matrimonial home with the children of the marriage, if any. The second situation is where the husband subsequently leaves the matrimonial home on a permanent basis, and the wife and the children, if any, continue to reside in it, with or even without his consent. The third situation is where the marriage is later dissolved and the position with regard to residence in the former matrimonial home continues as before, often but not always pursuant to a court order, that is to say the ex-wife continues to reside in the home with the children, if any.

The present appeal relates only to the third of the three situations described above, but it seems to me that, in order to decide it, it is desirable to give preliminary consideration to the first and second situations as well.

The relevant facts of the present case fall into two parts: first, the history of the appellant's marriage; and, second, the history of the rating of the matrimonial home.

First, the history of the appellant's marriage. The appellant, Mrs Sonia Patricia Routhan (whom I shall call 'the wife') was formerly married to Mr Peter Arthur Routhan (whom I shall call 'the husband'). They had three children and lived together with them at a dwelling house known as 3 Lansdowne Way, Lansdowne Road, Angmering (which I shall call 'the house'). The husband was the sole legal owner of the house, subject to a

mortgage on it. By the summer of 1976 the marriage had broken down and divorce
a proceedings which I shall next describe followed. During the pendency of those
proceedings the husband lived for a considerable time a separate existence under the
same roof as the wife before finally leaving the house.

On 9th August 1976 the wife presented a petition for divorce based on the husband's
behaviour. On 1st March 1978 a registrar made an order that the husband should pay
maintenance pending suit to the wife at the rate of £5 a week and periodical payments
b for the children at the rate of £10 a week each. On 29th November 1976 a judge granted
the wife a decree nisi of divorce on her petition, and ordered that she should have the
custody of the three children of the marriage. On 21st December 1978 the same
registrar made a further order that, on the wife undertaking to be responsible for the
mortgage repayments in respect of the house, the husband should, within 28 days from
the date of decree absolute, transfer the house into the joint names of himself and the
wife, to be held by them on trust for sale in equal shares, and that such sale should be
c postponed until the first of the following events should occur: (a) the wife dying or
remarrying or cohabiting with a man other than the husband; (b) the youngest child of
the family reaching the age of 17; (c) the wife and the husband consenting to a sale; or
(d) further order of the court. The order further provided that, on the sale of the house,
the net proceeds of sale should be divided equally between the wife and the husband, and
d that from the date of decree absolute the husband should make periodical payments to
the wife at the rate of £5 a week. On 22nd December 1978 the wife's decree was made
absolute.

The husband had not, up to the time of the hearing before the Arundel magistrates,
complied with the registrar's order for the transfer of the house. At the hearing of the
appeal before this court, however, we were informed by counsel that he has now done
e so. Since 22nd December 1978, the date of decree absolute, the wife, together with the
three children of the family, has continued to reside in the house, while the husband has
resided elsewhere.

Second, the rating history of the house. At all times prior to 22nd December 1978, the
date of the decree absolute, the husband was treated by the respondents, who are the local
rating authority, as the sole rateable occupier of the house, and the rates were demanded
f from and, so far as we know, paid by him alone. As from that date, however, the rating
authority decided to treat the wife as the sole rateable occupier of the house, and
demanded from her the sum of £77·24 which is in issue in this appeal. That sum
represents an apportionment for the period from 22nd December 1978 to 31st March
1979 of the rates for the whole year to the latter date.

So far as the principles of law relevant to the case are concerned, the four necessary
ingredients of rateable occupation are not in doubt, having been established by this court
g in *John Laing & Son Ltd v Kingswood Assessment Committee* [1949] 1 All ER 224 at 228,
[1949] 1 KB 344 at 350. First, there must be actual occupation or possession; second, that
occupation or possession must be exclusive for the purpose of the occupier or possessor;
third, the occupation or possession must be of some value to the occupier or possessor;
and, fourth, the occupation or possession must not be for too transient a period.

For a person to be the actual occupier of a house for rating purposes, it is not necessary
h that he should reside in it himself. In most cases actual occupation by a person of a house
is achieved by his residing in it. Personal residence is not, however, necessary to give rise
to actual occupation. It can be achieved equally by some other use by a person of a house:
for example, the use of it by him for storing his furniture, or by requiring an employee
of his, as a term of his contract of employment, to reside in it.

So far as a husband and a wife are concerned, there is a long line of reported cases in the
j Divisional Court of the Queen's Bench Division dealing with what I described earlier as
the second situation, namely where a husband departs permanently from a matrimonial
home, leaving his wife and children, if any, still residing in it. Those cases are: *Cardiff
Corpn v Robinson* [1956] 3 All ER 56, [1957] 1 QB 39, *Malden and Coombe Corpn v Bennett*
[1963] 2 All ER 527, [1963] 1 WLR 652, *Des Salles d'Epinoix v Royal Borough of Kensington*

and Chelsea [1970] 1 All ER 18, [1970] 1 WLR 179, *Lister v Reigate Borough Council* [1970] RA 1, *Thurrock Urban District Council v Curtiss* [1970] RA 359, *Bromley London Borough Council v Brooks* [1973] RA 137, *London Borough of Hounslow v Peake* [1974] 1 All ER 688, [1974] 1 WLR 26 and *Harrow London Borough Council v Brady* [1980] RA 168.

All these cases proceed on two supposed principles of law of general application. The first supposed principle of law is that, in what I described earlier as the first situation, namely where a husband and a wife live together normally in a matrimonial home with their children, if any, the husband is the sole occupier of the home for rating purposes, and it is not possible for the husband and the wife to be joint occupiers for such purposes. This supposed principle is treated as applying not only when the legal and equitable interest in the home belongs to the husband but also where the legal or equitable interest in the house belongs to the husband and the wife jointly. Thus the principle was applied even in a case like *Des Salles d'Epinoix v Royal Borough of Kensington and Chelsea*, where the home was rented and the husband and the wife were joint tenants of it.

The second supposed principle of law is that, in what I have described earlier as the second situation, where a husband has deserted his wife, leaving her and their children, if any, still residing in the matrimonial home, he is to be treated as the sole occupier of the home for rating purposes on the ground that, by providing a home in it for his wife and children, if any, he is discharging in part at least his common law duty to maintain them, and is thereby turning the use of the home to his own account: see *Cardiff Corpn v Robinson* [1956] 3 All ER 56 at 58, [1957] 1 QB 39 at 45–46 per Donovan J.

None of the long line of cases in the Divisional Court to which I have referred above has so far been considered by this court, which is not bound by them. Since we are concerned in this appeal only with what I described earlier as the third situation, namely the position after the final dissolution of the marriage, it is not necessary to express a concluded view on the correctness of those cases, which relate and relate only to what I described earlier as the first and second situations.

For my part, however, I feel bound to express the considerable doubts which I entertain about the correctness of either of the two supposed principles of law on the basis of which this long line of cases proceeds.

So far as the first of the two supposed principles of law is concerned, it is, in my view, necessary to take account of the fact that, in the social and legal conditions of today, a husband and a wife are treated, for almost all purposes, as separate persons each entitled to the same rights, and subject to the same obligations, as the other. In a very large number of cases today a husband and a wife are joint owners of their matrimonial home, either at law or in equity, and the case where the husband is the sole owner of it, both at law and in equity, is becoming progressively less common.

That being so, I see no justification whatever for holding that, in what I described earlier as the first situation, where a husband and a wife are living together normally in a matrimonial home with their children, if any, the husband must always, irrespectively of the legal or equitable interests which either may have in the freehold of the house, or, if the home is rented, in the tenancy of it, be held to be the sole occupier of it for rating purposes. On the contrary, my provisional view is that, in cases where a husband and a wife have joint interests, either at law or in equity, in the freehold of their matrimonial home or, if the home is rented, in the tenancy of it, the husband and the wife should be held to be joint occupiers for rating purposes. I say that because, in such a case, the wife occupies the matrimonial home not only in her capacity as the wife of the husband and the mother of their children, if any, but also in her own right as a separate person having a legal or equitable interest in the home.

It may be that in the case, which is becoming progressively rarer, where a husband is the sole legal and equitable owner of the matrimonial home, with his wife having no legal or equitable interest in it at all, the husband should be held to be the sole occupier for rating purposes. Even in that case, however, I incline provisionally to the view that the husband and the wife should still be held to be joint occupiers for rating purposes,

because the other view, that the husband is the sole rateable occupier, involves treating
a the wife, not as a separate person with the same rights and obligations as an occupier of
the house as her husband, but rather as some sort of appendage of his with no separate
existence of her own.

It was said by Lord Parker CJ in *Malden and Coombe Corpn v Bennett* [1963] 2 All ER 527
at 529, [1963] 1 WLR 654 at 656 that the only known form of joint occupation for rating
purposes was that of partners, and that joint occupation for such purpose by a husband
b and a wife living together in a matrimonial home was, in effect, impossible. With great
respect to Lord Parker CJ, I consider that this view is not consistent with the general
principle existing today that a husband and a wife are separate persons each with the
same rights and obligations as the other, or with what was said by Lord Diplock on the
subject of joint occupation in *Northern Ireland Comr of Valuation v Fermanagh Protestant
Board of Education* [1969] 3 All ER 352 at 364, [1969] 1 WLR 1708 at 1728.

c Once it is accepted that the first supposed principle of law on which the long line of
cases in the Divisional Court to which I referred above is founded is incorrect, certainly
where a husband and a wife have joint legal or equitable interests in their matrimonial
home, and perhaps also even where a husband has the sole legal and equitable interest in
it, it follows that the second supposed principle of law on which those cases proceed must
also be regarded as incorrect.

d On the footing that a husband and a wife, so long as they live together normally in a
matrimonial home, are joint occupiers of it for rating purposes, if follows that the
departure of the husband from the home on a permanent basis cannot result in the wife,
who remains in actual occupation of it by continuing to reside there, ceasing to be a
rateable occupier of it. On the contrary, it seems to me that, whatever the liability of the
absent husband may be, the wife must continue to be in rateable occupation as before.

e In this connection it is right to observe, bearing in mind the basis on which *Cardiff
Corpn v Robinson* and the cases which followed it were decided, that the fact that a
husband departs permanently from a matrimonial home does not necessarily mean that
he has deserted his wife and is therefore under a common law obligation to maintain
her. The situation may well be that the husband has good cause for leaving the
matrimonial home, for example, if his wife has committed adultery or behaved towards
f him in such a way that she has constructively deserted him. In such cases the husband
would no longer be under any common law obligation to maintain her, and the basis on
which *Cardiff Corpn v Robinson* and the many decisions which followed it proceeded
would not apply.

The views which I have expressed above relate to what I described earlier as the first
and second situations, and are, as I hope I have made clear, provisional only. I now turn
g to consider what I described earlier as the third situation, namely that following the final
dissolution of a marriage, which is the situation which arises in the present case. In
relation to that situation there are four authorities, all again in the Divisional Court,
which it is necessary to consider.

The first authority is *Mourton v London Borough of Hounslow* [1970] 2 All ER 564, [1970]
2 QB 362. The facts of that case were as follows. From 1951 to 1962 a husband and his
h wife lived together with their children in a matrimonial home owned by the husband
and his father. The husband was shown in the rating authority's records as the sole
rateable occupier of the house and was charged with and paid the rates in respect of it
accordingly. In 1962 the husband left the matrimonial home on a permanent basis. The
wife and one of the children of the family continued to reside in it. Divorce proceedings
followed in which the wife obtained a decree absolute in 1963. In 1964 a divorce
j registrar made a consent order under which, on the basis that the ex-husband would
continue to pay the outgoings on the former matrimonial home and allow the ex-wife
and the child of the marriage to continue residing in it, it was ordered that the ex-
husband should pay only nominal maintenance to the ex-wife. Following the divorce
the ex-husband went to live in Italy but, until 1967, he continued to be shown in the
rating authority's records as the sole rateable occupier of the former matrimonial home

and he continued to be charged with and to pay the rates in respect of it. In 1967 the ex-
husband ceased to pay the rates, whereupon the rating authority amended its records to
show the ex-wife as the sole rateable occupier of the former matrimonial home in place
of the ex-husband and to charge her with rates accordingly. The ex-wife failed to pay the
rates demanded of her and the question arose, on an appeal by her by way of case stated
to the Divisional Court, whether she was liable to do so or not.

It was held by the Divisional Court that the principle on which *Cardiff Corpn v
Robinson* and the cases which followed it had been decided, namely that a husband, by
using the former matrimonial home as a home for his wife and their children, if any, was
in actual occupation of it, and therefore the sole rateable occupier in respect of it, did not
apply after the dissolution of their marriage.

Bridge J, who gave the judgment of the court, referred first to *Cardiff Corpn v Robinson*
and the other cases which had followed it and then to a passage from the speech of Lord
Upjohn in *National Provincial Bank Ltd v Ainsworth* [1965] 2 All ER 472 at 484–485, [1965]
AC 1175 at 1232. Having done so, he said ([1970] 2 All ER 564 at 568, [1970] 2 QB 362
at 371):

'It follows that if the wife acquires any right to continue in occupation of the
former matrimonial home after the marriage has been dissolved, it is a right of a
new and different character. It may arise under an order of the court or by
agreement. Superficially it may appear to resemble the former right, especially if
the dissolution of the marriage has been preceded by a period of separation during
which a similar order or agreement may have been operative. But to extend the
principle of the *Cardiff Corpn v Robinson* line of cases across the watershed of divorce,
although logically plausible on the widest view of what is meant by the obligation
to maintain to which those cases refer, would in our judgment be to introdue a large
and unjustifiable element of fiction into this branch of the law of rating.'

Later on in his judgment Bridge J added what he called one word of reservation. He said
([1970] 2 All ER 564 at 569, [1970] 2 QB 362 at 372):

'While the common law duties of a husband to his wife terminate on termination
of the marriage, the common law duties of a father to his children clearly do not.
It is certainly possible to envisage a situation where a father may, after divorce,
provide a home for his children in which the mother will live as the person having
either custody or care and control. In such a situation it might well be held that the
father was the rateable occupier. That, however, is not this case. It was not
suggested to us in argument that any significance was to be attached to the reference
in the 1964 order to the son, Ian James Mourton, or to his continued presence in the
house today. The case stated contains no finding of fact as to his present
circumstances. He may now well be, for all we know, a fully self-supporting adult.'

The second authority is *Chelmsford District Council v Carroll* [1979] RA 45. In that case
a husband and wife with two young children were divorced in 1974. After the divorce
a house was purchased for the purpose of providing accommodation for the ex-wife and
the two children of the marriage. There was a maintenance order in existence against
the ex-husband for the benefit of the ex-wife and the children. The rating authority
treated the ex-wife as the sole rateable occupier of the house, but the Chelmsford
magistrates refused to issue a distress warrant against her for non-payment of rates on the
ground that the ex-husband's common law obligation to provide accommodation for his
young children remained after divorce and he was therefore still the sole rateable
occupier. It seems fairly clear that the magistrates reached this decision in the light of
the reservation made by Bridge J in his judgment in *Mourton v London Borough of
Hounslow*, the relevant part of which I quoted above.

On an appeal by way of case stated by the rating authority to the Divisional Court, it
was held that the ex-wife had been rightly treated as the sole rateable occupier of the
house and that a distress warrant should accordingly have been issued against her. May J,

who gave a judgment with which the other two members of the court, Lord Widgery CJ
and Tudor Evans J, agreed, referred to the reservation made by Bridge J in *Mourton v
London Borough of Hounslow*, but said that the facts stated by the magistrates did not bring
the case within the terms of that reservation. It appears that the main fact considered to
be lacking was that the house in which the ex-wife and two children lived had been
provided by the ex-husband in discharge of his common law duty to maintain such
children.

The third authority is *Charnwood Borough Council v Garner* [1979] RA 49. In that case
a husband and wife had lived together with their one child in a matrimonial home of
which they were the joint owners. Subsequently the marriage broke down, the husband
left, and the wife and child continued to reside in the home. An order was then made
by a magistrates' court that the husband should pay to the wife maintenance at the rate
of £10 a week for herself and £6 a week for the child, on the basis that the wife would
accept liability for the payment of the rates and the mortgage payments on the former
matrimonial home. Eventually there was a divorce, after which the ex-wife married
another man, and she and her second husband and the child continued to reside in the
home. The rating authority charged the first husband for rates, not only during the
period of separation prior to the divorce, but also during the period after the divorce up
to the date of the ex-wife's remarriage. The ex-husband having failed to pay the rates
demanded of him, the rating authority appealed by way of case stated to the Divisional
Court. That court held that the ex-husband was liable for the rates both before and after
the divorce, and that neither the fact that the ex-husband and the ex-wife were joint
owners of the former matrimonial home nor the basis on which the magistrates' court
had made its order made any difference to the ex-husband's liability.

The fourth authority is *Enfield London Borough Council v Woolls* [1979] RA 399. In that
case a husband and wife had prior to 1972 lived in a matrimonial home which comprised
a house and garage attached to it. The husband was registered in the Land Registry as the
sole owner of the premises, but late in 1971 the wife caused a caution to be entered in the
Land Registry in order to protect the right of occupation of them which she claimed to
have. In June 1972, in divorce proceedings brought by the wife, she was granted a decree
nisi, and at or about the same time the court ordered that the wife's rights of occupation
of the premises were to continue. The husband then left the matrimonial home and
went to live elsewhere, while the wife and the children continued to reside in it. On 8th
September 1972 the wife's decree was made absolute.

In January 1973 the High Court made an order for the ex-husband to make periodical
payments for the children. He was not, however, ordered to make periodical payments
for the ex-wife, it being taken into account by the judge that the wife was residing in the
matrimonial home with the children free of expenses. The order for periodical payments
for the children was varied on 5th April 1974 as to the amount of money payable, but
otherwise it remained in force at all material times. On the same day the court ordered
that the ex-husband should forthwith transfer the premises to the ex-wife, on
undertakings by her to pay various sums of money to her former father-in-law and also
to the ex-husband on specified future dates. She did not make the payments concerned
on the dates specified, but ultimately on 24th June 1976 she paid the whole of the sums
ordered, whereupon the ex-husband transferred the premises to her.

After leaving the premises in June 1972 the husband had continued to use the garage
for stowing a considerable quantity of industrial equipment, and occasionally had also
made use of it as a workshop.

The rates in respect of the premises up to 24th March 1974 were paid by the ex-
husband. For the period from 5th April 1974 to 24th June 1976 the rating authority
sought to charge the ex-wife with the rates. She failed to pay them, whereupon the
rating authority applied to the Edmonton magistrates for a distress warrant to be issued
against her. The magistrates, however, accepted the ex-wife's contention that the ex-
husband was still in rateable occupation and dismissed the application. The rating
authority then appealed by way of case stated to the Divisional Court. That court

dismissed the appeal on the ground that, in the particular circumstances of the case, there was material on which the magistrates could properly hold that the ex-husband had the degree of beneficial occupation necessary for them to come to the conclusion that he was still the rateable occupier.

The four authorities above relating to what I described earlier as the third situation, where an ex-wife continues to live with the children of the marriage, if any, in the former matrimonial home after her marriage has been finally dissolved, are not altogether easy to reconcile with each other.

As I indicated earlier, my provisional view is that, where a husband departs permanently from a matrimonial home, leaving his wife and children still residing in it, it is the wife and not the husband who should, in most cases at any rate, be held to be the rateable occupier, even though the marriage of the husband and the wife is still subsisting. Assuming, however, that that view is wrong, and that the principles applied in *Cardiff Corpn v Robinson* and the numerous cases which followed it are correct, then I agree entirely with the opinion expressed by Bridge J in *Mourton v London Borough of Hounslow* that the liability of the husband to pay rates cannot continue once the marriage between him and the wife has been finally dissolved. I would not, however, adopt the reservation to that principle which he thought it necessary to make.

Being of that opinion, I would regard *Chelmsford District Council v Carroll* as having been correctly decided, though on wider grounds than those relied on by the Divisional Court, and I would regard *Charnwood Borough Council v Garner*, in so far at any rate as it decided that the ex-husband was liable for rates after the final dissolution of his marriage, as having been wrongly decided. With regard to *Enfield London Borough Council v Woolls*, I think that, while the decision appears at first sight to run contrary to *Mourton v London Borough of Hounslow*, it may be possible to justify it on its special facts, in particular the delay in the transfer of the premises to the ex-wife resulting from her failing to make at the proper times the payments which she had undertaken to make, and the ex-husband's continued use of the garage, which was an integral part of the premises, for his own benefit.

Having examined what can only be described as the tangled law with regard to the liability to pay rates of husbands and wives, both during the subsistence of a marriage and after the final dissolution of it, I must now apply the conclusions which I have reached to the facts of the present case as they were when it was before the Arundel magistrates.

The situation then was that the marriage of the husband and the wife had been finally dissolved and that, by virtue of a judge's order for the transfer of the former matrimonial home into joint names, the ex-wife had an equitable interest in one-half of it. Her right to occupy the home with the children of the marriage was not a right conferred on her by her ex-husband in the discharge of his common law obligation to maintain his children: it was, on the contrary, her own personal right resulting from the transfer of property order.

That being the situation, it seems to me quite clear that the ex-wife, as the person in actual occupation of the home, and having an equitable one-half share in it, was the sole rateable occupier of it.

That was the conclusion arrived at by the Divisional Court. I agree with it and would dismiss the appeal accordingly.

Appeal dismissed.

Solicitors: *Whitehouse, Gibson & Alton* (for the wife); *Sharpe, Pritchard & Co* (for the husband).

Mary Rose Plummer   Barrister.

R v Wells Street Magistrates' Court, ex parte Albanese

QUEEN'S BENCH DIVISION (DIVISIONAL COURT LIST)
RALPH GIBSON J
11th, 12th, 29th JUNE, 8th JULY 1981

Criminal law – Bail – Recognisance – Validity – Recognisance for continuous bail entered into by surety – Subsequent variation in conditions of bail – Bail as varied continued on surety's previous recognisance – Surety not notified of variation in conditions of bail – Failure of accused to appear in court – Whether recognisance valid – Whether failure to notify surety of variation in bail conditions a breach of natural justice – Whether variation of bail conditions and continuation of bail on previous recognisance invalid.

Criminal law – Bail – Recognisance – Forfeiture – Magistrates' court – Discretion to forfeit recognisance in whole or in part – Matters to be considered – Surety's culpability for accused's disappearance – Recognisance for continuous bail conditioned for appearance of accused before court – Subsequent variation in bail conditions – Surety not notified and ignorant of variation – Surety not to blame for ignorance – Accused absconding from country – Magistrate ordering forfeiture of whole of recognisance – Whether failure to notify surety of variation in bail conditions a matter affecting magistrate's discretion to forfeit recognisance – Whether order to forfeit recognisance should be quashed – Magistrates' Courts Act 1952, s 96(1).

On 9th April 1979 two accused were remanded to 5th July 1979 and were granted bail by a magistrates' court on conditions that they respectively deposited with the court £3,000 and £5,000, obtained sureties for £7,000 and £5,000 and surrendered their passports. The applicant, who was their employer or business associate, entered into continuous recognisances in the sums of £7,000 and £5,000 respectively to secure their appearance in court. On 5th July 1979 the accused were remanded to 26th September 1979 and the bail conditions were varied by the return to the accused of their passports. The applicant agreed to continue as surety but he was not aware of the changes in the conditions of bail until shortly before 15th September. On 26th September the accused were remanded to 10th October. On 27th September, on the application of the accused, £1,000 was returned to each of the accused out of the moneys they had deposited in court. Due to an error, that variation in the bail conditions was not entered in the court records and neither was the applicant aware of if. On 10th October the accused were remanded to 18th March 1980, but they absconded before that date. On 6th February 1981, on an application to forfeit the applicant's recognisances because of the non-appearance in court of the accused, the stipendiary magistrate exercised his discretion under s 96(1) and (3)[a] of the Magistrates' Courts Act 1952 to order forfeiture of the whole of the recognisances. Because of the defect in the court records the magistrate made that decision in ignorance of the variation in the bail conditions made on 27th September 1979 and in ignorance of the fact that the applicant had not been notified of the variation. The applicant applied for an order of certiorari to quash the magistrate's order on the grounds (i) that because he had not been notified of the variation made on 27th

---

Section 96, so far as material, provides:
    '(1) Where . . . any recognizance is conditioned for the appearance of a person before a magistrates' court . . . and the recognizance appears to the court to be forfeited, the court may . . . declare the recognizance to be forfeited and adjudge the persons bound thereby, whether as principal or sureties, or any of them, to pay the sum in which they are respectively bound . . .
    '(3) The court which declares the recognizance to be forfeited may, instead of adjudging any person to pay the whole sum in which he is bound, adjudge him to pay part only of the sum or remit the sum . . .'

September and was not given an opportunity to be heard on the variation, the order of
27th September varying the bail conditions and continuing bail on his recognisances was *a*
void, (ii) alternatively, that by analogy with the rule that a surety under a contract of
guarantee was discharged where there was a material change in the terms of the contract
between the creditor and the principal debtor, a surety under a bail recognisance was
discharged if there was a material change in the bail conditions without his knowledge
and consent, or in the further alternative the magistrate should in the circumstances have
exercised his discretion under s 96(1) and (3) by not forfeiting the whole of the *b*
recognisances. The applicant also applied for an order of mandamus directing a
magistrate other than the stipendiary magistrate to hear and determine the application
to forfeit the recognisances.

Held – (1) Although a surety under a continuous bail recognisance had an interest in the
bail conditions so far as they affected the likelihood of the accused surrendering to his bail *c*
or the effectiveness with which the surety could keep in contact with him, a court, when
varying the conditions of bail and directing that the bail as varied should continue on the
previous continuous recognisance of a surety, was not under a duty either by statute or
by implication to notify the surety of the variation or to hear him on the variation. Since
a surety's failure to fulfil the condition of his recognisance that he secure the accused's
appearance in court gave rise to a civil debt which, subject to the court's discretion under *d*
s 96 of the 1952 Act to remit forfeiture of the whole or part of the recognisance, was
enforceable like a fine, it was the duty of the surety himself to keep himself informed of
the bail conditions by, for example, entering into a recognisance only from one remand
to another and not into a continuous recognisance. It followed that the validity of a
continuous recognisance was not affected by a subsequent variation of bail conditions
made without notifying the surety and that a subsequent variation without notification *e*
did not automatically discharge the previous recognisance. Accordingly, the orders of
27th September 1979 varying the conditions of the accused's bail were valid and did not
impair the validity of the recognisances entered into by the applicant (see p 776 *c d* and
g to *j*, p 777 *c* to *e* and p 778 *c*, post); dictum of Lord Denning MR in *Schmidt v Secretary
of State for Home Affairs* [1969] 1 All ER at 909 considered.

(2) However, a variation in the conditions of bail without notice to a surety under a *f*
continuous bail recognisance could be a matter which the court was required to take into
account in exercising its discretion under s 96(1) of the 1952 Act to forfeit the whole of
the surety's recognisance, particularly when considering to what extent the surety had
been culpable for the accused's non-appearance in court. Thus, if it appeared to the court
that the surety might have refused to continue as surety if he had known of the variation
in the bail conditions and if he was not to blame for his ignorance of the variation, that *g*
was a matter which was to be taken into account in considering his culpability for the
accused's non-appearance. Since the return to each accused of £1,000 out of the moneys
they had deposited in court, under the variation made on 27th September 1979, might
have indicated to the applicant that the accused were planning to abscond and might
have caused him to withdraw his recognisance, that variation and the applicant's
ignorance of it were matters which the stipendiary magistrate ought to have taken into *h*
account in considering whether to forfeit the applicant's recognisances. Since the
magistrate had not done so, due to the variation not being entered in the court records,
his decision would be quashed and the application to forfeit the recognisances remitted
to a different magistrate for rehearing. It followed that the orders of certiorari and
mandamus sought by the applicant would be granted (see p 775 *g*, p 778 *e* to *h* and p 779
d to p 780 *b*, post); dicta of Lord Denning MR in *R v Southampton Justices, ex parte Green* *j*
[1975] 2 All ER at 1077–1078 and of Lord Widgery CJ in *R v Horseferry Road Stipendiary
Magistrate, ex parte Pearson* [1976] 2 All ER at 266 applied.

Per Curiam. (1) Although variation of bail conditions cannot affect the validity of a
recognisance for continuous bail, consideration should be given to explaining to a surety
before he enters into a recognisance, and expressly warning him when he does enter into
the recognisance (possibly by a clear note on the recognisance form), that the conditions

of bail may be varied by the court and that he should not enter into a continuous bail

a recognisance if he is concerned about the bail conditions. Furthermore, the conditions of bail should be recorded on the recognisance form so that the surety is aware of them (see p 777 e to j, post).

(2) It is a proper and just practice for a court when making a variation in bail conditions which it thinks might affect a surety's willingness to continue as surety, to decline to continue bail on the varied conditions unless the surety knows of the variation

b and agrees to continue as surety (see p 778 c d, post).

Notes

For forfeiture of a bail recognisance, see 29 Halsbury's Laws (4th Edn) para 445, and for cases on the subject, see 14(1) Digest (Reissue) 317, 2448–2449.

For the Magistrates' Courts Act 1952, s 96, see 21 Halsbury's Statutes (3rd Edn) 266.

c As from 6th July 1981 s 96 of the 1952 Act was replaced by s 120 of the Magistrates' Courts Act 1980.

Cases referred to in judgment

Bracegirdle v Oxley, Bracegirdle v Cobley [1947] 1 All ER 126, [1947] KB 349, [1947] LJR 815, 176 LT 187, 111 JP 131, 45 LGR 69, DC, 33 Digest (Repl) 313, 1360.

d *R v Horseferry Road Magistrates' Court, ex parte Pearson* [1976] 2 All ER 264, [1976] 1 WLR 511, DC, 14(1) Digest (Reissue) 317, 2449.

R v Southampton Justices, ex parte Green [1975] 2 All ER 1073, [1976] QB 11, [1975] 3 WLR 277, 139 JP 667, CA, 14(1) Digest (Reissue) 237, 1709.

R v Tottenham Magistrates' Court, ex parte Riccardi (1978) 66 Cr App R 150, DC.

Ridge v Baldwin [1963] 2 All ER 66, [1964] AC 40, [1963] 2 WLR 935, 127 JP 295, 61 LGR

e 369, HL, 37 Digest (Repl) 195, 32.

Schmidt v Secretary of State for Home Affairs [1969] 1 All ER 904, [1969] 2 Ch 149, [1969] 2 WLR 337, 133 JP 274, CA, 2 Digest (Reissue) 203, 1160.

Cases also cited

Breen v Amalgamated Engineering Union [1971] 1 All ER 1148, [1971] 2 QB 175, CA.

f *Pergamon Press Ltd, Re* [1970] 3 All ER 535, [1971] Ch 388, CA.

R v Gaming Board for Great Britain, ex parte Benaim [1970] 2 All ER 528, [1970] 2 QB 417, CA.

R v Knightsbridge Crown Court, ex parte Newton [1980] Crim LR 715, DC.

R v St Albans Crown Court, ex parte Cinnamond [1981] 1 All ER 802, [1981] QB 480, DC.

Sabey (H) & Co Ltd v Secretary of State for the Environment [1978] 1 All ER 586.

g *Wiseman v Borneman* [1969] 3 All ER 275, [1971] AC 297, HL.

Application for judicial review

Pucci Albanese applied, with the leave of Webster J given on 1st April 1981, for (i) an order of certiorari to quash the order made on 6th February 1981 by Mr C Besley, the metropolitan stipendiary magistrate sitting at Wells Street Magistrates' Court ('the

h respondents'), that Mr Albanese forfeit within 28 days, with six months' imprisonment in default, recognisances in the sums of £5,000 and £7,000 he had entered into on 5th July 1979 in respect of bail granted to Maurizio Fiori and Cesare Brichenzo who failed to appear before a magistrates' court on 18th March 1980 and (ii) an order of mandamus directed to the magistrates other than Mr Besley at Wells Street Magistrates' Court to hear and determine according to law the application that Mr Albanese should forfeit his

j recognisances. The facts are set out in the judgment.

Peter Martin for Mr Albanese.
Andrew Collins for the respondents.

8th July. **RALPH GIBSON J** read the following judgment: Mr Albanese applies, by
leave of Webster J given on 1st April 1981, for relief with reference to an order made by *a*
the respondents, Wells Street Magistrates' Court, on 6th February 1981 directing that he
should forfeit and pay the sums of £5,000 and £7,000.

The £5,000 was ordered to be paid under a recognisance entered into by him on 5th
July 1979 as a condition of the bail granted to the accused Maurizio Fiori. The £7,000
was ordered to be paid under a recognisance entered into by him on the same date as a
condition of the bail granted to the accused Cesare Brichenzo. Fiori and Brichenzo were *b*
remanded on various charges relating to drugs. The forfeitures were ordered because of
the failure by Fiori and Brichenzo to appear on 18th March 1980.

Mr Albanese appeared at Wells Street Magistrates' Court on 16th May 1980 and 6th
February 1981 to answer the summons and to show cause why the sums in which he was
bound under the two recognisances should not be forfeited. He was represented by
counsel (not counsel who has appeared in this court). The case was heard by Mr Besley, *c*
a metropolitan stipendiary magistrate.

This application for judicial review, of which the purpose is to secure the quashing of
the forfeitures, was served on the magistrate and on the chief clerk of the court. The
affidavit of the magistrate sworn on 21st May 1981 is before the court. There was at the
first stage of this hearing no appearance on behalf of the respondents. The course of the
hearing has been extended in an unfortunate way.   *d*

On 11th June 1981 counsel for Mr Albanese presented the application and his
argument in support of it. I reserved judgment until the next day. In considering the
case, it seemed to me that it was necessary for certain evidence of importance which
counsel for Mr Albanese had put before the court, but which was not in Mr Albanese's
affidavit as served on the respondents, to be served by fresh affidavit on the respondents.
I also asked that the respondents be represented on the resumed hearing.   *e*

The matter came back before me on 29th June. The evidence was then in order.
Counsel then appeared on behalf of the respondents. The argument was concluded and
I have reserved my judgment again until today. The delay which has occurred is
regretted by me. I have found the case, for reasons which will be apparent, to be of some
difficulty.

The history of the matter is as follows. The accused Brichenzo and Fiori appeared at *f*
Clerkenwell Magistrates' Court on 9th April 1979. They appeared with one Guido
Lanza, but this man need not be mentioned again. Bail for them was fixed on terms: as
to Brichenzo a deposit of £3,000 in cash, a surety of £7,000, a condition of residence at
a named address and reporting twice a day at Chelsea police station. He was required to
surrender his passport. The bail was marked 'continuous'. As to Fiori, a deposit of
£5,000 was required, a surety of £5,000 and otherwise with similar conditions to those *g*
for Brichenzo. They were remanded to 5th July 1979.

On 17th May 1979 Mr Albanese signed the recognisance in form 616 in the sum of
£7,000 for Brichenzo and £5,000 for Fiori. It was in the form of a 'continuous'
suretyship. The condition was that the accused appear before the magistrates' court at
Clerkenwell on Thursday, 5th July 1979 and appear at every time and place to which
during the course of the proceedings the hearing might be from time to time adjourned, *h*
unless the court otherwise ordered in the meantime, to answer to the charges made
against them.

The form which Mr Albanese signed did not recite the conditions of bail. It would
appear that he knew what they were. He did not attend the court where he might have
heard those conditions but signed the form at Chelsea police station.

The accused next appeared at Clerkenwell Magistrates' Court on 5th July 1979 when *j*
they were again remanded to 26th September 1979. The court record shows that bail
conditions were to remain as before, save that the requirements of reporting were
changed to reporting on Mondays only and it was thought right that the passports of
both these men should be returned so that they could go abroad, and the obligation to
report was suspended while they were abroad.

On the same day, 5th July 1979, at Chelsea police station Mr Albanese signed a new
a recognisance in the sum of £7,000 in respect of the accused Brichenzo. This was
conditioned on his appearance at Clerkenwell on 26th September and at every time and
place to which the hearing might be adjourned. It was noted on that form that Brichenzo
was to reside at a named address and to report every Monday. It said nothing else about
bail conditions.

On that date Mr Albanese also signed a new recognisance in the sum of £5,000 in
b respect of the accused Fiori. That form was in the same terms.

It was part of Mr Albanese's case in the court below that he was not aware of the fact
that he had signed a recogisance in continuous form but thought he had assumed
responsibility on 17th May 1979 only to 5th July, and on 5th July only to 26th
September. It was suggested to him that, although an Italian, he could read and
understand the form he had signed. Counsel for Mr Albanese has pointed out in this
c court that, if the recognisance of 17th May 1979 was intended and understood by
everyone to be continuous, there was no apparent reason for the signing of a new form
on 5th July.

When Mr Albanese signed that new form on 5th July he was not told of any changes
in the terms of bail. His evidence before this court is that when he first signed the
recognisances he was aware of the conditions relating to deposit of cash by both men in
d sums of £3,000 and £5,000 and to the deposit of passports and as to residence.

On 26th September the accused were again remanded to 10th October. There was no
variation in bail conditions. Mr Albanese's evidence is that just before 15th September
he learnt that the bail conditions had been varied to permit return to the accused of their
passports.

For that and other reasons Mr Albanese, therefore, went to Chelsea police station on
e 15th September and there informed the police of his desire to be released from his
recognisance.

He made a witness statement on 15th September which included the following:

> 'Due to their recent attitude since Fiori Maurizio came back from holiday in
> Rome where he bought a brand new Porsche car which I know he cannot afford, I
> now wish to withdraw my surety, as I think now that they will not go to court when
f > they next have to.'

On the same day he returned and reinstated his suretyship for both men in the sums
agreed by the court and he signed a statement to that effect. His evidence is that he
agreed to continue as surety because of assurances he received from the accused and that
he thought his suretyship ran only to 26th September.

g On 27th September, on the application of the accused, out of the £3,000 deposited in
court by Brichenzo as a condition of bail £1,000 was returned to him, and on the same
date out of his £5,000 the sum of £1,000 was returned to Fiori. The receipts recording
that transaction were produced to this court by counsel for Mr Albanese on 11th June.
But there is not in the court record, which was produced, any note of that variation of
bail conditions. Mr Albanese's evidence is that he did not know of that variation, and
h there is nothing to suggest that he did.

Those receipts constituted the evidence which had not been served on the respondents
and which I have already mentioned. There was, therefore, no explanation from the
court why, if it was correct, the conditions of bail had been thus varied and why the
court's records contained no reference to the variation.

The evidence has now been served in the form of an affidavit dated 16th June 1981
j sworn by Mr Mackenzie, a managing clerk with Hallinan, Blackburn Gittings & Co,
solicitors, who at the material time were acting for the accused in the proceedings against
them, and who applied for and obtained a return of the money on 27th September 1979.

It has been acknowledged by counsel for the respondents that there was a failure at the
court to record this variation of the terms of bail through some error or oversight.

On 10th October 1979 the accused were again remanded to 18th March 1980. They did not appear on that date and nothing has been seen of them in this country since then.

It is easy, when it is known that the two men eventually failed to appear, to find those *a* decisions on bail conditions to be surprising. The court of course, having regard to the provisions of the Bail Act 1976, was on each occasion forming the opinion that there was a risk of the two men not appearing unless conditions were imposed and that the conditions which were imposed reduced it to an acceptable risk.

On the hearing before the magistrate on 16th May 1980 and 6th February 1981 it is clear that Mr Albanese put forward some evidence and contentions which did not *b* impress the magistrate. Mr Albanese contended that he did not know that his recognisance was for continuous bail, although the documents were said to be in clear terms.

He also asserted that on 12th October 1979, after the last remand on 10th October 1979, Mr Gittings (the senior partner in Hallinan, Blackburn Gittings & Co) had made a telephone call to Chelsea police station from Mr Albanese's restaurant and, after doing *c* so, had then assured Mr Albanese that he was 'no longer a surety'. Mr Gittings gave evidence to that effect. It was entirely a matter for the magistrate to assess the weight to be given to those points.

Mr Albanese, however, also put forward the contention that the bail conditions of the accused had been varied without Mr Albanese being told of the variations and that the variations granted increased the likelihood of their decision to abscond and not appear *d* and were relevant to a fair assessment of his own actions with reference to the two men.

There is before the court a note of the reasons given by the magistrate for his decision. Omitting substantial parts of it and giving only those parts which indicate the nature of the decision, the reasons were as follows:

> 'There is a remarkable history to this matter . . . it involves the arrest of three men in January 1979 and they were initially in custody, but when granted bail the *e* matter was thought by the court to be so serious that, when bail was granted, it was granted only on the basis that each of the three accused men would deposit £10,000 in court. That court order was later varied to a security (deposit of money) of £5,000 and a surety in the sum of £5,000 and there is a record that ultimately the decision of the court was varied, so that in the ultimate Mr Brichenzo was granted bail with a security of £3,000 and a surety of £7,000 and Mr Fiori was granted bail *f* with a security of £5,000 and a surety of £5,000 and there is a record that . . . "continuous" was entered in the court register, and I think that that condition that there be a surety who is made continuous is a condition of bail and if on future occasions the register records "bail as before" that that includes the condition of "continuous" sureties.'

g

On 5th July matters changed and the defendants were allowed to have their passports returned to them for specific trips abroad, and certainly that does not seem to have worried Mr Albanese, as he also went on holiday and appears not to have worried that their passports were returned to them. Mr Albanese knew that they had their passports returned to them and they returned to this country, having been on holiday to Rome. It was obvious that Mr Albanese felt upset that the men might use their money in order *h* to abscond, but he did not appear to be worried as he himself went on holiday.

There is then reference to the visit by Mr Albanese to the police station on 15th September which I have already described.

Continuing with the reasons, the magistrate said that on 26th September the accused appeared at court and were remanded until 10th October. Mr Albanese had a conversation and became worried about the defendants turning up for their trial. The *j* magistrate then described the evidence about Mr Gittings telephoning the police station to which I have referred.

The magistrate then said:

> 'I cannot say if that is a proper way of investigating if a person is in fact a surety or not, but I think that Mr Albanese entered into what was a valid recognisance and

I think it is clear that the recognisance he entered into was a continuous order. I think the real issue is whether I ought to exercise my discretion in favour of Mr Albanese by looking at two matters, one of which is that Mr Albanese did not realise what he was signing and secondly whether Mr Albanese exercised due diligence. I do not believe that Mr Albanese did not read the form he signed . . . The only way I feel I could exercise my discretion is on the question of culpability and with reference to that I think that the position of Mr Albanese is curious.'

After mentioning parts of the evidence, the magistrate concluded:

'I think he should have gone to the police station and that would have been consistent with his worry, but I think he adopted a curious course of conduct. He did not go to the police station and I think he should have done. I do not think he acted properly at all and I think he should forfeit the amount in total.'

It might be thought that, if an Italian did in fact get a solicitor to telephone the police station and was told that he was no longer a surety, it is not surprising that he did not personally visit the police station to check again. But it was for the magistrate to assess the weight and the force of that evidence.

Next, it is clear from those reasons that the magistrate referred to and considered the alterations in bail conditions made before 27th September 1979 when the cash was returned to the accused in the sum of £1,000 each. There was no mention of this last variation. The reason for that is made clear by the affidavit of the magistrate which contains the following: 'There was no evidence before me that the bail conditions were varied after the 26th September 1979. The evidence was that they were not varied—see Court Registers exhibit "CB 6".' Unfortunately, as I have already explained, the court record was on that particular matter defective and incomplete.

As to the application to quash the forfeiture orders, the grounds put forward were, first, that Mr Albanese did not know that the two recognisances were continuous, second, that he had been told by the telephone call to Chelsea police station that he was no longer a surety, and, third, because of the breach of natural justice in the variation of bail conditions without notice to Mr Albanese or the affording to him of a chance to be heard.

In my judgment, this court can grant no relief on either of those first two grounds. The magistrate was not wrong in law in attaching little or no importance to the points about alleged ignorance of the continuous nature of the recognisances or about an alleged relief in being free of the suretyship because of the conversation with an officer in Chelsea police station by Mr Gittings. They were matters to be decided by him.

This court can only interfere with the exercise by the magistrate of the discretion given by s 96(1) of the Magistrates' Courts Act 1952 in declaring the recognisances to be forfeited if it is shown that he has failed to take into account some matter which he should in law have considered, or has taken into account some matter which in law is irrelevant or has gone wrong in law, or, lastly, if the conclusion reached is one which no reasonable magistrate could reach: see *Bracegirdle v Oxley* [1947] 1 All ER 126, [1947] KB 349; *R v Tottenham Magistrates' Court, ex parte Riccardi* (1978) 66 Cr App R 155. The magistrate was entitled to take the view that those matters afforded no ground for adjudging that Mr Albanese pay part only of the sums in which he was bound or that those sums be remitted entirely.

As to the point of the change in bail conditions, counsel for Mr Albanese was concerned to argue that the court should quash that order of the magistrates' court at Clerkenwell pursuant to which the recognisances were made to continue by the direction that the bail should continue on the occasions after changes were made in the bail conditions.

Counsel's main submission was that by the requirements of natural justice Mr Albanese was entitled to receive notice and to be heard on the making of the orders which varied the conditions of bail and then directed bail to continue on his recognisances. Since he had not received such notice, the orders were void ab initio and, being void, could not be revised by any subsequent waiver.

I accept that Mr Albanese as surety on a recognisance for continuous bail did have an interest in the conditions of bail in so far as they affected the likelihood of the accused surrendering or the effectiveness with which the surety would keep in touch with the accused. The surety also would have an immediate interest in knowing of a reduction in the number of sureties, for example, if one surety withdrew and bail was continued without that additional surety.

Counsel for Mr Albanese referred to *Schmidt v Secretary of State for Home Affairs* [1969] 1 All ER 904 at 909, [1969] 2 Ch 149 at 170. It is not necessary to refer to the facts of that case. Counsel cited it for one dictum in the judgment of Lord Denning MR where he said:

> 'The speeches in *Ridge v. Baldwin* ([1963] 2 All ER 66, [1964] AC 40) show that an administrative body may, in a proper case, be bound to give a person who is affected by their decision an opportunity of making representations. It all depends on whether he has some right or interest, or, I would even add, some legitimate expectation, of which it would not be fair to deprive him without hearing what he has to say.'

It is impossible, however, in my judgment, to hold that a court, in varying the conditions of bail and directing that bail then continue on a surety who has previously provided a recognisance for continuous bail, is under a duty to give notice to or to hear that surety so that the order of the court will be void if it does not. The court, of course, knows of the interest of the surety in the conditions of bail and that those conditions may affect both the risk of the bailed man not appearing and the surety's assessment of that risk. But that knowledge in the court can give rise to no obligation to give notice to the surety or to hear him on the question of conditions of bail.

The first point is that the public duty of the court is to grant bail unless, inter alia, it considers that there are substantial grounds for believing that the defendant would fail to surrender to custody. If there is thought to be a risk of his not surrendering, the court may, and will, impose such requirements or conditions as appear to the court to be necessary to secure that he surrender to custody: see s 3(6) of the Bail Act 1976.

Next, the surety on a bail recognisance, as counsel for the respondents submitted, undertakes a special obligation. He does so voluntarily. Failure to fulfil the condition (that is to say non-appearance of the man bailed) gives rise to a civil debt which is enforceable like a fine. At common law, if the condition was not fulfilled, the surety automatically forfeited the sum secured by the bond. Forfeiture is no longer automatic but is subject to the discretion given to magistrates by s 96(1) of the Magistrates' Courts Act 1952: see per Lord Denning MR in *R v Southampton Justices, ex parte Green* [1975] 2 All ER 1073 at 1077, [1976] QB 11 at 19.

Apart from that discretion in the court to order the surety to pay part only of the sum in which he is bound or to remit the whole sum, the obligation remains in nature the same as it has always been. It is the duty of the surety to stay in touch with the bailed prisoner to see that he will appear at court. The court, in considering the culpability of the surety in the event of the failure of the bailed man to surrender, will look to what the surety did to see that the man did surrender and what he did to alert the police if there was any known risk of his absconding: see *Riccardi's* case to which I have already referred.

The surety, by s 23 of the Criminal Justice Act 1967, is given the right to notify the police that the surety believes that the man bailed is likely not to appear as required, and for that reason the surety wishes to be relieved of his obligations as a surety. If the surety gives that notice, the police may then arrest the bailed man without warrant. It is therefore clear, as I see it, that it is the duty of the surety to keep himself informed of the bail conditions if he is concerned about them, and he can help himself to do that if he wishes by entering into the recognisance only from one remand to the next so that he will learn of any variations in bail conditions which the court may order on the occasion of any remand.

It is further to be noted, as counsel for the respondents has pointed out, that none of the statutory provisions relating to bail or to recognisances by sureties provides for notice to the surety as to any variation in bail conditions, save as noted below. Those provisions

include s 6 of the Magistrates' Courts Act 1952 and s 105(3) of that Act, which empowers
the court to direct that the recognisance for bail be conditioned for continuous bail for
a his appearance at any time and place to which the hearing may be adjourned.

Section 3(8) of the Bail Act 1976 gives or confirms the power of the court to vary
conditions of bail. Section 106 of the 1952 Act makes provision for enlarging the
recognisance of any surety for a bailed man to a later date on failure by that man to
appear because of illness or accident.

b The Magistrates' Courts Rules 1968, SI 1968 No 1920, make provisions with reference
to recognisances and bail. By r 71, if a magistrates' court enlarges the recognisance to a
later time under s 106 of the 1952 Act, it is required to give notice to any surety of that
fact. By r 75B, if there is a change of time for appearance by the bailed man, the court
must give notice of that change to any surety. By r 75D, when a magistrates' court has
committed a person on bail to the Crown Court for trial and the court subsequently
varies and conditions of bail, the court must give notice to the Crown Court of such
c variation.

There is, however, as stated, no express general requirement to notify a surety of the
variation of the conditions of bail, and it is impossible to conclude that any such general
obligation can be implied.

I am therefore unable to accept the submission of counsel for Mr Albanese that any
order of the court was void. The orders varying the conditions of bail were not void.
d They were effective to vary the conditions. The validity of the recognisance entered into
by Mr Albanese was not affected by the orders which varied the conditions of bail,
although Mr Albanese was not given notice of an intention to vary them or of the
making of the variation.

It seems to me that any question of possible injustice arising from an unnotified
variation in bail conditions must be considered, if it is relevant at all, by the court on
e exercising its jurisdiction under s 96 of the Magistrates' Courts Act 1952 on any
application for forfeiture of the recognisance.

Although, in my opinion, variation of bail conditions cannot affect the validity of a
recognisance for continuous bail, I think that consideration could usefully be given to the
need for warning sureties expressly, possibly by a clear note on the forms used, that the
f conditions of bail may be varied by the court and that the surety should not sign for
continuous bail if he is concerned about the conditions of bail.

In many cases such a warning will not be required, but in a case like this, where a
businessman stands bail for an employee or business associate, the conditions of bail
might be, and be regarded by the surety as, of very great importance. I also see no reason
why the conditions of bail should not be recorded on the form of the recognisance so that
the surety would know what they are. Such a provision is of particular importance
g where, as here, the surety signs the form of recognisance at a police station and has not
heard the proceedings in court.

It is noted in Archbold's Pleading, Evidence and Practice in Criminal Cases (40th Edn,
1979, p 142, para 297):

'Before a surety formally accepts the obligations imposed upon him it is the
h practice (i) to explain to him exactly what the obligations involve, (ii) to ensure that
he understands the obligations he is to undertake, (iii) to ensure that he is still
prepared to undertake the obligations and that he is worth the sum involved after
all his debts are paid, and (iv) to warn him of the consequences, which include
possible imprisonment, if the defendant fails to appear when required to.'

j Once again it seems to me to be desirable, after reading the facts of this case, that that
explanation should include reference when appropriate to the possibility that bail
conditions may be varied by the court without notice to the surety and an explanation
that the surety can, albeit with further trouble to himself, enter into recognisances from
remand to remand and not in continuous form.

Counsel for Mr Albanese next advanced an alternative submission. He argued that the position of the surety liable on a bail recognisance is similar in some respects to the position of a surety at common law under the normal contract of guarantee. I found this *a* submission at first to be attractive and encouraged counsel to develop that argument. He submitted that the surety liable on a bail recognisance should be treated in law in the same way as the surety liable under a contract of guarantee. Any material variations of the terms of the contract between the creditor and the principal debtor without the consent of the surety will discharge a surety under a contract of guarantee: see 20 Halsbury's Laws (4th Edn) para 253. Therefore, it was submitted that any material *b* variation of the conditions of bail without the knowledge and consent of the surety should discharge a surety or, alternatively, make it unjust under s 96 of the Magistrates' Courts Act 1952 not to remit the whole sum.

This point is met, as I think, so far as concerns any automatic discharge of the duty by the same answers as that given to the first point based on the argument of natural justice and failure to give notice. The validity of the recognisance is not affected by a subsequent *c* variation of the conditions of bail. The court is free to vary the conditions of bail without getting the consent of the surety. I do not, by that conclusion, mean to say that it would be wrong for a court, when making a variation in bail conditions which it thinks might affect the willingness of a surety to continue to be bound, to decline to continue bail on the varied conditions without seeing that the surety knows of the variations and agrees to continue. I believe that many courts do now take that course. It is part of the proper *d* concern of the court to accept only suitable sureties who fully understand the obligation they are assuming. It is clearly a wholly proper and just practice to follow.

Although a variation in conditions of bail does not affect the validity of a recognisance, the relevance of such a subsequent variation of which the surety had no notice for the purposes of s 96 of the Magistrates' Courts Act 1952 is a different question. Although for the reasons given the magistrates' court is free to vary the conditions of bail without *e* notice to the surety who has given a bail recognisance either to a fixed date only or in continuous form without effect on the validity of the recognisance, such a variation made may be, and in some cases would be, a matter for consideration by the court in exercising its discretion under s 96.

The surety is obliged in his own interests to stay in touch with the person granted bail and to keep himself informed of the bail conditions if they are of concern to him. In *f* many, if not most, cases variation of the conditions of bail are obviously irrelevant to the risk assumed by the surety and would be regarded as irrelevant by him. In some cases the conditions of bail would be highly relevant, for example, the deposit as security of a large sum under the Bail Act 1976. The provisions of s 3(5) of that Act authorise the requiring before release on bail of security of surrender to custody 'if it appears that the prisoner is unlikely to remain in Great Britain until the time appointed for him to *g* surrender to custody'. A surety in a case where such a deposit has been required would regard it as relevant to the risk assumed by him if a deposit, once required, was returned.

A return of part only, as in this case, is of much less certain relevance. It may be, as the magistrates clearly thought it was in varying the terms, merely the release of part of a large sum to enable the defendant to live or to use the sum returned for necessary purposes while leaving a sufficiently large sum still deposited; and, on the other hand, it *h* might be regarded, as in this case it turned out to have been, as the last effort to get back as much as possible before absconding.

The return of a passport, after a request that it be deposited, would probably also be thought to be relevant by a surety, but the degree of importance which he would attach to it would depend on his judgment of the chances of a man passing out of this country without a passport.

In exercising their discretion under s 96 of the 1952 Act the magistrates are required *j* to consider to what extent the surety was at fault. In the well-known passage in *R v Southampton Justices, ex parte Green* [1975] 2 All ER 1073 at 1077–1078, [1976] 1 QB 11 at 19 Lord Denning MR said:

'By what principles are the justices to be guided? They ought, I think, to consider a to what extent the surety was at fault. If he or she connived at the disappearance of the accused man, or aided it or abetted it, it would be proper to forfeit the whole of the sum. If he or she was wanting in due diligence to secure his appearance, it might be proper to forfeit the whole or a substantial part of it, depending on the degree of fault. If he or she was guilty of no want of diligence and used every effort to secure the appearance of the accused man, it might be proper to remit it entirely.'

b In Riccardi's case 66 Cr App R 150 at 153, to which I have already referred, Lord Widgery CJ, citing his own judgment in R v Horseferry Road Stipendiary Magistrate, ex parte Pearson [1976] 2 All ER 264, [1976] 1 WLR 511, said of that passage:

c 'I find it difficult, with all respect to Lord Denning M.R., entirely to follow the passage that I have read because the forfeiture of recognisance is in no sense a penalty imposed on the surety for misconduct. I do not doubt that the magistrate, before forfeiting the recognisance, must consider among other things the conduct of the surety and see whether it was open to criticism or not. But one must, I think, start all these problems on the footing that the surety has seriously entered into a serious obligation and ought to pay the amount which he or she has promised unless there are circumstances in the case either relating to her means or her culpability, which make it fair and just to pay a smaller sum.'

d Provided the magistrates look fairly at the conduct of the surety and consider to what extent he was culpable or open to criticism, they are entitled to form their own view of how to exercise their discretion. In performing that task they would be entitled to take into consideration the fact that the conditions of bail had been varied without the knowledge of the surety. In many cases, as I have said, the fact would carry no weight at all because it would not have affected the action of the surety. If it should seem to the

e court that if the surety had known of the variation he would or may have acted differently, the court would consider how far that different course of action would affect their view of the surety's conduct. If it seemed very important, for example, that the surety might well after that variation have refused to continue as surety, a further question would need to be considered, namely, is the surety in any way to blame, having regard to all the circumstances and his experience and understanding of such matters, for

f not knowing about the variation of which he complains? It might be that the surety can show no more than that if he had known of the variation (for example, a successful application as in this case to get back all or part of the deposit lodged allowed as to £1,000 for each man) he might have realised or suspected that they were planning to abscond and would have reported to the police station to withdraw his recognisance. It is to be noted that in this case this surety had done that on one occasion of anxiety.

g If the magistrates were satisfied of that, then, subject to inquiring into any fault in the surety for not knowing of the variation, it would seem to me that they would be bound to have regard to the fact in considering the matter, but again the weight and the consequence of it would be for them.

I have referred to these matters not because I wish to tell magistrates in detail how to assess a matter such as a variation of a bail condition but to show that, in my judgment,

h the fact of the variation of 27th September 1979 in this case was a matter which the magistrate should have considered when he dealt with the case on 6th February 1981. The fact that he did not consider it arose from an unfortunate combination of misfortunes which it is not necessary for me to unravel.

Mr Gittings gave evidence at the hearing that his firm had the receipts which proved the variation of the bail conditions. I do not know why they were not produced and it

j is irrelevant for me to consider the position of Mr Gittings who was advising or at least helping Mr Albanese on 12th October 1979 in the telephone call to the police station and whose firm had also obtained the return of the cash, £1,000 each, for the two men on 27th September 1979. The reason for the magistrate's ignorance of the fact is the failure to record it in the court records. I do not know what weight, if any, the magistrate would have attached to this fact, but I am sure that, since he reached his

decision in the mistaken belief that the variation had not occurred or at least in ignorance
that it had, the decision of 6th February 1981 ordering forfeiture of the full amounts of
both recognisances cannot stand. Through no fault whatever of the magistrate he did
not consider the matter which he should have considered in order to decide what weight,
if any, to give to it. The decision must be quashed.

Counsel for Mr Albanese asked me to quash the order and not to remit the matter to
the court for reconsideration. I have decided that it must be remitted. I emphasise,
although the court below would of course know it, that the matter is remitted for a
rehearing. I shall direct that it be heard by a different magistrate. That direction is again
no reflection whatever on Mr Besley, who will, I am sure, understand that the direction
is to relieve him of the difficult task of hearing the matter again, while putting out of his
mind the decision he first formed on the material before him. I think he will be grateful
to be so relieved.

The court which hears the matter afresh will be free to reconsider the matter entirely
and to decide what, under s 96 of the 1952 Act, it is just to do. To that extent this
application succeeds.

Application granted. Case remitted to different magistrate for rehearing.

Solicitors: *Proctor Gillett* (for Mr Albanese); *Treasury Solicitor.*

Sepala Munasinghe   Barrister.

Janov v Morris

COURT OF APPEAL, CIVIL DIVISION
DUNN AND WATKINS LJJ
17th JULY 1981

*Action – Dismissal – Abuse of process of court – Second action raising same cause of action as
earlier action – Second action commenced within limitation period for cause of action – Earlier
action dismissed for want of prosecution because of plaintiff's failure to comply with peremptory
order of court – Plaintiff not explaining failure to comply with order and not indicating whether
he would comply with orders made in second action – Whether court having discretion to strike
out second action for abuse of court's process – RSC Ord 18, r 19(1)(d).*

In 1978 the plaintiff brought an action against the defendant for damages for breach of
a contract for the sale of a yacht. There was unexplained delay by the plaintiff in
proceeding with the action and on 21st March 1980 the master ordered that the action
be dismissed for want of prosecution unless the plaintiff served a summons for directions
by 1st April 1980. The plaintiff failed to comply with the order without giving any
explanation. On 2nd July 1980 the action was dismissed for want of prosecution.
However, the limitation period for the cause of action did not expire until 1984 and on
9th September 1980 the plaintiff brought a second action against the defendant raising
the same cause of action as in the first action. There was no indication that the plaintiff
was likely to comply with court orders made in the second action. On the application of
the defendant the master struck out the second action as an abuse of the process of the
court, under RSC Ord 18, r 19(1)(d)[a]. On appeal by the plaintiff, the judge in chambers
allowed the appeal and rescinded the master's order. The defendant appealed, contending
that as a claim identical to that raised in the second action had been struck out by the
dismissal of the first action, it was an abuse of process to allow the claim to be prosecuted

---

[a]   Rule 19(1), so far as material, is set out at p 782 h, post

again in a second action. The plaintiff submitted that since the period of limitation for
the cause of action had not expired, he was entitled to bring a second action at any time
a within the limitation period notwithstanding that the first action had been struck out
because of his failure to comply with a peremptory order of the court.

Held – Where an action had been struck out on the ground of the plaintiff's disobedience
of a peremptory order of the court and the plaintiff commenced a second action within
b the limitation period raising the same cause of action, the court had a discretion under
RSC Ord 18, r 19(1)(d) to strike out the second action on the ground that it was an abuse
of the court's process. In exercising that discretion the court would have regard to the
principle that court orders were made to be complied with. Accordingly, because there
had been no explanation by the plaintiff for his failure to comply with the peremptory
order made in the first action and there was no indication that he was likely to comply
c with orders made in the second action, the commencement of the second action was an
abuse of the process of the court and the court would exercise its discretion under Ord 18,
r 19(1)(d) to strike it out (see p 784 *h* and p 785 *b* to p 786 *a*, post).
  Dictum of Lord Diplock in *Tolley v Morris* [1979] 2 All ER at 571 and *Samuels v Linzi
Dresses Ltd* [1980] 1 All ER 803 applied.
  Dicta of Lord Salmon and of Lord Edmund-Davies in *Birkett v James* [1977] 2 All ER
d at 813, 817–818 and of Lord Edmund-Davies in *Tolley v Morris* [1979] 2 All ER at 571–
572 not followed.

Notes
For striking out a pleading as an abuse of the process of the court, see 36 Halsbury's Laws
(4th Edn) para 74.

e
Cases referred to in judgments
*Allen v Sir Alfred McAlpine & Sons Ltd, Bostic v Bermondsey and Southwark Group Hospital
     Management Committee, Sternberg v Hammond* [1968] 1 All ER 543, [1968] 2 QB 229,
     [1968] 2 WLR 366, CA, Digest (Cont Vol C) 1091, 2262b.
Birkett v James [1977] 2 All ER 801, [1978] AC 297, [1977] 3 WLR 38, HL, Digest (Cont
f   Vol E) 666, 2698b.
Samuels v Linzi Dresses Ltd [1980] 1 All ER 803, [1981] QB 115, [1980] 2 WLR 836, CA.
Tolley v Morris [1979] 2 All ER 561, [1979] 1 WLR 592, HL, Digest (Cont Vol E) 666,
     2262(w)(ii).

Interlocutory appeal
g In an action (no 1978 J 4563) brought by the plaintiff, Arthur Janov, against the
defendant, Barry Morris, claiming damages for breach of a contract for the sale of a yacht
by the plaintiff to the defendant, the plaintiff failed to comply with a peremptory order
of the court, dated 21st March 1980, that unless he issued and served a summons for
directions by 1st April 1980 the action would be dismissed for want of prosecution. On
2nd July 1980 the action was dismissed for want of prosecution and judgment on the
h claim was entered for the defendant. On 9th September 1980 the plaintiff issued another
writ and statement of claim against the defendant (action no 1980 J 6213) raising the
same cause of action. The defendant applied to strike out the second action as an abuse
of the court's process, pursuant to RSC Ord 18, r 19. On 2nd March 1981 Master Elton
ordered that the writ and statement of claim in the second action be struck out under
Ord 18, r 19. The plaintiff appealed. On 1st April 1981 Smith J in chambers allowed the
j appeal and rescinded Master Elton's order. The defendant appealed from Smith J's order
on the grounds, inter alia, that the plaintiff's conduct in failing to comply with the
peremptory order dated 21st March 1980 made in the first action was contumelious, that
therefore he was debarred from commencing a fresh action raising the same cause of
action and that accordingly the second action should be struck out as an abuse of process
under Ord 18, r 19, even though the limitation period for the cause of action had not

expired when the second action was commenced. The facts are set out in the judgment of Dunn LJ.

Robin Miller for the defendant.
Mark Strachan for the plaintiff.

DUNN LJ. This is an appeal from an order of Smith J made in chambers on 1st April 1981 whereby he allowed an appeal from an order of Master Elton, who had struck out an action on the grounds that the action was an abuse of the process of the court.

The action, which is no J 6213 of 1980, arose out of a contract for the sale of a yacht which had been made in April 1978. On 7th August 1978 the plaintiff, the seller of the yacht, had brought an action, no J 4563 of 1978, claiming damages for non-acceptance of the yacht. A defence was delivered in October 1978 disputing the contract and setting up a counterclaim for damages for non-delivery. Various steps were taken in the action, and on 23rd May 1979 further and better particulars of the defence and counterclaim were delivered pursuant to a request which had been made on 1st February. No further step was then taken in the action until 10th March 1980, a period of very nearly ten months, when the defendant applied to strike out the action for want of prosecution. His solicitor swore an affidavit in support of that application. There was no affidavit in reply by the plaintiff, and on 21st March 1980 the master made an order that the action would be struck out unless the plaintiff served his summons for directions by 1st April 1980. There was no appeal by the plaintiff against that order; no explanation was given for the delay and no application was made to extend the time for service of the summons for directions. So accordingly, on 2nd July 1980, the master gave judgment on the claim for the defendant, but ordered the counterclaim to stand, and directed that proceedings should be issued under RSC Ord 14 in respect of the counterclaim. On 13th August 1980 the defendant filed an affidavit under Ord 14 in respect of the counterclaim.

On 9th September 1980, the plaintiff issued a second writ, which is the writ with which we are presently concerned, no J 6213, in which he relied on precisely the same cause of action as in writ no J 4563 which had been effectively struck out only two months before. The defendant then issued a summons under Ord 18, r 19 to strike out that new writ on the ground that it was an abuse of the process of the court.

Meanwhile, in the first action, the plaintiff filed an affidavit in the Ord 14 proceedings on 14th November 1980, and was given leave to defend the counterclaim on 5th December 1980. So the counterclaim in the first action is still alive, but if this second action is struck out, then effectively the plaintiff is debarred from proceeding with his claim for damages for non-acceptance.

The defendant's application to strike out came before the master on 2nd March 1981, when the master made the order striking out the second action, and on 1st April the judge rescinded that order, and it is against that order of the judge that the defendant now appeals. The defendant relies on para 1(*d*) of Ord 18, r 19 which provides:

> 'The court may at any stage of the proceedings order to be struck out ... any pleading or the indorsement of any writ in the action ... on the ground that—
> ... it is otherwise [ie otherwise than by virtue of paras (*a*), (*b*) or (*c*) of r 19(1)] an abuse of the process of the court.'

What is said, quite shortly, on behalf of the defendant is that this claim having been struck out once in an action raising an identical cause of action, it would be an abuse of the process of the court to allow it to be resurrected.

What is said on behalf of the plaintiff, effectively, is this, that since the period of limitation for the original cause of action does not expire until 1984, the plaintiff is entitled to bring a second action at any time within that limitation period, notwithstanding that his original claim was struck out by reason of his failure to comply with a peremptory order.

The judge accepted that, and we have been told that he accepted it primarily because

he relied on a dictum of Lord Edmund-Davies in the well known case of *Birkett v James*
a [1977] 2 All ER 801, [1978] AC 297. The difficulty in the case arises because there are
what were submitted to be inconsistent obiter dicta in *Birkett v James* and in the more
recent case of *Tolley v Morris* [1979] 2 All ER 561, [1979] 1 WLR 592.

It is important to remember that both *Birkett v James* and *Tolley v Morris* were
concerned with applications to strike out actions for want of prosecution on the ground
of inordinate and inexcusable delay. They were not concerned, as is this case, with an
b application to strike out under Ord 18, r 19, where there had been a failure by the
plaintiff to comply with a peremptory order in a previous action.

Ever since *Allen v Sir Alfred McAlpine & Sons Ltd* [1968] 1 All ER 543, [1968] 2 QB 229
it has been accepted that the power of the court to strike out actions for want of
prosecution should be exercised only where the court is satisfied either that there has
been an intentional and contumelious default, for example, disobedience of a peremptory
c order of the court, or that there has been inordinate and inexcusable delay. And
although *Birkett v James* was dealing with the second ground, there are obiter dicta
relating to the first ground which are, of course, of persuasive authority in this court,
although not binding on us.

In *Birkett v James* Lord Diplock said ([1977] 2 All ER 801 at 807, [1978] AC 297 at 321):

> 'The court may and ought to exercise such powers as it possesses under the rules
d > to make the plaintiff pursue his action with all proper diligence, particularly where
> at the trial the case will turn on the recollection of witnesses to past events. For this
> purpose the court may make peremptory orders providing for the dismissal of the
> action for non-compliance with its order as to the time by which a particular step in
> the proceedings is to be taken. Disobedience to such an order would qualify as
> "intentional and contumelious" within the meaning of the first principle laid down
e > in *Allen v McAlpine*. But where no question of non-compliance with a peremptory
> order is involved the court is not in my view entitled to treat as "inordinate delay"
> justifying dismissal of the action in accordance with the second principle in *Allen v
> McAlpine*, a total time elapsed since the accrual of the cause of action which is no
> greater than the limitation period within which the statute allows plaintiffs to start
> that action. To dismiss the action in such circumstances would, in my view, involve
f > an error in principle in the exercise of judicial "discretion" which it is the function
> of the appellate court to correct.'

Lord Salmon said ([1977] 2 All ER 801 at 813, [1978] AC 297 at 328):

> 'I agree with my noble and learned friend, Lord Diplock, that if an action is
> dismissed for want of prosecution or even for the contumelious failure to comply
g > with a peremptory order before the limitation period has elapsed, this would not
> empower the court to strike out a writ for the same cause of action subsequently
> issued within the limitation period. The fact that the plaintiff or his solicitor had
> behaved badly in the first action does not make him into a vexatious litigant barred
> from bringing any further proceedings without permission of the court. Nor does
> the dismissal of the first action without any decision on the merits constitute res
h > judicata.'

And Lord Edmund-Davies said ([1977] 2 All ER 801 at 817–818, [1978] AC 297 at 334):

> '. . . I respectfully concur with my noble and learned friend, Lord Diplock, that,
> where there appears any likelihood that a plaintiff will issue a second writ, the case
j > must be quite exceptional (and difficult to imagine) where the court should within
> the limitation period dismiss an action simply for want of prosecution. If it be
> complained that this places the defendant at the mercy of a dilatory plaintiff, a
> partial answer is that in a flagrant case, the defendant can always seek peremptory
> orders which, if disobeyed, render the plaintiff liable to have his action struck out
> on the ground of contumelious default; though there, too, a second writ can

properly be issued within the limitation period, unless the circumstances are such that it could, on other grounds, be regarded as frivolous or vexatious.'

Counsel for the defendant having conceded that there was no other ground on which this present action could be regarded as frivolous or vexatious, counsel for the plaintiff relies strongly on that obiter dictum of Lord Edmund-Davies, and submits that the mere fact the first action has been struck out, on the ground of contumelious default, is no reason for the court to strike out this action.

The matter was adverted to again by their Lordships in *Tolley v Morris*, where Lord Diplock said ([1979] 2 All ER 561 at 571, [1979] 1 WLR 592 at 603):

'Disobedience to a peremptory order would generally amount to such "contumelious" conduct as is referred to in *Birkett v James* and would justify striking out a fresh action for the same cause of action, as an abuse of the process of the court.'

Lord Edmund-Davies, while agreeing with Lord Diplock on the facts of the case then before him, said ([1979] 2 All ER 561 at 571–572, [1979] 1 WLR 592 at 604):

'But I must make one qualification. I am not presently persuaded that a person who starts an action within the limitation period is liable to have it struck out as constituting an abuse of the process of the court, for the sole reason that a previous suit instituted by him in respect of the same cause of action was itself struck out on the ground that his disobedience to the court's orders (peremptory or otherwise) amounted to contumelious default. Although not an issue in *Birkett v James*, the point was canvassed in the course of argument and I accordingly expressed, obiter, the view that even in such circumstances a plaintiff, *not* having been declared a vexatious litigant, could within the limitation period prosecute to trial a fresh action. Highly unfortunate though such a conclusion must be regarded, it appeared to me then to be logically inescapable in the light of our decision in that case. But the point no more arises for decision in the present appeal than it did in *Birkett v James*, and a final conclusion on the matter must await a case in which the point arises directly for determination.'

And it is accepted that in this case the point does arise directly for determination.

As was said in the course of argument in this court, one can well understand Lord Edmund-Davies's opinion that the conclusion which he preferred would be a highly unfortunate one, because it was conceded by counsel for the plaintiff that if it were right, a litigant could disobey and disregard orders of the court, have his action struck out, and provided he was within the limitation period, he could immediately start another action; and even if another peremptory order was made in the second action and that action dismissed, then if the logic is taken to its ultimate, he could start a third or any number of actions provided they were within the limitation period and none would be regarded as an abuse of the process of the court.

In view of the difference of opinion of their Lordships we must decide the question according to principle. We are concerned with Ord 18, r 19, and it is plain from the use of the word 'may' in that rule, that the court has a discretion whether to strike out the pleading or not, and whatever the breadth of the discretion, there is no doubt with regard to the rule that it exists.

An analogous though dissimilar situation was considered by this court in *Samuels v Linzi Dresses Ltd* [1980] 1 All ER 803, [1981] QB 115. That was a case where the defendants had failed to comply with a request for particulars, and an order was made that unless the particulars were delivered by a specified date, the defence and counterclaim would be struck out, a similar type of order to the order made in the first action in this case. This court held that the court had the power to extend time where an 'unless' order had been made, but the mode of exercise of the power was dealt with by Roskill LJ. He said ([1980] 1 All ER 803 at 812, [1981] QB 115 at 126–127):

'In my judgment, therefore, the law today is that a court has power to extend the

time where an "unless" order has been made but not been complied with; but that
it is a power which should be exercised cautiously and with due regard to the
necessity for maintaining the principle that orders are made to be complied with
and not to be ignored. Primarily, it is a question for a discretion of the master or the
judge in chambers whether the necessary relief should be granted or not.'

It seems to me that those words are to be applied, by analogy, to a situation such as this,
where an 'unless' order has been made and not complied with, the action has been struck
out and a second action started. The court then has to consider whether, in the exercise
of its discretion under Ord 18, r 19, that second action should be struck out. In my view,
the court should be cautious in allowing the second action to continue and should have
due regard to the necessity of maintaining the principle that orders are made to be
complied with and not to be ignored.

We were told that *Samuels v Linzi Dresses Ltd* was not brought to the attention of the
judge below, and he appears to have approached the matter on the basis that it was a
matter of law and that there was no room for the exercise of discretion, and it was for
him to choose between the obiter dicta of Lord Diplock on the one hand, and Lord
Salmon and Lord Edmund-Davies on the other.

Speaking for myself, I regard it as a matter of discretion to be exercised having regard
to the circumstances of the particular case. In this case there had, from first to last, been
no explanation whatever by the plaintiff why there was the 10-month delay before the
application to strike out the first action in March 1980. There was no explanation at all
why he failed to comply with the 'unless' order, and there has been no indication in this
present action that he intends to comply with the orders of the court any more than he
did in the first action. Indeed he is still in contempt of court.

In my judgment, the judge was in error in not approaching the matter as one of
discretion in that way. His approach, in my view, was wrong in principle. This is a case
in which the necessity for maintaining the principle that orders are made to be complied
with should be upheld, and in the absence of any explanation as to why the order was not
complied with in the previous action or any assurance as to the conduct of this action I
would strike out this present action and allow the matter to be litigated on the
counterclaim in the first action.

Accordingly, I would allow the appeal and restore the order of Master Elton of 2nd
March 1981.

WATKINS LJ. I agree. A prospective litigant must be deemed to know that on taking
out a writ indorsed with a claim for monetary or other relief, his conduct of the action
thereby brought into being will be governed thereafter by rules and orders of the court.
A failure to conform to any one of these may cause him to be penalised even to the extent
of having his action struck out.

In the event of his action being ordered to be struck out for failure to obey a
peremptory order, he may appeal against that order seeking, if necessary, an extension of
time within which to do so. The outcome of such an appeal will to some extent depend
on the excuse for failure preferably set forth in affidavit form provided for the court's
consideration. If a litigant neglects to avail himself of that procedure and brings a fresh
but precisely similar action to that ordered to be struck out, without any explanation
then or at any later time for a failure to obey the peremptory order, he should not be
surprised that the commencement of the second action is found to be an abuse of the
process of the court and for that reason it, too, is struck out.

To behave in such a way is in my judgment to treat the court with intolerable
contumely. This is a matter which can properly be taken into account in the exercise of
the court's discretion. This is how I judge this plaintiff to have conducted himself.

The judge below does not appear to have allowed this consideration to have formed
part of the discretion exercised by him in deciding to reverse the decision of the master.
If it was, then, like Dunn LJ, I am bound to say that he paid insufficient regard to it in
adjudging that this action be allowed to continue.

For the reasons given by Dunn LJ, and for those briefly expressed by me, I too would allow this appeal and make the order which Dunn LJ proposes.

Appeal allowed; order of Master Elton of 2nd March 1981 restored. Leave to appeal to the House of Lords refused.

Solicitors: *Park Nelson & Doyle Devonshire*, agents for *Lock, Reed & Lock*, Dorchester (for the defendant); *Myers, Ebner & Deaner* (for the plaintiff).

Diana Brahams   Barrister.

Re Hay's Settlement Trusts

CHANCERY DIVISION
SIR ROBERT MEGARRY V-C
12th, 13th, 14th, 15th JUNE, 30th JULY 1981

Power of appointment – Uncertainty – Unascertainable class of objects – Intermediate power vested in trustees – Discretionary power to appoint to anyone in the world except specified class – Whether power invalid as being too wide.

Power of appointment – Excessive execution – Delegation of power – Intermediate power – Settlement giving trustees power to appoint to 'such persons' as they thought fit – Trustees executing deed of appointment empowering them to appoint to 'such persons' as they thought fit – Whether deed of appointment a valid exercise of power of appointment in settlement.

Settlement – Power – Intermediate power – Validity – Settlement giving trustees power to appoint to 'such persons' as they thought fit – Trustees executing deed of appointment empowering them to appoint to 'such persons' as they thought fit – Whether deed of appointment valid.

By a settlement dated 7th May 1958 the trustees were directed to hold the trust fund for 'such persons or purposes' as the trustees should in their discretion appoint by deed within 21 years of the date of the settlement, and in default of appointment, for the settlor's nieces and nephews living at the date of the settlement in equal shares. Apart from the settlor, her husband and the trustees there was no restriction on the persons or purposes that could be the object of an appointment. The settlement further provided that prior to any appointment the income was to be paid or applied in the trustees' discretion to or for 'any niece or nephew of the settlor' or any charitable object. On 5th May 1969 the trustees executed a deed of appointment in which they appointed the whole of the trust fund to be held by themselves on a similar trust to that created by the settlement, namely for 'such person or persons and for such purposes' as the trustees should in their discretion appoint by deed within 21 years of the date of the settlement. The deed of appointment further provided that prior to any appointment the trustees were to hold the trust fund on trust to pay the income thereof to 'any person or persons whatsoever' or any charity as the trustees thought fit for a period until 21 years after the death of the last survivor of the settlor's nieces and nephews living at the date of the settlement. Following the expiration of a period of 21 years from the date of the original settlement the trustees instituted proceedings to determine (i) whether the power of appointment in the original settlement in favour of 'such persons or purposes' as the trustees should appoint was invalid as being too wide, and therefore the trust fund vested ab initio in the nieces and nephews living at the date of the settlement, (ii) whether, if the power of appointment in the original settlement was valid, the discretionary trust created by the deed of appointment was nevertheless invalid as being too wide and outside the power of appointment in the settlement, so that the nieces and nephews living at the date of the settlement became entitled to the trust fund on 7th May 1979 on the expiration of 21 years from the date of the settlement, or (iii) whether both the power of appointment in the original settlement and the deed of appointment were valid so that the trustees continued to hold on trust to pay the income to such persons or charities as they thought fit until 21 years after the death of the last surviving niece or nephew.

Held – (1) An 'intermediate' or 'hybrid' power of appointment vested in a trustee to appoint to anyone in the world except a specified number or class of persons was not, despite the fiduciary duties of the trustees, rendered invalid merely by the width of the power and the number of persons who were objects of the power, since in exercising such a power of appointment the duties of the trustee were (a) to ensure that any appointment was within the power, (b) to consider periodically whether to exercise the power, (c) to consider the range of objects of the power, and (d) to consider the appropriateness of individual appointments; and nothing in the nature of an intermediate power of appointment prevented trustees from discharging those duties. It followed that the power of appointment contained in the settlement was not void for uncertainty (see p 793 *f g*, p 794 *g* to *j* and p 795 *b c*, post); *Re Gestetner (deceased)* [1953] 1 All ER 1150, *Re Gulbenkian's Settlement Trusts* [1968] 3 All ER 785, *McPhail v Doulton* [1970] 2 All ER 228, *Re Baden (No 2)* [1972] 2 All ER 1304 and *Re Manisty's Settlement Trusts* [1973] 2 All ER 1203 applied; dictum of Buckley LJ in *Blausten v Inland Revenue Comrs* [1972] 1 All ER at 50 not followed.

(2) However, by requiring the trustees to hold the trust fund for 'such persons' as they should appoint, the deed of appointment had not, as the settlement itself required, designated the persons to whom the appointment was to be made, but had merely provided the mechanism whereby appointees might be ascertained in the future, and in so doing the deed of appointment offended against the rule, which applied to intermediate powers of appointment, that unless authorised to do so a trustee could not delegate his powers. It was immaterial that the appointors under the deed of appointment were the same persons as the trustees under the settlement. The deed of appointment was therefore void as being an excessive execution of the power to appoint contained in the settlement. It followed that the nieces and nephews living at the date of the settlement became entitled to the trust fund on the expiration of 21 years from the date of the settlement (ie on 7th May 1979) by virtue of the gift over in default of any valid appointment being made during the term of the settlement (see p 795 *e* to *j* and p 796 *a* to *d*, post); dictum of Viscount Radcliffe in *Re Pilkington's Will Trusts* [1962] 3 All ER at 630 applied.

Notes

For powers in relation to trusts, see 36 Halsbury's Laws (3rd Edn) 535–540, paras 808–814, for uncertainty in relation to powers, see ibid 540, para 815, and for cases on those subjects, see 37 Digest (Repl) 401–404, *1309–1332*.

Cases referred to in judgment

Baden's Deed Trusts (No 2), Re, Baden v Smith, Pearson v Smith [1972] 2 All ER 1304, [1973] Ch 9, [1972] 3 WLR 250, CA, Digest (Cont Vol D) 1005, *317a*.

Blausten v Inland Revenue Comrs [1972] 1 All ER 41, [1972] Ch 256, [1972] 2 WLR 376, 47 Tax Cas 549, [1971] TR 363, 50 ATC 278, CA, Digest (Cont Vol D) 485, *1569a*.

Gestetner (deceased), Re, Barnett v Blumka [1953] 1 All ER 1150, [1953] Ch 672, [1953] 2 WLR 1033, 37 Digest (Repl) 411, *1400*.

Gulbenkian's Settlement Trusts, Re, Whishaw v Stephens [1968] 3 All ER 785, [1970] AC 508, [1968] 3 WLR 1127, HL, Digest (Cont Vol C) 806, *1330b*.

Hunter's Will Trust, Gilks v Harris [1962] 3 All ER 1050, [1963] Ch 372, [1962] 3 WLR 1442, 37 Digest (Repl) 371, *1066*.

Manisty's Settlement Trusts, Re, Manisty v Manisty [1973] 2 All ER 1203, [1974] Ch 17, [1973] 3 WLR 341, Digest (Cont Vol D) 728, *1332a*.

McPhail v Doulton [1970] 2 All ER 228, [1971] AC 424, [1970] 2 WLR 1110, HL; *rvsg* sub nom *Re Baden's Deeds Trusts, Baden v Smith* [1969] 1 All ER 1016, [1969] 2 Ch 388, [1969] 3 WLR 12, CA, Digest (Cont Vol C) 805, *1324a*.

Morris's Settlement Trusts, Re, Adams v Napier [1951] 2 All ER 528, CA, 37 Digest (Repl) 264, *217*.

Park, Re, Public Trustee v Armstrong [1932] 1 Ch 580, [1931] All ER Rep 633, 101 LJCh 295, 147 LT 118, 37 Digest (Repl) 403, *1328*.

Pilkington's Will Trusts, Re, Pilkington v Inland Revenue Comrs [1962] 3 All ER 622, [1964] AC 612, [1962] 3 WLR 1051, 40 Tax Cas 433, [1962] TR 265, 41 ATC 285, HL, 28(2) Digest (Reissue) 785, *1139*.

Triffitt's Settlement, Re, Hatt v Hyde [1958] 2 All ER 299, [1958] Ch 852, [1958] 2 WLR 927, 37 Digest (Repl) 264, *219*.

Originating summons

By an originating summons dated 11th September 1980 the plaintiffs, David Coventry Greig and Colin Henry Oliver, who were trustees of a settlement dated 7th May 1958 and of a deed of appointment made thereunder on 5th May 1969, sought the determination of the court on the question whether on the true construction of the settlement and in the events which had happened the trust fund subject to the trusts of the settlement and the income thereof (a) had at all times since the date of the settlement been held on trust for such of the nieces and nephews of the settlor, Dame Isobel Rose Hay, as were living at the date of the settlement, (b) was from the expiration of 21 years from the date of the settlement held on trust for such of the nieces and nephews of the settlor as were living at the date of the settlement, or (c) was to be held on the discretionary trust of income specified in the deed of appointment until the expiration of 21 years after the last survivor of such of the nieces and nephews of the settlor as were living at the date of the settlement and subject thereto on trust for such nieces and nephews absolutely. The defendants were the nieces of the settlor, Roxana Mary Jocelyn McGregor, Anne Coventry Ruck Keene, Elizabeth Rose Gimpel, and the Attorney General representing the interests of charity. The facts are set out in the judgment.

John Child for the first, second and third defendants.
John Mummery for the Attorney General.
T D Baxendale for the plaintiffs.

Cur adv vult

30th July. **SIR ROBERT MEGARRY V-C** read the following judgment: This originating summons raises difficult questions on a settlement dated 7th May 1958 and a deed of appointment thereunder made on 5th May 1969. The settlor, Lady Hay, had two brothers and a sister; and each of them had children. Mr Child appears on behalf of the first three defendants, who are all nieces of the settlor (one from each stirps); and a representation order is sought for them to represent all the settlor's nieces and nephews, and the estates of those deceased. Mr Mummery appears for the Attorney General, as representing the interests of charity, and Mr Baxendale appears for the plaintiffs, the trustees of the settlement. The settlor is still living, I may say.

By cl 1 of the settlement, 'the Trust Fund' is defined as meaning the initial £100 settled and any additions made to it. In April 1980 the trust fund consisted of a property in Edinburgh and investments worth over £140,000, with an annual income of over £11,000. Clause 2, when read with cl 6, confers wide powers of investment on the trustees, and then cl 3 makes the first of the provisions for beneficial interests. For five years from the date of the settlement (called 'the accumulation period') the trustees were given power to pay or apply the whole or any part of the income of the trust fund 'to or for the benefit of all or any person or persons or of any Charity appointed by them under Clause 5 hereof'. The reference to cl 5, I should say, is plainly a slip for cl 4. The trustees are then required to accumulate any part of the income not so paid or applied, and to hold the accumulation as an accretion to the trust fund.

Next, there is cl 4; and I must read a large part of it. The clause is not a model of clarity, but I think that it becomes rather more lucid if it is approached with the realisation that it may be divided into six parts. There is an introduction, two main limbs, a provision as to revocability and two provisos. The introduction is short:

'Subject as aforesaid the Trustees shall hold the trust fund . . .'

Then there is the first main limb:

'on trust for such persons or purposes for such interests and with such gifts over and (if for persons) with such provisions for their respective maintenance or advancement at the discretion of the Trustees or of any other persons as the Trustees shall by any deed or deeds revocable or irrevocable (but if revocable not after the expiration of twenty one years from the day hereof) executed within twenty one years from the date hereof appoint (but so that all interest under any such appointment shall necessarily vest during the lives of the Settlor's nieces and nephews now living or within twenty one years of the death of the last survivor of such nieces and nephews).'

In this, I may say, I have supplied the bracket after 'if for persons' in the second line that is missing in the original. The second main limb is short:

'and in default of such appointment in trust for the nieces and nephews of the Settlor now living in equal shares among them.'

The provision as to revocability merely lays down that an appointment that is expressed to be revocable is to be revocable by the trustees for the time being, whether or not they are the same persons as those who made the appointment. The first proviso states that any niece or nephew who (or whose issue) takes any part of the trust fund under an appointment under the power shall (in default of appointment to the contrary) bring the share so appointed into hotchpot. The second proviso precludes any appointment being made to the settlor, any husband of hers and any trustee or past trustee of the settlement.

Clause 5 deals with the income of the trust fund for the period beginning with the end of the accumulation period and ending when the power of appointment has been finally exercised or ceases to be exercisable: the maximum length of the period is thus the 16 years which lie between 5 years and 21 years from the date of the settlement. During that period, the clause provides that the trustees shall—

'pay or apply any part of the income of the Trust Fund to which no person is for the time being entitled under any partial or revocable appointment in manner following that is to say to or for the benefit of any niece or nephew of the Settlor as aforesaid or to or for such charitable objects in such shares and proportion and in such manner as the Trustees shall in their absolute discretion think fit.'

The rest of the deed of settlement may be summarised briefly. Clause 6, as I have indicated, deals with the trustees' powers of investment; cl 7 is a professional charging clause; cl 8 gives the settlor the power to appoint new trustees; and cl 9 provides for the settlement to be interpreted according to the law of England.

I turn to the deed of appointment. This was made by the trustees, who are described as 'the Appointors'. It recites, inter alia, that the appointors 'have determined to make such irrevocable appointment of the Trust Fund as is hereinafter contained'. The deed then witnesses that the appointors, in exercise of the power conferred on them by cl 4 of the settlement, 'Hereby Appoint' as follows; but neither there nor anywhere else does the deed state in terms whether the appointment is revocable or irrevocable. Clause 1 of the deed then proceeds to repeat in substance the first main limb of cl 4 of the settlement with a number of minor variations. The trustees are to 'stand possessed of the Trust Fund and of the income thereof upon trust' (in place of 'hold the Trust Fund on trust'). The trust is 'for such person or persons and for such purposes' (instead of 'for such persons or purposes'). 'Maintenance and advancement' replace 'maintenance or advancement', and the date of the settlement is preserved by replacing 'day hereof' and 'date hereof' in the settlement with 'date of the settlement'. Finally, the phrase 'settlor's nieces and nephews now living' is replaced by 'nieces and nephews of the Settlor and the survivor of them living at the date of the Settlement'. This leaves unchanged the requirement that all interest under any appointment must necessarily vest within 21 years after the death of the last survivor of the nieces and nephews living at the date of the settlement. The general effect of this clause of the deed of appointment is thus much the same as the first main limb of cl 4 of the settlement: it confers a power of appointment exercisable until 7th May 1979. However, the second main limb of the settlement, the provision as to revocability, and the two provisos are all without counterpart in this clause of the appointment.

The next clause of the deed of appointment, cl 2, like cl 5 of the settlement, deals with undisposed-of income: but the two provisions differ materially. Under the settlement, the income was to be paid or applied as the trustees thought fit between the nieces and nephews and charitable objects, whereas under the deed of appointment the class of objects of the discretionary trust is enlarged to any person or persons whatsoever (with only the very limited exception under cl 3), or any charity. Further, the duration of the trust under the deed of appointment is much greater. Instead of lasting for only 21 years from the date of the settlement (ie until 7th May 1979), it continues until 21 years after the death of the last survivor of the nieces and nephews living at the date of the settlement. Clause 2 reads as follows:

> 'PENDING the execution of an effective and irrevocable appointment of the whole of the capital and income of the Trust Fund and so far as any appointment thereof shall not for the time being and from time to time extend the trustees shall hold the Trust Fund upon trust until the lastest [sic] date for the vesting of the trust funds under the last preceding Clause hereof to pay the income of so much of the Trust Fund as is for the time being unappointed to or for the benefit of any person or persons whatsoever (save as hereinafter provided) whether or not related to Lady Isobel Rose Hay or to any Charity in such manner and in such shares and proportions as the trustees shall think fit.'

There are only two other clauses in the deed of appointment. Clause 3 prohibits any 'appointment under any power' in the deed, or 'under any other power exercisable by the trustees in relation to the Trust Fund', to be made in favour of the settlor, any husband of hers or any existing or former trustee of the settlement. In view of the words 'save as hereinafter provided' in cl 2, I think that the words 'any other power' in cl 3 must be read as including any discretion under any trust, and so as applying to cl 2.

Clause 4 reads as follows:

> 'SUBJECT as aforesaid and from and after the date for vesting provided by Clause 2 hereof the trustees shall stand possessed of the capital of the Trust Fund upon the trusts in default of appointment declared in Clause 4 of the Settlement but subject to the proviso for hotchpot therein contained.'

The 'date for vesting provided by Clause 2 hereof' is 'the lastest date for the vesting of the trust fund' under cl 1: and that is 21 years after the death of the last survivor of the nieces and nephews living at the date of the settlement. The 'trusts in default of appointment declared in Clause 4 of the Settlement' consist of the trust for the nieces and nephews living at the date of the settlement, in equal shares, under what I have called the second main limb.

Two provisions of these instruments are at the centre of the dispute. They are, first, the power of appointment conferred by what I have called the first main limb of cl 4 of the settlement; and, second, the discretionary trust of income under cl 2 of the deed of appointment. Under the power of appointment the trustees were to hold the trust fund on trust for 'such persons or purposes' as the trustees should appoint before 7th May 1979, subject to excluding the settlor, her husband and trustees or former trustees, by virtue of the second proviso. Such a provision raises obvious questions about the enormous class of persons who were possible objects of the power: everyone in the world

is included save for a handful of persons. If that power is invalid, then of course the
a   appointment made under it must also be invalid, and no other appointment could ever
have been valid. The result would therefore be that the second main limb of cl 4 would
take effect, and the nieces and nephews living at the date of the settlement would have
become entitled to the trust fund in equal shares ab initio. That is the solution put by
para 1(a) in the originating summons; and it is the result that counsel for the defendants
puts forward on behalf of the nieces and nephews, but only as his second and alternative
b   choice.

The first choice of counsel for the defendants is the solution put forward by para 1(b)
of the originating summons. That is that the nieces and nephews living at the date of the
settlement became entitled to the trust fund on 7th May 1979, at the expiration of 21
years from the date of the settlement. This has the fiscal attraction for the nieces and
nephews that it could not then be said that they had been entitled to past income which
c   in fact they have not received. This result is reached if the power of appointment under
cl 4 of the settlement is held to be valid, but the discretionary trust created by cl 2 of the
deed of appointment is held to be void. If that is the case, then on 7th May 1979 it
became impossible for any valid appointment ever to be made, for the 21 years' period
for appointments then expired. The discretionary trust under cl 2 being void, the
combined operation of cl 4 of the deed of appointment and the second main limb of cl 4
d   of the settlement would carry the trust fund to the nieces and nephews living at the date
of the settlement, in equal shares. In order to arrive at this result, the amplitude of a class
consisting of the whole world except a handful of individuals had to leave unaffected the
power of appointment given to the trustees by the first main limb of cl 4 of the
settlement, but at the same time bring to grief the discretionary trust created by cl 2 of
the deed of appointment. This was the path which by preference counsel for the
e   defendants trod, though he had an alternative ground for contending that cl 2 of the
deed of appointment was invalid. This was that the power was not wide enough to
authorise the appointment made by cl 2. Counsel for the Attorney General, on the other
hand, contended that both the power and the discretionary trust created by cl 2 of the
deed of appointment were valid; for only in that way could charity receive any benefit.

The starting point must be to consider whether the power created by the first limb of
f   cl 4 of the settlement is valid. The rival arguments were presented by counsel for the
defendants in his primary contention, and by counsel for the Attorney General, in favour
of validity, and by counsel for the defendants, in his alternative contention, against
validity. The essential point is whether a power for trustees to appoint to anyone in the
world except a handful of specified persons is valid. Such a power will be perfectly valid
if given to a person who is not in a fiduciary position: the difficulty arises when it is given
g   to trustees, for they are under certain fiduciary duties in relation to the power, and to a
limited degree they are subject to the control of the courts. At the centre of the dispute
there are *Re Manisty's Settlement Trusts* [1973] 2 All ER 1203, [1974] Ch 17 (in which
Templeman J differed from part of what was said in the Court of Appeal in *Blausten v
Inland Revenue Comrs* [1972] 1 All ER 41, [1972] Ch 256); *McPhail v Doulton* [1970] 2 All
ER 228, [1971] AC 424 (which I shall call *Re Baden (No 1)*); and *Re Baden's Deed Trusts
h*   *(No 2)* [1972] 2 All ER 1304, [1973] Ch 9, which I shall call *Re Baden (No 2)*. Counsel for
the defendants, I may say, strongly contended that *Re Manisty's Settlement* was wrongly
decided.

In *Re Manisty's Settlement* a settlement gave trustees a discretionary power to apply the
trust fund for the benefit of a small class of the settlor's near relations, save that any
member of a smaller 'excepted class' was to be excluded from the class of beneficiaries.
j   The trustees were also given power at their absolute discretion to declare that any person,
corporation or charity (except a member of the excepted class or a trustee) should be
included in the class of beneficiaries. Templeman J held that this power to extend the
class of beneficiaries was valid. In *Blausten v Inland Revenue Comrs* which had been
decided some eighteen months earlier, the settlement created a discretionary trust of
income for members of a 'specified class' and a power to pay or apply capital to or for the

benefit of members of that class, or to appoint capital to be held on trust for them. The settlement also gave the trustees power 'with the previous consent in writing of the *a* settlor' to appoint any other person or persons (except the settlor) to be included in the 'specified class'. The Court of Appeal decided the case on a point of construction; but Buckley LJ ([1972] 1 All ER 41 at 49, [1972] Ch 256 at 271) also considered a contention that the trustees' power to add to the 'specified class' was so wide that it was bad for uncertainty, since the power would enable anyone in the world save the settlor to be included. He rejected this contention on the ground that the settlor's prior written *b* consent was requisite to any addition to the 'specified class'; but for this, it seems plain that he would have held the power void for uncertainty. Orr LJ simply concurred, but Salmon LJ expressly confined himself to the point of construction, and said nothing about the power to add to the 'specified class'. In *Re Manisty's Settlement* [1973] 2 All ER 1203 at 1213, [1974] Ch 17 at 29, Templeman J rejected the view of Buckley LJ on this point on the ground that *Re Gestetner (deceased)* [1953] 1 All ER 1150, [1953] Ch 672, *Re* *c* *Gulbenkian's Settlement Trusts* [1968] 3 All ER 785, [1970] AC 508 and the two *Baden* cases did not appear to have been fully explored in the *Blausten* case, and the case did not involve any final pronouncement on the point. In general, I respectfully agree with Templeman J.

I propose to approach the matter by stages. First, it is plain that if a power of appointment is given to a person who is not in a fiduciary position, there is nothing in *d* the width of the power which invalidates it per se. The power may be a special power with a large class of persons as objects; the power may be what is called a 'hybrid' power, or an 'intermediate' power, authorising appointment to anyone save a specified number or class of persons; or the power may be a general power. Whichever it is, there is nothing in the number of persons to whom an appointment may be made which will invalidate it. The difficulty comes when the power is given to trustees as such, in that the *e* number of objects may interact with the fiduciary duties of the trustees and their control by the court. The argument of counsel for the defendants carried him to the extent of asserting that no valid intermediate or general power could be vested in trustees.

That brings me to the second point, namely, the extent of the fiduciary obligations of trustees who have a mere power vested in them, and how far the court exercises control over them in relation to that power. In the case of a trust, of course, the trustee is bound *f* to execute it, and if he does not, the court will see to its execution. A mere power is very different. Normally the trustee is not bound to exercise it, and the court will not compel him to do so. That, however, does not mean that he can simply fold his hands and ignore it, for normally he must from time to time consider whether or not to exercise the power, and the court may direct him to do this.

When he does exercise the power, he must, of course (as in the case of all trusts and *g* powers) confine himself to what is authorised, and not go beyond it. But that is not the only restriction. Whereas a person who is not in a fiduciary position is free to exercise the power in any way that he wishes, unhampered by any fiduciary duties, a trustee to whom, as such, a power is given is bound by the duties of his office in exercising that power to do so in a responsible manner according to its purpose. It is not enough for him to refrain from acting capriciously; he must do more. He must 'make such a survey of *h* the range of objects or possible beneficiaries' as will enable him to carry out his fiduciary duty. He must find out 'the permissible area of selection and then consider responsibly, in individual cases, whether a contemplated beneficiary was within the power and whether, in relation to the possible claimants, a particular grant was appropriate': per Lord Wilberforce in *Re Baden (No 1)* [1970] 2 All ER 228 at 240, 247, [1971] AC 424 at 449, 457.   *j*

I pause there. The summary of the law that I have set out above is taken from a variety of sources, principally *Re Gestetner (deceased)* [1953] 1 All ER 1150, [1953] Ch 672, *Re Gulbenkian's Settlement* [1968] 3 All ER 785 at 787, 592–594, [1970] AC 508 at 518, 524–525 and *Re Baden (No 1)* [1970] 2 All ER 228 at 246, [1971] AC 424 at 456. The last proposition, relating to the survey and consideration, at first sight gives rise to some difficulty. It is now well settled that no mere power is invalidated by it being impossible to ascertain every object of the power; provided the language is clear enough to make it possible to say whether any given individual is an object of the power, it need not be possible to compile a complete list of every object: see *Re Gestetner (deceased)* [1953] 1 All ER 1150 at 1155, [1953] Ch 672 at 688; *Re Gulbenkian's Settlement* [1968] 3 All ER 785, [1970] AC 508; *Re Baden (No 1)* [1970] 2 All ER 228, [1971] AC 424. As Harman J said in *Re Gestetner (deceased)* [1953] 1 All ER 1150 at 1056, [1953] Ch 672 at 688, the trustees need not 'worry their heads to survey the world from China to Peru, when there are perfectly good objects of the class in England'.

That brings me to the third point. How is the duty of making a responsible survey and selection to be carried out in the absence of any complete list of objects? This question was considered by the Court of Appeal in *Re Baden (No 2)*. That case was concerned with what, after some divergences of judicial opinion, was held to be a discretionary trust and not a mere power; but plainly the requirements for a mere power cannot be more stringent than those for a discretionary trust. The duty, I think, may be expressed along the following lines: I venture a modest degree of amplification and exegesis of what was said in *Re Baden (No 2)* [1972] 2 All ER 1304 at 1310, 1315, [1973] Ch 9 at 20, 27. The trustee must not simply proceed to exercise the power in favour of such of the objects as happen to be at hand or claim his attention. He must first consider what persons or classes of persons are objects of the power within the definition in the settlement or will. In doing this, there is no need to compile a complete list of the objects, or even to make an accurate assessment of the number of them: what is needed is an appreciation of the width of the field, and thus whether a selection is to be made merely from a dozen or, instead, from thousands or millions. (Incidentally, in order to avoid the relevant passage in the judgment of Sachs LJ being self-contradictory I think a comma needs deletion: the words 'it refers to something quite different, to a need to provide . . .' should read 'it refers to something quite different to a need to provide . . .', or, preferably, 'it refers to something quite different from a need to provide . . .': see [1972] 2 All ER 1304 at 1310, [1973] Ch 9 at 20). Only when the trustee has applied his mind to 'the size of the problem' should he then consider in individual cases whether, in relation to other possible claimants, a particular grant is appropriate. In doing this, no doubt he should not prefer the undeserving to the deserving; but he is not required to make an exact calculation whether, as between deserving claimants, A is more deserving than B: see *Re Gestetner (deceased)* [1953] 1 All ER 1150 at 1155, [1953] Ch 672 at 688, approved in *Re Baden (No 1)* [1970] 2 All ER 228 at 243–244, [1971] AC 424 at 453.

If I am right in these views, the duties of a trustee which are specific to a mere power seem to be threefold. Apart from the obvious duty of obeying the trust instrument, and in particular of making no appointment that is not authorised by it, the trustee must, first, consider periodically whether or not he should exercise the power; second, consider the range of objects of the power; and third, consider the appropriateness of individual appointments. I do not assert that this list is exhaustive; but as the authorities stand it seems to me to include the essentials, so far as relevant to the case before me.

On this footing, the question is thus whether there is something in the nature of an intermediate power which conflicts with these duties in such a way as to invalidate the power if it is vested in a trustee. The case that there is rests in the main on *Blausten v Inland Revenue Comrs* which I have already summarised. The power there was plainly a mere power; and it authorised the trustees, with the settlor's previous consent in writing, to add any other person or persons (except the settlor) to the specified class.

In that case, Buckley LJ referred to the power as being one the exercise of which the trustees were under a duty to consider from time to time, and said ([1972] 1 All ER 41 at 50, [1972] Ch 256 at 272):

'If the class of persons to whose possible claims they would have to give consideration were so wide that it really did not amount to a class in any true sense at all no doubt that would be a duty which it would be impossible for them to perform and the power could be said to be invalid on that ground. But here, although they may introduce to the specified class any other person or persons except the [settlor], the power is one which can only be exercised with the previous consent in writing of the [settlor] ... Therefore on analysis the power is not a power to introduce anyone in the world to the specified class, but only anyone proposed by the trustees and approved by the [settlor]. This is not a case in which it could be said that the [settlor] in this respect has not set any metes and bounds to the beneficial interests which he intended to create or permit to be created under this settlement.'

After referring to *Re Park* [1932] 1 Ch 581 at 583, [1931] All ER Rep 633 at 634, Buckley LJ went on ([1972] 1 All ER 41 at 50, [1972] Ch 256 at 273):

'... this is not a power which suffers from the sort of uncertainty which results from the trustees being given a power of so wide an extent that it would be impossible for the court to say whether or not they were properly exercising it and so wide that it would be impossible for the trustees to consider in any sensible manner how they should exercise it, if at all, from time to time. The trustees would no doubt take into consideration the possible claims of anyone having any claim on the beneficence of the [settlor]. That is not a class of persons so wide or so indefinite that the trustees would not be able rationally to exercise their duty to consider from time to time whether or not they should exercise the power.'

It seems quite plain that Buckley LJ considered that the power was saved from invalidity only by the requirement for the consent of the settlor. The reason for saying that in the absence of such a requirement the power would have been invalid seems to be twofold. First, the class of persons to whose possible claims the trustees would be duty-bound to give consideration was so wide as not to form a true class, and this would make it impossible for the trustees to perform their duty of considering from time to time whether to exercise the power.

I feel considerable difficulty in accepting this view. First, I do not see how mere numbers can inhibit the trustees from considering whether or not to exercise the power, as distinct from deciding in whose favour to exercise it. Second, I cannot see how the requirement of the settlor's consent will result in any 'class' being narrowed from one that is too wide to one that is small enough. Such a requirement makes no difference whatever to the number of persons potentially included: the only exclusion is still the settlor. Third, in any case I cannot see how the requirement of the settlor's consent could make it possible to treat 'anyone in the world save X' as constituting any real sort of a 'class', as that term is usually understood.

The second ground of invalidity if there is no requirement for the settlor's consent seems to be that the power is so wide that it would be impossible for the trustees to consider in any sensible manner how to exercise it, and also impossible for the court to say whether or not they were properly exercising it. With respect, I do not see how that follows. If I have correctly stated the extent of the duties of trustees in whom a mere power is vested, I do not see what there is to prevent the trustees from performing these duties. It must be remembered that Buckley LJ, though speaking after *Re Gulbenkian's Settlement* and *Re Baden (No 1)* had been decided, lacked the advantage of considering *Re Baden (No 2)*, which was not decided until some five months later. He thus did not have before him the explanation in that case of how the trustees should make a survey and consider individual appointments in cases where no complete list of objects could be compiled. I also have in mind that the settlor in the present case is still alive, though I do not rest my decision on that.

From what I have said it will be seen that I cannot see any ground on which the power in question can be said to be void. Certainly it is not void for linguistic or semantic uncertainty; there is no room for doubt in the definition of those who are or are not objects of the power. Nor can I see that the power is administratively unworkable. The words of Lord Wilberforce in *Re Baden (No 1)* [1970] 2 All ER 228 at 247, [1971] AC 424 at 457 are directed to discretionary trusts, not powers. Nor do I think that the power is void as being capricious. In *Re Manisty's Settlement* [1973] 2 All ER 1203 at 1211, [1974] a Ch 17 at 27 Templeman J appears to be suggesting that a power to benefit 'residents in Greater London' is void as being capricious 'because the terms of the power negative any sensible intention on the part of the settlor'. In saying that, I do not think that the judge had in mind a case in which the settlor was, for instance, a former chairman of the Greater London Council, as subsequent words of his on that page indicate. In any case, as he pointed out earlier, this consideration does not apply to intermediate powers, where no class which could be regarded as capricious has been laid down. Nor do I see how the

b power in the present case could be invalidated as being too vague, a possible ground of invalidity considered in *Re Manisty's Settlement* [1973] 2 All ER 1203 at 1208, [1974] Ch 17 at 24. Of course, if there is some real vice in a power, and there are real problems of administration or execution, the court may have to hold the power invalid: but I think that the court should be slow to do this. Dispositions ought if possible to be upheld, and the court ought not to be astute to find grounds on which a power can be invalidated.

c Naturally, if it is shown that a power offends against some rule of law or equity, then it will be held to be void: but a power should not be held void on a peradventure. In my judgment, the power conferred by cl 4 of the settlement is valid.

With that, I turn to the discretionary trust of income under cl 2 of the deed of appointment. Apart from questions of the validity of the trust per se, there is the prior question whether the settlement enabled the trustees to create such a trust, or, for that

d matter, the power set out in cl 1 of the deed of appointment. The power conferred by cl 4 of the settlement provides that the trustees are to hold the trust fund on trust 'for such persons or purposes for such interests and with such gifts over and (if for persons) with such provision for their respective maintenance or advancement at the discretion of the Trustees or any other persons' as the trustees shall appoint. Clause 2 of the deed of appointment provides that the trustees are to hold the trust fund on trust to pay the

e income 'to or for the benefit of any person or persons whatsoever . . . or to any charity' in such manner and shares and proportions as the trustees think fit. I need say nothing about purposes or charities as no question on them has arisen. The basic question is whether the appointment has designated the 'persons' to whom the appointment is made.

Looked at as a matter of principle, my answer would be 'No'. There is no such person

f to be found in cl 2 of the deed of appointment: instead, there is merely the mechanism whereby a person or persons may be ascertained from time to time by the exercise of the discretion given to the trustees. If that mechanism is operated, then persons may emerge who will be entitled: but they will emerge not by virtue of any exercise of the power in the settlement but by virtue of the exercise of the discretion in the deed of appointment. That seems to me to be a plain case of delegation: the power in the

g settlement is not being exercised by appointing the persons who are to benefit but by creating a discretionary trust under which the discretionary trustees will from time to time select those who will benefit. True, the appointor under the settlement and the trustees under the discretionary trust are the same persons: but I do not think that this affects the matter. The power in the settlement is a power to appoint to persons and not a power to nominate those (whether the appointors or anyone else) who will select

h persons who are to benefit; and I do not see how identity between the appointors and nominators can alter the fact that the mechanism set up by the deed of appointment differs from anything authorised by the settlement. I can see nothing whatever in the power conferred by the settlement which even contemplates that an appointment should designate no appointees but instead should set up a discretionary trust under which the trustees could determine who should benefit.

j Counsel for the defendants relied on *Re Hunter's Will Trusts* [1962] 3 All ER 1050, [1963] Ch 372 as supporting his contention that cl 2 of the deed of appointment was void. There, Cross J felt constrained by the decision of the Court of Appeal in *Re Morris's Settlement Trusts* [1951] 2 All ER 528 to hold that a special power to appoint to children and remoter issue did not authorise the imposition of protective trusts on appointments made to children, even though the power was to appoint to the objects 'with such trusts for their respective benefits' as might be appointed. It appears that apart from authority Cross J ([1962] 3 All ER 1050 at 1055, [1963] Ch 372 at 381) would have held that the power did authorise the imposition of protective trusts; but, significantly, he added 'though not the creation of an immediate discretionary trust'.

Now it is clear that in these authorities the rule delegatus non potest delegare was in issue. Does this rule apply to intermediate powers? This was not explored in argument, but I think that it is clear from *Re Triffitt's Settlement* [1958] 2 All ER 299, [1958] Ch 852 that the rule does not apply to an intermediate power vested in a person beneficially. Here, of course, the power is an intermediate power, but it is vested in trustees as such, and not in any person beneficially; and the rule is that 'trustees cannot delegate unless they have authority to do so': per Viscount Radcliffe in *Re Pilkington's Will Trusts* [1962] 3 All ER 622 at 630, [1964] AC 612 at 639. Accordingly, I do not think that the fact that the power is an intermediate power excludes it from the rule against delegation. On the contrary, the fact that the power is vested in trustees subjects it to that rule unless there is something in the settlement to exclude it. I can see nothing in the settlement which purports to authorise any such appointment or to exclude the normal rule against delegation. In my judgment, both on principle and on authority cl 2 of the deed of appointment is void as being an excessive execution of the power.

That, I think, suffices to dispose of the case. I have not dealt with the submission which counsel for the defendants put in the forefront of his argument. This was that even if the power had been wide enough to authorise the creation of the discretionary trust, that trust was nevertheless bad as being a trust in favour of 'so hopelessly wide' a definition of beneficiaries 'as not to form anything like a class so that the trust is administratively unworkable': see per Lord Wilberforce in *Re Baden (No 1)* [1970] 2 All ER 228 at 247, [1971] AC 424 at 457. I do not propose to go into the authorities on this point. I consider that the duties of trustees under a discretionary trust are more stringent than those of trustees under a power of appointment (see *Re Baden (No 1)* [1970] 2 All ER 228 at 247, [1971] AC 424 at 457), and as at present advised I think that I would, if necessary, hold that an intermediate trust such as that in the present case is void as being administratively unworkable. In my view there is a difference between a power and a trust in this respect. The essence of that difference, I think, is that beneficiaries under a trust have rights of enforcement which mere objects of a power lack. But in this difficult branch of the law I consider that I should refrain from exploring without good reason any matters which do not have to be decided. In my opinion, the question whether an appointment is within a power is anterior to the question whether, if the appointment is within the power, it is inherently good or bad; and having decided the first question against the validity of the appointment, I leave the second question undecided.

Subject to anything counsel may wish to say, I propose to answer para 1 of the originating summons in sense (b), and I make the representation order sought by para 2.

Order accordingly.

Solicitors: *Bircham & Co* (for the plaintiffs); *Lawrence, Graham, Middleton Lewis* (for the defendants); *Official Solicitor* (for the Attorney General).

Azza M Abdallah   Barrister.

Swain and another v Law Society

COURT OF APPEAL, CIVIL DIVISION
STEPHENSON, OLIVER AND FOX LJJ
15th, 16th, 17th, 18th, 19th JUNE, 31st JULY 1981

Insurance – Liability insurance – Professional indemnity insurance – Solicitors – Law Society's group scheme – Law Society authorised to 'take out and maintain insurance with authorised insurers' – Law Society arranging master policy with specified insurers – Law Society requiring all solicitors to participate in group scheme and pay premiums set under master policy – Whether scheme within Law Society's authority to take out and maintain insurance with authorised insurers – Solicitors Act 1974, s 37(2)(b).

Trust and trustee – Profit from trust – Account of profits – Commission – Professional indemnity insurance – Solicitors – Law Society's group scheme – Law Society arranging master policy with specified insurers through brokers – Law Society and brokers agreeing to share commission – Whether Law Society accountable to individual solicitors for commission received – Whether Law Society in a fiduciary relationship with solicitors when making commission agreement with brokers.

By virtue of s 37[a] of the Solicitors Act 1974 the Law Society was empowered to make rules for compulsory professional indemnity insurance against claims made against solicitors in respect of civil liability for professional negligence or breach of duty. Under s 37(1) the society had a general rule-making power to make rules concerning indemnity against loss arising from claims in respect of civil liability incurred by solicitors, while s 37(2) specified that 'for the purpose of providing such indemnity' such rules could (a) authorise the society to establish and maintain its own indemnity fund, or (b) authorise the society to 'take out and maintain insurance with authorised insurers', or (c) require solicitors to take out and maintain insurance individually with authorised insurers. The society opted for a group scheme whereby it arranged indemnity insurance through a particular firm of brokers and then required solicitors to participate in the scheme or else risk being refused a practising certificate. Accordingly, the society entered into a contract with specified insurers in November 1975 and later made the Solicitors' Indemnity Rules 1975 which provided for the society to take out and maintain with authorised insurers a 'master policy' and required solicitors to pay the premiums prescribed under that policy and to produce a certificate of insurance issued under the master policy when applying each year for a practising certificate. By s 37(3)(c) of the 1974 Act the society was authorised to require solicitors to 'make payments by way of premium on any insurance policy maintained by the Society [under s 37(2)(b)]'. The master policy, which was deemed to form part of the indemnity rules, was arranged by the society with specified insurers. The policy recited that the insurers agreed 'with the Law Society on behalf of all solicitors . . . required to be insured' by the indemnity rules to provide such insurance and provided for fixed premiums according to whether a solicitor was a partner or sole practitioner and later according to whether a solicitor practised in Inner London or elsewhere. A specified firm were to act as sole brokers under the scheme and all claims were required to be submitted to them. The brokers agreed that in return for being appointed sole brokers they would share with the society commission received by them from the insurers, and in fact the society received substantial amounts of revenue from this source. This agreement ('the commission arrangement') was made in May 1976 following renegotiation by the society and the brokers of an earlier commission agreement made in February 1975 in respect of the voluntary insurance scheme which the society ran in conjunction with the brokers prior to the compulsory scheme set up in November 1975. The February 1975 agreement provided for such renegotiation at the

---

a   Section 37 is set out at p 801 *d* to *j*, post

request of either party in the event of the introduction of a compulsory indemnity
insurance scheme. As a result of the renegotiation the society received a much greater *a*
share of the commission than before.

The plaintiffs were two practising solicitors who considered that given freedom of
choice they could obtain better insurance cover at a lower premium than that available
under the society's scheme. The plaintiffs took no action in the matter until 1979 when
they took out an originating summons seeking declarations (i) that the society had no
power under s 37 to make the indemnity rules, which were therefore null and void, and *b*
(ii) that the society was not entitled to retain for its own purposes commission received
by it from the brokers in respect of premiums paid by individual solicitors but was
instead accountable to them for the commission.

The judge ([1980] 3 All ER 615) refused to grant the first declaration sought, on the
grounds that the rules had been properly implemented and the society's scheme was
intra vires s 37(2)(b). The judge also refused to grant the second declaration sought, on *c*
the ground that although the society had entered into the contract with the insurers as
trustee for the solicitors concerned and therefore a fiduciary relationship came into
existence between the society and the solicitors when the contract was concluded, the
society owed no duty to solicitors when negotiating the contract from which the
arrangement relating to the commission arose, and accordingly the society was not
bound to account to the plaintiffs for any part of the commission received by them. The *d*
plaintiffs appealed.

Held – (1) Section 37(2) of the 1974 Act was exhaustive of the rule-making power
conferred on the Law Society for the purpose of providing indemnity insurance for
solicitors and covered all permissible methods for providing a compulsory insurance
scheme. However, by virtue of the powers contained in ss 37(2)(b) and 37(3)(c) those *e*
permissible methods included making group arrangements with insurers, and on the
true construction of s 37 the society was authorised to take out and maintain insurance
against loss incurred by solicitors and not just loss incurred by the society itself.
Furthermore, r 2 of the indemnity rules authorising the society to take out and maintain
with insurers a master policy and to arrange for the issue to solicitors of certificates of
insurance was within the power contained in s 37(2)(b), and r 3 requiring every solicitor *f*
to whom the rules applied to pay premiums under the master policy and certificate of
insurance was within the power contained in s 37(3)(c). The appeal would therefore be
dismissed in so far as it related to the first declaration (see p 802 c to f, p 803 b to d and h,
p 811 j to p 812 d and p 821 b c, post).

(2) Neither the compulsory payment of premiums by individual solicitors under the
Law Society's contract with the insurers nor the retention by the society of commission *g*
received by it in respect of the premiums were unlawful or ultra vires the powers
conferred on the society by s 37 or assumed by it under the rules, since both came within
an 'arrangement' which the society considered 'necessary or expedient for the purpose of
indemnity' and which the society was empowered by s 37(5) to carry into effect (see
p 804 a to d, p 811 j to p 812 d and p 821 b c, post).

(3) It was a strict rule of equity that a person who owed a fiduciary relationship to *h*
another was accountable to that person for any profit or advantage derived from the
relationship. The Law Society, by entering into the master policy arrangement with the
insurers on behalf of all solicitors and with the object of holding the benefit of the
insurers' obligations as trustee for individual solicitors, thereby established a fiduciary
relationship between itself and individual solicitors, and since the opportunity to obtain
commission was derived from the master policy arrangement the society had therefore *j*
obtained the commission by reason of its fiduciary position, notwithstanding that the
contract between the society and the insurers was concluded before the fiduciary
relationship arose or that the society had acted bona fide throughout. Furthermore, in
agreeing to receive the commission the society had placed itself in a position where its
duty as trustee arising out of the fiduciary relationship and its own interest in receiving
commission might conflict. It followed that in principle the society was accountable to

individual solicitors who paid premiums under the scheme for the commission received
a by it (see p 805 *f* to p 806 *b*, p 809 *a* to *e*, p 810 *a* to *f*, p 814 *a* to *c*, p 817 *d* to *f*, p 819 *e* to
h, p 820 *h* and p 822 *j* to p 823 *c* and *j* to p 824 *h*, post); *Regal (Hastings) Ltd v Gulliver*
[1942] 1 All ER 378 applied.

(4) However, the plaintiffs were debarred by acquiescence from enforcing their right
to their share of the commission received by the Law Society prior to 1979 (when the
plaintiffs issued their summons), because the plaintiffs along with all other solicitors had
b from the outset been informed and consulted by the society about the master policy and
the arrangements for commission and until 1979 had not questioned the society's right
to retain the commission. The issue of the summons, however, brought the plaintiffs'
acquiescence to an end, and a declaration would be made that the society was bound to
account to the plaintiffs for commission received by it after 1978. To that extent the
appeal in relation to the second declaration sought would be allowed (see p 810 *e f*, p 811
c *h j*, p 820 *h*, p 821 *b* and p 825 *d* to *h*, post).

Decision of Slade J [1980] 3 All ER 615 reversed in part.

Notes

For professional indemnity insurance, see 25 Halsbury's Laws (4th Edn) paras 719–724.
d For the accountability of a trustee arising out of a fiduciary relationship, see 38
Halsbury's Laws (3rd Edn) 957, para 1658, and for cases on the subject, see 47 Digest
(Repl) 364–367, 3275–3298.

For the Solicitors Act 1974, s 37, see 44 Halsbury's Statutes (3rd Edn) 1508.

Cases referred to in judgments

e *Aberdeen Railway Co v Blaikie Brothers* (1854) 1 Macq 461, (1852) 15 Dunl (Ct of Sess) 20,
3 Digest (Reissue) 53, *176.
Beswick v Beswick [1967] 2 All ER 1197, [1968] AC 58, [1967] 3 WLR 932, HL, 12 Digest
(Reissue) 50, 256.
Boardman v Phipps [1966] 3 All ER 721, [1967] 2 AC 46, [1966] 3 WLR 1009, HL; *affg*
[1965] 1 All ER 849, [1965] Ch 992, [1965] 3 WLR 839, CA; *affg* [1964] 2 All ER 187,
f [1964] 1 WLR 993, Digest (Cont Vol B) 732, 3295.
Bray v Ford [1896] AC 44, [1895–9] All ER Rep 1009, 65 LJQB 213, 73 LT 609, HL, 51
Digest (Repl) 856, 4070.
Dover Coalfield Extension Ltd, Re [1908] 1 Ch 65, [1904–7] All ER Rep 161, 77 LJ Ch 94,
98 LT 31, 15 Mans 51, CA, 9 Digest (Reissue) 488, 2912.
English v Dedham Vale Properties Ltd [1978] 1 All ER 382, [1978] 1 WLR 93, 35 P & CR
g 148, Digest (Cont Vol E) 529, 344a.
Huntington Copper Co v Henderson (1877) 4 R 294.
Keech v Sandford (1726) Sel Cas Ch 61, 2 Eq Cas Abr 741, Cas *temp* King 61, 25 ER 223,
LC, 47 Digest (Repl) 104, 749.
Macadam, Re, Dallow v Codd [1945] 2 All ER 664, [1946] Ch 73, 115 LJ Ch 14, 173 LT
395, 62 TLR 48, 47 Digest (Repl) 366, 3293.
h *Mulholland's Will Trusts, Re, Bryan v Westminster Bank Ltd* [1949] 1 All ER 460, [1949] LJR
1078, 31(1) Digest (Reissue) 165, 1431.
New Zealand Netherlands Society 'Oranje' Inc v Kuys [1973] 2 All ER 1222, [1973] 1 WLR
1126, [1974] RPC 272, [1973] 2 NZLR 163, PC, Digest (Cont Vol D) 135, 485a.
Reading v Attorney General [1951] 1 All ER 617, [1951] AC 507, HL; *affg* sub nom *Re
Readings Petition of Right* [1949] 2 All ER 68, [1949] 2 KB 232, CA; *affg* [1948] 2 All ER
j 27, [1948] 2 KB 268, 34 Digest (Repl) 149, 1028.
Regal (Hastings) Ltd v Gulliver [1942] 1 All ER 378, [1967] AC 134, HL, 9 Digest (Reissue)
532, 3181.
Shaw v Applegate [1978] 1 All ER 123, [1977] 1 WLR 970, 35 P & CR 181, CA, Digest
(Cont Vol E) 336, 235a.
Tito v Waddell (No 2), Tito v Attorney General [1977] 3 All ER 129, [1977] Ch 106, [1977]
2 WLR 496, Digest (Cont Vol E) 636, 15a.

Cases also cited

Brocklebank Ltd v R [1925] 1 KB 52, CA.   *a*
Brown v Inland Revenue Comrs [1964] 3 All ER 119, [1965] AC 244, HL.
Dale v Inland Revenue Comrs [1953] 2 All ER 671, [1954] AC 11, HL.
Dean v Wiesengrund [1955] 2 All ER 432, [1955] 2 QB 120, CA.
Department of Trade and Industry v St Christopher Motorists Association Ltd [1974] 1 All ER
    395, [1974] 1 WLR 99.
Hagedorn v Oliverson (1814) 2 M & S 485, 105 ER 461.   *b*
King, Re, Robinson v Grey [1963] 1 All ER 781, [1963] Ch 459, CA.
Lyell v Kennedy (1882) 20 Ch D 484, CA.
North Stafford Steel, Iron & Coal Co (Burslem) Ltd v Ward (1868) LR 3 Exch 180.
Plowright v Lambert (1885) 52 LT 646.
Powell & Thomas v Evan Jones & Co [1905] 1 KB 11, CA.
Steele v Williams (1853) 8 Ex Ch 625.   *c*
Watson v Swann (1862) 11 CBNS 756.
West Wake Price & Co v Ching [1956] 3 All ER 821, [1957] 1 WLR 45.
Williams v Barton [1927] 2 Ch 9, [1927] All ER Rep 751.

Appeal

The first plaintiff, James Midwood Swain, appealed against the decision of Slade J ([1980]   *d*
3 All ER 615, [1980] 1 WLR 1355) on 17th March 1980 dismissing an originating
summons issued by the first plaintiff and the second plaintiff, Alan Stephen McLaren,
against the Law Society seeking (1) a declaration that on the true construction of s 37 of
the Solicitors Act 1974 and the Solicitors' Indemnity Rules 1975, the Solicitors' Indemnity
Rules 1978 and the Solicitors' Indemnity Rules 1979 the Council of the Law Society had
no power to make all or any such rules, which were accordingly null and void, and (2) the   *e*
determination of the question whether, on the true construction of the 1974 Act and the
indemnity rules and in the events which had happened, the Law Society was entitled to
retain for its own purposes the commission received by it from London Assurance
Brokers Ltd in respect of premiums paid by individual solicitors pursuant to the society's
Solicitors' Indemnity Insurance Scheme, or whether it was accountable for such
commission to individual solicitors or otherwise. The second plaintiff did not appeal.   *f*
The facts are set out in the judgment of Oliver LJ.

John Bowyer for the plaintiff.
Robert Alexander QC, Patrick Phillips QC and *Clifford Smith* for the Law Society.

Cur adv vult   *g*

31st July. The following judgments were read.

STEPHENSON LJ. In this appeal two practising solicitors of the Supreme Court
challenge two things done by the Law Society: first, the validity of the Solicitors'
Indemnity Rules which regulate a solicitor's professional indemnity insurance scheme of   *h*
the Law Society; second, the Law Society's right to retain for its own purposes
commission received under the scheme. On 17th March 1980 Slade J in a reserved
judgment of nearly 30 pages, reported in [1980] 3 All ER 615, [1980] 1 WLR 1355,
answered both challenges in favour of the Law Society. Counsel for the first plaintiff
(whom I will refer to hereafter simply as 'the plaintiff') has renewed the plaintiffs'
challenges and attacked the judge's decision on both questions.   *j*
    If the importance of the case to the whole solicitors' profession and the pains taken by
the plaintiff's counsel to present his case to this court in 26 grounds of appeal supported
by the fullest argument were my only guide, I should find it necessary to give a
judgment at least as long as that of the judge and probably a great deal longer and less
lucid. But we have the advantage of his full, clear and correct statement of all the
relevant matters, facts and issues, and it would be idle to repeat, and impossible to

improve, what he has done so well. I can therefore confine my opinion to stating where

a I am in agreement with his judgment and where and why I have the misfortune to differ from it, even though I may thereby fail to discuss every point taken in argument before us.

The first of the two questions raised by the plaintiffs' originating summons was whether 'upon the true construction of Section 37 of the above-mentioned Act [that is, the Solicitors Act 1974] and of the Rules hereinafter mentioned the Council of the Law

b Society had no power to make all or any of The Solicitors' Indemnity Rules 1975, the Solicitors' Indemnity Rules 1978 and the Solicitors' Indemnity Rules 1979 and the said Rules are accordingly null and void'. I agree with the judge's general approach to this question, with the answer he gave and with his reasons for refusing the first declaration requested by the plaintiffs.

The recommendations of a special committee of the Law Society made in 1972 were

c finally implemented in the Solicitors Act 1974. That Act provided for, inter alia, the maintenance and administration of a compensation fund (by s 36 and Sch 2) and for professional indemnity (by s 37). It is in the latter section, if anywhere, that must be found the Law Society's authority for the single compulsory professional indemnity insurance scheme, including the Solicitors' Indemnity Rules, which is the subject of this appeal. I therefore set out s 37, which provides:

d
'(1) The Council, with the concurrence of the Master of the Rolls, may make rules (in this Act referred to as "indemnity rules") concerning indemnity against loss arising from claims in respect of any description of civil liability incurred—(a) by a solicitor or former solicitor in connection with his practice or with any trust of which he is or formerly was a trustee; (b) by an employee or former employee of a

e solicitor or former solicitor in connection with that solicitor's practice or with any trust of which that solicitor or the employee is or formerly was a trustee.

'(2) For the purpose of providing such indemnity, indemnity rules—(a) may authorise or require the Society to establish and maintain a fund or funds; (b) may authorise or require the Society to take out and maintain insurance with authorised insurers; (c) may require solicitors or any specified class of solicitors to take out and

f maintain insurance with authorised insurers.

'(3) Without prejudice to the generality of subsections (1) and (2), indemnity rules—(a) may specify the terms and conditions on which indemnity is to be available, and any circumstances in which the right to it is to be excluded or modified; (b) may provide for the management, administration and protection of any fund maintained by virtue of subsection (2)(a) and require solicitors or any class

g of solicitors to make payments to any such fund; (c) may require solicitors or any class of solicitors to make payments by way of premium on any insurance policy maintained by the Society by virtue of subsection (2)(b); (d) may prescribe the conditions which an insurance policy must satisfy for the purposes of subsection (2)(c); (e) may authorise the Society to determine the amount of any payments required by the rules, subject to such limits, or in accordance with such provisions, as may be prescribed by the rules; (f) may specify circumstances in which, where

h a solicitor for whom indemnity is provided has failed to comply with the rules, the Society or insurers may take proceedings against him in respect of sums paid by way of indemnity in connection with a matter in relation to which he has failed to comply; (g) may specify circumstances in which solicitors are exempt from the rules; (h) may empower the Council to take such steps as they consider necessary or

j expedient to ascertain whether or not the rules are being complied with; and (i) may contain incidental, procedural or supplementary provisions.

'(4) If any solicitor fails to comply with indemnity rules, any person may make a complaint in respect of that failure to the Tribunal.

'(5) The Society shall have power, without prejudice to any of its other powers, to carry into effect any arrangement which it considers necessary or expedient for the purpose of indemnity under this section.'

A heavier sanction for complying with indemnity rules is introduced by s 10 of the Act, which provides:

a

'(1) Subject to sections 11 and 12, the Society shall issue a practising certificate to a person who applies for one, if it is satisfied, within 21 days of receipt of his application . . . (*e*) that he is complying with any indemnity rules or is exempt from them.'

Read with s 1(*e*) of the Act, this provision debars a solicitor (unless exempted) from practising if he does not comply with these rules. Their validity is thus of the greatest importance.

b

It is common ground that the rule-making powers of the Council of the Law Society are to be found in sub-ss (1), (2) and (3) of s 37 and that the only provisions which can authorise the Law Society's scheme and rules are sub-ss (2)(*b*) and (3)(*c*). So, as the judge said ([1980] 3 All ER 615 at 621, [1980] 1 WLR 1335 at 1341), the present dispute as to the construction of the Act substantially concerns the meaning and effect of those two subsections. The judge thought ([1980] 3 All ER 615 at 619, 621, [1980] 1 WLR 1335 at 1338, 1340) that this rule-making power should be construed narrowly and restrictively in the light of the severity of the sanction against non-compliance. Counsel for the Law Society has submitted that on the contrary a practising certificate is a privilege qualifying its holder to serve the public, and the protection of the public calls for a more generous interpretation of the power. I do not think it matters; on any reasonable construction of the relevant provisions of s 37 the scheme and rules are, in my judgment, well within them, as the judge held.

c

d

More important is the judge's construction of sub-s (2) as exhaustive of the power conferred by sub-s (1). I reject the submission of counsel for the Law Society that this was an error and agree with the judge for the reasons that he gave ([1980] 3 All ER 615 at 621, [1980] 1 WLR 1335 at 1340) that it is improbable that the legislature should have intended to give the council a free hand to select whatever method of providing indemnity the council liked, subject only to the concurrence of the Master of the Rolls, and that if the legislature had intended that sub-s (2) should operate 'without prejudice to the generality of subsection (1)' it would have said so. That it expressly made the provisions of sub-s (3) operate 'without prejudice to the generality of subsections (1) and (2)' tells in favour of the judge's view, not, as counsel for the Law Society subtly argued, against it.

e

f

I agree also with the judge ([1980] 3 All ER 615 at 629, [1980] 1 WLR 1335 at 1350) that commonsense suggests that the legislature had in mind three obvious possible alternative routes for providing a compulsory insurance scheme for solicitors: (1) the establishment and maintenance by the Law Society of its own fund; (2) a direction to solicitors to take out and maintain insurance policies with authorised insurers; and (3) group arrangements with insurers under which insurers bound themselves to grant insurance to individual solicitors, who paid a specified premium, and individual solicitors were required to pay the premiums and take up the insurance rights which had been arranged for them. I agree also that it would have been a strange omission if the section had provided for route number (1) in sub-ss (2)(*a*) and (3)(*b*) and route number (2) in sub-ss (2)(*c*) and (3)(*d*), but failed to provide for route number (3), and I agree that sub-ss (2)(*b*) and (3)(*c*) did provide for this third route.

g

h

Counsel for the plaintiff has asked us to read s 37(2) not only as exhausting the methods of implementing the purpose of sub-s (1) (with which I agree) but as omitting the third route and providing for the first and second routes only. Subsection (2)(*b*) is to be read (he submits) with sub-s (2)(*a*) as authorising or requiring the Law Society to take out and maintain insurance for itself against loss which it incurs itself; either loss if its fund were inadequate to meet claims on it, or loss on an undertaking to pay claims against solicitors, the first being the sort of insurance contemplated by para 5 of Sch 2 in relation to the compensation fund. Subsection (2)(*b*) cannot be read as authorising or requiring the Law Society to take out and maintain insurance for individual solicitors

j

because the same words in sub-s (2)(c) refer to the insured persons taking out and maintaining insurance for themselves and must in sub-s (2)(b) refer to the Law Society insuring itself, not somebody else. Subsection (3)(c) reinforces this construction, for 'payments by way of premium' are not payments of premium by a solicitor insured under the master policy, but payments to the Law Society of premiums payable by the Law Society on its own policy.

I cannot accept these arguments or their result. I do not see why a person cannot make payments by way of premiums under a policy taken out on his behalf or why one person cannot take out and maintain insurance for others. The first is what solicitors like the plaintiffs are now doing. The second is what in the ordinary meaning of its language sub-s (2)(b) allows the Council of the Law Society to do by indemnity rules; and that is what it has in fact done in taking the third route. The argument of counsel for the plaintiff ignores the purpose of the section and the loss against which professional indemnity is required. That loss is clearly defined in sub-s (1) as loss arising from claims in respect of civil liability incurred by solicitors or their employees, past and present, and the rules are to be directed to 'such indemnity', as you would expect and the judge twice pointed out ([1980] 3 All ER 615 at 619–620, [1980] 1 WLR 1335 at 1338–1349): sub-s (1) refers to loss suffered by solicitors, not loss suffered by the Law Society.

If the judge's construction of s 37(2)(b) and (3)(c) is right, as I think it is, I would have thought the question whether the Solicitors' Indemnity Rules 1975–79 are ultra vires the section was unarguable had I not heard the arguments of counsel for the plaintiff. He has not, I am afraid, persuaded me that any construction of those rules takes them outside the section as I would construe it. They authorise the Law Society to take out and maintain with authorised insurers a master policy in the form set out in the schedule thereto and to arrange for the issue to solicitors of certificates of insurance in the form set out in the schedule (r 2). They require every solicitor to whom they apply to pay the premiums payable under the master policy and certificate of insurance (r 3).

By cl 1 of the scheduled master policy—

'The Insurers agree with The Law Society on behalf of all solicitors from time to time required to be insured by Indemnity Rules made under s. 37 of the Solicitors Act 1974, and on behalf of former solicitors, to provide such insurance in accordance with the terms of the Certificate attached hereto. Subject as hereinafter appears in respect of former solicitors, such Certificate will be issued annually on request on receipt of the premium payable in accordance with Clauses 2 and 3 hereof.'

Clause 2 provides for annual extensions of the master policy with annual increases of the rates of premium. Clause 3 defines the premium payable. Clause 4 requires all claims and notices to be given by the assured (not, of course, to the assured as printed in [1980] 3 All ER 615 at 623, [1980] 1 WLR 1335 at 1343) under the terms of the certificate of insurance to the brokers, London Insurance Brokers Ltd ('LIB').

By cl 6 the insurers give authority to the brokers to issue on behalf of the insurers to solicitors certificates of insurance in the scheduled form. The scheduled certificate certifies the grant by the insurers subscribing the master policy to the individual solicitors of insurance in consideration of the premium stated in the schedule to the certificate.

I shall have to return to cl 1 of the master policy when I consider the second question raised by the plaintiffs' summons and this appeal. But I can find nothing in the rules and scheduled master policy and certificate which is not authorised by s 37, and I agree with the judge ([1980] 3 All ER 615 at 631, [1980] 1 WLR 1335 at 1352) that the plaintiffs' first claim to a declaration fails accordingly.

The judge did, however, answer the question of commission in the Law Society's favour by declaring:

'Upon the true construction of the above-mentioned Solicitors Act 1974 and the above mentioned Solicitors' Indemnity rules 1975 to 1979 and in the events which have happened that the Defendants are not bound to account to either of the Plaintiffs for any part of any commission received by the Defendants or by Law

Society Services Limited from London Insurance Brokers Limited in respect of
premiums paid by individual Solicitors pursuant to the Solicitors Indemnity *a*
Insurance Scheme.'

I have found this second question more difficult than the first and counsel for the
plaintiffs' attack on the judge's answer to it more formidable. In so far as his attack was
mounted on the invalidity of the Solicitors' Indemnity Rules or the judge's construction
of them, or on the failure of the Law Society to implement the rules if valid, it was in my
opinion unsuccessful. I agree with the judge's conclusions and his reasoning on both *b*
these points. There is nothing in s 37 which makes the payment of premiums by
individual solicitors under their contracts with insurers, or the retention of commission
received by the Law Society from LIB in respect of those premiums, unlawful as outside
the power conferred on the Law Society by the section, or assumed by the Law Society
under the rules. The payment of premiums and commission would be an arrangement
which the Law Society considers necessary or expedient for the purpose of indemnity *c*
under the section and is therefore within the power conferred by s 37(5). I do not agree
with the submission of counsel for the plaintiff that it would not come within the wide
concluding words of the subsection, or that it did not carry out the scheme propounded
in the rules incorporating the provisions of the scheduled master policy and certificate of
insurance, because no master policy as such was ever issued.

But is the retention of this commission unlawful because it offends against the *d*
inflexible rule of equity that a person who owes a fiduciary duty to others is accountable
to them for any profit or other advantage he may obtain from his fiduciary position?

What is said on behalf of the plaintiff is that the Law Society took out this indemnity
insurance as agent and/or in a fiduciary capacity by taking out the master policy on
behalf of individual solicitors, including the plaintiffs, and maintained such insurance as
agent and/or in a fiduciary capacity by negotiating the master policy and by requiring *e*
them to pay premiums on their individual policies in accordance with the master policy,
and the Law Society was accordingly bound to account to the plaintiffs and other
solicitors who have paid such premiums for the commission received by Law Society
Services Ltd ('LSS') in respect of those premiums. In support of this contention the
plaintiff relied on certain parts of the judge's judgment.

The judge rejected the contention put forward at one time by both sides that the Law *f*
Society acted as agent for the plaintiffs and other individual solicitors in favour of the
alternative that it acted as trustee for them. According to him ([1980] 3 All ER 615 at
625, [1980] 1 WLR 1335 at 1345–1346):

'. . . the pattern of the form of master policy and certificate of insurance scheduled
to the 1975 rules was, in my judgment, this. The Law Society was to enter into a *g*
contract with the insurers on the terms of the master policy, on the footing that it
would hold the benefit of the contract as trustee for the persons referred to in cl 1
of the master policy, and that the contract would entitle such persons, as beneficiaries
under the trust, on paying the designated premium, to require the insurers to issue
them a policy on the terms specified in the certificate of insurance. By virtue of cl
6 of the master policy, LIB would possess authority from the insurers to issue, on *h*
their behalf, such a certificate to any solicitor seeking insurance in accordance with
cl 1 of the master policy. Whenever an individual solicitor should pay to the
insurers through LIB the appropriate premium and receive his certificate of
insurance, a further contract would come into being between him and the insurers,
quite separate from that between them and the Law Society.'

j

He founded his opinion that the Law Society would hold the benefit of the contract
with the insurers on the terms of the master policy as trustee for all solicitors required to
be insured by the indemnity rules primarily on the opening words of cl 1 of the master
policy which he regarded as of crucial importance ([1980] 3 All ER 615 at 624, [1980] 1
WLR 1335 at 1343). In its respondent's notice the Law Society reaffirmed its contention

that it entered into the master policy as agent for such solicitors; but counsel for the Law Society abandoned that contention in the course of argument before us and deleted it from his amended notice. The words of cl 1 suggest agency, as does their compressed version in a circular of 15th October 1975, by which the President of the Law Society commended to the profession the method of implementing the indemnity insurance scheme by 'A master policy taken out by the Society on behalf of all practising solicitors'. But in my judgment the Law Society was acting as a principal, not an agent, in contracting with insurers, as was each practising solicitor in contracting with the insurers. The practising solicitors could not sue the insurers on the Law Society's contract with them, but only on their own contracts with them.

I am accordingly in agreement with the judge that the Law Society was acting not as agent but as a trustee for the solicitors described in cl 1 of the master policy to hold the benefit of its contract on the terms of the master policy, and that a fiduciary relationship was thereby established between the Law Society and them, which entitled them to call for the Law Society's co-operation in enforcing their rights (as beneficiaries under the trust created by the contract) to obtain insurance cover from the insurers: see [1980] 3 All ER 615 at 637, [1980] 1 WLR 1335 at 1360. It is the next two pages of the judgment which lead to the judge's conclusion that the Law Society is not accountable for commission, and which I have found more difficult and less convincing than the rest of his judgment.

The judge held that as soon as the contract between the Law Society and the insurers had been concluded, there existed a fiduciary relationship between the Law Society and the solicitors concerned, but that the Law Society had not acted in a fiduciary relationship to such solicitors in negotiating the contract. True, the Law Society showed in cl 1 of the master policy that it made that contract 'on behalf of all' such solicitors, but that phrase, the judge held, 'by itself by no means necessarily imports that the Law Society was acting in a fiduciary capacity vis-à-vis the individual solicitors concerned in negotiating contracts': see [1980] 3 All ER 615 at 639, [1980] 1 WLR 1335 at 1362. It merely imports that the Law Society was to hold the benefit of those contracts when concluded as trustee for the individual solicitors concerned. To hold otherwise would be to hold that it acts in such a fiduciary capacity whenever it exercises its general powers for the good of the profession which it exists to serve.

I regret that I cannot dispose of the words of cl 1 so easily, or limit the consequences of the Law Society's holding the benefit of the contract as trustee so narrowly. The benefit of the contract is the contractual rights of indemnity which individual solicitors are to have. They are to have those rights in return for paying premiums. LIB's commission comes out of those premiums. The Law Society's commission comes out of that commission. It is agreed that its receipt by LSS is to be treated as receipt by the Law Society. It is not trust money or property, but it is money or property acquired by the Law Society by using its fiduciary position as trustee. The Law Society obtains the commission under its agreement of 11th May 1976 with LIB, but it obtained both agreement and commission by reason of its fiduciary position. If the Law Society had agreed to take commission out of premiums without the intervention of LIB, secretly or openly, it would surely be accountable for it to the solicitors as beneficiaries. You can have a contract which creates rights before a fiduciary relationship arises and which a trustee is not precluded from subsequently asserting against beneficiaries: *Re Mulholland's Will Trusts* [1949] 1 All ER 460. But there the pre-existing contract was not entered into on behalf of any beneficiaries. You can have a person in a fiduciary position quoad part of his activities, but not quoad other parts: *New Zealand Netherlands Society v Kuys* [1973] 2 All ER 1222 at 1225–1226, [1973] 1 WLR 1126 at 1130 per Lord Wilberforce. But here the retention of commission received through LIB from solicitors' premiums is, in my judgment, an integral part of the Law Society's activity in providing compulsory indemnity insurance. It need not have been, nor need the Law Society have appointed itself trustee for the benefit of its contract with insurers and the solicitor beneficiaries. But it chose to make the contract on their behalf and to contract with LIB for a share of the commission which came from the premiums paid by the solicitors. Once the original contract establishes a fiduciary relationship, whether of agency (which the judge rightly rejected) or of trusteeship (which the judge rightly accepted) or of some other legal species (as counsel for the Law Society submitted in part of his argument), it seems to me to cover the retention of commission and I cannot agree that the relationship arose so late after the contract as not to cover it.

Counsel for the Law Society has sought support for the judge's decision and the Law Society's right to retain commission on additional grounds, formulated in a respondent's notice, the first of which is that there was no fiduciary relationship established between the Law Society and any solicitor, including the plaintiffs. This submission came in as part of an amendment allowed in the course of argument and taking this form:

> 'The learned judge ought not to have held that there was any fiduciary relationship established between the Law Society and any solicitor, including the plaintiffs and each of them, *sufficient to sustain the application of the rule of equity next mentioned to the receipt by the Law Society of a share of commission earned by the brokers to the insurers under the Master Policy,* alternatively if there was any such fiduciary relationship it existed not between the Law Society and any individual solicitor but between the Law Society and the body of solicitors as a profession as a whole',

to which was added in manuscript: 'or alternatively that the commission was not received by the Law Society in the fulfilment of any fiduciary duty or in its capacity as a fiduciary'.

Counsel for the Law Society agreed that the words I have emphasised introduced what was really a further alternative better stated in the manuscript addition, and his first submission was an unqualified submission of no fiduciary relationship.

There is, he contended, no fiduciary relationship because the Law Society negotiated the master policy arrangement for and in the interests, not of the solicitors referred to in and identified by cl 1, but of the public and the profession as a whole in discharge of its general duty to them. This submission accords with the judge's view, which I have rejected, of what the Law Society was doing in negotiating the contract and leads easily into the first alternative argument of counsel for the Law Society that any fiduciary relationship which was created was between the Law Society and the whole body of solicitors as a profession. I do not deny the duty owed to the whole body, but if the whole body is owed a fiduciary duty in respect of the master policy arrangement and the rule of equity applies to the commission, the Law Society would be accountable to every member of that body and its last state would be worse than its first. But does the rule apply? Is counsel's third 'alternative' right that the commission was not received by the Law Society in fulfilment of any fiduciary duty or in its capacity as a fiduciary?

It is, he submits, not easy to fit this tripartite arrangement into the rule or the cases where it has been laid down and applied. The premiums from which the commission is derived by LIB are not paid under the master policy. The Law Society's opportunity to obtain commission arises from its ability to persuade LIB to give up part of what would otherwise go to them, but the Law Society obtains commission, not under the master policy but by virtue of its agreement with LIB in 1976, and it is not a trustee for the benefit of that agreement. It derived its opportunity to enter into that agreement not from its fiduciary position as trustee for the benefit of contracts under the master policy but from negotiating the master policy and making rules which required solicitors to pay premiums. But this conclusion rests on the two premises which I have rejected: (1) that the Law Society did not negotiate the required contract in a fiduciary capacity, and (2) that the 1976 agreement was not made an integral part of the indemnity insurance scheme.

I find some support for my opinion that a fiduciary relationship was established between the Law Society and the solicitors when it negotiated the original contract in the judgment of the Court of Appeal in *Re Reading's Petition of Right* [1949] 2 All ER 68, [1949] 2 KB 232 which was approved on appeal by every member of the House of Lords:

Reading v Attorney General [1951] 1 All ER 617, [1951] AC 507. In giving the judgment
of the Court of Appeal, Asquith LJ ([1949] 2 All ER 68 at 70, [1949] 2 KB 232 at 236)
concluded from a consideration of the authorities that—

> 'for the present purpose a "fiduciary relation" exists . . . (*b*) whenever the plaintiff
> entrusts to the defendant a job to be performed, for instance, the negotiation of a
> contract on his behalf or for his benefit, and relies on the defendant to procure the
> best terms available.'

The present purpose was to see whether a secret profit received by a servant or agent in
the course of his employment was recoverable by his master or principal; but the
judgment stresses the comprehensive sense in which the term 'fiduciary relation' is used
in such a context and does, I think, increase the difficulty of accepting either the judge's
conclusion or the first submission of counsel for the Law Society on this part of the
case. The Law Society was not entrusted by the plaintiffs with the negotiation of its
contract with insurers nor was the Law Society's commission secretly received; but it is
nevertheless held on trust for the plaintiffs and its retention cannot, in my opinion, be
supported on the new grounds introduced into the respondent's notice.

There remains to be considered one more answer to this part of the plaintiffs' claim
before the Law Society is driven back to rely on acquiescence; that is the fourth ground
in the original notice:

> 'The learned judge ought to have held that the rule of equity whereby one who
> by use of a fiduciary position, derives a profit from a third party, must account to his
> principal or beneficiary for the profit so obtained had no application to the
> relationship between the Law Society and solicitors as such rule is based upon the
> consideration of potential conflict and no such potential conflict existed between the
> Law Society and solicitors.'

This requires a short re-examination of the rule.

With certain exceptions, neither directly nor indirectly may a trustee make a profit
from his trust. This rule is part of the wider principle that in order to protect a trustee
against the fallibility of human nature he may not put himself in a position where his
duty and his interest may conflict. This has been a rule of equity at least since the leading
case of *Keech v Sandford* (1726) Sel Cas Ch 61: see Snell's Principles of Equity (27th Edn,
1973, pp 235–236). It is not only trustees who need this protection against fallibility.
Similar principles apply to all other persons who occupy a fiduciary position. They must
refund with interest all profits which they have made by means of their position unless
they made them with the full knowledge and approval of the persons to whom they owe
a fiduciary duty: see Snell, p 241.

The highest authorities have made it plain that the application of the rule imputes no
dishonesty to the person who has made the profit but that it is no answer to its
application to establish that the person to whom the duty is owed has benefited from the
transaction which made the profit. In applying the rule to an agent's discharge of his
fiduciary duty to his principal, Lord Cranworth LC in *Aberdeen Railway Co v Blaikie
Brothers* (1854) 1 Macq 461 at 471 said:

> '. . . it is a rule of universal application, that no one, having such duties to
> discharge shall be allowed to enter into engagements in which he has, or can have,
> a personal interest conflicting, or which possibly may conflict, with the interests of
> those whom he is bound to protect. So strictly is this principle adhered to, that no
> question is allowed to be raised as to the fairness or unfairness of a contract so
> entered into. It obviously is, or may be, impossible to demonstrate how far in any
> particular case the terms of such a contract have been the best for the interest of the
> cestui que trust, which it was possible to obtain. It may sometimes happen that the
> terms on which a trustee has dealt or attempted to deal with the estate or interests
> of those for whom he is a trustee, have been as good as could have been obtained
> from any other person—they may even at the time have been better. But still so

inflexible is the rule that no inquiry on that subject is permitted. The English authorities on this head are numerous and uniform . . .'

In considering the fiduciary position of the vice-chairman of a college who had charged the college with remuneration for his services as its solicitor, Lord Herschell said in *Bray v Ford* [1896] AC 44 at 51, [1895–9] All ER Rep 1009 at 1011:

'It is an inflexible rule of a Court of Equity that a person in a fiduciary position, such as the respondent's, is not, unless otherwise expressly provided, entitled to make a profit; he is not allowed to put himself in a position where his interest and duty conflict. It does not appear to me that this rule is, as has been said, founded upon principles of morality. I regard it rather as based on the consideration that, human nature being what it is, there is danger, in such circumstances, of the person holding a fiduciary position being swayed by interest rather than by duty, and thus prejudicing those whom he was bound to protect. It has, therefore, been deemed expedient to lay down this positive rule. But I am satisfied that it might be departed from in many cases, without any breach of morality, without any wrong being inflicted, and without any consciousness of wrong-doing. Indeed, it is obvious that it might sometimes be to the advantage of the beneficiaries that their trustee should act for them professionally rather than a stranger, even though the trustee were paid for his services.'

In *Regal (Hastings) Ltd v Gulliver* [1942] 1 All ER 378 at 386, [1967] 2 AC 134 at 144 Lord Russell said:

'The rule of equity which insists on those, who by use of a fiduciary position make a profit, being liable to account for that profit, in no way depends on fraud, or absence of *bona fides*; or upon such questions or considerations as whether the profit would or should otherwise have gone to the plaintiff, or whether the profiteer was under a duty to obtain the source of the profit for the plaintiff, or whether he took a risk or acted as he did for the benefit of the plaintiff, or whether the plaintiff has in fact been damaged or benefited by his action. The liability arises from the mere fact of a profit having, in the stated circumstances, been made. The profiteer, however honest and well-intentioned, cannot escape the risk of being called upon to account.'

In that case directors of a company were held accountable to the company for the profit made on the sale of shares which should have been the property of the company and preserved for it. In *Boardman v Phipps* [1966] 3 All ER 721, [1967] 2 AC 46 the facts were even further from the instant case: a solicitor to the trustees of a will and one beneficiary under the will were held accountable to another beneficiary for the profit made on shares which they purchased for themselves in a company in which the trustees owned some shares. The majority applied the rule with citations such as those I have quoted. Lord Upjohn ([1966] 3 All ER 721 at 757, [1967] 2 AC 46 at 123), who disagreed with its application to the facts of the case, described it as—

'the fundamental rule of equity that a person in a fiduciary capacity must not make a profit out of his trust, which is part of the wider rule that a trustee must not place himself in a position where his duty and his interest may conflict.'

and believed the rule to be best stated in the speech of Lord Herschell which I have quoted from *Bray v Ford*. Lord Guest ([1966] 3 All ER 721 at 753, [1967] 2 AC 46 at 118), in applying the rule, based his opinion on the fact that the two persons held accountable placed themselves in a special position which was of a fiduciary character in relation to negotiations relating to the trust shares and—

'Out of such special position and in the course of such negotiations they obtained the opportunity to make a profit out of the shares and knowledge that the profit was there to be made.'

Two questions have to be answered: (1) Did the Law Society place itself in a position

a where its duty and its interest might conflict in agreeing to receive the commission? (2) Did the commission and its receipt arise out of the fiduciary position in which the Law Society had placed itself by negotiating the contract with the insurers and arranging for the insurers' contracts with individual solicitors? The Law Society's answers are in the negative: (1) There was no potential conflict of interest. (2) The commission and its receipt arose out of the Law Society's agreement with LIB.

b   I regret that I cannot accept those answers.

(1) There must, of course, be 'a real sensible possibility of a conflict': see, for example, *Boardman v Phipps* [1966] 3 All ER 721 at 756, [1967] 2 AC 46 at 124 per Lord Upjohn. It is forcibly contended that any conflict is inconceivable between this responsible society's duty to the solicitors concerned with the scheme and any private interest of its own. But its interest is the interest of all members of the Law Society or of the whole

c solicitors' profession, and it is to the interest of the Law Society acting on behalf of them to get as much commission as it can, not from any selfish motive to benefit particular individuals, but from its desire to do its duty of advancing the interests of its members or the whole profession, including the solicitors insured under the scheme but also at their expense. For the more commission the Law Society is paid the higher the premiums the solicitors pay. It is no answer to accountability that the commission is

d taken and used for those solicitors' benefit, or (as counsel for the Law Society at one time suggested) that it would not be inequitable for the Law Society to retain the commission. The contention ignores the possibility of a conflict between the interests of those solicitors who are concerned with the scheme and those who are not, to say nothing of the admittedly remote possibility that the Law Society or its council or some member of it might fall short of the high standard of responsibility which they are known to maintain. To ignore these possibilities is to forget that it is temptation to misuse a

e fiduciary position against which the rule has been established.

(2) There must be a nexus between the fiduciary position and the money made 'out of' it: see per Lord Guest in *Boardman v Phipps* ([1966] 3 All ER 721 at 753, [1967] 2 AC 46 at 118, quoting passages from the Lord Ordinary's judgment in *Huntington Copper Co v Henderson* (1877) 4 R 294 at 308 and from Lord Wright's speech in *Regal (Hastings) Ltd*

f *v Gulliver* [1942] 1 All ER 378 at 392, [1967] 2 AC 134 at 154, respectively referring to the trustee obtaining an advantage 'through the execution of the trust' and a trustee or person in an analogous fiduciary position acquiring profits 'by reason of his fiduciary position and by reason of the opportunity and the knowledge, or either, resulting from it'.

In *Reading v R* [1948] 2 All ER 27 at 28, [1948] 2 KB 268 at 275 Denning J, in a part

g of his judgment cited with apparent approval in the judgment of the Court of Appeal ([1949] 2 All ER 68 at 70, [1949] 2 KB 232 at 235), said:

'In my judgment, it is a principle of law that, if a servant takes advantage of his service by violating his duty of honesty and good faith, to make a profit for himself, in the sense that the assets of which he has control, the facilities which he enjoys, or the position which he occupies, are the real cause of his obtaining the money as

h distinct from merely affording the opportunity for getting it, that is to say, if they play the predominant part in his obtaining the money, then he is accountable for it to his master.'

Later in his judgment ([1948] 2 All ER 27 at 29, [1948] 2 KB 268 at 276–277) Denning J distinguished 'the mere fact that his [Reading's] service gave the opportunity for getting the money' from 'the wearing of the King's uniform and his position as a soldier' which

j was 'the sole cause of his getting the money', and stated that the first fact would not entitle the master to the money, whereas the other two matters would. I do not think that the opportunities of gain provided by a fiduciary position can *never* of themselves render the person who has them accountable for the gain, or that Denning J intended so to hold. All the facts and circumstances of the particular case must be taken into account before accountability for the particular pecuniary advantage is established.

When the facts and circumstances of this case are considered the commission is seen plainly to come to the Law Society from, or by virtue, or by reason, or by means of, its *a* fiduciary position. It is because the Law Society, empowered by Parliament to arrange for indemnity insurance, has appointed itself a trustee for the benefit conferred on solicitors by their contracts under the terms of the master policy that it has put itself in a position, or acquired the opportunity, to arrange with LIB to be paid commission. The Law Society's own use of its fiduciary position to make the bargain of 11th May 1976 with LIB cannot prevent the fruits of that bargain from being derived in reality from the *b* use of that position.

I cannot break up the Law Society's arrangement or scheme in the way found possible by the judge or in the manner advocated by counsel for the Law Society. I accordingly conclude that whatever the merits of the commission agreement and whatever the practical problems which may ensue, the Law Society is not entitled to retain for its own purposes the commission received by it from LIB and is accountable for it to the *c* individual solicitors who pay premiums pursuant to the solicitors' indemnity insurance scheme, except in so far as the plaintiffs may have acquiesced in the Law Society's retention of the commission.

Upholding as he did the Law Society's right to the commission, the judge did not have to decide, and did not decide, whether these two plaintiffs were debarred by acquiescence from enforcing an equitable right to a share of the commission. But he pointed out that *d* it was common ground that such a right might be lost if 'it would be dishonest, or unconscionable, for the plaintiff, or for the person having the right sought to be enforced, to continue to seek to enforce it', as stated by Buckley LJ in *Shaw v Applegate* [1978] 1 All ER 123 at 131, [1977] 1 WLR 970 at 978; and he gave compelling reasons for attributing 'considerable force' to the defence of acquiescence (see [1980] 3 All ER 615 at 639, [1980] 1 WLR 1335 at 1363). They compel me to go as far as to hold that the defence succeeds *e* to some extent.

I do no more than repeat as briefly as I can the facts which, in my judgment, make it unconscionable for the plaintiffs to participate in the commission received by the Law Society in the first years of the master policy scheme.

1. A circular issued by the Council of the Law Society in May 1975 made full disclosure in the following manner to solicitors, including the plaintiffs, that if and when *f* the scheme was introduced the Law Society would be receiving a share of the brokers' commission on the relevant policies. The circular included the question: 'What arrangements are proposed under the Scheme for commission on premiums?' The answer given was as follows:

> 'The brokers to the Scheme (L.I.B.) will be remunerated on the usual commission basis from which they will meet the major cost of operating the Scheme and *g* handling claims. Hitherto the Society, through the Insurance Advisory Service, has received a share of the brokers' commission and as regards solicitors' professional indemnity business this amounted to approximately £46,000 gross in 1974 (the equivalent of nearly £2 on a practising certificate fee). The existing arrangements with L.I.B. require the Society to provide premises and defray certain quite substantial costs in relation to staff. Under the Scheme it is likely that if the existing *h* arrangements are continued the commission income to the Society will be of the order of £250,000 per annum gross. The benefit of the net excess receipts will inure for the profession as a whole, but, subject to taxation and other important considerations, the Council will consider whether the surplus can be appropriately earmarked for possible future improvements in the Scheme. The surplus, however, it is generally applied, will correspondingly reduce future calls upon the practising *j* members of the profession.'

2. In October 1975, the President of the Law Society sent to all solicitors with practising certificates a letter setting out the council's arguments in favour of the master policy scheme as recommended by it and enclosing a voting card asking for a 'Yes' or 'No'

answer to the question whether the recipient was in favour of the scheme. This letter
a contained the following paragraph:

> 'Although individual solicitors will no longer receive the benefit of commission,
> it will be payable by the Insurers, and The Law Society will receive a share after
> operating expenses have been deducted. This will enure for the benefit of the
> profession, thus mitigating future increases in the Practising Certificate Fee.'

b 3. Every set of the consolidated annual accounts of the Law Society and LSS has
disclosed the existence of the commission and its receipt by LSS.

4. Implicit in the statement in the circular that the benefit of the net excess receipts
would inure for the profession as a whole was the information that the Law Society did
not intend to account for the commission to the solicitors concerned individually, as the
judge pointed out ([1980] 3 All ER 615 at 639, [1980] 1 WLR 1335 at 1363). And the
c evidence shows that the net excess receipts have in fact been applied or allocated for the
benefit of the whole profession.

5. The plaintiffs have never suggested that they were not aware of the contents of the
council's circular, the president's letter and the Law Society's successive accounts and of
the manner in which the receipts were dealt with by the Law Society. The correspondence
in evidence shows that they complained about the existence of a compulsory insurance
d scheme and having to pay premiums to insurers selected for them by the Law Society;
but there is no evidence that they ever questioned the Law Society's right to participate
in the commission and to apply it for the benefit of the whole profession until 2nd
January 1979 when they gave notice by letter that they might claim repayment of
premiums. They did not know of the percentage agreed with LIB, but as they were not
interested enough to inquire, that ignorance does not assist them.

e It was suggested by counsel for the plaintiff that by not challenging the annual
commission retained when it approximated to the estimated £250,000, the plaintiffs had
not lost their right to call the Law Society to account when the annual receipt soared
above that figure: acquiescence in a minor invasion of a right did not debar enforcement
of the right after a major invasion. The accounts show the commission receivable as
amounting to £412,864 for the year ended 31st December 1976, £365,000 for the year
f ended 31st December 1977, and £670,185 for the year ended 31st December 1978, of
which, according to the evidence, £648,000 was received in respect of the master policy
scheme and used for the benefit of the profession. The size of the last figure may have
led the plaintiffs to issue their summons, but it does not relieve them of the consequences
of their having accepted the retention of the earlier sums without question. The
acceptance of the practice in the years 1976 to 1978 would not, however, prevent the
g plaintiffs from questioning the practice and asserting their right to call the Law Society
to account for the commission in 1979 and future years. The summons of October 1979
put an end to their acquiescence and I did not understand the contrary to be argued.

Indeed, counsel for the Law Society wanted a decision which would answer all
solicitors' claims in favour of the Law Society, not one which would defeat these plaintiffs
only and for a short time only. I would therefore, subject to any submissions by counsel,
h substitute for the second declaration made by the judge a declaration that on the true
construction of the Solicitors Act 1974 and the Solicitors' Indemnity Rules 1975 to 1979
and in the events which have happened, the Law Society *is* bound to account to the
plaintiffs and each of them for any commission received after 1978 by the Law Society
or by Law Society Services Ltd from London Insurance Brokers Ltd in respect of
premiums paid by the plaintiffs and each of them pursuant to the Solicitors' Indemnity
j Insurance Scheme. To that extent I would allow the appeal.

OLIVER LJ. I agree that as regards the first point, that is to say, the validity of the
scheme, this appeal should be dismissed. Essentially the argument of counsel for the
plaintiff founds itself on two propositions. First, he contends that the expression in s
37(1) of the Solicitors Act 1974 'loss arising from claims' etc includes not only loss to the

person by whom the liability is incurred but loss to the Law Society. Second, he suggests
that the 'insurance' authorised by sub-s (2)(b) to be taken out and maintained by the Law   a
Society means, and can only mean, an insurance policy under which the Law Society is
the insured person and which indemnifies it against the loss to the Law Society comprised
in his construction of sub-s (1). Neither of these propositions, in my judgment, bears
examination. Counsel for the plaintiff was unable to suggest any way in which a civil
liability incurred by an individual could result in loss to the Law Society in the absence
of some contractual or statutory liability on the Law Society to meet it, and he was   b
therefore constrained to submit that the loss envisaged in sub-s (1) against which the
indemnity is to be provided is a loss to the fund established and maintained under sub-
s (2)(a) for the express purpose of providing that very indemnity. This involves a mental
gymnastic through which, speaking for myself, I have not felt able to follow him; but
even assuming that he is able, as it were, to lift himself this far by his own bootlaces, I
find his next step equally unacceptable, for it involves reading sub-para (b) of sub-s (2) as   c
integral with, and subsidiary to, sub-para (a) so that together they form a single alternative
to sub-para (c). I find this a most unnatural construction and I would reject it for the
same reasons as those stated by the judge in his careful judgment, with the whole of
which, so far as this part of the case is concerned, I respectfully agree.

Turning now to the question raised with regard to the Law Society's accountability for
brokerage commission on the premiums paid under the master policy, it is important   d
first to see how this arose. The facts as they emerge from the evidence are set out in the
judgment of the judge but they convey very little information as to the course of any
negotiations between the Law Society and London Insurance Brokers ('LIB').

LIB had, before the scheme had come into being, been appointed to be the Law
Society's brokers for the purposes of an insurance advisory service which it then
conducted. That position was regulated by an agreement entered into in February 1975   e
and made between the Law Society, its wholly owned company, Law Society Services Ltd
('LSS'), LIB, and LIB's two controlling shareholders, which provided that LSS should be
entitled to receive a proportion of the brokerage earned by LIB from insurances effected
under the service and which also contained a provision to the effect that any party should
be entitled to require the terms to be renegotiated if a compulsory professional indemnity
insurance scheme came into operation. The final form of the master policy was agreed   f
between the insurers and the Law Society in November 1975 and the first rules (the 1975
rules) were approved by the Master of the Rolls on 12th December 1975. After the
scheme had come into operation, a new agreement was entered into between the same
persons as had been parties to the agreement of February 1975. It was dated 11th May
1976 and it provided that LIB should be appointed as from 1st October 1975 the
insurance broker to LSS in respect of all 'solicitors' business' (which included the   g
professional indemnity insurance) and as managing broker to the 'service', which was
defined to include both the insurance advisory service and the professional indemnity
insurance scheme. The Law Society was to provide office accommodation in return for
a licence fee; the duties of LIB as managing broker (subject to the supervision of a joint
committee) were defined, and it was agreed that LSS should be paid by LIB a commission
equal to 40% of what was defined as 'the net brokerage' which broadly amounted to the   h
brokerage commission received or retained by LIB after accounting to the insurers for
premium income less operating expenses.

The arrangement thus made was, as the judge observed, a very sensible commercial
arrangement, designed to provide funds to enable the Law Society to fulfil its functions,
funds which might otherwise have had to be raised by, for example, increasing the cost
of practising certificates. Additionally, it should be said that the circulars leading to the   j
adoption of the scheme made it perfectly clear that there was to be a commission-sharing
arrangement as part of the scheme so that there was no question whatever of non-
disclosure. That is not disputed; nor is there the slightest suggestion, nor, indeed, could
there be, of any want of propriety or candour on the part of those who negotiated this
arrangement. The argument in favour of the Law Society's accountability has been put

by counsel for the plaintiff, as it was put before the judge by counsel then appearing for
a the plaintiffs, on three alternative grounds, two of which amount to substantially the
same argument but based on different hypotheses. It is unnecessary, on the view which
I take of the case, to do more than mention the first two. Both were based on the
proposition that one who has been compelled to pay money by an excessive or improper
use of statutory powers, or of powers attached to an office, can recover it; and they rested
on two alternative hypotheses: first, that the whole scheme was ultra vires and second
b that, even if the rules were intra vires, the scheme actually introduced did not comply
with them. As stated above, I can find no fault with the judge's conclusion that the
scheme was intra vires and valid. He likewise rejected the contention that the rules had
not been complied with, for reasons which are fully set out in his judgment. With those
reasons I respectfully agree and no purpose would be served by repeating them.

It is the third argument advanced by counsel for the plaintiff which has given me most
c concern. Shorn of any refinements it comes to this, that in entering into the agreement
with the insurers the Law Society was acting either as agent or trustee for those who
ultimately became bound by the scheme; that the premiums from which the commission
was earned were paid under the scheme; and that the Law Society, as an agent or trustee
which has made a profit out of its position without the assent of the principal or
beneficiary, is therefore accountable on the well-known principle of equity exemplified,
d in perhaps its most severe form, in *Boardman v Phipps* [1966] 3 All ER 721, [1967] 2 AC
46.

That principle is too well-known and well-established to need restating. It has been
expressed in various cases in different ways, sometimes as a branch of the rule that a
trustee must not put himself in a position in which his own interests and those of his
beneficiary conflict, and sometimes as merely an application of the principle that that
which is the fruit of trust property or of the trusteeship is itself trust property. For
e myself I prefer the latter. Lord Sankey in *Regal (Hastings) Ltd v Gulliver* [1942] 1 All ER
378 at 381, [1967] AC 134 at 137 puts it thus:

> 'The general rule of equity is that no one who has duties of a fiduciary nature to
> perform is allowed to enter into engagements in which he has or can have a personal
> interest conflicting with the interests of those whom he is bound to protect. If he
f > holds any property so acquired as trustee, he is bound to account for it to his *cestui*
> *que trust*.'

It is this last sentence which appears to me, at any rate, to be the kernel of the matter. A
trustee may be, and frequently is, in a position where his personal interest may conflict
with that of his beneficiaries and, to be accurate, the rule is not so much that it is
improper for him to put himself in that position but that, if he does so, he is obliged by
g his trust to prefer the interest of the beneficiary. Lord Russell, in the same case ([1942]
1 All ER 378 at 385, [1967] 2 AC 134 at 143), expressed the principle in these terms:

> 'Nevertheless, they may be liable to account for the profits which they have made,
> if, while standing in a fiduciary relationship to Regal, they have *by reason and in*
> *course of that fiduciary relationship made a profit*.'

h and again ([1942] 1 All ER 378 at 389, [1967] 2 AC 134 at 149):

> '. . . having obtained these shares *by reason and only by reason of the fact that they*
> *were directors of Regal and in the course of* the execution of that office, [they] are
> accountable for the profits which they have made out of them.'

Finally, Lord MacMillan ([1942] 1 All ER 378 at 391, [1967] 2 AC 134 at 153) after
j adverting to the fact that the transaction in question was in good faith, went on:

> 'However, that does not absolve them from accountability for any profit which
> they made, if it was *by reason and in virtue of their fiduciary office* as directors that they
> entered into the transaction.'

(The emphasis is mine in each case.)

It seems to me therefore, as it seemed to the judge, that what one has to do is to ascertain first of all whether there was a fiduciary relationship and, if there was, from *a* what it arose and what, if there was any, was the trust property; and then to inquire whether that of which an account is claimed either arose, directly or indirectly, from the trust property itself or was acquired not only in the course of, but by reason of, the fiduciary relationship.

If it is found as a result of that inquiry both that there is a fiduciary relationship and that the fiduciary has derived from it a profit which has not been made available to his *b* beneficiary, then it matters not that that profit is one achieved openly and in the utmost good faith nor, in the absence of consent, that it has been fully and frankly disclosed: the principle of equity is inflexible and the fiduciary must hold it for the benefit of the person for whom his fiduciary duty was undertaken or assumed.

The first question, therefore, is whether, having regard to the statutory provisions, the framework of the scheme and the circumstances in which the scheme came to be put *c* into operation, the Law Society came under any fiduciary duty to those solicitors who, under the rules, became bound to insure under the scheme.

There are, I think, two approaches to this question. The narrow approach is to scrutinise the constituent elements of the scheme itself for the purpose of seeing whether, at any stage, there arose any trust or other fiduciary duty owed to individuals. The broad approach is to regard the scheme as a whole against the background that it is something *d* compulsively imposed under statutory powers upon individuals otherwise free to make their own arrangements and to ask whether it is a necessary implication from the statute that the body invested with those powers owes some and, if so what, duty to those affected by their exercise.

I will consider the broad approach first. In doing so, I leave aside for the moment any question of an express assumption of a fiduciary duty to individuals or of a duty arising *e* by necessary implication from the terms or framework of the scheme actually adopted. Such considerations apart, there does not appear to me anything in the adoption of the mechanism of a master policy to which solicitors become individually party or in the circumstances in which that method of dealing with the matter was in fact adopted which can legitimately be said to have created any fiduciary duty between the Law Society and the solicitors compelled to become party to the scheme under the rules.   *f*

One is tempted initially, when confronted with a scheme such as the present, constituted under statutory powers by a public or semi-public body which can have no personal or individual interest in the matter, to describe that body loosely as 'the trustee of the scheme'; but that is not, I think, a phrase which, on analysis, has any legal significance. 'The scheme' is not property which can be held on trust for anybody and one is reduced, therefore, to seek either some specific property held on trust for *g* ascertainable beneficiaries or some duty of a fiduciary nature and owed to ascertainable individuals which can be discerned as arising, impliedly or expressly, from the statutory provisions or from the framework or constitution of the scheme established under those provisions. Now, in my judgment, there is nothing in the statutory provisions which can be said to create or import any fiduciary relationship; nor is there anything in those provisions which would suggest that the Law Society, simply from the point of view of *h* the exercise of its statutory powers, could not quite properly enter into the sort of agreement into which it has entered with LIB. Such an agreement would, as the judge held, appear to be authorised under sub-s (5) of s 37 if, indeed, a statutory authority for it is required.

The primary object of this particular part of the legislation is, I think, quite clearly the protection of members of the public from loss which might otherwise be sustained by *j* reason of solicitors against whom legitimate civil claims are established failing to meet them through being uninsured or under-insured. That object does not compulsively require any private fiduciary duty owed to individual solicitors by the body charged with carrying into effect the statutory purpose. At the same time, however, it does not negate the creation of such a duty if the statutory powers are exercised in such a way as to cause

it to arise, for there is nothing necessarily inconsistent between a duty owed to the public
a and an independent and unrelated duty owed to individual solicitors.
     The most favourable way in which, as it seems to me, the matter can be put from the
point of view of the plaintiff is as follows. Under s 37 there were three general methods
authorised for giving effect to the indemnity at which the section was directed. The first
was the creation of a fund to which compulsory contributions could be directed by the
rules. That would no doubt involve the Law Society's being a fiduciary as regards the
b contributions received to the extent of applying them for the particular purpose for
which they were paid, but it is not easy to see how it could have involved any fiduciary
duty to individual contributors as regards the fund itself, its investment or, for example,
the disposition of any share of brokerage on changes of investment. A second possibility
was the framing of rules which would require solicitors, or solicitors of a specified class,
to insure with authorised insurers, laying down the extent and terms of insurance. It is,
c I think, common ground that there is nothing in the section which would authorise the
nomination of specific authorised insurers under such a scheme, much less the
channelling of insurance through specified brokers. If this had been adopted, then
solicitors would have been free to choose their own insurers and brokers and to make
their own arrangements for sharing with brokers any commissions earned on such
insurance. The third method was that in fact adopted, of negotiating the terms of a
d master policy and requiring solicitors to become party to it. That of course, has the effect
of depriving the individual solicitor of the opportunity which he would otherwise have
under the second option mentioned above of making his own financial arrangements
with brokers. The argument, then, may be expressed thus: a body invested by statute
with a power to compel individuals to subscribe to a scheme which has the effect of
depriving those individuals of financial benefits which they could otherwise provide for
e themselves is impliedly under a fiduciary duty to those individuals to hold for their
benefit any benefits which that body may derive as a result of the exercise of such a
power. Expressed thus the proposition is a novel one but it has a certain attraction in the
light of the length to which some of the authorities have gone in the creation of equitable
duties. If, as a result of its ability to command individual solicitors to place their
compulsory insurance business through the scheme's brokers, the Law Society is able to
f obtain by virtue of the premium payments, a benefit which, if the scheme had taken
another form, might have gone to the individual solicitors themselves, ought not that
benefit to be held on trust proportionately for the individual payers and accounted for
accordingly?
     Counsel for the plaintiff points to *Reading v Attorney General* [1949] 2 All ER 68, [1949]
2 KB 232 (affirmed by the House of Lords [1951] 1 All ER 517, [1951] AC 507) as
g indicating the freedom with which the courts may infer the existence of a fiduciary duty
from the nature of the transaction or the circumstances surrounding any given
transaction. And indeed the judge who decided the instant case at first instance has
stated (in *English v Dedham Vale Properties Ltd* [1978] 1 All ER 382 at 398, [1978] 1 WLR
93 at 110) that the class of fiduciary relationships is never closed. But in *Reading's* case,
of course, the relationship of master and servant existed already and what the court did
h was to hold the servant accountable for the use of property entrusted to him for his
master's service. In the instant case what is sought to be done is to imply the relationships
from the use of statutory powers where no previous relationship existed. The argument
is not altogether dissimilar to that which was advanced in *Tito v Waddell (No 2)* [1977] 3
All ER 129 at 232, [1977] Ch 106 at 230, and which was rejected by Sir Robert Megarry
V-C in the following terms:

j
     'I cannot see why the imposition of a statutory duty to perform certain functions,
     or the assumption of such a duty, should as a general rule impose fiduciary
     obligations, or even be presumed to impose any. Of course, the duty may be of such
     a nature as to carry with it fiduciary obligations: impose a fiduciary duty and you
     impose fiduciary obligations. But apart from such cases, it would be remarkable

indeed if in each of the manifold cases in which statute imposes a duty, or imposes
a duty relating to property, the person on whom the duty is imposed were thereby *a*
to be put into a fiduciary relationship with those interested in the property, or
towards whom the duty could be said to be owed.'

Now I ask myself here, is the duty imposed, or in this case the power conferred, on the
Law Society of such a nature as in itself to carry fiduciary obligations? To begin with,
one has to bear in mind the purpose of s 37, which appears to me to be simply that of *b*
providing, in the most effective manner that the Council of the Law Society sees fit to
adopt and in the interests of the general public, a proper indemnity against loss arising
from civil liability. In so far as it imposes a duty it seems to me to be one which is owed
to the public. Subsection (5) gives a wide power to carry into effect such arrangements
as the Law Society considers necessary or expedient and sub-s (3)(c) gives a general power
to determine 'the amount of any payments required by the rules, subject to such limits, *c*
or in accordance with such provisions, as may be prescribed by the rules'. None of this
seems to me to point in the least to the imposition on the Law Society of any fiduciary
duty to individual solicitors.

Is there, then, anything in the type of scheme itself or in the circumstances leading up
to its adoption which might lead to the conclusion that the Law Society, in adopting such
a scheme was impliedly *assuming* any fiduciary duty to the individual participants? The *d*
evidence shows that it was adopted after prolonged and elaborate consultation and as a
result of a majority vote for this type of scheme in preference to other options, and that
the making of a commission-sharing agreement was contemplated as part of the
arrangement and disclosed in the consultative document. That, in itself, does not
suggest that the Law Society was itself consciously and voluntarily assuming any
fiduciary obligation to participants. If, then, such an obligation is to be inferred merely *e*
from the method employed of providing indemnity it has, I think, to be inferred as a
natural, and perhaps almost inseparable, consequence of the nature of the scheme itself;
and in the ultimate analysis it comes down to this, that the inference has to be drawn
simply from two factors, that is to say, first, the fact that a block scheme was adopted in
preference to individually arranged insurance, and secondly, that the commission in
question comes to the Law Society as a result of the payment by individuals of the *f*
premiums payable under such a scheme.

Neither of these factors appears to me, without more, to justify a conclusion of the
existence of an implied fiduciary relationship and if the matter rested on this argument
alone, I should feel myself unable to reach such a conclusion, although the matter is, even
then, not free from difficulty.

But one has to look at the picture as a whole and, in particular, one has to consider, in
the context of that picture, the narrower question of the form and contents of the *g*
individual scheme in fact adopted. Now here counsel for the plaintiff submits that he
does not have to rely on implication. His first submission was that the words 'on behalf
of all solicitors from time to time required to be insured', which are contained in the
master policy, indicated that the Law Society was acting as an agent and, as such, owed
a fiduciary duty to its principals. The judge rejected that contention because of the
difficulty of finding, not only an ascertained, but an ascertainable, principal at the date *h*
of the agreement. I agree with his judgment in this respect. At the material time the
rules were not in being and there was no certainty about the qualifications which were
going to be required for inclusion in the scheme. It seems to me impossible, therefore,
to regard the Law Society, vis-à-vis the insurers, as negotiating and entering into the
master policy as anything but a principal. But that does not exclude the notion that the *j*
principal may be a fiduciary and the judge held that once the agreement was negotiated
the Law Society held the benefit of it upon trust for the solicitors from time to time
required by the rules to be insured under it. Counsel for the Law Society suggests that
the judge was in error in so holding because he assumed that in effecting the master
policy the Law Society must have been either an agent or a trustee and he ignored the

third possibility that it was neither; it was simply effecting the policy pursuant to its
a statutory power. That that third possibility exists I do not doubt; but I would not, for my
part, be disposed to quarrel with the judge's conclusion that the Law Society did in fact
hold the benefit of the master policy as a trustee. First, that is what is suggested by the
words 'on behalf of' etc. Those words cannot just be treated as a descriptive declaration
that the Law Society was representing the profession generally and indeed the agreement
defines the class of persons on whose behalf the agreement is made by reference to the
b requirements of the rules. They define, and must I think have been intended to define,
the particular class of individuals for whom the benefit of the agreement was to be held
and for whom anything to be performed by the Law Society was to be performed. The
agreement was, after all, one in which, by its very nature, the Law Society was not itself
to have any beneficial interest or right to insurance. Secondly, the whole way in which
the scheme was constructed suggests that the intention was that every solicitor required
c to be insured should have an enforceable right, on paying the requisite premium, to have
the insurance cover offered by the scheme without the risk of the insurers declining
cover, for instance, on the ground of a multiplicity of previous claims. It should perhaps
be said, however, that such a concept, whilst it was in fact the preferred machinery
adopted, was not the only or an essential mechanism for producing the result which the
statute envisaged, although it was a natural one. It might, for instance, have been
d equally effective from the Law Society's point of view if there had been no right of
enforcement conferred on individual solicitors by the creation of an equitable interest in
them, reliance being placed simply on the Law Society's own right of enforcement
against the insurers (see, for instance, *Beswick v Beswick* [1967] 2 All ER 1197, [1968] AC
58). But the express declaration of trust was the method in fact adopted and I take as the
starting point that, as a matter of machinery, the scheme itself involved the consequence
e that the Law Society held the benefit of the master policy on trust for those solicitors
designated by the rules as persons required to be insured. That, of course, does not entail
that the Law Society became 'the insured', for the so-called 'master policy' was not in fact
itself a policy of insurance at all but an irrevocable engagement by the insurers to offer
insurance on the terms of agreed certificates to those qualified persons who tendered
premiums to the brokers. What was held on trust therefore was the benefit of that
f engagement, and it is that trust and, on a narrow view of the matter, that trust alone,
which gave rise to any fiduciary relationship between the Law Society and the solicitors
required to be insured. Was, then, the opportunity to earn the shared commission under
the agreement with LIB, the amount of which must admittedly depend upon the
amount of the premiums paid to the insurers to secure the insurance irrevocably offered
under the master policy, something which came to the Law Society either directly or
g indirectly as a result of the fiduciary relationship created as part of the machinery of the
scheme?
     The judge answered this question in the negative because, although, as he had held,
the Law Society was a trustee of the benefit of the master policy, when entered into, for
those solicitors who became subject to the scheme under the rules, he attributed the
ability to negotiate the commission agreement with LIB to the negotiation of the
h contract with the insurers which, in his view, took place at a time before any fiduciary
relationship arose. For my part, I am not persuaded of the correctness of this reasoning
if, as might appear to be suggested by the analogy which the judge drew with the case of
a settlor-trustee who stipulates for an advantage before the creation of the settlement, he
was treating as crucial the existence of the fiduciary relationship at the date when the
opportunity to negotiate the personal profit or advantage arose. Plainly, for instance, one
j who is contemplating becoming a trustee of a settlement cannot escape accountability
for a personal advantage deriving from his trusteeship (for instance, a share of brokerage
on changes of investment of the trust fund) on the ground simply that he negotiated it
before he had actually become a trustee. But I do not think that, on analysis, the judge
can have intended to suggest this and he did, as it seems to me, ask himself the right
question, that is to say, was the opportunity to obtain the share of commission an

advantage which arose from the Law Society's position as trustee of the benefit of the agreement? There are, I think difficulties in the way of accepting his analysis but of course that does not necessarily invalidate his conclusion. In one sense, of course, the commission earned arose not simply from the trusteeship but from the trust property itself. The commission was and is directly related to the amount of the premiums paid by the beneficiaries of the benefit of the agreement and, but for the agreement, they would not have paid those premiums to LIB; LIB would not have earned its commission from the insurers; and the Law Society would not have received, through its wholly owned company, the payments which it did in fact receive. Those payments are therefore very directly connected with, and may be said to stem from, the trust property. On the other hand, it may be argued that the payments cannot be said to have been received by the Law Society *by virtue* of a fiduciary position which arose simply from the holding, as trustee for the individuals affected, of the benefit of an irrevocable offer by a third party, not so much because, as the judge found, the principle of commission-sharing with the brokers was negotiated before the creation of the fiduciary relationship, but because the opportunity to negotiate such an agreement was something which existed entirely independently of the actual terms of the master policy no matter when it was negotiated.

Whether the obligation of the insurers to accept applications for insurance was retained by the Law Society as sole beneficial owner, or whether it was made available to applicants for insurance through the medium of a trust, was entirely immaterial either to the opportunity to earn commission or to the amount of the commission earned. The fiduciary relationship assumed can be said to be purely mechanical and what enabled the Law Society to persuade the brokers to share the commission earned was not the Law Society's position as trustee but its position as the responsible statutory body empowered to set up, through rules effectively binding practising solicitors, a scheme which involved, and quite properly involved, the appointment of a single broker as part of the administrative machinery. Counsel for the Law Society has referred to *Re Mulholland's Will Trusts* [1949] 1 All ER 460 as an example of a case where a trustee was permitted to keep a benefit which had accrued to him quite independently of the trust. Another case in point is *Re Macadam, Dallow v Codd* [1945] 2 All ER 664 at 672, [1946] Ch 73 at 82, where the result was the other way but where the matter is succinctly expressed by Cohen J where he said: 'I think that the root of the matter really is: Did the trustee acquire the position in respect of which he drew the remuneration by virtue of his position as trustee?'

Judged by this test and assuming the only fiduciary duty to be that arising from the fact that the benefit of the master policy was held on trust for participants in the scheme, it is arguable that the claim for a declaration of accountability against the Law Society is not substantiated, for the opportunity to negotiate a commission-sharing agreement had no necessary connection with the adoption, as part of the scheme, of the machinery of a trust.

Nor, it may be said, is that affected by the fact that the premiums on which the commission is calculated are paid as a result of the adoption, the compulsory adoption in fact, of the benefit of the agreement by the participants in the scheme as a result of which they enter into a direct contractual relationship with the insurers. That connection does not mean that the commission is in any real sense the fruit of the trust property any more than, for instance, were the directors' fees the fruit of the qualifying shares held by the trustees in *Re Dover Coalfield Extension* [1908] 1 Ch 65, [1904–7] All ER Rep 161.

There appear to me to be two difficulties about accepting this analysis. In the first place, it appears to me to place too narrow an interpretation on the concept of fiduciary duty. It is not easy, as I have mentioned above, to see how such a duty can arise simply from the existence and use of the statutory powers and in one sense the opportunity to share the brokers' commission was simply a fortunate by-product of those powers. But it cannot be ignored that, in the way in which the powers were actually exercised, it could never have been intended that the agreement negotiated with the insurers, whether or not any actual trust was then in existence, should be entered into except on *a* the basis that it was to be held beneficially for solicitors to be insured under the scheme. There may not have been a fully constituted trust at that stage but there could be no doubt that the policy was being negotiated for the ultimate benefit of whoever might turn out to be the compulsorily insured solicitors. It was not for the Law Society's benefit and it was not the Law Society which was to pay the premiums: but the commission which the Law Society subsequently negotiated arose from, and was directly *b* related to, those premiums. The opportunity to obtain it was in a very real sense related to the trustee mechanism which was contemplated as the method of operating the Law Society's statutory power. What made it peculiarly effective was the Law Society's ability to compel the proposed beneficiaries to join the scheme: but the fact remains that it was the adoption of this scheme in which the Law Society interposed itself as the trustee and negotiating intermediary between insurers and insured which enabled it to make the *c* arrangements which it did with the brokers. Secondly, even if it were possible to avoid the conclusion of a fiduciary relationship in relation to the master policy in October 1975, the terms of that policy appear to me to rule out any suggestion that, as to the future, the Law Society was acting, or could act, in anything but a fiduciary capacity. Clause 2 provides a scale for the calculation of the premiums for the first two years of the operation of the master policy. It continues in these terms:

d
> 'This Policy can be extended for successive periods of one year on each 1st day of September subject to the rates of premium for each renewal being agreed by the Insurers and The Law Society at least six months before such renewal. In the event of any failure so to agree such rates of renewal premium all cover under this Policy shall cease on . . . the expiry of the period for which the Policy was last extended.'

e Now it is, in my judgment, the benefit of the agreement as a whole, and not merely the benefit of the insurers' obligation to provide insurance under cl 1, which is held by the Law Society as trustee for the specified class of solicitors. The obligation to insure, the payment of the premiums and the ascertainment of the rate of premium are all interdependent. If this is right then it seems to me inescapable that, whatever may have been the position prior to October 1975, the Law Society, in any subsequent negotiations *f* for the renewal of the insurance and the agreement of the premiums, must have entered into those negotiations as trustee for the persons entitled to the benefit of the agreement under which they took place. The subsequent entry, in 1976, into the new commission-sharing agreement with the brokers therefore involved an immediate conflict of interest, for it was in the beneficiaries' interest to keep the premiums as low as possible, if necessary by negotiating a lower rate of commission with the brokers, and in the Law *g* Society's interest to keep them as high as possible in order to increase the amount of its share of commisson although there is absolutely no foundation for any suggestion that such a calculation was in anybody's mind for a single moment. But the equitable rule is a strict one and the necessary consequence, it seems to me, is that at least as regards the commission received in respect of the years 1978 and 1979 the Law Society became accountable to its beneficiaries subject, of course, to any question of consent, acquiescence *h* or estoppel.

Three things are said about this. First, it is submitted that there was no conflict because the commission fell into the general funds of the Law Society and was applicable for (and applied for) the benefit of the profession. But that cannot be right. 'The profession' was not the beneficiary and the fact that the trustee's profit was made with the utmost bona fides and applied for the most beneficial public purposes cannot affect the *j* application of what is, I apprehend, an inflexible equitable principle.

Then it is said that the intention to share commission was fully disclosed in the documents leading up to the scheme, and indeed it was. But that could affect the matter only if the beneficiaries consented. No doubt those who voted in favour of the scheme did consent and cannot now complain. But it was not a unanimous vote, and I can see no way in which the consent of the majority of the beneficiaries who approved the scheme can bind those who did not assent to it but were nevertheless compelled to join it.

Finally it is said that the matter is largely academic because, if the Law Society had not raised the money it required for its purposes in this way, it would have been obliged to raise the fees payable for practising certificates, so that what the plaintiffs have lost on the indemnity insurance swings they have gained on the practising certificates roundabout. There are two answers to this. In the first place, the beneficiaries of the master policy and solicitors requiring practising certificates are not identical classes so that if, as I believe, the Law Society is accountable, it is no answer to say that A's money has been used to subsidise A and B, however deserving B may be. Secondly, and in any event, the commission has gone into and forms part of the general funds of the Law Society (or rather of its wholly owned company). An equivalent sum raised by increasing the fees for practising solicitors would have had to be made the subject of a special account in accordance with s 11(4) of the Act. The sums raised from these two quite distinct sources cannot, therefore, be equated.

I find myself, therefore, driven to the conclusion that, as regards this part of the case the plaintiffs are right, although I recognise that that conclusion is an extremely inconvenient one for the Law Society and it is not one which I embrace with any enthusiasm. Nevertheless the principle is universal and if the Law Society has chosen the mantle of a fiduciary, as in my judgment it did by the express terms of the arrangements into which it entered, it cannot at the same time disclaim the concomitant consequences. As to this part of the case, therefore, I would, albeit reluctantly, allow the appeal.

That raises a question which the judge was not, on the view which he took of the case, required to answer, namely the form of the relief to be granted under para 2 of the summons. The evidence on this aspect of the case is jejune and I feel some concern that the relevant facts were not, as they evidently were not, thought worthy of a rather fuller investigation than they in fact received. Speaking for myself I should have preferred this question to have been properly pleaded and, if necessary, to have been tried with cross-examination. Nevertheless it was an issue distinctly raised in the case, argued by counsel and, by common consent, submitted to the judge and to this court for decision on the footing that the evidence before the court contains all the material facts. It is a point raised directly by the respondent's cross-notice and it must, therefore, be decided on such material as is before the court.

The nub of the Law Society's case, as it seems to me, is that the plaintiffs have throughout known what was being done and did not seek to challenge it prior to 1979, apart from a letter in September 1978 expressing dissatisfaction with the amount of premium charged. Quite apart from the fact that during this period the commission earned was expended on the Law Society's lawful purposes, the objection was not raised until it was, in any event, too late for any alternative arrangements to be made for raising the finance necessary to provide for those purposes, for instance by increasing the fees for practising certificates. It would, I think, clearly be inequitable for the court to order the Law Society to account to the plaintiffs for commission received prior to 1979 in respect of which no challenge was made until the Law Society had irrevocably altered its position on the footing that no objection was being taken to the validity of the scheme or anything done under it. Commission received in respect of the policy effected in 1979, however, is in my judgment on a different footing. It is perfectly true, as counsel for the Law Society has pointed out, that no challenge to the commission as such was raised until very late in the day, and even then it was originally based only on the invalidity of the scheme as a whole. Nevertheless, it is clear from the correspondence that the Law Society knew from January 1979 onwards that it was at risk of proceedings and that in those proceedings the plaintiffs were proposing to claim back the premiums which they had paid. It was, I think, a necessary implication from this that they would be laying claim also to the commission, albeit perhaps not directly. The 1979 rules were not brought into force until July of 1979 so that it follows that when they were brought into force and

a operated, and when the Law Society received commission on the premiums paid under those rules, it must be taken to have been aware that the whole basis for payment was being challenged. If, therefore, they changed their position they cannot be said to have done so in reliance on any acquiescence by the plaintiffs, for the one thing that was perfectly plain by that stage was that the plaintiffs were not only dissatisfied but were threatening action. I would therefore hold any claim to an account of commission by the plaintiffs barred in respect of all years up to the year 1979, but would order an account
b in respect of the commission received in respect of the master policy effected in that year and any subsequent year.

FOX LJ. I agree that the appeal on the question of the validity of the scheme should be dismissed for the reasons given by Stephenson and Oliver LJJ and the judge.

I come to the question of the accountability of the Law Society for commission
c received in respect of the premiums paid under the master policy.

On 12th December 1975 the Law Society made the 1975 indemnity rules. Rule 1 authorised the Law Society to take out and maintain a master policy in the form scheduled to the rules and to arrange for the issue to solicitors of certificates of insurance in the form there set out. Rule 2 required that every solicitor to whom the rules applied should pay the premiums payable by him under the master policy and the certificate as
d soon as they fell due. The scheme became compulsory on 1st September 1976.

The crucial provisions of the master policy scheduled to the 1975 rules are these. By cl 1 of the policy—

> 'The Insurers agree with the Law Society on behalf of all solicitors from time to time required to be insured by Indemnity Rules made under s. 37 of the Solicitors' Act 1974 . . .'

e Clause 2 provided:

> 'This policy commences on the 12th day of December, 1975, and shall be extended on the first day of September 1976, and the first day of September, 1977, for a further 12 months' period in each case. At each extension date the rates of premiums payable in respect of the year next following shall be the annual rates of
f premium applicable in respect of the immediately preceding period as increased by [and then specified percentages are set forth]. This Policy can be extended subsequently for successive periods of one year on each first day of September subject to the rates of premium for each renewal being agreed by the Insurers and The Law Society at least 12 months before such renewal. In the event of any failure to agree such rates of renewal premium all cover shall cease on the expiry of the period for which the policy was last extended.'

g The forms of the master policy annexed to the 1978 and 1979 rules are not materially different, for present purposes, from that annexed to the 1975 rules.

The insurers first accepted the risk under the master policy in November 1975, which was before the 1975 rules were made. By an agreement of 6th February 1975 the Law Society and LSS had appointed LIB as insurance brokers to LSS and to operate the Law
h Society's existing indemnity advisory service on terms (inter alia) that if a compulsory professional indemnity insurance scheme should be introduced for solicitors, the provisions of the agreement could be renegotiated at the request of either party.

After the Law Society decided to adopt the scheme for compulsory insurance based on the master policy, but before the 1975 rules were made, the Law Society sent a circular to solicitors which indicated that under the scheme, if the existing commission
j arrangements were continued, the commission income of the Law Society would be about £250,000 p a gross. That was in May 1975. The estimate, of course, was on the basis of the rate of premiums then prevailing: the commission income per annum is now very much larger.

In October 1975 the Law Society wrote to solicitors setting out the case for the scheme as the council saw it. The Law Society's letter stated:

'Although individual solicitors will no longer receive the benefit of commission, it will be payable by the Insurers and The Law Society will receive a share after operating expenses have been deducted. This will enure for the benefit of the profession, thus mitigating future increases in the Practising Certificate Fee.'

Every set of the Law Society's consolidated annual accounts has disclosed the existence of the commission and its receipt by LSS. There was a majority vote of solicitors in favour of the scheme.

On 11th May 1976 the Law Society, LSS, LIB and others entered into a written agreement which, after reciting the wish of the Law Society and LSS to terminate the appointment of LIB as brokers to LSS under the agreement of 6th February 1975, and to enter into a new agreement, it was provided that the Law Society and LSS thereby appointed LIB with effect from 1st October 1975 as insurance brokers to the Law Society in respect of 'solicitors' business' (which included the scheme). The agreement went on to provide for the actual rate of commission to be paid to LSS.

The plaintiff's case in respect of the commission is put on three separate grounds. The first is that the scheme was ultra vires and that the commission was, in effect, an unlawful exaction under a pretence of statutory authority. That contention fails since, as I have indicated, the scheme was in my view valid.

The second is based on the proposition that the scheme was intra vires, but that the Law Society has not given effect to the rules because, it is said, the insurers had never actually issued a document in the form of the master policy or contractually bound themselves to do so; again it is said that there was an unlawful exaction. The judge rejected that contention. I agree with him and with his reasons for doing so.

The third ground is that, assuming the scheme was valid and was, in fact, implemented, the Law Society is liable to account for the commission as a fiduciary in accordance with the equitable principle stated in *Boardman v Phipps* [1966] 3 All ER 721, [1967] 2 AC 46 and *Regal (Hastings) Ltd v Gulliver* [1942] 1 All ER 378, [1967] 2 AC 134. Lord Russell in the latter case stated the principle thus ([1942] 1 All ER 378 at 385, [1967] 2 AC 134 at 143):

'Nevertheless, they may be liable to account for the profits which they have made, if, while standing in a fiduciary relationship to Regal, they have by reason and in course of that fiduciary relationship made a profit.'

It was described by Wilberforce J at first instance in *Boardman v Phipps* [1964] 2 All ER 187 at 202, [1964] 1 WLR 993 at 1010 as 'a broad principle of equity developed by this court in order to ensure that trustees or agents shall not retain a profit made in the course of or by means of their office'.

The first question then is whether the Law Society stood in a fiduciary relationship to the plaintiff at all. It is suggested that a fiduciary relationship arose because the Law Society entered into the master policy arrangements with the insurers either as agent or as trustee on behalf of all solicitors required to be insured by rules under s 37 of the Solicitors Act 1974. I do not feel able to accept that the Law Society did so as agent. If there is to be an agency by a principal on behalf of another person, that person must be in existence and ascertainable. I agree with the judge that when the provisions of the master policy took effect many solicitors required to be insured by rules under the Act would neither be ascertained nor capable of ascertainment. The rules in fact, were not in being at the material time.

The position as to trusts is, however, different. An enforceable trust can be created for the benefit of persons as yet unborn or unascertained. The problem is whether such a trust as is asserted was in fact created.

There was not, in my view, any trusteeship of the scheme. Trusts are concerned with property, property which is impressed with equitable interests and is held by the trustee subject to equitable duties and obligations. The scheme was not property and I do not think that there was any property which was held upon trusts declared by the scheme.

It seems to me, however, that there was a trust, of which the Law Society was the

trustee, of the benefit of the insurers' obligations under the master policy. It is quite clear
a that the Law Society did not enter into the master policy arrangement on its own
behalf. That is evident from the words 'for and on behalf of all solicitors from time to
time required to be insured' etc. In my judgment the only sensible effect which can be
given to those words is to treat them as indicating a trust. The words must have been
intended to have some effect and I do not think that it in any way stretches their ordinary
meaning in the context so to treat them. If the Law Society is treated as entering into the
b arrangement on its own behalf (which is unlikely anyway) the words have no meaning.
And if they are treated as indicating agency they have no effect. As words imposing a
trust they have a sensible meaning.

The result, in my view, is that the Law Society held the benefit of the master policy as
trustee for a class of persons of whom the plaintiffs are two.

The next question is whether the Law Society obtained the benefit of the commission
c by reason of, and in the course of, that trusteeship.

There are two preliminary matters to which I should refer. First, the judge said
([1980] 3 All ER 615 at 637, [1980] 1 WLR 1336 at 1360):

'However, proof of a post-contract fiduciary relationship would not itself suffice
to entitle the plaintiffs to invoke the equitable principles exemplified in *Boardman
v Phipps* unless it were shown that the profits in question had been received by the
d Law Society as a result of the use of this post-contract fiduciary position. I do not
think that this has been shown. True it is that the 1976 agreement was in point of
time actually entered into long after the contract between the Law Society and the
insurers had been concluded in 1975. The Law Society, however, found itself in a
position in 1976 to conclude the advantageous arrangement relating to commission,
not by virtue of its then subsisting fiduciary relationship to the solicitors affected by
e the scheme, but because of the negotiation of the original contract with the insurers.'

I am not sure that the judge is suggesting the contrary, but for clarity I should say that
I do not think that the fact that the contract under which a fiduciary received a benefit
by virtue of his trust was a contract which ante-dated the trust, would affect his obligation
to account. If a man enters into an agreement under which he is entitled to a commission
f in certain circumstances and subsequently accepts a trusteeship under which he enters
into such transactions and obtains a commission he would still, I apprehend, be obliged
to account to the trust.

Second, the judge refers to the fact that if a grandfather entered into a contract with
insurers whereunder he was to hold certain benefits as trustee for his infant grandchild,
it could not be suggested that he was acting in a fiduciary relationship to the grandchild
g in negotiating the contract. I agree. The case postulated is, however, concerned with the
situation which arises before the trust is established; the settlor can set up a trust with
such benefits to himself as he thinks fit.

The question is whether the Law Society obtained the commission by reason and in
the course of its fiduciary relationship. As to that, it may be said that the fiduciary
relationship and the source of the commission were unrelated; the trust property was the
h benefit of the undertaking by the insurers in the master policy and, it may be said, the
benefits obtained by the Law Society in the form of commission did not derive from any
dealing with the trust property or from any exercise of the trustee's powers as trustee.
It would in fact have been possible for the Law Society to have produced a workable
scheme without the interposition of any trust or agency in respect of the benefit of the
master policy. The Law Society itself could have been left to enforce the policy against
j the insurers. The Law Society could still have obtained the commission. The Law
Society obtained the commission not because it was a trustee but because, in effect,
solicitors were compelled to insure if they were to continue to practise.

I think that is too narrow a view. First, whatever the Law Society might or might not
have done, it did in fact constitute itself a trustee (on my interpretation of the master
policy). Second, I do not think that the fact that a trustee receives a benefit otherwise

than from some direct dealing with the trust property or from the exercise of a trust power is conclusive of the question whether he has to account to the beneficiaries for the benefit he has received. If, for example, a trustee propounds a tax saving scheme to beneficiaries under which they are required to effect at their own expense policies on their own lives, I apprehend that if the trustee took commission from the insurers in respect of such policies he would be liable to account for the commission even though he received the commission without any exercise of his powers as a trustee and even though the commission did not derive from a dealing with the trust fund itself. Third, it was in no sense the purpose of the statute or the rules that the scheme should confer benefits on the Law Society. The purpose was the protection of the public. The mechanism was insurance for which the individual solicitors had to pay.

Fourth, the Law Society's opportunity to obtain the commission derived from the existence of a master policy, the benefit of which it held as trustee, which was the source of the individual insurances effected by solicitors and the premiums on which were the direct source of the commission received by the Law Society. I think that in the end the position is this. The Law Society put itself in a position to obtain the commission because it entered into the master policy; and it entered into the master policy as a trustee. In my view the two things are too closely linked to enable one to avoid the conclusion that the Law Society obtained the commission by virtue of its fiduciary position. The matter becomes very clear in relation to the renewals of the policy after 1977. Clause 2 of the master policy provides for extensions after 1977 for successive periods of one year at rates of premiums to be agreed between the insurers and the Law Society.

In my view the property of which the Law Society became a trustee was the entire benefit of the master policy including the provision whereunder the rate of premiums was to be settled by agreement between the insurers and the society. Consequently on the renewals after 1977 the Law Society must have negotiated the rate of premiums as a trustee. But, having regard to the agreement with LIB for the sharing of commission, that placed the Law Society in a position where its duty as a trustee and its own interest in respect of commission were in direct conflict. As a trustee its duty was to keep the premiums as low as possible while its own pecuniary interest would be served by an increase in premiums. I do not suggest for a moment that the Law Society preferred its own interest to that of its solicitor beneficiaries. But that is of no consequence. Lord Sankey in *Regal (Hastings) Ltd v Gulliver* [1942] 1 All ER 378 at 381, [1967] 2 AC 134 at 137 said:

> 'The general rule of equity is that no one who has duties of a fiduciary nature to perform is allowed to enter into engagements in which he has or can have a personal interest conflicting with the interests of those whom he is bound to protect. If he holds any property so acquired as trustee, he is bound to account for it to his *cestui que trust*.'

The result, in my judgment, is that, apart from any question of acquiescence, the Law Society is accountable to the plaintiffs for the commission because of its fiduciary relationship. I do not think that conclusion is affected in any way by the fact that the Law Society disclosed, from the first, that it intended to take the commission if the scheme came into operation. The Law Society indeed was entirely honest at every stage. But, as I understand it, the rule of equity is in no way concerned with good faith. Lord Russell in the *Regal* case [1942] 1 All ER 378 at 386, [1967] AC 134 at 144 said:

> 'The rule of equity which insists on those, who by use of a fiduciary position make a profit being liable to account for that profit, in no way depends on fraud, or absence of *bona fides*; or upon such questions or considerations as whether the profit would or should otherwise have gone to the plaintiff, or whether the profiteer was under a duty to obtain the source of the profit for the plaintiff ... The liability arises from the mere fact of a profit having, in the stated circumstances, been

a   made. The profiteer, however honest and well-intentioned, cannot escape the risk of being called upon to account.'

As it seems to me, the fact is that the rule of equity is a severe one. Full disclosure may be relevant to acquiescence or to consent. But it is not otherwise material to the liability to account in the present case. Acquiescence I shall come to later. There is no question of consent by the plaintiffs.

There are two other matters to which I should refer on this aspect of the case. First, it
b   is said that there was no conflict of interest because the commission obtained by the Law Society was applicable for the general benefit of the profession. The answer to that proposition is that the Law Society's obligation is to account to the beneficiaries under the trust who are not the same as the profession generally.

Second, our attention was drawn to the fact that, if the Law Society had not obtained the commission, it would have had to raise funds in other ways, probably by raising the
c   annual fees for practising certificates. This cannot, I think, be an answer to the problem of the basic liability to account (though it may be relevant to acquiescence). The right, if any, to commission and the right to increase fees for practising certificates are quite separate things. The Law Society is not entitled to displace the rule of equity as to the obligation of a fiduciary to account by saying that it could have extracted the money from the beneficiaries in another capacity and in some other way.
d   I come lastly to the question of acquiescence; it was not necessary for the judge to decide that on the view of the law which he took. It seems to me that a case of acquiescence is made out in respect of the period down to the effecting of the 1979 policy. Prior to that, the position seems to me to be this: the Law Society, before the commencement of the scheme, made clear its intention to share the commission. It is not disputed that the plaintiffs had seen the relevant documents and were aware of the
e   Law Society's intention; equally, it is not disputed that the plaintiffs saw the Law Society's annual accounts disclosing the commission. Prior to 1979 there was no protest by the plaintiffs, express or implied, as to the taking of commission. It would, in my view on the evidence before us, be inequitable now to hold the Law Society accountable in respect of the previous period. In respect of that period the Law Society proceeded on the basis that it was entitled to the commission; that was a reasonable assumption in the
f   absence of protest from the plaintiffs or anybody else. If a protest had been made the Law Society would have been in a position to consider whether it should raise equivalent revenue from other sources (for example, by increasing the fee for practising certificates).

In 1979 the position altered. The correspondence indicates that from January 1979 the Law Society must have known that it was at risk of proceedings which might involve a claim, direct or indirect, in respect of commission. The 1979 rules came into force in
g   July 1979. After they came into force and the Law Society received commission in consequence of their existence, the Law Society could not maintain that it did so in reliance on any acquiescence of the plaintiffs, because the Law Society was already under threat of an action.

In the circumstances I would hold that the plaintiffs cannot maintain any claim in respect of commission for the years down to 1979, but that an account should be ordered
h   in respect of commission received in respect of the master policy effected in 1979 and subsequent years.

Appeal allowed to the extent indicated in judgment of Stephenson LJ. Leave to both parties to appeal to the House of Lords.

j   Solicitors: *Lovell Son & Pitfield*, agents for *Pethybridges*, Great Torrington (for the plaintiff); *Slaughter & May* (for the Law Society).

Patricia Hargrove   Barrister.

R v Chief Constable of the Devon and Cornwall Constabulary, ex parte Central Electricity Generating Board

COURT OF APPEAL, CIVIL DIVISION

LORD DENNING MR, LAWTON AND TEMPLEMAN LJJ

22nd, 23rd, 24th, 25th SEPTEMBER, 20th OCTOBER 1981

Police – Powers – Removal of persons from private land – Removal of protesters – Actual or apprehended breach of peace – Protesters obstructing survey of site for nuclear power plant – Protest peaceful and non-violent – Whether police having power to remove or assist in removal of protesters.

The Central Electricity Generating Board was a statutory body empowered under s 35(1) of the Electricity Act 1957 and s 280 of the Town and Country Planning Act 1971 to enter and survey land for the building of power stations. The board, in the exercise of their powers, wished to enter a site on private land in Cornwall in order to carry out a survey of the site to assess its suitability for a nuclear power station. However, when employees of the board attempted to carry out the survey they were obstructed by a group of protesters who occupied the site. The protest, although disruptive of the board's attempts to carry out the survey, was peaceful and non-violent and took the form of obstructing the board's employees and plant. The board sought the assistance of the Chief Constable of the Devon and Cornwall Constabulary to prevent further obstructions, but he refused to intervene on the grounds that he had no statutory power of arrest in the circumstances nor any common law power of arrest since there had been no breach of the peace, nor was any anticipated, nor was there any unlawful assembly to be dispersed. The board applied for an order of mandamus directed to the chief constable requiring him to remove, or assist the board's employees or agents in removing, persons who obstructed the board's work. The Divisional Court refused the application and the board appealed.

Held – (1) Notwithstanding that the protest and obstruction took place on private land, the board, having a statutory right to be on the land, were entitled in the circumstances to use the common law remedy of self-help to remove obstructing protesters, and the police had power to enter on the land at the invitation of the board and assist the board in removing the protesters either in order to prevent actual or apprehended breaches of the peace occurring when the removal took place or (per Lord Denning MR) because the conduct of the protesters in unlawfully obstructing the board's survey was itself a breach of the peace (see p 832 f to j, p 834 d to g, p 837 h, p 838 f to j and p 839 b to j, post).

(2) However, since it was for the police at the site and not the court to decide when and how to exercise that power, mandamus would not be issued against the chief constable (see p 833 f to j, p 837 d and p 840 d e, post).

Per Lord Denning MR. (1) There is a breach of the peace whenever a person who is lawfully carrying out his work is unlawfully and physically prevented by another from doing it (see p 832 g h, post).

(2) An unlawful assembly is an assembly of three or more persons with intent to commit a crime by open force (see p 833 c, post).

Per Lawton LJ. The presence of violence or tumult is an essential element of the offence of unlawful assembly and the offence is not committed merely when three or more persons gather to commit a crime (see p 834 h to p 835 a, post).

Notes

For mandamus against public officers to enforce statutory duties, see 11 Halsbury's Laws *a* (4th Edn) paras 1521, 1523–1527, and for cases on the subject, see 16 Digest (Reissue) 365–366, 3866–3874.

For the Electricity Act 1957, s 35, see 11 Halsbury's Statutes (3rd Edn) 1048.

For the Town and Country Planning Act 1971, s 280, see 41 ibid 1893.

Cases referred to in judgments

b *Cole v Thomas* (1704) Holt KB 108, 6 Mod Rep 149, 90 ER 958, NP, 46 Digest (Repl) 418, 615.

Holmes v Bagge (1853) 1 E & B 782, 22 LJQB 301, 21 LTOS 256, 17 JP 631, 17 Jur 1095, 118 ER 629, 15 Digest (Reissue) 1192, *10,231*.

Hubbard v Pitt [1975] 3 All ER 1, [1976] QB 161, [1975] 3 WLR 201, [1975] ICR 308, CA, Digest (Cont Vol D) 538, *152c*.

c *Kamara v Director of Public Prosecutions* [1973] 2 All ER 1242, [1974] AC 104, [1973] 3 WLR 198, 137 JP 714, 57 Cr App R 880, HL, 14(1) Digest (Reissue) 121, *811*.

Sedleigh-Denfield v O'Callagan (trustees for St Joseph's Society for Foreign Missions) [1940] 3 All ER 349, [1940] AC 880, 109 LJKB 893, 164 LT 72, HL, 36(1) Digest (Reissue) 486, *633*.

R v Metropolitan Police Comr, ex parte Blackburn [1968] 1 All ER 763, [1968] 2 QB 118, [1968] 2 WLR 893, CA, 16 Digest (Reissue) 344, *3615*.

d

Cases also cited

Albert v Lavin [1981] 1 All ER 628, [1981] 2 WLR 1070, DC.

Beatty v Gillbanks (1882) 9 QBD 308, [1881–5] All ER Rep 559.

Cohen v Huskisson (1837) 2 M & W 477, 150 ER 845.

e *Duncan v Jones* [1936] 1 KB 218, [1935] All ER Rep 710.

Field v Metropolitan Police Receiver [1907] 2 KB 853, [1904–7] All ER Rep 435.

Gelberg v Miller [1961] 1 All ER 291, [1961] 1 WLR 153.

Glasbrook Brothers Ltd v Glamorgan County Council [1925] AC 270, [1924] All ER Rep 579, HL.

Humphries v Connor (1864) 17 ICLR 1.

f *Ingle v Bell* (1836) 1 M & W 516, 150 ER 539.

McGowan v Chief Constable of Kingston upon Hull [1967] Crim LR 34, DC.

O'Kelly v Harvey (1883) 15 Cox CC 435.

R v Caird (1970) 54 Cr App Rep 499, CA.

R v Dewhurst (1820) 1 State Tr NS 529.

R v Hodges [1974] Crim LR 424, DC.

g *R Howell* [1981] 3 All ER 383, [1981] 3 WLR 501.

R v Hunt (1820) 3 B & Ald 566, 106 ER 768.

R v Metropolitan Police Comr, ex parte Blackburn (No 3) [1973] 1 All ER 324, [1973] QB 241, CA.

R (Feeham) v Queen's County Justices (1882) 10 LR Ir 294.

Rice v Connolly [1966] 2 All ER 649, [1966] 2 QB 414.

h *Thomas v Sawkins* [1935] 2 KB 249, [1935] All ER Rep 655.

Webster v Watts (1847) 11 QB 311, 116 ER 492.

Wershof v Comr of Police for the Metropolis [1978] 3 All ER 540.

Wise v Dunning [1902] 1 KB 167, [1900–3] All ER Rep 727.

j **Appeal**

The Central Electricity Generating Board appealed against the decision of the Divisional Court (Hodgson and McCullough JJ) dated 28th July 1981 dismissing the board's application for an order of mandamus directed to the respondent, the Chief Constable of Devon and Cornwall, requiring him to instruct police officers under his control to remove or to assist the board's servants or agents in removing persons obstructing the

board's works at Luxulyan, Cornwall. The facts are set out in the judgment of Lord
Denning MR.   *a*

A T Hoolahan QC and *Andrew Caldecott* for the board.
Alan Rawley QC and *Phillip Mott* for the chief constable.

                                                                   Cur adv vult
                                                                                 b
20th October. The following judgments were read.

LORD DENNING MR. The coast of Cornwall is beautiful. Much of the inland is
ugly. It is despoiled by china clay workings. Not far from them there is open farmland
with small villages dotted around. Pleasant enough but not outstanding. The Central
Electricity Generating Board view this as a possible site for a nuclear power station. They *c*
wish to survey it so as to compare it with other possible sites. The farmer objected to the
survey. So did the villagers. They took up a stand against it. But on being told by the
courts that it was unlawful for them to obstruct the survey, they desisted. They moved
off the site. They obeyed the law. But then groups of outsiders came in from far and
wide. They had no local connection with the place. They came anonymously. They
would not disclose their identity. They would not give their names and addresses. They *d*
flouted the law. They wilfully obstructed the survey. Can these newcomers be moved
off the site so that they obstruct no more? Can the board move them off? Or, if the
board cannot do it, can the police be called in to help? The chief constable feels that he
cannot use his force for the purpose. It would put his men in a bad light with the local
inhabitants. What then is to be done?
                                                                                 e
The need for electricity
    The whole of our country is now dependent on electricity. It is the driving force of
industry. It is the source of light for homes. It is generated in huge power stations. At
one time it was fuelled by coal. Afterwards by oil. In the future it will be by nuclear
power. We are concerned here with its provision for the South-West of England.
    To ensure this vital supply, Parliament has set up the Central Electricity Generating *f*
Board, which I will call 'the board'. At present they have five power stations to supply
Cornwall and Devon. But these will not last for ever. The board, looking to the future,
feel that they should in time be replaced by one nuclear power station to supply the
whole of the South-West of England. They have five sites under consideration. Any one
of them might be suitable. But it is necessary for the board to survey each of the sites so
as to see if it will take the weight. They have had no difficulty in surveying four of the *g*
possible sites. But they have met with intense opposition in surveying the fifth site. It
is near Luxulyan in Cornwall, on a farm owned by Mr and Mrs Searle. The survey would
only take a few more days. It involves drilling a few holes and making a few seismic tests
with explosives so as to see the nature of the subsoil. After the survey is finished the site
would be left afterwards exactly as it was before. It would be entirely without prejudice
to the future. If the board did eventually think that this site would be the most suitable *h*
of the five, there would have to be a public inquiry at which all objectors could be heard
and a decision by a minister responsible to Parliament. In short, there would be no
nuclear power station built there unless Parliament was satisfied that it was in the
interests of the consumers of electricity in the whole of the South-West of England,
including as they do many industries of much importance.
    This sort of problem is recurrent in modern society. The country as a whole needs to *j*
be provided with reservoirs for water, with military areas for defence, with airports for
travel, with prisons for criminals, and so forth. The local inhabitants object most
strongly. But still it does happen from time to time that their objections have to be
overruled. It is much to be regretted, but, if the national interest so demands, they must
give way, remembering that they are to be fully compensated, so far as money can do it,

a for any property that is compulsorily acquired or any injurious effect to persons or property.

The board met opposition

The board here acted throughout in complete accord with their statutory powers and obligations. They gave due notice to the farmers, Mr and Mrs Searle, and sought their consent to the survey. It was not forthcoming. The board informed them of the
b statutory provision which authorised entry to their land. They gave them notice that they were coming on 24th February 1981. News of it got through to the television people and the newspapers. On 24th February 1981 three of the board's staff and three surveyors approached the site. They had written authority to enter. They found the way blocked by about 60 people, including Mr and Mrs Searle and a group known as 'Luxulyan against Nuclear Development'. The television people were there. Also
c newspaper reporters. Five policemen were present. Two of them controlled the crowd and the traffic. The representatives of the board said to Mr Searle: 'It is obvious that you do not intend to let us on the land.' Mr Searle said: 'That is correct.' So the board's representatives withdrew to the boos of the crowd.

The board got injunctions

d Now this opposition by Mr and Mrs Searle and their supporters was clearly unlawful. There is a section in the Town and Country Planning Act 1971 which makes it a criminal offence. Section 280(9) gives the board power not only to enter land to survey it but also to search and bore so as to ascertain the nature of the subsoil and the presence of minerals thereunder. Section 281(2) says that:

e 'Any person who wilfully obstructs a person acting in the exercise of his powers under section 280 of this Act shall be guilty of an offence and liable on summary conviction to a fine not exceeding £20.'

This has since been increased to £50.

The statute does not, however, contain any power of arrest. But it is clear law that the board can enforce it either by issuing summonses before the magistrates or by applying
f for an injunction in the High Court.

On 4th March 1981 the board issued writs against Mr and Mrs Searle and neighbouring farmers, Mr and Mrs Lawton, asking for an injunction to restrain them from preventing or interfering with the entry of the board onto their land. On 16th March 1981 Boreham J granted the injunction.

The farmers obeyed the injunctions. They no longer blocked the way. On 26th
g March 1981 the board's contractors entered on the land of Mr and Mrs Searle. They did quite a lot of survey work. They were not obstructed until the middle of May 1981. Then several local objectors appeared and sought to obstruct the operations. The contractors brought in drilling rigs and men to operate them. Then local objectors came in motor cars and blocked the entrances. On 19th May 1981 one rig got into the field. Mr John St John Bamford from Bodmin tried to stop it. He held onto it. He had to be
h manhandled clear of the moving rig or he would otherwise have been severely injured, if not killed. Mrs Varcoe and Mr and Mrs Miller threw themselves under an approaching rig and had to be lifted clear of it. On 20th May 1981 drilling was started but objectors then started to climb on the rig and to interfere with the gear levers. This was so dangerous that drilling had to be stopped. One woman chained herself to the rig, and when she left a substitute took her place. The police took the names and addresses of the
j obstructors and the numbers of the cars. They were mainly local people from Luxulyan and places fairly near.

On 22nd May 1981 the board issued a writ against 32 named persons and on the same day Talbot J granted an injunction against them. They too obeyed the injunction and moved off the site. They marched round the roads preceded, it is said, by the Lostwithiel Silver Band.

You might have thought that that would be the end of the matter: and that the rule of law had prevailed. But no. Groups of interlopers then came from far and wide and *a* tried to stop the work. One group, calling itself the Cornish Republican Movement made an overnight attack on another drilling rig at Nancekuke. Another group calling itself the Cornwall Anti-Nuclear Alliance started a systematic campaign of obstruction. They set up headquarters in a caravan. They had seven posts on the farm manned by 17 persons. They took up position in relays. As one party went off, another came on. And so forth. They called one another by their Christian names, Tom, Dick or Harry, or *b* Susan, Mary or Jane, so that no one could discover their true names and addresses. Their organisers issued a leaflet giving instructions to volunteers who came to help them. I will quote part of it so that you may see what they were told to do:

'WELCOME . . .

'1. It is peaceful and friendly—it must be kept that way—if at any time you feel unable to respond in such a way, please walk away from the situation . . . *c*

'5. The Drillers are basically friendly but have a job to do; be "nice" but clear about why you are there.

'6 . . . c) . . . If a rig gets inside the field lie down in front of it, but ALWAYS WARN THE DRIVER FIRST (he cannot see in front of his wheels from the cab) . . . Always explain to them that your actions are NON-VIOLENT . . . (f) . . . If an attampt [sic] is made to move the drill INTO the field, two people must chain themselves to the *d* rig. (You will be told where the keys are kept). NO attempt can legally be made to man-handle you. DO NOT PANIC if the Drillers arrive—they often come to service the Machinery . . .

'7. If you see a seismic team crossing onto the land, follow them . . . If possible, put your foot (umbrella . . .) under the hand-drill to stop a hole being drilled, or otherwise if you are too late for this—Sit on the hole . . . *e*

'10. Do not bring illegal substances onto the site or break the Law in any way— it would only be an excuse for the CEGB to call the Police in and have us all removed . . .'

The board approached the police

These newcomers made things so difficult for the board that they approached the *f* police for help. The difficulty is best described in a letter they wrote to the chief constable:

'Unfortunately, those injunctions have not prevented further interference. Although the local demonstrators have obeyed them and withdrawn, other anti-nuclear objectors from much further afield have now moved on to the Searles' land *g* and are being equally obstructive. Their action has stopped all work on one of two rigs. To try to use it in present circumstances would expose the demonstrators in its immediate vicinity to serious risk of injury. The Board also still have to carry out the survey's final phase, a seismic test, involving a number of controlled explosions. This again would be too dangerous to carry out while demonstrators remain on the land. I understand that the present demonstrators have ignored all *h* requests from Mr. Searle to leave. Although the Board will continue to seek injunctions against any person obstructing the work whom it is able to identify, such action will not end the interference, because the new demonstrators are unknown in the area and their identification is therefore becoming increasingly difficult. Moreover, further replacements appear to be readily available. On the other hand, the Board should only need approximately seven more days of *j* uninterrupted work to complete all aspects of the survey. It is against this background that we seek your assistance. Wilful obstruction of the Board's exercise of its powers under S. 35(1) of the Electricity Act 1957 is a criminal offence under S. 280(2) of the Town and Country Planning Act 1971. All other works in relation to the survey of this site and of the other four sites have been completed . . . We *a* therefore write to ask you for your assistance in enabling the Board to carry out its statutory duties by preventing further unlawful obstruction.'

The chief constable's reply

The chief constable felt, however, that neither he nor his men could do anything to remove the demonstrators. They had no power of arrest. In a letter of 11th June 1981 he said:

b 'I am sure you will appreciate that contentious issues such as the work at Luxulyan place the local officers in an unenviable and sensitive position. We have endeavoured to give the Board every possible assistance and we will continue to do so. The legal position is complicated and the public opposition genuinely and vociferously voiced. Against this background, without a more definitive legal mandate, the police inevitably must maintain their low-key presence to preserve the peace.'

c *The board's application*

Now the board feel that they cannot ask their own staff, or the contractors' men, to turn these people off the site. They want the police to do it. The chief constable says No. He thinks he has no lawful authority to do it. He also thinks that it would harm the relationship of his men to the public.

The board feel that the chief constable is mistaken. On 8th July 1981 they applied for *d* a mandamus to compel him. It was for—

'An order of mandamus directed to the Chief Constable of the Devon & Cornwall Constabulary, requiring him to instruct police officers under his control to remove or assist the Applicant's servants or agents to remove persons obstructing the Applicant's works at Luxulyan in the County of Cornwall.'

e *The law*

Much discussion took place before us about the law. It is common ground that, although the statute gives no power to arrest obstructors, nevertheless the police have power to arrest them if there is a breach of the peace or the reasonable apprehension of it. Also that the police have power to disperse an unlawful assembly. But the question is whether the obstructors were guilty of a breach of the peace, or whether there was any *f* apprehension of it; or whether there was an unlawful assembly.

Breach of the peace

In our present case the police have taken the view that there has been no breach of the peace, nor that there is any apprehension of it, nor that there is an unlawful assembly. This is shown by these extracts from the papers:

g The chief constable in his letter of 11th June 1981:

'Police have remained on private land during the demonstrations at Luxulyan expressly to ensure the preservation of the peace. The demonstrations so far have been of such a nature that possible breaches of the peace and instances of criminal damage have not occurred. Had they done so there would have been a clear *h* opportunity for police to act and they would have done so . . .'

The most detailed report is one made by the Chief Inspector Bradley, who made a report on 2nd July 1981, in which he says:

'The officer with responsibility for Community Policing in the area is Constable 994 Penlerick who has an excellent local knowledge and is a valuable asset in such *j* a situation as he provides me information which gives a clear indication as to attitudes of demonstrators and other local persons . . . You appreciate there is no power of arrest and the Police have the same powers as the CEGB to take the demonstrators' names and report them . . . I would suggest that if we involved ourselves in this context our whole community relationship, which at the present time is second to none, and has taken a considerable length of time to establish, would be in jeopardy ... to date I fail to see that a Breach of the Peace has been occasioned or is likely to be occasioned ...'   *a*

And in the affidavit of the chief constable of 22nd July 1981:

'I am not satisfied that the demonstrators have any intention whatsoever of using violence or committing breaches of the peace or threatening to do so. Their whole behaviour so far has been perfectly peaceful and my Officers have been assured on a number of occasions by various demonstrators that they have no intention or desire to breach the criminal law by the use of violence or by threatened or actual breaches of the peace ...'   *b*

And in the affidavit of Chief Inspector Bradley:

'In the circumstances there is no reason whatsoever for the Police to suspect or have any grounds to believe that a breach of the peace is anticipated; the demonstrators are acting in a very "passive" manner and in no way are they committing a breach of the peace.'   *c*

The conduct of the obstructors

Now I am afraid that I cannot share the view taken by the police. English law upholds to the full the right of people to demonstrate and to make their views known so long as all is done peaceably and in good order (see *Hubbard v Pitt* [1975] 3 All ER 1, [1976] QB *d* 161). But the conduct of these demonstrators is not peaceful or in good order. By wilfully obstructing the operations of the board, they are deliberately breaking the law. Every time they lie down in front of a rig, or put their foot or umbrella down to stop a hole being drilled, or sit on the hole, they are guilty of an offence for which they could be fined up to £50 for every occasion. They must know it is unlawful. They must know of the injunctions granted against the farmers and the local residents. Yet they persist in *e* going on with their unlawful conduct, knowing full well that it is unlawful. Is the law powerless to stop them? Can these people avoid the process of the law by not giving their names and addresses, so that neither a summons nor a writ can reach them? Can they avoid it by bringing in one group after another? I think not. These obstructors should not be in any better position than those against whom injunctions have been obtained. The arm of the law is long enough to reach them despite their attempts to *f* avoid it.

In the first place, I must say that the leaflet issued by the organisers is completely erroneous. The board and their contractors are entitled to manhandle the obstructors so as to move them out of the way. Every person who is prevented from carrying out his lawful pursuits is entitled to use self-help so as to prevent any unlawful obstruction: see *Holmes v Bagge* (1853) 1 E & B 782 at 786–787, 118 ER 629 at 631 per Lord Campbell *g* CJ. He must, of course, not use more force than is reasonably necessary; but there is no doubt whatever that he can use force to do it.

I go further. I think that the conduct of these people, their criminal obstruction, is itself a breach of the peace. There is a breach of the peace whenever a person who is lawfully carrying out his work is unlawfully and physically prevented by another from doing it. He is entitled by law peacefully to go on with his work on his lawful *h* occasions. If anyone unlawfully and physically obstructs the worker, by lying down or chaining himself to a rig or the like, he is guilty of a breach of the peace. Even if this were not enough, I think that their unlawful conduct gives rise to a reasonable apprehension of a breach of the peace. It is at once likely that the lawful worker will resort to self-help by removing the obstructor by force from the vicinity of the work so that he obstructs no longer. He will lift the recumbent obstructor from the ground. *j* This removal would itself be an assault and battery, unless it was justified as being done by way of self-help. Long years ago Holt CJ declared that 'the least touching of another in anger is a battery' (see *Cole v Turner* (1704) Holt KB 108, 90 ER 958). Salmond on Torts (17th Edn, 1977, p 120) adds that even anger is not essential. An 'unwanted kiss may be a battery'. So also the lifting up of a recumbent obstructor would be a battery

unless justified as being done in the exercise of self-help. But in deciding whether there
a is a breach of the peace or the apprehension of it, the law does not go into the rights or
wrongs of the matter, or whether it is justified by self-help or not. Suffice it that the
peace is broken or is likely to be broken by one or another of those present. With the
result that any citizen can, and certainly any police officer can, intervene to stop breaches.

If I were wrong on this point, if there was here no breach of the peace or apprehension
of it, it would give a licence to every obstructor and every passive resister in the land. He
b would be able to cock a snook at the law as these groups have done. Public works of the
greatest national importance could be held up indefinitely. This cannot be. The rule of
law must prevail.

Unlawful assembly

Beyond doubt these groups are guilty of a criminal conspiracy. By combining together
wilfully to obstruct the survey, they are liable to prosecution, provided that the Director
c of Public Prosecutions consents (see ss 1 and 4(1) of the Criminal Law Act 1977).

But were they guilty of an unlawful assembly? The old authorities, going back to
Coke, Blackstone, Stephen and Archbold, all say that an unlawful assembly is an assembly
of three or more persons with intent to commit a crime by open force. I think this case
comes within that statement and I think it is still the law. But I need not go into it
d further, in view of my holding that their conduct is also a breach of the peace.

The authority of the police

I would add one further word. It is to my mind within the authority of the police to
intervene to prevent any criminal offence being committed in their presence, even
though it is only a summary offence, where the offender fails or refuses or avoids giving
his name and address. Even though the statute does not give a power of arrest, the law
e says that a police officer can do whatever is necessary by way of restraint to prevent a
criminal offence being committed or continued. So here the police would in my opinion
be acting within the law if they cleared these obstructors off the site. If any resisted, or
returned afterwards, the police would be entitled to take them before a justice of the
peace who could require them to enter into a recognisance to be of good behaviour.

f ### Mandamus

Notwithstanding all that I have said, I would not give any orders to the chief constable
or his men. It is of the first importance that the police should decide on their own
responsibility what action should be taken in any particular situation. As I said in *R v
Metropolitan Police Comr, ex p Blackburn* [1968] 1 All ER 763 at 769, [1968] 2 QB 118 at
136:
g
'. . . it is for the Commissioner of Police, or the chief constable, as the case may be,
to decide in any particular case where enquiries should be pursued, or whether an
arrest should be made, or a prosecution brought. It must be for him to decide on
the disposition of his force and the concentration of his resources on any particular
crime or area. No court can or should give him direction on such a matter. He can
also make policy decisions and give effect to them, as, for instance, was often done
h when prosecutions were not brought for attempted suicide; but there are some
policy decisions with which, I think, the courts in a case can, if necessary, interfere.'

The decision of the chief constable not to intervene in this case was a policy decision
with which I think the courts should not interfere. All that I have done in this judgment
is to give the 'definitive legal mandate' which he sought. It should enable him to
j reconsider their position. I hope he will decide to use his men to clear the obstructors off
the site or at any rate help the board to do so.

The board's position

It is plain that the board can use self-help so as to get rid of this wilful obstruction. To
me the obvious solution would be to erect a fence around their place of work, a barbed-

wire entanglement if need be, so as to prevent the obstructors getting anywhere near the operations. This is just common sense, so that they should not be a danger to themselves *a* or to others. If they should try and break through the fence, or rush it, the battle would be on. There would be the clearest possible breach of the peace. The police would move in, arrest them, and take them before the magistrates. So I would say to the board, put up a fence and get on with your work. Stand no more of this obstruction.

For the reasons I have given, however, I would make no order against the police. The appeal should be dismissed.   *b*

LAWTON LJ. This appeal has two aspects, the general and the particular. The general can be described as follows: can those who disapprove of the exercise by a statutory body of statutory powers frustrate their exercise on private property by adopting unlawful means, not involving violence, such as lying down in front of moving vehicles, chaining themselves to equipment and sitting down where work has to be done. Such means are *c* sometimes referred to as passive resistance. The answer is an emphatic No. If it were otherwise, there would be no rule of law. Parliament decides who shall have statutory powers and under what conditions and for what purpose they shall be used. Those who do not like what Parliament has done can protest, but they must do so in a lawful manner. What cannot be tolerated, and certainly not by the police, are protests which are not made in a lawful manner.   *d*

A statutory body can use the minimum of force reasonably necessary to remove those obstructing the exercise of their statutory powers from the area where work has to be carried out. This is the common law remedy of abatement by self-help; but it would involve the statutory body taking the law into its own hands and is, as Lord Wright said in *Sedleigh-Denfield v O'Callagan* [1940] 3 All ER 349 at 369, [1940] AC 880 at 911, much to be discouraged. There are many reasons why self-help should be discouraged. *e* Disputes are likely to arise whether the minimum amount of force reasonably necessary was used. In my judgment, based on my understanding of human nature and a long experience of the administration of criminal justice, the most important reason for not using self-help, if any other remedy can be used effectively, is that as soon as one person starts to, or makes to, lay hands on another there is likely to be a breach of the peace. Those obstructing may assert that they will allow themselves to be removed without *f* resisting; but, when the manhandling starts, particularly if a man has to lay hands on a woman, struggling and uproar are likely to begin. I should have expected most police constables to appreciate that this is so; and as they have a duty to deal with breaches of the peace which actually occur or which they have reasonable cause for suspecting are about to occur, those who see what is happening should act either by trying to persuade those obstructing to stop doing so or arresting them if they persist in their unlawful conduct. *g* In many cases those who persist to the point of having to be arrested will commit some other offence in doing so, such as obstructing or assaulting police officers in the execution of their duty: see s 51 of the Police Act 1954. If no other offence is committed, the police constable making the arrest should take the person arrested before the local magistrates to show cause why he should not be bound over, with or without sureties, to keep the peace and be of good behaviour: see s 115 of the Magistrates' Courts Act 1980.   *h*

If the obstructors are three or more in number and by conduct show an intention to use violence to achieve their aims or otherwise behave in a tumultuous manner, any police constables present have the duty to disperse them because those present and forming part of the gathering will be committing the offence of unlawful assembly. I do not accept counsel's submission on behalf of the Central Electricity Generating Board (to whom hereafter I shall refer as 'the board') that an unlawful assembly comes about *j* whenever three or more persons gather to commit any crime. Unlawful assembly is one of a number of common law crimes designed to uphold public order and to protect the public generally against lawlessness and disorder: see the speech of Lord Hailsham LC in *Kamara v Director of Public Prosecutions* [1973] 2 All ER 1242 at 1248. Comments in 3 Co Inst 176 and 4 Bl Com (14th Edn, 1803) 146 which seem to show that an unlawful assembly can occur without the factor of either violence or tumult do not accurately state

a the modern law.

So much for the broad aspect of this appeal. I turn now to the particular. By letter dated 1st June 1981 the chairman of the board told the chief constable how they had been obstructed in carrying out their statutory duties, what steps they had taken by way of civil proceedings to stop the obstruction and what prevented the further effective use of civil remedies. The penultimate paragraph of the letter ended with these words:

b
'We therefore write to ask you for your assistance in enabling the Board to carry out its statutory duties by preventing further unlawful obstruction. We would be grateful if you would let us know when the police assistance will be available, so that the Board can arrange for a suitable programme for the completion of the survey.'

The chief constable answered by letter dated 11th June 1981. He described the board's

c difficulties as being of a quasi-private nature. They were not. He ended his letter as follows:

'The demonstrations so far have been of such a nature that possible breaches of the peace and instances of criminal damage have not occurred. Had they done so there would have been a clear opportunity for police to act and they would have done so. I am sure you will appreciate that contentious issues such as the work at Luxulyan

d place the local officers in an unenviable and sensitive position. We have endeavoured to give the Board every possible assistance and we will continue to do so. The legal position is complicated and the public opposition genuinely and vociferously voiced. Against this background, without a more definitive legal mandate, the police inevitably must maintain their low-key presence to preserve the peace.'

The drafting of this letter can be criticised; but I can see no useful purpose in subjecting

e it to critical analysis. The chief constable's stance was reasonably clear: he was saying, as he was entitled to do, that on the information then available to him he did not anticipate any breaches of the peace.

The board were dissatisfied with the chief constable's answer to their request for help and applied to the Divisional Court for an order of mandamus directed to the chief constable requiring him to instruct police officers under his control to remove or assist

f the board's servants or agents to remove persons obstructing their works at Luxulyan in the county of Cornwall. That application, in my judgment, showed a misconception of the powers of chief constables. They command their forces but they cannot give an officer under command an order to do acts which can only lawfully be done if the officer himself with reasonable cause suspects that a breach of the peace has occurred or is imminently likely to occur or an arrestable offence has been committed. In July 1981

g the Chief Constable of Devon and Cornwall could have, and probably did, order some of his constables to watch what was going on in the field where the board wanted to exercise their statutory powers; but what he could not do was to give unqualified orders to his officers to remove those who were obstructing the board's work. Any orders he gave would have to have qualifying words to the effect that those obstructing should be removed if, but only if, there was a breach of the peace or an imminent likelihood of one

h or an unlawful assembly formed.

The issue between the board and the chief constable got befogged by conflicting evidence which each received at the beginning of July 1981. By letter dated 2nd July 1981 the board's agents on the site, a firm of consulting engineers, made the following report:

j
'As you know we have at all times been very careful to pull back from the point of actual physical contact with the protesters. There have been a number of occasions when relatively harmless jostling has reached the point where to have continued was obviously going to lead to more serious violence, and potentially the most dangerous situation was the time when Mr. Bamforth had to be manhandled clear of the moving rig when he would otherwise have been severely injured if not

killed. A similar situation arose with Mrs. Varco and Mr. & Mrs. Millar when they
threw themselves under the rig approaching B.H.26. These incidents and the many *a*
discussions we have had with the protesters make it abundantly clear that certainly
the more militant of them are keen to provoke a violent confrontation, which we
most certainly wish to avoid.'

Counsel for the chief constable told us that the police had not witnessed anything which
could be described as a breach of the peace. On the same day, a chief inspector stationed
at St Austell made a report to his superintendent at Launceston, giving a history of what *b*
had happened and his assessment of the situation. This report was forwarded to the chief
constable. In a paragraph of it describing what had happened at the end of April 1981
he stated: 'It was obvious that any move by the CEGB would be met by resistance from
the demonstrators present and also reinforcements obtained locally.' He made it clear
that in his opinion the board could not protect itself by injunctions since it was obvious
to him that 'the intention would be to replace persons served with injunctions with new *c*
demonstrators'. Towards the end of his report came this passage:

'I would suggest that if we involved ourselves in this context our whole
community relationship, which at the present time is second to none, and has taken
a considerable length of time to establish, would be in jeopardy. Likewise, to date,
I fail to see that a Breach of the Peace has been occasioned or is likely to be
occasioned, and if it had, our powers are such that we could only place the defendants *d*
before the Court, who in turn only have limited powers of dealing with them for
a period of time, during which time they would be replaced by others as has
happened with the service of injunctions. We must not take sides in this dispute.
I do not feel we should act as agents for the C.E.G.B and our relationship with the
local community should remain untarnished. To date, no arrests have been made
and no persons have been reported for any offence in connection with these *e*
demonstrations. The demonstrators have behaved in a most law abiding manner
and seem to be fulfilling their intentions of keeping their demonstrations within
the criminal law.'

I was surprised to read, and I would like to think that the chief constable was too, that a
senior police officer could have been of the opinion that the situation which he described *f*
was not likely to cause a breach of the peace. The demonstrators were not behaving in
a most law-abiding manner, nor were they keeping their demonstrations within the
criminal law. They were all committing offences under ss 280 and 281(2) of the Town
and Country Planning Act 1971. What matters, however, is not the chief inspector's
errors in law but his assessment of what was likely to happen. The unlawful obstruction
was going on in his area; his officers were reporting to him what they had seen; he may *g*
himself have watched what was happening. Although he may have put too much stress
on keeping on good terms with those in the area who did not want a nuclear power
station built there, there is nothing in his report or in the other evidence to suggest that
his assessment of the situation was not his honest opinion. The chief constable was
entitled to accept it and he did. This led him to state in the affidavit which he swore in
opposition to the board's application for an order of mandamus that he was not satisfied *h*
that the demonstrators had any intention of using violence or committing breaches of
the peace.

The issue was further befogged by the chief constable averring, on legal advice, first
that he was not satisfied 'that force should be used in the present circumstances either by
the Board or by anyone else' and, second, that the board should deal with the problem by
taking further proceedings. If the chief constable was purporting to tell the board when *j*
they could use self-help, he had no right to do so any more than the board had any right,
if they ever thought they had, to call on the chief constable to provide muscle power to
remove those who were obstructing the exercise of their statutory powers. Police
constables are no one's lackeys; but they do have a duty to preserve the peace no matter
how unpopular that may make them with some sections of the community.

Both sides in this dispute now know the other's point of view. The chief constable
a knows that the board's consulting engineers anticipate that some of those obstructing
their work are keen to provoke a violent confrontation. The board know that any police
officers who may be watching what is going on cannot act unless they see a breach of the
peace or have reasonable cause for suspecting that there is a real and imminent risk of one
occurring or that those present, being three or more in number, by their conduct show
an intention to use violence or behave in a tumultuous way. If those obstructing do
b allow themselves to be removed without struggling or causing uproar (which to me
seems unlikely, but I may be wrong) the police will have no reason for taking action, nor
should they.

On the evidence it seems likely that the board will have to use self-help if they are to
perform their statutory duties at Luxulyan. Civil proceedings have been ineffective.
Prosecutions for offences under ss 280 and 281(2) of the Town and Country Planning Act
c 1971 would serve no useful purpose. When they do decide to use self-help and fix a day
for doing so, they should inform the local police who will no doubt be present in
sufficient numbers to ensure as best they can that breaches of the peace do not occur and,
if they do, that those responsible are removed from the site.

In my judgment this is not a case for making an order of mandamus against the chief
constable. It is a case for co-operation between the board and the chief constable and the
d use of plenty of common sense by all concerned, including those who are on the site
obstructing the board's functions.

I would dismiss the appeal.

TEMPLEMAN LJ. The CEGB seek the help of the police in removing obstructors
who are preventing the board from surveying a possible site for the construction of a
e nuclear power station.

A protest against the construction of a nuclear power station has lasted for six months
and the obstructors intend to continue the protest, if possible, until the board abandon
their attempts to survey the site.

By s 35(1) of the Electricity Act 1957 and s 280 of the Town and Country Planning Act
1971 as applied to the 1957 Act, the board have power and are seeking to exercise power
f to survey part of a farm in Cornwall owned by Mr and Mrs Searle and to make bore holes
and to carry out controlled explosions to test the subsoil with the object of discovering
whether the land is a suitable site for the construction of a nuclear power station.

Section 281(2) of the Town and Country Planning Act 1971 provides: 'Any person
who wilfully obstructs a person acting in the exercise of his powers under section 280 of
this Act shall be guilty of an offence.'

g The police have no powers of arrest for an offence against this statutory provision of
the criminal law. Any person who wilfully obstructs the board in the exercise of their
powers also commits a tort for which the board may exercise their civil remedies. The
police have no powers to arrest anyone for breach of this civil law.

Thus the board have the legal right to enter on the farm and to conduct operations in
order to determine whether the land is suitable for the site of a nuclear power station and
h any person who interferes with the exercise by the board of their rights commits a breach
of the criminal and the civil law. The obstructors believe that the construction of a
nuclear power station on this site would be a national and local disaster. Other people
may believe that the construction of a nuclear power station is essential and that the
advantages of building such a power station on this site will outweigh the
disadvantages. Other people may have no opinion at all about the matter or vaguely
j dislike or favour the construction of a nuclear power station on this site without any
strong feeling one way or another. The judges and the police are not asked to decide
whether a nuclear power station on this site would represent progress or catastrophe.
The tasks of the judges and the police are to uphold the law and maintain order.

Those who oppose the construction of a nuclear power station on the site are entitled
to demonstrate their disapproval and to organise opposition. The obstructors have

carried their opposition further. They have occupied the site with the object of forcibly preventing the board from exercising their statutory rights. The interference of the obstructors is forcible because they intrude themselves so that the board cannot exercise their statutory rights without endangering limbs and lives. The obstructors lie on the ground in front of vehicles, handcuff themselves to machinery and place themselves in proximity to explosive charges. The board in these circumstances are prevented from exercising their rights until the board have removed or procured the removal of the obstructors from the site. The obstructors assert that they are passive resisters, that is to say they claim that they will not offer physical violence to prevent the board from removing them; but they will not remove themselves and can only be removed bodily by others. If they are removed bodily, they have every intention of returning unless they are subjected to physical or legal restraints and each obstructor who is removed knows that another obstructor will if possible replace him as an obstacle in the path of the exercise by the board of their rights.

The board possess a legal remedy against each obstructor. The board can obtain and in some cases have obtained an injunction restraining a defendant from interfering with the exercise by the board of their statutory rights. Disobedience to such an order involves contempt of court for which the defendant can be fined or committed to prison. But there is no evidence that any breach of an injunction has been committed or threatened. In any event, the remedy does not avail the board to establish conditions under which they can exercise their rights. A defendant must be identified and served with legal proceedings and evidence must be produced that the defendant interfered or threatens to interfere with the rights of the board. In the same way as any obstructor removed bodily from the site will be replaced by another, so every obstructor restrained by injunction will be replaced by another obstructor against whom proceedings have still to be launched. The organisation of a state of affairs under which every obstructor who is removed or restrained is replaced by another obstructor constitutes a conspiracy to prevent the board from exercising their statutory rights. But such a conspiracy only gives further grounds for the grant of an injunction against an identified conspirator.

The board possess the remedy of self-help. The board are entitled to exercise that remedy by forcibly clearing the site of obstructors and by preventing obstructors from returning to the site or from entering the site. The board may only use the minimum of force reasonably necessary for the purposes of asserting their rights. The board, as a responsible public authority, are in practice unable to help themselves without the help of the police. The board may be faced with abuse or propaganda and with violence despite the protestations of the campaign leaders. The board may be falsely accused of excessive force in removing or restraining the obstructors.

In these circumstances the board are entitled to ask for the assistance of the police. The police are entitled to assist the board by supervising and controlling the clearance of the site by the board and by approving the steps proposed and taken by the board to prevent obstructors from returning to the site or entering the site by means of manned fences or other reasonable means.

The police are also entitled to assist the board by the police themselves arresting or removing or restraining the obstructors if there is an imminent danger of a breach of the peace or if a breach of the peace is committed in consequence of the resistance, threatened or actual, passive or violent, of an obstructor to his own removal and restraint.

It was suggested that the police have no powers in relation to passive resisters on private land. This is not the case. In addition to other powers possessed by the police, they are entitled to enter on private land at the invitation of the owner or at the invitation of any person who himself has a right to be on the land. The board are entitled to enter on the site and to complete the survey and they are entitled to invite the police to enter on the site to assist the board to establish conditions under which the board will be able to complete the survey without any outbreaks of violence taking place.

It was also suggested that the powers of the police to deal with passive resisters are limited, that the obstructors have discovered a loophole in the law and that, if action is to be taken against passive resisters, Parliament must pass further legislation. In my

a   judgment, the common law is sufficiently robust and sufficiently sensible to be able to put an end to a six month campaign of lawlessness characterised by physical interference with the rights of others, whether in a good cause or a bad cause and whether in the form of passive resistance or any other form of resistance. There is no need for further statutory extensions of police powers which at present balance the rights of individuals and protesters against the policy of the state and the requirements of law and order and

b   provide a workable compromise between these considerations.

The police have ample power to supervise the clearance of the site by the board and to assist the board by the police themselves arresting or removing and restraining the obstructors in order to prevent breaches of the peace which are reasonably apprehended or which are committed by any person as a result of the insistence by the obstructors in remaining on the site or entering on the site or returning to the site. The police, like the

c   board, may only use the minimum of force reasonably necessary to enable the board to establish and maintain conditions under which they will be able to complete the survey. The police may be faced with abuse or propaganda or with violence despite the protestations of the protest campaign leaders and may need to prevent or terminate violence provoked by the presence or by the activities of the obstructors. The police, like the board, may be falsely accused of excessive force in removing or restraining the

d   obstructors. The duties of the police frequently involve similar problems which must be faced.

Without the assistance of the police, the board have been inhibited from employing their remedy of self-help so that they might assert their rights and perform their duties of completing the survey for fear of resistance and misrepresentation on the part of the obstructors. The police have been reluctant to assist because they were afraid of

e   unpopularity, uncertain of their powers and reluctant to exercise their powers for fear of resistance and misrepresentation on the part of the obstructors.

The board and the police may instruct the obstructors to leave the site and warn them that if they do not leave the site and remain off the site the obstructors will be liable to be forcibly removed or arrested. If after such a warning the board enter the site with the object of completing the survey, the possibility of a confrontation with the obstructors

f   will at once raise a danger of breaches of the peace when the board's workmen seek to carry out their work and find the obstructors lying in their path. An obstructor who will not leave the site unless he is forcibly removed presents a threat and danger of a breach of the peace even if he disclaims any intention of causing a breach of the peace. The board have only acquiesced in six months' interruption of the survey because they rightly fear violence if they persist. The police are only present at the site because they

g   rightly fear violence if the board resume their work. Even Mahatma Gandhi discovered to his sorrow that in the conduct of ordinary mortals passive resistance only remains passive so long as the resistance is successful.

The police on the spot must decide when to intervene. I consider that they will be fully justified in intervening if the board enter the site with the intention of completing the survey and the obstructors decline to leave. But in any event the police will be

h   entitled to intervene if an obstructor resists being carried away from the site or runs to another part of the site or tries to enter the site or tries to return to the site, thus obliging the board's representatives to seize him so that he may be permanently excluded. Such conduct by an obstructor, whether he calls himself a passive resister or not, will create an imminent and serious danger of a breach of the peace for which the obstructor will be responsible and liable to arrest or removal by the police.

j   The present campaign has been successful for six months and the campaigners seek a permanent success flouting the civil law and the criminal law. The success of the campaign to date has been made possible by the physical interference of the obstructors with the lawful activities of the board, by the reluctance of the board to perform their functions in the face of opposition and the reluctance of the police to carry out their duty for fear of unpopularity, recriminations, assaults and misrepresentations. The board and the police have difficult tasks to perform and their interventions may be exploited and misrepresented, but, if persuasion fails, action must follow.   *a*

The police are not bound in all circumstances to act every time there is a breach of the law, criminal or civil. In the present case, if the obstructors had chosen to occupy the site for a short period to demonstrate the strength of their feelings and the amount of support for their views, I would not have expected the board or the police to take any action. The distinguishing and disturbing feature of the present case is the undisguised intention of the obstructors by physical interference to deprive the board permanently of their power   *b* to perform functions which Parliament has imposed on the board and by an organised campaign of passive resistance, which constitutes both force and a threat, to infringe the civil rights of the board and the criminal code of the Town and Country Planning Act 1971 until the board, and the police representing law and order, are driven to admit defeat.

The present litigation is due partly to the understandable desire of the police to be   *c* certain of the extent and limitations of their powers and partly to the understandable desire of the board to obtain the assistance of the police in the unpleasant task of removing and restraining the obstructors so that the board can complete their survey. In my judgment, the powers of the police and the board are adequate to ensure that the law prevails.

But it is for the police and the board to co-operate and to decide on and implement the   *d* most effective method of dealing with the obstructors. The court cannot tell the police how and when their powers should be exercised, for the court cannot judge the explosiveness of the situation or deal with the individual problems which will arise as a result of the activities of the obstructors. This court can and does confirm that the police have powers to remove and arrest passive resisters in the circumstances which prevail at the site when the board resume their work to complete their survey. This court can and   *e* does indicate that the time has come for the board and the police to exercise their respective powers so that the survey may be completed.

Appeal dismissed. No order as to costs in Court of Appeal or Divisional Court.

Solicitors: *Hywel M Thomas* (for the board); *Neville B Jennings* (for the chief constable).   *f*

Diana Procter   Barrister.

R v Folkestone and Hythe Juvenile Court, ex *g* parte R (a juvenile)

QUEEN'S BENCH DIVISION
LORD LANE CJ, KILNER BROWN AND MCCULLOUGH JJ
6th OCTOBER 1981   *h*

*Magistrates – Committal for sentence – Committal with view to borstal sentence – Power to commit – Legislation conferring power to commit replaced by later legislation – Proceedings commenced before new legislation in operation – Committal required to be made under old legislation – New and old legislation in similar terms – Minute of adjudication and copy sent to Crown Court stating committal made under new legislation – Court rules not requiring minute   *j* or copy sent to Crown Court to state statute under which committal made – Whether committal void – Magistrates' Courts Act 1980, s 37(1), Sch 8, para 2.*

Proceedings charging criminal offences against the applicant, a juvenile, were commenced in a magistrates' court before 6th July 1981, ie before the date of commencement of the Magistrates' Courts Act 1980, which consolidated certain enactments relating to

magistrates' courts, including the Magistrates' Courts Act 1952. By virtue of para 2[a] of
a Sch 8 to the 1980 Act, the 1952 Act continued to apply to proceedings commenced
before 6th July 1981. On 6th July 1981 the applicant pleaded guilty to the charges and
on 27th July the magistrates convicted him and made an order committing him to the
Crown Court with a view to a borstal sentence. Power to make such a committal order
was conferred on magistrates by s 28(1) of the 1952 Act, which was replaced by s 37(1)[b]
of the 1980 Act. The minute of the magistrates' adjudication entered in the court
b register pursuant to r 54 of the Magistrates' Courts Rules 1968 and the copy of the
minute sent to the Crown Court pursuant to r 16(1) of those rules were accurate in all
respects save that they stated that the committal was made under s 37(1) of the 1980 Act
whereas, by virtue of para 2 of Sch 8 to the 1980 Act, the committal was made under the
powers conferred by s 28(1) of the 1952 Act. The 1968 rules did not, however, require
either the minute of adjudication entered in the court register or the copy of the minute
c sent to the Crown Court to state the statute under which a committal for sentence was
made. On 17th August 1981 the Crown Court sentenced the applicant to borstal
training. The applicant applied for an order of certiorari to quash the committal order
on the ground that the error in stating that the committal was made under the 1980 Act
vitiated the committal order and made it a nullity.

d **Held** – Since the magistrates had power under s 28(1) of the 1952 Act to commit the
applicant to the Crown Court for sentence and it was unnecessary under the 1968 rules
for the minute of adjudication or the copy sent to the Crown Court to state the statute
under which the committal was made, the statement that the committal had been made
under the 1980 Act in the minute of adjudication and in the copy sent to the Crown
Court had been a mere error of surplusage which could be disregarded. Accordingly, the
e committal was valid and the application would be dismissed (see p 846 *d* and p 847 *e f*
and *h j*, post).

Meek v Powell [1952] 1 All ER 347 and *R v Kent Justices, ex parte Machin* [1952] 1 All ER
1123 distinguished.

R v Huntingdon Justices, ex parte Simpkin and Coombes (1959) 123 JP 166 considered.

Notes
f For committal with a view to borstal sentence, see 29 Halsbury's Laws (4th Edn) para
400, and for cases on procedure under summary jurisdiction, see 33 Digest (Repl) 195–
203, 383–435.

For the Magistrates' Courts Act 1980, s 37, Sch 8, see 50(2) Halsbury's Statutes (3rd
Edn) 1476, 1603.

g **Cases referred to in judgments**
Meek v Powell [1952] 1 All ER 347, [1952] 1 KB 164, 116 JP 116, 50 LGR 247, DC, 33
Digest (Repl) 202, 430.
R v Cockshot [1898] 1 QB 582, [1895–9] All ER Rep 253, 67 LJQB 467, 78 LT 168, 62 JP
325, 19 Cox CC 3, 14(1) Digest (Reissue) 148, 1033.
R v Edgar, R v Parr, R v Pontika, R v Rooney [1958] 2 All ER 494, 122 JP 342, 42 Cr App
h R 192, CCA, 14(1) Digest (Reissue) 226, 1621.
R v Gee, R v Bibby, R v Dunscombe [1936] 2 All ER 89, [1936] 2 KB 442, 105 LJKB 739, 155
LT 31, 100 JP 227, 34 LGR 265, 30 Cox CC 432, 25 Cr App R 198, CCA, 14(1) Digest
(Reissue) 226, 1618.
R v Grant [1944] 2 All ER 311, 30 Cr App R 99, CCA, 14(2) Digest (Reissue) 660, 5355.
R v Huntingdon Justices, ex parte Simpkin and Coombes (1959) 123 JP 166, DC.
j *R v Kent Justices, ex parte Machin* [1952] 1 All ER 1123, [1952] 2 QB 355, 116 JP 242, 36
Cr App R 23, DC, 14(2) Digest (Reissue) 715, 6006.
R v Wharmby, Lindley and Lindley (1946) 31 Cr App R 174, CCA, 14(1) Digest (Reissue)
226, 1619.

---

a   Schedule 8, para 2 is set out at p 843 *b c*, post
b   Section 37, so far as material, is set out at p 842 *h j*, post

Cases also cited

R v Octigan [1966] Crim LR 622, CCA.

R v South Greenhoe Justices, ex parte Director of Public Prosecutions [1950] 2 All ER 42, sub nom *R v Norfolk Justices, ex parte Director of Public Prosecutions* [1950] 2 KB 558, DC.

Application for judicial review

R, a juvenile, applied, with the leave of the Divisional Court granted on 6th October 1981, for an order of certiorari to quash an order made by the Folkestone and Hythe Juvenile Court on 27th July 1981 committing him to the Crown Court with a view to a sentence of borstal training pursuant to s 37 of the Magistrates' Courts Act 1980, and that all proceedings on the order be stayed until after the hearing of the application or further order. The ground of the application was that the committal order was wrong in law because the juvenile court had no power to make it under s 37 of the 1980 Act, because the proceedings against the applicant had been commenced prior to 6th July 1981, the date on which the 1980 Act came into operation, and it ought to have been made under s 28 of the Magistrates' Courts Act 1952. The facts are set out in the judgment of Lord Lane CJ.

John Hazan QC and *Robert Cooney* for the applicant.
Michael Hill QC and *Allan Green* for the prosecutor.

LORD LANE CJ. This is an application by leave by way of judicial review praying for an order of certiorari to remove into this court and to quash an order made by a lower court in respect of the committal to the Crown Court for sentence purportedly under s 37 of the Magistrates' Courts Act 1980. It is said that the proceedings by which the applicant was committed to the Crown Court with a view to a sentence of borstal training were a nullity.

It is a case which, if I may respectfully say so, has been argued with great clarity and skill by counsel on each side, and we understand that it is a matter which is likely to affect a very large number of cases up and down the country where a similar error to the one committed in this case has taken place.

The facts which lie behind the case are these. The applicant was at the material times a youth of 15. On 31st May 1981 he was arrested for a breaking and entering offence at Sainsbury's in Folkestone. He was released to the custody of his father. The offence was committed some time between 29th May and 1st June.

He was rearrested on 30th June and charged with an offence at the Globe public house, Folkestone, and another offence at the premises of a concern called Spain & White. Those were counts 1 and 2 eventually laid against him.

On 1st July he made his first appearance in court in respect of these matters and he was remanded to a place called Oakhurst Home. On 3rd July he was charged with the first offence which I have already mentioned, the Sainsbury's offence.

He appeared at court on 6th July and pleaded guilty to all three offences. On 27th July he was committed for sentence, purportedly, as I say, under s 37 of the 1980 Act, and 17th August saw him before the Crown Court where he was sent to borstal training.

The terms of the Magistrates' Courts Act 1980, s 37(1) are as follows:

'Where a person is convicted by a magistrates' court of an offence punishable on summary conviction with imprisonment, then, if on the day of the conviction he is not less than 15 but under 21 years old and is a person who under section 1(2) and (4) of the Criminal Justice Act 1961 may be committed for a sentence of borstal training, the court may commit him in custody or on bail to the Crown Court for sentence in accordance with the provisions of section 20 of the Criminal Justice Act 1948.'

That particular section is in words which, to all intents and purposes, are precisely similar to those of the Act which preceded it, the relevant provision being s 28(1) of the Magistrates' Courts Act 1952, as amended. The only difference between the two Acts is

simply a transposition of certain words which deal with the section of the Criminal
a Justice Act 1961; it is a distinction without any difference. The words are the same.

But the difficulty arises in this case in the following way. The appointed day for the
coming into operation of the 1980 Act was 6th July 1981. That was the very day of
course on which this young man pleaded guilty to the charges in the magistrates'
court. There are tucked away in the Act transitional provisions which are to be found in
Sch 8, para 2, and those read as follows:

b
> '(1) Where proceedings were commenced before the appointed day, the old
> enactments relating to the proceedings continue to apply and nothing in this Act
> affects those enactments.
> '(2) Without prejudice to the generality of sub-paragraph (1) above, the old
> enactments relating to proceedings which continue in force by virtue of it include
> any provision of those enactments which creates an offence, which relates to civil or
c
> criminal procedure, which relates to the punishment for an offence, or which relates
> to enforcing, appealing against, questioning, varying or rescinding anything ordered
> or done in the proceedings.'

Those provisions relate to penalties and also to procedures. They relate both to trial
and to disposal of the offender after trial.
d Happily, in this case we do not have to enter onto the vexed territory of what
'proceedings were commenced' means. There is a wealth of authority on that subject,
but it is conceded by both counsel, and indeed is clear, that, whatever meaning may be
given to the words 'Where proceedings were commenced', proceedings here had certainly
commenced before 6th July because not only had this young man been charged with the
various offences before that date, but he had also made his first appearance before the
e magistrates on 1st July, which was five days before the 1980 Act came into force.

The way in which the minute of adjudication was sent forward to the Crown Court
was as follows. The name of the informant or complainant in each of the three cases was
Det Con Lloyd. The name of the defendant was NJR in each case. There set out
accurately in each case is: the nature of the offence; the Theft Act 1968 and the correct
section and subsection of the 1968 Act which it was alleged had been broken; the date of
f offence accurately set out in each of the three cases; plea or consent to order in each case,
'Admits F.J.C. [ie the Folkestone and Hythe Juvenile Court] 6.7.81'; and then finally, in
the final column 'Minute of Adjudication' (and this is the material part of course),
'Committed in custody to Crown Court for sentence of Borstal Training (MCA. 1980,
section 37). Legal Aid granted.'

It is plain, having read the transitional provisions and having set out the chronology
g of events, that that was the incorrect way of stating what the justices had done. In fact
what they should have done to get the matter correct was to have used exactly the same
words in all the columns, including the final column, save for the words in brackets. The
words in brackets should have read 'MCA. 1952, section 28(1)'.

It is submitted by counsel for the applicant that that error vitiates the committal,
which thereby becomes a nullity. He would submit, and does submit, that in those
h circumstances the applicant is entitled to succeed and entitled to have held in his favour
that these proceedings were void and should be quashed.

The way he puts the matter is this. He submits that the magistrates' court in the
exercise of their powers are creatures of statute. They must operate strictly in accordance
with the terms of their statute, and, if they deviate from that straight and narrow way,
what they do is without jurisdiction and will be held to be null and void. Moreover, he
j says, statutes dealing with the disposition of offenders must be strictly construed.

He points correctly to the mistake procedure which exists under the new Act in s 142,
which there is no need for me to read, imposing a 28-day limitation on the correction of
mistakes by the magistrates, and to its precursor, which was s 41 of the Criminal Justice
Act 1972, which originally gave the same power but to a lesser extent because 14 days
was originally the period during which the mistake had to be rectified, but that was
enlarged a little later in 1972 to a period of 28 days.

He points out that those provisions show that, where there has been an error of this sort, then the power to amend the error is one which itself is limited very strictly by the statute which gives the power.

The various authorities on which counsel for the applicant relied can perhaps be rather more briefly dealt with even than he himself dealt with them, because there are certain of them which appear to me not to be relevant at all. There are, however, two in his list of authorities to which it is necessary to refer.

The first one of those is *R v Kent Justices, ex parte Machin* [1952] 1 All ER 1123, [1952] 2 QB 355. In that case the applicant had consented to be dealt with summarily and was convicted by a court of summary jurisdiction of obtaining credit by fraud and of larceny, and was committed to quarter sessions for sentence under the Criminal Justice Act 1948. The error which the court made there was the failure to explain to the applicant that he might be so committed, as was required by statute, and on the basis of that error he applied for an order of certiorari.

It was held by this court under the presidency of Lord Goddard CJ that the provisions of the statutes were peremptory, and, therefore, the convictions were bad because the justices, although with the consent of the applicant, had dealt with the cases summarily without complying with those provisions, and the order for certiorari was accordingly granted and the conviction quashed.

There is one passage of the report which is rewarding to read. It reads as follows ([1952] 1 All ER 1123 at 1124, [1952] 2 QB 355 at 360):

'Following the reasoning of the court in *R. v. Cockshott* ([1898] 1 QB 582, [1895–9] All ER Rep 253), we think we must give effect to the provisions of sched. IX to the Act of 1948, and we must, therefore, hold that the order for certiorari must go and these convictions must be quashed because the justices took on themselves, although with the consent of the applicant, to try the cases summarily without a strict compliance with all the statutory provisions which now allow an indictable offence to be dealt with summarily. It was a very venial offence in the justices and one can well understand their overlooking a provision tucked away in a schedule as this one is, but the applicant is entitled to take advantage of it, and, therefore, we hold the committal and the convictions to be bad.'

In that case the justices had omitted in the course of their trying of the applicant, and in the course of their procedural behaviour had failed, to take a step which the statute demanded that they must take before exercising their powers. Although in the circumstances of that particular case it may have been something of a technicality because the man had consented to be dealt with in that way, yet, nevertheless, an important procedural step had been omitted.

That is not the case here. It is conceded on all hands that everything done by the justices was done strictly according to the book until it came to the very last minute, namely the recording of the Act under which they were purporting to proceed. It seems to me that that case can easily be distinguished on that basis.

The next case is another decision of this court, *Meek v Powell* [1952] 1 All ER 347, [1952] 1 KB 164. In that case the respondent was convicted by a court of summary jurisdiction on two informations charging him with offences under the Food and Drugs Act 1938. That section was repealed by, but re-enacted in identical terms in, s 9 of the Food and Drugs Act 1950, which came into force on 1st January 1951. The respondent appealed against the convictions to quarter sessions, who held the informations to be bad as charging an offence under a repealed statute. They refused to amend them and quashed the convictions.

It was held by the Divisional Court, consisting of Lord Goddard CJ again, Byrne and Parker JJ, that the informations were not validated by the provisions of s 36 of the 1951 Act, that the convictions were bad for the reason given by quarter sessions and that quarter sessions had power to amend an information only in cases where the court of summary jurisdiction had that power, and the latter court had no power so to do when

once it had recorded a conviction on the information. Quarter sessions therefore had no
a choice but to quash the convictions.

Byrne J, who delivered the leading judgment, had this to say ([1952] 1 KB 164 at 167):

> 'But, it is nevertheless of importance that a conviction should be obtained under
> the correct statute, although the wording of the provision repealed may be
> reproduced in a later statute.'

b There again, although there are similarities between the present case and *Meek v
Powell*, yet in that case it was a case of the information being laid under the wrong Act
and therefore the man, on the face of it, had been convicted under a non-existent Act.
Conviction is one thing, but disposal for sentence seems to me to be something entirely
different.

We were referred by counsel for the applicant to four cases, the names of which I will
c give simply for the purposes of completeness: *R v Gee* [1936] 2 All ER 89, [1936] 2 KB
442, *R v Wharmby* (1936) 31 Cr App R 174, *R v Edgar* [1958] 2 All ER 494 and *R v Grant*
[1944] 2 All ER 311. But it seems to me that those cases do not really help us in coming
to a conclusion whether his arguments are to be supported or not.

On the other side, counsel for the prosecutor submits to us that, where the magistrates
have exercised a jurisdiction, which they undoubtedly have, and do not go beyond the
d power which that jurisdiction gives them, an error in the recording of the order does not
vitiate either the proceedings or the order itself.

The way in which he puts it is this. What is required from the justices in circumstances
such as this? When considering what it is that is required, one bears in mind that not
only is the old enactment in precisely the same terms as the new to all intents and
purposes but the old rules are also identical with the new. He submits that the justices
e have to do this. They have to hear the evidence. They have to consider the circumstances
and then they either deal with the young man, as they did in this case, there and then,
or they say, 'We are committing you in custody to the Crown Court with a view to
borstal training.' That is all they have to do.

But certain procedural matters emerge from a consideration of the rules. For the
purposes of convenience, we have been referred to Stone's Justices' Manual (113th Edn,
f 1981, vol 3), and that is a course which I shall adopt. I turn first to the rules as to the
register of convictions, r 54 of the Magistrates' Courts Rules 1968, SI 1968 No 1920,
which read as follows (see pp 6070–6071 of Stone):

> '(1) The clerk of every magistrates' court shall keep a register in which there shall
> be entered—(*a*) a minute or memorandum of every adjudication of the court; (*b*) a
> minute or memorandum of every other proceeding or thing required by these
g > Rules or any other enactment to be so entered.
> '(2) The register shall be in the prescribed form, and entries in the register shall
> include, where relevant, such particulars as are provided for in the said form . . .'

One then turns to the prescribed form, form 146 (set out in Stone at p 7445) which has
eight columns. Column 1 is 'Number'; column 2 is 'Name of informant or complainant';
h column 3 is 'Name of defendant. Age, if known'; column 4 is 'Nature of offence or
matter of complaint'; column 5 is 'Date of offence or matter of complaint'; column 6 is
'Plea or consent to order'; column 7 is 'Minute of adjudication'; column 8 is 'Time
allowed for payment and instalments'.

It is to be noted that, in so far as those various columns are relevant, they were all
correctly filled in by the justices, with a possible exception of column 7 as already
j mentioned. But there is no mention there of any requirement that the statutory
authority for doing what the magistrates did had to be mentioned under the minute of
adjudication heading, or indeed under any other heading.

That takes me to the next provision, which is also to be found in Stone (at p 6039).
This is r 16(1) of the 1968 rules, which provides that, where a magistrates' court commits
an offender to the Crown Court under various provisions, one of which is s 28 or s 29 of

the 1952 Act, the clerk of the magistrates' court shall send to the appropriate officer of the Crown Court a copy signed by the clerk of the magistrates' court of the minute or *a* memorandum of the conviction entered in the register, which is precisely what he did; and once again there is no mention of the necessity to put in the name of the statute under which the magistrates say they are acting.

It seems to me that, without further authority on the point, the magistrates could properly in this case have simply said in their judgment to this young man, 'You are committed in custody to the Crown Court for consideration of a sentence of borstal *b* training', and that would have been a perfectly proper exercise of their powers to which no exception could properly have been taken anywhere.

Likewise it seems to me that, in form 146 sent off to the Crown Court, if they chosen under 'Minute of adjudication' to do exactly the same, namely to have said what they did on that form without the words in brackets, that is to say 'Committed in custody to Crown Court for sentence of borstal training. Legal Aid granted', that, likewise, would *c* have been a perfectly proper exercise of their powers and jurisdiction, to which again no possible exception could have been taken. They had the power. They acted on it properly. They had the power to commit and it was unnecessary for them to state whether it was under Act A or Act B that they were acting.

The fact that they did so, subject to the case which I am about to cite, seems to me to make no difference. The use of the words 'Magistrates' Courts Act 1980' was unnecessary; *d* it was surplusage and can be disregarded.

But our attention was drawn, and very properly drawn by counsel for the prosecutor as was his duty, to a decision of this court in 1959, which at first blush appears to be contrary to the point of view which I have been endeavouring to express. The case is *R v Huntingdon Justices, ex parte Simpkin and Coombes* (1959) 123 JP 166. What happened there is this. *e*

The two applicants were charged before the magistrates on two informations, the first of which alleged theft and the second receiving of certain motor car or lorry spares, a wheel and tyre. The justices dismissed the theft information but convicted on the receiving and committed the applicants to quarter sessions for sentence under s 29 of the Magistrates' Courts Act 1952. Their clerk then put an entry in the register, which under r 54 of the Magistrates' Courts Rules 1952, SI 1952 No 2190, it was the duty of their clerk *f* to make. That entry was correct in respect of the adjudication on the information for larceny, but on the information with regard to the receiving in column 5, which provided for the date, what they put was the word 'ditto', indicating that the date was the same as that for the larceny charges which had been dismissed. Under 'Nature of offence' the words entered were 'Received from some persons unknown a Bedford lorry spare wheel complete with tyre [of a certain size] knowing the same to have been stolen'. The *g* minute of adjudication was 'Committed to quarter sessions for sentence in accordance with s. 29 of the Criminal Justice Act 1948'. The clerk of the justices sent to the clerk of the peace a copy of both adjudications (that is the acquittal and the conviction) and the latter contained the aforementioned inaccuracies and omissions. On motion on behalf of the applicants to bring up and quash the record of the conviction on the ground that the record did not comply with r 54, it was held that the contention of the applicants was *h* right and that the entry must be quashed.

One turns then to the judgment of Lord Parker CJ, which was the leading judgment, to see on what basis the court came to that conclusion so far as one can, and this is what he said (at 168):

> 'In my judgment, it is imperative that convictions should be fully and accurately *i* recorded, and this was not. In particular [note those words] there was no specific entry of the date of the offence. It was also suggested that the nature of the offence was not properly described in that it did not state where the receiving had taken place or whose property the spare wheel was. I find it unnecessary to say whether those two matters should or should not have been entered, but there is no doubt that r. 54(3) does provide that a description of the offence should be set out, and clearly

that must be with sufficient detail so that it can be seen exactly in respect of what charge the prisoners were convicted. At any rate, in regard to the date of offence this record is not complete and not in accordance with the rules. The effect of that not being in order was this. It is provided by r. 20 that in sending the case forward to quarter sessions, the clerk of the justices shall send to the clerk of the peace a copy signed by the clerk of the justices' court of the minute or memorandum of the conviction entered in the register. What went forward to quarter sessions in the present case was a copy of the two adjudications in the register. If the clerk had sent forward the second adjudication, which was the one of conviction, it was clearly incomplete because it had no date, and in order that he should make it complete he had to send what I may call an omnibus copy, namely, a copy of both adjudications, the acquittal and the conviction. He also in that copy perpetuated the error which had already crept in of a committal under s. 29 of the Criminal Justice Act, 1948.'

In the short supporting judgment Donovan J said (at 169):

'I agree. This case illustrates the difficulties which can arise through entries in the court's register being abbreviated in order to save an insignificant amount of time, and the clerk to the justices will, no doubt, be on guard to avoid any similar trouble in the future.'

In that case not only had there been an error in the statement of the provision under which the justices were purporting to act, but there had also been (and this is underlined by what Donovan J said) material errors in the way in which the particulars had been set out in the document sent to quarter sessions.

One asks oneself what would have been the judgment of the court in that case had there only been the error which had crept in relating to s 29 of the 1948 Act. I cannot help feeling that in those circumstances the result would have been different and the court would have come to the same conclusion as that which I have come to in the present case, namely that this was an error which was an error of surplusage, one which can be disregarded, and that accordingly, in my judgment, the committal here was perfectly valid and the appeal by way of judicial review fails.

KILNER BROWN J. I agree entirely.

McCULLOUGH J. I agree. A statutory offence cannot properly be described without reference to the statute creating the offence; hence the decision in *Meek v Powell* [1952] 1 All ER 347, [1952] 1 KB 164, where an offence was described as being contrary to a statute which had been repealed. No criminal offence can properly be described without reference to the date on which the offence was committed. This no doubt is why form 146 in the Magistrates' Courts Rules 1968 contained a column headed 'Date of offence or matter of complaint'. This, to my mind, explains the decision in *R v Huntingdon Justices, ex parte Simpkin and Coombes* (1959) 123 JP 166.

I do not in the circumstances here see any difficulty in distinguishing either of those cases. There is no doubt about the offences of which the applicant was convicted; nor is there any doubt that he was committed for borstal training exactly as the magistrates had power to commit him. All that has happened is that an error was made in the magistrates' clerks' office when the completion of the column headed 'Minute of adjudication' was made and reference was made to the wrong statute. I see no need for there to have been any reference to any statute at all and I would regard the mistake here as immaterial and having no more consequence than had a wrong digit appeared by a typing error.

Application dismissed. The court refused leave to appeal to the House of Lords but certified, under s 1(2) of the Administration of Justice Act 1960, that the following points of law of general public importance were involved in the decision: (1) whether in cases covered by the transitional provisions of the Magistrates' Courts Act 1980 proceedings in the magistrates' court are rendered null and void if the memorandum of the finding of guilt entered in the register shows that the committal for sentence purports to be under s 37 of that Act; and (2) if the proceedings are not null and void, does the Crown Court have jurisdiction to deal with the offender on receipt of such memorandum of finding of guilt?

12th November. The Appeal Committee of the House of Lords (Lord Wilberforce, Lord Russell of Killowen and Lord Bridge of Harwich) dismissed a petition by the applicant for leave to appeal.

Solicitors: *Rootes & Alliott*, Folkestone (for the applicant); *Director of Public Prosecutions.*

Dilys Tausz   Barrister.

Practice Direction

SUPREME COURT

Practice – Tape recorders – Use of tape recorders in court – Leave of court – Discretion – Factors relevant to exercise of court's discretion – Contempt of Court Act 1981, s 9.

1. Section 9 of the Contempt of Court Act 1981 contains provisions governing the unofficial use of tape recorders in court. Among other things it provides that it is a contempt of court to use in court, or bring into court for use, any tape recorder or other instrument for recording sound, except with the leave of the court; and it is also a contempt of court to publish a recording of legal proceedings or to use any such recording in contravention of any conditions which the court may have attached to the grant of permission to use the machine in court. These provisions do not apply to the making or use of sound recordings for purposes of official transcripts of proceedings, on which the Act imposes no restriction whatever.

2. The discretion given to the court to grant, withhold or withdraw leave to use tape recorders or to impose conditions as to the use of the recording is unlimited, but the following factors may be relevant to its exercise: (a) the existence of any reasonable need on the part of the applicant for leave, whether a litigant or a person connected with the press or broadcasting, for the recording to be made; (b) in a criminal case, or a civil case in which a direction has been given excluding one or more witnesses from the court, the risk that the recording could be used for the purpose of briefing witnesses out of court; (c) any possibility that the use of a recorder would disturb the proceedings or distract or worry any witnesses or other participants.

3. Consideration should always be given whether conditions as to the use of a recording made pursuant to leave should be imposed. The identity and role of the applicant for leave and the nature of the subject matter of the proceedings may be relevant to this.

4. The particular restriction imposed by s 9(1)(b) of the 1981 Act applies in every case, but may not be present to the mind of every applicant to whom leave is given. It may, therefore, be desirable on occasion for this provision to be drawn to the attention of those to whom leave is given.

5. The transcript of a permitted recording is intended for the use of the person given leave to make it and is not intended to be used as, or to compete with, the official transcript mentioned in s 9(4) of the 1981 Act.

LANE CJ
DENNING MR
JOHN ARNOLD P
R E MEGARRY V-C

19th November 1981

R v Reynolds

COURT OF APPEAL, CRIMINAL DIVISION
SHAW LJ, TUDOR EVANS AND SHELDON JJ
2nd APRIL, 21st JULY 1981

Jury – Majority verdict – Practice – Statement of number of assenting and dissenting jurors – Number of dissenting jurors – Failure to comply with requirement that number of dissenting jurors be stated by foreman in open court – Foreman stating number of assenting jurors in open court – Judge accepting majority verdict and defendant convicted – Validity of verdict – Whether mandatory to state number of dissenting jurors – Whether failure to comply with requirement rendering verdict nugatory – Juries Act 1974, s 17(3).

At the appellant's trial for theft before a jury of 12 the trial judge, pursuant to s 17[a] of the Juries Act 1974, decided to accept the majority verdict of at least ten of the jurors. The clerk of the court in taking the jury's verdict of guilty asked the foreman of the jury how many of them were agreed on the verdict, to which the foreman answered that ten were agreed. The clerk failed to ask the foreman how many were opposed to the verdict. The judge accepted the verdict of guilty and the appellant was convicted and sentenced. She appealed against conviction on the ground that because the foreman of the jury had failed to state in open court the number of jurors who dissented from the verdict, as required by s 17(3) of the 1974 Act, there was a material irregularity in the trial and the conviction should be quashed.

Held – The requirement in s 17(3) of the 1974 Act that where there was a majority verdict the foreman of the jury should state in open court how many agreed and how many dissented from the verdict was mandatory, the purpose of stating how many dissented being to preclude a majority verdict being accepted where one or both of the remaining jurors had not formed a final view on the case. Accordingly, the requirement that the foreman should state the number of dissenting jurors was to be meticulously followed and it was the trial judge's duty to see that that was done. Failure to follow that requirement would result in the verdict not being properly taken and would constitute a material irregularity in the trial. It followed that the appellant's conviction would be quashed (see p 851 g to p 852 a, post).

R v Barry (Christopher) [1975] 2 All ER 760 applied.

Per Curiam. Failure to observe the practice direction regarding the directions to be given by the trial judge in respect to a majority verdict (see [1967] 3 All ER 137) will not of itself vitiate a majority verdict (see p 851 b, post).

Notes

For majority verdicts, see 11 Halsbury's Laws (4th Edn) paras 317–319, and for cases on the subject, see 30 Digest (Reissue) 336–337 513–524.

For the Juries Act 1974, s 17, see 44 Halsbury's Statutes (3rd Edn) 576.

Case referred to in judgment

R v Barry (Christopher) [1975] 2 All ER 760, [1975] 1 WLR 1190, 139 JP 558, 61 Cr App R 172, CA, Digest (Cont Vol D) 573, 524a.

---

a   Section 17, so far as material, provides:
    '(1) Subject to subsections (3) and (4) below, the verdict of a jury in proceedings in the Crown Court or the High Court need not be unanimous if—(a) in a case where there are not less than eleven jurors, ten of them agree on the verdict . . .
    '(3) The Crown Court shall not accept a verdict of guilty by virtue of subsection (1) above unless the foreman of the jury has stated in open court the number of jurors who respectively agreed to and dissented from the verdict . . .'

Appeal

On 7th December 1979 in the Crown Court at Cambridge before his Honour Judge Wild   *a*
and a jury the appellant, Janice Elizabeth Reynolds, was convicted on indictment on
three counts of theft contrary to s 1 of the Theft Act 1968, in each case by a majority
verdict of ten jurors. On each count she was conditionally discharged for two years, the
sentences to run concurrently. She appealed against the convictions on the ground, inter
alia, that there was a material irregularity in the trial because the foreman of the jury did
not state in open court the number of jurors who dissented from the verdicts in breach   *b*
of the provision in s 17(3) of the Juries Act 1974 which was mandatory. The facts are set
out in the judgment of the court.

David Iles (assigned by the Registrar of Criminal Appeals) for the appellant.
Peter Crane (who did not appear below) for the Crown.

c

At the conclusion of the hearing of the appeal the court announced that it would quash
the convictions because of the defect in the mode of returning the jury's verdict but
stated that it would give its reasons for that decision at a later date.

21st July. **SHAW LJ** read the following judgment of the court: The appellant was tried   *d*
in the Crown Court at Cambridge on three charges of shoplifting alleged to have been
committed on different occasions. The defence was that she had taken the articles which
were the subject matter of the charges in a state of 'clouded consciousness' which caused
her to be unaware of some of her actions. The case was one in which a verdict of guilty
might well have been justified; but, on the other hand, as she went into the witness box,
a jury might have come to the view that she was the sort of person who could at times   *e*
be oblivious of what she was doing.

On the second day of the trial, the judge having concluded his summing up, the jury
(which remained at its full complement) retired at 2.20 pm. At 3.25 pm they were
brought back into court as they appear to have sent a note to the judge indicating that
they could not agree. The transcript does not record the text of the note as it was not read
out in court, but counsel on both sides saw it. After an appropriate exhortation by the   *f*
judge the jury again retired.

At 4.33 pm they were once more brought into court on the direction of the judge. He
then told the jury that he could accept a verdict on which at least ten agreed. He went
on to ask the foreman whether it was possible to reach such a verdict. The foreman
intimated that it was possible, indeed more than possible. Thereupon the judge stated
that he would take such a verdict there and then. After an unavailing intervention by   *g*
counsel for the Crown calling attention to the Practice Direction ([1967] 3 All ER 137,
[1967] 1 WLR 1198) in this regard, the clerk of the court addressed the foreman of the
jury. There followed this colloquy:

'*The clerk.* Mr Foreman, will you please answer my first question either Yes or
No. On count 1 of the indictment have at least ten of you agreed upon a verdict?   *h*
The foreman. Yes.
'*The clerk.* On count 1 of the indictment do you find [the appellant] guilty or not
guilty? *The foreman.* Guilty.
'*The clerk.* Is that the verdict of you all or by a majority? *The foreman.* By a
majority.
'*The clerk.* How many agreed and how many opposed? *The foreman.* Ten agreed.   *j*
'*The clerk.* And two against. On count 2 of the indictment, do you find her guilty
or not guilty? *The foreman.* Guilty.
'*The clerk.* Is that the verdict of you all or by a majority? *The foreman.* By a
majority.

a   '*The clerk.* How many agreed the verdict and how many opposed? *The foreman.* Ten agreed.

'*The clerk.* On count 3 of the indictment, do you find her guilty or not guilty? *The foreman.* Guilty.

'*The clerk.* Is that the verdict of you all or by a majority? *The foreman.* By a majority.

b   '*The clerk.* How many agreed the verdict and how many opposed? *The foreman.* Ten agreed.'

It is unfortunate that the practice direction relating to majority verdicts in crime was not followed. The failure to observe it would not of itself vitiate the verdict, but, had the judge taken time to follow it, more meticulous attention might have been given to what ensued. Counsel for the appellant complains that, apart from neglect of the practice *c* direction, the statutory requirements as to the taking of a majority verdict were not observed. Those requirements are to be found in s 17 of the Juries Act 1974. That section re-enacts, with immaterial variations, the provisions of s 13 of the Criminal Justice Act 1967. It is necessary to recall that the earlier statute introduced for the first time into the criminal jurisprudence of this country the concept of a majority verdict. In so far as it made conviction possible by a verdict that was not unanimous, it eroded in *d* some measure one of the historical liberties of the subject. It is not surprising that the operation of this innovation was made subject to stringent conditions. Section 17 of the 1974 Act enacts in sub-s (3) that the Crown Court—

'shall not accept [a majority verdict] unless the foreman of the jury has stated in open court the number of jurors who respectively agreed to and dissented from the *e*   verdict.'

The requirement could not be more explicit or stated in more peremptory terms. In *R v Barry (Christopher)* [1975] 2 All ER 760, [1975] 1 WLR 1190 the foreman of the jury was asked, after an appropriate lapse of time, whether the jury had reached a verdict on which at least ten were agreed. The foreman replied, 'Yes'. When asked whether they *f* found the defendant guilty or not guilty, he said, 'Guilty'. The clerk of the court then said, 'And that is the verdict of ten of you', which utterance concluded the process of taking the verdict of the jury. Counsel urged the judge to ask the foreman how many had agreed on their verdict but the deputy judge thought this a superfluous formality. The Court of Appeal took a different view and quashed the conviction on the ground that the majority verdict taken in the manner which has been recounted did not comply with *g* the statutory provisions and could not be allowed to stand.

The requirement that where there is a majority verdict the foreman of a jury should state in open court how many dissented is neither more nor less imperative than stating how many agreed. It was argued in the present case that since the foreman had stated in open court that ten agreed, it was superfluous to go further. The number who dissented became a matter of the simplest arithmetic. This is a fallacious argument. As has been *h* said already, s 17, like its precursor, is in peremptory and mandatory terms. Its insistence on requiring a statement in open court by the foreman of how many dissented is to preclude a verdict being accepted where ten had agreed but one or both of the remaining jurors had not formed a final view at all. On hearing the foreman say that two dissented, that one or those two would have the opportunity of demurring publicly to the foreman's assertion. Otherwise, the verdict might operate against a defendant when only ten of the *j* jury had made up their minds one way or the other.

The statutory requirements are plainly stated and they must be meticulously followed if a majority verdict is to be legitimately accepted. It is the duty of the presiding judge to see that they are followed. In the present case, counsel very properly sought to alert the judge to the irregularity but his intervention was regrettably ignored.

The irregularity is fatal as no verdict was properly taken, and it is irrelevant to consider the application of the proviso to s 2(1) of the Criminal Appeal Act 1968. Accordingly, we were constrained to quash the conviction.

Appeal allowed ; convictions quashed.

Solicitors: *Williams & Co*, Bedford (for the Crown).

N P Metcalfe Esq   Barrister.

Croke (a minor) and another v Wiseman and others

COURT OF APPEAL, CIVIL DIVISION
LORD DENNING MR, SHAW AND GRIFFITHS LJJ
21st, 22nd JULY, 15th OCTOBER 1981

Damages – Personal injury – Loss of future earnings – Child – Irreparable brain damage resulting in total incapacity – Shortened expectation of life – Whether young child entitled to damages for loss of future earnings – Whether damages restricted to period of likely survival – Whether damages should include additional sum for lost years.

Damages – Personal injury – Pain, suffering and loss of amenity – Young child insensible of loss of amenity due to severity of injury – Award offering no solatium to child – Whether arbitrary conventional award appropriate.

Damages – Personal injury – Nursing – Cost of future nursing – Desirability of uniformity in multiplier applied – Mother giving up career to care for young child – Loss of pension rights – Whether sum for mother's loss of pension rights to be added to damages for cost of future parental nursing.

In December 1973 a normal infant boy aged 21 months was admitted to a hospital for treatment for an illness. During the treatment he suffered a cardiorespiratory arrest which resulted in irreparable brain damage. In consequence the infant's brain ceased to function, he became blind and unable to speak and was paralysed in all four limbs. He would never have an earning capacity. He came from a good home. His parents cared for him at home and his mother gave up her full-time career as a teacher to care for him. The infant claimed damages for negligence against the hospital authority, which admitted liability, and the quantum of damages was the only issue at the trial of the action in 1979. The trial judge, in awarding damages, took the infant's life expectancy to be, on the evidence, 40 years, and therefore at the date of the trial, when the boy was aged 7, his life expectancy was 33 years. The judge awarded him total damages of £269,698, which included the following sums: (1) £45,000 for loss of future earnings which the judge arrived at by assuming that the boy would, from the age of 18, have earned the national average wage (in 1979) for a young man of £5,000 a year, and applying to that figure a multiplier of 9 years; (2) £35,000 for pain, suffering and loss of amenities; and (3) £137,000 for the future cost of nursing care made up of (a) £100,000 for professional nursing care based on £6,000 per annum, to which the judge applied a multiplier of 16 to 17 years, and (b) £30,000 for parental nursing care based on £1,850 per annum for such care, to which the judge applied the same multiplier, and, in addition, £7,000 for the mother's loss of her pension rights as a teacher. The hospital

authority appealed, submitting (i) that the awards for loss of future earnings and for pain,
a suffering and loss of amenity were too high, (ii) that the multiplier applied in estimating
the cost of future nursing care was too high, and (iii) that the mother's loss of pension
rights was not recoverable as part of the infant's damages.

Held – (1) (Lord Denning MR dissenting) A gravely injured child who would live for
many years into adult life was entitled to a sum for his loss of future earnings during the
b period of his likely survival, and (per Shaw LJ) compensation for that loss was not to be
treated as being so speculative that it could not be assessed and nor was it a relevant
consideration that a plaintiff might not be able personally to benefit from the damages
awarded for such loss.   Accordingly, although the infant had been awarded a sum for the
cost of his future professional and parental nursing care, he was also entitled to an award
for loss of future earnings during the period of his likely survival.   It could not be
c assumed that his parents would remain able throughout his life to house, feed and care
for him and the award for loss of future earnings was required to provide a home for him
in the future and for his care and such extra comforts as he could appreciate.   If, however,
the award for future nursing care had included the full cost of residential care, the award
for loss of future earnings would have had to be small to avoid awarding the infant his
future living expenses twice over.   The infant was not, however, entitled to any
d additional sum for loss of earnings in the lost years, namely the years beyond the period
of his likely survival.   In assessing the sum to be awarded for loss of future earnings the
judge's figure of £5,000 per annum was in all the circumstances the correct multiplicand,
but his multiplier of 9 years would be reduced to 5 years to take account of the
accelerated payment of a capital sum for loss of future earnings and the fact that the
infant might never have become an earner.   The award for loss of future earnings would
e therefore be reduced from £45,000 to £25,000 (see p 861 *a b* and *e* to p 862 *g* and p 863
a to *h*, post); *Oliver v Ashman* [1961] 3 All ER 323 and *S v Distillers Co (Biochemicals) Ltd*
[1969] 3 All ER 1412 applied; *Pickett v British Rail Engineering Ltd* [1979] 1 All ER 774 and
Gammell v Wilson [1981] 1 All ER 578 considered.

(2) (Lord Denning MR dissenting) The judge's award of £35,000 for pain, suffering
and loss of amenity was not too high, because damages under that head of damage were,
f within conventional limits, to be measured against the extent of the plaintiff's
deprivation and were not to be a wholly arbitrary assessment even though as a result of
his injury the plaintiff was insensible of any loss of amenity and the award offered him
no solatium.   An injury of the gravest kind where there was total loss of amenity from
the outset of life would attract the highest conventional award.   In all the circumstances,
therefore, and having regard to current money values, £35,000 was the right figure to
g award to the infant for pain, suffering and loss of amenity (see p 859 *e* to *h* and p 863 *h*
to p 864 *a*, post); *Walker v John McLean & Sons Ltd* [1979] 2 All ER 965 applied; dictum
of Lord Scarman in *Lim Poh Choo v Camden and Islington Area Health Authority* [1979] 2 All
ER at 920 considered.

(3) Whilst the multiplicands taken by the judge in assessing the damages for the cost
of future nursing care were justified, his multiplier of 16 to 17 years was too high, since
h there ought to be a reasonable degree of uniformity by judges in the multiplier they
applied and (per Lord Denning MR) it was the Court of Appeal's function to assist in
attaining such uniformity, and furthermore (per Griffiths LJ) the judge's multiplier
made no allowance for the possibility that the infant's life might be terminated by
accident before he achieved his estimated life expectancy.   Accordingly (per Shaw and
Griffiths LJJ) the multiplier would be reduced to 14 years (Lord Denning MR being of
j the opinion that it should be reduced to 12 years) and that head of damage would
therefore be reduced to £119,000 (see p 858 *g* to *j*, p 860 *c* to *f* and *j* and p 864 *a* to *c*,
post); *Lim Poh Choo v Camden and Islington Area Health Authority* [1979] 2 All ER 910
applied.

(4) Although the mother had no separate cause of action and could not herself claim
for any loss of her pension rights, the judge had been entitled (Lord Denning MR

dissenting) to add a further sum of £7,000 for the loss of her pension rights to the damages awarded to the infant for the future cost of parental nursing care since it was an *a* element to take into consideration in deciding the fair sum to award for that cost and it should form part of the sum available to pay the parents for their future nursing care (see p 860 *g* to *j* and p 864 *c*, post).

Per Curiam. The law of damages for personal injuries is in urgent need of reform (see p 856 *e f* and p 862 *g* to *j*, post).

Notes

For the measure of damages in personal injuries cases, see 12 Halsbury's Laws (4th Edn) pages 1145–1157, and for cases on the subject, see 17 Digest (Reissue) 113–117, 168–193 and 36(1) ibid 313–318, 1265–1285.

Cases referred to in judgments *c*

Benham v Gambling [1941] 1 All ER 7, [1941] AC 157, 110 LJKB 49, 164 LT 290, HL, 36(1) Digest (Reissue) 383, 1544.

Clark v Essex Area Health Authority (1981) Times, 28th January.

Cunningham v Harrison [1973] 3 All ER 463, [1973] QB 942, [1973] 3 WLR 97, CA, 17 Digest (Reissue) 116, 191.

Gammell v Wilson [1980] 2 All ER 557, [1980] 3 WLR 591, CA; *affd* [1981] 1 All ER 578, *d* [1981] 2 WLR 248, HL.

Kandalla v British Airways Board (formerly British European Airways Corpn) [1980] 1 All ER 341, [1981] QB 158, [1980] 2 WLR 730.

Lim Poh Choo v Camden and Islington Area Health Authority [1979] 2 All ER 910, [1980] AC 174, [1979] 3 WLR 44, HL; *varying* [1979] 1 All ER 332, [1979] QB 196, [1978] 3 WLR 895, CA, Digest (Cont Vol E) 457, 1285a. *e*

Oliver v Ashman [1961] 3 All ER 323, [1962] 2 QB 210, [1961] 3 WLR 669, CA, 36(1) Digest (Reissue) 313, 1267.

Pickett v British Rail Engineering Ltd [1979] 1 All ER 774, [1980] AC 136, [1978] 3 WLR 955, [1979] 1 Lloyd's Rep 519, HL, Digest (Cont Vol E) 459, 1314b.

S v Distillers Co (Biochemicals) Ltd, J v Distillers Co (Biochemicals) Ltd [1969] 3 All ER 1412, [1970] 1 WLR 114, 17 Digest (Reissue) 115, 188. *f*

Shildrick v Clarence Erection Co (3rd April 1981, unreported), QBD at Teesside.

Walker v John McLean & Sons Ltd [1979] 2 All ER 965, [1979] 1 WLR 760, CA, Digest (Cont Vol E) 460, 1330b.

Cases also cited

Davies v Powell Duffryn Associated Collieries Ltd [1942] 1 All ER 657, [1942] AC 601, HL. *g*

Mallett v McMonagle [1969] 2 All ER 178, [1970] AC 166, HL.

Appeal

By a writ dated 27th October 1976 indorsed with a statement of claim the first plaintiff, James Patrick Croke, a minor suing by his father and next friend, James Croke, and the *h* second plaintiff, Bridget Teresa Croke, the first plaintiff's mother, claimed damages for negligence against, inter alios, the second defendants, the Brent and Harrow Area Health Authority, in respect of injuries sustained by the first plaintiff while he was receiving treatment in Northwick Park Hospital. The second defendants admitted liability and the quantum of damages was the only issue at the trial of the action. On 5th November 1979 Michael Davies J awarded the first plaintiff total damages of £269,698·63. The *j* second defendants appealed.

John Davies QC and *Michael Baker* for the second defendants.
John Byrt QC and *Nicholas Medawar* for the plaintiffs.

Cur adv vult

15th October. The following judgments were read.

LORD DENNING MR. James Croke was born in March 1972. So he is now nine years old. He was a lovely little baby, as bright as a button. But when he was only 21 months he became feverish with symptoms of croup. He was taken to the Northwick Park Hospital. There something went wrong in the treatment. Whilst the doctors were examining his throat, he suffered a cardiorespiratory arrest. That means he could not get his breath and his heart stopped. The blood stopped flowing to his brain. He was put into intensive care. He was brought back to life. But the cardiac arrest had destroyed his brain beyond repair. His brain does not function at all. He is blind. He is paralysed in all four limbs. He cannot stand. He cannot talk. He can only lie on his mother's lap or on the floor. Just like a baby of less than a year old. He has to wear nappies all the time, for he is doubly incontinent. There is no hope of any improvement. He does know his mother's voice and shows he loves her, just as a baby does. He is totally dependent on her for everything, for feeding, washing, changing and dressing, just like a little baby. Yet, whilst his brain does nothing, his body grows just as if were a normal boy. For some years now he has been taken each day to a school for disabled children, the Whittlesea School at Harrow, where the headmistress says:

> 'He is greatly loved by all the staff at Whittlesea and we have tried to give him a quality of happiness in his life, as his disabilities are so great that he will need constant care and attention for the rest of his life.'

He is not likely to live long. The doctors put his expectation of life as between 20 and 40 years.

Such is the tragic story of James Croke. By his father as his next friend he has sued the hospital authorities for negligence. They have admitted liability, but have left the quantity of damages to the courts. The judge took his life expectancy at 40. He has awarded the boy £269,698·63. The hospital authorities appeal to this court.

The present state of the law

Cases of this kind have increased much in recent years. It is largely due to the advances in medical science. The victims of accidents have their brains destroyed but their bodies are kept alive. They are helpless and need constant care and attention. Sometimes they are unconscious and feel nothing. At other times they are just conscious of their surroundings but happiness or sorrow mean nothing to them. I stated the principle on which, in my view, damages should be awarded in *Lim Poh Choo v Camden and Islington Area Health Authority* [1979] 1 All ER 332 at 341, [1979] QB 196 at 217:

> 'It is a modern problem, the impact of modern science, in prolonging life in a body destitute of mind. To my mind on principle fair compensation requires that there should be ample provision in terms of money for comfort and care during the lifetime of the sufferer such as to safeguard him or her in all foreseeable contingencies, including the effect of inflation; that, if he or she has any dependants, they should be compensated for any pecuniary loss which they suffer by reason of his or her incapacity and inability to earn, just as if he or she had died and compensation was being awarded under the Fatal Accidents Acts. Beyond that there can be conventional sums for pain and suffering and loss of amenities, but these should not be too large, seeing that they will do her no good, and can only accumulate during her lifetime to benefit others who survive after her death. This is reinforced by the views of Lord Pearson's commission (Report of the Royal Commission on Civil Liability and Compensation for Personal Injury (1978, Cmnd 7054–I), paras 391–392). Half of them thought there should be a statutory maximum of £20,000. The other half thought that there should not be a statutory maximum but that the Court of Appeal should exercise a restraining hand.'

But this principle was not accepted by the House of Lords. They declared that, even in these cases, we must go by the current method of itemising the various heads of damages. We must assess the cost of future care, loss of future earnings, pain, suffering *a* and loss of amenities as if they were separate causes of action. Then we must add the items together and award the total sum as damages, irrespective of any overlapping so long as it does not look outrageously high. But they did agree with me that—

> 'a radical reappraisal of the law is needed ... such a reappraisal calls for social, financial, economic and administrative decisions which only the legislature can take. The perplexities of the present case ... emphasise the need for reform of the *b* law.'

(See [1979] 2 All ER 910 at 913–914, [1980] AC 174 at 182.)

That was over two years ago. But nothing has been done since. No such reappraisal has been undertaken.

Meanwhile, the imperative need for reappraisal has been shown by two subsequent *c* decisions of the House of Lords. They are about one particular item, namely loss of future earnings. The House has held that where a man is fatally injured (see *Pickett v British Rail Engineering Ltd* [1979] 1 All ER 774, [1980] AC 136) or is killed outright (see *Gammell v Wilson* [1981] 1 All ER 578, [1981] 2 WLR 248) his personal representatives can recover damages for the loss of earnings that he would have received if he had lived and worked all his expected working life. Not only for the shortened period during *d* which he lived on, incapacitated by his injuries, but also for the 'lost years' after he dies of his injuries. Such damages do him no good at all. He is dead. They only go to benefit other people. In *Gammell v Wilson* the House of Lords, for once, confessed its error. It put on a white sheet. Lord Diplock observed significantly ([1981] 1 All ER 578 at 583, [1981] 2 WLR 248 at 253):

> 'I join with your Lordships in thinking that it is too late for anything short of *e* legislation to bring the like sense and justice to the law relating to damages for death recoverable by the estate of the deceased.'

That was six months ago. But nothing has been done. The same story could be repeated in many branches of the law. The judges repeatedly say: 'The law is unjust, but we can do nothing. It is for Parliament, not for us.' Then Parliament does nothing. It *f* makes me wring my hands with despair. I would say to the judges: 'Ye fearful saints fresh courage take.'

Loss of future earnings

The judge awarded £45,000 to this baby for loss of future earnings. To my mind there is something odd about giving this tiny baby two separate items of damages: one *g* for cost of 'future care'; the other for loss of 'future earnings'. 'Future care' is awarded on the footing that he is completely incapacitated and has to be kept at great expense all his future life. 'Future earnings' are awarded on the footing that he was not incapacitated at all and would be earning all his future life. I cannot think it right in principle that he should have both.

Never before has a child of two years claimed for loss of future earnings or received *h* any. In *Benham v Gambling* [1941] 1 All ER 7, [1941] AC 157 a baby of 2½ years was fatally injured in a motor accident and died the same day. He was unconscious from the moment of the accident till his death. A House of Lords of unusual strength awarded the child's estate £200 for loss of expectation of life. They said unanimously ([1941] 1 All ER 7 at 13, [1941] AC 157 at 167):

> 'Of course, no regard must be had to financial losses or gains during the period of *j* which the victim has been deprived. The damages are in respect of loss of life, not of loss of future pecuniary prospects.'

In *Oliver v Ashman* [1961] 3 All ER 323, [1962] 2 QB 210 a boy of 20 months was seriously injured in a motor accident. His brain was so affected that he became a low-

grade mental defective incapable of work. His expectation of life was reduced from 60
a years to 30 years. He was awarded £11,000 general damages, but this sum was not
itemised. Something may have been included for his loss of earnings during his 'lost
years' but it was so small as to be negligible. The Court of Appeal did not interfere.
Those cases were much considered in two recent cases in the House of Lords. Their
Lordships indicated in the clearest terms that with a baby of two years there should be
no award for loss of future earnings. In *Pickett v British Rail Engineering Ltd* [1979] 1 All
b ER 774 at 781, [1980] AC 136 at 150 Lord Wilberforce said: 'In that of a young child (cf
Benham v Gambling) neither present nor future earnings could enter into the matter ...'
Lord Salmon said ([1979] 1 All ER 774 at 786, [1980] AC 136 at 156) of *Oliver v
Ashman*:

> '... in the case of a child of such tender years, the amount of the earnings which
> he might have lost was so speculative and unpredictable that the sum in the award
c
> attributable to that element must have been minimal and could therefore be
> disregarded.'

Lord Scarman said ([1979] 1 All ER 774 at 797, [1980] AC 136 at 169):

> '... the plaintiff may be so young (in *Oliver v Ashman* he was a boy aged 20
d > months at the time of the accident) that it is absurd that he should be compensated
> for future loss of earnings.'

In *Gammell v Wilson* [1981] 1 All ER 578 at 593, [1981] 2 WLR 248 at 265 Lord
Scarman said:

> 'In the case of a young child, the lost years of earning capacity will ordinarily be
e > so distant that assessment is mere speculation. No estimate being possible, no
> award, not even a "conventional" award, should ordinarily be made.'

It is said that those observations only apply to cases of 'lost years'. But even so, it seems
to me that they apply also to cases where a baby of two years is killed in a motor accident
or dies after a few days. All its years are 'lost years'. Why on earth should such a baby be
f given damages for loss of future earnings? It is dead. Any amount of damages would go
to its parents, or, if its parents are dead, to some remote relative. That would be absurd.
If the English law were like Scottish law, they could be given a solatium. But not
damages for loss of earnings. Such loss is far too speculative.
If this be so, then it must follow that if a baby of two years is not killed but is deprived
of all brain power so that it can do nothing and earn nothing whatever, then that baby
g also has no claim for damages for loss of earnings either during its shortened life or for
the 'lost years' thereafter. The loss of future earnings, over the whole period, is just as
great or as small as if the baby were killed outright or fatally injured and dies after a few
days. The process of assessment is just as speculative. No logical distinction can be
drawn between the two cases.
This result is to my mind entirely satisfactory. It brings the case of these babies into
h the realm of the general principle which I stated in *Lim's case* [1979] 1 All ER 332 at 343,
[1979] QB 196 at 218–219:

> 'In my opinion when a plaintiff is rendered unconscious or insensible, fair
> compensation should not include an item for loss of earnings as such ... provided
> also that full compensation is also given for every expense that may be incurred on
> his behalf and every service that may be rendered to him by relatives and friends.
j > The cost of keeping the plaintiff for the rest of his days will exceed by far the salary
> or wages that he would have earned if he never had been injured. It is not fair to the
> defendants to make them pay both.'

In my opinion therefore the claim for loss of earnings should not be allowed. £45,000
should be struck off.

Loss of pension, £7,000

The boy's mother says that, as a result of the accident, she has not been able to return   **a**
to her work as a teacher as soon as she would otherwise have done, and that this has
meant that when she retires she will receive less pension than she otherwise would have
done. It is a long time ahead but the judge has awarded £7,000 on this head.

I cannot think this is right. It must be remembered that the mother has no cause of
action on her own account. She cannot claim for the loss of her pension. Her claim must
come under the umbrella of the boy's claim. The boy can recover compensation for the   **b**
value of the services she renders to him and must account to her for it: see *Cunningham
v Harrison* [1973] 3 All ER 463, [1973] QB 942. I cannot regard this loss of pension as
properly within the value of her services. The judge assessed those separately. He ought
not to have added on the £7,000 in addition.

Pain, suffering and loss of amenities, £35,000   **c**

This is a head of claim which is impossible to quantify in money terms. The only
thing that can be said is that it is some solace to the injured person when he is aware of
his loss. But, when he is not aware of it, money is no solace at all. It does him no good.
It is a benefit to those who succeed to his estate. It is assessed by the judges on a
conventional basis. What then should the conventional basis be?

In *Lim's* case the judge awarded £20,000. This was upheld in the House of Lords.   **d**
Lord Scarman said ([1979] 2 All ER 910 at 920, [1980] AC 174 at 190):

> 'As long, therefore as the sum awarded is a substantial sum in the context of
> current money values, the requirement of the law is met. A sum of £20,000 is,
> even today [June 1979], a substantial sum.'

To this I would add the observations of the Royal Commission over which Lord Pearson   **e**
presided (Cmnd 7054–I). In paras 391–392 half of them thought there should be an
upper limit as well as a lower limit. 'They consider that the maximum should be set at
five times average annual industrial earnings [about £20,000 in 1977].' On the basis in
this case two years later in 1979 I would consider that the maximum should be
£25,000. You must remember that whatever sum we approve in this case will act as a
precedent for future cases. It will become the conventional award. For this reason I   **f**
think we should interfere with the judge's award of £35,000. It is too high. It should
be reduced to £25,000.

Cost of future care

As I have said earlier, if loss of future earnings is out, there should be ample provision
for the cost of keeping this boy in the future so that he should have the best possible care   **g**
for the rest of his expected life. This is always done by finding first the 'multiplicand' and
afterwards the 'multiplier'. In this case the judge did not specify his multiplicand but we
can find it by deduction. He accepted the evidence of the plaintiff's doctor that he might
live to the age of 40. I would not interfere with this. For nursing care (other than the
parents') the judge awarded him a total of £100,000, for which the judge used a
multiplier of 16 or 17 years' purchase. That gives a multiplicand of about £6,000 a year.   **h**

For the parents' care the judge awarded £30,000, for which the judge used the same
multiplier of 16 or 17 years' purchase. That gives a multiplicand of about £1,850 a year.

Adding together the £6,000 and £1,850, it looks as if the judge took the total
multiplicand for future care at £7,950 a year. I would not interfere with this. It seems
to be about right.

But I am afraid I do not agree with the multiplier that he has used. He used a   **j**
multiplier of 16 or 17. I think that is far too high. The multiplier in these cases is of
much importance. It makes many thousands of pounds' difference to the award. There
should be a reasonable degree of uniformity in the approach by the judges, and it is the
function of the Court of Appeal to assist in attaining it. In *Lim's* case (which presented a
comparable problem) the House of Lords reduced the multiplier from 18 to 12. In this
case I think we should follow their example. We should reduce the multiplier from 16
or 17 down to 12.

This means that the total figure for future care is £7,850 (the multiplicand) multiplied
a by 12 (the multiplier). That comes to £94,000 instead of the £130,000 awarded by the
judge.

Conclusion
   I would therefore knock off these sums: £45,000 for future loss of earnings; £7,000
for loss of pension; £10,000 off pain, suffering and loss of amenities; and £35,800 off
b future care. That means a deduction in all of £97,800.
   That leaves a total of £156,524·72 to which interest is to be added, bringing it up to
about £170,000. That is still a very large sum. If it is made into a trust fund for the
benefit of the boy and well invested by the trustees on his behalf, it should be enough to
keep him in care and comfort for the rest of his days. It will not, of course, compensate
his father and mother for the tragedy which has befallen them. No money could do
c that. But I am sure they are not the sort of people who want to make money out of this
misfortune. All the courts can do is to award a fair compensation, fair to both sides, and
the figure I have suggested is, I believe, fair.
   I would allow the appeal and vary the award in the way I have stated. I would also,
exceptionally, allow the parents the costs of the appeal because I do not wish the award
to be reduced by their having to pay costs.
d   I will ask Griffiths LJ to give his judgment before I read the judgment of Shaw LJ
because Shaw LJ refers back to the judgment of Griffiths LJ.

GRIFFITHS LJ.
Pain, suffering and loss of amenity
e   The injury suffered by this child was catastrophic. The loss of amenity was total.
Although pain does not appear to have been a significant feature, I would suppose that
as the child grows to manhood in his present helpless condition he must inevitably suffer
much discomfort. Such an injury must attract the highest conventional award for loss
of amenity. The judge awarded £35,000. This award is in line with the guidance of the
Court of Appeal in *Walker v John MacLean & Sons Ltd* [1979] 2 All ER 965, [1979] 1 WLR
f 760 and is comparable with other current awards by judges at first instance: see *Clark v
Essex Area Health Authority* (1981) Times, 28th January, an award of £50,000 for loss of
amenity approved for a girl of 13 years of age, and *Shildrick v Clarence Erection Co* (3rd
April 1981, unreported), a case of severe brain damage to a man of 40 in which the award
for pain, suffering and loss of amenity was assessed at £30,000. I do not read Lord
Scarman's speech in *Lim Poh Choo v Camden and Islington Health Authority* [1979] 2 All ER
g 910, [1980] AC 174 as approving a sum of £20,000 as an appropriate standard award for
this head of general damages in such catastrophic injuries. He was in fact saying no more
than £20,000 in the context of the huge damages awarded in that case was not so low
that the court should interfere with that particular head. By the same token I do not
think that £35,000 is so high that this court should interfere with it. Indeed I would go
further and say that having regard to today's value of money it is the right figure for the
h gravest injuries.

Life expectancy
   The judge was fully entitled to base his assessment of this child's life expectancy on the
evidence of Professor Holt, who was the doctor who had seen the child regularly since the
accident over a period of five years. One of the defendants' doctors had not seen the child
j at all and the other had only seen him once. The judge had to choose between widely
different estimates of life expectancy given by the plaintiff's doctor on the one hand and
the doctors called by the defendants on the other. It was suggested that he should have
split the difference, but I can see no reason why he should have adopted this approach.
Judges are constantly faced with the difficult task of deciding which body of expert
evidence they prefer. This court should be very slow to interfere with the judge's choice
and should only do so if it is possible to point to some obvious feature of the evidence
which the judge has failed to take into account or the significance of which he has

apparently misapprehended. No such criticism can be made in this case and the judge was entitled to accept the view of Professor Holt that the probability was that this child *a* will survive to the age of 40.

The future cost of nursing care

This child was seven at the date of the trial; he therefore had a life expectancy of 33 years. The judge used a multiplier of 16 to 17 years. The actuarial tables produced by the defendants show that this is the appropriate multiplier to use when making a lump *b* sum award which by using both interest and capital will be exhausted at the end of 33 years. But Professor Holt in giving a probable life expectancy of 40 was, as I understand his evidence, doing so on the assumption that if the child suffered no untoward accident he would probably have the innate strength to survive to that age. This estimate makes no allowance for the possibility that some untoward chance such as a motor car accident or fire or so forth might terminate his life at an earlier date. I think the multiplier of 16 *c* to 17 years is too high, and this is particularly so when one bears in mind that in *Lim's* case the House of Lords, working on an expectation of life of another 36 years, approved a multiplier of 12. It is desirable that on comparable life expectation there should not be too great a disparity between the multipliers used in the different cases, although complete uniformity can never be expected because different circumstances will affect different cases. Bearing these factors in mind, I would reduce the multiplier in this case *d* to 14 years.

The multiplicand

For future professional nursing care the judge awarded a total sum of £100,000. That means that he assessed the cost of nursing care if he took a multiplier of 16 years at a total of £6,250 per annum and if he took a multiplier of 17 years at a cost of £5,582 per *e* annum. The schedules showing the cost of nursing care provide ample support for either of these figures. On the assumption that nursing care consists of a state enrolled nurse coming five hours a day for five days a week and a nursing auxiliary coming in for four nights a week, the total cost per annum is approximately £6,000. On the assumption that after the child leaves school and goes to a day centre at which he is not happy so that he is at home much more and requires more help from a state enrolled *f* nurse the total annual cost comes to nearly £8,000 per annum. In round figures the judge took a figure of approximately £6,000 per annum for the cost of this extra professional nursing and it seems to me fully justified.

The judge awarded £30,000 for future nursing care from the parents and, if one adds in the pension of £7,000 as a part of the cost of future nursing care, the total comes to £37,000. *g*

Although the judge allowed the £7,000 for loss of pension, it was under the head of the cost of future nursing care provided by the parents. In my view, he was entitled to take into account the fact that Mrs Croke would lose her pension rights as a teacher as a result of devoting herself to the care of her son. It was an element to take into consideration when deciding what was a fair sum to award as the cost of the nursing care provided by Mrs Croke. The judge did not award the £7,000 to Mrs Croke; it was *h* awarded to the infant plaintiff as a part of the sum of £37,000 which would be available to pay the parents for their future nursing care. This means that in round terms he valued the nursing services provided by the parents at £2,250 per annum. The parents will in fact be on duty for longer hours every week than the professional nurses, and they will have the whole of the weekends to cope with. When this accident occurred the mother was a full-time teacher. She has given up this career in order to be able to look *j* after this child. All the doctors stress the high quality of the nursing care provided by the parents and, in my view, the judge was entitled to assess the value of their care at a figure of the order of £2,500 a year. Taking the judge's figure for nursing care of £8,500 per annum in round figures and applying a multiplier of 14 produces a sum of £119,000. The judge's figure came to a total of £137,000. For the reasons I have given, I think this was too high and accordingly I would reduce this head of damage to £119,000.

Loss of future earnings

a   Under this head the judge awarded the sum of £45,000. He arrived at this figure by assuming that this child would earn the average wage which he took at £5,000 and he applied a multiplier of nine years' purchase. Counsel for the defendants attacked this figure as too high, but I did not understand him to submit that there should be no award under this head. I must express my respectful dissent from the view expressed by Lord Denning MR that in the case of a young child there should be no award for loss of future

b   earnings. It is, of course, a task of the greatest difficulty to assess an appropriate sum to award a young child for future loss of earnings, but it is not right to say that the courts have never before done so. The courts are frequently doing so. Take the tragic case of all the thalidomide children. Their cases have now all been settled on the basis of an award made by Hinchcliffe J to two children who were born with grave deformities as a result of their mother taking the drug thalidomide during pregnancy. At the time the

c   case came before him the children were respectively seven and eight years old, the same age as the child in this case. Their injuries had been received at birth; this child's injuries were received when he was 20 months old. In the case of one child the judge assessed the damages on the basis that there would be a large loss of earning capacity; in the other case he assessed it on the basis that the child would never have any earning capacity. In each case the award for future loss of earnings was over £10,000. That case was, of course,

d   decided in 1969: see *S v Distillers Co (Biochemicals) Ltd* [1969] 3 All ER 1412, [1970] 1 WLR 114. That case has been taken as the yardstick for assessing the damages for all the other thalidomide children, nearly four hundred of them.

   In *Oliver v Ashman* [1961] 3 All ER 323, [1962] 2 QB 210 the award was expressed to include a sum for future loss of wages. In the Court of Appeal it was never doubted that this was a proper head of damage to award so long as the child might be alive. The

e   argument was concentrated on whether any award should be made for the lost years after death. It is in this context that Lord Salmon's observations in *Pickett v British Rail Engineering Ltd* [1979] 1 All ER 774 at 786, [1980] AC 136 at 156 must be read.

   I do not read those passages in the speeches of their Lordships in *Pickett's* case and in *Gammell v Wilson* [1981] 1 All ER 578, [1981] 2 WLR 248 in which they stress the difficulty of assessing an award of damages for the lost years in the case of a child as

f   having general application to the claims of all children whose earning capacity has been diminished. In attempting to assess the value of a claim for the lost years, the court is faced with a peculiar difficulty. Not only does it have to assess what sum the plaintiff might have been earning, but it also has to make an assessment of the sum that would not have been spent on the plaintiff's own living expenses and would have therefore been available to spend on his dependants. In the case of a living plaintiff of mature years

g   whose life expectation has been shortened and who has dependants, there are compelling social reasons for awarding a sum of money that he knows will be available for the support of his dependants after his death. It was this consideration that led to the result in *Pickett's* case. As a consequence of the decision in *Pickett's* case, the House of Lords in *Gammell's* case felt compelled to apply the same principle to a claim brought on behalf of the estate of the deceased person. If it could be shown that part of the deceased's income

h   was available to be spent on his dependants, then a claim for that part of the income was available to cover the lost years of working life. In the case of a child, however, there are no dependants, and if a child is dead there can never be any dependants and, if the injuries are catastrophic, equally there will never be any dependants. It is the child that will be dependent. In such circumstances, it seems to me entirely right that the court should refuse to speculate whether in the future there might have been dependants for

j   the purpose of providing a fund of money for persons who will in fact never exist. It was this consideration that led me in *Kandalla v British Airways Board* [1980] 1 All ER 341, [1981] QB 158 to refuse to assess a sum for the lost years in respect of two unmarried doctors by speculating whether or not in the future they would have married and set aside some part of their income for husbands or children. I refused to enter into the realm of speculation about an impossible and hypothetical situation.

   However, when one is considering the case of a gravely injured child who is going to live for many years into adult life, very different considerations apply. There are compelling social reasons why a sum of money should be awarded for his future loss of *a* earnings. The money will be required to care for him. Take the present case: the cost of future nursing care has been assessed on the basis of nurses coming in to care for him for part of the day and night. It is not a case where damages have been awarded which will provide a sufficient sum for him to go into a residential home and be cared for at all times. Damages awarded for his future loss of earnings will in the future be available to provide a home for him and to feed him and provide for such extra comforts as he can *b* appreciate. It cannot be assumed that his parents will remain able to house, feed and care for him throughout the rest of his life. If of course damages have been awarded on the basis of the full cost of residential care so that they include the cost of roof and board, any award for future loss of earnings will be small because there will be a very large overlap between the two heads of damage. The plaintiff must not be awarded his future living expenses twice over; this would be unfair to the defendants. *c*

I would therefore award this child a sum to compensate him for his loss of earnings during the period that he will live but I would not award any additional sum to compensate him for the lost years.

The judge assessed the future loss of earnings at £5,000 per annum. He arrived at this figure by taking the national average wage for a young man. In my view, he was justified in doing so. This child came from an excellent home, the father is an *d* enterprising man starting his own business and the mother is a qualified teacher; they have shown the quality of their characters by the care they have given their child and their courage by the fact they have continued with their family even after this disaster befell them. The defendants cannot complain that they are unfairly treated if against this background the judge assumes the child will grow up to lead a useful working life and be capable of at least earning the national average wage. *e*

Assuming the child was able to start work at 18 and lived to the age of 40, his maximum working life would be 22 years. According to the actuarial tables put in at the trial, the appropriate multiplier to apply for such a period was 8·876. But that is a mathematical figure based on the certainty that earnings would have continued over that period. It makes no allowance for the large discount that must be given for the immediate receipt of the capital sum at least 11 years before earnings would commence; *f* nor does it allow a discount for the possibility that the child might never have become an earner. Taking these factors into account, I think there should be a substantial further discount on the multiplier which I would reduce to five years. Accordingly, I would reduce the judge's award under this head from £45,000 to £25,000.

I would therefore reduce the total award by £37,000 which will reduce it before interest to the sum of £215,724·72. *g*

In conclusion I should say that I also agree that our law of damages for personal injuries is in urgent need of reform. In this judgment I have sought to apply the law as I believe it to be and not as I would wish it.

SHAW LJ (read by Lord Denning MR). I respectfully agree with much that Lord Denning MR said in regard to the illogicality and irrationality of the principles which *h* govern the award of damages for loss of amenity and loss of future earnings in such cases as the present, where a victim of negligence suffers a catastrophe of such dimensions that he is utterly insensible of any loss of amenity and can have no beneficial use for his potential earnings. An award of damages in those regards offers no solatium to him. In a practical sense such an award does the victim no good; in a moral sense it may not be easy to justify. As the law stands, however, there is an entitlement to compensation *j* under both heads. If the victim has a glimmer of sensibility, he may get some satisfaction from such additional luxury or comfort as a greater financial resource may bring; and, if by some freak of nature or advance in medicine there is an unforeseen measure of recovery, the use of the damages awarded will have a realised impact on the condition in which the victim lives or exists. Furthermore the principle of compensation which pervades the law of damages for tort ought apart from statutory modification or well-

established authority to be consistently and uniformly applied. That the victim may not
a be capable of using for his personal benefit the damages awarded for loss of earnings or
loss of amenity is in a real sense irrelevant. A multi-millionaire who loses a leg in a road
accident will get no comfort or support, which his existing resources do not provide,
from a conventional award of damages. The money will mean little or nothing to him,
but this is no ground for denying him his damages. They are the law's sometimes futile
recompense for that of which a victim of negligence has been deprived.

b   Starting from this position, which has not really been disputed by counsel for the
defendant authority, the next question that arises is whether any different principle
applies in relation to loss of future earnings where the victim is a very young child as in
this case. For my part, I fail to see why there should be any difference in the principles
which determine what are the bases for the recovery of damages whatever the age of the
victim. The assessment of the measure of damages may be more or less difficult but the
c right of the plaintiff to an assessment of damages for that element of damage cannot be
brushed aside. The obligation of the court to make the best assessment it can is not to be
avoided by treating compensation for loss of future earnings in the case of a young child
as being so speculative as not to deserve to be considered at all. On an actuarial basis a
healthy child of two in a caring and comfortable home has a life expectation of some
seventy years. I can see no valid reason for assuming that such a child is unlikely to reach
d adulthood or to achieve the capacity to earn a livelihood. I would adopt the approach of
the judge. He assumed a life expectancy of 40, which was founded on the evidence of
Professor Holt. Some criticism has been directed towards the acceptance of that evidence
inasmuch as two expert witnesses spoke to a considerably shorter period as the probable
expectation. Having read the respective testimonies of the witnesses on both sides, I see
no reason for differing from Michael Davies J in this regard. I would support also the
e figure of £5,000 as representing the average annual earnings the plaintiff would have
achieved if he had not been rendered incapable. Where I part from the judge is in regard
to the adoption of a multiplier of nine. With a life expectancy of 40, the plaintiff's
conjectural working life would be about twenty years at the most. The judge's multiplier
virtually divided that by two. This would have been appropriate if, at the time of the
trial, the plaintiff was at the threshold of his working career; but he was then not eight
f years old and many years away from it.

In his meticulous judgment, to which I pay respectful tribute, Michael Davies J said
that he had 'considered this particular aspect of the case very carefully'. In my view,
however, he had not given due weight to this factor of doubly accelerated payment.
Taking it into account I would adopt a multiplier of five so that the figure for loss of
future earnings would become £25,000.

g   This takes no account of the 'lost years'. I recognise the philosophical anomaly but will
not seek to resolve it. I have had the advantage of reading in draft the judgment about
to be delivered by Griffiths LJ and am content to adopt his exposition of the practical
justification. As Lord Denning MR has said in trenchant terms, there is a high measure
of artificiality in the principles which are applied to this intractable area of compensation
for injuries which are destructive of personality.

h   I turn to the damages for pain and suffering and loss of amenity. It seems to me that,
as there is a tenable claim in this regard which the law recognises, it must, within
conventional limits, be measured against the victim's circumstances and in particular the
extent of his deprivation. A wholly arbitrary assessment does not to me carry any echo
of justice. In *Lim Poh Choo v Camden and Islington Area Health Authority* [1979] 2 All ER
910, [1980] AC 174 an award under this head of £20,000 was upheld in the House of
j Lords. The plaintiff in that case was a lady in early middle age who had had a professional
status as a doctor for some years. She had not been deprived of the enjoyment of life
from its outset. In the present case the plaintiff had no opportunity of enjoying any
significant part of his life at all. Not the innocent joys of childhood or the awkward
pleasures of growing up, of adolescence or of young manhood or of achievement. His
life was made barren when it had hardly begun. I do not see how for the loss of that
measure of living £35,000 can be said to be too much. It is in these days no more than

the price of the more expensive sort of motor car which is a standard amenity of most popular public entertainers.

Next as to the cost of nursing care and its incidentals. The judge adopted a multiplier of 16 years. It is universally accepted that in the assessment of damages in this field where no fixed mathematical basis exists it is not right to apply a slide-rule examination to the determination of the trial judge. In *Lim*'s case the House of Lords approved a multiplier of 12 on the basis of a life expectancy of 36 years, which corresponds in broad terms to the residual life expectancy of the present plaintiff. Dr Lim was, however, approaching 40. Physically and physiologically she was on the down side of life. James Croke was not quite eight at the time of the trial of this action. Physically he was developing and getting stronger despite the damage to his nervous and cerebral systems. His then expectation of life according to Professor Holt, whose opinion commended itself to Michael Davies J, was some 32 years. A multiplier of 16 does appear to me, as to Griffiths LJ, to be too high. Like him I would substitute 14.

While I respectfully agree with the reasoning of Lord Denning MR as to the award of £7,000 for loss of the mother's pension, I would support that sum as part of the overall award as a bolster for the cost of parental care in the way Griffiths LJ does in his judgment, with which in the result I agree.

I would allow the appeal in the respects I have indicated.

Appeal allowed; total award reduced by £37,000. No order as to costs.

Solicitors: *J Tickle & Co* (for the second defendants); *Stiles, Breen & Partners*, Harrow (for the plaintiffs).

Diana Procter   Barrister.

Practice Direction

QUEEN'S BENCH DIVISION (COMMERCIAL COURT)
PARKER J
9th NOVEMBER 1981

Commercial Court – Practice – Urgent matters – Revised practice – Fridays to be devoted to dealing with summonses and other short but urgent matters – Tuesdays ceasing to be summons days – New system to be operated flexibly to avoid difficulties – Parties to notify Commercial Court office of changes in estimated lengths of summonses etc – Counsels' clerks to notify office where counsel involved in more than one summons listed for a particular date – Existence of and suggestions for dealing with difficulties arising from new practice to be notified to Commercial Court Committee or Commercial Court office.

PARKER J gave the following direction at the sitting of the court: As is stated in the Supreme Court Practice 1982 (vol 1, p 1199, para 72/8/3) the Commercial Court has always sought to adapt its procedure to the continually changing needs of the commercial community and there has for some time existed, as a means of communication between the court and that community, the Commercial Court Committee.

One of the principal functions of the court has been and still is to deal swiftly with urgent matters. This it has done by bringing on for trial swiftly cases in which for one reason or another justice requires such a course to be taken, and by disposing as quickly as possible of other urgent matters such as applications for summary judgment, for orders continuing or discharging interlocutory injunctions, for interlocutory orders of various kinds, for orders to arbitrators to state a special case under the Arbitration Act 1950 or, now, motions for leave to appeal under the Arbitration Act 1979 and so on.

a Recently the volume of such urgent matters requiring early disposal has very considerably increased. In 1978, for example, 1,180 summonses occupying 115 judge-days were heard, whilst in the year to July 1981 the comparative figures were 2,106 summonses and 277 judge-days.

The result has been that return dates for such urgent matters have had to be put further and further ahead. In order that earlier return dates may be given for such matters which are likely to occupy less than one day, it has been decided, after discussion b in the Commercial Court Committee, to introduce, initially for an experimental period only, a new system.

As from Friday, 20th November 1981 all five Commercial Judges will normally sit on Fridays solely for the purpose of dealing with summonses and other short but urgent matters, and Tuesdays will cease to be summons days.

I say normally, for it is recognised (1) that such a practice might involve the parties to c a case part heard on a Thursday in unjustifiable extra expense if the case were adjourned to Monday in order to enable the judge to deal with short matters on Friday, (2) that there may be short matters which for one reason or another cannot be heard on a Friday and must be heard on a Tuesday or some other day, and (3) that if all judges are taking short matters on Fridays there may be insurmountable difficulties for both sides of the profession in having more than one matter in which they are involved coming on on the d same day.

The new system will therefore be operated on a flexible basis so as to obviate, or at least to reduce to a minimum, the foregoing difficulties and any others which may be found to arise when it is in operation.

In order that the new system can operate efficiently two essential requirements must be fulfilled. They are: (1) parties must notify the Commercial Court office of any change e in the estimated lengths of their summonses or other matters immediately such changes become known; (2) where counsel are involved in more than one summons listed for a particular date, notification of that fact must be made to such office by counsels' clerks not later than 9.30 am on the day prior to the return date.

In anticipation of the possible introduction of this system, the number of matters listed for Tuesdays has recently been kept down to a minimum but there are some which f are still so listed. The parties involved should, if they possibly can, apply for the matter to be refixed for a Friday. This need not involve any delay.

The new system will make it possible for some at least of matters which are presently fixed for dates more than two months in the future to be refixed for earlier dates. Parties with such late return dates, who wish their matters to be heard earlier, should make application to Mr Bird, the clerk to the Commercial Court, for earlier dates.

g In conclusion I should stress two points. (1) The purpose of the system is to accelerate urgent matters. Applications for leave to appeal under the 1979 Act are normally regarded as being in this category. I should, however, mention that there are several hundred applications for leave to appeal or other matters arising out of arbitration awards which were issued more than a year ago but for which no return date has yet been sought. Such, and other, dormant applications, although coming within a category h normally regarded as urgent, will, if hereafter proceeded with, not be regarded as urgent in the absence of some convincing argument for sudden urgency being shown. It may be that many of them are in fact dead. If they are it would be of the greatest assistance to the court if that fact could be notified as soon as possible. (2) It may be that the benefit to litigants which the new system is designed to produce will produce difficulties not presently envisaged. It will be of the greatest assistance if the existence of, and any j suggestions for dealing with, any such difficulties are promptly communicated to the Commercial Court Committee in accordance with the open invitation which appears in the Supreme Court Practice 1982 (vol 1, p 1199, para 72/8/3) or to the Commercial Court office.

K Mydeen Esq   Barrister.

Aspinall v Sterling Mansell Ltd

QUEEN'S BENCH DIVISION AT MANCHESTER
HODGSON J
21st JULY 1978

Practice – Stay of proceedings – Medical examination of plaintiff at defendant's request – b
Examination involving risk – Refusal to submit to examination – Reasonableness of plaintiff's
refusal – Plaintiff suffering from industrial dermatitis – Defendant seeking examination involving
patch testing of plaintiff – Patch testing involving minimal but real risk of recrudescence of
dermatitis – Whether plaintiff's objection reasonable – Whether plaintiff should give evidence of
reasons for objection – Whether proceedings should be stayed pending patch testing of plaintiff.

c
The plaintiff brought an action against the defendants claiming damages for industrial
dermatitis which she alleged was contracted during her employment by the defendants
and as a result of their fault. The plaintiff's solicitors offered the defendants' insurers the
usual facilities for a medical examination of the plaintiff. The insurers accepted the offer
and instructed a skin disease consultant to examine the plaintiff. The consultant
proposed to carry out some skin tests, known as patch tests, on the plaintiff. Such tests d
involved a minor, but real, risk of recrudescence of dermatitis. The plaintiff objected to
undergoing patch testing. The defendants then sought an order that all further
proceedings in the action be stayed unless and until the plaintiff submitted to the
examination and to patch testing.

Held – Although a defendant in an action for damages for personal injuries had a right e
to defend himself in the litigation as he and his advisers thought fit, that did not give him
a right to choose the method by which his expert medical witnesses could examine the
plaintiff where that method extended beyond an ordinary examination and included a
procedure such as patch testing. A distinction was to be drawn between an ordinary
medical examination of a plaintiff and an examination which involved 'experimenting'
or a diagnostic procedure such as patch testing. The difference between a medical f
examination which included manual interference with the patient's body and such
procedures as patch testing, the use of a hypodermic syringe, the administration of a drug
or anaesthetic and, at the far end of the scale, exploratory operations was one of kind and
not degree. In such circumstances the plaintiff's right to personal liberty had to prevail.
It was not the reasonableness of the defendant's request which was in question but the
reasonableness of the plaintiff's refusal, and it could not be unreasonable for a plaintiff to
refuse to undergo a procedure which carried with it a risk, however minimal, so long as g
it could be called real, of serious injury. It followed that the defendant's application for
a stay of proceedings would be dismissed (see p 868 *a* to *c* and *g* to *j*, post).

Dictum of Scarman LJ in *Starr v National Coal Board* [1977] 1 All ER at 249 applied.

Per Curiam. A plaintiff is entitled to instruct his legal advisers to contest an application
by the defendant for a stay of proceedings pending medical examination of the plaintiff h
without himself giving evidence of his reasons for his objection to undergoing the
examination (see p 869 *a b*, post).

Notes

For the circumstances in which an action may be stayed, see 30 Halsbury's Laws (3rd
Edn) 407, para 768, and for cases on the subject, see 51 Digest (Repl) 1003–1008, 5374– j
5404.

For disclosure of medical evidence, see 13 Halsbury's Laws (4th Edn) para 53.

Cases referred to in judgment

Edmeades v Thames Board Mills Ltd [1969] 2 All ER 127, [1969] 2 QB 67, [1969] 2 WLR
668, [1969] 1 Lloyd's Rep 221, CA, Digest (Cont Vol C) 1102, 5371*a*.

Lane v Willis, Lane v Beach (executor of estate of George William Willis (deceased)) [1972] 1 All

a ER 430, [1972] 1 WLR 326, CA, Digest (Cont Vol D) 1068, 5371c.

Pickett v Bristol Aeroplane Co Ltd (1961) Times, 17th March, [1961] Court of Appeal
Transcript 114.

Starr v National Coal Board [1977] 1 All ER 243, [1977] 1 WLR 63, CA, Digest (Cont Vol
E) 670, 5354c.

Interlocutory appeal

b The defendants, Sterling Mansell Ltd, appealed against the decision of Mr District
Registrar Gavin on 26th May 1978 whereby he dismissed an application by the
defendants for an order that all further proceedings in an action commenced by a writ
dated 21st February 1977 and brought against the defendants by the plaintiff, Edna
Aspinall, for damages for personal injury and/or physical harm occasioned to her by the
negligence of the defendants while she was employed by them at their premises at

c Mansell Way, Horwich, Bolton, in Greater Manchester, be stayed unless and until the
plaintiff submitted to a medical examination by Dr Anne Maguire and to patch testing.
The appeal was heard in chambers. The case is reported by permission of Hodgson J.
The facts are set out in the judgment.

Simon Fawcus for the defendants.

d *Janet Smith* for the plaintiff.

At the conclusion of the hearing Hodgson J announced that the appeal would be
dismissed and that he would send his written reasons to the parties' solicitors at a later
date.

e **HODGSON J.** The plaintiff is claiming damages for industrial dermatitis which was,
she alleges, contracted during her employment by the defendants and due to their fault.

As long ago as 24th June 1975 the plaintiff's solicitors wrote to the defendant's insurers
offering them 'The usual facilities for a medical examination on your behalf'. Eighteen
months later the insurers wrote accepting this offer and saying that they proposed to
instruct Dr Anne Maguire. On 14th January 1977 the solicitors instructed by the

f plaintiff replied to the insurers and in so doing, took the stand which has led to this
appeal. 'While there is no objection to Doctor Maguire examining this client,' they
wrote, 'There would be every objection to patch tests being carried out.'

The correspondence continued, and it is not, I think contested by the plaintiff's
counsel that her case is argued primarily as a matter of principle, rather than as stemming
from any strongly held personal objection of the plaintiff's to patch testing.

g As a result of the continued objection of the plaintiff to undergoing patch testing the
defendants sought from the district registrar an order that all further proceedings in the
action be stayed unless and until the plaintiff submits to a medical examination by Dr
Anne Maguire, at Blackburn, and to patch testing. There is not, nor has there ever been,
any objection to an examination by Dr Anne Maguire, and this case therefore is solely
concerned with the question whether the plaintiff should be shut out from the seat of

h justice or compelled against her will to be subjected to patch testing.

The district registrar in a careful judgment dismissed the defendants' application.
From that dismissal they appeal.

Affidavits from Dr Anne Maguire and Dr Benjamin Portnoy, the doctor instructed by
the plaintiff's solicitors, were before the registar and are before me. Counsel for the
defendants contends that I should not concern myself with questions as to the efficacy

j and conclusiveness of patch testing as an aid to diagnosis in cases of industrial dermatitis.
I think that is right. It is well known that there is a difference of opinion between
eminent dermatologists on the matter, as is amply demonstrated by the two affidavits in
this case, and it is not something on which one could properly express a judicial opinion
merely on the evidence provided in two affidavits.

I do not, therefore, go behind the affidavits. All I take from them is that on which
they are not in disagreement. Dr Anne Maguire says: 'In the applying of patch tests there

is a minor risk of very slight irritation where a positive result is obtained . . . The risk involved is considered by all Patch Testing Units to be minimal.' It is agreed that, in this *a* second sentence, Dr Maguire is speaking of the risk of a major recrudescence of dermatitis. Dr Portnoy says: 'With regard to the dangers of patch testing, I agree that such dangers are minimal but the risk of recrudescence undoubtedly exists . . .'

If, therefore, I allow this appeal I shall be either exposing the plaintiff to an admittedly very slight risk of a major recrudescence of dermatitis or denying her the right to pursue her claim for damages. In any event I shall be exposing her to something which, in my *b* judgment, goes significantly further than an ordinary medical examination. The district registrar drew the distinction between 'examining' someone and 'experimenting' on someone. I think that it is a valid distinction. Counsel for the defendants has urged that it is 'but a short step' from an ordinary medical examination, with its necessary interference with the plaintiff's personal liberty, to an examination which involves a diagnostic procedure such as patch testing. I disagree. In my judgment the difference *c* between medical examination including, as it must, manual interference with the patient's body and such procedures as patch testing, the use of a hypodermic syringe, the administration of a drug or anaesthetic and, at the far end of the scale, exploratory operations is one of kind not of degree.

The decision of the Court of Appeal in *Starr v National Coal Board* [1977] 1 All ER 243, [1977] 1 WLR 63 has been cited to me. This case, and the line of cases which culminated *d* in it were all concerned with the identity of the doctor who the defendants wanted to examine the plaintiff. Scarman LJ outlined the principles to be applied by a court in the exercise of its discretion in those cases ([1977] 1 All ER 243 at 249, [1977] 1 WLR 63 at 70–71):

> 'So what is the principle of the matter to be gleaned from those cases? In my judgment the court can order a stay if, in the words of Lord Denning MR in *e* [*Edmeades v Thames Board Mills Ltd* [1969] 2 All ER 127 at 129, [1969] 2 QB 67 at 71], "the conduct of the plaintiff in refusing a reasonable request [for medical examination] is such as to prevent the just determination of the cause". I think that those words contain the principle of the matter. We are, of course, in the realm of discretion. It is a matter for the discretion of the judge, exercised judicially on the facts of the case, whether or not a stay should be ordered. For myself, I find talk *f* about "onus of proof" in such a case inappropriate. There is, I think, clearly a general rule that he who seeks a stay of action must satisfy the court that justice requires the imposition of a stay. In the exercise of the discretion in this class of case, where a plaintiff has refused a medical examination, I think the court does have to recognise (and here I think [*Pickett v Bristol Aeroplane Co Ltd* (1961) Times, 17th March] is helpful) that in the balance there are, amongst many other factors, two *g* fundamental rights which are cherished by the common law and to which attention has to be directed by the court. First, as mentioned in *Pickett's* case by Willmer and Donovan LJJ, and by Sachs LJ in [*Lane v Willis* [1972] 1 All ER 430 at 435–436, [1972] 1 WLR 326 at 333], there is the plaintiff's right to personal liberty. But on the other side there is an equally fundamental right—the defendant's right to defend himself in the litigation as he and his advisers think fit; and this is a right *h* which includes the freedom to choose the witnesses that he will call. It is particularly important that a defendant should be able to choose his own expert witnesses, if the case be one in which expert testimony is significant.'

Applying those principles to this case, can it be said that a defendant has a right to choose the way in which his witness can examine a plaintiff where that way extends *j* beyond an ordinary examination and includes a procedure such as patch testing? I think not. In my judgment in this situation the plaintiff's right to personal liberty must prevail. It is not, in my opinion, the reasonableness of the defendant's request which is here in question but the reasonableness of the plaintiff's refusal. And I do not think it can ever be unreasonable for a plaintiff to refuse to undergo a procedure which carries with it a risk, however minimal, so long as it can be called real, of serious injury.

a It has been strongly urged on me that, before I refuse to stay the plaintiff's action, I should have an affidavit from the plaintiff herself setting out her personal objections to patch testing. I do not agree. In my judgment a plaintiff is entitled to instruct her legal advisers to contest an application such as the defendants' in this case without herself giving evidence. Whether her objection is taken as a matter of principle or because of a personal aversion the result of my ordering a stay would be the same. It would be an interference with her personal liberty, which, in the exercise of my discretion, I am not
b prepared to enforce.

Appeal dismissed. Leave to appeal granted.

Solicitors: *Keogh, Ritson & Co*, Bolton (for the defendants); *Brian Thompson & Partners*, Manchester (for the plaintiff).

c
M Denise Chorlton   Barrister.

d

Prescott v Bulldog Tools Ltd

QUEEN'S BENCH DIVISION AT MANCHESTER
WEBSTER J
e 21st, 22nd JULY 1980

Practice – Stay of proceedings – Medical examination of plaintiff at defendant's request – Examination involving discomfort and risk – Refusal to submit to examination – Reasonableness of plaintiff's refusal – Reasonableness of refusal to be balanced against reasonableness of defendant's request – Reasonableness to be considered in light of information or advice received
f *from parties' advisers – Matters to be considered – Plaintiff suffering from industrial deafness – Employer seeking examination to see if deafness related to employment – Plaintiff contending examination would involve discomfort, radiation hazard and danger of infection – Whether proceedings should be stayed pending examination of plaintiff.*

The plaintiff brought an action against the defendants, his employers, claiming damages
g for noise-induced industrial deafness attributable to the negligence of the defendants. The plaintiff claimed that he had developed nerve deafness in both ears with the maximal loss in the high tone frequencies and that he had tinnitus and episodes of vertigo. The defendants denied liability for any deafness which the plaintiff had developed. The plaintiff underwent three medical examinations arranged by his own solicitors. Those examinations revealed that the deafness in the plaintiff's right ear, the tinnitus and the
h left-side vestibular disorder were probably not noise-induced. The reports were sent to the defendants' solicitors, who also arranged to have medical examinations of the plaintiff carried out. The defendants' solicitors arranged four such examinations, two of which were carried out by ear, nose and throat consultants, one by a consultant physician of occupational medicine and one by a neurologist. The reports of those four examinations were not sent to the plaintiff's solicitors. The defendants wished to have the plaintiff
j examined a fifth time. The examination would take between three and five days to carry out and involve a number of tests, including a caloric test (which involved running water 4° above or below body temperature into the outer ear canal), a polytomography (which was an X-ray of the inner ear) and an electrocochleography (which involved placing a very fine needle through the ear-drum). The tests were designed to see if the deafness in the plaintiff's left ear had some connection with the deafness in his right ear. The defendants did not contend that an opinion could not be given on the matter without the

tests being carried out, but they asserted that the tests would enable an opinion on the matter could be given with greater confidence. The plaintiff objected to the tests, contending, inter alia, (i) that it was unreasonable for the defendants to wish to have him examined a fifth time, and (ii) that it was reasonable for him to refuse to undergo the tests because the caloric test caused discomfort, giddiness and nausea, was frightening and caused some patients to vomit, the polytomography involved a radiation hazard to the brain and eyes which should be avoided if possible, and the electrocochleography was unpleasant and frightening and involved a danger that the ear membrane could be punctured, which could result in damage to the ear by infection. The defendants applied for the proceedings to be stayed unless and until the plaintiff submitted to the examination.

Held – (1) In general the decision whether to grant a stay pending medical examination of the plaintiff involved the exercise of the court's discretion, in which it was necessary for the court to balance a plaintiff's right to personal liberty against a defendant's right to defend himself in the litigation as he thought fit, and there was no reason in principle why one right should be regarded as more important than the other. In determining whether either party was being reasonable the question for the court was not whether the plaintiff's objection was objectively reasonable nor whether the defendant's request was objectively reasonable but whether the objection or the request was reasonable in the light of the information or advice which the respective parties received from their advisers. Furthermore, where the defendant's request for an examination was reasonable, the court could grant a stay if the plaintiff's refusal of that request would be such as to prevent the just determination of the cause, and the court would normally treat the fact that the defendant would be deprived of the expert of his choice as something which would prevent the just determination of the cause (see p 874 b to h and p 875 c and f g, post); dicta of Scarman and of Geoffrey Lane LJJ in *Starr v National Coal Board* [1977] 1 All ER at 251, 254 applied.

(2) In deciding whether the plaintiff's objection to undergoing the examination in question was reasonable, a distinction had to be made between (a) an examination which did not involve any serious technical assault but which only involved an invasion of privacy, (b) an examination which involved some technical assault, such as a palpation, (c) an examination involving a substantial assault but without involving discomfort and risk, (d) an examination involving a substantial assault which also involved discomfort and risk, and (e) an examination which involved risk of injury or to health. Where the defendant genuinely believed that he could not defend a case which might cost him personally in damages much more than he was worth unless the plaintiff were to submit to an examination which involved a real but minimal risk of some short-term injury to the plaintiff's health and where the defendant agreed to compensate the plaintiff for any such injury, the question whether the plaintiff's refusal to submit to that examination was reasonable was to be determined by the court by examining objectively the weight of the reasonableness of the defendant's request as seen by him and the weight of the reasonableness of the plaintiff's objection as seen by him, and balancing the one against the other to ensure a just determination of the cause as between the parties, taking into account their reasonable requirements and objections at the time of the exercising of the discretion (see p 874 j to p 875 a and c to g, post); *Aspinall v Sterling Mansell Ltd* [1981] 3 All ER 866 not followed.

(3) In all the circumstances the defendants' request for a fifth examination and the plaintiff's objection to the three tests were both reasonable, but the weight of the reasonableness of the plaintiff's objections to the electrocochleography and the polytomography outweighed the reasonableness of the defendants' request for those two tests, while the weight of the reasonableness of the defendants' request for a caloric test outweighed the reasonableness of the plaintiff's objection to that test (see p 875 h j, p 876 e to h and p 877 g, post).

Notes

a   For the circumstances in which an action may be stayed, see 30 Halsbury's Laws (3rd Edn) 407, para 768, and for cases on the subject, see 51 Digest (Repl) 1003–1008, 5374–5404.

For disclosure of medical evidence, see 13 Halsbury's Laws (4th Edn) para 53.

Cases referred to in judgment

b   *Aspinall v Sterling Mansell Ltd* [1981] 3 All ER 866, QBD at Manchester.

Smith v British Rail Engineering Ltd (1980) Times, 27th June, CA.

Starr v National Coal Board [1977] 1 All ER 243, [1977] 1 WLR 63, CA, Digest (Cont Vol E) 670, 5354c.

c   **Interlocutory appeal**

The defendants, Bulldog Tools Ltd, appealed against the order of Mr District Registrar Evans dated 11th February 1980 whereby he refused an application by the defendants for an order that all further proceedings in an action commenced by a writ dated 29th July 1976 and brought against the defendants by the plaintiff, James Prescott, for damages for personal injury be stayed unless and until the plaintiff submitted to a medical examination on behalf of the defendants by Professor Ronald Hinchcliffe, consultant

d   neuro-otologist to the Royal National Throat, Nose and Ear Hospital, professor of audiological medicine at the University of London. The appeal was heard in chambers but judgment was given by Webster J in open court. The facts are set out in the judgment.

e   *L D Lawton QC* and *G W Wingate-Saul* for the defendants.

Richard Clegg QC and *Janet Smith* for the plaintiff.

WEBSTER J. In this case the plaintiff is claiming damages for alleged industrial deafness attributable to the alleged negligence of the defendants, his employers. He issued his writ on 29th July 1976 and on 8th February 1977 he served a writ accompanied

f   by a statement of claim, in which he alleged that he had developed nerve deafness in both ears with the maximal loss in the high tone frequencies and that he had tinnitus and episodes of vertigo.

The defence was served on 7th April 1977. In it liability and damage were denied. The Limitation Act was pleaded, and in addition it was alleged that any damage (which was not admitted) had been sustained as a result of the plaintiff's contributory negligence

g   in failing to make any proper use of the ear muffs and/or protective wool which were readily available for his use.

On 14th June 1977 the order for directions was made, including the usual order for the mutual disclosure of medical reports, and on 28th June the case was set down for trial.

Both sides have had medical examinations of the plaintiff. The plaintiff's adviser's first had him examined by Mr Devine, who produced a report dated 2nd September 1976 in

h   which he expressed the opinion that there was no doubt that the plaintiff—

> 'has sustained noise-induced hearing loss and I would regard the loss in the left ear as being entirely attributable to this cause. Consideration of the right ear, however is considerably more complicated. It is in no way suggested that [the plaintiff] has tried to conceal any information, but the fact is that there has been inflammatory
>
> j   disease in the middle ear in the past with a perforation of the eardrum. It is quite probable that this may have occurred in early childhood and he would have then no recollection of the incident. He has a virtual total deafness in this right ear and it would indeed be extremely rare to find a loss of this severity as a result of noise trauma . . . It is impossible to be sure to what degree noise trauma has operated in

the case of the right ear. Taking the balance of probabilities it would seem reasonable to conclude that a similar degree of loss from noise trauma has operated *a* in the right ear as in the left ear and that it would seem reasonable to agree a bilateral loss of forty-eight decibels attributable to noise-induced hearing loss.'

On 25th August 1977 Dr Siddiqui, the plaintiff's general practitioner, wrote a report, to which I need not refer.

On 1st December 1977 Professor Coles carried out, or had carried out for him, a *b* number of examinations, and he wrote a report. Again, I quote from his opinion. He said:

> 'The hearing loss on the right cannot be attributed to noise; that is, although he may at some time have had some noise-induced hearing loss on that side, he would probably be no less deaf in that ear now if he had never been noise exposed. Likewise, the tinnitus is probably not due to noise exposure. The cause of the *c* hearing loss on the right side is uncertain. It may have been present for years. But the relatively recent hint of onset of his deafness, and more definite onset of tinnitus, coupled with his corneal hypoaesthesia and taste threshold elevation both on the right side, raise suspicion of a possible VIII nerve neuroma which, medically, cannot be ignored . . . The vestibular function test results were most unexpected. They explain his imbalance symptoms of 1976, but do not fit the right-sided *d* auditory lesion since the canal paresis is of the left ear. The left sided vestibular disorder cannot, however, be attributed to noise.'

By 14th June 1978 those three reports to which I have referred had been sent to the defendants' solicitors. The defendants have also had examinations carried out: first in March 1977 by a Mr Farrington, a consultant specialist in ear, nose and throat; second in *e* December, jointly by Mr Clarke, also an ear, nose and throat consultant, and Professor Atherley, a consultant physician of occupational medicine; and finally in October 1978 by Dr Evans, a neurologist. None of the reports of these examinations have been sent to the plaintiff's solicitors.

The present issue arises because the defendants want the plaintiff to be examined a fifth time, this time by Professor Hinchcliffe. *f*

On 11th August 1978 the defendants first asked for facilities for the plaintiff to be examined by Professor Hinchcliffe, and at first the plaintiff's solicitors agreed. Shortly before 3rd November 1978 the plaintiff attended at a hospital for that examination but he was told, or at any rate he thought he was told, that the examination would take five days. As he had been expecting only to spend one night at the hospital, perhaps not surprisingly he came away. *g*

There followed an exchange of correspondence about the length of the examination which Professor Hinchcliffe wanted to carry out and its nature. On 27th December the defendants' solicitors sent to the plaintiff's solicitors a copy of a letter dated 20th December 1978 from Professor Hinchcliffe to them, in which he set out the tests or examinations which he proposed to carry out. The last three were an electrocochleography, a vestibular function study with electrical recordings (which are referred to *h* hereafter as 'the caloric test') and X-ray studies of the ears (which I refer to hereafter as 'the polytomography'). The caloric test involves running water which is either 7° above or 7° below body temperature into the outer ear canal. Professor Hinchcliffe says that this test could be carried out with water 4° above or below body temperature. Polytomography is an X-ray of the inner ear. Electrocochleography involves placing a very fine needle through the ear-drum to abut the inner bony wall of the middle ear. *j*

Counsel for the defendants summarised the object, from the point of view of the defendants, of carrying out each of those tests. So far as the caloric tests were concerned, he said the object was to indicate the nature and the extent of the damage to the balance mechanism of the plaintiff's ears. As to the polytomography, the object was to show any

defect to the inner ear, and as to the electrocochleography the object was to ascertain
a whether any internal ear disorder existed.

On 24th April 1979 the plaintiff's solicitors wrote to the defendants' solicitors saying
they had no objection to Professor Hinchcliffe undertaking a medico-legal examination
of the plaintiff on the following terms: '1. the investigation is to take no more than ¾ of
a working day. 2. following investigations are not to be done a. electrocochleography
(ECOG) b. polytomography c. caloric tests, investibula investigation.'

b   Why do the defendants want these examinations? As already appears in Professor
Coles's report, the right-side deafness is not attributable to noise, the tinnitus is probably
not attributable to noise, and the left-side vestibular disorder is not attributable to
noise. Therefore, say the defendants, some other factors, if they are playing a part in the
deafness of the right ear, may also be playing a part in the deafness of the left ear. The
same considerations apply to the vestibular disorder and, therefore, they want an
c investigation of the right ear and the vestibular disorder. All this is in order to ascertain
the extent of the deafness in the left ear, the reason for it and the date of its onset.
Counsel for the defendants does not suggest, nor does Professor Hinchcliffe's affidavit
state, that an opinion on these matters, at least to the extent of the right ear deafness or
the reasons for the right ear deafness or the date of its onset, cannot be given without the
carrying out of Professor Hinchcliffe's examination, but counsel says that with such an
d examination the opinion on those issues can be given with greater confidence. In
addition, he says that Professor Hinchcliffe, as appears from his affidavit, will not have
any restriction imposed on any examinations he wishes to carry out.

The plaintiff by his counsel has given his reasons for resisting these examinations.
First he says that, already having had the examination of four experienced doctors, it is
unreasonable for the defendants to want him examined by a fifth, particularly as they
e have not disclosed any reports so far received by them from the first four, and as the trial
has already been delayed. Second, it is said on behalf of the plaintiff that the defendants'
request for three particular examinations is unreasonable and the plaintiff's refusal to
undergo them is reasonable: so far as the caloric test is concerned, because it causes
discomfort, it is frightening to some patients, it causes giddiness and nausea in many if
not most cases, and it causes some patients to vomit; so far as the polytomography is
f concerned, because it involves radiation dosage to the brain and eyes, a radiation hazard
which should be avoided if possible; and so far as the electrocochleography is concerned,
because it is somewhat unpleasant and frightening to some patients and is not without
danger in that occasionally the ear membrane is punctured, as a result of which damage
to ear from infection could follow. Moreover, Professor Coles doubts the utility and the
necessity of each examination. And the third reason on which the plaintiff relies is that
g the examinations may involve him in total in a loss of liberty of between three and five
days, although the defendants are willing to compensate him for the loss of his earnings
during that period.

On the plaintiff's refusing to submit to the examinations, the defendants applied to
stay the proceedings. An application came before the registrar on 10th December 1979
which was adjourned part heard to 29th January 1980, and a reserved judgment was
h given by the registrar on 11th February. In his judgment he decided that the defendants'
request for the plaintiff to submit to a fifth examination taking between three and five
days was reasonable. If this were the only issue, it is clear that he would have allowed the
defendants' application, but he upheld the plaintiff's objections to two out of the three
specific tests.

Because of the conflict of evidence on the affidavits before him, he did not decide the
j question of whether any of the tests were necessary or useful, but, although he found that
the polytomography, if carried out as Professor Hinchcliffe proposed and if it had been
the only examination proposed, was not objectionable, he found as a matter of fact on the
evidence contained in the affidavits that the caloric test induces a certain degree of
discomfort and that the electrocochleography test involves risk and discomfort, and he

therefore dismissed the defendants' application. The defendants now appeal against that decision. They say not only that it was wrong but that the registrar should not have *a* decided an issue of fact on the affidavits as he did, and they apply for leave to adduce the evidence of Professor Hinchcliffe in support of their appeal.

I look now at the decided cases, beginning with the decision of the Court of Appeal in *Starr v National Coal Board* [1977] 1 All ER 243, [1977] 1 WLR 63. Neither in that case nor in any of the cases considered by that court, I am told, had the party objected to the examination because of any risk or discomfort associated with it. No opinion was *b* expressed by the court in *Starr's* case on the considerations which should be taken into account in such a case. I ask myself, therefore, whether it is possible to deduce any principles of general application from that case, that is to say, of general application which may be relevant to the decision in the present case. In my view, it is possible to deduce three general principles: first that the decision whether or not to grant a stay involves the exercise of the court's discretion, second that in exercising that discretion it *c* is necessary for the court to balance the right of one party, the plaintiff, to personal liberty, against the right of the other party, the defendant, to defend himself in litigation as he thinks fit, and third that in determining whether either party is being reasonable the question is not whether in the case of the plaintiff his objection is objectively reasonable, or in the case of the defendant whether his request is objectively reasonable, but whether the objection or the request as the case may be is reasonable in the light of *d* the information or the advice which the respective parties receive from their respective advisers (see [1977] 1 All ER 243 at 251, 254, [1977] 1 WLR 63 at 72, 75 per Scarman and Geoffrey Lane LJJ.)

I cannot deduce any principle as to whether it is for the plaintiff to satisfy the court that his objection is reasonable, or whether it is for the defendants to satisfy it that it is not, because Scarman and Geoffrey Lane LJJ appear not to have been at one on that point (cf *e* [1977] 1 All ER 243 at 251, 254, [1977] 1 WLR 63 at 72, 75).

There is one further principle of general application to be derived from *Starr's* case, where there was no question of risk or discomfort, and that seems to be that where the defendant's request for an examination is reasonable the court can grant a stay if the plaintiff's refusal of that request would be such as to prevent the just determination of the cause, and that the court will normally treat the fact that the defendant would be *f* deprived of the expert of his choice as something which would prevent the just determination of the cause within the meaning of that expression as the Court of Appeal used it.

Then I ask myself the question: what principles apply when the plaintiff relies on the contention that there is risk or discomfort attached to the examination in question? First, as I have already said, in my view the principle to be derived from *Starr's* case is that *g* the issue is not whether there is ground for the plaintiff's objection but whether he reasonably apprehends that there is a risk in the light of the advice and the information that he has received. Beyond that, the decision and the judgments in *Starr's* case do not at first sight enable one to go.

I look next, therefore, at the judgment of Hodgson J in *Aspinall v Sterling Mansell Ltd* [1981] 3 All ER 866. In that case Hodgson J first of all distinguished between an *h* examination or a pure examination on the one hand and a test on the other. He also said (at 868): '. . . I do not think it can ever be unreasonable for a plaintiff to refuse to undergo a procedure which carries with it a risk, however minimal, so long as it can be called real, of serious injury.' On any matter and in particular a matter of this kind I naturally attach great weight to the judgment of Hodgson J, but, with respect, for my part I would approach those two matters, each of which can be said to arise in the present case, with *j* a slightly different emphasis.

For my part I would only distinguish between the following examinations: first, an examination which does not involve any serious technical assault, but involving only an invasion of privacy; second, an examination involving some technical assault, such as a *a* palpation; third, an examination involving a substantial assault but without involving discomfort and risk; fourth, the same, that is to say a substantial assault, but involving discomfort and risk; and fifth, an examination involving risk of injury or to health.

It seems to me that the weight of the reasonableness of the plaintiff's objections (to which I will refer later) must bear a very close correlation to the order in which I have listed those distinctions.

b On the second point, the passage from Hodgson J's judgment which I have just quoted, although in practice it seems to me that it is extremely unlikely that a court would ever hold it to be unreasonable for a plaintiff to refuse to undergo a procedure which carries with it the risk of *serious* injury (I emphasise the word serious) it seems to me that in the light of *Starr's* case the court must always consider the matter without introducing any presumption one way or the other; for Scarman LJ contemplated that one or other of the parties might have to accept an infringement of a fundamental

c human right cherished by the common law (see [1977] 1 All ER 243 at 250, [1977] 1 WLR 63 at 71), and I can see no reason in principle why one right should be regarded as more important than another. Suppose that a defendant genuinely believed that he could not defend at all a case which might cost him personally, in damages, much more than he was worth unless the plaintiff were to submit to a particular examination. Suppose that the examination involved a real but minimal risk of some short-term injury

d to the plaintiff's health; suppose that the defendant agreed to compensate the plaintiff for any such injury, and suppose that the plaintiff refused. Is it to be said without question that the plaintiff's refusal is necessarily reasonable?

In my view, in cases involving similar considerations the court should examine objectively the weight of the reasonableness of the defendant's request as seen by the defendant and the weight of the reasonableness of the plaintiff's objections as seen by

e him, and balance the one against the other in order to ensure a just determination of the cause in the way most just to the parties, taking into account their reasonable requirements and objections at the time of the exercising of the discretion. This approach, it seems to me, is a logical conclusion, when the question is considered in the context of an adversarial rather than an inquisitorial procedure; in an inquisitorial context, it might well be that the court would have to decide objectively whether an examination was necessary, as distinct from determining whether a defendant reasonably

f thought it to be necessary.

How, then, should these conclusions be applied to the present case? Taking first the plaintiff's general objection to any fifth examination at all, the answer to the question just posed depends on the following subsidiary questions. First, is the defendants' request for a fifth examination reasonable as seen by them? Second, are the plaintiff's objections to a fifth examination reasonable as seen by him? Third, what is the weight

g of the reasonableness of the defendants' request as compared with the weight of the reasonableness of the plaintiff's objections?

Although there is a clear inference to be drawn, as counsel for the defendants agrees, from the circumstances that the defendants do not at present intend to rely on or to call as witnesses those experts who have previously examined the plaintiff on their behalf,

h none the less, in my view, they are perfectly entitled to seek a fifth examination, particularly in such a relatively new field as that of industrial deafness in which I infer, from the evidence and from the report of *Smith v British Rail Engineering Ltd* (1980) Times, 27th June, there are new techniques of examination under development, and particularly since in this case, according to the advice of the plaintiff's own medical advisers, some of his complaints are not attributable to noise. I note also that the defendants did not

j receive Professor Coles's report until after Mr Farrington and Mr Clarke and Professor Atherley had examined the plaintiff. In my judgment, therefore, the defendants' request is, in the light of the information they have, reasonable.

The plaintiff's first objection is that the defendants failed to disclose the reports already received by them, and he complains of the delay which a further examination would cause. As to the failure to disclose the reports, it does not seem to me that that constitutes any failure on their part, so long as they are not proposing to call those expert witnesses. As to the delay, the matter has to be seen, in my view, as at August 1978, when the defendants first asked for the fifth examination. As at that date, it does not seem to me that the delay caused by a further examination would have been prejudicial to the plaintiff, and I do not think that that conclusion has been substantially altered by the lapse of time between August 1978 and today, a lapse for which I do not understand either party is accusing the other party of having been responsible.

Although I do not find that the plaintiff's first objection is unreasonable, when comparing the weight of the reasonableness of that objection with that of the reasonableness of the defendants' request, in my judgment the scales come down heavily on the defendants' side and I would not uphold the plaintiff's first objection.

What of his second objection, namely to the three tests? Here again, I pose the same questions and answer them in the following way. In my judgment, the defendants, as they see their case, reasonably require each of the three examinations. But they do not suggest that opinions on the extent and cause of the plaintiff's deafness cannot be given without the benefit of those tests: they require them for two reasons: first so that they can have the benefit of Professor Hinchcliffe's opinion and expert testimony, which he will not provide unless he is allowed to carry out the tests; and second so that the diagnosis can be provided with greater confidence or precision.

I deal with the first of those two reasons later in this judgment. As to the second reason, it is necessary to balance its objective weight with that of the plaintiff's objections to each of the examinations. He objects to them because he is advised and informed that one of them, the caloric test, involves discomfort (which I have already mentioned) and because the others, as he is advised, involve a risk of injury or injury to health. I am satisfied that on the evidence he reasonably apprehends a risk, which is substantial, of discomfort, which is not insubstantial, from the first test. And, I am satisfied that he reasonably apprehends risks from the other two which, though minimal, are real and which are risks of not insubstantial and possibly serious injury or injuries to health.

In my judgment, on the evidence, his objections to each of the three tests are reasonable, but the question then arises: how does the reasonableness of those objections compare in weight with the reasonableness of the defendants' requests that they should be carried out. In my judgment, the weight of the reasonableness of his objections to the electrocochleography and to the polytomography outweighs the weight of the reasonableness of the defendants' requests for each of these two examinations, albeit that those two requests are reasonable.

On the other hand, it seems to me, and I have so found, that the reasonableness of the defendants' request for their expert to carry out a caloric test outweighs the reasonableness of the plaintiff's objection to that test being carried out. He had it done once for the purpose of being examined by his own expert and it could, it seems to me, fairly be said that there would be one law for plaintiff and another for defendants if he refuses to have a similar test carried out by the defendants' expert, although it is a pity that it was not possible for arrangements to be made for a joint test to be carried out.

As to the plaintiff's third objection, that the loss of liberty for three to five days would be an unreasonable interference with his liberty, the question does not now arise. If it were a live issue I would uphold the registrar's decision on the ground that the reasonableness of the defendants' request just outweighs the reasonableness of the plaintiff's objection, taking into account the fact that, as counsel for the defendants says, the whole process of litigation necessarily involves the parties and their witnesses in invasion or loss of liberty of various kinds. I would have been happier about this particular issue if the defendants had offered something, and I mean something more than a mere token, to compensate for the long medical examination requested, in addition to compensating the plaintiff for the loss of wages which would have been involved.

a In view of the way in which I have approached the issues it does not seem necessary to me to deal at length with the defendants' contention that restrictions should not be placed by the courts on medical men carrying out investigations for the purpose of litigation, or with the question whether these men should or should not distinguish between such examinations and examinations for the purpose of treatment; but I would just say this, that the court imposes no restrictions on such examinations of any kind. If defendants go to a particular expert and if he says that he will only carry out an *b* examination in a particular way, it is for those defendants to decide whether to request a plaintiff to be examined on those terms, and if the question arises and if the plaintiff objects to those terms it is for the court to weigh the reasonableness of that objection against the reasonableness of the defendants' request for that examination. If the reasonableness of the plaintiff's objection outweighs the reasonableness of the defendants' request, then it is probable that the examination will not be carried out at all, not because *c* the court imposes its terms on the expert but because the expert (I am not suggesting improperly for a moment) seeks to impose those terms via the defendants on the plaintiff, who has no medical or contractual relationship with him, and because the plaintiff objects to those terms, ex hypothesi reasonably.

As to the distinction between examination for the purpose of litigation and examination for the purpose of treatment, I would be surprised if any medical man *d* would seek to treat, or even to examine for the purpose of treatment, a person who was not his patient, although I can quite understand that he might refuse to carry out his examination, or to carry it out in a particular way, if he thought it might be contra-indicated as a matter of treatment, unless, possibly, he had the consent both of the party in question and of the doctor or doctors responsible for this treatment.

The last question with which I should deal is the defendants' application for leave to *e* call Professor Hinchcliffe. I will assume that there is a discretion to allow a witness to be called for examination-in-chief as distinct from the discretion to allow a deponent to be examined. For the reasons which I have given for the decision I have already reached, it has not been necessary for me to determine any factual conflict between the evidence of the plaintiff and that of the defendants. All it is necessary for me to determine is the reasonableness of the defendants' request as reasonably seen by them, and the *f* reasonableness of the plaintiff's objections as seen by him (by which, of course, I mean as reasonably seen by him), and then to compare the weight of the reasonableness of the request with that of the reasonableness of the objection. For that purpose it does not seem to me (at any rate, in this case) to be necessary to resolve such conflicts as there are between the various deponents, and I accordingly dismiss that application.

It follows that whilst differing from the registrar as to the polytomography one way *g* and as to the caloric tests the other, in substance I uphold his decision.

Appeal dismissed. Leave to appeal granted.

Solicitors: *Keogh, Ritson & Co*, Bolton (for the defendants); *Brian Thompson & Partners*, Manchester (for the plaintiff).

M Denise Chorlton   Barrister.

Albert v Lavin

HOUSE OF LORDS

LORD DIPLOCK, LORD SIMON OF GLAISDALE, LORD KEITH OF KINKEL, LORD SCARMAN AND LORD ROSKILL

18th NOVEMBER, 3rd DECEMBER 1981

Criminal law – Breach of the peace – Arrest – Accused committing disturbance in bus queue – Accused restrained by off-duty police officer in plain clothes – Accused honestly but unreasonably believing police officer to be a private citizen – Accused assaulting officer in what he believed to be self-defence – Accused convicted of assaulting police officer in the execution of his duty – Whether belief that police officer was a private citizen a good defence.

The appellant caused a disturbance in a bus queue while attempting to board a bus. He was restrained by an off-duty police officer who was in plain clothes. A struggle ensued between the appellant and the officer, in the course of which the officer told the appellant that he was a police officer, a statement which the appellant in his excited state honestly but unreasonably disbelieved. The appellant continued to hit the officer and was arrested and charged with assaulting a police officer in the execution of his duty. The appellant was convicted by magistrates on that charge. He appealed, contending, inter alia, that his belief that he was being subjected to an unjustified assault because of his genuine, albeit mistaken, belief that the officer was not a policeman was a good defence to the charge. The Divisional Court ([1981] 1 All ER 628) dismissed his appeal, holding that it was not a defence to a charge of assault that the accused honestly but mistakenly believed that his action was justified as being reasonable self-defence if there were no reasonable grounds for his belief. The appellant appealed to the House of Lords.

Held – The well-established principle that to detain a man against his will without arresting him was an unlawful act and a serious interference with a citizen's liberty was subject to an equally well-established exception (which was not confined to detention effected by a police constable in the execution of his duty) that it was the right and duty at common law of every citizen in whose presence an actual or reasonably apprehended breach of peace was being or about to be committed to make the person who was breaking or threatening to break the peace refrain from so doing and, in appropriate cases, to detain him against his will. It followed therefore that, even if the appellant's belief that the officer was a private citizen and not a constable had been correct, it would not have made his resistance to the officer's restraint of him lawful. The appeal would accordingly be dismissed (see p 880 c to e f and h to p 881 b, post).

Decision of the Divisional Court of the Queen's Bench Division [1981] 1 All ER 628 affirmed on other grounds.

Notes

For powers of arrest at common law and arrest for breach of the peace, see 11 Halsbury's Laws (4th Edn) paras 107–108, and for cases on the subject, see 14(1) Digest (Reissue) 199–202, 1434–1468.

Appeal

Cleeve Albert appealed by leave of the Appeal Committee of the House of Lords granted on 18th February 1981 against the decision of the Divisional Court of the Queen's Bench Division (Donaldson LJ and Hodgson J) dated 27th November 1980 ([1981] 1 All ER 628, [1981] 2 WLR 1070) dismissing his appeal by way of case stated against his conviction by the magistrates for the Middlesex area of Greater London acting for and in the petty sessional division of Brentford on 6th November 1979 of an offence under s 51 of the Police Act 1964 of assaulting a constable of the Metropolitan Police, namely the

respondent, John Lavin, in the execution of his duty. The facts are set out in the opinion
a of Lord Diplock.

On the opening of the appeal, the chairman of the Appellate Committee, Lord
Diplock, said that their Lordships thought that the case had been argued below on a
mistaken view of the law. The questions on the appeal did not arise unless it was
accepted that the appellant would have been entitled to free himself if the respondent
b had not been a constable. Lord Diplock said that that seemed to be contrary to established
law. Their Lordships were not prepared to hear the appeal argued on a wrong premise
of law, and the appellant should consider whether he wished to argue that the premise
was right. Counsel for the appellant then conceded that on a correct view of the
applicable law he could no longer pursue the appeal, and the appeal was not argued
further.

c *Ronald J Walker* and *Roger McCarthy* for the appellant.
John Hazan QC and *John L Reide* for the respondent.

Their Lordships took time for consideration.

3rd December. The following opinions were delivered.

d
LORD DIPLOCK. My Lords, this is a very much simpler case than it was made to
appear to the magistrates who tried it and to the Divisional Court to which an appeal by
way of case stated was brought by the appellant (Albert) against his conviction by the
Brentford Magistrates' Court of an offence under s 51 of the Police Act 1964 of assaulting
a constable (the respondent, Lavin) in the execution of his duty (see [1981] 1 All ER 628,
e [1981] 2 WLR 1070).
The relevant facts can be stated in three sentences. As a result of incidents that
occurred when Albert tried to 'jump the queue' at a bus stop, Lavin, a police constable
who, at the time, was at the head of the queue, off duty and in plain clothes, had, as the
magistrates found, reasonable grounds for believing a breach of the peace to be imminent
unless he obstructed Albert from boarding the bus out of turn. Albert's conduct
f thereafter, while he was being restrained by Lavin, during the course of which Lavin had
said that he was a constable, was found by the magistrates to amount to a continuing
breach of the peace. After being told that Lavin was a constable, a statement which the
magistrates found that Albert in his excited state honestly but unreasonably disbelieved,
Albert struck him five or six blows in the stomach. This constituted the assault on a
constable in the execution of his duty for which Lavin arrested him and of which he was
convicted by the magistrates.
g
On those facts and findings the magistrates' court stated a case that raised the two
following questions of law for the opinion of the High Court:

'THE questions for the opinion of the High Court are whether: (i) a constable who
reasonably believes that a breach of the peace is about to take place is entitled to
detain any person without arrest to prevent that breach of the peace in circumstances
h which appear to him to be proper (ii) a person being detained in the circumstances
set out above but who does not accept that the person detaining him is a constable
may be convicted of assault on a constable in the execution of his duty if he uses no
more force than is reasonably necessary to protect himself for what he mistakenly
and without reasonable grounds believes to be an unjustified assault and false
imprisonment.'

j
My Lords, if in the first question the adverb 'reasonably' be treated as inserted before
the verb 'appear' (and it is apparent from the body of the stated case that this was the
magistrates' intention) the answer to each of these questions is Yes.
Unfortunately in the Divisional Court the appeal proceeded on the basis, apparently
undisputed by either party, that there was only one exception to what Hodgson J, who
gave the main judgment, called 'the well-established principle that to detain a man

against his will without arresting him is an unlawful act and a serious interference with
a citizen's liberty', and that the sole exception was where the detention was effected by a
constable in the execution of his duty. This led the learned judge into a lengthy and
erudite consideration of what must be the state of mind of a person charged with assault
in order to enable him to rely on the defence of a mistaken belief that facts existed that
justified the assault as the exercise of a lawful right of self-defence of which he would
have been entitled to avail himself if the belief had been correct. Consideration of this
question involved reference in the judgment to more than a score of reported cases on
mens rea, 'subjective' and 'objective' tests and related topics, which led Hodgson J to the
conclusion that there must be reasonable grounds for the mistaken belief, if it is to be
relied on, as a defence.

With the correctness or otherwise of this part of the judgment of Hodgson J your
Lordships are not concerned in this appeal. The question to which it was directed simply
does not arise. What had been overlooked in the argument in the Divisional Court and
in the written cases of both parties that were lodged in this House is that to the well-
established principle referred to by the learned judge there is an equally well-established
exception, not confined to constables, that is applicable to the instant case. It is that every
citizen in whose presence a breach of the peace is being, or reasonably appears to be about
to be, committed has the right to take reasonable steps to make the person who is
breaking or threatening to break the peace refrain from doing so; and those reasonable
steps in appropriate cases will include detaining him against his will. At common law
this is not only the right of every citizen, it is also his duty, although, except in the case
of a citizen who is a constable, it is a duty of imperfect obligation.

On the findings of the magistrates in the stated case this well-established exception was
plainly applicable to the instant case. It was drawn to the attention of counsel at the
opening of the hearing before your Lordships, when it was pointed out that this House
could not deal with the appeal on the basis of an erroneous assumption as to the
applicable law even though in the court below the case had been argued and decided on
the basis that the erroneous assumption was correct. After an adjournment to enable
counsel to verify the accuracy of the proposition as to the citizen's rights and duties at
common law when confronted with breaches or threatened breaches of the peace, which
I have stated above, counsel for the appellant conceded that on a correct view of the
applicable law he could no longer pursue the appeal. Even if Albert's belief that Lavin
was a private citizen and not a constable had been correct, it would not have made his
resistance to Lavin's restraint of him lawful.

The Divisional Court certified that the following question of law of general public
importance was involved in its decision:

'Whether a person charged with an offence of assault may properly be convicted
if the court finds that he acted in the belief that facts existed which if true would
justify his conduct on the basis of self-defence but that there were in fact no
reasonable grounds for so believing.'

My Lords, for the reasons I have given, the Divisional Court was mistaken in thinking
that that question of law was involved in the appeal that it was hearing. It is a
hypothetical question on which it has not been necessary, nor would it have been proper,
for your Lordships to hear argument; and your Lordships should decline to answer it.

I would dismiss this appeal.

LORD SIMON OF GLAISDALE. My Lords, I have had the privilege of reading in
draft the speech delivered by my noble and learned friend on the Woolsack. I agree with
it, and for the reasons given I too would dismiss the appeal.

LORD KEITH OF KINKEL. My Lords, I have had the benefit of reading in draft the
speech of my noble and learned friend Lord Diplock. I agree with it, and for the reasons
he gives I would dismiss the appeal.

LORD SCARMAN. My Lords, I have had the advantage of reading in draft the speech
a delivered by my noble and learned friend Lord Diplock. I agree with it, and for the
reasons he gives I would dismiss the appeal.

LORD ROSKILL. My Lords, for the reasons given by my noble and learned friend
Lord Diplock, whose speech I have had the benefit of reading in draft, I too would
dismiss the appeal.

b
Appeal dismissed.

Solicitors: *Somers & Leyne*, Ealing (for the appellant); *R E T Birch* (for the respondent).

Mary Rose Plummer   Barrister.

c

Din and another v London Borough of Wandsworth

d HOUSE OF LORDS
LORD WILBERFORCE, LORD FRASER OF TULLYBELTON, LORD RUSSELL OF KILLOWEN, LORD LOWRY
AND LORD BRIDGE OF HARWICH
5th, 6th OCTOBER, 26th NOVEMBER 1981

Housing – Homeless person – Person becoming homeless intentionally – Act or omission causing
e person to cease occupying accommodation available for him – Material date on which intentional
or unintentional homelessness to be determined – Applicant voluntarily vacating residential
accommodation before court order for possession made against him – Applicant's move prompted
by fear on receipt of distress warrant for rates – Applicant subsequently applying to local
authority for accommodation – Applicant likely to have been evicted from his accommodation in
any event by the time he applied for accommodation – Whether fact that applicant would have
f become unintentionally homeless had he not moved relevant in determining whether he was
homeless intentionally – Housing (Homeless Persons) Act 1977, s 17(1).

The appellants, a married couple with four children, occupied a flat in Wandsworth.
The appellants fell into arrears with their rent and rates and sought advice from the
Wandsworth housing authority which informed them that the authority could not assist
g them until a court order for possession was made against them. Shortly after, the
appellants received a distress warrant for rates and, alarmed by possible consequences,
they moved to temporary and overcrowded accommodation with a relative. When they
were forced to leave that accommodation they applied to the Wandsworth housing
authority for accommodation under s 4(5)[a] of the Housing (Homeless Persons) Act
1977. The authority, after making inquiries as required by that Act, decided that,
h although the appellants were homeless and in priority need, they had become 'homeless
intentionally' within the meaning of s 17(1) of the 1977 Act because they had voluntarily
left the Wandsworth accommodation while it was still available to them and when it
would have been reasonable for them to continue to occupy it. The authority accordingly
concluded that it was not under a duty to provide permanent accommodation for the
appellants under the 1977 Act. In reaching that decision the authority was aware that

j
_____

a   Section 4(5) provides: 'Where—(a) [a housing authority] are satisfied—(i) that [a person who has
applied to them for accommodation or for assistance in obtaining accommodation] is homeless,
and (ii) that he has a priority need, but (b) they are not satisfied that he became homeless
intentionally, their duty, subject to section 5 below, is to secure that accommodation becomes
available for his occupation.'

had the appellants stayed in the Wandsworth accommodation they would very likely have been evicted shortly thereafter by the landlord for failing to pay the rent, but the authority considered that possible events occurring after the appellants left their accommodation were irrelevant in reaching its decision. The appellants brought an action against the authority in the county court seeking, inter alia, a declaration that the authority's determination that the appellants were intentionally homeless was void. The judge granted the declaration sought on the ground that by the time the appellants made their application for accommodation they would have been evicted from the Wandsworth accommodation in any event and would have been homeless unintentionally. The Court of Appeal reversed that decision holding that the fact that the appellants would have been homeless by the date of the application was not relevant in determining the question whether their homelessness was initially intentional. The appellants appealed to the House of Lords.

Held (Lord Russell and Lord Bridge dissenting) – Having regard to the plain and unambiguous meaning of the 1977 Act and the context in which it was to be administered, namely that of competing priorities for available local authority housing which was in acutely short supply, the material date for determining whether a person had become homeless intentionally or unintentionally was the date on which he left his accommodation, and hypothetical events which might have occurred if the person had stayed in his accommodation and which might have caused him to become homeless unintentionally were irrelevant in considering an application by a homeless person for permanent accommodation under the Act. Although on the true construction of s 17[b] of the 1977 Act a housing authority could only decide that an applicant was intentionally homeless if there was a continuing causal connection between the deliberate act from which the homelessness resulted and the homelessness which existed at the time the authority made its inquiries, the appellants' homelessness at the time their application was considered was a direct consequence of their leaving the Wandsworth accommodation when they were not forced to do so. The local authority were therefore entitled to conclude that the appellants had become homeless intentionally within the meaning of s 17(1). The appeal would therefore be dismissed (see p 883 h to p 884 b, p 886 b to p 887 c, p 889 d to p 890 b and e f, p 892 d to f and j to p 893 d and f to h, p 895 h j and p 896 a b, post).

Dyson v Kerrier District Council [1980] 3 All ER 313 considered.

Notes

For a housing authority's duties to a homeless person, see 22 Halsbury's Laws (4th Edn) para 513.

For the Housing (Homeless Persons) Act 1977, ss 4, 17, see 47 Halsbury's Statutes (3rd Edn) 318, 330.

Cases referred to in opinions

Associated Provincial Picture Houses Ltd v Wednesbury Corpn [1947] 2 All ER 680, [1948] 1 KB 223, [1948] LJR 190, 177 LT 641, 112 JP 55, 45 LGR 635, CA, 45 Digest (Repl) 215, 189.

De Falco v Crawley Borough Council, Silvestri v Crawley Borough Council [1980] 1 All ER 913, [1980] QB 460, [1980] 2 WLR 664, 78 LGR 180, CA.

Dyson v Kerrier District Council [1980] 3 All ER 313, [1980] 1 WLR 1205, CA.

Jobling v Associated Dairies Ltd [1981] 2 All ER 752, [1981] 3 WLR 155, HL.

Appeal

By amended particulars of claim dated 25th March 1980 the appellants, Taj Din and Mansura Akther Din, sought as against the respondents, the mayor and burgesses of the

b   Section 17, so far as material, is set out at p 884 h to p 885 a, post.

a London Borough of Wandsworth, (i) a declaration that the respondents' determination of 4th January 1980 that the appellants were intentionally homeless was void, (ii) a declaration that the respondents owed the appellants a duty under s 4(5) of the Housing (Homeless Persons) Act 1977, (iii) a mandatory injunction requiring the respondents to secure that accommodation became available to the appellants, and (iv) damages limited to £2,000. On 24th June 1980 his Honour Judge White sitting in the Wandsworth County Court gave judgment for the appellants on their claim and awarded the first *b* appellant damages of £79·99 and the second appellant damages of £50. On 23rd June 1981 the Court of Appeal (Waller and Ackner LJJ, Donaldson LJ dissenting) reversed the decision. The appellants appealed to the House of Lords with leave of the Court of Appeal. The facts are set out in the opinion of Lord Wilberforce.

Stephen Sedley and *Nicholas Blake* for the appellants.
c *Anthony Scrivener QC* and *Geoffrey Stephenson* for the respondents.

Their Lordships took time for consideration.

26th November. The following opinions were delivered.

d **LORD WILBERFORCE.** My Lords, this appeal arises under the Housing (Homeless Persons) Act 1977. In December 1979 the appellants, who are husband and wife, applied to the London Borough of Wandsworth, the respondents, for housing as homeless persons entitled to priority under the provisions of this Act. The respondents refused their application on the ground that they were 'intentionally homeless'. The question is, or ought to be, whether the respondents in so doing erred in law. I say 'ought to be' *e* because the procedure adopted by the appellants was to sue the respondents in the Wandsworth County Court for damages and a mandatory injunction to house them; this resulted in a trial with witnesses of issues of fact. At the conclusion of this trial his Honour Judge White found for the appellants, awarded them damages, declared that the determination of the respondents was void, and made an order that the respondents should forthwith secure that accommodation become available for the appellants and *f* their family, subject to a stay pending appeal. The Court of Appeal by a majority reversed this order, and the appellants now seek its restoration. I shall comment on this procedure later in this opinion.

The 1977 Act was an important measure imposing for the first time on housing (sc local) authorities a duty to accommodate or to assist homeless persons. There had previously been legislative provisions for the benefit of the homeless through local *g* authority welfare departments, but these suffered from weakness of definition and of means of enforcement. The Housing Act 1957, s 113 placed certain obligations on local authorities as regards housing, including one of securing that in the selection of their tenants a reasonable preference should be given to persons occupying insanitary or overcrowded houses, having large families, or living in unsatisfactory housing conditions. The 1977 Act (s 6 (2)) made use of this provision by bringing homeless persons within it, *h* and by imposing on local authorities independent duties under that Act (see s 6(1)(b) and (c)).

In applying and interpreting the 1977 Act there are several important points to bear in mind. First, it is designed for the expressed purpose of bringing families together. Second, it forms part of a complex of duties which local authorities owe to categories of persons seeking housing. These persons are normally placed on a waiting list, in some *j* areas a very long one, and are given accommodation according to a points system of priority. Inevitably every allocation of priority housing to homeless persons must have the effect of deferring the hopes of persons in other categories, some of whom may have been waiting for a long time. Third, a decision against priority treatment under the Act does not mean that nothing can be done for the 'homeless' applicants. They can join the waiting list for a council tenancy (indeed Mrs Din did so in June 1979) or they can seek nomination to a housing association or, with the help of advice, they can seek private sector housing, with temporary accommodation meanwhile. Fourth, as the Act *a* recognises, conditions may (and do) differ greatly from one authority to another, and in administering its provisions, they may be taken into account. The Act must be interpreted in the light of these matters, with liberality having regard to its social purposes, and also with recognition of the claims of others and the nature and scale of local authorities' responsibilities. It should be noticed that the Secretary of State has power (by s 12) to give guidance to local authorities, and that he has done so through a *b* prescribed code of guidance. This emphasises that it is for the authority to satisfy itself whether an applicant became homeless intentionally and that careful and sensitive inquiries will be important (see Code of Guidance, para 2.19).

I can summarise fairly briefly the relevant statutory provisions. 'Homelessness' is defined in s 1. It is not confined to cases where the applicant himself is without accommodation but expressly includes the case where a person has no accommodation *c* which he, together with any other person who normally resides with him as a member of his family, is entitled to occupy. Subsection (3) adds that a person is 'threatened with homelessness' if it is likely that he will become homeless within 28 days.

Section 2 defines the homeless persons who are considered to have a priority need for accommodation. The housing authority must be satisfied either that the applicant has dependent children who are residing with him or who might reasonably be expected to *d* reside with him or that he comes within another of the categories stated in the section.

Section 3 imposes on local authorities, when faced with a case of possible homelessness, a duty to make appropriate inquiries. These relate to (i) the state of homelessness or threatened homelessness, (ii) the question of priority need, and (iii) inquiries necessary to satisfy them 'whether he [the applicant] *became homeless* or threatened with homelessness intentionally'. *e*

Section 4 defines in detail the duties (so expressed) of local authorities in the various cases. If they *are satisfied* that a person is homeless, or threatened with homelesssness, and that he has a priority need, but *are also satisfied* that he *became* homeless or threatened with homelessness intentionally, the duty is to furnish him with advice and appropriate assistance (see s 4(1) and (2)(*b*)).

If they *are satisfied*, as above, but not satisfied that he *became homeless* intentionally, the *f* duty is to secure that accommodation becomes available for him. (This is subject to certain considerations as to local connections with the authority's area: see s 5.)

The words 'are satisfied' must be noted; they leave the decision, on these issues of fact, to the local authority. On well-known principle, there is no appeal to a court against such a decision, but it may be subject to 'judicial review' for error in law including no doubt absence of any material on which the decision could reasonably be reached. *g*

Section 8 contains safeguards as regards any decision of a local authority. The applicant must be notified of it; and, in particular, if the authority notifies him that they are satisfied that he *became* homeless intentionally, they must notify him of their reasons.

Finally, there are the critical provisions regarding intentional homelessness. These are contained in s 16 or s 17, the relevant parts of which I must quote. I think it is more intelligible to do so in reverse order. Section 17 provides: *h*

'(1) Subject to subsection (3) below, for the purposes of this Act a person becomes homeless intentionally if he deliberately does or fails to do anything in consequence of which he ceases to occupy accommodation which is available for his occupation and which it would have been reasonable for him to continue to occupy . . .

'(3) An act or omission in good faith on the part of a person who was unaware of any relevant fact is not to be treated as deliberate for the purposes of subsection (1) *j* or (2) above.

'(4) Regard may be had, in determining for the purposes of subsections (1) and (2) above whether it would have been reasonable for a person to continue to occupy accommodation, to the general circumstances prevailing in relation to housing in a   the area of the housing authority to whom he applied for accommodation or for assistance in obtaining accommodation.'

Section 16 provides:

'For the purposes of this Act accommodation is only available for a person's occupation if it is available for occupation both by him and by any other person who might reasonably be expected to reside with him and any reference in this Act to
b   securing accommodation for a person's occupation shall be construed accordingly.'

On these provisions the case of Mr and Mrs Din has to be decided. Can they successfully challenge the decision of the local authority that it was satisfied that the appellants became homeless intentionally within the definition in s 17(1)? To answer this, we must consider the facts as they were before the local authority as the result of their inquiries.

The appellants are married with four children; there is no doubt that they would fall
c   into a potential priority class. In 1977 the whole family moved, from Croydon, into accommodation at 56 Trinity Road, Wandsworth, accommodation which was suitable for the whole family to occupy. This belonged, under a lease, together with a shop, to a relative, Mr Jaswail. Mr Din entered into a loose partnership with Mr Jaswail dealing with Pakistani food, but Mr Din retained his existing employment with Airfix Products Ltd. In April 1978 Mr Jaswail withdrew from the business. The landlord of the
d   premises accepted rent from Mr Din without prejudice, but arrears of rent mounted up and Mr Din came to be in financial difficulties. In June 1979 Mrs Din went to the housing aid centre in Wandsworth and was put on the waiting list for accommodation. She was advised that before she could be helped she would have to wait for a court order for possession to be made against her. Mr Din was similarly advised on 2nd July 1979. On 28th August 1979 the appellants vacated the premises; no court proceedings had
e   been initiated against them, and no demand for vacant possession had been made. I do not think that there is any doubt that this action was deliberate and intentional and fell within the provisions of s 17. They then went to live with Mr Jaswail in a flat at Upminster; this was crowded accommodation. Mr Din hoped to get employment with Ford Motors at Dagenham; in this he was unsuccessful. In November 1979 he returned to his previous job with Airfix and took a room in Wandsworth. In December 1979 the
f   appellants were asked to leave the Upminster flat. On 20th December 1979 the appellants applied to the respondents as homeless persons under the 1977 Act. The respondents made appropriate inquiries and on 4th January 1980 notified the appellants that they were satisfied that the appellants' homelessness was 'intentional'. The reasons given were that the appellants left 56 Trinity Road, Wandsworth after they had been advised on two occasions to remain in occupation until the owner sought a court order;
g   they disregarded this advice and moved to Upminster knowing this to be only temporary accommodation.

As I have stated, the appellants later started proceedings in the county court. As to this procedure I have reservations. The local authority is, under the Act, carrying out statutory functions, and is required to make a decision based on findings of fact (being 'satisfied' as set out above). Its decision can be the subject of judicial review (see above),
h   but county courts have no power to make this. A procedure achieving, in effect, the same result by county court action appears to have been approved by the Court of Appeal in *De Falco v Crawley Borough Council* [1980] 1 All ER 913, [1980] QB 460 and was not challenged in this case, so for the purposes of this appeal I will, under reservation, assume its validity. The evidence at the trial amplifies the facts in some respects and I am prepared to take it into consideration.
j   In his evidence Mr Din said that the only reason that compelled him to quit the place (56 Trinity Road) was the rate demand (he was scared) and said later that the main reason why he left was that he could also be at a new place but his move was prompted by his fear. Mr Godbold, an officer of the respondents, confirmed that this was what Mr Din told the housing centre. Mr Bruneau, head of the housing department, said that the

reason why the local authority generally insisted on a court order was because of the 'impossible shortage' of accommodation. A few weeks are of extreme importance on financial grounds and as affecting the pressure on the stock. He did not accept that it was inevitable for the applicant to leave 56 Trinity Road in June 1979. In December he 'accepted on the evidence that they had no chance of making the accommodation pay' and that 'on what I knew—whatever the time factor they would have had to have left.' In December 'I accepted there was no possibility of him staying'. The imprecision, as regards time, of this evidence is to be noted.

So how does the matter stand? If one takes the words of the statute, the local authority have to be satisfied that the applicant became homeless intentionally (s 17). Under s 4(2)(b) their duty is limited to advice and assistance if 'they *are* satisfied . . . that [the applicants] *became* homeless . . . intentionally'. The time factors here are clearly indicated: at the time of decision (the present), the local authority must look at the time (the past) when the applicants became homeless, and consider whether their action *then* was intentional in the statutory sense. If this was the right approach there could only be one answer: when the Dins left 56 Trinity Road their action was intentional within s 17, and the local authority were entitled to find that it would have been reasonable for them to continue to occupy 56 Trinity Road.

The appellants' argument against this is as follows. Whatever the position may have been in July 1979 when they left 56 Trinity Road, at the time of the decision in December 1979 they would have been homeless in any event; the original cause of homelessness (even if intentional) had ceased to operate. For s 17 to apply there must be a causal nexus between the intentional action and the homelessness subsisting at the time of the decision. On the facts of the case there was not, so that the decision was wrong in law. I am unable to accept this argument.

1. It cannot be reconciled with the wording of the Act. This is completely and repeatedly clear in concentrating attention on when the appellants became homeless and requiring the question of intention to be ascertained as at that time. To achieve the result desired by the appellants it is either necessary to distort the meaning of 'in consequence of which he ceases to occupy' (s 17(1)) or to read in a number of words. These are difficult to devise. Donaldson LJ suggests adding at the end of s 17(1) 'and still to occupy'; the appellants, as an alternative, 'to the date of his application'. Both are radical, and awkward, reconstructions of the section.

2. Such an interpretation, or reconstruction, of the Act is not called for by any purposive approach. As I have pointed out, the Act reflects a complex interplay of interests. It confers great benefits on one category of persons in need of housing, to the detriment of others. This being so, it does not seem unreasonable that, in order to benefit from the priority provisions, persons in the first category should bring themselves within the plain words. Failure to do so involves, as Mr Bruneau pointed out, greater expense for a hard pressed authority, and greater pressure on the housing stock.

3. The appellants' interpretation adds greatly to the difficulties of the local authority's task in administering this Act. It requires the authority, as well as investigating the original and actual cause of homelessness, to inquire into hypotheses as to what would have happened if the appellants had not moved, hypotheses involving uncertain attitudes of landlords, rating authorities, the applicants themselves, and even intervening physical events. The difficulty of this is well shown by the singularly imprecise and speculative evidence given as to what was likely to have happened in December 1979 set out above. This approach almost invites challenge in the courts, all the more if it is open to applicants to litigate the whole state of facts with witnesses, de novo, in the county court, but still significantly if the applicants are limited to judicial review. On the other hand the respondents' contention involves a straightforward inquiry into the circumstances in which the appellants became homeless.

4. The appellants' argument is not assisted by *Dyson v Kerrier District Council* [1980] 3 All ER 313, [1980] 1 WLR 1205. There (as here) the applicant intentionally surrendered available accommodation in order to go to precarious accommodation (a 'winter letting')

from which she was ejected and so became homeless. It was held (in my opinion,
a rightly) that she had become homeless in consequence of her intentional surrender. This
does not in any way support an argument that a subsequent hypothetical cause should be
considered to supersede an earlier actual cause. It merely decides that a disqualification
for priority by reason of an intentional surrender is not displaced by obtaining temporary
accommodation. As pointed out by Ackner LJ in the Court of Appeal, it can be displaced
by obtaining 'settled' accommodation.

b   5. It does not follow from accepting the respondents' argument that occupants who
move before a notice to quit takes effect will be held to be intentionally homeless. Such
cases are likely to be covered by s 1(3) referred to above.

I agree therefore with the majority of the Court of Appeal in holding that the present
case falls squarely within the provisions of the Act as to intentional homelessness and that
there is no justification for reading these provisions otherwise than in their natural sense.

c   In the result the local authority was entitled to decide, on the facts, and in law, that the
appellants became intentionally homeless. I would dismiss this appeal.

LORD FRASER OF TULLYBELTON. My Lords, the question in this appeal is
whether the appellants became homeless 'intentionally' in the sense of the Housing
d (Homeless Persons) Act 1977. One of the main purposes of that Act was to secure that,
when accommodation is provided for homeless persons by the housing authority, it
should be made available for all the members of his family together and to end the
practice which had previously been common under which adult members of a homeless
family were accommodated in hostels while children were taken into care, and the
family thus split up. The emphasis on treating the family as a unit appears from s 1
e which provides that a person is homeless for the purposes of the Act if he has no
accommodation, and that he is to be treated as having no accommodation if there is no
accommodation which he 'together with any other person who normally resides with
him as a member of his family . . . is entitled to occupy' (s 1(1)(a)). The particular
emphasis on families with children appears from s 2 which provides that a homeless
person has 'a priority need for accommodation' when the housing authority is satisfied
f that he is within one of certain categories, the first of which is that 'he has dependent
children who are residing with him or who might reasonably be expected to reside with
him' (s 2(1)(a)).

When a person applies to a housing authority for accommodation, the housing
authority, if they have reason to believe that he may be homeless (as defined in s 1) or
threatened with homelessness, have a duty under s 3 to make inquiries into three
g matters. The first of these is: (1) whether he is homeless or threatened with
homelessness. If the housing authority are satisfied that the answer to that question is in
the affirmative it has to go on to inquire into the other matters which are: (2) whether
he has a priority need, and (3) whether he has become homeless or threatened with
homelessness intentionally. If the housing authority are satisfied that he has a priority
need, but are not satisfied that he became homeless intentionally, they come under a
h duty 'to secure that accommodation becomes available for his occupation' (s 4(5)). If the
housing authority are not satisfied that he has a priority need, or if they are satisfied that
he became homeless intentionally they come under the lesser duty of furnishing him
with advice and appropriate assistance and of securing that accommodation is made
available for his occupation for long enough to give him 'a reasonable opportunity of
himself securing accommodation for his occupation' (s 4(3)), that is, to provide him with
j temporary bridging accommodation. The practical issue in this appeal is whether the
respondents, as housing authority, owed the higher duty to the appellants or were
entitled to be satisfied that they became homeless intentionally with the result that the
respondents owed them only the more limited duty.

The meaning of the expression 'becomes homeless intentionally' is explained by s 17
which provides as follows:

'(1) Subject to subsection (3) below, for the purposes of this Act a person becomes homeless intentionally if he deliberately does or fails to do anything in consequence *a* of which he ceases to occupy accommodation which is available for his occupation and which it would have been reasonable for him to continue to occupy . . .

'(4) Regard may be had, in determining for the purposes of subsections (1) and (2) above whether it would have been reasonable for a person to continue to occupy accommodation, to the general circumstances prevailing in relation to housing in the area of the housing authority to whom he applied for accommodation or for *b* assistance in obtaining accommodation.'

That section has to be read along with s 16 which provides as follows:

'For the purposes of this Act accommodation is only available for a person's occupation if it is available for occupation both by him and by any other person who might reasonably be expected to reside with him and any reference in this Act to *c* securing accommodation for a person's occupation shall be construed accordingly.'

This appeal brings out once more the distressing results of shortage of housing accommodation which exists in certain parts of the United Kingdom. So far as directly relevant to the appeal the facts here are simple. In 1977 the first appellant with his wife and four children moved from Croydon, where they had been living for some years, to *d* live in Trinity Road, Wandsworth, in a flat above a shop there. The tenant of the whole premises was the first appellant's brother-in-law and the appellants and their family were to assist the brother-in-law in running a takeaway food business from the shop premises, in return for which they were to occupy the flat above the shop rent free. Unfortunately, the takeaway food business was not successful and the brother-in-law fell into arrears with the rent. He left in April 1978 and went to live elsewhere where he got work. The *e* appellants and their family stayed on in the Trinity Road accommodation and tried to run the takeaway food business but they ran increasingly into debt. In the summer of 1979 the first appellant sought advice from the housing aid centre in Wandsworth and was advised that the housing authority could not help him until there was a court order for possession against him and that until such an order was issued he should stay on in the accommodation at Trinity Road. In July 1979 he received a distress warrant for rates. *f* This alarmed the first appellant and on 28th August, contrary to the advice received from the respondents' housing advice centre, he and his family left Trinity Road while the accommodation there was still available to them, and went to live with relatives at Upminster in the hope of his getting work at Dagenham. The accommodation at Upminster was much too small to be suitable for a prolonged stay by the appellants and their family. The first appellant failed to get work at Dagenham and in November 1979 *g* he himself returned to his previous job in Wandsworth and soon got temporary lodgings there. He left his wife and children at Upminster, but in December they were asked by their relatives to leave. On 20th December 1979 he applied to the respondents as housing authority for accommodation under the 1977 Act.

The respondents rejected his application for permanent accommodation on the ground that he had left the Trinity Road accommodation on 28th August while it was still *h* available for his occupation, and when it would have been reasonable for him to continue to occupy it. The respondents, or their officials, recognised that by December that accommodation would almost certainly have ceased to be available for the appellants, because the landlord would have evicted them for failing to pay the rent. But the respondents disregarded that fact (if it be a fact) as irrelevant on the ground that the accommodation had been available when the appellants became homeless in August, and *j* that they were not concerned with any change of circumstance in that respect occurring thereafter. The argument on behalf of the appellants was that the respondents had erred in that respect because by December 1978 the effective cause of their homelessness was no longer their having left in August but the fact that the accommodation would no longer have been available for them in any event.

Before I consider that matter I should mention another point which was disputed at an
a earlier stage of these proceedings but which is not now in dispute. The respondents'
decision that the appellants had become homeless intentionally involved their
determining two issues, viz (1) that the appellants had deliberately done something in
consequence of which they had ceased to occupy the accommodation at Trinity Road and
(2) that that was accommodation 'which it would have been reasonable for [them] to
continue to occupy' (s 17 (1)). The appellants now accept that the respondents were
b entitled to determine the latter issue against them. I think that is clearly right, although
the determination is one of exceptional difficulty because it requires the comparison of
things which are unlike. The appellants, quite rightly from their point of view, wished
to leave the accommodation at Trinity Road in July 1979, as soon as they recognised that
they could not run the takeaway food business profitably. They naturally wished to
avoid getting further into debt for arrears of rent and rates. The concern of the
c respondents was that persons with families such as the appellants, who were likely to
become homeless, should stay on in their accommodation as long as possible in order to
avoid swelling the number of those for whom they had a duty to secure accommodation,
and they were entitled to have regard to their obligation to other families in this regard
(s 17(4)). As Wandsworth is in Inner London it is within judicial knowledge that
housing in the respondents' area was very scarce. For that reason the respondents'
d determination that it would have been reasonable for the appellants to continue to
occupy the accommodation at Trinity Road after July 1979 was, in my view, one that
they were well entitled to make, although if the same issue had arisen in another part of
the country where accommodation was under less pressure the position might have been
different.

I return to the question whether the respondents were entitled to decide that the
e appellants had deliberately done something in consequence of which they ceased to
occupy accommodation which was available for their accommodation. I feel no doubt
that the respondents were entitled to do so. The 1977 Act contains various provisions
relating to persons who have 'become' homeless intentionally. In all these provisions the
word 'become' in one of its tenses is used and attention is thus concentrated on how the
condition of homelessness began. In s 17(1) itself the provision is that a person 'becomes'
f homeless intentionally if he 'ceases' to occupy accommodation which is available for
him; the word 'ceases' evidently assumes that he has been occupying the accommodation
up till the time when he 'becomes' homeless. Again, in s 3 the housing authority is
directed to inquire whether the applicant 'is' homeless (s 3(2)(a)) and, if so, whether he
'became' homeless intentionally (s 3(2)(b)(ii)). The same contrast between the question
whether the applicant 'is' homeless at the time of the housing authority's inquiry and the
g question whether he 'became' homeless, which must be looking to some earlier date, is
seen in s 4(3)(a), 4(2)(b), 4(5)(a)(i) and 4(5)(b). Perhaps the most striking example of such
a contrast is in s 11(1) which makes it an offence to give false information with intent to
make a housing authority believe that a person—

> '(a) *is* homeless or threatened with homelessness, or (b) *has* a priority need, or (c)
> *did not become* homeless or threatened with homelessness intentionally . . .'

h
In the face of such repeated emphasis it is, in my opinion, impossible to read the
provisions in the Act as to becoming homeless otherwise than literally, and as looking to
the date at which homelessness began. It is therefore irrelevant for an applicant who is
homeless at the date of his application, and who became homeless intentionally, to show
that he would have been homeless by that date in any event. The material question is
j why he became homeless, not why he is homeless at the date of the inquiry. If he
actually became homeless deliberately, the fact that he might, or would, have been
homeless for other reasons at the date of the inquiry is irrelevant.

There can, in my opinion, be no doubt that that is the plain meaning of the statutory
provisions. But it is said that it produces a result which is harsh and which ought to be
ameliorated by some benevolent reading of the Act in favour of the applicant. No doubt

there may be cases in which such an argument is admissible, but in my view this is not
one of them. Although the parties to this appeal are, on the one side, homeless persons   *a*
with a family including dependent children and, on the other side, a public authority,
circumstances which might perhaps be urged in favour of a benevolent construction in
favour of a homeless applicant, the true competition is between the appellants and the
many other persons with families in the respondents' area who are homeless or
threatened by homelessness. That is recognised by s 17(4). In these circumstances of
competition between too many homeless persons chasing too little accommodation I   *b*
would not consider it proper to depart from the plain and unambiguous meaning of the
statutory provisions.

The view that I take appears to me to be entirely consistent with the decision of the
Court of Appeal in *Dyson v Kerrier District Council* [1980] 3 All ER 313, [1980] 1 WLR
1205, where the plaintiff became homeless in consequence of her deliberate act in
ceasing to occupy accommodation at Huntingdon in October 1978. She subsequently   *c*
obtained other accommodation, which she knew would be only temporary, under a
'winter let' which expired on 31st March 1979. The court held that her homelessness
after 31st March 1979 was in consequence of her original act in ceasing to occupy
permanent accommodation in October 1978. I respectfully agree, because on the facts
of that case the original cause of her homelessness was still in operation at and after 31st
March 1979. That, I think, was what Brightman LJ, who delivered the judgment of the   *d*
Court of Appeal, had in mind when he said ([1980] 3 All ER 313 at 318, [1980] 1 WLR
1205 at 1213): 'If the plaintiff had not left the Huntingdon flat in October 1978 she
would not have found herself threatened with homelessness in March 1979.' Counsel
for the appellants sought to apply that language to the circumstances of this appeal and
argued that even if the appellants had not left the Trinity Road accommodation on 28th
August 1979 they would nevertheless have been homeless by the date of the respondents'   *e*
inquiry. Be it so. The fact remains that the appellants' homelessness in December 1979
was a consequence of their deliberate act of moving out on 28th August. I accept that for
s 17(1) to be applicable there must be a continuing causal connection between the
deliberate act in consequence of which homelessness resulted and the homelessness
existing at the date of the inquiry. Such a causal connection exists in this case, and that
being so it is immaterial to inquire whether they might in other circumstances have   *f*
been homeless then for other reasons.

I would dismiss the appeal.

LORD RUSSELL OF KILLOWEN. My Lords, the facts and circumstances of this
appeal have been sufficiently stated in the opinions of others of your Lordships. The
correct conclusion in law turns on a short point.   *g*

The authority conclusively determined that when Mr Din on 2nd August 1979 left 56
Trinity Road it would have been reasonable for him and his family to continue to occupy
that accommodation beyond that date. It would follow that if Mr Din had then applied
as a homeless person it would have been a correct conclusion by the authority that his
then condition of homelessness was attributable to his voluntary withdrawal (unreasonably) from Trinity Road, and accordingly that for the purposes of ss 4 and 17(1) of the   *h*
1977 Act he became homeless intentionally.

But that is not what happened. Mr Din applied under the Act, claiming to be
homeless and having a priority need (as to both of which the authority was satisfied),
towards the end of December 1979. The crucial question in this appeal is raised by the
fact that by that date the Din family would in any event have been evicted from the
Trinity Road accommodation.   *j*

The county court judge heard evidence from the appropriate official of the housing
authority, of which we have only his notes. In his judgment he made the following
comments and findings. (1) 'It is not in dispute . . . that it was only a matter of time
before the Dins would have had to leave the premises in any event.' (2) 'Mr Bruneau [the
official above-mentioned] said he considered there was no reason in the short period of
weeks before an [eviction] order would be made why Mr Din should run down the

[takeaway food] business completely.' (3) 'By the end of December the plaintiffs [the

a Dins] would in any event, whether or not they had followed the defendant's [the housing authority's] advice, have been homeless.'

There were several other passages in the judgment to the same effect, which I need not trouble to set out. In short the judge found on the evidence that the Dins' condition of homelessness, albeit that it had started in August by their voluntary move in August 1979, was not at the time of the late December application and its determination by the

b authority any longer attributable to their voluntary departure in August, and could no longer bear the badge of intentional.

I make at this stage the comment that *Dyson v Kerrier District Council* [1980] 3 All ER 313, [1980] 1 WLR 1205 was different in a vital respect. There the applicant had a secure council house tenancy in Huntingdon which she voluntarily surrendered to take temporary (winter let) accommodation in Cornwall. When that ended she became

c homeless because she had voluntarily surrendered her secure tenancy in Huntingdon, without which act she would still (at the time of application) have been there: therefore her homelessness was intentional. In that respect the case is the opposite of the present case.

What then of the present case? I entirely understand the reasoning behind the conclusions of those of your Lordships with whom I am about to differ: Mr Din in

d August 1979 became homeless intentionally within the explanation afforded by s 17(1) of what is involved in becoming homeless intentionally, and when the authority made its inquiries at the end of December they were then entitled to say that he became homeless (in August) intentionally and that the statutory language was satisfied. But I prefer to consider the statute more broadly, though not seeking to add to the language. The inquiries and conclusions of the authority fall to be made at (or after) the

e application. Is the applicant now homeless? Has he now a priority need? In my opinion the investigation of the question whether he became homeless intentionally, which is to be made at the same time, is directed to the cause of his present homelessness. Why is he homeless now? If in the past he has become homeless intentionally and but for that he would not now be homeless (as in the *Dyson* case) well and good: that is why he is homeless now. But if on the facts as established in the present case he would be homeless

f now in any event, the past circumstances in which the homelessness originated appear to me to be no longer of any relevance; the past actions of the applicant are spent.

I recognise, of course, that questions not easy of solution may arise in any given case. There may well be situations which are neither within the *Dyson* case at one end and the instant case at the other. Those will fall for decision by the authority under s 4, and normally will be unassailable. But in the instant case in my opinion the facts are clear

g and the authority failed to consider whether the present homelessness was attributable to the applicant's actions in August 1979.

I would allow the appeal and restore the decision of the county court judge.

LORD LOWRY. My Lords, the learned county court judge put it well in his admirable judgment when he said:

h   'The background to the case, which has important undertones, is the acute shortage of accommodation in this part of London, the unbearable pressures that homelessness must inevitably bring to individual families however it may be that they have become homeless and the difficult and at times almost impossible burden placed on local authorities in trying fairly to discharge the various duties that Parliament has imposed on them.'

j The Housing (Homeless Persons) Act 1977 has given rise to a volume of cases which is remarkable, having regard to the short time it has been in force, the extent of the discretion it confers and the absence of an ordinary right of appeal: the courts cannot, whatever the procedure, upset a decision under ss 3 and 4 except within the bounds prescribed by *Associated Provincial Picture Houses Ltd v Wednesbury Corpn* [1947] 2 All ER 680, [1948] 1 KB 223, remembering that one way of 'contravening the law' is to misapply a statutory provision. The frequency with which judicial opinion has been divided is also notable, and the appeal now before your Lordships provides the latest example. As in other cases, the real contest here is not between the homeless citizen and the state: the duty of the housing authority is to hold the balance fairly among all homeless persons and to exercise a fair discretion according to law, while your Lordships' task is to declare the law relevant to this case.

Taj Din and Mansura Akther Din ('the appellants'), together with their four children, left 56 Trinity Road, Wandsworth on 28th August 1979, and in consequence ceased to occupy accommodation there which was available for their occupation and which it would have been reasonable for them to continue to occupy. Thereby, as they admit, the appellants became homeless intentionally within the meaning of s 17(1) of the Act. They went to stay with a brother-in-law, Mr Jaswail, in his small flat in Upminster above a Kentucky Fried Chicken shop. This accommodation was far too small for them all to live in for any length of time and it was common ground, as set out in the appellants' particulars of claim in the county court action, that there was a continuing state of homelessness at all material times from 28th August 1979. As Ackner LJ said in the Court of Appeal: 'There was no break in the homelessness, as the accommodation to which they went in the brother-in-law's flat was intended to be, and could only have been, for a short temporary period.' It must also be accepted, for the purpose of these proceedings, that the appellants, if they had not left Trinity Road in August, would inevitably have become homeless in any event through having to leave there before 20th December 1979, the date of their housing application.

On these facts, my Lords, I agree with the majority in the Court of Appeal and with my noble and learned friends Lord Wilberforce and Lord Fraser that the respondents were in law entitled to be satisfied that the appellants became homeless intentionally in a way which was relevant to their housing application and that accordingly the respondents were only subject to a duty towards the appellants (by virtue of s 4(2)(b) of the Act), to give them advice and appropriate assistance and to secure that accommodation was made available for their occupation for such period as the respondents considered would give the appellants a reasonable opportunity of themselves securing accommodation for their occupation.

I might be content to say no more, but out of respect for those of your Lordships who take a different view I would add some observations of my own, first summarising the main points of the appellants' argument.

They contend that, although they became homeless intentionally on 28th August 1979, this original cause of their homelessness was rendered a spent cause by the fact that, through having to leave the Trinity Road accommodation, they would in any event have become homeless by 20th December 1979, the date of their housing application; therefore, it is submitted, by the latter date that fact was the real cause of their homelessness, and one must, they say, consider the real cause of the homelessness at the time when the application is made. Or, as the learned county court judge said: 'I cannot think it was Parliament's intention that if an applicant has made himself intentionally homeless earlier than he need be he must be barred from help after he would have been made homeless unintentionally in any event.'

The appellants say that the 'intentional homelessness' which occurred in August cannot be taken into account so as to deprive them of their priority unless the act of becoming intentionally homelessness is causally linked to the homelessness existing in December, and they further contend that the intentional homelessness is *not* causally linked to the December homelessness if the appellants would in any event have been homeless in December.

On the other hand, my noble and learned friend Lord Wilberforce has pointed out that these arguments cannot be reconciled with the actual wording of s 17(1) and that what would be required to sustain them is a reconstruction of the Act. I concur, and I further agree that the appellants' interpretation is not required by reference to the purpose of the Act. I readily adopt the view of my noble and learned friend Lord Fraser that all the provisions which relate to becoming homeless concentrate attention on *how*

the homelessness began and look unambiguously to the *date on which* homelessness
a began. I also agree with both of my noble and learned friends that *Dyson v Kerrier
District Council* [1980] 3 All ER 313, [1980] 1 WLR 1205 does not help the appellants'
cause. I shall, however, have something to say about that case.

I accept that for s 17(1) to bite, the act of becoming homeless intentionally, as the
appellants did, must be causally linked to homelessness at the time of the housing
application. It would, for example, be absurd if a priority applicant who became
b homeless intentionally in September and obtained good accommodation in October for
other than temporary occupation and then lost that accommodation 'unintentionally' in
November could lose his priority for a housing application made in December. Avoiding
this result in construing the Act, does not need words to be implied: it merely recognises
the obvious fact that, when the housing authority make appropriate inquiries under
s 3(1), they will inquire into the origin of the homelessness (which I shall call 'the
c relevant homelessness') on which the applicant relies. The relevant homelessness in my
example originated in November and the applicant did not *then* become homeless
intentionally. In the present case, on the other hand, inquiries showed that the relevant
homelessness began in August 1979 when the appellants became homeless intentionally.

Their argument necessarily disregards this aspect of causation and concentrates on
something else: what would have been the position if the deliberate act which caused the
d relevant homelessness had not occurred. They then say that the real cause of their
homelessness is not the act which caused it but something which did not cause it, namely
the fact that they would have been homeless unintentionally by December if they had
not already become homeless intentionally in August.

The appellants have prayed in aid a fallacious analogy with the rule governing
responsibility for damages in tort by referring to cases like *Jobling v Associated Dairies Ltd*
e [1981] 2 All ER 752, [1981] 3 WLR 155. The principle there discussed is that the effect
of a subsequent event may be to limit or terminate an earlier tortfeasor's liability, and the
victim's entitlement, to damages. It has nothing to do with the interpretation of
s 3(2)(*b*)(ii) and 17(1) of the 1977 Act or with the type of causation with which your
Lordships are now concerned.

My point is clearly illustrated by the observation of Waller LJ in the Court of Appeal:
f
> 'The question which has to be considered is not "What would have caused him to
> become homeless if he had not intentionally become homeless?", nor is it "Would
> he have become homeless or been threatened with homelessness if he had not
> already become homeless?" ... the real question for the housing authority was:
> "Were they satisfied that he became homeless intentionally?" ... I do not myself
> see how the addition of another cause, whether it be real or hypothetical, can break
g > the chain of causation which still exists.'

The appellants say that their homelessness in December was due not to their leaving
Trinity Road in August but to the fact that they *would have been* evicted by December; it
seems clear, however, that the cause of their being homeless in December *was* their
leaving in August; if they had *not* left then, the cause of their homelessness in December
h would have been their later eviction (which did not occur), but to say that they would
have become homeless from a cause which did not occur does not extinguish the actual
cause.

With regard to statutory interpretation, I think the appellants would need to read into
the Act a provision that 'when it appears that an applicant who became homeless
intentionally would have been rendered homeless in any event before the date of his
j application, then he shall be deemed not to have become homeless intentionally'.

I have had the opportunity of reading in draft the thoughtful and challenging speech
of my noble and learned friend Lord Bridge who takes the view that, although it is
common ground that the appellants were continuously homeless since August 1979,
they were, having regard to the terms of s 1 of the Act, not homeless while living in the
Upminster accommodation, from which it would follow that their relevant homelessness
began only in December. It was, moreover, not a *Dyson* situation at that time, because

in that case the Huntingdon flat was treated as available to the plaintiff when she became homeless in Helston, whereas the Trinity Road accommodation was not available to the appellants in December. Lord Bridge does not require to consider the case on this footing, because his view of the Act leads to a conclusion in favour of the appellants, even if they are assumed to have been continuously homeless since August. But I have to deal with the point because, on my view of the law, the result would be different if the appellants' relevant homelessness began in December.

The appellants' pleadings in the county court alleged continuous homelessness and this situation has been accepted as common ground. I cannot say in point of law that this could not be right. At best, from the appellants' point of view, it was a question of fact and degree whether at any time after leaving Trinity Road the appellants ceased to be homeless within the meaning of s 1(1). When a person becomes homeless, he remains homeless for so long as he has no accommodation, that is 'if there is no accommodation which', in this case, 'he, together with any other person who normally resides with him as a member of his family . . . has . . . an express or implied licence to occupy'. I consider that to be homeless and to have found some temporary accommodation are not mutually inconsistent concepts. Nor does a person cease to be homeless merely by having a roof over his head or a lodging, however precarious.

My Lords, when one studies ss 3 and 4 of the Act, one finds different duties: under s 3(4) to 'secure that accommodation is made available for his occupation pending any decision which they may make . . .'; under s 4(3) to 'secure that accommodation is made available for his occupation for such period as they consider will give him a reasonable opportunity of himself securing accommodation for his occupation'; under s 4(4) to 'take reasonable steps to secure that accommodation does not cease to be available for his occupation'; and under s 4(5) 'to secure that accommodation becomes available for his occupation'. It is clear from the context and the words used that the accommodation referred to in ss 3(4) and 4(3) is intended for temporary occupation and that the accommodation mentioned in s 4(4) and 4(5) is for other than temporary occupation, since there is no temporal adverbial qualification of the word 'occupation'. There is a similar absence of qualifying words in s 1(1) and in s 5(3) and 5(5) (both of which are linked with s 4(5) by reference), but s 5(6) is different: it speaks of securing that accommodation is available 'until it is determined whether subsection (3) or (5) above applies to him'. Sections 16 and 17, on the other hand, are concerned with occupation other than temporary occupation. It follows from this analysis that a person continues to be homeless while he enjoys temporary occupation. Section 3(4) deals with a special case where it is uncertain whether the person is then homeless, but it is clear that a person is not homeless when he is in occupation under ss 1(1)(a), 4(4), 4(5), 16 and 17. Section 1(1)(b) would arise in relation to non-temporary occupation. The anomalous case, however, is occupation 'by virtue of . . . an order of a court' under s 1(1)(a)(i), since this could occur in relation to any kind of accommodation.

There will be difficult questions of fact and law, but an obviously temporary letting or licence to occupy will not, in my opinion, cause homelessness to cease. For example, the housing authority would not be discharging their duty under s 4(5) by securing that accommodation on such precarious terms was made available for a person's occupation. It is also, in my view, still a matter for debate whether the terms 'occupation' and 'occupy' are appropriate to describe the position of a person sharing a house as a guest without having any portion of the accommodation definitely allotted to him.

My Lords, I now have to come back to *Dyson v Kerrier District Council* [1980] 3 All ER 313, [1980] 1 WLR 1209, the case which Donaldson LJ cited in the Court of Appeal in support of the argument that the Act could not be construed literally, since *Dyson's* case could be regarded as an example of deliberately leaving available accommodation, acquiring a new home and then being held to have become homeless intentionally on having to give up that home, thus proving that on the construction of the Act supported by the respondents 'a person who became homeless intentionally could never redeem himself but would always bear the mark of Cain'.

a   I do not consider, my Lords, that without the benefit of argument I should go down a side road to analyse *Dyson's* case, but I am far from satisfied that it was correctly decided. It could well be that the plaintiff, having become homeless intentionally when she left the Huntingdon flat, was continuously homeless during the temporary winter letting and therefore rightly lost her priority. That is a result which I would understand and accept. But that was not the basis of decision in *Dyson's* case. The court held that the plaintiff became threatened with homelessness at Helston on 19th March and actually

b   homeless on 25th May when she had to leave the flat. On this basis I find it very hard to accept the complete rewriting of s 17(1) and (2) (see [1980] 3 All ER 313 at 319–320, [1980] 1 WLR 1209 at 1214–1215). I agree with the observation of Brightman LJ that sub-ss (1) and (2) of s 17 should not be construed in such a way that different results are reached before and after homelessness (see [1980] 3 All ER 313 at 319, [1980] 1 WLR 1209 at 1214), and I cannot accept a construction of s 17(2) according to which the

c   plaintiff in *Dyson's* case became threatened with homelessness intentionally on 19th March at Helston because she did something at Huntingdon, namely, surrender the tenancy, the likely result of which was that she would be *forced* to leave accommodation at Huntingdon. I mention this aspect of *Dyson's* case only to explain an anomaly which Donaldson LJ (quite justifiably, I think) sought to recruit in favour of the appellants' case.

d   My Lords, the appellants relied strongly on the policy of the Act in order to displace its literal meaning. The legislation aims to remedy the mischief of lack of accommodation and the splitting up of families to which it leads. To achieve the remedy, heavy burdens are placed on housing authorities, but s 17 relieves those authorities by describing circumstances in which a person can become homeless or threatened with homelessness 'intentionally'. No one really becomes homeless or threatened with homelessness *intentionally*; the word is a convenient label to describe the result of acting or failing to act

e   as described in s 17. The result of the housing authority's inquiries under s 3(1) will define their obligation to the homeless person under s 4. Clearly Parliament did not intend to *punish* persons for becoming homeless intentionally: the object was to lay down conditions for retaining priority and thereby to discourage persons from so acting as to increase the already heavy burden on housing authorities. The method was to postpone the claims of those who so acted and to give their places in the queue to those who did

f   not. Housing authorities were further helped by the arbitrary definition of 'threatened with homelessness' in s 1(3). The housing authority may properly decide that it would have been reasonable for a person to continue to occupy accommodation, even when it would also have been reasonable to leave, and finally s 17(4) confers for the purpose of sub-ss (1) and (2) an administrative discretion which depends on the general circumstances prevailing in relation to housing in the area. Indeed, so wide is this administrative

g   discretion and so untypical of a judicial proceeding in its exercise, that I wonder whether certiorari could ever lie, regardless of the actual form of the housing committee's written decisions.

It does not make sense, against this background, for a person to become homeless intentionally and yet regain his lost priority as soon as the accommodation which he ceases to occupy becomes unavailable, as it will inevitably do where shortage of

h   accommodation is the problem. The use of s 17(1) and (2) to adjust priorities will then be meaningless.

In practice homeless persons will be advised in their own interests by housing staffs, as these appellants were, and most people will accept the advice tendered. It is the sad misfortune of the appellants that, through panicking about the debt for rates (which they have now most creditably discharged), they became intentionally homeless contrary to

j   advice.

My noble and learned friend Lord Bridge has rightly pointed to the waste of time and money on proceedings which arises from the policy of housing authorities based on the prevailing interpretation of s 17. It also seems unacceptable that anyone should have to cling to accommodation and defend hopeless cases of ejectment for tactical reasons and thus be compelled by the law to misuse court procedure lest his claim to a house be irretrievably prejudiced. I have already commented on the volume of litigation resulting from decisions of housing authorities in their administration of the Act. All this strongly indicates the need for Parliament to review the legislation in the light of experience.

There is, to my mind, no question here of queue jumping or other unmeritorious conduct. But, applying the law, as I see it, to the facts, I am coerced to hold that the appellants lost their priority by becoming homeless in a relevant way. Therefore I would dismiss this appeal.

LORD BRIDGE OF HARWICH. My Lords, the Housing (Homeless Persons) Act 1977 confers an important and valuable right on a homeless person who has a priority need for accommodation. The categories who can claim a priority need are set out in s 2 of the Act. The nature of those categories, including those with dependent children, pregnant women, and the disabled, gives some indication of the social policy underlying the Act. A homeless person who has a priority need can look to the relevant housing authority to secure that accommodation becomes available for his occupation. This throws a heavy burden on already hard-pressed housing authorities in areas, of which Wandsworth is undoubtedly one, where there is a desperate shortage of housing accommodation and a long housing waiting list. It may also no doubt engender a sense of grievance among those on that list who either have no priority need or cannot claim to be homeless, although their existing accommodation is far from satisfactory, to see others going to the head of the queue. But the Act embodies an important safeguard against abuse, in that the authority's duty to secure accommodation for the homeless person with a priority need is only for a limited period if they are satisfied that he became homeless intentionally (see s 4(3)). It is only if they are not so satisfied that they must house him indefinitely (see s 4(5)).

Against this background it is not surprising that many authorities adopt a general policy under the Act in relation to those whose circumstances render their continued occupation of their existing home precarious, of advising them to wait until a court order is made for their eviction. This may involve the expenditure of unnecessary legal costs by somebody but, from the authority's point of view, it postpones the evil day when the expense of providing accommodation, whether temporary or permanent, will fall on the ratepayers. Even after a court order for possession has been made, if its operation is suspended, a person does not become formally 'threatened with homelessness', a condition which also imposes a duty on the authority, until 28 days before the order will take effect.

This appeal raises the question of how the Act applies to a person with a priority need who voluntarily leaves accommodation prematurely. I use the expression 'leaves accommodation prematurely' as a convenient shorthand to describe the action of a person whose tenure of accommodation has become so precarious, due to circumstances for which he cannot be held responsible, that it can be foreseen that within some reasonably short period (exceeding 28 days) he will have to leave in any event, but who chooses to move out at a time when the housing authority can properly conclude that it would have been reasonable for him to continue in occupation. I will return to the facts of the instant appeal later in this opinion, but to illustrate graphically the problem of construction of the Act which arises when a person leaves accommodation prematurely I take the example of a person who receives a summons for possession with a hearing date two months ahead, who recognises that he will have no defence to the claim, and moves out immediately. On a date, say, four months later, being homeless and in priority need, he applies to the housing authority for accommodation under the Act. The housing authority take the view that on receipt of the summons it would have been reasonable for him to continue in occupation at least until the hearing of the summons but that when the summons was heard an order for possession to take effect within at most six weeks would have been made. What is their duty?

Under ss 3 and 4 of the Act there are three questions, relevant for present purposes, which the housing authority must ask and answer in relation to an applicant for accommodation. They are: (i) is he homeless? (ii) has he a priority need? (iii) did he

become homeless intentionally? The formula to be applied in deciding whether a
person became homeless intentionally is found in s 17(1), which provides:

> '. . . a person becomes homeless intentionally if he deliberately does or fails to do
> anything in consequence of which he ceases to occupy accommodation which is
> available for his occupation and which it would have been reasonable for him to
> continue to occupy.'

In answering the first two questions, the authority are clearly concerned with the
applicant's circumstances at the date of application. Is he *presently* homeless? Has he
presently a priority need? It seems to me to be equally clear that the question whether
'he became homeless intentionally' imports an inquiry as to the cause of his *present* state
of homelessness. To reach this conclusion I do not, with respect, find it necessary, as was
suggested in the Court of Appeal, to read any words into s 17(1) which are not there.
Section 17 is simply concerned to define what is meant by becoming homeless
intentionally. But in construing the phrases 'whether he became homeless intentionally'
and 'that he became homeless intentionally' in the context in which they are found in
ss 3 and 4, it would be absurd to hold that the housing authority are at liberty to rely on
any past act or omission on the part of the applicant which satisfies the s 17 formula but
which is not causally related to the applicant's present state of homelessness.

Thus, on the true construction of ss 3 and 4 and in the application of s 17(1), the third
question the housing authority must ask and answer may be expanded into the following
form: is the applicant's present homelessness the result of a deliberate act or omission on
his part in consequence of which he ceased to occupy accommodation which was
available for his occupation and which it would have been reasonable for him to continue
to occupy? Asking that question in the circumstances of my illustrative example of the
person who left accommodation prematurely when he received the summons for
possession, the housing authority must necessarily give it a negative answer. By the time
he applies to the authority for accommodation the fact that he left prematurely has no
causal connection with his present homelessness. He would now be homeless in any
event.

In the light of the arguments addressed to your Lordships on behalf of the respondent
authority, it is appropriate to add two further observations on the application of this
construction of the Act to different circumstances in which it may be said that an
applicant for accommodation under the Act has left prematurely accommodation which,
by the time he makes his application, would in any event no longer have been available
for his occupation. First, if this construction is correct, it can make no difference to its
application whether the applicant for accommodation, during the period intervening
between the time when he left previous accommodation prematurely and the making
of his application under the Act, was continuously homeless or found some temporary
accommodation for himself which in its turn has ceased, through no fault of his, to be
available to him. In the latter case it is perhaps the more obvious that his premature
leaving of the previous accommodation is quite irrelevant to his present homelessness
because, in this instance, his homelessness first began when he had to leave the temporary
accommodation and ex hypothesi by this time the former accommodation would no
longer be available. In the former case there is a certain plausibility in the proposition
that, the applicant having become homeless intentionally in the first place and having
remained so ever since, this is sufficient to establish the necessary chain of causation
between becoming intentionally homeless and the present state of homelessness. But it
requires no profound philosophical analysis to demonstrate the fallacy in this
proposition. Provided always that it can be demonstrated (or is accepted by the authority)
that by a certain date a man was bound to be evicted from his home, it offends
commonsense to hold that the cause of his homelessness after that date was that he chose
to leave of his own volition before that date.

The second observation arises from the submission that the authority, in deciding
whether an applicant became homeless intentionally, cannot be expected to take account
of what might have happened in a hypothetical situation which in fact did not arise.

Thus, if the authority find that the applicant voluntarily left accommodation which, on the face of it, remained available for his occupation and which it would have been *a* reasonable for him to continue to occupy, they cannot be expected or required to consider the hypothetical question for how long the accommodation would have remained available if he had not left. I see the force of this and certainly accept that if an applicant vacates accommodation which he had an indefinite right to continue to occupy in circumstances in which there is no reason to anticipate a threat of eviction the authority are entitled to treat that as a continuing cause of homelessness without *b* considering the mere possibility that some other cause might have supervened. This is the situation, the very converse of that involved in the present appeal, illustrated by the Court of Appeal's decision in *Dyson v Kerrier District Council* [1980] 3 All ER 313, [1980] 1 WLR 1205. The plaintiff in that case occupied a council flat in Huntingdon in which, in practice, she could expect to remain as long as she wished. She chose to move to Helston to a privately rented flat on terms which gave her no statutory protection in *c* possession. Some eight months after the move she was evicted from the new accommodation. The immediate cause of her homelessness was clearly that eviction. But the Court of Appeal held that the relevant deliberate act on which the housing authority were entitled to rely under s 17(1) in finding that she became homeless intentionally was vacating the Huntingdon flat. The essential basis of the decision was that the voluntary surrender of her Huntingdon tenancy was the cause of her *d* homelessness which arose on eviction from the flat in Helston. Brightman LJ, giving the judgment of the court, put it thus ([1980] 3 All ER 313 at 319, [1980] 1 WLR 1205 at 1215):

> 'The local authority were entitled to reach the conclusion that the plaintiff became homeless on 25th May intentionally because she deliberately had done something (surrendered the Huntingdon tenancy) in consequence of which she ceased to *e* occupy accommodation (the Huntingdon flat) which was available for her occupation and which it would have been reasonable for her to continue to occupy; and that, therefore, *if she had not done that deliberate act she would not have become homeless on 25th May.*' (My emphasis.)

But if a housing authority are minded to rely against an applicant on the fact that he *f* voluntarily left accommodation on some date in the past as the cause of his present homelessness and to make that the basis of their conclusion that he became homeless intentionally, I do not see how the question how long the accommodation would otherwise have continued to be available for his occupation, hypothetical though it may be, can in all cases be avoided. In a sense perhaps it is a matter of degree. At one end of the spectrum, as already indicated, is the case (as in *Dyson's* case) where there was no *g* reason to anticipate eviction from the vacated accommodation and the housing authority could properly assume that it would have remained available indefinitely. At the other end is the case where a court order for possession has already been made but the applicant, for some reason, leaves voluntarily more than 28 days before the date named in the order when, in the authority's view, it would have been reasonable for him to remain. But between these two extremes there may be an almost infinite variety of *h* circumstances in which an occupier of residential accommodation will find himself in more or less obvious and more or less imminent danger of eviction on grounds which cannot be attributed to any earlier deliberate act or omission on his part and where he may choose to leave voluntarily rather than wait for a court order for possession to be made against him. In any such case, the housing authority, on considering a later application for accommodation under the Act, assuming they find that he left the *j* previous accommodation prematurely, having ascertained the relevant facts, must ask themselves the question: if the applicant had not left his previous accommodation, is it likely that he would now be homeless? If they answer that question in the negative, and that conclusion is one which a reasonable authority could reasonably reach on the facts, their conclusion that the applicant became homeless intentionally will, of course, be beyond challenge in the courts. But if they simply ignore the question, they fail to take

account of the relevant issue which arises as to the cause of his present homelessness and
a thus proceed on an erroneous construction of the Act.

In the instant case the appellants and their four children, in summer 1979, occupied
56 Trinity Road, Wandsworth, which comprised a shop with living accommodation
over. Their occupation was under licence from the lessee, a relative, who had moved
elsewhere. The business carried on in the shop was not prospering and the appellants
found themselves under an ever-increasing burden of debt for unpaid rent and rates.
b They twice consulted the respondent housing authority and were told that the authority
could not help them before there was a court order for possession against them. They
left in July 1979 and went to live with the same relative in accommodation at
Upminster. In December 1979 they were required to leave this accommodation and
made their application to the respondent authority for accommodation under the Act.

In notifying (as required by s 8 of the Act) their decision on the application and the
c reasons for it, the respondents wrote, on 4th January 1980, to the appellants in the
following terms:

'Further to your interview on 28th December, and subsequent investigations, it
has been decided that you are homeless and in priority need but your homelessness
is regarded as intentional. The reasons for this decision are that you left your
accommodation at 56 Trinity Road SW17 after you had been advised on two
d occasions by the Wandsworth Housing Aid Centre to remain in occupation of 56
Trinity Road SW17 until the owners sought a Court Order. You disregarded this
advice and moved to your relations, Mrs. Ahmad at 197 St. Mary's Lane, Upminster,
Essex, knowing this to be only temporary accommodation.'

The case was pleaded and has been argued throughout on the basis, accepted as common
e ground between counsel, that the appellants became homeless in July 1979 when they
left 56 Trinity Road. But 'homeless' is defined in s 1 of the Act, and a person who has an
express or implied licence to occupy accommodation is not homeless within that
definition. It is plain from the undisputed primary facts that, from July to December
1979, the appellants and their children had at least an express or implied licence to
occupy the accommodation which they in fact occupied at Upminster and therefore were
f not 'homeless' within the definition. I should not myself think it right to decide an
appeal on a basis accepted as common ground which involved an erroneous conclusion
of law from undisputed facts. But for reasons which I have indicated earlier I do not
think it makes any difference in principle whether the appellants' homelessness began in
July or December.

The county court judge has found that the respondents properly concluded that the
g appellants in July 1979 deliberately ceased to occupy accommodation (56 Trinity Road)
which was available for their occupation and which it would have been reasonable for
them to continue to occupy. This view is not challenged. The judge had before him
both affidavits and oral evidence from two officers employed in the housing department
of the respondent authority who had investigated the circumstances relevant to the
appellants' application and who, in consultation with their superior officer, to whom the
h authority's statutory function of making decisions under the Act was delegated, had been
responsible for formulating the authority's reasons for deciding that the appellants had
become homeless intentionally. On the basis of this evidence the judge was, in my view,
amply justified in reaching the conclusion which he expressed in the following terms:

'Put simply on the facts of this case the question that the defendants should have
asked themselves was, even if the Dins had complied with the advice given to them
j in June and July and had remained where they were would they, by the time of
their application, have been homeless in any event. The defendants clearly did not
consider the point. Had they asked themselves the question the answer on the
evidence would have had to be Yes.'

No one disputes that the court's jurisdiction to review the decision of a housing
authority under the Act is supervisory, not appellate. The court can only intervene on

the well-known principles which find their classic expression in the judgment of Lord Greene MR in *Associated Provincial Picture Houses Ltd v Wednesbury Corpn* [1947] 2 All ER 680 at 682–683, [1948] 1 KB 223 at 228–229. It was not suggested in argument that a case otherwise within the jurisdiction of the county court was taken outside that jurisdiction because it raised an issue as to the legality of a housing authority's decision under the Act. Here the form of the action was a claim for damages for breach of statutory duty (within the county court limit) coupled with claims for declarations and an injunction. Without hearing argument on the jurisdiction issue, it would no doubt be wrong for your Lordships' House to make any considered pronouncement on it. But, if the appellants are entitled to succeed on the merits, to dismiss the appeal on the ground that the wrong procedure was followed would merely force the appellants to institute fresh proceedings by way of an application for judicial review in which, unless the respondents introduced fresh evidence contradicting that given in the county court, the appellants would be bound to succeed. In the light of this I do not think that a doubt about a question of jurisdiction which was never argued should inhibit your Lordships' House from allowing the appeal.

In the short passage which I have quoted above from his judgment, the learned county court judge, in my view, formulated with precise accuracy the proper test to be applied by the respondent authority in deciding whether the appellants had become homeless intentionally and demonstrated the error vitiating their decision which entitled the court to treat it as invalid.

I am not at all sorry to reach this conclusion. It would seem to me a great injustice if a homeless person in priority need having once left accommodation prematurely, no matter how short the period for which the accommodation would have remained available and in which it would have been reasonable for him to continue to occupy it, may thereafter be treated as intentionally homeless for an indefinite period and thus disqualified from claiming the major benefit which the Act confers. Ackner LJ thought this a just penalty for what he called 'unfair queue jumping'. But I can detect no trace of any attempt to jump the queue in the circumstances in which these appellants left 56 Trinity Road. He pointed out further, no doubt quite rightly, that a person categorised as intentionally homeless can throw off that status when he again achieves 'a settled residence'. But I wonder what chance the class of homeless person in priority need who is driven to rely on the housing authority's assistance under the Act has of finding 'a settled residence' by his own efforts. If the respondent authority put the appellants on the street, as presumably they will if the appeal fails, the most likely outcome must surely be that the family will be broken up and the children taken into care.

I would only add that nothing I have said should be taken as encouraging housing authorities to adhere to a rigid policy of refusing help to those threatened with eviction until a court order for possession has been made against them. I understand such a policy to be widely followed. It must involve a great expenditure of unnecessary legal costs. I fully appreciate the pressures to which housing authorities are subject and the reasons why they are loath to accept the burden of providing accommodation until it is irresistibly forced on them. But in cases, of which there must be many, where eviction in due course can be foreseen as inevitable, it would surely be more reasonable for the housing authority to accept their rehousing responsibility voluntarily, possibly on a date to be agreed with the landlord who is entitled to recover possession, without putting him to the expense of litigation.

I would allow the appeal, set aside the order of the Court of Appeal, and restore the order of Wandsworth County Court.

Appeal dismissed.

Solicitors: *Fisher, Meredith* (for the appellants); *Susan G Smith*, Wandsworth (for the respondents).

Mary Rose Plummer   Barrister.

Islam v London Borough of Hillingdon

HOUSE OF LORDS

LORD WILBERFORCE, LORD FRASER OF TULLYBELTON, LORD RUSSELL OF KILLOWEN, LORD LOWRY AND LORD BRIDGE OF HARWICH

5th, 6th, 7th, 8th OCTOBER, 19th NOVEMBER 1981

Housing – Homeless person – Person becoming homeless intentionally – Act or omission causing applicant to cease occupying accommodation available for him – Applicant coming from Bangladesh and settling in England – Applicant's wife and children residing at his parents' home in Bangladesh – Wife and children subsequently coming to England – Applicant's accommodation inadequate to house him and them – Applicant and family having no accommodation because of inadequacy of his accommodation – Whether applicant entitled to be permanently housed by local authority – Whether applicant homeless intentionally – Housing (Homeless Persons) Act 1977, ss 4(2)(b), 16, 17(1).

The appellant came to England from Bangladesh (then East Pakistan) in 1965 and thereafter lived and worked in the London Borough of Hillingdon. From time to time he revisited Bangladesh and he married there in 1968 and had four children. His wife and children lived with his parents in Bangladesh. Although his Bangladesh passport issued in August 1974 showed his permanent and present address as that of his parents, he was ordinarily resident in the United Kingdom and settled there 'with indefinite leave to remain' under the provisions of the Immigration Act 1971. In 1974 the appellant applied for a visa to permit his wife and children to enter the United Kingdom and had an entry certificate indorsed on his passport. Also in 1974 his wife applied for entry clearance for herself and the children but an entry visa was not granted to them until February 1980. Meanwhile, in August 1979, the appellant moved from his existing one-room accommodation in Hillingdon to new accommodation in Hillingdon which consisted of one shared room which was inadequate to house him and his family. On 27th April 1980 the appellant's wife and children arrived in England. The appellant's landlord accommodated them temporarily but in July 1980 he served on them notice to quit and on 8th September he ejected them. The appellant applied to Hillingdon council for accommodation as a homeless person under the Housing (Homeless Persons) Act 1977. The council determined (i) that he was homeless but was not in priority need of accommodation within s 2(1)[a] of that Act, because his children were not persons who might reasonably be expected to reside with him as they had lived apart from him (ie in Bangladesh) for the previous seven years, and (ii) that, even if he were in priority need, he was to be treated as having become homeless intentionally within s 17(1)[b] of the 1977 Act because he had deliberately arranged for his wife and children to leave accommodation in Bangladesh which it would have been reasonable for them to continue to occupy. Accordingly, the council decided that the appellant and his family were not entitled under the 1977 Act to be permanently housed by the council. The appellant applied for judicial review of the council's decision by way of, inter alia, an order of certiorari to quash the decision. The judge held that the appellant was in priority need of accommodation within s 2(1) but that, in bringing his wife and family to England from Bangladesh without ensuring there was permanent accommodation available for them in England, he had rendered himself and them intentionally homeless within s 17(1). The appellant appealed to the Court of Appeal ([1981] 2 All ER 1089), which dismissed his appeal on the ground that he had become homeless intentionally within s 17(1) of the

---

a   Section 2(1), so far as material, provides: 'For the purposes of this Act a homeless person or a person threatened with homelessness has a priority need for accommodation when the housing authority are satisfied that he is within one of the following categories:—(*a*) he has dependent children who are residing with him or who might reasonably be expected to reside with him . . .'

b   Section 17(1) is set out at p 906 *g h*, post

1977 Act because (i) (per Lord Denning MR) by arranging for his wife and children to come to England he did something in consequence of which he and his family ceased to *a* occupy accommodation in Bangladesh which was available for his and their occupation or (ii) (per Sir Denys Buckley) by bringing his family to England he deliberately did something in consequence of which he ceased to occupy accommodation, ie his shared room, which was available for his occupation, or, alternatively, the accommodation in England and Bangladesh taken together constituted available accommodation and by giving up the Bangladesh accommodation he ceased to occupy accommodation which *b* was previously available for occupation by himself and his family and which it would have been reasonable for him to continue to occupy. The appellant appealed to the House of Lords.

Held – The decision of the council that the appellant had become homeless intentionally was invalid because the room which the appellant shared in Hillingdon had never been *c* accommodation which was 'available' for his occupation within the meaning of s 17(1) of the 1977 Act read with s 16^c thereof because it had not been available for occupation by both the appellant and his family in view of its inadequacy and neither would it have been reasonable for them to occupy it. Furthermore, the appellant could not be treated as having occupied in any sense recognised by law a portion of his parents' house in Bangladesh through the agency of his wife and children, having regard to the fact that *d* he had been ordinarily resident in England for 15 years, and therefore he could not 'cease to occupy' it for the purposes of s 17(1). Moreover, the accommodation in England and in Bangladesh could not be taken together so as to constitute 'available' accommodation occupied by the appellant. It followed therefore that the appellant had never had any available accommodation which he could have given up and which it would have been reasonable for him to have continued to occupy, and accordingly the council were not *e* entitled to be satisfied under s 4(2)(b)^d of the 1977 Act that he had become homeless intentionally. The appeal would therefore be allowed (see p 904 *b c* and *g* to p 905 *a* and *c* to *e*, p 907 *a* to *e*, p 909 *b* to *j*, p 910 *d* to *j*, p 911 *a* and p 912 *b* and *e f*, post).

Decision of the Court of Appeal sub nom *R v London Borough of Hillingdon, ex parte Islam* [1981] 2 All ER 1089 reversed.

f

Notes
For a housing authority's duty to house homeless persons and the inquiries into possible homelessness a housing authority must make, see 22 Halsbury's Laws (4th Edn) paras 511–513.

For the Housing (Homeless Persons) Act 1977, ss 2, 4, 16, 17, see 47 Halsbury's Statutes (3rd Edn) 317, 318, 330.

g

Cases referred to in opinions
De Falco v Crawley Borough Council, Silvestri v Crawley Borough Council [1980] 1 All ER 913, [1980] QB 460, [1980] 2 WLR 664, 78 LGR 180, CA.
Din v London Borough of Wandsworth [1981] 3 All ER 881, HL.
Dyson v Kerrier District Council [1980] 3 All ER 313, [1980] 1 WLR 1205, CA. *h*
Edwards (Inspector of Taxes) v Bairstow [1955] 3 All ER 48, [1956] AC 14, [1955] 3 WLR 410, 36 Tax Cas 207, [1955] TR 209, 34 ATC 198, 48 R & IT 534, HL, 28(1) Digest (Reissue) 566, 2089.
Lewis v North Devon District Council [1981] 1 All ER 27, [1981] 1 WLR 328, 79 LGR 289.

---

c Section 16 provides: 'For the purposes of this Act accommodation is only available for a person's *j* occupation if it is available for occupation both by him and by any other person who might reasonably be expected to reside with him and any reference in this Act to securing accommodation for a person's occupation shall be construed accordingly.'

d Section 4(2), so far as material, provides: 'Where ... (b) [a housing authority] are satisfied that [a person who has applied to them for accommodation or for assistance in obtaining accommodation] has a priority need but are also satisfied that he became homeless or threatened with homelessness intentionally, their duty is to furnish him with advice and appropriate assistance.'

R v Hillingdon Borough Council, ex parte Streeting [1980] 3 All ER 413, [1980] 1 WLR 1425,
a   DC and CA.
R v Northumberland Compensation Appeal Tribunal, ex parte Shaw [1952] 1 All ER 122,
[1952] 1 KB 338, 116 JP 54, 50 LGR 193, 2 P & CR 361, CA, 35 Digest (Repl) 817, *104.*
R (Martin) v Mahony [1910] 2 IR 695.

Appeal

b   By a notice of motion dated 21st October 1980, the appellant, Tafazzul Islam, applied,
with leave of the Divisional Court granted on 20th October 1980, for judicial review of
the decision of 2nd October 1980 of the homeless families panel of the respondents, the
London Borough of Hillingdon, made pursuant to the Housing (Homeless Persons) Act
1977. The relief sought by the motion was: (1) an order of certiorari to quash those parts
of the panel's decision whereby it was decided that (a) the appellant was not in priority
c   need of accommodation pursuant to s 2(1) of the 1977 Act and (b) that if he was in
priority need he was intentionally homeless pursuant to s 17 of the Act; (2) an order of
mandamus directed to the respondents requiring them to make appropriate inquiries
pursuant to s 3 of the 1977 Act; and/or alternatively (3) a declaration that the panel did
not validly determine that the appellant was not in priority need of accommodation; and
(4) a declaration that it did not validly determine that the appellant was intentionally
d   homeless pursuant to s 17 of the 1977 Act; and (5) a declaration that the respondents
were under a duty to secure that accommodation became available for occupation by the
appellant and his family pursuant to s 4(5) of the 1977 Act; (6) an injunction ordering the
respondents to provide accommodation for the appellant and his family. An interim
injunction was granted on the hearing of the application for leave to apply for judicial
review ordering the respondents to provide accommodation for the appellant and his
e   family. On 30th January 1981 Glidewell J, hearing the Divisonal Court List, dismissed
the application. The appellant appealed. On 22nd May 1981 the Court of Appeal (Lord
Denning MR and Sir Denys Buckley, Ackner LJ dissenting) (sub nom *R v London Borough
of Hillingdon, ex parte Islam* [1981] 2 All ER 1089, [1981] 3 WLR 109) dismissed the
appeal and granted the appellant leave to appeal to the House of Lords. The facts are set
out in the opinion of Lord Lowry.

f
Derek Wood QC and *Andrew Arden* for the appellant.
John Samuels QC and *Robin Barratt* for the respondents.

Their Lordships took time for consideration.

g   19th November. The following opinions were delivered.

LORD WILBERFORCE. My Lords, this case also arises under the Housing
(Homeless Persons) Act 1977. I have referred to the relevant provisions of the Act in
dealing with the appeal in *Din v London Borough of Wandsworth* [1981] 3 All ER 881 and
I shall not repeat them. The facts are as follows; it is important to appreciate their
h   particularity.
Mr Taffazul Islam came to this country from Bangladesh (then East Pakistan) in
1965. He obtained employment, and from 1965 until August 1979 lived at 5 Cowley
Mill Road, Uxbridge, with the right only to occupy a single room. This residence, and
his place of work, were within the borough of Hillingdon, the respondents. This
borough, as is well known, includes Heathrow Airport, through which a number of
j   persons arrive in this country who have no accommodation, so presenting great problems
to the respondents, but that is quite coincidental to the present appeal. The appellant's
is not an 'airport' case; it could have arisen in the area of any other local authority.
In 1968 the appellant went to Bangladesh and married; his wife remained in that
country, living with the appellant's parents. On four subsequent visits by the appellant
his wife conceived the four existing children of the family; they all lived with the
appellant's parents.

In 1974 application was made for entry clearance for the appellant's wife and the then two children to come to this country to live with the appellant. It is important to appreciate that, since the appellant came to this country before 1973, this application could be made and entertained without the necessity of showing that accommodation here was available, as must be shown in post-1973 cases.

In August 1979 the appellant moved from 5 Cowley Mill Road to 120 Cowley Mill Road where he had the right to share one room with one other man.

Late in 1979 or early in 1980 the appellant's wife was issued with a Bangladeshi passport for herself and her four children and soon afterwards it was indorsed with an entry certificate; this was only valid for presentation within six months. In April 1980 the appellant heard that his wife and children were arriving in this country immediately. The appellant never had any accommodation in this country which could qualify as accommodation within the meaning of s 1 of the 1977 Act. The family spent one night at 5 Cowley Mill Road and then some time at 120 Cowley Mill Road, until in September 1980 they were summarily evicted. The appellant then applied to the respondents for accommodation under the 1977 Act as a homeless person.

On 2nd October 1980 the respondents' homeless families panel resolved as follows:

'(1) That the applicant be considered homeless, but not in priority need, as his dependent children might not reasonably be expected to reside with him having lived apart for the past seven years. (2) That, even if he were in priority need, the applicant be considered to have become homeless intentionally, having deliberately arranged for his wife and children to leave accommodation which it would have been reasonable for them to continue to occupy. (3) That accommodation continue to be secured for the applicant and his family up to and including 16 October 1980.

The appellant applied for an order for judicial review. The Divisional Court, after rejecting ground (1) above (and this part of their decision has not been appealed against) held that, in bringing his wife and family to England from Bangladesh without ensuring that there was permanent accommodation available to them, the appellant rendered himself, and them also, homeless 'intentionally'. The appellant appealed to the Court of Appeal, having obtained leave, to contend that he was not intentionally homeless because he had not left accommodation available for his occupation within the meaning of the Act.

The Court of Appeal by majority (Lord Denning MR and Sir Denys Buckley, Ackner LJ dissenting) ([1981] 2 All ER 1089, [1981] 3 WLR 109) dismissed the appeal, holding that the appellant had become homeless intentionally, but the majority differed in their reasons for so holding. I regret that I am unable to agree with either of the reasons given. Lord Denning MR decided the case on the basis that the appellant was occupying 'available' accommodation in Bangladesh. But this approach, which might be possible in some cases, is not supported by the facts. There is no finding, or evidence, that the Bangladesh accommodation was ever 'available' to the applicant himself, or that he was ever in occupation of it.

Sir Denys Buckley disagreed with this approach but held that by bringing his family here the appellant deliberately did something which had the effect of rendering the shared room at 120 Cowley Mill Road accommodation no longer available for his occupation. This, however, with respect, overlooked the provisions of s 16 which was to be read into s 17. The room at 120 Cowley Mill Road was never accommodation (within s 1) available for occupation by him and his family, so s 17 could not be applied to it. Sir Denys Buckley's alternative ground was that the accommodation in Uxbridge and Bangladesh taken together could constitute 'available accommodation' occupied by the appellant. But I do not think that rooms in two separate continents can be combined in this way.

On the other hand, not without misgiving, but without any doubt, I have reached the conclusion that the judgment of Ackner LJ is correct and I am glad to adopt his reasons as my own. Put very briefly, the case is four square within the 1977 Act: the appellant was 'homeless', he was entitled to priority, he never had any 'available accommodation' within the meaning of s 16 which he could give up and s 17 could not be applied to his case. There is no answer to his claim.

While the result in this particular case may be considered acceptable, in view of the appellant's long residence in this country and his efforts to unite his family here, and I entirely accept that immigrants as such are not intended to be excluded from the Act, I share Ackner LJ's misgiving whether, in relation to persons coming from overseas (whether the EEC or otherwise), or indeed to some persons moving from one part of this country to another, the Act is as well considered as it is undoubtedly well intentioned.

The difficulties of the Act are certainly diminished to some extent by the decision of the Court of Appeal in *De Falco v Crawley Borough Council* [1980] 1 All ER 913, [1980] QB 460, where a whole family was held to have deliberately left accommodation which was available to them in Italy, which, having regard to the housing situation in Crawley, it was reasonable for them to have continued to occupy. But many foreseeable difficulties remain. It would serve no purpose to anticipate them here, but I venture to suggest the need for some reconsideration of the Act.

I would allow the appeal, and grant declarations as sought by the notice of motion dated 21st October 1980.

LORD FRASER OF TULLYBELTON. My Lords, in this case I have had the advantage of reading in draft the speeches prepared by my noble and learned friends Lord Wilberforce and Lord Lowry. I agree with them, and for the reasons stated in them I would allow the appeal.

LORD RUSSELL OF KILLOWEN. My Lords, for the reasons contained in the speeches of my noble and learned friends Lord Wilberforce and Lord Lowry I would allow this appeal.

LORD LOWRY. My Lords, the proceedings which are the subject of this appeal took the form of an application by the appellant under RSC Ord 53 for the judicial review of a decision dated 2nd October 1980 of the homeless families panel ('the panel') of the respondent, the London Borough of Hillingdon pursuant to the Housing (Homeless Persons) Act 1977 and arose in the following circumstances.

The appellant, aged 23, came to England from Bangladesh (then East Pakistan) in 1965 and thereafter has lived and worked in Hillingdon. He has returned at intervals to Bangladesh and married there in 1968. He has revisited Bangladesh five times since then. By 1980 the appellant and his wife had four children and after the marriage she and, in course of time, the children lived with his parents in Bangladesh. The appellant has a Bangladesh passport issued in August 1974 in which his 'permanent address in Bangladesh' and his 'present address' are shown as that of his parents. He was, however, ordinarily resident in the United Kingdom and 'settled' there 'with indefinite leave to remain' under the provisions of the Immigration Act 1971.

The appellant applied in 1974 for a visa to permit his wife and children to come to the United Kingdom and had an entry certificate indorsed on his passport. In the same year his wife applied for entry clearance for herself and her children, then two in number, to enter the United Kingdom, but it was only in February 1980 that an entry visa, valid for six months, was indorsed on her passport to entitle her and the children, now four in number, to join the appellant there, as being the dependants of a person already settled in the United Kingdom. Because the appellant was settled here before 1973, the immigration rules restricting the admission of dependants for settlement did not apply, and so he did not have to show that he could support or accommodate them.

The appellant had for 14 years lived in a room at 5 Cowley Mill Road, Uxbridge and had in August 1979 moved to the house of a Mr Rahman at 120 Cowley Mill Road, where he obtained a share of a room. As soon as the family had been granted clearance, he arranged for them to come to England and took an extra room from Mr Rahman.

Exactly what arrangements they then made is not clear, but it is not relevant to this appeal. The appellant's wife and children arrived on 27th April 1980, but Mr Rahman would not at first receive them and they stayed for three nights at 5 Cowley Mill Road, the address of the old lodgings.

On 29th April the appellant had sought help from the respondents' homeless families unit and, as a result, it may be, of their intercession, Mr Rahman agreed to accommodate the appellant and his family from 30th April for a few weeks on a temporary basis, but he served notice to quit on 9th July 1980 and ejected the Islams on 8th September. The respondents then provided them with bed and breakfast accommodation in Harrow pending an application by the appellant to Uxbridge County Court for an interim injunction to restrain Mr Rahman from evicting the Islams from his house. This application seems to have been designed, by arrangement with the respondents, to establish that the appellant was indeed homeless, and on the evening of the day on which it was dismissed, 2nd October 1980, the panel met, further considered his position and reached a decision in the following terms:

'RESOLVED—(1) That the applicant be considered homeless, but not in priority need, as his dependent children might not reasonably be expected to reside with him having lived apart for the past seven years. (2) That, even if he were in priority need, the applicant be considered to have become homeless intentionally, having deliberately arranged for his wife and children to leave accommodation which it would have been reasonable for them to continue to occupy. (3) That accommodation continue to be secured for the applicant and his family up to and including 16 October 1980.'

This is the decision which has to be judicially reviewed.

Pursuant to leave granted to apply for judicial review, the matter came before Glidewell J who decided that, on the facts disclosed and on the true construction of s 2(1)(a) of the Act, the appellant, as well as being homeless, had a priority need for accommodation and that accordingly the first part of the panel's decision was wrong, because the appellant had dependent children who were residing with him, and he held that the words 'who might reasonably be expected to reside with him' would apply only in a case where the children were *not* residing with the appellant. The respondents, who had always conceded that the appellant was homeless within the meaning of s 1(1) of the Act, did not cross-appeal against or otherwise challenge the learned judge's conclusion that the appellant had a priority need as defined by s 2(1). Accordingly, my Lords, the only question which had to be considered by the Court of Appeal (and now comes before your Lordships) was whether the appellant became homeless intentionally within the meaning of s 17(1) of the Act, which is in the following terms:

'Subject to subsection (3) below, for the purposes of this Act a person becomes homeless intentionally if he deliberately does or fails to do anything in consequence of which he ceases to occupy accommodation which is *available for his occupation* and which it would have been reasonable for him to continue to occupy.'

Section 16 defines the words which I have emphasised above as 'available for occupation both by him and by any other person who might reasonably be expected to reside with him'; thus, with the definition incorporated, the material words of s 17(1) read, in effect, as follows:

'. . . a person becomes homeless intentionally if he deliberately does or fails to do anything in consequence of which he ceases to occupy accommodation which is *available for occupation both by him and by any other person who might reasonably be expected to reside with him* and which it would have been reasonable for him to continue to occupy.'

Glidewell J did not mention s 16 either in reviewing the Act or when considering the question whether the appellant became homeless intentionally. From this omission and

from the amendment which the appellant sought in the Court of Appeal it may be
a inferred that neither side drew the learned judge's attention to this important provision
which, if taken into account, could have prevented an otherwise clear and logical
judgment from falling into error, as I respectfully think it did. As it was, the judge was
led to apply *De Falco v Crawley Borough Council* [1980] 1 All ER 913, [1980] QB 460, in
which s 16 was not important because the entire family had been living together in Italy
in accommodation which was suitable for them.

b In the present case, however, resort to s 16 has the effect of making it appear that the
judge has said that the appellant became homeless intentionally on 8th September 1980
because he deliberately sent for his wife and children, in consequence of which he ceased
to occupy accommodation in Mr Rahman's house which was 'available for occupation by
the appellant *and* by his family and which it would have been reasonable for the
appellant to continue to occupy'. And yet it is clear from the inadequacy of the
c accommodation in Mr Rahman's house that it was *not* available for occupation by the
appellant *and his family*. What Glidewell J actually said was that the unit (or panel) were
entitled to decide, on the facts known to them, that, in bringing his wife and family to
England from Bangladesh without ensuring that there was permanent accommodation
available to them, the appellant had rendered himself, and them also, homeless
intentionally.

d It must not be overlooked, as my noble and learned friend Lord Russell reminded
counsel for the respondents, that on 2nd October 1980 the panel found, and at all times
the respondents have conceded, that the appellant became homeless when he had to leave
120 Cowley Mill Road on 8th September, since they rightly treated the family, for the
purposes of s 1(1)(a) of the Act, as then normally residing with the appellant. Otherwise,
having regard to the accommodation which was available, he would not have been made
e homeless.

From the decision of Glidewell J the appellant appealed to the Court of Appeal (see
[1981] 2 All ER 1089, [1981] 3 WLR 109).

Lord Denning MR, having summarised the facts, observed that the appellant sought
to distinguish *De Falco's* case. He then noted the effect of s 16 and said ([1981] 2 All ER
1089 at 1092, [1981] 3 WLR 109 at 113):

f   'In the light of all these provisions, it seems to me that we should look in every
case at the family unit, and treat the words "person", "he", "him" and "his" as
referring to him as the head of the family unit. We should regard the home as the
home of the family unit. So that "he" is homeless when the family unit is
homeless. Applying this concept to s 17 it means that "a person" with a family
becomes homeless intentionally if he deliberately does or fails to do anything in
g   consequence of which he *or* [sic] his family cease to occupy accommodation which
is available for his *or* their occupation and which it would have been reasonable for
him *or* them to continue to occupy.'

This reasoning is derived from the proposition that from 1968 until 1980 the appellant
was occupying in Bangladesh accommodation in his father's home where his wife and,
h in their turn, his children were living as his father's guests and to which he had made five
visits in 12 years. Lord Denning MR held that the appellant '"occupied" [sic] the home
in Bangladesh by his wife and family even whilst he was in lodgings in England . . .' and
continued ([1981] 2 All ER 1089 at 1093, [1981] 3 WLR 109 at 113):

'Looking at s 17 in this way, it seems to me that, when the applicant arranged for
j   his wife and children to come to England, he deliberately did something in
consequence of which he and his family ceased to "occupy" [sic] accommodation in
Bangladesh which was available for his and their occupation and which it would
have been reasonable for him and them to continue to occupy. That accommodation
was available for occupation both by him and by any other person who might
reasonably be expected to *reside with him*.' (My emphasis.)

After pointing out that the object of the Act was 'to keep the family together, so far as possible, and not separate', Lord Denning MR concluded ([1981] 2 All ER 1089 at 1093, *a* [1981] 3 WLR 109 at 114):

'The moral of this case is that men from overseas should not bring their wives and children here unless they have arranged permanent and suitable accommodation for them to come to. The applicant is homeless intentionally. He is not entitled to permanent accommodation. He will not take priority over young couples here who are on the waiting list for housing accommodation.'   *b*

Sir Denys Buckley reached the same conclusion, although for different reasons. He pointed out that the appellant was not homeless until his family arrived in England, and continued ([1981] 2 All ER 1089 at 1096, [1981] 3 WLR 109 at 118):

'Until they reached this country the applicant's wife and children were certainly not residing with him in this country, nor were they then persons who might *c* reasonably be expected to reside with him, for until they obtained entry permits and could travel to this country they could not enter the country. But as soon as they arrived in this country as permitted immigrants they became, in my opinion, persons who might reasonably be expected to reside with him.'

He then proceeded by logical steps to conclude that the appellant became a homeless *d* person with a priority need, but he considered that the appellant became homeless intentionally ([1981] 2 All ER 1089 at 1096–1097, [1981] 3 WLR 109 at 118–119):

'By bringing his family here or by procuring that they came to join him here, the applicant, in my opinion, deliberately did something which had the effect of rendering the shared room at 120 Cowley Mill Road accommodation which was no longer available for his occupation within the terms of s 17(1). This would, it seems *e* to me, have been so even if the applicant in fact continued to occupy his share of that room himself, for this share of the room would nevertheless have ceased to be "available" for his occupation within s 17(1) by reason of s 16 of the Act. With deference to Lord Denning MR, I do not feel able to regard the applicant's home as having been in Bangladesh throughout the period down to April 1980. In my view, he was resident in England at all relevant times and had his home here, *f* notwithstanding that by force of circumstances he had to leave his wife and children in Bangladesh. What accommodation he then had was presumably adequate to his need, living on his own; but when his family arrived the position was completely changed. What had been adequate accommodation for himself alone was wholly unsuited for himself and his family as a family unit. He therefore ceased to occupy accommodation *available for occupation by that family unit*.' (My emphasis.)   *g*

Sir Denys Buckley then propounded 'a possible alternative view' that the appellant had accommodation available for himself and his family, taking into account both the English and the Bangladesh accommodation and that by giving up the Bangladesh accommodation he ceased to occupy accommodation which was previously available for occupation by himself and his family and which it would have been reasonable for him *h* to continue to occupy. He added percipiently:

'Considerations of this kind would have been equally germane if the applicant's family had lived in the North of England instead of Bangladesh, too far from Hillingdon to enable the applicant to live there with them and remain in his employment at Hillingdon.'

He continued: *j*

'It may be legitimate to regard the accommodation at Hillingdon and that in the North of England or in Bangladesh, as the case might be, as together constituting the home of the applicant and his family for the purposes of the Act. In such circumstances, in my view, the applicant would on vacating the accommodation in the North of England or in Bangladesh have ceased to occupy accommodation which had theretofore been available for occupation by himself and by other persons *who might reasonably be expected to reside with him* [my emphasis], leaving himself only with accommodation unsuitable and inadequate to accommodate his family unit and consequently not to be treated as "available" for his occupation (see s 16). If the removal of his family from the North of England or from Bangladesh were the applicant's deliberate act and it would have been reasonable for him to continue to occupy the vacated accommodation, he would have become "homeless intentionally" under s 17(1) of the Act.'

Before commenting on the reasoning of these judgments, which, with the greatest respect, I consider to be unsound, I would turn to the dissenting judgment of Ackner LJ with which (apart from his expressions of regret) I entirely agree but from which I shall be content to select some observations. I pick up the thread from Ackner LJ's judgment ([1981] 2 All ER 1089 at 1095, [1981] 3 WLR 109 at 116).

(1) The English accommodation was never available for occupation by the family unit, because it was at all times unsuitable, and by 2nd October 1980 the appellant's wife and children were persons who might reasonably be expected to reside with him.

(2) With reference to the Bangladesh accommodation, Ackner LJ said:

'Counsel seeks to justify the council's decision by what he accepts, quite frankly, is an artificial view of the facts. He contends that the accommodation in the parents' home in Bangladesh was available for occupation both by the applicant and his family. As I have already indicated, the evidence on this is sparse indeed, five visits of an undefined period and no description of the accommodation. Counsel submits that when the Act provides that "he ceases to occupy" such accommodation that must be read as including both the applicant and those who are residing with him. I would not seek to criticise such an interpretation, but can he be said in reality to have been "occupying" that accommodation? In the context of the Act, where there are frequent references to the word "reside", the word "occupy" must have some element of permanence. It cannot, in my judgment, be extended to rare visits.'

(3) Then he said:

'... where is the material to justify the conclusion that it would have been reasonable for him to continue to occupy the Bangladesh room or rooms? Significantly the decision of the council was that it would have been reasonable for *the wife* and *children* to continue to occupy those premises. They do not suggest that it would have been reasonable for the applicant as well to continue the occupy the Bangladesh premises. This is in no way surprising. There was no material to suggest that there was any opportunity for the applicant to make a gainful living in Bangladesh.'

(4) With reference to the respondents' circular argument, he said:

'Unless the applicant finds accommodation to house himself and his family before they come to this country, then it is said he is intentionally making himself and his family homeless. But it is not suggested that he failed to take any steps reasonably open to him to find such accommodation. So how is he ever to implement the permission and get his family to join him, unless he can qualify for assistance from the council?'

This proceeding, in origin, is not an appeal but an application for judicial review. The appellant must show that, on a proper construction of the Act and having regard to the facts, the panel had no right to be satisfied under s 4(2)(b) that he became homeless intentionally. This, I consider, is not a difficult task. The panel, as now conceded, were not entitled to find that the appellant had not a priority need, because he had dependent children residing with him in England. Incidentally, I cannot, in the circumstances, follow the reasoning by which the panel concluded that his dependent children might

not reasonably be expected to reside with him 'having lived apart for seven years'. But
I pass over this point and come to para (2) of the resolution of 2nd October 1980:

> 'That, even if he were in priority need, the applicant be considered to have
> become homeless intentionally, having deliberately arranged for his wife and
> children to leave accommodation which it would have been reasonable for *them* to
> continue to occupy.'

Again I pass over, in favour of more obvious infirmities, the failure to state that the panel
is 'satisfied' that the appellant became homeless intentionally, only noting that this
apparent deeming of intentional homelessness fits in well with the fiction later adopted
by the respondents that the appellant was occupying accommodation in Bangladesh.

My first point is that para (2), viewed as an expression of satisfaction under s 4(2)(*b*), is
bad on its face for another reason. It does not convey (even if one assumes that
'satisfaction' has been expressed) that the appellant has, in the words of s 17(1), deliberately
done anything in consequence of which *he* ceased to occupy accommodation which was
available for his occupation and which it would have been reasonable for *him* to continue
to occupy; and para (1) does not remove this difficulty.

I wish, however, to forestall the suggestion that the matter be remitted for a proper
determination, and therefore I examine the position further.

Three ways have been suggested whereby the appellant became homeless intentionally. The first was that, by bringing his family to England, he deliberately did something
which rendered the Cowley Mill Road accommodation no longer available for his
occupation. The inescapable flaw in this theory is that, because his family were residing
with him, the Cowley Mill Road accommodation was (by reference to ss 16 and 17) never
'available', nor, of course, would it have been reasonable for the appellant (scilicet the
family unit) to continue to occupy it; thus s 17(1) never came into play.

The second theory was that the appellant was occupying accommodation in his
father's house in Bangladesh, and again that, by sending for his family, he deliberately
did something in consequence of which he and his family ceased to 'occupy'
accommodation in Bangladesh which was available for his and their occupation and
which it would have been reasonable for him and them to occupy. I am using the words
of Lord Denning MR (see [1981] 2 All ER 1089 at 1092–1093, [1981] 3 WLR 109 at 113),
including the quotation marks round the word 'occupy', the addition of which indicates
to me that Lord Denning MR was conscious of using the word in an artificial sense
which, I very respectfully suggest, is quite inconsistent with its ordinary meaning and
with the probably narrower sense in which it is used in the Act. When it speaks of
occupying accommodation, the Act has in contemplation people who are residing in that
accommodation (see s 1) and residing in family units, where possible. Indeed, Lord
Denning MR truly points out that the object of the Act was 'to keep the family together,
so far as possible, and not separate' (see [1981] 2 All ER 1089 at 1093, [1981] 3 WLR 109
at 114). I also think that, on the facts proved, no one could reasonably conclude that the
appellant, who had been ordinarily resident in England for 15 years and had in the past
12 years made five visits to his family in Bangladesh, was occupying in any sense
recognised by our law a portion of his father's house through the agency of his wife and
children. If he had even been, at some time, ordinarily resident with his wife and
children in that house since his marriage, the concept could be more easily entertained.
I do not deny that, in Great Britain or elsewhere, a husband who had set up house with
his wife as a family unit could later leave his wife and children at home and continue to
be the legal occupier.

The third suggested method, Sir Denys Buckley's 'possible alternative', contemplated
occupancy both in England and in Bangladesh, but also requires the appellant to have
been occupying the Bangladesh accommodation, or else he could not 'cease to occupy'
it. This theory is therefore open to the objections I have already stated and to those of Sir
Denys Buckley (see [1981] 2 All ER 1089 at 1097, [1981] 3 WLR 109 at 118) when
rejecting the view of Lord Denning MR. *Lewis v North Devon District Council* [1981] 1 All
ER 27, [1981] 1 WLR 328 affords no help to the respondents on either the second or the

third method, when its facts are examined; nor, for similar reasons, do I find it necessary to discuss *Dyson v Kerrier District Council* [1980] 3 All ER 313, [1980] 1 WLR 1205.

My conclusion is that by no artificial or other expedient, however ingenious, can a finding of intentional homelessness be legally sustained. It is therefore idle for the respondents to suggest that your Lordships ought not to interfere with the panel's decision unless it is plainly unreasonable.

So far I have said little about the policy of the Act, which clearly includes the object of bringing and keeping families together, but there is little need to invoke parliamentary intention when the meaning is clear. But, even if the relevant provisions were ambiguous, I cannot readily adopt a strained construction which would frustrate the policy of the Act and would promote the object, which is not to be found there either expressly or by necessary implication, of postponing the otherwise valid claims of homeless persons and families who have their origins outside Great Britain.

The respondents have an unenviable and difficult task in administering the Act and their officials, let it be clearly proclaimed, have gone to the greatest lengths of compassion and industry to alleviate the lot of the Islam family; but, in the course of argument, they have still sought to restrict their liability to such people. I refer to the fifth reason in the respondents' case, which was that they would have concluded that the appellant and his family were not homeless had the panel directed themselves in accordance with the decision of the Court of Appeal, 'not binding on your Lordships' House', in *R v Hillingdon Borough Council, ex parte Streeting* [1980] 3 All ER 413, [1980] 1 WLR 1425. This statement amounts to a submission, which was ambivalently pursued before your Lordships and which I consider to be completely unsustainable, that a housing authority owes no duty under the Act to any family unit which has not previously occupied a family home in Great Britain. Such an argument is merely a special way of advancing the equally untenable general proposition that housing authorities owe no duty to 'foreigners' under the Act. It is linked to the unsound proposition, which would penalise some residents in Great Britain, that a 'local connection' is requisite; a straightforward reading of ss 5 and 18 disposes of that argument. I need not spend time on discussion but, in so far as it dispensed with the need for a previous Islam family home in Great Britain, *Ex parte Streeting* was, in my respectful opinion, rightly decided. The appellant, of course, had, in point of fact, two local connections through residence and employment.

In seeking to limit the respondents' liability, counsel relied on a presumption that the Act was intended to be given territorial effect and not to be construed extra-territorially. This doctrine is not apt to exclude residents such as the appellant from the benefit of the Act and is more likely to be relevant to the question, if it were ever raised, whether the accommodation mentioned in s 1 is accommodation in Great Britain.

Counsel for the respondents suggested that by allowing this appeal your Lordships would facilitate 'double moves' of families in Great Britain and thereby aggravate the already serious burden cast on housing authorities. I do not think this is correct. The principle of *De Falco's* case is the safeguard, since it can properly be decided that an applicant has become homeless intentionally whether the family moves as a unit or the husband, leaving suitable accommodation, comes first and then calls on the family to follow. There will be, of course, and in the interests of the mobility of labour ought to be, cases where the housing authority will under s 17(1) accept that it would not have been reasonable in the circumstances for the applicant to continue to occupy the accommodation which he has left.

The view which I have taken of the law makes it unnecessary to consider in detail the panel's decision but it appears to me to be one in which, as Lord Radcliffe has put it (see *Edwards (Inspector of Taxes) v Bairstow* [1955] 3 All ER 48 at 57, [1956] AC 14 at 36), 'the true and only reasonable conclusion contradicts the determination', which is another way of saying that there was *no* evidence to support the panel's decision and that it ought therefore to be reversed by judicial review and suitable declarations granted. My noble and learned friend Lord Bridge pointed in argument to the anomaly of conceding that the appellant's wife and family might reasonably, at least from the time they were permitted to come here, be expected to reside with him, while at the same time defending a finding that it would have been reasonable for them to continue to occupy accommodation in Bangladesh. As the appellant put it, the only fact contradicting the conclusion that his family were persons who might reasonably be expected to reside with him was the lack of accommodation to enable them to live together. This is a circular argument because that lack is the very circumstance which s 16 and the Act are designed to relieve.

I would allow the appeal and grant the three declarations sought by the notice of motion. I would, however, be most reluctant to consider an order of certiorari in this particular case. This is not because of the nature of the body to which the order would go: there are precedents to justify it and the attitude of the courts in this respect is, rightly I consider, more flexible than it used to be. But, although para (2) is fit to be quashed, I do not think that the panel's *decision* is bad on the face of the record because para (1) cannot be attacked without extraneous aid in the way of evidence. It is Sphinx-like and not a speaking order and its infirmities are thereby concealed. To illustrate my point of view I need only refer to two very well-known and classic authorities, R (*Martin*) v *Mahony* [1910] 2 IR 695 at 734 and R v *Northumberland Compensation Appeal Tribunal, ex parte Shaw* [1952] 1 All ER 122 at 130, [1952] 1 KB 338 at 351.

I would defend myself against the charge of being over-technical in an enlightened age by pointing out that, if the requirements for certiorari are relaxed, many orders of the magistrates' courts, and of the Crown Court in England and Wales and the county courts in Northern Ireland in their appellate capacities, will become vulnerable to review on grounds which would not lead to a declaration or injunction in either jurisdiction. My second point is that the introduction of judicial review under RSC Ord 53 has already provided the proceedings with the flexibility the absence of which was formerly a cause of injustice and expense to a litigant with right on his side.

LORD BRIDGE OF HARWICH. My Lords, I have had the advantage of reading in advance the speeches of my noble and learned friends Lord Wilberforce and Lord Lowry. I agree with their reasons for concluding that on the true construction of the relevant provisions of the Housing (Homeless Persons) Act 1977 as applied to the facts of this appeal the respondents' conclusion that the appellant became homeless intentionally cannot be sustained and that the appeal should therefore be allowed.

I am not sure what prompted Ackner LJ to express regret and reluctance at having to reach the conclusion he did in his dissenting judgment in the Court of Appeal. Like Lord Lowry, I do not share that regret. On the contrary, I should be hard put to it to formulate any defensible principle to justify denying the benefits conferred by the Housing (Homeless Persons) Act 1977 to immigrants who, like the appellant, have acquired under the relevant legislation controlling immigration the unrestricted right not only to live and work in this country but also to bring their families to live with them here. Different considerations may apply to immigrant workers from EEC countries, who, in general terms, enjoy unrestricted freedom of movement within the Community and equal rights with nationals of member states in matters of housing: see arts 48 to 51 of the EEC Treaty and art 9(1) of EEC Council Regulation 1612/68. But, if these are at all likely to impose a substantial addition to the domestic burden which housing authorities have to bear, the problem would seem to arise rather from the relevant Community law itself than from any shortcomings in the 1977 Act.

Appeal allowed. Declarations in terms sought in paras (4) and (5) of the notice of motion dated 21st October 1980 granted, a declaration in the terms sought in para (3) being unnecessary by virtue of an undertaking given by the respondents.

Solicitors: *Edward Mackie & Co*, Greenford (for the appellant); *J A Kosky*, Uxbridge (for the respondents).

Mary Rose Plummer   Barrister.

End of Volume 3